DATE DUE

			PRINTED IN U.S.A.

Literature Criticism from 1400 to 1800

Guide to Gale Literary Criticism Series

For criticism on	Consult these Gale series
Authors now living or who died after December 31, 1959	*CONTEMPORARY LITERARY CRITICISM (CLC)*
Authors who died between 1900 and 1959	*TWENTIETH-CENTURY LITERARY CRITICISM (TCLC)*
Authors who died between 1800 and 1899	*NINETEENTH-CENTURY LITERATURE CRITICISM (NCLC)*
Authors who died between 1400 and 1799	*LITERATURE CRITICISM FROM 1400 TO 1800 (LC)* *SHAKESPEAREAN CRITICISM (SC)*
Authors who died before 1400	*CLASSICAL AND MEDIEVAL LITERATURE CRITICISM (CMLC)*
Authors of books for children and young adults	*CHILDREN'S LITERATURE REVIEW (CLR)*
Black writers of the past two hundred years	*BLACK LITERATURE CRITICISM (BLC)*
Short story writers	*SHORT STORY CRITICISM (SSC)*
Poets	*POETRY CRITICISM (PC)*
Dramatists	*DRAMA CRITICISM (DC)*
Major authors from the Renaissance to the present	*WORLD LITERATURE CRITICISM, 1500 TO THE PRESENT (WLC)*

For criticism on visual artists since 1850, see
MODERN ARTS CRITICISM (MAC)

Volume 24

Literature Criticism from 1400 to 1800

Excerpts from Criticism of the Works
of Fifteenth-, Sixteenth-, Seventeenth-, and
Eighteenth-Century Novelists, Poets, Playwrights,
Philosophers, and Other Creative Writers,
from the First Published Critical Appraisals
to Current Evaluations

James E. Person, Jr.
Editor

Michael Jones
Michael Magoulias
Zoran Miderović
Associate Editors

Gale Research Inc. · *DETROIT* · *WASHINGTON, D.C.* · *LONDON*

STAFF

James E. Person, Jr., *Editor*

Michael Magoulias, Zoran Minderović, Lawrence J. Trudeau, *Associate Editors*

George H. Blair, Kathryn Horste, *Assistant Editors*

Jeanne A. Gough, *Permissions & Production Manager*
Linda M. Pugliese, *Production Supervisor*
Donna Craft, Paul Lewon, Maureen Puhl, Camille P. Robinson, Sheila Walencewicz, *Editorial Associates*

Jill Johnson, Elizabeth Anne Valliere, *Editorial Assistants*

Sandra C. Davis, *Permissions Supervisor (Text)*
Maria L. Franklin, Josephine M. Keene, Michele M. Lonoconus, Shalice Shah, Kimberly F. Smilay,
Permissions Associates
Jennifer A. Arnold, Brandy C. Merritt, *Permissions Assistants*

Margaret A. Chamberlain, *Permissions Supervisor (Pictures)*
Pamela A. Hayes, Arlene Johnson, Keith Reed, *Permissions Associates*
Susan Brohman, Barbara A. Wallace, *Permissions Assistants*

Victoria B. Cariappa, *Research Manager*
Maureen Richards, *Research Supervisor*
Robert S. Lazich, Mary Beth McElmeel, Donna Melnychenko, Tamara C. Nott, Jaema Paradowski, *Editorial Associates*
Maria Bryson, Julie Leonard, Stefanie Scarlett, *Editorial Assistants*

Mary Beth Trimper, *Production Director*
Catherine Kemp, *Production Assistant*

Cynthia Baldwin, *Art Director*
Barbara J. Yarrow, *Graphic Services Supervisor*
C. J. Jonik, *Desktop Publisher*
Willie Mathis, *Camera Operator*

Library of Congress Catalog Card Number 86-645085
ISBN 0-8103-8462-0
ISSN 0362-4145

Printed in the United States of America
Published simultaneously in the United Kingdom
by Gale Research International Limited
(An affiliated company of Gale Research Inc.)
10 9 8 7 6 5 4 3 2 1

I(T)P

The trademark **ITP** is used under license.

Contents

Preface   vii

Acknowledgments   xi

Preface

*L*iterature Criticism from 1400 to 1800 (LC) presents criticism of world authors of the fifteenth through eighteenth centuries. The literature of this period reflects a turbulent time of radical change that saw the rise of drama equal in stature to that of classical Greece, the birth of the novel and personal essay forms, the emergence of newspapers and periodicals, and major achievements in poetry and philosophy. Much of modern literature reflects the influence of these centuries. Thus the literature treated in *LC* provides insight into the universal nature of human experience, as well as into the life and thought of the past.

Scope of the Series

LC is designed to serve as an introduction to authors of the fifteenth through eighteenth centuries and to the most significant interpretations of these authors' works. The great poets, dramatists, novelists, essayists, and philosophers of this period are considered classics in every secondary school and college or university curriculum. Because criticism of this literature spans nearly six hundred years, an overwhelming amount of critical material confronts the student. *LC* therefore organizes and reprints the most noteworthy published criticism of authors of these centuries. Readers should note that there is a separate Gale reference series devoted to Shakespearean studies. For though belonging properly to the period covered in *LC*, William Shakespeare has inspired such a tremendous and ever-growing corpus of secondary material that the editors have deemed it best to give his works extensive coverage in a separate series, *Shakespearean Criticism*.

Each author entry in *LC* attempts to present a historical survey of critical response to the author's works. Early criticism is offered to indicate initial responses, later selections document any rise or decline in literary reputations, and retrospective analyses provide students with modern views. The size of each author entry is intended to reflect the author's critical reception in English or foreign criticism in translation. Articles and books that have not been translated into English are therefore excluded. Every attempt has been made to identify and include the seminal essays on each author's work and to include recent commentary providing modern perspectives.

The need for *LC* among students and teachers of literature was suggested by the proven usefulness of Gale's *Contemporary Literary Criticism (CLC)*, *Twentieth-Century Literary Criticism (TCLC)*, and *Nineteenth-Century Literature Criticism (NCLC)*, which excerpt criticism of works by nineteenth- and twentieth-century authors. Because of the different time periods covered, there is no duplication of authors or critical material in any of these literary criticism series. An author may appear more than once in the series because of the great quantity of critical material available and because of the aesthetic demands of the series's *thematic organization*.

Thematic Approach

Beginning with Volume 12, all the authors in each volume of *LC* are organized in a thematic scheme. Such themes include literary movements, literary reaction to political and historical events, significant eras in literary history, and the literature of cultures often overlooked by English-speaking readers.

Organization of the Book

Each entry consists of the following elements: author or thematic heading, introduction, list of principal works (in author entries only), annotated works of criticism (each followed by a bibliographical citation), and a bibliography o further reading. Also, most author entries contain author portraits and others illustrations.

- The **Author Heading** consists of the author's full name, followed by birth and death dates. If an author wrote consistently under a pseudonym, the pseudonym is used in the author heading, with the real name given in parentheses on the first line of the biographical and critical introduction. Also located here are any name variations under which an author wrote, including transliterated forms for authors whose native languages use nonroman alphabets. Uncertain birth or death dates are indicated by question marks. The **Thematic Heading** simply states the subject of the entry.

- The **Biographical and Critical Introduction** contains background information designed to introduce the reader to an author and to critical discussion of his or her work. Parenthetical material following many of the introductions provides references to biographical and critical reference series published by Gale in which additional material about the author may be found. The **Thematic Introduction** briefly defines the subject of the entry and provides social and historical background important to understanding the criticism.

- Most *LC* author entries include **Portraits** of the author. Many entries also contain illustrations of materials pertinent to an author's career, including author holographs, title pages, letters, or representations of important people, places, and events in an author's life.

- The **List of Principal Works** is chronological by date of first book publication and identifies the genre of each work. In the case of foreign authors whose works have been translated in to English, the title and date of the first English-language edition are given in brackets beneath the foreign-language listing. Unless otherwise indicated, drama are dated by first performance, not first publication.

- **Criticism** is arranged chronologically in each author entry to provide a useful perspective on changes in critical evaluation over the years. For the purpose of easy identification, the critic's name and the composition or publication date or the critical work are given at the beginning of each piece of criticism. Unsigned criticism is preceded by the title of the source in which it appeared. All titles by the author featured in the critical entry are printed in boldface type. Publication information (such as publisher names and book prices) and parenthetical numerical references (such as footnotes or page and line references to specific editions of works) have been deleted at the editors' discretion to provide smoother reading of the text.

- Critical essays are prefaced by **Annotations** as an additional aid to students using *LC*. These explanatory notes may provide several types of useful information, including: the reputation of a critic, the importance of a work of criticism, the commentator's individual approach to literary criticism, the intent of the criticism, and the growth of critical controversy or changes in critical trends regarding an author's work. In some cases, these notes cross-reference the work of critics within the entry who agree or disagree with each other.

- A complete **Bibliographical Citation** of the original essay or book follows each piece of criticism.

- An annotated bibliography of **Further Reading** appears at the end of each entry and suggests resources for additional study of authors and themes. It also includes essays for which the editors could not obtain reprint rights.

Cumulative Indexes

Each volume of *LC* includes a cumulative **Author Index** listing all the authors that have appeared in *Contemporary Literary Criticism, Twentieth-Century Literary Criticism, Nineteenth-Century Literature Criticism, Literature Criticism from 1400 to 1800, and Classical and Medieval Literature Criticism,* along with cross-references to the Gale series *Short Story Criticism, Poetry Criticism, Children's Literature Review, Authors in the News, Contemporary Authors, Contemporary Authors Autobiography Series, Contemporary Authors Bibliographical Series, Dictionary of Literary Biography, Concise Dictionary of Literary Biography, Something about the Author, Something about the Author Autobiography Series, and Yesterday's Authors of Books for Children.* Readers will welcome this cumulative author index as a useful tool for locating an author within the various series. The index, which includes authors' birth and death dates, is particularly valuable for those authors who are identified with a certain period but whose death dates cause them to be placed in another, or for those authors whose careers span two periods. For example, F. Scott Fitzgerald is found in *TCLC,* yet a writer often associated with him, Ernest Hemingway, is found in *CLC.*

Beginning with Volume 12, *LC* includes a cumulative **Topic Index** that lists all literary themes and topics treated in *LC, NCLC* Topics volumes, *TCLC* Topics volumes, and the *CLC* Yearbook. Each volume of *LC* also includes a cumulative **Nationality Index** in which authors' names are arranged alphabetically under their respective nationalities and followed by the numbers of the volumes in which they appear.

Each volume of *LC* also includes a cumulative **Title Index,** an alphabetical listing of the literary works discussed in the series since its inception. Each title listing includes the corresponding volume and page numbers where criticism may be located. Foreign-language titles that have been translated followed by the tiles of the translation—for example, *El ingenioso hidalgo Don Quixote de la Mancha (Don Quixote).* Page numbers following these translated titles refers to all pages on which any form of the titles, either foreign-language or translated, appear. Title of novels, dramas, nonfiction books, and poetry, short story, or essays collections are printed in italics, while individual poems, short stories, and essays are printed in roman type within quotation marks.

A Note to the Reader

When writing papers, students who quote directly from any volume in the Literary Criticism Series may use the following general forms to footnote reprinted criticism. The first example pertains to material drawn from periodicals, the second to material reprinted from books.

T. S. Eliot, "John Donne," *The Nation and the Athenaeum,* 33 (9 June 1923), 321-32; excerpted and reprinted in *Literature Criticism from 1400 to 1800,* Vol. 10, ed. James E. Person, Jr. (Detroit: Gale Research, 1989), pp. 28-9.

Clara G. Stillman, *Samuel Butler: A Mid-Victorian Modern* (Viking Press, 1932); excerpted and reprinted in *Twentieth-Century Literary Criticism,* Vol. 33, ed. Paula Kepos (Detroit: Gale Research, 1989), pp. 43-5.

Suggestions Are Welcome

In response to various suggestions features have been added to *LC* since the series began, including a nationality index, a Literary Criticism Series topic index, thematic entries, a descriptive table of contents, and more extensive illustrations.

Readers who wish to suggest new features, themes or authors to appear in future volumes, or who have other suggestions, are cordially invited to write to the editor.

Acknowledgments

The editors wish to thank the copyright holders of the excerpted criticism included in this volume, the permissions managers of many book and magazine publishing companies for assisting us in securing reprint rights, and Anthony Bogucki for assistance with copyright research. We are also grateful to the staffs of the Detroit Public Library, the Library of Congress, the University of Detroit Library, Wayne State University Purdy/Kresge Library Complex, and the University of Michigan Libraries for making their resources available to us. Following is a list of the copyright holders who have granted us permission to reprint material in this volume of *LC*. Every effort has been made to trace copyright, but if omissions have been made, please let us know.

COPYRIGHTED EXCERPTS IN *LC*, VOLUME *24*, WERE REPRINTED FROM THE FOLLOWING PERIODICALS:

COPYRIGHTED EXCERPTS IN *LC*, VOLUME *24*, WERE REPRINTED FROM THE FOLLOWING BOOKS:

Daniel's Masque 'The Vision of the Twelve Goddesses'," in *Essays and Studies: 1971*. Edited by Bernard Harris. John Murry, 1971. © The English Association 1971. All rights reserved. Reprinted by permission of The English Association.—Cruttwell, Patrick. From "The Love Poetry of John Donne: Pedantique Weedes or Fresh Invention?" in *Metaphysical Poetry*. By Patrick Cruttwell and others. Edward Arnold, 1970. © Edward Arnold (Publishers) Ltd., 1970. Reprinted by permission of the publisher.—Dyson, A. E., and Julian Lovelock. From *Masterful Images: English Poetry from Metaphysicals to Romantics*. The Macmillan Press Ltd., 1976. © A. E. Dyson and Julian Lovelock 1976. All rights reserved. Reprinted by permission of Macmillan, London and Basingstoke.—Eliot, T. S. From "What Is Minor Poetry," in *On Poetry and Poets*. Farrar Straus and Cudahy, 1957, Faber & Faber, 1957. Copyright 1944 by T. S. Eliot. Renewed © 1985 by Valerie Eliot. Reprinted by permission of Farrar, Straus and Giroux, Inc. In Canada by Faber and Faber Limited.—Emerson, Ralph Waldo. From *The Early Lectures of Ralph Waldo Emerson: 1833-1836, Vol. 1*. Edited by Stephen E. Whicher and Robert E. Spiller. Cambridge, Mass.: Harvard University Press, 1959. Copyright © 1959 by the President and Fellows of Harvard College. Renewed 1987 by Elizabeth T. Whicher. Excerpted by permission of the publishers.—Fish, Stanley E. From *Self-Consuming Artifacts: The Experience of Seventeenth-Century Literature*. University of California Press, 1972. Copyright © 1972, by The Regents of the University of California. Reprinted by permission of the publisher.—Gardner, Helen. From an introduction of *The Elegies and the Songs and Sonnets*. By John Donne, edited by Helen Gardner. Oxford at the Clarendon Press, 1965. © Oxford University Press 1965. Reprinted by permission of the publisher.—Grant, Patrick. From *Images and Ideas in Literature on the English Renaissance*. The Macmillan Press Ltd., 1979, Amherst: The University of Massachusetts Press, 1979. Copyright © Patrick Grant 1979. All rights reserved. Reprinted by permission of Macmillan, London and Basingstoke. In North America by University of Massachusetts Press.—Grant, Patrick. From *Literature and the Discovery of Method in the English Renaissance*. The Macmillan Press Ltd., 1985. © Patrick Grant 1985. All rights reserved. Reprinted by permission of Macmillan, London and Basingstoke.—Hammond, Gerald. From an introduction to *Richard Lovelace: Selected Poems*. Edited by Gerald Hammond. Fyfield Books, 1987. Copyright © 1987 Gerald Hammond. Reprinted by permission of the publisher.—Hulse, Clark. From *Metamorphic Verse: The Elizabethan Minor Epic*. Princeton University Press, 1981. Copyright © 1981 by Princeton University Press. All rights reserved. Reprinted by permission of the publisher.—LaBranche, Anthony. From "Samuel Daniel: A Voice of Thoughtfulness," in *The Rhetoric of Renaissance Poetry: From Wyatt to Milton*. Edited by Thomas O. Sloan and Raymond B. Waddington. University of California Press, 1974. Copyright © 1974 by The Regents of the University of California. Reprinted by permission of the publisher.—Lewalski, Barbara Kiefer. From *Protestant Poetics and the Seventeenth-Century Religious Lyric*. Princeton University Press, 1979. Copyright © 1979 by Princeton University Press. All rights reserved. Reprinted by permission of the publisher.—Martz, Louis L. From "The Action of the Self: Devotional Poetry in the Seventeenth Century," in *Metaphysical Poetry*. Arnold, 1970. © Edward Arnold (Publishers) Ltd., 1970. Reprinted by permission of the publisher.—Marvell, Andrew. From *The Poems of Andrew Marvel*. Edited by James Reeves and Martin Seymour-Smith. Barnes & Noble, Inc., 1969. Reprinted by permission of the publisher.—McCoy, Richard C. From *The Rites of Knighthood: The Literature and Politics of Elizabethan Chivalry*. University of California Press, 1989. © 1989 by The Regents of the University of California. Reprinted by permission of the publisher.—McGowan, Margaret M. From " 'As through a Looking-glass': Donne's Epithalamia and Their Courtly Context," in *John Donne: Essays in Celebration*. Edited by A. J. Smith. Methuen, 1972. © 1972 Methuen & Co. Ltd. Reprinted by permission of the publisher.—McNees, Eleanor J. From *Eucharistic Poetry: The Search for Presence in the Writings of John Donne, Gerard Manley Hopkins, Dylan Thomas, and Geoffrey Hill*. Bucknell University Press, 1992. © 1992 by Associated University Presses, Inc. All rights reserved. Reprinted by permission of the copyright holder.—Nuttall, A. D. From *Overheard by God: Fiction and Prayer in Herbert, Milton, Dante, and St. John*. Methuen, 1980. © 1980 A. D. Nuttall. All rights reserved. Reprinted by permission of Routledge and the author.—Parfitt, George. From *English Poetry of the Seventeenth Century*. Longman, 1985. © Longman Group Limited, 1985.—Parrish, Paul A. From "The Feminizing of Power: Crashaw's Life and Art," in *"The Muses of Common-Weale": Poetry and Politics in the Seventeenth Century*. Edited by Claude J. Summers and Ted-Larry Pebworth. University of Missouri Press, 1988. Copyright © 1988 by The Curators of The University of Missouri. All rights reserved. Reprinted by permission of the publisher.—Proctor, Johanna. From " 'The Queenes Arcadia' (1606) and 'Hymens Triumph' (1615): Samuel Daniel's Court Pastoral Plays," in *The Renaissance in Ferrara and Its European Horizons*. Edited by J. Salmons.

Richard Crashaw

1612?-1649

English poet and translator.

INTRODUCTION

Crashaw was one of England's Metaphysical poets. Although not widely read, his works are known for their lavish and unusual images, with some passages possessing a quality and vision that stands with the best of Metaphysical poetry.

Crashaw was born in London; his father, William Crashaw, was a well-known Puritan minister and antipapist. He was educated at the Charterhouse school, going on to Pembroke Hall, Cambridge, as a Greek scholar, and receiving a B. A. in 1634. Two years later, he migrated to Peterhouse, Cambridge, where he was elected a fellow in 1637 and received an M. A. the following year. While at Cambridge, he spent much time in the church of Little St. Mary's, where he contemplated spiritual matters and wrote poetry in that vein. In fact, Crashaw wrote most of his poetry in Latin, Greek, and English, during his time at Cambridge, later revising and republishing these works in various collections. He also became active in Nicholas Ferrar's Anglican retreat at Little Gidding, and a devout ascetic. Unfortunately, with the occupation of Cambridge by Oliver Cromwell's Parliamentarian forces, Crashaw, a Royalist, lost his fellowship at Peterhouse; after a short time he emigrated to France, where he was presented to the exiled Catholic Queen Henrietta Maria in Paris in 1644. At about this time or shortly afterwards, he converted to Catholicism, devoting the rest of his writing career to religious themes. Eventually, upon the recommendation of Henrietta Maria, he became a member of Cardinal Palotta's household in Rome; but after criticizing the manner and conduct of the cardinal's staff, Crashaw was removed—for reasons of his own safety—and made a curate at the Shrine of Our Lady of Loretto, where he died within months of his arrival in 1649.

Crashaw's first published work was *Epigrammatum Sacrorum Liber* (1634)—a collection of religious epigrams. In 1646 he published *Steps to the Temple*, a wide-ranging collection of poetry, which primarily included sacred epigrams and poems, especially the controversial "The Weeper," wherein Mary Magdalene is compared to a picked rose—a metaphorical way of branding her a prostitute. "In the Holy Nativity of Our Lord," a more thematically conventional poem, enthusiastically explores the meaning of the birth of Christ as the defining moment of God's salvation for humankind. *The Delights of the Muses*, published that same year, includes the secular "Music's Duel," which contrasts the music of man with that of the nightingale, as well as several epitaphs and homages to dead friends. In 1652 *Carmen Deo Nostro*, a collection of religious works, was published posthumously and contains such well-known Crashavian poems as "To the Name Above Every Name, The Name of Jesus" (a hymn), a revised "In the Holy Nativity of Our Lord," hymns in honor of St. Teresa of Avila, and a poetic address to his patroness, "Letter to the Countess of Denbigh," regarding the spiritual necessity of the countess's conversion to Roman Catholicism. Though Crashaw's oeuvre was small and lacked the stature of the other Metaphysical poets of his time, his works were periodically republished, most recently in *The Complete Works of Richard Crashaw* (1983).

Scholars hold many differing views on Crashaw's poetry. While Edmund Gosse and some critics recognize a compelling style in much of Crashaw's poetry, they also insist that his true genius can only be found in a few passages widely scattered throughout his canon. Most critics maintain that his emblems and conceits are often outlandish and inappropriate, lacking logic and maturity of expression, such as the image of Mary Magdalene's tears flowing upward in "The Weeper," or the sun feeling guilty for its past sins of accepting worship from humankind in "Epiphany Hymn." Yet other critics focus upon Crashaw's elaborate and exaggerated imagery as found in the effusive descriptions of Jesus in the "Hymn to the Name Above Every Name," or the imaginative descriptions of the love between a man and woman in the secular "Love's Horoscope." While some of these same critics find these examples to be a reflection of the Metaphysical style and the poetic sensibilities of the age in which Crashaw lived, other commentators find marked similarities between the structure of many of Crashaw's poems and the classical poetry of Martial, Ovid, and Catullus, thus suggesting a cohesive link between Crashaw's poetry and the ancient poetic past.

A majority of scholars, however, focus primarily upon Crashaw's many religious poems and how he uses Biblical themes and quotes, the prayers of the Roman Breviary, and Roman Church liturgical practices in developing the themes of some of his more popular hymns, odes, epigrams, and poems. Some of these scholars explore the thematic influences of various Catholic saints and holy people on his works—particularly St. Ignatius Loyola, St. Augustine of Hippo, St. Francis de Sales, St. Teresa of Avila, and the capuchin poets. Others, however, contend that Crashaw's religious poems are the result of his own mystical experiences, which is evident from the use of so many fantastic and other-worldly religious images. Examples of this fantastic imagery can be found in "Hymn to the Nativity," "Epiphany Hymn," "In the Glorious Assumption of Our Lady," and in "Our Lord in his Circumcision to his Father." Finally, several critics probe Crashaw's obsession with martyrdom on a psychological level, and his seemingly unconscious melding of erotic imagery with the love of God, as in "The Flaming Heart," where St. Teresa receives the divine-love dart through the hands of a Seraph, and in the other St. Teresa poems, where the image of God is often that of a promiscuous divine lover. These and other instances, critics contend, are telling signs of Crashaw's inner turmoil.

Because Crashaw's poetic style and themes remain so enigmatic, his poetry has continued to give rise to a wide variety of criticism. As J. R. Tutin, in his edition of *The Poems of Richard Crashaw*, states: "Crashaw was gifted with the fervour of a devout enthusiast; and so it comes about that although he has occasionally fine poetry which is not religious, and too often ardent religious verse which is not poetry, yet his most exalted verse is that in which both influences meet."

PRINCIPAL WORKS

Epigrammatum Sacrorum Liber (epigrams) 1634
Steps to the Temple. Sacred poems with other Delights of the Muses (poetry) 1646; revised edition, 1648
Carmen Deo Nostro (poetry) 1652
*A Letter from Mr. Crashaw to the Countess of Denbigh (poetry) 1653
Richardi Crashawi Poemata et Epigrammata . . . Edition Secunda, Auctior et emandation (poetry and epigrams) 1670
Steps to the Temple, The Delights of the Muses, and Carmen Deo Nostro (poetry) 1670
The Poems—English, Latin, and Greek of Richard Crashaw (poetry) 1927
The Complete Works of Richard Crashaw (poetry, and epigrams) 1983

*First published in *Carmen Deo Nostro,* then expanded and printed as a separate work.

CRITICISM

Thomas Car (poem date 1652)

[*An English poet as well as a contemporary and admirer of Crashaw, Car wrote a poetic introduction to a collection of Crashaw's poems. In the following poem, originally published in 1652, Car expounds on Crashaw's passionately religious devotion to God.*]

  . . . . being pleas'd with all things, he pleas'd
    all.
Nor would he give, nor take offence; befall
What might; he would possess himself: and live
As dead (devoid of interest) t'all might give
Disease t'his well composed mind; forestall'd
With heavenly riches: which had wholly call'd
His thoughts from earth, to live above in th'air
A very bird of paradise. No care
Had he of earthly trash. What might suffice
To fit his soul to heavenly exercise,

Sufficed him: and may we guess his heart
By what his lips bring forth, his only part
Is God and godly thoughts. Leaves doubt to
  none
But that to him one God is all; all's one.
What he might eat or wear he took no thought.
His needful food he rather found then sought.
He seeks no downs, no sheets, his bed's still
  made
If he can find a chair or stool, he's laid,
When day peeps in, he quits his restless rest.
And still, poor soul, before he's up he's drest.
Thus dying did he live, yet lived to die
In th'virgin's lap, to whom he did apply
His virgin thoughts and words, and thence was
  styl'd
By foes, the chaplain of the virgin mild
While yet he lived without: His modesty
Imparted this to some, and they to me.
Live happy then, dear soul; enjoy the rest
Eternally by pains thou purchasedest,
While Car must live in care, who was thy friend
Nor cares he how he live, so in the end,
He may enjoy his dearest Lord and thee;
And sit and sing more skillful songs eternally.

             (pp. 10-11)

Thomas Car, in a poem in The Verse in English of Richard Crashaw, *The Grove Press, 1949, pp. 10-11.*

Abraham Cowley (poem date 1656)

[*Cowley was a seventeenth-century English poet. In the poem below, originally published in 1656, he eulogizes Crashaw's life and work, emphasizing his intensely religious devotion to God and the Virgin, which he describes as an inspiration for his own life and poetry.*]

  Poet and *Saint!* to thee alone are given
  The two most sacred Names of Earth and Heav-
    en.
  The hard and rarest Union which can be

Next that of Godhead with Humanity.
Long did the Muses' banished slaves abide,
And built vain Pyramids to mortal pride;
Like Moses Thou (though Spells and Charms
  withstand)
Hast brought them nobly home back to their
  Holy Land.
Ah wretched We, Poets of Earth! but Thou
Wert living the same Poet which thou'rt Now,
Whilst Angels sing to thee their airs divine,
And joy in an applause so great as thine.
Equal society with them to hold,
Thou need'st not make new Songs, but say the
  Old.
And they (kind Spirits!) shall all rejoice to see
How little less then They, Exalted Man may be.
Still the old Heathen Gods in Numbers dwell,
The Heavenliest thing on Earth still keeps up
  Hell.
Nor have we yet quite purg'd the Christian
  Land;
Still Idols here, like Calves at Bethel stand.
And though Pan's Death long since all Oracles
  broke,

Title page of Crashaw's first published work.

Yet still in Rhyme the fiend Apollo spoke:
Nay with the worst of Heathen dotage We
(Vain Men!) the Monster Woman Deify;
Find Stars, and tie our Fates there in a Face,
And Paradise in them by whom we lost it, place.
What different faults corrupt our Muses thus?
Wanton as Girls, as old Wives, Fabulous!
Thy spotless Muse, like Mary, did contain
The boundless Godhead; she did well disdain
That her eternal Verse employ'd should be
On a less subject then Eternity;
And for a sacred Mistress scorn'd to take
But her whom God himself scorn'd not his
   Spouse to make.
It (in a kind) her Miracle did do;
A fruitful Mother was, and Virgin too.
How well (blest Swan) did Fate contrive thy
   death;
And made thee render up thy tuneful breath
In thy great Mistress' Arms? thou most divine
And richest Offering of Loreto's Shrine!
Where like some holy Sacrifice t'expire,
A Fever burns thee, and Love lights the Fire.
Angels (they say) brought the famed Chapel
   there,
And bore the sacred Load in Triumph through
   the air.

'Tis surer much they brought thee there, and
   They,
And Thou, their charge, went singing all the
   way.
Pardon, my Mother Church, if I consent
That Angels led him when from thee he went,
For even in Error sure no Danger is
When joined with so much Piety as His.
Ah, mighty God, with shame I speak't, and
   grief,
Ah that our greatest Faults were in Belief!
And our weak Reason were even weaker yet,
Rather then thus our Wills too strong for it.
His faith perhaps in some nice Tenets might
Be wrong; his Life, I'm sure, was in the right.
And I myself a Catholic will be,
So far at least, great Saint, to Pray to thee.
Hail, Bard Triumphant! and some care bestow
On us, the Poets Militant Below!
Opposed by our old Enemy, adverse Chance,
Attacked by Envy, and by Ignorance,
Enchain'd by Beauty, tortur'd by Desires,
Expos'd by Tyrant-Love to savage Beasts and
   Fires.
Thou from low earth in nobler Flames didst rise,
And like Elijah, mount Alive the skies.
Elisha-like (but with a wish much less,
More fit thy Greatness, and my Littleness)
Lo here I beg (I whom thou once didst prove
So humble to Esteem, so Good to Love)
Not that thy Spirit might on me Doubled be,
I ask but Half thy mighty Spirit for Me.
And when my Muse soars with so strong a
   Wing,
'Twill learn of things Divine, and first of Thee
   to sing.

(pp. 12-13)

Abraham Cowley, in a poem in The Verse in
English of Richard Crashaw, *The Grove Press,
1949, pp. 11-13.*

Alexander Pope (letter date 1710)

[*Called the greatest English poet of his time, Pope was
also a critic and satirical commentator on eighteenth-
century England. In the following letter, originally written in 1710, Pope concludes that Crashaw's poetry has
"only pretty conceptions, fine metaphors, glittering expressions, and something of a neat cast of verse considering the age he lived in."*]

To Mr. Cromwell:

It seems that my late mention of Crashaw, and
my quotation from him, has mov'd your curiosity. I therefore send you the whole author, who
has held a place among my books for some years;
in which time having read him twice or thrice,
I find him one of those whose works may just deserve that trouble. I take him to have writ like
a Gentleman, that is at leisure hours, and more
to keep out of idleness than to establish a reputation: so that nothing regular or just can be expected from him. All that regards design, form,
fable, (which is the Soul of Poetry) all that concerns exactness or content of parts, (which is the
body) will probably be wanting; only pretty con-

ceptions, fine metaphors, glittering expressions, and something of a neat cast of verse considering the age he lived in, (which are properly the dress, gems, or loose ornaments of poetry) may be found in these verses. This is indeed the case of most poetical writers of miscellanies; nor can it be otherwise, since no man can be a great Poet, who writes for diversion only. These authors should be considered as Versifiers, and witty men, rather than as Poets; and under this head will only fall the particular thoughts the expressions, and the numbers; those parts of poetry which may be judged of at a view, and comprehended all at once: such whole coloring only entering the sight, but the Lines and Life of the picture are not to be inspected too narrowly.

This author form'd himself upon Petrarch, or rather upon Marino. His thoughts one may observe, in the main are pretty; but oftentime farfetch'd, and too often strained and stiffened to make them appear the greater: For men are never so apt to think a thing great, as when it is odd or wonderful; and inconsiderate authors would rather be admir'd than understood. This ambition of surprising a reader, is the true natural cause of all fustian, or bombast in poetry. To confirm what I have said, you need but look into his first Poem call'd the **"Weeper,"** where several of the Stanza's are so sublimely dull, as others of the same copy, are soft and pleasing: and if these last want anything, it is an easier and more unaffected expression: the remaining thoughts in that poem might have been spared, being either but repetitions, or very trivial and mean. And by this example in the first, one may guess at all the rest, to be like this, a mixture of tender gentile thoughts and suitable expressions, of forc'd and inextricable conceits, and of needless fillers-up to the rest. From all which it is plain, this author writ fast, and set down what came uppermost: A reader may skim off the froth, and use the clear underneath; but if he goes too deep, will meet with a mouthful of dregs: either the top or bottom of him are good for little, but what he did in his own natural, middle way is best.

To speak of his Numbers is a little difficult, they are so various and irregular, and mostly Pindaric. 'Tis evident his heroic verse (the best example of which is his **"Music's Duel"**) is carefully made up; but one may imagine from what it now is, that had he taken more care it had been musical and pleasing enough, not extremely majestic, but sweet: and the time consider'd of his writing, he was (ev'n as uncorrect as he is) none of the worst Versificators.

I will just observe, that the best pieces of this Author are, a Paraphrase on **"Psalm XXIII,"** on **"Lessius," "Epitaph on Mr. Ashton," "Wishes to His Suppos'd Mistress,"** and the **"Dies Irae."**

(pp. 13-15)

Alexander Pope, in a letter to Henry Cromwell on December 17, 1710, in The Verse in English of Richard Crashaw, *The Grove Press, 1949, pp. 13-15.*

William Hazlitt (lecture date 1819)

[*One of the most important critics of the Romantic age as well as a deft stylist and master of the prose essay, Hazlitt was a leader of the school of "impressionist criticism" which forged a reinterpretation of Shakespeare's characters and the revival of a number of Elizabethan dramatists such as Thomas Heywood. In the following excerpt from a lecture originally delivered in 1819, Hazlitt criticizes Crashaw's religious devotion and hyperbolic imagery.*]

Crashaw was a writer . . . whose imagination was rendered inflammable by the fervors of fanaticism, and who having been converted from Protestantism to Popery (a weakness to which the "seething brains" of the poets of this period were prone) by some visionary appearance of the Virgin Mary, poured out his devout raptures and zealous enthusiasm in a torrent of poetical hyperboles. The celebrated Latin Epigram on the miracle of our Savior, **"The water blushed into wine,"** is in his usual *hectic* manner. His translation of the contest between the Musician and the Nightingale is the best specimen of his powers.

William Hazlitt, in an extract from a lecture in The Verses in English of Richard Crashaw, *The Grove Press, 1949, p. 15.*

Samuel Taylor Coleridge (essay date 1834?)

[*Coleridge, famous poet and philosopher, recognized as the intellectual center of the Romantic movement, is one of England's greatest literary critics. In the following excerpt, written sometime before his death, Coleridge suggests that Crashaw's poetry utilizes a wide variety of conventional poetic images that at the same time exhibit a certain lack of selectivity.*]

Crashaw seems in his poems to have given the first ebullience of his imagination, unshapen into form, or much of, what we now term, sweetness. In the poem **"Hope,"** by way of question and answer, his superiority to Cowley is self-evident. In that on the name of Jesus equally so; but his lines on St. Theresa are the finest.

Where he does combine richness of thought and diction nothing can excel, as in the lines you so much admire—

> Since 'tis not to be had at home,
> She'l travel to a martyrdome.
> No home for her confesses she,
> But where she may a martyr be.
> She'l to the Moores, and trade with them
> For this invalued diadem,
> She offers them her dearest breath,
> With Christ's name in't, in change for death.
> She'l bargain with them, and will give
> Them God, and teach them how to live
> In Him, or if they this deny,
> For Him she'l teach them how to die.
> So shall she leave amongst them sown
> The Lord's blood, or, at least, her own.
> Farewell then, all the world—adieu,
> Teresa is no more for you;
> Farewell all pleasures, sports and joys,
> Never till now esteemed toys—
> Farewell whatever dear'st may be,

Mother's arms or father's knee;
Farewell house, and farewell home,
She's for the Moores and martyrdom.

These verses were ever present to my mind whilst writing the second part of "Christabel"; if, indeed, by some subtle process of the mind they did not suggest the first thought of the whole poem.—Poetry, as regards small poets, may be said to be, in a certain sense, conventional in its illustrations; thus Crashaw uses an image:—

As sugar melts in tea away;

which, although *proper then*, and *true now*, was in bad taste at that time equally with the present. In Shakspeare, in Chaucer there was nothing of this. (pp. 612-13)

> *Samuel Coleridge, "Poetry," in his* Coleridge on the Seventeenth Century, *edited by Roberta Florence Brinkley, Duke University Press, 1955, pp. 612-14.*

A. C. Swinburne (essay date 1862)

[*An English lyric poet and critic renowned for his skill and technical mastery as well as his rebellion against the Victorian age, Swinburne championed "pure poetry," whose key requisites are imagination and harmony. In the excerpt below, from an essay originally written in 1862, Swinburne contends that Crashaw's poetry possesses "fancy and melody" as well as being "ingenious and elaborate."*]

Theophile in France and Crashaw in England had many merits and faults in common. Crashaw is a Christianized Theophile, steeped in Catholic sentiment and deformed by fantastic devotion; he is a far smaller figure, a much weaker and perverser man; but in fancy and melody, in grace and charm of exquisite words and notes, he may rank next him and near him. He is far more ingenious and elaborate; if elaboration and ingenuity be qualities commendable in a poet. His studies are more fleshless and formless. . . . (pp. 15-16)

> *A. C. Swinburne,* The Verse in English of Richard Crashaw, *The Grove Press, 1949, pp. 15-16.*

George MacDonald (essay date 1868)

[*In the following excerpt, MacDonald explores Crashaw's "Easter Day" and other poems, asserting their poetic musicality, sentimentalism, and "strangeness of expression."*]

I come now to one of the loveliest of our angel-birds, Richard Crashaw. Indeed he was like a bird in more senses than one; for he belongs to that class of men who seem hardly ever to get foot-hold of this world, but are ever floating in the upper air of it.

What I said of a peculiar Æolian word-music in William Drummond applies with equal truth to Crashaw; while of our own poets, somehow or other, he reminds me of Shelley, in the silvery shine and bell-like melody both of his verse and his imagery; and in one of his poems, **"Music's**

Duel," the fineness of his phrase reminds me of Keats. But I must not forget that it is only with his sacred, his best poems too, that I am now concerned. (p. 238)

There is much in his verses of that sentimentalism which is rife in modern Catholic poetry. I will give from Crashaw a specimen of the kind of it. Avoiding a more sacred object, one stanza from a poem of thirty-one, most musical, and full of lovely speech concerning the tears of Mary Magdalen, will suit my purpose.

> Hail, sister springs,
> Parents of silver-footed rills!
> Ever-bubbling things!
> Thawing crystal! Snowy hills,
> Still spending, never spent!—I mean
> Thy fair eyes, sweet Magdalene!

The poem is called **"The Weeper,"** and is radiant of delicate fancy. But surely such tones are not worthy of flitting moth-like about the holy sorrow of a repentant woman! Fantastically beautiful, they but play with her grief. Sorrow herself would put her shoes off her feet in approaching the weeping Magdalene. They make much of her indeed, but they show her little reverence. There is in them, notwithstanding their fervour of amorous words, a coldness like that which dwells in the ghostly beauty of icicles shining in the moon.

But I almost reproach myself for introducing Crashaw thus. I had to point out the fact, and now having done with it, I could heartily wish I had room to expatiate on his loveliness even in such poems as **"The Weeper."**

His *Divine Epigrams* are not the most beautiful, but they are to me the most valuable of his verses, inasmuch as they make us feel afresh the truth which he sets forth anew. In them some of the facts of our Lord's life and teaching look out upon us as from clear windows of the past. As epigrams, too, they are excellent—pointed as a lance. . . .

I value the following as a lovely parable. Mary is not contented: to see the place is little comfort. The church itself, with all its memories of the Lord, the gospel-story, and all theory about him, is but his tomb until we find himself.

"Come, See The Place Where The Lord Lay."

> Show me himself, himself, bright sir!   Oh show
> Which way my poor tears to himself may go.
> Were it enough to show the place, and say,
> "Look, Mary; here see where thy Lord once lay;"
> Then could I show these arms of mine, and say,
> "Look, Mary; here see where thy Lord once lay."

From one of eight lines, on the Mother Mary looking on her child in her lap, I take the last two, complete in themselves, and I think best alone.

> This new guest to her eyes new laws hath given:
> 'Twas once *look up,* 'tis now *look down to heaven.*

And here is perhaps his best.

"Two Went Up Into The Temple To Pray."

> Two went to pray?   Oh rather say,

One went to brag, the other to pray.
One stands up close, and treads on high,
Where the other dares not lend his eye.
One nearer to God's altar trod;
The other to the altar's God.

This appears to me perfect. Here is the true relation between the forms and the end of religion. The priesthood, the altar and all its ceremonies, must vanish from between the sinner and his God. When the priest forgets his mediation of a servant, his duty of a door-keeper to the temple of truth, and takes upon him the office of an intercessor, he stands between man and God, and is a Satan, an adversary. Artistically considered, the poem could hardly be improved. (pp. 239-41)

The following is a world-wide intercession for them that know not what they do. Of those that reject the truth, who can be said ever to have *truly* seen it? A man must be good to see truth. It is a thought suggested by our Lord's words, not an irreverent opposition to the truth of *them*.

> *But now they have seen and hated.*

> *Seen?* and yet *hated thee?* They did not see—
> They saw thee not, that saw and hated thee!
> No, no; they saw thee not, O Life! O Love!
> Who saw aught in thee that their hate could
>   move.

We must not be too ready to quarrel with every oddity: an oddity will sometimes just give the start to an outbreak of song. The strangeness of the following hymn rises almost into grandeur.

"Easter Day."

> Rise, heir of fresh eternity,
>   From thy virgin-tomb;
> Rise, mighty man of wonders, and thy world with thee;
>   Thy tomb, the universal East—
>   Nature's new womb;
> Thy tomb—fair Immortality's perfuméd nest.

> Of all the glories make noon gay
>   This is the morn;
> This rock buds forth the fountain of the streams of day;
>   In joy's white annals lives this hour,
>   When life was born,
> No cloud-scowl on his radiant lids, no tempest-lower.

> Life, by this light's nativity,
>   All creatures have;
> Death only by this day's just doom is forced to die.
>   Nor is death forced; for, may he lie
>   Throned in thy grave,
> Death will on this condition be content to die.

When we come, in the writings of one who has revealed masterdom, upon any passage that seems commonplace, or any figure that suggests nothing true, the part of wisdom is to brood over that point; for the probability is that the barrenness lies in us, two factors being necessary for the result of sight—the thing to be seen and the eye to see it. No doubt the expression may be inadequate, but if we can compensate the deficiency by adding more vision, so much the better for us.

In the second stanza there is a strange combination of images: the rock buds; and buds a fountain; the fountain is light. But the images are so much one at the root, that they

slide gracefully into each other and there is no confusion or incongruity: the result is an inclined plane of development.

I now come to the most musical and most graceful, therefore most lyrical, of his poems. I have left out just three stanzas, because of the sentimentalism of which I have spoken: I would have left out more if I could have done so without spoiling the symmetry of the poem. My reader must be friendly enough to one who is so friendly to him, to let his peculiarities pass unquestioned—amongst the rest his conceits, as well as the trifling discord that the shepherds should be called, after the classical fashion—ill agreeing, from its associations, with Christian song— Tityrus and Thyrsis.

"A Hymn Of The Nativity Sung By The Shepherds."

Chorus. Come, we shepherds, whose blest sight
Hath met love's noon in nature's night;
Come, lift we up our loftier song,
And wake the sun that lies too long.

To all our world of well-stolen joy
    He slept, and dreamed of no such thing,
While we found out heaven's fairer eye,
    And kissed the cradle of our king:
Tell him he rises now too late
To show us aught worth looking at.

Tell him we now can show him more
    Than he e'er showed to mortal sight—
Than he himself e'er saw before,
    Which to be seen needs not his light:
Tell him, Tityrus, where thou hast been;
Tell him, Thyrsis, what thou hast seen.

Tityrus. Gloomy night embraced the place
    Where the noble infant lay:
The babe looked up and showed his face:
    In spite of darkness it was day.
It was thy day, sweet, and did rise
Not from the east, but from thy eyes.
    Chorus. It was thy day, sweet, &c.

Thyrsis. Winter chid aloud, and sent
    The angry north to wage his wars:
The north forgot his fierce intent,
    And left perfumes instead of scars.
By those sweet eyes' persuasive powers,
Where he meant frosts, he scattered flowers.
    Chorus. By those sweet eyes', &c.

Both. We saw thee in thy balmy nest,
    Young dawn of our eternal day;
We saw thine eyes break from the east,
    And chase the trembling shades away.
We saw thee, and we blessed the sight;
We saw thee by thine own sweet light.
    Chorus. We saw thee, &c.

Tityrus. "Poor world," said I, "what wilt thou do
    To entertain this starry stranger?
Is this the best thou canst bestow—
    A cold and not too cleanly manger?
Contend, the powers of heaven and earth,
To fit a bed for this huge birth."
    Chorus. Contend, the powers, &c.

Thyrsis. "Proud world," said I, "cease your
   contest,
   And let the mighty babe alone:
The phœnix builds the phœnix' nest—
   Love's architecture is his own.
The babe, whose birth embraves this morn,
Made his own bed ere he was born."
   Chorus. The babe, whose birth, &c.

Tityrus. I saw the curl'd drops, soft and slow,
   Come hovering o'er the place's head,
Offering their whitest sheets of snow
   To furnish the fair infant's bed:
"Forbear," said I; "be not too bold:
Your fleece is white, but 'tis too cold."
   Chorus. "Forbear," said I, &c.

Thyrsis. I saw the obsequious seraphim
   Their rosy fleece of fire bestow;
For well they now can spare their wings,
   Since heaven itself lies here below.
"Well done," said I; "but are you sure
Your down, so warm, will pass for pure?"
   Chorus. "Well done," said I, &c.

Full Chorus. Welcome all wonders in one
   sight!
   Eternity shut in a span!
Summer in winter! day in night!
   Heaven in earth, and God in man!
Great little one, whose all-embracing birth
Lifts earth to heaven, stoops heaven to earth!

               * * * *

Welcome—though not to those gay flies
   Gilded i' th' beams of earthly kings—
Slippery souls in smiling eyes—
   But to poor shepherds, homespun things,
Whose wealth's their flocks, whose wit's to be
Well read in their simplicity.

Yet when young April's husband showers
   Shall bless the fruitful Maia's bed,
We'll bring the firstborn of her flowers
   To kiss thy feet, and crown thy head:
To thee, dear Lamb! whose love must keep
The shepherds while they feed their sheep.

To thee, meek Majesty, soft king
   Of simple graces and sweet loves,
Each of us his lamb will bring,
   Each his pair of silver doves,
At last, in fire of thy fair eyes,
Ourselves become our own best sacrifice.

A splendid line to end with! too good for the preceding
one. All temples and altars, all priesthoods and prayers,
must vanish in this one and only sacrifice. Exquisite, however, as the poem is, we cannot help wishing it looked less
heathenish. Its decorations are certainly meretricious. (pp.
242-46)

     George MacDonald, "Crashaw and Marvell,"
     in his England's Antiphon, *Macmillan & Co.*
     Publishers, 1868, pp. 238-50.

Edmund Gosse (essay date 1883)

[*A distinguished nineteenth-century English literary historian, critic, and biographer, Gosse wrote extensively on
seventeenth– and eighteenth-century English literature.
In the following excerpt, Gosse decries Crashaw's use of
"every extravagant and inappropriate image" in his poetry. Still, he maintains that Crashaw's "Hymn to St.
Teresa" and other poems exhibit a fresh and true genius
in style, wording, and theme.*]

Crashaw's English poems were first published in 1646,
soon after his arrival in Paris. He was at that time in his
thirty-fourth year, and the volume contains his best and
most mature as well as his crudest pieces. It is, indeed, a
collection of juvenile and manly verses thrown together
with scarcely a hint of arrangement, the uncriticised labour of fifteen years. The title is ***Steps to the Temple, Sacred Poems, with other delights of the Muses***. The sacred
poems are so styled by his anonymous editor because they
are "steps for happy souls to climb heaven by;" the ***Delights of the Muses*** are entirely secular, and the two divisions of the book, therefore, reverse the order of Herrick's
similarly edited *Hesperides* and *Noble Numbers*. The ***Steps
to the Temple*** are distinguished at once from the collection
with which it is most natural to compare them, the *Temple*
of Herbert, to which their title refers with a characteristic
touch of modesty, by the fact that they are not poems of
experience, but of ecstasy—not of meditation, but of devotion. Herbert, and with him most of the sacred poets of the
age, are autobiographical; they analyse their emotions,
they take themselves to task, they record their struggles,
their defeats, their consolation.

But if the azure cherubim of introspection are the dominant muses of English sacred verse, the flame-coloured
seraph of worship reigns in that of Crashaw. He has made
himself familiar with all the amorous phraseology of the
Catholic metaphysicians; he has read the passionate canticles of St. John of the Cross, the books of the Carmelite
nun, St. Teresa, and all the other rosy and fiery contributions to ecclesiastical literature laid by Spain at the feet of
the Pope during the closing decades of the sixteenth century. The virginal courage and ardour of St. Teresa inspire
Crashaw with his loveliest and most faultless verses. We
need not share nor even sympathise with the sentiment of
such lines as these to acknowledge that they belong to the
highest order of lyric writing:—

    Thou art Love's victim, and must die
    A death more mystical and high;
    Into Love's arms thou shalt let fall
    A still-surviving funeral.
    His is the dart must make thy death,
    Whose stroke will taste thy hallowed breath—
    A dart thrice dipped in that rich flame
    Which writes thy spouse's radiant name
    Upon the roof of heaven, where aye
    It shines and with a sovereign ray
    Beats bright upon the burning faces
    Of souls which in that name's sweet graces
    Find everlasting smiles. So rare,
    So spiritual, pure, and fair,
    Must be the immortal instrument
    Upon whose choice point shall be spent

A life so loved; and that there be
Fit executioners for thee,
The fairest first-born sons of fire,
Blest seraphim, shall leave their choir,
And turn Love's soldiers, upon thee
To exercise their archery.

Nor in the poem from which these lines are quoted does this melodious rapture flag during nearly two hundred verses. But such a sustained flight is rare, as in the similar poem of **"The Flaming Heart,"** also addressed to St. Teresa, where, after a long prelude of frigid and tuneless conceits, it is only at the very close that the poet suddenly strikes upon this golden chord of ecstasy:—

Let all thy scattered shafts of light, that play
Among the leaves of thy large books of day,
Combined against this breast at once break in,
And take away from me myself and sin;
This gracious robbery shall thy bounty be,
And my best fortunes such fair spoils of me.
O thou undaunted daughter of desires!
  By all thy dower of lights and fires,
  By all the eagle in thee, all the dove,
  By all thy lives and deaths of love.
  By thy large draughts of intellectual day,
And by thy thirsts of love more large than they,
By all thy brim-filled bowls of fierce desire,
By thy last morning's draught of liquid fire,
By the full kingdom of that final kiss
That seized thy parting soul and sealed thee His;
  By all the heaven thou hast in Him,
  Fair sister of the seraphim!
  By all of thine we have in thee—
  Leave nothing of myself in me;
  Let me so read thy life that I
  Unto all life of mine may die.

If Crashaw had left us nothing more than these two fragments, we should be able to distinguish him by them among English poets. He is the solitary representative of the poetry of Catholic psychology which England possessed until our own days. . . . (pp. 168-71)

One of the largest pieces of work which he undertook was the translation of the first canto of the *Strage degli Innocenti,* or "Massacre of the Innocents," a famous poem by the Neapolitan Cavaliere Marini, who had died in 1625. Crashaw has thrown a great deal of dignity and fancy into this version, which, however, outdoes the original in ingenious illustration, as the true Marinists, such as Achillini, outdid Marini in their conceited sonnets. Crashaw, in fact, is a genuine Marinist, the happiest specimen which we possess in English, for he preserves a high level of fantastic foppery, and seldom, at his worst, sinks to those crude animal imagings—illustrations from food, for instance— which occasionally make such writers as Habington and Carew not merely ridiculous but repulsive.

In criticising with severity the piece on Mary Magdalene which stands in the forefront of Crashaw's poems, and bears the title of **"The Weeper,"** I have the misfortune to find myself at variance with most of his admirers. I cannot, however, avoid the conviction that the obtrusion of this eccentric piece on the threshold of his shrine has driven away from it many a would-be worshipper. If language be ever liable to abuse in the hands of a clever poet, it is

surely outraged here. Every extravagant and inappropriate image is dragged to do service to this small idea— namely, that the Magdalen is for ever weeping. Her eyes, therefore, are sister springs, parents of rills, thawing crystal, hills of snow, heavens of ever-falling stars, eternal breakfasts for brisk cherubs, sweating boughs of balsam, nests of milky doves, a voluntary mint of silver, and Heaven knows how many more incongruous objects, from one to another of which the labouring fancy flits in despair and bewilderment. In this poem all is resigned to ingenuity; we are not moved or softened, we are merely startled, and the irritated reader is at last appeased for the fatigues he has endured by a frank guffaw, when he sees the poet, at his wits' end for a simile, plunge into the abyss of absurdity, and style the eyes of the Magdalen

Two walking baths, two weeping motions,
Portable and compendious oceans.

These are the worst lines in Crashaw. They are perhaps the worst in all English poetry, but they must not be omitted here, since they indicate to us the principal danger to which not he only but most of his compeers were liable. It was from the tendency to call a pair of eyes "portable and compendious oceans" that Waller and Dryden, after both of them stumbling on the same stone in their youth, finally delivered us. It is useless to linger with indulgence over the stanzas of a poem like **"The Weeper,"** simply because many of the images are in themselves pretty. The system upon which these juvenile pieces of Crashaw are written is in itself indefensible, and is founded upon what Mr. Matthew Arnold calls an "incurable defect of style."

Crashaw, however, possesses style, or he would not deserve the eminent place he holds among our poets. The ode in praise of Teresa, written while the author was still among the Protestants, and therefore probably about 1642, has already been cited here. It is an exquisite composition, full of real vision, music of the most delicate order, and imagery which, although very profuse and ornate, is always subordinated to the moral meaning and to the progress of the poem. The **"Shepherd's Hymn,"** too, is truly ingenious and graceful, with its pretty pastoral tenderness. **"On Mr. G. Herbert's Book sent to a Gentleman"** evidently belongs to the St. Teresa period, and contains the same charm. The lyrical epistle persuading the Countess of Denbigh to join the Roman communion contains extraordinary felicities, and seems throbbing with tenderness and passion. We have already drawn attention to the splendid close of **"The Flaming Heart."** There is perhaps no other of the sacred poems in the volume of 1646 which can be commended in its entirety. Hardly one but contains felicities; the dullest is brightened by such flashes of genius as—

Lo, how the thirsty lands
Gasp for the golden showers with long-stretch'd
    hands!

But the poems are hard, dull, and laborious, the exercises of a saint indeed, but untouched by inspiration, human or divine. We have to return to the incomparable **"Hymn to St. Teresa"** to remind ourselves of what heights this poet was capable.

There can be very little doubt that Crashaw regarded the second section of his book, the secular **Delights of the Muses**, as far inferior in value and importance to the **Steps to the Temple**. That is not, however, a view in which the modern reader can coincide, and it is rather the ingenuity of his human poems than the passion of his divine which has given him a prominent place among poets. The **Delights** open with the celebrated piece called the "**Muse's Duel**," paraphrased from the Latin of Strada. As one frequently sees a reference to the "Latin poet Strada," it may be worth while to remark that Famianus Strada was not a poet at all, but a lecturer in the Jesuit colleges. He belonged to Crashaw's own age, having been born in 1572, and dying in the year of the English poet's death, 1649. The piece on the rivalry of the musician and the nightingale was published first at Rome in 1617, in a volume of *Prolusiones* on rhetoric and poetry, and occurs in the sixth lecture of the second course on poetic style. The Jesuit rhetorician has been trying to familiarise his pupils with the style of the great classic poets by reciting to them passages in imitation of Ovid, Lucretius, Lucan, and the rest, and at last he comes to Claudian. This, he says, is an imitation of the style of Claudian, and so he gives us the lines which have become so famous. That a single fragment in a school-book should suddenly take root and blossom in European literature, when all else that its voluminous author wrote and said was promptly forgotten, is very curious, but not unprecedented.

In England the first person who adopted or adapted Strada's exercise was John Ford, in his play of *The Lover's Melancholy*, in 1629. Dr. Grosart found another early version among the Lansdowne MSS., and Ambrose Phillips a century later essayed it. There are numerous references to it in other literatures than ours, and in the present age M. François Coppée has introduced it with charming effect into his pretty comedy of *Le Luthier de Crémone*. Thus the schoolmaster's task, set as a guide to the manner of Claudian, has achieved, by an odd irony of fortune, a far more general and lasting success than any of the actual verses of that elegant writer. With regard to the comparative merits of Ford's version, which is in blank verse, and of Crashaw's, which is in rhyme, a confident opinion has generally been expressed in favour of the particular poet under consideration at the moment; nor is Lamb himself superior to this amiable partiality. He denies that Crashaw's version "can at all compare for harmony and grace with this blank verse of Ford's." But my own view coincides much rather with that of Mr. Swinburne, who says that "between the two beautiful versions of Strada's pretty fable by Ford and Crashaw, there will always be a diversity of judgment among readers; some must naturally prefer the tender fluency and limpid sweetness of Ford, others the dazzling intricacy and affluence in refinements, the supple and cunning implication, the choiceness and subtlety of Crashaw." Mr. Shorthouse, on the other hand, suggests to me that "Crashaw's poem is surely so much more full and elaborate, that it must be acknowledged to be the more important effort." There can be no doubt that it presents us with the most brilliant and unique attempt which has been made in our language to express the very quality and variety of musical notation in words. It may be added that the only reference made by Crashaw in any

part of his writings to any of the dramatists his contemporaries is found in a couplet addressed to Ford:—

> Thou cheat'st us, Ford, mak'st one seem two by art;
> What is *love's sacrifice* but *the broken heart*?

After "**Music's Duel**," the best-known poem of Crashaw's is his "**Wishes to his Supposed Mistress**," a piece in forty-two stanzas, which Mr. Palgrave reduced to twenty-one in his *Golden Treasury*. He neglected to mention the "sweet theft," and accordingly most readers know the poem only as he reduced and rearranged it. The act was bold, perhaps, but I think that it was judicious. As Crashaw left it, the poem extends beyond the limits of a lyric, tediously repeats its sentiments, and gains neither in force nor charm by its extreme length. In Mr. Palgrave's selection it challenges comparison with the loveliest and most original pieces of the century. It never, I think, rises to the thrilling tenderness which Donne is capable of on similar occasions. Crashaw never pants out a line and a half which leave us faint and throbbing, as if the heart of humanity itself had been revealed to us for a moment; with all his flying colour and lambent flame, Crashaw is not Donne. But the "**Wishes**" is more than a charming, it is a fascinating poem, the pure dream of the visionary poet, who liked to reflect that he too might marry if he would, and choose a godly bride. He calls upon her—

> Whoe'er she be
> That not impossible She
> That shall command my heart and me;
>
> Where'er she lie
> Locked up from mortal eye
> In shady leaves of destiny—

to receive the embassy of his wishes, bound to instruct her in that higher beauty of the spirit which his soul demands—

> Something more than
> Taffata or tissue can,
> Or rampant feather, or rich fan.

But what he requires is not spiritual adornment alone; he will have her courteous and accomplished in the world's ways also, the possessor of

> Sydneian showers
> Of sweet discourse, whose powers
> Can crown old Winter's head with flowers;

and finally,

> Life, that dares send
> A challenge to his end,
> And when it comes say, 'Welcome, friend.'
>
> I wish her store
> Of worth may leave her poor
> Of wishes; and I wish—no more.

The same refined and tender spirit animates the "**Epitaph upon Husband and Wife, who died and were buried together**." The lovely rambling verses of "**To the Morning, in satisfaction for Sleep**," are perhaps more in the early manner of Keats than any other English lines. In some of those sacred poems which we have lately been considering, he reminds us no less vividly of Shelley, and there are not a few passages of Crashaw which it would require a very quick ear to distinguish from Mr. Swinburne. We may safely conjecture that the latter poet's "Song in Season" was written in deliberate rivalry of that song of Crashaw's which runs—

> O deliver
> Love his quiver;
> From thine eyes he shoots his arrows,
> Where Apollo
> Cannot follow,
> Feathered with his mother's sparrows.

But perhaps the sweetest and most modern of all Crashaw's secular lyrics is that entitled **"Love's Horoscope."** The phraseology of the black art was never used with so sweet and picturesque an ingenuity, and the piece contains some of the most delicately musical cadences to be found in the poetry of the age:—

> Thou know'st a face in whose each look
> Beauty lays ope Love's fortune—book,
> On whose fair revolutions wait
> The obsequious motions of Love's fate.
> Ah! my heart! her eyes and she
> Have taught thee new astrology.
> Howe'er Love's native hours were set,
> Whatever starry synod met,
> 'Tis in the mercy of her eye
> If poor Love shall live or die.

It is probable from internal and from external evidence also that all these secular poems belong to Crashaw's early years at Cambridge. The pretty lines **"On Two Green Apricocks sent to Cowley by Sir Crashaw"** evidently date from 1633; the various elegies and poems of compliment can be traced to years ranging from 1631 to 1634. It is doubtful whether the **"Wishes"** themselves are at all later than this. Even regarding him as a finished poet ten years before the publication of his book, however, he comes late in the list of seventeenth century lyrists, and has no claims to be considered as an innovator. He owed all the basis of his style, as has been already hinted, to Donne and to Ben Jonson. His originality was one of treatment and technique; he forged a more rapid and brilliant short line than any of his predecessors had done, and for brief intervals and along sudden paths of his own he carried English prosody to a higher refinement, a more glittering felicity, than it had ever achieved. Thus, in spite of his conceits and his romantic colouring, he points the way for Pope, who did not disdain to borrow from him freely.

It is unfortunate that Crashaw is so unequal as to be positively delusive; he baffles analysis by his uncertain hold upon style, and in spite of his charm and his genius is perhaps most interesting to us because of the faults he shares with purely modern poets. It would scarcely be unjust to say that Crashaw was the first real poet who allowed himself to use a splendid phrase when a simple one would have better expressed his meaning; and in an age when all but the best poetry was apt to be obscure, crabbed, and rugged, he introduces a new fault, that of being visionary and diffuse, with a deliberate intention not only, as the others did, to deck Nature out in false ornament, but to represent her actual condition as being something more "starry"

and "seraphical" than it really is. His style has hectic beauties that delight us, but evade us also, and colours that fade as promptly as the scarlet and the amber in a sunset sky. We can describe him best in negatives; he is not so warm and real as Herrick, nor so drily intellectual as the other hymnists, nor coldly and respectably virile like Cowley. To use an odd simile of Shelley's, he sells us gin when the other poets offer us legs of mutton, or at all events baskets of bread and vegetables. (pp. 173-82)

> *Edmund Gosse, "Richard Crashaw," in his*
> Seventeenth Century Studies, *1883. Reprint*
> *by William Heinemann, 1913, pp. 157-90.*

Francis Thompson (essay date 1889)

[*Thompson was one of the most important poets of the Catholic Revival in nineteenth-century English literature, and is often compared to Crashaw. In the following excerpt from an essay originally published in 1889, Thompson contends that Crashaw's use of conceits and florid imagery often detracts from the power of his poetry, as in "St. Teresa," "The Nativity," "The Weeper," "The Horoscope," and other poems.*]

Crashaw's genius, in spite of his often ecstatic devotion, is essentially a secular genius. He writes on religious themes; but he writes of them as Milton wrote in the "Ode on the Nativity," or Rossetti in the "Ave." Milton speaks with the gravest, Rossetti with the warmest reverence; yet they are allured, not by the religious lessons, but by the poetical grandeur or beauty of their subject; and it is the same with Crashaw. He sings the tears of Magdalen. But he sings them much as Shelley sings his "Skylark"; stanza following stanza in a dropping rain of fancies, as Shelley expands, lustred plume by plume, the peacock splendor of his imagery. He sings the Stable of Bethlehem. But he does not sing its lessons of humility, poverty, self-abnegation; he sings of the Divine light shining from the Child, of the snows offering their whiteness and the seraphim their roseate wings, to strew the heavenly Infant's couch. The themes are religious, the poetry beautiful; but it is not what people are accustomed to understand by religious verse.

Apart, however, from a disadvantage compatible with unblemished excellence, there is, it must be conceded, a just reason for Crashaw's unpopularity; a reason which excludes the charge of unmerited neglect. He has written no perfect poems, though some perfect poetry, and *that* is discontinuous. His faults are grave, exasperatingly prominent, and—throughout large portions of his work—are not merely present as flaws, but constitute an intimate alloy. The consequent vitiation of his nevertheless great beauty alienates general readers, and—unless they come prepared to give him special attention—discourages even poetical readers. For there are, in regard to verse, two classes of readers. The general reader, attracted by the accidents rather than the essence of poetry, regards the poet much as a barrel-organ to reel off *his* (the reader's) favorite tunes, or is affected by him in proportion as he mirrors the broad interests common to all humanity. But the poetical reader, as we have called him, is of kin to the poet. He is born with the lyre not in his hand, but in his bosom; not

The shrine of Loretto, where Crashaw died in 1649.

for his own touch, but to thrill in sympathy with the swept chords of all singers. He loves poetry for its poetry. To the first class, Crashaw, were he as faultless as he is faulty, could never be of interest, owing to his deficiency in the human element, to the ethereal insubstantialities of his genius. But poetical readers unfamiliar with him may be stimulated to make a pleasant acquaintance, if we bring together some typical specimens of his excellence dismantled, so far as possible, of its parasitic growths.

Since because of this plan his defects will not come conspicuously before the reader, it is all the more necessary to explain in what these defects consist; and to warn the intending student that in the original they will confront him intermittently, demanding that habitual allowance which we make for infantile deficiencies of technical knowledge in early Italian painters. The explanation is simple. Crashaw riots in conceits. Originally the word "conceit" signified merely a detached cameo-like image, such as form the bulk of Shelley's "Skylark." An Elizabethan critic would have styled that "an excellent conceited poem," and he would have been right. But we use the term in its modern and opprobrious sense, according to which it means an image marked by high-wrought ingenuity rather than beauty or appropriateness. From Donne to Dryden most of our poets indulged in this vice; and

Crashaw only followed the fashion of his day. But he sublimated his errors as he sublimated his poetry, beyond the level of his brother-singers. . . . The perverted ardor of his devotion to the false fashion, no less than its contrast with his exquisite powers, render it peculiarly intolerable. It corrupted his judgment so that years but rooted the fault more deeply; and in his maturest poems he cannot write twenty consecutive lines without lapsing from finished delicacy to errors of taste which make the reader writhe. Trailing in exasperating profusion over his most charming verse are lines of which the following present a perhaps extreme example. They refer to the weeping eyes of St. Mary Magdalen.

And now where'er He strays,

He's followed by two faithful fountains

Two walking baths, two weeping motions,
Portable and compendious oceans.

When the reader has recovered, he may take this, which is not an extreme example.

Does thy sweet-breathed prayer
Up in clouds of incense climb?
Still at each sigh, that is each stop,
A bead, that is a tear, does drop.

It *might* have been a fair image; but the hard elaboration of detailed touch ruins it in the expression. And here, finally, is a specimen of the high-raised conceits in which he abounds; high-raised to such a degree that one editor, Dr. Grosart, quotes it with admiration. To us it appears so essentially fantastic in its fancy, and strained in expression, as to merit only the phrase which we have applied to it.

> Heavens thy fair eyes be;
> Heavens of ever-falling stars.
> 'Tis seed-time still with thee;
>   And stars thou sow'st whose harvest dares
> Promise the earth to countershine
> Whatever makes Heaven's forehead fine.

To the foregoing indictment we must add, that there is often a feminine effusiveness, and almost hysterical fantasy in his religious raptures, which is a weakness complementary to his sensitive tenderness.

These disfigurements lie thick on Crashaw's poetry; or its wine would need no bush. But there is rich compensation for those who will move aside the rank undergrowth. Every now and then the rare genius of the man shines away the infectious vapors of contemporary influence which stain it with eclipse; and he is transfigured before our eyes. His very faults

> Suffer a sea-change
> Into something rich and strange;

his conceits into fancies of delicate grace, his tortured language into the most refined sorcery of expression, his emotional femineity into rarefied ethereality of sentiment. Fancy, expression, lofty ideal sentiment—these sum sufficiently fairly the qualities which we claim for him at his best. It is perhaps his abundant fancy which has caused his admirers to compare him with Shelley, a comparison to which we do not entirely adhere, while we admit some resemblance, stronger in certain moods than in others. His fondness for stringing together a series of images on a given subject, which often makes a whole poem a veritable air with variations, recalls Shelley's habit of weaving similar chaplets. But Crashaw's imagery is fragile and lily-like, the offspring of fancy; Shelley's rich and glowing, the offspring of imagination. Dr. Grosart, however, who strongly upholds the theory of Crashaw's resemblance to Shelley, credits the elder poet in the highest measure with this very quality of imagination; and if we could agree in such a judgment, we should have no difficulty in accepting the theory. It is partly because we regard imagination as one of Shelley's most essential attributes, but hold Crashaw's dominant faculty to be fancy, that we dissent from the current view. Yet since Shelley's fancy is hardly less striking than his imagination, there still remains ground for comparison.

Another reason for our dissent is to be found in Crashaw's expression. If it be remembered that we are now treating of him *at his best*, we may say unhesitatingly that it is perfect in its kind. But that kind belongs, we think, to another school than Shelley's, a school of which the supreme modern example is Coleridge. All great poets at their finest are perfect in expression; but as the colorist's gift may in itself reach genius, so a small number of poets are so unique in expression that their diction alone is almost poetry. These masters of diction may be divided into two classes. The first class aim at enthralment by the display of their art; the second, by its concealment. (pp. 131-40)

Crashaw's diction, when most excellent, belongs to the latter school; and in this quality he is often as nearly akin to Coleridge as a lyric can be to a narrative poet. It is the true wonder-working diction; and when his ideas free themselves from conceit sufficiently to give his diction a chance, the combination is unsurpassable for sweet felicity. Take as a specimen a selection of stanzas from the poem on St. Mary Magdalen called **"The Weeper."** We have so arranged them as to form a continuous whole; while the reader will perceive by the numbering of the stanzas how many we have omitted.

VII

> The dew no more will weep,
>   The primrose's pale cheek to deck;
> The dew no more will sleep,
>   Nuzzled in the lily's neck;
> Much rather would it be thy tear,
> And leave them both to tremble here.

X

> Not in the Evening's eyes,
>   When they red with weeping are
> For the Sun that dies,
>   Sits Sorrow with a face so fair.
> Nowhere but here did ever meet
> Sweetness so sad, sadness so sweet.

XI

> Sadness, all the while
>   She sits in such a throne as this,
> Can do nought but smile,
>   Nor believes she Sadness is:
> Gladness itself would be more glad
> To be made so sweetly sad.

XV

> Well does the May that lies
>   Smiling in thy cheeks confess
> The April in thine eyes;
>   Mutual sweetness they express.
> No April e'er lent kinder showers,
> Nor May returned more faithful flowers.

XXIII

> O precious prodigal!
>   Fair spendthrift of thyself! thy measure
> (Merciless love!) is all,
>   Even to the last pearl in thy treasure:
> All places, times, and seasons be
> Thy tears' sweet opportunity.

XXIV

> Does the day-star rise?
>   Still thy tears do fall and fall.
> Does Day close his eyes?
>   Still the fountain weeps for all.
> Let Night or Day do what they will,
> Thou hast thy task: thou weepest still.

XXVIII

Not "so long she livèd,"
  Shall thy tomb report of thee;
But, "so long she grievèd:"
  Thus must we date thy memory.
Others by moments, months, and years,
Measure their ages; thou, by tears.

The way in which the beautiful opening lines of stanza VII. are marred by the concluding conceit to which they lead up, is unfortunately characteristic of Crashaw. But stanza X. is lovely throughout, perfect both in fancy and expression to the charmingly phrased final couplet. The secular cast of Crashaw's genius is well illustrated in these excerpts; and the more strikingly to enforce it we will show the reader, by a parallel treatment of a love-poem, how entirely the difference between the two is a difference of subject. The **"Wishes to a Supposed Mistress"** is one of his few secular poems, and of his only two love-poems: it is, moreover, as happy an inspiration as he has left us, with a smaller proportion of conceits than usual. (pp. 142-45)

A typical specimen of his best religious work is that **"Hymn of the Nativity,"** to which we alluded in the opening of our article. We can only, in our remaining space, draw together three or four of the most admirable stanzas, which we place before the reader without further preface. They are sung by the shepherds in alternate verses.

BOTH
We saw Thee in Thy balmy nest,
  Young dawn of our eternal Day!
We saw Thine eyes break from Their East
  And chase the trembling shades away.
We saw Thee; and we blessed the sight;
  We saw Thee by Thine Own sweet light.

* * * * *

TITYRUS
I saw the curled drops, soft and slow,
  Come hovering o'er the place's head;
Offering their whitest sheets of snow
  To furnish the fair Infant's bed:
Forbear, said I, be not too bold,
  Your fleece is white, but 'tis too cold.

THYRSIS
I saw the obsequious Seraphim,
  Their rosy fleece of fire bestow,
For well they now can spare their wing,
  Since Heaven itself lies here below.
Well done, said I; but are you sure
  Your down so warm will pass for pure?

BOTH
We saw Thee in Thy balmy nest,
  Bright dawn of our eternal Day!
We saw Thine eyes break from Their East
  And chase the trembling shades away.
We saw Thee; and we blessed the sight;
  We saw Thee by Thine Own sweet light.

FULL CHORUS
Welcome, all wonders in one sight!
  Eternity shut in a span!
Summer in Winter, Day in Night!
  Heaven in Earth, and God in man!

Great little One! Whose all-embracing birth
Lifts Earth to Heaven, stoops Heaven to Earth.

Notice that most apt epithet, "curled drops." Of all the poets who have described snow, we do not recollect one besides Crashaw who has recorded this characteristic trait of snow-flakes. They *are* curled. Pluck one of the inner petals from a rose, lay it with its concavity uppermost, and you have a sufficiently close resemblance to the general form of a snowflake when falling through the air. It is easy to see the reason of this form. The pressure of the atmosphere on the lower surface of the descending flake necessarily tends to curve upward its edges. But Crashaw alone has thought of noting the fact.

This notice would be incomplete did we not refer to our poet's metre. . . . Chaucer, of course, founded English rhyming heroics; while Spenser, Collins, and Coleridge are masters of metrical combination. Crashaw is a worthy companion to these great names; not, it is true, as regards the invention and treatment of irregular metres, but in the cunning originality with which he manipulates established forms. He is unequal even here: it would be easy to cite examples of harshness and want of finish: but when he does himself justice, it is not too much to say that his numbers are unsurpassed by anything of the kind in the language. His employment (in the **"Hymn to St. Teresa"** and its companion, **"The Bleeding Heart"**) of those mixed four-foot Iambics and Trochaics so often favored by modern poets, marks an era in the metre. Coleridge (in the *Biographia Literaria*) adopts an excellent expression to distinguish measures which follow the changes of the sense from those which are regulated by a pendulum-like beat or tune—however *new* the tune—overpowering all intrinsic variety. The former he styles *numerous* versification. Crashaw is beautifully numerous, attaining the most delicate music by veering pause and modulation—a

Miser of sound and syllable, no less
Than Midas of his coinage.

We have said advisedly that the **"St. Teresa"** marks an era in its metre. For Coleridge was largely indebted to it, and acknowledged his debt. He had, he said, those lines constantly in his mind when writing the second part of "Christabel"; if, indeed, by some inexplicable mental process, it did not suggest the first idea of the whole poem. The student who reads in the light of this declaration those portions of the second part which are composed in ordinary couplet-rhyming Tetrameters, Iambic and Trochaic, will perceive how true it is. Both expression and metre have manifestly been closely studied by the modern writer. The diction of the two poets is here markedly akin; and the versification is not so much akin as identical. The greatest metrical master of the nineteenth century was for once content to imitate such exquisite lines as these:—

Scarce has she learned to lisp the name
Of martyr; yet she thinks it shame
Life should so long play with that breath
Which spent can buy so brave a death.
She never undertook to know
What Death with Love should have to do;
Nor has she e'er yet understood
Why to show love she should shed blood;

Yet though she cannot tell you why,
She can love, and she can die.

Coleridge has done as well; better even Coleridge could
not do. For fuller conviction, compare the lines which we
are about to quote with those lines on the dreaming Christabel terminating in the lovely phrase

Both blue eyes, more bright than clear,
Each about to have a tear.

This phrase is essentially identical in its art with a line of
Crashaw's which we italicise. Each is singularly felicitous
in its expression; and each, if carried one step further,
would have been a conceit.

All thy old woes shall now smile on thee,
And thy pains sit bright on thee,
All thy sorrows here shall shine,
All thy sufferings be divine:
Tears shall take comfort, and turn gems,
And wrongs repent to diadems.

Let us end by quoting in its entirety Crashaw's second and
very charming love-poem, the **"Horoscope."** It is more
nearly free from conceit than any other complete poem.
Indeed the very motive of it is so essentially a slight fantasy that a little fantasy in the execution appears almost per-
missible, because harmonious with the central idea. The
last two stanzas of the fanciful trifle could not well be improved in their airy grace: the subtle music and the subtle
expression seem to beget each other:—

Love, brave Virtue's younger brother,
Erst hath made my heart a mother;
She consults the conscious spheres
To calculate her young son's years.
She asks, if sad, or saving powers,
Gave omen to his infant hours;
She asks each star that then stood by,
If poor Love shall live or die.
Ah, my heart, is that the way?
Are these the beams that rule thy day?
Thou know'st a face in whose each look
Beauty lays ope Love's fortune-book;
On whose fair revolutions wait
The obsequious motions of man's fate:
Ah, my heart, her eyes and she
Have taught thee new astrology;
Howe'er Love's native hours were set,
Whatever starry synod met—
'Tis in the mercy of her eye
If poor Love shall live or die.

If those sharp rays putting on
Points of death, bid Love be gone:
(Though the Heavens in council sat
To crown an uncontrollèd fate,
Though their best aspects twined upon
The kindest constellation,
Cast amorous glances on his birth,
And whispered the confederate Earth
To pave his paths with all the good
That warms the bed of youth and blood)
Love hath no plea against her eye:
Beauty frowns, and Love must die.

But if her milder influence move,
And gild the hopes of humble Love:
(Though Heaven's inauspicious eye

Lay black on Love's nativity;
Though every diamond in Jove's crown
Fixed his forehead to a frown:)
Her eye a strong appeal can give,
Beauty smiles, and Love shall live.

O, if Love shall live, O where
But in her eye, or in her ear,
In her breast, or in her breath,
Shall I hide poor Love from Death?
For in the life ought else can give,
Love shall die, although he live.

Or, if Love shall die, O where
But in her eye, or in her ear,
In her breath, or in her breast,
Shall I build his funeral nest?
While Love shall thus entombèd lie,
Love shall live, although he die!

The melody of those two final stanzas is bewitching. Were
six more delectably-modulated lines ever written for the
ravishment of all sensitive ears? No less noticeable are
they as an example of delightful repetition, in which (as
in nearly all judicious echoing) the verbal repetition corresponds to a repetition of idea. So artfully precise is the iter-
ation of cadence, that in the respectively parallel lines of
the two verses, the very position of the *caesurae* is exactly
preserved.

Those who are able and willing to sift the gold in so rich
a stream as that from whose sands we have washed these
few handfuls, will assuredly experience no disappointment
in the work of the Catholic whom even the Protestant
Cowley could address as "Poet and Saint." (pp. 150-60)

> *Francis Thompson, "Crashaw," in his* A Rene-
> gade Poet and Other Essays, *The Ball Pub-*
> *lishing Co., 1910, pp. 129-60.*

T. S. Eliot (essay date 1928)

[*Perhaps the most influential poet and critic to write in
the English language during the first half of the twentieth century, Eliot is closely identified with many of the
qualities denoted by the term Modernism: experimentation, formal complexity, artistic and intellectual eclecticism, and a classicist's view of the artist working at an
emotional distance from his or her creation. In general,
he upheld values of traditionalism and discipline, and
in 1928 he annexed Christian theology to his overall conservative world view. Of his criticism, Eliot stated: "It is
a by-product of my private poetry-workshop: or a prolon-
gation of the thinking that went into the formation of my
verse." The following excerpt is taken from a review,
originally published in the* Dial *in 1928, of L. C. Martin's edition of Crashaw's Latin and Greek poems. Here,
Eliot takes issue with several statements made by Martin
in his introduction (wherein he compares Crashaw with
Shelley and Keats) and expresses his own high valuation
of Crashaw's accomplishment.*]

'When we survey' says Professor Martin, 'the remarkable
development of Crashaw's genius close up to the end of
his life, in circumstances that must often have been trying
and distracting in the extreme, his "unfulfilled renown"
becomes indeed comparable with that of those other two

English poets whose work his own in some ways strangely foreshadows, and who, like him, found in Italy a retreat and a final resting place.' (I wish Mr. Martin had saved a line or two by saying Keats and Shelley straight out, instead of searching for a fine phrase.) Now this remark might lead to several false inferences. Crashaw lived to be about thirty-seven; so he had some good years more than Keats or Shelley in which to develop. A man can go far between twenty-seven and thirty-seven. Mr. Martin is therefore unfair to Keats and Shelley. But moreover Crashaw's verse is, as one would expect, far more mature than that of either of these poets; and I do not find in the poem on which he bases this suggestion, the **'Letter to the Countess of Denbigh'**, the evidence of *promise* that Mr. Martin finds in it. It is indeed a fine poem, but it is the work of a mature master, and promises nothing but more of the same kind. Crashaw is, I believe, a much greater poet than he is usually supposed to be; Keats and Shelley

are, in their actual accomplishment, not nearly such great poets as they are supposed to be. But nothing that Crashaw wrote has the *promise* that is patent in *Hyperion* or *The Triumph of Life.* We must try of course always to distinguish promise from performance; both must be taken into account in judging a poet, and they must be kept separate. We can only say that Keats and Shelley would *probably* have become greater poets, poets on a much greater scale, than Crashaw; judging them on their accomplishment only, Crashaw was a finished master, and Keats and Shelley were apprentices with immense possibilities before them.

So much for one question. Next, in what way can Crashaw be said to 'foreshadow' Keats and Shelley? As for Keats, I simply do not know what Mr. Martin means, I see so little resemblance. With Shelley, there are obvious and striking resemblances, though I think very superficial ones. To suggest, as Mr. Martin's words seem to me to suggest, that Crashaw was in any way a forerunner or 'prophet' of Shelley, is quite off the rails. The obvious parallel is between **'The Weeper'** and 'The Skylark', rather than between their uses of the octosyllabic couplet, which are wholly different. . . . I doubt whether the *sound* of two poems can be very similar, when the *sense* is entirely different. At any rate, I have found that the more I studied the meaning of Crashaw's verse, and his peculiar use of image and conceit, the less resemblance the music of it seemed to have to Shelley's. Take one of Crashaw's more extreme and grotesque figures, from **'The Tear'**:

> Faire Drop, why quak'st thou so?
> 'Cause thou streight must lay thy Head
>   In the Dust? o no;
> The Dust shall never bee thy Bed:
> A pillow for thee will I bring,
> Stuft with Downe of Angels wing.

This imagery is almost the quintessence of an immense mass of devotional verse of the seventeenth century. But it has nothing to do with Shelley. Crashaw's images, even when entirely preposterous—for there is no warrant for bringing a pillow (and what a pillow!) for the *head* of a *tear*—give a kind of intellectual pleasure—it is a deliberate conscious perversity of language, a perversity like that of

the amazing and amazingly impressive interior of St. Peter's. There is brain work in it. But in 'The Skylark' there is no brain work. For the first time perhaps in verse of such eminence, sound exists without sense. Crashaw would never have written so shabby a line as 'That from heaven or near it' merely to provide an imperfect rhyme for *spirit.*

> Keen as are the arrows
>   Of that silver sphere
> Whose intense lamp narrows
>   In the white dawn clear,
> Until we hardly see, we feel that it is there.

I should be grateful for any explanation of this stanza; until now I am still ignorant to what Sphere Shelley refers, or why it should have silver arrows, or what the devil he means by an intense lamp narrowing in the white dawn; though I can understand that we could hardly see the lamp of a *silver* sphere narrowing in *white* dawn (why dawn? as he has just referred to the pale purple even). There may be some clue for persons more learned than I; but Shelley should have provided notes. Crashaw does not need *such* notes.

And when Shelley has some definite statement to make, he simply says it; keeps his images on one side and his meanings on the other:

> We look before and after,
>   And pine for what is not:
> Our sincerest laughter
>   With some pain is fraught;
> Our sweetest songs are those that tell of saddest thought.

This is a sweeping assertion, and is rather commonplace in expression; but it is intelligible. And it is not in the least like Crashaw.

I call Crashaw a 'devotional' poet, because the word 'religious' is so abused. Shelley even has been called religious, but he could not be called devout; he is religious in the same sense as when we say that Dean Inge or the Bishop of Birmingham is religious. Devotional poetry is religious poetry which falls within an exact faith and has precise objects for contemplation. Crashaw is sometimes called erotic in his devotion. 'Erotic' is an abused word, but in any case ought not to be an offensive word. In one aspect it may be applied to Crashaw. Dante, for instance, always seems perfectly aware of every shade of both human and divine love; Beatrice is his means of transition between the two; and there is never any danger of his confounding the two loves. But just as Crashaw is deficient in humanity, and yet is neither quite in the world nor out of it, and so is neither a Dante nor an Adam of St. Victor, so we feel at times that his passion for heavenly objects is imperfect because it is partly a substitute for human passion. It is not impure, but it is incomplete.

Yet Crashaw is quite alone in his peculiar kind of greatness. He is alone among the metaphysical poets of England, who were mostly intensely English: Crashaw is primarily a European. He was saturated still more in Italian and Latin poetry than in English. Indeed Mr. Mario Praz, who has probably read more than anybody of the Latin poetry and the continental poetry of the seventeenth century, puts Crashaw above Marino, Góngora, and everybody else, merely as the *representative* of the baroque spirit in literature. (pp. 119-25)

T. S. Eliot, "A Note on Richard Crashaw," in his For Lancelot Andrewes: Essays on Style and Order, *Faber & Gwyer*, 1928, pp. 117-25.

Rev. Thomas Foy (essay date 1933)

[*In the excerpt below, Foy discusses the elaborate imagery and conceits in Crashaw's religious poetry, asserting that they often spoil his works, "which had greater potentialities than that of many other poets who had maintained a higher level" of self-critical poetic control.*]

Crashaw's religious poetry cannot be properly understood without an appreciation of the poet's own large tolerance. His **"Epitaph Upon the Death of Mr. Ashton, a Conformable Citizen"** contains these lines:—

> He was a Protestant at home
> Not only in despite of Rome
> He loved his father; yet his zeal
> Tore not off his mother's veile.

Again, his **"Treatise on Charity,"** though suppressed in 1646, had the following ending:—

> Nor shall our zealous ones still have a fling
> At that most horrible and horned thing,
> Forsooth the Pope; by which black name they
>   call
> The Turk, the Devil, Furies, Hell and all,
> And something more; oh! he is Anti-Christ;
> Doubt this, and doubt—(say they) that Christ is
>   Christ;
> Why, 'tis a point of faith, whate'er it be,
> I'm sure it is no point of Charity.
> In sum, no longer shall our people hope,
> To be true Protestants but to hate the Pope.

Crashaw's happiest vein is his **"Address to the Noblest and Best of Ladies, the Countess of Denbeigh, Against Irresolution and Delay in Matters of Religion."** He suggests that the lady addressed is sure to come over later to Catholicism, and so is now guilty of the sin of delay. Crashaw subtly expresses it:—

> Who grants at last, a great while tried
> And did his best to have denied.

He assumes that Catholicism is her destined refuge and he gently chides her for not doing at once what she knows she cannot avoid doing later on. The climax of the poem is the suggestion of reasons for man's reluctance to be saved. Ironically he asks:—

> What magic bolts, what mystic bars
> Maintain the will in these strange wars
> What fatal, yet fantastic, bands
> Keep the heart free from his own hands?
> Say, lingering Fair, why comes the birth
> Of your brave soul so slowly forth?
> Love that lends haste to heaviest things
> In you alone hath lost his wings.
> Mark with what faith fruit answer flowers
> And knows the call of Heaven's kind showers
> Mark how the curled waves work and wind

> All hating to be left behind—
> The aery ration of weak doves
> That draw the chariot of chaste Loves
> Chide your delay.

Finally he bursts into a passionate outburst of praise of the great love of God for man—the love which prompted the Incarnation:—

> All things swear friends to fair and good,
> Yea, suitors; man alone is wooed,
> Tediously wooed and hardly won;
> Only not slow to be undone;
> As if the Bargain had been driven
> So hardly betwixt Earth and Heaven
> Our God would thrive too fast, and be
> Too much again and by 't, should we
> Our purchased selves too soon bestow
> On Him who had not loved us so.
> When Love of all called him to see
> If we'd vouchsafe his company;
> He left his Father's court and came
> Lightly as a lambent flame,
> Leaping upon the hills, to be
> The humble King of you and me.

This passionate and devotional poetry is the first of its kind, and in it Crashaw ascends into real fervour.

"Here Crashaw is at his best," says L. C. Martin, "some of the new lines being the most remarkable of their kind ever written. And when we survey the remarkable development of Crashaw's genius, close up to the end of his life, in circumstances that must often have been trying and distracting, his "unfulfilled renown" becomes comparable with that of two other English poets, whose work his own in some way strangely foreshadowed, and who, like him, found in Italy a retreat and final resting-place." Francis Thompson feels, too, that "though the crest of the tide was not to come," Crashaw "marks an epoch, a turn of the tide in English lyric."

The best-known of Crashaw's religious poems is the **"Hymn to the Name and Honour of the Admirable St. Teresa,"** which has been praised by almost every critic. The canonization in 1622 of St. Teresa produced much literature about her, and her books were widely circulated. "While he was yet among the Protestants," he tells us, her writings moved him to passionate utterance:—

> Thine own dear books are guilty; for from
>   thence
> I learned to know that love is eloquence.

Crashaw knew that his interest in the Spanish mystic would seem strange to his English readers, but he boldly claims St. Teresa for his "soul's countryman":—

> O 'tis not Spanish, but 'tis Heaven she speaks.

St. Teresa is a woman, but she is more than a woman in her "angelical height of speculation, and in her masculine courage of performance," for while yet a child she "outran maturity and did plot a martyrdom."

The poem can scarcely be praised too highly. The poet's inspiration never flags from the beginning to the end. He passes from the tender pathos and humour in which the child's love of martyrdom is told, to the glorious picture of the mystical martyrdom that awaited her, and finally to the peaceful bliss of the Beatific Vision.

In the poem are to be found the most beautiful delicacies of language—and the metre is peculiar to Crashaw. Love, the "absolute sole lord of life and death," makes his—

> mansion in the mild
> And milky soul of this sweet child,

and urges her on to do great things for her "Lords' glorious name."

Speaking of Teresa's childish attempt to run away and become a martyr among the Moors, he says:—

> Scarce had she learnt to lisp the name
> Of Martyr; yet she thinks it shame
> Life should so long play with that breadth
> Which spent can buy so brave a death.
> She never undertook to know,
> What Death with Love should have to do;
> Nor has she e'er yet understood
> Why to show Love, she should shed blood;
> Yet though she cannot tell you why
> She can love and she can die.
>
> Love is the great driving-force;
> 'Tis love, not years that can
> Make the martyr or the man.

The tenderness Crashaw displays in his farewell to St. Teresa going to Martyrdom would atone for many faults:—

> Farewell then, all the world, adieu!
> Teresa is no more for you.
> Farewell, all pleasures, sports and joys
> (Never till now esteemed toys)
> Farewell, whatever dear may be,
> Mother's arms or father's knee;
> Farewell house, and farewell home,
> She's for the Moors and Martyrdom.

Crashaw's ardent temperament gave a warmth to his devotional writings which scarcely any English writer before him possessed, and his knowledge of Spanish brought the writings of all the Spanish mystics, as well as those of St. Teresa, within his reach. His deep knowledge of Italian literature also affected not only the matter, but the manner of his poetry—for it contains much of the luscious sweetness and hyperboles of Marino.

The **"Hymn to St. Teresa"** is superior even to the **"Wishes,"** which is regarded by many as the most delicate of his secular poems. **"Wishes"** is playful, but the **"Hymn to St. Teresa"** is intense with passion. In the secular love poems there is "dainty trifling," but in most of the divine poems, there is the "very outgoings of his soule." In the **"Hymn to St. Teresa"** we find passionate outbursts, which results in rapid-moving lines, and his ardent, glowing, religious spirit is in this poem everywhere in evidence. The poem is full of vision. It has music of the most delicate kind, and although the imagery is ornate and profuse, it is always subordinated to the meaning of the poem:—

> Blest powers forbid, thy tender life
> Should bleed upon a barbarous knife;
>   O No,
> Wise Heaven will never have it so,

> Thou art Love's victim, and must die
> A death more mystical and high.

Love, he continues, is the dart which

> must make the death

> Whose stroke shall taste thy hallowed breath;
> O dart; thrice dipped in that rich flame
> Which writes thy spouse's radiant name
> Upon the roof of Heaven, where aye
> It shines; and with a sovereign ray
> Beats right upon the burning faces
> Of souls which in that name's sweet graces
> Find everlasting smiles.

Some critics hold that he uses the language of Love poetry too freely.

"In soaring imagination," writes Gilfillan, "in gorgeous language, in ardent enthusiasm, and in ecstasy of lyrical movement, Crashaw very much resembles Shelley:—

> His raptures are
> All air and fire

Yet, you often hear the language of earthly instead of celestial love, and discover a certain swooning, languishing, voluptuousness of feeling as in St. Teresa:—

> O what delight, when revealed Life shall stand,
> And teach thy lips Heaven with His hand;
> On which thou now may'st to thy wishes
> Heap up thy consecrated kisses,
> What joys shall seize thy soul, when she
> Bending her blessed eyes on Thee,
> (Those second smiles of Heaven) shall dart
> Her mild rays through Thy melting Heart.

Gilfillan objects to such expressions as "consecrated kisses" and "*melting*" heart, and regards it as the language of earthly love. Yet, in reading the poem, we cannot fail to realise that Crashaw's devotion is a noble, chivalrous one, and it is his chivalrous ideas that prompt him to call St. Teresa "his rosy love," and the Blessed Virgin his "rosy princess." "We may remark, in passing," continues Gilfillan, "how different and how far superior Milton's language in reference to women is, to that of Crashaw's school. How respectful, how dignified, yet modest and delicate are all Milton's allusions to female beauty. How different from the tone of languishment, of everlasting talk of 'sighs' and 'kisses' and 'bosoms,' found in some part of our poet." It must be remembered, however, that Milton was a Puritan, and one of his critics has acknowledged frankly that it was a "hard thing to be Milton's wife or daughter." To appreciate a poet's work fully one must be in sympathy with the writer, and Gilfillan, in discussing Crashaw's mysticism, attacks very vehemently the Catholic Church, of which Crashaw was a member, and concludes with the trite, dogmatic expression, "Catholicism is not Christianity." One can understand, then, his serious objections to what others call Crashaw's "manly, chivalrous devotion."

Crashaw ends his poem on a note of hope. He contemplates his beloved saint walking through Paradise in the footsteps of her Lord and loving Him with a heart that was, if possible, "purer, and more spiritual" than it was on earth.

> Thou, with the Lamb, thy Lord shalt go,
> And wheresoever He sets His white
> Steps, walk with Him those ways of light;
> Which who in death would live to see
> Must learn in life to die like thee.

This is the true mystic's contemplation; it is also the thought that occupies the minds of the saints—the infinite love of God for the creatures He has made. "Crashaw has written, and written beautifully on general subjects, but is always most at home in the field of sacred poetry. His muse is never herself till she hears the organ of the Roman Catholic Church. To this music and to these litanies which swell up upon it, like strong eagles, riding on mighty winds, Crashaw seems to write, and we question if man ever appreciated better the poetical elements which abound in the Catholic Faith."

Coleridge said that the **"Hymn to St. Teresa"** was present to his mind while he was writing the second part of "Christabel," if, indeed, by some subtle process of the mind, it did not suggest the first thought of the whole poem. In reading "Christabel," it is very difficult to discover any direct influence of Crashaw on the poem, and it is suggested that Coleridge may have been referring to the second part of "Christabel," which was never written. Coleridge, however, sometimes recalls Crashaw by the richness of his lines, as Shelley does by his smooth and limpid flow; but at his best Crashaw has more radiance than either."

"It may be doubted," writes Herbert Read, "whether there are any lines so sincere and passionate, and yet so direct and impressive, in the whole of English poetry."

The poem is followed by an "Apology"—an "Apology," first of all, because the poet was a Protestant when he wrote the poem; and, secondly, an "Apology to Englishmen" for praising a Spaniard. To this "Apology" was later added a poem called **"The Flaming Heart,"** and for seventy lines of "frigid, lifeless conceits" the poet treats with an evident want of taste of a picture of St. Teresa "with a seraphim beside her," to the effect that the saint is the better seraph of the two. Later, twenty-four lines were added, which are a passionate invocation of the saint herself and have no connection with the picture. The first eight lines of this final addition seem to have been written to connect the new with the old, but they are far superior to the old. His **"Golden Chord of Ecstasy"** is not as well known as it deserves to be—. . . . (pp. 50-8)

"These glowing verses may well be recognised as the highest achievement of the muse of Religious Poetry." With justice it has been called by Saintsbury "a marvellous rocket of song." "And then in a moment," he writes (evidently thinking that the concluding lines of **"The Flaming Heart"** formed part of the original poem) "and then in a moment in the twinkling of an eye, without warning of any sort, the metre changes, the poet's inspiration catches fire, and there rushes up into the heaven of poetry, this marvellous rocket of song." It is "one of the most astounding things in English or in any other literature." It has all the

ardour and brave soaring transport of the highest lyrical inspiration.

The most ambitious of Crashaw's religious poems is the **"Hymn to the Name above every Name—the Name of Jesus."** This is the poem Crashaw himself ranked highest, probably because of its appeal to all the voices of Nature to join with him in giving thanks to God for his wonderful gifts. The passages about music are especially beautiful:—

> Wake, lute, and harp, and every sweet-lipped
>   thing
> That talks with tuneful string
> Start into life, and leap with me
> Into a hasty, fit-tuned harmony,

and again:—

> O you, my soul's most certain wings,
> Complaining pipes and prattling strings;
> Bring all the store
> Of sweets you have, and murmur that you have
>   no more.

Later, wood and stringed instruments are described as:—

>   Such
> As sigh with supple wind
> Or answer artful touch.

The opening of the final invocation is the most touching of all.

> Come, lovely name! Appear from forth the
>   bright
>   Regions of peaceful light;
> Look from thine own illustrious home
>   Fair King of names and come;
> Leave all Thy native glories in their gorgeous
>   nest
> And give Thyself awhile the gracious guest
> Of humble souls, that seek to find
>   Thy hidden sweets
>   Which man's heart meets
> When thou art master of the mind.
> Come, lovely name; Life of our hope!
> Lo, we hold our hearts wide ope!
> Unlock Thy cabinet of Day,
>   Dearest Sweet, and come away,
>   Lo, how thy thirsty lands
>   Gasp for thy golden showers! with long-
>   stretched hands.
>
> Lo, how the labouring Earth
>   That hopes to be
>   All Heaven by Thee
> Leaps at Thy birth!

The passage about the martyrs at the close of the poem is an instance of the fire which Crashaw, notwithstanding his gentle nature, could put into his verse:—

> When Thy old friends of fire, all full of Thee,
> Fought against frowns with smiles; give glorious
>   chase
> To persecutions, and against the face
> Of Death and fiercest dangers dost, with brave
> And sober pace, march on to meet a grave.
> On their bold breasts, about the world they bore
>   Thee
> And to the teeth of Hell stood up to reach Thee,

In centre of their inmost souls they wore Thee;
Where racks and torments strived, in vain to
    reach Thee,
Little alas! thought they
Who tore the fair breasts of Thy friends,
Their fury but made way
For Thee, and served Them in Thy glorious
    ends.

The poem has many merits and yet, like many of
Crashaw's poems, it is not a success. He is too fluent, and
there are many repetitions, not only of ideas, but even of
phrases. The word "nest," for instance, is used five
times—and always as a rhyme. The poem contains two
hundred and forty verses, and, owing to its length, it was
almost impossible to avoid repetitions. Its length is also responsible for many "conceits" which spoil the effect of
what would otherwise be a very musical poem. For instance, speaking about the joy of the world on the birth
of Christ he says:—

The attending World, to wait thy rise
First turn'd to eyes;
And then, not knowing what to do
Turn'd them to tears, and spent them, too.

The subject of the poem was one on which nothing except
a short lyric could be written, if the writer wished to ensure a good poem—and the metre which Crashaw used
tended to longwindedness, rather than conciseness. Speaking of the "vagueness" of this poem, Canon Beeching
writes: "One cannot help wishing that Crashaw had been
born a few years earlier, so that at Cambridge he might
have formed a friendship with Milton, instead of with
Cowley. He would have been attracted, we cannot doubt,
to the "Lady of Christ's," and Milton's zealous care that
the word, the phrase, the paragraph should be perfect as
choice could make them, would have been invaluable to
Crashaw, if he could have learned it. There might also
have been reciprocal influence in matters of temperament,
which was as sorely needed." **"Charitas Nimia,"** or the
"Dear Bargain" is, perhaps, the only religious poem of
Crashaw which is not spoiled either by glaring conceits or
by being too long. It is, perhaps, also the only one which
shows any influence of his contemporary—the "Divine
Poet," Herbert:—

Lord, what is man? why should he cost Thee
So dear? What has his ruin lost Thee?
Lord, what is man, that thou hast ever bought
So much a thing of naught?

Love is too kind, I see; and can
Make but a simple merchantman.
'Twas for such sorry merchandise
    Bold painters have put out his eyes.
Alas! sweet Lord, what were 't to Thee
If there were no such worms as we?
Heaven ne'er the less still Heaven would be
    Should mankind dwell
    In the deep Hell;
What have his woes to do with Thee?

The plea at the end of the poem shows Crashaw's deep
love for God and the Mystics' passionate desire to realise
fully the price Christ paid for man's redemption:—

O my Saviour, make me see

How dearly Thou hast paid for me,
That lost again, my life may prove,
As then in death, so now in love.

The hymns, **"In the Holy Nativity of our Lord; a Hymn
as sung by the Shepherds,"** and **"In the Glorious Epiphany of our Lord; a hymn sung as by the Three Kings,"** although alike in theme, are of very different merit. The Nativity hymn is full of happy expressions and ideas. (pp. 59-
63)

One cannot help comparing this poem with Milton's great
"Ode," and though it is a very different poem to Milton's,
it has, nevertheless, its own characteristic beauty. A note
of warm tenderness pervades the whole hymn—a note
which is absent from many of his sacred poems and which
is lacking, too, in much of the sacred poetry of the seventeenth century. Milton's "Ode" has dignity and sincerity,
nor does it lack touches of a gentler grace, too often lacking in his greater works. . . . (p. 64)

One feels, however, in reading Crashaw's **"Ode"** that it
has more sincerity—perhaps because it is more simple.
Milton's "majesties, his splendours, his august solemnities" keep his poetry out of our reach; "he could not forget, nor can we, that he was Milton." Speaking of this
hymn, Fr. Thompson says, "There is one note of
Crashaw—the human and lover-like tenderness which informs his sacred poem, differentiating them from the conventional style of English sacred poetry with its solemn
aloofness from celestial things. In the curled drops, etc.,
is shown the happiness of his diction." "It is truly ingenious and graceful, with its pretty, pastoral tenderness."

In the hymn on the Epiphany, on the other hand, notwithstanding the loftiness of the theme, Crashaw fails. One
might think that the visit of the Magi would have set
Crashaw's imagination on fire, but it did not. The poem
is full of dull "conceits," and it has nothing of the charm
or devotion of the Christmas hymn:—

To Thee, thou Day of Night! thou East of West!
Lo we at last have found the way
To Thee the world's great Universal East,
The general and indiff'rent Day.

The poem is turgid and, in composition, is too artificial.
Yet Courthope says that it has more of central idea and
organic unity than is usual in Crashaw. "The prophecy of
the Magi, who are represented as sunworshippers, of the
approaching eclipse of their deity by the Sun of Righteousness, is most musically elaborated in an antiphon full of
skilfully combined verbal harmonies."

Many of Crashaw's religious poems are paraphrases of the
old church hymns. They are very elaborate paraphrases,
and cannot compare with the simplicity and directness of
the Latin originals. Nevertheless, he never goes outside
the particular subject he is dealing with, and notwithstanding their flamboyancy, many of them have been admired, especially the **"Dies Irae"** and the **"Lauda Sion,
Salvatorem."**

The opening verses of the **"Dies Irae,"** the hymn of the
Church in meditation for the day of judgment, are perhaps
the best of the whole poem:—

> Hears't thou, my soul, what serious things
> Both the psalm and Sybil sings
> Of a sure Judge, from whose sharp ray
> The world in flames shall fly away.
>
> O that fire! before whose face
> Heaven and Earth shall find no place
> O those eyes! whose angry light
> Must be the day of that dread night.

The last verse of the translation partakes somewhat of the plaintiveness of the original, though notwithstanding its "many beauties and fine touches," the whole poem "fails to represent the masculine strength of the Latin":—

> O hear a supplicant heart, all crushed
> And crumpled into contrite dust,
> My hope, my fear, my Judge, my Friend,
> Take charge of me, and of my end.

"What he did in his own natural way is best," writes Pope, and among the best pieces of the author, he mentions, "the paraphrase of **'Psalm Twenty-three,'** the epigram on **'Mr. Ashton,' 'Wishes,'** and the **'Dies Irae.'**"

The **"Lauda Sion,"** in praise of the Blessed Sacrament, is a passionate plea for Christ to come and take possession of his heart and soul. . . .

"Crashaw, one must admit," writes A. Q. Couch, "is often terribly at his ease in Sion—and if one must contrast him with Herbert, often so gently familiar too with God, the difference is that Herbert had, with modesty, a breeding that made him at home with any company." But, one is inclined to ask, why should he not be at his ease in Sion? Is it not the privilege of the Mystic to speak in familiar terms with the One Person he really loves, and by Whom he knows he is loved in return?

> Jesu, Master, just and true!
> Our food and faithful shepherd too!
> O by Thyself vouchsafe to keep,
> As with Thyself Thou feed'st Thy sheep.

Although it is steeped in mediaeval scholasticism, he has succeeded in breathing poetry into it, while at the same time, keeping closer to the original than he did in the other paraphrases:—

> Lo, the Bread of Life, this day's
>
> Triumphant text, provokes thy praise;
> The living and life-giving bread,
> To the great twelve distributed;
> When Life, Himself at point to die
> Of Love, was His own legacy.

But the most elaborate of all Crashaw's paraphrases is **"The Office of the Holy Crosse."** We may form a good idea of Crashaw's method of procedure by comparing one stanza of this with the stanza in the original. The hymn in the "Office for the Third Hour" runs:—

> Crucifige clamitant hora tertiarum:
> Illusus induitur veste purpurarum;
> Caput ejus pungitur corona spinarum;
> Crucem portat humeris ad locum paenarum.

Crashaw renders it thus:—

> The third hour's deafened with the cry

> Of Crucify Him, crucify,
> So goes the vote (nor ask them why!)
> Live Barabas, and let God die!
>
> But there is wit in wrath, and they will try
> A "Hail" more cruel than their "Crucify."
> For while in sport He wears a spiteful crown
> The serious showers along His decent Face run
>   down.

One of the psalms translated by Crashaw deserves particular mention, and may be taken as an example of Crashaw's insight into the meaning of a particular phrase. Anyone familiar with Crashaw's greater poems could not fail to detect the touch of his hand in the following translation of "He leadeth me in the paths of righteousness":—

> He expounds the weary wonder
> Of my giddy steps, and under
> Spreads a path, clear as the day
> Where no churlish rub says nay
> To my Joy-conducted feet,
> Whilst they gladly go to meet
> Grace and peace to learn new lays
> Turn'd to my great Shepherd's praise

These translations, though they have great merit, have not, nevertheless, the particular merit of the originals. Even **"Vexilla Regis"** cannot escape his favourite phrase, a "full nest of loves." His warm, sensuous imagination kindles with his subject, and he passes only too easily into a "sweet inebriated ecstasy."

The longest of all Crashaw's translations is the **"Sospetto d'Herode," "The Suspicion of Herod."** It consists of sixty-six stanzas, with Crashaw's usual licence, and is a translation from Marino's "Strage degli Innocenti." Crashaw was influenced to a great degree by the "conceits" of Marino, and perhaps this influence is nowhere so much in evidence as in **"The Suspicion of Herod."** The stanza, with its triple rhyme, is very well managed. Many of its passages recall the lofty dignity of the style of Milton who, very probably, profited by its perusal. Courthope, however, regards Crashaw as being so much inferior to Milton, that the latter could learn nothing from his work. He feels that Crashaw, of himself, is able to do very little. "In these (i.e., **'Music's Duel,' 'Suspicion of Herod,' 'St. Teresa'** and **'The Flaming Heart'**) and, indeed, in most of Crashaw's poems, the inspiring motive comes from the thought of others, rather than from his own. And the cause of this phenomenon is not difficult to understand. Poetry was not to Crashaw what it was to Herbert, a vehicle of metaphysical thought, enabling him to mount by an intellectual process into the presence of God, and therefore under the control of judgment and reason; it was a musical instrument which gave forth its notes like an Aeolian harp, at the breath of each mystical emotion. His artistic temperament, combined much of the genius of the musician and the painter, and his imagination was swayed more through his senses than through his intellect. Hence his methods of composition were more proper to painting and music than to poetry. What he admired in the work of other poets was richness of descriptive detail, and nothing is more noticeable in his own than the number of images it contains, raising associations of sight, sound and even smell. For example, he was evidently attracted to

Marino's 'Strage degli Innocenti,' for the sake, not of the action, in which the poem is very deficient, but of the vividness of the descriptions. Marino, like all poets of the second class, seeks to produce a feeling of the sublime by piling up images, and Crashaw endeavours to surpass his master."

In the following description of Satan in Hell the words in italics are additions to the conceptions of the Italian poet:—

> His eyes, the *sullen dens* of Death and Night
> Startle the *dull air* with a *dismal* red;
> Such his fell glances as the fatal light
> Of staring comets, that look Kingdoms dead.
> From his *black nostrils* and *blue lips* in *spite*
> Of *Hell's own stink, a worser stench is spread.*
> His breath Hell's lightning, is; and each deep groan
> Disdains to think that Heaven thunders alone.
>
> His flaming eyes' dire exhalation
> Unto a dreadful pile gives fiery breath;
> Whose unconsumed consumption preys upon
> The never-dying life of a long death.
> In this sad house of slow destruction
> *(His shop of flames) he fries himself beneath
> A mass of woes*; his teeth for torment gnash,
> While his steel sides sounds with his tail's strong lash.

"In the minds of those who have familiarised themselves with great poetry," writes Courthope, "this materialistic imagery, whether in Marino or Crashaw, produces not horror, but disgust, and the justice of Pope's criticism can be verified by anyone who chooses to compare with the above description the consummate art which Milton in *Paradise Lost* contrives by means of simile and comparison to suggest rather than to describe the colossal stature of Satan. It is needless to say that such an organic distribution of imagery is beyond the reach of poets like Marino and Crashaw."

Such a criticism of Crashaw is, perhaps, too general and sweeping. The passage which Courthope quotes may be inferior to Milton's, but yet, who can fail to see the resemblance in dignity of style between Milton and Crashaw in the following, from the speech of Satan in the same poem:—

> He has my heaven (what would He more?) whose bright
> And radiant sceptre this bold hand should bear;
> And for the never-fading fields of light,
> My fair inheritance, he confines me here
> To this dark house of shades, horror and night,
> To draw a long-lived death, where all my cheer
> Is the solemnity my sorrow wears
> That mankind's torments waits upon my tears.

Beeching thinks that Milton learned a good deal from Crashaw. Speaking of his poem, he says, "As a piece of writing, it is excellent, the stanza with its triple rhyme is well managed, and there are not a few passages which recall Milton who had undoubtedly profited by its perusal."

Hazlitt, on the other hand, treats with contempt the suggestion that Milton could learn anything from Crashaw.

Milton's description of Satan is so much superior to Crashaw's that it is impossible that the one could be modelled on the other. As an example of Crashaw's descriptive powers, he takes the following two stanzas:—

> Below the bottom of the great Abyss
> There where one centre reconciles all things,
> The world's profound heart pants; there placed is
> Mischief 's old Master; close above him clings
> A curled knot of embracing snakes, that kiss
> His correspondent cheeks; these loathsome strings
> Hold the perverse prince in eternalties
> Fast bound, since first he forfeited the skies.
>
> The judge of torments, and the king of tears,
> He fills a burnished throne of quenchless fire;
> And for his old fair robes of light he wears
> A gloomy mantle of dark flames; the tire
> That crowns his head on high appears;
> Where seven tall horns (his empire's pride) aspire;
> And to make up Hell's Majesty each horn
> Seven crested Hydras horribly adorn.

"This portrait of monkish superstition," writes Hazlitt, "does not equal the grandeur of Milton's description. His form:—

> Had not yet lost
> All her original brightness, nor appeared
> Less the Archangel ruin'd, and the excess
> Of glory obscured.

Milton had got rid of the horns and tails, the vulgar and the physical insignia of the Devil, and clothed him with great and intellectual terrors, reconciling beauty and sublimity, and converting the grotesque and deformed into the ideal and the classical. Milton's mind rose superior to all others in this respect, on the outstretched wings of philosophic contemplation."

Nobody is likely to dispute the fact that Milton's Satan has more "intellectual terror" than Crashaw's, and while all critics agree that Milton's description is the better, they do not fail, as Hazlitt does, to see the resemblance. Hazlitt, whom somebody calls "an untrustworthy critic" even misses the sweetness of Crashaw's best verses, for he writes without any qualification, "Crashaw was a hectic enthusiast in religion and poetry, and was erroneous in both."

Marred as it is by the grotesque images of stanzas nineteen and twenty-one, **"The Weeper"** remains alike in its exuberance of expression and in its delicacy of spiritual aspiration, the most typical poem ever Crashaw wrote. "Amid stanzas of the most frigid conceits," says Francis Thompson, "are others of the loveliest art in conception and expression." The Weeper is St. Mary Magdalene:—

> "Her wounded heart and bleeding eyes conspire—
> Is she a flaming fountain, or a weeping fire?"

The theme, seemingly a narrow one, is enriched by inexhaustible imagination and fancy. The poem consists of thirty-three stanzas, each of six lines, and notwithstanding its beauty it has been said that **"The Weeper"** was probably the poem Pope had particularly in mind when criticising Crashaw. "No metrical composition," writes Courthope, "in the English language contains so much imagery and so little thought." Its professed subject is the tears of the Magdalene. The poet's intention was to exhibit this subject in a different light in each stanza. The underlying idea is that the tears of the Magdalene, which are spoken of in Scripture, never ceased to flow, "and he ransacks heaven and earth to illustrate his idea by a string of hyperboles." He addresses the Saint's eyes thus:—

> Hail! sister springs!
> Parents of silver-footed rills!
> Ever bubbling things!
> Thawing crystals! snowy hills!
> Still spending! never spent!   I mean
> Thy fair eyes, sweet Magdalene!
>
> Heavens thy fair eyes be;
> Heavens of ever falling stars
> 'Tis seed-time still with thee;
> And stars thou saw'st whose harvest dares
> Promise the earth to countershine
> Whatever makes heaven's forehead fine.

These opening verses of **"The Weeper"** have been often severely criticised. Yet, the reader is inclined to forget how far-fetched the imagery is, while listening to the exquisite music of the verse. (pp. 64-74)

The poem, however, is spoiled by its ingenuities, which are often in bad taste and even ludicrous. Crashaw shows himself in this poem to be lacking in self-criticism, and had he a little more of it, he might have saved himself from the "metaphysical vagaries then in fashion." Comparing the tears of the Magdalene to the milky way (which comparison serves as an introduction to the exquisite verses quoted above) he writes:—

> But we are deceivèd all;
> Stars indeed they are too true;
> For they but seem to fall,
> As Heaven's other spangles do;
> It is not for our Earth and us,
> To shine in things so precious.
>
> Upwards thou dost weep,
> Heaven's bosom drinks the gentle stream,
> Where the Milky rivers creep,
> Thine floats above and is the cream
> Waters above the Heavens, what they be
> We are taught best by thy tears and thee.
>
> Every morn from hence,
> A brisk cherub something sips,
> Whose sacred influence
> Adds sweetness to his sweetest lips;
> Then to his music, and his song
> Tastes of this breakfast all day long.

"We are indignant and disgusted at these frigid ardours." Proceeding with his idea of the stellification of the tears, he says:—

> Yet let the poor drops weep
> (Weeping is the ease of Woe);
> Softly let them creep,
> Sad that they are vanquished so.

> They, though to others no relief,
> Balsam may be for their own grief.
>
> Such the maiden gem
> By the purpling vine put on,
> Peeps from her patient stem
> And blushes at the bridegroom sun.
> This watery blossom of thy eyne,
> Ripe, will make the richer wine.
>
> When some new bright gust
> Takes up among the stars a room,
> And Heaven will make a feast;
> Angels with crystal phials come
> And draw from these full eyes of thine
> Their Master's water, their own wine.

"In anyone but Crashaw," says Courthope, speaking of the last stanza, "we might suspect an intention of humour in such imagery. But that the suspicion in his case would be entirely groundless is proved by the imagery of his "**Answer**" to Cowley's lines on "Hope":

> Thy golden growing head never hangs down
> Till in the lap of Love's full noon
> It falls and dies!   Oho!   It melts away,
> As doth the down upon the day;
> *As lumps of sugar lose themselves and twine*
> *Their subtle essence with the soul of wine.*

Whenever Crashaw gives offence in **"The Weeper,"** it is invariably of the gaudy colouring of these "outrageous conceits," or by "straining an idea which has been squeezed dry." In **"The Weeper,"** more than in any other poem, this lack of sureness of touch is evident. "His defective power of self-criticism," writes Beeching, "makes him one of the most unequal of our poets"—and it has been proved that most of the verses which offend are additions to the original version.

Gosse, while frankly admitting that he is at variance with almost all Crashaw's critics, on the merits of **"The Weeper"** gives a scathing criticism of the poem. The extract deserves quoting in full; it is another proof of how impossible it is, even for the great literary critics, to arrive at a definite idea of Crashaw's work as a poet.

"In criticising with severity the piece on Mary Magdalene, which stands on the forefront of Crashaw's work, and bears the title **'The Weeper,'** I have the misfortune to find myself at variance with most of his admirers. I cannot, however, avoid the conviction that the obtrusion of this eccentric piece on the threshold of his shrine, has driven from it many a would-be worshipper. If language is ever liable to abuse in the hands of a clever poet, it is surely outraged here. Every extravagant and inappropriate image is dragged to do service to this small idea, that the Magdalene is for ever weeping. Her eyes, therefore, are 'Sister springs,' 'parents of rills,' 'thawing crystals,' "hills of snow,' 'heavens of ever-filling stars,' 'eternal breakfasts for brisk cherubs,' 'nests of milky doves,' 'a voluntary mint of silver,' and Heaven knows how many more incongruous objects, from one to another of which the labouring fancy flits in despair and bewilderment. In this poem all is resigned to ingenuity. We are not moved or softened; we are merely startled, and the irritated reader is at last appeased for the fatigues he has endured, by a frank guffaw, when he sees the poet, at his wits' end for a simile, plunge into the abyss of absurdity and style the eyes of the Magdalene:—

> Two walking baths, two weeping motions
> Portable and compendious oceans.

These are the worst lines in Crashaw. They are, perhaps, the worst in all English poetry. These pieces of Crashaw are founded upon what Arnold called "an incurable defect of style!"

It must be admitted that **"The Weeper,"** placed as it is in most editions at the beginning of ***Steps to the Temple***, has proved a stumbling-block to many would-be worshippers. Gosse finds it "distressing" and "humiliating"; to him it is merely a "string of preposterous conceits." Yet these "preposterous conceits" are evident in only nine stanzas, and if these are excised, "there remains a poem, which, if its topic be once allowed—a rosary of devotion to St. Mary Magdalene—should give nothing but delight to the lover of poetry." First, however, it is required that the reader should not be out of sympathy with the subject. If he starts with the idea that the theme is trifling and "very small" he is likely to be more and more provoked as the poem draws out in length. "It is the first duty of a critic," says Beeching, "to renounce prejudice, and one would imagine that in reading the works of a Catholic poet for aesthetic purposes it might be pardonable to abate something from the rigour of Protestantism." Surely it is not difficult to find music in such poetry as this:—

> There's no need at all
> That the balsam-sweating bough
> So coyly should let fall
> Her med'cinable tears; for now
> Nature hath learned to extract a dew
> More sovereign and more sweet from you.
>
> Golden though he be,
> Golden Tagus murmurs though;
> Were his way by thee,
> Content and quiet he would go,
> So much more rich would he esteem
> Thy silver than his golden stream.
>
> Well does the May, that lies,
> Smiling in thy cheeks confess
> The April in thine eyes;
> Mutual sweetness they express.
> No April e'er lent kindliest showers
> Nor May returned more faithful flowers.
>
> Not, "so long she lived"
> Shall thy tomb report of thee
> But, "so long she grieved";
> Thus must we date thy memory.
> Others by moments, months and years
> Measure their ages; thou by tears.

Although some of the comparisons are not exactly those which would be made in ordinary conversation, yet, with the exception of the nine verses of "preposterous conceits," none of the similes are altogether inapt. It seems strange, however, that such musical, if sometimes "startling" imagery should be followed by such a prosaic, even ludicrous, conceit as this:—

> So do perfumes expire
> So sigh tormented sweets, opprest
> With proud unpitying fire,
> Such tears the suffering rose, that's vext
> With ungentle flames, does shed
> Sweating in a too-warm bed.

He continues, evidently unconscious of the outrageous conceits:—

> Whether away so fast?
> For sure the sordid earth
> Your sweetness cannot taste,
> Nor does the dust deserve your birth.
> Sweet, whither haste you then?   O say
> Why you trip so fast away?

As she sighs at prayer:—

> Still at each sigh, that is, each stop
> A bead, that is, a tear, does drop.

The poem ends with a verse which, perhaps, makes amends for the conceits which introduce it:—

> We go not to seek
> The darlings of Aurora's bed,
> The rose's modest cheek,
> Nor the violet's humble head.—
> Though the field's eyes two Weepers be,
> Because they want such tears as we.
>   We go to meet
> A worthy object, Our Lord's feet.

Ernest Rhys thinks that the "painted stucco" of the Weeper pales before the glory of Vaughan's Mary Magdalene—a "melody which evades analysis." (pp. 75-80)

It may be readily admitted that the opening of most of Vaughan's verses are delightful, but generally they flag at the end. Only sometimes does he attain to the starry "chrystaline" perfection at which he aimed. One must "add to Vaughan's note of adoring and deploring innocence, wondering at its own fall, a something of personal passion, and an accent intensive, and even dramatic," before an idea of the temper of Crashaw—so evident in all his work—can be obtained.

The stanzas of **"The Weeper"** are admirably fashioned. The thought in each is complete in itself, though there is very little consecutive thought. Intoxicated by the flow of words, he loses all sense of proportion, and occasionally even the organisation of his metrical harmonies is bewildering. Each stanza opens with a short line, probably meant to give a trochaic effect, emphasising each new beginning, and concludes with a couplet which emphasises the close. "The only other poem in English that for a similar contemplative effect can be compared with it, is Rossetti's 'Staff and Scrip,' but in that case the separate roundness of each stanza is not so completely an advantage, as the poem tells a continuous tale. It will be observed how much variety of rhythm Crashaw obtains within each stanza, without violating the metre, by merely shifting the pause."

Although Pope's criticism of Crashaw is generally too severe, he relaxes a little when treating of **"The Weeper."**

"His thoughts, one may observe, are in the main pretty,

but oftentimes far-fetched, and too often strained and stiffened to make them appear the greater. For men are never so apt to think a thing great as when it is odd or wonderful, and inconsiderable authors would rather be admired than understood. This ambition of surprising the reader is the true natural cause of all bombast in poetry. To confirm what I have said, you need but look into his first poem of **"The Weeper,"** where the second, fourth, sixth, fourteenth and twenty-first stanzas are as sublimely dull as the seventh, eighth, ninth, sixteenth, seventeenth, twentieth, and twenty-third stanzas of the same copy are soft and pleasing; and if these last want anything, it is an easier and more unaffected expression. The remaining thoughts of that poem might have been spared, being either repetitions or very trivial and mean. And by this example in the first, one may guess all the rest to be like this—a mixture of tender, gentle thoughts, and suitable expressions, of forced and inexpressible conceits, of needless fillers-up to the rest. From all of which it is plain that this author writ fast, and set down what came uppermost. A reader may skim off the froth, and use the clear underneath, but if he goes too deep, will meet with a mouthful of dregs."

In view of all Pope has learned from Crashaw, this criticism is not a very generous one, and though it be admitted, with Warton, that his borrowings are "much heightened and improved," there are occasions when Crashaw, as a poet, is on a much higher level than Pope. Yet his analysis of **"The Weeper"** is fairly accurate, but one would be inclined to think that the following stanza which Pope mentions in his analysis, is something more than merely "soft and pleasing":—

> Does the day-star rise?
> Still thy tears do fall and fall.
> Does Day close his eyes?
> Still the fountain weeps for all.
> Let Night or Day do what they will,
> Thou hast thy task; thou weepest still.

Notwithstanding the many fine qualities of his poetry, the fact remains that Crashaw never succeeded in winning the popular ear. This fact is inexplicable, unless the mystical qualities of his work are taken into account. "That such poetry as this (Crashaw's) should have been ignored by a long succession of English critics and anthologists shows how little chance the mystic singer, chant he never so wisely and sweetly, has in finding recognition in a world devoted to tangibilities. And the genuine Catholic mystic, needless to say, must now and then count on being handicapped by his creed. But it was a peculiarly hard fortune for Crashaw that his merits should be minimised by a compeer like Thompson—a brother in faith, mysticism and poetry."

In his "Essay on Shelley," Thompson calls Crashaw "a Shelley *manquê*." In order to understand the full significance of Thompson's criticism of Crashaw, it is necessary to know exactly Thompson's idea of Shelley as a poet, for in this "bewitching Essay" he may be said to have done justice to all poets besides Shelley; scarcely even Homer or Shakespeare had any such rainbow shower of brilliant appreciations poured upon him.

"Coming to Shelley's poetry," he writes, "we peep over the wild mask of revolutionary metaphysics, and we see the winsome face of a child. Perhaps none of his poems is more purely Shellian than 'The Cloud,' and it is interesting to note how essentially it springs from the faculty of make-believe. . . . The Universe is his box of toys. He dabbles his finger in the day-fall. He is gold-dusty from tumbling amongst the stars. He dances in and out of the gates of Heaven—this "creature of ebullient heart."

For astounding figurative wealth, he yields only to Shakespeare, and not even to Shakespeare in absolute fecundity, but in range of figures. Suspended in the dripping well of his imagination, the commonest objects become encrusted with imagery—Imagery was to him not a mere means of expression, not even a means of adornment; it was a delight, for its own sake." It is in this delight in imagery for its own sake that Thompson sees the likeness between the two poets. "Herein," he continues, "we find the trail by which we would classify him. He belongs to a school of which, not impossibly, he may hardly have read a line— the metaphysical school. To a large extent he is what the metaphysical school should have been. That school was a certain kind of poetry trying for a range. Shelley is the range found. Crashaw and Shelley sprang from the same seed; but in the one case the seed was choked with thorns, in the other case it fell on good ground. The metaphysical school was in its direct results an abortive movement though, indirectly, much came of it.

"Crashaw was a Shelley *manquê*; he never reached the promised land, but he had fervid visions of it. The metaphysical school, like Shelley, loved imagery for its own sake." This criticism of the "beautiful and ineffectual angel beating in the void his luminous wings in vain," is indeed the criticism of one who writes with a "quill plucked from the eagle's wing." But if the "Essay" is a tribute to Shelley, and if it dazzles us into forgetting our points against Shelley, at the same time it does formal injustice to Richard Crashaw. This love of imagery is only evil—"when the poets, on the straight way to a fixed object, lags continually from the path to play. The metaphysical school failed, not because it toyed with imagery, but because it toyed with it frostily." It is scarcely ever sound criticism to blame a poet for not being more like some other poet, and in the present instance, it seems an error to think that Crashaw had any business to be like Shelley. In many particulars he is quite different—yet he is not different in the way Thompson suggests, by being "cold," "frosty," and "artificial." "You may toy with imagery," he says, "in mere intellectual ingenuity, and then you might as well go into acrostics; or you may toy with it in raptures, and then you may write a 'Sensitive Plant.' " Thompson here seems to exaggerate the import of what Crashaw, in his worst moments, had in common with Donne, Herbert and Cowley. "In fact," Thompson continues, "the metaphysical poets, when they went astray, cannot be said to have done anything so dainty as is implied of 'toying' with imagery. They cut it into shapes with a pair of scissors."

There is another point in which Thompson says the "bubbling genius" of Shelley touches the metaphysical school. It is the power to "give to airy nothing a local habitation and a name." The metaphysical poets were habitually pursuing abstractions and "they failed in that pursuit from the one cause omnipresent with them, because in all their poetic smithy they had left never a place for a forge. They laid their fancies chill on the anvil. Crashaw partially anticipated Shelley's success—and Crashaw, Collins and Shelley were three ricochets of the one pebble, three jets from three bounds of the one Pegasus."

To speak of "cold," or "frost," or laboured artificiality in connection with the intense and glowing **"Hymn to St. Teresa,"** the sublime **"Hymn on the Holy Name,"** the playfully-earnest and loving **"Hymn on the Nativity,"** or the splendid outburst at the close of the **"Flaming Heart,"** is simply to recall certain superficialities while closing one's heart and eyes to essentials.

Crashaw's poetry had, of course, its failings—failings which are, perhaps, made too much of by critics. The fact that he was a mystic appears a failing only to those who cannot understand what true mysticism is. For them, "the Urania of the Mystic haunts the icy and untrodden splendours of Himalayan summits. She eludes their gaze amid remote clouds, or in loftiest ether," and perhaps even the greatest lovers of mystic poetry would be more pleased with Crashaw's work, if it "maintained a little more friendly relation with the valleys." But it must be remembered that if we are unable to follow Crashaw's "soaring discants," the fault lies, not with Crashaw, but with ourselves. Yet, with the Tennysonian shepherd, we might wish that poetry should generally "haunt the lower atmospheres of colour and music":—

> Come down, O Maid, from yonder mountain
>   height
> What pleasure lives in height (the Shepherd
>   sang)
> In height and cold, and splendour of the hills?
> But come, for love is of the valley, come
> And find him; by the happy threshold, he,
> Or hand in hand with plenty in the maize
> Or foxlike in the vine; nor cares to walk
> With Death and Morning on the silver horns.

Poetry should be familiar with the heights. Yet it is her function to be their "perpetual intermediary and interpreter to the valleys." In this Crashaw fails, or, at least, never obtains perfect success. In his greatest work he is often too abstract, subtle and contemplative.

Of Crashaw's chief weakness—the most obvious and the most often complained of—his "metaphysical" subtleties and conceits, perhaps too much has been made. These conceits were the fashion of the time. It was the Metaphysical Age for England and for Europe, and it is scarcely fair to judge him by modern canons. At the same time the defects in his poetry are so obvious that one wonders how it was he could not see them himself. Crashaw did not seem born for these "fashionable extravagances," and yet he falls into them more frequently and more unhappily than almost any of his contemporaries. According to Milton, sublime poetry should be "simple, sensuous, passionate." Crashaw evidently does not achieve great success under this canon. "He knows and feels but he does not interpret and conciliate." It was perhaps this sense of the

lack of sensuous charm in his poetry that made him fall into these extravagances. He felt its "desperate remoteness, the impalpably spiritual character of its inspiration, and he clutched at popularity by the most obvious way. He would be as subtly fantastic and quaintly ingenious as the best of them—as Donne, or Cowley, or the gentle euphuist, George Herbert, and the result is that he gives us the oddest contrasts and jumbles. The delicate and devout poet who writes us perfectly lovely verses on the penitent sorrows of the Magdalene, tells us in the very next stanza that her eyes are

> Two walking baths, two weeping motions,
> Portable and compendious oceans.

A little later he describes her tears as " 'cream,' bottled up daily to supply breakfasts for the Cherubim." Even the beautiful **"Poem On the Assumption of Our Lady"** contains the "wretched pedantic pun" that "no Assumption shall deny us!" It appears all the more pedantic because of the delicate setting in which it is placed:—

> Hail! she is call'd, the parting hour is come;
> Take thy farewell, poor world, Heaven must go
>   home.
> A piece of Heavenly Earth, purer and brighter
> Than the chaste stars whose choice lamps come
>   to light her
> While through the crystal orbs clearer than they
> She climbs and makes a far more Milky Way.
> She's call'd! Hark, how the dear immortal
>   Dove
> Sighs to his silver mate: "Rise up, my love!"
> Rise up, my fair, my spotless one!
> The winter's past, the rain is gone:
> The Spring is come, the flowers appear,
> No sweets but thou, are wanting here.
>   Come away, my love!
>   Come away, my dove!
>   Cast off delay;
> The court of Heaven is come
> To wait upon thee home
>   Come, come away.

In the midst of such delicate poetry as this the "pedantic pun" appears, and Crashaw is evidently unconscious of how much out of tone it is with its delicate surroundings. It is impossible to understand how a man with such delicate and refined taste and such a musical ear as Crashaw possessed could not immediately detect the want of harmony when a false note was struck. It has been said that Crashaw's age was an age of very wavering aesthetic principles—that it was even an age of bad taste. It would then, it is urged, be too much to expect from Crashaw, to soar above the bad taste of his time. Perhaps the best explanation is that given by O'Neill, though even that explanation is very weak. "By such eccentric and tasteless conjuring with ideas and words did this naturally elevated, refined and intense poet seek to win the crowd of his day, seeing that he possessed no other bait to draw them to his feet." Crashaw was not qualified to make this popular appeal, either by pathos, or fury, and sentimentality. A mystic, "dwelling habitually in rarefied and impalpable soul regions," notwithstanding his "nimble and alert fancy," was not likely to win the favour of the multitude by these "extraordinary acrobatics in thought, imagery, and style."

The faults in Crashaw's sacred poetry are much more apparent than those of his secular poems, because they occur in a finer setting. His failures "are peculiarly exasperating, because they spoil work which had greater potentialities than that of many other poets who had maintained a higher level. There are inspired moments when he outdistances all his rivals." Yet immediately after one of those "inspired moments" he could compare—what Herbert with all the familiarity which he imparted to the metaphysical style, would scarcely have ventured to have done—the blood and water flowing from the Saviour's side to the casks of Massic and Falernian wine celebrated by Horace. (pp. 81-9)

> *Rev. Thomas Foy, in his* Richard Crashaw, *"Poet and Saint," 1933. Reprint by Folcroft Library Editions, 1971, pp. 50-89.*

Austin Warren (essay date 1939)

[*Warren was an English scholar and authority on Crashaw's poetry. In the following excerpt from a work originally published in 1939, Warren examines Crashaw's symbolism, contending that his religious faith*

Plate used in an early edition of Crashaw's "In the Holy Nativity of Our Lord God. A Hymn Sung as by the Shepherds."

contributed to its "phantasmagorical" and "miraculous" imagery.]

Crashaw, sensuous of temperament, wrote a poetry mellifluously musical, lavishly imagistic. At first acquaintance it seems the song of the nightingale hovering over her skill, "bathing in streams of liquid melody"; later, it seems the passage work, the cadenzas, the glissandi of an endowed and much-schooled virtuoso. Yet his life shows him to have been an ascetic, denying his senses all save their homage to God. In turning to religion and religious poetry, he "changed his object not his passion," as St. Augustine said of the Magdalen: the images of his secular poetry recur in his sacred. He loves his God as he might have loved his "supposed mistress."

Not a preacher or prophet, Crashaw had no "message" to announce. He had suffered and exulted, and exulted in suffering; but his experiences did not tempt him to philosophy or other prose formulation. His was to be a poetry in which the rhythms and images would tell their own tale.

To his symbolism he supplied no chart of prose equivalents. Yet no reader has long studied his poems without feeling that their imagery is more than pageant; that, rather, it is a vocabulary of recurrent motifs.

Nor is this symbolism really undecipherable. In the main it follows traditional Christian lines, drawing on the Bible, ecclesiastical lore, and the books of such mystics as St. Bernard and St. Teresa. Even when it is "private"—as, in some measure, every poet's will be—it yields to persistent and correlating study. Not widely ranging, Crashaw's images reappear in similar contexts, one event elucidating another. No casual reader of his poems, for example, but has been arrested by the recurrence of "nest," usually in rhyming union with "breast"; and, surely, no constant reader has long doubted its psychological import, its equivalence to shelter, refuge, succor.

It need not be maintained—it is, indeed, incredible—that Crashaw constructed a systematic symbolism. It is unlikely, even, that he knew why certain images possessed, for him, particular potence. Obviously much concerned with his technique, given to revision, a lover of the arts, he seems, as a man, ingenuous, free from self-consciousness, imaginatively uncensored.

In his steady movement from secular poetry to an exclusive pre-occupation with sacred, from Latin to the vernacular, he relinquished—deliberately, it would seem—the Renaissance decoration of classical mythology. As a schoolboy he had written hymns to Venus, poems on Pygmalion, Arion, Apollo and Daphne, Aeneas and Anchises; and in his Latin epigrams, and in **"Music's Duel,"** there occur classical embellishments. From the English sacred poems, however, such apparatus is conspicuously absent. Giles Fletcher, of his English predecessors closest to him in temper and idiom, had compared the ascending Christ to Ganymede, snatched up from earth to attend upon Jupiter; but no such bold correlation of pagan and Christian finds place in Crashaw's poetry. Donne and Herbert, also erudites, had made a similar surrender of their classicism; and to Herbert's example in particular he may have been indebted.

Otherwise, Crashaw makes no attempt to differentiate his sacred from his secular imagery; many characteristic figures and metaphors, "delights of the Muses," are renlisted in the service of Urania. For example, the familiar paradox of the Incarnation, whereby Jesus is at once the son and the father of the Blessed Virgin, is anticipated in the apostrophe to Aeneas carrying Anchises: "Felix! *parentis* qui *pater* diceris esse tui!" The persistent motif of the mystical poems first appears in **"Wishes"**:

> A well tam'd heart
> For whose more noble smart
> Love may bee long chusing a Dart.

Unlike Herbert, Crashaw rarely recollects homely images of market place and fireside; and allusions to the polities and economies of the Stuart world come but seldom. Christ, dying, is called "his own legacy." With the Blessed Virgin, Crashaw, who, too, has set "so deep a share" in Christ's wounds, would draw some "dividend." To these financial metaphors, one may add what at first view seems Herbertian—the angels with their bottles, and the breakfast of the brisk cherub. Yet, though "breakfast" Herbert would surely not have disdained, such intimacy with the habits of cherubs is peculiarly alien to the Anglican spirit of *The Temple*. It is Mary's tears which, having wept upwards, become, at the top of the milky river, the cream upon which the infant angel is fed, adding "sweetnesse to his sweetest lips"; and this context, by its extravagant lusciousness, reduces the blunt word to but a passing grotesquerie.

Some feeling for Nature, especially the dawn and flowers, the young Crashaw undoubtedly had; but even the early poems evince no botanical niceness, no precision of scrutiny. The first of the Herrys poems develops a single metaphor, that of a tree whose blossoms, ravished by a mad wind, never deliver their promised fruit; but unlike Herbert's "orange tree," this is a tree of no specific genus. Crashaw's habitual blossoms are the conventional lily and rose.

These flowers, which appear briefly, in his earliest poems, as outward and visible creatures, do not disappear from his later verse; but they soon turn into a ceremonial and symbolical pair, a liturgical formula, expressive of white and red, tears and blood, purity and love. Already in the panegyric on the Duke of York, lines which begin with a delicate naturalism, end with a reduction to liturgical red and white, in a prefiguration of Crashaw's final style.

> So have I seene (to dresse their Mistresse *May*)
> Two silken sister flowers consult, and lay
> Their bashfull cheekes together, newly they
> Peep't from their buds, shew'd like the Gardens eyes
> Scarce wakt: like was the Crimson of their joyes,
> Like were the Pearles they wept. . . .

In the "Bulla," or "Bubble," the flowers have become antithetic colors in shifting transmutations.

If Crashaw's *flora* soon turn symbols, his *fauna* have never owed genuine allegiance to the world of Nature. The worm; the wolf, the lamb; the fly, the bee; the dove, the eagle, the "self-wounding pelican," and the phoenix: all derive their traits and their significance from bestiary or Christian tradition, not from observation; and their symbolism is palpable. In their baseness men are "all idolizing worms"; in their earthly transience and fickleness and vanity, foolish wanton flies. The bee, a paragon of industry, is still more a creator, preserver, or purveyor of mystic sweetness. The Holy Name of Jesus is adored by angels that throng

> Like diligent Bees, And swarm about it.
> O they are wise
> And know what *Sweetes* are suck't from out it.
> It is the Hive,
> By which they thrive,
> Where all their Hoard of Hony lyes.

The dove and lamb, of frequent appearance, betoken innocence and purity; they are also meet for votive offering. Sometimes the doves emblemize elect souls, whose eyes should be "Those of turtles, chaste, and true"; sometimes, the Holy Ghost. The *Agnus Dei*, the white lamb slain before the foundation of the world, was Crashaw's favorite symbol for Christ and for him, among all symbols, one of the most affecting.

"By all the Eagle in thee, all the dove": so Crashaw invokes the chaste Teresa, the mystic whose wings carried her high, whose spiritual vision was unflinching and acute.

> Sharpe-sighted as the Eagles eye, that can
> Out-stare the broad-beam'd Dayes Meridian.

Meditating her books, the responsive reader finds his heart "hatcht" into a nest "Of little Eagles, and young loves."

To the phoenix, Crashaw devoted a Latin poem, a **"Genethliacon et Epicedion,"** in which the paradox of a fecund death shows its expected fascination for him. The fragrant, unique, and deathless bird reappears in the Latin epigrams, and in the English poems, both secular and sacred. It occurs twice in the sequence of Herrys elegies; it is belabored at length in the panegyric to Henrietta Maria, **"Upon her Numerous Progenie,"** where it becomes a symbol of supreme worth. In the sacred poems, it assumes its traditional Christian office as sign of the God-man, virginborn, only-begotten, and immortal.

With most artists, the pleasures of sight are pre-eminent; with Crashaw, in spite of his interest in pictures and emblems, the fullerbodied and less sharply defined senses would appear to have afforded richer, more characteristic delight.

His colors are elementary, chiefly conventional, readily symbolic. In his religious poetry, but three occur: red (or purple ⊄ *purpureus*), with its traditional relation, through fire and the "Flaming Heart" to love; black; and white. Black is, for him, the sign not of mourning or penitence but of sin and, still more, of finiteness, of mortality: "Dust thou art, and to dust thou shalt return." In his translation of Catullus, men are "dark Sons of Sorrow." Augmented, the phrase reappears in **"The Name of Jesus"** as "dark Sons of Dust and Sorrow." Elsewhere in the religious poems, man is "Disdainful dust and ashes" or "Darke, dusty Man."

White, perhaps as the synthesis of all colors, perhaps as

the symbol of luminous purity, is the most exalting adjective in Crashaw's vocabulary. It occurs in his secular verse, especially in his panegyrics upon the royal family. But it is more frequent in his *carmina sacra*, used customarily of the Blessed Virgin or Christ, and most strikingly of Christ as the Lamb.

> Vain loves, avaunt! bold hands forbear!
> The Lamb hath dipp't his white foot here.
> **["Hymn to Saint Teresa"]**

The absence from the religious poetry of green, the color of nature, and blue—in the tradition of Christian art, the color of truth and of the Blessed Virgin—is conspicuous; so is the absence of chiaroscuro. By other means, he produces a sensuous luxuriance; but, in respect to the palette, he turns, like the Gospels, to bold antithesis of black and white.

For evidence that Crashaw was a lover of music, one need not appeal to **"Music's Duel."** **"On the Name of Jesus,"** among his four or five masterpieces, calls to celebration all sweet sounds of instrument—

> Be they such
> As sigh with supple wind
> Or answer Artfull Touch. . . .

These flutes, lutes, and harps are the "Soul's most certain wings," Heaven on Earth; indeed, in a moment of quasi-Platonic identification of reality with highest value he equates "All things that Are" with all that are musical. Assuredly, Crashaw intended his own poetry to be—what by virtue of his mastery of vowel and consonant sequences and alliteration it habitually is—sweet to the ear, Lydian. But, for him, it is also true, human music was an initiation into an archetypal music, the harmonious concert of the spheres "which dull mortality more feels than hears." The ears are "tumultous shops of noise" compared with those inner sensibilities which, properly disciplined, may hear, as from afar, the inexpressive nuptial hymn.

Crashaw's favorite adjectives, "sweet" and "delicious," mingle fragrance and taste. His holy odors are chiefly traditional—those of flowers and of spices. "Let my prayer be set forth in Thy sight as the incense," said the Psalmist; but the simile finds its analogy in the ascent of both. The fragrance of spices pervades that manual of the mystics, the *Song of Songs*. To the Infant Jesus, the magi brought frankincense and myrrh. The Magdalen dies as "perfumes expire." The Holy Name is invoked as a "cloud of condensed sweets," bidden to break upon us in balmy and "sense-filling" showers. In his ode on Prayer, the most mystical of his poems, Crashaw bids the lover of God, the virgin soul, to seize the Bridegroom

> All fresh and fragrant as he rises
> Dropping with a baulmy Showr
> A delicious dew of spices. . . .

Sometimes Crashaw's gustatory delights, like those of the

> sweet-lipp'd Angell-Imps, that swill their throats
> In creame of Morning Helicon . . .
> **["Music's Duel"]**

remain innocently physical. But customarily the pleasure of the palate, too, becomes symbolic, as it is when the Psalmist bids us "taste . . . how good the Lord is." The angels who swarm about the Holy Name are wise because they "know what Sweetes are suck't from out of it." This palatal imagery might be expected to culminate in apostrophes to the Blessed Sacrament; but not so. For Protestants, the Holy Communion is a symbolic as well as commemorative eating and drinking; to Crashaw, who believed in Transubstantiation, the miraculous feast seemed rather the denial of the senses than their symbolic employment. His expansive paraphrases of St. Thomas' Eucharistic hymns are notably sparse in sensuous imagery. It is not the Blood of Christ on the altar but the redeeming blood on the cross which prompts him to spiritual inebriation.

Crashaw's liquids are water (tears, penitence); milk (maternal succor, nutrition); blood (martyrdom on the part of the shedder, transference of vitality to the recipient); wine (religious inebriation, ecstasy). Fluid, they are constantly mixing in ways paradoxical or miraculous. In one of his earliest poems, a metrical version of Psalm 137, blood turns into water. In one of the latest, **"Sancta Maria,"** "Her eyes bleed Teares, his wounds weep Blood." From the side of Christ, crucified, flowed an "amorous flood of Water wedding Blood." The angels, preparing for a feast, come with crystal phials to draw from the eyes of the Magdalen "their master's Water: their own Wine." Milk and blood may mingle, as when maternal love induces self-sacrifice; water turns to wine when tears of penitence become the happy token of acceptance and union; wine is transubstantiated into blood in the Sacrament; blood becomes wine when, "drunk of the dear wounds," the apprehender of Christ's redeeming sacrifice loses control of his faculties in an intoxication of gratitude and love.

The last of the senses is at once the most sensuous and the least localized. To it belong the thermal sensations of heat and chill. Fire, the cause of heat, is, by traditional use, the symbol of love; its opposites are ordinarily lovelessness and—what is the same—death. The "flaming Heart" of Christ or of the Blessed Virgin is the heart afire with love. St. Teresa's ardor renders her insensitive to love's antonym and opposite, the chill of the grave. Crashaw is likely to unite the opposites. Since she is both Virgin and Mother, Mary's kisses may either heat or cool. Lying between her chaste breasts, the Infant Jesus sleeps in snow, yet warmly.

The supremities of touch, for Crashaw's imagination, are experienced in the mystical "wound of love," in martyrdom, and in nuptial union. In the former states, torment and pleasure mix: the pains are delicious; the joys, intolerable. In his mystical poems, Crashaw makes free use of figures drawn from courtship and marriage. Christ is the "Noble Bridegroom, the Spouse of Virgins." Worthy souls are those who bestow upon His hand their "heaped up, consecrated Kisses," who store up for Him their "wise embraces." The soul has its flirtations, its "amorous languishments," its "dear and divine annihilations." St. Teresa, love's victim, is sealed as Christ's bride by the "full Kingdom of that final Kiss"; and her mystic marriage has made her the mother of many disciples, many "virgin-births."

In the spirit of St. Ignatius' *Exercitia Spiritualia,* Crashaw performs an "Application of the Senses" upon all the sacred themes of his meditation. God transcends our images as He transcends our reason; but, argues the Counter-Reformation, transcension does not imply abrogation. Puritanism opposes the senses and the imagination to truth and holiness; for Catholicism, the former may be ministering angels. "How daring it is to picture the incorporeal," wrote Nilus Scholasticus in the *Greek Anthology;* "but yet the image leads us up to spiritual recollection of celestial beings." Not *iconoclasts,* some censors would grant that visual imagery, emanating from the "highest" of the senses, may point from the seen to the unseen; there they would halt. Crashaw, like one persistent school of mystics, would boldly appropriate the whole range of sensuous experience as symbolic of the inner life.

Studied case by case, Crashaw's striking imagery will yield its symbolic intent. But its most characteristic feature emerges only when image is collated with image. Poetic symbolism may constantly devise new alliances of sense and concept; indeed, the poet Emerson objected to Swedenborg's "Correspondences" on the precise ground of their fixed and systematic character. With Crashaw, though rigidity is never reached, his metaphors yet form a series of loosely defined analogies and antitheses and cross references, a system of motifs symbolically expressive of themes and emotions persistently his.

Associated images recur like ceremonial formulas. In the secular poems, the lily and the rose have appeared, singly and together. The association continues into the religious poems, but the metaphorical character of the flowers has become explicit. In the epigram on the Holy Innocents, the mother's milk and the children's blood turn, for Crashaw's pious fancy, into lilies and roses. A characteristic later juxtaposition, in the **"Hymn for the Circumcision,"** gives the metamorphosis: "this modest Maiden Lilly, our sinnes have sham'd into a Rose."

A similar ritual coupling is that of the pearl and the ruby. Sometimes these symbols appear singly, sometimes together. In the same **"Hymn for the Circumcision"** Crashaw sees Christ's drops of blood as rubies. The tears of the Magdalen are Sorrow's "richest Pearles." They are united in the eighteenth stanza of **"Wishes."** Still united, they reappear in the religious poetry: When men weep over the bloody wounds of Christ,

> The debt is paid in *Ruby*-teares,
> Which thou in Pearles did'st lend.
> **["On the Wounds of our Crucified Lord"]**

Another frequent union—and this not of contrasts but of contradictories—couples fire and water, an oxymoron of images. Already, in an early poem, the sun is represented as paying back to the sea in tears what, as fire, it borrowed. When the Magdalen washes Christ's feet with tears, wiping them with her hair,

> Her eyes flood lickes his feets faire staine,
> Her haires flame lickes up that againe.
> This flame thus quench't hath brighter beames:
> This flood thus stained fairer streames.

The Blessed Virgin is the "noblest nest Both of love's fires

and floods." The tears of contrition or of sorrow, so far from extinguishing the fire of love, make it burn more ardently.

But one cannot thus far have surveyed Crashaw's imagery without perceiving how the whole forms a vaguely defined but persistently felt series of inter-relations. There are things red—fire, blood, rubies, roses, wine—and things white—tears, lilies, pearls, diamonds: symbols of love and passion; symbols of contrition, purity, innocence.

On its sensuous surface, his imagination sparkles with constant metamorphosis: tears turn into soft and fluid things like milk, cream, wine, dew; into hard things like stars, pearls, and diamonds. Beneath, the same experiences engage poet and poem.

All things flow. Crashaw's imagery runs in streams; the streams run together; image turns into image. His metaphors are sometimes so rapidly juxtaposed as to mix—they occur, that is, in a succession so swift as to prevent the reader from focusing separately upon each. The effect is often that of phantasmagoria. For Crashaw, the world of the senses was evidently enticing; yet it was a world of appearances only—shifting, restless appearances. By temperament and conviction, he was a believer in the miraculous; and his aesthetic method may be interpreted as a genuine equivalent of his belief, as its translation into a rhetoric of metamorphosis. If, in the Gospels, water changes to wine and wine to blood, Crashaw was but imaginatively extending this principle when he turned tears into pearls, pearls into lilies, lilies into pure Innocents.

Style must incarnate spirit. Oxymoron, paradox, and hyperbole are figures necessary to the articulation of the Catholic faith. Crashaw's *concetti,* by their infidelity to nature, claim allegiance to the supernatural; his baroque imagery, engaging the senses, intimates a world which transcends them. (pp. 253-62)

Austin Warren, "Symbolism in Crashaw," in Seventeenth-Century English Poetry: Modern Essays in Criticism, *edited by William R. Keast, Oxford University Press, 1962, pp. 252-63.*

George N. Shuster (essay date 1940)

[In the excerpt below, Shuster contends that Crashaw ensured the "longevity of the English ode" by giving its neoclassical style a modern reworking, as seen in his "Hymn of the Nativity" and other poems.]

Like Spenser, Richard Crashaw was suspended halfway between religion and aesthetic. Perhaps the bridge between the two was supplied by music, which the poet often praised. One of his ablest recent critics, Ruth Wallerstein [in her *Richard Crashaw: a Study in Style and Poetic Development,* 1935], believes as a matter of fact that his metrical arrangements were suggested by melodies, and there is much to be said for her point of view. For the moment it is well to remember that, while Miss Wallerstein may be right, music and verse had greatly changed by the middle years of the century. The Elizabethans had been passionately fond of song, but none of them had written "**The Weeper**." Under Charles I, royal patronage was accorded to music on a scale worthy of great things, and the ancient rights of the musicians' guild were confirmed. Even more important was the regard in which the art was held by the cultivated and the genteel. The "metaphysical" poets are inseparable from the lute, or whatever other instrument they may have preferred to the lute. Donne's rugged songs had been set to music; and we are informed [in *Letters Written by Eminent Persons in the Seventeenth and Eighteenth Centuries: to Which Are Added ... Lives of Eminent Men, by John Aubrey, Esq.*, 1813] that Herbert "had a very good hand at the lute, and sett his own lyrics or sacred poems." Crashaw was an able performer, as Milton may have been. In every department of versemaking the same addiction to tunes prevailed. Carew's songs, Waller's lyrics, the ditties of Lovelace, Benlowes' rhapsodies, the simpler strains of the Fletchers—all were grist to the composer's mill. The habit of singing was widespread. Aubrey maintains, for example [in *Letters Written by Eminent Persons*, 1813], that Hobbes kept a book of "prick-song" on his table. Then "at night, when he was abed, and the dores made fast, and was sure nobody heard him, he sang aloud." The author of *Leviathan* was unexpectedly considerate. But he fancied that the music "did his lunges good, and much prolonged his life." Even Cromwell possessed a fondness for the art. (pp. 93-5)

It is likewise quite probable that Crashaw also swam for a time in the orbit of Stanley. It may well be that he owed to this passionate student what he knew of Italian and Spanish literatures. For left to himself Crashaw was preminently a classical scholar and a liturgist. His Greek verse is probably the best ever written by an English poet of any importance; his Latin poems are highly commendable; and his versions of the great lyrics of the Roman Hymnal are still unsurpassed. It is, therefore, at least highly probable that it was Crashaw who brought Pindar to the attention of Cowley, and not the other way around, as has been suggested. No one in the middle seventeenth century could have been as fine a Greek scholar as Crashaw undoubtedly was without being tempted to look into Pindar; and yet he may have failed—as Milton also may have failed—to grasp the principle of Pindaric ode construction. Much may have depended upon how the Greek text was printed in the editions at hand. These texts apparently retained the tripartite divisions, but erred in their reading of lines. In so far as Cowley is concerned, everything we know about him as a young poet indicates that he was by temperament and training a Latinist. At any rate, the relationship between the two poets was intimate enough to be important; and though Crashaw termed none of his metrical irregularities Pindaric or Greek, he might conceivably have done so with some show of reason.

Crashaw's was a baroque Muse. The point has been duly noted in connection with his manifest faults, primarily that of bizarre overstatement. It is easy to pick from his earlier work, as Kane does [in his *Gongorism and the Golden Age*, 1928], phrases or tropes which illustrate "the extreme of the grotesque and the bizarre." Whether this tendency was the result of his reading in Italian and Spanish

literatures, or whether it must be traced in the first instance to the stylistic injunctions of [Johannes] Buchlerus, is a moot question which need be raised here only to point out that it is largely by reason of his departures from the normal imagistic perspective that Crashaw is attuned to a certain twentieth-century prosodic practice. Here we must, however, be concerned with his patterns and meters, since these are in several ways landmarks in the history of the ode.

None of Crashaw's lyrics is, to be sure, called an "ode," probably for the reason that he, the product of Little Gidding and Catholicism, still associated that word with amorousness. Moreover, the form of his "hymns" often suggests the Italians. Thus **"A Hymn of the Nativity"** is a forerunner of what would later be termed the "cantata ode" and may have been based upon either the new "opera" or the Oratorian "Cantata Spirituale." The music for such a stanza as this would necessarily have been florid and Italianate:

> I saw th' officious angels bring
>   The down that their soft breasts did strow,
> For well they now can spare their wings,
>   When Heaven itself lies here below.
> "Fair youth," said I, "be not too rough,
> Your down, though soft's, not soft enough."

Even so it is not possible to say with certainty whether Crashaw was following a specific Italian practice. He may have been attempting to serve the same liturgical purpose to which the "broken form" of **"The Office of the Holy Cross"** is dedicated. All these poems have their counterparts in the downpour of odes, written for orchestral accompaniments, which marked the eighteenth century, though it must immediately be added that any direct influence of Crashaw upon the writers of that time cannot be assumed. In general, however, Crashaw was less dependent upon the Italian models in vogue than is commonly supposed. Thus he translated Marini and Strada, but they taught him nothing of moment about form.

He was obviously also a close reader of the English poets. Miss Wallerstein is correct in saying that "at twenty-four or twenty-five, Crashaw had mastered the Spenserian manner." Likewise he learned to use variants of the Jonsonian ode stanzas, and to write his own kind of *terza rima* ode. No doubt the patterns of Herbert, the admired teacher, made the deepest impression of all, suggesting the form of such poems as **"Sancta Maria Dolorum"** and, above all, the magnificent **"In the Glorious Epiphany of Our Lord God."** There is reason to feel that the influence of Milton also counted for something; and, of course, the younger Crashaw shone principally as a writer of epigrams. Accordingly his place in English verse is secure, regardless of how exotic his diction may be. For he began where others had left off and added something of his own to the history of the poetic adventure.

Crashaw's best skill was lavished on meter. His first notable feat is, perhaps, skipping unstressed syllables and thus making his verse depend upon the stresses. From this point of view **"The Weeper"** is a triumph as signal as Shelley's "Skylark." Indeed, I think the exordium of

Crashaw's poem richer in every sense than is that of Shelley's:

> Hail sister springs,
> Parents of silver-forded rills!
>   Ever bubbling things!
>
>   Thawing chrystal! snowy hills!
> Still spending, never spent; I mean
> Thy fair eyes sweet Magdalen.

That, being concerned with woman's tears, naturally seems grossly exaggerated; and of course it is. But can one truthfully say (the question of taste being beyond solution) that it is much more outlandish than Shelley's transformation of a skylark into a heavenly spirit? And, proceeding now to the world of language, where is there a more captivating use of the "i" sound or a more artful arrangement of stresses than is here provided by Crashaw?

One is led to believe that he must have possessed an unusually deep insight into what may be termed the quantitative possibilities of English speech—that is, the use of pauses to create effects similar to those produced in classical verse by the substitution, for example, of spondees for dactyls. Crashaw's feeling for these things is Greek. And his second memorable feat—his success with poems written in irregular stanzas—can likewise be accounted for easily only on the basis of what he had learned from reading Greek verse. **"On a Prayer-Book Sent to Mrs. M. E."** is, for example, more than a *tour de force,* though it is that, too. Opening with a quatrain akin to the *In Memoriam* stanza, the poem rises gradually through varying stanzaic patterns to that magnificent lyric passage beginning "O fair! O fortunate!" which out-does Shelley two hundred years before Shelley's time. The pattern, *5 4 3 2 2 2 4 4 4 3 2 2 4 3 3,* suggests nothing so much as a cascade of verbal music; and the deft additions of feminine rhyme and trochaic rhythm leave one wondering how it was that so much illustrious artistry could virtually be ignored for centuries.

"A Hymn to the Name and Honour of the Admirable Saint Teresa" is, after Milton's Nativity ode, the most illustrious blending of art and hymnody in seventeenth-century verse. It is the model after which Francis Thompson and his disciples consciously or unconsciously wrote. Crashaw errs here, as elsewhere, by scattering his jewels with too lavish a hand. The poem is exordium, encomium, doctrine, prayer, all in one; it storms Heaven with venturesome antitheses, hyperboles, and variations on the muted strings; and the mood shifts from sententious reflection to lyric ecstasy. The sole constants are the four-stress lines and the couplet rhymes, and they show off to greater advantage the highly subtle and melodious prosodic structure. Certainly few poets have ever bedecked a profane love with more splendor than Crashaw here throws round the Immortal Eros. To the writers of the 1650s, this poem must have seemed what it really was—the culmination of one great English poetic adventure. I am quite sure that its influence persisted throughout later elaborate hymnody, just as I feel that the incentive given to Cowley was decisive. (pp. 99-106)

George N. Shuster, "Crashaw, Cowley, and the Pindaric Ode," in his The English Ode from Milton to Keats, *Columbia University Press, 1940, pp. 93-122.*

Basil Willey (essay date 1949)

[In the excerpt below, Willey presents Crashaw's work as a true example of the Baroque style, contending that he "is most fully himself, where fire and sweetness and ecstatic love are fused together in the pure passion of prayer."]

[The] Counter-Reformation baroque, of which [Crashaw's] poetry is the distillation, represents a mode of feeling and expression as far removed as possible from the native sentiment and tradition, or at any rate from the standards, whether religious or aesthetic, which on the whole dominated the eighteenth and nineteenth centuries. If not his conceits and paradoxes, or his tropical lushness of imagery, then his exotic vein of religious ecstasy would be sure to give offence. The sober protestantism and neo-classicism of the Hanoverian epoch were repelled by the art whereby the Counter-Reformation sought to exploit the Renaissance, the art which, whether by the grandiose or the pathetic, whether by melodrama or ecstasy, by the lachrymose or the erotic, tried to win back an apostate world to the Faith. The nostrils of the eighteenth century, and most of those of the nineteenth, were allergic to the smell of incense, and Crashaw's poetry exhaled its very attar. Moreover, intermingled with the aroma of frankincense and myrrh, there seemed to be also the heavy scent of lilies and tuberoses, and the taint of carnality and corruption. English religious sentiment had inherited from Puritanism and Evangelicalism a distrust of the senses, and Crashaw, who fixes his attention continually upon the physical manifestations of Christianity—the wounds of the crucified Christ, the blood and water, the tear-drops of the Magdalene, the love-pierced heart of St Teresa—could evoke little response but distaste and suspicion. Even the Catholic revival of the nineteenth century brought little enhancement to his reputation; he was felt to be sickly, unmanly and foreign; and the Catholicism of more recent times has looked rather to St Thomas Aquinas and Dante than to Ignatius Loyola, Teresa or Marino. Crashaw was described in his own time as a second Herbert, but his prevailing mood, at once inflamed and relaxed, denied him the representative quality which Herbert has for the seventeenth century, Watts and Charles Wesley for the eighteenth, and Keble for the nineteenth. Charles Wesley, indeed, refers constantly to the redeeming blood of Christ, and longs to feel its cleansing flow, but with him the physical reference is of the slightest, his thought being fixed upon contrition and the forgiveness of sin. In Crashaw the conviction of sin, though not absent, counts for little; his concern is with the roses and raptures, the lilies and languors, the intolerable joys and the delicious wounds of mystical experience; he deals, in fact, with just those spiritual luxuries enumerated by Sir Thomas Browne at the end of *Urn Burial:* 'Christian annihilation, ecstasies, exolution, liquefaction, transformation, the kiss of the spouse, gustation of God, and ingression into the divine shadow.' And if he thereby gains 'a handsome anticipation of heaven', it is on the whole a heaven too warm, roseate and honeyed for most English tastes. Let us take from his poem "Prayer: an Ode which was Praefixed to a little Prayer-book given to a young gentlewoman," an example of the sort of rewards promised by Crashaw to the devout vestal. Prayer, he has been saying, gives access to a 'sacred store of hidden sweets and holy ioyes'; he continues:

> WORDS which are not heard with EARES
> (Those tumultuous shops of noise)
> Effectuall wispers, whose still voice
> The soul it selfe more feeles then heares;
> Amorous languishments; luminous trances;
> SIGHTS which are not seen with eyes;
> Spirituall & soul-peircing glances
> Whose pure & subtil lightning flyes
> Home to the heart, & setts the house on fire
> And melts it down in sweet desire
>   Yet does not stay
> To ask the windows leaue to passe that way;
> Delicious DEATHS; soft exalations
> Of soul; dear & diuine annihilations;
>   A thousand vnknown rites
> Of ioyes & rarefy'd delights;

—all these the 'dear spouse of spirits' will bring with his embraces,

> All fresh & fragrant as he rises
> Dropping with a baulmy Showr
> A delicious dew of spices; . . .

and the 'selected dove', the initiate soul, shall discover

>   What ioy, what blisse,
> How many Heau'ns at once it is
> To haue her GOD become her LOVER.

Or notice how, in another poem, he contemplates the wounds of our crucified Lord:

> O these wakefull wounds of thine!
>   Are they Mouthes, or are they eyes?
> Be they Mouthes, or be they eyne,
>   Each bleeding part some one supplies.
>
> Lo! a mouth, whose full-bloom'd lips
>   At too deare a rate are roses.
> Lo! a blood-shot eye! that weepes
>   And many a cruell teare discloses.

Then, thinking as so often of his Magdalene, he adds,

> O thou that on this foot hast laid
>   Many a kisse, and many a Teare,
> Now thou shal't have all repaid
>   Whatsoe're thy charges were.
>
> This foot has got a Mouth and lippes,
>   To pay the sweet summe of thy kisses:
> To pay thy Teares, an Eye that weeps
>   In stead of Teares such Gems as this is.
>
> The difference only this appeares,
>   (Nor can the change offend)
> The debt is paid in *Ruby*-Teares,
>   Which thou in Pearles did'st lend.

This type of sensuous brooding and emblem-making, static because it leads to nothing beyond itself, is an Ignatian

'spiritual exercise' in the 'application of the senses' to one of the central themes of Christianity [as noted in Austin Warren, *Richard Crashaw*, 1939] A comparison of this poem, so pictorial, so ingenious, and thus so limited in its range, with Isaac Watts's 'When I survey the wondrous Cross', in which the *contemplatio crucis* leads on, without any fanciful elaboration or sensuous unction, to the thought of self-dedication, reveals the gulf that separates Crashaw's religious sensibility from the more characteristically English varieties. Note, too, the imagery with which he celebrates the Name of Jesus, in the Hymn **"To the Name above Every Name"**:

> O dawn, at last, long look't for Day!
> Take thine own wings, and come away.
> Lo, where Aloft it comes!   It comes, Among
> The Conduct of Adoring SPIRITS, that throng
> Like diligent Bees, And swarm about it.
>   O they are wise;
> And know what SWEETES are suck't from out it.
>   It is the Hiue,
>   By which they thriue,
> Where All their Hoard of Hony lyes. . . .
>
> O dissipate thy spicy Powres
> (Clowd of condensed sweets) & break vpon vs
>   In balmy showrs;
> O fill our senses, And take from vs
> All force of so Prophane a Fallacy
> To think ought sweet but that which smells of
>   Thee. . . .
>
> SWEET NAME, in Thy each Syllable
> A Thousand Blest ARABIAS dwell;
> A Thousand Hills of Frankincense;
> Mountains of myrrh, & Beds of spices,
> And ten Thousand PARADISES
> The soul that tasts thee takes from thence.

Christianity is a religion of paradoxes, and Crashaw—in this respect like Donne and other 'metaphysical' poets, though in general so unlike them—loves to let his subtle fancy play upon them. God and man, life and death, east and west, day and night, fire and water, pain and ecstasy— all these and other contraries he constantly unites, sometimes with epigrammatic point, sometimes on a larger scale. He speaks, for instance, of how

> Three Kings (or what is more) three Wise men
>   went
> Westward to find the worlds true *Orient;*
>   ["**Sospetto D'Herode**," 17]

and declares, of the face of the weeping Magdalene, that

> No where but here did euer meet
> Sweetnesse so sad, sadnesse so sweet.
>   ["**The Weeper**," VI.]

The tears of this divine Weeper, to which this, one of his best-known poems, is wholly devoted, fall, not downwards, but upwards, and he adds to this thought a typically sensuous expansion:

> Vpwards thou dost weep.
>   Heau'n's bosome drinks the gentle stream.
> Where th'milky riuers creep,
>   Thine floats aboue; & is the cream.
> Waters aboue th'Heauns, what they be

We'are taught best by thy TEARES & thee.
                          [Ibid. IV.]

The **"Epiphanie"** hymn is the best large-scale example of this method; it shows, moreover, a degree of intellectual concentration rare in Crashaw, who usually glides rapidly from one image to another. The three Kings, conceived as converted sunworshippers, worshippers of a sun of darkness, have come to adore the true Sun, who through the shades of mortal flesh has dispelled the darkness of paganism. They prophesy how the natural sun, essentially a shadow, will at length, by his eclipse at the crucifixion, do penance for his long usurpation,

> Proud to haue gain'd this pretious losse
> And chang'd his false crown for thy CROSSE. . . .

> That forfeiture of noon to night shall pay
> All the idolatrous thefts done by this night of day.

The whole poem is one long elaboration of this paradox; it is, indeed

> A mutuall trade
> 'Twixt sun & SHADE,
> By confederate BLACK & WHITE
> Borrowing day & lending night.

It becomes evident, I think, in considering these examples, why the romantic revival of the nineteenth century, and our own century's renewed interest in the 'metaphysical' poets, though they have rescued Crashaw from the neglect he suffered in the eighteenth century, have not produced a more startling revaluation. The romantics and Victorians, indeed, developed a gusto for the Elizabethans, Jacobeans and Carolines, found them more congenial than the Augustans, and often valued seventeenth century poets as alleged 'forerunners' of romanticism. Thus Vaughan and Traherne were good because they 'anticipated' Wordsworth, and Crashaw, similarly, was supposed to show something of Keats's sensuousness and Shelley's fire. But Crashaw's world is utterly different from theirs, and though (for example) his images from taste or smell, and his fondness for the luxuries of pain and death, may remind us of Keats's longing for rich death, or his afflatus remind us of Shelley's, we now see that the resemblances are superficial, that to be a harbinger of romanticism would in any case be no ground, in itself, for unthinking praise, and that the critic's task is rather to sharpen than to blur distinctions. Crashaw's nature-images, for instance, his roses and lilies, dew-drops, dawns and sunsets, turn out on inspection to be mostly non-naturalistic: they are there for emblematic rather than romantic reasons; and his intolerable joys, sweet and subtle pains and delicious deaths, belonging as they do to the context of Teresan mysticism, turn out to have nothing to do with Keats's desire to cease upon the midnight or to glut his sorrow on a morning rose. In these days the Baroque style, of which (as Mr Eliot has truly said) Crashaw is the leading English representative, can be appreciated for its own sake, without apology, and without pretending that it is like something else. . . . [However], the modern taste for Donne has not greatly helped Crashaw, for he lacks, in general, that toughness and sinew, that blend of logic and passion, and

that tumult of spirit, which our generation has found congenial in Donne. If we wanted now to praise him for affinities with other poets, we might be more inclined to say that his couplets are sometimes like Pope's, or that he can sometimes achieve the noble valiancy of a Shakespearean cadence:

> O 'tis not spanish, but 'tis heau'n she speaks!

But [it is in the concluding section of **"The Flaming Heart"** where] Crashaw is most fully himself, where fire and sweetness and ecstatic love are fused together in the pure passion of prayer, and where, transcending all sensuous fancies, he soars on eagle-wings straight towards the sun. (pp. 16-25)

> *Basil Willey, in his* Richard Crashaw (1612/13-1649), *1949. Reprint by The Folcroft Press, Inc., 1969, 25 p.*

George Walton Williams (essay date 1963)

[*In the following excerpt, Williams reviews Crashaw's use of red and white colors, and light and dark imagery, asserting that there "is a pattern which is peculiarly Crashavian."*]

White and red are for Crashaw the primary colors of poetry. Mr. Warren has observed that one cannot survey Crashaw's imagery "without perceiving how the whole forms a vaguely defined but persistently felt series of interrelations. There are things red—fire, blood, rubies, roses, wine—and things white—tears, lilies, pearls, diamonds: symbols of love and passion; symbols of contrition, purity, innocence" [in Austin Warren, *Richard Crashaw*, 1939]. There are indeed two groups of things opposed in color and opposed in symbolic values; their member images recur with almost tedious frequency in the poetry. This chapter will examine these images and symbols and clarify their interrelations, vaguely felt and persistently defined, by a judicious rearranging and supplementing of Mr. Warren's list of things white and red. So there are flowers—lilies and roses—and there are gems—pearls or diamonds and rubies—and there are liquids—tears or water and blood or wine. After an excursus into sources, the following pages will notice first the flowers and then the gems. The most conspicuous set of color images is that involving the liquids; as it is extensive and as it has its own integrity, it appears separately in Chapter V. There are other white substances and liquids—snow, silver, milk, cream, crystal—but they do not regularly stand in color opposition and they may conveniently be noticed in the poems as they occur; there is fire, which is red only occasionally and which does not stand in color opposition. There is, however, one other thing white and red—the blush; it neatly and appropriately combines the two colors. Finally there are many adjectives of color which Crashaw uses to expand the pattern. In line after line, he joins substantives and attributives in a manner which demonstrates unmistakably that he is thinking in terms of the white and red contrast and of its symbolic values.

To speak of sources for the white/red color distinction is perhaps to mislead; it is more nearly accurate to trace traditions or to cite suggestions. The white/red contrast was very much in the air when Crashaw began to write. It occurs, occasionally, for example, in Southwell, and with regularity in the poems of d'Aubigné; it is a marked characteristic of many of the painters of the baroque. The result of Crashaw's interest in these colors—the poet was also a painter—is a pattern which is peculiarly Crashavian, which Crashaw uses with consummate skill to considerable effect, and of which the reader must be aware to understand the nuances of the poetry.

The first suggestion for the contrast and the one which reflects the most important theological significance comes from Isaiah and the Passion and underlies many images in the sacred poetry of the Renaissance. The Prophet refers to the remission of the red sins of man by the cleansing power of the whiteness of divinity: "Come now and let us reason together, saith the Lord: though your sins be as scarlet, they shall be white as snow; though they be red like crimson, they shall be as wool." Donne follows the tradition:

> Oh make thy selfe with holy mourning blacke,
> And red with blushing, as thou art with sinne;
> Or wash thee in Christs blood, which hath this
>   might
> That being red, it dyes red soules to white.
> [*Holy Sonnets*, IV]

So does Herbert:

> Thy bloudy death and undeserv'd, makes thee
>   Pure red and white,
> ["*Dulnesse*"]

and Vaughan writes:

> [Christ's] pure blood did flow
> To make stain'd man more white then snow.
> ["*Ascension-Hymn*"]

The second suggestive source for the contrast is the colors of the bread and wine of the Eucharist. This source does not yield the wealth of connotation that the former does, but in some passages the poet is evidently thinking of the color distinctions of the creatures of the Mass. The third suggestive source is the natural color of the dawn or Homer's observation of that color (unless Nature and Homer are the same). The pink pastels of the dawn's light, recalling the lushness of Rubens, form one of the family of reds. The fourth suggestive source is the Petrarchan tradition of amorous poetry. The color contrast appears as a commonplace in sixteenth- and seventeenth-century secular lyrics, and it weaves a meaningful strand in *Venus and Adonis*.

The color distinction pervades a rich and highly involuted complex of symbols, and its powers of suggestion and connotation are among the most extensive in Crashaw. White represents purity and the effect of cleansing. The purest soul or person shares the divine purity of absolute white, but there are off-whites to suggest the innocence of others. Whites perhaps most frequently color tears. Tears are white because they are the evidence of repentance and contrition; they symbolize the first step that the sinner must take up the ladder of perfection to the blessedness of pure white. Red is basically the blood of the sacrificed

Lamb, and it symbolizes the great love of God and His Son as revealed in the Passion. Through the image of the blush, however, red stands also for the fleshly shame and the sinfulness of man. Hence the typical Christian paradox: the red blood (divine love) can wash white as snow the red sins of man (mortal shame). The love of God comes to man as the dawn comes, and Crashaw has a ramified set of images to suggest this manifestation. The contrast between these two colors figures in almost every poem; any interpretation of Crashaw must consider it.

The first of the symbolic contrasts predicated on the distinction between white and red is composed of flowers: lilies and roses. It is well to recall the Biblical references to these flowers. The first occurs in Isaiah (35.1) in a passage foretelling the birth of the Messiah. The Vulgate and the King James versions provide differing translations:

> et exsultabit solitudo, et florebit quasi lilium;
> and the desert shall rejoice, and blossom as the
>   rose.

A second well-known mention of the lily, in Matthew 6.28-29, describes its native and undecorated beauty and compares it favorably to Solomon in all his glory: "Considerate lilia agri quomodo crescunt . . . Dico autem vobis, quoniam nec Salomon in omni gloria sua coopertus est sicut unum ex istis." This expression of the simplicity and beauty of the lily Crashaw paraphrased in one of his epigrams.

> Candide rex campi, cui floris eburnea pompa est,
>   Deque nivis fragili vellere longa toga;
> Purpureus Solomon impar tibi dicitur. esto.
>   Nempe (quod est melius) par fuit ille rosis.

Crashaw's comment on the passage characteristically contributes the rose to complete the color pattern. Solomon is said to have been unlike the lily; he must consequently have been like the rose. And how much more fitting this is! The whiteness of the lily implies its complete purity, its nearness to God; the redness of the rose associates it with the color of carnality. Solomon, purple in his raiment and his flesh, is but a mortal sinner. The third reference to roses and lilies is familiar in the King James version (Song of Solomon 2.1): "I am the rose of Sharon, and the lily of the valleys." Herbert and Vaughan both were moved by this verse—the former declared the presence of God in His created world (and rejected secular love poetry):

> *Roses* and *Lillies* speak thee; and to make
>   A pair of Cheeks of them, is thy abuse;
> ["Sure Lord there is enough"]

and the latter addressed Christ Himself:

> O rose of *Sharon!*   O the Lilly
>   Of the valley!
> How art thou now, thy flock to keep,
> Become both *food*, and *Shepheard* to thy sheep.
> ["Holy Communion"]

Jesus is referred to as a lily in order to represent poetically His purity and His unadorned beauty. The drops of blood shed at the Circumcision transform this unstained whiteness into unstained redness (divine love) or stained redness (mortal sin):

> Ah ferus, ah culter! qui tam bona lilia primus
> In tam crudeles jussit abire rosas.

The lily Christ comes into this world and begins almost immediately to be tainted with the redness of man's sins; He is " . . . this modest maiden lilly / Our sins haue sham'd into a rose." The purity of the Infant Christ illuminates the Infant Martyrs who died in consequence of Herod's proclamation (Matthew 2.16). As Herod was searching for Christ, it is only just that the Innocents who were slaughtered in His place should receive their reward. Crashaw liked the story of the infant martyrdom and treated it several times. Twice he compared the mothers' milk and the infants' blood to lilies and roses.

> To see both blended in one flood
> The Mothers Milke, the Childrens blood,
> Makes me doubt if Heaven will gather,
> *Roses* hence, or *Lillies* rather.
>
> ["Hymnus Epiphaniae"]

The red rose decks the birthplace of the Infant Christ, and Crashaw implies that the Babe emits the beauty of the flower.

> Cernis ut illa suo passim domus ardeat auro?
> Cernis ut effusis rideat illa rosis?
> Sive aurum non est, nec quae rosa rideat illic;
> Ex oculis facile est esse probare tuis.

And in a grim paradox at the death of Christ, the crown of thorns causes drops of blood (roses) to bloom on Christ's head.

The second of the symbolic contrasts is formed of gems: pearls or diamonds and rubies. A gem has its own individual worth, but it often combines with others to form a diadem. This action raises the gems to a power of circular perfection, a crown of glory. The rhyme assists.

White gems in general partake of either the purity of heavenly virtue or the contrition of mortals. The water of baptism with which John baptized Christ was imaged as a gem and a tear. The little white drop of water on the tip of Lazarus' finger was a pearl containing quantities of heavenly Grace. Pearls and diamonds are the images most closely and frequently associated with tears, the sign of an humble and a contrite heart. The image of the tear as a pearl is a commonplace in Renaissance poetry. Shakespeare writes:

> The liquid drops of tears that you have shed
> Shall come again, transformed to orient pearls.
> [*Richard III*, IV, iv. 321-22]

The small teardrop, "the liquid jewell of a teare," possesses much more value than would be expected of so small an object. Tears are "Sorrowes best Iewels" [**"The Weeper"**] and the best decoration that contrition can assume. The tears of the Magdalene are the most distinctive tears in the canon; they are often described as pearls. Teardrops, as another sort of pearl, represent the dew of morning or evening.

> Such a Pearle as this is

> (Slipt from *Aurora's* dewy Brest)
> The Rose buds sweet lip kisses.
>
> ["**The Teare**"]

> The purest Pearles, that wept her Evening Death.
>
> ["**Upon the Death of Mr. Herrys**"]

In these lines the pearls replace the dewdrops for ornamental effect. The meaning is straightforward and figurative without being complex, though, as the dew was thought to be heaven-sent, these pearls might contribute the whiteness of divine grace. The diamond is an alternative to the pearl.

> What bright soft thing is this?
> Sweet *Mary* thy fair Eyes expence?
> A moist sparke it is,
> A watry Diamond; from whence
> The very Terme, I think, was found
> The water of a *Diamond.*
>
> ["**The Teare**"]

Or the diamond may stand for the eye, with a cluster of connotations. The Madonna and Child look at one another:

> Shee 'gainst those Mother-Diamonds tryes
> The points of her young Eagles Eyes.
> ["**A Hymn of the Nativity**"]

One more white "gem" of great value concludes the list, ivory, though the image is rare. Christ is described as "Virgineüm hoc . . . ebur," and the color reflects His purity. In an epigram already cited, the adjective colors the "pomp" of the lily ("Candide rex campi, cui floris eburnea pompa est").

Of red gems Crashaw distinguishes only the ruby. The drops of red blood shed at the Circumcision are compared to the bright red coloring of the morning.

> Bid thy golden GOD, the Sun, . . .
> Put all his red-ey'd Rubies on;
> These Rubies shall putt out their eyes.
> ["**New Year's Day**"]

Christ's blood is brighter and more beautiful than the red streams in the firmament; it represents strikingly His love for mankind.

The contrast between white and red gems occurs frequently. Though no specific gem is mentioned, Dives' purple clothing, bejeweled, so to speak, with ruby flames in Hell, presents the difference effectively.

> Rich *Lazurus*! richer in those Gems, thy Teares,
> Then *Dives* in the Roabes he weares:
> He scornes them now, but o they'l sute full well
> With th'Purple he must weare in Hell.

The white tears of poor Lazurus typify greater wealth than the purple clothing of opulent Dives. The white drop on Lazurus' pearl-tipped finger and the white drops of his tears both represent divine favor.

The epigram **"On the wounds of our crucified Lord,"** juxtaposing the blood of Christ's feet nailed on the cross and the tears of Mary Magdalene, incorporates the imagery of white and red flowers and gems. Seeing Mary at the Crucifixion (Mark 15. 40), Crashaw recalls the earlier episode (Luke 7. 36-50) when she had kissed Christ's feet and washed them with her tears. The feet of the crucified Christ must pay back these kisses and tears through the wounds made by the nail. Hence (stanza ii) the wounds must be both mouth and eye.

> Lo! a mouth, whose full-bloom'd lips
>   At too deare a rate are roses.
> Lo! a blood-shot eye! that weepes
>   And many a cruell teare discloses.

The first two lines are red—"mouth," "bloom'd," "lips," "roses"; the second two are white—"eye," "tear." But the eye, being bloodshot, is itself a concentrated image of the white/red contrast. Stanza iv:

> This foot hath got a Mouth and lippes,
>   To pay the sweet summe of thy kisses:
> To pay thy Teares, an Eye that weeps
>   In stead of Teares such Gems as this is.

The purpose of these paradoxes is now apparent. The Magdalene's kisses from her lips and tears from her eyes are both to be repaid (v),

> The difference onely this appeares
>   (Nor can the change offend)
> The debt is paid in *Ruby*-Teares,
>   Which thou in Pearles did'st lend.

In the third line of this stanza the red blood and the white tears condense into the phrase, "*Ruby*-Teares"; the red gems which are drops of blood from the mouth-wound assimilate with the white gems which are tears from the eye-wound. In a commercial image, Christ pays the debt of tears in blood; He satisfies the obligation, though He makes the payment in currency of another color. . . . Unfortunately, at this point Crashaw deserts the logic of the structure which has been promising a fair apportionment to both tears and kisses, and, in the sudden condensation, he forgets the kisses. Crashaw assures us that Mary "shal . . . have all repaid,/Whatsoe're [her] charges were," but he fails to repay the kisses in the contract.

The blush is another of the Crashavian substantives which depend on the relationship of red and white. The image is common in Renaissance poetry, and Shakespeare employs it with full cognizance of its red and white contrasts.

> The roses fearfully on thorns did stand,
> One blushing shame, the other white despair.

It occurs as well in Spenser:

> The ioyous day gan early to appeare,
> And faire *Aurora* from the deawy bed
> Of aged *Tithone* gan her selfe to reare,
> With rosie cheekes, for shame as blushing red.
>   [*Faerie Queene* I, XI. ll]

Crashaw uses the blush in two distinct senses. One blush is the blush of modesty. This coloring flushes the cheeks of maidens and those of unquestioned purity. The second blush is the blush of shame—"the burnish of . . . sin"—and results from the attempt to conceal a sin. Miss Wallerstein [in her *Richard Crashaw*, 1935] has pointed out the progression in the development of the image from the juvenilia of an ingenious schoolboy to the final poems with

their rich symbolic significances, but she has not indicated this distinction. The simplest use of the term is for the purpose of showing a red color; a field of battle red with the blood of soldiers is a "blushing ground." Generally, the image describes the cheek of an individual or a personification. Cheeks begin as white as snow, and they may become "nests of new roses."

The blush of modesty is applied to infants and to those of pure character. Brides—as traditionally—blush modestly. Mary's modesty reveals itself in a blush which, though red, does not stain her purity. It contrasts, however, with the white light of the moon (another chaste goddess) and the stars.

> Whose blush the moon beauteously marres
> And staines the timerous light of starres.
>   ["O Gloriosa Domina"]

And the little lips of the infant Christ blush the pure red of the rosebud: "the red leaves of thy Lips, / That in their Buds yet blushing lye." ["A Hymn of the Nativity"] A particular example of the blush of modesty has been much commended. It occurs in the epigram on the Water Changed to Wine, as the first miracle that Christ wrought in Cana of Galilee (John 2. 1-11).

> Unde rubor vestris, & non sua purpura lymphis?
>   Quæ rosa mirantes tam nova mutat aquas?
> Numen (convivæ) præsens agnoscite Numen:
>   Nympha pudica Deum vidit, & *erubuit.*

The quatrain has been translated many times, but no translator has captured the beauty of the original nor done so well as Crashaw himself in animating Grotius' account:

> Drinke fayling there where I a guest did shine
> The Water blush'd, and started into Wine.

The blush of shame is applied to those who have something to hide or who recognize that they are guilty of sin. It is in this explication of the blush that the major symbolic significance exists.

> With blushing Cheek & bleeding ey,
> The conscious colors of my sin
> Are red without and pale within.
>   [**"Hymn of the Church in Meditation of
>   the Day of Judgement"**]

Crashaw expresses the conflict in the colors of white and red three times in these lines: the white cheek has blushed to red, the white tears of the eye are bleeding red, and the heart, conscious of its guilt, is ashen white in contrition, sending its red blood into the cheeks.

Less spectacularly—almost playfully, one might say—the image colors St. Teresa's youthful voyage to the Moors and martyrdom. Crashaw commends the child but notes practically,

> Scarse has she Blood enough to make
> A guilty sword blush for her sake
>   [**"Hymn to St. Teresa"**]

The conscious colors of man's sins are white and red, and they show that they are by appearing in flushed cheeks. It is only the whiteness of the broken body and the redness of the Redeemer's blood in the Eucharist which together can wash the scarlet sins of man and make him white as snow (Psalm 51.7).

Whiteness has several tints and several attributive adjectives. Uncomplicated or pure *white* symbolizes primarily divine purity and is closely associated with the "light" of the next chapter which is basically the Good. Pure white pertains most frequently to the Godhead. Crashaw uses the adjective for Christ himself and in a spirit of devout humility aspires no higher than to Christ's feet. The final destination of mankind is the Lord's white feet. Crashaw advises that man "crowd for kisses from the LAMB's white feet"; that mankind walk with Christ "whereso'ere he setts his white/ Stepps." The Virgin Mary is St. Teresa's "white/ MISTRESSE." The raiment and feathers of angels are white. The Resurrection of Christ is recorded in "joyes white Annals." *Snowy* is another shade of whiteness. The dove which represents the Holy Ghost has a snowy back; the company of heaven surrounding the Virgin is her "snowy family;" the pure maiden's bosom is a "snowy fortresse of defence." Another adjective of white is *silver*. In devotional and secular poems it describes a mountain stream, the tears of Cupid, and the hairs of old age. But its important symbolic use in Crashaw is in the expression of the purity of mortals and saints. It shares with white gems the connotations of value. In the **"Ode"** prefixed to a prayer book, Mrs. M. R. is termed a "silver breasted dove." The Virgin is also described as silver: "the dear immortall doue / Sighes to his syluer mate." *Milky* is yet another adjective of whiteness. In the religious poetry it refers often to the Milky Way in a punning pattern found, for example, in the next paragraph. But it can represent mortal penitence or purity. The eyes of the Magdalene are "nests of milky doues" in **"The Weeper"**; hence it is hardly surprising in the same poem to find also cream, the most excellent and desirable part of milk.

A more important variant of white is *crystal*. Like silver it is at once a color of purity and a substance of value. It partakes of the purity of whiteness in that it is the substance from which are made the Heavens (Revelation 21.11) and the concentric spheres. Spenser describes the sphere of Heaven in "The Hymne of Heavenly Beautie":

> And last, that mightie shining christall wall,
> Wherewith he hath encompassed this All.

Crashaw's cosmos too is built of this substance; heaven is "the Christall globe," and the harmonious spheres are crystalline. In the **"Hymn in the Glorious Assumption,"** the Virgin mounts "through the crystall orbes, clearer then they / . . . and makes a farre more milkey way." On earth by an extension of the image, a pure soul in a pure body may be "sheath'd in a christall shrine." Only the building material of heaven is pure enough for the mortal flesh of the pure and temperate Christian. The waters of the River Jordan like those of the River of Life (Revelation 22.1) are melted crystal. *Pearly* shares with crystal connotations of purity and value. It occurs rarely, though the noun is frequently met.

"The Weeper" contains all of these shades of white. There are touches of red which flash occasionally also, but the poem is essentially a study and impressionistic painting in whites. It is as well an extraordinary example of the con-

cept of liquidity, but this aspect of the poem belongs in Chapter V. The white characteristics of Mary's tears are symbolic of the fact that, as she has been purified by her contact with Jesus, her weeping is the evidence of her contrition. Her tears witness to divine mercy, showing mankind the importance of repentance. The symbols of whiteness begin with the opening lines: the eyes of the Magdalene are "Parents of syluer-footed rills! [the Lamb is white-footed] / . . . Thawing crystall! snowy hills" (i). Her tears are the cream that "floates aboue" the "milky riuers" of heaven (iv). Paralleling the redness of the morning, here "the euening's eyes / . . . Red with weeping are"—a white/red concentration (vi). The Magdalene's tears are Sorrow's "proudest pearles" (vii). The white dew prefers serving as the Saint's tears to adorning two white flowers: "The primrose's pale cheek" and "the lilly's neck" (viii). The "watry Blossom" of the Saint's eyes—her white tears—when ripe (i. e., red) "will make the richer wine": white tears bloom to red wine (xi). The same color contrast occurs in the next stanza; angels fill their "crystall violls" (cf. Revelation, *passim*) with "Their master's Water: their own Wine" (xii).

Stanza xiv implies a color combination based on the image of the blush. The cheeks of the Magdalene in which the "faithfull flowres" of May lie smiling—she is blushing—agree with her eyes from which the "kinder showres" are falling (xiv). The white April showers bring (red) May flowers; the Saint has "Fountain & Garden in one face" (xv). This white and red concentration reveals the subtlety of the image. The repentance of the Magdalene has earned the forgiveness of Christ.

> The lamb hath dipp't his white foot here.
>
> (xviii)

The Saint is a mint; she coins "syluer shoures" (xxi); then she spends—"Still spending, neuer spent" (i)—her wealth prodigally, "Euen to the last Pearle" in her treasury (xxii).

The poem concludes with two stanzas in which the tears respond to the poet's direct questions. In the first one the tears will not become dew again for two red and blushing (?) flowers (having previously left two white flowers in stanza viii): "The rose's modest Cheek / Nor the violet's humble head" (xxx). Nor will they become "gemmes" or even "Diadems." They go, as in the epigram "On the wounds of our crucified Lord," to meet

> A worthy object, our Lord's FEET.
>
> (xxxi)

"Mary in the New Testament is always found at the feet of our Lord," [notes J. N. Davies in the *Abingdon Bible Commentary,* 1929].

The ramifications of white are matched by shades of red; *red, purple, ruby,* and *rosy* are the principal colors, but *ruddy, crimson,* and *vermillion* occur also. *Red* is the basic color. Examples of this adjective are too numerous and obvious to require explication; one will suffice: "Every red letter / A wound of thine" now spells salvation for man. *Purple* is a shade of red which adds the concept of royalty to the divine love, or, by transference, it may heighten the sense of sinfulness. It may refer simply to the grape, the vine, and the blood of humans; it may signify the royal blood of Christ in the Circumcision; and with connotations of the magnificence of the sacrifice, it may figure the Crucifixion itself.

> Larg throne of loue!   Royally spred
> With purple of too Rich a red.
>
>   ["Vexilla Regis"]

The consummate image suggests the red blood of Christ's death, the royalty of the death and its magnificence, and the redness of man's sin for which only the absolute whiteness of Christ can atone:

> Why should the white
> Lamb's bosom write
> The purple name
> Of my sin's shame?
>
>   ["Charitas Nimia"]

The color ruby refers on its simplest level to a bright red sunrise. Crashaw speaks of "the Ruby portalls of the East." It conveys connotations of great wealth also, as in the epigram **"On the wounds of our Crucified Lord."** The contrast with white is natural, but Crashaw might have found it in Lamentations 4.7.

One admirable passage includes all these reds and introduces the fourth one, rosy. In the **"Hymn to the Name of Jesus,"** Crashaw discusses the persecution by the Roman gladiators of the Christian martyrs, Christ's "old Friends of Fire" whose blood is "That impatient Fire":

> What did their Weapons but sett wide the
>   Doores
> For Thee: Fair, purple Doores, of loue's deuising;
> The Ruby windowes which inrich't the EAST
> Of Thy so oft repeated Rising.
> Each wound of Theirs was Thy new Morning;
> And reinthron'd thee in thy Rosy Nest,
> With blush of thine own Blood the day adorning.

The passage is a brilliant succession of reds. The wounds of the martyrs made by the swords of the gladiators are first "purple Doores" suggesting the royalty of the martyrs' deaths, then "Ruby windowes" suggesting the richness and the value of their deaths, and then the "Rosy nest" of Christ, suggesting the protection and salvation secured through His blood which has ignited the blood of the martyrs with the red fire of love. But most striking in the conceits is the idea, clear throughout, that the wounds of the martyrs testify to the dawn of a new day, the day of the true light (a red / white contrast). This dawn / day concept is suggested through the images of doors and windows, magic casements opening to something new, and through the adjective traditional for the dawn, "rosy." Crashaw has given the ancient Homeric color rich Christian significance. This "rosy MARTYRDOME" leads in the dawning of the new day of Christ.

Though Crashaw uses the adjective rosy also to describe wine, Saints, angels, and the Virgin, he thinks regularly of the inescapable link between rosy and the dawn and feels in each use of the word infant beatings of some great promise to be fulfilled. This close association predicates a concept of things becoming, a dynamic nascent symbol.

As the dawn leads in the day, so the promise is fulfilled, the earnest expectation is manifested, hope is satisfied and defined, types yield to truths, and Law submits to Grace. Christ, *cuius nomen est Oriens*, is the dawn, the day-spring (*Vulgate*: "Oriens") from on high who "hath visited us, To give light to them that sit in darkness and in the shadow of death, to guide our feet into the way of peace" (Luke 1. 78-79). The Incarnation is

> The day-break of the nations; their first ray
> When the Dark WORLD dawn'd into Christian
>   DAY.
>
>   ["To the Queen's Majesty"]

So the Virgin's "healthfull womb" was "the Rosy DAWN that sprung the Day." [**"O Gloriosa Domina"**] The old law yields to the new truth when it "spyes loue's dawn." The poet appeals to the Messiah: "O dawn, at last, long look't for Day!" [**"Hymn to the Name of Jesus"**].

The image of the dawn suggests the East; and the richness of the East, seen specifically in the magnificence and opulence of the Kings in the **"Epiphany Hymn,"** is summed up in the image of Arabia, a land vastly wealthy in spices and redolent of rare perfumes: "exceeding rich in all those things which we esteem most precious." Crashaw sings a **"Hymn to the Name of Jesus"**:

> SWEET NAME, in Thy each Syllable
> A Thousand Blest ARABIAS Dwell;
> A Thousand Hills of Frankincense;
> Mountains of myrrh, & Beds of spices,
> And ten Thousand PARADISES.

The reference to Paradise, to the Garden in Eden, accounts for some part of the value of Arabia, but Arabia was traditionally always a place of riches and astonishing creatures; not the least remarkable of the latter was the 'rare Arabian bird," the phoenix.

> Bring hither all the BLEST
> ARABIA, for thy Royall Phœnix' nest.
>
>   ["Office of the Holy Cross"]

The symbolic significances of this bird are manifold. Some part of the richness of the East lies in its spices and perfumes. The nest of the phoenix (another nascent symbol) is made of cinnamon and frankincense, and when the image is transplanted to a Christian society and literature, the scent comes too. Religion is instructed to bring with it "whatsoe're perfum'd thy *Eastern nest*." The tomb of Christ is called "faire Immortalities perfumed Nest." As He rises, Christ is enveloped in a mandorla of perfuming exhalations "Dropping with a baulmy Showr / A delicious dew of spices." But the most luscious of the images of scent and perfume is the long passage in **"The Hymn to the Name of Jesus"** (ll. 165-182).

> O thou compacted
> Body of Blessings: spirit of Soules extracted!
> O dissipate thy spicy Powres
> (Cloud of condensed sweets) & break vpon vs
>   In balmy showrs;
> O fill our senses, And take from vs
> All force of so Prophane a Fallacy
> To think ought sweet but that which smells of
>   Thee.
> . . . In none but Thee

And Thy Nectareall Fragrancy,
    Hourly there meetes
An vniuersall SYNOD of All sweets;
By whom it is defined Thus
    That no Perfume
    For euer shall presume

To passe for Odoriferous,
But such alone whose sacred Pedigree
Can proue it Self some kin (sweet name) to Thee.

Other rich associations with the dawn are suggested by the two meanings of "spring," vernal season and water source, both senses of the word connoting the nascent symbol. The latter sense employs the synonyms "fount" and "fountain." The fertile season betokens the abundant harvest which is to follow; the water source develops into a stream of great size.

Water'd by the showres they bring,
    The thornes that thy blest browes encloses
(A cruell and a costly spring)
    Conceive proud hopes of proving Roses.

The crown of thorns planted on Christ's head, produces drops of blood which are roses. The thorns bring showers, the showers of April; and the image is primarily one of the spring season. But as the stanza appears in the early version of one of Crashaw's most "liquid" poems, the idea of the stream is appropriate also. The drops of blood become a river. A clear instance of the image of the water source is the vision of Christ's eyes as "The blissfull springs of joy" ["**Office of the Holy Cross**"] from which sun and stars drink their luminosity. Spring, the season, "All the yeare doth sit and sing," a characteristic which is reminiscent of Christ's "so oft repeated Rising," each martyr's death being a new morning of the revelation of love. Another example recalls the color contrast which is behind the symbolic interpretation of the dawn and the spring. Jesus is "The rich & roseall spring of those rare sweets." The word "spring" is intentionally an ambivalent nascent symbol. Jesus is the spring because he is the source of all sweet things and because he is the climate that promises the harvest. He is the rich spring, because he promises them continuously and abundantly. He is the roseal spring because he has shed his red blood for mankind and because like the dawn he foretells the wonder, beauty, and fulfillment of the new, rich day.

Yet another facet of the nascent symbol exists in the image of the bud of the rose. It is readily seen that the blowing bud is at once the sign of spring and the cognate of the dawn.

And, through the *Night* of error and dark doubt,
Discerne the *Dawne* of Truth's eternall ray,
As when the rosie *Morne* budds into Day.
    ["**On the Frontispiece of Isaacson's
    Chronologie**"]

At Christ's birth the "babe's bright face" is "the purpling Bud / And Rosy dawn of the right Royall blood ["**To the Queen's Majesty**"]." As the bud image is applicable at the birth of Christ, which is the beginning of His earthly ministry, so is it at the Resurrection, which is the beginning of His heavenly intercession for man. The tomb of Joseph of Arimathea is the rock which "buds forth the fountaine of the streames of Day." In the same way that Moses' rod brought water from the rock and rescued the Israelites thirsting in the wilderness (Numbers 20.11), here from the rock which has entombed Him, Christ in two nascent images rises as a fountain of light or unfolds as a white, perfumed bud. He is also a stream of light and love to the thirsting world which can be satisfied only through his sacrifice.

The Feast of the Circumcision of Christ is celebrated on the first of January. By virtue of this date the Feast Day is a nascent or beginning time. Furthermore, the blood of the Circumcision by its color suggests the red dawn, or beginning, imagery. In addition, the little drops of blood, in themselves evidencing the abundance of God, prefigure the greater shedding of blood at the Crucifixion and, therefore, like the dawn or the rosebud, herald greater things to come. The concept of growing informs the structure of one of Crashaw's epigrams on the Circumcision: from death to life, youth to maturity, hope to realization, dawn to day, weeping to dying, buds to tree, knife to spear.

To thee these first fruits of my growing death
(For what else is my life?) lo I bequeath. . . .
Now's but the Nonage of my paines, my feares
Are yet but in their hopes, not come to yeares.
The day of my darke woes is yet but morne,
My teares but tender and my death new-borne.
Yet may these unfledg'd griefes give fate some
    guesse,
These Cradle-torments have their towardnesse.
These purple buds of blooming death may bee,
Erst the full stature of a fatall tree.
And till my riper woes to age are come,
This knife may be the speares *Praeludium.*
    ["**Our Lord in his Circumcision to his
    Father**"]

The splendid image of the bud of the purple rose, which is figured in the drops of blood shed by the Infant, growing to a full-blooming and full-bleeding tree, the cross, is one of Crashaw's more effective epigrammatic conceits. The thoroughness of the growth image, it should be noted, is developed after the publication of the Latin original of the poem, which has no lines that can pass for a source for most of it. This development is an example of the maturing of Crashaw's imagery and symbolism.

"In the Holy Nativity of our Lord God A Hymn Sung as by the Shepheards" utilizes the color of rose and the imagery of the dawn with the particular liturgical purpose of celebrating the Feast of the Nativity; its closely related companion piece, **"In the Glorious Epiphanie of our Lord God, A Hymn. Sung as by the Three Kings,"** celebrates the Feast of the Epiphany. Mr. Warren notes that the relationship of the two hymns invites speculation. It does, indeed, and one aspect of that relationship is the imagery of color which reflects their historical and theological backgrounds. The two poems express two states. In the **"Nativity Hymn"** Christ's birth is sung by the Hebrew shepherds to whom He has been shown in His first manifestation (the day spring from on high hath visited us): it is the dawn, the promise of a new beginning. Christ is the glory of His people Israel. In the **"Epiphany Hymn"** Christ's epiphany is sung by the Gentile Kings to whom He has been shown in His second manifestation (to give light to them that sit in darkness): it is the day, the fulfillment of a new life to the Gentiles. Christ is a light to lighten the Gentiles (Luke 2.32). The two states are figured in the imagery: the **"Nativity Hymn"** is rich in imagery of the dawn and the Orient—white and red; the **"Epiphany Hymn"** is rich in imagery of the day—white and black.

St. Luke recounts that after worshiping the Christ child "the shepherds returned, glorifying and praising God for all the things that they had heard and seen" (2.20) and that "they made known abroad the saying which was told them concerning this child" (2.17). Crashaw supposes the shepherds returning from their tremendous midnight enlightenment and awakening the morning sun to sing their dawn song to him [in **"Hymn of the Nativity"**].

> Come we shepheards whose blest Sight
> Hath mett loue's Noon in Nature's night;
>   Come lift we vp our loftyer Song
> And wake the SVN that lyes too long.
> (1-4)

> Tell Him He rises now, too late
> To show vs ought worth looking at.
> (9-10)

In its rise, the supernatural sun has superseded the natural, a theme which is to be more fully developed in the **"Epiphany Hymn,"** a hymn of the noonday sun. Forgetting the sun now, the two shepherds sing alternate verses describing the effects of the Babe's eyes. Tityrus sings that even in the night these eyes emanated light; the new day of Christianity

> was THY day, SWEET! & did rise
> Not from the EAST, but from thine EYES.
> (21-22)

The day that rises is a new kind of dawn; Christ is his own East. Like Venus, Aurora must go shift. The promises of this new dawn will be kept. Thyrsis, the second shepherd, extends the metaphor; the eyes are not only the dawn, they are also the spring. So in the dead of winter

> The North forgott his feirce Intent;
>   And left perfumes in stead of scarres. . . .
> Where he mean't frost, he scatter'd flowrs.
> (26-29)

The flowers of spring—though no color is specified—are probably red to contrast with the white of the frost and to recall that the stable has elsewhere been decked with roses. **"The Weeper"** has already described the flowers of May as red, and these same flowers bloom at the end of this poem. The flowers of spring bring their own perfumes, and "perfume" is one of the words associated with the imagery of the East.

The two shepherds combine to sing the glory of yet another nascent image, Mary.

> We saw thee in thy baulmy Nest
>   Young dawn of our aeternall DAY!
> We saw thine eyes break from their EASTE
>   And chase the trembling shades away.
> (31-34)

Mary's womb has already been noted as the rosy dawn;

she is herself here the "Nest"—a symbol of becoming—from which the fledgling will fly to His own tree. The nest is "baulmy" for several reasons: it is surrounded by the fragrant perfumes of the benignant North Wind; it exudes its own sweet savor of the Orient; it drops balm, a healing restorative and an attribute suitable to the Virgin; and specifically it is made of spicy and aromatic twigs, for it is the nest of the phoenix.

> The Phœnix builds the Phœnix' nest.
>   Love's architecture is his own.
> (46-47)

The Incarnation and the Resurrection compress into this single, striking image, "symbol at its purest and richest, concentrated and clarified . . . by the now mature integration of the imagination of its maker."

"He that made all things, had not done," Crashaw writes, "Till he had made Himself thy son" [**"O Gloriosa Domina"**].

> The BABE whose birth embraues this morn,
> Made his own bed e're he was born.
> (48-49)

The next section of the poem contrasts neatly the colors of white and red, reconciling their differences in the Child and His Mother. Christ has built His own nest, but Nature wishes to supply Him with gifts. The snow offers itself as sheets, but its offer is rejected:

> Your fleece is white But t'is too cold.
> (56)

The whitest natural object on earth though perfectly white is too cold. It possesses perhaps something of the quality of sterility. It is too pure; it is not sufficiently vital. At the other extreme is the gift of "the obsequious SERAPHIMS" who wish to bestow "Their rosy fleece of fire." Once again the offer is rejected:

> are you sure
> Your down so warm, will passe for pure?
> (62-63)

The reddest natural object in heaven though perfectly red is too hot. It possesses perhaps something of passionate carnality. Its color is impure; it is not sufficiently divine. What will serve? Nothing but the Virgin.

> See see, how soon his new-bloom'd CHEEK
>   Twixt's mother's brests is gone to bed.
> Sweet choise, said we! no way but so
> Not to ly cold, yet sleep in snow.
> (67-70)

The Christ lays His red cheek between the white breasts of His Mother. She alone has all the cool, white purity and all the warm, red love required for

> Æternity shutt in a span.
> Sommer in Winter.   Day in Night.
> Heauen in earth, & GOD in MAN.
> (80-82)

She alone has the gift of divine abundance in her maternity. Her breasts are full of cool, pure, white milk; her lips give warm, pure, red kisses. Hence:

WELCOME.　Though nor to gold nor silk.

> To more then Caesar's birthright is;
> Two sister-seas of Virgin Milk,
> 　With many a rarely-temper'd kisse
> That breathes at once both MAID & MOTHER,
> Warmes in the one, cooles in the other.
> 　　　　　　　　　　　　　　　　(85-90)

The shepherds conclude their Hymn of welcome with a reminder of the spring:

> Yet when young April's husband showrs
> 　Shall blesse the fruitfull Maja's bed
> We'l bring the First-born of her flowrs
> 　To kisse thy FEET & crown thy HEAD.
> 　　　　　　　　　　　　　　　(97-100)

The shepherds' crown will be one of flowers—not of thorns—which will kiss with their red lips the Lamb's white feet. The following passage recalls the reader deftly to the shepherds and their flocks and brings him back to the fields of Palestine on Christmas morning.

> To thee, dread lamb! whose loue must keep
> 　The shepheards, more then they the
> 　　sheep. . . .
> Each of vs his lamb will bring
> 　Each his pair of syluer Doues;
> Till burnt at last in fire of Thy fair eyes,
> 　Our selues become our own best SACRIFICE.
> 　　　　　　　　　　　　　　　(101-109)

The final quatrain suggests the fulfillment of the New Covenant, replacing the old tradition of animal sacrifice with the revealed experience of human and personal sacrifice; and the last couplet, through its paraphrase of the Prayer of Consecration in the Holy Eucharist, includes all sinners, inviting them to participate in the Oblation, to reject the silver doves and to burn in the red fire of Christ's eyes. The fire is the fire of divine love which illuminates those eyes symbolically with the light of the dawn of the Christian Day and with the warmth of the spring of the New Year. (pp. 33-56)

> *George Walton Williams, in his* Image and Symbol in the Sacred Poetry of Richard Crashaw, *second edition, 1963. Reprint University of South Carolina Press, 1967, 151 p.*

Joseph H. Summers (essay date 1970)

[*In the following excerpt, Summers discusses Crashaw's religious imagery and how his "hyperboles and ardours of ordinary lovers' language" become "a triumphant new language for a new and supreme [spiritual] love."*]

Richard Crashaw, the son of an eminent Puritan clergyman, was twenty years younger than Herrick, Carew, King and George Herbert, and the exact contemporary of that best-selling poet John Cleveland. His *Epigrammatum Sacrorum Liber,* the only volume that he saw through the press, was published in 1634, the year after *The Temple.* His first volume containing English poems did not appear until 1646, after Crashaw, a recent convert to Rome, had left England for Paris. The preface to that volume, probably written by Crashaw's friend and contemporary Joseph

Beaumont, explains the title given to the English sacred poems: 'Reader, we style his Sacred Poems, *Steps to the Temple*, and aptly, for in the Temple of God, under his wing, he led his life in St. *Mary's* Church near St. *Peter's* College . . . There, he penned these Poems, *Steps* for happy souls to climb heaven by.' Although Crashaw had indeed been a Fellow at Peterhouse, Cambridge, the explanation seems a little disingenuous. Surely the more likely reason for the title (probably provided either by Beaumont or the publisher rather than the poet) is suggested earlier in the Preface: 'Here's *Herbert's* second, but equal, who hath retrieved poetry of late, and returned it up to its primitive use; Let it bound back to heaven gates, whence it came.' *The Temple* had been remarkably popular. Christopher Harvey had published *The Synagogue: Or, The Shadow of The Temple* (including within it 'A Stepping Stone to the Threshold of Mr. Herbert's Church-Porch') as early as 1640, and by 1646, Herbert's volume had already gone through six or seven editions. To present a friend's new volume of religious verse under a title related to *The Temple* was simply to attempt to attract a wide and ready audience.

A poem within *Steps to the Temple* makes almost equally clear Crashaw's knowledge of Herbert's volume and his general independence of its influence:

> **"On Mr. G. Herbert's booke intituled the Temple of Sacred Poems, sent to a Gentlewoman."**
>
> Know you Fair on what you look?
> Divinest love lies in this book:
> Expecting fire from your eyes,
> To kindle this his sacrifice.
> When your hand unties these strings,
> Think you've an Angel by the wings.
> One that gladly will be nigh
> To wait upon each morning sigh,
> To flutter in the balmy air,
> Of your well perfumèd prayer.
> These white plumes of his he'll lend you,
> Which every day to heaven will send you:
> To take acquaintance of the sphere,
> And all the smooth faced kindred there.
> And though *Herbert's* name do owe
> These devotions, fairest; know
> That while I lay them on the shrine
> Of your white hand, they are mine.

That mixture of gallant compliment and decorative devotion is not at all like Herbert: there are no flutterings in 'balmy air' or 'well-perfumèd prayers' in *The Temple.* And that mixture of seven- and eight-syllable couplets is also unlike Herbert's verse. As Austin Warren pointed out [in his *Richard Crashaw*, 1962], only one of Crashaw's poems, **"Charitas Nimia, or The Dear Bargain"** (not published until the second edition of *Steps to the Temple* in 1648) seems to owe a substantial debt to Herbert.

The two poets' poetic treatments of St. Mary Magdalene demonstrate in a dramatic fashion their essential differences. . . . Crashaw's poem is the notorious **"Saint Mary Magdalene, or The Weeper,"** which begins,

> Hail, *Sister Springs*,
> Parents of silver-forded rills!
> Ever bubbling things!

Thawing Christall!   Snowy Hills!
Still spending, never spent; I mean
Thy fair Eyes sweet *Magdalene.*

Austin Warren has described the poem as 'a free fantasia': 'From his poem Crashaw has excluded the story, the character, the psychology, and the moral. Mary has no part in her poem; it should be called not **"The Weeper"** but "Tears" . . . It is a theme with variations—only the variations lack much variety: they do not change timbre or increase in resonance; and though they are all ingenious even their ingenuity is not climactic.' If Crashaw took the phrase 'crystal viols' from Donne, it is surely all that the poem owes to him. And with this poem, in contrast to the little poem on sending *The Temple* to a 'gentlewoman,' one can hardly imagine a debt to Jonson or even the minor Jonsonians. Although there are lines and phrases that remind one of Spenser or the Spenserians, the chief literary indebtednesses here are, for an English poet of the time, more unusual: to the Jesuit Latin poets, Francis Remond, Baudouin Cabilliau of Ypres, and Herman Hugo, and particularly to that poet of the astounding, Giambattista Marino. If William Drummond of Hawthornden, who had to listen to Ben Jonson tell him that his verses were old-fashioned, read Crashaw's book and still cared about such things, he must have taken some satisfaction in seeing a brilliantly 'new' young poet turn from the once-fashionable Donne and the dictatorial Jonson to one of the Italian poets Drummond had admired and translated.

Crashaw became the chief English poet of the Counter Reformation. His poems do not usually invite us primarily to rational understanding or even the appreciation of a performance, but to rapt participation in ecstatic joys and sufferings or delight in decorative and sensuous ornament. We are not expected to *judge* such poetry but to identify with its emotional states, to become entranced by its mellifluous sounds, to be shocked delightfully by its conceits and its occasionally outrageous epithets. Douglas Bush [in his *English Literature in the Early Seventeenth Century, 1600-1660,* 1962] has suggested that 'poetry like Crashaw's' may serve as the simplest definition of what most people mean when they talk about 'baroque poetry'; he also remarked that its motto might be, 'Over-ripeness is all.' This is the Crashaw who called 'un-English,' sometimes with the tone of shocked propriety appropriate to an occasion when a child with the wrong blood lines inherits a valuable familial estate—or even with the moral indignation which often accompanies the phrase, 'un-American.'

Crashaw is unusual, and he does present problems for both the critics and the literary historians. I think that one can identify the responses of two partisan groups, both of which strike me as mistaken: those who do not much like Crashaw's poetry and tend to attribute what they consider its failings to ignorance (he didn't know what he was doing), or to incompetence (he couldn't do anything else), or to his corruption by the Italians and Roman Catholics; and those who are such ardent defenders that they admit no shortcomings whatsoever and claim that he was always in control of his forms and images, that his language was never unusually sensual or sexual, and that any impression to the contrary is only the result of our incompetence in reading and responding to traditional religious symbolic language. Those extremes tend to obscure not only some of the radical problems but also some of the unusual possibilities of Crashaw's poetry.

Since one can glimpse most of the problems within *The Delights of the Muses,* the separately titled secular poems which were printed along with *Steps to the Temple* in both 1646 and 1648, I think it is best to begin there, undistracted by the special and complicated issues raised by the religious verse. One poem in that collection, **"Upon two green Apricocks sent to Cowley by Sir Crashaw,"** probably written when he was in his early twenties, shows that Crashaw could, when he wished, achieve impressive mastery of the sort of ingenious, witty, tightly-organized seventeenth-century poem so admired in the first half of the twentieth century. Cowley had published his *Poetical Blossoms* in 1633, when he was only fifteen years old. (Three years later he dared to apologize for the immaturity of one of the poems on the grounds that it had been written when he was only ten.) Crashaw was five years older than Cowley, already a fellow at Peterhouse when Cowley went up to Trinity. Crashaw turned his two green apricots into a graceful comment on his own late poetic immaturity in comparison to Cowley's astonishingly early fruits and flowers:

> O had my wishes
> And the dear merits of your Muse, their due,
> The year had found some fruit early as you;
> Ripe as those rich composures time computes
> Blossoms, but our blest taste confesses fruits.
> (ll. 10-14)

The poem ends with lines of elegance and power that go quite beyond conventional compliment:

> How then must these,
> Poor fruits look pale at thy Hesperides!
> Fain would I chide their slowness, but in their
> Defects I draw mine own dull character.
> Take them, and me in them acknowledging,
> How much my summer waits upon thy spring.
> (ll. 29-34)

If anyone wishes further evidence of Crashaw's abilities in this direction, he can find it, again in relation to Cowley, in the poem **"On Hope,"** printed among the sacred poems in *Steps to the Temple.* There, in alternate stanzas, Cowley attacked the hope that appears in the guises of worldly anticipation, greed, and coxcombry, and Crashaw defended the theological virtue that goes under the same name. In that poem Crashaw equalled Cowley in wit and neatness and far surpassed him in warmth and imaginative range. The final couplet is one of Crashaw's finest:

> True *Hope's* a glorious Huntress, and her chase
> The God of Nature in the field of Grace.

Wit and economy were of the essence in most of the Latin epigrams. If Crashaw did not write more poems like these it was because he preferred to write another kind of poetry.

One finds other and stranger things in *The Delights of the Muses.* The author of those poems shared much of the typical seventeenth-century young man's interest in decorative amatory poetry. (In addition to Marino and some of the Italian madrigalists, Crashaw used the fairly, standard classical texts: Moschus's 'Cupid's Crier,' Ausonius, Catullus's 'Seize the Day' once again.) One of the more memorable couplets in this vein is from the epigram "Upon *Venus* putting on *Mars* his Arms":

> Mars thou hast beaten naked, and o then
> What need'st thou put on arms against poor
>   men?

But if almost anyone might have tried his hand at adapting another epigram from the Greek Anthology (although seldom with such neatness), I think there is a good deal more than the usual literary taste and sensual susceptibility in Crashaw's translation of a passage from Virgil's Georgics, **"In the praise of the Spring"**:

> All trees, all leavy groves confess the Spring
> Their gentlest friend, then, then the lands begin
> To swell with forward pride, and seed desire
> To generation; Heaven's Almighty Sire
> Melts on the bosom of his love, and pours
> Himself into her lap in fruitful showers.
> And by a soft insinuation, mixt
> With earth's large mass, doth cherish and assist
> Her weak conceptions; No lone shade, but rings
> With chatting birds' delicious murmurings.
> Then *Venus'* mild instinct (at set times) yields
> The herds to kindly meetings, then the fields
> (Quick with warm *Zephyr's* lively breath) lay
>   forth
> Their pregnant bosoms in a fragrant birth.
> Each body's plump and juicy, all things full
> Of supple moisture. . . .
>
>   (ll. 1-16)

The rhythms of those fervent, astonishingly enjambed lines, are not those associated with witty point; they anticipate some of Milton's. I think it most unlikely that the young man who wrote those lines would ever make unconscious or unintentional use of a large amount of sexual imagery or allusion.

In the forty-two triplets of **"Wishes. To his (supposed) Mistress"** (the poem that begins: 'Who e'er she be,/ That not impossible she / That shall command my heart and me') one can see another of Crashaw's individual qualities: his tendency towards copious, almost infinite, variations. A version of that poem containing only ten triplets was published earlier, in the second edition of *Wits Recreations* (1641); it has a clearer shape than the 1646-1648 version and it is nearer to what we ordinarily think of as 'a poem' (even, perhaps, a 'Jonsonian' poem), but it is less interesting and much less a characteristic poem by Crashaw. Reading the full version, one can imagine that, as with the first version of **"The Weeper,"** still more additional stanzas could have been added or these stanzas rearranged with very little harm—or improvement—to the poem. Related to the multiplication of variations is Crashaw's tendency to expand greatly his models or originals. That is clear enough in **"Music's Duel,"** the poem about a contest between a nightingale and a lutanist, where Crashaw turned Famianus Strada's 58 Latin lines into 168 English ones, expanding the 14-line description of the actual 'duel' to 100 lines. That poem also demonstrates Crashaw's fascination with the emotional effects of

sounds, and his agility (and delight) in moving rapidly from one image or sensory response to another, mixing or confusing them to the point that, while the mind can sometimes hardly disentangle the 'prose meanings' (which often seem to cancel each other), the lines powerfully suggest an ardent voice, excess, and ecstasy:

> Then starts she suddenly into a throng
> Of short thick sobs, whose thund'ring volleys
>   float,
> And roll themselves over her lubric throat
> In panting murmurs, 'stilled out of her breast
> That ever-bubbling spring; the sugared Nest
> Of her delicious soul, that there does lie
> Bathing in streams of liquid Melody;
> Music's best seed-plot, whence in ripened Aires
> A golden-headed harvest, fairly rears
> His honey-dropping tops, plowed by her breath
> Which there reciprocally laboureth
> In that sweet soil.
>
>   (ll. 62-73)

There was a time when I confidently judged effects such as those in **"Wishes to his (supposed) Mistress"** and **"Music's Duel"** to be somehow illegitimate, but I now attribute my prejudiced response to youthful conservatism Why, after all, should there not be a poetry of excess as well as ecstasy? Why should we tie everything to logical or rhetorical schemata or notions of necessarily obvious beginnings and middles and ends? What is wrong with the idea of an open-ended form? As the American poet Elizabeth Bishop once casually remarked, why shouldn't Western poetry, like Eastern music, explore the possibilities of theoretically infinite variations? (Of course eventually we would get tired; and then the poem might stop or we might, individually, stop reading it.) Such questions are likely to disturb our few, hard-won concepts concerning a coherent poetics, and they may prove particularly upsetting if we have tried to make literature into a surrogate for religion. But we should try not to be afraid of unusual ideas, and it is just such possibilities that Crashaw's poetry suggests. If we read **"Wishes to his (supposed) Mistress"** with such queries in mind rather than with the assumption that the poem intends (or should intend) to 'build' and fails to do so, we may find that we enjoy nearly all of those occasionally repetitious triplets, and we may come to question the assumption that every poem should be 'built' as if it were a house. There are other things that we can do with poems besides try to live within them, and there are other possible constructions besides houses—or even temples. As Crashaw remarked in some of his finest lines, 'The phoenix builds the phoenix' nest./ Love's architecture is his own.'

From the secular poems it seems obvious that by temperament and desire Crashaw was early destined to be an unusual kind of English poet. He was fortunate, I think, to find in the Italian Jesuit poets and in the Catholicism of the Counter Reformation sustaining traditions, guides, and perhaps restraints. His religious poems present more problems for the modern reader—and many more rewards. It is within them that Crashaw developed most fully both his voice of exclamatory apostrophe (whether addressed to an absent lady, a book, a saint, or the name of Jesus) and his dithyrambic movements of mixed meters (suggesting the suddenly shifting movements characteristic of intense emotion) which Cowley was to popularize as the 'English' or 'irregular' Pindaric ode. Crashaw is not always surely in control. He falters, I think, when he concentrates on one desired meaning or effect so intensely that he fails to anticipate (and prevent) the possibility of a disastrous secondary one. That seems to be the problem when in **"The Weeper"** he means to emphasize the relations between the precious, nourishing tears and the angelic music, but unfortunately says that the angel's song 'Tastes of this breakfast all day long'; and also when he means to relate the precious essence of roses to the fires of its distilling process, but mistakenly describes the rose as 'Sweating in a too warm bed.' But I think Crashaw knew exactly what he was doing and was fully in control in **"On a prayer book sent to Mrs. M. R.,"** a poem that ends with the lines,

> Happy soul, she shall discover,
>   What joy, what bliss,
>   How many heavens at once it is,
> To have a God become her lover.

Crashaw clearly intended there, as elsewhere, to devote the language of sexual love to the higher spiritual ecstasy, and it is no accident that, as Bush has noted, one can find in that poem a number of the same images that one finds in Carew's erotic masterpiece, 'The Rapture.' No one can make us like such effects, of course, but we have no right to avoid the issue either by claiming that the mystical tradition had eliminated in advance all the sexual implications of Crashaw's language, or by assuming that the effects are the result of an inadvertent slipping of the poet's ordinary mask from his unconscious. Crashaw's strain of love is at its best, I think, in the St. Teresa poems. **"A Hymn to the Name and Honor of the Admirable Saint Teresa"** is consciously controlled and carefully revised, and it is an astonishing poem.

I cannot read Crashaw every day, and I cannot ordinarily read many of his poems at a sitting. Some of the poems which my friends admire seem to me to go on a good deal longer than they need to. (Occasionally, however, and with other works besides Crashaw's, I find it useful to remind myself of Stephen Crane's judgement on *War and Peace*: it was too long.) When for whatever reason one discovers that he cannot share at all in the excitement, Crashaw's rhapsodies can seem both tedious and tasteless. It may be a mark of my generally conservative taste that the poem which strikes me as most fully successful as a whole should be **"An Hymn of the Nativity, sung by the Shepherds,"** where the traditional materials and the formal divisions between two shepherds and the chorus provide an obvious and firm structure for the poem. At any rate, it is a lovely poem, and one of those which Crashaw carefully improved by his revisions. Its most dramatic moment (in the 1648 version) occurs when, after Thyrsis and Tityris have joined together in the repetition of an earlier stanza celebrating their sight of the Child, the full chorus repeats the stanza once again and goes on to the magnificent beginning of their welcome to Him and all the paradoxes that He represents.

BOTH

> We saw thee in thy balmy nest
>   Bright *Dawn* of our eternal *Day*,
> We saw thine eyes break from their *East*
>   And chase the trembling shades away
> We saw thee, and we blest the sight,
> We saw thee, by thine own sweet light.

CHORUS

> We saw thee, and we blest the sight,
> We saw thee, by thine own sweet light.

FULL CHORUS

> Welcome, all *wonders* in one sight!
>   Eternity shut in a span,
> Summer in winter, day in night,
>   Heaven in earth, and God in man;
> Great little one! whose all embracing birth
> Lifts earth to heav'n, stoops heav'n to earth.

Fine as those stanzas are, though, I do not think they are quite Crashaw's greatest lines. I would judge those to be the concluding lines of **"The Flaming Heart: Upon the Book and Picture of the seraphical Saint Teresa (as she is usually expressed with a Seraphim beside her)"** lines which appeared only in the *Carmen Deo Nostro* version of the poem, published in 1652 after Crashaw's death in Loreto. Within them, I think that Crashaw most successfully transformed the hyperboles and ardours of ordinary lovers' language into a triumphantly new language for a new and supreme love. The lines may remind us in some respects of Blake. Neither Blake nor any other English poet has ever been able to sustain for long such incandescence:

> O thou undaunted daughter of desires!
> By all thy dower of *Lights* and *Fires;*
> By all the eagle in thee, all the dove;
> By all thy lives and deaths of love;
> By thy large draughts of intellectual day,
> And by thy thirsts of love more large than they;
> By all thy brim-fill'd Bowles of fierce desire;
> By thy last morning's draught of liquid fire;
> By the full kingdom of that final kiss
> That seiz'd thy parting soul, and seal'd thee his;
> By all the heav'ns thou hast in him
> (Fair sister of the Seraphim!)
> By all of *Him* we have in *Thee;*
> Leave nothing of my *Self* in me.
> Let me so read thy life, that I
> Unto all life of mine may die.

(pp. 102-15)

Joseph H. Summers, "A Foreign and a Provincial Gentleman: Richard Crashaw and Henry Vaughan," in his The Heirs of Donne and Jonson, *Oxford University Press, Inc., 1970, pp. 102-29.*

John Tytell (essay date 1971)

[*In the essay below, Tytell identifies erotic imagery in Crashaw's sacred and secular poetry, contending that he is "unaware of the larger implications of the sexual terms integral to his celebration of a union with God."*]

Certain of Crashaw's poems, especially those addressed to women, include sexual allusions and images which do not

The Countess of Denbigh, friend and patroness of Crashaw.

directly support the religious subjects of those poems. Several passages are so manifestly erotic as to seduce the reader from the immediate argument to a distracting sexual metaphor that has little apparent function when the context of the poem is considered.

The initiated reader of Crashaw knows that the poet is never as ribald as Herrick, nor as candidly sexual as Suckling (in such a poem as "A Candle"); he knows that there is almost no appearance of a seduction or "carpe diem" appeal in Crashaw, nor is there an hedonistic sensuality or a cynical attitude to sexuality as is often found in Donne (in a poem such as "The Flea," which parodies sexual union through the corrupt vehicle of the dung-eating flea, in which "our two bloods mingled bee"). Crashaw, as Austin Warren has observed:

> never sang the sexual passions; he wrote none of those at once exact and honorific descriptions of the female body such as one finds in Spenser, in Sidney, in the "Compliment" and "Rapture" of his contemporary, Carew. [in his *Richard Crashaw: A Study in Baroque Sensibility*, 1939]

Allusions to sexual activity do not appear even when the subject of the poem warrants such appearances. And when sexuality is included in a secular poem, it is almost always hinted at modestly or understated. There are, for example, no startlingly sexual images in **"Loves Horoscope,"** a poem reminiscent of Donne's intellectual tendencies without the complementing balance of his direct and concrete imagery. There are, as well, neither overt nor covert allusions of any exciting quality in Crashaw's one poem in the "to my mistress" genre—**"Wishes. To his (supposed) Mistresse."** The title of the poem is significant because the personal pronoun suggests a personna; and even if a personna is more suitable for the expression of a poet's own erotic fantasies, Crashaw's "wishes" are disappointing. The woman's beauty is rendered in restrained and conventional terms; her appeal is genteel, coy and sisterly rather than erotic:

> Smiles, that can warme
> The blood, yet teach a charme,
> That Chastity shall take no harme.
>
> Blushes, that bin
> The burnish of no sin,
> Nor flames of ought too hot within.

Crashaw permits very few allusions to the sexual act itself. In **"Wishes,"** he mentions the loss of the bride's virginity with an unrealistic calm that is remarkably inconsistent with his treatment of the same subject in the religious poems. In a poem in the "debat" genre, **"On Hope,"** he writes of "deflour'd virgins" and marital "Spousal rites." His most graphic allusion to the sexual act appears in **"To Pontius washing his blood-stained hands,"** a poem about Pontius's rape of an innocent virgin:

> Harke how at every Touch she does complaine
>   her:
> Harke how she bids her frighted Drops make
>   hast,
> And with sad murmurs, chides the Hands that
>   stain her.

(94)

The drops can refer both to the virgin's tears, and more subtly to her bleeding; the picture of sexual transgression is more direct than any other in Crashaw, and the circumstances surrounding the encounter, those of the plundered virgin, are indicative of Crashaw's unusual use of sexual imagery.

Crashaw frequently alludes to virginity, a time for the female when the still unrealized sexual act is connected with the anticipation of the pain, mystery and ecstasy of the sundered hymen. His one poem in the epithalamic genre, a poem left in manuscript form, becomes more an elegy for "this sweet maydenhead" which "alas is dead" than a celebration of marriage. The first half of the poem describes the mythological phoenix, and the self-immolation of the bird is compared to the virgin bride's sacrifice. The choice of the phoenix as symbol is peculiar, however: the symbol is narcissistic, the creation by the phoenix is inhumanly solipsistic, without the dual physical involvement necessary for procreation among mammals. The phoenix resurrects itself from its ashes, and is reborn after its self-inflagration; the pattern is that of martyrdom and close to the example of Christ. The choice of this particular symbol as the appropriate one for lost virginity can best be understood within the context of Crashaw's religious celebration of martyrdom and devotion to Christ. The ecstatic and painful surrender of the virgin was the closest approximation that Crashaw would invent for the sacrifice on the cross, and for his own personal desire and longing which was presumably fulfilled in mystic vision resulting from meditation.

The full significance, however, of the poem cannot be appreciated until what follows the phoenix symbol is examined. The surprising result is that the reader realizes that the sexual ecstasy anticipated for the virgin has been transferred to the ritualistic sphere of the phoenix. The **"Epithalamium,"** however, is a secular poem. The actual description of the sexual encounter following the sacrifice of the phoenix is strangely without passion.

> With many pretty peevish tryalls of angry
>   yeelding, faint denyings,
> melting No's, and milde denyalls, dying
>   liues, and short liued dyings;
>   with doubtful eyes,
>   halfe smiles, halfe teares,
>   with trembling joyes,
>   and jocund feares;
> Twixt the pretty twilight strife
> of dying maide and dawning wife;
> twixt raine, and sun-shine, this sweet mayden-
>   head alas is dead:
>   (407-8)

The description is ordinary, quite untransfigured by any but completely expected emotions. The bridegroom is determined; conquest is inevitable but has its rewards for the fearful bride. Crashaw filters nature images through the rest of the poem and makes it a healthy paean of fertility, full of traditional associations of early spring and regeneration.

The sexual imagery in the second half of the poem is not striking or subtle, and it seems conscious. The poem, however, was left in manuscript. It dealt, perhaps, too directly with emotions Crashaw was to use indirectly, possibly more unconsciously than consciously, and to celebrate different ends than human propagation. The **"Epithalamium"** can be taken as representative of Crashaw's secular poems; like **"Wishes,"** it deals with human love in conventional terms which are not especially sexual. This characteristic in itself is not unusual. What Crashaw does or does not do in the secular poems is of significance only when compared with the religious poems. When passages of torrid sexuality appear in the religious poems with a freedom obviously not present in the secular poems, then the reader is entitled to question in order to try to explain so unexpected a transference.

These questions should be postponed until a further examination of the secular poems is completed. Another poem in the "debat" genre, **"Musicks Duell,"** illustrates the quality of Crashaw's language which creates the basis for a sensual interpretation of much of the poetry. The lines, for example, which describe the singing of the nightingale, full of "short thicke sobs" and "panting murmurs," are particularly erotic. Crashaw compares the nightingale's

exertion to the plowing of a wheat field. The nightingale, who "Heaves her soft Bosome," then

> . . . opes the floodgate, and lets loose a Tide
> Of streaming sweetnesse, which in state doth
>   ride
> On the wav'd backe of every swelling straine,
> Rising and falling in a pompous traine.
> And while she thus discharges a shrill peale . . .
>   (151)

The rhythmical rise and fall, the release and discharge of pent-up notes seen metaphorically as fluids, as part of a sea wave, correspond to the emotions relieved through sexual orgasm. As a result, Crashaw writes:

> Her little soule is ravisht: and so pour'd
> Into loose extasies, that shee is plac't
> Above her selfe, Musicks Enthusiast.
>   (151-2)

The nightingale has attained, as in that elusive moment of highest sexual release, the transcendence and obliteration of the self.

These comments are not intended as interpretation. Nightingales are loath to mate with lute-players. The point is that the exultant and supreme effort of the bird (similar to the phoenix) is patently couched within a potently sexual analogy. This analogy, born out of the very choice of language by Crashaw, adds a measure of physical excitement to the poem, but it also creates a typical source of ambiguity.

Ambiguity, usually, has been understood to add levels of richness to poems, in the sense of multiplicity of meaning. Crashaw's type of ambiguity, however, occurs through the use of a series of images which evoke an action not directly expected or conceivable, given the ideological or thematic context of the poem. The result, frequently, is confusing.

The best example of this ambiguity occurs in Crashaw's famous poem, **"The Weeper."** The poem celebrates Mary Magdelene's agony over the death of Christ. In the second, expanded version of the poem, the following lines appear:

> So doe perfumes expire.
> So sigh tormented sweets, opprest
> With proud vnpittying fire.
> Such Teares the suffering Rose that's vext
> With vngentle flames does shed,
> Sweating in a too warm bed.
>   (313-14)

This is the first mention of "Rose" in the poem; the only possible antecedent is the use of some nature imagery, as the "balsom-sweating bough." On the immediate and apparent level, Crashaw is creating an analogy ("so doe," "so sigh") between Mary's remorse and sorrow and that of a rose which is wilting in its flower-bed because of the merciless sun.

But Crashaw, of course, was aware of Magdelene's history, and of the fact that she had experienced carnal knowledge. The choice of the rose now seems deliberate. Crashaw himself indicated an awareness of the almost archetypal situation of this flower in English poetry, in his poem **"An Himne for the Circumcision day of our Lord"**:

> . . . this modest Maiden Lilly,
> Our sinnes have sham'd into a Rose.
>
> (141)

The rose, then, stands for the fallen woman, it helps to identify the weeper more precisely; and the passage can well stand as the symbolic correlative for Magdalene's thoughts. Each line contains a physical basis which becomes a sexual analogy for the act of copulation. The "perfumes" suggest the particular aroma emitted by the female during intercourse; the following lines suggest the sighing of the woman who is experiencing the greatest possible mixture of pleasure and pain under the weight of the relentless, heated male. The final line is almost too naturalistic a conclusion. In this case, the sexual imagery can be understood since Magdelene, as a former prostitute, can be expected to perceive the world in sensual terms. But, the reader may justifiably query, isn't her vision of Christ to be interpreted as redemption from her former slavery to the perceptions of the body? Is Crashaw suggesting through the very nature of his word choices that her transformation is incomplete? This question becomes even more pressing when the sexuality in Crashaw's poems about virgins and Saint Teresa seems to contradict the state of ideal beatitude which the content of these poems urges.

This passage did not exist in the originally published, 1646 version of the poem. Certain revisions in the 1648 text indicate that there was some sensitivity on Crashaw's part to the implications of his own words. In the original version, in the twenty-first stanza, Crashaw had the phrase "fertile Mothers," which was later amended to "fruitful," "wombes of sorrow" (for Mary's eyes) was revised to "nests," and "sluttish Earth" became "sordid." The sexual quality was not eliminated by the changes but rendered less obvious, more private in meaning.

The general ambiguity arises from the difficulty of accepting the metaphor of God as lover, of Christ as "Noble Bridgroom," when the terms of comparison are as vivid and graphic as Crashaw's often become. Catholicism, as Austin Warren has written

> . . . has persistently affirmed that, as the body,
> the senses, the affections, and the imagination
> are integral parts of man, they must all collabo-
> rate in God's service; that the lower may offici-
> ate as instruments to the higher.

But there are reasonable limits. The whole problem—as Basil Willey has urged—is that Crashaw's "intollerable joys, sweet and subtle pains and delicious deaths" need appreciation within a "context of Teresan mysticism" [in his *Richard Crashaw: A Memorial Lecture*, 1949]. The question is whether readers—in a society which anyway largely denies the validity of the mystical experience—can grasp so intense an anthropomorphic transfer of human love to spiritual exultation. Whether this transfer is esthetically satisfactory (outside a surrealistic framework), valid or even possible, is a question open for speculation. Nevertheless, this paradoxical dependence of transcen-

dant spirit on the imagery of physical passion reveals the essential Crashaw.

The last line of Crashaw's **"On a prayer booke sent to Mrs. M.R."** reads "to have a God become her lover." This concept, actually more pagan and classical in origin than Christian, becomes the basis of the poem and all of Crashaw's religious poetry. His woman is faced with the alternative of offering possession of her "sacred store/Of hidden sweets, and holy joyes" to a "Noble Bridegroom" or to one of the "gay mates of the god of flyes." The central ambiguity of the poem is that *either* seems able to produce an effect in the woman which is described in terms of the sexual analogy:

> Delicious deaths, soft exhalations
> Of soule; deare, and divine annihilations.
>   A thousand unknown rites
>   Of joyes, and rarifyed delights.
>
> (129)

If the cohorts of the god of flyes can cause the same result—and syntax and structure in the poem supports this observation—then how can that result be merely an account of spiritual love? The divine lover, the "spouse of Virgins," is unusually fickle and indiscriminately promiscuous because if the woman is not receptive:

> Doubtless hee will unload
> Himselfe some other where,
>   And powre abroad
>   His precious sweets,
> On the faire soule whom first hee meets.
>
> (129)

The words "unload," "powre" and "sweets" suggest connotations of male sexual climax. Later allusions to a "balmy showre" and to "rifle and deflour" are too obviously physical to exist on a purely spiritual level.

The Saint Teresa poem, **"In memory of the Vertuous and Learned Lady Madre de Teresa that sought an early Martyrdome,"** creates similar difficulties. The poem can be interpreted on two levels. Teresa, a virgin, does not know:

> Why to show love shee should shed blood,
> Yet though shee cannot tell you why,
> Shee can love and shee can dye.
>
> (131-2)

Teresa is reserved for martyrdom, a special sacrifice. Upon the "choice point" of an "immortal instrument," her life must be "spent." The expense, as described in the poem, is so physical as to remind the reader constantly of the "little death" of sexual activity:

> O how oft shall thou complaine
> Of a sweet ad subtile paine?
> Of intollerable joyes?
> Of a death in which who dyes
> Loves his death, and dyes againe,
> And for ever so be slaine!
> And lives and dyes, and knowes not why
> To live, but that he still may dy.
>
> (134)

To study the numerous examples of overt sexual reference which occur in this poem would only belabor the point. Crashaw, who could conceive of only virginity for the women in his poems, (who himself "would be married to a single life") was able to deflower them in his religious poems with more passion than found in many poets. As he advised yet another woman, in the **"Countesse of Denbigh"** poem:

> Yield then, o yeild, that loue may win
> The Fort at last, and let life in.
>
> (238)

The result is the incongruity of a "carpe diem" message within an intentionally religious context. Is this fort like the "usurpt towne" in Donne's "Batter my heart" sonnet? Can the labor necessary for the admission be entirely intellectual or spiritual; or is a more primary passion implied by the language itself?

This physical basis, perhaps, is clearest in Crashaw's most famous poem, **"The Flaming Heart."** The poem does much to clarify the kind of love that is Crashaw's main subject. In the poem, after a reversal of role in which the masculine Teresa is awarded the phallic love dart, Crashaw explains:

> For in loue's feild was neuer found
> A nobler weapon than a WOVND.
>
> (326)

This wound (is it Christ's wound or the female vulva?) precedes lines which equate primitivistic sexuality with the martyr's act:

> Liue here great HEART; & loue and dy & kill;
> And bleed & wound; and yeild and conquer still.
>
> (326)

Shafts of light "break in" and despoil, "brim-filled Bowles of feirce desire" overflow with an oxymoronic "liquid fire" (the male discharge?). The result is an annihilation of self, the "Leave nothing of my SELF in me," which is the purpose of physical union.

Cowley was wrong when, in his elegy, he implied that all but Crashaw deified women:

> Nay with all the worst of Heathen dotage
> We (vain men!) the Monster woman
> Deifie.

Crashaw's peculiar deification outstripped them all. Women were placed on an ideal plane of everlasting virginity; however, the context in which they were placed did not promise to preserve this virginity. Whether Crashaw was aware of this, whether he realized the extent to which his own use of sexual metaphor threatened and ultimately compromised his virgins, is doubtful.

Unfortunately, there exists no way of proving whether Crashaw's use of sexual imagery was deliberate. If it was conscious, the resulting contradictions might exist within the seventeenth century tradition of paradox: the craving demands of the bridegroom who can be nourished on purely Platonic broth. Yet the terms of this nourishment are so tactile, so sensuous and frequently sensual, so completely unethereal, that the reader may be confused and perhaps misled.

It is always tempting to attribute such uses of sexual metaphor to the unconscious. The thesis, briefly, would be that the saintly communicant of the Little Gidding group was innocent of the effect of his choice of language, naive and pure in his intentions. Due to certain emotional deprivations, of which there is inadequate biographical evidence, Crashaw could not imagine sexuality in its proper, normal and expected context, and so transferred it to an impossible plane. What his virgins and his God reveal about his own youth is impossible to determine, but Joan Bennett has noticed a repellent element in Crashaw's repeated "collocation of torture and erotic emotion"; she has argued that the images spring directly from his emotional needs [in her *Four Metaphysical Poets*, 1934].

The contours of Crashaw's poems are like landslides: momentum builds and increases. The sexual language usually occurs near the end of the poems, just as Crashaw's fervor, perhaps his unconscious frenzy, was at its height. There is no equivalent frenzy in the secular descriptions of love; the ecstasy is exclusively reserved for love between virgin and her god. The ambiguity of a poem such as **"On a prayer booke sent to Mrs. M.R."** raises the possibility that Crashaw's expression of love was not merely to express union with the divine force, but actually the imaginative release of mundane desires for human love that he could not realize in any other manner. This, of course, is offered only as speculation; but the hypothesis does serve to explain the disparity in the sexual content of the secular and religious poetry.

Divine love is translated in the religious poems into the terms readers best understand, the physical ones describing the process of their own method of procreation. Esthetically this results in a kind of emotional sensationalism. Yet some emotions are abstract, more generalized than others; and some emotions need to be independent of, perhaps transcendent of, physical sensations. Much religious poetry does imply the sexual connection which is evident in Crashaw's poetry; Crashaw's very bluntness, however, separates him from most poets who write for the glory of a higher being. No value judgment is necessary to determine the quality of Crashaw's result. The kind of ambiguity which this essay has revealed is basic to that of unsuccessful attempts in art: an apparent theme which is not supported by the language or images presented by the poet. To call this a deliberate "baroque" dislocation, in Crashaw's case, would mean that a sense of irony would have to be present. There is no evidence of this. Crashaw's attempt seems to have been a genuine one; he seems on the whole, unaware of the larger implications of the sexual terms integral to his celebration of a union with God. (pp. 21-7)

> *John Tytell, "Sexual Imagery in the Secular and Sacred Poems of Richard Crashaw," in* Literature and Psychology, *Vol. XX, No. 1, 1971, pp. 21-7.*

Paul G. Stanwood (essay date 1979)

[*In the excerpt below, Stanwood examines the liturgical elements of Crashaw's work, asserting that by a "perversity of language" dealing in extremes, he successfully*

explores the religious themes of "incarnation, penitence,
martyrdom and mystical death."]

Between Richard Crashaw and his older contemporary
Donne, it is difficult to see any real affinity, as Douglas
Bush [in his *English Literature in the Earlier Seventeenth
Century 1600-1660*, 1962] observes when he suggests that
the motto of Crashaw's poetry might be "Over-ripeness is
all." While Crashaw's themes and interests are less wide
ranging than Donne's, the two poets nevertheless share a
similar intensity and excitement, and as with Donne, so
Crashaw's sense of time is compacted and concentrated on
a single point. Their poetry employs different figures, but
both poets move toward the same end into which and out
of which everything spins and radiates in the oneness of
worshipper and the object of worship. Consecration, ceremony, unity of experience, and publicly formalized yet
personal feeling—all features of the liturgical mode—
belong as much to Crashaw as to Donne.

The popular view of Crashaw is not one I share. This is
expressed, for example, not only by Bush, but by
Crashaw's most recent editor, who says: "Richard
Crashaw may be considered the most un-English of all the
English poets. As his native poetic genius developed, it absorbed continental influences, both sacred and secular, to
such a degree that Crashaw eventually removed from Puritanism and England to Roman Catholicism and Rome."
This statement mixes truth with fantasy. While Crashaw
certainly moved easily in Tridentine devotion, he wrote in
ways common to many other Englishmen of his time, but
in a richer and better informed manner. Crashaw should
not be read in isolation (though he usually is) from Giles
and Phineas Fletcher, Henry Hawkins, Joseph Beaumont,
Edward Benlowes, William Chamberlayne, Katherine
Philips, Abraham Cowley, and from such prose writers as
Robert Shelford for whose *Five Pious and Learned Discourses* (1635) he wrote a commendatory poem, and Anthony Stafford, author of *The Femall Glory: or, the Life,
and Death of our Blessed Lady, the Holy Virgin Mary,
God's owne immaculate Mother* (1635). Puritanism and
England spawned much that was exotic and unlike what
we might have expected. Crashaw's ceremonial, adora-
tional mode of expression, his passion, and his alleged
Catholic flamboyance are familiar in other and non-
Roman writers contemporary with him, as well as in
Donne and in earlier English poets such as Sidney and
Spenser.

Above all, Crashaw is concerned with the experience of
faith and only secondly with doctrine. Like Donne, he
seeks to describe complete moments in a continuously
moving world but in more explicitly Christian terms
where the end of time is its beginning with "aeternity shutt
in a span." The urgency of Crashaw's devotion is single-
minded and heated, as much public as it is private. He is
as if present at the altar of God, offering his poetry and
our aspirations to be a fit and sufficient thanksgiving and
sacrifice. Crashaw is a poet of the liturgical mode, where
the Incarnation informs his every gesture and speech:
word and world, preacher and sermon, offering and receiving, going and returning, history and eternity meet in
the point around which all else turns. Here ceremony is
performed not for its own sake, but for the sake of liturgical rightness.

Crashaw illustrates best—or most prominently—the features of these paradoxes and the qualities of this worship
in the **"Hymn of the Holy Nativity."** He writes from the
standpoint of a rapt observer in the period of a literal time
past, but one which is currently and continuously present:

> We saw thee in thy baulmy Nest,
>   Young dawn of our aeternall day!
> We saw thine eyes break from their EASTE
>   And chase the trembling shades away.
> We saw thee; & we blest the sight
> We saw thee by thine own sweet light.
>   (ll. 31-36, p. 249)

> Wellcome, all WONDERS in one sight!
>   AEternity shutt in a span.
> Sommer in Winter.   Day in Night.
>   Heaven in earth, & GOD in MAN.
> Great little one! whose all-embracing birth
> Lifts earth to heaven, stoopes heav'n to earth.

> WELLCOME.   Though nor to gold nor silk.
>   To more than Caesar's birthright is;
> Two sister-seas of Virgin-Milk,
>   With many a rarely-temper'd kisse
> That breathes at once both MAID & MOTHER,
> Warmes in the one, cooles in the other.

>   (ll. 79-90)

Crashaw's carefully controlled and restrained breathlessness, his use of antithesis, of oxymora, of homoioteleuton,
and of other rhetorical figures, urge us to abandon ordinary time in preference to another higher and paradoxical
time. This new time describes the world correctly, being
of an infinite dispensation, and it provides for and clothes
the earthly order in a liturgical setting, where the poet portrays himself in the role of worshipper at an eternal scene
demanding total attention.

"The Weeper" is generally felt to be Crashaw at his worst;
but while I would not claim that it is among his very best
poems, even the most "celebrated" stanzas have power
and integrity. Crashaw stretches the resources of poetic
language as far as he can; his subject is, indeed, nothing
less than the exaltation of penitential tears into an independent and autonomous world. We may not like to think
of tears in this way, but that is the way Crashaw intends
us to see them and this was a convention of his time. We
may wonder over the details of their metamorphosis:

> Hail, sister springs!
> Parents of sylver-footed rills!
> Ever bubling things!
> Thawing crystall! snowy hills,
> Still spending, never spent!   I mean
> Thy fair eyes, sweet MAGDALENE!
>   (st. 1, ll. 1-6)

> Upwards thou dost weep.
> Heavn's bosome drinks the gentle stream.
> Where th'milky rivers creep,
> Thine floates above; & is the cream.
> Waters above th'Heavns, what they be
> We'are taught best by thy TEARES & thee.

Every morn from hence
A brisk Cherub somthing sippes
Whose sacred influence
Addes sweetnes to his sweetest Lippes.
Then to his musick.   And his song
Tasts of this Breakfast all day long.

Not in the evening's eyes
When they Red with weeping are
For the Sun that dyes,
Sitts sorrow with a face so fair,
No where but here did ever meet
Sweetnesse so sad, sadnesse so sweet.
(sts. 4-6, ll. 19-36)

But can these fair Flouds be
Friend with the bosom fires that fill thee
Can so great flames agree
AEternal Teares should thus distill thee!
O flouds, o fires! o suns ô showres!
Mixt & made freinds by love's sweet powres.

Twas his well-pointed dart
That digg'd these wells, & drest this Vine;
And taught the wounded HEART
The way into these weeping Eyn.
Vain loves avant! bold hands forbear!
The lamb hath dipp't his white foot here.

And now where're he strayes,
Among the Galilean mountaines,
Or more unwellcome wayes,
He's follow'd by two faithfull fountaines;
Two walking baths; two weeping motions;
Portable, & compendious oceans.
(sts. 17-19, ll. 97-114)

The tears of the penitent Magdalen take on a life of their own, and later in the poem begin to speak. But they are not merely the result of devotion; they are themselves objects of devotion, and they offer themselves for a devotional end, which is to wash *our Lord's feet*. Here is a new world made of tears which worship and ask for worship. I see nothing inherently different about Crashaw's ambition in this poem and Donne's in "A Nocturnall," since both poems make preposterous statements and claim to be complete and encompassing experiences. Finally both are liturgical poems, and both demand our wholehearted assent.

Some commentators have dismissed **"The Weeper,"** and especially these stanzas of it, as a collection of mere *bon-bons* and not even delectable ones. But Crashaw nearly always knew what he was doing; he was a constant reviser of his work and this version of **"The Weeper,"** for example, contains thirty-one stanzas as opposed to an earlier version of twenty-three. Crashaw is right in expanding his effects, in urging us in ceremonial yet familiar terms to wonder at the singleness of devotion. His exotic fantasies turn out to be no different in kind, let us say, from Donne's invitation at the end of **"Death's Duell"**—his last sermon—where he urges us to climb the Cross and suck at the bloody wounds of Christ, a conceit which seems not to have troubled anyone as either outrageous, tasteless or atypically English. T. S. Eliot [in his "A Note on Richard Crashaw," in *For Lancelot Andrewes*, 1928] was right in saying that Crashaw was a poet with intelligence: "Crashaw's images . . . give a kind of intellectual plea-

sure—it is a deliberate conscious perversity of language, a perversity like that of the amazing and amazingly impressive interior of St. Peter's. There is brain work in it."

Crashaw writes of extremes and carries them as far as metamorphosis and consuming passion will permit. His intensity is both a credit and a shortcoming—helpful in producing highly colorful performances but limiting since it narrows the range of possible subjects. Incarnation, penitence, martyrdom, mystical death—these are Crashaw's principal topics, and these he offers in a variety of ritualized forms. The Magdalen is one saint who engaged his imagination, while Teresa of Avila is a second. The last lines of **"The Flaming Heart"** are well known, but they should be recalled in view of the theme of time and liturgy. Here Crashaw joins himself to St. Teresa and hopes that he may become one with her in order to defeat the corruption of common time and space. As well, he celebrates her ecstasy both for her sake and for his own and suggests that in her life and death we may see the true and sufficient pattern of all life. The poem may be witty, baroque and metaphysical, but it is definitely liturgical:

O thou undanted daughter of desires!
By all thy dowr of LIGHTS & FIRES;
By all the eagle in thee, all the dove;
By all thy lives & deaths of love;
By thy larg draughts of intellectuall day,
And by thy thirsts of love more large then they;
By all thy brim-fill'd Bowles of feirce desire
By thy last Morning's draught of liquid fire;
By the full kingdome of that finall kisse
That seiz'd thy parting Soul, & seal'd thee his;
By all the heav'ns thou hast in him
(Fair sister of the SERAPHIM!)
By all of HIM we have in THEE;
Leave nothing of my SELF in me.
Let me so read thy life, that I
Unto all life of mine may dy.
(ll. 93-108)

Crashaw intends this conclusion as a litany, where there is a perfect meeting of public ritual and personal desire. His language reminds us of Cranmer's Litany in *The Book of Common Prayer*, which of course Crashaw knew: "By the mystery of thy holy Incarnation; by thy holy Nativity and Circumcision; by thy Baptism, Fasting, and Temptation, *Good Lord, deliver us*. By thine Agony and Bloody Sweat; by thy Cross and Passion; by thy precious Death and Burial; by thy glorious Resurrection and Ascension; and by the Coming of the Holy Ghost, *Good Lord, deliver us*. . . ." In such forms are particular desires offered in one common prayer. Crashaw recalls one ritual in performing another, and in his triumph he writes liturgically. "It is the world of man's inner life at its mystical intensity," writes Austin Warren, "the world of devotion expressing itself through the sacraments and ceremonial and liturgy; it is a world which knows vision and rapture, tears and fire; it is a world of the supernatural, wherein the miraculous becomes the probable; and this world manifests itself to the senses in a rhetoric brilliant, expressive, and appropriate." [in his *Richard Crashaw: A Study in Baroque Sensibility*, 1939] It is also a world comparable in many ways to Donne's: the flames of passion sometimes rise higher in Crashaw, but the desire is similar in both writers; for in both, the literary creation contains the world and is one world, and we are bound to this world by admiration and prayer. (pp. 98-102)

> *Paul G. Stanwood, "Time and Liturgy in Donne, Crashaw, and T. S. Eliot," in* Mosaic: A Journal for the Comparative Study of Literature and Ideas, *Vol. XII, No. 2, Winter, 1979, pp. 91-105.*

Patrick Grant (essay date 1979)

[*Below, Grant contends that Crashaw's religious poetry was heavily influenced by Gallican Capucin poetry techniques, making Crashaw "a cool manipulator of effects, and . . . [giving us] a sense too of a man aware of himself in the spiritual life."*]

Richard Crashaw is a most peculiar poet who tends to stimulate among his critics either extremes of revulsion or of deliberately argued admiration. This sharp division in taste tends to correspond also to a methodological distinction between 'modern' and 'historical' approaches to his work. To those who read his poems without concern for devotional conventions the images of wounds and mouths and blood and nests are soon revolting and the sense grows strong of something awry in the poet's sensibility, something smacking of perverse eroticism. Those who wish to defend Crashaw nearly always begin by acknowledging the lurid and sensuous qualities and then, producing a range of examples from contemporary Baroque devotional practice, go on to say that the sensuality must be understood not literally, but as emblematic of certain spiritual states. One critic [Julius D. Locke, "Images and Image Symbolized in Metaphysical Poetry with Special Reference to Otherworldliness," Diss. University of Florida, 1958] claims that the images should be read with no corporeal significance attached to them at all, and in this light Crashaw becomes less an enraptured mystagogue and more a careful and intellectual manipulator of conventional materials: a cool and aloof arranger of brightly coloured beads, not a febrile and over-excited case of arrested development. (p. 89)

It is attractive, if bland, when faced with this kind of polarity to attempt to take the middle road, but with Crashaw the problem is that he pulls us so strongly in one direction or the other. John Donne's *A Litanie*, on the other hand, gives us lines like these:

> My heart is by dejection, clay,
> And by selfe-murder, red.

The image is striking, but we do not experience a great deal of perplexity about how, basically, to read it. We are never tempted to imagine the speaker's heart as literal *terra cotta,* or to think of a literal suicide. Rather we see a reference to the Fall of Man: the word 'dejection' contains the latinate implication of throwing down, the clay heart suggests the melancholy humour, cold and dry, which follows upon the human realisation of fallenness, and the self-murder confirms the general theological interpretation by referring to the original transgression by which man, by his own hand, brought death into the world. The further combination of 'clay' and 'red' suggests

a pun on the Hebrew *adom* or 'red earth' from which, by tradition, the first man was moulded and which the poem develops in the following line, 'From this red earth, O Father, purge away/All vicious tinctures'. Thus the clay heart and the red colour are effective because they are such enlivening ways to deepen our understanding of original sin.

But when Crashaw writes of, say, the wounds of his crucified Lord, the relationship of image to concept is much less readily ascertained:

> Lo! a mouth, whose full-bloom'd lips
> At too deare a rate are roses.
> Lo! a blood-shot eye! that weepes
> And many a cruell teare discloses.

The transpositions are obtrusively anatomical. The body's integrity is violated, both by crucifixion and by the distortion of normal physical functions which follow on it as wounds become lips ('full-bloom'd') and eyes ('blood-shot'). Our first reaction is to recoil from the physical horror as the poem shows us, presumably, Magdalene ('O thou that on this foot hast laid/Many a kisse') who is kissing a mouth and commiserating with a weeping eye, actions which the poem depends on us seeing as normal—except that these consolations have for their objects the physical distortions caused by the maiming of Christ's body. Magdalene, we come to see, is licking Christ's wounds, and with an ardour of erotic concern.

On reflection, however, it may seem that the poem operates by playing deliberately with our attitudes to harsh physical facts. We have to note and accept that kisses and tears are normal manifestations of pity in order to appreciate the abnormality of Magdalene's actions, in physical terms. In our recoil, and partly dependent on it, we begin to reconsider what we have been reading, for the suffering of Christ, in theological terms, is the act which uniquely causes us to take stock again of the meaning of all human suffering. The eloquence of grief in those wounds, theologically understood, will direct us to the significance of the event which is the poem's true subject. There is a clue in the last stanza:

> The difference onely this appeares,
> (Nor can the change offend)
> The debt is paid in *Ruby*-Teares,
> Which thou in Pearles did'st lend.

The word 'difference' is ambiguous. On one level (the actual-physical) it indicates that Christ's weeping is in blood while Magdalene's is in water. But on another (the imaginative-symbolic), it has to do with the value of rubies and pearls in relation to the implied theme of payment for the 'debt' of the third line. The transformation from blood and water to rubies and pearls, things familiarly physical, fluid and impermanent to things rare and more enduring, suggests a scale of values rising towards the eternally transforming and redeeming act of the crucifixion itself, whereby human and physical suffering is endowed with meaning in relation to the most enduring, because spiritual, values.

Crashaw's poem is thus about the spiritually transforming effects of the crucifixion, but the sense of what the crucifixion means in spiritual terms depends on our reaction away from the grotesquerie of the sheer anatomical actualities which the poem evokes. On this point, the critics who argue that we should not visualise Crashaw's images are on weak ground, and their very insistence tells against them. There is clearly little need to argue in this way about the degree to which we should or should not visualise Donne's clay heart in the lines I have quoted earlier, and the same would go for much that we have read, for example, in Spenser. When the two trees, Fradubio and Fraelissa, talk, do they have mouths? How does Amoret recover so swiftly from the incisions into her heart by Busyrane? How does Florimel breathe under the sea? Spenser critics do not waste time on questions like these because they are the wrong sorts of questions. The 'dark conceit' does not work that way, and neither do the lines from Donne's *A Litanie.* But Crashaw's critics argue about this kind of question all the time, and the insistence of some of them that we should not actualise the images underlines the fact that the images cry out for us to do so.

At this point the historians will often adduce examples from Baroque tradition, to assure us that Crashaw wrote in a milieu where aesthetic tastes and expectations were less ready to be revolted by such physical actuality than is the case today. By this argument they attempt to reduce the full impact of the physical component, and I am unconvinced. In a great deal of Crashaw, as in the poem **'On the wounds of our crucified Lord'** revulsion from physical grotesquerie remains essential and should not be explained away. Nor will it do to say that Crashaw is aware in a particularly acute manner of the physical in relation to the spiritual life, and that the poems show how peculiar as a result are his perceptions of things. His poetry shows more than that too. Crashaw rather attempts to convince us that the physical seen by itself really is horrid, and a very important dimension of his spiritual meaning involves our recognising, simply, the distortion of a physical world seen without God.

The technique of spiritualising the physical by 'referring' the creatures to their divine source is an age-old convention of Christian devotion which Crashaw would have known very well. We 'refer the things that we use', as St Augustine says 'to the enjoyment of the goodness of God', and proper enjoyment is the key to charity, against which the love of creatures without referral—the 'worshiping of any creature or any part of any creature as though it were God'—is idolatry or cupidity. Thus the famous canticle to the sun, in which St Francis addresses the creatures, attempts to draw us to a heightened awareness of the divine glory and confirms the Augustinian principle of using things to praise the creator. The same insight underlies a poem like George Herbert's 'The Starre', where the starbeam is praised as an analogue of the source of all light, physical as well as spiritual. The star referred to its maker 'wilt joy, by gaining me/To flie home like a laden bee', as its 'use' in creation is appreciated by man praising its beauty in God. As I have argued elsewhere, George Herbert writes within a Franciscan tradition, the roots of which extend mainly through the English religious lyrics of the Middle Ages, and he is partly nourished also by continental sources through the Franciscan-based writings of Juan de Valdés who was highly valued by the Little Gidding community. Crashaw, clearly enough, has a place here; he was a dedicated admirer of George Herbert, and the title of his first volume, **Steps to the Temple,** is a compliment and avowal of deference to the author of *The Temple,* whose poems were formative for the younger writer. Crashaw, moreover, joined practice to precept, for he became intimate with the Gidding community and his spiritual life at Peterhouse was moulded on what he learned from the Ferrars. But however much Crashaw seems influenced by *The Temple,* there are striking differences. Certainly there is nothing in Herbert of that technique which I am claiming for Crashaw of using the traditional doctrine of creatures to stimulate our revulsion from the physical object seen as an end in itself.

At this point I can suggest a means of reconciling my critical conclusion (that Crashaw's poems attempt to give us a sense of the distortion of the physical world seen without God), and what seems to make sense historically (that Crashaw uses physical things emblematically, as signs to be referred in the conventional Augustinian manner to a higher spiritual reality). Crashaw, I suggest, does stay faithful to the main traditions of Augustinian devotion, but develops them in a form consistent with his leanings to Roman Catholicism as well as his debt to Herbert. A type of spirituality which enabled him to do this had evolved in France among the counter-Reform branch of the Franciscans, *Ordinis Sancti Francisci Cappuccinorum,* better known as the Capucins, and was readily available to Crashaw in England during his most active period as a poet.

A number of advantages attend this suggestion. First, it helps to relate Crashaw to the traditions of English devotional poetry in his period: both George Herbert and the community of Little Gidding shared an inheritance of native English Franciscan devotion which they attempted to adapt to the needs of a reformed church. Crashaw follows in their path, developing their insights in a direction separate from, and yet continuous with, theirs. Second, it demonstrates the extent and energy of Capucin influence in England: the concern of French spirituality in *le grand siècle* in relation to English devotion is almost entirely unwritten, but, as I shall suggest in this and in a subsequent chapter, is of signal importance for clarifying the concern expressed in English devotional literature for the new philosophy of Locke and the eighteenth century. Third, it helps to explain Crashaw's path Romewards: Capucin thought has certain close links with England so that the path by that route from Anglicanism to Romanism could be taken without suggesting that Crashaw's sensibility is basically European and not English. Fourth, an allied but minor point, has to do with Crashaw's biography. His eventual end at Loreto assumes a particular significance because the Holy House at Loreto was given to the Capucins in 1608 as a special favour acknowledging their missionary zeal. Loreto is also sacred to St Mary Magdalene who is said to have died there after the pilgrimage of her long penitential life, and in giving Loreto to the Capucins, the Holy See was acknowledging not only the success of the new movement, but also the special Capucin devotion to Mary Magdalene. It is fitting, and to a degree poignant, to think that Crashaw, himself so warmly espousing such devotion, should in his last days be directed towards one of its most hallowed shrines. Perhaps Cardinal Palotto, who is said to have been a good man though his corrupt servants endangered the life of the saintly English exile, saw the appropriateness of finding Crashaw a place there among the Capucin fathers.

Lastly, and most important, my suggestion clarifies Crashaw's special use of the doctrine of referring the creatures. In Capucin devotion the central act of the will, the Augustinian *conversio* or turning towards the good, is developed through a unique emphasis on the horrors of physical nature seen literally, and without God. The Capucin referral of the creatures thus assumes peculiar mystical overtones by exploiting the actualising powers of imagination, and the results are strikingly similar to Crashaw's poems. In light of this point my argument provides a way for reconciling the divergent tendencies of the two camps of Crashaw criticism. We *should* visualise the images, and even recoil from them, but we should not too simply think Crashaw uncontrolled on that account: his aim is to edify by exposing us to a certain kind of horror, and his technique is wholly characteristic of a devotional tradition to which, I have suggested, he might well be expected to show sympathy. (pp. 90-5)

Crashaw inherits a native English and Augustinian spiritual tradition which he is at pains to adapt and interpret for a new age. Yet the chaste and chiselled style of other writers who took up the same challenge, for instance Valdès, Ochino, or Herbert, is not that of Crashaw, or the Capucins. I suggest, therefore, a more direct line of influence between Crashaw and seventeenth-century Gallican spirituality. (p. 117)

Crashaw's poems try, centrally, to arouse in the will a desire for God and for annihilation by His infinitude. The way is through 'Delicious deaths, soft exhalations/Of soule; deare, and divine annihilations/ . . . /An hundred thousand loves and graces,/And many a mysticke thing' (**'On a Prayer Booke'**, 129). In his evocations of mystic theocentricism, the language of transcendence, fraught with highly abstract metaphors and paradoxes, recurs frequently, and Crashaw's debt to Dionysius the Areopagite is plain. One poem even directly addresses 'The right-ey'd Areopagite' who teaches the path to 'mystick day' through obscure explorations of 'negatiue light' (**'Epiphanie'**, 259), and elsewhere we catch the characteristic Dionysian language of superlatives and negative intuitions, abstractions and conceptual paradoxes cryptically challenging us with the limits of what language can say. So, for instance, God is the 'vnbounded NAME' (**'To The Name Above Every Name . . .'**, 239) at the soul's centre where 'Aeternall worlds' have their seat (**'To the Countesse of Denbigh'**, 238), and here the poet finds 'bottomlesse treasures' both 'Boundlesse and infinite' (**'On a Prayer Booke . . .'**, 130), but beyond the limits of language: 'O what! aske not the tongues of men,/Angells cannot tell' (**'In memory of . . . Lady Madre de Teresa'**, 134). Yet a way can be found towards this 'faire Center' (**'Psalme 23'**, 104); it lies both in love and in self-annihilation, and especially in realising that the 'whole SELF' (240) of God makes the personal ego both nothing and empty

(240). Man is a 'Hyperbolized nothing!' (**'Upon Mr. Staninough's Death'**, 175) given definition by God (**'On Hope'**, 143) whose 'incomparable Light' (**'On the Assumption'**, 141) he must seek with dedication and self-consuming love. The aspiration to die for love is itself the essence of love's 'hard command' (**'Sancta Maria Dolorum'**, 285) and, as mystics from Dionysius to Benet confirm, it involves the annihilation of personal will before the all-consuming refulgence of God's 'full fac't Glories' ('It is better to go into Heaven with one eye, etc.', 93):

> That lost again my LIFE may proue
> As then in DEATH, so now in loue.
>   (**'Charitas Nimia'**, 282)

The nature of true desire, both uncompromisingly theocentric and demanding an abandonment of self-will, is expressed in Crashaw's punning and epigrammatic commentary on Matt. 6:22:

> Yet if thou'lt fill one poore Eye, with thy Heaven and Thee,
> O grant (sweet Goodnesse) that one Eye may be All, and every whit of me.
>   (93)

The biblical image of entering heaven with a single eye suggests the one-pointedness of mystical vision and the absorption of partial sight in the 'All' of God's light. Also, by the two senses of 'Eye' (indicating the organ of sight and the ego, 'I'), the surrender of self-regard to God's will also becomes central to the poem's meaning.

Such preoccupation with theocentric self-abandonment draws Crashaw especially to St Teresa and Mary Magdalene, in whom the combination of devotion and self-abnegation produces unusually striking examples of 'death more misticall and high' (**'In memory of Lady Madre de Teresa'**, 133). Even the Preface to ***Steps to the Temple*** makes clear how fundamental to Crashaw is his 'Copernican' focus, not only for dictating his choice of subject matter, but for the language of poetry itself. All his poems, he says, direct us to 'that other state' (75), and poetic language attempts merely to approximate the higher and intuitive language of angels—'the Quintessence of Phantasie and discourse center'd in Heaven'. (75)

In describing the dynamics of the soul's transformation into this higher state, Crashaw, like his Capucin forebears, draws heavily on images of fluidity in which literally-apprehended meanings change into symbolic evocations of eternity and in which the mortification of carnal passion is accompanied by an enlivening of spiritual affect. As in Benet, Zacharie, and Remi, the sea for Crashaw is a favourite image for representing the absorption of ego into Godhead. Thus the streams of Christ's blood blend into 'a generall flood' and a single mystical red sea: 'I counted wrong; there is but one/But ô that one is one all o're'. In the midst of an overwhelming tide the blood itself is transfused to blessed and 'living Waters' (**'On the bleeding wounds . . .'**, 102). Elsewhere, Crashaw tells us that by reading St Teresa his exposure to a 'Faire sea of holy fires' has totally 'transfused' his spirit (**'An Apologie . . .'**, 136). Again he becomes 'a melting sacrifice' (**'To the**

Morning', 185) as partial intimations of God's high mysteries are absorbed in an ocean of mystical awareness:

> Tast this, and as thou lik'st this lesser flood
> Expect a Sea.
>
> ('**Our Lord in his Circumcision**', 98)

In the famous meditations on Mary Magdalene's tears Crashaw, like Remi, is fascinated by the multifold transmutations of 'milky rivers' (**'The Weeper'**, 79), alternately dew and wine and amber and gold, flowing towards the 'Christall Ocean' (79) of sweet Heaven. Such images, in which tears and blood mingle and blend 'in one flood' (**'Upon the Infant Martyrs'**, 95) and where bitterness is transformed to an inebriating joy remain favourites, and with all of them at the centre we observe, as in an emblem, the literal sense become symbolic. Thus the water of Christ's baptism, in washing 'Is washt it selfe' (**'On the water . . .'**, 85); by the miracle of the loaves 'food it selfe is fed' (**'On the miracle of multiplied loaves'**, 86); when we think of Christ's sepulchre, we see that 'the Grave lies buried' (**'Vpon the Sepulchre . . .'**, 86). In these literal objects spiritually observed the subtle miracle of divine grace enacts an enlivening metamorphosis: things, as Crashaw puts it,

> Are in another sence
> Still legible;
> Sweet is the difference.
>
> ('**On the still surviving markes of our Saviours wounds**', 86)

In attempting to express something of this 'difference', Crashaw's poetry fully exploits the implications also of 'sweet'. His indulgence of spiritual eroticism is well known, and he draws often on the canticles to convey a sense of 'Amorous Languishments' (**'On a Prayer Booke'**, 128) which accompany the mystical state. The 'divine embraces' of the 'deare spowse' (129) are an inebriating blend of 'sweet Light' (**'An Hyme of the Nativity'**, 107), perfume (106), and seas of virgin's milk (107). Here belongs the music that sings tears to sleep (108), chastened 'With many a rarely-temper'd kisse', and all in the snug warmth of a 'perfumed' or 'Balmy Nest' (107), incomparably delicious and full of 'An hundred thousand loves and graces,/And many a misticke thing' (**'On a Prayer Booke'**, 129). In such lavish exploitations of the full range of sensual experience for spiritual ends, Crashaw achieves effects as peculiar and remarkable as those of the French Capucin fathers.

In all this, Crashaw remains acutely aware of the ambivalence of the human being challenged by God's love in a world given over to distractions and falsity. The condition of man, 'Whose DEFINITION is a doubt/Twixt life and death, twixt in and out' (**'To the Countesse of Denbigh'**, 236) is never far from his mind as he writes of the 'strange warres' (237) of spiritual life. Christ's wounds in particular are symbols of the relationship Crashaw constantly sees between self-mortification and spiritual joy. Thus the extended meditations on the cross do not involve a strenuous composition of place prior to self-scrutiny as in the typical 'Ptolemaic' devotion. Rather, as with the Capucins, they are directed at a 'Copernican' realisation of how the *'purple Rivers'* (**'On the bleeding wounds'**, 101) can

wash away and dissolve the puny assertions of self-will in a sea of cosmic consciousness. Crashaw devotes a series of poems to the Office of the Holy Cross and he writes also on the *Stabat Mater Dolorosa*, a traditional Franciscan theme which especially heightens the ambivalent human suffering of the Virgin at the crucifixion. Love's trials for her are especially 'sweet bitter things' (**'Sancta Maria Dolorvm'**, 287), and Crashaw is fascinated by the mixture of pleasure and pain which accompanies the *via mystica* in light of the paradox of the 'sad, sweet TREE!' (**'Evensong'**, 273). His poems feature plentiful sweet woundings and there is a special stress on arrows. St Teresa's heart will 'Kisse the sweetly-killing dart' and deeply embrace its 'delicious wounds' (134). The dart is itself dipped in a rich flame (133) which melts the sweet mansion of her soul 'Like a soft lumpe of Incense' (134). She experiences 'sweet deaths of Love' (137), full of 'subtile paine' (134) and 'intollerable joyes' (134). The Countess of Denbigh also is wounded by love's dart, an 'arrow of light' and 'healing shaft' (237) that penetrates her soul's centre (238). Love's martyrdoms are an entire 'sweet inciendary' of 'mystick DEATHS' (**'The Flaming Heart'**, 326) where blood becomes purifying water, fire becomes ardour, and pain pleasure. Substances mix in extraordinary ways, and like the snow that blends with fire to express the mystery of the Incarnation, they give us a sense of the puzzle of human nature itself: 'Aeternity shutt in a span' (**'In the Holy Nativity'**, 250).

This leads to my final point, namely Crashaw's exploitation of our recoil from many of these images literally conceived, so that our initial shock may be read in 'another sence' (**'On the still surviving markes . . .'**, 86) and thereby even seemingly repugnant things find meaning in God. The technique of the poem already discussed on the wounds of his crucified Lord represents Crashaw's standard procedure on this kind of subject matter. Take as another example the divine epigram on Luke II, **'Blessed be the paps which Thou has sucked'**:

> Svppose he had been Tabled at thy Teates,
> Thy hunger feeles not what he eates:
> Hee'l have his Teat e're long (a bloody one)
> The Mother then must suck the Son.
>
> (94)

The poem assumes a conventionally acceptable analogy between Mary's nourishment of Christ's vulnerable human flesh at the nativity, and his sustaining of our weak spiritual natures at the crucifixion. But we are asked to take this symbolism literally. The first line makes a hypothesis which we should imagine in actual terms: the concrete and domestic 'Tabled' enforces this sense, and the reader takes the place, momentarily, of a nursing mother. But when Christ himself grows a teat which gives blood (presumably the wound in his side) we are repelled, partly because wounding mars the body's integrity, and partly because our literal imagination forces us to see the unnaturalness of a man with a teat. When the mother now undertakes to suck the son, the literal imagination is pushed beyond endurance, and our mixed revulsion from the image of Christ's side turns to shocked rejection. We can actually imagine and perhaps accept ourselves as mothers, or that Christ's side-wound is like a teat. But we balk, and I think Crashaw intends us to, at Mary consoling herself at Christ's side literally in the manner suggested. As we thus refuse to see the traditional image as a literal 'worke in itself', we acknowledge again, with relief, the spiritual meaning of what, in literal terms, involved only an escalation of horrors. The poem, after all, turns out to be an affirmation of spiritual nourishment, redemption, and the paradox of the Incarnation which uses Mary's dependent and weak flesh as a vehicle for the triumphant cross to extend divine love to men. So, for instance, tasting the blood of circumcision and desiring then to drink seas of it (**'Our Lord in his Circumcision'**, 98), ceases to be upsetting as we reject the actual implications in favour of the spiritual sense. And the blood of the 'self-wounding Pelican' (**'Adoro Te'**, 293) which transfuses its 'benign flood' to the gasping heart also becomes increasingly difficult to accept 'in itself' if we move away from the spiritual reference to the cleansing action of grace on the sinful soul. In all these examples the traditional symbol, if simply reified, becomes as Crashaw says, a 'Brooding Horror' (**'Psalme 23'**, 103) which must be transformed again by referral to the 'faire Center' (104),

> Fresh from the pure glance of thine eye,
> Lighting to Eternity.
>
> (104)

Yet the perspective on eternity must not blind us either to actual sufferings attendant on the human condition, and, paradoxically, the engendering of a spiritual awareness in Crashaw's poetry confirms also the obtrusive facticity of physical realities. The impact of things remains 'still legible' even in the spiritual sense ('On the still surviving markes . . .', 86), and Crashaw's insistence on avoiding complete otherworldliness remains, as in other aspects of his poetic technique, close to the Capucin example.

Crashaw's **'The Weeper'** combines most of the characteristics which I have now exemplified from the poems in general. He is indebted to a variety of sources in this famous work, but his treatment, like Remi's, shows Mary Magdalene yielding to passionate longings for her lover, as her penitence and self-abasement triumph over the world by absorbing its coarse sensuality and referring it 'Vpwards' (309) to Heaven. The image of transcendant 'Waters aboue th'Heauns', represents the ineffable source in God to which other images of fluidity in the poem strive to blend. Crashaw indeed uses almost the same repertoire of metamorphoses as the Capucin poet, as tears become pearls, spring showers, cosmic principles of regeneration, crystals, streams of gold, rivers, wine, and the food of angels. The literal significance of these comparisons of course is transformed as they become symbols of penitence redeeming the world, and the abandonment of herself to God in sorrow and longing thus allows Magdalene unselfconsciously to draw the physical world towards God. They are a great many references to 'sweetness' in the images which describe this referral, from the 'sweetest Lippes' (309) of the cherub to 'clouds of incense' (313), dew 'Nuzzel'd in the lilly's neck' (310) and the coy droppings of balsam-sweating boughs (310). Such spiritual joys also reduce temporal reality to a simple, delightful eternity enjoyed in contemplation. The anguished round of sunrise and sunset (309), changing minutes into hours and months

into seasons, is measured by tears but then transformed in turn by penitence into the ineffable mystery of the timeless ocean: 'Waters aboue th'Heauns' (309). Yet Mary remains human throughout her bittersweet joy: the word 'sorrow' recurs almost as often as 'sweet', and the poem suggests the fair penitent is exemplary in her ambivalent 'Sweetnesse so sad, sadnesse so sweet' (309). In such a context we are *meant* to discriminate between the inappropriateness of comparisons literally conceived when they show the anomaly of things-in-themselves, and then move to the relief which spiritual significance provides. Thus the famous 'walking baths; two weeping motions;/Portable, and compendious oceans' (312) are intended to suggest cleansing tears in relation to the absorbing cosmic sea, but I am not sure that we are not meant to notice (as throughout Remi's poem) how outlandish the comparison would be in itself. Crashaw gives a hint when, after the opening two stanzas of similarly outlandish conceits ('Euer bubling things!/Thawing crystall snowy hills!' (308) and among other things, stars), he writes:

> But we are deceiued all,
> Starres indeed they are too true,
>   For they but seem to fall,
>   As Heauen's other spangles doe:
> It is not for our Earth and vs,
> To shine in Things so pretious.
>
> (309)

The conceits have not been actual comparisons at all, and our earthbound imaginations are too literal-minded. Yet the poetic imagery is not without actual foundation, for in a sense the eyes are even more star-like than stars, and this we can see if we look spiritually. The argument here may not seem anything more than the old mediaeval convention that analogies are real, but there is one important difference: Crashaw deliberately manipulates our reaction to move us away from a nominalist interpretation to a realistic one. He depends on the powers of our reason to diagnose the unacceptability of the actualising imagination, and thus to move us to the spiritual sense. Such a view of the physical world is the characteristic contribution of Capucin spirituality to the Augustinian tradition: it is a striking innovation, with far-reaching implications.

In attempting to explicate Crashaw's poetry in light of French Capucin spirituality I do not hope to reduce his work to dependency on a particular source, or to denounce critical views which relate Crashaw to other aspects of his culture. Mainly, I hope to clarify Crashaw's place in the history of English devotional poetry, and to suggest that his work shows, in one way, how the new materialism affected the use of traditional images in devotional literature. I have stressed the continuities extending to Donne and Herbert because their tradition precipitates the very departures which Crashaw makes from it. In attempting to maintain the techniques of Franciscan devotion through the pressures of seventeenth-century secularism, Crashaw resembles these earlier writers, seeking a timely solution to traditional problems. Yet he is more willing also to risk new departures, and in this he resembles Henry Vaughan, who, to the same end, looked to the novel insights of Hermetic philosophy, or Thomas Traherne, whose highly personalised and radiant thought is a unique departure from a tradition which nonetheless continued to nourish his work. But the important point for the present study is that Crashaw found in the Gallican spirituality of the Capucins a unique prescription for interpreting St Augustine in the age of Descartes. From Little Gidding, where the influence of Franciscan reformed devotion was already felt, to the atmosphere of Peterhouse and the influence of the court and the Capucin mission, a series of relationships can be established to suggest how readily Crashaw could have found a path from George Herbert's *Temple* to the concerns of Père Zacharie, until at the end of his life he made his way to the Capucin house of Loreto itself. At the centre, however, is simply the question of whether or not the main Capucin emphases—the theocentricism, the self-abandonment, the debt to Dionysius, the evocation of the spiritual senses, the fluid images of transformation, the devotion to the cross, the concentration on the ambivalence of ecstatic experience, and the technique of stimulating a reaction away from the thing-in-itself to centre the will on God—seem sufficiently peculiar and clearly enough shared by Crashaw and his Capucin antecedents to compose a tradition, as I believe they do.

My argument, if thus accepted, helps also to establish the place of Crashaw in the scheme of this study. The world of materiality is experienced by him in a manner new to English poetry. As Ruth Wallerstein [in her *Richard Crashaw: A Study in Style and Poetic Development*, 1959] some time ago pointed out, Crashaw learned a great deal from Spenser, but Crashaw is a much more deliberate and calculating writer. There is a sense in his poetry of a cool manipulator of effects, and there is a sense too of a man aware of himself in the spiritual life in a new way standing over and against a world of thwarting materiality. The thing-in-itself never appears in Spenser, but in Crashaw it is recognised and exploited for particular effects as we have seen. His poetry exists partly because in the world of ideas a critical dislocation had occurred, and was increasingly affirmed in complex ways by society at large, between our images and material substance. I have tried to show how such an innovation was pertinent for Crashaw's poetry: certainly his effectiveness depends greatly on how we interpret his treatment of images in relation to material things. As we have seen, his works exploit traditional types and images so that we first see them literally, and then we move, driven by the reified image itself, as it were, to seek relief in reaffirming the spiritual significance which absorbs us with a sense of affective participation in the mysteries. This act of 'vertical transcendence' to which Crashaw so unremittingly forces us, requires a special technique whereby the spiritual meaning of images is rescued in the end by giving them first a desperate injection of concreteness. Augustine's 'spiritual vision' here has become self-conscious to the point where the corporeal element must be *forced* to reveal the intellectual truth. So we are recalled to our awareness of the spirit by the very fact that the split between object-in-itself and the image as acceptable spiritual sign is made the ground of the poem. Crashaw's indebtedness to the Capucins for this technique therefore carries over into his poems something of their concern to meet the challenge presented by scientific ma-

terialism to the older, traditional ways of knowing the world. (pp. 119-28)

Patrick Grant, "Richard Crashaw and the Capucins: Images and the Force of Belief," in his Images and Ideas in Literature of the English Renaissance, *Amherst: The University of Massachusetts Press, 1979, pp. 89-128.*

Loriane Roberts (essay date 1987)

[*Below, Roberts asserts that the faith theme in Crashaw's "Epiphany Hymn" is not emotionally excessive, but rather strives for an "intellectual depth [through] the consummate control of the poet over all aspects of his poem."*]

Of all the important English religious poets of the seventeenth century, Richard Crashaw has generally received the least sympathetic response from readers and critics. He is likely to be attacked on three grounds: his use of ingenious imagery allegedly operates at the expense of thought, his development of themes is often found wanting in logic or dramatic progression, and his expression of emotion is thought to be too flamboyant. But when one examines the critical commentary on Crashaw's sacred poetry, one discovers that these three negative judgments arise from a consideration of only a few poems, rather than from a consideration of all. Thus, the comments may apply to **"The Weeper"** or some of the sacred epigrams; they do not, however, apply to excellent poems such as the Nativity or Epiphany Hymns. The latter poem in particular serves well to discredit the three negative generalizations about Crashaw's poetry, for it demonstrates that Crashaw is consciously in control of the poem's structure, imagery, and theme, and that his intent is not only emotional but rational as well.

Not all readers agree, however, that a conscious control of structure and theme is manifested in the **"Epiphany Hymn."** While the four-part division that George Walton Williams outlines for the poem elicits no disagreement, the logic underlying the four parts has not gone unquestioned. The choral poem opens with the arrival of the Magi to worship Christ, the new day in night (ll. 1-41); it then moves to a rejection of former pagan religions that falsely worshiped the sun as God (ll. 42-133); from this past time it projects into the future to the moment of the Crucifixion and the sun's eclipse, interpreted as a sign of the sun's reparation for having accepted the false worship of men (ll. 134-233); the poem closes with the conversion and the obeisance of men and nature, represented by the figures of Dionysius the Areopagite, the Magi, and the sun (ll. 234-54).

One is not surprised by the convergence of all planes of time in the poem—past, present, future, eternity—for the liturgical basis of the poem naturally allows for it. Nor is one surprised by the section that banishes religions that falsely worshiped the sun, for Milton anticipated Crashaw with such an account in his Nativity poem. Nor in fact is one surprised by the presence of the Passion in a poem about the manifestation of Christ to the Gentiles. Rosemond Tuve has reminded us that this alignment had its inception in Scripture and its flowering in poets and painters through the ages. The presence of the Crucifixion in a poem about the Epiphany completes the theological significance of the Incarnation, a significance one would expect to be the climactic moment of the poem. Yet in the **"Epiphany Hymn"** more action follows this moment, namely, the conversion of Dionysius the Areopagite, and it is his presence in the third division that has elicited questions about the structure and the theme of the poem.

Ruth Wallerstein, for example, believing there is a disjunction between the light-dark imagery of the first part of the hymn and the attention given to Dionysius later, declares that "the statement of the concept [of the *via negativa*] does not flower from the vision of the poem as a whole, but seems added to it" [in her *Richard Crashaw: A Study in Style and Poetic Development*, 1935]. Austin Warren sees a disjunction between Crashaw's earlier interest in Teresian mysticism, with its emphasis on "picture thinking" about the spiritual world, and his seemingly radical shift to the *via negativa* of Dionysian mysticism, with its emphasis on the voiding of sense perceptions and intellect in order to apprehend God.

If the **"Epiphany Hymn"** were primarily about mysticism, as both Warren and Wallerstein—indeed, most critics—presume, then their questions and objections would inevitably follow. But the **"Epiphany Hymn"** is not primarily about the mystical way; it is about faith—about the way of belief that exists for those beyond the time of the historical Christ in the darkened natural world.

In a poem whose scene of action is the manifestation of God in the Christ Child, that is, the spiritual becoming material, why would Crashaw advocate the *via negativa*, the conscious voiding of the material to know the spiritual? Dionysius is not present in the poem primarily as an advocate of the *via negativa*, but rather as one whose example shows us the way to epiphany. The poem contains not just one illumination or epiphany, that is, that of the Magi, but two, that of Dionysius also. The reason for the presence of the great mystic in this poem becomes clearer when one recognizes that the structure of the poem embodies a comparison of sorts between the conversion of the Magi and that of Dionysius, the first taking place in the presence of the human Christ, the second in the darkness of the Crucifixion.

With careful artistry Crashaw emphasizes imagery of the "face" in the first conversion—the face of God as well as the face of the natural sun, along with all the features contained therein—eyes, cheek, lips. Facial imagery is so prevalent that it cannot be ignored, yet only one critic has called attention to it—and merely to suggest that Warren is incorrect in saying the poem lacks sensuous imagery. This frequent use of facial imagery, however, helps to underscore the contrast between the earlier epiphany of the Magi and the later one of Dionysius, and thus the overall theme and intellectual content of the poem.

Perhaps the more obvious and traditional paradoxes of light and dark in the poem obscure the emphasis meant to be placed on the "face" of God as it displaces the "face"

of the natural sun as the light of the world. Yet the opening of the poem announces this theme and action:

> (1. Kinge.) Bright BABE! Whose awfull beau-
> tyes make
> The morn incurr a sweet mistake;
> (2.) For whom the' officious heavns devise
> To disinheritt the sun's rise,
> (3.) Delicately to displace
> The Day, and plant it fairer in thy face.
>
> (ll. 1-6)

These lines echo several biblical passages that compare Christ's face with the sun, such as "his face shone like the sun" [Matt. 17:2]. It is appropriate, indeed traditional, when speaking of events surrounding the Incarnation to do so in terms of human imagery. God has become man and is manifested to the Gentile world, represented by the Magi. He has thus the physical attributes of man—face, eyes, smile, cheeks, lips, all of which and more are part of the imagery of the face in the hymn.

Yet this concrete imagery is balanced by some very abstract imagery as well. A prime example of this balance is Crashaw's "depiction" of Christ:

> (1.) All-circling point. All centring sphear.
> The world's one, round, AEternall year.
> (2.) Whose full and all-unwrinkled face
> Nor sinks nor swells with time or place;
> (3.) But every where and every while
> Is One Consistent solid smile.
>
> (ll. 26-31)

Nothing could be more concrete than for Crashaw to evoke God's "full and all-unwrinkled face," his "One Consistent solid smile," lines reminiscent of one in Herbert's "To all Angels and Saints": "See the smooth face of God without a frown" (l. 2). On the other hand, nothing could be more abstract than "All-circling point. All centring sphear." This technique of balancing the concrete and the abstract is appropriate for, even emblematic of, the God-Man being described. Ultimately, however, in this most metaphysical of Crashaw's poems, the conceit or intellectual idea, not the visualization of images, is important. Thus, this passage asserts that God is changeless and loving, unlike the sun, which—the poem emphasizes—changes daily and yearly and leads men astray. When Christ is no longer in men's presence, his changelessness, his love continue as sources of illumination.

The ways that men find God are central to the poem. As Robert V. Young has noted [in his *Richard Crashaw and the Spanish Golden Age*, 1982], the word *way* is used as a rhyme in the **"Epiphany Hymn"** seven times, underscoring this concept. In the opening of the poem the Magi are fortunate to see the "glory of God in the face of Christ" (2 Cor. 4:6). After a life spent in the false worship of the sun, the Magi are "illuminated" by a star that directs them to the manger, where they have the privilege of seeing God in the flesh.

> (1.) We, who strangely went astray,
> Lost in a bright
> Meridian night,
> (2.) A Darkenes made of too much day,
> (3.) Becken'd from farr

By thy fair starr,
Lo at last have found our way.

(ll. 15-21)

Both the natural and spiritual worlds—that is, the human
Christ and the "illumination" produced by the star, a star
less material than spiritual—combine to produce their
epiphany, although one could say the natural dominates,
because the Magi have before them the human figure of
Christ. This somewhat greater emphasis on the human
Christ parallels the liturgy from Christmas up to Epiphany, which also stresses Christ's humanity. The feast of the
first Epiphany celebrates equally Christ's humanity and
his divinity, while the following four epiphanies of the liturgical calendar emphasize Christ's divinity, recounting,
in fact, some of his first miracles. This same movement
from an emphasis on Christ's humanity in the epiphany
of the Magi to a greater emphasis on his divinity in the
epiphany of those who live after the death of the historical
Christ is reproduced in the **"Epiphany Hymn."**

This movement is provided for us by the wise men, who
have visionary powers that allow them to foresee the eventual death of Christ on the cross and the darkening of the
natural world in response. The sun, guilty of having accepted the worship of men, is glad to be free of its sin and
does penance by bowing its head at midday for three
hours. Crashaw describes the eclipse in sensuous "face"
imagery:

(3). That forfeiture of noon to night shall pay
All the idolatrous thefts done by this night of
day;
And the Great Penitent presse his own pale lipps
With an elaborate love-eclipse
To which the low world's lawes
Shall lend no cause
(Cho.) Save those domestick which he borrowes
From our sins and his own sorrowes.

(ll. 149-56)

The human attributes of the sun serve to connect the subservience and obeisance of nature to those of men. For in
doing penance for its past sins, the sun, the world of nature, becomes a means of leading men to God:

(2.) And as before his too-bright eye
Was Their more blind idolatry,
So his officious blindnes now shall be
Their black, but faithful perspective of thee.

(ll. 168-71)

The natural world of the sun—transformed by the supernatural eclipse—will lead men to a belief in the supernatural world, for they will be unable to explain the eclipse by
natural laws.

The power of God to become man on the one hand or to
subdue the natural world on the other is the means to produce epiphany. Thus, when the wise men foresee the darkening of the sun at the Crucifixion, they predict the relationship of the sun and the future believers in these words:

(1.) Three sad hour's sackcloth then shall show
to us
His penance, as our fault, conspicuous.
(2.) And he more needfully and nobly prove
The nations' terror now then erst their love.

(3.) Their hated loves changd into wholsom
feares,
(Cho.) The shutting of his eye shall open Theirs.

(ll. 157-62)

Dionysius himself says, in an account of his conversion
after witnessing the eclipse,

. . . both of us at that time, at Heliopolis, being
present, and standing together, saw the moon
approaching the sun, to our surprise (for it was
not appointed time for conjunction); and again
from the ninth hour to the evening, supernatu-
rally placed back again into a line opposite the
sun. . . . So great are the supernatural things of
that appointed time, and possible to Christ
alone, the Cause of all, Who worketh great
things and marvellous, of which there is not
number.

The Magi in Crashaw's **"Epiphany Hymn"** contrast their
experience in the presence of the new-born Christ with the
spiritual illumination of Dionysius. Whereas the Magi are
led to Christ by the light of the star, Dionysius will find
illumination in darkness at the supernatural eclipse of the
sun:

(2.) By the oblique ambush of this close night
Couch't in that conscious shade
The right-ey'd Areopagite
Shall with a vigorous guesse invade
And catche thy quick reflex; and sharply see
On this dark Ground
To descant THEE.
(3.) O prize of the rich SPIRIT! with what feirce
chase
Of his strong soul, shall he
Leap at thy lofty FACE,
And seize the swift Flash, in rebound
From this obsequious cloud.

(ll. 189-200)

This difference in arriving at the same faith—to see "face
to face" or "through a glass darkly"—is of ultimate importance to the theme of the poem.

Most critics emphasize the contrast between the sun-son
worship and the banishment of paganism by the new faith,
but then fail to see the comparison between the illumination of those present at Christ's birth and of those who
come after his death. It is this comparison that occasions
the figure of Dionysius in the poem, not the *via negativa*;
it is his example as one who saw in darkness and believed,
who saw the natural world controlled by the supernatural,
rather than his method of contemplation, that fulfills the
poem's theme. Just as the sun's darkness taught men to see
the true god—"The shutting of his eye shall open
Theirs"—so too shall Dionysius's example of conversion
teach the rest of mankind how to know God in darkness:

(1.) Thus shall that reverend child of light,
(2.) By being scholler first of that new night,
Come forth Great master of the mystick day;
(3.) And teach obscure MANKIND a more close
way
By the frugall negative light
Of a most wise and well-abused Night

To read more legible thine originall Ray,

(Cho.) And make our Darknes serve THY day.
(ll. 205-12)

I do not deny that this passage is charged with terms and concepts suggestive of Dionysian mysticism. But I do not believe that it functions as an advocacy of this mysticism, that is, as it is understood by many, a rejection of the material world. Rather, the passage functions as a symbol of submission and faith for those who are left with only this material world, but who see in its darkness a sign of divine power and divine love. To Crashaw, mystical union with God is of course the acme of Christian experience, yet he does not seem to suggest that such union is beyond the sincere Christian's spiritual ken. Life on earth for Crashaw is always related to life in heaven. The **"Epiphany Hymn"** makes this connection explicit. Asking for a "commerce" between "thy world and ours," "A mutual trade / 'Twixt sun and SHADE" (ll. 215-16), the Magi, as representatives of mankind, wish to make their darkness serve God's day.

Having been taught by Dionysius's example that their "noble powres" of sight and intelligence will not bring them "the blissfull PRIZE" of "fastening on Thine eyes," they offer to all mankind an alternative to dependence on human faculties. Like the sun, they submit themselves to God: "(Cho.) Now by abased liddes shall learn to be / Eagles; and shutt our eyes that we may see" (ll. 231-32). This passage does not suggest the descriptions of mystical experience given by the saints or even by Crashaw in other poems; this is no "luminous trance" or "divine annihilation." It is mystical only in the sense that any epiphany or conversion or spiritual illumination is mystical. The emphasis in the passage is on the "confederacy" of man and God in Christian time. But it is not a confederacy of equals.

Thus in the last stanza, the poem elaborates on the correct order of the natural world and of man in relationship to the heavenly one. The sun bows in adoration to God at the same time that it is to be the "golden index" to man, "Pointing us Home to our own sun / The world's and his HYPERION" (ll. 252-53). Man must use the natural world and its right order to see through it to the divinity of Christ. Even Dionysius in *The Divine Names* speaks to this role of the sun:

> this great, all-bright and ever-shining sun, which is the visible image of the Divine Goodness, faintly re-echoing the activity of the Good, illumines all things that can receive its light while retaining the utter simplicity of light, and expands above and below throughout the visible world the beams of its own radiance. . . . I say not (as was feigned by the ancient myth) that the sun is the God and Creator of this Universe, and therefore takes the visible world under his special care; but I say that the "invisible things of God from the creation of the world are clearly seen, being understood by the things that are made, even His eternal power and Godhead."

The fact is that Dionysius did not write only of a negative way to God, that is, the shutting down of human eyes and mind as a means of knowing God in exchange for passive emptiness that hopefully is filled by the divine presence. Dionysius also wrote of an affirmative way, suggested by the passage quoted above. That way stresses the use of human eyes and mind in experiencing God (imperfectly of course), for both natural and ecclesiastical signs and symbols are present in the universe to testify to the presence of the divine. While this way does not lead to mystical ecstasy, it can lead to faith in Christ, as Dionysius himself so effectively shows us by his own example. Christ is the supreme representation of the affirmative way, the material sign of a higher divinity, even more, the perfect union of the human and the divine. Surely the affirmative way is more appropriate than the negative way in a poem that celebrates the Incarnation and the manifestation of Christ to all mankind.

The theme of the **"Epiphany Hymn"** is, thus, very carefully structured around the illumination of the Magi and of Dionysius the Areopagite. The refrain that ends both the submission of the sun and the submission of the ordinary believer serves to tie together these different conversions. The fact that we are dependent on the world of nature, as well as God's intervention in that world through the supernatural star and the unnatural eclipse of the sun, teaches what faith is. With a consciously and artistically crafted imagery meant to emphasize the humanity of God and the limitation of human knowledge, Crashaw works out with great control the paradoxes and the full significance of the Epiphany. At no point in the poem are our emotions engaged excessively; what strikes us instead is the intellectual depth and the consummate control of the poet over all aspects of his poem.

If Crashaw's **"Epiphany Hymn"** is not representative of *all* his work, it is representative of a larger portion than is popularly supposed. A number of the poems have been analyzed structurally and thematically with profitable results: we need only remind ourselves of Louis L. Martz's study [in his *The Poetry of Meditation*, 1954] of **"Hymn to the Name of Jesus,"** of Kerby Neill's analysis [in his "Structure and Symbol in Crashaw's 'Hymn in the Nativity," *PMLA* 63, 1948] of the three versions of **"Hymn in the Holy Nativity,"** of A. R. Cirillo's examination of the whole cycle of Christmas-tide poems [in his "Crashaw's 'Epiphany Hymn,' The Dawn of Christian Time," *Studies in Philology* 67, 1970], of Marc Bertonasco's defense even of **"The Weeper"** [in his *Crashaw and the Baroque*] The present-day reader should not forget that Crashaw is in fact a very learned poet, aware of classical forms, biblical tradition, meditative methods, liturgical rites, and Continental trends—all of which to some degree inform his poetry. Some recent critics who have not ignored this fact— Diana Benet, Eugene R. Cunnar, Paul A. Parrish, and Robert V. Young, Jr.—have all argued successfully for a rationality behind a number of the poems. Thus to approach Crashaw's poetry free of the popular censures and aware of its intellectual dimension undoubtedly elicits new insights as well as lends a more balanced assessment of his work as a whole. (pp. 134-44)

Loriane Roberts, "Crashaw's 'Epiphany Hymn': Faith Out of Darkness," in "Bright Shootes of Everlastingnesse": The Seventeenth-Century Religious Lyric, edited by Claude J. Summers and Ted-Larry Pebworth, University of Missouri Press, 1987, pp. 134-44.

Paul A. Parrish (essay date 1988)

[*In the following essay, Parrish examines the masculine/feminine dialectic in Crashaw's poetry, asserting that he challenges many conventional gender-related assumptions.*]

William Winstanley's brief but sympathetic portrait of Richard Crashaw [in his "Mr. Richard Crashaw," *The Lives of the Most Famous English Poets*, 1687] and William Prynne's snarling denigration [in his *Legenda lignea*, 1653] are admittedly an odd coupling, yet each points to a dimension of Crashaw we have long accepted as characteristic: his love for privacy and the quiet, contemplative life and his remarkable attachment (in his poetry, at least) to women. A rehearsal of the life and a review of the poetry confirm an essential truth in each of these observations. Furthermore, it might be argued that these characteristics are only two facets of a "feminine" personality type, one that prefers privacy and intimacy to more public arenas, and prefers more gentle, tender, or emotional virtues to more physical, bolder, or logical "masculine" ones. This association, suggesting a consistency and harmony between Crashaw's life and art, is revealing because it points to numerous occasions in the life and in the poetry that demonstrate Crashaw's allegiance to private, feminine virtues; it is inadequate, however, because it fails to acknowledge the complex relationship between these values and their antitheses. Preferring a life of solitude, Crashaw nonetheless was a committed Royalist who paid dearly for that public stance; his poetry, demonstrating his extraordinary devotion to femininity, also confronts the language and expectations of masculine conduct in which power, courage, and aggression are virtues. (pp. 148-49)

Crashaw's poetry has characteristically been regarded with grudging or qualified praise, and there are three principal reasons for the depreciation of his work. First, Crashaw is judged to be more Continental than his contemporaries; thus when measured against the more "English" quality of Donne or Herbert, Crashaw typically suffers. Second, his poetry is seen as too obsessed with a limited range of experiences and images, especially images of liquefaction—water, milk, blood—and thus as unusual, strange, or grotesque. In the 1950s Robert M. Adams [in his "Taste and Bad Taste in Metaphysical Poetry: Richard Crashaw and Dylan Thomas," *Hudson Review 8*, 1955] made perhaps the most damning assessment of Crashaw in finding some of his poetry representative of "bad taste" and in viewing some illchosen images as revolting and grotesque. The third reason is not so openly acknowledged. We find Crashaw's poetry discomforting because it so obviously focuses on feminine figures and feminine qualities. Over and over we read of soft breasts, of milk-white doves, of well-fledged nests and winged loves. Such concerns fail to be tough, concise, direct, and precise—in a word, manly.

Mario Praz [in his *The Flaming Heart*, 1958], for example, commenting on Crashaw's paraphrases of the Psalms, remarks that a "study of Crashaw's versions shows how incapable he is of a concise style, of rendering severe and manly feelings in a few strokes; how, on the contrary, he makes capital out of whatever lends itself to florid divaga-

tions and to description of tender and delicate emotions. Grace is not denied to him, but Strength is beyond his reach." Praz's evaluation of the **"Hymn to the Name of Jesus"** is less pejorative, but Crashaw's achievement is again seen in terms of its feminine qualities, its "feminine tenderness," which is contrasted to the "heroic note" of which Crashaw is only rarely capable. Warren, [in his *Richard Crashaw*, 1939] remarking on the sacred verse of Donne, Herbert, and Crashaw, observes that Donne's "Divine Poems have more passion, more intensity, than Herbert's; but their masculinity, their dialectic, their abrupt rhythms, their range of figures, separate them from Crashaw."

To say it simply, we have at times clearly brought a masculine bias to our reading of Crashaw's poetry, and when it fails to meet the implicit criteria, it is judged to fail, or to succeed only occasionally. Taking this stance, however, we are critically begging the question and, more significantly, neglecting the quality of Crashaw's achievement that will be more apparent if we look at his poetry anew, with an eye toward its attention to power and gender roles. Intensely concerned about power and submission, activity and passivity, masculinity and femininity, Crashaw nonetheless is unwilling to accept conventional alignments and traditional expectations. In the poetry I will examine here—which includes occasional and more private verse, both secular and sacred—he characteristically acknowledges the virtues usually associated with the two sides of the human dialectic—the masculine figure of power, strength, and courage, the feminine figure of grace, emotion, and passivity—but also challenges and subverts those conventional roles and audience expectations, achieving in some of his most powerful poems a "cultural androgyny" that denies easy conceptions of the masculine and the feminine.

Crashaw's **"Panegyricke"** is the royal poem most apt for this study and, significantly, it focuses on the queen. Among the other poems discussed here two important features are evident: in each there is an open or implicit contest between masculinity and femininity, and each encourages a revaluation of what masculinity and femininity, power and courage, activity and passivity, finally mean. Just as Crashaw's life calls into question easy choices between contemplative and active modes, so his poetry reveals a constant effort to rethink and to transform conventional assumptions about meaningful action and gender roles.

Crashaw's **"Panegyricke"** was printed in two versions, the first celebrating the birth of the Duke of York in October 1633 and the second a longer celebration of the royal family with attention to several of the children and the queen. The second version, which I will discuss here, was published in a volume of poems celebrating the birth of Prince Henry and published at Cambridge; that version was later printed in the 1648 edition of ***Delights of the Muses***. The poem reminds us of the parentage of the children celebrated and, in particular, of the two "Grandsires," Henry IV of France and James I of England. Henry was a warrior and is called Mars in the poem; James is associated with softer virtues and is Phoebus, "Wisdomes God." The young prince Charles is praised as a descendant of both and thus as a "full mixture of those mighty souls / Whose vast intelligences tun'd the Poles / Of peace and warre" (39-41). Later, the youngest child, newborn prince Henry, is portrayed as one whose presence frightens away the manly virtues imaged as war, blood, and death:

> Rebellion, stand thou by; Mischief, make room:
> Warre, Bloud, and Death (Names all averse
>   from Joy)
> Heare this, We have another bright-ey'd Boy:
> That word's a warrant, by whose vertue I
> Have full authoritie to bid you Dy.
>
>   (ll. 83-87)

While neither ignoring the conventional flattery involved in this occasional tribute nor arguing for Crashaw's originality in seeing a royal prince as one who will overcome the forces of rebellion and war, I would emphasize the language and values evident at this point, where a male heir is in opposition to traditional masculine virtues and where *his* virtues are those of peace and calm and felicity. Crashaw leaves his portrayal of the newest of Charles's progeny by reiterating his strengths—and they are feminine ones—in contrast to the qualities recognizably associated with the political world of power and conquest. The prince, a "sweet supernumerary Starre," is urged to

> Shine forth; nor fear the threats of boyst'rous
>   Warre.
> The face of things has therefore frown'd a while
> On purpose, that to thee and thy pure smile
> The world might ow an universall calm;
> While thou, fair Halcyon, on a sea of balm
> Shalt flote; where while thou layst thy lovely
>   head,
> The angry billows shall but make thy bed:
> Storms, when they look on thee, shall straight
>   relent;
> And Tempests, when they tast thy breath, re-
>   pent
> To whispers soft as thine own slumbers be,
> Or souls of Virgins which shall sigh for thee.
>   Shine then, sweet supernumerary Starre;
> Nor feare the boysterous names of Bloud and
>   Warre:
> Thy Birthday is their Death's Nativitie;
> They've here no other businesse but to die.
>
>   (ll. 99-114)

The considerable attention to the queen over the final section of the poem adds to its emphasis on feminine virtues, as the queen is praised for her fruitfulness and her chastity. In a poem that on one level is overtly political, the principal values enumerated stand in contrast to power and authority and war.

The male is strong and triumphant in Crashaw's **"Epithalamium,"** written in celebration of the marriage of Sir John Branston and Alice Abdy in 1635, but in that poem winning and losing, being powerful and being passive become more complex and point us toward the more androgynous roles of later poems. Opening stanzas mildly denigrate the independence and aloofness of the woman about to be married, and she is figured through the "matchlesse maydenhead / that now is dead" (ll. 11-12). Virginity and independence are a "fine thin negative

thing," "a nothing with a dainty name," "a selfe crownd King," and a "froward flower" with "peevish pride." Further imaged as a phoenix "chaced by loves revengefull arrowes," the feminine figure, in her independence, is said to oppose nature by freezing "the fruite of faire desire / which flourisheth in mutuall fire, / 'gainst nature."

Finding contentment and "rest" in the "soft breast" of Alice Abdy, the phoenix-maidenhead is nonetheless eventually won over by the forces of love "in noble Brampstons eyes," and the catalog of responses of the feminine suggests the uneasy vacillation of the conquered:

> With many pretty peevish tryalls
>   of angry yeelding, faint denyings
> melting No's, and milde denyalls
>   dying lives, and short lived dyings;
>   with doubtful eyes,
>   halfe smiles, halfe teares,
>   with trembling joyes,
>   and jocund feares;
> Twixt the pretty twylight strife
> of dying maide and dawning wife;
> twixt raine, and sunshine, this sweet mayden-
>   head
>   alas is dead.
>
>   (st. 7)

These images are not remarkable, nor are the portraits of the two participants in the premarital contest. More interesting are the images associated with the couple newly married. The male is the "faire oake" being embraced by the "Vine" of the female, but the stanza in which these conventional images are conveyed leaves ambiguous the relative strength of each:

> Nor may thy Vine, faire oake, embrace thee
>   with ivy armes, and empty wishes,
> but with full bosome enterlace thee,
>   and reach her Clusters to thy kisses;
>   safe may she rest
>   her laden boughes,
>   on thy firme breast,
>   and fill thy vowes,
> up to the brimm, till she make even
> their full topps with the faire eyed heaven,
> And heaven to guild those glorious Hero's birth
>   stoope and kisse earth.
>
>   (st. 10)

The feminine figure is, if not the agent of power, at least the agent of opportunity and possibility, and the opening priority given the "faire oake" in contrast to the "Vine" is mitigated through the full and circuitous entwining of the "laden boughs." Active verbs are associated with the feminine, as she is seen to "embrace," "enterlace," "reach," "fill," and "make even" in her association with the masculine figure. Attention to this dominant activity of the feminine largely subverts our initial acceptance of the strength and authority of the masculine.

"Epithalamium" evolves from conventional portraits of masculine strength and feminine softness but also encourages rethinking of conventional associations. Crashaw's poems addressed to women work even more decisively to reveal the poet's allegiance to the feminine and the strength and control the feminine ultimately exercises.

Two epigrams Crashaw wrote on the woman of Canaan as recorded in Matthew 15:21-28 (in Williams's edition, poems 182 and 183) provide fitting headnotes to the discussion that follows. In the biblical account the woman engages in a verbal contest with Jesus, asking him to heal her sick daughter. The disciples urge his refusal, and Jesus reminds the woman that his mission is to the house of Israel, not Canaan. Her steadfast pleas win him over, however, and the daughter is healed. Crashaw's two Latin poems on the episode reveal that through passivity and surrender there may be victory, and in the feminine there is strength. The first is exemplified not by the woman but by Jesus, who, in yielding to the strength ("vires") of the woman, actually gains a greater victory by seeing faith spread. The woman's strength, in turn, demonstrates the power of the feminine. Crashaw plays on the feminine gender of the Latin "fides," remarking, "A woman, and of such strong faith? now I believe that faith is / more than grammatically of the *feminine gender*" (Phyllis S. Bowman's translation in Williams's edition).

These controlling images, strength through yielding and strength in the feminine, find their principal display in Crashaw's poems addressed to contemporary women and to St. Teresa. The **"Ode on a Prayer-booke Sent to Mrs. M. R.,"** "To the Same Party Councel concerning her Choise," and the **"Letter to the Countess of Denbigh"** all argue for decisiveness, for control, and for strength, but in each instance these are to be realized through submission to a "dearer Lord."

The poem to Mrs. M. R. "concerning her Choise" and the **"Letter to the Countess of Denbigh"** develop from similar situations, with the poet as friendly counselor advising the woman to choose an eternal mate and thereby reject "the Sonnes of Men." Mrs. M. R. has apparently been unfortunate in love, and Crashaw takes advantage of the occasion to counsel her on behalf of his "dearer LORD." The poem unites secular marriage and sacred commitment but does not explore the erotic potential of that linkage. Mrs. M. R. is urged to avoid the "painted shapes, / Peacocks and Apes, / Illustrious flyes, / Guilded dunghills" and "glorious LYES" of this world in favor of a "braver love," "a farre more worthy SPOUSE / Then this world of Lyes can give ye." Indeed, the poet suggests that this "Mighty lover" has had a hand in the failure of worldly love so that he might woo her for himself. In view of more active roles assigned feminine figures in other poems, the role of Mrs. M. R. here is strikingly static. She is still suffering from crossed love, is unable or unwilling to act, and is receiving—happily or not we do not know—advice from one who knows her. The final lines suggest that in this poem the feminine is inactive, not because of gender but because of a sense of momentary defeat:

> Your first choyce failes, o when you choose agen
> May it not be amongst the sonnes of Men.

The **"Letter to the Countess of Denbigh"** is in two versions, the first of which is more personal and more directly challenges the woman addressed. Apparently unsettled about her ecclesiastical commitment, she is encouraged, as the first version has it, "to render her selfe without further delay into the Communion of the Catholick Church."

To be decisive is, in this instance, to forego refusal and to give up what seems to be the strength of independence but is in fact "peevish strength / Of weaknes" (1652, ll. 41-42). Genuine strength results from a decision to yield:

> Raise this tall Trophee of thy Powre;
> Come once the conquering way; not to confute
> But kill this rebell-word, IRRESOLUTE
> That so, in spite of all this peevish strength
> Of weakness, she may write RESOLV'D AT
>   LENGTH.
>
> (1652, ll. 38-42)

The second version of the poem urges yielding on impersonal, philosophical grounds, in less intimate language than the first version. The "Dart of love" and, contrastingly, the "well-meaning Wounds" of "Allmighty LOVE" will be aimed at the feminine heart that should yield to its force. But yielding is itself strength, and both versions of the poem close with that crucial paradox:

> Disband dull Feares, give Faith the day:
> To save your Life, kill your Delay.
> 'Tis Cowardise that keeps this Field;
> And want of Courage not to Yield.
>   Yield then, O yield, that Love may win
> The Fort at last, and let Life in.
>
> (1653, ll. 81-86)

The **"Ode on a Prayer-booke,"** also in two versions, is the longest and most provocative of the three, and it most fully mingles imagery of love, war, and religion in its invitation to a young woman to be steadfast in love. Steadfastness in love means resisting earthly lovers and keeping oneself pure for Christ, the "noble BRIDEGROOM." The prayer book serves as "love's great artillery" (l. 15) in defense against those who would storm "the hold of your chast heart" (l. 20). The heart, duly admonished by the words of the prayer book, is sufficient to stand and "be strong" (39). Avoiding "the gay mates of the god of flyes" (51) and forsaking the temptation of the "devill's holyday," the pure soul will be a fitting mate for the eternal spouse. As we would expect, the woman is to receive the advances of her spiritual lover, who will "poure abroad / His pretious sweets / On the fair soul whom first he meets" (ll. 93-95). But it is also left to the woman to assert her independence from the world and to seek aggressively the alliance that will empower her She must "meet," "Seize," "tast," "rifle and deflour," and "discover" in her determination to be victorious through yielding. The final twenty lines of the poem focus on the aggressive action of the feminine in acquiring the pleasures and sweets of the masculine. Indeed, the almost startling fusion of influences as diverse as the Song of Songs, St. Teresa, and Thomas Carew's erotic poem "A Rapture" results in a near reversal of conventional gender roles, as the feminine figure forcefully acquires the "delicious dew of spices" yielded by "her sweet prey." The closing stanza and a half make clear the reversal of values and the consequent portrayal of the feminine as the aggressor, the masculine as the passive yielder. The "thrice happy" soul

> Makes hast to meet her morning spouse
> And close with his immortall kisses.
> Happy indeed, who never misses
> To improve that pretious hour,

And every day
Seize her sweet *prey*
All fresh and fragrant as he rises
Dropping with a baulmy Showr
A delicious dew of spices;

O let the blissfull heart hold fast
Her heavnly arm-full, she shall *tast*
At once ten thousand paradises;
She shall have *power*
To *rifle* and *deflour*
The rich and roseall spring of those rare sweets
Which with a swelling bosome there she meets
Boundles and infinite
Bottomles treasures
Of pure inebriating pleasures
Happy proof! she shall *discover*
What joy, what blisse,
How many Heav'ns at once it is
To have her GOD become her LOVER.
(ll. 102-24 italics added)

The poems discussed thus far suggest Crashaw's interest in exploring and transforming conventional views of victory and strength, of masculine and feminine, of activity and passivity. They also point to an ultimately androgynous portrait of humanity that has its fullest treatment in the poems on St. Teresa. Perhaps in part because the historical Spanish saint so easily yielded such a portrait—though certainly a woman, St. Teresa was strong, aggressive, and powerful—and no doubt because he was personally and emotionally comfortable with such a portrait, Crashaw paints a Teresa who is gloriously free from the restrictions of being solely masculine or solely feminine.

The **"Hymn to St. Teresa"** rejects the conventional roles of both gender and age, as St. Teresa is both masculine and feminine, a child and mature. The full title announces these paradoxes: **"A Hymn to the Name and Honor of the Admirable Sainte Teresa, Foundresse of the Reformation of the Discalced Carmelites, both men and Women; A Woman for Angelicall height of speculation, for Masculine courage of performance, more then a woman. Who Yet a child, out ran maturity, and durst plott a Martyrdome."** The poem rejects traditional martyrdom with its masculine features in favor of a softer martyrdom embodied in a woman-child. Gone are the "old Souldiers, Great and tall, / Ripe Men of Martyrdom, that could reach down / With strong armes, their triumphant crown, / Such as could with lusty breath / Speak lowd into the face of death / Their Great LORD'S glorious name" (ll. 4-9). "Spare blood and sweat," Crashaw urges, and see instead love make "his mansion in the mild / And milky soul of a soft child" (ll. 13-14).

Throughout the poem Teresa is the feminine child embodying extraordinary power, never abandoning her femininity, never limited by it. Her heart is touched and burns with "brave heates" (l. 36); "she breathes All fire" (l. 39); and "Her weake brest heaves with strong desire" for something more than "her MOTHER's kisses" (ll. 40-42). Her determination to be a martyr leads her to "travail," to "labor" as would a woman and to "travel" as would a man to realize that goal. The "milder MARTYRDOM" (l. 68) that she is called to embrace is not that of conventional victims but one more apt for a victim of love. The "death

more mysticall and high" is both the experience of religious ecstacy and the image of sexual union, and the description fits one who receives and who is strengthened in that reception:

O how oft shalt thou complain
Of a sweet and subtle PAIN.
Of intolerable JOYES.
Of a DEATH, in which who dyes
Loves his death, and dyes again.
And would for ever so be slain.
And lives, and dyes; and knowes not why
To live, But that he thus may never leave to DY.
How kindly will thy gentle HEART
Kisse the sweetly-killing DART!
And close in his embraces keep
Those delicious wounds, that weep
Balsom to heal themselves with.
(ll. 97-109)

The power of the saint is apparent as Crashaw anticipates the physical death of Teresa and her admission into heaven. There, all her works and all those "Thousands of crown'd Soules' (l. 166) whom she has made will greet her and bless her, as will be "soveraign spouse" who has, the poet says, "Made fruitfull thy fair soul" (ll. 168-69).

The **"Hymn to St. Teresa"** announces its androgynous aim at the beginning, but the interest in the inadequacy of conventional human gender roles is abandoned halfway through the poem in favor of a setting in heaven where gender designations are matters of language and convenience, not predictive or authoritative, where there would be, as St. Paul says, "neither male nor female." **"The Flaming Heart"** is similarly concerned with "manliness" and femininity but maintains that focus until the final twenty lines, where the poet's desire for religious ecstasy supersedes his determination to understand the true nature of the saint who is his subject. Here, as in the earlier **"Hymn to St. Teresa,"** Crashaw is unwilling to accept conventional gender roles and turns St. Teresa into a figure at once feminine and masculine, passive and active, submissive and powerful. **"The Flaming Heart"** challenges our understanding of masculine and feminine qualities and argues against the usual portrayal of Teresa as a "weak, inferiour, woman saint" (l. 26). Rather, she is the aggressor and the wielder of power. For Crashaw, of course, the source of such power is spiritual, and it flows from private experience, as the closing lines of the poem confirm.

The poem is a reaction to one or more paintings of Teresa and the angel who brought the flaming arrow (the "Dart") that inflamed the heart of the ecstatic woman. In traditional portrayals, Teresa is the submissive recipient, the angel the active provider. Crashaw urges a reversal of roles in language that confronts both power and sexuality.

Give her the DART for it is she
(Fair youth) shootes both thy shaft and THEE
Say, all ye wise and well-peirc't hearts
That live and dy amidst her darts,
What is't your tastful spirits doe prove
In that rare life of Her, and love?
Say and bear wittnes. Sends she not
A SERAPHIM at every shott?

What magazins of immo tall ARMES there shine!
Heavn's great artillery in each love-spun line.
Give then the dart to her who gives the flame;
Give him the veil, who kindly takes the shame.

(ll. 47-58)

The "flaming heart," the most visible symbol of the private experience of ecstasy, is imaged in terms drawn from both sexual and military conquest and in language that challenges, indeed subverts, conventional notions about femininity and masculinity, the passive and the active, the submissive and the conquering. Love and devotion and ecstasy—"feminine" qualities that Teresa so vividly displays—are shown to be powerful and transforming virtues in the poem. As Crashaw puts it, "Love's passives are his activ'st part" (l. 73), and the "great HEART," which, true to the private, emotional experience of the poem, loves, dies, bleeds and yields, is nonetheless a powerful and evident influence over others, as Crashaw's litany of the heart's achievements makes clear:

> Live here, great HEART; and love and dy and
> *kill;*
> And bleed and *wound,* and yeild and *conquer*
> still.
>
> (ll. 79-80, italics added)
> (pp. 152-61)

The poetry confirms his commitment to the private, "feminine" virtues of love, compassion, and feeling and his simultaneous recognition of the worldly attraction of power, conquest, and might. Indeed, one of the obvious ironies in Crashaw's subversion of conventional power is that the world of masculine, public conduct, though dispraised and rejected, inevitably yields the language through which the usually secondary feminine virtues can be elevated to primacy. Unwilling to be no more than a distant observer in the ongoing political and religious skirmishes, Crashaw was incapable of endorsing many of the conventional values associated with the political life. His answer was to moderate the prominence of power and force in a poem such as the **"Panegyricke,"** where they might have been expected, and to heighten those same images in his poems on contemporary women and St. Teresa, where they would be least expected. Both poetic strategies reveal his deep allegiance to feminine virtues. In the public world of religious controversy and political warfare, masculine qualities are, in Crashaw's hands, minimized and subdued; in the imaginative world of saints and idealized feminine figures these same qualities function as images—forceful, original, provocative and disturbing—to remind us that devotion and loyalty and love are also powerful and conquering. (pp. 161-62)

> Paul A. Parrish, "The Feminizing of Power: Crashaw's Life and Art," in "The Muses of Common-Weale": Poetry and Politics in the Seventeenth Century, edited by Claude J. Summers and Ted-Larry Pebworth, University of Missouri Press, 1988, pp. 148-62.

R. V. Young, Jr. (essay date 1990)

[*In the following excerpt, Young assesses Crashaw's liberal use of the Holy Scriptures, asserting that "they are*

Teresa of Avila in ecstasy—a favorite subject of several of Crashaw's poems.

central to the development of [*his sacred poetry's*] *complex structure of meaning."*]

Recent years have witnessed a surge of interest in the Bible as a literary inspiration for the devotional poetry of the seventeenth century. Scholars have come to recognize in Sacred Scripture—especially the Psalter and the other poetical books—a source of generic and metaphorical models, as well as of traditional typological symbolism. This literary interest in Scripture has been almost exclusively associated with the Reformation, and biblical poetics is widely regarded simply as a major component of Protestant poetics. An examination of continental literature in the era of the Counter-Reformation, however, reveals a distinct Catholic interest in the Bible as a literary work and model; and this interest bore fruit in England in the poetry of Richard Crashaw.

The earliest verse we have by Crashaw consists of paraphrases of the Psalms in Latin and English and the Latin epigrams of *Epigrammatum Sacrorum Liber* (1634), which are based on the Sunday Gospel readings from *The Book of Common Prayer.* More important, a lively responsiveness to the Psalms and to Gospel narrative is a recurrent feature in his sacred poetry. Crashaw's **"Hymn to the Name of Jesus,"** the culminating work of his biblical poetry, has its generic roots in Scripture and displays a deep sensitivity to what Barbara Lewalski [in her *Protestant Po-*

etics, 1979] has called "the poetic texture of Scripture." An examination of this poem, especially, in such terms is helpful both in understanding the complexities of its tone and structure and in suggesting ways in which Protestant and Catholic poets of the seventeenth century still shared, for all their differences, a common Christian culture centered on the person of Jesus. Finally, the scriptural elements of Crashaw's poetry provide a revealing insight into the intellectual dynamic of biblical poetics: the poet seeks to rewrite the Word of God in his own imitation or version of "scripture," thus inscribing the Word—Christ's name and presence—in his own soul in the blood of the Lamb. (pp. 30-1)

Within this context, the biblical elements of Crashaw's hymns begin to emerge. It is important to recall that Christian liturgical hymns are scriptural in inspiration and draw their form from the Psalms and biblical canticles. Crashaw's feastday hymns are all attempts to combine an imitation of liturgical celebration with private meditation, and in that sense have a scriptural basis. His English translation of the *Stabat Mater* is a revealing example of how he reorients a public hymn, by means of an "application of the self," toward private meditation, without losing its liturgical overtones. It is generally overlooked that devotion to the Blessed Virgin constitutes an identification on the part of the faithful with a figure from Scripture; hence, in the *Stabat Mater*, Mary becomes a "type" of the faithful Christian at the foot of the Cross. In Crashaw's version, this sense of reexperiencing the scriptural event in one's own life is paramount:

> By all those stings
>   Of love, sweet bitter things,
> Which these torn hands transcrib'd on thy true
>   heart
>   O teach mine too the art
> To study him so, till we mix
> Wounds; and become one crucifix.
>
> (stanza 10)

Crashaw's entire ten-line stanza (of which the last six lines are here quoted) is woven from a single line of the Latin original: "Fac me plagis vulnerari" (Make me be wounded with the blows). Throughout the poem, Crashaw's method is thus to adapt the inner life of Mary, developed from hints in Scripture and Latin hymns, to the spiritual situation of his own time.

In the Gospel according to Luke (2:35), Mary is told by Simeon that a sword will pierce her soul, and in John (19:35) she is placed at the site of the Crucifixion. The original hymn is, of course, a meditation on the latter verse, and the former is mentioned in its first stanza. What Crashaw does is to elaborate the scriptural passages into a "scripture" of blood and wounds written in the soul. Scripture is "applied" to the self as the Passion of Christ is "written" not only in the words of the Gospels but also in the heart of his mother. In stanza 3, "His Nailes write swords in her," and as the poem draws to a close Christ's very wounds have "transcrib'd" his sufferings in her heart. It is this experience that the poet would share in order to "mix / Wounds" with the crucified Christ and become "one crucifix" with him. In Crashaw's vision Jesus, the Word of God is, by the wounds of his Passion, written—

"transcrib'd"—in the heart of the Blessed Virgin, who thereby becomes the model for all Christians. In this way, biblical narrative and image are rewritten in the soul of the believer, and the Bible becomes the book in which the salvation of the individual is inscribed even as he is joined with the communion of the saints.

In much the same way, Crashaw's meditation on the Gospel narrative of the finding of the Christ Child by the Wise Men (Matthew 2:1-12) becomes an account of the mystical discovery of Christ in the soul of the individual believer. Despite its elaborate format alternating the voices of the "Three Kings" and the "Chorus," the **"Hymn in the Glorious Epiphanie"** is as much a personal reflection on the meaning of the search for Christ as T. S. Eliot's "The Journey of the Magi." It is also a poem deeply involved with the text of Scripture, interpreting one passage by juxtaposing it with another. The significance of the coming of the kings is suggested by their prophecies, first of the eclipse of the sun during the Crucifixion of Christ (Matthew 27:45, Mark 15:33, Luke 23:44) and then of the conversion of Dionysius the Areopagite (Acts 17:34), traditionally as a result of this miraculous eclipse. Once again scriptural passages become the occasion—the pre-text, as it were—for a rewriting of Scripture in the heart and soul of the believer. For those who once worshiped the sun of this world, the "elaborate love-eclipse" (l. 152) at the time of the Crucifixion makes it their duty

> To'injoy his Blott; and as a large black letter
> Use it to spell Thy beautyes better;
> And make the night it self their torch to thee.
>
> (ll. 186-88)

"The right-ey'd Areopagite" (l. 191), in Crashaw's day still generally identified with the author of the sixth-century *Mystical Theology*, will interpret this mysterious writing:

> And teach obscure MANKIND a more close way
> By the frugall negative light
> Of a most wise and well-abused Night
> To read more legible thine originall Ray
>
> (ll. 208-11)

As in the translation of the *Stabat Mater*, here in the Epiphany meditation a poem in the form of a liturgical hymn deploys a set of scriptural passages in order to explore the most intimate relations of Christ and the individual soul. The collocation of biblical verses is interpretive: the discovery of the Savior of Israel by the heathen Magi, the enlightening darkness of the eclipse at the hour of Christ's death, and the conversion of Dionysius are arranged as a pattern of significance for the reader of Scripture. The reader must reenact this pattern in his own spiritual life. Crashaw, like the Areopagite, seeks to make the written Word more "legible," to help the individual to "read" the "Ray" of God's grace in the dark recesses of his own soul.

In addition to his paraphrases of Psalms 23 and 137, Crashaw also uses implicit allusions to Psalm 1 in poems that explicitly treat New Testament themes. The continuity of the two testaments is thus affirmed, and their interrelationship establishes a means of reciprocal interpretation. The device is fairly obvious in **"Charitas Nimia,"** in which, as George Williams points out, the opening stanza echoes the Prayer Book version of Psalm 144:3-4.

> Lord, what is man?   why should he coste thee
> So dear?   what had his ruin lost thee?
> Lord what is man?   that thou hast overbought
>   So much a thing of nought?
>
> (ll. 1-4)

The purpose of Crashaw's poem is to create a New Testament context for this psalm motif, and his approach is similar to Cardinal Bellarmine's. In the commentary of the latter, the psalmist's wondering exclamation about the mercies of God serves as provocation to even greater admiration and gratitude among us who have benefited from the Incarnation:

> Et si David dicit, & tanto sensu pietatis dicit, quid nos facere, sentire, & dicere par esset, quibus Deus non solùm innotuit, sed formam serui accepit, & in ea forma humiliauit semetipsum factus obedies vsque ad mortem, mortem autem crucis.

> (And if David says these things, and says them with such a feeling of piety, what would be suitable for us to do, to feel, to say, whom God has not only noticed, but for whom he took the form of a servant and humbled himself in that form made obedient even to death, even death on the cross.)

Crashaw uses the same phrases of wonder from the psalm to make the same point about the enormity of Christ's sacrificial passion and death recorded in the Gospels. In **"Charitas Nimia,"** as in Crashaw's version of the *Stabat Mater*, the wounds of the slain Christ become implements of writing. The wounds are literally inscribed in Christ's hands and feet; however, by a metaphorical reversal, they become instruments of power. In **"The Flaming Heart"** there "was never found / A nobler weapon than a WOUND," and "The wounded is the wounding heart" (ll. 71-72, 74). Just so, in **"Charitas Nimia"** the ink in which man's sin is inscribed is the blood of the Lamb, pouring out of his wounds:

> If my base lust
> Bargain'd with Death and well-beseeming dust,
>   Why should the white
>   Lamb's bosom write
>   The purple name
>   Of my sin's shame?
>
> (ll. 55-60)

Sin is thus dissipated in discourse; the incarnate Word takes sin upon himself by setting it down in his own blood. Old and New Testament expressions converge in this "writing" of Christ, read in the soul of the redeemed Christian.

Like **"Charitas Nimia," "Hymn to the Name of Jesus"** is a biblical poem tying together specific texts from the Old and New Testaments, but the procedure here is more oblique and sophisticated. There is, further, an intriguing parallel with Henry Vaughan's poem beginning "And do they so?"—recently accepted as a Protestant exemplar of biblical poetics. In place of a title, the heading of this piece is a quotation of Romans 8:19, in Beza's Latin version.

Here is the verse in the King James version, along with verses 21-23:

> For the earnest expectation of the creature, waiteth for the manifestation of the sonnes of God. . . . Because the creature itselfe also shall be delivered from the bondage of corruption, into the glorious libertie of the children of God. For wee know that the whole creation groaneth, and travaileth in paine together untill now. And not only they, but our selves also which have the first fruites of the spirit, even we our selves groane within our selves, waiting for the adoption, to wit, the redemption of our body.

Vaughan's meditation on this passage leads him to reflect upon his own unworthy attitude toward divine grandeur. The scriptural image of the entire creation longing for Christ is an expression of his glory, which inspires the poet to love God with the constancy of the lesser creatures:

> O let me not do lesse! shall they
>   Watch, while I sleep, or play?
> Shall I thy mercies still abuse
>   With fancies, friends or newes?

Even as Vaughan's poem is a direct meditative response to the eighth chapter of Romans, so Crashaw's **"Hymn to the Name of Jesus"** is a meditation on the text of Philippians 2:9-10: "Wherefore, God also hath highly exalted him, and given him a name which is above every name, That at the name of Jesus every knee should bow, of *Things* in heaven, and *things* in earth, and *things* under the earth." In its form the hymn resembles a number of the poems by Pedro Espinosa called *salmos*, which, like Crashaw's poem, are written in an irregular alternation of long and short lines with plentiful rhymes but no fixed rhyme scheme. Espinosa's "Psalm calling for the coming of God to the soul of the poet" seems especially close to Crashaw's poem in form and conception. It begins with an allusion to Psalm 129 (King James Version 130) and includes further references to Psalm 148 (King James Version 149) and the Canticles. Like Crashaw's hymn, Espinosa's "Psalm" involves a meditation on the creatures and many personal invocations of God and the angelic powers. The following passage conveys some sense of Espinosa's lush imagery and exalted rhetoric:

> Levanta entre gemidos, alma mìa,
> el grito afectuoso,
> pidiendo amor, pues Dios te lo ha mandado.
> ¡Oh mi esperanza, oh gloria, oh mi alegrìa,
> oh mi Esposo gentil, oh dulce Esposo,
> querido mìo, amante regalado,
> más florido que el prado!
> Ven, ven, no tardes; ven, sabroso fuego,
> no tardes: luego, luego,
> tu rayo me deshaga.

> (Lift up among groans, soul of mine, the impassioned cry, seeking love, since God has commanded it of you. Oh my hope, oh glory, oh my joy, oh my gentle Spouse, oh sweet Spouse, oh my desired one, delicate lover, more flowered than the meadow! Come, come, do not delay; come delicious flame; do not delay: then, then, may your ray melt me.)

Espinosa's verses, like Crashaw's, are psalm-like in their free, chanting quality and in the use of impassioned address to the Deity, and both poets weave into their own poetic texture the actual language of the scriptural Psalms as well as other books of the Bible. Both poems are biblical in theme, mood, and style.

There are also similarities of detail between Crashaw's **"Hymn to the Name of Jesus"** and Vaughan's "And do they so?" Like Vaughan, Crashaw dwells upon the parallel longing of man and of nature for the coming of Christ. The third of the seven sections of the poem is "An address to other creatures, asking their help," and it is only after he has dealt with the natural creatures as a means to God that the poet effects a "Return to self-address, with greater confidence," preparatory to the "invocation" and "Celebration of the Name [in Louis L. Martz, *The Poetry of Meditation: A Study in English Religious Literature of the Seventeenth Century*, 1962]" It is only as the choirmaster of the earthly creation that the poet dares to join with the heavenly hosts in the celestial harmony of praise to the name of Jesus:

> May it be no wrong
> Blest Heavns, to you, and your Superiour song,
> That we, dark Sons of Dust and Sorrow,
> A while Dare borrow
> The Name of Your Delights and our Desires,
> And fitt it to our farr inferior LYRES.
>
> (ll. 97-102)

"To the Name of Jesus," then, is an example of biblical poetics at work in two senses. It is a hymn both of praise and of personal reflection, in the manner of the Psalms, and it is a meditation on the personal implications of a scriptural text for the poet. Just as Vaughan asks in his poem, "What does this passage of the Epistle to the Romans mean to me?" so Crashaw shows how individual Christians might respond to the Pauline injunction that every knee must bend at the name of Jesus.

Further, he shows himself to be a biblical poet in his use of allusion to the Bible and of biblical language in his own text. At the very center of his poem, as the Name itself is invoked, he recalls the passage from the Epistle to the Romans that inspired Vaughan:

> Lo how the thirsty Lands
> Gasp for thy Golden Showres! with long
>   stretch't Hands
> Lo how the laboring EARTH
> That hopes to be
> All Heaven by THEE,
> Leapes at thy Birth.
>
> (ll. 129-34)

George Williams has pointed out the echo of Psalm 143:6 (in the version of the English prayer book) in the phrase "thirsty Lands / Gasp"; in addition, the phrase "laboring EARTH" suggests that the entire passage is inspired by the "creature" in travail of Romans 8:22. Crashaw intimates that the "creature," the earth, will be delivered of its travail only when the name, Jesus, is born into glory. The pregnancy and womb imagery in this poem is linked to the messianic Psalm 109 (King James Version 110): "The people shall be willing in the day of power; in the beauties of holiness from the womb of morning, thou hast the dew of thy youth." Crashaw plainly echoes this verse in his hymn:

> WELCOME to our dark world, Thou
>   Womb of Day!
> Unfold thy fair Conceptions; and display
> The Birth of our Bright Joyes.
>
> (ll. 161-64)

The ultimate scriptural source of this hymn is, of course, the account of the bestowal of the name *Jesus* at the time of the Lord's circumcision (Luke 2:21), but the allusions to Romans and Psalm 109 embedded within the poem have the force of prophecy. The implicit juxtaposition of these diverse scriptural passages conveys an expectation of the final apocalypse, which will redeem the entire creation from its labor.

> O see, so many WORLDS of barren yeares
> Melted and measur'd out in Seas of TEARES.
> O see, The WEARY liddes of wakefull Hope
> (LOVE'S Eastern windowes) All wide ope
>   With Curtains drawn,
> To catch The Day-break of Thy DAWN.
>
> (ll. 143-48)

This apocalyptic element explains how the apparent digression on the martyrs (ll. 197-224) fits into the structure of the poem as a whole, and it prepares for the vision of Judgment Day with which the poem concludes. The passage on the martyrs, in addition, suggests how man redeemed by Christ can imitate him by writing out the Word in his own bloody script. A "martyr" is literally a "witness," and what the martyrs witness to is Christ; he is what they *reveal*: "What did their Weapons but sett wide the Doores / For Thee: Fair, purple Doores, of love's devising" (ll. 216-17). Just as Christ's wounds are "written" in the heart of his mother and of all the faithful, so his name is inscribed in the blood of the martyrs. They are thus a "book" of Scripture: in revealing Christ through their wounds, the martyrs anticipate the final Revelation—another term for "Apocalypse." Indeed, the poem as a whole reflects the next to last verse of the Book of the Apocalypse: "He which testifieth these things saith, Surely I come quickly. Amen. Even so, come, Lord Jesus" (Revelation 22:20). The key to it all is love: the "Doores" are "Of love's devising." This theme has been already established by the allusion to the eighth chapter of Romans. In explicating the typological "name of Christ" from Isaiah 5:1, "well-beloved" (*amado*), Fray Luis de León adduces the same verses from Romans that are cited explicitly by Vaughan, implicitly by Crashaw. "All things, guided by a secret motion," says the Spanish friar, "loving their own good, also love Him and pant with their desire and moan for his coming in the manner the Apostle writes of it. . . . This is nothing at all except an appetite and a desire for Jesus Christ, who is the author of this liberty, as St. Paul says, and for whom all clamor" ("Porque todas las cosas, guiadas de un movimiento secreto, amando su mismo bien, le aman tambien a Él y suspiran con su deseo y gimen por su venida en la manera que al Apóstol escribe. . . . Lo cual no es otra cosa sino un apetito y un deseo de Jesucristo, que es el autor de esta libertad, que San Pablo dice, y por quien todo vocea").

The allusions to Scripture in Crashaw's **"Hymn to the Name of Jesus"** are not, therefore, merely adventitious or decorative; they are central to the development of its complex structure of meaning. In meditating upon the mysterious grandeur of the Holy Name, as set forth in the Epistle to the Philippians (and suggested in Luke), Crashaw makes use of the messianic prophecy of Psalm 109 and the enigmatic intimations of a text from Romans. This cross-referencing of Scripture requires a profound sense of the typological unity of the Bible. **"To the Name of Jesus"** is, then, biblical in its psalm-like form, in its meaning, and in its metaphoric texture.

It would be misleading to ignore the very sharp differences between Reformation and Counter-Reformation, but they have been overemphasized in recent literary studies. Poetry is not, after all, a good medium for polemics; and there is a vast area of experience and concern shared by Catholics and Protestants. Surely the Bible is one of the things they shared. When Crashaw converted to the Catholic Church, he did not abandon the love of Holy Scripture fostered by his Protestant upbringing; and there was, as we have seen, ample interest among other Catholic poets to encourage him further. Although one can identify significant discrepancies between Catholic and Protestant practice and belief, the devotional poetry of the seventeenth century, with its scriptural foundation, represents an area in which the unity of Christendom survived, in some measure, the ecclesiastical breakup of the Reformation. (pp. 37-48)

> *R. V. Young, Jr., "Crashaw and Biblical Poetics," in* New Perspectives on the Life and Art of Richard Crashaw, *edited by John R. Roberts, University of Missouri Press, 1990, pp. 30-48.*

A. D. Cousins (essay date 1991)

[*In the following excerpt, Cousins asserts that Crashaw's poems about Christ and the Virgin "illustrate a variety of forms" as well as "a mastery of the baroque [style] in devout guise."*]

Crashaw's religious verse is dominated by study of the love descending from God to man, of that reaching from man to God, and of those loves' intermingling. His poems' pervasive studying of sacred love is characterized by several concerns. He focuses often on illuminative and on unitive experience, more often than do any of the other Catholic poets (with the possible exception of Beaumont). He examines how sacred love transforms human perception and identity, how it perfects or transcends human reason; he presents it as transforming, extending, traditional modes of religious discourse. In so considering sacred love, then, his poems emphasize its intensity, generosity - and wit ("O wit of loue!"). Furthermore they almost constantly, and always memorably, manifest what Austin Warren finely described as Crashaw's "baroque sensibility" [in his *Richard Crashaw: A Study in Baroque Sensibility*, 1939]. One might add finally that his poems surpass in

stylistic sophistication those of his Catholic predecessors and study virtually all the spiritual interests of their verse with a subtlety that they could seldom equal.

What has been suggested above of Crashaw's religious verse could be illustrated by reference to either his English or his Latin poems. Though in the following discussion mention will necessarily be made of the Latin poems, it is of course those in English which will be given most attention, especially those in **Carmen Deo Nostro** (the final collection of Crashaw's verse). In offering an account of the English poems one needs to begin with the poems which are directly centred on Christ: there Crashaw identifies the source and the end of sacred love; there he most thoroughly considers its nature. They indicate, moreover, that his English poems as a whole, for all their frequent and ardent celebrating of female saints, are undoubtedly Christocentric. Examining Crashaw's **"To the Name above Every Name, the Name of Iesvs. A Hymn"** and some of his poems on, or connected with, Christ as the Good Shepherd will suggest that his poems directly centred on Christ do indeed help to set in perspective those others wherein he studies sacred love. In addition, to examine the poems is to show that Crashaw could fashion interestingly contradictory (if nonetheless convergent) images of Christ, for the **"Hymn"** uses the Holy Name to represent Christ as the all-encompassing Word, the Logos—and so to emphasize his incomprehensible, as well as loving, divinity—whereas the Good Shepherd poems tend to picture Christ as the protector of and the provider for individual souls—stressing the immediacy of his humanity.

The **"Hymn"** to the name of Jesus images both celebration of that "Name above Every Name" (the poem's title alluding to *Philippians* 2,9) and invocation of its presence. The poem begins with Crashaw's visionary speaker praising and interpreting the Name, in doing which he represents it as the source, focus, and end of sacred love, the centre of the Church Triumphant. Later in the **"Hymn,"** the speaker pleads that the Name become present within the Church Militant and so grant to the faithful on earth a foretaste (see ll.154—158) of heavenly beatitude. The speaker's invocation of the Name, and his subsequent account of its appearance in the world, resplendently affirm and develop his initial perception of it as sacred love's embodiment. To convey something of the richness and comprehensiveness with which Crashaw's poem thus studies sacred love, one must now look more closely at the work itself.

The **"Hymn"** opens with topoi of humility (see especially ll.1—2, 1.6), Crashaw's speaker beginning to celebrate the Name, but at the same time acknowledging his innate unworthiness, and inability, to do so. Amidst his hesitancy, however, he tells much of the Name, for in starting to praise it he indicates what he sees as its significances. The speaker interprets the Name as signifying the spiritual life and fulfilment of humanity (because of Christ's self-sacrificial love); he implies, moreover, that it signifies the focal point of true human love. He sings of the Holy Name as "The Name of our New PEACE; our Good: / Our Blisse: & Supernaturall Blood: / The Name of All our Liues & Loues" (ll.3—5). In so interpreting the Name,

Crashaw's speaker emphasizes that Christ's selfless love encompasses, as well as completes, human existence ("our New PEACE" alluding to God's redemptive scheme to history). He also stresses that Christ is true human love's ultimate desire ("Our Blisse"; "The Name of All our . . . Loues"). That initial, compressed explication of the Holy Name is then elaborated into a luminous vision of unitive experience when the speaker climactically prays for aid from, and describes the members of, the Church Triumphant:

> Hearken, And Help, ye holy Doues!
> The high-born Brood of Day; you bright
> Candidates of blissefull Light,
> The HEIRS Elect of Loue; whose Names belong
> Vnto The euerlasting life of Song;
> All ye wise SOVLES, who in the wealthy Brest
> Of This vnbounded NAME build your warm
>   Nest.
>
> (ll.6-12)

The passage images the beatitude of the Church Triumphant, and represents it as the immaculate, incandescent (ll.7-8) existence of the Many in the One, of "Names" (l.9) in the "vnbounded NAME" (l.12) of the Word made flesh; that blessedness is indicated to be sacred human love's fulfilment in the ineffable (at least, here—for the name of Jesus remains unuttered throughout the "Hymn"—cf. l.2), all-encompassing (l.12) Holy Name, whose primal love (ll.7-9) has gathered those who are now the "holy Doues" (l.6)—wise in their love of the Name (l.11)—into "The euerlasting life of Song" (l.10). In thus closing the introduction to the "Hymn," the passage amplifies and extends the interpretation of the Name implied in the poem's opening lines, thereby concluding their analysis of sacred love. Many ideas and images in that analysis pervade Crashaw's religious verse. As can be seen recurrently in his poems, but most notably in those to or about women, he implies that Christ, having physically manifested God's love in the world and having redemptively shaped history, embodies primal love that encompasses all human experience; just so, Crashaw again and again depicts heavenly beatitude, or anticipatory sensation of it, as spiritual union with Christ, the ecstasy of that oneness often being suggested through images of incandescence or of musical harmony. He centres his studies of love, that is to say, on Christ as the embodiment of total life, at once the divine source of sacred love (insofar as he directly expresses God's saving love for mankind), the focus of sacred human love, and its final goal.

The Christocentrism of Crashaw's religious verse is also indicated in the immediately following sections of the "Hymn" (ll.13-114), wherein the speaker proceeds from contemplation of the Holy Name to reflection on himself and then to evocation of universal harmonies. There the speaker in effect explains the hesitancy that he revealed in the poem's introduction, for he asks whether the "fair WORD" (l.14), "SOVL" (l.13), could be applied to his spirit in the poverty of its selfcentredness (ll.19-23), implicitly contrasting his spiritual state with the rich Christcentredness of the blessed "Names"—see ll.9-12), and he wonders how as "empty" (l.21) a creature as himself, to whom the term for spiritual identity may not have applica-

bility, can become sufficient to celebration (and invocation) of the Name which signifies Being and embraces all things. His need of spiritual sufficiency impels him subsequently to summon the musical harmonies of nature, art, and heaven to join with him in concordant celebration of the Name to which all true love is directed:

> Come, here to part,
> NATVRE & ART!
> Come; & come strong,
> To the conspiracy of our Spatious song.
>   Bring All the Powres of Praise
> Your Prouinces of well-vnited WORLDS can
>   raise;
> Bring All your LVTES & HARPS of HEAVN &
>   EARTH;
> What e're cooperates to The common mirthe
>   Vessells of vocall Ioyes,
> Or You, morè noble Architects of Intellectuall
>   Noise,
> Cymballs of Heau'n, or Humane sphears,
> Solliciters of SOVLES or EARES;
>   And when you'are come, with All
> That you can bring or we can call;
>   O may you fix
>   For euer here, & mix
>   Your selues into the long
> And euerlasting series of a deathlesse SONG;
> Mix All your many WORLDS, Aboue,
> And loose them into ONE of Loue.
>
> (ll.68-87)

In seeking sufficiency to praise the "Rich WORD" (l.95), that is, the Name of the incarnate Logos, he aptly evokes a universal symphony, *concordia discors*. But his doing that is not what justifies him as the poet of the Name which is at once his theme and his muse. Rather, he finds himself justified in his role because the "WORD" generates and subsumes all words that are in its service:

> Powres of my Soul, be Proud!
> And speake lowd
> To all the dear-bought Nations This Redeeming
>   Name,
> And in the wealth of one Rich WORD proclaim
> New Similes to Nature.
>
> (ll.92-96)

Moreover, he knows that the "WORD" lovingly condescends to accept the words directed to it in love by even the lowliest creature:

> Our Murmurs haue their Musick too,
> Ye mighty ORBES, as well as you,
>   Nor yeilds the Noblest nest
> Of warbling SERAPHIM to the eares of Loue,
> A choicer Lesson then the ioyfull BREST
>   Of a poor panting Turtle-Doue.
> And we, low Wormes haue leaue to doe
> The Same bright Busynes (ye Third HEAVENS)
>   with you.
>
> (ll.103-110)

The speaker's quest for, and finding of, justification of his poetic role suggests that fallen humanity and its words can act in the divine service because both are empowered and made acceptable by the Word. Throughout Crashaw's religious poems his speakers insistently allude to Christ's making sufficient those who want to serve him but are weak, or unworthy as well as weak (representative instances, and ones interestingly comparable to the instance in this poem, occurring in the hymn to St Teresa, ll.1-80, and **"The Weeper,"** *passim*); they stress, furthermore, that Christ is the ultimate source of and the authority behind his servants' words (whether, for example, those words are in St Teresa's *Life* or in "a *little Prayerbook*"). It is indeed on the Word, not on the mediating figures and words of saints or of anyone else, that Crashaw's personae and their words are centred.

The speaker of the **"Hymn,"** having discerned his sufficiency to put words in the service of the Word, prays that the Holy Name descend from the Church Triumphant and manifest itself within the members of the Church Militant. In praying for (ll.115-150) and in witnessing (ll.151-196) the descent of the Name, he resplendently affirms and develops his initial perception of it as the source, focus, and goal of sacred love. When the speaker invokes the Name he requests, in effect, a pacific Second Coming:

> Come, louely NAME! Appear from forth the
>   Bright
>   Regions of peaceful Light
> Look from thine own Illustrious Home,
> Fair KING of NAMES, & come.
> Leaue All thy natiue Glories in their Gorgeous
>   Nest,
> And giue thy Self a while The gracious Guest
> Of humble Soules, that seek to find
>   The hidden Sweets
>   Which man's heart meets
> When Thou art Master of the Mind.
> Come, louely Name; life of our hope!
> Lo we hold our HEARTS wide ope!
>
> (ll.115-126)

Asking that the Holy Name express again the accommodating love revealed in the Incarnation (see ll.115-121, with their allusion to humility), the speaker elaborates upon his earlier perception of the Name as the divine source of sacred love. His prayer emphasizes too (most obviously in ll.121-126) that the Name is the focus of sacred human love, but more interesting seems to be his inversion—to stress that the Holy Name is sacred human love's goal—of the image of beatitude with which his song began (ll.6-12). Now he asks that the One dwell in the Many, the Name in its servants (the reverse being depicted in ll.11-12), and allow momentarily (l.120) the Church Militant to know that unitive experience which is the blessedness of the Church Triumphant. Sensuously vehement in its incandescence and its luxuriance, the speaker's invocation confronts the reader with a compelling representation of the Holy Name as the Alpha and Omega of sacred love.

If the speaker's invocation of the Name resplendently amplifies his initial interpretation of it, his witnessing of its descent does so with even greater brilliance. When the Name appears, he cries:

> Lo, where Aloft it comes! It comes, Among
> The Conduct of Adoring SPIRITS, that throng
> Like diligent Bees, And swarm about it.
>   O they are wise;
> And know what SWEETES are suck't from out it.
>   It is the Hiue,

> By which they thriue,
> Where All their Hoard of Hony lyes.
>
> (ll.151-158)

The richly sensuous and astute image of the hive, an *audacia* which accords with Gracián's idea of the first species of conceit, suggests the Name to be the soul's nourishment, delight, and home (cf. ll.11-12): the total life of the soul. Having identified the Name as total life, the speaker then pictures it as total love—again in luxuriantly sensuous imagery: "Lo where it comes, vpon The snowy DOVE'S/ Soft Back; And brings a Bosom big with Loues" (ll.159-160). Affirming and developing his earlier association of the Name with spiritual illumination, the speaker here declares, "WELCOME to our dark world, Thou / Womb of Day!" and prays, "Vnfold thy fair Conceptions" (ll.161-163). The Name of the incarnate Logos is the radiant origin of spiritual light. As the speaker subsequently implies, the Name is every Good: "O thou compacted / Body of Blessings: spirit of Soules extracted!" (ll.165-166). Hence his initial depiction of beatitude as union with the Name is also amplified, in fact receiving amplification upon amplification. Praying that the Church Militant may now know something of the blessedness experienced by its triumphant counterpart, he asks: "O dissipate thy spicy Powres / (Clowd of condensed sweets) & break vpon vs / In balmy showrs;/ O fill our senses . . . " (ll.167-170). He goes on to celebrate union with the Name not merely in such intensely sensuous terms but by overgoing, and so indirectly repudiating as inadequate, the ecstatically sensuous language of the *Song of Solomon,* traditionally taken to be an allegory of the Spiritual Marriage:

In his paraphrase of psalm 23 Crashaw of course identifies the Father as the Good Shepherd but nonetheless places the Son at the poem's centre: it is through the Son that the Father, as Shepherd, is shown to feed his flock. Crashaw more forcefully images God as the immediate protector of and provider for the individual soul, however, when he depicts the Son himself as the Good Shepherd. Christ appears in that guise in several of Crashaw's poems (for example, see **"Lavda Sion Salvatorem. The Hymn for the BL. Sacrament,"** sts XIII-XIV; cf. "On the miracle of multiplyed loaves"), yet it could reasonably be suggested that the most forceful and the ultimate instance in which Crashaw presents Christ as the Good Shepherd can be seen in his paraphrase of **"Dies Irae":** **"The Hymn of the Chvrch, in Meditation of the Day of Ivdgment."** That poem has been criticized because, as the claim runs, Crashaw brings into it both more concern for the individual soul than is apparent in the original and a tone of intimacy that the original lacks. Neither part of the criticism could be denied, but one could reply that the things objected to are, in fact, basic to the poem's success, for **"The Hymn of the Chvrch . . . "** is a subtle and ambitious paraphrase unfolding an eschatological vision in which sacred love is seen to transform the persona's perception of Christ, and hence *"Dies Irae"* and the biblical texts from which it comes.

As has been often remarked, though never closely considered, **"The Hymn of the Chvrch . . . "** juxtaposes two images of the returned Christ. The first is an icon of Christ the Judge, an image which Crashaw makes far more force-ful than that from which it derives in *"Dies Irae."* Follow-ing the original, and thus the Bible, he describes the Day of Judgment in terms of a trumpet blast, fire, a book, and the rising of the dead (sts 1-5). He gives those motifs an imaginative scope and vividness that they do not always have in their Latin source (compare, however, 3,1-2 of *"Dies Irae"* with 3,1-2 of the paraphrase). Yet it is not only their amplification that makes them affective, for Crashaw frequently represents the experience of beatitude in terms of musical harmony, of burning love, and thus here, in heightening the apocalyptic motifs of trumpet blast and corrosive fire he also strikingly (if necessarily) inverts mo-tifs that elsewhere in his works suggest heavenly bliss. Through amplifying the conventional detail of his origi-nal, Crashaw foregrounds his icon of Christ the Judge with a distinctness and, in the main, an emotional empha-sis greater than those given its counterpart in *"Dies Irae."* Moreover, his icon of Christ is in itself far more powerful-ly affective than that in the Latin hymn. In fashioning the icon Crashaw uses a visual effect not present in his original but drawn from Scripture (see Revelation 1,14 and 19,12): the "sharp Ray" (1,3), the "angry light" of Christ's "eyes" (2,3). Christ the Judge appears as terrible, because Crashaw portrays him as the Divine Intellect (the Logos) penetrating and purging all things with the unendurable light of his omniscient gaze (1,3-4 and 5,3-4). Crashaw's presentation of Christ in judgment is, then, a remarkable recreation of that in *"Dies Irae."*

The juxtaposed icon of Christ as Good Shepherd counters the image of him as judge by indicating him to be the soul's loving, attentive guardian, the Shepherd who will look to his flock even at the end of all things when he is also fulfilling another role and scrupulously weighing souls' good deeds against their bad. Crashaw's persona prays to Christ:

> Dear, remember in that Day
> Who was the cause thou cams't this way.
> Thy sheep was stray'd; And thou wouldst be
> Euen lost thy self in seeking me.
>
> (8)

He adds:

> Though both my Prayres & teares combine,
> Both worthlesse are; For they are mine.
> But thou thy bounteous self still be;
> And show thou art, by saving me.
>
> O when thy last Frown shall proclaim
> The flocks of goates to folds of flame,
> And all thy lost sheep found shall be,
> Let come ye blessed then call me.
>
> (14-15)

Of importance here, however, are not only that the second icon of Christ counters its predecessor, and that it does so by implying a Christocentric view of sacred love, but also the way in which the occurrence of that Good Shepherd icon has been managed in the poem, for Crashaw's strate-gy in making it appear tells one as much about the nature of sacred love in his verse as does its symbolic detail.

Crashaw's fashioning of two different images of Christ in

his poem is an elaboration on a strategy of the original hymn. The speaker of **"Dies Irae"** prays to Christ the Judge: *"Rex tremendae maiestatis, / Qui salvandos salvas gratis, / Salva me fons pietatis"* (8). Then, using that latter trope as the basis for addressing Christ as a more accessi-bly human figure, he pleads: *"Recordare, Iesu pie / Quod sum causa tuae viae: / Ne me perdas illa die"* (9). Yet (and the ninth stanza of **"Dies Irae"** illustrates this point as well) Crashaw additionally derives from the Latin original his idea of giving **"The Hymn of the Chvrch . . . "** a tone of intimacy and a concern for the individual soul, an anxi-ety for the self—and it is through them that he introduces the Good Shepherd icon into his poem. Crashaw struc-tures his poem as a meditation offering from the start a dramatically individual response to the overwhelming phenomenon of the Apocalypse. His persona begins, "Hears't thou, my soul, what serious things / Both the Psalm and sybyll sings" (1,1-2), a note of urgent self-communion which makes the start of Crashaw's hymn dif-ferent at once from that of **"Dies Irae."** After presenting the icon of Christ the Judge, his persona reflects:

> Ah then, poor soul, what wilt thou say?
> And to what Patron chuse to pray?
> When starres themselues shall stagger; and
> The most firm foot no more then stand.
>
> (6)

The persona's self-concern, then, implicitly pervades the hymn's initial image of Christ, and also explicitly frames it in his communings with his own soul. In the latter part of the hymn, however, whilst his self-concern remains per-vasive and whilst intimacy of tone is still an intrinsic quali-ty to his speech, both have revealingly altered.

Having asked his soul as to "what Patron" it will "chuse to pray" (6,2) when it is on the verge of meeting with judg-ment, the persona subsequently addresses the very figure who will be the apocalyptic judge and says:

> But thou giu'st leaue (dread Lord) that we
> Take shelter from thy self, in thee;
> And with the wings of thine own doue
> Fly to thy scepter of soft loue.
>
> (7)

The lines suggest that the persona, who has been anxiously anticipating his need for an ultimate defender (see, in the sixth stanza, his play on the biblical topos of "standing"), now remembers with sudden relief the fact that his "dread Lord" (l.1) is simultaneously his Redeemer (ll.1-4, espe-cially l.4). To put the point another way, the persona's anxious self-communing on the Apocalypse confronts him with the recollection of Christ as sacred love's divine ori-gin, and hence with the paradox that Christ the Judge is simultaneously his refuge from judgment: his self-concern and self-communion evoke his remembrance of Christ's redemptive love, that remembrance and the sacred love in turn evoked by it (7,3ff.) then transform his perception of Christ, enabling him to see Christ the Judge as also, at the same time, the Good Shepherd (sts 8-16), and in the whole process his self-concern and self-communion are them-selves changed, for the first becomes a mingling of fear with hope, and the second is transformed into intimate colloquy with the embodiment of that hope. But

Crashaw's hymn indicates that the metamorphic power of sacred love does not effect only those transformations, for in manifesting them the text necessarily expresses others. By presenting the argument that, on the Day of Wrath, Christ the Judge will yet be the Good Shepherd, the hymn forms a radical rewriting of its original, a canonical text of the early Church. It therefore implicitly becomes a re-writing of a greater canonical text: the biblical account of the Apocalypse (on which of course it directly draws in stanzas 1, 2, and 5). Through astute direction of his persona's anxious self-communing, Crashaw fashions his hymn as a spectacularly comprehensive affirmation of sacred love's metamorphic power, and as affirmation indeed of the idea that "Loue [is the] Absolute sole lord / Of LIFE & DEATH."

The two hymns and the paraphrase of psalm 23 suggest a Christ-centred vision of sacred love that is variously re-stated or alluded to throughout Crashaw's religious verse. Before different forms of, or references to, that vision are considered, however, something should be said of what the three poems reveal also about the spirituality of Crashaw's writing—the more so because the paraphrase is an early and minor work, whereas the hymns are later works and undeniably major ones. Moreover, the paraphrase pre-dates (apparently by quite some time) Crashaw's conversion, whilst the hymns seem almost certainly to have been written after he became a Catholic.

The paraphrase and the hymn on the Holy Name image spiritual states, of illumination and of union, that are depicted frequently in Crashaw's religious verse; some of his most famous poems celebrate the states themselves and the spirituality able to achieve them. The natures of those states, as represented here and generally by Crashaw, can perhaps best and most concisely be indicated by quotations from authors for whom he had from quite early on, or came to have, a special fondness. The paraphrase of psalm 23 images the experience of illumination. St Teresa, in her autobiography, describes an aspect of illumination as follows: "This quiet and recollectedness in the soul makes itself felt largely through the satisfaction and peace which it brings to it, together with a very great joy and repose of the faculties and a most sweet delight." Not all that she says immediately before or after those words could be applied to Crashaw's imaging of illumination in his paraphrase; nonetheless, her words seem well to express the spiritual temper of his poem, and thus to imply that Crashaw's religious verse, even when not aspiring to depict the heights of mystical experience, can yet have an affinity with her spirituality (although *here* that affinity may be accidental). By contrast to his version of psalm 23, Crashaw's hymn on the Holy Name images unitive as well as illuminative experience. The nature of the latter, as it appears there and in other of his poems, can be indicated by two quotations from St Francis de Sales. In his *Introduction to the Devout Life* the saint writes:

[T]hose who love God can never stop thinking about him, longing for him, aspiring to him, and speaking about him. If it were possible, they would engrave the holy, sacred name of Jesus on the breasts of all mankind. All things call them to this and there is no creature that does not pro-

claim the praises of their Beloved. As St. Augustine, following St. Anthony, says, all things in this world speak to them in a silent but intelligible language in behalf of their love. All things arouse them to good thoughts, and they in turn give birth to many flights and aspirations to God.

In a letter to the Baronne de Chantal he writes:

I am so hard pressed that the only thing I have time to write to you is the great word of our salvation: JESUS, O, my daughter, if we could only for once really say this sacred name from our heart! What sweet balm would spread to all the powers of our spirit! How happy we should be, my daughter, to have only Jesus in our understanding, Jesus in our memory, Jesus in our will, Jesus in our imagination! Jesus would be everywhere in us, and we should be all in him. Let us try this, my very dear daughter; let us say this holy name often as best we can. And even if at present we can only say it haltingly, in the end we shall be able to say it as we should. But how are we to say this sacred name well? For you ask me to speak plainly to you. Alas, my daughter, I do not know; all I know is if we are to say it well our tongue must be on fire, that is, we must be saying it moved only by divine love which alone is capable of expressing Jesus in our lives and of imprinting him in the depths of our heart. But courage, my daughter, surely we will love God, for he loves us. Be happy about this and do not let your soul be troubled by anything whatever.
I am, my dear daughter, I am in this same Jesus, most absolutely yours . . .

Whilst the paraphrase suggests, then, illuminative tranquility, the hymn on the Holy Name suggests a fervent illumination looking toward unitive ecstasy—those seeming to be the most recurrently imaged aspects of that level of mystical experience in Crashaw's verse.

Reference to the same Counter-Reformation saints helps to elucidate the nature of unitive experience as it is depicted in the hymn and elsewhere by Crashaw. In the letter from St Francis de Sales which was just cited, the saint describes unitive experience in these passionate terms: "O, my daughter, if we could only for once really say this sacred name from our heart! What sweet balm would spread to all the powers of our spirit! How happy we should be, my daughter, to have only Jesus in our understanding, Jesus in our memory, Jesus in our will, Jesus in our imagination! Jesus would be everywhere in us, and we should be all in him." St Francis' ardent, exclamatory and, at one point, richly sensuous description of utter unity with Christ concisely (if not of course completely) characterizes the desire for unitive experience that pervades the climax of the hymn (ll.159-196; cf. ll.120-126). But another form or phase of unitive experience is pictured in the conclusion to the hymn (ll.197-239), and its nature is indicated by St Teresa's account of "Divine union": "The soul that has experienced . . . union . . . is left so full of courage that it would be greatly comforted if at that moment, for God's sake, it could be hacked to pieces. It is then that it makes heroic resolutions and promises, that its desires become full of vigour . . ." [The Life of Teresa of Avila]. Using terms similar to Crashaw's yet more comprehensive than his (for his are historically specific), St Teresa makes explicit what he chooses rather to imply: that union is a source of transcendently heroic virtue. As the hymn represents unitive experience, so Crashaw's other poems depict it.

Whilst those poems reveal much about the spiritual states predominantly imaged by Crashaw, they—and the **"Hymn of the Chvrch"**—also imply that the spiritualities of his personae who undergo mystical experience, or who, at the least, are shown as devout and questing for beatitude, are not necessarily unproblematic. Furthermore, they imply that forming a clear view of the degrees to which Crashaw's poems deliberately suggest flaws or difficulties in the spiritualities of his personae can itself be far from easy. In the paraphrase of psalm 23 (to start with that early work) his persona says to God the Father, at the poem's climax:

> At the whisper of thy Word
> Crown'd abundance spreads my Bord:
> While I feast, my foes doe feed
> Their rank malice not their need,
> So that with the self-same bread
> They are starv'd, and I am fed.
> How my head in ointment swims!
> How my cup orelooks her Brims!
>
> (ll.49-56)

Echoes of the biblical original are distinct here (notably in ll.50-51 and ll.55-56) and, as regards Communion, the passage seems theologically orthodox. The problem is, though, that the persona's words can be read with equal plausibility as expressing assured faith, illuminative calm that verges on ecstasy, or as manifesting a sense of triumph, of dismissive complacency. The original rightly celebrates, in the contexts of Davidic story and of Old Testament values generally, triumph over enemies; and such a note can be heard repeatedly, on the basis of such precedents and values, in Reformation and Counter-Reformation controversial literature. For all that, the climatic lines of Crashaw's paraphrase concern taking Communion: being in charity with one's (erstwhile) enemies was, when Crashaw wrote—as it is now—a doctrinal prerequisite for participation in Communion, and Crashaw's persona can quite reasonably be perceived as uncharitable in his description of his enemies' lack of charity, of the "rank malice" (l.52) which vitiates their participation in Communion and leaves them "starv'd" while he is "fed" (l.54). There seems to be nothing in the paraphrase that prepares the reader for the ambiguous spirituality at its climax, nor does anything in or after the climactic lines themselves seem to signal that the persona is being deliberately revealed as a problematic figure. As a result, if the paraphrase does not raise doubts about the nature of illumination, it certainly raises doubts about Crashaw's imaging of that state.

The hymn on the Holy Name also has a persona whose mystical experience is, to an extent, curiously problematic; as is the case with the paraphrase, one cannot *know* whether or not Crashaw deliberately portrayed his persona's mystical experience so that it would reveal Christian paradoxes of unusual kinds. The title of Crashaw's poem openly announces it to be a hymn in honour of *the Name of* IESVS. The poem's author proclaims, then, that *Name above Every Name* which the poem's persona does not utter. At the outset, the persona declares, "I sing the NAME which None can say / But touch't with An interiour Ray . . ." (ll.1-2), and thereafter he alludes to the Holy Name yet never speaks it. Having made that initial declaration he goes on (as has been discussed in detail above) to seek virtually universal aid, that he might overcome his unworthiness to celebrate the Name and subsequently both to celebrate the Name and to request its presence on earth—that request being answered. In other words, the persona who at first sees himself as unworthy even to say the Name later comes to recognize that he may not only celebrate it—and, in fact, "speake lowd / To All the dear-bought Nations This Redeeming Name" (ll.93-94)—but invoke its descent from heaven, though of course he still does not say the Name. The first paradox, that of the author's proclaiming the Name which his devout and spiritually enabled (see ll.44-153) persona does not utter, could perhaps be explained as the expression of a distinction between writing and speech: the author feels able to pen what his persona, apparently from humility, cannot allow himself actually to say, speaking the Name being given by Crashaw implicit pre-eminence over writing it. If that explanation were correct, such a distinction would itself nonetheless involve theological difficulties, and if one were to propose that the incongruity rather expresses a contrast between unconscious authorial self-assertion and the persona's humility, then the paradox would merely take on another aspect. In either case, moreover, the persona's humble reticence would remain problematic when related to his clear recognition of his spiritual enablement. That second paradox is the more important of the two. Crashaw's persona is obviously not unable to speak the Holy Name (compare ll.1-2 with ll.93-94, and l.118 with 1 Corinthians 12,3); his revelation of spiritual enablement (ll.93-94 are especially relevant here) makes his devout refusal to speak the Name seem a graceful, if not quite intelligible, act of adoration. The persona's reticence should possibly be seen as suggesting that to become a servant of the Name is to devote oneself to that which is holy beyond human expression—which would make his reticence appear no less problematic. It may be that one should see the persona's refusal to say the Name as an act of adoration at once decorous and beyond questions of logical consistency. Whatever conclusions are drawn about its function in the hymn, the persona's humble avoidance of speaking the Holy Name implies that the representation of his spirituality by Crashaw is not simply harmonious.

Unlike the other two poems, **"The Hymn of the Chvrch"** has a persona whose paradoxicality of spirit is, beyond doubt, deliberately fashioned by Crashaw and designed to be representative rather than merely specific (for Crashaw elaborates upon the image of a communal spirituality in the liturgical source of his poem). His persona knows both fear and hope: fear cannot overcome his hope, yet neither can his hope cease to be troubled. Crashaw creates his persona, that is to say, as an affective image of spiritual self-division, but of a self-division in which another element—faith—finally predominates (that being the case also in

"Dies Irae") and makes the persona's paradoxical spirituality fruitful:

> O hear a supliant heart; all crush't
> And crumbled into contrite dust.
> My hope, my fear! my Iudge, my Freind!
> Take charge of me, & of my END.
>
> (st. 17)

Unable, of course, to resolve the contradictoriness that he experiences (as the *chiasmus* of 17,3 suggests), the persona brings at the last his hope and fear openly before Christ, acknowledging that they are in fact hope in and fear of Christ—and as he does so he resigns himself utterly to Christ's will, in faith which rises above (without escaping from) his spiritual conflict.

In Crashaw's poems on Christ, as the two hymns and the paraphrase imply, can be seen a comprehensive vision of sacred love and varieties of illuminative, as well as of unitive, experience. It has been suggested above that what those poems reveal of sacred love and of mystical experience is elemental to Crashaw's other religious verse. To confirm that, one need turn only to his poems on (usually triumphant) female spirituality: there one sees his ideas on sacred love and on the mystical ways informing, or indicated by, works which are among his best and best known.

Most of the attention given to Crashaw's poems on female spirituality has been focused on those about St Teresa or St Mary Magdalen. His poems about the Virgin have not been ignored, but they seem to have been regarded as inferior to, or at the least, as less challenging than the Teresa poems and "The Weeper." Individually the poems on the Virgin are probably not the equals of "A Hymn to . . . Sainte Teresa" or "The Weeper"; however, "In the Gloriovs Assvmption of Ovr Blessed Lady. The Hymn " is certainly one of Crashaw's major works and, moreover, the poems on Christ's mother are important within the Crashaw canon because of their diversity: they interpret with ingenious variety the Virgin's relation to the Godhead, and so her receiving and manifesting of sacred love.

A useful place to begin suggesting how astutely Crashaw can image the Virgin is "Luke 2. Quaerit Jesum suum Maria." The source of the poem is of course St Luke's brief account of the Christ child's separation from his parents after the Holy Family had celebrated the Passover in Jerusalem. The gospel story from which Crashaw develops his poem has to do with the Christ child's revelation of himself as Logos and Son of God, with his parents' anxiety at his separation from them, and with their incomprehension of his self-revelation (Luke 2,41-51). Here Crashaw omits reference to St Joseph and concentrates on the relationship between mother and child, the result being a study of the Virgin as mother of God which simultaneously and indirectly is a study of Christ.

Throughout the poem, Mary laments the immensity of her loss; in doing so she describes herself and, necessarily, Christ. To consider first Crashaw's representation of what the Christ child means (in general terms) to the Virgin—and, by implication, to mankind—makes it easier for one to appreciate Crashaw's representation of the grieving Virgin herself. All that Mary says of her son accords with what other personae suggest of him in the poems which Crashaw directly focuses on Christ; for example, she calls the Christ child her "soules sweet rest" (l.6), and the focus of her "joy" (l.3, ll.8-11, and *passim*). A more important instance than those, however, occurs when she says:

> Oft haue I wrapt thy slumbers in soft aires,
>   And stroak't thy cares.
> Oft hath this hand this morning silken casements kept,
>   While their sunnes slept.
> Oft haue my hungry kisses made thine eyes
>   Too early rise.
>
> Dawne then to me, thou morne of mine owne day,
>   And lett heauen stay.
>
> (ll.31-36, ll.45-46).

There the Virgin climactically reveals why the Christ child's loss causes her so much grief (cf. ll.9-18). He is, she effectually suggests, at once her son and the sun of her life (her words remind the reader of Christ's being the Sun of Righteousness): her description of the Christ child indicates him to be the centre of her life and the power that sustains as well as illuminates it (see ll.17-18, and l.48—where she calls him her "bosome God"). Her description of her son/sun affirms the idea, evident in the poems on Christ which were discussed above, that he is total life (cf. ll.41-42).

To have looked initially at the poem's images of Christ reveals how comprehensive the Virgin's sense of loss is, and thereupon one can more readily perceive what that sense of loss reveals of the Virgin herself. Those lines in which the Virgin implies that Christ is the focal point of her universe suggest that, in losing her son/sun, she has not only lost her "joy" (l.3, l.8, and *passim*) but has herself become displaced: the sustaining principle of order in her life has gone; she has lost her telos (cf. "My soules sweet rest," "My bosome God"). Hence in expressing her loss the poem pervasively expresses her confusion. More important, though, those lines cited above also suggest the Virgin's incomprehension of the Christ child, and that too pervades the poem's telling of her loss. In the Lucan narrative, Mary and Joseph fail to understand the boy Jesus' explanation of his disappearance ("How is it that you sought me? Did you not know that I must be in my Father's house?"). In "Luke 2. Quaerit Jesum . . . " Crashaw indicates instead Mary's incomprehension of who and what her son actually is. She knows him to be her delight, the vital centre of her being, and her God—knowledge gained experientially or from divine revelation; however, she seems to have no real idea of why her son cannot be entirely hers, of his role on earth (which his separation from her, to teach in the Temple, foretells):

> Oh, would'st thou heere still fixe thy faire abode,
>   My bosome God:
> What hinders, but my bosome still might be
>   Thy heauen to thee?
>
> (ll.47-50)

Thus whilst the loss of her son evokes intense grief, it also evokes loss of self, confusion—and reveals the necessary failure of her reason to understand Christ.

That failure is amplified by the poem's approximation to

the form of a deliberative oration. The opening couplets act as an introduction or *exordium* (ll.1-4), and then the poem continues as if with *narratio* (ll.5-14), *aversio/obsecratio* (ll.15-18), *confutatio* (ll.19-24), *confirmatio* (ll.25-44), *obsecratio/conclusio* (ll.45-50). Whether or not that deliberative pattern was consciously imposed by Crashaw, the point is that his poem unfolds as a carefully organized argument and, in doing so, does not lead to resolution of the Virgin's incomprehension (see ll.46-50), but rather, by the very fact of its lucid, reasonable, powerless unfolding, emphasizes the Virgin's inability to understand her son through reason (Mary will find him when he is manifesting himself in the Temple as Logos). Highlighting individual rationality's limitations in dealing with Christ, the poem suggests indirectly the failure of all human reason to understand him. Yet the poem's stress on Mary's incomprehension has a function more direct than that: it emphasizes her capacity to love. It seems that in amplifying Mary's incomprehension, Crashaw's poem also amplifies the importance of her total, loving devotion to Christ. Reason being depreciated, love is given distinct primacy in her relationship with her son, and thus Crashaw represents her as typifying the soul truly focused on Christ—the soul utterly and lovingly centred on him as its God, whose ability to apprehend him rationally matters far less than its capacity for devotion to him—and as the type of maternal love.

If **"Luke 2. Quaerit Jesum suum Maria"** celebrates the Virgin by imaging her as a figure in whom sacred love far transcends human reason, **"Sancta Maria Dolorvm"** honours her in a complementary way. Whereas the former poem cunningly plays reason against sacred love, the latter implies that the Virgin's love for her son transcends notions of ideal secular love. In the third stanza of **"Sancta Maria Dolorvm,"** Crashaw's persona says wittily:

> O costly intercourse
> Of deaths, & worse,
> Diuided loues.   While son & mother
> Discourse alternate wounds to one another;
> Quick deaths that grow
> And gather, as they come & goe:
> His Nailes write swords in her, which soon her
>   heart
> Payes back, with more then their own smart;
> Her SWORDS, still growing with his pain,
> Turn SPEARES, & straight come home again.

There, as in the poem looked at a moment ago, the Virgin is pictured grieving for her son—but the differences between the images of her are immense. In **"Luke 2. Quaerit Jesum . . ."** she appears as the imperfectly comprehending mother of the Christ child, grief-stricken by (temporary) loss of him; in this poem, she is shown grieving as her son dies on the cross, and paradoxically to be at one with him throughout the time she is losing him. The second of those images is certainly the more sophisticated and that can be seen immediately in the lines quoted above. There Crashaw's persona suggests the unity of mother and son by allusion to prophecies about them—Simeon's of the Virgin (Luke 2,35) and Christ's of himself (as in Luke 9,22)—which the Crucifixion both fulfils and reveals to have been interwoven, but he uses Simeon's

symbol of the sword (l.9) and the accoutrements of the Crucifixion (l.7, l.10) to imply that, during the Crucifixion, the Virgin and Christ are connected not merely by the simultaneous fulfilment of prophecies. In declaring, "[S]on & mother / Discourse alternate wounds to one another" (ll.3-4), then using the scriptural "Nailes" (l.7), "SWORDS" (l.9), and "SPEARES" (l.10) to describe that process, Crashaw's persona implies that the Virgin and Christ, though being separated by death, so love each other that they interchange pain and grief—and become virtually one in suffering. The concept that ideal secular love is the sharing of existences, but the achievement of emotional and intellectual oneness rather than of physical oneness, was often and variously formulated in the Renaissance. Crashaw's persona indicates in this poem, however, that the Virgin's love for Christ transcends that secular ideal. True, she and her son appear to be emotionally and almost physically at one during the Crucifixion, but it is that context of their oneness which of course makes all the difference. The Virgin is pictured as being, in effect, "crucified with Christ": Crashaw's meditative persona images her as enacting Galatians 2,20 (if not precisely in the Pauline sense) and so as going beyond the secular ideal of achieving unity in love, self-sacrificially achieving unity in sacred love with God himself. She sees "her life [that is, Christ] dy," and retains "only so much Breath / As serues to keep aliue her death" (4,8-10); she loses herself in him and becomes an archetype of Christocentric existence that Crashaw's persona wishes he could imitate (sts 5-11).

Far different from the icons of the grieving Virgin is the triumphant image of her in the haunting **"In the Gloriovs Assvmption of Ovr Blessed Lady. The Hymn."** That poem does not picture her as focused on Christ but as the spouse, the "syluer mate" (l.8), focused upon by the Holy Spirit, who now summons her to heaven. She is imaged as the "doue" (l.14) of the Holy Dove, called by him to her virtual apotheosis (cf. "O Mother turtle-doue!" in **"Sancta Maria Dolorvm,"** 5,1). In so depicting her, Crashaw's speaker presents her in accord with conventional exegesis of episodes in The Song of Solomon. The speaker imagines that he hears:

> Rise vp, my fair, my spottlesse one!
> The winter's past, the rain is gone.
>   The spring is come, the flowrs appear
> No sweets, but thou, are wanting here.
>   Come away, my loue!
>   Come away, my doue! cast off delay,
> The court of heau'n is come
> To wait vpon thee home; Come come away!
>   (ll.9-16)

As those lines clearly imply, Crashaw interprets the Assumption as a celebration of Mary's unique role in the redemptive pattern of history (cf. l.41). Yet his poem may have something further to suggest. Near its end Crashaw's speaker says to the Virgin, "LIVE, rosy princesse, LIVE" (l.60). The words remind one of **"The Authors Motto"** in *Steps to the Temple*, "Live Jesus, Live, and let it bee / My life to dye, for love of thee," and that likeness seems to indicate a similarity—if by no means an equality—of importance to Crashaw between the Virgin and Christ.

To have examined Crashaw's poems on Christ and on the

Virgin is to have studied a fair range of his religious verse, and so it would seem reasonable now to consider what those poems tell of his style. Most discussion of Crashaw's style in his religious verse has been concerned primarily with his links to the devotional literary traditions of the Counter-Reformation. That issue certainly has to be looked at here; however, a couple of remarks need to be made beforehand.

First, Crashaw's literary relations with the Counter-Reformation are diverse and cannot be restrictively described. Finally, since the Counter-Reformation does not provide the only stylistic models for his religious verse, the use that he makes of others—such as the medieval religious lyric and Herbert's poems—has to be considered too.

Perhaps the best way to begin is by considering Crashaw's youthful paraphrase of psalm 23 and then his later **"Charitas Nimia."** **"Psalme 23"** clearly indicates major continuities of style in Crashaw's sacred verse. There he interplays a Christian plainness—and the influence of his father—with some catachrestic, sensuous conceits (see, for example, ll.13-15) and moments of ecstatic exclamation (l.1, ll.55-56). Thus the poem suggests that (presumably) long before he became a Catholic, Crashaw had a marked interest in elements of style which were, as he could hardly not have known, prominent in Counter-Reformation writings. The elaborate, vividly sensuous conceits and tendency to fervent exclamation which pervade his subsequent work can be seen initially in the paraphrase, whose plain style he would thereafter all but forsake and central tenets of whose eucharistic theology he would come to abandon. To glance at **"Psalm 23,"** in other words, is to see at once that Crashaw's English religious verse had from the start affinities with Counter-Reformation artistry, and hence that its strengthening as well as broadening of those affinities expressed not only his movement toward Catholicism but the development in him of long-established aesthetic interests.

Turning from the paraphrase to **"Charitas Nimia"** affirms and complements what has just been argued. From the poem's very opening one hears the echo of a familiar voice:

> Lord, what is man?   why should he coste thee
> So dear?   what had his ruin lost thee?
> Lord what is man?   that thou hast ouerbought
> So much a thing of nought?
>
> Loue is too kind, I see; & can
> Make but a simple merchant man.
> 'Twas for such sorry merchandise
> Bold Painters haue putt out his Eyes.
>
> (ll.1-8)

The rhythms, imagery, and tone of the poem (especially in ll.5-6) unmistakably bear the impress of Herbert; Crashaw carefully recreates his predecessor's mingling of Christian plainness with strong lines (in which dramatically plain speech is often, in any case, an element). Crashaw greatly admired Herbert's verse, the style of this poem and the title *Steps to the Temple* respectively expressing the specificity and the scope of his admiration. Nonetheless, if Herbert's verse offered Crashaw models of style that he clearly found attractive throughout his liter-

ary career—as the publication date of **"Charitas Nimia"** suggests—those models seem to have strongly influenced almost none of his important poems; they were, moreover, increasingly supplanted in his favour by Counter-Reformation models of style, with which, in his early days as a poet, they had arguably held at least equal value. To consider **"Charitas Nimia"** after **"Psalme 23"** is to be reminded that the limited influence of Herbert's poems on Crashaw's highlights simultaneously the closer relations between Crashaw's poems and Counter-Reformation writings, and the distance that Crashaw moved from contemporary Anglican poetic modes.

The flamboyance, the occasional strangeness, of those poems which express Crashaw's interest in Counter-Reformation artistry have frequently been noted, much attention having been given necessarily to his fashioning of conceits. The devout aspect of the baroque in Crashaw's verse, then, has indeed been studied, often innovatively and learnedly; even so, the variety and subtlety of his religious poems' baroque strategies—used to represent, for the most part, the diversity and the nuances of spiritual illumination or union, and of sacred love's transforming power—invite further discussion. Yet once more, **"Psalme 23"** seems the place to begin. In describing and celebrating the experience of illumination, Crashaw's speaker says:

> At my feet the blubb'ring Mountaine
> Weeping, melts into a Fountaine,
> Whose soft silver-sweating streames
> Make high Noone forget his beames. . . .
>
> (ll.13-16)

There, as sometimes elsewhere in the poem, the speaker images illumination in terms not merely pastoral, but luxuriantly pastoral. He does not, however, suggest only in doing so that sacred love (cf. ll.3-4) has radically transformed the conditions of his soul's existence. He traces an elaborately sensuous process of transformation (the mountain's metamorphosis into a fountain) to suggest sacred love's radical transformation of his illumined soul's perceptions. In accord with the poetic theory and practice of the Counter-Reformation, Crashaw fashions vividly physical and extreme conceits (*conformatio* and *audacia*) to make transcendent spiritual experience sensuously apprehensible—and to convey the wonder of it. It may be that the stylistic affinities of **"Psalme 23"** with Counter-Reformation poetry and poetics reflect the sensibility of the young Crashaw rather than his imitation of Counter-Reformation texts, but the affinities are there, and they foreshadow the sophistication with which, as well as basic functions for which, baroque strategies (that were certainly used quite deliberately) appear in his later poems.

Crashaw's more sophisticated and more ambitious use of those strategies can be seen in his hymn on the name of Jesus, in which can also be seen the resplendence of his baroque style at its most impressive. The poem does not, of course, reveal the full range of his achievement in the baroque; it does, however, show the greater sophistication, higher ambition, and resplendence with which he could use that style in connection with a central concern of his religious verse—spiritual union. When perceiving the descent of the Holy Name to the world, Crashaw's persona cries:

> Lo, where Aloft it comes!   It comes, Among
> The Conduct of Adoring SPIRITS, that throng
> Like diligent Bees, And swarm about it.
>   O they are wise;
> And know what SWEETES are suck't from out it.
>   It is the Hiue,
>   By which they thriue,
> Where All their Hoard of Hony lyes.
>
> (ll. 151-158)

The lines celebrate the Name by identifying union with it as heaven's bliss. Their main strategy is the conceit, and their conceits function much as do those in lines 13-16 of **"Psalme 23"**: they seek to make transcendent spiritual experience intelligible in sensuously affective terms (see especially l.155), and to communicate the marvellousness of it. In other words, although the conceits here are used to a more ambitious end than the ones considered above from **"Psalme 23,"** they seem nonetheless to function similarly and thus to have no greater sophistication than the conceits of the earlier work. The only significant difference between them appears to be that whereas the mountain/fountain conceits of the paraphrase image sacred love's transforming of individual perception, the bees/hive conceits from the hymn act primarily as an Augustinian accommodation of the divine to the human (that is, of divine truth to the human mind). Yet if lines 151-158 of the hymn suggest continuities between the baroque strategies of that poem and those of the earlier paraphrase, a subsequent passage tends rather to emphasize discontinuities.

Describing what the earthbound soul will experience in union with the Name, Crashaw's speaker rhapsodizes:

> SWEET NAME, in Thy each Syllable
> A Thousand Blest ARABIAS dwell;
> A Thousand Hills of Frankincense;
> Mountains of myrrh, & Beds of spices,
> And ten Thousand PARADISES
> The soul that tasts thee takes from thence.
> How many vnknown WORLDS there are
> Of Comforts, which Thou hast in keeping!
>
> (ll. 183-190)

Like the preceding passage, this one is dominated by sensuously affective conceits that seek to communicate the wonder of spiritual union. The main stylistic difference between the two would seem to be that here Crashaw fashions his conceits both to mediate the divine to the human—to impress something of the transcendent upon the human—and to intimate the tremendous strain placed on language in that role. In attempting to suggest experience of the infinite, of the Name of the Word, in human words, Crashaw's speaker gestures rather than depicts. His conceits imply the visual, yet defy visualization. Moreover, they indicate union with the Name to be the satiety of pleasure and complete felicity, yet call attention by their labouring extravagance to the fact that they can do no better than to indicate such ecstasy. Their extraordinary multiplication of the historically unique ("A Thousand Blest ARABIAS"; "ten Thousand PARADISES"), their use of the plurality of worlds motif (ll. 189-190), and their multiplication of images from The Song of Solomon ("A Thou-

sand Hills of Frankincense;/ Mountains of myrrh, & Beds of spices") reveal Crashaw's speaker as striving necessarily to overgo the limits of language—the language of ordinary signification and also that of Scripture. (As is apparent, Crashaw's speaker expresses himself in hyperboles; Puttenham calls hyperbole the "Ouer reacher.") Those extravagant and luxuriant conceits reveal, that is to say, the inexpressibility topos as implicit in the speaker's attempt at representing unitive ecstasy. Implicitly connecting affective conceits with that topos is a strategy recurrent in Crashaw's developed baroque style, which means (among other things) that his Counter-Reformation artistry sometimes both represents the divine and indirectly acknowledges its own, as well as all human words', unavoidable failure to do so adequately.

The baroque strategies in that moment of the hymn on the Holy Name certainly aspire higher, are more resplendent, and are more subtle than those in **"Psalme 23"** or in lines 151-158 of the hymn itself. One could continue to examine the linking of the inexpressibility topos to the conceit in Crashaw's religious verse, for example in the hymn to St Teresa (ll. 105—121), the ode on a prayer book (ll. 76-86), the hymn in the Assumption (ll. 64-69), and **"The Weeper"** (sts 6-14. Cf. **"Lavda Sion Salvatorem,"** st. 1, and **"The Hymn of Sainte Thomas . . . ,"** *passim*). More significant at this point, however, might be to consider how the strategies studies so far, and yet others, are used by Crashaw in relation to larger units of design—of which he draws on a range familiar in seventeenth-century religious verse.

The poems on Christ and on the Virgin that have been discussed above illustrate a variety of forms: most are hymns; some are both hymns and meditations; one is a biblical paraphrase; another is a complaint. Many reflect Crashaw's interest in the epigram. None, for all the applicability of those terms, can be contained in a simple generic description (nor, of course, do the poems instance quite all the forms employed in Crashaw's religious verse). Something of how Crashaw uses the conceit and the inexpressibility topos in relation to the meditation and the hymn has already been considered with regard to the hymn on the Holy Name. Relations between the conceit, the meditation, and revision of a canonical hymn have been looked at in discussion of **"The Hymn of the Chvrch . . . "**; Crashaw's paraphrase of **"Psalme 23"** has been studied in much the same way. His astute interplay of the conceit, the inexpressibility topos, the hymn, and the meditation will be focused on later and anew in the contexts of the hymn to St Teresa and **"The Weeper."** Here, though, one can further illustrate the rich diversity of Crashaw's baroque strategies and, in doing so, consider particularly how he seeks to use musicality in relation to a larger form, by returning to **"Luke 2. Quaerit Jesum. . . . "**

One of that poem's most attractive strategies is the conceit. Sometimes delicately sensuous, sometimes passionately so, its conceits are always elegant. For example, consider:

> Oft hath this hand those silken casements kept,
>   While their sunnes slept.
>
> (ll. 33-34)

> Oft from this breast to thine my loue¢tost heart
> Hath leapt, to part.
>
> (ll.39-40)

> Dawne then to me, thou morne of mine owne
> day. . . .
>
> (l.45)

Perhaps the most interesting feature of those lines, however, is that they illustrate the subtlety with which Crashaw can connect the conceit and the emblem, connection of the two being a more recurrent strategy in his religious verse than the linking of the conceit to the inexpressibility topos. At some points in his religious verse Crashaw displays emblems directly, manifesting them in single or throughout several conceits (see, for an instance of the latter, **"Sancta Maria Dolorvm,"** XI,1-4—as that passage also shows, he may add individual touches to such conventional images); at others, he rather alludes to emblems through one or more conceits. Here, through the conceit of the "sunnes" (l.34) and that of the "morne" (l.45), he does not directly present but cunningly alludes to the emblem of Christ as the Sun of Righteousness (cf. ll.35-36). His cunning lies partly in the fact that the figure of the grieving Virgin who utters those conceits, emphasizing her son's vital centrality to her existence, does not of course know that she is thereby obliquely identifying her son in profound, scriptural terms. Yet Crashaw's connection of the conceit and the emblem is more sophisticated than that. The conceit of the "sunnes" comes from the Petrarchan tradition; the "morne" conceit, too, has Petrarchan associations. Through images related to secular love verse, Crashaw at once communicates the sacred love of the Virgin for the Christ child and evokes a great emblem representing the majesty of Christ.

Although Crashaw's linking of the affective conceit and the emblem is one of the more important baroque strategies in his religious verse, and although he uses it at the climax of **"Luke 2. Quaerit Jesum . . . ,"** it apparently occurs only once, and is an indirect presence, in the poem. A strategy (other than that of the conceit itself) which both openly pervades the lyric and which Crashaw develops astutely from the start as an element of the lyric's design is the creation of musical effects. The suggestion was made earlier that **"Luke 2. Quaerit Jesum . . ."** approximates to the form of a deliberative oration, and that it does so not to reveal the Virgin's lament for her son as coherently reasoned but to emphasize instead the failure of her reason to understand the Christ child. Against the unfolding failure of reason in the poem, Crashaw plays an elaborately patterned musicality, using the affective power of music to amplify the Virgin's expression of grief and to arouse the reader's sympathy with—to make the reader share in—her extreme emotion: to contribute, that is to say, to the poem's implicit privileging of sacred love over human rationality. The following lines well illustrate the poem's intricate harmony of repetitions and contrasts, its finely controlled modulation of cadence and of tone:

> And is he gone, whom these armes held but
> now?
> Their hope, their vow?

> Did ever greife, & joy in one poore heart
> Soe soone change part?
> Hee's gone. the fair'st flower, that e're bosome
> drest,
> My soules sweet rest.
> My wombes chast pride is gone, my heau'en-
> borne boy;
> And where is joy?
> Hee's gone. & his lou'd steppes to wait upon,
> My joy is gone.
> My joyes, & hee are gone; my greife, & I
> Alone must ly.
> Hee's gone. not leaving with me, till he come,
> One smile at home.
> Oh come then. bring thy mother her lost joy:
> Oh come, sweet boy.
> Make hast, & come, or e're my greife, & I
> Make hast, & dy.
>
> (ll.1-18)

Through the elaborate musicality of his verse, Crashaw in effect makes the Virgin's lament an aria at the same time as, by other means, he virtually (and perhaps consciously) makes it a deliberative oration. There indeed one sees what Pontanus could have called *"compositissima oratio."*

To consider even briefly the style of Crashaw's religious verse is to recognize the subtlety, resplendence, frequent ambitiousness, and diversity of his Counter-Reformation artistry, and thus how well his artistry realizes many of the ideals of style proposed by Pontanus and by Gracián. If his style at times reflects his admiration for Herbert, or suggests his interest in medieval religious poetry, Herbert's influence on his important poems seems rare, and it is apparent that he tended not only to imitate but to recreate those aspects or instances of medieval religious verse that drew his pen to paper (as **"Luke 2. Quaerit Jesum . . . ,"** **"The Hymn of the Chvrch . . . ,"** **"The Hymn of Sainte Thomas . . . ,"** and **"Sancta Maria Dolorvm"** notably attest). What one recognizes, in other words, when considering Crashaw's style in his religious verse is a mastery of the baroque in its devout guise unequalled in England by any other poet during the first half of the seventeenth century. (pp. 127-59)

> *A. D. Cousins, "Richard Crashaw," in his* The Catholic Religious Poets from Southwell to Crashaw: A Critical History, *Sheed & Ward, 1991, pp. 126-76.*

FURTHER READING

Bertonasco, Marc F. *Crashaw and the Baroque*. University: University of Alabama Press, 1971, 158 p.

Explores Crashaw's use of emblems and the influence of St. Francis de Sales's life and writings on the development of his religious poetry. Bertonasco also reexamines "The Weeper."

Cirillo, A. R. "Crashaw's 'Epiphany Hymn': The Dawn of

Christian Time." *Studies in Philology* LXVII, No. 1 (January 1970): 67-88.

    Contends that the "Epiphany Hymn" possesses a liturgical quality in its celebration of the Incarnation, and "contains a richness of detail and evocation, [and] a pattern of careful orderly development."

Davis, Walter R. "The Meditative Hymnody of Richard Crashaw." *ELH* 50, No. 1 (Spring 1983): 107-29.

    Compares various editions of the St. Teresa hymns, "To the Name Above Every Name," and many of Crashaw's sacred poems, contending that they are meditative by design and were written for actual devotional use.

Hammill, Graham. "Stepping to the Temple." *South Atlantic Quarterly* 88, No. 4 (Fall 1989): 933-59.

    Explores the psychological perspective of "jouissance" (joy and delight), especially as it pertains to the divine/human relationships found in Crashaw's poems.

Martz, Louis Lohr. "Richard Crashaw: Love's Architecture." In his *From Renaissance to Baroque: Essays on Literature and Art*, pp. 194-217. Columbia: University of Missouri Press, 1991.

    Examines "The Flaming Heart" and "A Hymn to the Nativity" as examples of popular baroque conceits.

McCanles, Michael. "The Rhetoric of the Sublime in Crashaw's Poetry." In *The Rhetoric of Renaissance Poetry*, edited by Thomas O. Sloan and Raymond B. Waddington, pp. 189-211. Berkeley and Los Angeles: University of California Press, 1974.

    Examines Crashaw's poetic hyperbole against Kantian notions of reason and imagination.

Neill, Kerby. "Structure and Symbolism in Crashaw's 'Hymn in the Nativity'." *PMLA* LXIII, No. 1 (March 1948): 101-13.

    Comprehensive assessment of Crashaw's theological images and themes in "Hymn to the Nativity."

O'Brien, Edward J. "The Inspiration of Crashaw." *Poet Lore* XXI, No. V (September/October 1910): 397-400.

    Comments on Crashaw's religious emotionalism and lyrical style, noting that the poet "grasps the eternal realities, and the melody of their expression."

Parrish, Paul A. "Crashaw's Two Weepers." *Concerning Poetry* 10, No. 3 (Fall 1977): 47-9.

    Compares two versions of Crashaw's "The Weeper."

Peter, John. "Crashaw and 'The Weeper'." *Scrutiny* XIX, No. 4 (1953): 258-72.

    Contends that Crashaw handles his imagery in "The Weeper" as a device for establishing tone as it leads "the reader into unfamiliar and unusual areas of feeling."

Quiller-Couch, Sir Arthur. "Traherne, Crashaw, and Others." In his *Studies in Literature, first series*, pp. 137-57. Cambridge: Cambridge University Press, 1937.

    Investigates many of Crashaw's exaggerated and emotionally charged images, focusing on those which exemplify his poetic genius.

Schleiner, Louise. "Song Mode in Crashaw." In her *The Living Lyre in English Verse*, pp. 85-101. Columbia: University of Missouri Press, 1984.

    Contends that the "vivid pictorial images" of Crashaw's hymn poems were substantially influenced by the songs and music of his time.

Schwenger, Peter. "Crashaw's Perspectivist Metaphor." *Comparative Literature* XXVIII, No. 1 (Winter 1976): 65-74.

    Contends that Crashaw's elaborate images in "The Weeper" raise "Magdalene's tears from a literal level to a level of apotheosis."

Strier, Richard. "Crashaw's Other Voice." *Studies in English Literature* IX, No. 1 (Winter 1969): 135-51.

    Asserts that several of Crashaw's religious poems exhibit "tension and doubt" despite their deeply devotional character.

Willy, Margaret. "Richard Crashaw." In *British Writers and Their Work*, Vol. 4, by Frank Kermode, T. S. Eliot, and Margaret Willy, pp. 89-103. Lincoln: University of Nebraska Press, 1964.

    Assesses Crashaw's use of conceits, emblems, and impressa, as well as the development of religious themes and the musical quality of his poetry.

Samuel Daniel

1562/63-1619

English poet, dramatist, historian, and translator.

INTRODUCTION

During his own lifetime Daniel was a respected literary figure whose sonnets and dramatic entertainments attracted the notice of important patrons. The demands of his royal and aristocratic sponsors required Daniel to produce original works in a variety of literary modes, and his repertory included love sonnets, verse epics, poetic epistles, court masques, dramatic tragedies and tragicomedies, histories in verse and prose, and occasional verse to commemorate special events. Daniel's poetry, for which he is best remembered today, is most often described as dignified and affecting, perfectly constructed, and marked by what Joan Rees has called "an exquisite poetic decorum."

Little written record exists for the early life of Daniel. He was born in the county of Somerset in 1562 or 1563 and educated at Magdalen Hall (now Hertford College), Oxford, without obtaining a degree. Probably in 1592 Daniel came under the patronage of the second Earl of Pembroke and his famous wife Mary (née Sidney), Countess of Pembroke. The countess, herself an accomplished author, was the sister of the writer and politician Sir Philip Sidney, and was patroness of an important literary circle that included Michael Drayton and Edmund Spenser. Rees and other scholars believe it was the environment of this circle and the encouragement of its members that persuaded Daniel to pursue a literary life. After Daniel left the Pembroke household in 1594, a succession of notable patrons supported his writing, among them Lady Margaret, Countess of Cumberland, who in 1599 engaged Daniel to tutor her young daughter, the Lady Anne Clifford. With the benefit of enlightened patrons, this was a fruitful period in Daniel's life, during which he completed his long philosophical poem *Musophilus; or, Defense of All Learning* and his critical prose treatise *A Defense of Rime.*

After the accession of a new monarch, James I, in 1603, Daniel was commissioned to write a masque—*The Vision of the 12 Goddesses*—for Queen Anne and her court. Shortly afterward King James appointed Daniel licenser to the acting company called the Children of the Queen's Revels. In January 1605 the company presented Daniel's *The Tragedy of Philotas,* a play that dramatized treason at the court of Alexander the Great. As the result of this performance, Daniel was called before the Privy Council and charged with sedition. There is no record of further legal actions against him, but he resigned his post at court in April 1605. The support of the Earl of Hertford subsequently allowed the writer to retire to a farm in Wiltshire and finish his verse epic *The Civile Wares between the Howses of Lancaster and Yorke,* published in complete

form in 1609. From 1607 to 1619 Daniel was called upon to produce further dramatic works for the court's entertainment, but most of his attention during these years was directed to his second great historical work, *The Collections of the Historie of England from the Conquest to the Reign of Edward III,* dedicated in 1618 to Queen Anne. He died in 1619 at Beckington.

Daniel's first original work, *Delia,* has been identified as the earliest published body of sonnets in the English form (defined as four separate quatrains followed by a couplet). Critics have suggested from an early date that the *Delia* poems may have influenced Shakespeare in choosing his own sonnet form, although Daniel's sonnets are usually seen as distinct from those of other Elizabethan poets because of their gently meditative, sometimes brooding, tone: the sonnets to Delia dwell on melancholy themes of regret or of beauty and its inevitable ruin by time. Daniel's long poem *The Complaint of Rosamond,* a romantic lament told in the voice of Rosamond Clifford, mistress of Henry II, was widely praised and was Daniel's best-known work in his own day. In *Delia* and *The Complaint of Rosamond,* as critics have pointed out, Daniel introduced himself as the Elizabethan poet most sensitive and sympathetic to the social plight of women. He elaborated these sympathies in his verse epistles contained in *Epistles with a Panegyric Congratulatory to the Kings' Majesty,* which form an important category of his poetical works. In the earliest one, *A Letter from Octavia to Marcus Antonius* (first published in *The Poetical Essays of Samuel Daniel*), the Roman matron Octavia delivers an eloquent protestation against the double moral code of male privilege. In addition to his love sonnets and epistles, in 1599 Daniel published *Musophilus,* an extended treatise in verse framed as a debate between two allegorical personages—Musophilus, who defends the value of knowledge, art, and the contemplative life, versus Philocosmus, spokesman of the active life.

In the category of theatrical works, Daniel produced court masques, pastorals, and a tragedy, *The Tragedy of Cleopatra.* When he first composed the drama in 1594, Daniel was unfamiliar with the plays of his contemporary, Shakespeare; in 1607, however, he published a major revision of *Cleopatra* which shares some elements with Shakespeare's *Antony and Cleopatra* and which has since been the subject of much critical speculation regarding the mutual influence of the two authors. Most of Daniel's other dramatic works were written as entertainments for the court. Those conceived in the form of the masque—*The Vision of the 12 Goddesses* and *Tethys Festival; or, The Queenes Wake*—were allegorical and offer a highly idealized image of the court, equating it with the mythical Mount Olympus of the Greek gods and goddesses. Daniel's greatest contribution to Jacobean drama was his introduction of the Italian pastoral into the English-language theater as a genre of tragicomedy, beginning with *The Queenes Arcadia: A Pastoral Tragi-Comedy* (first performed under the title *Arcadia Reformed* in 1605). *The Queenes Arcadia* was closely based on the immensely popular *Il Pastor Fido* (1590; *The Faithfull Shepherd,* 1647) by the celebrated poet Giovanni Battista Guarini, whom Daniel had met during a journey to Italy in 1590-91. Drawing on a standard topos, Daniel's play contrasts a sophisticated society, false and corrupt, with a pastoral arcadia of honest shepherd folk.

Daniel's fascination with history, particularly that of England's dynastic wars, revealed itself early in his career, when he published the first four books of his verse epic *The Civile Wares.* Today it is widely regarded as one of the first examples of modern historical writing in England. Critics have pointed out that the originality of Daniel's approach lies in his comparative objectivity as an observer, an attitude rare among his Elizabethan contemporaries. Arthur B. Ferguson has noted that Daniel's attitude is part of "a new scholarship marked by a realistic and systematic examination of evidence, a willingness to stay within the area of what is credible and humanly knowable, and, perhaps most significantly, a recognition of cultures, customs, and institutions, of society." *The Civile Wares* deals with themes of kingship and dynastic succession, and the mythical Pandora plays a significant role: she is sent to England by Providence to introduce science and knowledge to the island, along with two inventions Daniel portrayed as disastrous, the printing press and firearms. Daniel likewise published a prose chronicle, *The History of England,* in in-

stallments between 1612 and 1618. Scholars have been most intrigued by the sympathetic attitude toward the Middle Ages that Daniel exhibits in this work. No Protestant historian of Daniel's era had assumed such a stance, since the Middle Ages were almost uniformly regarded as a dark time of ignorance and superstition.

Critical esteem for Daniel's work has fluctuated over time. In his own lifetime it was above all his ability to compose masques, dramas, and other royal theatrical entertainments that brought Daniel a livelihood. Nevertheless, his sonnets were more highly regarded among his literary contemporaries than either his plays or his histories. Spenser, perhaps the most respected poet of his day, addressed a complimentary stanza to the young Daniel in his *Colin Clouts Come Home Againe* (1595), encouraging him to be more adventurous and predicting that he would excel in a poetry of "tragic plaints and passionate mischance." A modern authority on Daniel's work, Cecil Seronsy, has described Daniel's *The Complaint of Rosamond* as a tour de force in its own day, one that launched the fashion of joining a narrative poem with a sonnet sequence. The poem was highly praised by such contemporaries of Daniel as Spenser, John Marston, and Drayton, and Shakespeare imitated its rime royal stanza in his *Rape of Lucrece* (1594). Yet, although certain of his works were admired, Daniel has been viewed as a figure decidedly of second rank among his contemporaries. In the nearly four centuries since his death, his work has been most admired by the English Romantic writers and enjoyed a literary revival through the attentions of William Wordsworth, Samuel Taylor Coleridge, and Charles Lamb. It was Daniel's histories rather than his sonnets that attracted the Romantics, with Coleridge comparing Daniel's verse style in *The Civile Wares* to Wordsworth's in its modernity. Daniel's method of writing history has also been one of the favorite subjects of twentieth-century commentators, who have pointed to the author's detached and non-judgmental way of recounting historical events as a capacity that distinguishes him from most Elizabethan writers. Critic William Blissett has called Daniel "the Elizabethan poet with the most fully and justly developed sense of the past." Modern readers have also been particularly struck by Daniel's uncommon sympathy for women and his interest in conveying their processes of thought in his works. Scholars generally agree that, within a system of support for the arts that depended upon aristocratic and court patronage, Daniel can be seen as one of those numerous literary figures who enriched, without reinventing, the poetry and theater of the Elizabethan age, but whose historical works belong to a genuinely new way of composing history.

PRINCIPAL WORKS

The Worthy Tract of Paulus Jovius, contayning a discourse of Rare Inventions both Militarie & Amorous called Imprese [translator; from *Dialogo dell' imprese militari et amorose* by Jovius] (prose) 1585
Delia (poetry) 1592
†*Delia & The Complaint of Rosamond* (poetry) 1592

‡*Delia & Rosamond Augmented; The Tragedy of Cleopatra* (poetry and drama) 1594

The First Fowre Bookes of the civil warres betweene the two houses of Lancaster and Yorke (poetry) 1595; also published as *The Civile Wares between the Howses of Lancaster and Yorke, corrected and continued* [enlarged edition], 1609

Musophilus; or, Defense of All Learning (poetry) 1599

§*The Poetical Essays of Samuel Daniel* (poetry) 1599

A Defense of Rime (prose) 1603

‖*Epistles with A Panegyrike Congratulatorie to the Kings' Majesty* (poetry) 1603

The Vision of the 12 Goddesses (masque) 1604

#*Certain Small Poems* (poetry) 1605

A Funeral Poem upon the Death of the . . . Earl of Devonshire (poetry) 1606

The Queenes Arcadia: A Pastoral Tragi-Comedy (drama) 1606
[first performed as *Arcadia Reformed,* 1605]

Tethys Festival; or, The Queenes Wake (masque) 1610

The Ist Part of the History of England (prose) 1612

Hymen's Triumph (drama) 1615

The Collection of the Historie of England from the Conquest to the Reign of Edward III (prose) 1618

---

*First authorized edition, which includes fifty sonnets. In 1591 twenty-seven of Daniel's love sonnets were appended by Thomas Newman to his pirated edition of Sidney's *Astrophel and Stella.*

†Includes fifty-four sonnets.

‡Includes fifty-five sonnets.

§Includes *A Letter from Octavia to Marcus Antonius.*

‖Includes the *Epistles* to T. Egerton, H. Howard, Margaret Countess of Cumberland, Lucy Countess of Bedford, Anne Clifford, and H. Wriothesly.

#Includes *The Tragedy of Philotas* and *Ulisses and the Syren.*

CRITICISM

Thomas Fuller (essay date 1662)

[*The capsule biography of Daniel reprinted here is taken from Fuller's witty and well-known* The Worthies of England, *published in 1662, in which the author chronicled notable persons of the seventeenth century according to their respective professions. Fuller praises Daniel as both poet and historian.*]

Samuel Daniel was born [1562] not far from Taunton in this country; whose faculty was a master of music, and his harmonious mind made an impression on his son's genius, who proved an exquisite poet. He carried in his Christian and surname two holy prophets, his monitors, so to qualify his raptures, that he abhorred all profaneness.

He was also a judicious historian; witness his lives of our English kings, since the Conquest until King Edward the Third; wherein he hath the happiness to reconcile brevity with clearness, qualities of great distance in other authors;

a work since commendably continued (but not with equal quickness and judgment) by Mr. Trussell.

He was a servant in ordinary to Queen Anne, who allowed him a fair salary. As the tortoise buried himself all the winter in the ground, so Mr. Daniel would lie hid at his garden-house in Old Street, nigh London, for some months together (the more retiredly to enjoy the company of the Muses) and then would appear in public, to converse with his friends, whereof Doctor Cowel and Mr. Camden were principal.

Some tax him to smack of the old cask, as resenting of the Romish religion; but they have a quicker palate than I who can make any such discovery. In his old age he turned husbandman, and rented a farm in Wiltshire nigh the Devizes. I can give no account how he thrived thereupon; for though he was well versed in Virgil, his fellow husbandman poet, yet there is more required to make a rich farmer than only to say his *Georgics* by heart; and I question whether his Italian will fit our English husbandry. Besides, I suspect that Mr. Daniel's fancy was too fine and sublimated to be wrought down to his private profit.

However, he had neither a *bank* of *wealth* or *lank* [the editor translates *lank* in a footnote as scarcity or leanness] of *want,* living in a competent condition. By Justina his wife he had no child; and I am unsatisfied both in the place and time of death, but collect the latter to be about the end of the reign of King James. (pp. 500-01)

> *Thomas Fuller, in a biography in his* The Worthies of England, *edited by John Freeman, George Allen & Unwin Ltd., 1952, pp. 500-01.*

Samuel Taylor Coleridge (letter date 1808)

[*A prolific poet and critic, Coleridge was the preeminent theorist of the English Romantic movement. Among his major contributions to nineteenth-century English letters, Coleridge revolutionized Shakespearean criticism. In the following letter addressed to his friend, the English critic and essayist Charles Lamb, Coleridge commends Daniel's* Civile Wares.]

Dear Charles,

You must read over these *Civil Wars* again. We both know what a *mood* is. And the genial mood will, it shall come for my sober-minded Daniel. He was a Tutor and a sort of Steward in a noble Family in which Form was religiously observed, and Religion formally; & yet there was such warm blood & mighty muscle of substance within, that the moulding Irons did not distort tho' they stiffened the vital man within. Daniel caught & recommunicated the Spirit of the great Countess of Pembroke, the glory of the North (he *formed* her mind, & her mind inspirited him). Gravely sober in all ordinary affairs, & not easily excited by any—yet there is one, on which his Blood boils—whenever he speaks of English Valour exerted against a foreign Enemy. Do read over—but some evening when we are quite comfortable, at your fire-side—& O! where shall I ever be, if I am not so there—that is the last Altar, on the horns of which my old Feelings hang, but alas! listen & tremble) Nonsense!—well! I will read it to you & Mary. The 205, 206, and 207th page [of Daniel's *Poetical Works,* 1718, Vol. II] (above all, that 93rd * Stanza) what is there in description superior even in Shakspere? only that Shakespere would have given one of his *Glows* to the first Line, and flatter'd the mountain Top with his sovran Eye—instead of that poor "a marvellous advantage of his years"—but this however is Daniel—and he must not be read piecemeal. Even by leaving off, & looking at a Stanza by itself, I find the loss.

S. T. Coleridge

* and in a different style the 98th stanza, p. 208: and what an Image in 107, p. 211. Thousands even of educated men would become more sensible, fitter to be members of Parliament or Ministers, by reading Daniel—and even those few who, quoad intellectum only gain refreshment of notions already their own, must become better Englishmen. O, if it be not too late, write a kind note about him. (pp. 511-12)

> *Samuel Taylor Coleridge, in a letter to Charles Lamb on February 10, 1808, in* Coleridge on the Seventeenth Century, *edited by Roberta Florence Brinkley, Duke University Press, 1955, pp. 511-12.*

Samuel Taylor Coleridge   (essay date 1817-34)

[*In the following excerpt from a collection of Coleridge's comments on Daniel written between 1817 and 1834, Coleridge discusses Daniel's poetic style.*]

In Daniel's Sonnets there is scarcely one good line; while his *Hymen's Triumph,* of which Chalmers says not one word, exhibits a continued series of first-rate beauties in thought, passion and imagery, and in language and metre is so faultless, that the style of that poem may without extravagance be declared to be imperishable English.

Read Daniel—the admirable Daniel—in his *Civil Wars,* and *Triumphs of Hymen.* The style and language are just such as any very pure and manly writer of the present day—Wordsworth, for example—would use; it seems quite modern in comparison with the style of Shakspeare. . . .

Samuel Daniel, whose diction bears no mark of time, no distinction of age, which has been, and as long as our language shall last, will be so far the language of the to-day and for ever, as that it is more intelligible to us, than the transitory fashions of our own particular age: A similar praise is due to his sentiments. No frequency of perusal can deprive them of their freshness. For though they are brought into the full day-light of every reader's comprehension; yet are they drawn up from depths which few in any age are priviledged [*sic*] to visit, into which few in any age have courage or inclination to descend. If Mr. Wordsworth is not equally with Daniel alike intelligible to all readers of average understanding in all passages of his works, the comparative difficulty does not arise from the greater impurity of the ore, but from the nature and uses of the metal. A poem is not necessarily obscure, because it does not aim to be popular. It is enough, if a work be perspicuous to those for whom it is written, and,

Fit audience find, though few.

(p. 507)

Daniel is a superior man; his diction is pre-eminently pure;—of that quality which I believe has always existed somewhere in society. It is just such English, without any alteration, as Wordsworth or Sir George Beaumont might have spoken or written in the present day. (p. 508)

On the contrary to how many passages, both in hymn books and in blank verse poems, could I (were it not invidious) direct the reader's attention, the style of which is most *unpoetic, because,* and only because, it is the style of *prose?* He will not suppose me capable of having in my mind such verses, as

> I put my hat upon my head
> And walk'd into the strand;
> And there I met another man,
> Whose hat was in his hand.

To such specimens it would indeed be a fair and full reply, that these lines are not bad, because they are *unpoetic;* but because they are empty of all sense and feeling; and that it were an idle attempt to prove that an ape is not a Newton, when it is evident that he is not a man. But the sense shall be good and weighty, the language correct and dignified, the subject interesting and treated with feeling; and yet the style shall, notwithstanding all these merits be justly blameable as *prosaic,* and solely because the words and the order of the words would find their appropriate place in prose, but are not suitable to *metrical* composition. The *Civil Wars* of Daniel is an instructive, and even interesting work; but take the following stanzas (and from the hundred instances which abound I might probably have selected others far more striking) . . .

> Ten kings had from the Norman conqu'ror reign'd
> With intermixt and variable fate,
> When England to her greatest height attain'd
> Of power, dominion, glory, wealth, and state.
> After it had with much ado sustain'd
> The violence of princes with debate
> For titles, and the often mutinies
> Of nobles for their ancient liberties.
>
> For first the Norman, conqu'ring all by might,
> By might was forced to keep what he had got;
> Mixing our customs and the form of right
> With foreign constitutions, he had brought;
> Mastering the mighty, humbling the poorer wight,
> By all severest means that could be wrought;
> And making the succession doubtful rent
> His new-got state and left it turbulent.

Will it be contended on the one side, that these lines are mean and senseless? Or on the other, that they are not prosaic, and for *that* reason unpoetic? This poet's well-merited epithet is that of the *"well-languaged Daniel;"* but likewise and by the consent of his contemporaries no less than of all succeeding critics, the "prosaic Daniel." Yet those, who thus designate this wise and amiable writer from the frequent incorrespondency of his diction to his metre in the majority of his compositions, not only deem them valuable and interesting on other accounts, but willingly admit, that there are to be found throughout his poems, and especially in his *Epistles* and in his *Hymen's Triumph,* many and exquisite specimens of that style which, as the *neutral ground* of prose and verse is common to both. (pp. 508-09)

Samuel Taylor Coleridge, "Samuel Daniel," in Coleridge on the Seventeenth Century, *edited by Roberta Florence Brinkley, Duke University Press, 1955, pp. 506-19.*

Mrs. Jameson [Anna Brownell Jameson]   (essay date 1829)

[*Mrs. Jameson (as she signed her publications) had a distinguished and prolific career as a critic and essayist on art history, biography, theology, the Middle Ages, travel, and social issues. In the following excerpt from a work published in 1829, she briefly discusses Daniel's sonnets to Delia, praising his plaintive poetic style.*]

Daniel, who was munificently patronized by the Lord Mountjoy, . . . was one of the most graceful sonnetteers of that time; and he has touches of tenderness as well as fancy; for *he* was in earnest, and the object of his attachment was real, though disguised under the name of Delia. She resided on the banks of the River Avon, and was unmoved by the poet's strains. Rank, with her, outweighed love and genius. Daniel says of his sonnets—

> Though the error of my youth in them appear,
> Suffice they show I lived, and loved thee dear

The lines

> Restore thy tresses to the golden ore,
> Yield Citherea's son those arcs of love,

are luxuriantly elegant, and quite Italian in the flow and imagery. Her modesty is prettily set forth in another Sonnet—

> A modest maid, deck'd with a blush of honor,
>   Whose feet do tread green paths of youth and
>   love,
> The wonder of all eyes that looked upon her,
>   Sacred on earth, designed a Saint above!

After a long series of sonnets, elaborately plaintive, he interrupts himself with a little touch of truth and nature, which is quite refreshing:

> I must not grieve my love! whose eyes should
>   read
>   Lines of delight, whereon her youth might
>   smile;
> The flowers have time before they come to seed,
>   And she is young, and now must sport the
>   while.
> And sport, sweet maid! in season of these
>   years,
>   And learn to gather flow'rs before they wither;
> And where the sweetest blossom first appears,
>   Let Love and Youth conduct thy pleasures
>   thither.

If the lady could have been won by poetical flattery, she must have yielded. At length, unable to bear her obduracy,

and condemned to see another preferred before him, Daniel resolved to travel; and he wrote, on this occasion, the most feeling of all his Sonnets.

> And whither, poor forsaken! wilt thou go?

Daniel remained abroad several years, and returning, cured of his attachment, he married Giustina Florio, of a family of Waldenses, who had fled from the frightful persecutions carried on in the Italian Alps against that miserable people. With her, he appears to have been sufficiently happy to forget the pain of his former repulse, and enjoy, without one regretful pang, the fame it had given him as a poet. (pp. 201-03)

Mrs. Jameson [Anna Brownell Jameson], "Court and Age of Elizabeth," in her Memoirs of the Loves of the Poets, *Ticknor and Fields, 1865, pp. 200-17.*

George Saintsbury   (essay date 1880)

[*Saintsbury is considered one of the most influential historians and critics of English literature writing at the turn of the century. As a critic of poetry and drama, Saintsbury was a pure formalist, and this prevailing interest shows itself in the following excerpt, where he briefly evaluates Daniel as poet.*]

There are few poets, not of the first class, to whose merits a stronger consensus of weighty opinion can be produced than that which attests the value of Samuel Daniel's work. His contemporaries, while expressing some doubts as to his choice of subjects, speak of him as 'well-languaged,' 'sharp-conceited,' and as a master of pure English. The critics of the eighteenth century were surprised to find in him so little that they could deem obsolete or in bad taste. The more catholic censorship of Hazlitt, Lamb, and Coleridge was delighted with his extraordinary felicity of expression, and the simple grace of his imagery and phrase. There can be no doubt however that his choice of historical subjects for his poetry was unfortunate for his fame. The sentence of Joubert is not likely to be reversed: 'Il faut que son sujet offre au génie du poëte une espèce de lieu fantastique qu'il puisse étendre et resserrer à volonté. Un lieu trop réel, une population trop historique emprisonnent l'esprit et en gênent les mouvements.' This holds true of all the Elizabethan historians; and it holds truer perhaps of Daniel than of Drayton. For the genius of the former had a tender and delicate quality about it which was least of all applicable to such work, and seems to have lacked altogether the faculty of narrative. Daniel's one qualification for the task was his power of dignified moral reflection, in which, as the following extracts will show, he has hardly a superior. This however, though an admirable adjunct to the other qualities required for the task, could by no means compensate for their absence; and the result is that the *History of the Civil Wars* is with difficulty readable. *The Complaint of Rosamond* is better.

It is however in the long poems only that the 'manner better suiting prose,' of which Daniel has been accused, appears. His minor work is in the main admirable, and displays incessantly the purity and felicity of language already noticed. His "Sonnet to Sleep" became a kind of model to younger writers, and imitations of it are to be found in the sonneteers of the time, sometimes with the opening epithet literally borrowed. The whole indeed of the **Sonnets to Delia** are excellent, and throughout Daniel's work single expressions and short passages of exquisite grace abound. The opening line, for instance, of the Address to Lady Anne Clifford,

> Upon the tender youth of those fair eyes,

is perfect in its kind. So is the distich which begins one of the Sonnets:—

> The star of my mishap imposed this pain,
> To spend the April of my years in grief;

and the invocation of Apollo:—

> O clear-eyed rector of the holy hill.'

It is in such things as these that the greater part of Daniel's charm consists, and they are scattered abundantly about his works. The rest of that charm lies in his combination of moral elevation with a certain picturesque peacefulness of spirit not often to be found in the perturbed race of bards. The **Epistle to the Countess of Cumberland** is unmatched before Wordsworth in the expression of this.

His two tragedies and his **Defence of Rhyme,** though neither of them falling strictly within our limits, are too important in connection with English poetry to be left unnoticed. **Cleopatra** and **Philotas** are noteworthy among the rare attempts to follow the example of Jodelle and Garnier in English. They contain much harmonious verse, and the choruses are often admirable of their kind. The **Defence of Rhyme,** directed against the mania which for a time infected Spenser and Sidney, which Webbe endeavoured to render methodic, and of which traces are to be found in Milton, is thoroughly sound in principle and conclusion, though that conclusion is supported by arguments which are as often bad as good. (pp. 467-68)

> *George Saintsbury, "Samuel Daniel," in* The English Poets: Chaucer to Donne, Vol. I, *edited by Thomas Humphry Ward, 1880. Reprint by The Macmillan Company, 1920, pp. 467-68.*

Thomas Lodge pays tribute to Daniel's *Delia*:

Kisse Delia's hand for her sweet Prophets
    sake,
  Whose, not affected but well couched,
    teares
Have power, have worth a marble minde to
    shake;
  Whose fame no Iron-age or time out
    weares:
Then lay you downe in Phillis lappe and
    sleepe,
Untill she weeping read, and reading weepe.

Thomas Lodge, in his Phillis, *1593.*

Henry Hallam   (essay date 1882)

[*Hallam's vast four-volume survey of the literature of Europe treats every genre of literary production of the fifteenth, sixteenth, and seventeenth centuries—from philosophy, jurisprudence, poetry, and drama, to scientific writings. In the following excerpt, the critic looks at Daniel's two most important works of history, viewing them primarily from a stylistic standpoint.*]

[One of the earliest poets of historical narrative] is Daniel, whose minor poems fall partly within the sixteenth century. His **History of the Civil Wars between York and Lancaster,** a poem in eight books, was published in 1604. Faithfully adhering to truth, which he does not suffer so much as an ornamental episode to interrupt, and equally studious to avoid the bolder figures of poetry, it is not surprising that Daniel should be little read. It is, indeed, certain that much Italian and Spanish poetry, even by those whose name has once stood rather high, depends chiefly upon merits which he abundantly possesses,—a smoothness of rhythm, and a lucid narration in simple language. But that which from the natural delight in sweet sound is enough to content the ear in the Southern tongues, will always seem bald and tame in our less harmonious verse. It is the chief praise of Daniel, and must have contributed to what popularity he enjoyed in his own age, that his English is eminently pure, free from affectation of archaism and from pedantic innovation, with very little that is now obsolete. Both in prose and in poetry, he is, as to language, among the best writers of his time, and wanted but a greater confidence in his own power, or, to speak less indulgently, a greater share of it, to sustain his correct taste, calm sense, and moral feeling. (p. 250)

Daniel's **History of England from the Conquest to the Reign of Edward III.,** published in 1618, is deserving of some attention on account of its language. It is written with a freedom from all stiffness, and a purity of style, which hardly any other work of so early a date exhibits. These qualities are indeed so remarkable, that it would require a good deal of critical observation to distinguish it even from writings of the reign of Anne; and, where it differs from them (I speak only of the secondary class of works, which have not much individuality of manner), it is by a more select idiom, and by an absence of the Gallicism or vulgarity which are often found in that age. It is true that the merits of Daniel are chiefly negative; he is never pedantic or antithetical or low, as his contemporaries were apt to be: but his periods are ill-constructed; he has little vigor or elegance; and it is only by observing how much pains he must have taken to reject phrases which were growing obsolete, that we give him credit for having done more than follow the common stream of easy writing. A slight tinge of archaism, and a certain majesty of expression, relatively to colloquial usage, were thought by Bacon and Raleigh congenial to an elevated style; but Daniel, a gentleman of the king's household, wrote as the court spoke; and his facility would be pleasing if his sentences had a less negligent structure. As an historian, he has recourse only to common authorities; but his narration is fluent and perspicuous, with a regular vein of good sense, more the characteristic of his mind, both in verse and prose, than any commanding vigor. (p. 258)

Henry Hallam, "History of Poetry from 1600-1650," in his Introduction to the Literature of Europe in the Fifteenth, Sixteenth, and Seventeenth Centuries, Vol. III, *revised edition, J. Murray, 1882, pp. 221-70.*

William Minto   (essay date 1885)

[*Minto was a professor of logic and English literature at the University of Aberdeen (Scotland). In the following excerpt, he assesses the place of Daniel in English literary history.*]

Had Daniel lived in the present day, his destiny probably would have been to write scholarly and elegant articles in the magazines, ripe fruits of leisurely study, cultivated taste, and easy command of polite English. His was not one of the stormy irregular natures that laid the foundation and raised the structure of the English drama: the elements of his being were softly blended, and wrought together mildly and harmoniously. In the prologue to **Hymen's Triumph,** he declares that he has no rude antique sport to offer—

> But tender passions, motions soft and grave
> The still spectators must expect to have.

He wrote for Cynthia, and therefore his play—

> Must be gentle like to her
> Whose sweet affections mildly move and stir.

He might have said the same about all his poetry. He was no master of strong passions: he never felt them, and he could not paint them. Between his Cleopatra and Shakespeare's there is a wide gulf. But he is most exquisite and delicate in pencilling "tender passions, motions soft and grave."

Without being strikingly original, Daniel has a way and a vein of his own. He fills his mind with ideas and forms from extraneous sources, and with quietly operating plasticity reshapes them in accordance with the bent of his own modes of thought and feeling. He had not the Shakespearian lightning quickness in adaptation and extension; the process in him was more peaceable and easy. The diction of his poems is choice; the versification easy and flowing. He often puts things with felicitous terseness and vigour, and his words almost invariably come together happily and harmoniously.

The publication of Daniel's sonnets in 1592 is an epoch in the history of the English Sonnet. This was the first body of sonnets written in what is sometimes called by preeminence the English form—three independent quatrains closed in by a couplet. Daniel also set an example to Shakespeare in treating the sonnet as a stanza, connecting several of them together as consecutive parts of a larger expression. Apart from their form, there is not very much interest in the sonnets to Delia. They have all Daniel's smoothness and felicity of phrase, and are pervaded by exceedingly sweet and soft sentiment. Though they rouse no strong feelings, they may be dwelt upon by a sympathetic reader with lively enjoyment. One of them, with somewhat greater depth of feeling than most of the others, the sonnet beginning—"Care-charmer Sleep, son of the sable Night,"

is ranked among the best sonnets in the language. But their most general interest is found in their relation to Shakespeare's sonnets, several of which seem to have been built up from ideas suggested by the study of those to Delia. In the following [sonnet], for example, readers familiar with Shakespeare's will not fail to remark a certain similarity of idea, although the two series of sonnets differ as widely as the genius of the two poets.

Sonnet 37.

> But love whilst that thou mayst be loved again,
>   Now whilst thy May hath filled thy lap with
>   flowers;
> Now whilst thy beauty bears without a stain:
>   Now use the summer smiles, ere winter low-
>   ers:
> And whilst thou spreadst unto the rising Sun
>   The fairest flower that ever saw the light,
> Now joy thy time before thy sweet be done;
>   And, Delia, think thy morning must have
>   night,
> And that thy brightness sets at length to west,
>   When thou wilt close up that which now thou
>   show'st,
> And think the same becomes thy fading best,
>   Which then shall most inveil and shadow
>   most.
> Men do not weigh the stalk for that it was,
> When once they find her flower, her glory pass.

(pp. 191-93)

Daniel's genius is best shown in the expression of bereaved love in the **Complaint of Rosamond,** and in **Hymen's Triumph**— as Spenser said, "in tragic plaints and passionate mischance." In the expression of courtship love, his imagination is cold and acts artificially and mechanically: but when the beloved object is taken away, he is moved to the depths, and pours forth his strains with genuine warmth. The passion has still a certain softness in it: his lovers have not the inconsolable fierce distraction of Shakespeare's forsaken lover, "tearing of papers, breaking rings atwain:" they do not shriek undistinguished woe: but they sigh deeply, and their voices are richly laden with impassioned remembrance. The plaintive sorrow of Thyrsis is sweet and profound. But nothing that Daniel has written flows with surer instinct and more natural impulse than the agonised endearments of Harry over the body of Rosamond. Wholly different in character from the frantic doting of Venus over her lost Adon, these verses are hardly less perfect as the utterance of a milder and less fiercely fond passion. The deep heart's sorrow of the bereaved lover makes itself felt in every line—

> Then as these passions do him overwhelm
> He draws him near my body to behold it;
> And as the vine married unto the elm
> With strict embraces, so doth he enfold it:
> And as he in his careful arms doth hold it
> Viewing the face that even death commends
> On senseless lips millions of kisses spends.
>
> "Pitiful mouth," said he, "that living gavest
> The sweetest comfort that my soul could wish:
> O be it lawful now, that dead thou havest,
> This sorrowing farewell of a dying kiss.
> And you, fair eyes, containers of my bliss,

Motives of love, born to be matched never,
Entomb'd in your sweet circles, sleep for ever."

(p. 194)

*William Minto, "Elizabethan Sonneteers:
Daniel," in his* Characteristics of English
Poets from Chaucer to Shirley, *second edition,
1885. Reprint by Ginn & Company, 1889, pp.
191-95.*

Edmund K. Chambers   (essay date 1893)

[*An English scholar highly regarded for his studies of
medieval and Elizabethan plays, particularly those of
Shakespeare, Chambers described himself as an "im-
penitent Victorian." In the following excerpt, Chambers
surveys the literary output of Daniel, with particular attention to his sonnets and poetical epistles.*]

"Read Daniel, the admirable Daniel," said Coleridge. The
very exhortation itself, the presumed need for it, may help
us to place the subject thereof. One does not say, "Read
Shakespeare," or "Read Tennyson." And, as a matter of
fact, probably very few do read Daniel. It must be a disappointment to his shade, an unexpected reversal of contemporary criticism. There is a passage in one of his prologues
in which he appears quite serenely confident of immortality. "I know," he says,

I know I shall be read among the rest
So long as men speak English, and so
    long
As verse and virtue shall be in request,
Or grace to honest industry belong.

The audacity of this is as sublime as that of Horace's
"Exegi monumentum ære perennius," and surely with less
excuse. Indeed, if the longevity of poetry depended either
upon "virtue" or upon "honest industry," Daniel's vaunt
would be fairly justified. The innumerable and minute alterations which he made in successive issues of his works
bear witness to the latter; and the former is no less undeniable. His sentiments are always ethically correct, even
where they lack distinction or force of expression.
"Moral" Daniel he is called, and "well-languaged" Daniel, and "sharp-conceited" Daniel. If the third title implies
vividness and intensity of imaginative power it is a misnomer; the second may well pass; the first is entirely deserved. But in truth Daniel, like many others, was praised
by the men of his own day with less discrimination than
fervour. One cannot but think that the custom of commendatory verses (and his were much in request) must
have led to what the Americans call "log-rolling." Meres,
Lodge, Carew, Drummond, Harington vie in his honour.
Nash, no gentle-tongued critic, wrote thus in his *Piers
Pennilesse* (1592): "You shall find there goes more exquisite pains and purity of wit to the writing of one such rare
poem as **Rosamond,** than to a hundred of your dimistical
sermons." Spenser, in *Colin Clout's Come Home Again*
(1591), mentions Daniel by name, with terms of high commendation.

And there is a new shepherd late up sprong,
The which doth all afore him far surpass;
Appearing well in that well tuned song,

Which late he sung unto a scornful lass.
Yet doth his trembling Muse but lowly
    fly,
As daring not too rashly mount on height,
And doth her tender plumes as yet but
    try
In love's soft lays and looser thoughts
    delight.
Then rouse thy feathers quickly, Daniel,
And to what course thou please thyself
    advance:
But most, me seems, thy accent will excel
In tragic plaints and passionate mischance.

Daniel's success must have been rapid, for Spenser's poem
was published only a few months after the first batch of
the sonnets to Delia had been surreptitiously given to the
world. Equally complimentary, ten years later, is the reference in the *Return from Parnassus* (1601).

Honey-dropping Daniel doth wage
War with the proudest big Italian
That melts his heart in sugared sonneting.

But there were dissentient voices. Bolton, the author of
Hypercritica, and Drayton, in his *Epistle on Poets and
Poesy,* depreciate Daniel as flat and prosaic. He certainly
had in him but few of those "brave translunary things" in
which Drayton delighted. A still greater name is upon the
same side. Ben Jonson, a Triton among the minnows of
Elizabethan criticism, said to Drummond of Hawthornden, "that Daniel was a good honest man, had no children, but no poet"; "that he wrote **Civil Wars,** but yet had
not one battle in all his book." There appears to have been
some jealousy between Jonson and Daniel, springing perhaps out of their rivalry as providers of court-masques:
and although Jonson stated that the ill-will was all upon
the other side, we are not bound to assume that his opinion
was an absolutely unprejudiced one. He seems to have ridiculed Daniel in some lines to the Countess of Rutland,
and also, if we may trust Mr. Fleay's investigations into
the Aristophanic element in the English drama, upon the
stage. Hedon in *Cynthia's Revels* (1600), and Littlewit in
Bartholomew Fair (1614), are both, says Mr. Fleay, carica-
tures of Daniel.

Perhaps, however, we may be allowed to form our opinion
of Daniel for ourselves, without undue deference either to
Jonson or to Spenser. It is gentlemanly poetry, but one
does not quite see why an Elizabethan should have written
it. There is none of that flush and fervour, that red-hearted
passion and irregular genius, which we are accustomed to
regard as characteristics of Renascence work. The note is
pitched low throughout; the beauty is that of a sober, chastened style; the sentiments are irreproachable and set in
well-turned phrase. Grave, serene, and dignified, Daniel
might belong rather to the company of Crabbe and
Wordsworth than to that of the turbulent, full-blooded
poets of the sixteenth century. His habitual chastity and
reticence of speech contrasts oddly with their outspoken-
ness and ethical audacities. They are his superiors, Mar-
low and Sidney and Donne, in the great essentials of poetry, in imagination and the gift of song. And yet Coleridge
was right when he said, "Read Daniel." He is an admirable companion with whom to pass a bookish hour. His fe-

licities of expression do not sting the mind, but they gratify the taste. His lofty idealism and crystal purity of thought have "ample power to chasten and subdue." The kindly nature of the man shines through his limpid verse; and, like so many dead writers, he has the genius of friendship with the living. (pp. 433-34)

The sum of Daniel's poetical achievement is not very considerable; sixty sonnets, two tragedies and four masques, eight books of versified history, two dramatic elegies, and a bundle of letters in verse. It is in the first and last of these that the finest fragrance of his poetry is to be found.

The **Sonnets to Delia** form one of those great groups of sonnets which mark the last twenty years of the sixteenth century. Like Sidney's *Astrophel and Stella,* they became in some degree a model for later writers. Sidney's "Come, Sleep! Oh Sleep, the certain knot of peace," for instance, and Daniel's "Care-charmer, Sleep, son of the sable night," were the first blows in a tournament of sonnets on the subject, whereof Shakespeare's lines in *Macbeth* are an obvious reminiscence. Indeed "Care-charming Sleep" or "Care-charmer, Sleep" became a traditional opening for such a sonnet.

Daniel's sonnets are written throughout in a melancholy vein. They are a series of laments against a cruel fair, who has rejected his love and set his tears at naught. The same situation continues throughout; there is no change of attitude, no development, as in Shakespeare's sonnets, from crisis to crisis. Perhaps, therefore, the total effect is a little monotonous. This is a fair specimen:

> If this be Love, to draw a weary breath,
> To paint on floods, till the shore cry to
>   th' air;
> With downward looks, still reading on the
>   earth
> These sad memorials of my Love's despair;
> If this be Love, to war against my soul,
> Lie down to wail, rise up to sigh and
>   grieve;
> The never-resting stone of Care to roll,
> Still to complain my griefs, whilst none
>   relieve.
> If this be Love, to clothe me with dark
>   thoughts,
> Haunting untrodden paths to wail apart;
> My pleasures' horror, music, tragic notes,
> Tears in mine eyes, and sorrow at my
>   heart.
> If this be Love, to live a living death,
> Then do I love and draw this weary
>   breath.

Two secondary ideas introduce a little variety. One is the famous comparison of woman's beauty to the fading glories of the rose, which nearly every lyrist, from Ausonius downwards, has handled. Daniel's version of it is one of his most graceful efforts. The other is the consolatory thought that, when the fate of the rose overtakes his mistress, her beauty will still dazzle the world in his verse. Though she love him not, he can confer an immortality upon her. Daniel does not share the want of chivalry which a modern writer has imputed to the foiled Elizabethan lover. He does not "turn upon the adamantine fair,

roundly tell her that henceforth he shall repay scorn with scorn, and altogether behave with a degree of incivility which the occasion does not seem to require." (pp. 436-37)

If the range of the thought in the sonnets is not very wide, one may yet linger with delight upon their cameo-like phrasing. Such lines as

> Oh clear-eyed Rector of the holy Hill,

or

> Th' eternal annals of a happy pen;

such quatrains as,

> A modest maid, decked with a blush of honour,
> Whose feet do tread green paths of youth and
>   love,
> The wonder of all eyes that look upon her:
> Sacred on earth, designed a Saint above:

such recur throughout, and give a peculiar air of distinction to the whole.

As with Shakespeare, as with Sidney, so with Daniel, the inevitable question rises: Is this genuine love-poetry, expressive of real emotions, or is it merely artificial, a literary man's exercise in a recognised mode of song? The question is a perennial one, and will always be answered rather by the temperament of the reader than in accordance with any exact rules of criticism. In all such cases there must be a certain element of art. Verse can never be the direct reflex of feeling; it does not flow from present emotion, but, as Coleridge said, from "emotion remembered in tranquillity." And the act of recollection must needs transform; a subtle mental state cannot be exactly reproduced; the processes of imagination and fancy insensibly colour it. Therefore, even if your Elizabethan love-sonnet rings at times a little unreal, that is no reason for supposing that there is no reality behind it. We have no doubt that there was a real Delia, that she rejected the poet, and that it caused him real grief, a grief that found expression, and not impossibly solace, in writing these sonnets. Nor can we regard it as illegitimate to speculate who Delia may have been. When a bit of romance is cast up to us from the wreckage of time, it were inhuman not to feel a desire to know what little may be to be known of the actors therein. The identities of Delia, of Stella, of Rosalind, of Shakespeare's "Mr. W. H." and "his Dark Woman," appear to us subjects eminently worthy of serious literary research. In the case of Delia there are not many hints to be of service to us. The only definite fact we are told is that she had her seat upon

> Avon, rich in fame, though poor in waters.

Mr. Fleay, with his accustomed ingenuity, suggests that she was Elizabeth Carey, daughter of a certain Sir George Carey, who had a house upon the Lower Avon near Bath. Nash, writing of this lady in 1594, in the dedication to his *Terrors of the Night,* says, "The wittiest poets of our age have vowed to enshrine you as their second Delia." The first Delia would be, one supposes, Elizabeth the Queen. Another possible, though not very probable, theory is that the poems were written to Mary Countess of Pembroke. They are dedicated to her, and one of them, for some reason or other, is headed "To M. P." Those critics who say that this cannot refer to the Countess, because it would be audacious for a dependent to address her as M. P., have overlooked the seventy-sixth stanza of the eighth book of the *History of the Civil War,* which opens thus:

> Here, Mary Pembroke,. . . . could I show.

But if she is the subject of the sonnets, they can hardly be regarded as anything more serious than a graceful poetic tribute.

Before leaving the sonnets, it is worth while to notice the fact that Shakespeare took them for a model. The distinctive Shakespearian form of the sonnet, the three independent quatrains followed by a "clinching" couplet, occurs here for the first time; and the idea of the memory of the loved ones being eternalised by the verse of the lover, is also common to the elder and the younger poet.

In the 1601 folio of his poems Daniel included a little sheaf of *Certain Epistles after the manner of Horace,* addressed to the nobles and great ladies of his acquaintance. These show him at his best, in the display of his unrivalled talent for ethical exposition. They might have been called *Sermons in Verse.* To the Lord Chancellor he discourses upon equity and its place in the State; to the Countess of Cumberland upon the advantage of the philosophic mind; to his pupil Lady Anne Clifford, on the text of *noblesse oblige;* to Lord Southampton on the uses of adversity. His tone throughout is dignified and gracious, didactic without asperity, courteous without flattery. (pp. 437-38)

With the Epistles we may class, as belonging to the same order, the Ovidian **"Letter from Octavia to Antonius,"** **Musophilus, or, A Defence of Learning,** the **Panegyrick Congratulatory** to the King, and the *Funeral Poem* on the Earl of Devonshire.

The poem which Daniel doubtless regarded as the chief work of his life is the one which has most lost its savour for a modern reader. "Ætas prima canat Veneres, postrema tumultus," he wrote on the title-page of his *History of the Civil War* between the Houses of York and Lancaster. But we have distinguished more accurately the spheres of prose and poetry, and care little for versified accounts of rebellions and the rise and fall of kings. The chronicle was apparently intended to stretch as far as the coming of the Tudors; but it remains unfinished. The eight books which we have extend from the accession of Richard the Second to the middle of the reign of Henry the Sixth. The quatrains are flowing, the narrative easy, but monotonous. Daniel often takes a hint or a phrase from Shakespeare; and, like Shakespeare, he is not pedantic about accuracy. He uses the "poetical license of framing speeches to the persons of men, according to their occasions," quoting for his practice the example of Livy and Sallust; and, for emotional effect, he advances by some years the age of Richard's child-wife Isabella. One of the few telling episodes in the work is the scene where Isabella goes forth to meet the King on his return from Flint Castle. Mr. Grant White states that the verbal parallels with Shakespeare's *Richard the Second* occur mainly in the later editions of the *Civil History,* and thinks that the play had not appeared when the first edition was published in 1595. Daniel's only other narrative poem is the *Complaint of Rosamond,* modelled on the tales in Lydgate's *Fall of Princes,* and in *The Mirror for Magistrates.*

The masques and pastoral comedies we must pass over lightly. Both Lamb and Coleridge call our attention to *Hymen's Triumph;* but perhaps Daniel's muse was hardly playful and fanciful enough for such trifles. They compare but ill with Lyly on the one side and Ben Jonson on the other. And in the masques, at least, the wit of the poet was ever subordinate to the ingenuity of the architect. The tragedies have more interest for us, though indeed it is rather for their historic position than their literary merit. They are academic and colourless enough. Daniel's Cleopatra looks but a pale and wan ghost beside the "infinite variety" of Shakespeare's impassioned queen. Yet they come to us with a sound of thunder heard remote, the last reverberations of a subsiding storm. In form they retain the limitations of the Senecan tragedy, the unities of time and place, the machinery of chorus and messenger. Only at the time they were written, *Cleopatra* in 1594, *Philotas* in 1604, the Senecan tragedy was already out of date. A decade or two earlier it had very nearly succeeded in imposing its cast-iron rules upon the future of the theatre. It was the darling of the Court; Sidney wrote a brilliant tract in its defence; Sackville and Ferrers united their talents in the production of *Gorboduc.* But the vitality of the popular drama of romanticism triumphed; the pseudo-classic spirit vanished, leaving to its conqueror the glorious inheritance of blank verse. Only Daniel, standing aside from the main stream of poetic development, careless, as he himself says, "of Thames or theatres," persists in producing these two forlorn and solitary experiments, pale garlands plucked from the gardens of the past. A comparison, however, of the earlier and later versions of *Cleopatra* reveals a tendency even in Daniel to become less strict in his observance of the classical rules. He almost entirely recast the play, adding long scenes and re-arranging the whole. The unities are violated, and incidents previously narrated only are now acted on the stage. The date of these alterations is apparently about 1607, and their motive the appearance of *Anthony and Cleopatra* at the Globe about that period. The curious thing is that, by a kind of fatality, Daniel failed to grasp the one point in which the classic drama had got the better of the earlier romanticists; he writes not in blank verse, but in rhyming quatrains. This at least is the case in *Cleopatra:* in *The Defence of Rhyme* he accepts the theory of blank verse for tragedy; and in *Philotas* he introduces unrhymed lines in the midst of others that rhyme. In this matter of rhyme, indeed, Daniel parts company with Sidney and his pedantic Areopagus. When Thomas Campion in 1602 attempted to reintroduce the heresy of "English versifying," the sapphics and anacreontics and licentiate iambics beloved by Gabriel Harvey, Daniel was one of the first to enter the field against him. This he did in *The Defence of Rhyme* (1603), wherein he laid down the eternal principles which separate English from classical verse. None the less, Daniel is by way of being a metrical reformer. He has a dislike to the monotony of the heroic couplet in long poems, and introduces devices of his own for avoiding it. Let him speak for himself:

I must confess that to mine own ear those continual cadences of couplets used in long and continued poems are very tiresome and unpleasing, by reason that still, methinks, they run on with a sound of one nature, and a kind of certainty which stuffs the delight rather than entertains it. . . . Beside, methinks sometimes to beguile the ear with a running out and passing over the rhyme, as no bound to stay us in the line where the violence of the matter will break through, is rather graceful than otherwise. . . . And to avoid this over-glutting the ear with that always certain and full encounter of rhyme, I have essayed in some of my epistles to alter the usual place of meeting, and to set it further off by one verse, to try how I could disuse my own ear, and to ease it of this continual burden, which indeed comes to surcharge it a little too much, but as yet I cannot come to please myself therein; this alternate or cross rhyme holding still the best place in my affection.

Daniel's practice squares with his theory. The alternately rhymed quatrain is his mainstay. Sometimes he attempts other arrangements of alternate rhymes; and in **Philotas,** as we have said, and in the comedies, he introduces unrhymed lines.

Ben Jonson, by the way, told Drummond of a design which he seems never to have carried out, to confute both Campion and Daniel in a pamphlet defending the couplet. If he had actually written this pamphlet, as Drummond says, it must have perished with others of his papers. (pp. 438-40)

> *Edmund K. Chambers, in an originally unsigned essay titled "Samuel Daniel," in Macmillan's Magazine, Vol. LXVIII, No. 408, October, 1893, pp. 433-40.*

Edmund Spenser's reaction to Daniel's *Sonnets to Delia*:

And there is a new shepherd late up sprong,
The which doth all afore him far surpass:
Appearing well in that well-tuned song,
Which late he sung unto a scornful Lass.
Yet doth his trembling Muse but lowly fly,
As daring not too rashly mount on height,
And doth her tender plumes as yet but try
In love's soft lays and looser thoughts'
   delight.
Then rouse thy feathers quickly, Daniel,
And to what course thou please thyself
   advance:
But most, me seems, thy accent will excel
In tragic plaints and passionate mischance.

> *Edmund Spenser, in his* Colin Clouts
> Come Home Againe, *1595.*

May McKisack (essay date 1947)

[*McKisack is known today as an historian, through her* The Parliamentary Representation of the English Boroughs *during the Middle Ages (1962) and* The Fourteenth Century, 1307-1399 *(1991), among other works. In the following excerpt, she examines Daniel's attitudes toward the past, describing him as one of the few Elizabethans to write about the Middle Ages with a sense of loss.*]

Popular history has a long ancestry in England. Its roots may be traced in the Middle Ages, and ever since the printing-press began to bring literature within the reach of a widening circle of readers 'General' or 'Complete' histories of England have found a steady market; nor have authors been wanting to satisfy the public taste. Sometimes, like Robert Brady, these have been scholars who deliberately set themselves to present their knowledge in readable form: sometimes they have been indefatigable compilers, like Thomas Carte; sometimes men of affairs, like Sir William Temple; sometimes poets, like Milton, or novelists, like Smollett; sometimes philosophers, like Hume. If the majority of them made little or no original contribution to knowledge, if their facts were not always accurate, their works are none the less interesting because in them we find preserved those generally held historical conceptions which were in part productive of and in part consequent on the political thinking of their several generations. Samuel Daniel has his place in this long succession of historical writers. Poet and man of letters, he, like Milton, was moved to attempt an essay in English history in his latter years. His unpretentious volume which to-day has passed into oblivion was among the first of many attempts at concise and readable treatment of a vast subject. As a pioneer work in this field it is well worth re-examination and, as I hope to show, it possesses intrinsic merits which go far to uphold and explain the reputation it enjoyed in the seventeenth century.

Daniel made no great claims for himself as historian, and his **History of England,** though it was widely appreciated in the century following his death, has been little read or commended since that time. Daniel is classed with the poets, not with the antiquaries, and by the standards of the latter he was not, indeed, a deeply learned man. Though, if Wood is to be believed, his interest in English history went back to his undergraduate days at Magdalen, it was not until he was in his fifties that he published his **History of England,** his last important prose work. It is a slim and modest volume by contrast with the weighty folios of Holinshed and Speed. Daniel brought no new material to light and though he had access to some of Cotton's manuscripts the bulk of his work is derived from printed sources many of which had been first published in his own lifetime. In his prefaces he makes it clear that his object is not to disclose the hitherto undiscovered but to interpret what is already familiar to the learned and to present this interpretation in concise form to the general reader. He is concerned with 'the obseruation of those necessary circumstances and inferences which the History naturally ministers' and with the weaving together of material which has long lain 'dispersed in confused pieces'. The qualifications which the author claims for himself are, first, a lifelong interest in the subject, 'hauing spent much of my best understanding in this part of humane Learning, Historie'; secondly, knowledge of men and affairs, 'it hath bene in my fortune (besides conference with men of good experience) to haue seene many of the best discourses, negotiations, instructions and relations of the generall affaires of the World'; and, thirdly, respect for truth, 'the Reader shall be sure to be payd with no counterfeit Coyne but such as shal haue the Stampe of Antiquity, the approbation of Testimony and the allowance of Authority, so farre as I shall proceed herein'. Daniel's motive was patriotic. He desired to serve his country by preserving the names of her great men and, in particular, of her great men of action from undeserved oblivion. There is, he writes, no nation

> whose Ancestors haue done more worthy things, both at home and abroad; especially for matter of war. For since the Romans, no one people hath fought so many battailes prosperously. And therefore out of the tender remorse to see these men much defrauded of their glory so deerely bought and their affaires confusedly deliuered, I was drawne (though the least able for such a worke) to make this aduenture . . . and perhaps, by my example induce others of better abilities to undergoe the same.

The sentiments are commonplace enough; and the modesty of Daniel's disclaimers must be held partly responsible for the otherwise almost inexplicable neglect of his historical work. For he was no mere collector and abbreviator of other men's opinions. Though much less deeply read than many of his learned contemporaries he was what few of them could claim to be—a natural historian, endowed with a rare sense of the past and with an intuitive understanding (almost unique in that age) of the limitations of historical knowledge. The shrewd judgements of character and lucid analyses of historical situations which are packed into his one small volume suggest that the poet Daniel was an historian *manqué* who found his vocation too late in life to develop his talents to the full.

Daniel planned a History of England in three sections. The first was to cover the period from the earliest times to the end of the reign of Stephen; the second was to run from 1154 to 1485; the third to deal with the Tudor age. Since the book was intended to be easily readable by men who were not scholars, 'seeing it concernes them most to know the generall affaires of England who haue least leasure to read them', since it was to furnish 'an uninterrupted deliuery of the especiall Affaires of the Kingdome (without imbroyling the memory of the Reader)', documentary evidence was to be reserved for an Appendix which was to contain 'all Treaties, Letters, Articles, Charters, Ordinances, Intertaynments, prouisions of Armies, businesses of Commerce, with other passages of State appertayning to our History'. The project was unfortunately never brought to completion. The first section to 1154, with a dedication to Rochester, was printed in small quarto by Nicholas Okes in 1612 and reprinted in the following year for the Company of Stationers. A new edition, dedicated to Queen Anne, with a continuation to 1377, appeared in folio in 1617 or 1618, some two years before Daniel's death. The remainder of the *History* was never printed nor, so far as is known, written and, apart from several references to it in the printed text, there is no trace of the promised Appendix. What we have is a continuous

History of England to the end of the reign of Edward III. (pp. 226-28)

The *History* is the work of a courtier but not of a sycophant; and the balance between servile flattery and injudicious criticism is, on the whole, nicely held. If praises of King Cnut and of the valorous Scots were well calculated to please the ears of the reigning monarchs, neither was without warrant in history; and references to the 'confusion and mischiefe' attending the advancement of 'unworthy minions' and to the 'vaine expences of apparell, (the note of a diseased time)' must have been less acceptable. The independence of mind which led Daniel to withdraw from Court from time to time and 'lye hid at his Gardenhouse in Old Street nigh London for some months together the more retiredly to enjoy the company of the Muses doubtless made it distasteful to him to distort his historical judgements in order to flatter kings.

The early seventeenth century was a propitious period for the composition of such a History as Daniel had in view. The past century had seen a great revival of antiquarian studies and the publication, both in England and abroad, of many of the sources indispensable to the historian of medieval England. (pp. 229-30)

[By] the time that Daniel came to write his *History,* a substantial number of medieval Latin chronicles was available in print and it was from these chronicles, supplemented by Lord Berners's Froissart published in 1525, that he drew the bulk of his material. For the Saxon and Norman periods his principal literary authority is William of Malmesbury, but he draws also from Hoveden and Henry of Huntingdon. The early history of Normandy and the Normans is taken mainly from William of Jumièges. Hoveden and Wendover (whose chronicle was incorporated in that of Matthew Paris) are his main sources for the reigns of Henry II and Richard I, though he draws freely on Giraldus for the story of the conquest of Ireland. The history of the reigns of John and Henry III is taken mainly from the St. Albans chroniclers, Wendover and Paris, that of Edward I from 'Matthew of Westminster'. From 1299 Daniel begins to use Walsingham who, together with Froissart and Geoffrey le Baker, continues to be his principal authority for the reigns of Edward II and Edward III. The only unprinted chronicle on which he seems to have relied to any great extent is that of Rishanger, and for access to this he, like Speed, was almost certainly indebted to Cotton.

His project for an Appendix of *pièces justificatives* shows that Daniel recognized the importance of official and semiofficial documents as well as of chronicles, and, though the Appendix was never printed, there is enough documentary material in the body of the *History* to show the lines upon which he worked. Many letters are transcribed in full. They are, writes Daniel, 'the best peeces of History in the world and shewe vs more of the inside of affayres then any relations else'. Much of the Becket correspondence, for example, is quoted *in extenso* from Hoveden. There are many references in the early chapters of the book to Lambarde's *Archaionomia*. From Cotton Daniel probably gained access to the *Dialogus de Scaccario,* then generally believed to be the work of Gervase of Tilbury.

Daniel, who uses it freely for the Norman and early Angevin periods, refers to it consistently as *Tilburiensis,* and the Cotton manuscript which he probably consulted bears in a contemporary hand the memorandum 'This booke was made by G. Tilburiensis'. References to the Statute Rolls are probably to Tottel's *Antiqua Statuta* (1556), this being the edition of early statutes then most generally in use.

For foreign affairs and Anglo-French relations in particular, Daniel supplemented Froissart and the Latin chronicles by reference to three well-known sixteenth-century French histories, the *De Rebus Gestis Francorum,* compiled by Paolo Emilio and first published in 1516; the *Chronicon de Regibus Francorum* of Jean du Tillet, first published in 1551; and Haillan's *Histoire de France,* first published in 1576. These were the stock French histories of the day and Daniel's references show that he, like Speed, drew freely upon them. He had made no independent study of foreign sources, and for details relating to French history he relies mainly upon secondary authors.

Daniel was inevitably familiar with the standard Tudor histories though it was not his habit to rely on them to the neglect of original authorities. In his preface he refers to the collections of Polydore Vergil, Fabian, Grafton, Holinshed, Stow, and Speed, but his indebtedness to them appears to have been slight. From Speed he takes details of the marriages of King John's children; from Holinshed, the profits drawn by Edward I from his silver-mines in Devon; from Stow, figures relating to some of the subsidies. The critical temper of the whole work may have owed something to the example of Polydore Vergil, though Daniel is not very ready to borrow opinions from his contemporaries and immediate predecessors. His historical judgements are his own and are based on independent reading of the sources. There is clear proof that he had seen Cotton's *Short View of the Long Life and Reign of Henry III,* which was finished in 1614 though not published till 1627. From it he took some references to the Close Rolls and to a royal charter; but it is noteworthy that Daniel's treatment of this reign as a whole is quite independent of and much fuller than Cotton's.

As has already been suggested, it is the quality of his mind rather than the depth of his reading that lends Daniel distinction as an historian. Among his learned contemporaries few possessed any glimmerings of historical imagination or any notion of historical criticism. Their curiosity was boundless, their power of discrimination feeble indeed. Turning the pages of their immense folios we find ourselves confronted with a strange mingling of legend and history. The activities of the mythical British kings occupy hardly less space than those of Henry II or Edward I; the minutiae of antiquarian learning find a place beside strange tales of fiery comets, human monstrosities, and mystic prophecies culled from Geoffrey of Monmouth or from popular folk-lore. The Tudor historians have a charm of their own for the modern reader, but, though their superstitions are of a different character from those of their medieval predecessors, it is difficult to contend that their historical method is much farther advanced. The annalistic arrangement is maintained; the past is still judged in the light of the present; and in many of the writers of the period, most notably in Hall and Holinshed, misunderstanding of the Middle Ages is further enhanced by violent Protestant prejudice. There are, of course, exceptions. Polydore Vergil had learnt to read the more extravagant of the medieval chroniclers with a critical eye, though the reception given to his History shows how little his scepticism was to the liking of his contemporaries. Stow's *Annales* are dispassionate, if dull. Speed had some notion of criticizing his sources but, though he rejects Brutus and the wilder of the Arthurian legends, he is at one with his predecessors in accepting the story of Joseph of Arimathaea's visit to Britain and in his belief that Ambrosius Aurelianus built Stonehenge.

It was not, indeed, easy, even had it been thought necessary, for the subjects of Elizabeth and James I to arrive at any true understanding of the Middle Ages. The men of the Renaissance had their own doubts and perplexities, but when they looked back with uncertain longing to a happier past it was, if not to some mythical Age of Gold, to the world of classical antiquity or of the primitive Church. The popularity of the Shakespearian cycle of historical plays may well have helped to deepen the tendency, for which Hall was largely responsible, to identify the whole medieval period with the recent past, with that age of civil discord from which England had emerged under the wise guidance of her Tudor sovereigns. The man of letters looked askance at the supposedly obscurantist period which preceded the dawn of humanism: the Puritan took a no less gloomy view of the age of superstitious enslavement to Rome. Only among a few lawyers and antiquaries was there some dim recognition of the legal and constitutional achievement of medieval England.

The originality of Daniel's approach to medieval history cannot be fully appreciated from his ***History of England*** alone. In the best known of his prose works, ***A Defence of Ryme,*** published in 1602, he had made an eloquent plea for more intelligent understanding of the period that lay between the fall of the Roman Empire and the dawn of the Renaissance: 'Is it not a most apparent ignorance', he asks,

> both of the succession of learning in Europe, and the generall course of things to say, that all lay pittifully deformed in those lacke-learning times from the declining of the Romane Empire, till the light of the Latine tongue was reuiued by Rewcline, Erasmus and Moore. . . . And yet long before all these . . . was not our Nation behind in her portion of spirite and worthinesse, but concurrent with the best of all this lettered worlde: witnesse venerable Bede, that flourished aboue a thousand yeeres since: . . . What should I name Walterus Mape, Gulielmus Nigellus, Geruasius Tilburiensis, Bracton, Bacon, Ockam and an infinite Catalogue of excellent men, most of them liuing about foure hundred yeares since and haue left behinde them monuments of most profound iudgement and learning in all sciences. So that it is but the clowds gathered about our owne iudgement that makes vs thinke all other ages wrapt vp in mists and the great distance betwixt vs, that causes vs to imagine men so farre off, to be so little in respect of our selues. . . . The distribution of giftes are vniuersall and all seasons hath them in some sort. We must not

thinke, but that there were Scipioes, Caesars, Catoes and Pompeies, borne elsewhere then at Rome. . . .

The medieval legacy in the sphere of government speaks for itself:

> . . . they had the learning of Gouernment and ordring their State, Eloquence inough to shew their judgements. . . . Let us go no further, but looke vpon the wonderfull Architecture of this state of England and see whether they were deformed times that could giue it suche a forme. Where there is no one the least piller of Maiestie but was set with most profound iudgement and borne vp with the iust conueniencie of Prince and people. No Court of Iustice but laide by the Rule and Square of Nature, and the best of the best commonwealths that euer were in the world. So strong and substantial as it hath stood against al the storms of factions, both of beliefe & ambition, which so powerfully beat vpon it and all the tempestuous alterations of humorous times whatsoeuer.

Daniel's whole thesis, in itself a fine expression of humanist belief, implies a protest against the intellectual snobbery born of the Renaissance:

> Nor can it be but a touch of arrogant ignorance to hold this or that nation Barbarous, these or those times grosse, considering how this manifold creature man, whersoeuer hee stand in the world, hath always some disposition of worth. . . .

With this remarkable readiness to judge the past on its own merits Daniel combines some understanding of historical development and of historical method. In his *History of England* he censures 'those narrow conceits as apprehend not the progresses in the affaires of mankind' as well as those who argue about the past 'from the example and Idea of the present customes they see in vse'. 'Pardon us, Antiquity,' he writes after passing severe judgement on Richard I,

> if we mis-censure your actions which are euer (as those of men) according to the vogue and sway of times and haue onely their upholding by the opinion of the present: we deale with you but as posterity will with us (which euer thinkes it selfe the wiser) that will iudge likewise of our errors according to the cast of their imaginations.

In the preface to the first section of the *History* Daniel shows his lively awareness of some of the common pitfalls that lie in the path of the medievalist:

> Now for the errors herin committed . . . I must craue Pardon, of course. It is a Fate common to Bookes and Book-men and wee cannot auoyde it. For besides our owne faylings we must heere take up many things upon other mens credits, which often comes imperfect to our hands: As the summes of Monies, numbers of Souldiers, Shippes, the slayne in Battaile, Computation of Times, differences of Names and Titles etc. Wherein our Authors agree not.

From the spectacle of myth masquerading as history Dan-

iel derives neither artistic nor intellectual satisfaction. True knowledge of the past is his aim and where truth does not seem to him to be attainable he will leave his pages blank, he will accept what in his fine poem, *Musophilus,* he calls 'the misery of darke forgetfulnesse' rather than take what is offered by ignorance with fabulous discourse'. In his *History,* he declares himself to be

> So greedy of doing well, as nothing suffices the appetite of my care heerein. I had rather be Maister of a small peece handsomely contriued then of vaste roomes ill proportioned and unfurnished.

His natural scepticism is, perhaps, best illustrated from that part of the *History of England* which relates to the earliest period. All the legendary material with which historians from Geoffrey of Monmouth to Holinshed and Stow had elaborated their historical narrative is rejected by Daniel out of hand. He is bolder than Polydore Vergil who, while recognizing that 'ther is nothinge more obscure, more uncertaine, or unknowne then the affaires of the Brittons from the beginninge', yet thought it a necessary part of his task as historian to 'brefelie passe through the life of those kinges'. Daniel tells us that it had been his hope to begin his *History* with an account of the early kings of Britain but 'finding no authenticall warrant' for their existence he abandoned the attempt—with a shrewd comment on such legendary origins:

> The beginnings of all people and States were as vncertaine as the heads of great Riuers . . . considering how commonly they rise from the springs of pouerty, pyracie, robbery and violence, howsoeuer fabulous Writers (to glorifie their nations) striue to abuse the credulity of after ages with heroycall or miraculous beginnings.

(pp. 231-36)

Daniel's mistrust of legends does not, however, lead him to belittle the medieval historians as such. His understanding of the nature of evidence is much too acute for him not to appreciate the value of contemporary witness. He is by no means uncritical of the monastic writers, rejecting not only their legendary glorification of the remote past but also certain of their comments on current affairs. He thinks, for example, that William I's reputation for harshness may be partly the result of his reign having been chronicled by members of the religious houses on which he laid heavy burdens of military and other service; and he anticipates the most recent historical criticism in his suggestion that the defects of [King] John's character and the sufferings of the clergy in his reign may have been exaggerated by the St. Albans chroniclers. But, on the whole, he is ready to take the medieval historians seriously and to select from the best of them the material which enables him to build up a convincing historical narrative, free from legendary embellishments. Daniel is very far from sharing the view of Milton, who dismissed all the monastic historians, Bede not excepted, as 'dubious relaters . . . blind, astonished and struck with superstition as with a planet; in one word, Monks', and was prepared to stigmatize the works of Florence of Worcester, Henry of Huntingdon, and even Hoveden as 'volumes of rubbish' [John Milton, *History of Britain*]. Indeed, Daniel's freedom from the unintelligent Protestant bias of most of his contemporaries is one of his most valuable qualities as an historian. It may have been partly responsible for the rumour that he was *in animo catholicus.* Fuller [in *The Worthies of England,* 1662] rejects the suggestion that Daniel was an adherent of the 'old religion' and Sir Sidney Lee is doubtless right in dismissing it as 'worthless gossip' but, whatever the truth of the matter, it can be said in Daniel's favour that the nature of his ecclesiastical allegiance cannot be deduced from the pages of his ***History of England.***

Ecclesiastical affairs are, in the main, regarded by Daniel as outside the scope of his work and one cannot but regret his failure to use Bede and the scant attention paid to the conversion of the English. Yet his historical sense forces him to perceive that to omit such an episode as the Becket controversy would be to distort his picture of twelfth-century England. 'This businesse of the Church', he tells his readers,

> I haue the more particularly deliuered (according to the generall report of the Writers of that time) in regard it lay so chayned to the Temporall affaires of the State and bewrayed so much of the face of that Age with the constitution both of the Soueraignty and the rest of the body as it could not well bee omitted.

The Papacy comes in for its fair, but not more than its fair, share of criticism, directed chiefly against the rapacity of its agents in the thirteenth century. The Crusades are presented as a papal device to weaken opponents, particularly the Emperors, and Daniel sees the whole movement as infinitely wasteful, both spiritually and materially, and as productive of grave dangers to Christendom. Yet he deprecates a cynical view of the ordinary crusader's motives in taking the Cross. A more sceptical age may interpret these motives to be 'rather of Policy then Piety', but, in Daniel's opinion,

> it were since to thinke they disguised their ends or had other couerings for their designes then those through which they were seene; their spirits seeme to haue bin warmed with a Nobler flame.

In this last and most revealing sentence Daniel betrays his nostalgia for a world that has passed away. He is one of the few Elizabethans to write of the Middle Ages with a sense of loss.

In passing judgement on secular rulers Daniel accepts the political theories of his own age. Monarchy, bounded by law and intent on the preservation of internal peace, is the norm of good government; and it is interesting to find Henry II's action in securing the coronation of his son during his own lifetime stigmatized as an attempt to 'communicate the Crowne and make the common-wealth a Monster with two heads'. High qualities are demanded of the Prince. 'Deuotion and mercy' are 'the brightest Starres in the Spheare of Majesty'; the administration of justice is 'that Diuine and Almighty worke of Kings'. 'Quietnesse and generall content are the blessings of the State. Yet, if Daniel's ideals are high his sense of reality is also strong,

and the verdicts that he passed on the rulers of England have, for the most part, stood the test of time. Thus, of Henry I he writes:

> His gouernment in peace was such as rankes him in the list amongst our Kings of the fairest marke: holding the Kingdome so well ordered as during all his reigne, which was long, he had euer the least to do at home. . . .

Henry II was 'this mightie King of England, the greatest of all the Christian world in his time or that the Kingdome euer saw', but he met his match in Becket, for it was

> his ill Fortune to grapple with a man of that free resolution as made his sufferings his glory; had his ambition beyond this World; set vp his rest, not to yeelde to a King; was onely ingaged to his cause; had opinion and beleefe to take his part.

Richard I was, in Daniel's view, over-rated by his contemporaries, particularly by those ecclesiastics who wrote the history of his reign.

> This was the end of this Lyon-like King when he had reigned nine yeares and nine moneths; wherein hee exacted and consumed more of this Kingdome then all his predecessors . . . and yet lesse deserued then any, hauing neyther liued here, neither left behind him Monument of Piety or of any other publique worke or euer shewed loue or care to this Common-wealth but onely to get what hee could from it. Neuer had Prince more giuen with lesse adoe and lesse noyse than hee, The reason whereof was his vndertaking the Holy wars . . . that made the clergy, which might then doe all, to deny him nothing; and the people fed with the report of his miraculous valour . . . were brought to beare more then euer otherwise they would haue done.

John is seen as an unjust and violent ruler, not as the stout anti-papalist of Bale and Holinshed: but he is rightly credited with a wise and far-seeing policy in Ireland: the rumours about his excesses are regarded sceptically ('for the point of offering to forgoe the Christian faith we may in charity forbeare to make it a part of ours:'), and it is recognized that he was not without his supporters 'whose names are recorded in Mat. Par. and other Writers'. Henry III was a king 'lightly seduceable and neuer did good to the Kingdome, either in expelling or repressing enemies or amplifying the bounds thereof'. Admiration for Edward I is qualified in this good subject of King James I by reservations on the point of his Scottish policy such as are nowhere found in the sixteenth-century historians. Lengthy tribute is paid to the valour of the Scots. Edward I, for all his merits, remains guilty of having fomented something not far removed from civil war:

> A Prince of a generous spirit wherein the fire held out euen to the very last; borne and bred for action and Militarie affaires which he managed with great iudgement: euer wary and prouident for his own businesse: watchfull and eager to enlarge his power: and was more for the greatnesse of England then the quiet thereof. And this we may iustly say of him, that neuer King before or since shed so much Christian blood within this

Isle of Brittaine as this Christian warrior did in his time and was the cause of more in that following.

Edward II was one whose 'Nature agrees not with his Office', contrasting sadly with both his father and his son to whom for the first forty years of his reign 'Fortune neuer yet shewed her back, neuer was retrograde', but the 'last ten yeares present vs with a turning of the Beame, a declination from that height of glory'.

Few modern historians would find much to quarrel with in these judgements which afford striking evidence both of Daniel's eye for character and of his capacity for grasping the essentials of an historical situation.

Like Shakespeare and nearly all his contemporaries, Daniel regards civil discord as the deadliest evil that can befall a state. Stephen's reign is described as a period

> wherein wee are to haue no other representations but of reuolts, beseeging of Castles, surprizings, recouerings, losings againe, with great spoiles and destruction; in briefe, a most miserable face of a distracted State. . . .

From the tyrannical acts of King John there grew

> the beginning of a miserable breach betweene a King and his people, being both out of proportion and dis-joynted in those just Ligaments of Commaund and Obedience that should hold them together. . . .

So, too, on the delicate subject of the deposition of kings Daniel's opinion is soundly Elizabethan. Orleton's argument, before the deposition of Edward II, that when the kingdom has an aching head it should be removed, is condemned as

> a most execrable Doctrine and repugnant to the Sacred Word which in all corrupted times is euermore produced to abuse mens Credulity and iustifie Impiety in whatsoeuer Ambition or Malice shall attempt: a sinne beyond all other that can bee committed vpon earth.

Like so many of his generation, Daniel sees in this impious act of deposition the *fons et origo* of the Wars of the Roses. Edward III was not personally responsible for the deposition and does not suffer personally, but divine judgement works itself out in the reign of his grandson and in the century that follows:

> The deposing of foure kings and fiue vsurpations: which in the end so rent the State as all the glory of forraine greatnesse which that line brought, expired with it selfe.

—a theme which Daniel had already developed in his long poem on the Civil Wars between Lancaster and York.

Throughout the *History* runs a lively interest in law and justice. The importance of the great legal reforms of both Henry II and Edward I is clearly recognized and the measures for which they were responsible are carefully summarized. Daniel shares the pride of his generation in the antiquity of English Common Law while deploring its intricacies and obscurities and the use of Norman-French in the courts. For many years after the Norman Conquest

> Law . . . still held forraine and became in the ende wholly to be inclosed in that Language: nor haue we now other marke of our subiection and invassalage from Normandie but onely that, and that still speakes French to us in England.

Only law has the power to restrain the impulses of princes. Daniel, for all his respect for monarchy, is no advocate of newfangled theories of absolutism, and William Rufus, John, and Henry III are all alike censured for their attempts 'to breake out into the Wildnesse of their wills from those bounds wherein by the law of the State they are placed'.

Like all historians, Daniel makes his mistakes, but when he errs it is usually in good company. He follows Polydore Vergil and the majority of the Elizabethans in crediting William I with the institution of the office of Justice of the Peace and in regarding Henry I as the founder of parliamentary representation. The succession of popes is not altogether clear to him, though his worst blunder (Innocent IX for Innocent III) may be a printer's error. Failure to distinguish between the Old English *borh* and *burh* leads him astray on the origin of the borough as it had led Cowell before him. But, on the whole, he is accurate in detail; and his errors in interpretation are mainly the result of working in a pre-scientific age on limited materials.

Samuel Daniel came to the writing of history late in his life. In his youth and early maturity he had turned to poetry as the mode best suited to the expression of his emotions and ideas. This was natural enough in an age which gave a ready hearing even to the indifferent poet, and it may well have been the Elizabethan bias in favour of poetry which led Daniel to give a verse form to his first long historical essay on the Civil Wars between the Houses of Lancaster and York. For this poem Daniel had read much less widely than for the prose *History;* he seems to have relied mainly on the sixteenth-century historians, with a few references to Froissart and Walsingham. Though it contains many fine passages and much subtle analysis of historical problems, the *Civil Wars* was generally deemed a failure. In the well-known words of Drayton,

> . . . Some wise men him rehearse
> To be too much historian in verse;
> His rhymes were smooth, his metre well did
> close
> But yet his manner better fitted prose.
>   ["To Henry Reynolds, of Poets and Poesy."]

Whether or not he recognized the justice of such criticisms, Daniel decided to use prose for his general *History of England.* It was a wise decision; for the critic, Langbaine, was probably right in thinking that whatever his talent for poetry it was as a prose historian that he reached his greatest heights [Langbaine, *Dramatick Poets* 1691]. Yet his early apprenticeship to poetry stood him in good stead in his historical work. If so many years spent in the study and writing of verse meant that he was of necessity less well read in history than many of his contemporaries, it meant also that he was able to write with a discreet economy of words sadly wanting in the work of the great Tudor antiquaries. The study of poetry had quickened his imagination, stimulated his powers of reflection, and enabled him to set the details of his subject against a spacious background. Nor does it detract from the interest and value of his *History* that Daniel was so deeply infected with the poet's sense of the transitoriness of things. Edward I 'dyes at Borough vpon the Sands, as if to shew on what foundation hee had built all his glorie in this world'. Philip VI overtakes Edward III at 'a village called Arenes, a name remarkable (signifying the Sand) to shew on what vnstable earth all the trust of humaine forces and the designes of the great are founded.' The epilogue to Edward III's reign with which the published part of the *History* concludes affords a fair example of the dignity of this poet's handling of the historical theme:

> Thus haue we seene the end of this great King: who, how he came to the Crowne, we know and now how he left it wee see: In both are considerations of importance. His stepping ouer his Fathers head to come to his throne, though it were not his fault, yet had it a punishment and that in a most high kinde: For hauing so plentifull and so able an Issue Male, he had not yet a sonne of his owne to sit on his Seate; but left the same (worse than he found it) to a Childe of eleuen yeares of age, exposed to the Ambition of Vncles, which ouer weighed him: to a factious and discontented State at home: to broken and distracted inheritances abroad: Himselfe hauing seene all his great gettings, purchased with so much expence, trauaile and blood-shed, rent cleane from him and nothing remayning, but onely the poore Towne of Calais. To show that our Bounds are prescribed vs; and a Pillar set by Him who beares vp the Heauens, which we are not to transpasse.

Between the antiquaries, so large in appetite, so weak in digestion, and the playwrights for whom historical exactitude must necessarily be subordinated to the demands of the stage, there was room enough and to spare for a judicious interpreter of England's past, endowed with taste, imagination, and care for truth, for one who desired not only knowledge but also understanding of the history of his own country. It cannot be claimed for Daniel that he was a great historian. The circumstances of his age, the limitations of the material at his disposal, the inadequacy of his own scholarship, all made it inevitable that he should succeed only imperfectly in the difficult task he had set himself. But his achievement is impressive enough to earn him a more honourable place than has been accorded him in modern times among the pioneers of historical writing in England. (pp. 237-43)

> *May McKisack, "Samuel Daniel as Historian," in* The Review of English Studies, *Vol. XXIII, No. 91, July, 1947, pp. 226-43.*

Theodore Spencer   (essay date 1948)

[*A Harvard professor of literature and a poet in his own right, Spencer is the author of* Death and Elizabethan Tragedy *(1936) and the widely read* Shakespeare and the Nature of Man *(1942). His scholarly criticism ranges broadly from Chaucer, the Elizabethans, and Montaigne, to Yeats and T.S. Eliot. In the following ex-*

cerpt from an essay published in 1948, Spencer describes Daniel as "not a great poet" but a craftsman, and points to Delia *as evidence that Daniel was strongly influenced by the poetry of Sir Philip Sidney.*]

In his own day, Daniel's reputation was high, and from 1591 until his death at the age of 57 in 1619 he is continually referred to as one of the leading contemporary poets. He is "sweet, honey-dropping Daniell;" his rhymes "were smooth, his meters well did close;" he is a shepherd who "doth all afore him far surpasse." Sir John Davies, at the end of his *Orchestra* (1596), lists him, with Homer, Virgil, Chaucer, and Spenser as one of the poets whose qualities he envies:

> O that I could old Geoffrey's muse awake,
> Or borrow Colin's fair heroic style,
> Or smooth my rhymes with Delia's servant's
>   file.

Yet his contemporaries were not satisfied with him. He ought, they say, to have more self-confidence; smoothness, they imply, is not enough. His "trembling muse" should not be afraid to soar. "Then rouze thy feathers quickly, Daniell," says Spenser,

> And to what course thou please thyself advance;
> But most me seemes thy accent will excell
> In tragic plaints and passionate mischance.

Ben Jonson was more blunt. He told Drummond that Samuel Daniel "was a good honest man, had no children, but no poet." After Daniel's death he was not often read, and when Elizabethan poetry was being rediscovered at the end of the eighteenth century Gray condemned him by saying that in "all he has left us, there are two defects (perhaps of his nature) very conspicuous, the want of imagination, and the weakness of expression."

Daniel is not a great poet, but it would be unfair thus to take away from him the two characteristics without which he would not be a poet at all. His range of feeling may have been narrow and within its limits not very deep; his imagination may have swung too inertly in the hammock of its traditional themes; his diction may have fitted too glibly into the lull of a conventional incantation. Those faults are easily recognizable. But at its best Daniel's poetry is musical, serious, convincing. As a craftsman he is among the most careful of the Elizabethans. A. C. Sprague, in his well-chosen selection of Daniel's poems [Samuel Daniel, *Poems and a Defence of Ryme,* ed. A. C. Sprague, 1929], gives many interesting examples of Daniel's minute and painstaking revisions, of the labor (some of it misdirected) he expended throughout his life on making his lines as smooth and correct, according to his own strict canons, as possible. And when he had a congenial subject, this devoted attention to technique helped to produce poetry from which all poets may learn.

Daniel's poetic vein, not being very robust, gave out some years before his death; a lifetime of revision is not one of the signs of vitality. He is not one of those poets, like Dryden or Yeats, who go on developing. Daniel was a shrinking soul—"as the tortoise burieth herself all the winter in the ground, so Mr. Daniel would lie hid at his garden house in Old Street, near London, for some months together, the more retiredly to enjoy the company of the Muses"—he did not attack life, he accepted it, wailing gracefully over the speed of its passing. Both his poetry and his prose reflect a personality unassuming, charming, diffident, courteous. Daniel's age was an age of patrons; patrons need people to patronize; Daniel was a born patronee. He was emotionally at home in that role. Never servile, conventionally sensible, keeping his intellectual independence quite intact, he clearly liked to write from a position, and the position of a patronee was socially a parallel, in a conventional society, to the intellectual and emotional traditionalism which is to be found in his writing. Daniel's life and expression are all of a piece. The extremely dim figure of Delia that emerges (or fails to emerge) from his sonnets is that of a patroness, not a mistress. We feel that Daniel would have been profoundly embarrassed, even horrified, if his lady had ever succumbed to the suggestions his conventional words were continually urging upon her. It is not surprising that the melody of Daniel's poetry, its keyboard once tuned, never changed. His younger contemporaries had no effect on it; the innovations of Donne, of Marston, of the later dramatists, passed him by; Daniel's late pastoral play, *Hymen's Triumph* (1614), might have been written at the same time as the sonnets to Delia a quarter century before. The versification is as smooth, as musical, in one as in the other; the timbre of emotion is the same. Throughout his poetic career Daniel remained what under the Countess of Pembroke's patronage he had originally become: the disciple, in versification, of Sir Philip Sidney; in narrative poetry, of Ovid and Sackville; in drama, of the Countess herself.

Daniel came under the influence of the Sidney circle at an early age. In addressing his *Defence of Rhyme* to Sidney's nephew, William Herbert, Earl of Pembroke, he speaks of how he had been first "encouraged and framed" to versification by "your most worthy and honorable mother, receiving the first notion for the formal ordering of those compositions at Wilton, which I must ever acknowledge to have been my best school." The first time Daniel's poems were printed was when twenty-eight of his sonnets to Delia appeared as part of that "indiscretion of a greedy printer," the wretched first (pirated) edition of Sidney's *Astrophel and Stella* (1591). The whole collection of fifty, together with *The Complaint of Rosamund,* appeared the next year, dedicated to the Countess of Pembroke.

It is obvious at a glance that the author of *Delia* had studied Sidney with care; that great innovator and master of technique had a devoted pupil in his sister's protégé. The alternation between feminine and masculine rhymes in sonnets 6, 7, 8, the exclusive use of feminine rhymes in 26 and 27, are experiments based on similar ones throughout Sidney's work. The variation on the iambic pentameter in such lines as

> Paint on floods, till the shore, cry to the air . . .
> (Sonnet 9)

> Which cheers the world, joys each sight, sweetens the air . . .
> (*Rosamund,* 1, 133)

> Pleasure's plague, beauty's scourge, hell to the fair . . .

> (*Rosamund,* 1, 265)

is clearly in imitation of Sidney's experiments, as is the use of spondees in the familiar rhetorical figure at the end of sonnet 11:

> Yet will I weep, vow, pray, to cruel She;
> Flint, frost, disdain, wears, melts, and yields we see.

In this particular case the technique fails to produce poetry; and in fact a critical reader has difficulty in finding over a dozen of the Delia sonnets (though there are lovely single lines in more) which are worth preserving entire. The subject matter is everywhere conventional, frequently borrowed directly from the French or Italian, and there are only these relatively few occasions when the conventional thought and the carefully polished expression sing together; mostly there is either no sound, or a hollow one.

Spenser, trying to give Daniel encouragement, suggested that his accent might excel in "tragic plaints and passionate mischance." As usual with Spenser, the words are loose, but the general intention is correct: "tragic" and "passionate" are not appropriate adjectives for anything that Daniel could handle, but "plaints" and "mischance" describe the kind of subject matter he was at home with. The best of Daniel's sonnets are "plaints"; laments about his relation to Delia or objurgations to Delia to contemplate the universal subject of lament, the destructive passage of time. Perhaps the most characteristic of them is the forty-second, familiar in all the anthologies, but worth regarding again as illustrating a most happy marriage between technique and theme; the feminine ending in the second quatrain giving its delicate impetus to the incantation, the trochees substituted in five of the first feet gently rapping the rhetorical emphasis, the final couplet adding the break that is so effective as conclusion—all these things contributing to the melodious portrayal of the sad platitude it seems so consoling for the poet to contemplate.

> Beauty, sweet love, is like the morning dew,
> Whose short refresh upon the tender green,
> Cheers for a time but till the sun doth show,
> And straight 'tis gone as it had never been.
> Soon doth it fade that makes the fairest flourish,
> Short is the glory of the blushing rose;
> The hue which thou so carefully dost nourish
> Yet which at length thou must be forc'd to lose.
> When thou surcharg'd with burden of thy years,
> Shalt bend thy wrinkles homeward to the earth,
> When time hath made a passport for thy fears,
> Dated in age the Kalends of our death—
> But ah no more; this hath been often told,
> And women grieve to think they must be old.

This is Daniel's happiest tone. The drama that so frequently makes Sidney's sonnets active, the range and resonance of Shakespeare, are lacking, but within its limits Daniel's music—an andante for muted strings—is entirely successful ("Daniel's father was a master of music, and his harmonious mind made an impression on his son's genius"), producing a tranquil hypnosis which is one of the pleasures of such verse. Daniel is unsurpassed among the Elizabethans in the kind of poetry which is withdrawn from its emotional object and contemplates it reflectively from a distance. It is a kind of writing, to use Daniel's own words,

> Wherein no wild, no rude, no antic sport
> But tender passions, motions soft and grave,
> The still spectators must expect to have.

Daniel's emotional equipment was elegiac; elegiac is the mood of all the good sonnets; elegy is the essence of the old regretful sigh of the hopeless victims in the *Mirror for Magistrates* to which Daniel gave new music in the **Complaint of Rosamund.** Beauty contemplated in its inevitable change, the pathos of time and death, these are the subjects that move Daniel most, and produce the emotional overtones and twilight colors which he so gracefully controls:

> No April can revive thy with'red flowers,
> Whose blooming grace adorns thy glory now;
> Swift speedy Time, feath'red with flying hours,
> Dissolves the beauty of the fairest brow.
> O let not then such riches waste in vain,
> But love whilst that thou may'st be lov'd again.

It is, of course, among the oldest of poetic themes:

> Interea, dum fata sinunt, iungamus amores;
>   iam veniet tenebris Mors adoperta caput;
> iam subrepet iners aetas, nec amore decebit,
>   dicere nec cano blanditias capite.

Indeed Tibullus, who also addressed love poems to a Delia, is, with Ovid, one of the closest of the Latin poets to Daniel. His poetry has more concrete images than Daniel's, but it is equally melodious, equally tranquil, equally undramatic and resigned.

Daniel wrote much poetry in his thirties; his most ambitious attempt failed. In the early 1590's, under the patronage of Lady Pembroke and Fulke Greville, he was committed to being a professional poet; tradition and contemporary example (Tasso, Spenser, and others) demanded that he center his career around a big poem of public importance. Daniel's **Civil Wars,** in four books, was published in 1595; he added four more books later, but never finished the story. The artistic failure of the poem was not implicit in the subject, for the Wars of the Roses had recently given Shakespeare his first resounding success; Daniel failed for temperamental reasons. He loved history, and being conservative and traditional, he was happy in the past; in this one respect his subject was congenial and its choice auspicious. But to feel moved by the fact that history has occurred is not the same thing as being able, like Shakespeare, to describe it, movingly and actively, as occurring. Furthermore, the training Daniel had given himself as an imitator of the *Mirror for Magistrates*—the training toward which his temperament directed him—was also bad for a writer who had fixed on a subject demanding an active narrative rather than a lament. Daniel's deficiencies outweighed his advantage; he could not describe action, he could not dramatize. He never lifted his subject from the ground. One of his contemporaries complained that he was "too much Historian in verse." "Daniel wrote *Civil Wars,*" said Ben Jonson, "and yet hath not one battle in his book." The judgment is harsh but sound.

Daniel returned to history at the end of his life, but by then he had given up trying to make poetry of it; the **Collection of the History of England,** written under the patronage of Queen Anne, "under her roof," is in prose. He also, at various times in his life, tried the drama, but, as might be expected, his drama fits the closet not the stage: **Cleopatra, Philotas, The Queen's Arcadia,** and **Hymen's Triumph** are highly neoclassical performances, the first two very strictly Senecan, and though some of them were acted, they have little dramatic vitality. They belong to a backwater, they are not part of the main current of Elizabethan drama.

But they are not to be ignored. **Cleopatra,** the earliest (written under the patronage of the Countess of Pembroke in 1593 as a companion piece to her *Antony*), is also the best; its design is well adapted to the mood in which Daniel is poetically most at home. The action takes place after Antony's death, and consists of a series of graceful, polished, and mostly static laments and narratives; Cleopatra bewails the loss of Antony, Rodon and Seleucus bewail their betrayal of Cleopatra, the messenger narrates Cleopatra's lamentable death. Everyone speaks in heroic quatrains, and the five acts are divided by choruses, in shorter lines, commenting on the situation and drawing moral lessons out of it. It sounds archaic and cold, so described, and compared with Shakespeare's Titian-like dash and splendor it is indeed a pale little water color of a piece. But its design is clean and its colors pure; there is nothing to be ashamed of in **Cleopatra,** and much that is genuinely pleasurable. There are many passages which sound with eloquence Daniel's familiar note of lament over the passing of time and love; the following lines spoken by Philostratus (3, 1) over the decline of Egypt offer an example:

> O thou and I have heard, and read, and known
> Of like proud states, as woefully encumber'd,
> And fram'd by them, examples for our own:
> Which now among examples must be number'd.
> For this decree a law from high is given,
> An ancient canon of eternal date,
> In consistory of the stars of Heaven,
> Enter'd the book of unavoided Fate;
> That no state can in height of happiness
> In th'exaltation of her glory stand;
> But thither once arriv'd, declining less,
> Ruin themselves, or fall by others' hand . . .
> When yet ourselves must be the cause we fall,
> Although the same be first decreed on high;
> Our errors still must bear the blame of all;
> This must it be; earth, ask not heaven why.

The quatrains, at first sight so apparently hopeless a medium for dramatic declamation, turn out to be not so inappropriate after all. Their stiffness gives a formal dignity to the sentiment, and the highly starched puppets that speak them are seen to move in a somewhat human way so that we share their lament and respond to their music.

Conservative, traditional, diffident, always with a patron (or more often a patroness) to hold on to—a donlike spirit, timorous and slow—Daniel, especially if we think of Marlowe or Donne, is apparently the reverse of a typical Elizabethan. But when we look beneath the surface this seems less true: in one sense Daniel's traditionalism is actually more typical than either Marlowe's range or the probing of Donne. Both in thought and technique Daniel's best work represents a tradition, a lowest common denominator, a norm, which acts as a basis for higher and deeper excursions than a poet like Daniel can manage himself, but which needs to be maintained if such excursions are not to go crazy. When Daniel reflects about life, he expresses those neo-stoic platitudes that underlie all Elizabethan thought about human wisdom, which everyone kept referring to and coming back to and relying on, and expresses them in a style whose quiet sway underlies all Elizabethan poetic technique. He is classical in both content and form. He is at his best in such a poem as the consolatory epistle to the Countess of Cumberland, where none of the advice is new—Cicero, Seneca, and the horde of their sixteenth-century imitators in consolation had all given it before—but where the expression is so purified to limpidity, and the rhythm in such perfect harmony with the sense, that something new is made. It begins:

> He that of such a height hath built his mind,
> And rear'd the dwelling of his thoughts so
>   strong
> As neither Fear nor Hope can shake the frame
> Of his resolved powers, nor all the wind
> Of vanity and malice pierce to wrong
> His settled peace, or to disturb the same,
> What a fair seat hath he from whence he may
> The boundless wastes and wilds of man survey!

The familiar theme continues—the exaltation of the remote ataraxic ideal which to so many sixteenth-century minds seemed more congenial than the Christianity which had once supplanted it:

> And whilst distraught ambition compasses
> And is encompass'd, whilst as craft deceives
> And is deceiv'd, whilst man doth ransack man
> And builds on blood, and rises by distress,
> And th'inheritance of desolation leaves
> To great expecting hopes, he looks thereon
> As from the shores of peace with unwet eye
> And bears no venture in impiety.

Indeed, as we read a poem like this, as we read all of Daniel's best work, we think of him not merely as an Elizabethan classicist, but as a classicist in terms of English literature as a whole. In a sense he is the typical English poet: "his diction," said Coleridge, "is pre-eminently pure—of that quality which I believe has always existed somewhere in society." And what is true of his diction is true of his rhythm and his tone: the union of native Anglo-Saxon melancholy with Latin sonority, a mood of gentle reflec-

tion, of pathos not tragedy, which is like a kind of pedal point sustained throughout English poetry, finds a most lucid, perhaps its most unadulterated, expression in him. His style can be felt as the ground swell of English poetry, the movement that is always there, by him never tossed to tempests as by others, but to the rhythm of which, in calm moments, like him they congenitally swing.

In illustration we may choose a few single lines almost at random:

> The wailing Iliads of my tragic woe . . .
> And all the marvel of the golden skies . . .
> Those titles vanish and that strength decay . . .
> The guilty goddess of my harmful deeds . . .
> The famous warriors of the antique world . . .
> O clear-eyed rector of the holy-hill . . .

The first and the last of these lines are by Daniel; the others, respectively, are by Arnold, Wordsworth, Shakespeare and Spenser.

A poet like Daniel is at his best when writing about generalities, and his chief danger is that his work may become, in off moments, toothless from abstraction. The "plaints" which emotionally attract him may produce a boneless lamenting, the final impression of his work be that of remoteness from life. But at his best Daniel avoids these dangers, and it would be false to think of him as a poet who merely repeats, in a polished style, commonplaces that are mostly sad or negative. On one subject he is far from negative, the subject which his patronee's life gave him the needed leisure to devote himself to, the practice of his art. When Campion attacked his art of rhyming, Daniel immediately wrote his famous and admirable defense of it, beginning with words that draw an accurate self-portrait:

> And though irresolution and a self-distrust be
> the most apparent faults of my nature, and that
> the least check of reprehension, if it savor of rea-
> son, will as easily shake my resolution as any
> man's living; yet in this case, I know not how,
> I am grown more resolved, and before I sink,
> willing to examine what those powers of judg-
> ment are, that must bear me down, and beat me
> off from the station of my profession, which by
> the law of nature I am set to defend.

It is characteristic of Daniel's devotion to his craft that he should use such a strong expression as "the law of nature" in referring to it. He speaks with equal strength in *Musophilus:* even if what he writes should not please a single reader, that fact, he says,

> cannot undo
> The love I bear unto this holy skill;
> This is the thing that I was born to do,
> This is my Scene, this part I must fulfill.

And because so devoted a conviction runs through the poem, it has a much more positive energy than his other writings, an energy which justifies our calling it his masterpiece. Nor is the poem merely an eloquent personal credo; it helps document, to our admiration, the mind of the English Renaissance.

Musophilus, Containing a General Defense of All Learn-

ing, is a one-sided dialogue of more than 1,000 lines between Philocosmos, the lover of the world, and Musophilus, the lover of the Muses (Daniel), who does most of the talking. Philocosmos argues that it is a waste of time to practice "ungainful art," since people are too busy to pay attention to it, fame is an illusion, and it is wiser not to be odd but to do as other men do; man is made for action and if poetry is to be written at all, it should be a spur to worthy deeds. To this, the hero of the poem replies (as the contemplative man has always replied to such arguments) that it is the time's fault if his song is unseasonable, that he, not his opponent, is on the side of true being, and—in a memorable phrase—

> if I may attain but to redeem
> My name from dissolution and the grave,
> I shall have done enough, and better deem
> T'have liv'd to be, than to have died to have.

The rest of Daniel's long discourse is a series of variations on this and similar traditional themes, ending with an admirable invocation to the

> Power above powers, O heavenly Eloquence,

whose mother is poetry, whose subject is knowledge, the soul of the world, and who, flourishing now in northern climates, may in time go further still:

> And who in time knows whither we may vent
> The treasure of our tongue, to what strange shores
> This gain of our best glory shall be sent
> T'enrich unknowing nations with our stores?
> What worlds in the yet unformed Occident
> May come refin'd with th'accents that are ours?
> Or who can tell for what great work in hand
> The greatness of our style is now ordain'd?

The poem ends with an address to Fulke Greville, who had calmed Daniel's doubts as to whether it was proper to argue ("discourse") in poetry, and whose "mild grace and gentle hand" first made Daniel's infant muse "partaker of the light."

Musophilus has many obvious faults: it is uneven, too long, too rambling, and too bare of images. The problem of versified argument is by no means satisfactorily solved, for sometimes the demands of the argument deaden the verse and sometimes the demands of the verse obscure the argument. Compared to other examples of versified rationalization, compared to the rationalistic poetry of Pope or even to that of Sir John Davies, *Musophilus,* as far as the presentation of ideas is concerned, is the work of an untrained mind. The sequence of thinking is not very logical, and there are some long passages during which Daniel seems to be pushing his subject ahead of him with a perfunctory hand. But these are outweighed by the passages that succeed—by no means always spoken by Musophilus himself. An Elizabethan, even so retiring an Elizabethan as Daniel, was bound to feel that the claims of the life of action, disputing the worth or possibility of literary fame, had a strong case against the claims of the contemplative life, arguing the worth of art and the assurance of literary immortality. The lamenting side of Daniel's temperament, his gift for nostalgically deploring, could make him as elo-

quent in putting forth the first set of claims as his positive devotion to his art could make him eloquent in opposing them, and the lines given to Philocosmos are among the best written in the poem. But the positive affirmation is in the long run the most poetically successful, not merely because Daniel's *mind* wanted it to be so, but because the conviction which made his life so devoted, urged the want.

And yet (and this is perhaps the reason why eloquence informs both sides of the argument) the conflict between the two views of man's good is basically an artificial one, and to take Daniel at his ostensible word and treat it as if it were real, is actually to falsify the poem; the opposition is not so real as it seems. The recording of action for remembrance, as both disputants agree, is itself one of the noblest forms of action, just as Daniel's own retirement from the life of action was itself a positive act. And though this act did not produce, in the *Civil Wars,* a successful example of what Philocosmos says he wants from poetry—the singing of "great heroical deserts / Of brave renowned spirits" as "models for posterities"—it did produce, in *Musophilus,* a generalized statement, expressed in Daniel's finest classical style, of the humanistic union between thought and deed which Daniel's first poetic master, Sidney, so nobly exemplified and which is at the heart of Renaissance belief:

> Soul of the world, knowledge, without thee,
> What hath the earth that truly glorious is?
> Why should our pride make such a stir to be,
> To be forgot? What good is like to this,
> To do worthy the writing, and to write
> Worthy the reading, and the world's delight?
>
> (pp. 100-12)

Theodore Spencer, "Two Classic Elizabethans: Samuel Daniel and Sir John Davies," in his Selected Essays, *edited by Alan C. Purves, Rutgers University Press, 1966, pp. 100-22.*

E. M. W. Tillyard   (essay date 1954)

[*A Cambridge scholar of Renaissance literature, Tillyard produced major studies of Milton and of Shakespeare's plays, as well as the highly influential essay* The Elizabethan World Picture *(1943). His debate with C.S. Lewis about the value of a writer's work as a key to his psychological state was published in 1939 as* The Personal Heresy: A Controversy. *In the following excerpt, Tillyard perceives a common political philosophy in Daniel's* The Civile Wares *and Shakespeare's history plays.*]

In calling his *Civil Wars* 'my Homer-Lucan', Daniel implied a double truth. Spenser wanted to be looked on as the English Virgil, and in some ways he was. But the form of his epic was anything but Virgilian. Poetically Daniel may have less right to invoke comparison with the classical epics but in the matter of form he is their first true imitator in English. And this makes him a landmark in the history of the English epic. Further, he is a sincere classiciser. While the dullness of *Gorbuduc* is due partly to its conscientious imitation of Senecan tragedy, any dullness in the *Civil Wars* is unconnected with its neo-classicism. On the contrary, Daniel thrives on his care to construct

neatly and economically and to maintain an austere rhetoric. To imitate the classical epic is for him an inspiration.
Although as much an Elizabethan as Spenser and Shakespeare, he genuinely looks forward to May and Cowley
and to the neo-classic side among all the many sides of
Milton, and in doing so he showed himself a poet of uncommon resolution and initiative.

The second truth contained in his Homer-Lucan claim
will take longer to set forth. Though the theme of civil war
occupies most of the poem's contents, it was not the final
theme, while the ethical temper went beyond Lucan's stoical resistance in a world of despair. Through the contrast
with the Wars of the Roses Daniel intended to make the
peace of the Tudors more striking. The Homeric analogy
pointing to this intention is not too obvious, but Daniel
may have been thinking of the reconciliation at the end of
the *Odyssey*. Anyhow, through mentioning Homer Daniel
rightly claims to go beyond Lucan's narrow ethical temper. Unfortunately the claim is not fully verifiable, for
Daniel wrote only eight out of his projected twelve books:
but he leaves us in no doubt that he would have celebrated
the peace of the Tudors. After beginning with the words
'I sing the Civil Wars' and deploring the madness of Englishmen in earlier days, he writes as follows in his third
stanza:

> Yet now what reason have we to complain,
> Since hereby came the calm we did enjoy,
> The bliss of thee, *Eliza?* Happy gain
> For all our losses; when as no other way
> The Heav'ns could find, but to unite again
> The fatal sever'd families, that they
> Might bring forth thee: That in thy peace might
>   grow
> That Glory, which few times could ever show.

At the end of the second book, which deals with Bolingbroke's triumph over Richard II, there occurred in the
original edition (1595) a picture of what England's fate
might have been had Bolingbroke's genius been given a
virtuous outlet. Civil war would have been averted; England would have dominated western Europe; and even
now the Earl of Essex might have been leading an expedition against the Turk. Naturally the passage had to be cut
after the fall of Essex, but it shows that Daniel while describing the wars of the Roses had his eye all the time on
the present too. Near the beginning of Book Six there is
the strange and powerful episode where Nemesis, seeing
and envying the prosperity of a Europe divided into many
small states and afflicted only by small, domestic, quarrels,
prompts the invention of printing and artillery. Through
the first, seditious doctrines are easily spread; through the
second, war becomes more horrible. With these inventions
Daniel associates the climax of English civil wars in the
breach between York and Lancaster. But Nemesis, who
describes these happenings in a speech, ends with the accession of the Tudors. England will in the end recover and
be able to look back on her past sorrows as if they were
a play. (pp. 322-23)

Finally, in his Epistle Dedicatory to his second edition
(1609) of the ***Civil Wars,*** enlarged now from four to eight
books, Daniel writes of his plan for the complete poem.
It is:

Title page with portrait of Daniel from the 1609 edition of his Civil
Wars; *engraved by T. Cockson.*

To show the Deformities of Civil Dissension,
and the miserable events of rebellious Conspiracies and bloody Revengements which followed
(as in a Circle) upon that Breach of the due
Course of Succession by the usurpation of Henry
iv; and thereby to make the blessings of peace
and the happiness of an established government
in a direct line the better to appear. I trust I shall
do a grateful work to my country to continue the
same unto the glorious Union of Henry vii, from
whence is descended our present Happiness.

It is clear therefore that if he had finished his poem Daniel
would have celebrated the Tudors as well as presented the
Wars of the Roses.

That Daniel discriminated between the methods of Lucan
and of Homer in the way I have indicated, making one
poet stand for the tragic happenings to be shunned and the
other for the deeds to be emulated, appears from a fine and
interesting passage at the beginning of the fifth book. He
has come to the accession of Henry V, but he has clearly
decided not to interrupt the course of England's decline
by a full narrative of Henry's victories. So he pictures the
ghost of Henry appearing to him and chiding him fiercely
for failing to do justice to his deeds and, incidentally, for
omitting one half of the epic function. Speaking of the
great deeds of himself and his officers, Henry said:

What everlasting matter here is found,
Whence new immortall *Iliads* might proceed!
That those, whose happie graces do abound
In blessed accents, here may have to feed
Good thoughts; on no imaginarie ground
Of hungry shadowes, which no profite breed;
Whence, musick-like, instant delight may
   growe;
Yet when men all do knowe, they nothing
   knowe.

And why dost thou, in lamentable verse,
Nothing but blood-shed, treasons, sinne and
   shame,
The worst of times, th'extreame of ills, rehearse;
To rayse old staynes, and to renew dead blame?
As if the mindes of th'evill and perverse,
Were not farre sooner trained from the same,
By good example of faire vertuous acts,
Then by the shew of foul ungodly facts.

Daniel here confesses that he knows that he has been a
Lucan rather than a Homer and that he intends to omit
the present excellent chance of fulfilling the prime epic
function (according to Renaissance theory) of instructing
through the example of heroic deeds. And this confession
should strengthen our opinion that Daniel intended to
make good his deficiency elsewhere.

I have spent so long over Daniel's intention to praise the
Tudor settlement because without it his claim to be Hall's
successor and the nearest analogy to the Shakespeare of
the Histories would be much less cogent. Granted that intention, Daniel's *Civil Wars* is the most successful rendering in narrative of the theme of Hall, since 1588 once more
relevant, if in somewhat different guise, as the true epic
theme of the age.

To a modern reader one of the chief interests of Daniel's
Civil Wars is that its subject matter and its political temper are close to the great cycle of Shakespeare's History
Plays. Both poets begin with the prosperity of Edward III
with his seven sons; both make the murder of Woodstock
a prominent cause of Richard II's misfortunes: both make
Bolingbroke's usurpation and disposal of Richard the supreme crime that only the full horrors of civil war could
expiate; both make Margaret of Anjou, wife of Henry VI,
a dominant character but England's evil genius; both
make the death of the Talbots prominent; both make the
Battle of Towton the culminating horror of the Wars of
the Roses, with Henry watching it from a little hill. Daniel
broke off at a point corresponding to the middle of *Henry
VI, Part 3,* the point where Warwick, indignant with Edward IV for withdrawing from the French match he had
gone to France to negotiate, changed his allegiance to
Lancaster from York. There is no doubt that if he had finished his poem Daniel would have treated events up to the
Battle of Bosworth much as Shakespeare did.

Common to Shakespeare and Daniel is a solemn political
philosophy. It is a philosophy, much like that of Aeschy-
lus, of the visiting of a crime on future generations but
with the hope of ultimate expiation. The whole cycle of
events from Richard II to Henry VII is a classic and awe-
inspiring illustration of the process. Daniel, a more academic poet than Shakespeare, is naturally more definite

and explicit; and partly because he supplemented poetry
by history. His unfinished *History of England,* extending
from where history as against myth begins, and ending
with the death of Edward III, is a useful gloss on the *Civil
Wars.* In it Daniel claims no originality of matter, but admits that he draws general conclusions from known fact;
as he says in his preface "To the Reader,"

> For the Worke it selfe, I can Challenge nothing
> therein but onely the sowing it together, and the
> observation of those necessary circumstances,
> and inferences which the History naturally min-
> isters.

There is no need to read all history for general truths: a
sample will serve, because

> We shall finde still the same correspondencies to
> hold in the actions of men: Vertues and Vices the
> same, though rising and falling, according to the
> worth or weaknesse of Governors: the causes of
> the ruines, and mutations of States to be alike.

And when he comes to the end of his book he writes a
paragraph that sets forth not only his philosophic conception of history but the historical position from which the
events described in the *Civil Wars* took off:

> Thus have we seene the end of this great *King:*
> who, how he came to the Crowne, we know, and
> now how he left it we see: In both are consider-
> ations of importance. His stepping over his Fa-
> thers head to come to his throne, though it were
> not his fault, yet had it a punishment, and that
> in a most high kinde: For, having so plentifull,
> and so able an Issue Male, he had not yet a sonne
> of his owne to sit on his Seate; but left the same
> (worse then he found it) to a Childe of eleven
> yeares of age, exposed to the Ambition of Un-
> cles, which over weighed him to a factious and
> discontented State at home: To broken and dis-
> tracted inheritances abroad: Himselfe having
> seene all his great gettings, purchased with so
> much expence, travaile and blood-shed, rent cl-
> eane from him, and nothing remayning, but
> onely the poore Towne of *Calais.* To show that
> our Bounds are prescribed us; and a pillar set by
> him who beares up the Heavens, which we are
> not to trespasse.

Such was the ordinance of heaven: though Edward III was
a fine king in every way with a wife to match and sons of
the lucky number of seven, his initial irregularity could
not escape divine vigilance, although we may think that
it could have been expiated with comparative ease. Unex-
piated it led to crimes vastly greater. In the *Civil Wars*
Daniel enunciates this same great principle as a prelude
to the reign of Henry VI (as Shakespeare had implied it
through Henry V's prayer on the eve of Agincourt that
God should suspend vengeance for his father's crime).
There were various reasons why things should have gone
wrong in the reign of Henry VI: but the profoundest reason was

> the now ripe Wrath (deferd till now)
> Of that sure and unfayling *Justicer,*
> That never suffers wrong so long to growe,
> And to incorporate with right so farre,

As it might come to seeme the same in showe,
(T'incourage those that evill minded are
By such successe) but that at last he will
Confound the branch, whose root was planted
    ill.

Else, might the impious say, with grudging
    spight,
Doth God permit the Great to riot free,
And bless the mightie though they do unright,
As if he did unto their wrongs agree?
And only plague the weake and wretched wight,
For smallest faults, ev'n in the high'st degree?
When he, but using them for others scourge,
Likewise of them at length the world doth purge.

Whether Daniel would have resembled Shakespeare in making Richard III the scapegoat of the accumulated sins of both parties we cannot say, but the probabilities are that he would. Some expiation he finds in the innocent sufferings of Henry VI; but plainly more is needed before Lancaster and York can be united, and Richard III offered the obvious motive. But it is not the details that matter but the steady and coherent moral that runs through the whole of Daniel's poem and unites him to Shakespeare as to no other contemporary poet.

Daniel then had a great and living theme; the question remains what he made of it. Much more, I think, than is commonly allowed. Readers have praised Daniel for his smaller poems and his *Defence of Ryme;* scarcely anyone has a good word for the *Civil Wars.* Its most distinguished advocate was Coleridge, who wrote a letter to Lamb on it in Lamb's own copy of Daniel. After his exhortation to Lamb to acquire the right mood for the *Civil Wars* NB‡. . . ,Coleridge went on:

> Gravely sober on all ordinary affairs, and not easily excited by any, yet there is one on which his blood boils—whenever he speaks of English valour exerted against a foreign enemy. . . . He must not be read piecemeal;—even by leaving off and looking at a stanza by itself, I find the loss. . . . Thousands even of educated men would become more sensible, fitter to be members of parliament, or ministers, by reading Daniel; and even those few who, *quoad intellectum,* only gain refreshment of notions already their own, must become better Englishmen.

I do not think Coleridge right in suggesting that the only subject that fired Daniel was 'English valour exerted against a foreign enemy', for much of his political moralising is impassioned. But he makes one essential point which other writers on Daniel fail to make or deny: 'he must not be read piecemeal'. He did grasp that the *Civil Wars* is a continuity and not a compilation. It is for this reason that it must be seriously considered as an epic.

In a martial poem, such as the *Civil Wars* professes to be, readers naturally expect some kind of pattern to be made out of the fighting. Tasso had constructed his *Jerusalem Delivered* in this way. It was Daniel's failure to do this that is at the bottom of his contemporaries' doubts of his success as an epic writer. He was considered too much of a historian and too little of a poet. Ben Jonson went further and complained that there was not a battle in the book.

Literally he was wrong—Daniel includes more battles than Shakespeare—but impressionally he was right. The active, heroic side leaves no impression. But this does not mean that there are not impressions, and powerful ones, of another kind. Daniel is a reflective poet, who is above rather than in the battle, and he is powerfully aware of the great processes of which the battles are the expression. And if we follow our author and not our expectations of what a poet writing on an exceptionally active period of history ought to be doing, we shall find that Daniel had some definite and comprehensive things to say.

Now the 'processes' of which I have just spoken are of two different kinds. There are the great processes of mind through which the actors come to do what they do. It is in these two types of process that Daniel's interest lies.

Of some of God's processes as conceived by Daniel I have just written in course of comparing him with Shakespeare. But Daniel's conception included more than Shakespeare, with his power of presenting action at close quarters, found convenient. In the first place it took more of the world and more of history into its ken. This enlarged vision is found outside the poetry. Take that splendid section of his *Defence of Ryme* where he begins by protesting that 'all our understandings are not to be built by the square of *Greece* and *Italie*'. Whatever the use men have made of them, God distributed potentialities for good or ill evenly to the different ages. It is thus vain to exalt one age to the exclusion of another:

> The distribution of giftes are universall, and all seasons hath them in some sort. We must not thinke, but that there were Scipioes, Caesars, Catoes and Pompeies, borne elsewhere then at *Rome,* the rest of the world hath ever had them in the same degree of nature, though not of state.

Moreover, we must judge the quality of ages not on the narrower ground of articulateness but on the wider ground of successful government:

> It is not the contexture of words, but the effects of Action that gives glory to the times: we finde they had *mercurium in pectore* though not in *lingua,* and in all ages, though they were not Ciceronians, they knew the Art of men, which onely is, *Ars Artium,* the great gift of heaven, and the chiefe grace and glory on earth; they had the learning of Government, and ordring their State, Eloquence inough to shew their judgements.

Through this wider rule of humanity instead of the narrower one of culture Daniel had an unprejudiced view of history rare in his time. It led him to defend the Middle Ages and to allow some qualities to the barbarian conquerors of the Roman Empire. It is a view remarkably commanding and philosophic, in itself propitious to the epic reach. Coming to the providential principle governing actions of men upon this uncommonly capacious stage, Daniel puts the decisive weight on the soundness of the beginning. If the foundations are good, if the core is sound, great results will follow. Contrariwise, if the core is unsound, no amount of added virtue or wisdom will secure them. The Roman Republic was well founded, with the result not only that it achieved great things but that the

Roman state lasted in spite of the many abuses that should have caused its ruin. The opposite case has already been illustrated from the *History of England.* Edward III succeeded to the throne of England in a not completely lawful manner; and, though he had every virtue and achieved great things, his prosperity could not last. His achievements were neutralised by the time of his death, and a boy-king was his successor.

Both this comprehensive vision and this ruling principle of history, set forth in the *Defence of Ryme,* appear in the *Civil Wars.*

In his History Plays Shakespeare related the stretch of English history he chose for his great cycle to the current philosophy of order or 'degree'. He did not relate it (and in the drama why should he?) to any theory of world history. Within this stretch, however, he did, to my thinking, indicate his sense of the differences between the more formal and ceremonious England of the Middle Ages and the England of his own day. Daniel too is aware of the brilliance of medieval England, but unlike Shakespeare he reveals a conception of medieval history far wider than his insular subject strictly demanded, just as he divagated from tragic fact by conjecturing the course of world events had Bolingbroke used his great powers in a righteous cause. (I mentioned this divagation above, and I must add here that it included the notion that Spain would not have become an imperial power but have remained in provincial Castilian tranquillity.) Daniel's conception of medieval history comes in a striking episode at the beginning of the sixth book. The political situation at this point is the beginning of Yorkist action. York for the first time has raised an army. He has taken it to London, halts outside the city on the Kent side, 'and there, intrenched, plants his Artillery'. And the mention of artillery causes him to embark on his episode by pondering on medieval Europe before this dreadful invention:

> It was a time when fair *Europa* sate
> With many goodlie Diadems addrest
> And all her parts in flourishing estate
> Lay beautiful, in order, at their rest:
> No swelling member, unproportionate,
> Crowne out of forme, sought to disturbe the rest:
> The less subsisting by the greaters might;
> The greater, by the lesser kept upright.

For greater emphasis Daniel added this footnote:

> The principal Part of *Europe,* which contain'd the most flourishing State of *Christendom,* was at this time in the Hands of many several Princes and Commonwealths, which quietly governed the same: For being so many, and none over-great, they were less attemptive to disturb others, and more careful to keep their own, with a mutual Correspondence of Amity. As *Italy* had then many more Principalities and Commonwealths than it hath. *Spain* was divided into many Kingdoms: France consisted of divers Free Princes, Both the Germanies, of many more Governments.

There may have been minor broils, but 'no eruption did in general Break down their rest with universal sin'. Seeing this prolonged peace, fierce Nemesis, 'word-bearer of

th'eternal Providence', who had been busy afflicting the Christians of Asia with the incursions of 'foul impious Barbarism', turns her attention to the West. She calls Pandora to her aid, knowing that mankind can be tricked and made to suffer by the offer of gifts. Her account of the pious and innocent peace of western Europe is remarkable:

> Devotion (mother of Obedience)
> beares such a hand on their credulitie,
> That it abates the spirit of eminence,
> And busies them with humble pietie,
> For, see what workes, what infinite expence,
> What monuments of zeale they edifie;
> As if they would, so that no stop were found
> Fill all with Temples, make all holy ground.

Pandora is to break the peace of these simple, pious cathedral-builders by the old temptation of enlarged knowledge; she is indeed Eve tempting Adam, as well as Pandora bearing her box with its fatal gifts to mankind. And the new knowledge is of the two arts of printing and artillery. Both arts, by giving power to base men, upset the soundness of the old hierarchy. Printing is an art,

> Whereby all quarrels, titles, secrecies,
> May unto all be presently made knowne;
> Factions prepar'd, parties allur'd to rise;
> Seditions under faire pretensions sowne;
> Whereby, the vulgar may become so wise,
> That (with a self-presumption over-growne)
> They may of deepest mysteries debate,
> Controule their betters, censure actes of State.

And artillery is the means of making the confusion wrought by printing more horrible and more extensive,

> For by this stratagem, they shall confound
> All th'antient forme and discipline of Warre:
> Alter their Camps, alter their fights, their
>   ground,
> Daunt mighty spirits, prowesse and manhood
>   marre:
> For, basest cowards from a far shall wound
> The most couragious, forc't to fight a farre;
> Valour wrapt up in smoake (as in the night)
> Shall perish without witnesse, without sight.

In preparation for the mischief to be spread by the two inventions Nemesis orders Pandora (but without indicating by what means) to upset the existing balance of large and small states in western Europe and to make great states swallow up the lesser. Then let her breed factions in the 'Fairest Land', that is, England. When these things have been done, printing and artillery will be able to produce a general chaos.

Obviously we must not inquire too nearly into Daniel's version of the facts of history. The relevant and remarkable thing is that he sets the Wars of the Roses into a large context: that of western Europe and Byzantium at one end and the wars of religion at the other, for the chaos to which the Wars of the Roses are prelude can only be that which prevailed in parts of Europe in the sixteenth century.

It is in the course of this enlarged picture of history that Daniel presents an enlarged picture of God's way with nations: something that goes beyond the Aeschylean scheme of the Wars of the Roses, common to himself and Shakespeare. It is that in this world God cannot allow perpetual prosperity. The Nemesis that upset the simple life and the virtuous pieties of the earlier Middle Ages was God's agent. It may be true that the Roman state, founded honestly, was allowed a long span; but even so there is a tragic and unalterable law of necessary change. The reason for this (though Daniel does not state it) would surely have been that the condition of earth must not be allowed to compete with that of heaven, for that would upset God's order and scheme. Whether in making Nemesis God's agent Daniel meant that men would always discover the reasons for their own decline from prosperity or whether he conceived her as an interposition of God is not clear, nor need the question be decided. All that matters here is that Daniel showed a conception of God's processes remarkably comprehensive for a poet of his day.

I come now to the other 'process' in which Daniel was interested: that of men's minds on the way to action. It will be recalled that in the passages quoted from the *Defence of Ryme* Daniel referred to the unknown Scipios and Caesars of the inarticulate nations and how, though they wee not Ciceronians, they knew 'the Art of men, which onely is *Ars Artium*'. In his *Civil Wars* he seeks to demonstrate this art of men by describing less their actions than their motives for action; and his literary eminence consists mainly of this demonstration. Indeed, the only way to read Daniel aright is to agree with the spirit of Ben Jonson's pronouncement that there is not a battle in the book, and to expect the high places not in the acts themselves but in the preparation for them. A good example of Daniel's interest and of his method occurs in the third book: the conspiracy of the Abbot of Westminster, Surrey, Exeter, and others. He lets us know he sets store by the episode because he invokes the Muse at its beginning. Richard II is now a prisoner and the conspirators plan to murder Henry IV and restore Richard to the throne. The Abbot invites the likely men to a feast ('For when Men will have fed, th'Blood being warm / Then are they most improvident of Harm') and makes an equivocal speech, feeling his way.

> This open-close, apparent-dark discourse,
> Drew on much speech: and everie man replies:
> And every mad addes heate: and words enforce,
> And urge out wordes. For, when one man espies
> Anothers mind like his, then ill breedes worse:
> And out breaks all in the'end what closest lies.

The conspirators become clamorous, and one vows himself ready to kill Henry. Then they plan a concerted scheme to kill him at a masque and take an oath of secrecy. There is, however, one of the band who is more cautious and perceptive, Sir Thomas Blount. He wants the rest to realise what they are in for, and recounts the dangers before and after the deed. He does not want to back out, though he would have preferred open war. He is committed, and the great thing now is success.

> This sayd, a sad still silence held their mindes,
> Upon the fearful project of their woe;
> But that, not long, ere forward Furie findes
> Incouraging perswasions on to goe.
> We must (sayd they) we will; our honour bindes,

> Our safety bids; our fayth must have it so.
> We know the worst can come, 'tis thought upon:
> We cannot shift; being in, we must goe on.

Thus far, the scene is clear and forceful, and it corresponds aptly to our notions of human nature. Men do indeed act, we say, on such motives. But the event itself, the betrayal of the conspiracy by Aumerle, is recounted with a flatness that astonishes if we expect the stress to be on the climax of action and not on the preliminaries to it.

> And on in deed they went; but O! not far;
> A fatal stop traverst their headlong course;
> Their drift comes knowne, and they discovered
>   are:
> For, some of many will be false, of force.
> *Aumarle* became the man, that all did marre,
> Whether through indiscretion, chance, or worse;
> He makes his peace with offring others blood,
> And shewes the King, how all the matter stood.

And after two or three more weak stanzas the episode closes.

I will give one more out of many possible examples of Daniel's preference for the preliminaries of action over action itself. It comes from the eighth book, at the end of what Daniel completed of his poem. The Earl of Warwick was deeply offended by Edward IV's going back on the French match he went to France to promote. But he concealed his feelings on his return, resolving to retire to his own estates to meditate and then set about revenge. So he goes to Warwick Castle and visits his estates. His confessor guesses what is passing in his mind: and there ensues a debate; the confessor setting forth the advantages of moderate ambition and the ordered life in the sphere allotted by God, and Warwick answering in the vein of Renaissance restlessness. If, says Warwick, he could get free from the sphere in which he is fixed, he would rather wish his palace to be 'that Sheepcot, which in yonder Vale you see / Than any roof of Proudest Majesty'. But honour forbids, or

> I knowe, that I am fixt unto a Sphere,
> That is ordayn'd to move. It is the place
> My fate appoints me; and the region where
> I must, whatever happens, there, imbrace,
> Disturbance, travaile, labor, hope and feare,
> Are of that Clime ingendred in that place;
> And action best, I see, becomes the Best:
> The Starres that have most glorie, have no rest.

The confessor is of course a fiction, and the poet uses him to express the real conflict in Warwick's mind. And he does express it nobly. Into this conflict, the preliminary to action, action breaks in with the customary frigidity. The Reverend Father would have replied,

> But that a speedy messenger was sent
> To shewe, the Duke of *Clarence* was hard-by.
> And thereupon, *Warwicke* breaks-off, and went
> (With all his Train attending formally)
> To intertaine him with fit complement;
> As, glad of such an opportunitie
> To worke upon, for those high purposes
> He had conceiv'd in discontentedness.

This stanza ends the book and all we have of the *Civil Wars.*

Daniel's philosophy of history and his solemn concern with the motives of great political action are the two things that most give his poem an epic tinge. They are worthily answered by the simple and solid sententiousness of his verse. His metre, the *ottava rima*, was, I should guess, borrowed from Tasso direct rather than from Harington's *Orlando Furioso.* He probably thought of it as the proper form for a modern classicising epic, the form hallowed by the two greatest recent practitioners. His style, that middling near-prose style admired by Coleridge, is all his own. It is extremely direct, uses a high proportion of very simple words, is hardly metaphorical at all except through occasional similes, and yet, though often dull, hardly ever lacks dignity. Though not great verse, it has a decided character and could have been evolved only by a severe effort. Its dullness is of the right kind, negative not positive; the index of not having a great deal to say just then without being worried by the deficiency. It is worry that breeds the harmful kind of positive dullness. Daniel knows serenely that he will not be dull for long and is content. At its best his verse rises to a passionate but controlledly passionate eloquence; but its characteristic vein is one of even dignity.

These matters of thought and style give Daniel's poem some share of epic quality. It is of course vain to seek in him the amplitude and variety that mark the great epics. Daniel's mind was not flexible and it shows no humour. What gives most relief from the pervading moral solemnity or stark matter-of-factness is a sense of pity. In describing the misfortunes of Richard II he alters his position of philosophic remoteness and takes his stand near the doomed king. There is an exquisite passage (iii. 64) where Richard from his prison sees the traffic of the ordinary world outside:

> The Morning of that day, which was his last,
> After a weary rest rysing to paine,
> Out at a little grate his eyes he cast
> Upon those bordering hills, and open Plaine,
> And viewes the towne, and sees how people past:
> Where others libertie makes him complaine
> The more his owne, and grieves his soule the
>   more;
> Conferring captive Crownes, with freedome
>   poore.

Then there is the equally pathetic picture of his queen watching for him from a window as the procession goes through London and thinking she sees him in the place of honour:

> Thus does false joy delude her wrongfully
> (Sweete Lady) in the thing she held so deare.
> For, nearer come, she findes she had mistooke;
> And him she markt was *Henrie Bullingbrooke.*

Daniel showed considerable strength of will in carrying through the *Civil Wars* to the end of the eighth book. It is a surprise, as well as a pity, that he did not write the last third. He may have felt that the emotional strength of his great subject was slipping away after the death of the last of the Tudors. His architectonic power, corresponding to the power of his will, was not of the greatest: there is no sign of his keeping the total shape fluid till the very end. He seems to have composed slowly, piece by piece. But he had a plan, and a well-shaped one; and he stuck to it with determination. An example of resolute plotting has occurred already: his subordination of the reign of Henry V to his theme of civil war. His plan was to present the beginning, development, and issue of the dynastic curse; and he refused to be diverted by the brilliant intrusion of Henry V's successes. He allows himself a panegyric (and a splendid one), but he describes none of Henry V's triumphs, military or other, in France. That he has done all this deliberately should be evident from the care and thoughtfulness of all his work; but he confirms what we should in any case have inferred by the statement that follows his account of the death of Henry IV. Instead of turning to the triumphs of Henry V, he wrote:

> And now, into the *Ocean* of new toyles;
> Into the stormie Maine (where tempestes growe
> Of greater ruines, and of greater spoyles)
> Set foorth my course (to hasten on my vow)
> Ov'r all the troublous Deepe of these turmoyles,
> And if I may but live t'attaine the shore
> Of my desired end, I wish no more.

The Wars of the Roses themselves are his main theme, and the preceding troubles lead up to them. And within the Wars Towton is the culminating horror. The gradual leading up to this culmination is nobly contrived; it is the more remarkable for having been contrived in a literary age when copiousness was far commoner than order.

Did Daniel speak for a large body of men? No: he was too academic and too little concerned with men at large. On the other hand his high political subject was in itself the age's true epic subject: there he was absolutely central. And in his treatment of it he did represent a most important minority. Daniel speaks for the political aristocracy of England, and most for the statesmen of the Cecil type, the sage and conscientious servants of the crown. His terribly exacting standards for the ruling aristocracy found superb expression in his "Epistle to the Lady Margaret Countesse of Cumberland," surely as worthy an expression of the theme of *noblesse oblige* as exists in literature. The *Civil Wars* should be read in the light of this epistle. Both poems come out of the heart of that extraordinary governing class of Elizabethan England: a class which combined high passions with peculiarly exacting consciences; wildnesses with extravagantly humble loyalty. Daniel was the epic successor of the political side of Sidney's *Arcadia* and he enjoyed the favour of Fulke Greville, the friend and biographer of Sidney and the man who has best described the essentially political theme of his friend's masterpiece. He was of course the spectator not the participant of the political life which was his essential subject; and he was thus at a disadvantage compared with a man who was poet and doer equally. But that he watched and wrote of the states of mind that were truly paramount in his age was sufficient cause to make him produce a poem with a partial claim to epic dignity. (pp. 324-37)

E. M. W. Tillyard, "The Chronicler-Poets," in his The English Epic and Its Background, *Oxford University Press, 1954, pp. 320-37.*

Laurence Michel and Cecil C. Seronsy   (essay date 1955)

[*In addition to his publications on the theory of tragedy from Shakespeare to William Faulkner, Michel has devoted monographs to two of the major literary works of Daniel,* The Tragedy of Philotas *(1949) and* The Civil Wares *(1958). Seronsy has also made a specialty of Daniel's works, with his studies of Daniel as historian, Daniel and Wordsworth, and Daniel's epic poem,* The Complaint of Rosamond. *Here, Michel and Seronsy present a summary and critique of the relationship between Daniel and Shakespeare.*]

Harold Jenkins, in his survey of History-Play criticism within Nicoll's *Shakespeare Survey 6,* remarks that "the whole question of the sources, now that it has proved less simple than used to be supposed, is in need of fresh survey and synthesis;" his citations of work already done indicate that such synthesis will build chiefly on "fresh scrutiny of the chronicles." In the belief that Daniel's part as an intermediary between Hall and Shakespeare deserves some of the scrutiny, the present article attempts a summary and critique of estimates of the Daniel-Shakespeare relationship on a factual basis, to get the record straight. Jenkins says that

> Daniel's *Civil Wars,* long known to have resemblances with Shakespeare, was established as a source for *Henry IV* by F. W. Moorman [in *Shakespeare Jahrbuch,* XL, 1904] and, after Hardin Craig's 'Tudor' *Richard II,* for that play also.

It hasn't been as simple as this (necessarily) laconic statement might imply. And since "within recent years the History Plays have been rapidly coming into their own", the time seems ripe for a re-examination of the whole matter.

While it is true that Daniel, unlike Shakespeare, was university-bred and wrote ostensibly to please the tastes of small and cultivated courtly circles at the same time that Shakespeare as playwright, actor, and manager was addressing himself to a larger and more popular audience, yet the aims and materials of the two poets were by no means altogether divergent. Both wrote sonnets and both experimented successfully with the erotic poem. Daniel in his epic poem *The Civil Wars* and Shakespeare in several of his plays utilized the same historical matter, and both

wrote "classical" plays with Plutarch as a common source. More significantly, they seem to have been "illustrating" the same general philosophy of history in some of these latter works.

The likelihood that Daniel knew Shakespeare or any of his works before about 1604 is small. There is no evidence, and what similarities can be mustered—the sonnets, *Rosamond* and *Lucrece,* plays on classical subjects, the *Civil Wars* and the History Plays—are all instances of one-way influence, if any, from Daniel to Shakespeare. Agreement is general that Daniel's *Complaint of Rosamond* (1592) clearly influenced some of Shakespeare's earlier dramatic and non-dramatic work. With regard to the *Civil Wars* and the History Plays, the parallels undoubtedly exist, but the conclusions drawn by commentators as to indebtedness have in most cases been dictated by a prior conviction concerning the dates of Shakespeare's plays. Thus Probst and Moorman [Frederic W. Moorman, "Shakespeare's History Plays and Daniel's 'Civile Wars,'" *Shakespeare Jahrbuch,* XL (1904), and A. Probst, *Samuel Daniels "Civil Wars between the two Houses of Lancaster and York" und Michael Draytons "Barons Wars." Eine Quellenstudie,* 1902], following a line of critics going back to Malone in the belief that *Richard II* was written in 1593, are forced to find a radical difference between the connection of the *Civil Wars* (1595) with that play and its connection with *Henry IV* (1599). These considerations, and all aesthetic arguments based upon them, would lose cogency with the successful advent of a different theory of dates, *e.g.,* that of another group of critics culminating with Dover Wilson, that *Richard II* was written in 1595.

We proceed, then, with a set of assumptions based on broad probabilities, to survey factual and bibliographical evidence, together with resemblances in language, style, and idea.

Daniel's reputation was well established by 1595; he was giving authoritative literary expression to material and attitudes well known in the chronicles and the *Mirror for Magistrates;* he was following Spenser's lead as a poet historical; it is therefore probable that Shakespeare, who had previously drawn upon *Rosamond* and possibly Daniel's sonnets, now read the *Civil Wars* (and possibly *Cleopatra,* 1594-5) while contemplating or writing his series of plays covering the same historical period. Daniel, a purist and scornful of the popular stage, probably did not see or read Shakespeare's dramatic works until his appointment as a licenser of plays in 1604. Thereafter it seems that he in turn was influenced by Shakespeare in his revision of *Cleopatra* in 1607 and in the changed attitudes reflected in his extensive revision of the *Civil Wars* in 1609. (pp. 549-51)

· · · · ·

The over-all philosophical conception lying behind both Daniel and Shakespeare in their studies of English history has been well described by Tillyard, and further attention will be given it later in this article. For the present, it should be noted that the attitudes of the two poets, and of course most of the details of the action they treat, are to be found in the chronicle sources used by both, so that it is chiefly material not to be found in these sources which is relevant for a discussion of influence. R. M. Smith [in his *Froissart and the English Chronicle Play,* 1915] adduces twelve such parallels which he says differ from the chronicle sources. The present discussion therefore begins with a summary and brief evaluation of all these parallels and offers new information on some of them.

Several of the resemblances alleged by Smith have little or no value:

1. Bolingbroke's popularity with the common people is given as the reason for his banishment.
5. Bolingbroke courts the favor of the common people, and his growing power is contrasted with Richard's decline in day-night, rising- and setting-sun imagery.
6. Similar portents in the heavens.
7. Adoption of the familiar name "Bullingbrooke," and the spelling "Herford."
9. The plotters against Henry reassure each other by swearing on the sacrament.

These are not sufficiently independent of common "sources" to have any significance as parallels.

However, the remaining instances cited by Smith merit more attention.

4. Isabel watches Richard enter London, is dismayed at his aspect, and later procures a meeting with him.

There is no warrant for any of this in any source. Apart from the incident itself, there do not appear to be many resemblances in language or ideas between the corresponding passages in the two works; this need not, however, militate against the theory of influence: Daniel's passage is an elaborated show-piece of his characteristic mode; Shakespeare finds the incident fruitful for dramatic purposes, and reserves pathos for his characterization of Richard.

2. Queen Isabel is presented as a mature woman, exhibiting understanding and passion beyond the scope of a lass of eleven.
3. Bolingbroke and Richard enter London tandem-style, the one triumphantly in the lead, the other following unnoticed or reviled.
8. Richard delivers the crown to Bolingbroke with his own hand.
10. Hints are given by Henry IV for the murder of Richard by Sir Piers of Exton.

Although clues for these resemblances *can* be found in the chronicles, Daniel and Shakespeare both provide much sharper dramatization of the incidents, and the likenesses are often remarkable, in detail and sentiment. Thus Shakespeare's use of "rid" and "fear" in Henry's remark, quoted by Exton, "Have I no friend will rid me of this living fear?" seems to indicate that he was drawing upon Daniel more heavily than has been hitherto recognized. First comes Daniel's reflection on how Richard is at the mercy of his enemies, "And they rid quite of feare, he of the Crowne." (II. 47) Later the same idea, similarly phrased, suggests itself to Henry who "wisht that some would so

his life esteeme / As ridde him of these feares wherein he stood." (III. 57)

11. Richard muses on kings and commoners in his cell, just before a servant [perhaps Ienico d'Artois, of whom Daniel makes so much?] rushes in to warn him, followed by Exton and his fellow-assassins.

Here again is a scene with many resemblances heretofore unnoticed. The scene is set,

In *Civil Wars,* III. 64

> The morning of that day, which was his last,
> After a wearie rest rysing to paine,
> Out at a little grate his eyes he cast
> Vpon those bordering hils, and open Plaine,
> And viewes the towne, and sees how people past:
> Where others libertie, makes him complaine
> The more his owne, and grieues his soule the more;
> Conferring captiue-Crownes, with freedom poore.

In *Richard II,* V, v:

> I haue beene studying how I may compare
> This prison where I liue, vnto the world: . . .
>
>   sometimes I am a King,
> Then treasons make me wish my selfe a beggar,
> And so I am: then crushing penurie
> Perswades me I was better when a king, . . .

There are some tantalizing echoes, difficult to fit in but insistent to the ear, as is again the case in *Civil Wars,* III. 65

> O happie man, sayth hee, that lo I see
> Grazing his cattle in those pleasant fieldes!
> If he but knew his good (how blessed hee,
> That feeles not what affliction Greatnes yeeldes!)
> Other then what hee is, he would not bee,
> Nor change his state with him that Scepters wieldes—

which recalls the last line of Shakespeare's Sonnet XXIX, "That then I skorne to change my state with Kings." Indeed, it recalls the whole tenor of Sonnets XXIX and XXX—and the echo chain goes on from the latter's "And with old woes new waile my deare times waste," to "I wasted time and now doth time waste me" in line 49 of this scene in *Richard II.* Stanza 66 of *Civil Wars,*

> Thou sitst at home, safe, by they quiet fire,
> And hear'st of others harmes; but feelest none:
> And there thou telst of Kings, and who aspire,
> Who fall, who rise, who triumphs, and who do mone:
> Perhaps thou talkst of me, and dost inquire
> Of my restraint, why here I lieu alone,
> And pittiest this my miserable fall:
> For, pittie must haue part; enuie, not all,

and the incantatory use of the word "Death" spoken of in 69 and 70, seem to find a counterpart in the famous speech of *Richard II,* III, ii, 155 ff.:

> For Gods sake let vs sit vpon the ground,
> And tell sad stories of the death of Kings, . . .

for within the hollow crowne
That roundes the mortall temples of a king,
Keeps death his court, . . .

and in Richard's valediction to Isabel (V, i, 38 ff.):

Thinke I am dead, and that euen here thou tak-
est
As from my death bed thy last liuing leaue;
In winters tedious nights sit by the fire,
With good old folkes, and let them tell the tales,
Of woeful ages long agoe betidde:
And ere thou bid good night to quite their
griefes,
Tell thou the lamentable tale of me,
And send the hearers weeping to their beds: . . .

We are on slippery ground here, and indeed perilously close to the quicksands of the sonnet-dating question and the influence of Daniel's *Delia;* perhaps it is safest to say that both poets are curiously caught up in corresponding imagery bearing on the same dramatic situation.

12. Exton is repudiated by Henry IV after the murder ["Shakespeare must have taken this from the *Civil Wars*" (according to Smith in *Froissart and the English Chronicle Play*].

Here Smith has fallen into the error (which Wilson appears not to have noticed) of assuming that Daniel's passage was in the 1595 edition. The parallel is close, there is no mention in the chronicles; but this is one instance where it seems incontrovertible that Daniel borrowed from Shakespeare rather than *vice versa.* The 1595 version does not raise the point of Exton's relationship with Henry; the 1601 version revises, substituting a stanza on the theme of Exton's infamy with posterity, but still not advertising to his repudiation by Henry; the 1609 version revises again, taking this out to make room for the repudiation idea. It seems probable that by 1609 Daniel had been forced to recognize Shakespeare as a serious writer on historical subjects, and revised, especially those parts of his poem concerning Henry IV, in the light of Shakespeare's treatment.

(As for Shakespeare's precedent in this matter, no one seems to have remarked the very close similarity between Henry-Exton-Richard, and John-Hubert-Arthur in *King John,* although somewhat the same impulse is found behind the two plays written very close together (and Wilson notes similarities in imagery, going back ultimately to Daniel!): John leers and hints to Hubert that he would be glad to have Arthur out of the way, and repudiates him when he thinks Arthur is dead). (pp. 552-57)

To complete the record, the following parallels have been noticed by the present writers or others.

The idea of a Nemesis dogging Henry IV for his impiety in rebelling against and usurping the crown of an anointed king is an important point of contact, but difficult to pin down. It, and horror at the vision of the wounds of civil war which are its instruments of revenge, are pervasive in both the whole *Civil Wars* and Shakespeare's cycle, transcending the bounds of any reign because the curse works itself out in the whole Lancastrian dynasty. The link in *Richard II* is Carlisle's speech, with its insistence on the invalidity of subjects' passing sentence on a king. In Daniel's poem the Bishop of Carlisle protests against the deposition of Richard and abhors the thought that the lawful king

Should here be judg'd, unheard, and unar-
raigned;
By Subjects too (Judges incompetent
To judge their King unlawfully detained)
And unbrought-foorth to plead his guiltless
Cause;
Barring th'Annoynted, libertie of lawes.

(III, 23)

Shakespeare's bishop speaks in similar language:

What subiect can giue sentence on his King:
And who sits here that is not Richards subiect?
Theeues are not iudgd but they are by to heare,
Although apparant guilt be seene in them,
And shall the figure of Gods Maiesty,
His Captaine, steward, deputy, elect,
Annointed, crowned, planted, many yeares
Be iudgd by subiect and inferiour breath,
And he himselfe not present?

(IV, i, 121-9)

The whole speech abounds in echoes of Daniel: perhaps the most striking one is

Peace shall go sleepe with turkes and infidels,
And in this seat of peace, tumultuous warres,
Shall kin with kin, and kinde with kind con-
found.

(IV, i, 139-41)

This argues for Shakespeare's recognition of Daniel as a spokesman for the central idea, by borrowing from his thematic opening stanza:

I sing the ciuill Warres, tumultuous Broyles,
And Bloody factions of a mightie Land:
Whose people hautie, proud with forraine
spoyles,
Vpon themselues turn-backe their conquering
hand;
Whil'st Kin their Kin, Brother the Brother
foyles;
Like Ensignes all against like Ensignes band;
Bowes against Bowes, the Crowne against the
Crowne;
Whil'st all pretending right, all right's throwne
downe.

(I. 1)

Tillyard [*Shakespeare's History Plays*] has assembled a number of points of overall resemblance between Daniel's poem and Shakespeare's two tetralogies beginning with *Richard II* and ending with *Richard III* (if we accept his authorship of all or most of the Henry VI trilogy). Both poets (as do Hall and the *Mirror for Magistrates*) begin at the same point in the reign of Richard II, and in political philosophy they are identical, showing the evils of civil dissension and the curse of rebellion. Tillyard further points out that they are "at one in their sense of history repeating itself, of history educating through the example, of one crime leading to another," and that they agree in seeing all this misery as prelude to the glorious times of the Tudors. These common aims, along with the surprising concurrence of their choice of incidents, whatever their difference in execution, are probably more than mere coincidence. Speculating on the three English epic models before Shakespeare in 1595 (*Arcadia, The Faerie Queene,* the *Civil Wars*), Tillyard observes that these were the products of the poets whose ideas Shakespeare shared, although he worked in another medium, and adds, "He must have wanted to be one of them, to compete with them . . . Daniel's poem, using Shakespeare's most essential source, Hall, and treating of identical material, must surely have put it into Shakespeare's mind to achieve in his own medium the epic intentions translated into the above three great fragments. Further, Daniel's failure to animate his material thoroughly may have encouraged Shakespeare to do better."

An interesting correspondence is shown by the way in which both poets envisage woe and destruction as a consequence of Bolingbroke's ambition and ultimate usurpation of the crown. Daniel has the Genius of England first sound the ominous note to Bolingbroke as he returns from exile:

> The babes unborne, shall (ô) be borne to bleed
> In this thy quarrell, if thou do proceede.
>
> (I. 89)

And when the usurpation is accomplished, the poet exclaims,

> What mourning in their ruin'd houses now!
> How many children's plaints, and mothers cryes!
> How many wofull Widowes left to bow
> To sad disgrace! What perisht families!

Shakespeare seems to elaborate on this theme of general bloodshed and slaughter that awaits those yet unborn. Richard foretells the fate that the conspirators are bringing down upon England:

> Yet know, my maister God omnipotent,
> Is mustering in his cloudes on our behalfe,
> Armies of pestilence, and they shall strike
> Your children yet vnborne, and vnbegot, . . .
>
> But ere the crowne he lookes for, liue in peace,
> Ten thousand bloudy crownes of mothers sonnes,
> Shall ill become the flower of Englands face, . . .
>
> (III. iii, 85-8, 95-7)

And later in the play, after the deposition, the Bishop of Carlisle prophesies:

> The woe's to come, the children yet vnborne,
> Shall feele this day as sharp to them as thorne.
>
> (IV, i, 322-3)

The resemblances in circumstance and, to some extent, in language between the poem and the play in these prophecies of woe to come are not found in Holinshed and Hall. Characteristically, Daniel exploits the pathos and sentiment of the situation, in "children's plaints," "mothers cryes," and "wofull Widowes." All these touches are neglected by Shakespeare, who seizes upon the "babes unborne" phrase as a means to intensify his account of the iron tragedy of war.

Gaunt's famous speech, celebrating England's insularity

as defense against foreign infection, has echoes of Daniel's apostrophes to Neptune in Book IV, and the sea-spurning-shore imagery (a link, incidentally, with *King John*) may have come from Daniel's description of the ambush of Richard II in Book II.

The image of a river in flood running over its banks is, of course, common in both poets; but an influence seems pretty certain here since the image is employed to describe the same thing—the freshet of rebellion that greeted Bolingbroke when he returned to England from exile—and since both poets employ this image to pun on the name of the usurper. After showing how Henry's forces have been augmented like the river Thames, Daniel adds,

> So flocke the mighty, with their following trains,
> Unto the all-receiving *Bullingbrooke*.
>
> (II. 8)

And Shakespeare offers a somewhat more furious and dynamic punning image:

> So high aboue his limits swels the rage
> Of Bullingbrooke couering your fearful land.
>
> (III, ii, 109-10)

Richard's reproaches to Northumberland, his prophecy of Bolingbroke's spurning Northumberland once he has used him for a ladder to the throne, and the vision of ensuing corruption (V, i, 55,-68) are very close to the sentiments inaugurated by Daniel in II. 2 ff. This may serve as one more illustration of the different quality of the two poets: Daniel first moralizes in his own person, then transfers the theme to Richard as a "complaint" soliloquy; his image is suggestive rather than concrete:

> Th'aspirer once attaind vnto the top,
> Cuts off those meanes by which himselfe got vp.

Whereas Shakespeare has Richard blurt out his bitter lines as a direct response to being "checked and rated" by the blunt Northumberland; he makes the image simultaneously concrete and insulting: "Northumberland, thou ladder. . . ." And he thought well enough of the idea to re-use it (and in a rare direct quotation) in the new dramatic situation of the prophecy's apparent operation in *Henry IV Part II* (III, i, 57 ff.).

The reiteration of the idea that Richard was betraying his patrimony by not prosecuting glorious foreign conquests, and the impiety of England's "shameful conquest of itself," find a continuous counterpart in Daniel, from the beginning of his poem.

Richard's "senseless conjuration" of the stones of the castle when he returns from Ireland,

> This earth shall haue a feeling, and these stones,
> Proue armed souldiers ere her natiue King,
> Shall faulter vnder foule rebellions armes,
>
> (*Henry IV,* Part II, III, ii, 24-6)

may well derive from Salisbury's eloquent plea, in Daniel, that Richard should stay where he is:

> Here haue you craggie Rocks to take your part;
> That neuer will betray their faith to you: . . .
>
> If men will not, these verie Cliffes will fight,

And be sufficient to defend your right.
                    [*The Civil Wars,*] (II. 29)

The present writers are convinced that the totality of evidence presented here makes it certain that the two treatments of Richard II are intimately connected. The verbal coincidences take on incomparably greater importance (than if they were found in isolation) because they occur in the same contexts. And indeed, once it were established that Shakespeare followed Daniel, it would be more than likely that even much of the treatment for which there is precedent in the sources common to both men would have taken its shaping impulse from the poet rather than the chronicler: as Wilson puts it, "Shakespeare had his head full of the poem while he was engaged upon the play". In establishing the question of indebtedness, clearing up the date-muddle helps considerably, but final conviction still rests on the broad probabilities mentioned at the beginning. The net result, it is hoped, is that the **Civil Wars** will be recognized as the most illuminating background reading yet found for a full appreciation of *Richard II,* and a companion-piece not unworthy to stand beside it.

. . . .

Once it has been accepted (as now seems universally the case) that *Henry IV* was written around 1597-98, and that it has unmistakable links of continuity with *Richard II,* there is not much need for argument that here Daniel's contribution is clear. Daniel often appears to anticipate Shakespeare in introducing many changes from the chronicle sources. In both poets the idea of Nemesis plays a prominent part: a retributive justice works through all the political action and forces Henry to express remorse over his past conduct. (It is interesting to realize that Shakespeare was later to build his character of Claudius much upon the pattern of King Henry IV.) Daniel, it has been well said, "furnished his great disciple with the interpretation of the character of King Henry IV, as he had done in the case of the same man as Bolingbroke in the earlier play." Daniel and Shakespeare agree in making Hotspur a contemporary of Prince Henry, whereas historically he was older even than the king, and again they concur in having the Prince become a glorious knight of war at seventeen, encounter Hotspur in the battle of Shrewsbury, and save his father from death or capture by the Douglas. Glendower and the Welsh forces fail to appear at Shrewsbury: the usual chroniclers say they were there; Daniel derived his information from some other source as yet undescried; Shakespeare took it from him; modern historians bear them out.

Henry's interview with the Prince shortly before he dies is to be found in the chroniclers, but Daniel introduced the theme of regret for the "blot of foul attaining" on the crown he was about to pass on to his son, and for not having been able to erase it by the crusade he had vowed at the close of *Richard II.* When Daniel introduces the narrative of the downfall of the house of Lancaster (with York beginning to "looke / Into their right"), he enters a reservation:

Neere three score yeeres are past since Bulling-
    brooke

Did first attaine (God knows how just) the
    Crowne.
                                            (V, 45)

In Shakespeare the remorse is more directly felt by the king:

God knowes (my sonne)
By what by-paths, and indirect crookt waies,
I met this crowne, . . .
                        (Pt. II, IV, v, 184-6)

This, and the advice he gives the Prince to keep his subjects in hand by busying them with foreign conquest, may be confidently assigned as taken by Shakespeare from Daniel. A rather striking piece of evidence that he followed very closely at times is the image both poets use to describe the bodily feebleness of King Henry just before the arrival of death:

Whose harald sicknes, being sent before
With full commission to denounce his end,
And paine, and griefe, enforcing more and more,
Besiegd the hold that could not long defend,
And so consum'd all that imboldning store
Of hote gaine-striuing bloud that did contend,
Wearing the wall so thin that now the mind
Might well looke thorow, and his frailty find.
                        [*The Civil Wars,* III. 116]

No, no, he cannot long hold out these pangs,
Th'incessant care and labour of his mind
Hath wrought the Mure, that should confine it
    in,
So thin that life lookes through [and will break
    out].
                        [*Henry IV,* Pt. II, IV, iv, 117-20]

There is much mention, in *I Henry IV,* of gunpowder, shot, artillery, cannon, culverins, pistols (possibly even the use of explosives to change the course of the river Trent), at the time of Homildon Hill and Shrewsbury. This anachronism was avoided by Daniel; in his long fanciful derivation of the arts of printing and artillery (VI. 26 ff.) he puts the first use of both, properly, in the time of Henry VI. However, his vivid description of the devilish provenance of artillery, and its instrumentality in the decline of personal valor in battle, may well have so impressed itself upon Shakespeare's mind as to be the source of Hotspur's angry paraphrase of the pestering popinjay:

And that it was great pitty, so it was,
This villanous saltpeeter, should be digd
Out of the bowels of the harmeless earth,
Which many a good tall fellow had destroyed
So cowardly, and but for these vile guns
He would himselfe haue been a souldior.
                            (Pt. I, I, iii, 59-64)

It may be some corroboration that Milton also seems to have been struck by this passage in Daniel.

King Henry's nocturnal soliloquy, followed by his justification of his actions to Warwick and Surrey,

ô sleepe! o gentle sleep!
Natures soft nurse, how haue I frighted thee,

and

(Though then (God knowes) I had no such in-
    tent,
But that necessitie so bowed the state,
That I and greatnesse were compeld to kisse.)
    [Shakespeare, *Henry IV,* Pt. II, III, ii]

may owe something to Daniel's having the Genius of England appear to Bolingbroke in a nocturnal vision, and to
his defending Bolingbroke's action in breaking exile; Daniel himself comments,

    And let vnwresting charitie beleeue
    That then thy oth with thy intent agreed,
    And others faith, thy faith did first deceiue,
    Thy after fortune fore'd thee to this deed:
    And let no man this idle censure giue
    Because th'euent proues so, twas so decreed:
    For ô what counsels sort to other end
    Then that which frailty did at first intend?
    [*The Civil Wars,* I, 98]

Mention has been made above of the pervasive presence
of Nemesis in Daniel's account of the struggle between the
rival Houses of York and Lancaster. The fact that Nemesis is named for the first time in the poem in Book V (printed after 1595 and some time before 1599) has induced
scholars to regard Daniel's explicit idea of Nemesis as having been available as a suggestion to Shakespeare for use
in the later *Henry IV* and not for the earlier *Richard II.*
Yet Daniel's earlier use of the idea in *Cleopatra* (1594),
which may well have been read by Shakespeare, seems to
have been hitherto overlooked. The chorus at the end of
Act III thus apostrophizes:

    O Fearefull-frowning Nemesis,
    Daughter of Iustice, most severe.

Here already is the kernel of Daniel's (and Shakespeare's)
conception of English history, as the chorus, elaborating
on the necessity of righting wrongs and of reversing evil
trends and insisting on the alternate course of weal and
woe, points the way to the philosophic notion behind the
Civil Wars. And the idea is worked out in some detail in
Daniel's tragedy. For instance, there is the speech of Caesario just before he goes to his death:

    And thou Augustus that with bloody hand,
    Cutt'st off succession from another's race,
    Maist find the heavens thy vowes so to with-
        stand.

And Caesario then looks ahead to the time when Augustus himself will have no issue to succeed him, and the
wheel of retribution will have come full cycle. The tone
and form of this prophetic utterance is not unlike that in
Richard's warning to Bolingbroke, though the actual
prophecy takes a different turn.

The direction of the Daniel-Shakespeare influence seems
to have been reversed in Daniel's revision of the **Civil
Wars** in 1609. Possibly he was attracted to Shakespeare's
work earlier, after his appointment as a licenser of plays
in 1604, particularly in his drastic revision of **Cleopatra**
in 1607. In the 1609 **Civil Wars** the considerable amount
of new and revised material indicates that Daniel checked
back over his presentation of Henry IV and Richard II
after having seen Shakespeare's. Book III was split into III

and IV, and much matter expanded: III. 82, which had announced that with Richard's death Henry was now secure,
was changed to introduce 24 new stanzas showing that the
deed did *not* free Henry from care or fear. This theme is
the burden of the opening scene of *Henry IV Part I*—the
link with *Richard II.* Stanzas 17-19 of Book IV, added at
this time, describe the friction between Henry and the Per-
cies treated in I, iii of the play; Daniel confuses the two
Mortimers, as had Shakespeare; 26-27 introduce the Per-
cies' bill of complaint; 49-52 shift the emphasis from the
two Blunts at the battle of Shrewsbury to Douglas' difficulties in encountering so many King Henrys. Stanza 56,
added, tells of Douglas' capture and his pardon for "noble
valour" shown, and introduces 26 new stanzas which
summarize the political content of *Henry IV Part II.* Two
new stanzas (IV. 41-42) give the circumstances of Worcester's concealing from Hotspur the king's peace proposal
and urge that Henry, by conceding much in making the
peace overture, was moved to do so by a real horror of
bloodshed. Daniel's shift from an earlier and harsher view
of Henry, noticeable in a few such passages as these, may
well have been influenced by Shakespeare.

This is not to say that Daniel could not have found all
these things in the chronicles, and the fact that he does not
describe a meeting between Prince Henry and Hotspur is
indicative that he was not copying Shakespeare. However,
the bulk of new material is impressive, and fits extremely
well with what Daniel would have found treated by Shakespeare, if he had become familiar with the play by 1609.
It is perhaps significant that nine-tenths of the whole-line
substitutions, and all of the complete-stanza additions, in
the whole poem of 1609 concern Henry IV.

No less interesting than Daniel's re-touching of the events
of Henry IV's reign in 1609 is his omission of several stanzas that are sympathetic to the cause of Richard II. Thus
stanza 21 of Book II of the 1601 edition had concluded
Richard's "complaint" with his bemoaning his fall and
had suggested an innocent Richard victimized by his
council; stanzas 58-61 presented a righteous Richard solil-
oquizing on the difficulties of ruling and pleasing all. All
these stanzas were removed in 1609. Here and in many
other places throughout Books III and IV it is evident that
Daniel felt in 1609 that he had allowed Richard altogether
too much wisdom and good intention, in earlier versions
of the poem. In confirmation of this more sober view, he
added in 1609 a "character" of Richard at the end of Book
III, in which Richard's engaging manners, his generosity,
and his personal charm are balanced against the excesses
and defects of his character which had been dealt with
rather lightly in the earlier editions. There had already
been some toning-down of his early sympathies for Richard, in successive editions, but the shift of view is considerably more extensive in 1609.

    . . . . .

Since the controversy over the authorship of *Henry VI* is
still undecided, our discussion of influence is perforce tentative. Relying on the "basic probability" asserted above,
we may assume that Daniel did not know the original
plays of which *The Contention* and *The True Tragedy* are
generally considered to be some kind of distorted versions.

Consequently, it is only the Folio version of *Henry VI* (and especially *Part III,* which, it has been argued, Shakespeare revised) that concerns us. The difficulty is that there is no indication whatever of when this revision, if any, took place. Daniel's Book VIII was first published in 1609, and we can be reasonably certain that Shakespeare would not be concerned with rehashing an old play on *Henry VI* after that date, and consequently that he was not the debtor in this instance; but when Daniel got hold of it must remain a matter of conjecture. If the supposition that he became interested in Shakespeare after 1604, and made use of him in the revision of 1609, be good, then we may further suppose that he sought out the same dramatist's treatment of material he was about to work up for the first time: the incidents of Book VIII. (Incidentally, while this sheds no light on the time of the "Shakespeare revision," it may strengthen the argument that the ascription to Shakespeare is true—Daniel was a very discriminating critic, and having recognized Shakespeare's value in *Henry IV,* he might very well have turned to a version of *Henry VI* by the same pen when he continued his poem in 1609.)

Probst [in his "Samuel Daniel's *Civil Wars*"] has pointed out some of the resemblances, although he seems unaware of any difference between the Folio version of *Part III* and *The True Tragedy.* Two scenes afford similarities: (1) King Henry on the molehill ("little hill" in Daniel, VIII. 22) at Towton (*3 Henry VI,* II, v, 20-54), which, in its general scheme of a slighted monarch comparing his situation with that of a common man and its preoccupation with the time-image of dials, minutes, and hours, harks back to (or was the exemplar for?) Richard's soliloquy; and (2) the wooing of Lady Grey by Edward IV. The first scene is without detailed precedent in the chronicles: and the second, while reported rather fully by Hall and Holinshed, is still further elaborated by the play in details which are picked up by the poem—such as the *double entendre* on "pleasure," for example. Incidentally, Daniel's estimate of Edward's character underwent some change in 1609—he omitted a whole stanza of glowing praise of the new King Edward IV (VI. 113) first introduced in 1601—but this fact need not be attributed solely to the influence of Shakespeare's unflattering presentation of Edward. Other concomitances, cited by Probst, such as the reference to Margaret as a modern Helen, and giving Warwick the epithet "kingmaker," are doubtful; the elaboration of the Amazon-like character of Margaret, however, and especially having her upbraid the weak Henry on behalf of herself and their son, are strikingly similar in the poem and the play—and it is just these passages that are not to be found in *The True Tragedy.* However, on the whole, the evidence that in 1609 Daniel drew upon *3 Henry VI* is less extensive and convincing than that he adapted some of *Richard II* and *Henry IV* to his own purposes in his revisions of that date. Again one can applaud his discrimination.

· · · · ·

Did Shakespeare in writing *Antony and Cleopatra* (usually dated 1606-07) make any use of Daniel's *Cleopatra* (1594, revised in 1599 and 1601), and did Daniel in his drastic revision of *Cleopatra* in 1607 have recourse to Shake-speare's play? While the evidence for such a two-way influence is still far from conclusive, the connections are too extensive to be summarily dismissed. The 1594 version of **Cleopatra** was a Senecan tragedy in the manner of Garnier, the chief model of the group of writers, including Daniel, around the Countess of Pembroke. These writers sought to reform English tragedy along the lines laid down by Sidney in his *Defense of Poesy.* Characteristically absent from the Garnier-type of play are sensational themes of violence and sexual love. It avoids anachronisms and short dialogues. Typical are the long soliloquies with corresponding lack of action, the chorus in each act that plays an integral part in the drama itself, and stichomythic dialogue in rhymed couplets. The members of this group sought above all for dignity and refinement in their plays. Daniel's **Cleopatra** of 1594 exhibits all these qualities. Cleopatra is herself a mature woman, possessed of regal dignity and of a beauty already in decline, and has no touch of the girlishness and moodiness of Shakespeare's temptress. The play adheres to the unities of time and action, but not of place. It deals only with those events in Cleopatra's life subsequent to Antony's death. Daniel greatly expands Plutarch's account of Cleopatra's son Caesario, and exhibits the queen's mother-love to deepen the pathos. All the principal action of the tragedy—Cleopatra's affectionate leave-taking of her son, the son's going to his execution, and finally the queen's own suicide—is reported.

In point of structure this play is vastly different from *Antony and Cleopatra.* In Shakespeare's tragedy the action extends over years of time and continents of space, and all the important events are fully dramatized. Yet certain parallels in situation and language have been noted by those who contend that Shakespeare made some use of Daniel's play. These resemblances will be discussed below. Daniel's revisions of **Cleopatra** in 1599 and 1601 chiefly concerned rhyme and diction, and these changes were inconsiderable beyond Act I. However, in 1607 the play was greatly altered, and from the revised dedication it appears that he intended the 1607 version to stand as the final one. The principal changes in this new version of the play are additions to the original text, the introduction of new scenes and some rearrangement of old ones, the substitution in some cases of dialogue for long soliloquies and of dramatic action for narrative, and the introduction of several new characters who, instead of having their conversation reported, now speak for themselves. From this heightening of dramatic effect it has been generally felt that perhaps Daniel was forced to compromise with the popular drama and that this play shows the influence of romantic tragedy. From what appear to be the marks of Shakespeare's influence on the 1607 edition of Daniel's play, there has been some argument for dating *Antony and Cleopatra* prior to 1607. The evidences for mutual indebtedness therefore need to be reviewed and summarized.

First, as to the probability that Shakespeare drew upon the 1594 **Cleopatra.** R. H. Case first pointed out a few resemblances in expression (not in Plutarch) between the two plays, [in his *The Tragedy of Antony and Cleopatra,* 1906 and again in the 8th edition, 1938], of which the more significant ones are referred to here. Daniel's queen says (1. 54), "I have both hands and will, and I can die;" Shakespeare's says (IV, xv, 49), "My resolution and my hands I'll trust." Both poets have Cleopatra envisage the humiliation of passing as a captive queen before Octavia at Rome (Daniel, ll. 67-70; Shakespeare, V, ii, 52-55). This circumstance is not altogether independent of Plutarch, who mentions Octavius' desire to take Cleopatra back to Rome to set out his triumph. It is significant, however, that Plutarch omits any mention of Octavia in this connection. Case admits that these resemblances could have been accidental, and H. H. Furness believed that Shakespeare could have found no *dramatic* aid whatever in Daniel's play [in *A New Variorum Edition of Shakespeare*]. However, Furness does concede the possibility that Daniel's aid may have been levied on in two or three small things, such as Cleopatra's calling Antony "demi-Atlas" (I, v, 23; "my Atlas" in Daniel, l. 15), and her reference to Cydnos (V, ii, 228; Daniel, ll. 1473-80) as she prepares for death. A resemblance hitherto unnoticed is the reference to the asp: in Daniel it is "the fairest creature that faire Nylus feeds" (l. 1511); in Shakespeare it is "the pretty worm of Nilus" (V, ii, 243).

Some of the above parallels are cited by Willard Farnham in a recent study of Shakespearean tragedy [*Shakespeare's Tragic Frontier,* 1950]. He adds one important pair of corresponding passages to support his brief that Shakespeare followed Daniel's play: those lines in *Antony and Cleopatra* where Proculeius, in answer to Cleopatra's assertion that she asks for nothing from Caesar but the kingdom of Egypt for her son, replies that Caesar will be full of grace if that grace is kneeled to. To this Cleopatra returns, "Say, I should die." (V, ii, 21-8, 70). Mr. Farnham observes that Plutarch makes no reference to Caesar's "grace" or to Cleopatra's desire to die. The passage, he believes, was derived from Proculeius' account to Caesar in Daniel's play:

> But through a Grate at th'entry of the place
> Standing to treate, I labour'd to advise her,
>
> To come to Caesar and to sue for grace.
> Shee saide, she crav'd not life, but leave to die,
> Yet for her children, prayd they might inherite.
>   (ll, 287-91)

There is no evidence that Daniel's play in any way influenced Shakespeare's handling of plot and situation beyond what might be suggested in the verbal parallels themselves. The presence of Nemesis and the strong note of retributive justice in *Cleopatra* alluded to above, while it may have helped shape the historical purpose behind *Richard II* and *Henry IV,* seems to have exercised little or no force in *Antony and Cleopatra.* Another work of Daniel's, his *Letter from Octavia to Marcus Antonius* (1599), has been mentioned as a poem with which Shakespeare may have been acquainted. R. C. Bald ["Shakespeare and Daniel," *TLS,* November 20, 1924] first drew attention to the "Argument" prefixed to this *Letter,* in which "the fetters of Egypt" are mentioned, and compared the passage to Antony's resolve in the play,

> These strong Egyptian fetters I must break
> Or lose myself in dotage.
>   (I, ii, 119-20)

Farnham cites the possibility of another slight borrowing

by Shakespeare from the same "Argument" in Antony's remark, "I' the east my pleasure lies." Thus there persists the feeling that Daniel, in one or another of his writings, has exerted a slight influence on the making of *Antony and Cleopatra.*

What then of Daniel's use in turn of Shakespearean materials in his *Cleopatra* of 1607? Here Case is more certain; conceding that the parallels between the earlier version of Daniel's play and Shakespeare could be chance concomitances, he finds the resemblances between the later *Cleopatra* and Shakespeare too striking to be called accidental. For he notices the following circumstances in the later version: relation and soliloquy are to a great extent replaced by dialogue; the characters of Charmian, Eras, Directus, and Diomedes are a new feature; as are also the incident of Directus' bringing Antony's sword to Caesar, treated likewise by Shakespeare, and the narration of events preceding Antony's death [*Tragedy of Antony and Cleopatra,* 1906]. That Daniel so noticeably altered his play is in itself suggestive of Shakespeare's influence. However, some of these alterations can be accounted for in simpler fashion. For the scene of Directus' sword-bearing, Daniel's source could very well have been Plutarch. Furthermore, Daniel relates the events preceding Antony's death no more "along the lines followed by Shakespeare" than along the course laid out by Plutarch. The items that follow, comprising an outline of the action taken from Plutarch in both versions of Daniel's play, are here given in order to demonstrate to what extent the play was altered along lines independent of Plutarch. The order of events in Plutarch treated by Daniel is:

1. Antony is defeated and subsequently commits suicide.
2. Cleopatra receives Antony into the monument, where he dies.
3. Directus takes Antony's sword to Caesar and tells of Antony's death.
4. Cleopatra attempts suicide and is rescued by Proculeius.
5. Cleopatra interviews Caesar and Dolabella.
6. Caesar grants Cleopatra's request to visit Antony's tomb.
7. Cleopatra returns from the tomb of Antony. Her sumptuous meal and rich attire are described. A country fellow enters with figs. Cleopatra sends a letter explaining her suicide to Caesar.
8. Caesar's messengers find Cleopatra and her servants dead of poison. Various accounts are given of the poisoning.

It will be readily seen that these events comprise only about the last third of Shakespeare's play. In the 1594 *Cleopatra* the first three items were lacking, and (4) was preceded by Cleopatra's long soliloquy which reviews the antecedent action. In the 1607 version there is really only one rearrangement of the action. Rhodon's account of Cleopatra's parting with her son is moved from Act IV to Act I, Scene 1, where the leave-taking is directly presented. It should be noted that Plutarch gives little attention to this incident and that Shakespeare gives none. In fact, Plutarch relates that Caesario was put to death *after* his mother's suicide. Daniel in both versions of his play characteristically exploits the sentimental and pathetic aspects of the mother-son relation, but, oddly enough, in no way relates Caesario's death to Cleopatra's motives for suicide. The second scene of Act I is altogether new in the 1607 version. This comprises events (1), (2), and (3) listed above, dramatically treated in Shakespeare's play but here narrated by Dircetus. The order of events in the rest of the 1607 version follows closely the 1594 *Cleopatra,* except in Act IV, Scene 3, where Caesario is directly presented as he goes to his execution, and in the final scene of Act V, where Cleopatra's end is presented dramatically instead of being narrated as in the earlier version.

From this analysis of the action, two significant conclusions are reached. (1) That portion of new material added to the 1607 version of Daniel's play, material that might have been suggested by either Plutarch or Shakespeare, or both, is narrated rather than cast into dramatic form. (2) With the exception of the final scene, those portions of the early version of his play that are converted into direct dramatic presentation are almost entirely elements of the story to which Shakespeare gave no attention. The scenes between Caesario and Cleopatra and later, between Caesario and his guard, as he is conducted to his death, owe nothing to Shakespeare and very little to Plutarch. Daniel seems to have worked independently of his sources. And in both his versions he has Cleopatra *plan* the final catastrophe much more completely than in Plutarch and Shakespeare. The way in which this episode is handled by the two poets is instructive. After telling of Cleopatra's death, Plutarch offers several explanations of how the suicide took place, saying that some reported that the asp was brought in at Cleopatra's command and hidden in a basket of figs. Other reports, according to Plutarch, were that the serpent was hidden in a box and was pricked into biting the queen, or that she died by poison hidden in a hollow razor. Shakespeare chooses the first of these without much elaboration, though he does have Cleopatra hint darkly at her plot as she whispers to Charmian (V, ii, 195-6). Plutarch implies his choice of the first alternative also when he says that "they [the guards] believed he [the country fellow] told them truly" (II. 133), and a similar plot is further implied by Shakespeare in Cleopatra's question, "Hast thou the pretty worm of Nilus there?" (V, ii, 243). But in both versions of his play Daniel has Cleopatra carefully plot the whole catastrophe. Nothing is left to chance or mystery, and the second version does not differ materially from the first.

A point in which Daniel might have been guided by Shakespeare is his treatment of Thyreus, the messenger from Caesar whom Antony ordered whipped. No mention of him occurs in the 1594 *Cleopatra.* Shakespeare devoted two scenes to the incident (III. xii, xiii). Daniel adverts to it for the first time in the edition of 1607 (ll. 474-8), where he has Eras remind Cleopatra of how she might have profited by Caesar's offer of safety, made through this ambassador Thyreus. The incident is of course to be found in Plutarch.

In connection then with the problem of what guided Daniel in recasting his play, it is concluded that he may have derived suggestions from Shakespeare for introducing the second and final scenes of his new version, that the recasting of three scenes from narrated action to dramatic representation was probably influenced by the popular drama, but that these recast scenes show Daniel continuing to work in a manner independent of all sources, real or supposed. If he borrowed from Shakespeare—and the suspicion that he did so is strong—he showed great resourcefulness in concealing his obligation.

The "noticeable expressions" cited by Case at the beginning of Daniel's new scene, Act I, Scene 2, are not very pointed parallels to Shakespeare's play. It is clear that Case's argument rests mainly upon the larger structural changes made in the 1607 *Cleopatra.* The verbal resemblances adduced to date appear then to be negligible, although the present writers offer a few previously unnoticed instances which reinforce the notion of a Shakespeare influence, however elusive it may be. Two of these occur in connection with the circumstances of Antony's death (Shakespeare, IV, xv, and Daniel, I. ii), and it should be noted that at this point both poets are following Plutarch closely.

1. After Antony has been raised into the monument, Plutarch thus described Cleopatra's conduct:

> Then she dried up his blood that had berayed his face, and called him her Lord, her husband, and Emperor.
>
> (II, 123)

Shakespeare works independently of his source here and has his Cleopatra say,

> And welcome, welcome! die where thou hast lived:
> Quicken with kissing: had my lips that power,
> Thus would I wear them out.
>
> (II. 38-40)

Daniel, following Plutarch, possibly tones down the exuberance of Shakespeare's lines and retains the one detail of the kiss:

> Stops up his wound again that freshly bled,
> Calles him her Lord, her spouse, her Emperor,
> Forgets her owne distresse, to comfort his,
> And interpoints each comfort with a kisse.
>
> (ll. 87-90)

2. The dying Antony, as reported by Plutarch, advises Cleopatra as to her immediate course of action:

> . . . and persuaded her, that she should seek to save her life, if she could possibly, without reproach and dishonour: and that chiefly she should trust Proculeius above any man else about Caesar.
>
> (II, 123)

Shakespeare follows this passage closely and condenses a portion of it. Antony tells Cleopatra:

> Of Caesar seek your honour, with your safety.—O!
> CLEO. They do not go together.
> ANT.   Gentle, hear me.
> None about Caesar trust but Proculeius.
>
> (ll. 46-8)

In Daniel's play, as Dircetus reports it to Caesar, Antony suggests another motive to Cleopatra, but a portion of the speech is identical with Shakespeare's account:

> But rather ought she seeke her race to free;
> By all the meanes (her honour sav'd) she can;
> And none about Octavius trust, said he,
> But Proculeius; he's an honest man.
>
> (ll. 99-102)

These correspondences are close enough to suggest influence, even taking into account Plutarch as a source, and there is a slight indication that it is Daniel who is following Shakespeare. These seem to be the only significant verbal parallels. They add a little to the argument for the priority of Shakespeare's play—an argument that rests mainly, if uncertainly, on the structural changes Daniel made in the 1607 version.

In this article the attempt has not been made to survey the "whole question" of Shakespeare's sources in the History Plays as Jenkins suggests is needed. Instead, one very important contemporary source, Daniel, has been scrutinized, and the effort has been made to evaluate evidences of mutual influence. Their handling of corresponding and often identical materials reveals, along with the inevitable differences in two poets of such diverse talents, many important resemblances in fact, idea, and mood which cannot be dismissed as accidental or be relegated to their common sources. Hence Shakespeare's craftsmanship, and to some extent his conception of history, cannot adequately be appreciated without recognition of Daniel as a shaping force. Daniel in turn appears to have altered certain of his ideas (indubitably some historical ones, and possibly some dramatic ones) by the square of the writer whom he had influenced at an earlier day. (pp. 558-77)

> *Laurence Michel and Cecil C. Seronsy, "Shakespeare's History Plays and Daniel: An Assessment," in* Studies in Philology, *Vol. LII, No. 4, October, 1955, pp. 549-77.*

J.W. Lever (essay date 1956)

[*In the following excerpt, the critic examines Daniel's contribution to the form and imagery of the late Elizabethan love sonnet, as exemplified in his sonnet sequence, Delia.*]

In the last years of the sixteenth century a new spirit, elusive but all-pervading, appears in English literature. It was the age of Marlowe's *Faustus* and Bacon's *Essays,* of Nashe's pamphlets and Donne's lyrics; above all, the age of Shakespearean drama. What common qualities of thought or imagination, we ask, underlie works of such amazing variety? (p. 139)

Certain unifying trends stand out unmistakably. The old interlude play with its personified virtues and vices, its type figures and didactic utterances, makes way for dramas enacting the conduct of individuals. In narrative poetry, allegorical and moralistic themes are superseded by the frank sensuousness of Ovidian romance or by versified history and politics. The lyric, though maintaining pastoral conventions, acquires a new grace and vividness; satires

and epigrams, though imitating Roman models, show an acute observation of contemporary manners. No original system of ideas, no co-ordinating philosophy, is to be distilled from these works, which draw continually upon established precedents; but there is in fact a different mode of apprehension, a re-viewing of the old landscape from a changed perspective. The author took his theories wherever he found them, and preferably from the most ancient authorities; but whatever he borrowed was subtly transfigured. His approach might perhaps be described as a hyperacute curiosity concerning all forms of phenomenal behaviour, and especially of his fellow human beings; an eager desire to experience all knowledge upon his own nerve-endings. The metaphysical constructions of the universe, the moral categories of behaviour which were part of his intellectual inheritance, were constantly reaffirmed; but their hold on his imagination lay not so much in their intrinsic truth as in their power to illuminate the more obscure regions of personality. Man became in effect the measure of the universe and it is especially notable that a drama whose protagonists were characters in their own right should emerge as the most typical art-form of the age. (pp. 139-40)

[Paradoxically] the sonnet sequence, through which the Renaissance poets first came to voice personality, now proved the least amenable to new needs. By the end of the sixteenth century, the sonnet was no longer an excitingly modern form of lyric expression but a time-honoured institution. Practised by generations of writers for over two hundred years, modified by Serafino and his school, reconstituted in French by Ronsard and his fellows of the *Pléiade,* revived in Italy by the Neoplatonist poets, further rehandled by Desportes, and known in England since the time of Wyatt, the sonnet carried a vast accretion of concepts, images, and traditional phraseology. Every detail in the pattern of courtship, every simile portraying lover and lady, had already been prescribed. . . . Only through a major creative effort, comparable to that of Petrarch himself in his revitalization of the Troubadour inheritance, would the sonnet once more answer fully to the needs of the age. (pp. 143-44)

Daniel's sonnets were probably the first of [a] new school, twenty-three of them appearing with the 1591 edition of *Astrophel and Stella.* Desportes was at that time his principal model and from the French poet he learned the virtues of simplicity and grace. These sonnets show a smooth and accomplished handling of verse, an avoidance of extravagant conceit, and a fastidious choice of words. Where, for example, Desportes wrote—

> *Je verray par les ans, vangeurs de mon martyre,*
> *Que l'or de vos cheveux argenté deviendra,*
> *Que de vos deux soleils la splendeur s'esteindra,*
> *Et qu'il faudra qu' Amour tout confus s'en retire.*
>   *Cléonice* LXIII

—Daniel produced the chaster rendering in *Delia:*

> I once may see when yeeres shall wrecke my wronge,
> When golden haires shall chaunge to siluer wyer:
> And those bright rayes, that kindle all this fyer

Shall faile in force, their working not so stronge.

(xxx)

Martyre is toned down to 'wronge', and *vos deux soleils* to 'those bright rayes'; while the Petrarchan image of Love retreating from the face, already used by Surrey, is entirely omitted, at the cost of a rather awkward fourth line. The theme of Desportes in this sonnet, with its stress on the fading of beauty and its metaphors of sun and flowers, owed much to Ronsard. When in 1592 Daniel brought out the first independent edition of **Delia,** twenty-seven new sonnets were added to those published in the previous year, making up a sequence of fifty sonnets; and in the new poems it was evident that he had been led on to an earnest study of Ronsard's own work. Instead of the usual ardours and complaints of courtly love, his main concern was with the pathos of youth and beauty as victims of time. Women, like flowers, blossomed in the spring of their maidenhood and withered in the autumn of old age. The lady of the sonnets, however idealized by her lovers, was but mortal: the day would surely come when her beauty would decline and these very lovers forsake her—all save the poet, who would commemorate her as she once had been. Such reflections were, of course, no more than variations on the pagan theme of *carpe diem* to be found in Catullus and Horace; but in the last phase of the Renaissance they acquired a special relevance. The glories and frailties of the individual, consummation of all that was fair in the phenomenal world, yet subject, like all phenomena, to time's depredation, stirred the deepest sentiments of the age. Conceived in terms of this vision, the sonnet heroine appeared once more as an authentic being, endowed with poetic universality; while the poet who claimed to immortalize her in verse, instead of being a mere mouthpiece for decorative phrases, became the serious champion of positive human values. The best of Daniel's new sonnets were devoted to this conception. In the true sixteenth-century sense, he 'imitated' Ronsard—and Tasso, in so far as the Italian poet showed Ronsard's influence; subduing his own genius so completely to the spirit of his originals that their poetry virtually became his own. Every image, every turn of thought, was recreated and re-experienced. The result was a formal perfection unmatched in the work of any of his contemporaries, Shakespeare excepted. As mere fragmentary illustrations, we may note the subtle variations of metre, acting in sensitive accord with the inner implications of the theme, in the following verse:

No Aprill can reuiue thy withred flowers,
Whose blooming grace adornes thy glorie now:
Swift speedy Time, feathred with flying howers,
Dissolues the beautie of the fairest brow.

(XXXI)

When men shall finde thy flowre, thy glory passe,
And thou with carefull brow sitting alone:
Receiued hast this message from thy glasse,
That tells thee trueth, and saies that all is gone.

(XXXIII)

Care-charmer sleepe, sonne of the Sable night,
Brother to death, in silent darknes borne:
Relieue my languish, and restore the light,
With darke forgetting of my cares returne.

(XLV)

or these examples of metaphorical imagery, the effects of an equally penetrating insight by the visual sense and the inner eye:

A modest maide, deckt with a blush of honour,
Whose feete doe treade greene pathes of youth and loue

(VI)

Th'Ocean neuer did attende more duely,
Vppon his Soueraignes course, the nights pale Queene:

(XL)

In nearly all these sonnets, the diction is admirably simple and pure, based upon monosyllables chosen with fastidious regard for their sonorous quality. Daniel was a master in the evocative use of long vowels and in quiet harmonies of assonance and alliteration. Without looking beyond the verses quoted, we may note how the lines from XXXI range through a wide gamut of vowel sounds and link these in a subtle music; or listen to the iterative vowels of *flowre, thou, brow* in XXXIII as they collaborate with the f-, l-, and th- alliterations; or trace the interweaving of s- and r- consonants in XLV. Nor was Daniel a slave to mere euphony: if this last sonnet is read as a whole it will be seen what power he was able to convey by interposing such strong, highly suggestive words as 'shipwrack', 'torment', 'passions', 'lyers', in the lulling, smooth invocation to sleep.

In addition to all this, Daniel should be credited with two major contributions to the formal development of the late Elizabethan sequence. His grasp of metaphorical imagery led to its employment as a structural principle binding together a run of sonnets, where the rose image of Ronsard and Tasso expanded, as it were organically, through a sustained metaphorical treatment of flowers, sun, and summer-and-winter contrasts. The nucleus of sonnets thus created, numbered XXXI-XXXV in the 1592 edition, had a new formal coherence, reinforced by the device of echoing the last line of each sonnet as the first of that which succeeds it, and the consequent iterations of rhyme-pattern. The effect was to restore in some measure the integral character of the sonnet sequence, which was in danger of being lost with the contemporary decline of interest in its traditional themes. Secondly, Daniel revealed the latent potentialities of the Surrey verse-form. With the exception of two sonnets in the 1591 edition, and five added after 1592 under the influence of Spenser, he consistently adhered to this in the **Delia** sequence. Surrey's form had been the staple of the English sonnet from the time of its inception; but hitherto its appeal had rested chiefly on its simplicity of rhyme and logic. Only once, in Sidney's 'Leaue me, ô Loue', had its wider possibilities been explored. Now at last it was recognized as a great reversionary inheritance for the new generation of poets. Devised by a writer more concerned with detached observation than ideal concepts, Surrey's sonnet-form perfectly corresponded with the needs of the later Elizabethans. Their thought-processes, if more speculative than his, were likewise experiential; built upon sense-perception; and functioning on empirical lines through the logic of apposition and contrast. *When . . . Then . . .* were the great structural words of their sonnets. However wide the range of their imagination, however profound their intuition, its basis remained the solid ground of physical reality. Daniel was the first of his generation to appreciate the contemporary significance of Surrey's form, which supplied the necessary foundation for all future developments in the sonnet medium.

There can be no doubting the crucial importance of Daniel's work. It was to exercise a far-reaching influence upon his colleagues, who all benefited from one or another aspect of his achievement. But at the same time these sonnets had their shortcomings, which were clearly recognized by the poets of his day. The trouble was that Daniel, while proving his mastery in his own chosen field, had failed sufficiently to widen the scope of his subject-matter. *Delia*, apart from its residuary features, was a sustained elegiac lament on the passing of youth and beauty, coupled with a declaration of faith in the survival of the poet's vision. It was undoubtedly a theme that touched chords of Elizabethan sentiment; but the contemporary spirit was nevertheless too positive and restless to be contained within such limits. Brightness might fall from the air; but the Elizabethans at the end of the sixteenth century were not disposed to sum up their total attitude to experience in terms of finely modulated pathos. (pp. 150-54)

> *J. W. Lever, "The Late Elizabethan Sonnet," in his* The Elizabethan Love Sonnet, *Methuen & Co. Ltd, 1956, pp. 139-61.*

Joan Rees   (essay date 1964)

[*Rees is an English scholar who has published numerous books on British authors, specializing in the sixteenth and nineteenth centuries. In the following excerpt from her biography of Daniel, Rees discusses* The Tragedy of Cleopatra *and, in particular, the patronage of the Countess of Pembroke in fostering the play.*]

The background to the composition of *Cleopatra* can be filled in with considerably more certainty than the background to *Delia* and *Rosamond* because it belongs to literary rather than to personal history. *Cleopatra*, in fact, owed its origin to the Countess of Pembroke's intention to strike a blow in a literary crusade, a crusade which had been initiated by her brother [Sir Philip Sidney] in the *Apologie for Poetry* and which she had been prosecuting as best she could, since his death. The advent of Daniel, whose name had been linked with Sidney's in [Thomas Newman's edition of *Astrophel and Stella*], whose first volume had been received with acclaim as contemporary tributes show, and who not only had true poetic power but was also content to take up residence under the Pembroke roof and be educated by the Countess herself (Wilton was his 'best Schoole' we remember), must have seemed to her something of a godsend. To find not only a good poet but one amenable to instruction was the very thing she needed if her campaign was to make any ground at all.

Sidney had written the *Apologie for Poetry* in 1580 or 1581, probably while he was at Wilton. It is a plea, in general, that imaginative literature should be restored to the high esteem which, he argues, it enjoyed in ancient times, but

at the end it turns to a special theme, and Sidney urges the creation of a modern English literature to compare with the work which has been done on the continent. He reviews briefly but cogently the existing state of English writing and exposes its deficiencies, and he declares his faith that, in spite of the small harvest since Chaucer, 'our tongue is most fit to honor Poesie, and to bee honored by Poesie'. When, after his death, his sister took upon herself his function as literary patron, she seems to have felt that it also devolved on her to do what she could to bring about the literary resurgence that Sidney's *Apologie* called for. Sidney had singled out Spenser for praise on the showing of *The Shepheardes Calender* and since Sidney's death, Spenser's poetic career had gone from strength to strength. Spenser might be counted on to champion a high ideal of poetry in the field of non-dramatic verse but there was no comparable defender of Sidney's ideals in drama and the ground seemed to be giving way all round his position. It is to shore up this weak point that Daniel and his talents are seized upon and *Cleopatra* is 'the labour' imposed upon him by the Countess, whose influence 'predominated', as he says, his Muse. (pp. 44-5)

The scene is all set for the entry of Daniel as the new champion of the cause, one who, properly tutored by the Countess of Pembroke herself, will carry his spear against 'Grosse Barbarisme' with more conviction and a better sense of aim, one who, moreover, is a better poet than [Thomas] Kyd. His task is not mere translation, but the creation of an original English play, that 'exact model of all Tragedies' which Sidney desiderated, and for which the Countess of Pembroke has been carefully preparing the ground.

The lines on which he should work were fairly clearly laid down for him. His play was to be a companion-piece to the Countess's [translation of Garnier's play, *Marc-Antoine*]: he therefore had Garnier as an immediate model, and, further back, there was a handling of Cleopatra's story by the creator of French classical tragedy, the *Cléopâtre Captive* by Étienne Jodelle of which also he made some use. He had, of course, to write within the neo-classic formula.

It is remarkable, in all the circumstances, that anything of any individuality got written at all, and it is hardly surprising that many readers have been too much depressed by the form ever to find the individuality. Yet *Cleopatra* may still be read with pleasure, for there is life and humanity in it and considerable skill in the handling of the material. The play is conceived as a unity in the fullest, as distinct from a merely conventional sense: its theme is the character of Cleopatra and its whole purpose is to illuminate that character, chosen for attention at a moment of greatest crisis, from a variety of angles. To that end, the material of outward action is pared to a minimum. Jodelle chooses the same moment of crisis for his Cleopatra, but he includes more tangential material than Daniel, all of which tends to dissipate attention and by introducing extraneous emotions to weaken the concentration of interest and sympathy on Cleopatra at which Daniel very deliberately aims. Once the full power of the concentration on Cleopatra is realised, the essential coherence of the play is revealed. The Philostratus-Arius scene, for example, which Daniel works up from a hint in Garnier, gives him scope for the exercise of what Saintsbury called his 'almost unsurpassed faculty of ethical verse-writing', but its true purpose and its justification is to serve as a commentary on Cleopatra's resolve to die and to put the story of individuals into the wider context of society as a whole. Arius has saved Philostratus from death and Philostratus, a fellow philosopher, is a little ashamed that he has clung to life so eagerly in a time of disaster when his country's honour is laid low. Yet, he says, even amidst wretchedness:

> . . . yet we reckon life our dearest good.
> And so we live, we care not how we live:
> So deepe we feele impressed in our blood,
> That touch which nature with our breath did
>   give.

The pertinence of this to Cleopatra's situation and the contrast between the abjectness of the philosophers and her courage are obvious. Arius then takes up the discussion, agrees that 'Though we speake more then men, we are but men', and goes on to speak of the state of the whole country, to paint the wider background to the personal tragedy of Cleopatra and to draw more general morals:

> . . . never any age hath better taught,
> What feeble footing pride and greatnesse hath.
> How improvident prosperitie is caught,
> And cleane confounded in the day of wrath.
> See how dismaid Confusion keepes those
>   streetes,
> That nought but mirth and musique late re-
>   sounded,
> How nothing with our eye but horror meetes,
> Our state, our wealth, our pride, and al con-
>   founded.

It is instructive to compare this whole scene with the soliloquy which Garnier gives to his Philostratus. Daniel's philosophers are much more philosophical and it is noticeable that for the signs and wonders which Garnier retails from Plutarch, foretelling the downfall of Antony and Cleopatra, Daniel substitutes auguries of a different nature: pride and riot grown overweening, dissolute impiety seizing the minds of Prince and people, insolent security and wanton thoughts, all ministering to 'fat-fed pleasure'.

This scene has a legitimate place in the play then, not merely because it offers an example of Daniel exercising his gifts in a species of writing in which he excelled, but because, far from dispersing attention, it concentrates it even more firmly on the fate of Cleopatra and reveals implications as yet not touched on.

Another scene, that between Seleucus and Rodon, which may at first glance appear superfluous, is likewise revealed on closer examination to be deliberately contrived as an integral part of the development of the play. Jodelle made Seleucus repent of his betrayal of Cleopatra but the whole episode is treated by Jodelle half-comically and the interchange between Seleucus and the Chorus, though no doubt meant seriously, hardly escapes a hangover of comedy:

> Lors que la Roine et triste et courageuse
> Devant Cesar aux cheveux m'a tiré,

Et de son poing mon visage empiré:
S'elle m'eust fait mort en terre gesir,
Elle eust preveu à mon present desir . . .

Jodelle has Plutarch's authority that Cleopatra 'flew upon him (Seleucus) and tooke him by the heare of the head, and boxed him wellfavoredly', but Jodelle's treatment of the scene strikes a note out of harmony with the play as a whole. Daniel tones down the violence and preserves more dignity, and in the scene which follows between Seleucus and Rodon, he develops the theme of repentance after treachery more fully than Jodelle. Seleucus, tasting the bitterness of remorse, reveals the respect Cleopatra's servants have for her and his sense of obligation to 'such a bounteous Queene as she'. What is more important, he is, with his grief at his own baseness, a convenient and suitable confidant for Rodon, who introduces yet another aspect of Cleopatra's character, and weaves one of the strongest of its strands into the texture of the play.

In *Marc-Antoine* Garnier had made an interesting attempt to intensify the drama and emotion in his story by the introduction of a scene showing Cleopatra parting from her children. Daniel takes up this idea and makes a great deal more of it. He sticks closer to Plutarch and confines the parting to Caesario (Cleopatra's son by Julius Caesar) and he works up to Rodon's account of the parting, moreover, by a series of preparatory references so that, by the time the crisis is reached, the reader is sensitive to its full effect. In the opening speech of the play, the theme of Cleopatra's love and concern for her children is emphatically introduced:

> You lucklesse issue of an wofull mother,
> The wretched pledges of a wanton bed,
> You Kings designed, must subjects live to other;
> Or else, I feare, scarce live, when I am dead.
> It is for you I temporize with *Caesar,*
> And stay this while to mediate your safety:
> For you I faine content, and soothe his pleasure,
> Calamity herein hath made me crafty.

Immediately following these lines comes a hint of an emotional conflict involved in this love of her children:

> For come what will, this stands, I must die free.
> And die my selfe uncaptiv'd and unwonne:
> Blood, Children, Nature, all must pardon me,
> My soule yeelds Honor up the victory,
> And I must be a Queene, forget a mother;
> Though mother would I be, were I not I;
> And Queene would not be now, could I be other.

The same ideas are insisted on in the next scene, this time in Proculeius's account of his interview with Cleopatra. Cleopatra has been pleading for her freedom and pleads especially for her children, mentioning Caesario by name. She goes on:

> But if that with the torrent of my fall,
> All must be rapt with furious violence,
> And no respect, nor no regard at all,
> Can ought with nature or with blood dispence:
> Then be it so, if needes it must be so.

And Proculeius adds that she:

> There staies and shrinkes in horror of her state.

Here Daniel again, and with greater emphasis, points to the conflict between Cleopatra's instincts as a Queen and her instincts as a mother. There is no comparable preparation for the Garnier scene. When the moment for parting comes, the children are wailed over, consigned to Euphronius's care, Euphronius says, 'Allons, enfans' and the children dutifully reply, 'Allons'; we have scarcely had time so much as to recognise Cleopatra in maternal guise before it is all over. In Jodelle the children are even more briefly treated and any possible anxiety over their fate is quickly dismissed since before the end of the Caesar-Cleopatra interview Caesar has promised to spare them.

When in Daniel's play, Rodon tells his story, in the exchange of treacheries with Seleucus, the full significance of the earlier references to the children is revealed in the moving narrative of Cleopatra's parting from Caesario (the other children and their fates, having served Daniel's purpose, are allowed to remain obscure). Cleopatra's vacillations, as she tries to dismiss Caesario, for his own sake and for Egypt's, and struggles against a presentiment of doom, are traced with a humanity that makes the story genuinely poignant. At last she makes up her mind:

> But stay: there's something else that I would say:
> Yet nothing now. But O God speed thee well,
> Lest saying more, that more may make thee
>   stay.
> Yet let me speake: It may be tis the last
> That ever I shall speake to thee my sonne.
> Doe Mothers use to part in such post hast?
> What, must I end when I have scarce begunne?
> Ah no (deare heart) tis no such slender twine
> Wherewith the knot is tide twixt thee and me;
> That blood within thy veins came out of mine,
> Parting from thee, I part from part of me:
> And therefore I must speake. Yet what? O
>   sonne.

There is an echo of this scene later on, distorted, as echoes are, and used deliberately to recall this parting at the moment of Cleopatra's death as she dallies with the asp, procrastinating a little before the final deed:

> Looke how a mother at her sonnes departing
> For some farre voyage bent to get him fame,
> Doth entertain him with an ydle parling
> And still doth speake, and still speakes but the
>   same;
> Now bids farewell, and now recalles him backe,
> Tels what was told, and bids againe farewell,
> And yet againe recalles; for still doth lacke
> Something that Love would faine and cannot
>   tell;
> Pleas'd he should goe, yet cannot let him goe.

The rest of Rodon's account is concerned with the betrayal of Caesario and Caesario's lament on the irony of being born great only to suffer great miseries—a common theme in Senecan tragedy which, with its inverse, the virtues of mediocrity, finds a place also in Jodelle. In Daniel it demonstrates yet another implication of Cleopatra's fate and extends the story into the future when another generation will take up the old quarrels.

Daniel, then, from the slightest of hints in Plutarch, and with Garnier's tentative treatment of it before him, developed a theme which considerably enriches his play. In the scene between Seleucus and Rodon, he opens up a new vista in the character of Cleopatra and suggests that a passionate and tender devotion to her children is included in her personality. It is evident that Daniel became deeply interested in Cleopatra as he revolved the material for his play and his work takes its shape and impulse from that interest so that, ultimately, all his material, from whatever source, is used to give body and life to a conception which is entirely original.

The scene between Cleopatra and Caesar provides a good single example of Daniel's handling of his material. Daniel introduces Dolabella as a witness of the scene and this is a device which is effective in several ways. It serves to bind the play together, as it is Dolabella who is to send the important letter to Cleopatra warning her of Caesar's intention to send her shortly to Rome (in Jodelle, Dolabella's name is mentioned in connection with the letter but without any reference to him before or after); it serves, by paving the way for the Dolabella-Titius scene, to provide a means of linking the action between Cleopatra's last rites at Antony's tomb and the final narrative of her death; and most important of all, it throws still more light on Cleopatra by illustrating the powerful effect of her beauty and her personality even at this time of disaster. It shows, too, how Cleopatra, made more sensitive to true love and friendship in her sorrow, responds now with gratitude, whereas once she had thought that all men owed her love as a duty and she was bound to none.

What Daniel has done, then, is to evolve a closely integrated action out of his material and, above all, to produce a study of character remarkable for its sympathy and insight. Daniel recognised in 1594 that his Cleopatra was not much like the historical figure and in the dedication of the 1611 edition he defends himself in significant words. He has presented her tragedy, he writes:

> In th'habit I conceived became her care
> Which if to her it be not fitted right
> Yet in the sute of nature sure it is
> And is the language that affliction might
> Perhaps deliver when it spake distresse.

Political issues are firmly subordinated to this sympathy and there is even some inconsistency as far as the moral is concerned, for while the Chorus and the philosophers talk about lust and luxury, the Cleopatra who is portrayed is at least well on the way to being purified. In her first speech she recognises a new depth in her love for Antony and she can see now, too, the quality of his love:

> And yet thou cam'st but in my beauties waine,
> When new appearing wrinckles of declining
> Wrought with the hand of yeares, seem'd to de-
>   taine
> My graces light, as now but dimly shining,
> Even in the confines of mine age, when I
> Failing of what I was, and was but thus:
> When such as we do deeme in jealousie
> That men love for themselves, and not for us;
> Then, and but thus, thou didst love most sincere-
>   ly,
> O *Antony,* that best deserv'dst it better,
> This Autumne of my beauty bought so dearely,

For which in more than death, I stand thy
debter . . .

This passage is in direct contradiction to what Plutarch
says of Cleopatra's beauty: ' . . . Caesar and Pompey
knew her when she was but a young thing, and knew not
then what the worlde ment: but nowe she went to Antonius at the age when a woman's beawtie is at the prime, and
she also of best judgement'. The alteration enables Daniel
to illustrate the change he conceives to have taken place
in Cleopatra's character under the pressure of sorrow, her
ruthless examination of herself, and her new tenderness
towards Antony; but such touches make it difficult to
identify her with the sinful figure whom the Chorus de-
nounces.

The human touches, the vividness with which some scenes
and situations are realised, are among the by no means
negligible rewards offered to a sympathetic reading of this
play. Caesario makes the usual comments about the disad-
vantages of greatness and the retribution which overtakes
tyrants, but he adds, more feelingly:

> Yet in the meane time we whom Fates reserve,
> The bloody sacrifices of ambition,
> We feele the smart, what ever they deserve,
> And we indure the present times condition.
> The justice of the heavens revenging thus,
> Doth onely satisfie it selfe, not us.

The messenger, who takes the aspics to Cleopatra, tells
how he put them in a basket of figs, covered with leaves:

> And comming to the guard that kept the doore,
> What hast thou there? said they, and lookt
> thereon.
> Seeing the figges, they deem'd of nothing more,
> But said, they were the fairest they had seene.
> Tast some, said I, for they are good and pleasant.
> No, no, said they, goe beare them to thy Queene,
> Thinking me some poore man that brought a
> present.

And he describes Cleopatra in her last finery:

> Glittering in all her pompeous rich aray,
> Great *Cleopatra* sate, as if sh'had wonne
> *Caesar,* and all the world beside, this day.

As she sinks in death Charmion sets straight the crown on
her head

> That all the world may know she dide a Queene.

The verse itself labours at times but, as some of the quotations above have shown, when a congenial opportunity occurs it comes alight and takes the imagination. There are
many single lines and some longer passages which make
moments, if not immortal, yet certainly memorable. Daniel's eloquence has greater opportunities here than ever before and the development has now taken place which was
foreshadowed in **Rosamond,** his 'very pure and copious
English' (in Edmund Bolton's phrase) has been brought
fully into the service of his sensitive, reflective, and intelligent mind.

The Choruses deserve some separate discussion.

The members of the Chorus are 'all Egyptians' and although they do not participate in the action they are naturally deeply concerned about what is going on. At the end
of Act I, which has consisted solely of Cleopatra's soliloquy, they comment severely on the sins of the great:

> The scene is broken downe
> And all uncov'red lyes,
> The purple actors knowne
> Scarce men, whom men despise.

Cleopatra, they somewhat grimly point out, now sees
what lies at the end of 'the dangerous way' she took:

> Which led her to decay.
> And likewise makes us pay
> For her disordred lust,
> The int'rest of our blood:
> Or live a servile pray,
> Under a hand unjust,
> As others shall thinke good.
> This hath her riot wonne:
> And thus she hath her state, herselfe and us un-
> done.

Daniel uses a twelve-line stanza form, rhymed ababbcdbc-
dee, consisting of eleven lines of three iambic feet and a
final alexandrine. Far from being graceful, it is an inflexi-
ble form which imparts a peculiar harshness to the Chorus's judgements. At times they contrive a moral allegory
that sounds as though Daniel has been reading his Spenser
recently:

> Their conscience still within
> Th'eternall larum is
> That ever-barking dog that calles upon their
> misse.

> No meanes at all to hide
> Man from himself can finde:
> No way to start aside
> Out from the hell of minde.
> But in himselfe confin'd,
> He still sees sinne before;
> And winged-footed paine,
> That swiftly comes behind . . .

For the second chorus Daniel evolves another curious
stanza form, consisting this time of fourteen lines rhyming
abbaacddcceeff. The subject is the frustrations and miseries of the discontented mind which, whether it seeks the
objects of ambition or of lust, is never satisfied but finds
only 'destruction, envy, hate'. Even Cleopatra's resolution
to die is seen by the Chorus here as nothing more than a
last will o' the wisp:

> This is that rest this vaine world lends,
> To end in death that all things ends.

The lines are longer by a foot than those of the first chorus
but the high proportion of monosyllables and a certain
bleakness of statement, which is not unimpressive, make
them appear clipped. The third chorus has four-foot lines,
like the third, a twelve-line stanza, ababbccabadd, and,
what distinguishes it very markedly from either of the previous two, a very much richer vocabulary and fuller tone:

> O Fearfull-frowning Nemesis,
> Daughter of Justice, most severe;
> That art the worlds great Arbitresse
> And Queene of causes raigning here.

It gives strong lyric expression to the idea of 'inevitable destiny', the 'swift confusion' which will abase 'late proud mounting vanity' and it questions heavenly justice which includes 'The innocent poore multitude' in the punishment of great men's sins. But, resignedly, the Chorus conclude that in the cycle of human affairs, prosperity will ever grow overweening and will ever be punished:

> As we, so they that treate us thus,
> Must one day perish like to us.

The fourth chorus has a four-foot line and a fourteen-line stanza composed as three quatrains and a final couplet. It is again distinguished from all its predecessors this time by the fact that feminine rhyme endings are used throughout except in the final couplets. It is a languid, nerveless poem in which the chorus find slippery excuses for Egypt's humiliation—it is the decree of fate—it is the fault of their rulers—and only rouse themselves to hope that the conquerors will in time be corrupted by the weaknesses of the conquered:

> Fill full your hands, and carry home,
> Enough from us to ruine Rome.

The last chorus returns to the three-foot line of the first. The stanza has fourteen lines and is rhymed abcdabcddc-baee. The theme is the extinction of all hope for Egypt now that Cleopatra is dead, and the passion of the moment urges the chorus into symbolic language of some imaginative power:

> And canst O Nylus thou,
> Father of flouds indure,
> That yellow Tyber should
> With sandy streames rule thee? . . .
>
> Draw backe thy waters floe
> To thy concealèd head:
> Rockes strangle up thy waves,
> Stop Cataractes thy fall.
> And turne thy courses so,
> That sandy Desarts dead,
> (The world of dust that craves
> To swallow thee up all,)
> May drinke so much as shall
> Revive from vasty graves
> A living greene, which spred
> Far florishing, may grow
> On that wide face of Death,
> Where nothing now drawes breath.

It ends with unanswered questions to the gods:

> Are these the bounds y'have given
> Th' untranspassable barres,
> That limit Pride so short?
> Is greatnesse of this sort,
> That greatnesse greatnesse marres,
> And wrackes it selfe, selfe-driven
> On Rockes of her owne might?
> Doth Order order so
> Disorders overthrow?

The choruses, as this account of them has shown, combine commentary on the moral implications of the drama with statements appropriate to the individuals composing the Chorus, the ordinary Egyptian people. They are carefully worked in form and diction and each is devised to make a particular impression and an individual contribution to the play as a whole. Great care has evidently been devoted to them, but the result is only intermittently successful: perhaps, indeed, they try to do too much.

A great deal of effort has undoubtedly gone into the whole play. Daniel is forcing his poetic gifts to expand in the directions that Lady Pembroke and her friends wished, leaving the love-melancholy of **Delia** and **Rosamond** for the fall of kingdoms and the tragedies of the great, and for the cultivation of rarefied dramatic and lyric form. His poetry runs, naturally, more easily into some of the new channels than others. Some of the better passages have already been quoted and it is especially interesting to see the characteristics of the later Daniel emerging in such things as his patient and sympathetic elaboration of the character of Cleopatra, the reduction of the violence of the Seleucus scene in favour of a more adult and dignified treatment, and the serious reflection on human life and character, which leads him, for example, to reject a count of supernatural phenomena and replace it by a history of moral degeneration. As a work complete in itself Daniel's **Cleopatra** deserves much better than to be dismissed merely as an aberration from the path of true drama; in its relation to Daniel's career, it is a very important document, for in the composing of it Daniel developed the character by which he is now best known.

When he began **Cleopatra** he was 'Sweete hony-dropping Daniel'; by the time he finished it, he was Coleridge's 'sober-minded Daniel' and he knew much better than he had where his aptitudes and inclinations in this 'higher straine' lay. (pp. 49-61)

> *Joan Rees, in her* Samuel Daniel: A Critical and Biographical Study, *Liverpool University Press, 1964, 184 p.*

Edward Phillips on Daniel's reputation in the seventeenth century:

Samuel Daniel, an Author of good note and reputation in King *James* his Reign; whose **History of the II first Kings of England from the Norman Conquest,** though it be of all the rest of his Works most principally sought after and regarded, yet are not his Poetical writings totally forgotten, as namely his Historical Poem of the *Civil Wars* between the House of *York* and *Lancaster,* his **Letter of Octavia to Antoninus,** his **Complaint of Rosamund,** his Panegyric, &c. and of Dramatic pieces his Tragedy of **Philotas,** and **Cleopatra, Hymen's Triumph,** and the **Queens Arcadia** a Pastoral.

> *Edward Phillips, in his* Theatrum Poetarum; or, A Compleat Collection of the Poets, *1674.*

Geoffrey Creigh (essay date 1971)

[*In the following excerpt, Creigh focuses on Daniel's*

masques, highlighting the influence of Sir Philip Sidney's writings—in particular his Defence of Poetry*—in the formation of Daniel's own ideas about the function of poetic form.*]

Daniel's reputation as a deviser of masques, though never high, has progressively diminished in direct proportion to the increasing regard entertained for the masques and entertainments of Ben Jonson. We do not need to look very far for the reason for this; Jonson's cause was that of literary criticism and Daniel's was not. The genesis of the quarrel between Jonson and Daniel, a prologue to the feud conducted so long and so bitterly between Jonson and Inigo Jones, was Jonson's insistence that the masque is a poem while Daniel from the outset contended that the masque is a hybrid form of which poetry constitutes but one element. In recent years a great deal of critical attention has been focussed upon Jonson's aesthetic of the masque and the Jones-Jonson controversy has been fully documented and analysed. Daniel's masques, on the other hand, have been largely neglected or, at best, brought forward even by his apologists as inferior examples of the genre. An examination of Daniel's first masque, ***The Vision of the Twelve Goddesses,*** reveals a highly developed theory of the nature of masque executed with considerable skill, and the masque itself in no way justifies the critical contempt which has been poured upon it.

Critical debate about the validity of Daniel's method in this masque certainly pre-dates the publication of the first printed authorized edition of the masque in 1604. It is clear from the tone of Daniel's remarks in his preface that an attack upon his practice has already been initiated against which he is concerned to defend himself. This being so, it is unwise to accept his statements in this pamphlet, as they have often been accepted, as detached expressions of theory; Daniel's remarks constitute one side of an argument, and they have a context we can only infer. As Ben Jonson and Inigo Jones repeatedly overreach themselves in their later controversy, Jonson in particular adopting a position so extreme that it in no way reflects the true nature of his collaboration with Jones, so Daniel may here have misrepresented his true position in defending himself against his detractors. The factor of temperament is of relevance also. Whereas both Jones and Jonson were certainly volatile and probably irascible, Daniel was of a diffident and retiring nature, prone to take a depreciatory view of his own work, and generally lacking in self-confidence. A superficial reading of the preface to ***The Vision*** is misleading for it would appear to suggest that Daniel's view of masque is not far removed from that of Francis Bacon who was later to write of such entertainments that 'these things are but toys to come amongst such serious observations' ['On Masks and Triumphs', *The Essays* etc., ed. Samuel Reynolds 1890]. It is true that Daniel does write [in his preface] that he conceives the essential function of masque to be 'the decking and furnishing of glory and majesty as the necessary complements requisite for state and greatness', and adds in a statement surely directed against Jonson that 'whosoever strives to show most wit about these punctilios of dreams and shows are sure sick of a disease they cannot hide and would fain have the world to think them very deeply learned in all mysteries

whatsoever'. Quoted out of context these remarks suggest that Daniel was contemptuous of the form itself, but in their context, that of the total situation, they suggest nothing of the kind. The first statement, neutral in tone, describes the function of the masque without prescribing its nature, whereas the second is personal, angry and hostile, directed by one who no doubt saw himself as a courtier and a scholar against an arrogant and upstart, albeit gifted, bricklayer's son. Daniel's view of Jonson is certainly ungenerous, but as far as we can determine he was not the initiator of the quarrel. To arrive at a legitimate conception of Daniel's view of the nature of masque, it is better to examine his practice as a deviser than to attempt to deduce his theory from a preface apparently provoked by adverse criticism, the precise nature of which we cannot ascertain. Daniel's theory of masque is self-consistent, sophisticated and of a piece with his general aesthetic views; it derives ultimately from his early intellectual commitments and his earliest literary interests.

Among the principal influences in Daniel's intellectual development the work of Sir Philip Sidney has primacy. In later years Daniel was to speak of the time he spent at Wilton House under the patronage of Lady Pembroke, Sidney's sister, as one of the most optimistic and beneficial periods of his life. Sidney's *Defence of Poesie* impressed Daniel and there are a number of points of contact between this work and Daniel's own critical verse essay, ***Musophilus.*** Like Sidney, Daniel maintains poetry to be the servant of philosophy and as such concerned primarily with truth; and like Sidney, if we may judge from his practice, he conceived of poetry fulfilling this function in Aristotelian terms, by presenting an image of the truth more refined than any that is to be found in the world of nature. In *The Defence of Poesie* Sidney had written of the poet that:

> he yeeldeth to the powers of the minde an image of that whereof the *Philosopher* bestoweth but a wordish description, which doth neither strike, pearce, nor possesse the sight of the soule so much, as that other doth.

And further, of the function of poetry itself:

> the final end is, to lead and draw us to as high a perfection, a sour degenerate soules made worse by their clay-lodgings can be capable of.

Sidney's aesthetic is cast in the conventional Aristotelian terms and he regards poetry as mediating between the ideal reality of the form and the perceptive faculty capable of apprehending it. This notion is applied precisely by Daniel both in ***The Vision of the Twelve Goddesses*** and in his later masque, ***Tethys Festival,*** though in each of these cases the eye as the instrument of the soul performs an interpretative and mediating function logically prior but necessarily complementary to that of the understanding.

In a further important respect Daniel remained committed to his early interests in establishing the foundation for his theory of the masque. Daniel's masques are highly emblematical and his earliest publication, probably begun before he left Oxford in 1583, was his translation of Paolo

Giovio's treatise on *Imprese* or emblems, **The Worthy Tract of Paulus Iouius** (1585). To this translation Daniel prefixed a long essay in which he recounts the history of *Imprese* and also speaks of the rules to be followed in their composition. The importance of Giovio's treatise to the critic of the masque is that it is from this work that the terminology subsequently bandied in the Jones-Jonson controversy ultimately derives. Giovio discusses at length the balance to be maintained between device and motto in the composition of an emblem, stressing that the perfect emblem is characterized by an interdependence of the two parts, which he speaks of as body and soul.

> Knowe you then (Master *Iodouico*) that an inuention or *Impresa* (if it be to be accounted currant) ought to haue these fiue properties, First, iust proportion of body and soule. Secondly, that it be not obscure, that it neede a Sibilla to enterprete it, nor so apparent that euery rusticke may vnderstand it. Thirdly, that it haue especially a beautifull shewe, which makes it become more gallant to the vew, . . . Fourthly, that it haue no humane forme. Fifthly, it must haue a posie which is the soule of the body, which ought to differ in language from the *Idioma* of him which beareth the *Impresa,* to the ende the sence may bee the more couert. . . . And to make apparent these properties, you shal vnderstand that the body and soule aboue mentioned, is meant either by the mot or by the subiect, and an *Impresa* is accounted vnperfect when the subiect or body beare no proportion of meaning to the soule, or the soule to the body.
>
> [S. Daniel, trans., *The Worthy Tract of Paulus Iouius,* 1585].

That Daniel was profoundly influenced by Giovio's work and that his later support of Inigo Jones in his argument with Jonson is a matter of intellectual rather than personal commitment, is beyond doubt. For Daniel the composition of a masque was an undertaking similar in kind to the composition of an emblem, and the criterion of adequacy was the maintenance of a proper correspondence between the body or visual element and the soul, the poetry. Moreover, for Daniel in **The Vision of the Twelve Goddesses** as for Spenser in *The Masque of Cupid,* for the author of *The Masque of the Adamantine Rock,* and for Jonson in *The Entertainment at Highgate,* and to a lesser extent in *The Masque of Blackness,* the art of making a masque was an emblematical art, and the pleasure to be taken by the spectator in experiencing and interpreting the action was of the same kind as he would experience in reading an *Impresa.* Daniel, more consistent though infinitely less flexible than Jonson in his conception of the form, is deeply rooted in the emblematical tradition, and in neither of his masques does he permit, as Jonson increasingly does, the claim of dramatic poetry to disturb what he conceives to be the necessary balance between the visual and the poetic. The pleasure the spectator enjoys, as in the reading of *Imprese,* is the pleasure of recognition. The understanding meditates upon those images which enter at the eye and is assisted by the measure of prose or verse illumination judged appropriate to the occasion. The universal nature of such pleasure is described at length by Daniel in his preface to *The Worthy Tract of Paulus Iouius:*

Yet I say, that to represent vnto the sence of sight the forme or figure of any thing is more natural in act, and more common to al creatures then is hearing, and thereupon sayth Aristotle, that we loue the sence of seeing, for that by it we are taught and made to learne more then by any other of our sences, whereby we see that all men naturally take delight in pictures . . . in which facultie the Aegyptians were most singulare as the first authors of this *Hieroglyphicall* art: as well do witnesse their sacred Colomnes dedicated to *Mercurie,* whereon were diuers formes and pictures wrought and engrauen, contayning great knowledge, which they called *Hieroglyphi.* To which pillers Plato is sayde to haue gone and retourned with great profit. Yet notwithstanding, in my opinion their deuise was vnperfect, by reason of the diuersitie of the natures of beastes and other things which they figured. Whereupon they who drewe more neere vnto our time seemeth to haue brought this art to perfection, by adding mots or posies to their figures whereby they couertly disclose their intent by a more perfect order. Moreouer besides the figuring of things corporall and of visible forme, men haue also represented things incorporal. . . .

Clearly then, when in 1610, in his preface to **Tethys Festival,** Daniel makes his one substantial contribution to the Jones-Jonson controversy and forcibly argues the dependence of poet upon architect in the devising of masques, it is not simply because he is 'at Jealousies' with Jonson, nor can his comments be dismissed as 'testy and pedestrian'. It can be demonstrated that **The Vision of the Twelve Goddesses** reveals that as early as 1603 Daniel had conceived a theory of masque which was both intellectually respectable and dramatically viable; that he comprehended as fully as anyone the nature of the occasion on which the masque at Court was conventionally performed, and that he succeeded in providing the Court with an entertainment entirely appropriate to this occasion.

Critics of the masque have been severe with Daniel's first attempt in this genre and are more or less united in their dismissal of **The Vision** as a monument to dead ideas, a cumbersome emblematic procession amounting, in Orgel's view, to 'little more than pageantry' and lacking 'dramatic coherence'. Herford and Simpson considered the piece 'structureless and old-fashioned'. The masque is also ridiculed by Brotanek while Professor G. Bentley finds that Daniel fails to 'reveal the faintest hint of Jonson's high conception of the form and function of the masque'. Notwithstanding its current reputation, however, there is no doubt that Daniel's masque was well received by the Court and that it occasioned a great deal of contemporary interest. It appears to have been the first entertainment of its kind to have been independently printed, appearing in two editions, one authorized and the other surreptitious. A letter written by Dudley Carleton to his friend John Chamberlain testifies to the enthusiastic manner in which the entertainment was received at the Court.

Daniel's sense of the nature of the occasion of which the masque is the centre piece controls his conception of the form. It is clear that he thinks of the masque as a form in which the spectators participate, although their participation is mute. In *The Vision of the Twelve Goddesses* Daniel's principal concern is to provide the Court with the opportunity of celebrating its own proper identity; the dramatic centre piece, the masque itself, achieves its full significance only in terms of its successful interrelation with its specific context. In *The Vision of the Twelve Goddesses* Daniel sets out to represent to James, to the foreign ambassadors and the spectators at large, an idealized image of the English Court tactfully implying at the same time that with the accession of James the ideal and the real have become, or at least should have become, identified.

The Vision is essentially processional and emblematical in structure and the written speeches and songs are economical and interrelated with the total design. Though far from structureless, the scenario of the masque is simple. Daniel makes use of a dispersed setting having at one end of the Great Hall a mountain from which the goddesses descend in triadic procession and at the further end a Temple of Virtue and the Cave of Somnus. The plot is straightforward. Night awakes her son, Sleep, from his cave. Sleep carries two wands, one white to evoke meaningful and instructive visions and one black to promote confused dreams. The spectators are initiated into the ritual to follow when Sleep flourishes his white wand and retires to his cave. The dramatic action then begins. First Iris, the messenger of the goddesses, proceeds from the mountain to the temple to warn the Sibilla in attendance there of the approach of the goddesses, presenting her with a 'prospective' or telescope through which she may view them before they descend. This device serves the practical end of removing the necessity of interrupting the flow of the later action, for the Sibilla proceeds to identify the goddesses and to describe them prior to their descent into the Court. The goddesses then proceed in threes (each rank interspersed with a triad of torchbearers) from the mountain to the temple bearing emblems designating the particular virtues they are to be taken to represent, and these are deposited on the altar. Whilst this procession is in progress the three Graces further point its significance with their accompanying song. The Measures follow, after which the Graces sing once again before the masquers select their partners from the audience and dance with them. A short retiring dance performed by the masquers precedes their return to the mountain and thus the entertainment ends.

The basic simplicity of Daniel's design is admirable and it conceals a purpose which is both serious and sophisticated. Daniel's expressed intention in the masque [as stated in his preface] was to 'present the figure of those blessings, with the wish of their increase and continuance, which this mighty kingdom now enjoys by the benefit of his most gracious Majesty, by whom we have this glory of peace', a theme closely related to that of the *Panegyrike Congratulatorie* with which he had greeted James at Burley-on-the-Hill the previous year. For Daniel mere pageantry will not suffice. He clearly sees the occasion, that of James's first Christmas in London, as one of great political significance, and his consciousness of the nature of the occasion is reflected in the total design of the masque.

Daniel's first concern is to establish the ground upon which the masque is to be entertained, and it is to this end that the prospective or telescope is introduced. Somnus has already initiated the spectators into a mystery, and the telescope, the essential property of which is to distort vision by providing a point of view other than the natural, enables the Sibilla to proceed beyond the natural and to perceive a higher reality than that which is to be apprehended by the human eye. The goddesses discerned by the Sibilla on the mountain are revealed to her as the virtues they traditionally represent. It was therefore beside the point to object to Daniel's practice on the grounds that his figures were not 'drawn in all proportions to the life of antiquity'. Myth and history are not to be confused. When the goddesses descend from their mountain, they do so as:

> figures wherein antiquity hath formerly clothed them and as they have been cast in the imagination of piety, who hath given mortal shapes to the gifts and effects of an eternal power, for that those beautiful characters of sense were easier to be read, than their mystical *Ideas,* dispersed in that wide and incomprehensible volume of nature.

Daniel's manipulation of the nature of reality is deliberate and it enables him to pay an effective compliment to the Queen and the other ladies personating the goddesses. That they incarnate virtue, he suggests, is no more a fiction than to suppose that virtue was ever incarnate. The ladies of James's Court thus not only represent the goddesses; they are seen to be as real as the goddesses they represent. They embody those virtues they confer upon the Court into which they now formally descend. The use of the prospective glass is further justified in the conceit that their physical presence is so resplendent that it will 'bereave (the spectators) of all save admiration and amazement, for who can look upon such Powers and speak?' Their beauty dazzles the beholders but their correlative virtue has been defined and expressed by the Sibilla who discerns not only the outward show, but beyond this the true essences of things. The total conceit is entirely Platonic.

The progress of the goddesses from the mountain at the lower end of the Hall to the temple at the upper end is accompanied by the first of two songs sung by a chorus of three Graces. The song encapsulates much of the topical political significance of the entertainment and is entirely appropriate to the occasion. Daniel is drawing upon a rich tradition in presenting these figures, and his treatment of the Graces—not the conventional figures of the neoplatonic triad, *Pulchitrudo, Amor* and *Voluptus*—is nevertheless sanctioned by classical authority. For Daniel, as for the Florentine Neoplatonists, the ultimate source of information on the signification of this complex icon is Seneca; and in presenting the triad 'Desert, Reward and Gratitude', Daniel is following closely Seneca's account of Chrysippus's interpretation of the image. The relevant passage occurs in Seneca's *De Beneficiis* [I, III, 2-4]. . . . [Arthur] Golding's translation of 1578 renders the passage as follows:

> . . . why there bee three Graces, why they bee sisters, and why they go hand in hand: why they looke smyling, why they bee yoong, and why

they bee maidens, and appareled in looce and sheare raiment. Some would have it ment thereby, that one of them bestoweth the good turne [,] the other receiveth it, and the thirde requiteth it. Othersome meene that there bee three sortes of benefyting: that is too wit, of befreendyng, of requyting, and both of receiuyng and requyting together. But take whiche of these you list to bee trew. What dooth this maner of knowledge profite vs? Why walkes that knot in a roundell hand in hand? It is in this respect, that a good turne passing orderly from hand to hand, dooth neuerthelesse returne too the giuer: and the grace of the whole is mard, if it bee anywhere broken of: but is most beautifull, if it continew toogether and keepe his course.

Daniel's presentation of the Graces follows Seneca's account and elaborates upon it. As Ficino had seen in the configuration of the Graces the circle of divine love, the ultimate image of cosmic harmony, so Daniel turns the moral towards the Court, and presents the Graces in a social context in which they are seen as mirroring the circle of divine love in terms appropriate to society at large and the Court, the superior microcosm of that society, in particular:

> Desert, Reward and Gratitude,
> The Graces of society,
> Do here with hand in hand conclude
> The blessed chain of amity:
> For we deserve, we give, we thank,
> Thanks, gifts, deserts, thus join in rank.
>
> We yield the splendent rays of light,
> Unto these blessings that descend:
> The grace whereof with more delight
> The well disposing doth commend;
> Whilst Gratitude, Rewards, Deserts,
> Please, win, draw on, and couple hearts.
>
> For worth and power and due respect,
> Deserves, bestows, returns with grace
> The meed, reward, the kind effect
> That give the world a cheerful face,
> And turning in this course of right,
> Make virtue move with true delight.

The Graces' song is entirely appropriate to the action which it accompanies. As the goddesses lay emblems of the particular virtues they represent upon the altar of the temple, the Graces define the nature of the moral climate in which these gifts can most effectively flourish.

The emblematical gifts having been deposited upon the altar, the dancers perform their measures 'with great majesty and art, consisting of divers strains, framed unto motions circular, square, triangular, with other proportions exceeding rare and full of variety'. It is likely that the choreography was integral to the total concept of the masque, but unfortunately we possess no record of its precise nature. The measures, however, certainly symbolized in the traditional manner concord and harmony, thus celebrating the ideal nature of society which is to move in imitation of the greater cosmic harmony. The measures completed, the Graces again sing while the ladies symbolically initiate the Court at large into their own assumed higher reality as they select their partners from amongst the spectators and perform a further set of dances with them. Having thus once more symbolically conferred their favours or blessings upon the Court, they perform a final measure before Iris announces their departure and they reascend the mountain in the same order as that which marked their descent.

Iris's final speech sustains the underlying Platonic theme of the masque and provides further evidence of Daniel's self-conscious manipulation of overlapping layers of reality, so important an aspect of the world of masque. Daniel remains faithful to his earlier delimitation of the validity of myth and skilfully turns it to artistic advantage. As the goddesses of antiquity were themselves human representations of divine powers, 'characters of sense . . . easier to be read than their mystical *Ideas*', so do these Powers, represented by former times 'in the shape and name of women' now discover in the Queen and the ladies of her Court 'the best (and most worthily the best) of ladies . . . whose forms they presently undertook as delighting to be in the best-built temples of beauty and honour'. It is not enough that the Court of James has been shown to be comparable to Olympus; ultimately it has been shown to belong to a higher order of reality and is therefore to be preferred before it.

It is not really necessary, as has become fashionable, to decry Daniel in order to pay Jonson his proper due. The sophistication and quality of Daniel's mind are evident in his conception of this masque and here, as in *Tethys Festival,* his honesty and fairmindedness are revealed in his generous allowance of the claims of poet, choreographer and architect; and with characteristic modesty he did not exaggerate the claims of the poet. As a poet Daniel is not Jonson's inferior though he lacks Jonson's flexibility and dramatic skill. As an entertainment, however, **The Vision of the Twelve Goddesses** has its own unique merit, blending didacticism, spectacle and poetry in a pleasing and intelligent manner. It warrants greater respect than it has been paid. (pp. 22-35)

> *Geoffrey Creigh, "Samuel Daniel's Masque 'The Vision of the Twelve Goddesses'," in* Essays and Studies: 1971, *edited by Bernard Harris, John Murray, 1971, pp. 22-35.*

Anthony LaBranche   (essay date 1974)

[Here, LaBranche examines Daniel's poetic voice and the audience's reception of his poetry.]

Our first reaction, like Jonson's, to Samuel Daniel's poetry is that, regrettably, true poetic talent and a certain kind of honesty cannot coexist: "Samuel Daniel a good honest man, but no poet." Instead of persuasive techniques Daniel appears to have moments of sincere self-revelation, issuing through a voice of thoughtfulness, and we allow that these moments are eloquent, but not really poetic or poetically engaging. This is, of course, an oversight on our part, and on Jonson's. There is a poetry of sincere self-expression which manages to discover its own particular rhetorical techniques and can become as well the object of our study as the more exaggerated postures which poets habitually assume. But even this last assertion raises further questions, which Daniel in his prefatory poems to *Musophilus* recognized implicitly.

> But here present thee, onelie modelled
> In this poore frame, the forme of mine owne
>   heart.

Does thoughtfulness, or honesty, or the "forme of mine owne heart" search out a rhetoric proper to it, or *is* it its own rhetoric in the sense that it provides a mutual association between speaker and reader which forms the basis for further specific rhetorical conduct?

As poet and defender of learning Daniel respects the public image of honesty, the image that must be strengthened and guarded with weapons from the armory of persuasiveness. Like Sidney's Astrophil who lives in fear of words uttered mechanically, divorced from an "inward touch," Daniel's speaker is sensitive to the conflicting demands of well-speaking and truth-saying. Daniel's choice and handling of the speaking voice, consequently, are important aspects of his rhetorical technique which Jonson passed over and which, generally, we neglect in favor of a rather disjunctive examination of rhetorical figures according to criteria of persuading and delighting. The rhetorical procedures which we attach to these criteria I will call "accepted" or "recognized," for our discovery of them at work amplifying and advancing favorite poems has encouraged us to speak about Renaissance poetry too exclusively, I believe, in terms of epideictic and forensic argument. We neglect the difference between argumentation in verse and the poetic representation of an argument in a poem—the voice of the thinking, deliberating speaker. This last event is a dramatic rehearsal, and it has more to do with the speaker's tone of voice, his presentation of a recollected self to us, and our feeling of closeness to or distance from that voice, then it has to do with our mastery of "accepted" rhetorical procedures. I hope to show that Daniel's notion of a speaker confronts most sensitively the problem of just where persuasion lies, whence it issues, how it makes itself heard and takes on significance—problems which cannot be reduced to the choice and control of verbal technique, while excluding all consideration of the posture out of which the rhetorical figures emerge.

Given more time and patience, we might redress the imbalance of scholarly investigation by studying Kierkegaard's anguishings over direct and indirect communication, over the inward consistency of irony, and over the basically ironic vein of man's thinking. Moving closer to Daniel himself, as I hope to show presently, we can fight this oversimplification by remembering Montaigne's struggle to express *his* particular kind of "honesty." With what is the sincere or honest speaker keeping faith when he confronts his audience with a particular speaking voice which hardly says the whole truth about his own thoughtful abstraction from us? The whole autobiographical enterprise is evasive and misleading, even ironic, in its effort to represent through a particular speaking presence the thoughtful abstraction or absence of the speaker. For, "To be conscious is, among other things, to be somewhere else" [Maurice Merleau-Ponty, "Reading Montaigne," in *Signs,* trans. Richard C. McCleary, 1964].

Daniel offers a significant example in this perplexing mat-

ter of the dramatic speaker, for often we describe our relations to Daniel's speaker as "honest" rather than "poetic" or "dramatic," without recognizing that this "honesty" is first of all a careful poetic creation of the autobiographical speaker. The mode or manner of this voice is established by Montaigne and his imitators, freely-ranging and confessional, and we have seen that the basic irony of that voice arises from the problem of how to be both thoughtful to oneself and present to one's audience. This is the first and most basic problem of the poet who expresses himself through any speaker. But the problem requires, first that we recognize details of the poet's style and technique. I would like to examine, in this opening section, some of Daniel's favorite rhetorical strategies, just to make sure that we see how he is selecting and modifying the traditional figures to create a particular tone of speech. In a later part of my study I will try to describe the effort of creative imitation which lies behind Daniel's inventive use of "accepted" rhetorical procedure in his verse epistles. Although we cannot hope to answer all the general questions we have raised concerning the dramatic speaker, perhaps we may profit from a deeper experience of one poet's creation of the speaking voice.

. . . . .

The rhetorical figures which Daniel uses to proclaim those urgent moments when man must face some moral question, seem to operate in balanced periods of flow and interruption. Into the smooth river of his *thus . . . and, who, which* and *that* clauses, Daniel introduces exclamations, interrogations and word-repetition which, aided by rhyme, impose a new and heightened rhythm on the narrative. It is evident that the "moments" which we have mentioned are outbursts or emphatic underlinings which show through the otherwise regular and sober narrative.

> Percy, how soone, by thy example led,
> The household traine forsooke their wretched
>   Lord!
> When, with thy staffe of charge dishonoured,
> Thou brak'st thy fayth, not steward of thy word,
> And tookst his part that after tooke thy head;
> When thine owne hand had strengthned first his
>   sword
> "For, such great merits do upbraid, and call
> "For great reward, or thinke the great too smal.
>   (*Civil Wars,* 1609, II, 2)

The figures of exclamation and interrogation usually appear at those instants when the argument has reached a local climax or temporary dead-end; by adopting an excited attitude the speaker asks us to reconsider the irony, injustice or paradoxical nature of events. This technique applies often, as above, to the structure within a stanza as well as to the relatively large patterns of interruptive stanzas within whole sections of narrative. In the *Panegyrike Congratulatorie* (1602), for example, stanzas 17-21 operate markedly by this process of interruption. These are traditional figures of rhetoric exhorting to action or persuading to an opinion. But in Daniel they become a means of articulating second thoughts and calling to our attention a speaker who is definitely involved with moral issues. The dramatic situations of the first, second and fifth books of the *Civil Wars* (here given in the text of 1609) lend themselves to the amplifications and word-play which accompany such contemplative moments. The word-play indicates a deliberative effort as well as an emotional heightening of the incident. The poetic justice of Percy's reward, given above, is worked out in a series of ironic qualifications suggested by the words *brak'st, word, took'st, part, after tooke, head, hand, strengthned first,* and *sword.*

> Thou brak's thy fayth, not steward of thy word,
> And took'st his part that after tooke thy head;
> When thine owne hand had strengthned first his
>   sword.

It is this tone marking the presence of this particular speaker that critics have been at pains to define, but they have neglected to specify the origins of the tone. Terms such as "sober," "well-languaged Daniel" indicate a kind of dramatic presence, most carefully defined by particular moments of emphasis—or at times lack of emphasis. Ideally, as we move down the interminable list of rhetorical devices we might gradually grow to see them in a more organic, organizational light—something resembling the imaginative adaptation of an orator's emphatic stance rather than merely as tools of public address itself. One such trait, which operates very near to the ironies of word-play, is what Henry Wells discussed long ago as "sunken imagery" [*Poetic Imagery,* 1924]. Such imagery, in Daniel's hands, avoids witty similarities and resemblances while plunging down to a level of natural and unavoidable (rather than striking) association, and it creates often the tone of sober, tenacious contemplation. The breaking of the staff of steward, and the breaking of Percy's loyalty to Richard, the taking of parts and the taking of heads ("And took'st his part that after tooke thy head"), the acts of forsaking and of strengthening, all point to a seriously ironic level of association among events and imply a speaker who is reflecting upon his discourse before us, not merely declaiming a dissertation.

Especially in those poems where the poet appears to speak his mind, or where we are given a speaker deeply concerned with a continuing line of thought—the dedicatory pieces "To the Reader" (1607), the dedication of *Philotas* to Prince Henry, and in "To the Right Reverend . . . James Montague"—we hear the freely discursive, self-commemorating monotone which strikes many of Daniel's less patient readers as prosaic. Actually no prose or stance could be more ingratiating than this one, and too little attention has been given to the artful representation of second thoughts and qualifications through unusual syntax and word repetition.

> Though I the remnant of another time
> Am neuer like to see that happinesse,
> Yet for the zeale that I haue borne to rime
> And to the Muses, wish that good successe
> To others trauell, that in better place,
> And better comfort, they may be incheerd
> Who shall deserue, and who shall haue the grace
> To haue a Muse held worthy to be heard.
>   (Preface to *Philotas,* 66-73)

The word-repetition, to which our eyes have become accustomed, provides emotional shading as well as structure to the central portion of the passage. The uncertainty of the long opening appositive, "I the remnant of another time," is contradicted by the emphatic phrases of the dangling, ruminative construction that follows ("to rime / And to the Muses"; "that in better place, / And better comfort"; "Who shall deserue, and who shall haue the grace / To haue a Muse"). Among the further peculiarities of style which readers have noted in Daniel's use of the word *that*—possibly both as a demonstrative and a correlative conjunction intermixed in this case—"wish that good successe / To other trauell, that in better place . . . they may be incheerd." The same appearance of correlated or even "fused" thinking is achieved in the emphatic restrictive clauses at the end of our passage with their curious play on *deserue, haue, held* and *heard.* (pp. 123-28)

We might sum up by saying that Daniel's rhetoric is not really oratorical in purpose and tone, but it is a rhetoric of thoughtfulness, creating a poetry that presents habits of mind through certain rhetorical signals, a mind given in this case to tracing cause and effect, analogy, recapitulation and the like. This overall presence, when captured by the poem, is a truly rhetorical discovery. It is truly a tone of voice, not just the intrusion of a haphazard honesty into the argument of the poem—even when the speaker appears to be uttering the poet's own feelings. I mean that this speaking presence is a deliberate device no matter how closely the poet stands behind it—as in the memorable passages of *Musophilus* and of the various epistles and dedications. In fact the semblance of closeness to the poet's own mind and feelings, as well as the rhetorical mannerisms which reflect that mind, are embodiments of that "inward consistency" toward which Daniel (like his predecessor Sidney) is striving. This portrait of a mind discoursing, reconsidering, reacting, is Daniel's sober representation of the eternal struggle between truth of subject matter and the arts of persuasion by which the poet must present that matter. The arts of persuasion have come under scrutiny and have been submerged in favor of the speaker's recollection of himself. Out of Daniel's "imitation of a discourse" emerges not clear precepts or propaganda, but man's tenacious effort to persist in confronting truth, whatever that may be, in its many guises. This becomes what the rhetorician would call Daniel's *ethos.* Having glimpsed this, we may go on to our more specific task of describing Daniel's epistolary imitations.

· · · · ·

If we were to compare Jonson's "Epistle to Katherine, Lady Aubigny" which Wesley Trimpi [in *Ben Jonson's Poems: A Study of the Plain Style,* 1962] calls "plain, intimate and urbane" and Daniel's **"To the Ladie Lucie, Countesse of Bedford"** (1603), we would be struck by differences in the order and procedure which each poet deems appropriate to his poem. Jonson's strategy is to win the reader's belief in his sincerity at the outset by describing the setbacks he has suffered in praising virtue and condemning vice and his fiercer determination now to proceed in his encouragement of virtue, "Nor feare to draw true lines, cause others paint"(20). Jonson, or his speaker, can assure Lady Aubigny directly that his praise will be truth, not flattery, and there follows a list of qualities he will *not* praise (while mentioning how favorably they are disposed in her)—beauty, wealth and position (21-42). But what really concerns the poet is her mind, that is her virtues, and these virtues all reside in her resolution to shun the dissoluteness of court life (which 59-88 describe in variety and detail) and to embrace a chaste domestic life. This life is subject for celebration by the poet and will shower a reward of fruitfulness, domestic love and unity upon the happy pair (99-120). The Lady will see that her resolution promises a lasting and virtuous course by consulting the poet's "truest glasse" (122). We must agree with Trimpi that the poem is urbanely calculated and that the castigation of courtly vice and glorification of plain virtue are amalgamated into a single discourse. Jonson proceeds by vivid, even exaggerated illustration and assertion, not analytically; he seeks to move the emotions by praise and ridicule. The importance of cogent descriptive *exempla* in this operation cannot be overestimated; and other poems, for example the epistle to Sir Robert Wroth, proceed in much the same manner.

Daniel's **"Epistle to the Ladie Lucie, Countesse of Bedford,"** on the other hand, adopts an entirely different approach to its advisory or hortatory task, and the result is an entirely different kind of epistolary discourse. For the opening twenty-five lines the speaker remains on a level of generality as he describes the effectiveness of a virtue according to the position of its practitioner. The entire movement of the poem is toward the problem of virtue's "abilitie" to affect other people. Only then does the speaker bring his discourse to its particular application.

> And therefore well did your high fortunes meete
>   With her, that gracing you, comes grac't
>   thereby
>   And well was let into a house so sweete
> So good, so faire; so faire, so good a guest,
>   Who now remaines as blessed in her seate,
>   As you are with her residencie blesst.
>   (26-31)

The basis of this "vertue" is knowledge which is achieved through study, "the'onely certaine way that you can goe / Unto true glory, to true happiness" (34-35). The poet offers by way of development an excursus of false appearances (36-39), then a commendation of knowledge as the key to enfranchising the fair sex from the prison of false appearances (40-49), and an extraordinarily extended account (*aetiologia*) of how the mind is the seat of all good (50-82)—interrupted only in time for the conclusion which returns us to the subject of books as a directive to knowledge and the addressee's "cleerenesse" in choosing this "Rightest way" (83-97). As we consider this strange and unprepossessing structure we are struck by the truth that though Daniel appears digressive, even evasive, he is more tenaciously analytical than Jonson. Daniel's speaker continues to examine the worth of studies, their relation to the mind and to knowledge; Jonson's speaker leaps from example to example of praise or blame with an orator's persuasiveness of "application." In other words, the sum of Jonson's individual sections is a rather self-consciously cogent act of persuasion, whereas Daniel's more evasive and parallel lines of exposition (e.g. the emphatic "digressions" of 36-39 and 50-82) provide a more

subtle embodiment or reenactment of his cardinal feelings. He ends by capturing a "voice" somewhere nearby, not just a formal witty posture. One poem sets out wilfully to persuade by example, the other by repetition and parallel movement provides a contemplative structure which addresses the reader's attention and sympathy. This may be the moment, if ever, to venture that Jonson's epistle in the plain style is cogent and decorous, perhaps even moving, but not very thoughtful. This is one defect of his version of classical plain style and sufficient warning not to judge his attempts in the epistolary genre by the square of the poems alone.

Most of Daniel's rhetorical traits, his word-play, sunken imagery, and tenacious if syntactically loose-jointed pursuit of a theme, point to the welcoming of a thought process as the basic activity of his poetry—the poetic imitation of an argument rather than the argument itself. And to the purposefully-minded reader his poems may seem muted and removed, pre-occupied with an autobiographical working-out of favored ideas, rather than a full-blooded attempt to convince a worldly audience. They seem to do something slightly different from what they should be doing, and they owe greater allegiance to a single, continuing philosophical discourse within themselves than they do to the call of social need or of external occasion. In a sense they perform for themselves, or to themselves, and we are permitted to witness the show. Daniel's best passages are most profoundly passages of presence, illuminations of a highly imitative and allusive kind. And the highly "imitative" uses to which he puts the normal devices of apostrophe, exclamation and self-examination in shadowing forth a sincere and earnest speaker have discouraged our critical attention. It is this lack of rhetorical aggressiveness which has deceived us into describing Daniel's performances largely in negative terms. But we are far from describing that performance which we *are* called upon to witness and to complete.

Some light in this case may be thrown upon Daniel's poetic performance by sizing up the genre in which he is working. Where did Daniel find the impetus to an intimate, epistolary yet un-Horatian kind of poetry which presents alternately the personality of an immediate speaker and that lofty moral attitude "written from above" which Auerbach remarks of Tacitus [*Mimesis,* trans. Willard Trask, 1953]. This style or mode may be one more example of Renaissance imitation—that eclectic and contemporary recreation of classical and continental models which inspires so much of Renaissance poetry and which reveals indirectly much of the disposition of Renaissance poetic minds. Jonson himself observes that among Daniel's "pilferings" stands the ever-fashionable Montaigne, and modern scholars have detected some of those borrowings from Montaigne and, behind him, from Seneca. The interesting point which has remained unmentioned, however, is that Daniel's sense of organization also may owe something to Montaigne's loose, discursive intimate essay style—a version of the Senecan mode which affected matter over manner. Daniel appears to have caught the mainstream of the Senecan revolt with its insistence on "inward consistency" yet with its often contradictory passions to express a balanced overview of man's moral history. The progression from *Rosamund* (1952) to *Cleopatra* (1594) to the *Civil Wars* (1595) and on to the later *Epistles and Defense of Ryme* (1603) could bear some scrutiny for this trend.

Our immediate approach to this tone of voice is through Daniel's possible borrowing in 1603 from Montaigne . . . [in his Epistle to Iohn Florio]. Both Croll and Williamson describe Montaigne's mature style as "loose" or a combination of loose and curt elements whose "progression adapts itself to the movements of a mind discovering truth as it goes, thinking while it writes." Analogously, the structure of the essays avoids the oratorical and strives toward the organic. . . . This may be the reason behind the "troubled frame" which Daniel mentions in his poem to Florio, and it may be also the impulse by which he transforms his own more orotund "public" discourses, filled as they are with conditional and causal periods, into a more appealing, personal ruminative genre, "the forme of mine owne heart."

Montaigne's art of interior monologue (and in less rambling fashion Bacon's more curt *Essays*) offer an interesting analogy, then, to Daniel's adaptation of the *genus humile*—a concentrated effort to capture the new (in 1600) serious orientation to moral concerns and to capture the new (in 1600) serious orientation to moral concerns and to a responsible speaker, concerns traditionally assigned to the province of Jonson's plain style. In Book I. 38, [Montaigne's] "Of Solitarinesse," an essay which Himelick notes supplies background to some of Daniel's pronouncements on integrity, virtue and fit audience, there occurs the following passage. This passage does not move in the loose style of the later essays, and yet it shows (in Florio's version) something of the system of association and emphasis within an extended periodic structure which Daniel's ethical verse also creates.

> We should reserve a store-house for our selves, what need soever change; altogether ours, and wholly free, wherein we may hoard up and establish our true libertie, and principall retreit and solitarinesse, wherein we must go alone to our selves, take out ordinarie entertainement, and so privately that no acquaintance or communication of any strange thing may therein find place: there to discourse, to meditate and laugh, as, without wife, without children, and goods, without traine or servants; that if by any occasion they be lost, it seeme not strange to us to passe it over; we have a minde moving and turning in it selfe; it may keep it selfe companie; it hath wherewith to offend and defend, wherewith to receive, and wherewith to give.

The excesses of ornament and expansion which Matthiessen and Yates remark of Florio's translation are held to a minimum in our passage, but Florio's natural redundancy relieves some of the curtness of the original. The passage proceeds by appositions, associations, loosely conjunctive members: *what need soever, wherein, and, wherein, and so,* and the like. It is freely extended, yet sober and regular. The same rhythms and the appearance of extending his thoughts while he writes occur in Daniel's epistle **"To the Countess of Bedford."** Each unit of three or four lines is loosely conjoined to an earlier theme or concern

through the topics of definition, division (subject and adjuncts) and causality.

> *Since all* the good we haue rests in the mind,
>   *By whose* proportions onely we redeeme
>   Our thoughts from out confusion, and do finde
> The measure of our selues, and of our powres.
>   *And that* all happiness remaines confind
>   *Within* the Kingdome of this breast of ours,
> *Without whose* bounds, all that we looke on, lies
>   *In* others Iurisdictions, others powres,
>   *Out* of the circuit of our liberties.
> All glory, honor, fame, applause, renowne,
>   Are not belonging to our royalties.
>   But t'others wills, *wherein* th'are onely growne.
> *And that* vnless we finde vs all *within*,
>   We neuer can *without* vs be our owne:
> Nor call it right our life, *that* we liue *in*. . . .
>   (50-64)

The phrases I have put into italics are all means of furthering the discourse in a curiously additive manner; despite their gestures toward causality and definition, they give the appearance of a freely expanding rumination extending outwards and onwards. This loosely appositive expansion within a periodic framework *is* the essential progression of the passage. And the aim of this manner of progression is not just to offer precepts and example, but to show the self extending itself into a question, into a position facing the predicaments of life. The members of the passage are fairly regular, if isolated from each other; they create a feeling both of deliberateness and of associative freedom, of serious commitment to the "life we live *in*" and of speculative expansiveness regarding its challenges. And they create the presence of a speaker engaged in an expansion-discovery, such as is indicated by the series of *and that* clauses all relating to the *finde* of the third line. The use of word-play and of word-repetition (*within, without,* and the final relative *that* following upon the insistent *and that*) reveals a speaker who is anxious to describe himself, in his well-timed dilations, by the qualifications of balance, contrast and irony.

It is only too evident that Daniel's application of the ruminative manner, based on the premise "gentle Reader, myselfe am the groundworke of my booke," results in a curious compromise which for many readers robs Daniel's poetry of clarity and decisiveness. Daniel sees the poet's task as morally directive, through ancient authority, and this task demands an elevated, even orotund style, a voice issuing an overview, rather than an intimate, informal, ironic confession to the reader, like Montaigne's above. One might accuse Daniel's speaker of a certain doubleness or bad faith—he engages us at the level of argument, but ends by giving us autobiographical revelation. This doubleness creates a breach of contract in the rhetorical relationship which Daniel's speaker seems eager to acknowledge as the basis of clear and honest social intercourse.

In the passage we have selected for analysis, and throughout the *Epistles,* Daniel's style is essentially formal even though his speaker's presence is intimate, or as Coleridge remarks "grave and easy." This style is reminiscent in tone and rhythm of Hoby's *Courtier,* and, for 1603, it appears more Isocratean than Senecan. But I have stressed Daniel's new modification, his tendency to revise, extend and qualify the basic syntactic regularity out of a need to approximate in his own terms the "dramatic sentence of a mind thinking." As a result Daniel's epistolary style is both humble and formal, immediate and distant, intimate and authoritative, and I believe, in reply to Daniel's critics, that this was a poise or balance toward which he was striving, albeit with varying success. The *Epistles* and prefatory pieces, for that matter the longer poems too, present a test of true balance, perspective and insight which we must pass in order to qualify as morally sensitive beings. The curiously ambiguous intimacy of the speaker is the largest challenge of these addresses. We sense a less intimate personality in Daniel's speaker than we do in Montaigne's, perhaps to the extent that he doesn't quite carry off the autobiographical dimension of his discourses, but the speaker's voice is not really distant. The speaker appears so persistently concerned throughout the poem with thinking as a valid mode of action that we have the illusion of a close intellectual companionship with him, a familiarity with his "thinking" presence—precisely one concern of the loose mode. Here Daniel's style, as formal as we know it to be, is also truly plain in that it assumes the stance of having no artistic concern for itself.

· · · · ·

Our few insights into Daniel's style, alone or placed in the relief of Jonson's or Montaigne's, should guard us from too simple a notion of rhetorical procedure, and particularly from the notion that such a procedure when singled out by us could describe the style and principal direction of a poem. It is important that we allow ourselves to see Renaissance poetry as poetic representation rather than simply oratorical persuasion. Many of Daniel's rhetorical figures become meaningful only in context of the larger gestures of the poem. For example, his reiterative word-play stresses ironic contrasts of attitude, but also a certain continuity of concern in the poem, the concern embodied in a tone of voice and a presence which apply themselves gravely to the "topics" of life as they arise. That is, word-play may support certain ironic contrasts in local passages, but it also represents the continuing process of thought and commentary which is the major subject of the poem and which sets its "pitch" and tone. Such word-play is not merely ironic, interruptive and fragmenting, but indicates the continuing concern of the speaker for his subject, his continuing struggle to be present to life. It gathers together and harmonizes the individual addresses of thought, the transitions, extensions and reservations of attitude which extend the length of Daniel's poems.

The original, and larger question, however, is that of the dramatic speaker's presence to us and our presence to him—that bond of relationship which gives rise to our understanding the rhetoric of the situation. If the problem of communicating one's *thinking* to an audience is a problem of the absent-present, the nearby-distant, then the normal criteria of rhetorical description, expansion and argument are not exactly to the point, and we will not achieve through their terms an adequate description of Daniel's style and poetic accomplishment. Vividness and concreteness, for example, are only momentary accomplishments and smack of necessary falsification to the gravely speculative mind. Is "honesty" either vivid or concrete? There are other kinds of patience than the patience of careful illustration and clarity which Jonson epitomizes. The "plainer," more basic kind of patience may be a humility in pursuing the process of thinking itself, a feeling for the deep irony of its activities, and an autobiographical consciousness which bows to the limits placed on truth by man's preoccupation with living. This may be the organizing mentality of the honest or thoughtful style. The question posed by Daniel's version of the poetic speaker contrasted with Jonson's, for example, is not a superficial one of appeal to or intimacy with an audience. It is Montaigne's nagging question of why he should expose himself at all, why he should come forward, when the inevitable result will be the falsification of his most inward thinking and at the same time a failure to acquiesce in an audience's thirst for vivid entertainment and flashy argument. Daniel's answer strikes us as less maturely resolved or thought out than Montaigne's, but it is still too honest to answer the demand of many readers for vivid performance in poetry. The voice in Daniel's poetry is aware of this, but too often that voice gets no further than letting us share the biting irony of the thinker's predicament, fighting back despair with whatever arguments seem to offer some ray of hope.

The latter part of this study has tried to suggest the kind of imaginative effort required to seek out a style for the speaker whom Daniel was set on representing, a style which involves in its distant-engaged tone an ingenious imitation of the essay-style and of which we can note traces as early as *Cleopatra* (1594). In this deeper sense of imitation all of Daniel's maneuvers to present a sympathetic and persuasive speaker can be viewed as a fictionalization, and so an extension of the struggles of the autobiographical "I" to retain balance, self-awareness, and perspective. The term "dramatic" does justice only to the external features of this process, for the curious "presence" of Daniel's best poetry reveals that the speaking voice is an extension of psyche as well as a verbalization of it. This double activity—first, the extension of this active center within us, and second, the excitement inherent in its portrayal and verbalization—are the continuing actions in most of Daniel's poetry. I believe he shaped his style to reflect this activity. And so, as much as they are concerned with precept and discourse, his better "moral" passages also create the presence of a voice speaking near to us.

To speak, for Daniel, is to capture this predicament—or rather to reflect upon one's speech-act is to capture it. The sound of one's voice lends assurance that one is individual, yet savingly entangled in a network of human appositions, extensions, qualifications, antitheses. To speak is the first and, for Daniel, the most serious step toward our embodiment in the world. To this step or commitment the conventions of vividness and concreteness add little: "I know I shal be read, among the rest / So long as men speake english." This is why his poetry appears both engaging and forgettable, to many readers, and possesses at times the poignancy of a telephoned farewell which we soon feel to be "unreal" though it was terribly near to us while it was happening.

At the level of technique Daniel seems bent upon selecting and adapting rhetorical strategies so as to turn them from their normally emphatic clarifying role toward the non-public, personal and "directly expressive." Once again the sensitive reader may feel in Daniel a deep conflict—a respect for the presence of inward thoughtfulness crossed by the desire to imitate that thoughtfulness, and so publicize it, as carefully as his knowledge of literary devices permitted. His speakers are more deeply concerned with literary composition than with poetic effectiveness, the former being the more personal, the latter the more satisfying. We are hesitant to determine where the speaking voice is issuing *from,* and so we say it is the man himself. We must be getting the "poet himself." Or are we getting only his concern with the question of being present to himself and to the "questions" of living in the world? This latter concern would militate against a vivid sense of location, for all thinking is undeniably "here"—and elsewhere.

Rhetorically considered, the formation of this style depends on an eclectic mingling of figures, being as they are common tools, but always, hopefully, with that Sidneian "inward touch," that inspection of the relation of honest feeling to its artistic expression which so absorbed the attention of Astrophil. Such a style cannot be considered in Daniel's case a mingling of poetic figures with prosaic matter. Much of the rhetoric is directed to specific representations of the speaker's stance, balance, and manner of discourse, rather than to isolated vivid turns and "effective" argumentation.

My main interest has been to arouse our more imaginative instincts when approaching these signals, and to ask once again what is a speaker's "voice," out of what sense of our worldly entanglement does it issue, how does it draw us to it? One way to start on this problem is through a more sensitive observation of Renaissance imitation, such as that which is suggested by the various genres which Daniel methodically undertook from **Delia** to **Musophilus.** Although Daniel turned entirely to prose history after 1612, for the last ten years of his life, we should not let this pronounce the final word on his earlier accomplishments in verse-essay, beginning around 1594, which ask us to revise our notions of poetic rhetoric and behind that, of imitation—that deepest kind of imitation in which the novelty, energy, perhaps meaning of the Renaissance poem often reside. (pp. 128-39)

> *Anthony LaBranche, "Samuel Daniel: A Voice of Thoughtfulness," in* The Rhetoric of Renaissance Poetry: From Wyatt to Milton, *edited by Thomas O. Sloan and Raymond B. Waddington, University of California Press, 1974, pp. 123-39.*

Clark Hulse   (essay date 1981)

[*In the following excerpt from his book-length study of the Elizabethan minor verse epic, Hulse explores Daniel's* The Complaint of Rosamond *in light of the dichot-*

omy between history and imaginative invention which Hulse finds in Elizabethan historical poetry.]

The oblivion into which Samuel Daniel and Michael Drayton have sunk masks the fate of historical poetry generally. While writers have in practice always mixed invention and fact to make fiction, literature and history came to be thought of in the late sixteenth century as opposite in their goals, one dedicated to imaginative truth, the other to factual truth, and only recently have the theorists of the two disciplines dared to think otherwise. The revolution in historical and poetic theory in the sixteenth century produced for the poets of the Elizabethan minor epic a peculiar crisis of identity. Daniel and Drayton were born in the world of Holinshed's *Chronicles* and died in the world of Selden's *History of Tithes.* Each entered on the career of the poetic historian by employing that mixture of Petrarch and old chronicles that characterized the minor epic in the first half of the 1590s. Each progressed on the Vergilian path to write full-dress historical epics stuffed with dynastic propaganda and glances at contemporary politics. But for each, the struggle to reconcile chronicle to minor epic ended in doubts about the nature of historical fiction and the validity of his personal achievement. This thwarting of the poet's normal course of development is symptomatic of a deeper problem with which both grappled: at stake were nothing less than the definitions and uses of both poetry and history. Was poetry just lies or could the humanist dream of literature as a social force prove itself true? Was history just a chronological record of what happened or was it a narrative designed or even invented by the historian? (p. 195)

[A] revolution in English historical verse was in large part fought out in the back alleys of the minor epic, for the simple reason that vast poems like Daniel's **Civil Wars** or Drayton's *Barons Warres* take years to write and the brevity of the minor epic made it a natural arena for experiment. Perhaps the point is best illustrated by the case of Samuel Daniel, whose minor epic poem **The Complaint of Rosamond** marked the first step in his attempt to fashion himself into the English Lucan [historian of ancient Rome]. (pp. 198-99)

Lucan was born, Lucanists are made. Daniel grew slowly to his role in distant but stoical England. His first piece of historical verse, the minor epic **Complaint of Rosamond,** has . . . more of Petrarch in it than of the chronicles. The chronicle accounts of Rosamond barely mention her among the other domestic troubles that Henry II experienced with his wife, his sons, and his nobles. Typical is Caxton's *Chronicle* (i.e., Ranulf Higden's *Polychronicon,* translated by John of Trevisa and edited by Caxton):

> And he [Henry II] that hadde prysonned his wyf Elyanor the quene and was pryvely a spouche-breker / and lyved now openly in spousebrekyng and is not ashamed to mysuse the wenche Rosamund / To this fayre wenche the kyng made at Wodestoke a chambre of wonder crafte slyly made by dedalus werke / leste the Quene sholde fynde and take Rosamund / but the wenche dyed soone and is beryed in the chapyter hows at Godestow . . . This wenche had a lytel Coffre scarcely of twey fote longe made by a wonder

crafte that is yet seen there. / Therein it semyth
that geauntes fyghtyn / beestes startlyn / foules
fleyn / and fysshes leepe withoute ony mannes
moevynge /

Higden/Trevisa/Caxton are hardly bothered by the confusions in their account of Rosamond whereby Henry,
having imprisoned his wife Eleanor and lived openly in
adultery, seeks to conceal from her his affair with Rosamond. On one hand, they focus on remarkable objects and
events that are worthy of everlasting fame (or infamy),
while on the other, they observe a providential scheme of
six monarchies for the work as a whole. But there is little
attempt to show this providence at work in the reward or
punishment of individual deeds. They are concerned to
preserve truth in both divine and human terms without
much communication between the two. They ponder the
obscure way that history in the gross drifts into conformity with God's will, or rather, comes to reveal a divine plan
that is scarcely visible in any given particular.

To Daniel, it is precisely the area between the particular
and the universal that is of interest. He focuses on the
character of Rosamond rather than on marvelous events,
makes the labyrinthine architecture of Woodstock [home
of Eleanor of Aquitaine] and the Ovidian casket into emblems of her mental state, and turns her sudden death into
a murder at the hands of Eleanor. The result is to articulate a material and psychological level as the internal principle of organization for his poetic history. The chronicle
disintegrates events into facts: "this year a sow with two
heads was born in Surrey" or accumulates them into
schemes: "the troublesome reign of Henry IV" or "the
sixth age of man." Humanist history finds its truth in the
middle scale where fact becomes scheme and scheme can
be seen breaking down into its component events.

By inventing much of his *res* as well as his *verba* in **Rosamond,** Daniel has set out to vivify the past and make it
present. The middle scale of truth frees him from the timeless perspective of providence without binding him to the
particle of past time occupied by the single event. Hence
he has neither the wonder of the chronicles that the remote past can be known at all nor the despair of the
French historiographers at the paucity of good documentary evidence. To Daniel the remoteness of the past is
something to be overcome by the force of rhetorical elaboration, giving an order to words that reflects the material
and psychological orders of time. Like Petrarch, Boccaccio, and the authors of the *Mirror for Magistrates,* Daniel
imposes a poetic scheme, the rise and fall of tragedy, onto
a single episode from the chronicles while expanding that
episode into a "life" of its protagonists. He then makes the
tension between this orderly scheme and the flux of events
the subject of long commentary by his two main characters, Henry II and Rosamond. The invented speeches shift
Daniel's historical focus from the providential pattern
used by universalist historians from Eusebius to Ranulf
Higden, to the theatrical patterns of a political historian
like Thucydides or Guicciardini.

To compare Daniel to Thucydides or Guicciardini may
seem perverse, but his amorous verse and their practical
prose stand at the opposite poles of humanist history and

between them its nature and scope is defined. In the opening debates at Athens and Sparta in which the two states
decide to embark on their fatal war, Thucydides shows
men calculating the weight that chance and human cunning will have in its outcome. In the Melian dialogue,
which so raised the ire of Dionysius of Halicarnassus, he
breaks openly into a dramatic mode, assigning speeches
not to particular individuals but to two choruses labeled
"Athenians" and "Melians." In this passage
F. M. Cornford [in *Thucydides Mythistoricus,* 1907] found
the proof that the *Peloponnesian War* is Aeschylan in its
conception. Whether or not one accepts Cornford's arguments that the "real" causes of the war lay in imperialist
economics, he is clearly right that Thucydides wants to
show the fall of Athens through a combination of chance
(the death of Pericles), passion (the wrath of Cleon), and
misdirected reason (the disastrous expedition to Syra-
cuse).

Similarly, Guicciardini shows men struggling to master
the chaos of events in the tragedy that was Italian history
after the death of Lorenzo the Magnificent. The Emperor
Charles V is shown listening with unusual prudence to the
debates of his counselors, but more often Guicciardini
finds that the decisions of princes are based on ambition
and greed. Neither cunning nor virtue is a guarantee of
success, however, and Guicciardini points to the fortunate
career of the monstrous Roderigo Borgia to confound
those who think themselves able to sift the secrets of providence. Indeed, Felix Gilbert finds much of the difference
between Machiavelli and Guicciardini in the extent to
which Machiavelli still clung to the idea that Fortune
would sometimes yield to *virtú.*

Daniel's Rosamond operates in a humbler sphere, but in
her long speeches reflecting on how she came to sin and
imminent death she confronts the same inscrutable confusion of providence, chance, will, and misguided calculation. A long debate with a cunning old crone leads her to
yield to Henry's advances for two reasons, the calculated
desire to keep the favor of her ruler, and the promptings
of her own erotic nature, which has been roused by the lascivious scenes on the casket Henry has sent her. Once fall-
en and facing death, she acknowledges her responsibility
for what she has done, but sees herself to be, at least in
part, the scapegoat of a decadent society and the victim
of a capricious fate.

Still, there are important and obvious differences between
Daniel and the political historians. They are dealing with
public deeds in their own lifetimes or the lifetimes of their
fathers. He is telling of private actions in the distant past.
Thucydides and Guicciardini both are interested in eye-
witnesses more than in documents. For them the past is
alive in the memory of their informants and their purpose
is summarized by the "rule of Polybius": history aims at
political and military instruction and is best written by
those with political and military experience. Like them,
Daniel cannot tell exactly what happened. He must shape
his material according to the information available and
make plausible conjectures when it is not, as in the invented speeches recording what was likely to have been said
by the actual participants. Armed not with memory but

with old chronicles and a humanist-historical poetics of presence, Daniel must in **Rosamond** use far more violent rhetorical elaboration to overcome the greater obscurity of his subject. And whereas a Thucydides or a Guicciardini could assume the unparalleled importance of his subject matter, Daniel faces the further problem of giving public meaning to private actions. This he does by elaborating his speeches for emotional as well as analytical point. His desire to impress the human significance of his subject matter on his audience is witnessed by the incessant contemporary references to the sheer pathos of the poem.

If the histories of Thucydides and Guicciardini are self-conscious verbal imitations of a lost reality, then Daniel's extreme elaboration of his subject in **Rosamond** clearly makes his work not history, but a poetic imitation of history. It is fiction in the most perfect tradition of Plato's cave, an imitation of an imitation of a dubious reality. Such a mode is possible precisely because of the obscurity of his subject. He need not fear that any records will turn up to contradict him, or that any living soul recalls the matter differently, so he can freely invent his matter without telling lies. Poetic truth consists not of what can be proven true but of what has not been (or even cannot be) proven false. It colors in the blank spots in our knowledge of the past. (pp. 205-09)

> Clark Hulse, "Chronicle, History, Legend," in his Metamorphic Verse: The Elizabethan Minor Epic, *Princeton University Press, 1981, pp. 195-241.*

William Wordsworth on Daniel:

I ought to mention that the line 'And holy things of holy use unhallowed lie' is taken from the following of Daniel, 'Strait all that holy was unhallowed lies' [**Musophilus**, 1. 289]. I will take this occasion of recommending to you (if you happen to have Daniel's poems) to read the epistle addressed to the Lady Margaret, Countess of Cumberland, beginning 'He that of such a height hath built his mind.' The whole poem is composed in a strain of meditative morality more dignified and affecting than anything of the kind I ever read. It is, besides, strikingly applicable to the revolutions of the present times.

William Wordsworth in a letter to Lady Beaumont, 20 November, 1811.

Johanna Procter   (essay date 1984)

[In the following excerpt, Procter examines the importance of two court plays by Daniel for introducing conventions of Italian pastoral drama into the English theater. She further illuminates the context of the plays by connecting both to the patronage of Anne of Denmark, queen of James I of England.]

Although it is a matter of some dispute exactly when the influence of Italian pastoral drama entered the English theatre in the Renaissance, there is little doubt when it did

so formally. Samuel Daniel's **Arcadia Reformed,** performed 1605, and published in the following year as **The Queenes Arcadia,** marks the arrival on the English stage of the drama of Tasso and Guarini. Nearly nine years later, Daniel again wrote a pastoral play, **Hymens Triumph** (1614), published in 1615. The first was written for Anne of Denmark, wife of James VI of Scotland and I of England; the second was written at her behest; and both plays were performed before a courtly audience.

Samuel Daniel was particularly well suited to transmute this Italian, or rather, perhaps, Ferrarese, genre into English. He was an excellent Italianist, with a wide knowledge of Italian literature, including all the major Renaissance poets and many minor ones. As a professional poet, he spent his life in the service of the courtly class, numbering among the noble patrons who supported and encouraged his career some of the most cultured ladies and gentlemen of the age. He shared their interest in the 'new' literature of the Renaissance, and they shared his aims of establishing European traditions in English writing, and making them 'English'. Before his introduction of pastoral drama, Daniel had been associated with earlier innovations; he published the first emblem book in English, his sonnet sequence, **Delia,** was one of the heralds of the Elizabethan petrarchan vogue of the Fifteen nineties; and he had made contributions to neo-classical tragedy. Although these were ill fated for Daniel—**Cleopatra,** a closet drama, undertaken at the direction of the Countess of Pembroke, led to the breach between patron and poet; whilst **Philotas** resulted in the author being called before the Privy Council, and accused of seditiously commenting on the trial and execution of the Earl of Essex in 1601—he had gained experience of constructing plays with principles of composition related to those of pastoral drama.

Daniel's knowledge of Italian pastoral probably began in the early Fifteen eighties when, as a student at Oxford, he learnt Italian from John Florio. In 1580, seven years after its first performance, Tasso's *Aminta* was printed, and it is hard to believe that a copy of an early edition of so famous and popular a work did not find its way quickly into the hands of Florio and his eager young pupils. Tasso's influence is present in **The Queenes Arcadia,** and pervasively so in **Hymens Triumph**—beyond specific debts, the mood of the play implies that *Aminta* is a work long lived with and loved—, and the response of the English poet to Tasso's eclogue is earlier evidenced in a translation of the Chorus of Act I, 'O bella età de l'oro', which Daniel first published in his **Works,** 1601. **"O Happy Golden Age"** is not only a faithful rendering of Tasso's beautiful lines, but also of the haunting lyric form which evokes the difference between our world and the lost world of perfection and innocence even as it creates it:

> O Happy Golden Age
> Not for that Rivers ranne
> With streames of milke and hunny dropt from
>   trees:
> Not that the earth did gage
> Unto the husbandman
> Her voluntary fruites, free without fees:
> Not for no cold did freeze,
> Nor any cloud beguile,

Th' eternall flow'ring Spring,
Wherein liv'd everything,
And wherein liv'd everything,
And whereon th' heavens perpetually did smile:
Not for no ship had brought
From forraine shores, or warres or wares ill
    sought.

Daniel was not the only English Renaissance poet to respond to Tasso's Chorus, but he was the only one who attempted to capture its entire spirit in English verse—as befits the future writer of pastoral drama. 'O bella età de l'oro' is the quintessential expression of the vision of man which lies at the heart of the pastoral myth: man restless, 'cabin'd, cribb'd, confin'd' yearning, for peace, freedom and happiness; desiring perfection which he can only reach through the mystery of love, which alone can release him from a world where each day reminds him of his mortality:

Amiam, che 'l Sol si muore e poi rinasce:
a noi sua breve luce
s'asconde, e 'l sonno eterna notte adduce.
            [Tasso, *Aminta*]

Daniel certainly understood this spirit of Italian pastoral; and though he did not choose to reproduce Tasso's expression of it in his own plays, the influence is there informing his own approach.

The success and popularity of Tasso's *L'Aminta* was overtaken by *Il Pastor Fido* of Guarini, sometime, like Tasso, in the service of Alonso II of Ferrara; and shortly after the publication of Guarini's pastoral, Daniel met the poet whilst on a tour of Italy with his first patron, Sir Edward Dymoke, in 1590 or 1591. The talk must have included discussion of *Il Pastor Fido* and the critical controversy surrounding it, a work so much in the public eye; but clearly the range of literary topics covered more than pastoral drama. Ten years later, Daniel was to recall that visit in a sonnet addressed to Sir Edward Dymoke, which prefaced the first English translation of *Il Pastor Fido:*

I do reioyce learned and worthy Knight,
That by the hand of thy kinde Country-man
(This painfull and industrious Gentleman)
Thy deare esteem'd Guarini comes to light:
Who in thy loue I know tooke great delight
As thou in his, who now in England can
Speake as good English as Italian,
And here enioyes the grace of his owne right.
Though I remember he hath oft imbas'd
Vnto vs both, the vertues of the North,
Saying, your costes were with no measures
    grac'd,
Nor barbarous tongues could any verse bring
    forth.
I would he sawe his owne, or knew our store,
Whose spirits can yeeld as much, and if not
    more.

Guarini would, in fact, have to wait for Sir Richard Fanshawe's 1647 translation, *The Faithfull Shepherd,* before he could 'Speake as good English as Italian', but clearly the spirit of Renaissance emulation informs the sestet of the sonnet—Guarini's aspersions about the relative merits of Italians and English in the field of literature still rankle

after the lapse of ten years—and when Daniel writes his first pastoral play, it is the relation of *Il Pastor Fido* to **The Queenes Arcadia** that we notice, particularly as the model for the plot.

Daniel's pastoral plays have found little favour with the critics, even amongst those who value him; and adverse comment started early, with Ben Jonson's jibe in *Volpone* (1605): 'Here's PASTOR FIDO, says Lady Would-be, showing off her knowledge of Italian poets,

All our English writers,
I meane such, as are happy in th'Italian,
Will deigne to steale out of this author, mainely.

Modern critics, too, tend to emphasize Daniel's sources, usually extending discussion only to point out the dramatic deficiencies of plot and style. **The Queenes Arcadia** suffers most adverse criticism; it contains a strong satirical element which is generally ill regarded, as at odds with the pastoral, and the play is seen by Daniel's most sensitive critic as 'a hotch-potch of satire, high-flown romantic situation and solid common sense.' **Hymens Triumph** is more favourably received, partly on account of its simplicity of plot, partly because it is seen as more independent of models, and its poetry as having more lyric beauty. What is left out of modern critical discussion is the role of the pastoral play in the court world to which it belonged. Such an approach will not transform Daniel's plays into masterpieces, but it will, I hope, show that there is a unity to **The Queenes Arcadia,** and suggest where some of the strengths of **Hymens Triumph** lie.

Pastoral drama, like the heroic poem of the Renaissance, showed the court an idealized image of itself; indeed, pastoral presented the contemplative equivalent of the active life of virtue proclaimed by the heroic. In it the prince and courtier could observe those virtues of personal magnanimity, truth, sincerity and constancy which informed both inner and social behaviour, and therefore reached out to affect the health of the state itself. The aim was both complimentary and didactic: the timeless quality of the Golden Age told the court, 'These are the eternal values, and these are *your* values'; whilst at the same time the Arcadian setting, a landscape not only of pleasant plains but also of rugged mountains and dark woodland, was saying 'Keep faith with your values through all adversity'. The adversity of pastoral drama was generally presented through the sufferings of lovers, where endurance was finally rewarded with happiness and fulfilment, and suffering finally seen as an initiation into this state of perfection. Such is the ethos of the pastoral world out of which Daniel created his plays, and they too fulfil the dual roles of compliment and instruction.

The Queenes Arcadia is in itself a compliment to Queen Anne, as it was written specially for her, and performed by students at Oxford when King James and his wife visited the University in August 1605. Four plays were given during the four days of the visit, but only Daniel's was in English—the others were in Latin—and it was therefore the only one the Queen could understand. The play's much noticed dependence on Guarini for the complications of the love plot, with three pairs of lovers, a 'discovery' of a shepherdess in a cave by one, and a villainess whose forebear is Corsica, is also on one level part of that compliment—we know that Anne, in common with most ladies of Europe, was fond of Guarini's play—though this is subsidiary to the use Daniel makes of the complex plot model for the theme of his play. That, too, involves compliment—to King James, his Queen, and his court—, a message of congratulation at the outset of the new reign, and a warning to the courtiers of the need for constant vigilance to keep the new age undefiled.

The sense of a new era marks even the staging of the Oxford plays of 1605. The University had called on the services of Inigo Jones, just at the beginning of his own career in court entertainment, to devise the stage and scenery in Christ Church Hall; and Jones, described by one observer of the Oxford visit as 'a great Traveller', employed the periaktoi seen on his Italian tour in the creation of a perspective stage, the first time it was used for drama in England. Daniel's pastoral was presumably staged against a setting which corresponded to Vitruvius's third scene, the satyric, suitable for satyr plays and pastoral drama; from the text it is clear that rugged rocks should surround the playing area to mark the bounds of Arcadia, whilst there should be free standing bushes on each side of the stage to conceal Meliboeus and Ergastus on the one side, and Colax and Techne on the other. Costumes for all four of the Oxford plays were supplied from the wardrobe of the Children of the Queen's Revels; and amongst items listed for 'the English Pastorall' were '4 Sheppardes coates of Taffata of severall coulors', '7 Hatts of Taffata', and 'one yelowe Taffata Robe'. To the spectators, it must indeed have appeared that the theatre of Guarini and Tasso had arrived in every way, and the contemporary audience was apparently pleased with **Arcadia Reformed;** after the tedium of the Latin plays, John Chamberlain declared that it 'made amends for all, being indeed very excellent, and some parts exactly acted.'

'All the world's a stage', and the stage is a mirror of that world. James had been on the English throne only two years; long enough, however, to see his rule as the promise of stability and order, and also to take account of the kind of dangers which could undermine the Stuart Age of Gold. Pastoral always acknowledged its own vulnerability: to the pains of love, to invasion from the lawless, such as the brigands or pirates of Greek romance, or the savage beasts which threaten to ravage the land—but may be found more truly in the human breast:

> La selva se' tu, Silvio,
> e la fèra crudel, che vi s'annida,
> è la tua feritate.
>
> [Guarini, *Il Pastor Fido*]

Besides the dangers from within, there were those that came from the corruption of a sophisticated society, dressing appetite and selfishness up as pleasure, as Corisca shows us. 'Et in Arcadia ego' was a threat uttered by more than one kind of death; hence the appearance of satire within Renaissance pastoral from the eclogues of Petrarch on. The inclusion of the satiric in Daniel's **The Queenes Arcadia** is an extension of the role of satire in pastoral; but the very nature of the pastoral form, with its belief in the

unchanging truths, contains and finally banishes the threats to its stability.

The play opens with Ergastus and Meliboeus, 'two ancient Arcadians', asserting the old values of Arcadia even as they lament its change:

> The gentle region of plaine honestie,
> The modest seat, of vndisguised trueth,
> Inhabited with simple innocence
> And now, I know not how . . .
> Hath put off that faire nature which it had,
> And growes like ruder countries or more bad.

The list of ills affecting 'the body of [the] state' is extensive: faithlessness in love, slander and malice, mysterious ailments, disputes over land, the 'disguises' of cosmetics and fashion; and they retire to observe, if they can, the sources of the corruption. Ergastus and Meliboeus are both the watchers, the guardians of the Arcadian world who will restore order in the last act, and the Choric figures who emerge at the end of each act and movement of the plot to comment, and assess what has been observed. They thus present that watchfulness which, in the court world, statesmen should (and, the implication of pastoral, do) exercise over the body politic. The ancient shepherds make it clear that such watchfulness has to begin with the internal state of man.

The threat to 'the little world of man' comes from the two characters who jauntily take the place of the Choric figures, Colax (Flatterer) and Techne (Art). They are the corrupters of manners, in whose wake come the social evils which prey on the gullibility of those disorientated from their native condition of 'vndisguised trueth', Alcon the quack, Lincus the small-time lawyer, and, only revealed in the last act, Pistophoenax (Trusty Impostor) 'a disguiser of Religion'.

Colax and Techne are complementary characters. He is Arcadian born, but comes of aspiring stock—he is 'The sonne of *Nicoginus* of the Hill', and his restlessness has led him abroad to the court of Telos (the state of completeness; sophisticated accomplishment; complete manhood) from which sophisticated environment he has returned 'a corrupted traueller' like Guarini's Corisca. The false court is the source of all moral corruption, whilst 'plaine honesty' belongs to the pastoral world. From Telos Colax has fetched his philosophy, 'wrong is as men thinke it', and confirmed his own restlessness:

> we desire not what we haue,
> But what we would, our longings neuer stay
> With our attaynings, but they goe beyond.

He stands for that principle of change which strikes at the very heart of Arcadia, the virtue of constancy, which in his pursuit of pleasure with one woman after another he consistently undermines. He has already seduced Daphne, turned the head of Dorinda so that she has disregarded her vows to Mirtillus, and separated two faithful lovers, Palaemon and Silvia, by telling each lies about the other's inconstancy in order to win Silvia for himself. Activity is the hallmark of this philanderer, aided and abetted by his accomplice Techne.

As Colax is a product of the corrupt court, so Techne is

a product of the venal city. She is a purveyor of cosmetics and fashion, disguising body and face. Colax appeals to that part of human nature which wants to be knowing, whilst Techne plays on every girl's desire to be pretty, and converts this into vanity. She is an outsider in Arcadia, 'a subtle wench of Corinth', driven from her home by competition; and no wonder, since Corinth was a town with a reputation for women like Techne, who doubles as a bawd—Corinth bearing an additional meaning of brothel. Having worked as procuress for Colax before, she undertakes to use her influence for him with Cloris, and does so the more readily as she has 'a little leaning loue To sweet *Amyntas',* who is in love with Cloris. The parallel with Corisca is obvious.

In **The Queenes Arcadia,** the labyrinthine tangles of lovers at crossed purposes, true lovers separated, true love spurned and selfish passion pursued with no thought of the cost to others are not seen as the vagaries of the human heart or circumstances; malice and unbridled appetite instead of waywardness and fate affect each partnership or would-be partnership; they are not confined to the Corisca-type plot of Techne serving her own ends. One of the Guarini motifs which Daniel takes is that of the unresponsive lover spurning the girl who loves him. Carinus and Amarillis are modelled on Silvio and Dorinda (there is even the scene with the dog Laelaps to point the parallel), but Carinus does not reject Amarillis because his greater passion is hunting. Instead, Daniel complicates the situation by making Carinus follow the unattainable Cloris, and become the rival of Amyntas, to whom Cloris is beginning to incline. The angry exchanges of Carinus and the more noble responses of Amyntas in the 'rivals' scene, Act I, scene II, which Daniel took from Luigi Groto's *Pentimento Amoroso* (1575), makes Carinus appear at first cunning and spiteful; he tricks Amyntas into revealing what tokens of love Cloris has shown him, and then exultantly declares he will tell Cloris Amyntas has been boasting of her love. Moreover, Carinus bases his claim to Cloris's affection on the fact that he has saved her honour, and her love is a debt to be paid him:

> I sau'd her from the hands
> Of that rude satyre, who had else vndone
> Her honour vtterly; and therfore ought
> My loue of due raigne soueraigne in her thought.

At this point it seems that Carinus has something of the Satyr's cunning, and that it is a native malice he shows. However, at the end of the play, when Carinus happily takes Amarillis for his own, we find his earlier attitudes had been infected by Colax, and that Colax was behind his rejection of Amarillis too: 'Colax had persuaded me before Neuer t'accept or to beleeue the loue Of any Nimph'.

The poison is at work everywhere and there is constant need to be vigilant, as the Silvia and Palaemon complication shows. These two lovers have passed through the stage of modest rebuff of devotion, softened only by the imminent suicide of Palaemon, when, in the crisis, Silvia's reserve was cast away and she saved Palaemon's life. Theirs was the Aminta-Silvia story of Tasso, with lovers happily united—or so it seemed, before Colax spread his lies. Now that perfect devotion and perfect purity are impugned, the basis of all human love relationships is destroyed; in the eyes of each deceived lover, trust is gone for ever. The only prospect for both lovers is to find a darksome wood, and hide themselves away with their grief. But again the pastoral form will contain the threat of the death of love, and when in the denouement Silvia and Palaemon are summoned from their forest fastnesses to learn the truth, the result is a greater affirmation of the qualities of masculine devotion and female virtue. At this point in the play, the compliment to the court becomes overt, with Silvia and Palaemon both turning to the audience to make their apologies to the sex they berated:

> SILVIA: And now o pardon me you worthy race
> Of men, if I in passion vttred ought
> In preiudice of your most noble sexe;
> And thinke it was m'agrieued errour spake
> It knew not what, transported so, not I.
> PALAEMON: And pardon me you glorious company
> You starres of women, if m'inraged heat
> Haue ought profan'de your reuerent dignitie,

and here Palaemon addresses the Queen directly, by the name of the goddess of wisdom, the role played by Queen Anne in the masque Daniel wrote for the court at Christmas, 1603: *The Vision of the Twelue Goddesses*

> And thou bright Pallas sou'raigne of all Nimphes, . . .
> The royall Mistresse of our Pastorall Muse . . .
> Forgiue me mine offence . . . . :

Anne is the mistress of the pastoral muse in two senses; as Pallas, it is her wise virtue that the play celebrates; and as Queen Anne, she is the mistress of the pastoral poet, Daniel, in her employ. The poet and the pastoral mode have served their mistress well. The lovers can be forgiven because, though their faith in the other was shaken, their love for one another remains the same. The victory of Colax and Techne is not complete. Carinus, who starts the play as Amyntas's bitter, jeering rival, is magnanimous when he is told of Amyntas's attempted suicide; Cloris is fascinated by the cosmetic wonders of Techne's art and pretty headdresses, but she is not seduced by either Techne's pleading of Colax's cause, nor by that lady-killer's smart appearance and smooth impudence; and when Amyntas, who believes Techne's story that Cloris is false when he sees her running away from the cave to which the bawd has lured her for an assignation with Colax, prefers to die rather than live with the knowledge of Cloris's lightness, the Aminta story is being re-enacted yet again—Cloris, like Tasso's and Daniel's Silvia, yielding finally to her love to save her lover's life. The court of virtue, so different from that of Telos, is the pastoral world over which Pallas presides.

In the midst of the love complications and in the middle of the play, with trust and constancy undermined, the quack and the lawyer appear to compare how they have thriven since coming to Arcadia. Here the social satire is strongly apparent, and held to be out of place in the artifice of pastoral love motifs. Rather, the corruption of manners within an individual is taking its effect on the larger world of the community, allowing the con-men to disrupt the health of society and the organization of that society, its natural order.

Alcon the quack has considerable success to recount, since women are eager to try pleasant medicines, frequently discovering themselves to be ill to try Alcon's useless remedies. Their gullibility is matched by that of the men, who are equally delighted with the pernicious drug tobacco: 'Now do they nothing else, but sit and suck, And spit, and slauer, all the time they sit'. Lincus the pettifogger is less successful than his friend; the Arcadians' 'long and easy peace' has, contrary to the usual experience of the world, left them free from quarrels and the restless contention on which the lawyer thrives. The nature of Arcadia remains unviolated:

> this poore corner of *Arcadia* here,
> This little angle of the world you see,
> Which hath shut out of doore, all th'earth beside
> And [is] barrd vp with mountaines, and with
> rocks;
> Hath had no intertrading with the reste
> Of men, nor yet will have, but here alone,
> Quite out of fortunes way, and vnderneath
> Ambition, or desire, that waies them not,
> They liue as if still in the golden age,
> When as the world was in his pupilage.

It is an unfallen world, untempted as yet by the enticing but bitter fruit of knowledge,

> before men haue transform'd
> Their state of nature in so many shapes
> Of their owne managements, and are cast out
> Into confusion, by their knowledges.

Lincus has his hopes, however; he is busy stirring up avarice and a sense of property rights in two old shepherds, and sees this as the beginning of a possible successful career.

In the pastoral world, to make admission of the simple innocence, even if the outsiders do pour contempt or seem amazed by it, is to assert its value; and the virtue of Arcadian simplicity is stronger than the villains realize. Daphne, first seduced and then jilted by Colax, comes to Alcon for a potion to ease an aching heart or to help her to forget; Alcon, who knows her state, gives her a swift diagnosis in medical jargon, maliciously playing on the names of the lover Daphne threw over and the one who was false to her:

> you must first euacuate
> All those Colaxicall hote humour[s] . . .
> and then refrigerate
> Your bloud by some Menalchian Cordials . . .

Ironically this is the very advice Daphne needs; for, although Alcon's aim is to cast her out into confusion by her knowledge of her own falsehood, conviction of sin is the first step to salvation; and in the denouement, Daphne is sent on her way with the pastoral equivalent of 'Go and sin no more':

> Ergastus: looke more warily vnto your feete,
> Which if you doe, no doubt but all [this] will be
> well.

Alcon ministers false medicine to the spirit, but the force of religious corruption, Pistophoenax, does not appear until the last scene, when he enters with the villains, an unexpected addition to the company. He is a masque-like figure, visored, a beautiful appearance covering an ugly reality, which is revealed when the Arcadian guardians see through his disguise:

> Meliboeus: This man I found . . .
> Mayntayning hote dispute with *Titerus*
> About the rites, and misteries of *Pan.*

The forces of evil are banished from Arcadia by the wisdom of the ancient shepherds, but clearly will fight another day elsewhere; Colax and Techne join in marriage, in a parody of the union of the Arcadian shepherds and nymphs, whilst the three social evils of corrupt medicine, corrupt law, and corrupt religion band together undaunted, with Pistophoenax pointing out the mistake the others made in Arcadia:

> you should haue let
> Me ma[k]e the way, that I might haue dislinkt
> That chayne of Zeale that holds in amitie,

that is, attack the very foundations of Arcadian truth, and break the Great Chain of Being itself. Once again, the threat has been held back by the power of the pastoral truth and honesty, but it is a high note on which to dismiss the villains, and Meliboeus draws the play to its conclusion in a fittingly serious sententious manner; exhorting the Arcadians to banish the strains of the 'ill example' and thus be free from the tyranny of custom:

> who takes from us our priviledge
> To be our selues, rendes that great charter too
> of nature, and would cancell man.

It is a speech which, in its seriousness, includes not only the Arcadians on the stage but the Arcadians who are the courtiers; a plea for judgement, watchfulness and the virtues of honesty and truth which can withstand the forces of corruption.

The mundane evils of Alcon and Lincus, with the more serious threat of Pistophoenax, link the play world with the real world; with some of the evils which had and were to mark the reign of James. 1603, the year in which he came to the throne, suffered a particularly virulent outbreak of plague, a recurrent evil; and Ergastus's reference of Act I scene I to the climate, 'Our wholesome climate growne more maladiue', with the increase of ailments, bears more than a reference to the interest in quack medicine. It is at such a time, of course, that figures like Alcon flourish, preying on credulity and fear, bringing miracle cures from distant parts to deceive the gullible. Lincus, too, as the cunning lawyer, is a figure of topical reference; lawyers are always vulnerable to satire, but at this time, with the shifts in social mobility, litigation was rife; the season in London followed the legal terms, emphasizing dissension at the heart of society.

Pistophoenax is a more ominous figure. He is not anatomized in such full satiric fashion as his colleagues, partly because it was a theme which Daniel would see as too lofty for treatment in the 'low' literary form, and partly because it was too delicate politically. Pistophoenax reflects the divisive impulse in the Church of England, which had come into the open at the Hampton Court conference of 1604, where the polarization of King and Bishops on the one side and the puritan clergy on the other, over church discipline and liturgical practices, would indeed result in the dislinking of the social chain, revolution, and the execution of a king. But that belonged to a future reign. In Daniel's play, Arcadia is restored, and becomes the Queen's Arcadia.

The distinct tones of Daniel's pastoral, with the love tangles and victories of virtue on the one hand, and the social satire on the other, are not in fact antagonistic but complementary, just as are the masculine and feminine spheres; the concerns of a King and those of a Queen. The Queen's taste is served by Guarini, the King's by Alcon's tirade against tobacco—topically following from James's own *Counterblast to Tobacco* (1604); but the inner world of personal and the outer world of social behaviour equally depend on the Arcadian virtues which pastoral presents under attack, disorientated for a time, but ultimately victorious through endurance and patient, watchful truth.

Daniel's second pastoral play is concerned with a closer union of male and female; *Hymens Triumph,* as the title indicates, is a play of celebration of marriage. The occasion for this drama was the marriage of Jean Drummond to Robert Ker, Lord Roxborough, in February 1614; the Queen asked the poet to prepare a play, which was to serve both as compliment to the bridal pair—Jean Drummond had been a member of Anne's Household—and also a housewarming celebration, as the marriage took place at Somerset House which had been altered under Anne's direction, and the King was at the festivities as her guest.

By 1614, Daniel had ceased to write poetry. From the mid fifteen nineties his concern had been more and more with English history, particularly that period of the Wars of the Roses, and his major literary work of the period 1595—1609 was his unfinished *The Civil Wars.* The last ten years of his life saw a continuation of the serious subject of history, but in a different form; Daniel worked on a prose *History of England* (published 1612-1618), unfinished at his death in 1619. However, his position as Groom of the Queen's Privy Chamber meant that he was prepared to contribute to the entertainments that Anne loved, and in the case of *Hymens Triumph* probably the more readily as he and Jean Drummond had both been in the service of the Queen. *Hymens Triumph* is a wedding present from the poet as well as from the Queen, and Daniel gave the bride a presentation manuscript copy.

The occasion of the play, the combined wedding and house-warming celebrations, was both a domestic and state occasion; graced with the trappings of pomp and splendour, but also bringing together and focusing on people who had known, respected and liked one another over a number of years. Daniel's dedication to the Queen, 'Most lou'd, and most respected Maiesty', captures the atmosphere of the occasion: he refers to his play

> As being a piece of that solemnity,
> Which your Magnificence did celebrate
> In hallowing of those roofes (you rear'd of late)
> With fires and chearefull hospitality.

It is in *Hymens Triumph* that Daniel, who from the first had written with sensitivity and tenderness towards women, pays them his greatest compliments; and it is clear that Anne, royal lady presiding over the restoration of houses and over the wedding feast which would continue a house of a different kind, is the chief recipient of his praise:

> Know her [woman] to be th' especiall creature,
>   made
> By the Creator as the complement
> Of this great Architect the world; to hold
> The same together, which would otherwise
> Fall all asunder: and is natures chiefe
> Vicegerent vpon earth, supplies her state.

Woman as the living embodiment of Nature's fertility, creativity and continuity is a queen; in the person of Anne, she is *the* Queen. This is the symbolic expression of the grateful praise of the Danish Queen which closes the Dedication; she is seen as bringing gifts of noble alliance, peace, and the special blessing of an heir to assure the stability of the kingdom. Dynastic and political considerations are embodied in the historical Anne, whilst in the pastoral the benefits she bestows are the very principle of life itself—the cosmic realization of order. This is the kind of symbolism present in the court masques of Ben Jonson and Inigo Jones, and which the pastoral element in both literature and masque—masque especially, with its recourse to visual image and spectacular effects—conveys as part of its essence. The pastoral world reflects the court, and the court reflects the cosmos in its orderliness and harmony. Marriage itself is a reflection of that divinely ordained harmony, and the presence of King and Queen gracing a wedding feast offers another image of the cosmic significance of harmonious union: Daniel's hero, Thirsis, ends a speech proclaiming the sacredness of woman and love with an appeal to the royal couple:

> And I to great *Apollo* here appeale
> The soueraigne of the Muses, and of all
> Well tun'd affections, and to *Cinthia* bright
> And glorious Lady of cleere faithfulnesse;
> Who from aboue looke down with blisful beames
> Vpon our humble groues, and ioy the hearts
> Of all the world, to see their mutuall loues;
> They can iudge what worthinesse there is
> In worthy loue.

The masque element of *Hymens Triumph* is further seen in the Prologue, in which Hymen in pastoral dress defeats Envy, Avarice, and Jealousy, the three enemies of true affection and happy marriage; a triumph which is to be repeated in the action of the play.

Like *Il Pastor Fido,* **Hymens Triumph** celebrates a noble marriage; but, as the appearance of Hymen in pastoral costume suggests, recalling Cupid's shepherd's disguise in the Prologue to *L'Aminta,* it is Tasso's poem which is the inspiration of Daniel's. Although there are elements of Guarini's world in the play—Cloris and Lidia have something of Corisca's scheming to achieve her own ends—the play is predominantly Tassonian in atmosphere and focus. It centres on the sufferings and devotion of Thirsis, and Aminta-like figure, who establishes the truth of love and loving in the play. This concentration on the hero leads to a simpler plot structure than in *The Queenes Arcadia,* so that the central story of Thirsis being reunited with Silvia, the love whom he thought dead, is supplemented by each having an unwanted lover—Cloris pursuing Thirsis, Phillis pursuing Silvia (disguised as the boy Clarindo)—and this motif is repeated as Phillis is in turn followed by a jealous lover, Montanus, who sees Clarindo as his rival. All the action leads to Thirsis; Cloris sends Clarindo, so hauntingly like the lost Silvia, to woo for her; Lidia's scheme of revenge to repay Clarindo for spurning her charge, Phillis, leads to the attack of the jealous Montanus on Silvia which brings about the reunion of the lovers; and Thirsis is the tender concern of Silvia, Cloris, his friend Palaemon, and his father; he is talked of, sought after, argued with, and loved. Through all he remains absolutely constant to a dead girl, of whom he has only a torn veil and lock of hair. Such a theme, and such treatment, Daniel undoubtedly considered appropriate to the occasion—a St Valentine Day's wedding of a couple whose marriage had been postponed, delay and union being reflected in the play in a fable of separation and reunion through the power of love's truth. *Hymens Triumph* is an affirmation of the strength of constancy, and also a pattern for the newly married couple to observe.

The play sets out different attitudes to love through the different characters. Cloris's love is selfish, and artful in the instructions she gives her boy Clarindo:

> Nay but stay boy, wilt thou say nothing else?
> As of thysselfe, to waken vp his loue?
> Thou mayst say something which I may not say,
> And tell him how thou holdst me full as faire,
> Yea and more faire, more louely, more complea
>   ate
> Then euer *Silvia* was; more wise, more stai'd:
> How shee was but a light and wavering maid.

Phillis, who has hitherto rejected all the shepherds and herdsman that sought her love as resolutely as Tasso's Silvia, loves wildly and distemperedly, as shown by her passion for the disguised Silvia; and she has attracted a lover more violently extreme than herself, for the rough forester Montanus can be persuaded to disbelieve what his own eyes have seen and, as blind in judgement, he attacks and wounds Clarindo/Silvia. Medorus, Silvia's father, views marriage through the eyes of gain, until he learns from Thirsis's father how deeply Thirsis loved his daughter; whilst Palaemon, like old Charinus, the lover's father, cannot believe that love and women are worth devotion to the point of death. Montanus's forester friends, Dorcas and Silvanus, are even more convinced of this, as they reflect on the state of the world in Act II, scene I. Only Silvia and Thirsis present the ideal selflessness of love.

When the play opens, Silvia's time of trial is over. Her capture by pirates, her preservation of her virtue, her escape and return to Arcadia where she bides her time, waiting for Alexis, to whom she had been betrothed by her father's avarice, to marry his new bride before she reveals herself to Thirsis, is a history of patience; and she puts it to good use, by using her visits to Thirsis to woo for Cloris—which honourably she does—to encourage him to come out from the dark woods in which he withdraws as into himself, and to implant gradually in the grieving lover's mind the idea

that hope survives: here she is reporting her first visit, to her mistress Cloris:

> I besought him that he would not be
> Transported thus; but know that with the dead
> He should no more converse: and how his loue
> Was living, that would giue him all content,
> And was all his intire, and pure, and wisht
> To liue no longer then she should be so.

Ostensibly, she is talking of Cloris; but to Thirsis there is only one woman—'She only was a reall creature, she',—and the voice speaking and the face before him are those of Silvia, which he senses before he realizes. Yet for a man in such deep grief, the return to happiness must be gradual, by hint, by reviving memories of the living, not the lost girl; and finally, by the account of her own adventures in Act V, scene III. Silvia's tact and gentleness, her disguise as well as her being the emissary for her rival, recall Viola in *Twelfth Night,* that is, the motifs come from romantic comedy; whilst the random violence she receives from Montanus comes from the world of romantic tragedy or tragicomedy, *Philaster,* or *The Maid's Tragedy;* all are closely related to pastoral. Here, Clarindo must die that Silvia might live; and she wakes from her wound, as Thirsis from his death-like swoon, into a new life.

Thirsis is Daniel's Aminta, at times quite deliberately echoing his original:

> Ah I remember well . . . when first
> Our flame began, when scarce we knew what
>   was
> The flame we felt, when as we sate and sigh'd
> And look'd vpon each other, and conceiu'd
> Not what we ayld; yet something we did ayle,
> And yet were well, and yet we were not well;
> And what was our disease we could not tell.
> Then would we kisse, then sigh, then looke: and
>   thus
> In that first garden of our simplenesse
> We spent our child-hood. . . .

Echoing, but not simply reproducing his original. Thirsis is of a different cast of temperament; not passionately impulsive, but still loving deeply; and a man who finds his grief, which others think folly, rational, because he knows the virtue he has lost. When he speaks of his heart as one 'That knows, that feels, that thinks' he is defining his own quality. Tasso is the poet of the feeling heart, Daniel of the thinking heart; and it is through, and from, thought that Thirsis has to be saved.

At first the movement of the play takes him away from company into the solitariness of the dark wood, a kind of living death—scarcely living, for Thirsis's life is ebbing—where Palaemon's attempts to rouse him to 'come to life again' meet with no success. Silvia's presence and encouragement alone have that power, and in Act III scene III Thirsis, for the first time, is associated with images of light—the sun, which brings return of the anniversary of Silvia's death, brings day and hope—, but it is first the hope of release from life. However, the vigour which accompanies this hope in his argument with Palaemon goes against the death-wish: and Thirsis's arguments affirm life, in the qualities they uphold: 'To act one man, and do that part exact'; the worth of women; the sacredness of love. Yet he is right to trust the oracle's promise that he will find happiness the day he dies, for he must die to grief and rise to the bliss of pure and mutual love.

Hymens Triumph is a play about renewal, the renewal of that eternal process of life after death, in which love is the unchanging, fixed principle; the order and stately movement and harmony in the cosmos; the order, stability of succession which ensures the continuance of a kingdom, the harmony between man and woman in marriage; all reflect the eternal changelessness which is always being reborn. It is not a theme stated with great flourish, for Daniel is not a poet of grand gestures; he is by temperament thoughtful, philosophical; and he deliberately avoids extremes. His language is restrained, and his pastoral 'low' style lacking in rich ornament; there is no sensuous, passionate, let alone erotic writing, as Daniel seeks the purest language to evoke a state of complete simplicity. It is the greatest art to be natural; Daniel attempted to show his courtly audience this art which gave their lives its meaning. (pp. 83-106)

> *Johanna Procter, " 'The Queenes Arcadia' (1606) and 'Hymens Triumph' (1615): Samuel Daniel's Court Pastoral Plays," in* The Renaissance in Ferrara and Its European Horizons, *edited by J. Salmons, University of Wales Press, 1984, pp. 83-109.*

Richard C. McCoy   (essay date 1989)

[*In the excerpt below from his book on the Elizabethan revival of chivalry, McCoy detects in such works as* The Civile Wares *and* Philotas *a profound ambivalence on the part of Daniel toward warfare and peace, and toward sovereign authority.*]

The Earl of Essex inspired many writers both before and after his death, but one of his most ardent admirers was the poet Samuel Daniel. In the first edition of *The Civil Wars,* published in 1595, Daniel praised both Essex and Charles Blount, Lord Mountjoy, as the incarnation of contemporary chivalric heroism:

> You in whose actions yet the image shines
> Of ancient honor neere worne out of date,
> You that haue vertue into fashion brought
> In these neglected times respected nought.

Blount was Daniel's patron, and the poet says that Blount could reduce "Whole landes and Provinces" to "calme obedience." But his praise for Essex is more high-flown: the Earl could lead a second crusade "Against the strength of all the Eastern Powres":

> Thence might thy valor haue brought in
>   despight
> Eternall Tropheis to Elizas name,
> And laid downe at her sacred feete the right
> Of all thy deedes and glory of the same.
> All that which by her powre, and by thy might
> Thou hadst attained to her immortall fame
> Had made thee wondred here, admir'd a farre
> The Mercury of peace, the Mars of warre.
>
> (p. 103)

Daniel's imaginary triumph of Elizabethan chivalry was . . . disrupted by the misdeeds of his own time, in ways he did not anticipate. Instead of winning "Eternall Trophies to Elizas name," the Earl of Essex revolted against her rule. Within a few years the Earl's "image . . . of ancient honor" had become as dangerous as image as the engraving of Essex on horseback, and Daniel therefore omitted the stanzas praising Essex from the 1601 edition. Following Blount's fall from favor and subsequent death, he removed the entire section from the 1609 edition of *The Civil Wars.*

The difficulties of this passage are typical of Daniel's work as a whole. The chivalric compromise is shattered by the civil wars of the past and, still more dramatically, by the tumults and conspiracies of the present. Daniel was shocked by the Essex revolt, yet his reaction was profoundly ambivalent. Although he suppressed the stanzas praising Essex, he later addressed a verse epistle to a fellow conspirator, celebrating the Earl of Southampton's release from prison while comparing him to Cato, the noble opponent of Caesar's tyranny and paragon of republican virtue. He also wrote a play, *Philotas,* which many regarded as a defense of Essex, and he had to appear before the Privy Council to answer these suspicions. Despite his declared allegiance to authority and order, Daniel admired the noble rebel, and he could not decide which side he favored. Despite his praise for peace, he was fascinated by the energies unleashed by war, and he could not decide which of their virtues he preferred—order or honor.

In Daniel's case the literary text proved as vulnerable to the contradictions it sought to mediate as the social texts of Elizabethan chivalry. Indeed, these contradictions eventually overwhelmed his most ambitious undertakings and prevented their completion. Daniel's narrative breaks down, in the way described by Fredric Jameson in *The Political Unconscious,* as his "entire system of ideological closure [becomes] . . . the symptomatic projection of something quite different, namely of social contradiction." In *The Civil Wars* Daniel set out to write an epic account of England's turbulent history from the reign of Richard II down to the beginning of the Tudor dynasty under Henry VII. Despite sustained and recurrent efforts to complete the poem, Daniel failed to do so, ending it with the reign of Edward IV. A second attempt in prose, *The Collection of the History of England,* was even more ambitious, beginning with a brief account of Roman rule and proposing to include a survey of the reigns of the "fiue Soueraigne Princes of the Line of Tewdor," but it too fell short of the goal, ending with the reign of Edward III.

Daniel's failure to complete his major works is partially attributable to his own confusion and ambivalence. He may have regretted the diminished "virilitie" of his own age, when "more came to be effected by wit then by the sword," but his praise for aristocratic belligerence could not go too far. Yet while he could not oppose the "greater improuement of the Soueraigntie" of his own time, he could forestall its eventual triumph by resisting narrative closure. The result is a narrative impasse in which the opposing forces remain perpetually suspended, reflecting Daniel's inability to choose between them.

It was an expedient that proved more frustrating than satisfying. Daniel's unhappiness because of his failure to finish his most ambitious work is manifest in his dedication of another piece, *Philotas,* to Prince Henry in 1605. Referring to *The Civil Wars,* he announces that "I grieue for that unfinisht frame / Which thou deare Muse didst vow to sacrifice / Vnto the bed of Peace," and he complains that it must remain unfinished without further patronage. On the other hand, the difficulties *Philotas* caused him with the authorities prompt fears that he has "outliu'd the date / Of former grace, acceptance, and delight" as well as a desire that the verses inspired by Elizabeth's reign "had neuer come to light". Daniel's torturous ambivalence persisted. Although he declares in this dedication that he "has sung enow, / And more then will be heard," having decided it is better "not to write, as not be understood", he went on to complete one more book of *The Civil Wars* and published a revised edition in 1609.

Daniel's difficulties with his material can also be attributed to his choice of genre, epic history. He boasted of his commitment to historical verity, announcing in the opening stanzas of *The Civil Wars,* "I versifie the troth; not Poetize". This commitment to truth distinguished him, in his own eyes, from his contemporaries, most notably poets like Spenser who were caught up in the vain and fictive images of chivalric romance. He emphasized the contrast from the beginning of his career, writing in one of the *Delia* sonnets:

> Let others sing of Knights and Palladines,
> In aged accents, and vntimely words:
> Paint shadowes in imaginary lines,
> Which well the reach of their high wits records.

In dedicating *The Civil Wars* to Elizabeth in 1601, he also distinguishes his own labors from those who have "vainely entertained / Thy land, with ydle shadowes to no end." The contrast with the "historicall fiction" of *The Faerie Queene* could not be more pointed. Daniel's difficulty arises from his subordination of poetry to his conception of historic truth. His work becomes uniquely vulnerable to the conflicts and contradictions of past and present history partly because it is, in Sidney's words, "captived to the truth of a foolish world." Moreover, whereas Daniel insists that history's "acted mischiefs cannot be vnwrought" by poetry's "imagined good," the reverse effect occurs in his own poetry, which is "vnwrought" by its proximity to current events. Daniel's poetry finally failed to comprehend and mediate the conflicts of his period because it failed to provide him with the necessary detachment and distance.

In *The Civil Wars* Daniel's ambivalence and confusion about his subject is manifest in the split between his declared narrative scheme and its actual development. At several points near the beginning he earnestly sets forth his didactic design. In the dedication of the 1601 edition to the Queen he says that he intends to

> Bring here this worke of Warre, whereby was
>   gain'd
> This blessed vnion which these wounds redrest,
> That sacred Concord which prepar'd the way
> Of glory for thee onely to enjoy.

In the dedication of the 1609 edition to the Countess of Pembroke he says he plans

> to shewe the deformities of Ciuile Dissension, and the miserable euents of Rebellions, Conspiracies, and bloudy Reuengements, which followed (as in a circle) vpon that breach of the due course of Succession, by the Vsurpation of Hen.4; and thereby to make the blessings of Peace, and the happinesse of an established Gouernment (in a direct Line) the better to appeare: I trust I shall doo a gratefull worke to my Countrie, to continue the same, vnto the glorious Vnion of Hen.7: from whence is descended our present Happinesse.

Finally, in the opening stanzas, after lamenting the wasteful horrors of the civil wars, he poses this rhetorical question:

> Yet now what reason haue we to complaine?
> Since hereby came to the calme we did inioy;
> The blisse of thee Eliza; happie gaine
> For all our losse.

The historical scheme is initially teleological, based on the orthodox Tudor mythology, in which the discords of the fifteenth century are reconciled by the triumph of Henry VII and his marriage to Elizabeth of York. From this perspective the Wars of the Roses become a *felix culpa,* whose savage conflicts lead to the blessed harmony of Tudor rule.

Nevertheless, the actual narrative unfolds along entirely different lines, fatalistic and cyclical rather than progressive. History is seen as a sequence of transitory advances and inescapable declines. Peace is never a stable achievement nor an especially honorable or attractive goal; instead it is enervating and emasculating, making Daniel's own age a "time not of that virilitie as the former." In *The Civil Wars* England lurches and oscillates helplessly between the sluggish inertia of peace and the chaotic horrors of war. The belief in the inevitability of decay is deeply ingrained in Daniel's writings, and it is asserted early in *The Civil Wars* when he declares that he will show "How things, at full, do soone wex out of frame." This viciously circular pattern is repeated throughout *The Civil Wars,* and it is literally endless.

Daniel's fatalism wreaks havoc with his nominal moral design. *The Civil Wars* is supposed to be a simple tale of crime and punishment and redemption, but redemption is indefinitely deferred, and crime and punishment "as in a circle" are endlessly repeated. Indeed, the issue of guilt is muddled from the beginning by confusion about the origins and consequences of the crime. The opening stanzas of the poem reveal that the succession was breached long before Bullingbrook's supposedly original sin, with no dire results. The Norman conquest made "the succession doubtful, [and] rent / This new-got State, and left it turbulent." This turbulence continues through the reigns of ten kings, stirring up

> The violence, of Princes, with debate
> For titles, and the often mutinies
> Of Nobles, for their ancient liberties

(pp. 104-09)

When Daniel turns to the central conflict of *The Civil Wars,* his fatalism blurs the opposition between Richard II and Bullingbrook, undercutting the legitimacy of both sides. Certainly the latter's rebellion against legitimate authority is frequently rebuked. When Bullingbrook blames the King for provoking him by tyrannous abuse and presents himself as the champion of liberty and justice, a figure called the Genius of England dismisses these claims as the self-serving arguments of an ambitious mind. Similarly, the sympathy of the "multitude" for Bullingbrook's cause, which stems from their own afflictions, is derided as the fickle murmuring of "the malcontented sort" who seek change for its own sake. At the same time, Daniel takes a surprisingly jaundiced view of the reaction of the "grauer sort" who are prepared to endure the wrongs that princes do for the sake of social order: "Since wise men euer haue preferred farre / Th'vniustest peace, before the iustest warre." Their quietism is rejected as an empty and self-serving rationalization:

> Thus they considered, that in quiet sate,
> Rich or content, or else vnfit to striue:
> Peace-louer wealth, hating a troublous State,
> Doth willing reasons for their rest contriue:
> But, if that all were thus considerate,
> How should in Court, the great, the fauour'd
>   thriue?
> Factions must be, and these varieties:
> And some must fall, that other-some may rise.

Despite his professed allegiance to "the blessings of Peace," Daniel equates it here with sluggish inertia and complacency, contrasting it with the vigorous energies of factional opposition and "purging Warre." Yet Daniel's attitude toward both war and peace remains profoundly ambivalent: his equivocations are elaborated with no clear moral resolution in a series of paradoxes later in the work:

> O warre! begot in pride and luxurie,
> The child of malice, and reuengeful hate;
> Thou impious good, and good impietie,
> Thou art the foul refiner of a State;
> Vniust-iust scourge of mens iniquitie,
> Sharpe-easer of corruptions desperate.
> Is there no means, but that a sin-sicke Land
> Must be let bloud with such a boysterous hand?

Daniel sees history as a sequence of mechanical fluctuations between peace and war, and he clearly cannot decide which he prefers.

The Civil Wars offers occasional respites from this vicious circle of constant discord, moments when history promises to take another, healthier direction. The "actiue Raigne" of Henry V presents a far more heroic story of foreign conquests, one that constitutes an alternative to the poem's base plot of recurrent catastrophe. As in Shakespeare, Daniel's King succeeds in channeling his subjects' aggressions into foreign campaigns:

> He brings abrode distracted Discontent,
> Disperst ill humors into actions hie;
> And to vnite them all in one consent,
> Plac't the faire marke of glorie in their eye.

At home a true *discordia concors* is achieved since Henry "cherished the ofspring of his foes; / And his Competitors

to grace did bring." Unfortunately, Henry's reign is only a brief interlude, "so happy a meane-while," in the inexorable cycle of decay. Civil war persists because "the irritated blood, / Enduring not it selfe, it selfe assail'd." The organic forces of decay prove stronger than Henry's heroic triumphs.

The dead monarch himself appears to ask "great ELIZA" to commission a record of his deeds and to rebuke the poets of Daniel's "Vngrateful times" for neglecting them, in words that echo Daniel's own:

> Why do you seeke for fained Palladines
> (Out of the smoke of idle vanitie)
> Who may giue glory to the true designes,
> Of Bourchier, Talbot, Neuile, Willoughby?
> Why should not you striue to fill vp your lines,
> With wonders of your owne, with veritie?
> T'inflame their ofspring with the loue of good,
> And glorious true examples of their Blood.
>
> What euerlasting matter here is found,
> Whence new immortall Illiads might proceed!
> That those, whose happie graces do abound
> In blessed accents, here may haue to feed
> Good thoughts, on no imaginarie ground
> Of hungry shadowed, which no profite breed;
> Whence musicke-like, instant delight may
>   growe;
> Yet, when men all do knowe, they nothing
>   knowe.

This is clearly intended as a reproach to authors of chivalric romance, such as Spenser; but the King's next reproof is squarely aimed at Daniel himself:

> And why dost thou, in lamentable verse,
> Nothing but blood-shed, treasons, sinne and
>   shame,
> The worst of times, th'extreame of ills, rehearse?

Daniel's excuse is generic decorum. He is bound to the "sadder Subiect" of civil war rather than the heroic victories of foreign combat, a task he must complete before he undertakes "immortall Illiads." He never completes that task.

Yet Daniel resolves to finish in a section of Book VI added to the 1601 edition. He also attempts a kind of mythopoetic overview of the ceaseless discord of his narrative, allowing another temporary break from its otherwise inescapable antagonisms. He introduces the figure of Nemesis, who instructs Pandora to unleash havoc on the previously peaceful states of Europe. Her implements will be those two pernicious inventions of the late Middle Ages, the printing press and gunpowder:

> two fatall Instruments,
> The one to publish, th'other to defend
> Impious Contention, and proud Discontents.

Daniel then declares that Queen Elizabeth alone shall be exempt from the dire workings of Nemesis, and "no distresse shall touch her Diadem." Prophecies of a Tudor truce are reaffirmed, a time when "the conioyned aduerse powers" are united in "blessed vnion" and produce a "sacred branch" descending to Daniel's own day. The Tudor myth is once again invoked, but it remains shadowy and remote, a goal never attained by the narrative of the poem.

By looking backward to the Middle Ages rather than forward to his own times, Daniel provides a far more alluring escape from the poem's hostilities. According to his marginal note, medieval Christendom was "at this time in the hands of seuerall Princes, and Commonwealths, which quietly gouerned the same: for, being so many, and none ouer-great, they were lesse attemptiue to disturb others, & more carefull to keepe their owne, with a mutuall correspondence of amitie." These countries and their subjects lived

> At-one with their desires, friends with Debate,
> In peace with Pride, content with their owne
>   gaine,
> Their bounds containe their minds, their minds
>   appli'd
> To haue their bounds with plentie beautifi'd.

Here is a profoundly attractive, if highly implausible, vision of innocence and vibrant harmony: debate flourishes between friends, and pride coexists with peace.

A romantic primitivism colors Daniel's view of the Middle Ages, but there is more than mere nostalgia behind it. The same political yearnings that prompted the Elizabethan chivalric revival and the antiquarians' interest in feudalism are also at work here: the desire for a model of peaceful coexistence between sovereign authority and the privileged subject. For Daniel, it seems, the Middle Ages provided a more appealing model than his own age. Arthur Ferguson finds this odd, but he notes the most salient feature of Daniel's medievalism: "Curiously enough, Daniel admired the medieval unity of faith, yet felt that the civil virtues of the age stemmed from a de-centralized polity" ["The Historical Thought of Samuel Daniel," *Journal of the History of Ideas* 32 (1971)]. The absence of any central autocratic authority is essential, in Daniel's view, to the tranquil amity of the period. (pp. 110-14)

The work that most clearly betrays Daniel's lingering uncertainty toward the heroes and ideals of Elizabethan chivalry is his play **Philotas.** Suspicions that the play alluded to the Essex conspiracy were well founded, as Laurence Michel has shown, [in his introduction to the 1949 ed. of the play]. Philotas is a powerful and popular noble at the court of Alexander the Great. His worst offenses are careless indiscretion and noble arrogance. His slighting remarks about Alexander's pretensions are revealed by his mistress to his enemies, and Alexander is irritated that Philotas attributes his awards of high office and elevation over his peers "rather [to] his desarts, / Than the effects of my grace any way." Philotas's presumption recalls Essex's insistence on the power of his own inherent "active virtues . . . [to] draw on a prince to bestow a marshal's ofice." Philotas is driven by noble ambition and a sense of his own magnanimity, but he does not oppose Alexander's rule. Nevertheless, Daniel shows that "they that have power to hurt, and will do none," can provoke the fears of those above them regardless of what they do:

> But this is still the fate of those that are
> By nature of their fortunes eminent,
> Who either carried in conceit too farre,

Do worke their owne or others discontent,
Or els are deemed fit to be supprest,
Not for they are, but that they may be ill.

Caught up in the conspiracy forming against Alexander, Philotas is initially presented as an innocent bystander, but his failure to inform his sovereign is used against him. Following an unfair trial arranged by his enemies, Philotas is subjected to torture, which he endures bravely for a time until, according to the Nuncius (a character who functions as a chorus), he cravenly collapses, admitting his own guilt and accusing all his friends as well:

>   and so forgot
> Himselfe that now he was more forward to
> Confesse, than they to urge him thereunto.

Essex also shocked his supporters by his sudden change from "death-defying hero" to "abject penitent," accusing everyone, including his sister, of leading him astray. However, by placing his account of the protagonist's collapse in the mouth of the Nuncius, Daniel may have intended to cast doubt on the official versions of both deaths; for Philotas has warned us in his last speech to the court that

> what I here do speake, I know, my Lords,
> I speake with mine owne mouth, but other
>   where
> What may be sayd I say, may be the words
> Not of my breath, but fame that oft doth erre.

Nevertheless, Daniel's final attitude toward his protagonist and toward Essex is profoundly confusing. In the "Apology" that follows the play, he takes Philotas's confession of treason at face value and praises the "graue and worthy Councellors" who prosecuted Philotas so maliciously. As Joan Rees points out, such a conclusion "by no means squares exactly with the impressions which the play itself produces." Daniel could be simply attempting to placate the censorious authorities; he also wrote a letter to Robert Cecil, the "prime mover of the prosecution against Essex," offering to withdraw the play "yf it shall seeme sknendulous [*sic*] to any." The inconsistencies of the play may also derive from Daniel's characteristic ambivalence regarding the conflict between sovereign authority and noble ambition, an ambivalence aggravated by his personal feelings for Essex. He concludes his "Apology" by asking his readers not to draw any parallels between Philotas and "the late Earl of Essex. It can hold in no proportion but only in his weaknesses, which I would wish all that loue his memory not to reuiue." Even as he denies the association, he ends up reinforcing it.

Daniel's defense of himself and his play is characteristically contradictory. He declares rather disingenuously that the subject was "so farre from the time, and so remote a stranger from the climate of our present courses," that he "could not imagine that Enuy or ignorance could possibly haue made it, to take any particular acquaintance with vs, but as it hath a generall alliance to the frailty of greatnesse, and the vsuall workings of ambition, the perpetuall subjects of bookes and Tragedies." He asserts here that the play's treatment of the frailties and ambitions of the overmighty subject are matters of mere literary convention, "the perpetuall subjects of bookes and Tragedies," and that in any case he began writing it "neere halfe a yre before the late Tragedy of ours (where-unto this is now most ignorantly resembled) vnfortunately fell out heere in England." By calling the Essex revolt a tragedy, Daniel revives a resemblance he seeks to deny. He further undermines his own argument by declaring, "I thought the representing of so true a History, in the ancient forme of a Tragedy, could not but haue had an vnreproueable passage with the time, and the better sort of men, seeing with what idle fictions, and grosse follies, the Stage at this day abused mens recreations." Even as he defends himself, he cannot resist indulging in a variation of his familiar boast, "I versifie the troth; not Poetize." In Daniel's view, most poetry consists of little more than "idle fictions," which pale before the force of historical verity. His work deliberately subjects poetry to events, subordinating "the ancient forme of a Tragedy" to "so true a History" here and elsewhere. Thus, the incidents of past and present history inevitably encroach on his creations. He also fails to obtain any perspective on history's contradictions because his narrowly factual notion of truth and his subservient notion of poetry lead to works that are thoroughly muddled by the conflicts they represent.

Badly shaken by the controversy stirred up by **Philotas,** Daniel wrote a letter to Mountjoy, now the Earl of Devonshire, apologizing for reviving the painful memory of the Essex conspiracy. Protesting his innocence and loyalty to his patrons, he proclaims his earnest desire to protect his own reputation as well as theirs: "I know I shall liue inter historiam temporis as well as greater men." His determination to assert his own integrity is firm: "I will not leaue a stayne of villanie vppon my name whatsoeuer error els might skape me vnfortunately thorow mine indiscreation, & misvnderstanding of the tyme." "Misvnderstanding of the tyme" is a pregnant phrase for Daniel. It may imply a merely personal lapse, like his "indiscreation," or it may be a collective bias shared by all his contemporaries. In either case, in the letter written to Devonshire, he bravely resolves to transcend it. Nevertheless in the funeral poem he dedicates to Devonshire the next year he doubts his ability to do so, and in the preface to a collected edition of his poems published in 1607 he despairs completely of any escape from the "misvnderstanding of the tyme." That despair illuminates the weakness at the heart of Daniel's poetry.

In his *"Funerall Poeme Vpon the Earle of Deuonshire"* Daniel asserts his enduring loyalty and gratitude to his old patron, but Mountjoy's death reminds him yet again of the fall of Essex. Daniel cannot resist trying to exonerate himself one more time by justifying his own errors of judgment as opinions widely held:

> And if mistaken by the Parralax
> And distance of my standing too farre off
> I heretofore might erre, and men might tax
> My being so free of prayses, without proofe.
> But here it is not so, and yet the choyce
> Of those I made did yeald the greatest show
> Of honour and of worth, and had the voyce
> Of present times their virtues to allow.
> And if they haue not made them good, it
> No fault of mine.

He may have eventually realized the bad taste of excusing

excessive praise for one patron in a funeral tribute to another; in any case, he dropped the passage from later editions. Nevertheless, Daniel openly confesses his own vulnerability and that of his poetry to the "misvnderstanding of the tyme." The contrast with a comparable apology by Ben Jonson is striking. The latter justifies his errors in praising "some names too much" by declaring it was done "with purpose to have made them such." Jonson characteristically presumes almost absolute didactic control over his subjects; failure to live up to his praises is squarely theirs and not his. Daniel presents himself as the passive, helpless victim of contemporary consensus, who merely echoes "the voyce / Of present times."

Daniel finally subordinates everything, including his own work, to the vicissitudes of history. In the prefatory verses to **Certaine Small Poems,** a collection of his poetry, he acknowledges its dependence on changing customs:

> And since the measures of our tong we see
> Confirmed by no edict of power doth rest
> But onely vnderneath the regencie
> Of vse and fashion, which may be the best
> Is not for my poore forces to contest.

For Daniel, the "poore forces" of his verse and all poetry were no match for the powerful forces of history. His works were too closely engaged by the political controversies and complex celebrities of his age, and he never fully understood their essential conflicts. In Daniel's verse we hear "the voyce / Of present times" speaking with heightened urgency in all its confusing contradictions. (pp. 122-26)

> *Richard C. McCoy, "Samuel Daniel: 'The Voyce of Present Times'," in his* The Rites of Knighthood: The Literature and Politics of Elizabethan Chivalry, *University of California Press, 1989, pp. 103-26.*

FURTHER READING

OVERVIEWS AND GENERAL STUDIES

Courthope, W. J. "Spenser's Successors: Samuel Daniel." In his *A History of English Poetry,* Vol. III, pp. 9-26. London: Macmillan and Co., 1924.

> A survey of Daniel's career and poetical works; first published 1903.

Davis, Dick. "Samuel Daniel: A Neglected Elizabethan Poet." *Essays by Divers Hands* 44 (1986): 1-23.

> A thorough and up-to-date introduction to Daniel's poetical works, including his verse pastorals and *The Civile Wares.*

Quiller-Couch, Arthur. "Samuel Daniel." In his *Adventures in Criticism,* pp. 3-10. New York: G. P. Putnam's Sons, 1925.

> Pithy introduction to Daniel's work; first published 1896.

Seronsy, Cecil. *Samuel Daniel.* New York: Twayne Publishers, 1967, 198 p.

> Overview of the life and works of Daniel, focusing on the various literary genres in which he wrote.

DRAMA

Michel, Laurence. Introduction to *The "Tragedy of Philotas,"* by Samuel Daniel, pp. 1-35. New Haven: Yale University Press, 1949.

> Looks at Daniel's tragedy in the context of other plays written by members of the Wilton circle and discusses the relationship of *Philotas* to the Essex affair.

Norman, Arthur M. Z. "Daniel's *The Tragedie of Cleopatra* and *Antony and Cleopatra.*" *Shakespeare Quarterly* IX, No. 1 (Winter 1958): 11-18.

> Discusses the influence of Daniel's tragedy *Cleopatra* on Shakespeare's play on the same subject.

HISTORIES

Blissett, William. "Samuel Daniel's Sense of the Past." *English Studies* XXXVIII, No. 2 (April 1957): 49-63.

> Examines Daniel's expressed motives for writing history and the reasons for his sympathetic view of the Middle Ages.

Chang, Joseph S. M. J. "Machiavellianism in Daniel's *The Civil Wars.*" *Tulane Studies in English* XIV (1965): 5-16.

> Argues that Daniel's *Civile Wares* describes a world in which the rule of order is being undermined, even as the historian refrains from moral judgments in recounting the actions of individual statesmen.

Ferguson, Arthur B. "The Historical Thought of Samuel Daniel: A Study in Renaissance Ambivalence." *Journal of the History of Ideas* XXXII, No. 2 (April-June 1971): 185-202.

> Explains how Daniel achieved both maturity and the consciousness of the modern historian in his *The History of England.*

Hulse, S. Clark. "Samuel Daniel: The Poet as Literary Historian." *Studies in English Literature 1500-1900* XIX, No. 1 (Winter 1979): 55-69.

> Analyzes Daniel's disenchantment with the "modern" (Renaissance) movement in letters and his rejection of the belief in historical progress.

Michel, Laurence. Introduction to *The Civil Wars,* by Samuel Daniel, pp. 1-51. New Haven: Yale University Press, 1958.

> Discusses the sources for Daniel's epic in earlier English chronicles and the arguments for Shakespeare's reliance

on Daniel. Includes a collection of comments by Coleridge on *The Civile Wares.*

Seronsy, Cecil. "The Doctrine of Cyclical Recurrence and Some Related Ideas in the Works of Samuel Daniel." *Studies in Philology* LIV, No. 3 (July 1957): 387-407.

> Examines the doctrine of alternating progress and decay of cultures and empires in Daniel's philosophy of history.

POETRY

Maurer, Margaret. "Samuel Daniel's Poetical *Epistles,* Especially Those to Sir Thomas Egerton and Lucy, Countess of Bedford." *Studies in Philology* LXXIV, No. 4 (October 1977): 418-44.

> Notes a relationship between Daniel's ways of conveying meaning in his poetical epistles and the Renaissance theory of the emblem, or device.

Seronsy, Cecil. "Daniel and Wordsworth." *Studies in Philology* LVI (April 1959): 187-213.

> A systematic demonstration, primarily in stylistic terms, of the widely acknowledged indebtedness of Wordsworth to the poetry of Daniel.

————. "Daniel's *Complaint of Rosamond*: Origins and Influence of an Elizabethan Poem." *The Lock Haven Bulletin* 1, No. 2 (1960): 39-57.

> Identifies sources for *Rosamond* in stories from *The Mirror for Magistrates* and Thomas Churchyard's "Shore's Wife," and specifies the poem's influence on Shakespeare, Drayton, and Middleton.

Shackford, Martha Hale. "Samuel Daniel's Poetical *Epistles,* Especially That to the Countess of Cumberland." *Studies in Philology* XLV, No. 2 (April 1948): 180-95.

> Comments on the classical character of Daniel's epistles, which take the Roman epistles of Horatio as their antique model.

OTHER MAJOR WORKS

Himelick, Raymond. Introduction to *"Musophilus: Containing a General Defense of All Learning,"* by Samuel Daniel, pp. 9-59. West Lafayette, Indiana: Purdue University Studies, 1965.

> Argues that Daniel's treatise belongs to a movement among late Renaissance humanists and men of letters to justify the literary profession and its values.

Additional coverage of Daniel's life and career is contained in the following source published by Gale Research: *Dictionary of Literary Biography: Elizabethan Dramatists, Vol. 62.*

John Donne

1572-1631

English poet, epigrammatist, and sermonist.

INTRODUCTION

The following entry presents a selection of criticism from the last three decades. For additional information on Donne's life and works see *Literature Criticism from 1400-1800*, Vol. 10.

Often identified as the head of the metaphysical school of English poetry, Donne is best known for his controversial love poems, which depict an unbridled sensuality. His later poems and sermons, also well-known, and written while an Anglican divine, reflect a struggle for religious truth and authenticity and seek a balance between the sensual and spiritual elements of human life.

A distant relation of Sir Thomas More, Donne was born into a Roman Catholic family in London. He received his early education from the Jesuits; later he matriculated at Oxford, eventually studying law at the Inns of Court in London (1591-96). After a short term of military service, Donne became the personal secretary of Sir Thomas Egerton. Shortly thereafter, he married Egerton's niece, Anne More, without her family's approval, and this breach of etiquette lost him his secretarial position. Despite financial hardship, he and Anne managed to raise twelve children. Devoted to writing poetry, Donne eventually came under the patronage of Sir Thomas Morton; Lucy, Countess of Bedford; and Sir Robert Drury. After embracing the English Catholic Church, Donne wrote two anti-Roman Catholic works, *Pseudo-Martyr* (1610) and *Ignatius His Conclave* (1611), both of which condemn the authoritarian excesses and high-living ways of the Roman church leadership. These works caught the attention of James I, who insisted that Donne take Anglican orders, which he did in 1615. In 1621 Donne became dean of the Cathedral Church of St. Paul, London. Following his ordination, Donne's poetry and prose began to reflect his religious preoccupations, and he also became famous for his sermons, which were eventually collected and published in 1640. He died in 1631, a few weeks after preaching his own funeral sermon, and was interred in St. Paul's.

Most of Donne's early writings were love poems, written during his student years at the Inns of Court. These poems were first collected with others and published in 1633 in a volume called *Poems*. Among the most famous are the *Songs and Sonnets*—notably "The Canonization," "The Ecstasie," "The Flea," and "A Valediction: forbidding mourning"—and the *Elegies*, which are often characterized as provocative and sensual adventures into the realms of love, and reflective of Donne's rakish, ebullient youth. In 1611 and 1612, Donne wrote two long elegiac poems

widely known as the *Anniversaries*. These poems—"An Anatomie of the World," and "Of the Progresse of the Soule,"—recall the brief life and tragic death of Elizabeth Drury, the daughter of Donne's patron. They are noted for their extravagant flattery, as Donne describes in almost beatific terms a young girl he did not even know. Around this same time Donne also penned his famous *Satyres* which explore his many thoughts and feelings as he prepared to leave the Roman Catholic Church for the Anglican communion. In the years after his conversion to Anglicanism, Donne employed a distinctive religious casuistry in his poetry, prose, and sermonizing, especially as he defended his Anglican theological beliefs and moral ideals while struggling to find common ground between the material and spiritual worlds. This canonical approach toward the fulfillment of God's will through the exercise of his commandments and church laws can also be found in his *Holy Sonnets*, his Sermons, and "The Progresse of the Soule," as well as in his *Devotions upon Emergent Occasions* (1624), which is a somber collection of meditations that includes the famous prose work, "No man is an island." During his final years, Donne also wrote two poems of hopeful resignation, "Hymn to God the Father" and "Hymn to God my God in my sicknesse." Donne's most famous sermon, *Deaths Duell* (1632), was called Donne's "own Funeral Sermon" by Izaak Walton. It is Donne's last written and best-known reflection on life and death, on heaven and hell, and on Christian resignation to God's will. Various collections of his works were published after his death; among them the first collection of his poetry in 1633, his *LXXX Sermons* (1640), which reveals his casuistic focus on a wide variety of spiritual issues, *Biathanatos* (written in 1611 but withheld from publication until 1646) on the matter of suicide, and *Essayes in Divinity* (1652), exploring various aspects of religious belief.

Critical assessments of Donne's works began with his contemporaries such as Thomas Carew and Ben Jonson, who praised Donne's poetry for its wit; Jonson and others, however, criticized his occasionally obsequious manner, his profane subject matter, as well as his innovative meter. Throughout the nineteenth century interest in Donne's writings grew with the support of such favorable commentators as Samuel Taylor Coleridge, Robert Browning, and Thomas De Quincey, who described his works as brimming with life and filled with primeval emotion. With the advent of the twentieth century and H. J. C. Grierson's critically acclaimed edition of Donne's collected poems in 1912, writers such as T. S. Eliot, Lionel Trilling, and Cleanth Brooks have pointed out Donne's ability to poetically expose the primal instincts of mankind, revealing the joys, sorrows and dilemmas of flesh and faith in the human experience; some, like C. S. Lewis, have faulted his poetry as overrated and questionable in structure, subject matter, and meter.

Recent criticism has noted the kaleidoscopic nature of Donne's love poetry, which includes almost all of the various aspects of love relationships. However, some critics find that Donne's poetic images are obscure and disconnected because they are often drawn from classical and medieval sources, and this, they contend, unnecessarily intrudes on the presentation and clarity of his themes. Further, it is undeniable that there was a break between the younger Donne who wrote the gay *Songs and Sonnets*, the Donne of middle years who wrote to please his patrons and gain favor with influential readers, and the older Donne so much concerned with the meaning of sanctification. Then too, it has been emphasized that the modern reader of Donne's poetry and the interpreter of his life must take into account the cultural mores and atmosphere of Donne's age: a time when the fleshly and the solemnly spiritual were comfortably married in English life; a time of plagues in which a widespread sense of life's brevity and fleeting beauty was acknowledged; a time of schism and doubt as people in a once-Roman Catholic nation searched for certainty in a land now under the control of a state church of questionable authority. As a poet Donne served as the inspiration to an entire school of poets—"the school of Donne"—who collectively wrote some of the most accomplished religious poetry in English history. He is seen as the forerunner of many modern poets, notably those Modernist innovators of the first half of the twentieth century. Frank Kermode has praised Donne as "at least as original and idiosyncratic" as his near-contemporaries Edmund Spenser and William Shakespeare. Perhaps Carew wrote the most succinct and elo-

quent summary of Donne's accomplishment, concluding his elegy: "*Here lie two Flamens, and both those, the best. / Apollo's first, at last, the true Gods Priest.*"

PRINCIPAL WORKS

Pseudo-Martyr (essay) 1610

Ignatius His Conclave; or His Inthronisation in a Late Election in Hell: wherein many things are mingled by way of satyr; concerning the disposition of Jesuits, the creation of a new hell, the establishing of a church in the moone (essay) 1611

**The First Anniversarie. An Anatomie of the World. Wherein By Occasion Of the untimely death of Mistris Elizabeth Drury, the frailtie and decay of this whole World is represented* (poetry) 1611

**The Second Anniversarie. Of the Progres of the Soule. Wherein, By Occasion Of the Religious death of Mistris Elizabeth Drury, the incommodities of the Soule in this life, and her exaltation in the next, are Contemplated* (poetry) 1612

Devotions upon Emergent Occasions, and Severall steps in my sickness (devotions) 1624

Deaths Duell (sermon) 1632

Juvenilia; or, Certaine paradoxes, and problems (prose) 1633

†*Poems* (poetry) 1633

LXXX Sermons (sermons) 1640

BIAJANATOS. A declaration of that paradoxe or thesis that self homocide is not so naturally sinne, that it may never be otherwise. wherein the nature and the extent of all those lawes, which seeme to be violated by this act, are diligently surveyed (essay) 1646

‡*Essayes in Divinity* (essays) 1652

Works. 6 vols. (poetry, essays, sermons, devotions, epistles and prose) 1839

Selected Passages from the Sermons (sermons) 1919

The Showing forth of Christ: Sermons of John Donne (sermons) 1964

---

*These works were published together as *The Anniversaries* in 1963.

†In later centuries, this first edition of Donne's poetry was succeeded by other, more authoritative editions, notably those issued in 1895 and 1912. H. J. C. Grierson's 1912 edition is considered definitive and contains *Songs and Sonnets, Epigrams, Elegies, Heroicall Epistle, Epithalamions, Satyres, Letters to Severall Personages, An Anatomie of the World, Of the Progresse of the Soule, Epicedes and Obsequies upon the Deaths of Sundry personages, Epitaphs, Infinitati Sacrum, Divine Poems, Holy Sonnets,* Donne's Latin poems and translations, and poems of questionable authorship attributed to Donne in early editions.

‡This work was published with a 1652 printing of *Juvenilia; or, Certaine paradoxes, and problems.*

CRITICISM

Helen Gardner   (essay date 1965)

[*In the following excerpt, Gardner presents an overview of Donne's* Elegies *and* Songs and Sonnets, *laying particular emphasis on their various love themes.*]

Donne has a claim to the title of our greatest love-poet on two grounds. First, the range of mood and experience in his love-poetry is greater than can be found in the poetry of any single other nondramatic writer. We can find almost any and every mood of man in love with woman expressed memorably and vehemently in his poetry. The qualification is necessary because there is one range of feeling that he never touches and it is a range that has given us some of the most beautiful lyric poetry in the language. He never speaks in the tone of a man overwhelmed by what he feels to be wholly undeserved good fortune. Gratitude for love bestowed, the sense of unworthiness in face of the overwhelming worth of the beloved, self-forgetting worship of her as she is: these notes Donne does not strike. But his second claim to pre-eminence is that he has given supreme expression to a theme that is rarely expressed in lyric poetry, and finds expression in drama rather than in lyric, the theme of the rapture of fulfilment and of the bliss of union in love.

> She'is all States, and all Princes, I
>   Nothing else is.
> Princes doe but play us; compar'd to this,
> All honor's mimique; all wealth
>   alchimie. . . .

> Only our love hath no decay;
> This, no to morrow hath, nor yesterday,
> Running it never runs from us away,
> But truly keeps his first, last, everlasting day.

To match this note of passionate joy we have to turn to *Romeo and Juliet,* to *Othello,* or to *Antony and Cleopatra.*

> Let Rome in Tiber melt, and the wide arch
> Of the rang'd empire fall!   Here is my space.
> Kingdom's are clay.

The poems that Donne wrote on this theme of mutual love are charged with such a tone of conviction and expressed with such a naked and natural force of language that it is commonly assumed that they must directly reflect an actual experience of such a rapturous discovery of a new heaven and a new earth in love; and many critics have taken them as celebrating his love for Ann More and their reckless marriage. But Donne himself has warned us against making any simple equation between the truth of the imagination and the truth of experience. Writing to Sir Robert Carr in 1625, in apology for the feebleness of his poem on the death of Hamilton and the reward of the blessed in heaven, he said: 'You know my uttermost when it was best, and even then I did best when I had least truth for my subjects.'

The love-poetry of Donne is, in its limited sphere, like the plays of Shakespeare in being 'of imagination all compact'. As Shakespeare was stimulated by stories he read or plays he had seen to make a play, so Donne, I believe, was stim-

ulated by situations, some literary, some imagined, some reflecting the circumstances of his own life, by things seen on the stage or read in the study, or said by friends in casual conversation, to make poems. Whatever experiences literary or actual lie behind his poems have been transmuted in his imagination, which has worked on them to produce poems that are single and complete, as a play is single and complete. While other poets were producing sequences which, whether truly or not, at least purported to be based on their own fortunes in love, Donne produced a corpus of discrete poems. No links are suggested between them by the use of an imagined name or by connexion of circumstances. The literary sources of Donne's poems can be suggested. It is a fascinating study for he transforms whatever stimulates his imagination. Some actual experiences we may see reflected; others we may guess at, if we wish. And the personality of Donne that gives unity to all we know of his life and is so apparent in his letters, sermons, and other prose works, where he speaks in *propria persona* (whether as Jack Donne, the private man, or as Doctor Donne, the public figure) strongly informs his love-poems, and gives them much of their fascination. Nobody can doubt that all Donne's works are by Donne. He is highly inimitable. None of his followers catch more than a superficial trace of his accent; as none of the post-Shakespearians catch more than a faint echo of Shakespeare's voice. In the love-poems, because he was in every sense writing *con amore*, it might be claimed that his personality found its purest expression. But their strength is a strength of the imagination, which abandons itself wholly for the space of a poem to an imagined situation or mood. Donne's love-poetry has not the brooding tone of memory or the poignant note of hope. It has the dramatic intensity of present experience.

The situations that Donne's imagination dramatizes are bewilderingly varied. He has lost his mistress's token, a gold chain, and she demands that he buy another; his mistress has sent him a cheap favour, a jet ring—as he twirls it to put it on his finger he wonders what it signifies; his perfume has given him away to the father of a young girl he was clandestinely visiting; he is about to go abroad and his mistress has pleaded to be allowed to go with him as his page; he is about to go to the wars and gives her his picture, wondering whether he will look different when he returns; he is about to go abroad and, doubting his mistress's constancy, he scratches his name on a pane of glass as a charm; a flea hops from him to his mistress while he is urging her to yield to him; he has been dreaming and just at the moment he dreams that she is his, she enters and wakes him; he is in bed watching his mistress undress and urges her to hurry; he is in bed with his mistress and the sun wakes them; he and his mistress have been walking to and fro for three hours in the morning and now as they stand still it is high noon; a friend is reproaching him for sacrificing worldly advantages for love; he is alone and unhappy in a spring garden because his mistress is too true to love him; he is alone at midnight in midwinter and more desolate than the season because his mistress is dead; it is a year since they first saw each other, but their love has mysteriously remained unchanged in a world of change; it is spring and he loves her more than he did in winter and he wonders whether his vows in winter were therefore false; his mistress has given him a bracelet of her hair and it is a sign of the miraculous union of their souls which has been achieved without the help of their bodies; his mistress has given him a bracelet of her hair: it is a sign perhaps of her power over him, to preserve him from corruption, or perhaps of the cruelty by which she has enslaved him and condemned him to die.

Even when a poem is not strictly dramatic in that we cannot thus define the exact situation, the imagined moment, Donne assumes the role that a poem demands with dramatic zest and consistency. He can argue with a wild persistent logic that since it is the centric part that men love they should waste no time admiring women's faces, but start their voyage to the desired port from the foot; or that his friend will do far better to marry the hideous Flavia than to marry a beauty. He will declare that he can love any and every kind of woman, except a constant one; or explain the diet by which he has kept his love low; or bargain with the God of Love, offering to accept willingly later on the absurd role of an aged infatuate in return for freedom from love's servitude now. Or, if he wishes, he can play the despairing lover. In poems such as **'The Broken Heart'**, **'The Triple Fool'**, **'The Message'**, or **'The Legacy'** he is all made of tears and sighs and groans, faithful to a mistress who denies or betrays him.

To jumble the love-poems thus together, as they appear jumbled in the great majority of manuscript collections, is to make clear the variety of moods and attitudes to which Donne gave expression and reminds us that a tone of conviction, an accent of truth, is characteristic of his love-poetry whatever mood it expresses. On aesthetic grounds we cannot say, for example, that **'A Valediction: forbidding Mourning'** is more sincere than **'The Flea'**. If it is argued that no woman could possibly be persuaded to lose her honour by sophistries about flea-bites, it might with equal justice be argued that no woman would be comforted by analogies drawn from compasses. **'The Flea'** is persuasive because of its tone of impatient confidence sweeping aside all objections: **'A Valediction: forbidding Mourning'** is persuasive because of its tone of tenderness and absolute assurance. Each expresses its mood with that lack of hesitation, or equivocation, that purity of tone, that gives sincerity to a work of art and makes it appear veracious, or imaginatively coherent. If we are to value one poem more highly than the other it must be on the non-aesthetic ground that we value its mood and sentiments more highly. Nor can we legitimately assume that poems that express idealistic sentiments must have been written at a different period from those that express a cynical view of man's love and woman's virtue. If Shakespeare's imagination could give life at the same time to a Mercutio and a Romeo, to an Iago and an Othello, why should we think it impossible for Donne to turn from the mood of **'Love's Growth'** to the mood of **'Love's Alchemy'**?

Donne's vividly dramatic imagination transforms what are in many cases stock themes of European love-poetry and has disguised the extent to which his inspiration is literary and the nature of his originality. He is not original in writing about a flea; but he is not content, like many Renaissance poets in all countries, to write yet another grace-ful but tedious variation on 'Ovid's flea', envying the flea for the liberties it takes with his mistress's person, or its good fortune in dying at such hands and on her snowy bosom. The old Petrarchan theme of the love-dream—

> Thus have I had thee as a dream may flatter,
> In sleep a king but waking no such matter—

is transformed by the brilliant stroke of bringing the lady herself into the room just as the dream reaches its climax of joy; and for the sadness of waking there is substituted disappointment in actuality and a return to the pleasures of dreaming. Ovid's narrative of how Corinna came to him one hot noon and how he lay watching her undress, an erotic memory, becomes in Donne's hands an impassioned address by the lover in which the tide of mounting passion is rendered in splendid hyperboles. In the short compass of seventeen lines **'The Apparition'** modulates from what appears to be a conventional attack on a cruel mistress, through an original remaking of the classic theme that what she now refuses to enjoy with him she will when old long for in vain, to a surprising close that seems at first sight to contradict the opening; for if he no longer loves her why should her cruelty kill him? But the logic of the poem's movement is a logic of the heart, humiliated pride preferring the sweets of frustration and revenge to tamer satisfactions. When we praise Donne for his dramatic imagination we are paying tribute to his truth of feeling. The bright light of drama, which heightens and exaggerates, is fatal to weakness or falsity of feeling.

Puttenham [in his *The Art of English Poesie*] said of love-poetry that it required 'a form of Poesie variable, inconstant, affected, curious, and most witty of any others'. The versatility that makes Donne's love-poetry a kind of compendium of the poetry of classical, medieval and Renaissance Europe on the theme of love is matched by a corresponding virtuosity in the creation and handling of metrical forms. He achieves the effect of wholly natural speech in complex stanzas with demanding rhyme schemes. He spoke of 'Rimes vexation'; but there is no poet whose sense appears to be so little led by the exigencies of rhyming. He plainly strove for unobtrusive rhyme; he loves sliding rhymes, on vowels, or on liquids or nasals, and he frequently avoids hard rhyme by opening the following line with a vowel. But when he wishes his rhyme is emphatic. Similarly, while keeping the accent of ordinary speech, he is a master of placing and of repetition; as in **'The Expiration'** where the placing of the repeated 'Go' and the support given to it by assonance creates an exquisite musical effect. He is a master of concision and economy in language, seeming effortlessly to fill his lines, without waste of words or awkward condensation or inversion. And his use of rhetorical devices, like his handling of literary conventions, is so individual that we are usually unaware of the means by which he elicits our response. (pp. xvii-xxii)

The *Elegies* . . . form a homogeneous collection of poems, unified in style and in their handling of the couplet, and inspired in the main by two literary models, the classical love-elegy, particularly the *Amores* of Ovid, and the Italian Paradox. One can also see clearly reflected in them that the young Donne was 'a great frequenter of Playes'. The two strains, the Ovidian and the Paradoxical, blend very well since outrageousness and perversity mark Ovid's handling of the theme of love in the *Amores,* which are a constant offence against Roman *gravitas.* Obviously Ovidian are **'Jealousy'**, **'Tutelage'**, **'Love's War'** (though it recalls two Elegies of Propertius), and **'Going to Bed'**. Obviously Italianate in their paradoxical arguments are **'The Anagram'** (which overgoes Tasso's 'Sopra la Bellezza') and **'Love's Progress'**, though this may owe something to Nashe's indecent *A Choice of Valentines.* Influenced more I think by the stage than by reading are **'The Bracelet'** and **'The Perfume'**; and the influence of the stage is also felt in the beautiful Elegy **'On his Mistress'** which, like the other valedictory Elegy **'His Picture'**, transcends the world of Ovid. The *Elegies* are untouched by the idealization of women that distinguishes the courtly and Petrarchan traditions from the tradition of classical love-poetry. They are equally free of the dialectical subtleties of Neoplatonism. They show no trace of the conception of love as humble service or of the conception of love as a mystical union by which two souls become one. This is true even of the serious and impassioned valedictions. They speak of parting directly and unphilosophically without any attempt to prove that souls may remain united though bodies are parted. The brief **'Funeral Elegy'**, which appears linked by manuscript tradition to the Love Elegies, is in the same way content to dwell on the virtues of the dead man and the grief of his family. It makes no attempt at the elaborate panegyrical and theological conceits characteristic of the Epicedes that Donne wrote between 1609 and 1614.

It seems reasonable to regard the *Elegies* as fairly close to each other in date and from topical allusions in some they can be dated between 1593 and 1596 when Donne was a law student at Lincoln's Inn. They are thus contemporary with the first three Satires. Donne begins his poetic career by taking two Roman poets as his models: the Horace of the *Satires* and the Ovid of the *Amores.* He was no doubt attracted by the social realism of both and by the dramatic element in Roman satire and elegy. This last he develops in the *Elegies* far beyond what he found in his Roman models, following the bent of his temperament, stimulated one imagines by the flowering of the Elizabethan drama. His wit also far overgoes the wit of Ovid, drawing on medieval dialectic and legal disputations. Again for parallels we must turn to the logic-chopping of Elizabethan comedy.

The *Elegies* give an overwhelming impression of masculinity. The 'masculine persuasive force' of the language and the reckless, overbearing argumentativeness match an arrogance that in some of the poems amounts to a brutal contempt for the partner of his pleasures, in others issues in a confident assertion of the will to enjoy her, and even in the two valedictions appears in the lover's unquestioning assumption of superiority. The *Elegies* are the product of the 'youth, strength, mirth, and wit' that Walton saw portrayed in the Marshall engraving. The young man there, with his intellectual brow, his sensual lips, his powerful nose ('the rudder of the face') and his bold gaze, plainly regards the world as his oyster. English poetry provides no precedent for the adoption of so whole-hearted a rejection of all social, moral, and religious values in the

interests of youthful male desire, and none of the poets who followed Donne in writing love-elegies approached his masterful vigour.

To turn from the *Elegies* to the *Songs and Sonnets* is to exchange homogeneity for extreme diversity in theme, mood, form, and style . . . Even so, the effect of diversity remains. Donne is a tireless experimenter in the lyric.

So much praise has been given to Donne's colloquial vigour and so much, sometimes misconceived, praise has been given to his supposed metrical irregularity that it is worth stressing that although there are no sonnets in the *Songs and Sonnets* there are many songs and that Donne's songs run with a delightful lilting ease. Six of the poems in my first set are said to have been written to existing airs and song rhythms can be heard behind many of the others, as in the nursery-rhyme cadence of 'I can love her, and her, and you, and you' of **'The Indifferent'** and the beautiful rocking movement of **'Break of Day'**, set up by continual inversion of the first foot. Parody, in its now obsolete sense of the setting of fresh words to an old tune, was one of the ways in which the Elizabethans liberated themselves from the jog-trot of mid-sixteenth-century lyric verse and learned to trust their ears rather than their fingers. Sidney, before Donne, exercised himself in this way. If song is one root of Donne's art as a lyric poet, the classical love-epigram is another. Donne admired the witty brevity of Martial whom he quotes from seven times in the *Paradoxes and Problems.* The poems that I have placed after the songs have the brevity and point of the epigrammatic form, and the development of Donne's art might be described in one way as his learning how to expand and enrich epigrammatic themes without losing the point and pungency that is characteristic of epigram.

The norm of Donne's songs is the octosyllabic line, the old staple line of medieval verse. The norm of epigram is the decasyllabic line, the line that catches the rhythm of speech, the line of drama. A good many of the poems in this first set combine decasyllabics with octosyllabics, as if Donne were trying to combine the soaring of song with the force of speech. Or we might put it that he was trying to achieve a stanza that combined the weight of the decasyllabic with the lightness of the octosyllabic. Equally interesting and without precedent are the two dramatic monologues in verse-paragraphs, **'Woman's Constancy'** and **'The Apparition'**, where matter that might have been handled in the *Elegies* is given a form that corresponds more closely with fluctuating feeling than regularly rhyming couplets can.

Other poems in this first set handle themes and reflect moods that remind us of the *Elegies* and of the *Satires*, or are, like them, inspired by classical models. But in others the young man about town of the *Elegies* who takes his pleasure at will is replaced by another figure: the lover who loves without reward. This is the young man of the Lothian portrait, posed 'with folded arms and melancholy hat', asking in a parody of religious language that his lady would lighten his darkness. But whether Donne is bargaining with the God of Love in **'Love's Usury'**, or pleading with him for mercy in **'Love's Exchange'**, explaining to us how he keeps his heart free so that his body may reign in **'Love's Diet'**, or complaining of Love's unwarranted extension of his power in **'Love's Deity'**, it is the same voice that speaks. The licentious young amorist and the frustrated lover are the same person, as the same eyes look out at us from the Marshall engraving and the Lothian portrait. Donne infuses his own accent, his personal tone, into Ovidian licentiousness and Petrarchan frustration. He is not one to 'serve and suffer patiently' or to languish for love. He rebels against the tyranny of the God of Love, and blames and despises himself for his folly in accepting such bondage. If, as at the close of **'Love's Deity'**, he accepts that the lady cannot, if she is to be true, love him, it is with an ill grace and with only a grudging admission of the claims of virtue.

One song and two finely wrought love-epigrams, one employing the old conceit from the Greek Anthology that souls are breathed out in kisses, the other the conceit of the lover's image reflected in his mistress's weeping eyes, echo the two beautiful valedictory Elegies and, like them, point forward to the great theme of Donne's later love-poetry, the celebration of love as peace and not rage; but they do so without having recourse to 'mystical mathematics' and philosophic speculation and in simple metrical forms.

It is not the mark of the second set of the *Songs and Sonnets,* whose composition I place after 1602, that they all handle the theme of love as union. The set includes that bitter masterpiece **'Love's Alchemy'**, the sombre treatment of a Petrarchan theme in **'Twickenham Garden'**, the melancholy debate on the meaning of the 'subtle wreath of hair' that his mistress gave him in **'The Funeral'**, and the curious speculation on what is a 'true love' in **'The Primrose'**. Their distinction lies in their more subtle and complex conception of lyric form and style. Apart from the poems in quatrains and **'Image and Dream'**, which I put together, they are mainly in stanzas of some scope and complexity, and the creation of such stanzas enabled Donne to fuse into a single poem gifts that one would have thought incompatible: his gift for song, for pure melodic phrasing, his gift for creating the illusion of actual vehement speech, and his gift for arguing in verse. This last one would have thought as incompatible with the other two as they would seem to be incompatible with each other. This fusion of song, drama, and argument is unique in English poetry. None of Donne's followers equals him in his power to give weight and fullness to lyric stanzas without loss of pace where pace is needed and with variation of pace when feeling demands it.

But although this second group of lyrics is not confined to the theme of mutual love, it is in the poems on this theme that Donne has no model and no rival, is at his most original and at his greatest. These poems demand more than admiration for the poet's art; they express the most intimate and precious human feelings and communicate, to use words Henry James used of Browning, 'the seriousness of the great human passion'. I do not doubt that there is a connexion between Donne's love for Ann More and the appearance of this theme in his poetry, and that we can see reflected in these poems Donne's situation in the years that followed his marriage. But the poems themselves,

even the most idealistic, are too far from the reality we know of for us to speak of them as written to Ann More, or even about her. The bond they celebrate is not the bond of marriage, a contract entered into before the eyes of the world, bringing joys and griefs but also responsibilities. The husband of Ann More soon became the father of their children. His wife was often sick and ailing and so was he. The lovers in these wonderful poems need fear no sublunary consequences of their ecstatic unions any more than Lancelot or Guinevere, Tristan and Isolde, Troilus and Criseyde. The lovers of "**The Anniversarie**" cannot look to be buried together as married lovers may, and as Donne himself hoped to be buried with his wife: instead, 'Two graves must hide mine and thy corse'. The lady in **'A Valediction: forbidding mourning'** is told to hide her grief because 'the laity' must not know:

> So let us melt, and make no noise,
>   No teare-floods, nor sigh-tempests move,
> 'Twere prophanation of our joyes
>   To tell the layetie our love.

This is not an argument to use to a wife, who has no need to hide her grief at her husband's absence. The superb *égoisme à deux* of these poems, their scorn for the world of everyday and the duties of daily life, their stress on secrecy and insistence on the esoteric nature of love—a religion of which Donne and his mistress are the only saints, alone fit to give 'rule and example' to other lovers and communicating their mystery only to adepts, 'loves clergie'—make these poems a quintessence of the romantic conception of passionate love as the *summum bonum*. It is a lover and his mistress, not a husband and wife, who prefer to be blest 'here upon earth' rather than to share with others the full bliss of heaven, who

> dye and rise the same, and prove
> Mysterious by this love;

and tell the sun that his duty is done by warming them and that the bed they lie in is his centre.

As Donne's powerful and idiosyncratic temperament transformed the witty depravity of Ovid and the refined sentiment of Petrarch, so he turned to his own uses his reading in the Neoplatonists. Their concept of love as union his imagination seized on; the philosophic system of which it is a part he ignored. The union of lovers is an end in itself in Donne's poems, needing no justification and reaching to nothing beyond itself. This concept of love implies the worth of the beloved:

> For, Love is so noble, so soveraign an Affection,
> as that it is due to very few things, and very few
> things worthy of it. Love is a Possessory Affec-
> tion, it delivers over him that loves into the pos-
> session of that that he loves; it is a transmutatory
> Affection, it changes him that loves, into the
> very nature of that that he loves, and he is noth-
> ing else.

It is true that when distinction is made, either by metaphor as in 'She'is all States, and all Princes, I', or in argument as in **'Air and Angels'**, the superiority of the masculine is implied or conceded; but in general the 'He and She', the 'I and Thou' of Donne's earlier poetry are transformed into 'We' and 'Us'. Donne also found in the Neo-platonists many casuistical arguments to prove that bodily love was not incompatible with spiritual and that lovers united in soul should unite in body to make their union perfect. He is not original in declaring:

> Loves mysteries in soules doe grow,
> But yet the body is his booke.

But in poems such as **'The Good-Morrow'**, **'The Anniversarie'**, **'The Canonization'**, or **'Love's Growth'** no casuistry is needed to defend or excuse what the poems' whole tone affirms, the unity of the whole personality, of body and soul, in the union of love. To have imagined and given supreme expression to the bliss of fulfilment, and to the discovery of the safety that there is in love given and returned, is Donne's greatest glory as a love-poet. (pp. xxiii-xxx)

> *Helen Gardner, in an introduction to* The Elegies and the Songs and Sonnets by John Donne, *edited by Helen Gardner, Oxford at the Clarendon Press, 1965, pp. xvii-xlxii.*

Patrick Cruttwell   (essay date 1970)

[*In the following excerpt, Cruttwell examines Donne's* Songs and Sonnets, *asserting that these poems randomly cover "every aspect of love," thus mirroring the realities of life.*]

In their original order, the short poems [in Donne's ***Songs and Sonnets***, as published in the original 1633 edition and in H.J.C. Grierson's edition]—and the ***Elegies*** also, which differ in genre, not in material—come to one as a body of verse which says in effect that every aspect of love is liable to be present, in reality or in imagination, at any time, on any occasion: promiscuity, misogyny, hopeless adoration, intimate tenderness, bitter hate, Platonic adoration, frivolous cynicism, brothel-lust, monogamous devotion, all of them. What Swift wrote in *Cadenus and Vanessa* might serve as these poems' epigraph:

> Love why do we one passion call,
> When 'tis a compound of them all?
> Where hot and cold, where sharp and sweet,
> In all their equipages meet;
> Where pleasures mix'd with pains appear,
> Sorrow with joy, and hope with fear . . .

If this be the true total meaning of Donne's love poetry, then the order of the first editions, whether deliberate or haphazard, serves that meaning admirably. (pp.17-18)

The first poem is **'The Good-morrow'**, a poem which expresses tenderness and passion for one woman, and a vivid feeling of discovery: now, at last, after many false starts, they have found what real love is. Next comes the **'Song'**, **'Goe, and catche a falling starre . . .'**: a cynical, but not very serious, denial that any woman can be both 'true and faire'. Third is **'Womans Constancy'**, another piece of cheerful cynicism, which adds to the former the proposition that he himself is no better. Fourth is **'The Undertaking'**, a celebration of Platonic adoration, which declares that such love is a higher thing than 'the Hee and Shee' and claims moreover that the poet himself has experienced

it. After that, **'The Sunne Rising'**: a joyfully pagan, Ovidian hymn to a completely satisfactory love. Married? adulterous? mercenary?—one isn't told, and it doesn't matter (as far as the poem is concerned). Then, **'The Indifferent'**: back to cynicism, reinforced, in this, by an explicit mocking of the Petrarchan doctrine of eternal faithfulness, putting in its place the anti-morality which argues that constancy is a 'heresy' and that 'Love's sweetest part' is 'variety'. Seventh, **'Loves Usury'**, another Ovidian poem, addressed to the 'God of Love', asking him to give to the lover a freedom from all cerebration, all moral twinges, all emotional involvements, allowing his body alone to 'reign'. And if one adds, eighth, **'The Canonization'**, which is a quasi-serious, quasi-self-mocking poem on the theme directly opposite to that of **'The Indifferent'**, arguing that he and his lady are the ideal Petrarchan lovers, fit to be 'canonized' as saints in the religion of love and worshipped accordingly, then one has pretty well all the themes and moods this poetry plays with. And the collection continues in this style: indeed, the pack has been shuffled so thoroughly, the absence of any order which can be 'memorized' is so striking, that one begins to wonder if the original editor . . . didn't, perhaps, know what he was up to.

This question of the order of the ***Songs and Sonets*** is not just a question of scholarly pedantry—or of some long-standing reader, like myself, who has become incurably 'fixated' on Grierson. It does really touch on one's response to the poems. There is an interesting, though to my mind totally wrong-headed, attack on them by C. S. Lewis, which is relevant here. Lewis's response is very personal . . . ; he obviously disliked intensely the sexual personality which he deduced from the poems, and did so because the concept of love which he thought that personality held conflicted with his own.

> In one way, indeed, Donne's love poetry is less true than that of the Petrarchans, in so far as it largely omits the very thing that all the pother is about. Donne shows us a variety of sorrows, scorns, angers, disgusts, and the like which arise out of love. But if anyone asked 'What is all this about . . . ?', I do not know how we could reply except by pointing to some ordinary love-poetry. . . . He shows us amazing shadows cast by love upon the intellect, the passions, and the appetite; to learn of the substance which cast them we must go to other poets, more balanced, more magnanimous, and more humane. . . . In the main, his love poetry is *Hamlet* without the prince.

Lewis's objection is really theological (all his criticism was in essence theology); he is objecting because he believes that there is 'a thing called Love'—an ultimate reality of which all these symptoms or phenomena are mere 'imitations'. But suppose the whole point of Donne's love poetry is, not exactly to deny this proposition (I would have said that he has many poems which affirm it, for all readers except Lewis), but rather to suggest that if one's business is to make poems—and essentially dramatic poems—out of the 'amazing shadows cast by love', then each 'shadow' must be treated as if it were just as valid as all the others. Love, for this poetry, is not an entity above, apart from, distinct from, all these phenomena. Love is the sum of them, and no one can say that any item in the sum is worth more than any other.

Donne's love poetry, then, is a body of verse whose effect (rather than intention; I suspect it had no intention) is to present as total a knowledge of the experience of love as one imagination could compass. If we look at it like this, the question of 'personality' and 'sincerity' becomes irrelevant; Leishman's phrase, 'the dialectical expression of personal drama', puts very well the manner in which this poetry fuses three ingredients—the analytical, the autobiographical, and the dramatic—and does so with such completeness that it is vain and foolish to try to separate them. Of this experience of love there are only two limiting conditions. It is entirely human, not divine, however much it may play with philosophical and theological concepts. And it is entirely, even aggressively, masculine and heterosexual. There is no trace of that ambi-sexual strand which is in Shakespeare's sonnets and in so much more of the poetry and art of the earlier Renaissance.

This love-experience takes place in a definite setting, which is quite clearly registered though not self-consciously described. It is a setting of cultivated, sophisticated people. It is thoroughly urban. All round the lovers is the manifold variegated life of a great city: its furtive adulteries in domestic interiors; its music-making, play-going, whoring; its church-going, funerals, marriages; its plagues; its fashions; its traders, merchants, town-criers, porters at house-doors, lawyers, alchemists, schoolboys. And nearby is the court, with its royal hunts and 'progresses', its intriguing flattering courtiers, and its ladies of easy virtue. (pp.18-20)

Man and woman alike are members of a mature, complex, in some ways corrupt society. Therefore they don't behave in the least 'naturally'; they behave, as we all do, according to patterns characteristic of their age and situation—which means, for them, in the manner of educated English gentry during the last years of Queen Elizabeth and first years of King James. What, then, were these patterns, in the domain of sexual love?

There were three main patterns. The first was that made by Christian marriage, sacramental and monogamous. The surprising thing here—surprising, at least, to an unprepared modern reader—is its complete absence from the poetry. It never occurs, specifically. Some of the poems, such as **'The Good-morrow'**, the song **'Sweetest love, I doe not goe'**, **'Lovers Infinitenesse'**, or **'A Feaver'**, express feelings of tenderness, constancy and devotion with such power and beauty that one would 'like to think' they had something to do with Mrs. Anne Donne; and one of them, **'A Valediction forbidding Mourning'**, was said by Izaak Walton, Donne's first and almost contemporary biographer, to have been written for her before Donne's departure for the continent in 1611. But nothing in any poem identifies the status of the woman except those few (**Elegie I, 'Jealosie', Elegie XII, 'His Parting from Her'**) which identify her as the wife of another man. This exclusion of married love, specified as such, from the domain of love poetry was of course a commonplace of the medieval-Renaissance tradition; but it would be totally wrong to make any deductions from this about the poet's personal life or opinions. It was no more than a social-aesthetic convention; but it is worth remembering—since we tend to forget it—that because this major area of men's, and women's, real experience was excluded, the love poetry had almost always a certain element of fictional expression: which does *not* mean that it was untrue, still less that it was insincere, but does mean that because of this social-aesthetic convention, which was thoroughly understood by everyone, there existed this area where art and life did not meet. Life, for one thing, in that area at that time, included many things somewhat resistant to poetry—dowries, jointures, family negotiations about matters of status and money, incessant pregnancies and almost equally incessant deaths of infants and children—and Donne's own life, which included a marriage that wrecked his worldly career for years and resulted in twelve children of whom five died in childhood, taught him better than most men's the difference between the love one wrote poems about and the love one lived.

The second pattern was that of pagan libertinism. The literary ancestry of this was Roman, and its most powerful preacher was Ovid. Its basic dogma was that in some past Golden Age sexual love had been free, as it still is among the animals (**'Confined Love'**) and still could be among us if only we lived as Nature meant (**'Communitie'**). But Shame and Honour (i.e., the modesty and chastity expected of Christian women) and the possessive exclusiveness which went with these idols, had destroyed that happy and natural freedom. Women had become 'cold' and 'proud', and men, therefore, were engaged in an endless war against what **'The Dampe'** calls 'th' enormous Gyant, your Disdaine' and 'th' enchantresse Honor'. In this war they used all the weapons they could find—tears, flattery, rhetoric, casuistical arguments. And it was a war not only against the individual women whom the men desired, but also against society, which 'officially' disapproved of the men's assaults as an attack on sound morality—not to mention a frivolous waste of time. For the true lover was far too busy for 'business' (**'Breake of Day'**) or for any sort of career (**'The Canonization'**); he was contemptuous of the demands of the state, and proclaimed his intention (though for reasons hardly ideological) of 'making love, not war' in the best twentieth-century manner (**Elegie XX, 'Loves Warre'**). In many of the poems which show this lover successful, there is a vivid sense of the pair *excluding* the rest of the world, shutting themselves away from a society conceived as hostile or simply busy with affairs which it regards as more important than love (**'The Good-morrow'**, **'The Sunne Rising'**, **'The Canonization'**).

This lost freedom of love—however much society and morality may disapprove of it—is claimed to be what virtually all men (and quite a few women) would really like to return to. It has its mock morality, its anti-morality, whereby faithfulness and chastity and the rest are vices, and 'love's sweetest part' is 'variety' (**'Womans Constancy'**, **'The Indifferent'**); it proclaims too that many of the women who pretend to chastity do so only because respectability demands it: they would change sides if they dared, and after suitable treatment some of them do (**'The Flea'**, **'The Exstasie'**). Because of these cross-currents and oppositions, 'modern love' has become immensely more difficult than love used to be; it has become complex and agonized and all-demanding, for

> . . . every moderne god will now extend
>   His vast prerogative, as far as Jove.
> To rage, to lust, to write to, to commend,
> All is the purlewe of the God of Love . . .
>   ('Loves Deity')

And from this comes a bitter doubt if what one gains from it is worth the effort and agony, a suspicion that "tis imposture all', 'a vaine Bubles shadow' (**'Loves Alchimie'**), which only a fool would devote his life and art to (**'The Triple Foole'**); and out of that doubt, again, comes a fierce contempt for the women whom all the agony is about. They are silly creatures, after all: you needn't hope for 'mind' in them (**'Loves Alchimie'**); their love is always less 'pure', less intellectual, than men's (**'Aire and Angels'**); for all their talk about Honour and sentiment, they are not really interested in a 'naked thinking heart', only in 'some other part' of a man (**'The Blossome'**); and they are quite capable of bedding with one man after pretending impregnable chastity to another (**'The Apparition'**).

The third, and last, pattern of love was that formed by the Platonic-Petrarchan adoration of a woman accepted as eternally chaste, through whose cruelty the lover must die. This, of course, was the old tradition of courtly love, now in its dotage. By Donne's time, at least for someone of his intelligence and temperament, this ancient convention could no longer be taken quite straight; it had to be refreshed, either with some irony or with a new range of intellectual reference and imagery. Donne gives it both. But he is not at all inclined to abandon it. He uses it in many poems: **'The Undertaking'**, **'The Legacie'**, **'Twicknam Garden'**, **'The Nocturnall'**, **'The Funerall'**, **'The Relique'**. . . . There are variations within the convention. In some poems the lady, though still denying, is still alive and the poet is still besieging her; in others, she is dead and the poet is left alone to grieve; in others again, both she and poet are imagined as dead. Where the presence of death is felt, these poems take on a very strong theological colouring, and one which is specifically Catholic; I suspect, in fact, that the attraction of this convention for Donne was that it enabled him to make a poetry which bridged the passage between his two main subjects, sexual love and religion. These poems tend to be the most ambiguous in effect of all Donne's works, and also perhaps the most quintessentially Donne, since they include all his manners and are liable to change keys with bewildering rapidity. Take the first stanza of **'The Relique'**. It begins with a down-to-earth allusion to the fact that in the crowded church-yards of Donne's London the bodies were dug up after ten years or so, the bones thrown into a common pit, and the graves used again. This leads first to a cynical joke about women's fickleness, next to that famous line ('a bracelet of bright haire about the bone') which fuses with tremendous intensity images of beauty and death, after that to a Hamlet-like evocation of a simple-minded, superstitious gravedigger, then to the image of a pair of lovers still lying together in the grave, and finally to a picture of the Day of Judgement, seen in the literal medieval manner, with all the resurrected bodies standing beside their opened graves. (pp.22-6)

Patrick Cruttwell, "The Love Poetry of John Donne: Pedantique Weedes or Fresh Invention?" in Metaphysical Poetry *by Patrick Cruttwell and others, Edward Arnold, 1970, pp. 11-40.*

Margaret M. McGowan   (essay date 1972)

[*In the excerpt below, McGowan assesses the influences of courtly life and its preoccupations on the development of Donne's nuptial poem,* Epithalamia.]

Works written for a precise occasion, or composed to praise a particular patron, are frequently regarded by critics with some scepticism. They are dismissed as 'insincere' and 'inflated', or as 'not credible'. It is the purpose of this essay to suggest that works such as Donne's verse letters—and two of his *Epithalamia.* in particular—which have received relatively little attention precisely because they fall into this category of occasional verse, should be studied not as anomalous and extravagant pieces but as the natural expressions of a highly self-conscious and literate society which genuinely believed itself to be exactly as its spokesmen depicted it.

In the past, the *Epithalamia* have been subjected to rather narrow comparative studies. They have been examined in relation to other nuptial songs written for the same occasion, or precedents have been sought which might, or might not, have inspired Donne. Close study of parallels and influences has tended to state the obvious in terms of form and theme. For example, McPeek [in his *Catullus in Strange and Distant Britain*, 1939] argues lengthily the thematic influence of one poet upon another; while the influence of Catullus is remorselessly traced through the tradition of the Epithalamium by another scholar. Elsewhere, the reappearance of an image is thought to be significant; or the borrowing of a particular stanzaic form, or an order of treatment is remarked upon. These restricted approaches are unsatisfactory, since the individual character of Donne's own work disappears in a welter of learned and not altogether relevant comment. They also prove that the study of influences (even within one form) is too complex to be handled by tracing a theme, an image, or an author's subsequent fortunes. The criss-cross ramifications of inspiration which were consciously or unconsciously present in Donne's mind when he composed his two Epithamalia certainly owe something to classical examples, to Jonson's learning, and to the healthy spirit of competition which existed between fellow poets. (pp. 175-76)

In this essay, the intention is not to chart detailed influences, but rather, through the study of specific works, to convey an idea of the spirit of James I's Court, and of the criteria of expectation assumed by poet and audience alike. Donne's *Epithalamia* will be examined against the background of other poems, plays, and masques written to celebrate the same occasions, so that a composite picture of the literature of the Court and the kind of language current there might be built up. The analysis of the festivities for the marriage of the Elector Palatine and Princess Elizabeth (James I's only surviving daughter), and for that of the Earl of Somerset and Lady Francis Howard, might seem over-extended. But it is my contention that the closest attention to detail is first necessary to establish an accurate impression of the general context, and that *only then* should Donne's poems be considered. In this way, I hope that the individual character (if any) of his contributions will be more readily seen.

By 1612-13 King James's Court was well schooled in lavish ceremonial. Already, when the King and his Danish Queen Anne entered London in the spring of 1604, the time was described by a chronicler as 'Triumphant'. So great were the crowds thronging the streets to celebrate the arrival of a new king and the beginning of a new era, that the same observer commented: 'I can compare to nothing more conveniently than to imagine every grass to have been metamorphosed into a man in a moment, the multitude was so marvellous'. Wonder, triumph, and festivity naturally accompanied every public appearance of the King and his family, and they similarly dominated the life of the Court.

The masques and plays, arranged to present views of vigorous and beneficial kingship to an acquiescent Court and to critical foreign ambassadors, were rather different in character from those which had formed the image of Elizabeth I. As the focal point of every spectacle, the unattainable Virgin Queen had inspired poets to stress chivalric attitudes and ideas. She was the Lady of the Lake who released beleaguered knights (Kenilworth, 1575), and the August Queen who presided over tilts fought in her honour (Earl of Warwick's marriage, 1565; Kenilworth, 1575; and Count Palatine's Entertainment, 1578). She was Cynthia (Elvetham, 1591); Perfect Beauty (1581); Diana, Goddess of Chastity (Bisson, 1592); and the Fairy Queen who had power to dispel enchantments (1595). Although the centre of everything, Elizabeth had appeared as a still and lonely figure, whose very presence was sufficient to excite achievement. Her incredible loftiness of being was acutely expressed by poets who spoke the adoration felt by courtiers towards their monarch: an adoration which at first glance might seem mere flattery designed for self-profit, but which on closer examination is seen as the only means of describing the fervent emotions generated in subjects by a Queen who guides and orders their lives. (pp. 177-78)

Ostensibly, the relationship of monarch and subject had not altered under James I. He remains the fountainhead of social and political activity, and the principal source of inspiration to poets and artists. But the mood has changed. From his Court Festivals, we receive the impression of a much more dynamic personality. The King is depicted not so much as the aloof pinnacle of State, but as the busy centre towards which all eyes turn and from which all activity begins. He seems closer to his courtiers; and he literally fathers their peace and prosperity by organising their marriages. (p. 178)

If poets were 'the trumpetters of all praise', as Puttenham had called them [in G. Gregory Smith, *Elizabethan Critical Essays*, 1904] . . . then, when it came to displaying princely magnificence fit to publish the Union between two Protestant powers in Europe—England and the

Palatinate . . . King James and his Court *expected* a certain tone, in poems, plays and masques, reflecting not their aspirations to greatness but the glory they felt manifest in themselves every day. As Ben Jonson expressed it in *Neptune's Triumph* (1624) 'That were a heauy and hard taske, to satisfie *Expectation*'. (p. 182)

Let us then turn to the detailed calendar of magnificence which stretched out over a fortnight. Five hundred musketeers had been called into London where the bells rang 'generally in every church, and in every street bonfires blazed abundantly'. This was the spirited scene which Donne and his contemporaries experienced every time they walked out. Thursday 11th February witnessed the first of the Fireworks: ordnance pealed like thunder, rockets of fire burst from the water, and the sky seemed filled with blazing sparks. Artificially contrived, a flaming St George on horseback vanquished a dragon, and burning hunting hounds pursued a hart up and down the waters as realistically as if the hunt had been on land. As the smoke cleared, a Christian navy advanced upon Turkish territory, espying a Turkish fleet, and two towers of defence; and the ensuing sea-fight ended in triumph for the Christians when the towers were 'sacked, burned, and ruinated'. This was a mere prelude to an elaborate naval battle which took place on the Thames on Saturday 13th. Two hundred and fifty vessels guarded the bounds of the contest area where sixteen ships, sixteen galleys, and six frigates prepared to do damage. First, the Venetians and then the Spaniards unsuccessfully assailed the Turks, and, inevitably, it was left to the English Fleet to carry the day. The 'business' cost the King upwards of £9,000. And there were other costs, too: 'as one lost both his eyes, another both his handes, another one hande, with divers others maymed and hurt'. As one of the Captains, Mr Phineas Pett, complained, 'in which jesting business I runn more danger than if it had been a sea service in good earnest'.

The religious ceremony was conducted by the Archbishop of Canterbury. First, from the new Banqueting House specially built for the occasion, came the Palsgrave attired in garments of white satin, richly set with pearls and gold. Elizabeth came next in richly embroidered white, attended by virgin bridesmaids 'like a skye of caelestial starres, [attending] upon faire Phoebe'. The King wore jewels esteemed 'not to be less worth than six hundred thousand pounds', while Queen Anne's gems were valued at four hundred thousand pounds. The solemnities were done in due form in the presence of magnificently clothed princes, earls, barons, and their ladies, the Ambassadors of France, Venice, and the States. This splendid company, carefully observing the rules of precedence, then processed ceremoniously back to the Banqueting House where they 'fell to dancing, masking, and revelling, according to the custome of such assemblies, which continued all the day and part of the night'. It was well that the Spanish Ambassador had refused to be present for he would have had to stare at the wall of the Great Chamber decorated by a new set of Tapestries representing the defeat of the Spanish in 1588. (pp. 184-86)

Throughout the celebrations for this marriage the tone has been precisely that which James and his Court expected.

The occasion and the context naturally called forth certain effects, recognised forms, and a specific language. The wedding ceremonies followed a pattern of behaviour and a traditional ritual of service. Where Kings are 'the most conspicuous beings', [in Ben Jonson, His Panegyre, On the happie entrance of James . . . , 19 March 1603. Works] magnificence, rich apparel, and ceremony automatically attach themselves to them. They receive their most eloquent expression at particular moments in time (such as a princely marriage) when not only the Court, but the country as a whole, can contemplate a well-ordered, harmonious structure, working magnificently. The moment might be a particular one, but its significance is general. Marriages are public affairs, and princely ones are even more so. They act as a looking-glass reflecting the prosperity of the State. The songs of the masque 'ravish' and do not 'rave', however superlative our more democratic eyes might find the words. We interpret these songs as expressions of some kind of ideal state to which people merely aspired, but could never, in fact, attain; but for Donne's contemporaries the meaning was much more immediate: the state celebrated in these songs was an ideal, but it was one which could be attained by certain beings on certain occasions. James is the Sun of Britain, and he and his Court are self-consciously rejoicing *in that fact.* (p. 192)

While Donne was seeking secular preferment he came into daily contact with the kind of language used in Court Festivals. Since he was, during a major part of his career, a 'courtier', in the sense that he sought employment from the great and was willing to serve them for favours, he knew how to distinguish different levels of language for different occasions. Among his friends can be counted many writers of masques and related works dedicated to the glories of the Court: Ben Jonson, Samuel Daniel, Michael Drayton, George Wither, and Sir John Davies. He also had close connections with many successful diplomats of whom Sir Henry Wotton is, perhaps, the most outstanding. Among his patrons Lucy, Countess of Bedford 'the Queenes only favourite', who always danced at her side in every masque, can be singled out, together with the Countess of Huntingdon, Mrs Herbert (mother of George Herbert), Lord Hay, and the Earl of Somerset. Lady Lucy Donne addressed variously as 'unique', 'the good countess', 'the best lady', and 'the Happiest and Worthiest lady'; and to Sir Robert More he wrote, 'no man attends Court fortunes with more impatience than I do.' (p. 202)

The Epithalamium shared general similarities and many detailed characteristics with the Court Masque. It celebrated a specific occasion; it had similar religious, political, and social, as well as erotic, overtones; and its role was to praise the bridal pair and offer them tokens of good will. The language was suitably elevated in both forms, which depended in large part for their effects on recurrent images. Yet the Epithalamium is more limited. It lacks the flexibility of the masque, the harmonious effects of song and dance, and the spectacular wonder of the décor. To praise and celebrate without these aids, as one writer on Epithalamia has expressed it, has frequently been 'l'écueil des Potes'.

Donne's marriage song for Princess Elizabeth and Count

Frederick immediately draws attention to the general context in which this specific happening must be set. The union of these two princes is a significant human fragment of a universal structure built by Bishop Valentine,

> . . . whose day this is,
>   All the air is thy diocese,

A solemn, religious occasion, is the first suggestion of these words which are quickly underscored with tones of expansiveness, and filled with airy delight. The gaiety of a bird hastening to its mate is heightened by the knowledge that this ceremony is an eternal one, to be renewed every year; and yet, in spite of this eternity, the specific occasion which Donne celebrates has especial brilliance, capable of rebounding back upon Old Valentine and *enflaming even him.*

It is this uniqueness (in all senses of the word), only hinted at here in a general way, which forms the main source of inspiration, and the principal theme of the poem. The general happy mating of bird with bird, annually performed, according to religious rites, 'All that is nothing unto this'—the coupling of two Phoenixes. Now, as Donne well knew, legend decreed that the Phoenix, symbolising flames and passion, was the rarest bird. It was unique, and only reproduced itself by self-destruction—that is to say, out of its ashes a new Phoenix was born. This is how James I defined its nature:

> . . . my Phoenix rare, whose race,
>   Whose kynde, whose kin, whose offspring, they
>   be all
>   In her alone, whom I the *Phoenix* call
>   That fowle which only one at onis did live.

And the King's notes [in his *Poems,* 1955] suggest how widespread was the knowledge of this bird. Thus, by the second stanza, Donne's poem begins to turn on a deliberately contrived impossibility. As is his custom, he instantly acknowledges the paradoxical nature of the facts he presents, and stresses the artificial character of the occurrence, by suggesting that the Phoenix is being used here only metaphorically:

> Thou mak'st a taper see
>   What the sun never saw,

And yet, before we have absorbed the ingenuity of this, he insists:

> . . . what the Ark . . .
>   Did not contain, one bed contains, through thee,
>   Two phoenixes,

and a few lines later he affirms even more strongly that these two phoenixes shall produce,

> Young phoenixes, and yet the old shall live.

In these ways, the legend is broken twice: phoenixes multiply, while the old live on, and their qualities of love and courage overspill the confines of St Valentine's Day to embrace the whole year. The special character of the occasion increasingly takes on extraordinary overtones.

Flames, light, love, and courage—all these elements are contained in the notion of Phoenix, and the third stanza singles out the fair Phoenix Bride as a source of warmth, activity, and with the power to create of herself extensive constellations of jewels, of brightness, and light. One remembers the prose description of her at the wedding ceremony: 'shining like a constellation, her train supported by 12 young ladies in white garments so adorned with jewels that her passage looked like the milky way'. Donne himself has absolutely succumbed to her dazzling force. He assumes from the start an extraordinary power of light, inspiration, and passion; appeals of 'frustrate the sun' and of 'up', 'call', 'take', and 'make' (the last three gaining more urgency by echoing at the line-end) increase the impression of the active participation of the poet. He himself is personally touched by the vision he is re-creating. As he thinks about her brilliance, associated notions present themselves—'new star', 'new glory', portentous of 'Ends of much wonder'. And his mind moves from the sphere of the physical presence of light, passion, and riches, to the more exciting speculations about the consequences of such gifts.

The glorious flames grow larger and stronger, and the tone more impassioned and argumentative, as Donne imagines the meeting, mating, and union of Elizabeth and Frederick. Since they are both one and infinite (infinity being incapable of separation), they are doubly and irrevocably joined. The call to Church seems almost impatient, only one way of making one, among 'divers ways', the most urgent seeming 'yourselves to entwine'. Here, Donne brings to the fore a preoccupation which has been lurking throughout the poem: the physical joining of Elizabeth and Frederick. For three stanzas this interest had seemed dominated by more traditional St Valentine references, decorously covering the feather beds introduced at the end of stanza 1, and diverted by the paradox of two phoenixes in stanza 2. Yet, 'one bed contains two Phoenixes' is the central notion of that stanza. The interest was screened by the dazzling light of the Phoenix bride in stanza 3 where the subtle suggestion—'a great Princess falls, but doth not die'—seemed anticlimactic and even a rather exaggerated and not an entirely appropriate compliment, until one realises that sexual union is the main burden of the poem—and, incidentally, the one way that Donne can solve his paradox, making his two Phoenixes become One, and restoring Nature to herself again (stanza 8).

The traditional chronology of the Epithalamium is largely ignored, telescoped into one stanza to enhance the sense of urgency and unreasonable delay which Donne wishes to convey. He expostulates against the lingering sun— 'Stays he new light from these to get?'—and reprimands the slow steps of the bridal couple in procession from the Church. Food furnishes additional fodder for blame as he dwells lingeringly on its 'gluttonous delays'. Even the masquers are gently upbraided for prolonging their magic till cockcrow, like fairies. One would think it were Donne's own wedding night.

At last, relief and expectation are combined in stanza 6, for night is come. Yet, patience is stretched tauter as the formalities of disrobing the Bride are precisely and punctiliously performed,

> . . . (as though
> They were to take a clock in pieces,)

The incongruity of the simile is a measure of the poet's increased irritation, while his notion of how a bride should be bedded at once describes his ferment and tells us how extraordinarily precious she seems to him:

> A Bride, before a good night could be said,
> Should vanish from her clothes, into her bed,
> As souls from bodies steal, and are not spied.

This sense of spiritual uplift and exaltation while performing a physical act is maintained throughout the rest of the poem. The bridegroom passes 'through sphere after sphere', touching sheets, arms, anywhere and everywhere.

These two are mirrors to each other, reflecting their glories, sharing their riches and generosity, dazzling with truth and courage. A 'she sun', she has dominated the poem with light and warmth, and has communicated her brilliance to others so that they are filled with wonder and awe. Her groom, like the moon, takes all his strength from her. The famous and abused—'Here lies a she sun, and a he moon here'—sums up the purport of the poem. It points directly and precisely at a contained self-reflecting universe, where two privileged people enflamed with passion seem exemplary. They are models, capable of imparting to others the exhilaration they feel, and of giving such pent-up emotions a spiritual value. The overturning of our normal expectation of a 'she moon' only serves to emphasise the points further. The line appears unseemly and extravagant when wrenched out of the context which has been so carefully prepared for it.

Elizabeth and Frederick outdo all Valentine's birds in a blessed harmony which extends to the universe at large. The last two stanzas celebrate the unique nature of this event, and the poem comes full circle, back to Bishop Valentine and the mating season, back to the problem of the two Phoenixes:

> And by this act of these two phoenixes
> Nature again restored is,
> For since these two are two no more,
> There's but one Phoenix still, as was before.

Just as the golden statues of the bridal pair stared out at excited spectators in Campion's masque, so this sun and moon, these two phoenixes, arrest Donne's gaze as he expresses the enthusiasm of many. The context is the same, the atmosphere produced is identical, and yet, somehow, an individual voice seems to speak.

In the Court performances and in this poem we recognise the same spirit. We are the witnesses of men contemplating themselves and indulging their wonderment. It is not surprising that Elizabeth and Frederick appear as exemplary figures in both, for the enthusiasm which their union provokes can only be conveyed through heightened phrases where their particular marriage serves as a model for others to emulate. Consistent elevation of tone and images matches the feelings of formality and excitement. Poets of masque and epithalamium assume the active participation of an audience. Donne, for instance, is conscious that Epithalamia have rules of structure, tone, language, imagery, and chronology; he assumes that his readers have a similar knowledge of the rules; and his ingenuity depends upon that assumption. Chronology, as we have seen, he abandons, since he can highlight the impression of his own feelings of impatience by doing so. The tone is largely formal, as would be expected, though its harmonies are frequently broken by contorted syntax, as in stanza 2 when Donne wishes to set in relief 'one bed contains . . . two Phoenixes'—the main focus of the poem. The images of light, sun, moon, Phoenixes, and so on, belong to that vocabulary which customarily expressed praise and admiration; yet, in the image of the Phoenix he deliberately plays with the reader's normal expectation of its significance, only to restore the symbol to its rightful form by the end of the poem. Some readers might well have solved the riddle for themselves, long before the end; and it is arguable that, as a consequence, their participation is greater, and their appreciation of the poem is enhanced.

It is noticeable that the tapestry-like descriptions which delight us in Spenser's Epithalamium are nowhere in evidence here. As in the masque, magnificence of mind and body is self-evident: its impact is what is important. Nevertheless, the impact is given a different focus in the two forms. Public harmony, political and religious concord, and a ritual, public celebration were the main preoccupations of the masque. Donne, using similar means, and while speaking for all men ('us' occurs more than once in the poem), has created something much more private. He recognises the general reverberations of the union, is tempted by idealisation, but concentrates the attention of all—bridal couple, and readers alike—on the revelling of two bodies made one.

Expectation seems to play an even more significant role in Donne's second Epithalamium entitled '**Eclogue 1613. December 26**'—his contribution to the Somerset wedding—which straight-away strikes a strange and contentious note. 'Unseasonable' begins the poem, and raises doubts and questions. The thematic structure is founded on a complex set of contraries: the block 'East, Sun, Warmth, Light, King, and Heaven' opposes a second block 'Winter, West, North, Cold, Night, and Hell', and their contest extends itself through to the end of the poem. Such contraries, and such argument, are of course germane to the Eclogue form which Donne has chosen as the frame of his Epithalamuim. The form is loose and freer, allowing the poet considerable room to protect himself while performing his task of praise with due distinction. However, it is important to note that, from the beginning, Donne makes it clear to his alert reader that this is to be no ordinary eclogue. Already, a note of harshness introduces the poem. And then, the idylls of the countryside, the joys of pastoral life, that Arcadia of ease and delights which any reader anticipates with the very sound of the word Eclogue has been metamorphosed into the 'ice', the 'cold and decrepit time' which turns the landscape into a 'frieze jacket'. Allophanes (possibly Donne's friend Sir Robert Ker) remonstrates with Idios (a private man) who is mad enough to retire to such a region of frost, when the centre of heat is where the King is, at Court. From his generous light, so powerful and all pervading that it resembles that light which antedated both sun and moon, comes warmth, good desire, wisdom, honour, blessings, and spir-

itual expansion. From the beings, who walk in his radiant sphere, emanates the brilliance of stars, so from

> . . . the Brides' bright eyes,
> At every glance, a constellation flies,

which, in turn, kindles the lights of others. In this way, Allophanes persuasively argues the case for being at Court, at the wedding of the Earl of Somerset.

'No, I am there,' is Idios' paradoxical reply. The reader, who has already had his expectation punctured once, starts up perplexed, only to settle back comfortably once more as Idios asserts that Princes animate everything: the physical world of lights and warmth; and, more significantly, the mental world. They 'enlarge' narrow men, allowing them to feel effects from afar, and to surpass themselves in perception.

In the ensuing discussion, it becomes evident that these two are in no way disagreeing with each other. Apparently contrary arguments are used not to prove opposite cases, but to reinforce their shared view that the King is the source of all power and good,

> . . . all tinctures move
> From higher powers; from God religion springs,
> Wisdom, and honour from the use of kings.

There is something almost extravagant about the insistence on the wisdom, justice, trust, liberality, and virtue in the King; such statements extend over virtually the first hundred lines of the poem:

> Hast thou a history, which doth present
>   A Court, where all affections do assent
> Unto the King's, and that, that King's are just?
>   And where it is no levity to trust.
> Where there is no ambition, but to obey,
>   Where men need whisper nothing, and
>   yet may;
> Where the King's favours are so placed, that all
>   Find that the King therein is liberal
> To them, in him, because his favours bend
>   To virtue, to the which they all pretend.

Such lines as these elaborate views on James and kingship which had been adumbrated by Jonson and Dekker at his Entry into London in 1604; and they parallel his virtues so frequently extolled in pamphlets such as Marcelline's *The Triumphs of King James the First* (1610), and in the detail of the masques. . . . In order 'to know and feel all this' more deeply, Idios has retired from Court, to write; for words are a means of knowing and feeling more acutely—a way of rediscovering exhilaration in tranquillity.

In some ways the nuptial song strikes a great contrast with its lengthy prelude. It is extremely formal: eleven stanzas of eleven lines, each one given a title. It follows much more closely the conventional pattern for such poems than Donne's first 'Epithalamium,' adhering fairly strictly to a chronological sequence, which moves from the Time of Marriage through the church ceremony to the Going to Bed; declaring vows and blessings and, expostulating at delays in an attempt to imitate, or re-enact, the actual ritual of the ceremony. There is, however, thematic consistency between the 'Eclogue' and the nuptial song; the block 'East, Sun, Warmth, Light continues to provide the principal source of theme and metaphor, figuring, rather insistently, through the poem in the repetitive last line of each stanza with 'The fire of these inflaming eyes' and 'this loving heart'.

Since the content of each stanza is announced in advance, each stanza constitutes in a sense a specifically defined difficulty to be overcome. Expectation is screwed up tight as each successive verse challenges our credulity, proceeds through paradoxes, and turns received opinions upside down. In stanza 1 the Sun bows low and withdraws early on the most wintry of nights; but, amazingly, a mightier fire of Promethean strength prolongs its effects of warmth and love. The second stanza seeks ways of distinguishing the bride and groom; yet they both love equally, and their qualities are such that their persons seem interchangeable: the Bride 'Becomes a man' because of her manly courage which scorns unjust opinion, and 'the Bridegroom is a maid' by virtue of his beauty. Donne is asking a lot, even from his initiates, with this blunt proposition which seems not so much forced, as too startlingly and emphatically stated for the needs of the case. Beauty and courage, insufficiently attached to what Donne has told us about the bride and groom, remain abstract words. Even when we do contemplate the Bridegroom we are allowed no details of physical description. In a stanza, which leaps forward with gathering speed, we catch some glimpse of the strong urges of his passion, as he outstrips the sun with her 'red foaming horses'; and his surging inward flame obscures all other outer characteristics. The Bride is next presented in two stanzas where her coming and her apparelling are evoked. And her form, too, almost disappears behind lustrous radiance. She is akin to Phoebus, and her clothes of silk and gold serve merely to cloud her dazzling form and allow us to glimpse her,

> . . . since we which do behold,
> Are dust, and worms, 'tis just
> Our objects be the fruits of worms and dust;

It is difficult to see quite why Donne interpolates this moralising play on words; it certainly establishes a sense of distance between the onlookers and the Bride, whose ethereal and diaphanous nature has been delicately suggested. Her form is insubstantial, and filled with light; it is unreal, and perhaps Donne is implying that from her lofty height she scorns the golden silks she wears. Certainly the next lines serve to underline both her unreality and her distant purity:

> Let every jewel be a glorious star,
> Yet stars are not so pure, as their spheres are.

So we proceed through statement, qualification, or contradiction, on to the religious ceremony where these two suns—the bride and groom—meet, and become one. For two stanzas the contrary movements of statement and denial cease, as a climax of union in Church is reached, and vows for blessings are eloquently made. The King appears once more as the spring of riches, crowned (indeed almost overburdened) with wisdom and honour. The excessive nature of these blessings provides the link to the next verse, which seems strangely distorted with its many short lines of sharp complaint. The food is too abundant, the entire sphere of the world whirls in the dance, the sun is set,

eyes are weary, and the revels go on. These events are referred to again in the following stanza, but this time they are used metaphorically to describe the bride's wedding night.

The tone of the poem changes yet again. No longer are there the extravagant comparisons, seemingly unrelated asides, and insistent imagery. In stanzas 9-11 the poet generates the same passionate excitement which was a feature of his first Epithalamium, and which has so far been absent in this poem. The notion of abundance, of whirling dance and revels, readily anticipates the transports of the Bride and Groom as they discover each other, and the husband finds a warm and yielding wife. Joy's bonfire, kindling bright and strong, provided with fuel enough to last an eternity, rounds off this record of passion.

Although it was in Donne's interest at this time to be a committed supporter of the Earl of Somerset, the 'Epithalamium' which he wrote in his honour is not devoid of the sense of strain which Jonson displayed in his compositions for the same occasion. Both use a specific occasion as a way of expressing general notions and reactions. Both, at the outset, give pride of place to the King, introducing extended comment on his beneficence and his power to do good. In Donne's poem, however, the bride and groom figure very prominently. It is true that they might be any bride and groom—the theme is both topical and timeless—yet Donne is careful to write into his work references to the distasteful circumstances surrounding this particular wedding with the words 'unjust opinion' in stanza 2; and he dwells strangely on wisdom and honour (in stanza 7). It is as if he wants the reader to recognise that he himself is conscious that an extraordinarily difficult feat of persuasion is being undertaken, and that he is capable of accomplishing it.

One may, however, have reservations about the degree of his success. His presentation and evocation of the Bride seem especially laboured. By introducing so early in the **"Eclogue"** her 'bright eyes' which sow

> . . . the Court with stars, and doth prevent
> In light and power, the all-eyed firmament;

he has given himself the task of maintaining this luminous vision throughout the nuptial song. However ingenious his list of compliments—comparison with Phoebus, clothed in silk and gold to hide her dazzle (as well as to enhance it), pure as a sphere, and so on—they do not complement each other, or provide us with a convincing picture. He is not interested in her physical reality, but only in the sparkling impact she makes on him; and somehow, he has not managed to communicate that effect to us. He has only assumed that we agree with him, while making no effort to ensure this. Only when she seethes with excitement and arouses an answering passion does Donne's pen convey the authenticity of those feelings.

His treatment of the bride reflects his handling of the main theme—the passion of Somerset and Lady Frances for each other. Until he can dispense with particular identities, Donne reels from one extravagant effort to another, opposing contraries, arguing by extremes, while managing fairly successfully to keep the two opposing blocks 'East,

Sun', and 'West, Cold' moving consistently through the poem. In no way do the metaphors and superlatives transform these beings into exemplary figures like Elizabeth and Frederick. Such idealisation is either not achieved, through technical deficiency, or is not appropriate to a noble pair beneath the rank of prince.

A further problem arises from the thoroughly defensive stance which the poet assumes from the start. The nuptial song is lengthily prepared. Idios is any private man, not necessarily Donne (the 'me' of stanza 3 need not apply exclusively to him), and he has to be cajoled and persuaded into speech. He deliberately chooses to speak in a voice not his own; it is an unidentified voice, creating a pleasing ambiguity which both protects the speaker from potential attack, and provokes the reader, leading him into the poem while the poet can maintain (until the last three stanzas of the poem at least) a fairly objective stance. He calls his offering a sacrifice; and, he insists, both immediately before the 'Epithalamium' and after it,

> Read then this nuptial song, which was not
> made
>   Either the Court or men's hearts to invade.

There is an exhausted, rather exasperated note here, as he gives up his poem under pressure. It starts then as a private greeting, but by the end Allophanes has claimed it as part of a public worship,

> Whatever celebrates this festival
> Is common,

Donne seems to have associated his own feelings much less personally with this event than with the wedding celebrated on St Valentine's day; in **'Eclogue 1613. December 26'** his role as poet is much more stylised.

The relationship between poet, reader, and the work, is again extremely important, but seems much more complex in this poem, partly because there is so much advance preparation, partly because Donne has contrived ambiguities, and partly because the tone of the piece is so uneven. At two moments in particular, during the nuptial song, he seems to interrupt the natural flow of thoughts and events, and speaks in a different voice: in stanza 2 where the bride and groom temporarily change their sex; and in stanza 5 where there is a fairly gratuitous play on worms and dust. One is tempted to say that here is the voice of Donne himself who cannot resist an extravagance or a pun. Such manoeuvres certainly heighten the reader's awareness of what the poet is trying to do; but they seem also to work against the task he has set himself. Donne is perhaps indulging over-dangerously in what Greville called 'Ironia, wherein men commonly (to keep above their workes) seem to make Toies of the utmost they can doe'.

The general assumption behind this essay has been that a poet's individuality cannot be described in a vacuum. The particular character of Donne's *Epithalamia* emerges only when the poems are studied within the context which inspired them. In its turn, this context can only be defined with any accuracy by a study of the individual works which comprised it at any one moment of time. A more general survey might, for example, describe the language of the Jacobean masque, on those occasions when flattery

seems a dominating feature, as Petrarchist; or, at other times when Jonson argues his cosmic themes, as neoplatonist. But such descriptions are hopelessly superficial. They depict a succession of masques merely as variations on well-worn themes, elaborated in a familiar language of praise; and they can tell us little about the personal twists which different poets give to the same material, and which mark their work with an individual stamp. For example, the sun image, both in Donne's second **'Epithalamium'** and in Chapman's masque, concentrates a vast array of virtues relating to their ideas of kingship; whereas in the poem for Princess Elizabeth, the 'she sun' expresses for Donne the highest attributes possible in a private person.

Participation and celebration are key concepts for a proper understanding of any poetic work of this period when it was the social context, above all, which determined the form. Poet and reader consciously shared certain assumptions about language and metaphor, so that images could simultaneously provide not only a vehicle for general expression which could be immediately comprehended, but also a means of making more private comment. The phoenix legend, for instance, suggests notions of exception, rarity, and preciousness, and the use Donne makes of it both enlarges these qualities and allows him to include (and even to display) his personal emotion. Similarly decorum, a framework of appropriate formality, and fitting vocabulary, may encourage on the part of a reader or spectator general observations on a specific event; they do not, however, prevent him from feeling that his own thoughts are being expressed. The technique of generalising seems to me to be the principal way in which 'court' poets—and Donne is one of them—solved the problems posed by being bidden to write for a particular occasion. And such generalising was accomplished with comparative ease when the poet worked within commonly agreed assumptions about forms, words, and images. (pp. 204-18)

> *Margaret M. McGowan, " 'As through a Look-ing-glass': Donne's Epithalamia and Their Courtly Context," in* John Donne: Essays in Celebration, *edited by A. J. Smith, Methuen & Co. Ltd., 1972, pp. 175-218.*

A. E. Dyson and Julian Lovelock   (essay date 1976)

[*In the essay below, Dyson and Lovelock discuss the role of love in Donne's "The Sunne Rising," maintaining that the exaltation of physical love necessarily establishes a tension between the temporal and spiritual worlds.*]

The poem explodes into fiercely rhetorical argument, pursued through three stanzas of sustained exaltation. First the sun is rebuked as a kind of elderly voyeur; then sent about his business; then accused of vanity; then dispatched (unsuccessfully) to look for 'both the'India's'. Finally contempt gives way to patronage, and the sun is invited to perform his duties with the inertia more fitted to age, standing still.

Clearly, such an argument is provocative and, given the sun's normal role as king of the Heavenly bodies and divine emblem, even blasphemous; like Shakespeare's famous sonnet 130. 'My Mistres eyes are nothing like the

Sunne', only more outrageously, it reverses the tradition of hundreds of Petrarchan and Elizabethan love poems in which the sun is a touchstone of ecstatic tribute. As an emotional attitude to the sun it verges on derangement, or at least on that excess of fancy divorced from normal perception and judgement which helped to make metaphysical poetry so generally uncongenial to the eighteenth century, and which to Dr Johnson's tormented mind bore a fearful resemblance to insanity.

Where, then, might a critic start? On a fairly simple level the exaggeration of language mimes the assurance of love. Time becomes 'rags', change, decay, and diminution all recede. But we see at once that the poem works not directly but obliquely, by indirections finding directions out. The sun is not its true subject; contempt and patronage for the sun are not its true emotional charge. Its true subject is the lady; its true emotion love. Every insult to the sun is a compliment to the mistress, every assertion of the sun's weakness attests her power. This is in no simple manner a split between thought and feeling, since both are involved, in the equation, on either side. The literal argument is, in fact, a pseudo-argument (the term is I. A. Richards's): it uses an apparent subject and emotional attitude which relates to the real subject and emotional attitude by systematic inversion. The pseudo-argument generates an apparent logic (the sun's antics) and an appropriate emotion (contempt for the sun). The true argument is also logical, with the familiar and simple logic of love, and generates love's appropriate emotion, ecstatic homage.

It is precisely here, however, that we encounter the poem's central complexity and chief strategy. The literal argument is often more (though it is never less) than a pseudo-argument, and circles back even in the first stanza to make a kind of sense in its own right. If men are indeed exalted by love beyond the temporal, are they not entitled to 'look down' on the sun and on its 'spheare'?

> Busie old foole, unruly Sunne,
>   Why dost thou thus,
> Through windowes, and through curtaines call
>   on us?
> Must to thy motions lovers seasons run?
>   Sawcy pedantique wretch, goe chide
>   Late schoole boyes, and sowre prentices,
>   Goe tell Court-huntsmen, that the King will
>   ride,
>   Call countrey ants to harvest offices;
> Love, all alike, no season knowes, nor clyme,
> Nor houres, dayes, moneths, which are the rags
>   of time.

Any potentially comic effect is undercut by a note of seriousness, or perhaps overplayed by a note of exhilaration. Donne's imagery, though bizarre and exaggerated as pseudo-argument, asserts what every Platonist and Christian really believes. At certain moments, any man might be wrapt beyond mortality, in the eternal intimations of spiritual love. Statements like

> Love, all alike, no season knowes, nor clyme,
> Nor houres, dayes, moneths, which are the rags
>   of time

and (in the third stanza)

> She'is all States, and all Princes, I,
>   Nothing else is

ride triumphantly over their assumed contempt for the sun, attesting that the world fittingly symbolised in the 'schoole boyes, and sowre prentices', the 'Court-huntsmen' and 'countrey ants' is indeed tinged with illusion, and at one remove from the truth. In calling the material world (in normal speech, the 'real' world) unreal, the poem is saying, with Plato, that even the world's princes and potentates are mere shadows, an imitation in time of the timeless ideals. Such lines as

> Princes doe but play us; compar'd to this,
> All honor's mimique; All wealth alchimie
>
>   (stanza 3)

are not, on this showing, even paradoxical: Donne is a true Platonist, and perhaps unusually daring only in so far as he risks extending to earthly princes (indeed to James I himself, whose love of hunting is unflatteringly alluded to) the reminder that they, too, are shadows all.

In a similar manner the poem's questions are arranged, with dazzling sleight-of-hand, to confound any normal reading response. In the context of pseudo-logic, 'Must to thy motions lovers seasons run?' looks like a rhetorical question expecting the answer 'no'; but can it be less than a real and tragic question for men in time? Lovers who ignore external pressures and realities must surely be conquered by them: such is the theme of the great romantic tragedies; such is the underlying cause of the sterility of so-called 'free-love'. Yet the poem's strange power is to cancel, or transcend, or mock the obvious—it is hard to say which—perhaps through its suggestions that the sun and the lovers have actually exchanged roles (the 'seasons' are controlled by the lovers, while the sun is linked with the 'motions' of physical love).

Such complexities continue through the second stanza:

> Thy beames, so reverend, and strong
>   Why shouldst thou thinke?
> I could eclipse and cloud them with a winke,
> But that I would not lose her sight so long:
>   If her eyes have not blinded thine,
>   Looke, and to morrow late, tell mee,
>   Whether both the'India's of spice and Myne
>   Be where thou leftst them, or lie here with
>   mee.
>   Aske for those Kings whom thou saw'st yester-
>   day,
>   And thou shalt heare, All here in one bed lay.

The sun is accused of hollow boasts, but for dubious reasons; the poet could only 'eclipse and cloud' his 'beames' at a cost. If he closed his eyes, would a greater sun really light him, or would he merely be locked in a dream? Perhaps his love itself would disappear, along with all other values, as the uneasy excuse 'But that I would not lose her sight so long' more than half suggests. Once more, the poem's power pushes aside such doubts without wholly excluding them; the sun and the lovers again change roles, with the mistress for an instant becoming the sun, and her 'eye-beames' (cf. **'The Extasie'**, line 7) blinding the usurped lord of light.

The stanza ends with the claim that the countries and kings of the world have joined together in the lovers' bed. But, as the poem approaches its climax of supreme confidence, giddy with the richness of 'spice and Myne', it takes a further turn which is ultimately to undermine the warranty of that confidence. If love is indeed to be lifted up to the eternal world it must transcend the temporal; and such apotheosis requires something very different from the heavy sexual imagery of ruler and ruled and the basic language of the bedroom ('lie here with mee'; 'All here in one bed lay.'). The crowning irony, to which Donne would hardly have been oblivious, is that hierarchies sufficiently valid in spiritual contexts (cf. Book IV of *Paradise Lost*) become profoundly tainted when turned only to sexual ends.

In the third stanza the ideas hover explicitly between the exaggerated rhetoric of love, lost in lies or illusions, and the splendid platonic intimations of ultimate truth:

> She'is all States, and all Princes, I,
>   Nothing else is.
> Princes doe but play us; compar'd to this,
> All honor's mimique; All wealth alchimie.
>   Thou sunne art halfe as happy'as wee,
>   In that the world's contracted thus;
> Thine age askes ease, and since thy duties bee
> To warme the world, that's done in warming
>   us.
> Shine here to us, and thou art every where;
> This bed thy center is, these walls, thy spheare.

As we have suggested, the poet's declarations in the first four lines ring with the conviction of paradox apprehended as truth. But a taint of sexuality remains in the imagery, more dross to the poem (if another Donne image can be inverted) than allay. Such conviction could indeed be justified in some contexts, but not when love's 'contract' is 'contracted' along with the poem's world. If love is in truth to outlast 'seasons' it must be released from the shrinking and sexual connotations of 'contracted thus'; it requires a 'center' not in the bed, but in the soul.

Drawing together the complexities of **'The Sunne Rising'**, we immediately recognise their interdependence as they support, contradict and parallel each other, dictating in these tensions the poem's tone. Our sense that the poem allies love's psychology to the one metaphysic which ultimately validates it is strengthened by the fact that the mistress is always complimented, as it were, at one remove. There is no physical description of her beauty of the kind familiar in most Elizabethan love lyrics; the compliment exists wholly in what the poet feels. It is because she moves him to this dramatic urgency that we know her influence; in a manner wholly characteristic of Donne, it is the intensity of worship which guarantees worth. *Her* value is *his* veneration: and in as much as this does not leave her unbearably vulnerable to fickleness (a theme which Donne pursues in other, more cynical poems) we have to accept the superior truth of the spiritual world. Love is not a mere reflection of the lover's needs, subjective and transient; it is homage to beauty revealed and revered. Its habitat is a world where homage can be appropriate, and loyalty enduring; a world not yet caught in the egocentric snare. One could argue indeed that the outrageousness of

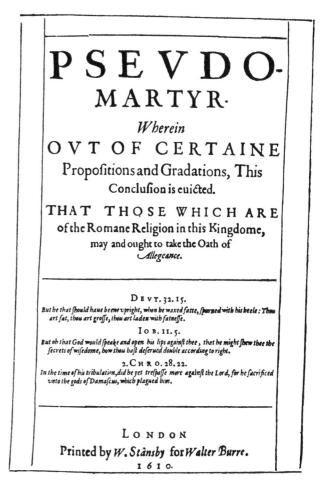

Title page from Donne's first published work.

the images goes hand in hand with their truth, even at the most literal level: if 'truth' is in their extreme of feeling, their exaggeration, this precisely attests the illusiveness and unimportance of the merely material world, and so of the sun, and of the great globe itself.

But the contempt for the sun which characterises the literal argument must undeniably affect our response to the poem in its own right (at least partially), and not simply as a signpost to the intensities of love. If so, it hints perhaps at a degree of unease surrounding the certainty, a residual anger as the poet makes statements which he feels should be true and even are true, but which must necessarily be dubious when made by mortal man. For so tormented a temperament, there must be a nagging fear that the sun might indeed shine on to mock lovers, as their intentions soil and their professions fade. And this poem is not in its essence serene and timeless; it is nothing like (say) Henry Vaughan's 'The Retreate' or T. S. Eliot's 'Little Gidding'. Rather it is violent, even in its unquestionable beauty, sweeping along moment by moment on currents of change.

It is at this point, no doubt, that we should take account of the poet's habitual cast of mind, which colours nearly everything he writes. Does the emotional charge of the poem relate after all more to the pseudo-argument, the rhetorical shadow-boxing, than to the still centre where the sun at last comes to rest? Donne is a poet who rushes into articulation, creating as he defines, initiating the reader into experience at its white heat. His soul seemingly knows itself in linguistic intensity—in this poem, in an extended conceit which is at once an elaborate game and an exploration, a supreme dramatisation of the whole man. On this aspect of Donne's poetry, T. S. Eliot's essay 'The Metaphysical Poets' is of course seminal, and remains valid as a definition of one poet's peculiar sensibility, even if we reject its extension to quasi-historical theorising, as we surely must.

The effect in **'The Sunne Rising'** is that statements and questions come alive with alternative meanings, none of which can be wholly suppressed. The poem thrives on extremes and quintessences, on paradoxes which look at one moment like intellectual scaffolding round simple emotions, at the next like internal complexities threatening the emotions themselves. We have to return in conclusion to the question of whether the ideas put forward in the poem are finally acceptable: or rather, to the question of what 'final acceptability', in such an instance, can be. If the poem's articulation is inseparable from the poet's experience, it must in an obvious sense be valid; yet the verbal construct remains, by any standards, bizarre. Few people would address the sun in this way seriously, or even fancifully; few would argue that human love can, in the manner asserted, defy time.

The problem turns on the relationship between erotic love and spiritual love; the poem yokes these two together, and apparently unites them, but are they fused, or confused, in the end? Human love naturally links with passionate needs for loyalty, which point, for a religious believer, to truths beyond time. The eternity demanded by love need not be mythic; the thoughts which dominate this poem can be directly and profoundly presented as truth:

> Thou, Lord, in the beginning hast laid the foundation of the earth: and the heavens are the work of thy hands.
> They shall perish, but thou shalt endure: they all shall wax old as doth a garment;
> And as a vesture shalt thou change them, and they shall be changed: but thou art the same, and thy years shall not fail.
> (Psalm 102, 25-7: Coverdale translation)

When Donne wrote later in the religious poetry and sermons of his love for God, the extraordinary intensity and deviousness of his conceits remained, but they linked there with the more normal and inescapable paradoxes of Christian faith. The sonnet **'Death be not proud'** expresses one of those grand Christian doctrines which separate believer from unbeliever irrevocably, in worlds too disparate for any bridges to link:

> Death be not proud, though some have called thee
> Mighty and dreadfull, for, thou art not soe,
> For, those, whom thou think'st, thou dost overthrow,
> Die not, poore death, nor yet canst thou kill mee.

> From rest and sleepe, which but thy pictures bee,
> Much pleasure, then from thee, much more must flow,
> And soonest our best men with thee doe goe,
> Rest of their bones, and soules deliverie.

For the Christian, death has lost all power to hurt, except for the deep and grievous, but temporary, anguish of bereavement. Such a triumph can scarcely be portrayed without extravagance or be seen as less than aggressive in its hope. In the most serious sense it is shocking: St Paul rightly associates it with the 'scandal' of the Cross, and celebrates it with famous verbal audacities of his own.

But such triumphs must belong, by their nature, to religion, and to hopes which transcend, if they do not exclude, the flesh. When Donne projects religious assurance into merely sensual experience, he sets up tensions hard to resolve. Love's triumph over time is convincingly asserted by Christian or Platonist only when certain other factors intervene. It is the promise beyond 'till death do us part' in the Christian marriage vows, the sacramental bond only half anchored to the body and to the world of time. But it must reach out beyond the bedroom if it is to carry conviction, to clearer loyalties, stronger renunciations of erotic possessiveness, than this poem affords.

It is because **'The Sunne Rising'** celebrates Eros as a true Immortal that it has a real, as well as rhetorical, nonsense at the heart. (pp. 21-8)

> *A. E. Dyson and Julian Lovelock, "Contracted Thus: Donne's 'The Sunne Rising',"* in their Masterful Images: English Poetry from Metaphysicals to Romantics, *1976. Reprint by Barnes & Noble Books, 1976, pp. 21-8.*

Barbara Kiefer Lewalski   (essay date 1979)

[*In the excerpt below, Lewalski maintains that Donne's religious poetry exhibits a view of Protestant Theology which is grounded in the Scriptures and includes a picture of God that is both witty and metaphorical.*]

Though Donne's sermons contributed vitally to the emerging Protestant poetics, not all of his ***Divine Poems*** are best explained in its terms. No doubt this fact helps explain why contemporaries referred to Herbert rather than Donne as the wellspring of the new school of English divine poetry. Nevertheless, though the dating of Donne's poems is often uncertain, in general his religious lyrics reflect the Protestant poetics more and more fully, from early work to late.

At first Donne seemed little concerned with the ideas about genre deriving from Protestant poetics. His genres for religious poetry were often derived from secular forms (sonnet, verse letter); or were variations on liturgical forms (litany, hymn); or were ostensibly meditations on major feast days, events of the liturgical cycle, or standard Ignatian themes. But he came to rely increasingly upon the genres important in Protestant devotion and in biblical poetics theory. He praised the Sidney-Countess of Pembroke version of the Psalms as a new revelation of the

Holy Spirit virtually equalling David's, and produced a close paraphrase of Lamentations. His *First Anniversary* is a complaint-elegy for a whole people in the Lamentations mode, and also a satire-cum-praise in the mode of the Mosaic hymn in Deuteronomy 32. The *Second Anniversary* is called a hymn, on the biblical poetics ground that it is an exalted praise of God—as revealed through his image in Elizabeth Drury. Donne also wrote three poems of "occasional" meditation upon experience, analyzing significant providential occasions in his own life—"Goodfriday 1613. Riding Westward," "Hymne to Christ," and "Hymne to God my God, in my sicknesse."

A comparable development took place in other areas. Donne's earliest poems—"**The Crosse,**" "**Upon the Annunciation and Passion,**" and the "**La Corona**" sonnets—treat the great theological mysteries in terms of sacred paradoxes and puns long familiar in the Fathers and the medieval poets, and the same early poems are also linked to traditional meditative and emblematic forms. By contrast the *Holy Sonnets* are characterized by echoes of the Psalms and of the Pauline Epistles as well as by extensive use of prominent biblical metaphors for the sinner's condition. And, though there is little conventional use of typology in Donne's religious verse at any time, the later poems exhibit to a marked degree the Protestant tendency to find biblical events and typological relationships re-enacted within the self. In the *Holy Sonnets* the speaker re-enacts within himself Paul's experience of the predicament of the Christian; in the "**Hymne to Christ**" the speaker is a new Noah about to encounter a new Flood; in the "**Hymne to God my God, in my sicknesse**" the speaker's soul becomes the stage for the embodiment of the typological drama of the Old Adam and the New. This characteristic Protestant typological and meditative focus upon the self helps explain Donne's pervasive self-dramatization in these poems, which critics find variously impressive or deplorable. Moreover, as we have seen, he manifests some heightening of consciousness about the problems of art and the sacred subject, moving from the comfortable assumption that the "**La Corona**" sequence is a proper fusion of "prayer and praise" devised in an appropriate devotional spirit ("my low devout melancholie"); to a recognition in "**A Litanie**" of the dangers of "excesse . . . Potiquenesse"; to the very self-conscious generic revisions in the "**Hymne to God my God, in my sicknesse.**" He also displays growing concern with biblical personae and models—Jeremiah, Moses, John of Patmos in the *Anniversaries* and, less overtly, David and Paul in the *Holy Sonnets.*

We can best comprehend these developments by considering Donne's divine poems in broad generic categories: emblematic poems, poems based upon liturgical forms, poems of complimentary address, biblical paraphrase, poems focusing upon the Protestant drama of regeneration, and occasional meditations. In all these categories many poems, early and late, display in heightened form the Protestant emphasis upon the "application to the self" of all scripture and doctrine.

One group of poems shows the strong impress of Donne's emblematic imagination. Ostensibly they are traditional meditations in the Catholic manner on religious symbols,

or on feast days, or on events in Christ's life. But Donne superimposes upon the meditative matter of these poems an overriding concern with the creation of or the analysis of a controlling emblem. Accordingly, the speaker does not approach his material as a meditator striving to understand and respond emotionally to his subject, but with the emblematist's wit and concern for formal design. Inappropriate expectations arising out of an approach to these poems as meditations accounts for some of the critical dissatisfaction with them.

"**The Crosse,**" perhaps Donne's earliest religious poem, is a variation on an emblem poem explaining the significance of and arguing the spiritual uses of the title emblem, the instrument of Christ's crucifixion. The poem relates to the controversy in the early seventeenth century over Puritan pressures to abolish the cross in the churches and the sign of the cross in baptism, as relics of Popish superstition; James I rejected those demands at the Hampton Court Conference in 1604, as does Donne in the lines, "no Pulpit, nor misgrounded law, / Nor scandall taken, shall this Crosse withdraw" (ll. 9-10). The poem is sometimes criticized as mere witty display, lacking in religious feeling, but this is to mistake its genre: it is not intended as a meditation upon the passion or upon Christ's cross itself, but rather (as with the emblem poems of Paradin or Peacham) it is an analysis and didactic interpretation of an abstract symbolic figure. Although the poem is hardly among Donne's masterpieces, it is much wittier and more artful than most emblem poems.

Donne's controlling argument, that the cross is and should be omnipresent in our lives, is in two parts. The first proposition is that crosses cannot in fact be abandoned, since they exist throughout nature:

> Who can deny mee power, and liberty
>
> To stretch mine armes, and mine owne Crosse to be?
> Swimme, and at every stroake, thou art thy Crosse,
> The Mast and yard make one, where seas do tosse.
> Looke downe, thou spiest out Crosses in small things;
> Looke up, thou seest birds rais'd on crossed wings;
> All the Globes frame, and spheares, is nothing else
> But the Meridians crossing Parallels. . . .
> And as thy braine through bony walls doth vent
> By sutures, which a Crosses forme present. . . .
>
> (ll. 17-24, 55-56)

This section of the poem seems directly dependent upon an emblem plate in Justus Lipsius' *De Cruce* which portrays most of these same natural crosses—a man praying with arms outstretched; a man swimming with arms extended; the mast of a ship; a cross-shaped handle of a shovel and a wheelbarrow ("Crosses in small things"); a bird flying with extended wings; a globe with meridians crossing parallels; a man's head (presumably with crossed skull sutures). The second proposition extends and transposes the usual didactic application of the emblem to derive a new argument on a higher plane—that in the spiritual order we should supply for ourselves spiritual crosses everywhere, on the analogy of their omnipresence in the material world. We should bear our crosses of tribulation and become other Christs crucified; we should cross our very joy in crosses lest it breed pride; we should cross all our senses in their craving for pleasure; we should cross our hearts in their undue dejections and exaltations; and we should cross our brain in its "concupiscence of witt." This last observation might well reflect with witty irony upon the excess this very poem seems to display, in its constant witty punning on "cross" as noun and verb and in several senses: "Crosse / Your joy in crosses"; "But most the eye needs crossing"; "crosse thy heart"; "Crosse no man else, but crosse thy selfe in all" (ll. 41-60). This wit is somewhat tempered by the analytic and didactic tone characteristic of discrete emblems that present "the creatures" or material objects as sources of moral and spiritual lessons. Donne's poem concludes on this note, though very wittily:

> Then doth the Crosse of Christ worke fruitfully
> Within our hearts, when wee love harmlessly
> That Crosses pictures much, and with more care
> That Crosses children, which our Crosses are.
>
> (ll. 61-64)

Another early poem, **"Upon the Annunciation and Passion falling upon one day. 1608,"** ostensibly celebrates the feast day but actually develops as a kind of emblem poem. It is not a meditation upon either or both events celebrated on the day, nor yet upon their Divine Actor. And though Jonathan Goldberg [in his "Donne's Journey East: Aspects of a Seventeenth Century Trope," *Studies in Philology,* 1971] is right to see typology in the background, the poem focuses upon conjunctions rather than foreshadowings. It treats the coincidence of these feasts upon a single day as an emblem of the perfect circularity and unity of the Christian vision, and to this end introduces the circle emblem immediately: this day shows Christ "man, so like God made in this, / That of them both a circle embleme is, / Whose first and last concurre" (ll. 3-4). This special day, in which opposites are conjoined and united even as they are in a circle or a globe, is accordingly "Th'Abridgement of Christs story, which makes one / (As in plaine Maps, the furthest West is East) / Of the 'Angels *Ave*,' and *Consummatum est*" (ll. 20-22). The circle thus supplies the governing figure for the all-pervasive and extremely witty paradoxes describing the Church's vision of circularity and unity on this day:

> Shee sees him nothing twice at once, who 'is all;
> Shee sees a Cedar plant it selfe, and fall,
> Her Maker put to making, and the head
> Of life, at once, not yet alive, and dead;
> Shee sees at once the virgin mother stay
> Reclus'd at home, Publique at Golgotha.
> Sad and rejoyc'd shee's seen at once, and seen
> At almost fiftie, and at scarce fifteene.
>
> (ll. 7-14)

Reflecting upon this emblematic day, the speaker perceives that the circularity and unity pertain not only to Christ's life but to human experience as well—"Death and conception in mankinde is one"—and that they also per-

tain to God's designing of Creation and Last Judgment as one period (ll. 34, 38). The poem concludes with the speaker's resolve to "uplay" the treasures of this day in gross, so that he may retail them to himself for future meditations.

A much more complex use of the emblem form is to be found in the seven interlinked **"La Corona"** sonnets, which are set forth as a "crowne of prayer and praise" offered to God. One source of Donne's conception evidently is, as Louis Martz [in his *Poetry of Meditation,* 1954] has suggested, the Corona rosary devotions, a special set of six decades with an appendage, devoted to the great events of the Virgin's life; in some versions, for instance that of Sabin Chambers, the subject matter corresponds rather closely to that of the last six sonnets in Donne's sequence. Martz calls attention to several specific precedents for Donne's sequence: the popular English "Corona of our Lord," which adapts the rosary devotions, as Donne does, to Christ; continental and English sequences of linked sonnets called "Coronas" by, e.g., Annibal Caro (1558), Gascoigne (1575), and Chapman (1595); and one Italian sequence combining the devotional and the poetic corona, called *Corona di laudi a Maria Vergine* (1617). Donne's poetic corona of linked sonnets, insofar as it is a sequence of meditations on specific events or mysteries of the Christian faith, has obvious debts to this tradition. But as an exercise explicitly undertaking to fuse two modes of devotion—"*Deigne at my hands this crown of prayer and praise*"—it has biblical analogues which Donne persistently cites as evidencing the circularity and inseparability of prayer and praise. One is the Psalms: Donne observes, for example, that the first and last verses of Psalm 38 are prayers and that thereby "*David* makes up his Circle." Another is the Lord's Prayer, which "being at first begun with glory and acknowledgement of his raigning in heaven, and then shut up in the same manner, with acclamations of power and glory, it is made a circle of praise, and a circle is infinite too, The Prayer, and the Praise is equally infinite." Looking to such models, Donne has created a sequence which is not so much meditation as emblem, a crown of prayer and praise with some resemblance to those emblem figures of olive, bay, and laurel wreaths, representing tributes of praise for notable poetic and military accomplishments and divine reward for Christian perseverance.

In the opening sonnet called **"La Corona"** this emblematic purpose is immediately announced: Donne relates the crown of prayer and praise he is constructing here for Christ to the crown of glory which he hopes will finally reward his poetry and his life; he also contrasts the crown of worldly honors with that crown of glory, seen as the direct consequence of Christ's crown of thorns:

> But doe not, with a vile crowne of fraile bayes,
> Reward my muses white sincerity,
> But what thy thorny crowne gain'd, that give
>   mee,
> A crowne of Glory, which doth flower always.
>
> (ll. 5-8)

Donne's imagery, opposing the true and false crowns to be won, derives from Isaiah (perhaps, as Helen Gardner suggests, by way of the Advent liturgy): "Woe to the crowne of pride, to the drunkards of Ephraim, whose glorious beauty is a fading flowre . . . / In that day shall the lord of hosts be for a crowne of glory, and for a diademe of beautie unto the residue of his people" (Isaiah 28: 1, 5). The lines allude also to the eternal crowns worn by the white-robed saints in Revelation 4:4, 11, which they cast down before the throne of God in praise.

The emblematic crown created by these sonnets undertakes to, and does, conjoin the two impulses of prayer and praise. The opening sonnet is in the mode of personal prayer to God, begging acceptance of the crown offered, and the reward of another; it modulates to praise at the end, echoing Isaiah 51: 4-5, "'Tis time that heart and voice be lifted high, / *Salvation to all that will is nigh*" (ll. 13-14). The next four sonnets, **"Annunciation," "Nativitie," "Temple," "Crucyfying,"** are in the mode of praise, though praise here does not mean hymnic praise but rather meditative wonder and admiration over the mysteries of redemption. The stylistic embodiment for this admiration and wonder is paradox—brilliantly pointed and witty formulations of the time-honored medieval paradoxes. Christ is he "Which cannot sinne, and yet all sinnes must beare, / Which cannot die, yet cannot chuse but die." The Virgin conceives him who conceived her; she is apostrophized as "Thy Makers maker, and thy Fathers mother"; and she has *Immensity cloysterd in thy deare wombe.*" The child lying in the manger at the Nativity is he "Which fils all place, yet none holds him"; the child in the Temple is the Word which "but lately could not speake, and loe / It sodenly speakes wonders." During the passion Christ's enemies "prescribe a Fate" to Christ, "Whose creature Fate is, . . . / Measuring selfe-lifes infinity to'a span, / Nay to an inch." Then Christ bears his cross, yet "When it beares him, he must beare more and die."

The turning point in the sequence comes with the reversion to prayer at the end of the fifth sonnet, **"Crucyfying"**: "Now thou art lifted up, draw mee to thee, / And at thy death giving such liberall dole / *Moyst, with one drop of thy blood, my dry soule*" (ll. 12-14). The sixth sonnet, **"Resurrection,"** is wholly in the prayer mode: the speaker does not meditate upon Christ's resurrection but prays for his own resurrection from sin through Christ's blood, and from death at the last day. The final sonnet, **"Ascension,"** weds the impulses of prayer and praise into perfect formal harmony: the octave is praise, extended to the public mode with the speaker exhorting all repentant sinners to *"Salute the last and everlasting day,* / Joy at the uprising of this Sunne, and Sonne." The sestet is again personal prayer to Christ, imaged as in Valeriano's emblems: "O strong Ramme . . . / Mild lambe . . . / Oh, with thine owne blood quench thine owne just wrath." The sequence ends as it began, though now with the recognition, before unexpressed, of the Spirit's necessary role in contriving acceptable prayer and praise:

> And if thy holy Spirit, my Muse did raise,
> *Deigne at my hands this crowne of prayer and praise.*

The poetic devices used in the construction of this corona are subtle rhetorical figures of poetic interlinking and in-

terweaving. Most obviously, the first and last lines of the entire sequence are identical, so that the sequence ends as it begins, as a crown or circle must; also, the last line of each individual sonnet is the first line of the next, so there is no hiatus to interrupt the circle's perfect continuity. And in addition to this, the constant use of ploce, repetition, and antithesis weaves lines and half-lines together—as, "The ends crowne our workes, but thou crown'st our ends, / For, at our end begins our endlesse rest, / This first last end, now zealously possest." The **"La Corona"** sequence is not, like **"The Crosse,"** an analysis of or a meditation upon an emblem, and neither is it primarily a meditative exercise upon specific mysteries. Rather, Donne here constructs a personal poetic emblem, even as he created his own *impresa* of the anchor-cross, and contrived an emblem *figura* of his own body on his deathbed. **"La Corona"** creates a poetic crown for Christ out of traditional meditative, liturgical, emblematic, and rhetorical materials.

Two poems adapted from liturgical forms are **"A Litanie"** and the **"Hymne to God the Father."** The first is an Anglican version of the Litany of the Saints—perhaps based upon Cranmer's version of 1544, which removed the long roll-call of individual Saints and retained only the headings of the major classes. The second is in the mode of the congregational hymn or anthem, so impressively developed by Luther and Coverdale. These poems are alike remarkable in that they transpose public forms into private devotions relating directly to the personal situation and experience of the speaker. Yet at the same time, that speaker sees his individual experience as presenting a paradigm of the Christian's situation in the world. (pp. 253-60)

Keeping to the major structural divisions of the Litany of the Saints—the initial invocations to the Trinity; praises of the saints but with Protestant care to avoid the *ora pro nobis* formula or the stance of invocation; petitions for deliverance and for God's hearing (*Libera nos, Domine, Audi nos, Domine*)—[Donne's **"A Litanie"**] analyzes a number of divine or saintly attributes in considerable detail, always applying them to his own circumstances. At the same time, his speaker moves out from an intimately personal posture to present himself as spokesman for, and his experience as typical of, a larger community.

In the first section, addressing the persons of the Trinity individually and collectively, the speaker in quasi-typological fashion proposes himself as a proper subject for the re-enactment of past divine actions. He begs the Father as creator to "re-create" him as a new Adam, out of the red earth to which his sins have reduced him: "My heart is by dejection, clay, / And by selfe-murder, red." He begs the Son, the redeemer, to re-enact the crucifixion within him: "O be thou nail'd unto my heart, / And crucified againe." He begs the Holy Ghost to purge and purify with his flame the sacrilegious temple of mud walls and condensed dust which he has become. And he prays the entire Trinity, with its united and distinguished functions of power, love, and knowledge, to work those effects within him: "Of these let all mee elemented bee, / Of power, to love, to know, you unnumbred three."

The following stanzas (v-xiii) on the Virgin Mary, the angels, and the various categories of saints do not petition them for their prayers, but rather pray God to let them play an important and often precisely appropriate role in the speaker's spiritual life. Mary's office is treated first, but cautiously, and in general rather than personal terms—as if Donne were unsure as to just how a Protestant should formulate the claim upon her assistance: "As her deeds were / Our helpes, so are her prayers" (ll. 43-44). The speaker prays to God regarding the angels, that "mine actions bee / Worthy their sight, though [I am] blinde in how they see" (ll. 53-54). He asks that the patriarchs' desire to see Christ "Be satisfied, and fructifie in mee," who often see less in the "fire" of Grace than they did in the "cloud" of the Law. And he would especially engage the prophets who sounded the heavenly harmony of the two Testaments, and the heavenly poets "which did see / Thy will, and it expresse / In rythmique feet" to pray for him, "That I by them excuse not my excesse / In seeking secrets, or Potiquenesse" (ll. 68-72). He prays God also to let the Apostles shape his biblical commentary, "that I goe / Th'old broad way in applying: O decline / Mee, when my comment would make thy word mine" (ll. 79-81). At this point the speaker assumes a more public stance, begging God to permit the other categories of saints to serve "us" in various ways: let the martyrs beg for us the patience neither to seek nor to avoid martyrdom; let the confessors pray that we, like them, may understand our temptations to be a kind of persecution. This sequence ends with two witty counter-examples: the virgins cannot pray that we be preserved as they were in our first integrity, but God can divorce sin in us "And call chast widowhead Virginitie"; and the doctors need to pray for our protection against themselves, that we may not adhere to "what they have misdone / Or mis-said."

Stanza xiv, introducing the deprecations (*"Libera nos, Domine"*), expresses the idea—implicit in the earlier stanzas—of the conjoined prayers of the saints in heaven and on earth, and wittily prays God's deliverance from trusting in such prayers rather than in God only. Subsequent petitions ask deliverance from excesses or inadequacies in regard to faith or works; they are spoken for the community (us) but obviously couched in terms personally felt. The overriding concern is to find mean ways, evenness in the practice of religion: "From being anxious, or secure / Dead clods of sadnesse, or light squibs of mirth, / . . . From needing danger, to bee good, / . . . From being spies, or to spies pervious, / From thirst, or scorne of fame, deliver us." Finally, the obsecrations beg (by the events of Christ's life) for deliverance from more customary evils—from death, from idolatry and hypocrisy, from evils in church and state, from plague or war or heresy, from all evil in the hour of death and on the eve of Judgment.

The final section, Supplications and Intercessions (*"Audi nos, Domine"*), develops with paradoxical wit all the problems of hearing—of God's hearing us, and of our own "labyrinthine" ears. The speaker begs God to hear himself in us—"Heare us, for till thou heare us, Lord / We know not what to say"; to hear us so "That we may heare" in scripture and nature God's promises and threats; to open

his ears so that we may lock ours against sinful speech; to lock his ears against just complaints against us so that we may open ours to profit from them. At length, as the speaker prays to be led to use all God's goods properly, a brilliant emblematic image of God as ear (analogous to that in Hugo and Quarles) together with a conceit of God as the cry which we weakly echo in our own prayers, resolves the problem of ears and hearing:

> That learning, thine Ambassador,
> From thine allegeance wee never tempt,
>   That beauty, paradises flower
> For physicke made, from poyson be exempt,
>   That wit, borne apt, high good to doe,
>   By dwelling lazily
> On Natures nothing, be not nothing too,
> That our affections kill us not, nor dye,
> Heare us, weake ecchoes, O thou eare, and cry.
>
>   (ll. 235-243)

The last stanza of the poem declines from this pitch of intensity to a conclusion perhaps over-witty and facile, though not without feeling—a prayer that sin, taken by Christ from us and unable to stick to him, may simply disappear: "As sinne is nothing, let it no where be" (l. 252).

The deceptively simple yet brilliantly witty and withal profoundly moving **"Hymne to God the Father"** almost defies description. This is not a hymn in the classical or biblical poetics sense of an exalted praise of God; it is more closely related to the anthem or congregational hymn—but with characteristic Donnean personalization. Walton's description of the intense personal emotion Donne felt upon hearing the public performance of this anthem may be partly apocryphal, but it does suggest Donne's special delight in creating poems which are at once public and very private:

> He caus'd it [this Hymne] to be set to a most grave and solemn Tune, and to be often sung to the *Organ* by the *Choristers* of St. *Pauls* Church, in his own hearing, especially at the Evening Service; and at his return from his Customary Devotions in that place, did occasionally say to a friend *The words of this* Hymne *have restored to me the same thoughts of joy that possess my Soul in my sickness when I composed it. And, O the power of Church-musick! that Harmony added to it has raised the Affections of my heart, and quicned my graces of zeal and gratitude; and I* observe, *that I always return from paying this publick duty of* Prayer *and* Praise *to* God, *with an unexpressible tranquillity of mind,* and a willingness *to leave the world.*

The speaker adopts a personal stance throughout, but in the first four lines of each six-line stanza the "I" may be universalized—each member of the congregation could make these interrogations and petitions in his own name, asking God to forgive various generalized categories of sins of which all are guilty. But the pun on done/Donne in the final lines of each stanza personalizes this congregational hymn in an altogether remarkable way—so that it has direct and unique reference to Donne himself, by name. Especially in the final stanza, as the speaker confesses his besetting sin of fear and finds the resolution of his problem in his characteristic sun/Son pun, are we aware of how completely personal the anthem is:

> I have a sinne of feare, that when I have spunne
> My last thred, I shall perish on the shore;
> Sweare by thy selfe, that at my death thy sonne
> Shall shine as he shines now, and heretofore;
> And, having done that, Thou hast done,
>   I have no more.

Yet even here the speaker can have it both ways: only the initiate need recognize that audacious pun on Donne's name, or know of his besetting sin of fear. Donne has contrived a congregational hymn which at one and the same time provides a form of simple devotion for all to sing, and a *tour de force* of wit which is the unique personal expression of its inordinately witty poet.

By common critical consent the most remarkable of Donne's *Divine Poems* are the nineteen *Holy Sonnets*, **"Goodfriday, 1613. Riding Westward,"** the **"Hymne to Christ,"** the **"Hymne to God my God, in my sicknesse,"** and a few occasional pieces. These are also the poems most profoundly affected by the Protestant poetics we have been tracing.

The *Holy Sonnets* pose a special problem because of the uncertainty, unresolvable from present knowledge, regarding the sequence in which they were written or were intended to be read. Louis Martz approaches them as discrete poems reflecting, some more and some less completely, the topics and structure to be found in typical Ignatian meditation—though his discussion indicates that the Ignatian three-part structure (preparation, analysis, colloquy) is present with any completeness only in two or three of them. Helen Gardner [in her introduction to the *Divine Poems*, 1965], on the basis of persuasive manuscript evidence and somewhat less satisfactory argument from internal evidence, has discriminated a set of six meditations on the Last Things (presumably sent with the dedicatory sonnet **"To the E. of D."**) and another set of six on the love of God for us and our love for him. These twelve sonnets appear—in the order in which Dame Helen reprints them—in the Group I and Group II manuscripts and in the first edition, 1633. In 1635, four new sonnets were added, interspersed among these; Dame Helen takes them to have been originally intended as a rather loosely organized sequence on the topic of penitence (though the first of them has virtually nothing to do with that matter). The final three are assumed to be separate occasional meditations, written later and available only in the Westmoreland manuscript until their late first printing in 1899. Other readers of the *Holy Sonnets* have suggested other thematic and structural patterns: the Anglican doctrine of contrition, involving a progress from fear to love to contrite sorrow; a penitential exercise deriving from Augustinian devotion as developed by the Franciscans; a spiritual progress in four meditative stages (adapted from Elizabethan love sonnet sequences), leading from religious doubt to assurance; an exploration, lacking sequence and progress, of several dramatic stances from lament to assurance which the speaker adopts in the continuing drama of Christian life. (pp. 260-64)

The first poem of the 1635 sequence is one of the interpolated sonnets. It is easy to see why it is so placed: it is linked thematically (by the references to creation and to the speaker's psychic condition of near-despair) to the following poem (the first sonnet in the 1633 sequence). It sounds the leitmotifs of the entire series—creation, decay, death, sin, reparation: "Thou hast made me, And shall thy worke decay? / Repaire me now, for now mine end doth haste, / I runne to death" (ll. 1-3). And it presents graphically the condition of anguish, terror, helplessness and despair accompanying the conviction of sin and guilt which is the first effect of God's calling—the mollifying of hard and sinful hearts with which the Protestant spiritual drama begins. The speaker, with echoes of the Psalmist's cry in Psalm 6:6-7—"I am weary with my groning. . . . / Mine eie is consumed because of griefe"—expects imminent death from sin's corruption, and is in an agony of helplessness: "I dare not move my dimme eyes any way, / Despaire behind, and death before doth cast / Such terrour." The sestet records a temporary relief through the remembrance of God, but this is undercut by the realization that the speaker cannot resist Satan's temptations "one houre." The only hope—effectual calling—is suggested in the final couplet, evoking a striking emblem from Georgette de Montenay of an iron heart drawn irresistibly by an adamant stone held out from heaven: "Thy Grace may wing me to prevent his art / And thou like Adamant draw mine iron heart." The second sonnet, "As due by many titles" (first in the 1633 series) focuses upon the problem of election. At the outset the speaker evokes a long series of biblical metaphors which establish the various titles by which God could claim ownership of him, and which might seem to "prove" his election: he is God's creature, he is bought by Christ's blood, he is son, servant, sheep, image, and temple of the Holy Spirit. But in the sestet he recognizes that Satan's conquest has undermined these legal titles: he cannot now be reclaimed unless God will actively fight for him. And he virtually despairs of election. His condition finds definition in the classic texts in Romans 8:28-30—"All things worke together for good . . . to them who are the called according to his purpose. / . . . Whom he did predestinate, them he also called"—in conjunction with the chilling warning in Matthew 20:16, "Many bee called, but fewe chosen." So Donne's speaker fears that he may not be among the elect: "thou lov'st mankind well, yet wilt'not chuse me."

The next three sonnets concern the speaker's grief for sin and efforts to repent: true repentance is the first outward sign of the working of God's grace in the soul though, as Perkins points out, even the reprobate may manifest some of these signs. Donne's speaker has as yet no confidence that his grief is a sign of true repentance. Two of these sonnets (III and V) are new in the 1635 volume. **"Sonnet III,"** **"O might those sighes and teares returne againe"** is about the condition of fruitless grief: the speaker desires now to "Mourne with some fruit, as I have mourn'd in vaine"—with reference to his former sinful agonies and miseries in his love-idolatries. The speaker longs for the "fruit" of repentance promised in Psalm 126:6, "He that goeth forth and weepeth, bearing precious seed, shall doubtlesse come again with rejoycing; bringing his sheaves with him," but he has no such fruit: "To (poore) me is allow'd / No ease; for, long, yet vehement griefe hath beene / Th'effect and cause, the punishment and sinne." Moreover, he is unable to distinguish essentially between his present and his past griefs, and so does not experience the effect of true sorrow described in 2 Corinthians 7:10—which could almost be the text for this sonnet: "For godly sorrow worketh repentance to salvation not to be repented of, but the sorrow of the world worketh death." In **"Sonnet IV"** the speaker finds his "blacke Soule" summoned by sickness, death's herald, and, like an exiled traitor or an imprisoned thief, he fears execution far more than present miseries. The essence of his spiritual state is summed up at the beginning of the sestet: "Yet grace, if thou repent, thou canst not lacke; / But who shall give thee that grace to beginne?" God of course must give that prevenient grace and the repentance itself: the speaker proposes to make himself *black* with mourning and *red* with blushing (as he is with sin), but recognizes that it is Christ's blood "which hath this might / That being red, it dyes red soules to white."

"Sonnet V," **"I am a little world made cunningly,"** perhaps received its place not only because of the continuation of the motif of grief and repentance, but also from the conception of the "blacke Soule" now threatened with imminent death: "black sinne hath betraid to endlesse night / My worlds both parts, and (oh) both parts must die." The inevitability of this result for his little world is indicated as the lines play off against various texts in Romans (5:12, 6:23): "By one man sinne entred into the world, and death by sin: and so death passed upon all men"; "For the wages of sinne is death." The speaker then envisions that death: he would drown his little world with the tears of his repentance if he could, but he recalls that after Noah worlds are not to be drowned any longer; so he offers hopefully to wash it. But that route of repentance seems not now available: instead he expects and deserves the other punishment established for the great world at the end of time—"But oh it must be burnt"—in punishment of previous burnings by lust and envy. Yet there is still a way to suffer burning which would be restorative and (almost paraphrasing Psalm 69:9) he prays for that: "burne me ô Lord, with a fiery zeale / Of thee and thy house, which doth in eating heale."

"Sonnet VI," **"This is my playes last scene,"** is something of a turning point: the speaker vividly imagines himself at the moment of death, but not by evoking a deathbed scene in the manner of an Ignatian *compositio loci*. Instead, the speaker calls upon the very familiar biblical metaphors of life as pilgrimage and as athletic race—"here heavens appoint / My pilgrimages last mile; and my race / Idly, yet quickly runne"—and evokes a traditional emblem in the image of a personified, "gluttonous death" unjointing the body. The means for dispelling the shaking fear of God's judgment this vision provokes is specified when the speaker cries out in the couplet, "Impute me righteous": the imputation of Christ's righteousness, forgiving and covering sins with his merits, is the result of justification, and this alone gives assurance of salvation. The speaker's cry indicates that he clearly understands his need and that his faith is now strong enough to formulate it, in terms suggestive of the long discussion in Romans 4:6-24 which begins by referring to the Psalmist's description of "the blessednesse of the man, unto whom God imputeth righteousnesse without works." The speaker hopes, with some-

what strained wit, that this justification might take place for him at the moment of death, for at that time (as not earlier) his soul will leave his body and his body will leave the world, so that if his sins will also (by justification) depart to the hell that bred them he can be said to leave "the world, the flesh, and devill."

"Sonnet VII," **"At the round earths imagin'd corners"** seems related to the preceding one, as the consideration of the moment of death leads logically to meditation upon the Day of Judgment. There is here some impress of the meditation upon the Last Things, and this sonnet is one of the two or three which exhibit the full Ignatian meditative structure. There is a vivid *compositio loci*: the first line (despite its witty reservation) evokes the scene in Revelation 7:1, "I saw foure Angels standing on the foure corners of the Earth"; and the octave fleshes out the details of the parade of souls arising and seeking their bodies. The dead include the primary categories the speaker considered in **"Sonnet V"** while anticipating his own death as microcosm—"All whom the flood did, and fire shall o'erthrow"—as well as other agents of death drawn in part from Revelation 6:8 and Ezekiel 14:21: war, famine, age, agues, tyrannies, despair, law, chance. The sestet provides a sharp *volte* as the speaker prays, "But let them sleepe, Lord, and mee mourne a space." Modifying the conclusion in his previous sonnet, in which he asks God to justify him at the very moment of death, the speaker here observes, "'Tis late to aske abundance of thy grace, / When wee are there." We might have expected him to say it was too late—but the formulation suggests the growth of the speaker's faith and his recognition that nothing is impossible to God. Now, however, he begs for more time to mourn his sins and asks specifically for the divine gift of true repentance, for that would be a trustworthy sign of his election and justification: "Teach mee how to repent; for that's as good / As if thou'hadst seal'd my pardon, with thy blood."

"Sonnet VIII," **"If faithfull soules be alike glorifi'd,"** is again interpolated, and was evidently placed here in evidence that the speaker has obtained the true repentance he sought. The poem turns on scholastic distinctions of modes of knowing: if the speaker's dead father knows as angels do, he will know his son's repentance to be sincere, but if those sainted souls can be misled by the appearances of grief or feigned devotions, he cannot know this. The speaker however is now confident enough of his repentance—"my mindes white truth"—to appeal directly to God to testify to it: "he knowes best / Thy true griefe, for he put it in my breast." **"Sonnet IX,"** **"If poysonous mineralls,"** enacts the speaker's true repentance and faith: after an almost blasphemous false start in the octave, he suddenly abandons all efforts to mitigate his guilt or to object to the sentence of damnation he deserves, throwing himself without reservation upon Christ's mercy in the earnest hope of justification. The entire sonnet shows the speaker defining himself against Job who maintained his integrity and righteousness before God, implying that God has unjustly dealt with him. By contrast, Donne's speaker admits readily that his sins deserve damnation but, in the octave, he too contends with God about the injustice of the threatened punishment: he protests that his reason unfairly subjects him to punishment not accorded to evils in nature or to vicious animals, and he argues that a God to whom mercy is easy should not show wrath. It is a specious argument, as he recognizes in his outcry, "But who am I, that dare dispute with thee?"—echoing Elihu's rebuke to Job and Paul's rebuke to one who would question God's incomprehensible will: "Therefore hath hee mercie on whom hee will have mercy, and whom he will, he hardeneth / . . . Who art thou that repliest against [disputest with, margin] God? Shall the thing formed say to him that formed it, Why hast thou made me thus?" The speaker finds his only hope in a "heavenly Lethean flood" made up of Christ's "onely worthy blood" and his own tears, to drown the very memory of those sins; in this he defines himself not only against Job, but also against the Psalmist who grounded his plea for God's mercy upon God's remembrance—"according to thy mercie remember thou me." The speaker of this sonnet finds his best hope in God's total forgetting: "That thou remember them, some claime as debt, / I thinke it mercy, if thou wilt forget." In Calvinist terms, this is precisely what justification means—that God will not see the sinner himself and his own sins, but will remember him only in Christ. This justification, evidenced by his true repentance and faith, brings the speaker a kind of victory over his sins.

That victory leads on to a conquest over death in the **"Death be not Proud"** sonnet (X), the first of several which focus upon the speaker's manifestation of saving faith—whereby in Perkins' terms he "doth particularly applie unto himselfe those promises which are made in the Gospel." In this sonnet the speaker, confident that he partakes of Christ's conquest over death, is able to face down the fear of death which has haunted him in the foregoing sonnets; moreover, in his tirade against the braggart Death (seemingly "Mighty and dreadfull" but in fact a powerless bully) he even enacts his own imitation of Christ's victory over death. The speaker can afford his condescension ("poore death") because he finds death no longer has power over him—"nor yet canst thou kill mee." And the apocalyptic terrors envisaged in **"Sonnet VII"** as the instruments of death are here wittily transposed into the unsavory masters of or companions to death: "Thou art slave to Fate, chance, kings, and desperate men, / And dost with poyson, warre, and sicknesse dwell." The whole sonnet, and especially the final lines, show the speaker recapitulating Paul's affirmation of the resurrection as an ultimate victory over death: "In a moment, in the twinckling of an eye . . . the trumpet shall sound, and the dead shall be raised incorruptible, and we shall be changed. / . . . Death is swallowed up in victorie. / O death, where is thy sting? O grave, where is thy victorie?" Donne's speaker proclaims: "One short sleepe past, wee wake eternally, / And death shall be no more, Death thou shalt die."

The next three sonnets are concerned with Christ's crucifixion, as the speaker exhibits his faith by applying the benefits of that crucifixion to himself. He begins by attempting a false application: in **"Sonnet XI,"** **"Spit in my face yee Jewes,"** he imagines himself undertaking the role of the crucified Christ in a surprising reversal of the mediator's usual stance before the crucified one. The speaker

seeks to arrogate to himself all the elements of Christ's passion, recognizing that his sins richly deserve them; but his faith reveals, of course, that the gesture is useless: "by my death can not be satisfied / My sinnes." Instead he finds, ironically, that he is one of the crucifiers—"They kill'd once an inglorious man, but I / Crucifie him daily, being now glorified." There is grave danger to the speaker in this recognition: Paul declared (Heb. 6:6) that those, once enlightened, who fall away, will not again be renewed, "seeing they crucifie to themselves the Sonne of God afresh, and put him to an open shame." The sestet resolves the problem through faith in Christ's infinite mercy. Although the speaker is not strong enough to put on the accoutrements of Christ's passion, Christ, as antitype of Jacob disguised in "vile harsh attire" puts on man's "vile flesh" to make himself "weake enough to suffer woe." **"Sonnet XII,"** **"Why are wee by all creatures waited on?"** examines the wonderful circumstance that sinful and weak man is served by purer elements, by stronger animals, and by a whole creation untarnished by sin, as a means to understand more fully the wonderful benefits of Christ's crucifixion: "But their Creator, whom sin, nor nature tyed, / For us, his Creatures, and his foes, hath dyed." The last sonnet on this theme, **"What if this present were the world's last night?"** (XIII), briefly recalls the Apocalypse, but now it is devoid of terror. The speaker now has "in my heart . . . / The picture of Christ crucified," and contemplation of that picture reinforces his faith that the suffering, loving Christ will save him. The sestet plays an almost scandalous variation upon the serious affirmation of faith in the octave: now the speaker begs Christ for reassurance of his mercy, arguing the Platonic connection between Beauty and Goodness which he used to cite in wooing his "profane mistresses"—"This beauteous forme assures a pitious mind." This whimsical wooing of Christ testifies to some confidence in the relationship, but at the same time to the wooer's constant need of reassurance: faith, like repentance, shows its variations and fluctuations over a whole lifetime.

"Sonnet XIV," **"Batter my heart, three person'd God,"** is explicitly about regeneration, "making new." Regeneration, or sanctification, is a process distinct from and yet accompanying justification (the imputing of Christ's merits to the elect), and involves the renovation of the soul by degrees, so that, progressively but never completely, the corruptions of sin are purged from it and the image of God is restored in it. Donne's speaker dramatizes his regeneration in uncompromising Calvinist terms, as solely the effect of God's grace upon his passive and helpless self. The imagery recalls several graphic descriptions and heart emblems representing the softening or mollifying of the heart as the first stage of regeneration:

> Batter my heart, three person'd God; for, you
> As yet but knocke, breathe, shine, and seeke to mend;
> That I may rise, and stand, o'erthrow mee,'and bend
> Your force, to breake, blowe, burn and make me new.

With characteristic dramatic imagination and application of this abstract doctrine to himself, the speaker invites the whole of God's power and force to be directed upon himself in a much more intense form than the biblical norm would seem to require. God usually calls men by knocking—"Behold, I stand at the doore, and knocke: if any man heare my voyce, and open the doore, I will come in to him (Rev. 3:20)"—but the speaker insists that God must break down his door. Or, God customarily gives his spirit to men by breathing upon them—at the creation to give life to Adam, in the upper room to give the Holy Spirit to the Apostles—but this speaker would have God blow upon him more fiercely. Likewise, God's people pray constantly that his face may shine upon them in blessing, but this speaker demands not shining but burning. Mere mending will not suffice to his regeneration: he must be made new by violence. The need for such violence is argued from his present situation, resembling a usurped town or a seduced spouse in the possession of an enemy. The speaker insists that his release must be worked by force, in paradoxical reversal of Christ's customary relationships with the soul—as liberator ("Stand fast therefore in the libertie wherewith Christ hath made us free, and bee not intangled againe with the yoke of bondage") and as Bridegroom:

> Take mee to you, imprison mee, for I
> Except you'enthrall me, never shall be free,
> Nor ever chast, except you ravish mee.

The Calvinist sense of man's utter helplessness in his corruption and total dependence upon God's grace in every aspect of his spiritual life could hardly find more powerful and paradoxical expression than in this declaration that Christ can be liberator of the soul only by becoming its jailer, and can be its Bridegroom only by becoming its ravisher.

The last two sonnets of the 1635 (and 1633) sequences focus upon the further ramifications of justification and regeneration. **"Sonnet XV," "Wilt thou love God, as he thee!"** invites the soul to meditate upon God's love shown especially in the matter of the speaker's adoption as a son of God. In the Calvinist paradigm adoption is the result of justification: it gives the believer Christian peace of mind and confidence that he is again a child of God, to whom the promise pertains, "And if children, then heires, heires of God, and joynt-heires [co-heires, Rheims] with Christ . . . that wee may be also glorified together (Rom. 8:17)." The speaker exhibits the confidence attendant upon adoption, and reviews all its benefits to himself, attributed variously to the three persons of the Trinity: "the Spirit . . . doth make his Temple in thy brest"; "The Father . . . / Hath deign'd to chuse thee by adoption, / Coheire to'his glory,'and Sabbaths endlesse rest"; the Son has achieved thy release from bondage, "unbinding" thee from Satan. The most spectacular evidence and cause of adoption is the Incarnation: "'Twas much, that man was made like God before, / But, that God should be made like man, much more."

The final sonnet in both the 1633 and 1635 sequences, "Father, part of his double interest," takes up the issue of how the regenerate Christian should serve God, how he should exhibit that "new obedience" to God's will that was understood to be the effect of regeneration and adop-

tion—especially in view of the Pauline/Protestant insistence that none can fulfill the Law laid down by God in the commandments. The speaker, conscious of the "interest" given him in the kingdom by his adoption, confronts the knotty issue of how to lay claim to his inheritance. Referring to the "two Wills" (the Old and New Testaments) wherein God has set out the terms of that inheritance, and recognizing that "None doth" fulfill the commandments of the Law, he appeals to the nature and the effects of the New Covenant: "all-healing grace and Spirit, / Revive againe what law and letter kill." These lines echo a medley of Pauline texts: "no man is justified by the Lawe in the sight of God"; "God / . . . hath made us able ministers of the New Testament, not of the letter, but of the spirit: for the letter killeth, but the spirit giveth life." The speaker finds his resolution in recalling that the New Covenant Law, the summary and epitome of the Old Law, is simply love of God and neighbor: "Thy lawes abridgement, and thy last command / Is all but love; Oh let that last Will stand!"

The remaining three sonnets from the Westmoreland manuscript are more strictly occasional pieces, all of them concerned with one or another of the exigencies of the regenerate Christian life. **"Sonnet XVII," "Since she whome I lovd, hath payd her last debt,"** must have been written after the death of Ann Donne (August 15, 1617). In it the speaker adopts a Platonic doctrine, viewing his love for his wife as the means which led him to seek God, "so streames do shew the head." Now he seeks God's love alone, but is still unsatisfied—"A holy thirsty dropsy melts mee yett." In the sestet, however, he admits that he has no grounds for complaint: God has offered all his own love in exchange for his wife's, and has every reason to be jealous of the speaker's propensity to give his love to others—not only to holy beings (angels, saints, his wife) but even to the world, the flesh, and the devil. The sonnet, especially its conclusion, seems less unified and effective than is usual with Donne.

"Sonnet XVIII," "Show me deare Christ, thy spouse," might have been conceived as a sequel to the above, moving from the speaker's love of his own spouse to his love of Christ's Spouse, the Church; as Ricks notes, we can read with the emphasis, "Show me deare Christ, *thy* spouse." The octave centers upon the problem of identifying that Spouse: one claimant is "richly painted" (Rome); another is "rob'd and tore" (the Reformed Church), and they are variously located "On one, on seaven, or on no hill." Their counterclaims are fraught with paradox: "Sleepes she a thousand, then peepes up one yeare? / Is she selfe truth and errs? now new, now outwore?" The resolution to these baffling paradoxes must rest with Christ's contriving a still more amazing and outrageous paradox. Christ must from Bridegroom turn pander, and so "Betray" his Spouse to the loves of others. And the Spouse, rather than exhibiting the undefiled purity of the Bride of Canticles and of Revelation, must in the necessary promiscuity of her love to many, turn harlot:

> Betray kind husband thy spouse to our sights,
> And let myne amorous soule court thy mild
>   Dove,
> Who is most trew, and pleasing to thee, then

When she'is embrac'd and open to most men.

Surely no one but Donne would so wittily seem to confuse the Bride with her antithesis in Revelation, the Great Whore of Babylon (Rev. 17:4-18), playing upon the contemporary Protestant term of opprobrium for Rome to point up the essential spiritual qualities God's church must display.

"Sonnet XIX," "Oh, to vex me, contraryes meete in one," could relate to virtually any stage of the Christian saga of regeneration, but it stands as a fitting summary of the vacillations and vicissitudes of the speaker's spiritual life. His changeable vows, his "humorous" contrition, his ague-like fits of devotion, his alterations between courting God in flattering speeches and quaking in "true feare of his rod" describe the varying moods of these sonnets and are a personal version of that perpetual internal warfare Paul describes, between the old man and the new, the body and the spirit. Donne's speaker does not cry as Paul does for deliverance—"Oh wretched man that I am: who shall deliver me from the body of this death?" (Rom. 7:24). Instead, like David the Psalmist, he perceives the special acceptability of a "broken and a contrite heart" and so prefers his agitated emotional state to complacency. His "true feare" may also partake of the quality praised in Job 28:28—"The feare of the Lord, that is wisdome"—affording sound theological basis for his paradoxical conclusion, "Those are my best dayes, when I shake with feare." The wit of these sonnets, though often very daring, is almost always in the service of serious theological analysis and profound emotional responses.

A few of Donne's *Divine Poems* in the genre of the verse letter testify explicitly to Donne's developing engagement with some of the issues important in Protestant poetics. The dedicatory sonnet to Magdalen Herbert, which probably accompanied the **"La Corona"** sequence, gives early evidence of such engagement, as much by the devices not used as by those employed. There is no sign here of the ubiquitous tears and passionate laments accompanying the Magdalen's dramatic conversion from harlot to penitent which was the topic of so much Counter Reformation art and poetry. Donne's poem is restrained and biblical; it holds the Magdalen forth not as a saint of penitence but as an exponent of the Protestant virtue of "active faith" (l. 3), in that, being made a herald of the Resurrection, she for a time knew more of Christianity than the Church itself. The verse letter **"To Mr. Tilman after he had taken orders,"** probably written after Tilman was ordained priest in March, 1620, is a thoughtful, restrained, and quite effective defense of the ministry as a noble calling; as several critics have noted, Donne's strongly urged complaints against the worldly gentry for their social discrimination against ministers says much more about Donne's own ambivalences in embracing that life than Tilman's. The defense is in distinctly Protestant terms: the speaker assumes that orders have somehow changed Tilman but he does not put his queries about such changes in sacramental terms, nor does he discuss the sacerdotal or even the liturgical functions of a priest. Instead the focus is upon preaching as the essence and the glory of the ministerial office: ministers, like angels, "beare Gods message, and proclaime his lawes" (l. 20). (pp. 266-75)

The finest flowering of Donne's growing commitment to . . . Protestant poetic concerns appears in the *Holy Sonnets,* in **"Goodfriday, 1613. Riding Westward,"** in the **"Hymne to Christ,"** and in the **"Hymne to God my God, in my sicknesse."** These last three poems have close generic affinities to Protestant occasional meditation upon experience. As developed by Joseph Hall, Richard Rogers, and Donne himself in his *Devotions upon Emergent Occasions,* such exercises explore the providential significance of a particular event or experience in the individual's life, usually in relation to a theological or biblical paradigm. Though the poems show the impress of such influences, they are among Donne's most magnificent and most original achievements.

Louis Martz considers **"Goodfriday, 1613"** to be a classic Ignatian meditation—the extended comparison in the opening lines presenting the preparatory stage; the long central section constituting an intellectual analysis of the crucifixion in terms of its manifold paradoxes; and the final lines containing a heartfelt colloquy or prayer to Christ emerging from the meditative exercise. Modifying this scheme, A. B. Chambers and Donald M. Friedman have usefully highlighted the poem's drama, in the course of which the speaker is led to correct an initial mistake. Chambers finds that mistake in the speaker's erroneous application of the analogy of the spheres with which the poem begins, in that, contradicting the traditional association of the western movement of the spheres with reason and the countermovement with irrationality, he assumes that his western direction is wrong and longs to make an immediate, irrational journey eastward. The rest of the poem corrects the error, as he learns that he does still "see" the crucifixion in memory; that such devotion is the business of a lifetime, not one day only; and that since west and east meet, the movement west will lead him to the east. Friedman finds an even more dramatic development, wherein a "naive" narrator begins with his spheres analogy as a facile excuse for failing to encounter the crucifixion, proceeds to the rather superficial repetition of pious paradoxes about it, but is finally led to an agonized confrontation, growing from the realization of his own inescapable implication in that crucifixion through his sins. Such dramatic emphasis unlocks much of the richness of the poem, but its special quality is perhaps best realized through consideration of the fusion of meditation and drama which Protestant occasional meditation encouraged and which Donne so brilliantly exploits.

The poem's primary subject is the speaker's failure to conduct a traditional "deliberate" Good Friday meditation because of an "emergent occasion" of business or pleasure which takes him away from what should be his devotional center of attention on this day, Jerusalem and Calvary. The somewhat facile opening analogy is not a preparation for a meditation so much as an explanation, by reference to the two distinct forces moving a sphere (its own intelligence and "forraigne motions"), as to why the expected deliberate meditation will not take place: "Hence is't, that I am carried towards the West / This day, when my Soules forme bends toward the East" (ll. 9-10). But the speaker does attempt to come to terms with the occasion of his apparent failure in proper religious devotion, and the poem becomes an occasional meditation on this circumstance. The second section resembles the analytic stage of an Ignatian meditation on the crucifixion in its review of the traditional paradoxes associated with Christ's death: "a Sunne, by rising set, / And by that setting endlesse day beget"; God dying "that is selfe life"; the hands that tune the spheres pierced with holes. But the speaker's paradoxical situation remains the true focus, for all these meditative paradoxes are controlled by a negative: though he should "see" (i.e., meditate upon) these things on this day, in fact he will not because his own occasions take him elsewhere. As he reviews these paradoxes the speaker responds with growing intensity to Christ and Mary, and to the recognition of his own sin as cause of the crucifixion, but still he does not, cannot, come to terms with the event and is almost glad that his occasions supply some color of an excuse: "Yet dare I'almost be glad, I do not see / That spectacle of too much weight for mee" (ll. 15-16).

The third section, appropriately, is not the colloquy of a meditation on the crucifixion, but the resolution of the problem posed by the occasion—the fact that the speaker has apparently turned his back on Calvary. That resolution does not, I believe, reside in the final identity of West and East: the speaker must finally "turne my face" rather than recognize that his journey has taken him to the right place after all. A first and partial resolution is supplied by memory: "Though these things, as I ride, be from mine eye, / They'are present yet unto my memory, / For that looks towards them" (ll. 33-35)—as indeed we have just seen in the speaker's review of what he should be visualizing and meditating upon. But the more adequate resolution grows out of the very position he has found himself in on this occasion, which he now sees to be providential and instructive for him: it signifies that God must initiate his renovation before he can make the appropriate meditative response. The imagined scene the speaker depicts of Christ looking toward his back and laying on "Corrections" to purge his deformities makes of his particular circumstance an emblem, recalling plates in Hugo and Quarles in which Divine Love lashes Anima across the back as she grinds in a mill. Donne's speaker has created his own emblem on similar lines with himself as central figure, his body turned away from the crucifixion scene but with back bared to Christ on the cross to receive "Corrections":

> . . . thou look'st towards mee,
> O Saviour, as thou hang'st upon the tree;
> I turne my backe to thee, but to receive
> Corrections, till thy mercies bid thee leave.
> O thinke mee worth thine anger, punish mee,
> Burne off my rusts, and my deformity,
> Restore thine Image, so much, by thy grace,
> That thou may'st know mee, and I'll turne my
>   face.
>   (ll. 35-42)

The **"Hymne to Christ, at the Authors last going into Germany"** is a deeply felt, and very great poem. The **"Hymne"** title is appropriate in that the stanzaic regularity and refrain-like close of each stanza are suggestive of the simple congregational hymn or anthem, though there is no record of a setting for it. In essence, however, this poem is an occasional meditation; as the title also indicates, it was composed in 1619 when Donne went to Germany as chaplain to the Earl of Doncaster's diplomatic mission. In the first stanza the speaker invests this occasion with complex emblematic and typological significance:

> In what torne ship soever I embarke,
> That ship shall be my embleme of thy Arke;
> What sea soever swallow mee, that flood
> Shall be to mee an embleme of thy blood;
> Though thou with clouds of anger do disguise
> Thy face; yet through that maske I know those
>   eyes,
>   Which, though they turne away sometimes,
>   They never will despise.
>   (ll. 1-8)

Donne here adapts a common emblem to his own purposes: his own ship becomes a tempest-tossed, flood-threatened vessel on the storm-wracked sea of life, recalling very similar emblem figures and explications in Montenay and Hulsius. In Donne's poem the Ark reference also has complex typological significance: his speaker imagines himself a new Noah about to experience a new Flood in a new Ark. Moreover, he recognizes himself as antitype of Noah, in that for him the figures will have New Testament significance. His flood will be an emblem of the first Flood's antitype, Christ's blood, and his ship will be (like the Ark's antitype, the Church) a vehicle of spiritual salvation, in that it will promote his personal spiritual growth by separating him from his familiar world. That personal world is not wicked or accursed as was the world from which Noah was saved by the Ark or mankind by the Church; but it is full of distractions from the love of God—fame, wit, other loves, other hopes. By sacrificing that world, divorcing it through this sea voyage, the speaker can center his love on God only, and so be more surely saved. The emblematic sea voyage with its dangers, its relinquishment of the world, and its exclusive search for God also takes on the character of a voyage to death undertaken in the "winter" of life, and finally signifies escape from the storms of life into eternity: "To see God only, I goe out of sight: / And to scape stormy dayes, I chuse / An Everlasting night" (ll. 30-32).

The **"Hymne to God my God, in my sicknesse"** is perhaps Donne's most brilliant and most moving religious poem. It has been much commented on, and much admired, though without full consideration of the way in which genre theory and typology contribute to its stunning effect. Obviously, it is an occasional meditation upon a personal and significant event, an illness expected to be terminal—probably that of 1623 and just possibly Donne's last illness in 1631. The title **"Hymne"** is a deliberate misnomer: the poem is neither a congregational anthem nor yet a lofty hymn of praise, and indeed the argument of the poem proceeds to redefine its genre by indicating heaven as the true ambience of the hymn of praise.

To begin with, the imagery of music suggests preparation for the **"Hymne"** of the title. The speaker on his supposed deathbed sees himself about to arrive where he will not only make music in the heavenly choir but will himself be music—part of the heavenly harmony. Therefore he does not sing now: he proposes instead to "tune the Instrument here at the dore" and this tuning involves not song but thought, meditation: "And what I must doe then, thinke now before" (ll. 4-5). Most of the poem is given over to this meditative tuning, during which the speaker transforms his imagined death scene (as later he will transform his actual death) into an emblem, a kind of anatomy lesson with the physicians poring over him like cartographers reading a map. He likens the circumstances of his illness to the circumstances of geographical exploration—" . . . this is my South-west discoverie / *Per fretum febris,* by these streights to die" (ll. 9-10). And this resemblance affords some hopeful analogues for his situation: as he is now a flat map in which the farthest west and east meet, "So death doth touch the Resurrection" (l. 15); moreover, his own "straits" of fever remind him that all the traditional locales for Paradise may be reached only through straits.

At this point he complicates the emblematic allegorical deathbed scene he has created with typological symbolism. Both Old Testament type and New Testament antitype are now seen to be embodied in him, as he finds himself to be the stage for the entire typological drama. Beginning from the geographical legend that Paradise and Calvary, Adam's tree and Christ's cross stood on the same site, the speaker discovers that this site is his dying self on his own deathbed, since now in one moment he suffers the death due to the sin of the first Adam, and experiences the conquest over death of the Second Adam:

> Looke Lord, and finde both *Adams* met in me;
> As the first *Adams* sweat surrounds my face,
> May the last *Adams* blood my soule embrace.
> (ll. 23-25)

Indeed, ambiguous pointing actually invites a fusion of the speaker and the Second Adam. In the line, "So, in his purple wrapp'd receive mee Lord" (l. 26), he at once petitions God for his salvation through Christ's blood, and declares confidently his own regal rights. Then the poem achieves its third and final generic identification: it is declared to be a sermon preached to the self on a text set forth formally, and wittily, as the final line of the poem—rather than at the outset, as we would expect of a sermon:

> And as to others soules I preach'd thy word,
> Be this my Text, my Sermon to mine owne,
> Therfore that he may raise the Lord throws
> down.

The speaker has, as it were, only realized as he completed the meditation that it was also a sermon upon a text God had provided, namely, the illness which brought him low but from which his resurrection is assured. This identification plays upon the near-affinity of sermon and meditation in Protestant theory. The poem, then, is an occasional meditation-cum-sermon, which provides the tuning necessary for the singing of true hymns, a genre Donne now identifies with the sublime praises of the choir of saints, and will not attempt to sing on earth.

Donne is the first major English poet in the devotional mode whose lyrics are influenced by a distinctive Protestant poetics. Though he is in some sense a transition fig-

ure, in that his earlier poems display liturgical and Counter Reformation influences, the later and finer poems are strongly imbued with characteristic Pauline themes, biblical allusions, Protestant meditative modes, and above all, the characteristic Protestant "application to the self" of typological, meditative, and emblematic patterns. Donne's poetic *œuvre* also displays a growing consciousness and self-consciousness about the uses of biblical models (the Psalms, Lamentations), and about the kind of art appropriate and possible to the religious poet. These concerns find their most complete articulation in Donne's sermons and **Devotions,** which contributed largely to the evolution of a body of Protestant theory on these issues. That theory, which informs many of Donne's poems, is grounded upon the proposition that the divine poet not only may but must imitate God's own method of creation, which, both in nature and in scripture, is supremely witty and artful and self-conscious. The divine poet's model is therefore the Bible, but the nature of that book is such that it stimulates, rather than restricts, his highest flights. The pillars of Donne's biblical, Protestant poetics are: that the scriptures are the most eloquent books in the world, that God is a witty and also "a figurative, a metaphoricall God," and that the religious lyric poet should endeavor to "write after . . . [his] *Copie.*" (pp. 277-82)

> *Barbara Kiefer Lewalski, "John Donne: Writing after the Copy of a Metaphorical God," in her* Protestant Poetics and the Seventeenth-Century Religious Lyric, *Princeton University Press, 1979, pp. 253-82.*

Camille Wells Slights   (essay date 1981)

[*Below, Slights examines Donne's use of religious casuistry not only in* Pseudo Martyr *and* Biathanatos, *but also in his secular* Songs and Sonnets.]

John Donne's interest in casuistry is well documented. His prose is sprinkled with references to such contemporary casuists as Juan Azor, Ludovico Carbo, and Robert Sayr, and, according to Izaak Walton [in his "The Life of Dr. John Donne" in *Lives,* 1927], he answered Thomas Morton's urging that he take holy orders with an appeal to the judgment of "the best of *Casuists*":

> . . . that *Gods Glory should be the first end, and a maintenance the second motive to embrace that calling;* and though each man may propose to himself both together; yet the first may not be put last without a violation of Conscience, which he that searches the heart will judge. And truly my present condition is such, that if I ask my own Conscience, whether it be reconcileable to that rule, it is at this time so perplexed about it, that I can neither give my self nor you an answer. You know, Sir, who sayes, *Happy is that man whose Conscience doth not accuse him for that thing which he does.*

In addition to studying the body of Roman Catholic casuistry and meeting personal crisis with casuistry, Donne wrote a collection of case. Walton testifies that Donne was in the habit of keeping his own solutions "of divers Letters and cases of Conscience that had concerned his friends," and Donne twice refers to a book of cases of conscience. Although this putative volume of cases has been lost, two surviving works, **Biathanatos** and **Pseudo-Martyr,** are in the casuistical tradition. Moreover, since the habit of mind with which Donne devoured contemporary theology and resolved cases of conscience also finds expression in his poems, his relation to the casuistical tradition provides an illuminating context for his poetry.

Besides maintaining the casuists' assumption that the individual conscience is the center of man's moral life, Donne also shared their absorption in the doubts and problems resulting from the conjunction of moral absolutes with the immediate circumstances of personal experience. In terms resembling Sanderson's warning that *"a mathematical certitude,* which is manifest by Demonstration, and impossible to be false, is in vain to be expected in *morals,"* Donne records his understanding of the problematical nature of experience: "Except demonstrations (and perchance there are very few of them) I find nothing without perplexities" [in Edmund Gosse, *The Life and Letters of John Donne,* 1899]. This vision of complexity, moreover, leads to positive emphasis on rigorous intellectual effort:

> To come to a doubt, and to a debatement in any religious duty, is the voyce of God in our conscience: Would you know the truth? Doubt, and then you will inquire: And *facile solutionem accipit anima, quae prius dubitavit,* sayes S. Chrysostome.

The attraction of intellectual inquiry, with its emphases on logical procedures, fine distinctions, and abstruse knowledge, does not absorb Donne either in the intricacies of doctrinal disputes or in incommunicable mystical experience. Rather, as poet and preacher, he insists on applying the truths the mind perceives to the practical difficulties of daily life. His exhortation to express knowledge of God in holy living could serve well as a motto for casuistry: "let us make *Ex scientia conscientiam,* Enlarge science into conscience: for, *Conscientia est Syllogismus practicus,* Conscience is a Syllogisme that comes to a conclusion" (**Sermons,** IX).

Throughout his life, Donne was intrigued with casuists' attempts to untangle knotty problems of conscience. He refers to their classification of kinds of conscience in an early letter (Gosse) and later, in one of his sermons, he explains the kinds of conscience and advises consulting a casuist in doubtful cases (**Sermons,** IV). In his sermons, he generally avoids detailed discussion of controversial religious and political cases, but he acknowledges their existence and attempts to teach his parishioners the general principles by which they can be solved. For example, this advice:

> Howsoever the affections of men, or the vicissitudes and changes of affairs may vary, or apply those two great axiomes, and aphorisms of ancient Rome, *Salus populi suprema lex esto,* The good of the people is above all Law, and then, *Quod Principi placet, lex esto,* The Pleasure of the Prince is above all Law, howsoever I say, various occasions may vary their Laws, adhere we to that Rule of the Law, which the Apostle prescribes, that we always make *Finem praecepti*

> *charitatem, The end of the Commandement charity.* (**Sermons,** III)

Donne devoted one sermon at least to a detailed discussion of what Geoffrey Bullough calls "one of those cases of conscience dear to Donne's heart." In a sermon on Esther 4:16, Donne uses the procedures of English case divinity to analyze what Esther did "in a perplexed and scrupulous case" (**Sermons,** V). He carefully sets up the problem, explaining the ethical questions that create doubt. When Esther learned that Haman had the king's permission to destroy the Jews, she went to the king, her husband, to plead that he save her people, in spite of the king's edict that no one enter his presence unsummoned on penalty of death. Donne emphasizes the difficulties that the decision to disobey the king presents:

> There is in every Humane Law, part of the Law of God, which is obedience to the Superior. That Man cannot binde the conscience, because he cannot judge the conscience, nor he cannot absolve the conscience, may be a good argument; but in Laws made by that power which is ordained by God, man bindes not, but God himself: And then you must be subject, not because of wrath, but because of conscience. . . . In all true Laws God hath his interest; and the observing of them in that respect, as made by his authority, is an act of worship and obedience to him; and the transgressing of them, with that relation, that is, a resisting or undervaluing of that authority, is certainly sinne. How then was Esthers act exempt from this? for she went directly against a direct Law, *That none should come to the King uncalled.* (**Sermons,** V)

In addition, by willingly risking death, Esther neglected the natural law of self-preservation.

Donne resolves these doubts and defends the rightness of Esther's decision on the basis of the casuistical concepts of the hierarchical nature of law, the intention of the law, and the significance of particular circumstances. "Whensoever divers Laws concur and meet together," he explains,

> that Law which comes from the superior Magistrate, and is in the nature of the thing commanded, highest too, that Law must prevail. If two Laws lie upon me, and it be impossible to obey both, I must obey that which comes immediately from the greatest power, and imposes the greatest duty. (**Sermons,** V)

Esther was bound by the king's law and also by "the fix'd and permanent Law, of promoting Gods glory." She would not have been justified in breaking a positive law on pretense of fulfilling her duty to God, Donne cautions, unless her conscience was completely satisfied that she was not violating the intention of the law. She considered carefully the purpose of the law, the exceptions mentioned in the body of the law, the imminence of the danger, and her relationship to the king. On the basis of these circumstances, she concluded that the law "intended only for the Kings ease, or his state, reached not to her person, who was his wife, nor to her case, which was the destruction of all that professed her Religion" (*Sermons*, V). Only then did she

> come to that, which onely can excuse and justifie the breaking of any Law, that is, a probable, if not a certain assurance, contracted *Bona fide,* in rectified conscience, That if this present case, which makes us break this Law, had been known and considered when the Law was made, he that made the Law would have made provision for this case. (*Sermons*, V)

Similarly, Donne justifies Esther's exposing herself to danger on the grounds of a higher duty and of attendant circumstances. She "was under two Laws, of which it was necessary to obey that which concerned the glory of God" (*Sermons*, V). She did not risk her life in a spirit of pride and reckless abandon but with humility and hope, prepared with prayer and fasting.

Donne's sermon on Esther 4:16, then, uses the tools of casuistry to provide a model of "what every Christian Soul ought to do, when it is surprised and overtaken with any such scruples or difficulties to the Conscience" (*Sermons*, V). This casuistical purpose and method, however, is unique among Donne's sermons. Although one could gather enough relevant passages from the sermons to construct a fairly comprehensive description of his theory of casuistry, the sermons, for all their learning and wit, are primarily directed to move the apostate will, not to enlighten the conscience. Donne's interest in the problems and methods of casuistry is more central to *Biathanatos* and *Pseudo-Martyr*, which are both extended discussions of traditional cases of conscience.

Biathanatos, Donne's demonstration that "Self-homicide is not so naturally Sin, that it may never be otherwise," clearly belongs to the body of casuistical literature, but just how it fits into that tradition is puzzling. Scholars have treated it variously as a bold challenge to traditional Christian thought, as a conventional case of conscience, and as a parody of casuistical reasoning and cases of conscience.

The question of whether causing one's own death is justified in any circumstances is a standard problem in casuistry, and Donne handles the problem with traditional casuistical methods, examining the doubtful action in relation to natural law, positive law, and divine law. He grants that natural law, man's knowledge as a rational being that he should avoid evil and seek good, ordinarily forbids suicide. But, he argues, since any law binds according to its intention, the "reason upon which it was founded," and binds only "so long as the reason lives," the natural law of self-preservation ceases to bind when man intends a greater good through his death.

His demonstration that human law does not make self-homicide wrong in all circumstances is similar. Acknowledging that civil legislation prohibits suicide, he argues that any human law may be broken when it conflicts with a higher law. Thus, although a man cannot lawfully kill himself to secure any physical or spiritual good for himself (for example, release from suffering or avoidance of temptation), he may take his own life when he intends "only or primarily the glory of God."

The strongest prohibition against self-homicide is divine law as set forth in scripture: Thou shalt not kill. Again, Donne argues that the general law does not apply in all circumstances and that the higher must take precedence over the lesser good. For example,

> If perchance a publique exemplary person, which had a just assurance that his example would governe the people, should be forced by a Tyrant, to doe an act of Idolatry, (although by circumstances he might satisfie his owne conscience, that he sinned not in doing it,) and so scandalize and endanger them, if the matter were so carried and disguised, that by no way he could let them know, that he did it by constraint, but [not?] voluntarily, I say, perchance he were better kill himselfe.

While this brief summary indicates Donne's debt to traditional casuistry, it overstates the argument for *Biathanatos* as an orthodox case of conscience. Donne explicitly criticizes the casuistical approach. He condemns the tortuous legalism of casuists "applying rules of Divinitie to particular cases: by which they have made all our actions perplex'd and litigious." In the Preface, he acknowledges that he has encumbered his prose with lengthy discussions of others' opinions and defends this "multiplicity of not necessary citations" as standard practice: "I did it the rather because scholastique and artificiall men use this way of instructing; and I made account that I was to deale with such." Indeed, Donne adopts the external characteristics of these "scholastique and artificiall men" with such zeal and with so little apparent connection with his actual reasoning process that he seems to be mocking the intricate legalism of the casuists. His prose is divided into numbered sections, his sentences are often compressed syllogisms, and logical connectives such as "therefore," "so," "for," and "since" are frequent. But the divisions and subdivisions in the text do not always correlate with the development of the argument, the logical steps do not appear in orderly sequence, and the argument itself seems in danger of collapsing under the weight of the lengthy citations of authorities and of the numerous and frequently bizarre examples. For example, since Donne argues that self-preservation, "the foundation of generall naturall Law," is simply man's innate preference for good and may admit of desiring death in certain circumstances, his long proof that suicide is common and therefore natural seems irrelevant, and such examples as "*Hippionas* the Poet rimed *Bubalus* the Painter to death with his Iambiques" appear as tongue-in-cheek spoofs of the legalistic marshaling of evidence.

The simultaneous use and mockery of the tools of casuistry reflect Donne's ambivalence toward contemporary Roman Catholic casuistry. Although he frequently cites casuists approvingly, Donne explicitly condemns the casuistical doctrine of probabilism as encouraging intellectual apathy and hypocrisy:

> . . . so many doctrines have grown to be the ordinary diet and food of our spirits, and have place in the pap of catechisms, which were admitted but as physic in that present distemper, or accepted in a lazy weariness, when men so

they might have something to rely upon, and to excuse themselves from more painful inquisition, never examined what that was. To which indisposition of ours the casuists are so indulgent, as that they allow a conscience to adhere to any probable opinion against a more probable, and do never bind him to seek out which is more probable, but give him leave to dissemble it and to depart from it, if by mischance he come to know it.

A. E. Malloch [in his "John Donne and the Casuists," *Studies in English Literature*, 1962] has shown that Donne's fundamental objection was to the probabalists' externalization of moral choice. While Donne believed that right action is necessarily based on personal assent, probabilism rests on the assumption that moral judgment can be made with reference to an external body of opinion and need not issue from personal conviction. Counter-Reformation casuistry, which separated lawful action from individual judgment, was quantitative and external, as Malloch explains:

> It claims in its treaties to be comprehensive, but it seeks comprehensiveness through a multiplying of the individual cases of conscience discussed. It copes with the variety and complexity of human existence not by speaking to the individual person and directing him how to proceed to moral judgment in whatever situation engages him, but by attempting to register and analyze as many "cases" (i.e., combination of circumstances) as possible. In this tendency we can again see moral action drawn out from the world of the self and reconstituted in a non-personal world where cases and their attendant probable opinions are multiplied almost indefinitely.

Donne, Malloch concludes, "insists that moral action must proceed from an assent of the self and yet he toys constantly with a literature of casuistry which sets moral action within a legal arena and allows little room for the self."

In *Biathanatos*, Donne's distrust of the externality of Roman Catholic casuistry takes two forms. He warns his readers directly against relying on authorities: "trust neither me, nor the adverse part, but the Reasons". He argues that one discovers what he should do in any particular situation through reason, not through the mechanical application of rules, and he insists on the inviolability of the individual conscience. Indirectly, he satirizes the legalism of the casuists by parodying their elaborate schemes for categorizing particular actions and their multiple citations of authorities and precedents. This combination of serious moral analysis with satire of an inadequate casuistical method is not wholly successful, in spite of Donne's acute grasp of casuistical procedures and his considerable satiric skill, because his central argument relies too heavily on the methods he condemns.

In *Biathanatos*, Donne's failure to distinguish his own casuistical method from the object of his satire is not the inevitable result of his ambivalence toward Roman Catholic casuistry. As Barbara Lewalski has demonstrated, the traditions of English Protestantism are generally more helpful in elucidating Donne than continental Roman Catho-

lic thought, and English Protestant casuistry departs from that of the Counter-Reformation along lines remarkably similar to those that Donne suggests. As we have seen, Jeremy Taylor also condemns Roman Catholic casuistry for its hair-splitting intellectuality and for its too accommodating morality. Like Donne, Taylor traces these weaknesses to probabilism, "the foundation on which their doctors of conscience rely," and insists that one must accept and act on the most probable conclusion.

Although the published casuistry that Donne knew was Roman Catholic, Malloch is wrong, I believe, in suggesting that Protestant casuistry cannot illuminate Donne's casuistry because it "avoided the legal complexity and the precision which seem for Donne to have been the fascinations of casuistry." Legal complexity and precision are essential to any casuistry, as Sanderson's cases and Taylor's *Ductor Dubitantium,* as well as Juan Azor's *Institutiones morales* will attest. Protestant casuists, who rejected probabilism for probabiliorism and insisted on the full assent of the self in right action, tried to show men how to proceed in their own moral dilemmas by stressing their reasoning process instead of by citing authorities. They presented individual cases not in an attempt to be comprehensive but in order to provide models of the process by which moral law can be applied to individual cases rooted in the unique circumstances of one particular moment in history. This emphasis does not relieve men of the intellectual effort to make fine distinctions among varying combinations of circumstances and to understand the complexities of moral law.

Donne's sermon on Esther's decision enunciates casuistical principles and resolves a case of conscience with logical clarity in a way similar to other Protestant casuists. But in *Biathanatos,* Donne does not construct a model case, nor does he systematically clarify the principles by which such a case can be solved. He relies instead on the methods of the despised probabilists, building his argument in terms of the body of opinion on the subject. The satiric impulse is inadequately integrated with the central intention of the work not because of Donne's ambivalence about the casuistical use of right reason in resolving moral dilemmas but because he was unable to resolve his ambivalence about the lawfulness of suicide.

What he really demonstrates with logical consistency is the orthodox casuistical judgment that, in certain circumstances—those of Christian martyrs, for example—causing one's own death is lawful and virtuous. Joseph Hall mentions such cases of legitimate self-homicide as dying to protect the sovereign's life, relinquishing the only plank to another survivor of a shipwreck, and those "infinite examples of deadly sufferings for good causes, willingly embraced for conscience' sake." The concrete cases Donne fully approves are similar. He cites the death of Samson:

> A man so exemplar, that not onely the times before him had him in Prophecy, (for of him it is said,) [*Dan shall judge his people,*] and the times after him more consummately in Christ, of whom he was a Figure, but even in his own time, other nations may seeme to have had some Type, or Copy of him, in *Hercules.*

And he adds,

> That hee intended not his owne death principal-
> ly, but accidentally . . . can remove no man
> from our side; for wee say the same, that this
> may be done onely, when the honour of God
> may bee promoved [sic] by that way, and no
> other.

But throughout *Biathanatos* there is the constant implication that Donne is justifying other kinds of suicide as well,
proving that there is nothing sinful in escaping the evils
of this world by fleeing to God with dispatch. The autobiographical remarks in the Preface suggest that his original
interest in the problem of self-homicide was of this sort:
"whensoever any affliction assailes me, mee thinks I have
the keyes of my prison in mine owne hand, and no remedy
presents it selfe so soone to my heart, as mine own sword."
By calling *Biathanatos* a paradox, Donne suggests that it
challenges conventional opinion, and modern readers usually interpret it as a defense against the orthodox condemnation of suicide.

The overall impression is that while Donne is strongly
compelled by the idea that man has within his power the
means to escape the pain of mortal existence and to find
eternal life he is simultaneously committed to the orthodox position that killing oneself to escape the burdens of
life is to despair of God and therefore is sinful. Because
this contradiction remains unresolved, Donne avoids
treating the personal problem directly, but it is always
there as a disrupting pressure on the logical consistency
of the argument. Thus, *Biathanatos* lacks the detailed attention to particular circumstances and rigorous distinctions evident in Donne's treatment of Esther's case of conscience. In the latter, he carefully explains that the principle by which honor to God takes precedence over human
law does not justify Puritan defiance of laws governing religious observances in England because the circumstances
differ. In *Biathanatos,* he declines to specify the kinds of
circumstances and conditions that make self-homicide
lawful:

> I abstained purposely from extending this dis-
> course to particular rules, or instances, both be-
> cause I dare not professe my self a Maister in so
> curious a science, and because the limits are ob-
> scure, and steepy, and slippery, and narrow, and
> every errour deadly, except where a competent
> dilligence being fore-used, a mistaking in our
> conscience may provide an excuse.

For all its intricacy, *Biathanatos* proceeds not by making,
but by blurring, distinctions. Donne, for example, offers
elaborate proof that we cannot judge whether suicide is
sinful because we cannot know other men's motives or
whether or not they are penitent. He argues for the ultimate identity of natural, positive, and divine law. Most
important, he obliterates the differences between wishes,
passive deeds, and direct action, so that the commonness
of the desire for death becomes proof of the compatibility
of suicide with natural law and so that the willingness to
risk death becomes equivalent to driving a knife through
one's heart. Donne concludes that we should be willing to
think about so complex a topic with open minds and that
we should be charitable to both the suicide and to those

who write books defending the suicidal act. But the constant blurring of distinctions and the repeated attacks on
the certainty of judgment have the further effect of suggesting the impossibility of clear perception or sure judgment by the individual conscience. Donne seems to be trying to establish some degree of probability for the lawfulness of suicide within the body of theological opinion rather than striving to provide the means for full assent by the
individual conscience. In this context, his attack on the externality of probabilistic casuistry weakens his argument;
satire becomes self-parody, and the case of conscience becomes paradox.

Pseudo-Martyr, probably written a year or so after *Biathanatos,* also deals with a recurrent casuistical problem.
Like Sanderson's "Ease of the Engagement," it attempts
to resolve the problems of conscience created by a loyalty
oath. After the discovery of the Gunpowder Plot, James
I imposed an Oath of Allegiance on all English Catholics
in order to make "a trew distinction betweene Papists of
quiet disposition, and in all other things good subjects, and
such other Papists as in their heartes maintained the like
violent bloody *Maximes,* that the Powder-Traitours did."
Initially many Catholics, including the archpriest George
Blackwell, complied, but the Pope subsequently issued
two breves condemning the oath. The Pope's prohibition
not only intensified the controversy between his Jesuit
supporters and several Catholic writers opposed to Papal
claims of temporal jurisdiction but it also created a moral
dilemma for many English Catholics. In *Pseudo-Martyr,*
Donne argues that English Catholics should take the Oath
of Allegiance to James I in spite of the Pope's prohibition
and that those who refuse the oath suffer not as Christian
martyrs but as disloyal subjects.

Pseudo-Martyr, then, is a political discussion carried on,
like most seventeenth-century political controversy, in
terms of conscience. Essentially Donne defends James's
position that it is improper for the Pope "to meddle betweene me and my Subjects, especially in matters that meere-
ly and onely concerne civill obedience," but Donne's casuistical habit of mind shapes his defense of the King's
rights in terms of the conscience of his Catholic subjects.
He violently attacks the leaders of the opposition to the
oath, the Jesuits, as:

> nourishing jelowsies in Princes, and contempt in
> Subjects, dissention in families, wrangling in
> Schooles, and mutinies in Armies; ruines of
> Noble houses, corruption of blood, confiscation
> of States, torturing of bodies, and anxious entan-
> gling and perplexing of consciences.

But he stresses his respect for the Roman Church, acknowledging it as for long "the head, that is, the *Principall*
and *most eminent, examplar member*" of the universal
Christian Church. He bases his argument against the temporal jurisdiction of the Pope, not on English law, but on
a detailed analysis of canon law and of the authority of
Papal breves, and he analyzes the wording of the oath to
show that it in no way "*violates the Popes spirituall Jurisdiction.*"

Donne's attitude toward casuistry is more straightforward
in *Pseudo-Martyr* than it is in *Biathanatos.* Again, he

both attacks and employs the methods of casuistry, but here he carefully distinguishes his own conception of the conscience from that of his adversaries. According to Donne, Jesuit casuistry incites men to suffer and die in a false martyrdom, but the roots of casuistry go deeper into Christian tradition than Jesuit sedition:

> For, their *Casuists,* which handle *Morall Divinitie,* and waigh and measure sinne (which for all that perplexitie and entangling, we may not condemne too hastily, since in purest Antiquitie there are lively impressions of such a custome in the Church, to examine with some curiositie the circumstances, by which sinnes were aggravated or diminished) . . . have filled their bookes with such questions as these, *How Princes have their jurisdiction, How they may become Tyrants, What is lawfull to a private man in such a case,* and of like seditious nature.

These casuists, he charges, instead of guiding and forming independent consciences, make endless rules that allow them to decide particular cases however they want. Thus they so obscure issues that in a particular case it is impossible to

> unentangle our consciences by any of those Rules, which their *Casuists* use to give, who to st[r]engthen the possession of the *Romane* Church, have bestowed more paines, to teach how strongly a conscience is bound to doe according to a *Scruple,* or a *Doubt,* or an *Opinion,* or an *Errour,* which it hath conceived, then how it might depose that *Scruple,* or cleare that *Doubt,* or better that *Opinion,* or rectifie that *Errour.*

He then sets out to show that, even according to their own rules of casuistry, taking the oath is lawful. The doctrine of probabilism, he argues, justifies taking the oath in spite of doubts or scruples:

> For when it comes to that, we shall finde it to be the *common* opinion of *Casuists,* which the same *Summist* [Ludovico Carbo] delivers, *That there is no matter so waighty, wherein it is not lawfull for me, to follow an opinion that is probable, though I leave the opinion which is more probable; yea though it concerne the right of another person:* as in our case of obedience to the *King* or the *Pope.* And then, wheresoever I may lawfully follow an opinion to mine advantage, if I will leave that opinion with danger of my life or notorious losse, I am guilty of all the damage I suffer. For these circumstances make that Necessary to me then, which was *indifferent* before: the reasons upon which *Carbo* builds this Doctrine of following a *probable* opinion, and leaving a more *probable,* which are, *That no man is bound, Ad melius & perfectius, by necessity, but as by Counsell:* And that this Doctrine hath this commoditie, *that it delivers godly men, from the care and solicitude, of searching out, which is the more probable opinion,* shew evidently, that these Rules give no infallible direction to the conscience, and yet in this matter of Obedience, considering the first native certaintie of subjection to the King, and then the damages by the refusall to sweare it, they encline much more to

Engraved title page of the first collection of Donne's sermons.

strengthen that civill obedience, then that other obedience which is plainly enough claimed, by this forbidding of the Oath.

While he is willing to construct this argument in the probabilists' terms, he is eager to distance himself from this kind of reasoning, and continues:

> So that in these perplexities, the *Casuists* are indeede, *Nubes Testium:* but not in that sense as the holy Ghost used the Metaphore. For they are such *clouds* of witnesses, as their testimonie obscures the whole matter. And they use to deliver no more, then may beget farther doubts, that so every man may from the *Oracle* of his *Confessors* resolution, receive such direction, as shall be fit at that time, when hee gives the aunswere.

In opposition to the intricate legalism that relieves man of the responsibility of searching out the truth and reduces him to dependence on his confessor's instructions, Donne's definition of conscience stresses the inseparability of knowledge and conscience, personal judgment and lawful action.

> Since the *conscience* is by *Aquinas* his definition, *Ordo scientiae ad aliquid,* and *an Act by which wee apply our knowledge to some particular thing,* the *Conscience* ever presumes *Knowledge:* and we may not, (especially in so great dangers

as these) doe any thing upon *Conscience,* if we doe it not upon *Knowledge.* For *it is not the Conscience itselfe that bindes us, but that law which the Conscience takes knowledge of, and presents to our understanding.*

His central argument is that men know on the basis of scripture and natural law that they owe obedience to their king, that searching examination of the oath and its political and religious context reveals nothing evil in the intention, matter, or consequences of the oath, and that therefore refusal to take the oath is sinful. Although Donne's demonstration that Roman Catholics might lawfully take the oath to a Protestant king is too complicated to treat adequately here, his primary strategy is to contrast the certain duty of civil obedience with the doubtful and debatable authority of Paul V's breves and of the Jesuit casuists' opinions. He consistently assumes that the *"Conscience,* which we must defend with our lives, must be grounded upon such things, as wee may, and doe not onely know, but know *how* we know them" and on this basis argues "That it is the *safest,* in both acceptations, both of *spirituall safety,* and *Temporall,* and in both *Tribunals,* as well of conscience, as of civill Justice, to take the Oath."

Pseudo-Martyr gives Donne's fullest exposition of his conception of casuistry and the most detailed application of these principles to a particular case. However, in spite of Donne's impressive analysis of the relevant ecclesiastical, political, and religious issues and of his sensitive understanding of the recusant conscience, *Pseudo-Martyr* is less engaging today than the casuistry of lesser writers. As a casuist, Donne is handicapped by his political position: he is not a priest advising his flock but rather an aspiring courtier supporting his king. He makes effective rhetorical use of the fact that he himself has gone through the process he advocates, surveying *"the whole body of Divinity, controverted betweene ours and the Romane Church"* before accepting the established Church of England. Still, this dual Roman Catholic and Anglican perspective prevents *Pseudo-Martyr* from having the economy and force that Sanderson's case achieves through the unrelenting drive of a single, logical progression. Donne's own position is that taking the Oath of Allegiance is a moral duty, but he spends much of *Pseudo-Martyr* merely trying to convince Catholic readers that taking the oath is not sinful. Because he concentrates on the legal complexities of one particular issue, his casuistry lacks the scope and general applicability of comprehensive discussions of principles like Taylor's and Baxter's. At the same time, by addressing himself variously to a heterogeneous audience whose assumptions differ from his own, he loses the implicit dramatic tension of cases of conscience addressing an individual problem and presenting a model of the decision-making process. (pp. 133-49)

Arguing correctly that the casuistical habit of mind need not be limited to religious subject matter, Dwight Cathcart [in his *Doubting Conscience: Donne and the Poetry of Moral Argument,* 1975] has investigated the broader implications of the casuistical tradition in Donne's *Songs and Sonnets,* showing how Donne's dual allegiance to the irreducible complexity of personal experience and to unified, harmonious truth from which moral certainty can be de-

rived parallels the casuists' attempts to bridge the gap between the unique particularity of individual experience and universal moral law. Cathcart demonstrates that much of the power of Donne's lyrics to disturb, excite, and delight comes from the speaker's assumption that truth is not self-evident and from his success in joining knowledge of universal law with knowledge of man's particular experience to discover truths about how to live that violate or transcend merely conventional morality and unthinking common sense. Cathcart overstates the case, however, when he claims that the "speaker is a doubting conscience" and that the "structure of the argument and the assumptions about truth and law and the resolution of doubt are the same in the cases of conscience and in the speaker's words in the *Songs and Sonnets.*"

In **"Womans Constancy,"** for example, Donne plays with sophistical arguments which plead that special circumstances create exceptions to moral law. When you break your promise and violate the law of fidelity, the speaker asks,

> Wilt thou then Antedate some new made vow?
>   Or say that now
> We are not just those persons, which we were?
> Or, that oathes made in reverentiall feare
> Of Love, and his wrath, any may forsweare?
> Or, as true deaths, true maryages untie,
> So lovers contracts, images of those,
> Binde but till sleep, deaths image, them unloose?
>   Or, your owne end to Justifie,
> For having purpos'd change, and falsehood; you
> Can have no way but falsehood to be true?
>   (Ll. 3-13)

But the poem does not exist for the sake of these parodies of casuistical reasoning; the parodies exist to dramatize the speaker's impudent cynicism. Characteristically Donne uses analysis and argument not to solve problems and to resolve doubt but to define and communicate emotion.

"Loves Growth" is typical. The poem opens with the speaker raising moral doubts about his own actions ("I scarce beleeve my love to be so pure / As I had thought it was . . . Me thinkes I lyed all winter, when I swore, / My love was infinite," ll. 1-2, 5-6) and ends with a promise to act well in the future ("No winter shall abate the springs encrease," l. 28). But while the opening lines seem to denigrate the speaker, the completion of the first sentence reveals that the problem Donne raises is not really about the quality of his love but about how to describe it accurately. His winter protestations of infinite love are called in doubt by its springtime growth.

> I scarce beleeve my love to be so pure
>   As I had thought it was
>   Because it doth endure
> Vicissitude, and season, as the grasse;
> Me thinkes I lyed all winter, when I swore,
> My love was infinite, if spring make'it more.
>   (Ll. 1-6)

The discrepancy between felt experience and verbal formulation creates doubt about the accuracy of traditional descriptions of love but not about the thing itself. While the casuist judges particular actions on the basis of general law, Donne judges general formulations against the authority of his own experience. The fact of his love's increase convinces him that Petrarchan attempts to limit love to an immutable, wholly spiritual union are misguided. Since the theory of love as pure essence has broken down, he poses an alternate theory.

> But if this medicine, love, which cures all sorrow
>   With more, not onely bee no quintessence,
>   But mixt of all stuffes, paining soule, or sense,
> And of the Sunne his working vigour borrow,
> Love's not so pure, and abstract, as they use
> To say, which have no Mistresse but their Muse,
>   But as all else, being elemented too,
>   Love sometimes would contemplate, sometimes
>   do.
>
> (Ll. 7-14)

Dissatisfied with his own description of love's mixed nature, in the second stanza, Donne qualifies his assertion that love, like everything else, is composed of various elements and thus capable of growth and action as well as of constancy and thought. The emotional experience he is trying to understand is not a matter of size or quantity but of perception.

> And yet not greater, but more eminent,
>   Love by the spring is growne;
>   As, in the firmament,
> Starres by the Sunne are not inlarg'd, but
>   showne.
>
> (Ll. 15-18)

But this image too is inadequate to capture the elusive sense that a love already strong and whole has grown, so he complements the idea of fuller manifestation with the idea of maturation.

> Gentle love deeds, as blossomes on a bough,
> From loves awaken'd root do bud out now.
>
> (Ll. 19-20)

While the blossom image corrects the static implications of the star image, it misleadingly fragments love into a sequential progression in time. The series of images—grass, medicine, stars, blossoms—all illuminate partial truths about growing love, but they also distort the wholeness of experience. The last attempt to find a suitable analogy succeeds in unifying love's multiplicity because it focuses on love's cause and object—the beloved.

> If, as in water stir'd more circles bee
>   Produc'd by one, love such additions take,
>   Those like to many spheares, but one heaven
>   make,
> For, they are all concentrique unto thee.
>
> (Ll. 21-24)

Because he has succeeded in finding a way to talk about his love that combines its past, present, and future, its physicality and spirituality, its movement and growth as well as its permanence, Donne can bring love back to the mundane world with lighthearted assurance that it cannot be damaged by time or political jokes.

> And though each spring doe adde to love new
>   heate,
> As princes doe in times of action get
> New taxes, and remit them not in peace,

No winter shall abate the springs encrease.

> (Ll. 25-28)

Like most of Donne's love lyrics, **"Loves Growth"** relates a particular human experience to general laws of behavior with the intellectual energy and subtlety characteristic of the best English casuistry. But Donne does not speak as a doubting conscience. He feels no doubt or confusion about whether to love, only about how to understand and describe his love. He argues not that his love's growth constitutes an exception to the law of love's immutability but that his experience reveals the true nature and operation of love. He analyzes his experience, pursuing the concept of growth through fine distinctions and intricate argument, not to resolve a moral dilemma but to compliment his beloved with the intensity and constancy of his love.

As preacher, political controversialist, and poet, then, Donne exhibits the "moral diligence" recommended by casuists, assuming with Taylor that "he that searches, desires to find, and so far takes the right course." In a broad sense, the casuistical habit of mind animates the intense self-exploration against a backdrop of the temporal and eternal conditions of men's lives in Donne's lyrics. But the lyrics are not casuistical in any precise, specific way; it is in the treatment of moral dilemmas in his verse satires that Donne is most significantly within the casuistical tradition. Indeed, the casuistical paradigm is more directly helpful in understanding Herbert's lyrics than Donne's. In the poetry of *The Temple,* Herbert devotes considerable attention to the moral theology that underlies casuistry as well as displaying a casuist's interest in particular, practical actions. Unlike the Donne of the lyrics, he uses the strategies of reasoned argument and self-analysis to resolve problems of moral doubt. Although Donne assumes a variety of roles in the ***Songs and Sonnets,*** neither a man struggling with moral doubt nor a casuist dispensing advice are among them. (pp. 178-82)

> Camille Wells Slights, "John Donne as Casuist," in her The Casuistical Tradition in Shakespeare, Donne, Herbert, and Milton, Princeton University Press, 1981, pp. 133-82.

Patrick Grant (essay date 1985)

[*In the excerpt below, Grant contends that Donne explores the theme of "the human heart disenfranchised by science . . . and Calvinism" in the* Anniversaries.]

The trouble with the ***Anniversaries*** was clear from the start, as we know from Ben Jonson's trenchant and famous observation on ***An Anatomy of the World (The First Anniversarie)*** that the poetry was 'profane and full of Blasphemies', and 'if it had been written of ye Virgin Marie it had been something'. Donne himself, in a letter, complains of 'many censures' upon his book, and it seems likely that contemporary readers felt uneasy at the embarrassing extravagance of the poet's praise for a dead fifteen-year-old girl whom he had never seen. It is hard not to share something of this reaction; it is just as hard, however, not to feel the massive distinction and disturbing power of the poetry.

The ***Anniversaries*** therefore place a special burden on criticism having to do with a certain, evident flaw which, because it is a matter of taste, threatens to vitiate the whole. Consequently, it is insufficient to claim that the poems are good in patches; the hyperbole remains problematic, and we must try to explain it. One way to do this is to provide some formula for 'understanding' Donne's treatment of Elizabeth Drury: perhaps we should see in her Astraea, or Queen Elizabeth, or Wisdom, or a Protestant version of the restored Image of God. Or perhaps we should remove her from the centre of the poems altogether, and allow the real subject - whether an Ignatian meditation on the soul, or a disquisition on scepticism or on the new science - to hold our attention.

These alternatives all require us, however, to take our eyes off the forlorn fifteen-year-old upon whose slight shoulders otherwise is placed the burden of the whole world's corruption as well as the significance of contemporary scientific discovery, and here we may well be reminded of the old schoolboy question about 'Lycidas', concerning the poem's 'digressions' and the relationship of the theme to its occasion. Yet Milton so elaborately formalises his subject that the particular friend, Edward King, all but disappears, taken up by the tropes and figures of classical, pastoral and elegiac conventions. The poem, in short, makes it easy for us to forget about him. Not surprisingly, Donne made a gesture at this kind of apology for his own practice when he said, replying to Jonson, 'that he described the Idea of a woman and not as she was'. One critic calls this 'undoubtedly the most acute defense of the poems ever made', but I am inclined to doubt it. Donne's reply is a predictable cliché: of course *The First Anniversarie* transcends its occasion, otherwise it would be no poem at all. But one very curious effect of the ***Anniversaries*** (unlike 'Lycidas') is that the hyperbole remains obtrusive: the poems refuse to allow us to free our minds from the fact that they are occasional, and that the girl's particular, faceless ordinariness is, somehow, what gives rise to the very disturbing energy we admire. (pp. 77-8)

There is, I think, no solution, no way in the end to readjust our thinking so that the poems will appear entirely satisfying. . . . The ***Anniversaries*** . . . communicate Donne's awareness that he must struggle to achieve significance for Elizabeth Drury, rather than depend upon the traditional, public content of his language to disclose allegorically the higher meaning of her life and death. The poems are, thus, partly about the difficulty itself of treating the girl as a symbol, and in this connection they can be especially well understood in terms of the human heart. Donne's claim that the world lost its heart with Elizabeth Drury's death indicates both a general human disorientation (which the poetry keenly records and links specifically with the rise of science), and also the human creature's peculiar, uncertain status as embodied spirit. Throughout his career, Donne's thinking about the heart is closely connected to his understanding of how the human being is, paradoxically, directed to a supernatural end while confined in a material body. In the ***Anniversaries*** his allusions to the heart consequently indicate a set of preoccupations which can help us to grasp what is most distinctive in his treatment of the dead girl. The word 'heart' occurs easily to Donne.

In the ***Songs and Sonnets*** it is the seat of the lover's emotions, and there is a conventional play of hearts given and lost, broken and mended, hardened and softened, devoted and cold. The heart thinks ('A naked thinking heart'—**'The Blossome'**, l. 27) and feels ('My ragges of heart can like, wish, and adore'—**'The Broken Heart'**, (l. 31); it is private ('The ground, thy heart is mine'—**'Loves Infiniteness'**, l. 21), and its affections can be physically visible ('true plaine hearts doe in the faces rest'—**'The Good Morrow'**, l. 16). Its affairs are personal and interior, but the impersonal, outside world impinges on it (**'Loves Infiniteness'**) both as seat of the soul ('in my heart, where my soule dwels'—**Elegie V: 'His Picture'**, l. 2) and as bodily organ ('When I had ripp'd me, and search'd where hearts should lye'—'The Legacie', l. 14). The heart is changeable ('And when I change my Love, I'll change my heart'—**Elegie XII: 'His Parting from Her'**, l. 98), equally subject to dark impulses ('Thou art not so black, as my heart'—**'A Jeat Ring Sent'**, l. 1) and to bright ('The fire of these inflaming eyes, or of this loving heart'—**'Epithalamion at the Marriage of the Earl of Somerset'**, l. 115), and its disequilibrium threatens the entire human organism ('Mad with much heart, then ideott with none'—**Elegie X: 'Image and Dream'**, l. 26). Donne's profane poetry clearly shows his fascination with the heart, man's central organ, symbol of his psycho-physical nature, and (following a well-tried tradition) microcosm of man as man is microcosm of the world: 'As man is of the world, the heart of man, / Is an epitome of Gods great booke / Of creatures' (**'Epithalamion'**, ll. 50-2). Donne likes to stress that, like man himself, the heart occupies a middle state between spirit and body: in the elegant language of **'The Dreame'**, it mediates between sense and understanding; in the ribald language of **'Loves Progress'**, between the non-physical love of 'barren Angels' (l. 23) and the instinctive physical urge for 'the Centrique part' (l. 36).

Much of this, of course, is conventional, but the quality of Donne's interest imparts to his descriptions a special concentration and relevance. The heart becomes a central, pervasive figure in his writing for that slightly nightmarish physicalism mixed with spiritual intuition which he saw as characteristic of the human predicament. (pp. 79-80)

On the one hand, as we see, the heart remains, throughout Donne's writing, a primordial symbol of the human being as a mysterious unity of body and soul. But, on the other hand, Donne's treatment of the heart as a devotional subject reflects a contemporary bias to differentiate its function as the seat of will and affection, from its relationships with understanding and memory. The heart's secrecy, the failure of understanding to compass it, the mystery of the will's dependence on grace, we might conclude, are not affirmed just by Protestantism; in some sense, these truths themselves helped to engender Protestantism as their adequate expression. Yet to insist to an extreme degree on the heart's hiddenness would be to deny the integrity of the 'subtile knot' which combines outer and inner reality. Elizabeth Drury's ordinariness is, clearly, incommensurate with the actual, hidden, state of her heart in which Christ's image dwells. But if the relationship were wholly incommensurate the poems could not record it. The treatment of Elizabeth Drury as a symbol can therefore even seem a kind of protest against the apparent injustice of this ordinary, wonderful child's death:

> Shee, shee is dead; shee's dead: when thou
>   knowst this,
> Thou knowst how lame a cripple this world is.
> And learnst thus much by our Anatomy,
> That this worlds generall sicknesse doth not lie
> In any humour, or one certaine part;
> But as thou saw'st it rotten at the hart . . .
>   (*FA* [*First Anniversarie*], ll. 237-42)

This could very well seem to say that her death calls into question the meaning of creation itself, 'rotten at the hart'. Protest atheism of course is not Donne's explicit intent; none the less, he was peculiarly attracted to forbidden lines of thought and sentiment, letting us be touched by them, just as in the *Songs and Sonnets* and *Elegies* we are made to feel the morbid, obsessive, vindictive and gloating divagations of those thwarted male egos the poetry dramatises, and which are in some sense Donne, but with which we cannot identify him tout court. William Empson [in his *Some Versions of Pastoral*, 1935] draws attention to Donne's 'secret largeness of outlook', which consists, partly, of the poet's willingness (and ability) to communicate the weight of opinions he does not fully endorse. *Biathanatos,* written just before the *Anniversarie* poems, is a conspicuous example, but it is so because the 'largeness of outlook' is less guarded there than usual.

In *Biathanatos,* Donne tells us straight out that he has often felt a 'sickely inclination' to suicide, and believes that insufficient charity and compassion are shown to those who kill themselves. The question, he argues, is complex, but there can be no healthy thinking about it until it is deliberately vexed, just as the pool at Bethesda brought no health until its waters were troubled. The author's deliberate pursuit of 'compassion' therefore depends on his ability to vex the question, as he does by providing some alarming insight into the ambivalence of human motivation and the fine points of distinction between commendation and condemnation. He thereby imparts to *Biathanatos* an unmistakable frisson of hypnotising doubt and existential terror, an effect immediately recognisable also in much of his best work.

Something of this effect certainly is present also in the *Anniversaries.* It comes, partly, from the way the hyperbole itself vexes us, communicating by its very outlandish excess how difficult it is to detect a providential order based on the facts as we know them, the main fact being the death of an ordinary child. On the question, for instance, of whether she is restored to heaven, the poet replies, 'Heaven may say this, and joy in't, but can wee / Who live, and lacke her, here this vantage see?' ('A Funerall Elegie', ll. 47-8). To our chagrin, we face yet a further question, a further uncertainty, for the world has grown mute trying to explain God's higher purposes in the teeth of darkly perplexing evidence. Such are the facts, and *The First Anniversarie*, with all its protracted analysis of the body's suffering and the soul's anguish, is a lament, but a lament touched with protest, and protest then crossed in turn by fear lest it tip too far into unseemliness. Jonson was right, after all, to detect blasphemy, but not because Donne praises Elizabeth Drury unduly; rather because the hyperbole itself carries the flavour of a rebuke to the powers that be for providing no better evidence of their benign purposes. And yet the hyperbole itself goes some distance towards neutralising its own protest because, simply, it so often strikes us as an extravagant game, a huge, witty display which can veer off, for instance, into odd moments of perplexing satire: 'One woman at one blow, then kill'd us all, / And singly, one by one, they kill us now' (*FA*, ll. 107-8). John Carey, indeed, thinks that the main point about the *Anniversaries* is their venal exaggeration, not their serious grappling with conceptual difficulties which Donne was trying to solve. And, although I find the poems more sincere than Carey, he is correct to point out that the complex tone has a way of deflecting us from any uniform high seriousness as distinct from a kind of unprincipled, dashing indulgence in exaggeration. The catalogue of the girl's perfections is, indeed, preposterous, a witty effort to make her more than we know her to be. But the very excess of wit none the less calls attention covertly to a kind of failure: to the fact that the poet here has his wheels spinning off the ground, as it were, because he cannot find purchase on a symbol adequate for teaching us about the girl's death: a symbol, in short, such as a poet could grasp and write about with confidence.

Of course, Donne does not say directly, This is a scandal, what kind of God is responsible? We should not exaggerate the 'atheist's protest', not just because the *Anniversaries* are at once so evidently Christian and so disconcertingly witty, but also because Donne knew the human psyche better than to think it could long be satisfied with such an attitude of protest, however pertinent. We are, on the contrary, specifically warned,

> except thou feed (not banquet) on
> The supernaturall food, Religion,
> Thy better Grouth growes withered, and scant;
> Be more than man, or thou'rt lesse than an Ant.
>   (*FA*, ll. 187-90)

These lines are less a promise of illumination than an acknowledgement that man is incurably a self-transcending creature; he is, as it were, a metaphysical animal, and in order to preserve his humanity needs metaphysical satisfaction. The last line is an imperative which does not promise but threatens: to seek comfort by ignoring the higher side of one's nature is to destroy one's nature, increasing its anguish. The opening lines of *The First Anniversarie* alert us again to this point: 'He who doth not this [celebrate Elizabeth Drury] / May lodge an In-mate soule, but 'tis not his' (ll. 5-6). We refuse the challenge of transcendence, it seems, at our peril.

The poetry cannot, therefore, without presumption declare upon the mystery of grace which makes Elizabeth Drury's inner life so remarkable, for how does the poet know she is blessed? Yet neither can it take refuge in the despair of straightforward materialism. And, if Protestantism, we might say, made Donne's problem as artist more acute in the first respect by emphasising God's transcendence and the imputation of Christ's merits to the elect, contemporary science made it more acute in the second, by declaring the incommensurability of the phenomena with conventional beliefs about the hierarchical order of creation.

The *Anniversaries,* consequently, are remarkable because they state so cogently the problem of dealing at all with the subject matter they address. In so doing, they raise once more the problem of the human heart, with its unified but dual allegiance to soul and body, to heaven and earth, to spirit and matter—a heart which is incurable, as Donne says, prone alike to spiritual pride and sensualist despair, never attaining final assurance, always to be tested, but capable of its own kind of heroism and honesty, and joy of itself in the midst of its own most terrible knowledge.

In some such fashion, Elizabeth Drury is the heart of *The First Anniversarie* just as she is, we are told explicitly, of the world, for, when mankind lost her, 'he lost his hart' (l. 174). His 'Carkas verses', Donne writes, would be sickly and short-lived whose soule is not shee' (**'A Funerall Elegie'**, l. 14). Soon after, he develops the idea:

> But those fine spirits, which doe tune, and set
> This Organ, are those peeces which beget
> Wonder and love; And these were shee.
>
> (ll. 27-9)

The heart is both immaterial and the physical organ producing 'fine spirits' which vitalise the blood. His verse lives because, through her, it has a material subject of spiritual consequence.

But what are we to make of the fact that, on the one hand, the girl's death causes corruption of the world's body ('This world, in that great earth-quake languished' and its 'vitall spirits' are drawn out when she dies—*FA*, ll. 11, 13), and, on the other, that the world's corruption causes her death (when Adam fell to the incitements of Eve, 'that first marriage was our funerall'—l. 105)? Harold Love [in his "The Argument of Donne's 'First Anniversary'," *Modern Philology* (1966)] deals with this problem specifically, again, in terms of the heart. *The First Anniversarie,* he suggests, is like a double fugue, in which Elizabeth Drury is spiritually the soul of the world and physically the heart of its body. The hard lesson, therefore, which Donne asks us to face about the body is that even such a piece of perfection as Elizabeth's could not escape the grave. This is helpful, even though Love tends to equate heart with body as distinct from soul, whereas for Donne, as we see, heart is body and soul in one. Elizabeth Drury as the world's heart is the physical means by which the world makes concrete what it loves, and the same is true when she is regarded as mankind's heart, and the heart of Donne's verse.

At the beginning of *The First Anniversarie,* for instance, when her soul goes to heaven, the world languishes. It gets a fever, forgets its name and loses its form. The world was 'Nothing but she, and her thou hast o'repast' (l. 32). Here she is the world's soul. Soon after we learn that her death teaches the world 'that thou art / Corrupt and mortall in thy purest part' (ll. 61-2), and here, presumably, she is the purest part of its body, later identified as its heart. When mankind lost her, we recall, 'he lost his heart'—that is, her immaterial virtue ('so much refin'd'—l. 177) in the form

of a physical body ('Shee tooke the weaker Sex'—l. 179). The poem assures us that 'The heart being perish'd, no part can be free' (l. 186): this goes for the world and for mankind and for verse, all of which require an interpenetration of confining form (the body) and a creative energy (spirit). The anatomy assures us that her significance is not just physical: the world's sickness 'doth not lie / In any humour, or one certaine part; / But as thou saw'st it rotten at the hart' (ll. 240-2). The 'hart' of the world clearly is not 'one certaine part' but a pervasive principle of the body's life. It is what 'she' stands for, she who 'should' (l. 220) reunite the parts in one, both as form (the 'first originall'—l. 227) and as physical being ('whose rich eyes, and brest / Guilt the West Indies'—ll. 229-30). But corruption of the 'inward' (l. 329) heart is not just spiritual either, for it poisons our 'actions' (l. 337) and puts us physically out of joint with the world. Thus the joys that possessed her 'hart' (l. 433) are alone worth our trouble and grief and perishing, for her body, as we learn in **'A Funerall Elegie'**, clearly encompassed her soul.

The *Second Anniversarie* begins by describing her as the lower world's and the 'Sunnes Sunne' (l. 4). Conventionally, sun is to cosmos what heart is to body, and here we find her again located so perfectly in the middle position, both physical and spiritual, that it is appropriate to say, 'her bodie thought' (l. 246). She was, after all, uniquely able (by divine grace, we are assured), to see God in nature itself, and in her heart she kept God's image. What this means, for practical purposes, is that the 'outward skin' (l. 505) as well as the 'mindes within' (l. 506) showed forth God's blessing.

We must not let go unconsidered, however, the implications of that crucially placed 'should' ('She that should all parts to reunion bow'—*FA*, l. 220). Elizabeth Drury should, but does not, in fact, hold 'the sundred parts in one' (l. 222). This of course is partly because as a symbol uniting heaven and earth she is hyperbolical and preposterous, and the poet who wrote those inflated descriptions of her perfectly elemented body, I suggest, knew himself to be having a hard time making her live up to what he conceived her to be—'the Idea of a woman'. But, since she is the heart of his verse, as of everything else, the poetry becomes in one respect a lament for the passing of a certain kind of symbolic mode of writing whereby physical events could, indeed, happily convey 'higher' spiritual meaning through a multi-levelled allegory. Elizabeth Drury is thus *allegory manqué,* and draws our attention alike to the limits of poetry's encroachment upon theology, and to the human difficulties of settling for a soulless world. In this she reflects, once more, the poet's fascination with the heart and the human predicament which it represents, even though it is a heart deeply troubled by the timely questions with which it must contend.

Indeed, throughout the *Anniversaries* Donne insists on timeliness: on how present circumstances have a crucial part to play in what we are to make of the dead girl. For instance, he repeatedly contrasts the world 'now' to what it was when mankind felt more at home in the universe, when he lived longer and in harmony with his surroundings, 'So spacious and large that every Soule / Did a faire

Kingdome, and large Realme controule' (*FA*, l. 124). 'There is not now that mankinde, which was then' (l. 112); 'If man were any thing, he's nothing now' (l. 171). The world, it seems, even though fallen, was once a happier place; it had more vitality, it was closer to God, and the designs of heaven were more clearly perceived by men on earth. But 'Where is this mankind now?' (l. 127). It has dwindled, and, as the poem also tells us, it has lost its heart, its capacity to see itself as mediator between heaven and earth, to feel at home in the world, to see the larger significance of temporal events, to appreciate how the girl's death has meaning. 'Now', with his shrunken and devitalised heart, man has extreme difficulty writing about such a subject at all, as the poem itself shows: the symbolism by which poetry can present metaphysical reality is, now, conspicuously arbitrary and full of strain: 'Up, up, for in that squadron there doth live / Shee' (*SA* [*Second Anniversarie*], ll. 356-7). The present times have, the poet complains, uniquely divided man from the heavens, body from spirit, corporeal images from informing ideas. We are assured on the one hand that the transcendent God operates by grace upon those he loves, but the operation has become hidden so that it threatens to elude poetry altogether; on the other hand, human knowledge—scientia, the advance of modern science—is sceptical about correspondences between physical fact and spiritual sense, and threatens poetry from precisely the opposite direction.

It is a cliché that *The First Anniversarie* records Donne's knowledge of contemporary scientific discoveries and how he found them disorienting. As C. M. Coffin [in his *John Donne and the New Philosophy*] has shown in detail, Donne was keenly sensitive to the discoveries of Kepler and Galileo in support of the Copernican thesis that the earth moved and that the heavenly bodies were both corruptible and irregular. In *Ignatius his Conclave*, for instance, Donne alludes twice to Galileo's *Siderius Nuncius,* and Copernicus is interviewed for a place in hell for deriding Ptolemy, thus joining the company of those whose innovations induced doubts and anxieties by having 'turned the whole frame of the world'. Kepler's name appears in Problem VIII of *Paradoxes and Problems*, as it does also in *Ignatius his Conclave*. The passage in *The First Anniversarie* on 'New starres' (l. 260) likewise seems to draw upon Kepler's *De Stella Nova* (and perhaps on the further discoveries of Tycho Brahe, Kepler's disciple). The *Anniversaries* allude besides to the earth's magnetism, as William Gilbert described it in *De Magnete* (1600) to account for the earth's diurnal movement (thereby undermining the old idea of the *primum mobile*): as world soul, Elizabeth Drury is thus able 'To draw, and fasten sundred parts in one' (*FA*, l. 222) like a 'magnetique force' (l. 221). Speculation on the plurality of worlds, a subject of antique origin but championed provocatively during the Renaissance (as by the unfortunate Giordano Bruno), would also have been known to Donne through Kepler and perhaps Thomas Digges, or through Bruno himself. Certainly, in *Holy Sonnet V*, Donne talks of 'new sphears' and 'new lands' beyond the heavens, and in *The Second Anniversarie* the moon is alluded to as a 'new world' (l. 196). He does not dwell on the idea or its consequences for theology, but his knowledge of current interest in the theory is at one with his appreciation of how radically the new science had dis-

turbed the traditional, providential conception of the universe by rendering (as William Empson suggests) Christ's incarnation perhaps not a unique event. Finally, Donne was an enthusiastic (though unsystematic) follower of Paracelsus, whose 'new principles' he praises as superior to the humoral theory of Galen and Hippocrates. Paracelsus is referred to in *Biathanatos* and, with Copernicus, makes an appearance in *Ignatius his Conclave*.

Scholars interested in Donne's concern for the new science are at pains to point out, however, that his treatment of such data is not systematic, but mainly expresses his sense of the instability of human knowledge. For instance, the lines in *The First Anniversarie* on the 'perplexed course' (l. 253) of the heavens constitute, according to Coffin, 'one of the most curious and significant utterances Donne ever made'. The poet's reaction to the new astronomy, Coffin explains, 'marks the birth of an idea in Donne's mind that a critical study of the new philosophy was bound to produce, that all systems of natural philosophy, traditional and new, are subject to modification and revision, and, therefore, will not suffice as a foundation for a satisfactory religious faith. The idea of the relativity of natural knowledge is essential to an understanding of the poem; but no less fundamental is an appreciation of the role of the new philosophy in bringing Donne to this conclusion. Donne is not merely echoing the medieval poet's contempt for the world.' In short, just as a Calvinist doctrine of imputed merit makes God inscrutably transcendent, so the extreme 'alterability' of the heavens destroys the sense of a world-order arranged by ascending degrees of perfection: ''Tis all in pieces, all cohaerence gone; / All just supply, and all Relation' (ll. 213-4). Man instead is thrown back upon the mystery of himself—'For every man alone thinkes he hath got / To be a Phoenix' (ll. 216-7)—and on the arbitrariness of his own imposition of significance upon the world as a creator, not just a receiver, of metaphysical truth:

> Man hath weav'd out a net, and this net throwne
> Upon the Heavens, and now they are his owne.
> Loth to goe up the hill, or labor thus
> To goe to heaven, we make heaven come to us.
> (ll. 279-82)

It seems that Donne very well knew his treatment of Elizabeth Drury reflected just this kind of arbitrariness, expressing the particular anguish of a mind constrained to achieve significance to satisfy its own metaphysical nature, rather than to disclose the *given* metaphysical significance of heaven and earth.

In light of these remarks, it is pertinent to look again at how, in *The Second Anniversarie*, Elizabeth Drury is the sun ('this lower worlds, and the Sunnes Sunne'—l. 4), and how the 'Eccentric parts' and 'overthwarts' and 'New starres' (*FA*, l. 260) so distort the heavens that this sun, disenfranchised, can no longer 'maintaine his way / One inche direct' (ll. 269-70) but is 'Serpentine: And seeming weary with his reeling thus' (ll. 272-3). As I have mentioned, it is a commonplace that the sun is to the heavens as the heart is to man. The idea occurs, for instance, frequently in blood-letting charts which divide the human body according to signs of the zodiac and consistently present the heart as Leo, pictured as a sun. Discussing 'the signe Leo'

Batman says that it especially 'helpeth in a man the . . . heart', and Cornelius Agrippa states plainly, 'Hinc veteres physici Solem ipsum cor coeli appellaverunt.' Shakespeare draws on the idea in *Henry V:* 'a good heart, Kate, is the sun and the moon, or rather, the sun, and not the moon, for it shines bright, and never changes, but keeps his course truly.' Robert Burton talks of the heart as 'the Sun of our body, the King and sole commander of it' and Samuel Purchas describes love's throne in 'the heart, the Sunne of this *Microcosme*'. In physiological terms, the heart was thought to produce body heat by a kind of combustion analogous to heat provided by the sun. 'The basic principle of life, "the divine spark",' a historian of the subject assures us, 'was said to enter the foetal heart in the fourth month as an occult ray via the sun' and the air of the lungs worked as a kind of bellows to fan and feed the heart's fire. As John Davies of Hereford explains, the '*Lunges* (breath's-forge)' are 'First to receaue the *Aire* that cooles the *Hart*'. The fiery hearts of sacred-emblem tradition are therefore not just metaphorical, but are depictions also of an actual physiological function. It thus seems clear that, when Donne compares Elizabeth Drury to the sun, and also to the world's heart, we are meant to see the relationship between new scientific theory having thrown the sun into disorientation in an eccentric universe, and the world having lost its heart because of the girl's death. The conventional symbolism no longer works as it ought to do to describe the relationship (qualitatively) of the inner man to outer world. The private, inner significance of Elizabeth Drury does not correspond in any immediately compelling way to the course of her public life. Just as, in the new science, the sun is materially (quantitatively) at the centre, but spiritually (qualitatively) imponderable, so with the girl herself in the poem: she like the sun is somehow out of place, suddenly become also extravagantly large, dangerously problematic. In this respect, Donne's emphasis differs sharply, for instance, from that of Paracelsus, who insists that a person's external appearance does reveal the inner life and, specifically, the heart's disposition: 'Physiognomies is the art of discovering what is within and hidden in man. . . . It tells us in what relation his heart stands to God'; 'the shape of a man is formed in accordance with the manner of his heart'. Donne's lament for the decay of the world is a lament for the loss of just this correspondence between the heart's condition and exterior appearances. In this sense man has indeed 'shrunk', for the extent of his discourse and the reality encompassed by his heart are confined and imprisoned increasingly within his own breast.

The hyperbole and sheer difficulty of the *Anniversaries* consequently derive partly from the fact that they are public poems. Donne is compelled to remake, if he can, a correlation between the world and God by way of the poem's chief symbol, the girl, 'Idea of a woman', the world's heart, at the same moment as he acknowledges the near-impossibility of doing so in the intellectual climate of his times. The *Anniversaries*, however, I repeat, are significant, less because of their obvious failure to make, as it were, a viable metaphysical symbol out of the girl's career, than for a kind of covert success, which comes from the sense they convey of why they cannot succeed, conveyed partly by a self-protective bravado and display of extrava-

gance for its own sake. 'Nor could incomprehensiblenesse deterre / Mee, from thus trying to emprison her' (*FA*, ll. 469-70), Donne writes. This remarkable statement partly acknowledges the poem's limits, but it is no mere gesture of respect to the mystery; it is an insistence also that the poem (like *Biathanatos*) has tried a task beyond its scope and has taken its very life from that trial. 'Incomprehensiblenesse' in this case offers a kind of release, a licence for wit to fill the gap between heaven and earth, even though Donne's inordinate, gratuitous wittiness itself calls attention to the absence which makes it free.

Throughout his career, then, Donne's fascination with the heart is clearly a fascination with the central paradoxes of the human condition; with the fact that man is neither angel nor beast, spirit nor body. The heart thus conceived becomes, for a critic, a particular means of approach to the larger scope of Donne's poetry, and my claim is not so much that the heart is, literally, Donne's subject as that Donne's subject is the middle state that the heart represents. Donne himself, however, as I have pointed out, treats the heart always as a metaphor carefully developed to expand our understanding of this middle state, and I therefore wish to maintain that it is indeed a key motif in his writing. Certainly the *Anniversarie* poems allude to the heart in such a sense to define and represent man's differences from what is above and below him. The poetry does not acquiesce in the radical disenchantment of sheer materialism, one consequence of the discovery of method pushed to an extreme whereby human experience is reduced entirely to the quantifiable. The mere 'cutting up a man that's dead' (*FA*, l. 435) discovers only a stinking carcass. The human corpse, rather, clutches at its soul-life. Just as the decapitated body twitches 'And seemes to reach, and to step forth to meet / His soule' (*SA*, ll. 16-17), so the poet also turns our eyes upwards, towards the heavens, where Elizabeth Drury is enshrined with God's image in her heart. That image, we are told, is present by grace, the imputation of God's mercy. But neither does the poem fall silent, struck dumb, as it were, by God's inscrutable, unmediated power. For here lurks another kind of tyranny, bound up, likewise, as we have seen, with the discovery of method in so far as new philosophy found it expedient to separate theology from science by stressing the imponderable distance between the first, originating cause and the created world. Spiritual absolutes are no less dehumanising than the material sort, and Donne self-consciously finds his subject between the two, refusing the temptations of both.

In this respect, it is interesting to reflect on how frequently the descriptions of Elizabeth Drury establish her middle condition by distinguishing it from what is above and below, rather than by stressing participation: 'heaven keepes soules,' Donne writes, 'The grave keeps bodies' (*FA*, ll. 473-4), but the girl, like his verse, 'hath a middle nature' (l. 473) distinct from both. When her 'rich soule' (l. 1) climbs to heaven, the earth languishes. But the poem's real subject is not heaven or earth, but rather, 'a perplexed doubt / Whether the world did loose, or gaine in this' (ll. 14-15). Man, we are told, has 'lost his hart' (l. 174) as part of a more general catastrophe which began in heaven, and first 'seis'd the Angels' (l. 195) and later the 'beasts and plants' (l. 200). But the 'rotten . . . hart' (l. 242) of 'The noblest part, man' (l. 199), removed from angels and beasts alike, is the poem's preoccupation. 'What is't to us, alas,' the poet asks, 'if there have beene / An Angell made a Throne, or Cherubin?' (**'A Funerall Elegie'**, ll. 49-50). The subject is not the grave or the angel, but lies in the very question, what 'vantage' (ibid.) can we take of her? 'In Heaven thou straight know'st all' (*SA*, l. 299), the poet assures his soul, but the earth is 'Our prison's prison' (l. 249). Meanwhile, the question presses: 'Poor soule . . . what do'st thou know?' (l. 254).

On the physical side, concerning 'matters of fact' (l. 285), not much: 'Knowst thou how blood, which to the hart doth flow, / Doth from one ventricle to th'other go?' (ll. 271-2). On the spiritual side, even less: 'Thou art too narrow, wretch, to comprehend / Even thy selfe' (ll. 261-2). But in the girl, heart of his world, the physical blood is 'eloquent' (l. 244). The poet's real subject is here, in the human heart disenfranchised by science on the one hand and Calvinism on the other, the mysterious 'knot' which it is the task of literature to describe, in all its pathos and magnificence. Donne thus attempts, in his treatment of Elizabeth Drury, to make of the deal girl a symbol adequate to his hope and faith and knowledge. But his deliberate metaphysical fabrication succeeds less in assuaging the fears and uncertainties of the human condition than in enabling the poetry to find its true subject by expressing those very fears and uncertainties. (pp. 89-101)

> Patrick Grant, *"John Donne's 'Anniversaries':*
> *New Philosophy and the Act of the Heart," in*
> his Literature and the Discovery of Method in
> the English Renaissance, *The Macmillan*
> *Press Ltd., 1985, pp. 77-101.*

Debora Kuller Shuger   (essay date 1990)

[*In the following excerpt, Shuger explores several theological themes in Donne's sermons, including the analogy between the power of God and that of the king; obedience and submission to God's will; predestination and punishment for sin; the interpretation of Scripture; and God's role in the dynamic between good and evil.*]

Donne's religious writings differ from those of his contemporaries primarily in the *degree* to which he stresses the analogy between God and kings. Even in the erotic poetry, he is fascinated by kingship. Often in the sermons, the analogy is quite casual, just indicative of a general habit of mind that perceives the divine in terms of royal and courtly associations. Thus he likes to point out that as one would never dare to offer the king a defective gift, so one should not presume to pawn damaged goods off on God. Elsewhere he notes in passing that "the Kings pardon flowes from his meere grace, and from his brest . . . [as] does faith from God," or, somewhat humorously, that God's coming to the individual resembles a visit by the king: "an honour . . . yet [not] without removes, and troubles, and charges." Occasionally one finds not unexpected traces of the ancient correspondences between sociopolitical and supernatural order. "God is a Monarch alone"; "Heaven is a kingdome, and Christ a King"; the "Heaven of Heavens" is "the Presence Chamber of God

himselfe"; as Christ is the mediator between God and man, so King's counselors are mediators "between Princes and People."

Donne's references to kings are frequently, however, more significant and more specific. Whether speaking about literal or metaphoric kings he almost invariably echoes the main themes of Jacobean royalism. Like Andrewes and James himself, he refers to the king as the image of God and as a god on earth. His authority therefore does not derive from the people but directly from God; like Christ, a true king is a hereditary not an elective monarch. Hence royal power does not simply inhere in a divinely sanctioned social *role,* but the king is in a real sense a sacred person, one who participates in the divine in such a way that "the Kings acts are Gods acts." Thus "Sedition and Rebellion [are] Sacriledge; for, though the trespasse seeme to be directed but upon a man, yet in that man, whose office (and consequently his person) is sacred, God is opposed, and violated." As in Andrewes and James, one sees the same connection between the Davidic priest-king and the royal headship of the Church of England. Like David, the king (Charles, in this case) "institutes those Orders, which the Church is to observe in the publique service of God" for "the King is King of men; not of bodies only, but of soules too." (pp. 165-66)

Donne's politicization of the divine image leads to a spirituality based on awe and subjection. One must have "a reverentiall feare" and "a fearfull reverence." Hence "no man may thinke himselfe to bee come to that familiar acquaintance with God, as that it should take away that reverentiall feare which belongs to so high and supreme a Majesty." A person comes before God with the "reverence" with which people come "to the Kings presence." Hence, Donne stresses the distance between God and man rather than their intimacy. He thus associates High Church ritual—kneeling at communion, genuflecting, baring the head—not with adoration or humble love but with the marks of submission to one's social superiors: "we must not be too familiar, too fellowly, too homely with God, here at home, in his house." Rather there must be "a due consideration of greatness, a distance, a distinction, a respect of Rank, and Order, and Majestie," not, apparently, unlike the reverential gestures required in the presence of the king. Along with "respect of Rank" God requires unquestioning obedience, the "silence of reverence, silence of subjection" that restrains one "from questioning any thing ordained by God."

It should be clear from the foregoing that Donne's theology is "absolutist" not by implication or inference but quite literally and explicitly. The sermons insist on the analogy between God and king and furthermore locate the point of contact in *power.* Kings are called gods "by participation of Gods power"—a power characterized by secret decrees, *potentia absoluta,* freedom from law, and the distant fearfulness of majesty. Moreover, as the following discussion will attempt to demonstrate, this analogy involves more than a simple comparison between temporal and spiritual centers of authority. It is a psychagogic rather than cosmological analogy; that is, Donne presses the absolutist qualities of divinity in order to generate terror, insecurity, and guilt. God is the utterly absolute monarch a Stuart could only dream of being.

The theological corollary of royal absolutism is radical monotheism, the total concentration of power into a single figure. Such a conception of God, as Donne is aware, verges on moral incomprehensibility and paradox. To the "naturall man" there is "no burden . . . so insupportable, no consideration so inextricable, no secret so inscrutable, no conception so incredible, as to conceive One infinite God, that should do all things alone, without any more Gods." If God does "all things alone," then He is responsible for all things; but "That that God that settles peace, should yet make warres . . . That the conquered God, and the victorious God, should be both one God, That that God who is all goodnesse in himselfe, should yet have his hand in every ill action, this the naturall man cannot digest, not comprehend." This final implication is the most significant. Donne's monotheism abolishes the mythic dualism of Andrewes's *Christus Victor* theology, in which responsibility for "ill action" devolves onto Satan and the powers of darkness, thus eliminating the paradox of a good God who directly causes evil. Donne, however, insists upon the paradox: "all the evill (that is, all the *penall* ill, all plagues, all warre, all famine,) that is *done* in the World, God doth." There is no cosmic battle between God and Lucifer but instead a "strange warre, where there are not two sides . . . for, God uses the Devill against us, and the Devill uses us against one another . . . so that God, and the Devill, and we, are all in one Army, and all for our destruction." God does not cause evil in the loose or deistic sense of establishing natural laws that may produce unpleasant side effects for some persons nor in the Catholic (and Arminian) sense of mere permission; rather, human suffering is "*penall* ill," it is intended to hurt and punish. If God requires man to keep his distance, yet God himself is painfully present in His "judgements . . . speedily enough executed upon thy soul and body together, every day." Donne's "Calvinism" is at work in the reiterated claim that "War, and Dearth, and Sickness, are the Weapons of Gods displeasure; and these he pours out of his Treasury, in this world," but Calvin himself tends to emphasize the comfort and safety to be derived from the notion of supernatural control rather than God's punitive capacity. In his stress on the latter, Donne seems closer to the English Calvinists and, perhaps, to Luther. (pp. 168-69)

Donne lays particular weight on man's utter vulnerability, both physical and psychological, to divine aggression. God can make people perish while they are in the middle of trying to repent. He can totally abandon them, forgetting all his prior "paternities," all his "filiations" to them. All human attempts at independence and rational control are illusory, since external events and psychic life are at the mercy of God, who can, with a word, "reduce them to *nothing* againe": "*Navyes* will not keepe off *Navies*, if God be not the *Pilot*, Nor *Walles* keepe out *Men,* if God be not the *Sentinell*. . . . as long as the Testimonies of GODS anger lye at the dore of the *Conscience*, no man can returne to peace there." The famous *pondus gloriae* passage from Donne's second Prebend sermon forms a nightmarish rhapsody on man's exposure to divine power. God

imposes intolerable burdens, "infinite waights of afflictions that oppresse us here." The prose stresses divine responsibility: "God calls in but the fly, to vexe Egypt, and even the fly is a heavy burden unto them. . . . It is not onely *Jeremy* that complains . . . That God made their fetters and their chains heavy to them, but the workmen in harvest complaine, That God had made a faire day heavy unto them. . . . all is waight, and burden, and heavinesse, and oppression." The pain is not just external. The psyche is likewise vulnerable to divine wrath, with the result that what appeared to be a proprietary selfhood can be ripped away and vanish in an instant:

> But when I shall trust to that, which wee call a good spirit, and God shall deject, and empoverish, and evacuate that spirit, when I shall rely upon a morall constancy, and God shall shake, and enfeeble, and enervate, destroy and demolish that constancy; when I shall think to refresh my selfe in the serenity and sweet ayre of a good conscience, and God shall call up the damps and vapours of hell it selfe, and spread a cloud of diffidence, and an impenetrable crust of desperation upon my conscience . . . except hee put in that *pondus gloriae,* that exceeding waight of an eternall glory, with his owne hand, into the other scale, we are waighed downe, we are swallowed up, irreparably, irrevocably, irrecoverably, irremediably.

And this is not deserved punishment for sin, but "still the best men have had most laid upon them." And, as Donne acutely notes, such agony is often not medicinal but produces aversion and drives us away from God, making us unable to hear His voice or He ours.

Although Donne generally depicts divine punishment as retribution for sin and therefore explicable, if terrifying, he also will play with the notion of undeserved suffering, or suffering that seems far in excess of the offense. He thus observes that first God hurts us and then punishes us for complaining; we "are whipt if we cry." Similarly, the fear that God is angry with us—a fear Donne makes every effort to inculcate—will make Him angry. In fact, this terror at inscrutable punishment guarantees its execution, since "nothing can alienate God more from thee, then to think that any thing but sin can alienate him." Divine logic operates with dilemmas and conundrums, rendering every human action potentially subject to penalty. Donne is, in fact, intrigued by all the things one can be punished for. If prayer is not made "in faith," if it is "discontinued, intermitted, done by fits," if "it be not vehement," such prayer "shall not only be ineffectuall, but even . . . *an abomination;* And not only an abomination to God, but destruction upon themselves." If one receives the Sacrament unworthily—and Donne inserts parenthetically that almost everyone does so—"at the last day, we shall be ranked with *Judas*." Similarly, if one loves God's creation in an ordinate manner and loves God "as a great and incomprehensible power," but does not love (because he does not know) Christ, then, Donne concludes, "let him be accursed, for all his love." The proximity of divine curse and human love seems particularly unsettling here. God's gifts of prayer and sacraments, His gift of His Son, turn out, in Donne's hands, to be snares and traps. With like rigorism, Donne dwells on the catastrophic results of dogmatic error. At the Last Judgment, the penalty for sins of "not cloathing, not visiting, not harbouring the poore" will be mild compared to that due for the "high treason . . . of denying or doubting of the distinct Persons of the holy, blessed, and glorious Trinity," without which "all morall vertues are but diseases." Indeed, "for matter of beleefe, he that beleeves not all, *solvit Iesum . . .* he takes Jesus in peeces." More explicitly, "He that beleeves not every Article of the Christian faith, and with so stedfast a belief, as that he would dye for it, *Damnabitur,* (no modification, no mollification, no going lesse) He shal be damned."

Donne also plays with the notion of damnation without personal guilt. His discussions of Original Sin and the condemnation of the invincibly ignorant underscore the mysterious and illogical implications of traditional doctrine on these matters. Thus in the second sermon he preached before Charles I, Donne begins by considering the economics of sin; sin is a sort of selling, a bad bargain whereby one gives up immortality and the love of God for temporal benefits. But as he attempts to apply this model to Original Sin, the analogy conspicuously breaks down: "But what had *I* for *Heaven*? *Adam* sinnd, and *I* suffer; *I forfeited* before I had any *Possession*, or could claime any *Interest*; I had a *Punishment*, before I had a *being*, And *God* was displeased with *me* before *I* was *I*." Original Sin fascinates Donne, but fascinates him because it is heteronomous and morally unintelligible. In other passages the illogic works itself into the rhythms of the prose. His funeral sermon for Lady Danvers, for example, contains the following passage: "For *his mercies are new every morning*; and his later mercies are his largest mercies. How many, how great *Nations* perish, without ever hearing the name of *Christ*." The space, the *aporeia*, between the first and second sentence seems intolerably large; the typographic relation between God's "mercies" and the fact that whole nations "perish" both demands and resists explanation. These are uneasy passages, exhibiting both an edge of moral revulsion and the determination to rub the hearer's nose in the terrifying reality of divine wrath and inexplicable rigor. They simultaneously force and forbid the perception of injustice. They assault the congregation with the destructive and alien power of God.

Yet however heteronomous, Donne's God never escapes the representational web of sociopolitical analogy. In His "psychological makeup," if the phrase may be used in this context, He strongly resembles a Renaissance nobleman. He is, above all, concerned to maintain His superiority. He thus jealously guards His honor, "which Honour consists much in our honouring of him," hence punishing people primarily to make them aware that they are being punished, to compel the acknowledgment of His power. Christ too "deliver[s] his own Honour, by delivering [a] . . . sinner to malediction." Like Calvin and almost all Reformed theologians, Donne holds that "Gods first purpose was his owne glory," a self-directed intentionality he associates with princes. In a thoroughly aristocratic manner, God resents whatever threatens to derogate from this glory. (pp. 172-75)

The relation between God and man in Donne thus oper-

ates along the axis of power and submission. God possesses ineluctable and overwhelming might designed to inspire fear and impel obedience. This relation recapitulates the structure of absolutist rule, as Donne makes perfectly clear, although intensifying precisely those aspects of royal absolutism that appalled members of Parliament and the common lawyers: sovereign will unconstrained by law, the taboo on probing the *arcana imperii,* the yawning distance between ruler and subjects. It is not enough to say that such power dynamics do not constitute the totality of Donne's theology. They are at the center of his conception of God, and an accurate understanding of that totality requires some comprehension of *why* Donne would choose to fashion divine/human relations along such harsh and politicized lines. (p. 176)

Donne attempts to stabilize the terrifying freedom of God vis-à-vis mankind by denying reprobation. He departs noticeably from Calvinist orthodoxy by claiming that Christ died for all persons and therefore damnation is not necessitated by any eternal decrees but is a consequence of sin. At times Donne moves close to the Catholic position that grace is offered equally to all, and people are then free to accept or resist it. More often, he seems to adhere to the position of moderate English Protestantism, which holds that divine condemnation is always with respect to sin, without affirming the universality of grace. (pp. 176-77)

Donne reinforces his rejection of the arbitrary deity implied in supralapsarian Calvinism by stressing the covenant or contract that places divine/human relations within a lawful, predictable context. By this contract "hath God expressed his love to us," since it has "manifested to us a way, to come to him." Since God is "*fidelis,* a faithful God," He will perform the covenant He has made; in other words, although God is an "absolute Lord," He will "proceed with us, according to that Contract which he hath made with us, and that Law which he hath given to us." God has *potentia absoluta* but governs the world according to His *potentia ordinata*—a distinction common to both the nominalists and the Stuarts. Insofar as the relation between God and human beings is contractual, it is also conditional. The condition on God's side is fidelity to His promise, on the human side, obedience: in Donne's words, "*If you obey you shall live, if you rebell you shall die.*"

This conditionality, however, undermines the attempt to establish the relation between God and humans on a predictable and workable footing. The divine promises remain contingent on obedience, for "all Gods promises have a *Si audieritis, si volueritis,* if *I* hearken, if *I* obey, I shall eat the good things of the land; otherwise I shall sterve, body, and soule." But Donne sets the standard of obedience so high that no one can perform his part of the bargain. As in Perkins, any fault is, in God's eye, a capital offense. Thus, for example, in an early sermon preached before Queen Anne, Donne argues,

> If thou hast lov'd thy self, or any body else principally; or so, that when thou dost any act of love, thou canst not say to thine own conscience, I do this for Gods sake, and for his glory; if thou hast loved so, thou hast hated thy self, and him

whom thou hast loved, and God whom thou shouldest love.

That is, if one does not love God to the exclusion of all else, then one hates God; there is no middle ground. This passage is typical of Donne's association of obedience with purity of motive. Although a firm moralist, he rarely makes the link between moral perfection and fulfilling the divine conditions on salvation. Instead, the connection between obedience and promise involves the more intangible and perhaps more impossible requirement of sincerity. That is, "if when we eat and drink, or sleep or wake, we do not all to the glory of God . . . he will divorce." Any trace of "selfness" totally contaminates an act or intention, no matter how good. Donne thus remarks, "If I would not serve God, except I might be saved for serving him, I shall not be saved though I serve him; My first end in serving God, must not be my selfe, but he and his glory." What is striking here is not the claim that one should intend God's glory—something no religious person would deny—but that the desire for one's own blessedness should be seen as a fatal perversion of saving love. Human action is viewed in black-and-white terms, and the "white" portion squeezed by a spiritual rigorism into nonexistence.

Hence, Donne's emphasis on covenants and contracts generally does not stabilize the relation between God and man. Since the human partner fails to fulfill his end of the bargain, the whole *instrumentum* falls to the ground. Instead such bilateral promises serve primarily to exculpate God while simultaneously incriminating man; "the justification of God . . . is accomplished at the expense of man." Donne describes God as setting up the Gospel so that "we might be absolutely inexcusable" if we continue to sin. God always does "all that is necessary"; our suffering is our fault. (pp. 176-79)

Donne freezes the posture of the individual before God into a tableau of remorse and self-reproach because spiritual relations, like economic ones, are governed by the law of scarcity; goodness and honor are limited commodities, always attained at another's expense. Hence the "literall sense" of Scripture always is "what may most deject and vilifie man, what may most exalt, and glorifie God." The mutual entailment of these upward and downward pressures becomes explicit in a similar passage from another sermon where Donne observes, "the more I vilifie my selfe, the more I glorifie my God." God's honor requires human guilt, for "*Adversum me*, is *Cum Deo*." Donne valorizes guilt because whatever "layes flat the nature of man" likewise "most exalts the Grace and Glory of God." But to the extent that guilt constitutes the proper attitude of a person with respect to God then Donne's contractualism is largely a fiction; if one could perform the conditions it would somehow detract from God's glory.

The spiritual importance Donne attributes to guilt also rests on his understanding of selfhood. The sermons come close to equating the self with sin. "All the imaginations of the thoughts of our hearts," he writes, "are only evill continually." All goodness comes from without the self, but "Our sins are our *own*." Donne thus represents the moment of spiritual *anagnorisis* as the discovery of the

monster behind the facade of moral decency. God's punishments bring a person "into company with himselfe," where he realizes, "Lord! how have I mistaken my selfe, Am I, that thought my selfe, and passed with others, for a sociable, a pleasurable man, and good company; am I a leprous Adulterer, is that my name? Am I, that thought my selfe a frugall man, and a good husband . . . am I an oppressing Extortioner, is that my name?" The devil occupies a surprisingly small place in Donne's theology seemingly because the self replaces Satan as the origin of evil. The two figures at times almost coalesce, the self becoming a *Spontaneus Satan*, a *Spontaneus Daemon*, for "every man hath a devill in himselfe," where "in" may mean not only "within," as if the devil were an alien presence inside the self, but also "intrinsically" (as in the phrase "lying is bad in itself "), with the implication that the devil is the self. (pp. 182-83)

These dynamics push Donne's conception of God close to the demonic or tyrannical, a conclusion he recognizes and resists—apparently successfully since he was not tried for heresy but became one of the most acclaimed preachers of his day. Donne always maintains with unequivocal clarity that God is not immoral or cruel. In fact, he precludes such an inference with a theological catch-22: it is the wicked who see God as a tyrant, and hence those who claim that God oppresses them unjustly prove, by their complaint, the justice of their punishment. But Donne's denial that God is a monster does not answer the problem of why he allowed such suspicions to arise.

At times, the threateningly absolute power of God in these sermons seems contained by the conventional Protestant Law-to-Gospel dialectic, where the God of the Old Testament is cast as punitive justice in contrast to Christ's love revealed in the New. Donne will therefore sometimes portray the relation between Christ and man in a wholly nonpolitical, nonanalogical fashion. For instance, he depicts the agon between Job and God in forensic terms, but as he starts to consider God as Christ the judicial analogy undergoes a sea change; Christ is the judge, but he is also the witness for the defendant, and he is not only judge and witness but the defendant himself:

> He that is my Witnesse, is my Judge, and the same person is my Jesus, my Saviour, my Redeemer; He that hath taken my nature, He that hath given me his blood. So that he is my Witnesse, in his owne cause, and my Judge, but of his owne Title, and will, in me, preserve himselfe.

When Donne speaks of Christ, he will begin to draw on the language of participation characteristic of Andrewes: "we are not onely His, but He"; "Christ is *Idem homo cum te*, the same man that thou art, so thou art *Idem spiritus cum Domino*, the same spirit that he is." In such passages, identity replaces power as the mode of relation.

But Donne's theology is not uniformly Christocentric in this sense. Rather, he portrays Christ in the context of absolutist power relations as often as those of paradox and participation. An early Lincoln's Inn sermon thus observes that "by Christs taking my sins, I am made a *servant of my God . . . a vassall*, a *Tributary* debtor to God."

Redemption thus entails enslavement. In general, Donne perceives Christianity as having increased man's moral burden, placing him under heavier obligations. In a late sermon preached at St. Dunstan's, he makes what appears to be an original claim (at least, I have never seen it elsewhere) that human suffering is a "re-crucifixion" imposed as a penalty for our crucifixion of Christ. Therefore, although "we think to enjoy" the death of Christ, "God would have us doe it over again. . . . All being guilty of Christs death, there lies an obligation upon us all, to fulfill his sufferings. And this is the *generality* of afflictions, as we consider them in their own nature." Guilt, pain, fear, domination, servitude are as much part of Donne's understanding of specifically Christian relations as they are of his theology as a whole. (pp. 186-88)

Guilt forces one into dependence on a power felt as both overpowering and personal and therefore as "aweful" in both its ancient and modern senses. The cultural basis for this apprehension of power manifests itself in James's quite conventional analogues for his own authority: father, husband, head. As noted previously, these metaphors all connote both absolute dominion over the other (child, wife, body) and loving care for that other. In particular, the father has both *patriae potestas*, the power of life and death, over his children and a deep natural affection for them; he cares for them more than for himself. The royal metaphors thus depict a power that is inherently ambivalent, a fusion of unlimited, fearful authority and protective love. But this cultural representation throws us back on the problem of bivalent co-option, for the particular ambivalence of Stuart absolutism was in no sense a Stuart invention but has a long history. Absolutist theology opens out on to what Rudolph Otto called the "idea of the holy." (pp. 191)

For Donne, sacred Power demands . . . submission. . . . Submission here is not a half-resentful, half-defiant obedience to an oppressive system, the master/slave model implicit in most modern discussions of power relations, but almost a mode of desire. The terror at divine power is bound up with a longing to be overpowered. The language of spiritual politics in Donne is thus suffused by an erotic and infantile affectivity. The self longs for a childlike passivity. Donne imagines God urging the self toward autonomy and independence, to which the self replies in horror, "*Domine Tu*, Lord put me not over to the catechizing of Nature . . . but take me into thine owne hands, do Thou, Thou, that is to be done upon me." This self (or soul), which Donne at times considers "female," desires dependence and submission because they entail "being mastered," being cared for by God: "God is the Potter: if God will be that, I am well content to be this: let me be any thing, so that I am be from my God. I am as well content to be a sheep, as a Lion, so God will be my Shepheard."

This desire for passivity at times modulates into a dramatic, and occasionally macabre, eroticism. Donne speaks of desiring to "awake at midnight, and embrace God in mine armes," although he immediately attempts to deny the sexual implications of this image by glossing "embrace" as "that is, receive God into my thoughts." Similarly he speaks of wanting to "Dye in [God's] . . . armes," where

the secondary, sexual meaning of "die" is heightened by the physicality of "armes." The longing to be almost sexually overcome is particularly associated with Christ's body. His body "covers me by touching me," "cover," like "die," frequently having erotic undertones in the seventeenth century. Christ covers sin, "by comming to me, by spreading himself upon me . . . Mouth to mouth, Hand to hand." Sometimes it is the soul that spreads itself on Christ: "so when my crosses have carried mee up to my Saviours Crosse, I put my hands into his hands, and hang upon his nailes, I put mine eyes upon his. . . . I put my mouth upon his mouth." Almost the same passage occurs at the end of Donne's final sermon, **Death's Duel:** "There wee leave you in that *blessed dependancy*, to *hang* upon *him* that *hangs* upon the *Crosse*, there *bath* in his *teares*, there *suck* at his *woundes*." With "suck," the erotic image of covering coalesces with that of infantile dependency. The desire to hang upon the beloved's mouth or to suck at his wounded side, the desires of the gendered anima and the infant, are parallel: cravings for submission to power, for intimacy and union with the dread beloved. (pp. 193-94)

In Donne, the idealization of power relations is never innocent. Andrewes's prose creates the impression that participation is an experiential given, an intuited relation rather than an explanation imposed on the contents of perception. This is not the case with Donne, who makes it quite clear that correct understanding of divine power depends on a prior interpretive act. The goodness of God is not a given but follows from a conscious mystification of power relations. Like Calvin—and like King James—he holds that absolute authority must be perceived as loving and caring. This perception is the premise of all patriarchal models of power—that the one who rules and therefore punishes also loves. If God slays his people, "yet, that God, their Father weepes over the slaughter." The *rex tremendae maiestatis* is also the *fons pietatis*, and Donne always insists on the identity of the God who strikes and the God of love and mercy. His punishments are always medicinal; "God strikes so, as that when he strikes, he strikes a fire, and lights him a candle, to see his presence by." (pp. 197-98)

Human suffering results from divine *caritas*, for the "Sharp arrowes" which wound us come "out of the sweet hand of God." God's arrows contain "a *Canticle*, a *lovesong*, an *Epithalamion*, a *marriage song* of God, to our souls, wrapped up, if wee would open it, and read it." Domination and punishment in theology are like objects approaching the speed of light; they lose their ordinary nature, and suddenly the relations of time and space, of power and pain, become paradoxical and unfamiliar. While Donne's radical Protestant monotheism leads him to see God as the cause of suffering, God's terrifying power, in turn, transmutes into tenderness. The torturer is also the healer, or, perhaps more accurately, one must see the torturer as the healer. Hence faith is largely a matter of being able to appreciate paradoxes: that God cuts us "into peeces" in order to sew us together again, that He breaks our bones "to set them strayter." While we "are fishes reserved for that great Mariage-feast," and therefore presumably designed to be consumed, each fish is "a ghest too," for "whosoever is served in at the table, sits at the table." Such paradoxes are rooted not only in the conviction that God controls all events, both good and bad, but also that all events are signs of His love and justice and mercy. God causes everything and everything He causes is significant. Thus Donne writes, "All comes from Gods hand; and from his hand, by way of hand-writing, by way of letter, and instruction to us." But if all events are divine messages—and in the passage immediately preceding this quotation Donne names the defeat of the Armada, the Gunpowder Plot, and the cessation of the plague—then there is no space left for the operations of natural law. Indeed, the attempt to propose natural explanations, as, for example, to "say the winds delivered us" from the Armada, implies a disbelief in God's power and "present judgements." (pp. 199-200)

A final implication of Donne's absolutist theology deserves mention. As noted previously, Donne tends to view God's self-communication as paradoxical, dark, as signs that require interpretation and decoding. This has consequences for both his exegetical and homiletic practice. Unlike most of his contemporaries, Donne seems curiously eager to point out the uncertainties of biblical interpretation, to bring up textual and interpretive problems without resolving them. For example, a sermon preached before King Charles in 1626 begins,

> There are occasions of Controversies of all kinds in this one Verse; And one is, whether this be one Verse or no; For as there are Doctrinall Controversies, out of the sense and interpretation of the words, so are there Grammatticall differences about the Distinction, and Interpunction of them: Some Translations differing therein from the Originall, (as the Originall Copies are distinguished, and interpuncted now) and some differing from one another.
>
> (p. 204)

The repeated references to textual difficulties, disagreements among the fathers, differences between ancient and modern expositors seem designed to erode belief in a single, accessible meaning of the holy text. Donne's own hermeneutic furthers this destabilization by replacing the spiritual senses of medieval exegesis with the principle of accommodation. The text has one genuine sense—the literal; but this sense can then be "accommodated" to various situations. Donne, however, never suggests that these applied meanings exist in any sense in the text as opposed to being useful inferences made *from* it. Discussing the first chapter of Acts, he observes, "*Christ* spoke the words of this *Text*, principally to the *Apostles* . . . but they are in their just extention, and due accomodation, appliable to our present occation of meeting heere." The accommodated meaning corresponds to the old tropological sense but relocated from the spiritual recesses of the text to the mind of the interpreter who applies the letter to the "present occasion." (pp. 205-06)

There is very little rationalistic softening here, little effort to substitute legal/contractual or ethical categories for personal and affective ones, despite Donne's awareness that religious perception involves an *interpretation* of the secularized contents of an already almost instinctive ratio-

nalism. Original Sin, the damnation of the heathen, and other manifestations of the apparent amorality of the divine will worry him, but he almost always chooses to accept these consequences rather than relax God's grasp on the world. It is only when the notion of power has been flattened into its present meaning, that such a grasp becomes intolerable—again both in politics and theology. This is obvious in Deism's revulsion from both forms of absolutism, its preference for legal structures over those based on personal power, and its neo-Stoic moralism. (p. 210)

> *Debora Kuller Shuger, "Absolutist Theology: The Sermons of John Donne," in her* Habits of Thought in the English Renaissance: Religion, Politics, and the Dominant Culture, *University of California Press, 1990, pp. 159-217.*

Eleanor J. McNees   (essay date 1992)

[*Below, McNees contends that Donne's move from the Roman to the Anglican Church influenced his presentation of the flesh and spirit in both his secular and sacred poetry.*]

The Anglican stance toward the Eucharist with its denial of transubstantiation but its assertion of Real Presence lends John Donne a model for the poetic paradoxes in both his secular and sacred lyrics. In the Eucharist human and divine intersect to create a sacramental presence. As the elements of bread and wine are not transubstantiated into body and blood but coexist with them, so the spirit does not deny flesh. Instead, the flesh is purged by penitential prayer, and the elements are changed in *use* after the Prayer of Consecration. The Anglican compromise in the early to midseventeenth century emphasized three elemental points to which Donne (after his ordination as an Anglican priest in 1615) adhered: (1) the eucharistic elements were not (as in transubstantiation or consubstantiation) changed in *substance* but rather in *use*; (2) the sacrament operated on the faithful as a seal of grace, not merely as a representational *sign*; (3) the celebration of Holy Communion was fundamentally a *sacrifice* recalling Christ's Passion and exacting contrition in the communicant.

The first of these points, the shift in *use* of the eucharistic bread and wine provided Donne with an analogy for his poetic mixture of sacred and secular images in the divine poems. The coexistence of flesh and spirit, however, precedes the divine poems; it runs throughout Donne's writing from his secular songs and sonnets to his divine poems and sermons. In the secular writings the equation of sacred and profane results in true paradox; in the divine writings paradox is undermined by a doctrinal belief in the sacramental connection between superficially disparate images.

One of Donne's most persistent themes, the ostensible paradox of death and resurrection, is grounded in the eucharistic ceremony with its recreation of Christ's Passion and the celebration of his resurrection in the act of communion. Donne's divine poems, however, rarely focus on the *act* of communion; rather, they are preoccupied with the repentance and confession of sins *before* participation in the act of Holy Communion. Conversely, Donne's secular lyrics frequently assert both transubstantiation and communion of body and soul with another human being. Donne freely uses Roman Catholic iconography throughout the secular lyrics partly to mock and partly to justify human love.

In his divine poems, particularly, Donne is concerned with confession and purification prior to death. His language is eschatological; it looks toward what he terms the "third resurrection" but only as a goal to be achieved after death. Throughout his sermons he spells out his doctrine of threefold resurrection: "There is a Resurrection from worldly calamities, a resurrection from sin, and a resurrection from the grave." Holy Communion embodies the second resurrection while pointing toward the third. It recalls the death and resurrection of Christ and symbolically dramatizes the death of sin in the communicant, a prerequisite for the final resurrection of the body and soul from the grave. Donne attempts to make his poems enact an analogous process. Following the method of Ignatian meditation, he conjures up a vivid picture of Christ's Passion, then tries to identify himself with Christ as victim. The poem is asked to function as a vehicle of conversion that will prepare the poet for colloquy with God. Death of sin can only be achieved by repentance and self-sacrifice, an emptying out of bodily evil. (pp. 33-4)

Although several critics have tried to demonstrate Donne's allegiance either to Calvinism or Roman Catholicism, Donne's poetry actually defies such labeling. Raised as a Roman Catholic, strongly influenced by Calvinist doctrine, and finally an Anglican priest, Donne advances toward Anglicanism as the most catholic of all religions. More recently critics have sought a synthesis between these two extremes, although few address Donne's particular breed of Anglicanism. In fact, the Anglican compromise between Roman Catholicism and Puritan Protestantism probably tempted Donne because of its ability (like paradox) to balance two extremes and renounce neither. Following article twenty-eight, "Of the Lordes Supper," Donne rejected the Roman Catholic belief in transubstantiation, which he thought bordered dangerously on the adoration of miracles. He frequently criticized the Roman church for its emphasis on visible spectacle over invisible faith. He chose instead to view the eucharistic ceremony as an unfolding of Christ's presence in a typological or hermeneutical sense, and thereby to avoid controversies over the nature of the Real Presence. Christ unveiled himself in the consecrated elements; one substance was not alchemically transmuted into another. Yet the sacrament with its specific ritual and liturgical language was a mandatory condition for such unveiling.

Donne's divine poems attempt to emulate the language and ritual of the sacraments, specifically of the Passion and its extension in the Eucharist. The poem's language offers the sacramental link between divine action and personal internalization of that action. One must devour the words—their rhythm, syntax, and secular and spiritual connotations—to realize presence. This presence fuses the poet with Christ and, by extension, the reader with the Christ-poet persona. Reading the poem is an exercise in figural fulfillment. The poet conjures up a picture of both Christ and his own struggling soul and through words links himself to that picture. The reader works back through the individual voice of the poet to the picture and thus to a personal identification with the picture. (pp. 37-8)

As an enactment of "Holy Communion" between two human souls, **"The Exstasie"** stands midway between Donne's secular and divine poems. Like the eucharistic ceremony, the poem moves from an emphasis on the physical presence of the elements—the two bodies—to the spiritual union of the souls. Although this latter union is contingent on the connection of bodies (the engrafted hands and twisted eye-beams), it demands their temporary relinquishment at the moment of the souls' union: "And whil'st our soules negotiate there, / Wee like sepulchrall statues lay. . . ." On earth, the physical senses of sight and touch are preconditions for the mysterious union of the souls. Like the bread and wine of Catholic transubstantiation, the bodies become mere accidents during the communion of the souls. Body and soul do not coexist.

In recounting the ecstasy of two earthly lovers, the poem uses the analogy of eucharistic communion to reinforce human union. Here, however, Donne subverts the divine process, making it serve human ends instead of vice versa. He thus mocks both human and divine love and reverses the hierarchical ascent of the human to the divine. The process the lovers go through closely resembles the position of the Roman Catholic communicant. The visible elements—bodies—become "sepulchrall statues" as they surrender their lives to a newly transubstantiated soul. Their bodies are like the eucharistic accidents of bread and wine. The transubstantiating agent is love that effects a permanent change:

> When love, with one another so
>   Interinanimates two soules,
> That abler soule, which thence doth flow,
>   Defects of lonelinesse controules.
>
> Wee then, who are this new soule, know,
>   Of what we are compos'd, and made,
> For, th'Atomies of which we grow,
>   Are soules, whom no change can invade.
>   [*Songs and Sonnets*] ll. 41-8)

Yet only through tangible connection and visible communion can the lovers advance to a more spiritual state. At this point Donne is unwilling to grant much weight to the bodies. The body is the book that reveals the sacramental and mysterious union of the souls. It is a precondition that instigates the spiritual union, then retires.

Like the eucharistic service, the poem turns narrative description to dramatic participation with "the device of the hypothetical listener." If the listener (prospective communicant?) were adequately prepared by "good love," he "Might thence a new concoction take, / And part farre purer than he came (*SS*, ll. 27-28)." Here Donne seems to imply the figural definition of "concoction" as digestion and "ripening, maturing, or bringing to a state of perfection" (*Oxford English Dictionary*). Similarly, the eucharistic concoction transforms the devout communicant from a sinful state to a state of grace. The poem demands a sacrifice of body to soul, whereas the eucharistic ceremony requires a sacrifice of *both:* "ourselves, our souls and bodies, to be a reasonable, holy, and lively sacrifice unto thee." The poem highlights the division between body and soul at the moment of the spiritual communion, whereas the Eucharist holds the two together. Donne seems here purposely to deny the conjunction of body and soul between human beings. That particular union he reserves for man with God.

Speaking of the eucharistic analogy in **"The Extasie,"** Robert Ellrodt emphasizes Donne's "frontier" between the body and the soul:

> Cette conception du sacrement suppose entre l'esprit et la chair un parallelisme qui rappelle curieusement la conception de l'amour exposé dans **"The Exstasie."** Donne et Herbert maintienent entre l'âme et le corps une frontière que ne franchissent pas ces esprits, engendrés par le sang, qui s'efforcent de se faire sembables à des âmes et n'y parviennent point.

Nevertheless, Ellrodt admits that "un lien indissoluble" exists between body and soul. This tie recalls Donne's conception of the Eucharist as a "conduit of grace." The eucharistic action provides the temporary meeting place for body and soul. Donne allows for spiritual transubstantiation of two souls but does not permit two bodies to be similarly transubstantiated. **"The Exstasie"** does not effect the coexistence of body and soul on a spiritual plane. It allows bodies, then souls, then bodies to unite in a deviation from either Anglican or Roman Catholic Eucharist:

> Transposé dans la doctrine eucharistique, ce mode de pensée supposerait plutôt que la grace divine se communique à l'âme du croyant par l'entremise et le detour des espèces sensibles.

The poem refuses to depict the lovers' union as exclusively spiritual or as literally transubstantial. Their communion is only partial, however, because bodies and souls are held apart throughout the poem. The end of the poem justifies the return from ecstatic union to separate bodies:

> To'our bodies turne wee then, that so
> Weake men on love reveal'd may looke;
> Loves mysteries in soules doe grow,
> But yet the body is his booke.
> And if some lover, such as wee,
> Have heard this dialogue of one,
> Let him still marke us, he shall see
> Small change, when we'are to bodies gone.
> (*SS*, ll. 69-76)

One must see and hear God through the visible sacrament and audible scripture. Roman Catholic emphasis on sacrament and sight must be balanced with Protestant stress on scripture. The body, like a book, is needed to narrate the drama of the *mysterious* union of the souls. The "weake" men need physical proof to anchor their belief. The actual mystery of the souls, like the eucharistic mystery, cannot be explained. **"The Exstasie"** presents a problematic view of eucharistic communion. It shows Donne playing with both Roman Catholic and Protestant doctrine but ulti-

mately refusing to make either transubstantiation or consubstantiation support the real presence of the lover's union. (pp. 40-3)

In reverse order in the secular poems Donne applies divine logic to justify secular actions. The result is an ironic gap between the limitless quality of divine language and severely limited (because temporal) mortal actions. In the secular lyrics too Donne plays more freely with the Roman Catholic doctrines of transubstantiation, sainthood, and visible ceremony. His conceits are more expansive than those of the divine poems, his logic often purposely subversive.

"The Canonization," "Twicknam Garden," and **"The Relique"** exaggerate specific eucharistic elements and reinforce Donne's complaint that Roman Catholics emphasize miracles over faith. These poems focus on the debate between "accidents" and "substance" instead of on the figural relationship between the two. In so doing, they deny the full presence of figural fulfillment. These secular lyrics are more dialectical than typological. They introduce transubstantiation to resolve the tension, but the transubstantiation appears to be too facile a reconciliation. One is left unconvinced by the announced union.

In **"The Canonization"** Donne employs the revelatory device to which Ricoeur refers (substantiation-death-birth of spirit) to expose the artificial quality of secular love. Stanza 3 describes the union of the lovers in the form of the neutral phoenix that rises from its ashes. Here the lovers have been transubstantiated into a fictitious substance that claims to be immortal. The choice of the phoenix with its miraculous overtones actually undermines the religious imagery of the poem. The stanza parodies both communion and canonization ceremonies. As in **"The Exstasie,"** liturgical language glorifies profane reality with such words as "tapers" (candles carried in the processional behind the cross by Taperers), the "phoenix" as a type of Christ able to die and be resurrected, and the "mysterious" quality that results from the union. Among the definitions of "mystery" in the *OED* is that of a "religious truth known only from divine revelation." Here the word strongly echoes the mystery of the Eucharist that symbolically reenacts Christ's death and resurrection. Beneath its liturgical veneer, the profane quality of the lovers' physical love forces the reader to see their transformation as miraculous rather than mysterious. Donne parodies Roman Catholic reverence for miracles by exaggerating the lovers' transformation.

Stanza 4 further undercuts the "mysterious" union of the previous stanza in its recourse to transubstantiation. The lovers dedicate themselves to immortality in the "pretty roomes" of sonnets instead of saints' chronicles. The sonnets are transmuted into hymns where "all shall approve / Us *Canoniz'd* for Love." (*SS*, ll. 35-36) The slight on the Roman Catholic tendency to multiply and revere saints is unmistakable. Also the effort to locate the *place* of immortality is a thinly disguised criticism of the Catholic focus on the how and the where of transubstantiation.

The punning on the word "love" that ends both first and last lines of each stanza reinforces Donne's distinction between visible secular love and divine love. The poem moves from the specificity of the lovers' love to a generalized quasi-religious love and finally to other earthly lovers' love. Divine love is actually obscured by secular love, although the latter purports to lead to the former. Through another exaggeration—repetition—the poem questions the efficacy of earthly love.

The last stanza further criticizes the earthly lovers' attempts to make their love holy. The canonized lovers are invoked by their earthly counterparts to "Beg from above / A patterne of your love!" (*SS*, ll. 44-45)—in other words, to implore the saints for a spiritual model. Donne is repeatedly adamant throughout his divine writings about the uselessness of saints as mediators. Thus, although the poem mimes a liturgical ceremony, it criticizes both Roman Catholic practices of transubstantiation and saint worship. In undermining these processes, it also satirizes the supernatural quality of the earthly lovers' love. What allegedly elevates the lovers actually makes them appear foolish. Canonization is not a route toward the achievement of Real Presence.

On a syntactical level, the monosyllabic rhymes—"wit," "it," "fit," in stanza 3—as well as the levity of tone further undercut the supposedly eschatological thrust of the poem. Donne's "limit-language" here involves parable transmuted to parody. He employs sacred language in the service of secular narrative. Although seeming to add spiritual authority to the secular lovers, he actually emphasizes the gulf between spiritual and secular. By making religious language praise mortal actions, Donne exposes the diminution of the spiritual to the secular. The words, particularly the constantly repeated "Love," ring hollow.

Throughout **"The Canonization,"** Donne pokes fun at the ease with which the Roman Catholics perform transubstantiation—"Call us what you will, wee'are made such by love" (l. 19)—and canonization—"And by these hymnes, all shall approve / Us *Canoniz'd* for Love." (*SS*, ll. 35-36) There is no hint of the precommunion penitence that pervades the divine poems. Instead of sacrificing themselves to spiritual love, the lovers have absorbed the world's soul into themselves and have abandoned others. They have proven inadequate models or mediators for other earthly lovers. The poem succeeds in wielding Roman Catholic imagery to criticize earthly or visible love.

"Twicknam Garden," like **"The Canonization,"** parodies the double meaning of secular and sacred love. Here, too, Donne employs eucharistic language to elevate a secular theme. In **"Twicknam Garden,"** however, love has already turned to rage and enacted a reverse transubstantiation:

> Blasted with sighs, and surrounded with tears,
>   Hither I come to seeke the spring,
>   And at mine eyes, and at mine eares,
>   Receive such balmes, as else cure every thing;
>   But O, selfe traytor, I do bring
>   The spider love, which transubstantiates all,
>   And can convert Manna to gall,
>   And that this place may thoroughly be
> thought
>   True Paradise, I have the serpent brought.
>   (*SS*, ll. 1-9)

As he will do in the later divine poems, Donne reactivates and personalizes a biblical narrative. Here, however, the drama of the Garden of Eden is denigrated to the agony of a lovesick individual who offers a sad communion to other lovers:

> Hither with christall vyals, lovers come,
>   And take my teares, which are loves wine,
>   And try your mistresse Teares at home,
> For all are false, that tast not just like mine;
>   Alas, hearts do not in eyes shine,
> Nor can you more judge womans thoughts by
> teares,
>   Then by her shadow, what she weares.
> O perverse sexe, where none is true but shee,
> Who's therefore true, because her truth kills
> mee.
>   (*SS*, ll. 19-27)

Here Donne reverses the upward movement of Christian typology from type to antitype to fulfillment in the Eschaton. By reversing this eschatological direction, he again emphasizes the gap between secular and spiritual worlds. The final couplet offers a paradoxical conceit ostensibly in the courtly love tradition. If viewed within the Christian narrative framework, however, the couplet may allude to Christ's Passion and the church's reenactment of that Passion in the Eucharist. Again Donne's theme of death as a prerequisite for eternal life surfaces. The poem ends with worldly death, completing the biblical cycle from creation to Christ's crucifixion. It is more pessimistic than either **"The Canonization"** or **"The Relique,"** both of which play with eschatological themes to emphasize human foibles. In **"Twicknam Garden"** Donne's persona is locked into an earthly hell by earthly love. Unlike Adam, he is doomed to remain in the garden transfigured into a mandrake or a fountain, robbed of his humanity.

The poem's eucharistic imagery—transubstantiation, manna, wine—provides an analogy with which to contrast the process of unhappy and unfulfilled love. That the "spider love" can transubstantiate manna into gall stresses Donne's tendency as in **"The Canonization"** both to support and to undercut human fallible love with Roman Catholic imagery. The seriousness of the imagery contrasts with the levity of the theme; it simultaneously undermines the religious allusions and elevates the earthly lovers' plight. Unlike the merging of the two souls in **"The Extasie,"** the act of transubstantiation here converts one substance into another and abolishes the first. The transforming agent—love—assumes a satanic quality in direct contrast to the divine love of the eucharistic Prayer of Consecration. Donne opposes human love to divine love in this poem. He employs the Eucharist as an authoritative model for the process of disintegration, not reintegration.

In the most eschatologically oriented of his secular lyrics, **"The Relique,"** Donne again personalizes a divine drama. Like **"Twicknam Garden,"** the movement reverses the typological process, focusing on the tangible quality of the lovers instead of their spiritual union on Judgment Day. As in **"The Canonization,"** Donne mocks the Roman Catholic focus on ceremony and the iconolatry of spiritual concepts. The "bracelet of bright haire about the bone" is construed by a gravedigger (one still alive, therefore not privy to the soul's whereabouts after death) as a lure to the dead lovers' souls to meet at the grave site on Judgment Day. Donne believed in the resurrection of the body and in the union of body and soul on that day. In **"The Relique"** he requests, however, a spiritual union *based* on a physical one (as in **"The Exstasie"**), not the reverse. Making a spiritual union contingent on (instead of coincident with) a physical one disrupts the eschatological thrust of Donne's sermons and divine poems. Here he seems to parody not so much the lovers' anticipated union of body and soul as the unorthodox speculations of the gravedigger who discovers the bracelet of hair.

In stanza 2, Donne overtly criticizes the Catholic reverence for relics and miracles by calling the craving for relics and miracles a time of "mis-devotion." In stanza 3, he parodies both secular love and miracle. After equating the lovers' love with miracles, he stipulates the precise nature of those miracles and thus robs them of any miraculous quality. He also implicitly criticizes the Catholic tendency to discover miracles outside of the Scriptures. If the lovers can proliferate miracles, anyone can:

> First, we lov'd well and faithfully,
> Yet knew not what wee lov'd, nor why,
> Difference of sex no more wee knew,
> Then our Guardian Angells doe.
>
> (*SS*, ll. 23-26)

Again, Donne uses a Catholic allusion as a satirical defense of the lovers' position. The lame comparison to the androgynous Guardian Angels promptly pokes fun at the Catholic emphasis on intermediaries—saints and angels—between man and God. These lines echo Donne's warning in his sermons to the communicants not to question the why and how of Real Presence in the Eucharist, but simply to believe in it. The final two lines, as in **"Twicknam Garden,"** undercut the superficial religious apparatus of the last stanza. They both reduce the definition of miracle to a synonym for the female lover and amplify it to suggest a definition beyond linguistic capacity: "All measure, and all language, I should passe, / Should I tell what a miracle shee was (*SS*, ll. 32-33)." A miracle defies language; like a mystery, it cannot be codified or explained. In this poem miracle is the secular counterpart of mystery, the latter a word much used by Donne to describe the unknowable union of Christ's body and spirit in the Eucharist.

In **"The Relique"** Donne seeks, . . . the existence of the lovers after death. Because he chooses to focus on earthly love throughout the poem, he opts for concrete Roman Catholic imagery—"such advancers of Images, as would throw down Christ rather than his Image" (*Sermons*, 8:433)—instead of the "limit-expressions" of parable or paradox. The poem criticizes Roman Catholic reverence for saints, relics, extrascriptural miracles and angels while at the same time it uses those images to reinforce earthly love. Emphasis falls on visible signs rather than on invisible faith.

Although some commentators have argued for either chronological or typological links between Donne's secular and divine lyrics, the reverse typology of the secular lyrics appears to refute any such figural relation. As in the eucharistic elements, the difference seems to be one of the *use* to which the words are put. The secular lyrics play with both spiritual and secular connotations, often using spiritual (particularly Roman Catholic dogma) to praise secular. The two are never in harmony; they form an unresolvable paradox. The divine lyrics, conversely, allow flesh and spirit to intersect and reinforce each other in a more traditional typological movement. On cursory perusal, the secular lyrics seem more Catholic in character, the divine poems more Protestant in their attention to spiritual union as an ultimate goal. Undermining this hypothesis, however, is the overtly sensual language of the divine poems and their emphasis on both body and soul. They illustrate Donne's effort to realize the second of his three resurrections on earth—the purification and purgation of the body through penitence and prayer. The divine poems still insist, however, on a balance between body and soul that is absent in Donne's conceptions of Catholic and Puritan faiths. In this sense, they are specifically Anglican in their refusal to indulge in Roman Catholic transubstantiation or to retreat to the abstract symbolism of Protestantism. The poems are neither transformed into icons nor made into Scripture signifiers. Liturgical ritual and Scripture mix with meditation to create a presence both personal and immediate. Often, it is true, that presence seems to be that of the persona instead of Christ or God. Always, however, it is the persona trying to realize Christ in words. (pp. 45-50)

In his longer divine poems, Donne is almost exclusively

Frontispiece of "Deaths Duell" (1632), reproducing the portrait of Donne in his burial shroud.

absorbed with the mystery of the Incarnation and Resurrection. His *Holy Sonnets* compact the persona's struggle toward death and resurrection into pleas to God to punish him so that he will be worthy of salvation, whereas the longer hymns and monologues protract that struggle. In these longer poems, Donne attempts to speak about the kingdom of God. To this end he uses the "limit-language" of paradox and parable. The speaker is less agonized, the poem less intensely personal than in the sonnets.

"The Crosse" and "Upon the Annunciation and Passion Falling Upon One Day. 1608," particularly, are miniature sermons occasioned by specific symbols or events. As he expands and explicates biblical texts in his sermons, so Donne takes the cross in "The Crosse" and pushes both thematic and linguistic capacities of the word to their limits. "The Crosse" insists on the ability of the Prayer of Consecration to put a word to another use or to make the natural sacred.

In a thickly textured criticism of the Puritan desire to remove the cross from church altars, Donne multiplies superficial paradoxes. He builds an argument that mimes the symbolic cross's bisection of time and eternity. Here the doubleness of which Ellrodt speaks becomes multiplicity: The argumentative strands intersect in the horizontal and vertical axis of the cross:

> From mee, no Pulpit, nor misgrounded law,
> Nor scandal taken, shall this Crosse withdraw,
> It shall not, for it cannot; for, the losse
> Of this Crosse, were to mee another Crosse;
> Better were worse, for, no affliction,
> No Crosse is so extreme, as to have none.
> Who can blot out the Crosse, which
>   th'instrument
> Of God, dew'd on mee in the Sacrament?
> Who can deny mee power, and liberty
> To stretch mine armes, and mine owne Crosse
>   to be?

Here metaphorical cross (cross of burden) meets symbolic cross (cross on the altar), which, in turn, leads back through the sacrament of the Eucharist to the actual cross on Calvary. All levels of the word are valid; the play of language illustrates Donne's refusal to allow one meaning to be swallowed up by another. All three coexist, loading the word with secular and spiritual presence. Yet Donne insists on the priority of the spiritual cross: "Materiall Crosses then, good physicke bee, / And yet spirituall have chiefe dignity" (*DP* [*Divine Poems*], ll. 25-26). The tight compression of "dew'd on me in the Sacrament" slices through time to capture the actual moment of Christ's blood falling from the cross. This blood is immediately turned to sacramental blood and gives the speaker strength to sacrifice himself in a mimesis of Christ. The sacrament leads inward until the speaker becomes his own cross or part of Christ. Acting as a seal of grace, the Eucharist guarantees the existence of the cross on these three levels. One must continually sacrifice oneself before partaking of the sacrament. Such an individual cross touches Christ's actual cross at the altar's cross in the Eucharist.

In addition to exegesis of the word "cross" on a semantic level, Donne internalizes the emblem of the cross to *re-*

present it, further advancing his belief in transformation as opposed to transubstantiation. Although Christ is already implanted in men and women, they must duplicate Christ's sacrifice to stand in sacramental relation to him. Otherwise the image, as in "Goodfriday, 1613. Riding Westward," grows tarnished and recedes. Such sacrifice involves a stripping away of false ceremony and imagery before Christ's presence can be realized:

> As perchance, Carvers do not faces make,
> But that away, which hid them there, do take;
> Let Christs, soe, take what hid Christ in thee,
> And be his image, or not his, but hee.
>   (*DP*, ll. 33-36)

These lines mark Donne's middle stance between Roman Catholicism and Protestantism. The cross is not mere icon to be adored for itself nor accidental symbol to be discarded when one reaches colloquy with God; internalized in a person, it demonstrates Real Presence, the intersection of divine and human natures. Such presence is contingent on mutual sacrifice. Missing in all the divine terminology of the secular poems is this realization of sacrifice.

Midway through the poem after disclosing the meanings of the *noun* cross, Donne switches to the *verb*. He does this only after enjoining the reader to recognize the emblem of the cross in himself. By entering into communion with Christ through imaginative participation in the crucifixion, the communicant reactivates the word. On a grammatical level this *presencing* of the noun parallels the activation of the elements of bread and wine to a different use after the consecration. In both, the focus shifts from stationary elements to active presence. The verb "cross" takes on different meanings: the first (to afflict), abstract; the second (making the sign of the cross), concrete. Crossing or afflicting oneself pushes one toward contrition where one learns forgiveness and is prepared to make the sign of the cross on his chest. Such penitential exercises must be constantly repeated as preparation for the final crucifixion of death. For Donne, the penitential offering is unending. The punning repetition of "cross" compresses sacrifice and redemption into a double image. It evinces Donne's ability to condense and explode several meanings in one major symbol. (pp. 51-3)

In "Upon the Annunciation and Passion Falling Upon One Day. 1608," Donne adopts the apparent paradox of the conception and death of Christ falling on the same day in the liturgical year. This coincidence allows him literally to equate life with death and to compress life on earth into a day. Furthermore, the paradox offers him the excuse to push language to its semantic limits to reconcile the mortal human world with God's eternal one. The poem echoes the paradoxes of the Annunciation sonnet in *La Corona*. In both, Donne is concerned with Incarnation—the point at which Christ enters human flesh and crosses his divine nature with man's human one. The simultaneous celebration of the Annunciation and Passion allows him to collapse time into a divinely charged present where Mary is "seen at once, and seen / At almost fiftie, and at scarce fifteene" (*DP*, ll. 13-14), and where "Gabrielle gives Christ to her, He her to John" (*DP*, l. 16). This collapsing of time triggers one of Donne's favorite paradoxical analogies—that of west meeting east—which becomes the main consolation of **"Goodfriday"**:

> All this, and all between, this day hath showne,
> Th'Abridgement of Christ's story, which makes one
> (As in plaine Maps, the furthest West is East)
> Of the'Angels *Ave*,' and *Consummatum est.*
>   (***DP***, ll. 19-22)

The liturgical coincidence has offered Donne an authoritative (if specious) resolution of the paradox of life and death: "This Church, by letting these daies joyne, hath shown / Death and conception in mankinde is one" (***DP***, ll. 33-34). This coincidence calls forth the eschatological connection between Incarnation and revelation, between the *idea* of the Redemption and the *fact* of the Incarnation. Chronological time defers to eternal time. Both Annunciation and Passion pinpoint this deference as the former enters chronological time, and the latter leaves it. Falling on the same day, these two events vividly exemplify the typological movement toward resurrection and revelation. Annunciation bows to Passion; the Eucharist that would ordinarily be celebrated at the Annunciation is denied by the Passion:

> Tamely fraile body'abstaine to day; to day
> My soule eates twice, Christ hither and away.
> She sees him man, so like God made in this,
> That of them both a circle embleme is,
> Whose first and last concurre; this doubtfull day
> Of feast or fast, Christ came, and went away;
> She sees him nothing twice at once, who'is all.
>   (***DP***, ll. 1-7)

Caught in time between conception and death, the body gives way to the soul that transcends both events. Ironically, the double presence of the Annunciation and the Passion denies the Real Presence of Christ or the conjunction of body and soul in the Eucharist. Although it provides Donne with a good argument for his doubled images and paradoxes, it prohibits mutual celebration of body and soul, the goal of many of Donne's later divine poems. Instead, Donne chooses the oddly physical image of the soul eating twice, once hither for the body and once away for death, as if to compensate for the body's abstention.

Stressing the intersection of vertical and horizontal (sacred and historical) time in the action of the Eucharist, Geoffrey Wainwright states that the ceremony signifies a "tension between the 'already now' and the 'not yet.' " Similarly, in his appendix to the 1559 *Book of Common Prayer* book, John Booty insists on the eschatological compression and transcendence of time in the Eucharist as a "dynamic view of time in the Holy Communion with its remembering (*anamnesis*) of events past, in the light of things to come (the messianic banquet), whereby Christ's presence is realized and human existence transformed in the present." In **"Upon the Annunciation and Passion"** Donne exposes this doubleness by mediating on the church and its primary sacrament. The poem looks back to the **La Corona** sequence that Helen Gardner notes was probably written in the same year. Although both poems are meditative and narrative, **"Upon the Annunciation and Passion"** thwarts narrative sequence, substituting simultaneity of events for linearity. Nevertheless, the poems

have the same hermeneutical quality as the sermons in their uncovering and explaining of liturgical acts. Their "limit-language" is sanctioned by the "limit-experience" of Christ's life as celebrated in the liturgical year. The church calendar's compression authorizes a similar linguistic compression.

In his later divine poems, Donne moves from description of liturgical "limit-experiences" to personal dramatizations of them. Language begins to mime experience as the priest's words during the Prayer of Consecration parallel his action with the eucharistic elements. The language of **"Goodfriday," "Hymne to God my God, in my Sicknesse,"** and the **Holy Sonnets** internalizes the public eucharistic and eschatological language of the previous poems to depict the persona's own private spiritual struggle. In a sense, as in his secular lyrics, Donne appears to convert Christ (antitype) to a type in a reversal of traditional typology. This conversion, however, serves a different purpose. In the secular lyrics, the lovers absorb the whole world into themselves and make universal drama subservient to their own personal drama. In the **Holy Sonnets** universal biblical drama narrows to an individual struggle to realize in both words and deeds the "limit-experience" of union with God. Rarely, however, do these poems succeed in effecting this union. Instead, they are like preliminary ceremonies designed to prepare the sinner for absolution and communion.

"Goodfriday, 1613. Riding Westward" internalizes the didactic, epigrammatic language of **"The Crosse"** and **"Upon the Annunciation"** to depict the persona's private spiritual struggle to realize Christ's presence within himself. Like **"The Crosse,"** it moves from conjured picture of the cross—Christ's crucifixion—to a plea for affliction and sacrifice before that presence can be realized. Because the internal struggle is more complex and personal, the language and logic of **"Goodfriday"** are also more complex. Donne abandons the repetitive pun for elaborate analogy and paradox, both of which collapse by the end of the poem. There is no easy resolution of the conflict between body and soul here: The two are at odds as the body initially refuses the challenge of **"The Crosse"** to look at the crucifixion.

The poem begins with an analogy of man's soul to a sphere moved by misguided intelligence. Here Donne blames the contrary westward direction of his journey on an analogical argument that lacks a solid ground. As in **"Upon the Annunciation"** he metaphorically assigns the soul concrete properties: "Let man's Soul be a Sphere, and then, in this, / Th'intelligence that moves, devotion is" (***DP***, ll. 1-2). Here Donne presents the already outdated Ptolemaic analogy as a superficial (and incorrect) rationalization of the speaker's willful action. This evidence—whether logical, pseudo-scientific, or theological—does not justify action. Instead it exposes the persona's willful tendency to snatch at visible excuses, to rely on false or inappropriate authority. In **"Goodfriday"** the gap between secular logic and faith is too great. One cannot be used to ratify the other.

The original superficial argument against riding eastward to face Christ is abandoned for a movement inward toward rhetorical self-examination. Donne moves from faulty analogy to a series of paradoxical questions that pit his own limited humanity against the godliness of Christ. The five questions concern the persona's reluctance to see God (Christ) humbled, humanized, and tortured. They compose a kind of negative meditation or epic catalog. As he repeats his inability to view Christ's wounds, the speaker perversely recalls vivid details of the Passion, thus substituting remembered scene for actual confrontation or *anamnesis.* Although his body is still turned away for multiple *reasons,* his *faith,* through sensuous contemplation of the Passion, has begun to pull him eastward toward identity with Christ. Will bows to memory as reason gives way to faith.

Yet the persona still struggles with the problem of Christ's dual nature. He is unable or unwilling to regard him as human:

> Could I behold those hands which span the
>   Poles,
> And tune all spheares at once, peirc'd with those
>   holes?
> Could I behold that endlesse height which is
> Zenith to us, and to'our Antipodes,
> Humbled below us? or that blood which is
> The seat of all our Soules, if not of his,
> Make durt of dust, or that flesh which was
>   worne
> By God, for his apparell, rag'd, and torne?
>   (*DP*, ll. 21-28)

Unsure of the relationship between Christ's blood and Christ's soul, Donne still appears reluctant to assert a eucharistic Real Presence, although he admits the presence of Christ's blood in man's soul in the sacrament. Intellectually, his questions echo the Puritan difficulty of realizing Christ simultaneously on earth and in heaven. Yet the emotional vividness with which Donne catalogs the crucified Christ's physical traits is indeed reminiscent of the first step of the Ignatian meditational method—composition of place. The carnal imagery suggests that Donne is conjuring up Christ's physical presence (albeit in conditional language) to identify himself with Christ's sacrifice and thereby become worthy of partaking in the eucharistic meal. Yet this process is backward. To achieve true conformity with the crucified Christ, the speaker must first suffer his own internal crucifixion through penitence.

The persona concludes in a tone reminiscent of the penitential sonnets for a wrathful Christ to

> . . . thinke mee worth thine anger, punish mee,
> Burne off my rusts, and my deformity,
> Restore thine Image, so much, by thy grace,
> That thou may'st know mee, and I'll turne my
>   face.
>   (*DP*, ll. 39-42)

The speaker's promise of future action is predicated on first action by Christ. By using memory, however, to revive a vivid sense of Christ's presence, Donne indicates his capacity to realize the physical presence of Christ within his own mind. Although communion has not occurred in the present moment of the poem, it has been both remem-

bered and promised. The poem demonstrates Donne's belief in the necessity of corrective affliction as a prerequisite for true realization of Christ's presence.

"Hymne to God my God, in my Sicknesse," possibly Donne's last poem, offers **"Goodfriday"** a destination. It adopts the familiar east-west debate and resolves it by planting the poles within the persona:

> I joy, that in these straits, I see my West;
>   For, though theire currents yeeld returne to
>   none,
> What shall my West hurt me?   As West and
>   East
> In all flatt Maps (and I am one) are one,
> So death doth touch the Resurrection.
>   (*DP*, ll. 11-15)

Unlike **"Goodfriday,"** **"Hymne to God my God"** uses analogical reasoning to argue toward, not away from, faith. Here analogies do not offer excuses for turning away; rather, they reinforce the speaker's final sacrifice—his acceptance of his own death. The simile incorporates the parenthetical metaphor "(and I am one)" and compresses geography, speaker, and spiritual event into an elaborate analogy. Man and world are sacramentally identified through Christ. The equation of a physical surface with a spiritual event forces the reader to jump from a literal to a spiritual plane. Prostrated by physical sickness, the speaker's body is horizontal while his soul awaits ascension. The formation of a cross by body and soul stresses the sacramental identification of the speaker with Christ. In addition, the horizontal meeting points of the map—east and west—create a cross as they intersect with the vertical typology of death and resurrection. West (death) and east (resurrection) act to double presence by retaining both their directional signification and their spiritual symbolism. The initial directional paradox is resolved by the deeper spiritual symbols of death and resurrection.

Stanza 5 pushes analogy toward typology. It forces the typological movement from Adam to Christ toward eschatological fulfillment in the speaker. In death the three are typologically united. The persona steals the "limit-language" of biblical typology to apply it to his own "limit-experience" of dying:

> We think that *Paradise* and *Calvarie,*
>   *Christs Cross,* and *Adams* tree, stood in one
>   place;
> Looke Lord, and finde both *Adams* met in me;
>   As the first *Adams* sweat surrounds my face,
>   May the last *Adams* blood my soule embrace.
>   (*DP*, ll. 21-25)

Here the speaker, on the brink of death, is about to partake of the communion previously denied him. Already a type of Adam in life, he will soon be united with Christ in death. The sweat of the sickness has afforded him the penitential affliction he requested as a prerequisite for union. Adam and Christ are equated by simile (which falls just short of metaphorical identification) to emphasize the figural relation among Adam, Christ, and the poet, and not their identity. As in the previous stanza, the first Adam is physical, met through sweat, whereas the second is both physical and spiritual, encountered in the meeting of

Christ's blood with man's soul. The extent of the sacrifice that links the two Adams also differs. The first is sweaty from struggle and hard work, the second bloody from death. The stanza ends conditionally, resting on an ontological base and begging for an eschatological one. The eschatological promise of communion with Christ at death allows the speaker to accept self-sacrifice as a precondition for resurrection.

In his letters, Donne frequently expresses a desire for a struggle with death so that it not ambush him unaware and unrepentant. This struggle is reminiscent of his constant hope in the poems that God will overpower him. It hints also at Donne's fear of his own inaction:

> I would not that death should take me asleep.
> I would not have him meerly seise me, and onely
> declare me to be dead, but win me, and over-
>   come
> me. When I must shipwrack, I would do it in a
> Sea, where mine impotencie might have some
>   excuse;
> not in a sullen weedy lake, where I could not
>   have
> so much as exercise for my swimming.

Likewise Donne writes to another friend, "I am afraid that Death will play with me so long, as he will forget to kill me; and suffer me to live in a languishing and useless age, a life, that is rather a forgetting that I am dead, than of living." It is as if Donne wishes to make violent language instigate personal action. By constantly beseeching God to punish him directly and forcefully, Donne pushes language to substitute itself for action.

It is, however, in his final sermon, *Deaths Duell,* that Donne explains the typology of his **"Hymne to God my God."** In counseling his congregation as to the necessity of preparing themselves for the sacrament of Holy Communion, Donne likens this penitential action to that of the dying man. The sacrament serves as a preliminary death where the communicant learns to mingle sweat and tears with blood. By meditating on Christ's Passion as the persona has done in **"Goodfriday,"** and by imaginatively participating in Christ's crucifixion as he has done in **"Hymne to God my God,"** the communicant has achieved conformity with Christ and is ready for communion or the further "limit-experience" of death:

> If that time were spent in a *holy recommendation* of thyself to *God,* and a *submission* of *thy will* to his, it was spent in a *comformity* to him. In that *time,* and in those *prayers,* was his *agony* and *bloody sweat.* I will *hope* that thou didst *pray;* but not *every ordinary* and *customary prayer,* but *prayer actually* accompanied with *shedding of tears* and *dispositively* in a readiness to *shed blood* for *his glory* in *necessary cases,* puts thee into a *conformity* with him.

Prayer and tears must mix with action and blood. Passive meditation does not equal self-sacrifice. Because the speaker of **"Hymne to God my God"** has experienced this agony, he has earned the right to commune with God through Christ:

> So, in his purple wrapp'd receive mee Lord,

> By these his thornes give me his other
>   Crowne;
> And as to others soules I preach'd thy word,
>   Be this my Text, my Sermon to mine owne,
> Therefore that he may raise the Lord throws
>   down.
>
>   (*DP*, ll. 26-30)

In his final stanza Donne the priest achieves the "limit-experience" of death and communion by making Christ's Passion his own. Unification with God depends first on unification with Christ at the moment of death. The language of the last two stanzas finds its counterpart in the end of **Deaths Duell**: " . . . and as *God breathed a soul into* the *first Adam,* so this *second Adam breathed his soul into the hands of God."* Whereas the sermon maintains the distinction between the meditative communicant and his biblical counterparts, the poem merges the two. As preacher, the persona has been the first Adam giving out God's word; in death, he returns this gift. Although the sermon prescribes and depicts, the poem dramatizes the union of man with God. The **"Hymne"** ends with a declarative cause-effect statement, not a conditional one. The last two lines survey the action of the poem—the "throwing down" of the speaker in death—and affirm the reason for this action: that God might raise man. Donne writes his own epitaph, circling back from his public life as a priest to his private one as faithful communicant. The sermon moves inward as the priest blesses himself. In death he has gained the authority to declare God's intention.

Like the **"Hymne,"** the *Holy Sonnets* press for the necessity of repentance and contrition as prerequisites to union with God. Also like the **"Hymne,"** they view identification with Christ's Passion as a route toward that union. To this end they continually seek affliction as a means of realizing Christ's presence. They dramatize the sinner's confrontation with his sin and his petition for grace to receive Holy Communion. The sonnets borrow liturgical language and rhythm to lend authority to the individual drama. The sonnet form, like the structured liturgical prayers, encloses the drama and imposes a familiar framework that both restrains and emphasizes the individual voice. Although most of these sonnets discuss the sinner striving for grace, several conclude with specifically eucharistic imagery. Blood and tears mingle in the sonnets as blood and sweat meet in the trinity of Adam, Christ, and the persona of the **"Hymne."**

"Oh my Blacke Soule," second in Gardner's 1633 sequence, initiates the soul's quest for purity through Christ's blood. Addressed to the sinful soul, the octet describes the death-in-life fate of an unrepentant soul. The sestet turns on the word "grace." Though still addressed to the soul and not to God, it suggests a course of action the static predicament of the octet lacked:

> Oh make thy selfe with holy mourning blacke,
> And red with blushing, as thou art with sinne;
> Or wash thee in Christs blood, which hath this
>   might
> That being red, it dyes red soules to white.
>
>   (*DP*, ll. 11-14)

Unlike the poems addressed to God, this sonnet charts the route toward personal self-sacrifice. It calls for individual action independent of God's command. Donne plays on the secular and sacred connotations of black and red throughout the sonnet. After the octet, these secular meanings are "consecrated" to spiritual ones; sinful black becomes the black of holy mourning; red shame washed in Christ's blood is transformed to pure white. Here, blood, part of the sacrament, is the "conduit of grace" that links man to God. On a syntactical level, the similes of the octet ("like a pilgrim," "like a thiefe") are transmuted to active metaphors in the sestet. This metaphorical action is based on the speaker's own penitential ability to "make" himself black with mourning and red with blushing in preparation for Christ's eucharistic offering—"dying red soules to white."

This concept of washing oneself in Christ's blood derives specifically from the Anglican liturgy of Holy Communion. The next-to-the-last prayer before actual communion runs thus:

> We do not presume to come to this thy table (O merciful Lord) trusting in our own righteousness, but in thy manifold and great mercies. We be not worthy so much as to gather the crumbs under thy table, but thou art the same Lord, whose property is always to have mercy. Grant us therefore (gracious Lord) so to eat the flesh of thy dear Son Jesus Christ, and to drink his blood, that our sinful bodies may be made clean by his body, and our souls washed through his most precious blood, and that we may evermore dwell in him, and he in us.

The sonnet's sestet depicts the process of the repentant communicant. After contritely offering up his sins, he is ready to participate in the Eucharist that offers to absolve the soul with Christ's blood. Like the precommunion prayer, the *Holy Sonnets* attest to the sinner's unworthiness and plead for cleansing. They transform the corporate language of the communion prayer into a private demand for absolution. As in **"Goodfriday,"** however, they fall short of realizing actual communion with God.

"At the Round Earths Imagin'd Corners" is the most explicitly eschatological of Donne's sonnets. The octet begins with a discursive description of the Last Judgment that includes both dead and living. The sestet shifts inward like that of the second sonnet, begging for the grace to begin repenting: "Teach mee how to repent; for that's as good / As if thou 'hadst seal'd my pardon, with thy blood" (*DP*, ll. 13-14). The couplet echoes Donne's belief in the sacrament as a "seal of grace"; if the persona learns to repent, he will be able to participate worthily in Holy Communion and have his pardon "sealed." Yet the conditional "as if" alerts the reader to the actual absence of pardon. God has neither taught the speaker how to repent nor has He sealed his pardon with Christ's blood. Furthermore, repentance does not constitute pardon. The conditional simile does not merge repentance with pardon as metaphor would. It holds the two apart by comparing the speaker's action to God's. Although God will not directly subdue the speaker's will, His tutelage may cause the speaker to subdue his own will, an action prior to receipt of grace.

Oddly, in both sonnets penitence does not join with communion. Rather, the two seem to offer separate routes toward redemption. The second sonnet balances the alternatives with the coordinate conjunction "or" instead of a subordinate conjunction or a conditional clause. The subordinate conjunction "for" of the fourth sonnet introduces a clause that emphasizes the unaccomplished subjunctive action: "As if thou 'hadst seal'd my pardon." In both sonnets, the imperative voice conveys the illusion of forceful action yet lacks a response. God is present only as a passive listener. The entire drama occurs within the speaker.

As in **"Goodfriday,"** and other *Holy Sonnets* the persona here and in the second sonnet is confounded by the problem of repentance. Being washed in Christ's blood is still only an anticipated reward. The prayer before the General Confession in the Anglican liturgy requires a personal response from the communicant before his communal participation in the Confession. The priest says to the congregation:

> You that do truly and earnestly repent you of your sins, and be in love and charity with your neighbors, and intend to lead a new life, following the commandments of God, and walking from henceforth in his holy ways: Draw near, and take this holy Sacrament to your comfort; make your humble confession to Almighty God before this congregation here gathered together in his holy name, meekly kneeling upon your knees.

The sonnets express the quandary of the communicant on the verge of confession. The prayer demands from the communicant a promise governing all his future actions. The persona of the sonnets lacks the faith in himself to make that promise. The third sonnet of the Westmoreland group describes precisely this predicament:

> Oh, to vex me, contraryes meete in one:
> Inconstancy unnaturally hath begott
> A constant habit; that when I would not
> I change in vowes, and in devotione.
> As humorous is my contritione
> As my prophane love, and as soone forgott:
> As ridlingly distempered, cold and hott,
> As praying, as mute; as infinite, as none.
> I durst not view heaven yesterday; and to day
> In prayers, and flattering speaches I court God:
> To morrow' I quake with true feare of his rod.
> So my devout fitts come and go away
> Like a fantastique Ague: save that here
> Those are my best dayes, when I shake with
>   feare.
>
>   (*DP*, ll. 1-14)

It is possible that having renounced Roman Catholicism for Anglicanism and having subsequently supported the *Articles of Religion,* Donne is wary of overpromising himself. Such a fear of possible recusancy could partially account for the overwhelming self-accusation in the sonnets. More likely, however, the struggle toward active repentance involves a personal battle with the speaker's individual will. He alone must subdue that recalcitrant will. (pp. 54-64)

The poem pits these two logics against each other and acknowledges the need for punishment as a prerequisite for redemption. The octet describes an Old Testament world—the Garden of Eden—with its nonhuman elements—the tree, the serpent which "cannot be damn'd." After comparing his own plight with the other elements' freedom from damnation, Donne asks, "And mercy being easie and glorious / To God, in his sterne wrath, why threatens hee?" (**DP**, ll. 7-8). The sestet charts the New Testament logic of superabundance based on Christ's Passion. The speaker chastises his own Job-like behavior as he realizes the need for mutual sacrifice:

> O God, Oh! of thine onely worthy blood,
> And my teares, make a heavenly Lethean flood,
> And drowne in it my sinnes blacke memorie.
> (DP, ll. 10-12)

Both the tears of repentance and the blood of communion combine to drown not the sins themselves but the memory of them. Donne stops short of Christian absolution; he mixes mythological and biblical references (Heaven and Lethean Hades' river of forgetfulness) into an orymoronic conceit. The speaker still quests for blind forgetfulness over remorse and contrition. Unlike more orthodox Christians who claim their sins' debts to be forgiven, he wishes God to forget instead of forgive.

"I am a little world made cunningly" deviates from the octetsestet divisions of the previously mentioned sonnets. Like the love lyrics, it plays on the microcosm-macrocosm connection between the seas and tears, asking God to "Powre new seas in mine eyes, that so I might / Drowne my world with my weeping earnestly, / Or wash it, if it must be drown'd no more (**DP**, ll. 7-9)." Again, the persona demands the motivation to repent through alternative actions separated by the conjunction "or." These alternatives, uncoupled with Christ's blood, fail. Next, the persona negates his previous petition by stating that his sinful world "must be burnt." He retracts this solution too and finally turns to God in the couplet, asking Him to "burne me ô Lord, with a fiery zeale / Of thee' and thy house, which doth in eating heale" (**DP**, ll. 13-14). Here Donne transfigures the word "burne" from its secular to sacred use by imploring God's intervention as opposed to that of the secular explorers. With this transformation he surrenders his temporal control over language to God's sacred control.

Although Helen Gardner cites David's Psalm 69 as a possible source for the final couplet ("For the zeal of thine house hath eaten me up; and the reproaches of them that reproached thee are fallen upon me"), it seems again that Donne is fusing Old Testament allusions with New Testament solutions. The psalm opens with David sinking in mire "where the floods overflow me." It ends with his assurance that God will save Zion. The sonnet is entirely personal and concerned less with life on earth than with preparation for death and salvation. It seems instead that Donne is converting David's lines to a request for fulfillment through participation in the eucharistic meal. David can only pray for salvation and deliverance from his enemies while the persona of the sonnet can participate in sacramental salvation. As in **"Oh My Blacke Soule,"** if he

has received the zeal (motivating grace) to repent, he can be healed by eating. (pp. 65-6)

Although the language of the secular and divine lyrics is similar, the real difference arises in the separate goals the words serve. The divine lyrics continually transform secular denotation to sacred connotation as the eucharistic ceremony transforms secular food into the spiritual food of Christ's body and blood. Within this sacramental framework, the divine lyrics are chary of such overtly Roman Catholic practices as miracles and transubstantiation. In his love lyrics, Donne is able both to parody Roman Catholic practices and make them appear to reinforce earthly love. In the divine poems he is less indulgent. Instead of seeking visible transformation, he focuses on the sinner's struggle for union with an invisible God. This struggle tends to make the human lovers' unions appear too easy.

The peculiarly Anglican quality of eucharistic Real Presence without transubstantiation offers Donne a foretaste of the kingdom of heaven on earth. This doctrine of Real Presence acts in the divine poems like a frequently frustrating lure to the sinner who has not yet learned how to repent. It is an example of a "limit-experience" that can only be described in the "limit-language" of paradox. Because of its sacramental character, it displaces linear logic; it amplifies instead of transforms the elements. Although transubstantiation also defies linear logic, it distances the bread and wine from the body and blood by relegating the bread and wine to accidents. The Anglican Real Presence forces the natural and spiritual elements to coexist and thus provides a model for Donne's compression of diverse images into an illusory paradox.

Donne's method of realizing such a presence in his poems is to multiply the meanings of words by playing on their secular and spiritual definitions and contexts. In this way he is able to effect a type of consecration that allows for a confabulation of meanings. Because he has not yet experienced death, Donne can use "limit-language" only to approximate the eschatological language of Christ in the parables, proverbs, and proclamatory sayings. Borrowing terms (wine, tears, body, blood) from the only earthly sacrament that merges human and divine, Donne is able to make his poems partial mimeses of the Anglican Eucharist. By incorporating eucharistic symbols into his poetry, he can juxtapose secular and sacred in the love lyrics and comingle them in his divine poems. (p. 67)

Donne looks toward the Eschaton heralded by Christ's death and resurrection, and typologically previewed by his own death. Because one can only experience pleromic Real Presence through kenotic death and self-sacrifice, Donne employs paradox as his chief poetic tool. Paradox forces death and resurrection (east and west) to clash, then erupt in a revelatory vision antithetical to linear logic. (p. 68)

Eleanor J. McNees, "The Eschatology of Real Presence: Donne's Struggle toward Conformity with Christ," in her Eucharistic Poetry: The Search for Presence in the Writings of John Donne, Gerard Manley Hopkins, Dylan Thomas, and Geoffrey Hill, *Bucknell University Press, 1992, pp. 33-68.*

Joshua Scodel   (essay date 1993)

[*In the following excerpt, Scodel assesses Donne's use of the classical Greek and Roman ideas of the "mean"— the middle ground between excessiveness and deficiency in conduct—in his search for religious truth, and denominational authenticity in his "Satyre 3."*]

The social and intellectual elite of early modern England generally accepted the Aristotelian definition of ethical virtues as habits that observe the mean between excess and deficiency. . . . Countless English moral treatises recommended the mean; ministers and politicians lauded the English church as the virtuous middle way between Catholicism and radical Protestantism; and clergymen, country gentlemen, and urban panegyrists celebrated the delights of belonging to the middle state between the humble and the great.

John Donne's early poetry uses the notion of the mean so central to his contemporaries in order to articulate a new ideological vision. His transformations of the mean emerge from his idiosyncratic classicism. Donne's spirited and independent engagement with ancient philosophy and literature gave him a vital critical distance from his culture's dominant habits of mind. Rejecting his contemporaries' use of the mean to justify prevailing religious and sociopolitical formations, he adapts the mean instead to enlarge the sphere of individual freedom. In **"Satire 3,"** he spurns the English church's self-description as the via media in order to advocate a mean of skeptical inquiry between rash acceptance and rejection of any of the rival Christian denominations; in his verse epistle to Sir Henry Wotton, "Sir, more than kisses," he eschews his contemporaries' use of the mean to glorify a fixed position in the social hierarchy—the middle state—and advances instead a mean that justifies a socially mobile self's freedom to maneuver.

At the time he composed these poems, Donne was unsure of his commitments. He wrote **"Satire 3"** during a period of religious crisis circa 1596, after he had abandoned the Catholicism of his parents but before he joined the English church. As an ex-Catholic without confessional allegiance, Donne was a religious deviant in an England that punished nonconformity. The epistle to Wotton was probably written in 1597 or 1598, around the time Donne began his court career as secretary to Lord Keeper Egerton. Though the son of a rich merchant, Donne often asserted his gentility with anxious pride and expressed contempt for the entrepreneurial and professional middle classes. Yet while he was drawn to the court as an avenue for gentlemanly advancement, he was also deeply aware of the precariousness of court careers and repelled by the subservience required to succeed. Both poems' transformations of the mean justify his lack of firm allegiances by celebrating transitional states between conventional religious and social identities.

Donne's use of the mean illuminates the relationship between early modern subjectivity and cultural institutions. New historicists and cultural materialists have portrayed Renaissance persons as subjects indelibly shaped by cultural forces rather than the autonomous selves that some Renaissance figures and some Burckhardtian critics have

celebrated. Stephen Greenblatt [in his *Renaissance Self-Fashioning from More to Shakespeare*, 1983], for example, discovers no instances of "pure unfettered subjectivity" in the English Renaissance but only "human subject[s]" who are "remarkably unfree." Donne's search for a middle way between the wholesale acceptance or rejection of prevailing norms invites one to rethink the binary opposition between autonomy and subjection and to examine the kinds of middle ground that some Renaissance figures themselves sought to articulate.

"Satire 3" is one of three poems in which Donne imitates Horatian satire by invoking the mean. Unlike Horace, however, Donne does not treat the mean as an unproblematic norm. Near the end of both his second and his fourth satires, he uses the mean-extremes polarity to treat issues or characters peripheral to the central issues that he confronts. Both passages allude nostalgically to Horace's secure stance, evoking a stable moral vision unavailable to Donne and incapable of explaining the most powerful evil forces of his world. By contrast, in **"Satire 3"** Donne transforms the mean to make it applicable to his search for "true religion" in a world of competing sects.

"Satire 3" opens with a burst of intense but conflicting emotions as the poet confronts mankind's sinfulness: "Kinde pitty chokes my spleene; brave scorn forbids / Those teares to issue which swell my eye-lids." In the third line, "I must not laugh, nor weepe sinnes, and be wise," the poet admonishes himself to control his strong feelings with an allusion to an ancient satiric topos concerning the proper response to the flaws of mankind. Juvenal's *Satire 10* commends both Democritus's laughter and Heraclitus's weeping as wise responses to human frailties. Juvenal presents laughter as more natural, however, thus implicitly associating his poem's stance with Democritus. In **"Satire 4,"** Donne similarly adopts the Democritean attitude when he claims that a fop would make even Heraclitus laugh (line 197). In one of his paradoxes, all of which were probably written during the same period as the satires, Donne also expresses a preference for laughter but notes that both responses are extreme: "The extremity of laughing, yea of weeping . . . hath been accoumpted wisdome: and Democritus and Heraclitus the lovers of these extremes have beene called lovers of wisdome." **"Satire 3,"** by contrast, deviates from both Juvenal and other Donnean works by suggesting that true wisdom will avoid such emotional extremes.

Donne's rejection of laughter and weeping sounds Stoic. Seneca [in *De tranquillitate animi*] argues that the wise man should "calmly" accept human faults without either laughing or weeping because he should not trouble himself with others' misfortunes. Seeking passionless detachment from the foolish world, the Stoics advised suppressing the emotions rather than bringing them to the mean, as Aristotle recommended. Yet like many of his contemporaries, Donne the satirist is more Aristotelian than Stoic regarding the emotions. He does not seek Stoic impassivity. Though he wants to avoid the extremes of laughter or weeping, he does not suggest that his "pitty" and "scorn" are themselves improper.

"Can railing then cure these worne maladies?" (line 4)

fully reveals that Donne seeks not Stoic detachment but rather an efficacious and therefore morally justifiable expression of emotion. "Railing" recalls Juvenal's most familiar stance [in his *Satire 1*], the angry abuse that stems from *indignatio*. Yet Donne does not simply vent his rage in a Juvenalian outburst; instead he weighs the propriety of giving expression to his anger. His sense that expressing rage might be the best response to sin runs counter to Stoic but not to Aristotelian norms. Seneca [in his *De ira*] argues that both Heraclitus's weeping and Democritus's laughter are better responses to folly than anger, the most violent emotion; Aristotle, by contrast, argues that there is a mean of virtuous anger. It is not clear what the implied answer is to Donne's question concerning "railing," or whether the rest of the verse paragraph is to be interpreted as virtuous "railing" or not. It is clear, however, that Donne desires not to suppress but rather to regulate his emotions properly as he confronts mankind's sins.

The rest of the verse paragraph continues to stress the dangers of extremism by depicting mankind's sins as Aristotelian extremes. Complaining that men neglect "our Mistresse faire Religion" in favor of secular pursuits (line 5), the poet berates as a "desperate coward," a "thou" who represents both himself and his fellow men (line 29). Donne often contrasts reckless desperation and cowardice as dual extremes opposed to courage. One Donnean paradox begins by noting that "extreames are equally removed from the meane: So that headlong desperatnes asmuch [sic] offends true valor, as backward cowardise"; another claims that "betweene cowardise and despayre valor is ingendred" [*Paradoxes and Problems*]. The satire's oxymoronic "desperate coward" is a new version of Aristotle's rash man. Although Aristotle contrasts rashness and cowardice as excess and defect on either side of courage, his detailed analysis of the rash man breaks down the distinction between these extremes by arguing that rash men are generally "rash cowards" (*thrasudeiloi, Nicomachean Ethics*, 3.7.9). The rash man "pretends to courage which he does not possess," is overly bold in situations that are not truly threatening, but is unable to endure truly frightening ones (*NE*, 3.7.8-9). Donne's "desperate coward" similarly collapses the distinction between the two extremes: he "seem[s] bold" in recklessly fighting in "forbidden warres" but is afraid to fight the spiritual battle "appointed" by God (lines 29, 32).

Donne's list of various kinds of "desperate coward" underscores their extremism. Reversing conventional depictions of military men as boldly active and lovers as meekly passive in order to emphasize the mad excesses of both, Donne opens with a soldier who entombs himself in "ships wooden Sepulchers," thus making himself a "prey," and ends with a gallant amorist who attacks others with sword or "poysonous words" (lines 18, 28). The imagery of hot and cold used to describe the middle figures, the explorers and buccaneers, also emphasizes their extremism, which ancient and Renaissance texts often describe in terms of the contraries of hot and cold. In a sonnet lamenting his own sinful mixture of opposite extremes, "Oh, to vex me, contraryes meete in one," Donne laments that he is "ridlingly distemperd, cold and hott." The explorers and adventurers who use their internal "fire to thaw the ice / Of

frozen North discoveries" (lines 21-22) and endure "fires of Spain, 'and the line" by being "thrise / Colder then Salamanders" (lines 22-24) seek out drastic situations in order to license their lack of moderation.

As he proceeds, Donne boldly revises the Aristotelian mean of courage. Aristotle argues that the courageous man has the proper amount of fear and can therefore face death in battle, the most terrifying thing (*NE*, 3.7.5, 3.6.6-9). Donne christianizes the ancient philosopher's formulation by suggesting that "great courage" demands a proper fear of damnation (lines 15-16) and that the truly courageous man dares to confront and combat the most terrifying things, damnation and the "foes" of God, the infernal triad of the devil, world, and flesh that the poet proceeds to describe (lines 33-42). In a paradox asserting that "only Cowards dare dye," Donne argues from the Aristotelian premise that courage is a mean between recklessness and cowardice to a radically non-Aristotelian conclusion. While Aristotle distinguishes between the brave man's willingness to die in battle and the coward's desire to escape from life through suicide (*NE*, 3.7.13), Donne's paradox deflates the norm of traditional military heroism by condemning all who court death as simultaneously reckless and cowardly suicides: whoever "run[s] to death unimportun'd" incurs "condemn'd desperatnes" and whoever "dares dye to escape . . . anguishes" is a coward unwilling to endure the "war-fare" of life. In **"Satire 3"** Donne broadens his rejection of traditional concepts of valor by condemning as rash and cowardly suicides all who risk killing or being killed in secular strife rather than fight the spiritual war demanded by God. Such people seek suicide in a deeper sense than Aristotle envisioned. They court damnation, the death of their souls.

Donne's image of the truly courageous man as one who would "stand / Sentinell in his [God's] worlds garrison" (lines 30-31) suggests how closely he identifies the "desperate coward" with the reckless and cowardly suicide. The image conflates Saint Paul's Christian soldier, who "stands" firm against his spiritual foes (Eph. 6:11-17), and a classical topos based on an influential mistranslation of a passage in Plato's *Phaedo*. Refusing to commit suicide, Socrates argues that man dwells in a "prison" (*phroura*) that he has no right to leave until God bids him to do so; ancient and Renaissance readers often gave *phroura* the contextually implausible meaning of "garrison." In critiques of suicide based directly or indirectly on this passage, Cicero, John of Salisbury, Erasmus, and Montaigne all compare man to a soldier who cannot leave his garrison.

The classical refusal of suicide is balanced by a refusal to cling to life. In the *Phaedo* Socrates refuses to avoid death by renouncing his philosophic mission, just as he refuses to embrace death; in *De senectute* Cicero introduces the prohibition of suicide by noting that old men should no more avidly seek than violently reject continued life. Donne christianizes this classical ideal of equilibrium as a standing guard in spiritual battle, a religious mean between the excess of attacking in "forbidden" wars and the defect of retreating from the "appointed" battle. In ***Pseudo-Martyr*** (1610), Donne suggests once more that such a stationary position is a religious mean. Attacking the Jesuits' supposed pursuit of martyrdom as a reckless impetus to suicide, Donne notes, "The way to triumph in secular Armies, was not to be slaine in the Battell, but to have kept the station. . . . As it was in the Romane Armies, so it ought to be taught in the Romane Church, *Ius legionis facile: Non sequi, non fugere.* For we must neither pursue persecution so forwardly, that our naturall preservation be neglected, nor runne away from it so farre, that Gods cause be scandaliz'd, and his Honour diminished." The satire's Christian sentry is Donne's earlier version of the "easy law of the legion"—"Not to pursue, not to flee"—that saves men from suicidal extremes.

While the first verse paragraph identifies religious devotion with the courage to fight traditional Christian enemies, the second verse paragraph identifies it with the courage to seek true Christianity in a world of warring, state-imposed sects. Those who simply accept one of the national churches provide Donne with satiric examples of how not to seek true religion. Some of the satiric portraits have Juvenalian models, but their careful arrangement recalls Horatian depictions of opposite deviations from the mean rather than Juvenal's looser mode of progression. Donne first presents a triad of characters who embrace Roman Catholicism, Genevan Calvinism, and the English church. Because the English church considered itself the mean between the excessive and deficient ceremonialism that it ascribed, respectively, to Catholicism and radical Protestantism, readers might have expected Donne to attack the first two characters' extremism and then praise the third's embrace of the English middle way. After satirizing the first two figures as extremes, however, Donne pointedly refuses to treat the third as the mean. Mirrheus chooses Catholicism, Crants his Calvinism on the basis of opposing "humors" (line 53) or irrational preferences for various contraries—old versus young, ornamented versus plain, courtly versus rustic. Their respective attachments to the "ragges" of a "thousand yeares agoe" (lines 46-47) and to a "yong" religion (line 51) recall the contrast between what the Elizabethan prayer book describes as those "addicted to their old customs" and those "so newfangled that they would innovate all things." Yet by comparing Mirrheus's fondness for Roman "ragges" with Englishmen's fawning at a monarch's "statecloth" (lines 47-48) and Crants's love for Genevan "plaine" simplicity to a "lecherous" preference for "country drudges" (lines 51, 53-54), Donne associates deviations from the English church's supposed mean with two extremes of English social life: the slavish life at court, which Donne attacks at length in **"Satire 4,"** and the brutish rustic life, where one "suck[s] on countrey pleasures, childishly," to quote **"The Good-morrow."** Moreover, Graius, the third figure, does not avoid extremes by staying "at home" (line 55) in the English church but instead mixes them through a perverse embrace of contraries. Impressionable and subservient, he obeys corrupt elders, preachers who act simultaneously like "Godfathers" and "bauds," and laws "Still new like fashions" (lines 56-57, 59), religious statutes that are as young as Crants's church and as devoid of substance as Mirrheus's rags.

While the name Mirrheus—that is, perfumed with myrrh—suggests an excessive concern for ceremonial, and Crants, a Dutch name, suggests the character's allegiance to Calvinism, Graius, the Latin for "a Greek," has puzzled commentators. This enigmatic name is probably intended to make the Englishman's allegiance to his national church seem literally alien. It also recalls Juvenal's Satire 3, which depicts the typical Greek as an empty sycophant who not only does whatever his patron commands but also derives his opinions and even his facial expressions from his patron. Donne's allusion underscores that the typical English conformist, who thinks precisely what the authorities "bid him thinke" (line 57), has forfeited his identity to the powers that be.

The first triad thus fails to locate a positive model. Having disposed of prevailing approaches to religious allegiance, Donne begins afresh with a second, unconventional triad composed of extreme figures who reject and accept all the religious sects, plus the poet's vision of the true mean adumbrated in the poem's final exhortative section. Unlike the preceding characters, the two extreme figures in this second triad, Phrygius and Graccus, do not evade the problem posed by religious diversity through superficial preferences for the various national churches:

> Careless Phrygius doth abhorre
> All, because all cannot be good, as on
> Knowing some women whores, dares marry
>   none.
> Graccus loves all as one, and thinkes that so
> As women do in divers countries goe
> In divers habits, yet are still one kinde,
> So doth, so is Religion; and this blind-
> nesse too much light breeds.
>
> [Lines 62-69]

Insofar as Graccus and Phrygius have genuine reasons for their views, they approach what Donne will reveal as the proper stance. Yet they reason themselves into opposite extremes. Phrygius is spiritually deficient in joining "none" while Graccus is excessive in regarding "all" sects as valid. Donne deepens his attack, moreover, by suggesting that both figures actually combine rather than avoid opposite extremes.

Phrygius is "careless" primarily in the sense of "heedless" or "reckless." He responds to the diversity of churches and the evident impurity of some with a rash decision to have "none." His "abhorre[nce]" implies dread as much as hatred, however, and he is not only rash but also cowardly in giving up the search for "true religion" out of excessive fear. Donne's comparison of Phrygius to one who "dares marry none" indeed makes him a "desperate coward" like those who "dare" to neglect religion in the first verse paragraph or those who "dare dye" in Donne's paradox concerning suicides: he rashly denies himself the possibility of finding salvation within a true church because he is overly afraid of the possibility of being damned by the choice of a false one.

The philosophical resonance of the epithet "careless" reveals the self-defeating nature of Phrygius's stance. Richard Strier has suggested that "careless" evokes *ataraxia* or tranquillity, the ancient philosophical ideal of being without care. Though Phrygius is too fearful actually to be "careless" in this sense, he clearly seeks personal tranquillity by avoiding religious commitment. Ataraxia was the goal of the major Hellenistic philosophical sects, Stoicism, Skepticism, and Epicureanism, all of which advocated ways of detaching oneself from the world and thereby gaining tranquillity. We have seen Donne eschew Stoic calm at the very opening of the verse, and the satiric portrait of Phrygius completes the poet's rejection of the ancient escapist ideal. Phrygius represents both a kind of Skepticism and a kind of Epicureanism, which the erotic analogy links as parallel and equally vain attempts to attain tranquillity by suppressing the desire for knowledge, whether cognitive or erotic. Responding to the epistemological uncertainty caused by the diversity of philosophical sects, the ancient Skeptics sought tranquillity by eschewing all doctrines; Phrygius responds to the diversity of religious sects by avoiding all churches. Epicureans sought tranquillity by avoiding pain and pleasures that could cause pain, such as erotic love; they consequently did not marry. Donne's erotic analogy suggests that, like the Epicureans, Phrygius seeks to avert possible pain by refusing to marry a (spiritual) mistress.

Through a pun Donne's epithet "careless" further associates Phrygius's spiritual deficiency with an Epicurean avoidance of love. Like its counterpart *cura* in Latin poetry, "care" in English Renaissance poetry can refer to a loved object, love itself, or the anxieties and pains of love. In sonnet 48, Shakespeare calls his beloved "mine only care." In *King Lear*, after Cordelia refuses to pledge all her love to her father, the enraged Lear exclaimed, "Here I disclaim all my paternal care, / . . . / And as a stranger to my heart and me / Hold thee . . . for ever." In **"A Lecture upon the Shadow,"** Donne recalls to his mistress their anxious "infant loves," when "Disguises did, and shadowes, flow / From us, and our care." Being "careless" thus can connote being without love and its attendant pains: a poem in *Tottel's Miscellany* presents a "carelesse" man "scorning" the servitude of love. In a poem ascribed to Virgil by Renaissance critics, the speaker reveals the Epicurean's emotional sacrifice when he bids farewell to his beloved, his "care of cares" (*o mearum cura . . . curarum*), so that he can pursue Epicurean *ataraxia*, a life "free of care" (*ab omni . . . cura*). In "Satire 3," Phrygius makes a far greater sacrifice in his quest for tranquillity: he is without care only to the extent that he is without spiritual love or beloved, having suppressed all attachment to "our Mistresse faire Religion." Yet his rejection of a specifically spiritual object of desire is itself true to Epicurean principles, for the Epicureans spurned traditional religion, just as they spurned erotic attachment, as a threat to tranquillity. They denounced conventional religion as superstitious fear, and critics accused them of escaping superstition only by going to the opposite extreme of "careless" irreligion. Plutarch claimed that the Epicureans, like Phrygius, foolishly spurned religious faith in order to be "fearelesse and carelesse." An Elizabethan moralist, who like many of his contemporaries felt that Epicurean disbelief was on the rise, similarly deplored the "careless cogitations" of the irreligious philosophical sect.

Donne's Graccus, by contrast, is described as a religious libertine: loving all sects, like all women, equally much and therefore equally little. Like Phrygius, he is both excessive and deficient: by "too much light," by seeking to be too enlightened or by blithely accepting the supposed "light" of all denominations, Graccus falls into "blindness," the inability to distinguish the light of "true religion." Since "breeds" activates the latent sense of "light" as "wanton, unchaste" (*OED*, 14b), the claim that "too much light breeds" Graccus's "blindness" recalls the Renaissance commonplace that sexual excess causes blindness and thereby suggests a physical analogue for Graccus's combination of spiritual excess and defect.

Like Phrygius, though in an opposite way, Graccus avoids difficult but necessary choices. By accepting all religious sects as valid on the grounds that, like women, they are still "one kinde" despite their "divers habits" (line 67), he avoids the superficial choices of the first three figures but evades the problem recognized by Phrygius, who "knows some women are whores." Donne bids his reader seek "true religion," not religion as such; and to be a "Religion" is not necessarily to be a "true religion" any more than to be a woman is necessarily to be an honest one. In **"The Indifferent,"** one of Donne's libertine lyrics, the speaker claims he can love any kind of woman as long as "she be not true" and not "binde" him to reciprocal fidelity. As a secular Graccus, Donne realizes that erotic license is irreconcilable with norms of truth and troth.

A further pun reenforces Graccus's self-serving suppression of crucial distinctions. Aristotle defines virtues and vices as hexeis, normally translated into Latin as *habitus* and in Renaissance English as "habits." Donne's elegy **"On his Mistris"** uses the pun when he begs his beloved not to follow him as a disguised page and not to "change / Thy bodies habit, nor mindes"; "habit" can apply to mind as well as body, constitutive ethical dispositions as well as superficial appearances. The pun on "habits" undercuts Graccus's love of all churches: while the dressing of a church or woman may not matter, their "divers habits" in the sense of divergent dispositions define them as good or bad.

The names Phrygius and Graccus clarify Donne's attitude toward their positions. Donne derived the names from an attack on Roman "effeminacy" in Juvenal's *Satire* 2. Juvenal ends a thirty-five-line section inveighing against men who shamefully participate in rituals traditionally restricted to women by comparing such ceremonies to the Phrygian rites of Cybele, at the climax of which men castrate themselves, and proceeds in the next twenty-six lines to mock the marriage of the once-virile transvestite Gracchus: "Why wait any longer," Juvenal rhetorically asks, "when it were time in Phrygian fashion [*Phrygio more*] to lop off the superfluous flesh? Gracchus . . . who is now arraying himself in the flounces and trailing habits and veil of a bride once carried the nodding shields of Mars!" Juvenal attacks the Phrygian rites and the Gracchian transvestite marriage as random examples of "effeminacy" without pursuing the relationship between such diverse ways of losing one's "manhood." Donne was clearly struck, however, by the contrast between the Phrygians' self-emasculation through the removal of what is essential, the far from "superfluous flesh," and Gracchus's self-emasculation through the addition of what is unnecessary, elaborate female finery. This contrast begins to explain why Donne gives Juvenalian names to religious extremists figured in terms of sexual deficiency and excess.

Though **"Satire 3"** rejects the association of courage with actual war, Donne's redefinition of courage in terms of spiritual battle and a male quest for "true religion" is conventional in its phallocentrism. Following Juvenal and other classical authors, Elizabethan satirists often attack those deemed effeminate by comparing them to, or labeling them as, emasculated Phrygians: Edward Guilpin sneers at a pederastic "Batchelour del Phrygio," while John Marston scornfully bids a cowardly "Phrigeo" not to fear a duel and mocks a "prettie Phrigio" who abases himself before his mistress. In his elegy **"The Perfume"** Donne claims that "to be call'd effeminate" is "the greatest staine to mans estate," and in **"Satire 3"** his choice of a name underscores that Phrygius, who fears to join a church, is "less" than a man. Donne's comparison of Phrygius to a marriage-shy bachelor makes the accusation of self-emasculation particularly apt: one may compare Erasmus's colloquy "Proci et Puellae," whose speakers agree that men who abjure marriage out of fear of carnal sin castrate themselves.

The name Phrygius is especially appropriate, moreover, as an indictment of one who fears religious commitment. Both pagan and patristic writers describe Phrygian eunuchs as, in Ovid's words, "nor man nor woman." Donne uses the name to construct a conceptual pun on a word not present in his text, "neuter," which in both Latin and Renaissance English had not only its modern meaning but also that of "taking neither one side nor the other" (*OED*, 2). William Perkins draws on the specifically religious application of "neuter" when he complains that "the world abounds with atheists, epicures . . . neuters that are of no religion." Donne's implicit pun reinforces the link between religious abstention and a deficiency of "manliness." (pp. 479-93)

Donne's allusion to the Juvenalian Gracchus is also suggestive. Since classical and Renaissance thinkers often treated a male's excessive interest in women as a loss of "manhood," there is a general appropriateness in Donne's implicit comparison of his libertine Graccus to the Roman poet's would-be woman. Furthermore, by recalling Juvenal's transvestite awaiting a husband, Donne underscores his own Graccus's extreme lability regarding objects of desire. In addition, Graccus's reasoning that women who go in "divers habits" are nevertheless of the same "kind" takes on redoubled irony when one remembers that the Juvenalian transvestite presented himself as a woman simply by wearing the "trailing *habits*" (*longos habitus*) of a bride. Donne's allusion to Roman cross-dressing undercuts his Graccus's "blind," self-indulgent confidence that he knows what "kind" actually lies hidden beneath the surface "habits" of diverse religious denominations.

Hence Donne advocates seeking a mean position between Phrygian abstention and Graccus's promiscuity. His claim that "thou / Of force must one, and forc'd but one allow" (lines 69-70) demands that his reader seek a mean between Phrygius's and Graccus's numerical extremes of

"none" and "all." The seeker must find the one true religion rather than remaining content with none, like Phrygius, and even under the force of persecution, he must not concede the validity of more than one religion, like Graccus.

Yet the poet promotes a mean position based, like Phrygian irreligion, on ancient Skepticism. Donne's exhortation "Be busie to seeke her, beleeve mee this, / Hee's not of none, nor worst, that seekes the best" (lines 74-75), his command that one "doubt wisely" (line 77), and his claim that "To stand inquiring right, is not to stray" (line 78) all use the vocabulary of Pyrrhonist Skepticism. Pyrrhonists were variously called "inquirers" (*skeptikoi*) and "seekers" (*zêtêtikoi*) because they professed to search ceaselessly for the truth and "doubters" (*aporêtikoi*) because they doubted all dogmatic claims. There is a crucial difference, however, between Phrygius's skeptical position and the one that Donne recommends. (pp. 494-95)

Donne thus presents the proper religious stance not only as a quantitative mean between Graccus's "all" and Phrygius's "none" but also as a skeptical mean between the extremes of positive and negative dogmatism: the seeker must neither rashly believe that he has already found the one true church, as the first three satiric figures do, nor rashly despair of the search, as Phrygius does. Lines 76-79 recapitulate the satire's movement from a triad consisting of the major churches' positions to one consisting of two extremes and the authentic mean of skeptical inquiry: "To'adore, or scorne an image, or protest, / May all be bad; doubt wisely; in strange way / To stand inquiring right, is not to stray; / To sleepe, or runne wrong, is." Donne's first triad hypothesizes that all the major churches' views concerning images might be in error: the Catholics' reverence; the Calvinist and radical Swiss reformers' iconoclasm; and the intermediate positions of the Lutherans, the original "protestants," and of the Elizabethan church, which self-consciously sought a "middle way" concerning images. Though such a possibility is hard to reconcile with the poet's firm conviction that one can eventually find the true church, Donne stresses that he is not advocating the easy adoption of a state-authorized compromise but a more fundamental conception of the via media between dogmas. By introducing the second triad with "in strange way," he signifies that his "middle way" is on an unexplored road that each man must find for himself. The exhortation to "stand inquiring right" appropriately recalls the Christian of the first verse paragraph who adheres to the mean by "stand[ing] / Sentinell," and Donne contrasts his skeptical mean with the two extremes of "sleep," that is, shirking the quest for true religion, and "runn[ing] wrong," that is, recklessly embracing a particular church or all churches. While Donne's warning against spiritual sleep echoes Pauline admonitions like "Let us not sleep, as do others" (1 Thess. 5:6), his warning against running recalls classical and humanist attacks on rash behavior that misses the mean. Horace's first satire claims that fools who seek to avoid a vice "run" (currunt) into its opposite; Boethius attacks a theologian who "has run" (cucurrit) from one heretical extreme to its equally heretical contrary; the Tudor translator of Erasmus's Adages notes the human "tendency to runne to[o] farre" in redressing abuses of the church. Donne's descriptions of "runn[ing] away" from spiritual perfection in *Pseudo-Martyr* and of "running to death unimportun'd" in his paradoxes similarly associate running with foolish extremism. (pp. 496-97)

Donne ends **"Satire 3"** explaining how to "Keepe the truth which thou'hast found" (line 89), whatever it might turn out to be. Yet Donne's directives continue to employ the notion of a skeptical mean. Holding fast to the truth requires a distancing from opposite extremes similar to the skeptical stance of "inquiring right." The Pyrrhonist suspends belief by opposing every dogmatic argument with a contradictory argument of apparently "equal strength," pitting arguments from authority against one another. Donne adapts this skeptical method to argue that the individual must not relinquish true religion by accepting either of the extreme "contraries" espoused by opposing (pseudo-)authorities: "Is not this excuse for mere contraries, / Equally strong? cannot both sides say so?" (lines 98-99).

Donne denies that men "stand / In so'ill case here" (lines 89-90) that temporal rulers can dictate the religious choices of their subjects. There is no legitimate authority besides God, he argues, in spiritual matters; rulers deserve obedience only in temporal affairs. While the first verse paragraph exhorts men to "know" the traditional enemies of mankind (line 33), the end of the poem exhorts men to "know" the limits of earthly power: "That thou may'st rightly'obey power, her bounds know; / Those past, her nature and name's chang'd; to be / Then humble to her is idolatrie" (lines 100-102). Donne's formulation returns to the theory of the mean in order to challenge state control over men's consciences. The famous description of the mean in Horace's first satire notes "fixed bounds" (*certi fines*) beyond which one must not stray. Donne's claim that exceeding "bounds" changes the "nature and name" closely resembles the assertion in one of his paradoxes that "exces . . . changes the natures and the names" of things. Just as near the beginning of **"Satire 3"** Donne suggests that excess changes courage into recklessness, so near the poem's end he claims that excess turns virtuous obedience into sinful "idolatry." Donne does not spell out the objective change in the nature of "power" when rulers exceed their "bounds"—the transformation of legitimate authority into tyranny—but instead focuses on the subjective consequences for the ruled—the change in the "nature and name" of a subject's obedience. He thereby underscores that for a subject to recognize the "bounds" of power entails his knowing the proper mean of response.

Donne ends with a powerful image of the dangers that subjects incur when they exceed their proper obedience:

> As streames are, Power is; those blest flowers that dwell
> At the rough streames calme head, thrive and prove well,
> But having left their roots, and themselves given
> To the streames tyrannous rage, alas, are driven
> Through mills, and rockes, and woods,'and at last, almost
> Consum'd in going, in the sea are lost:

> So perish Soules, which more chuse mens unjust
> Power from God claym'd, then God himself to trust.
>
> [Lines 103-10]

The poem returns to rash and cowardly suicides, souls that recklessly seek destruction because they fear to "stand" in their appointed station. The image of flowers and the stream is complex. The flowers who "perish" by giving themselves to the "streames tyrannous rage" represent souls who submit to a temporal power that exceeds its legitimate authority by claiming spiritual dominion. The image of a stream's flow suggests that rulers' movement from the proper rule of the "calme head" to the tyrannic excess of the "rough streame" is all too natural in the fallen world. Yet Donne's strikingly unnatural image of flowers, which normally have no power of self-motion, willfully leaving "their roots" suggests that persons who submit to tyranny perversely abandon and exceed their natural human capacities and dispositions. The initial positive image of the "blest flowers" that "thrive" at the "calme head" implies that human beings can be nurtured rather than destroyed by worldly authority simply by remaining in their natural place, aware of the proper minimum and maximum "bounds" of their obedience. Donne thus envisions both the objective inevitability of tyrannic excess and the subjective freedom of individuals, who can flourish by recognizing only legitimate rule or (conversely) can destroy themselves by accepting tyranny. Trusting in God as their spiritual master, and consequently aware of the limits on the allegiance they owe temporal powers, the blessed thrive. Instead of using the concept of the mean to defend the church and state of the Elizabethan settlement, Donne uses it to promote individuals' independence—but not isolation—as they seek and preserve the truth. In such an active, masculinist poem, it is striking that Donne ends with the passive and—according to Renaissance connotations of gender—feminized image of souls as flowers. He clearly wishes to persuade himself and his readers that after successfully completing the painful struggle for truth, it will be easy for individuals to maintain the truth, the mean, and their own "blest" souls.

Jonathan Dollimore [in his *Radical Tragedy: Religion, Ideology and Power in the Drama of Shakespeare and His Contemporaries*, 1984] has argued that the most important Renaissance thinkers, far from promoting individualism, "decentered" man. Adducing Donne as an example of the "corrosive scepticism" of a period that undermined conceptions of the free individual as much as cultural institutions, Dollimore cites "Oh, to vex me, contraryes meete in one" and other texts to exemplify Donne's sense of the "fragmentation of the self." The portrayal of suicidal extremism in **"Satire 3"** certainly reveals this sense of fragmentation, but the satire also uses skepticism reconstructively to imagine a self finally saved from self-destructive extremes. The poem's skepticism is not "corrosive" because it is limited. While Donne questions the validity of any given ecclesiastical and political formation, he does not doubt God's ultimate benevolence and man's eventual ability to find his proper place in the world. Dependent on God as he seeks a beneficent relationship to the world, the free, inquiring self that Donne invokes and thereby seeks to create is neither Dollimore's "decentered" subject nor the fully autonomous person imagined by the Enlightenment but rather a distinctive early modern *tertium quid*. (pp. 498-501)

> *Joshua Scodel, "The Medium Is the Message: Donne's 'Satire 3', 'To Sir Henry Wotton' (Sir, More than Kisses), and the Ideologies of the Mean," in* Modern Philology, *Vol. 90, No. 4, May, 1993, pp. 479-511.*

FURTHER READING

Baumlin, James S. *John Donne and the Rhetorics of Renaissance Discourse.* Columbia: University of Missouri Press, 1991, 333 p.

> Discusses the skepticism, sophism, and moral and religious beliefs found in Donne's *Satyres* and *Songs and Sonnets.*

Cathcart, Dwight. *Doubting Conscience–Donne and the Poetry of Moral Argument.* Ann Arbor: University of Michigan Press, 1975, 199 p.

> Explores the casuistic moral approach found especially in Donne's religious writings.

Ferry, Anne. "Donne." In her *The "Inward Language,"* pp. 215-46. Chicago: University of Chicago Press, 1983.

> Analyzes Donne's *Holy Sonnet* called "La Corona," focusing upon its mixture of spiritual love with physical love themes.

Gardner, Helen. Introduction to *John Donne: The Divine Poems,* edited by Helen Gardner, pp. xv-lv. Oxford: Clarendon Press, 1978.

> Presents an overview of Donne's religious poetry with a particular emphasis on the *Holy Sonnets.*

John Donne Journal: Studies in the Age of Donne I– (1982–).

> Biannual periodical edited since its inception by Donne scholar M. Thomas Hester. Each issue carries scholarly essays on Donne's work and on that of such contemporaries as William Shakespeare, Ben Jonson, Inigo Jones, and George Herbert, as well as reviews of recent books on the age of Donne.

Knights, L. C. "All or Nothing: A Theme in John Donne." In his *Explorations III,* pp. 95-100. London and Pittsburgh: University of Pittsburgh Press, 1976.

> Examines how Donne's poetry portrays the author's sense of self-worth as a man.

Marotti, Arthur F. "Donne and 'The Extasie'." In *The Rhetoric of Renaissance Poetry,* edited by Thomas O. Sloan and Raymond B. Waddington, pp. 140-73, Berkeley and Los Angeles: University of California Press, 1974.

> Discusses the marriage theme in Donne's "Extasie" and contends that the physical expression of love reinforces the spiritual ideal of marriage.

Morillo, Marvin. "Donne's 'The Relique' as Satire." *Tulane Studies in English* 21 (1974): 47-56.

> Contends that Donne's 'Relique' is really a satire on Platonic love.

Smith, A. J., ed. *John Donne: Essays in Celebration.* London: Methuen and Co., 1972, 470 p.

> Studies of Donne's work by Barbara Hardy, Sydney Anglo, and D. W. Harding among others.

Stampfer, Judah. *John Donne and the Metaphysical Gesture.* New York: Funk and Wagnalls, 1970, 298 p.

> Presents a brief examination of Donne's metaphysical literary genre, then explores these elements in both his sacred and secular poetry.

Summers, Claude J., and Pebworth, Ted-Larry, eds. *The Eagle and the Dove: Reassessing John Donne.* Columbia: University of Missouri Press, 1986, 333 p.

> Collects essays by James S. Baumlin, Walter Davis, Kathleen Kelly, and others, exploring Donne's poetry, his sermons, and the musical settings of his works.

——, eds. *"Bright Shootes of Everlastingnesse": The Seventeenth-Century Religious Lyric.* Columbia: University of Missouri Press, 1987, 240 p.

> Contains essays presented at a 1984 symposium by R. V. Young, Mary Ann Radzmowicz, M. Thomas Hester, and Summers.

Additional coverage of Donne's life and career is contained in the following sources published by Gale Research: *Concise Dictionary of British Literary Biography: Before 1600*; *Dictionary of Literary Biography*, **Vol. 121**; *Poetry Criticism*, **Vol. 1**; **and** *World Literature Criticism.*

George Herbert

1593-1633

Welsh-born English poet, essayist, and translator.

INTRODUCTION

Recognized as an outstanding figure in seventeenth-century English literature, Herbert was associated with the School of Donne poets, also known as the metaphysical school of English verse, whose most prominent members include John Donne, Andrew Marvell, Henry Vaughan, and Richard Crashaw. Reacting against the traditions of Elizabethan love poetry, the School of Donne poets avoided classical or romantic allusions, attempting instead to portray the complexities and uncertainties of everyday life. Their poetry is characterized by complex, witty conceits, sudden, even jarring paradoxes and contrasts, strong imagery that combines the ornate with the mundane, and contemplations melding the natural world with the divine. Unlike many of the other metaphysical poets, Herbert eschewed secular love lyrics, and his best known work, *The Temple: Sacred Poems and Private Ejaculations*, is a collection of approximately 160 poems on religious subjects. Although Herbert was once regarded as a relatively minor writer of popular didactic verse, an increasing number of studies from various critical perspectives have been devoted to his life and works, and *The Temple* is esteemed both as a profound exploration of humanity's relationship with God and as one of the most important literary works in the English language.

The fifth of ten children, Herbert was born in 1593 to a family of prominent political figures in Montgomery, Wales. After the death of Herbert's father in 1596, Herbert's mother moved the family to Oxford to supervise the education of her eldest son, Edward, who later became known for his philosophical writings. While at Oxford, Herbert's mother formed a friendship with John Donne, and Herbert might have met the poet at this time. In 1604, Herbert began studying at Westminster School in London, where he excelled as a student of Latin and Greek. He later earned one of three Westminster nominations to Trinity College at Cambridge University in 1609. The following year Herbert sent his mother two poems, "My God, Where Is That Ancient Heat toward Thee?" and "Sure, Lord, There Is Enough in Thee to Dry," and a letter in which he declared "my resolution to be, that my poor Abilities in *Poetry*, shall be all, and ever consecrated to Gods glory." During his years at Cambridge Herbert wrote poetry in both Latin and English, much of it remaining unpublished during his lifetime. After earning bachelor's and master's degrees, Herbert was elected a fellow of Trinity College in 1616, a position which required him to take holy orders within seven years.

Herbert held several positions at Cambridge, including lecturer in rhetoric and deputy orator. Elected to the position of university orator in 1620, he assumed responsibility for composing official correspondence and speaking on occasions of state. Four years later, Herbert applied to the Archbishop of Canterbury for a waiver of the usual probationary period for ordainment as a deacon. The date of Herbert's ordination is uncertain; however, it is known that he was installed as canon of Lincoln Cathedral in 1626. The following year, Herbert's first published work, *Memoriae matris sacrum*, a collection of Latin verse on the death of his mother, was printed with a funeral oration by John Donne. In 1630, he was appointed rector of Bemerton and ordained as a priest. During the next two years, Herbert revised many of his earlier poems and wrote *A Priest to the Temple; or, The Country Parson, His Character, and Rule of Holy Life*, a prose treatise on Anglican pastoral practice. Shortly before his death from tuberculosis in 1633, Herbert sent the final manuscript of

The Temple to his friend Nicholas Ferrar, who published it later in that year.

According to Izaak Walton's highly favorable and influential biographical study, *A Life of Mr. George Herbert,* first published in 1670, Herbert instructed the messenger bearing his manuscript to Ferrar in words "to this purpose": "Sir, I pray deliver this little Book to my dear brother *Farrer,* and tell him, he shall find in it a picture of the many spiritual Conflicts that have past betwixt God and my Soul, before I could subject mine to the will of *Jesus my Master:* in whose service I have now found perfect freedom; desire him to read it: and then, if he can think it may turn to the advantage of any dejected poor Soul, let it be made publick: if not, let him burn it: for *I and it, are less than the least of God's mercies.*" Although modern scholars have been unable to verify this account, most commentators agree that *The Temple* is to some extent autobiographical. Critics have also suggested several possible organizing principles to the arrangement of poems in *The Temple,* including the events of the Christian liturgical calendar and the progression of the soul from birth to death.

The arrangement of the poems in *The Temple* has been the subject of considerable controversy. Since the 1870s, modern editors of Herbert's poetry have relied primarily on the first issue of *The Temple* and two manuscript sources in compiling subsequent editions of the work. Discovered in the Dr. Williams Library in London by Alexander B. Grosart, the editor of the 1874 edition of Herbert's collected works, the Williams manuscript contains early versions of approximately half of the poems that appear in *The Temple* and two groups of Latin verse (*Lucus* and *Passio dicerpta*), all of which are generally thought to have been composed sometime between 1614 and 1630. The Bodleian manuscript, named for the library in Oxford where it has been held since the early eighteenth century, is a licenser's copy of *The Temple* produced for Cambridge University officials. The Bodleian manuscript and the first edition of *The Temple* closely resemble each other, and commentators generally agree that these two versions provide the best evidence of Herbert's final intentions for the work in the absence of his final manuscript, the location of which is unknown.

Most scholars of Herbert's poetry have accepted the division of *The Temple* into three major sections—"The Church Porch," "The Church," and "The Church Militant." Consisting of seventy-seven epigrammatic six-line stanzas, "The Church Porch" provides moral instruction on avoiding sin, conducting one's daily affairs, and the proper attitude of the worshipper towards the Church. Much critical attention has focused on the "Church" section of *The Temple,* which contains most of the individual pieces comprising the volume. The poems in this section display a wide range of metrical patterns and rhyme schemes. Two of Herbert's most frequently anthologized works, "The Altar" and "Easter Wings," are figure poems, the printed form of which resembles the outline of the object described by the poem. The closing section, "The Church Militant," provides an allegorical history of

Christianity as embodied by the Church from antiquity to Herbert's era.

During the seventeenth century *The Temple* was chiefly valued for the piety of its religious sentiments, and many of the poems in this work were adapted as hymns. Interest in the works of Herbert and other metaphysical poets declined during the eighteenth century, and no new editions of *The Temple* were issued between 1709 and 1799. During the following century, however, both Herbert's moral values and poetic skills came to be appreciated by such writers as Samuel Taylor Coleridge, Ralph Waldo Emerson, and George MacDonald. *The Temple* has served as an important influence on the metaphysical poets Vaughan and Crashaw as well as such noted nineteenth- and twentieth-century poets as Emily Dickinson, Gerard Manley Hopkins, and T. S. Eliot. Modern scholars have examined Herbert's works from diverse biographical, rhetorical, liturgical, and literary perspectives, thus establishing Herbert as a major figure in English literature. Commenting on the significance of Herbert's poetry, Eliot observed: "*The Temple* is not to be taken as simply a devotional handbook of meditation for the faithful, but as the personal record of a man very conscious of weakness and failure, a man of intellect and sensibility who hungered and thirsted after righteousness. And that by its *content,* as well as because of its technical accomplishment, it is a work of importance for every lover of poetry."

PRINCIPAL WORKS

Memoriae matris sacrum (poetry) 1627
The Temple: Sacred Poems and Private Ejaculations (poetry) 1633
Outlandish Proverbs [translator] (proverbs) 1640
Herbert's Remains; or, Sundry Pieces of that Sweet Singer of the Temple, Mr. George Herbert (prose and proverbs) 1652
Musae responsoriae (poetry) 1662
A Priest to the Temple; or, The Country Parson, His Character, and Rule of Holy Life (prose) 1671
The Poetical Works of George Herbert (poetry) 1853
The Complete Works in Verse and Prose of George Herbert. 3 vols. (poetry and prose) 1874

*This work was first published in *Herbert's Remains* (1652).

CRITICISM

Ralph Waldo Emerson (lecture date 1835)

[*Emerson was an American essayist and poet, who, as founder of the Transcendental movement, shaped a distinctly American philosophy which embraced optimism, individuality, and mysticism. His philosophy stresses the presence of ongoing creation and revelation by a god who exists in everyone, as well as the essential unity of all thoughts, persons, and things in the divine whole. Emerson was a decisive influence on the life and thought of Henry David Thoreau and is considered one of the most influential figures of the nineteenth century. In the following excerpt from a lecture originally delivered in 1835, he considers Herbert's poems as "the breathings of a devout soul reading the riddle of the world with a poet's eye but with a saint's affections."*]

George Herbert [was] the author of the ***Temple***, a little book of Divine songs and poems which ought to be on the shelf of every lover of religion and poetry. It is a book which is apt to repel the reader on his first acquaintance. It is written in the quaint epigrammatic style which was for a short time in vogue in England, a style chiefly marked by the elaborate decomposition to which every object is subjected. The writer is not content with the obvious properties of natural objects but delights in discovering abstruser relations between them and the subject of his thought. This both by Cowley and Donne is pushed to affectation. By Herbert it is used with greater temperance and to such excellent ends that it is easily forgiven if indeed it do not come to be loved.

It has been justly said of Herbert that if his thought is often recondite and far fetched yet the language is always simple and chaste. I should cite Herbert as a striking example of the power of exalted thought to melt and bend language to its fit expression. Language is an organ on which men play with unequal skill and each man with different skill at different hours. The man who stammers when he is afraid or when he is indifferent, will be fluent when he is angry, and eloquent when his intellect is active. Some writers are of that frigid temperament that their sentences always seem to be made with grammar and dictionary. To such the easy structure of prose is laborious, and metre and rhyme, and especially any difficult metre is an insurmountable bar to the expression of their meaning. Of these Byron says,

> Prose poets like blank verse
> Good workmen never quarrel with their tools.

Those on the contrary who were born to write, have a self-enkindling power of thought which never knows this obstruction but find words so rapidly that they seem coeval with the thought. And in general according to the elevation of the soul will be the power over language and lively thoughts will break out into spritely verse. No metre so difficult but will be tractable so that you only raise the temperature of the thought.

"For my part," says Montaigne, "I hold and Socrates is positive in it, that whoever has in his mind a lively and clear imagination, he will express it well enough in one kind or another and though he were dumb by signs."

Every reader is struck in George Herbert with the inimitable felicity of the diction. The thought has so much heat as actually to fuse the words, so that language is wholly flexible in his hands, and his rhyme never stops the progress of the sense. (pp. 349-50)

What Herbert most excels in is in exciting that feeling which we call the moral sublime. The highest affections are touched by his muse. I know nothing finer than the turn with which his poem on affliction concludes. After complaining to his maker as if too much suffering had been put upon him he threatens that he will quit God's service for the world's:

> Well, I will change the service and go seek
>   Some other master out
> Ah, my dear God, though I be clean
>   forgot
> Let me not love thee if I love thee not.

Herbert's Poems are the breathings of a devout soul reading the riddle of the world with a poet's eye but with a saint's affections. Here poetry is turned to its noblest use. The sentiments are so exalted, the thought so wise, the piety so sincere that we cannot read this book without joy that our nature is capable of such emotions and criticism is silent in the exercise of higher faculties. (pp. 352-53)

Ralph Waldo Emerson, "English Literature: Ben Jonson, Herrick, Herbert, Wotton," in his The Early Lectures of Ralph Waldo Emerson: 1833-1836, Vol. 1, *edited by Stephen E. Whicher and Robert E. Spiller, Cambridge, Mass.: Harvard University Press, 1959, pp. 337-55.*

George MacDonald   (essay date 1868)

[*A Scottish man of letters, MacDonald was a key figure in shaping the fantastic and mythopoeic literature of the nineteenth and twentieth centuries. Such novels as* Phantastes *(1858) and* The Princess and the Goblin *(1872) are considered classics of fantasy literature. In the following excerpt from his survey of English religious verse,* England's Antiphon *(1868), MacDonald provides an assessment of Herbert's artistic achievement, paying particular attention to the poet's use of symbols.*]

In George Herbert there is poetry enough and to spare: it is the household bread of his being. If I begin with that which first in the nature of things ought to be demanded of a poet, namely, Truth, Revelation—George Herbert offers us measure pressed down and running over. But let me speak first of that which first in time or order of appearance we demand of a poet, namely music. For inasmuch as verse is for the ear, not for the eye, we demand a good hearing first. Let no one undervalue it. The heart of poetry is indeed truth, but its garments are music, and the garments come first in the process of revelation. The music of a poem is its meaning in sound as distinguished from word—its meaning in solution, as it were, uncrystallized by articulation. The music goes before the fuller revelation, preparing its way. The sound of a verse is the harbinger of the truth contained therein. If it be a right poem, this will be true. Herein Herbert excels. It will be found impossible to separate the music of his words from the music of the thought which takes shape in their sound.

> I got me flowers to strow thy way,
>   I got me boughs off many a tree;
> But thou wast up by break of day,
>   And brought'st thy sweets along with thee.

And the gift it enwraps at once and reveals is, I have said, truth of the deepest. Hear this song of divine service. In every song he sings a spiritual fact will be found its fundamental life, although I may quote this or that merely to illustrate some peculiarity of mode.

"The Elixir" was an imagined liquid sought by the old physical investigators, in order that by its means they might turn every common metal into gold, a pursuit not quite so absurd as it has since appeared. They called this something, when regarded as a solid, *the Philosopher's Stone*. In the poem it is also called a *tincture*.

THE ELIXIR.

Teach me, my God and King,
  In all things thee to see;
And what I do in anything,
  To do it as for thee;

Not rudely, as a beast,
  To run into an action;
But still to make thee prepossest,
  And give it his perfection.

A man that looks on glass,
  On it may stay his eye;
Or, if he pleaseth, through it pass,
  And then the heaven spy.

All may of thee partake:
  Nothing can be so mean,
Which with his tincture—for thy sake—
  Will not grow bright and clean.

A servant with this clause
  Makes drudgery divine:
Who sweeps a room as for thy laws,
  Makes that and the action fine.

This is the famous stone
  That turneth all to gold;
For that which God doth touch and own
  Cannot for less be told.

With a conscience tender as a child's, almost diseased in its tenderness, and a heart loving as a woman's, his intellect is none the less powerful. Its movements are as the sword-play of an alert, poised, well-knit, strong-wristed fencer with the rapier, in which the skill impresses one more than the force, while without the force the skill would be valueless, even hurtful, to its possessor. There is a graceful humour with it occasionally, even in his most serious poems adding much to their charm. To illustrate all this, take the following, the title of which means *The Retort*.

THE QUIP.

The merry World did on a day
  With his train-bands and mates agree
To meet together where I lay,
  And all in sport to jeer at me.

First Beauty crept into a rose;
  Which when I plucked not—"Sir," said she,
"Tell me, I pray, whose hands are those?"
  But thou shalt answer, Lord, for me.

Then Money came, and, chinking still—
  "What tune is this, poor man?" said he:
"I heard in music you had skill."
  But thou shalt answer, Lord, for me.

Then came brave Glory puffing by
  In silks that whistled—who but he?
He scarce allowed me half an eye;
  But thou shalt answer, Lord, for me.

Then came quick Wit-and-Conversation,
  And he would needs a comfort be,
And, to be short, make an oration:
  But thou shalt answer, Lord, for me.

Yet when the hour of thy design
  To answer these fine things, shall come,
Speak not at large—say I am thine;
  And then they have their answer home.

Here is another instance of his humour. It is the first stanza of a poem to **"Death."** He is glorying over Death as personified in a skeleton.

Death, thou wast once an uncouth, hideous
  thing—
        Nothing but bones,
        The sad effect of sadder groans:
Thy mouth was open, but thou couldst not
  sing.

No writer before him has shown such a love to God, such a childlike confidence in him. The love is like the love of [the thirteenth-century religious poets]. But the nation had learned to think more, and new difficulties had consequently arisen. These, again, had to be undermined by deeper thought, and the discovery of yet deeper truth had been the reward. Hence, the love itself, if it had not strengthened, had at least grown deeper. And George Herbert had difficulty enough in himself; for, born of high family, by nature fitted to shine in that society where elegance of mind, person, carriage, and utterance is most appreciated, and having indeed enjoyed something of the life of a courtier, he had forsaken all in obedience to the voice of his higher nature. Hence the struggle between his tastes and his duties would come and come again, augmented probably by such austere notions as every conscientious man must entertain in proportion to his inability to find God in that in which he might find him. From this inability, inseparable in its varying degrees from the very nature of growth, springs all the asceticism of good men, whose love to God will be the greater as their growing insight reveals him in his world, and their growing faith approaches to the giving of thanks in everything.

When we have discovered the truth that whatsoever is not of faith is sin, the way to meet it is not to forsake the human law, but so to obey it as to thank God for it. To leave the world and go into the desert is not thus to give thanks: it may have been the only way for this or that man, in his blameless blindness, to take. The divine mind of George Herbert, however, was in the main bent upon discovering God everywhere.

The poem I give next, powerfully sets forth the struggle between liking and duty of which I have spoken. It is at the same time an instance of wonderful art in construction, all the force of the germinal thought kept in reserve, to burst forth at the last. He calls it — meaning by the word, *God's Restraint*—

THE COLLAR.

I struck the board, and cried "No more!—
         I will abroad.
What! shall I ever sigh and pine?
My lines and life are free—free as the road,
     Loose as the wind, as large as store.
         Shall I be still in suit?
Have I no harvest but a thorn
To let me blood, and not restore
What I have lost with cordial fruit?
         Sure there was wine
Before my sighs did dry it! There was corn
     Before my tears did drown it!
Is the year only lost to me?
     Have I no bays to crown it?
No flowers, no garlands gay? All blasted?
         All wasted?
Not so, my heart; but there is fruit,
     And thou hast hands.
Recover all thy sigh-blown age
On double pleasures. Leave thy cold dispute
Of what is fit, and not. Forsake thy cage,
     Thy rope of sands,
Which petty thoughts have made—and made to
     thee
     Good cable, to enforce and draw,
         And be thy law,
While thou didst wink and wouldst not see.
     Away! Take heed—
     I will abroad.
Call in thy death's-head there. Tie up thy
   fears.
     He that forbears
     To suit and serve his need,
     Deserves his load."
But as I raved, and grew more fierce and wild
     At every word,
Methought I heard one calling *"Child!"*
And I replied, *"My Lord!"*

Coming now to speak of his art, let me say something first about his use of homeliest imagery for highest thought. This, I think, is in itself enough to class him with the highest *kind* of poets. If my reader will refer to **"The Elixir,"** he will see an instance in the third stanza, "You may look at the glass, or at the sky:" "You may regard your action only, or that action as the will of God."

Again, let him listen to the pathos and simplicity of this one stanza, from a poem he calls **"The Flower."** He has been in trouble; his times have been evil; he has felt a spiritual old age creeping upon him; but he is once more awake.

     And now in age I bud again;
     After so many deaths I live and write;
     I once more smell the dew and rain,
     And relish versing. O my only light,
         It cannot be
         That I am he
     On whom thy tempests fell all night!

Again:

     Some may dream merrily, but when they
       wake
     They dress themselves and come to thee.

He has an exquisite feeling of lyrical art. Not only does he keep to one idea in it, but he finishes the poem like a cameo. Here is an instance wherein he outdoes the elaboration of a Norman trouvère; for not merely does each line in each stanza end with the same sound as the corresponding line in every other stanza, but it ends with the very same word. I shall hardly care to defend this if my reader chooses to call it a whim; but I do say that a large degree of the peculiar musical effect of the poem—subservient to the thought, keeping it dimly chiming in the head until it breaks out clear and triumphant like a silver bell in the last—is owing to this use of the same column of words at the line-ends of every stanza. Let him who doubts it, read the poem aloud.

AARON.

Holiness on the head;
     Light and perfections on the breast;
Harmonious bells below, raising the dead,
     To lead them unto life and rest—
         Thus are true Aarons drest.

Profaneness in my head;
     Defects and darkness in my breast;
A noise of passions ringing me for dead
     Unto a place where is no rest—
         Poor priest, thus am I drest!

Only another head
     I have, another heart and breast,
Another music, making live, not dead,
     Without whom I could have no rest—
         In him I am well drest.

Christ is my only head,
     My alone only heart and breast,
My only music, striking me even dead,
     That to the old man I may rest,
         And be in him new drest.

So, holy in my head,
     Perfect and light in my dear breast,
My doctrine turned by Christ, who is not dead,
     But lives in me while I do rest—
         Come, people: Aaron's drest.

Note the flow and the ebb of the lines of each stanza—from six to eight to ten syllables, and back through eight to six, the number of stanzas corresponding to the number of lines in each; only the poem itself begins with the ebb, and ends with a full spring-flow of energy. Note also the perfect antithesis in their parts between the first and second stanzas, and how the last line of the poem clenches the whole in revealing its idea—that for the sake of which it was written. In a word, note the *unity.*

Born in 1593, notwithstanding his exquisite art, he could not escape being influenced by the faulty tendencies of his age, borne in upon his youth by the example of his mother's friend, Dr. Donne. A man must be a giant like Shakspere or Milton to cast off his age's faults. Indeed no man has more of the "quips and cranks and wanton wiles" of the poetic spirit of his time than George Herbert, but with this difference from the rest of Dr. Donne's school, that such is the indwelling potency that it causes even these to shine with a radiance such that we wish them still to burn and not be consumed. His muse is seldom other than graceful, even when her motions are grotesque, and he is always a gentleman, which cannot be said of his master.

We could not bear to part with his most fantastic oddities, they are so interpenetrated with his genius as well as his art.

In relation to the use he makes of these faulty forms, and to show that even herein he has exercised a refraining judgment, though indeed fancying he has quite discarded in only somewhat reforming it, I recommend the study of two poems, each of which he calls **"Jordan,"** though why I have not yet with certainty discovered.

It is possible that not many of his readers have observed the following instances of the freakish in his rhyming art, which however result well. When I say so, I would not be supposed to approve of the freak, but only to acknowledge the success of the poet in his immediate intent. They are related to a certain tendency to mechanical contrivance not seldom associated with a love of art: it is art operating in the physical understanding. In the poem called **"Home,"** every stanza is perfectly finished till the last: in it, with an access of art or artfulness, he destroys the rhyme. I shall not quarrel with my reader if he calls it the latter, and regards it as art run to seed. And yet—and yet——I confess I have a latent liking for the trick. I shall give one or two stanzas out of the rather long poem, to lead up to the change in the last.

> Come, Lord; my head doth burn, my heart is
> sick,
>   While thou dost ever, ever stay;
> Thy long deferrings wound me to the quick;
>   My spirit gaspeth night and day.
>   O show thyself to me,
>   Or take me up to thee.
>
> Nothing but drought and dearth, but bush and
> brake,
>   Which way soe'er I look I see:
> Some may dream merrily, but when they wake
>   They dress themselves and come to thee.
>   O show thyself to me,
>   Or take me up to thee.
>
> Come, dearest Lord, pass not this holy season,
>   My flesh and bones and joints do pray;
> And even my verse, when by the rhyme and rea-
> son
>   The word is *stay*, says ever *come*.
>   O show thyself to me,
>   Or take me up to thee.

Balancing this, my second instance is of the converse. In all the stanzas but the last, the last line in each hangs unrhymed: in the last the rhyming is fulfilled. The poem is called **"Denial."** I give only a part of it.

> When my devotions could not pierce
>   Thy silent ears,
> Then was my heart broken as was my verse;
>   My breast was full of fears
>   And disorder.
>
> O that thou shouldst give dust a tongue
>   To cry to thee,
> And then not hear it crying!   All day long
>   My heart was in my knee:
>   But no hearing!
>
> Therefore my soul lay out of sight,

>   Untuned, unstrung;
> My feeble spirit, unable to look right,
>   Like a nipt blossom, hung
>   Discontented.
>
> O cheer and tune my heartless breast—
>   Defer no time;
> That so thy favours granting my request,
>   They and my mind may chime,
>   And mend my rhyme.

It had been hardly worth the space to point out these, were not the matter itself precious.

Before making further remark on George Herbert, let me present one of his poems in which the oddity of the visual fancy is only equalled by the beauty of the result.

THE PULLEY.

> When God at first made man,
> Having a glass of blessing standing by,
> "Let us," said he, "pour on him all we can:
> Let the world's riches, which dispersèd lie,
>   Contract into a span."
>
> So strength first made a way;
> Then beauty flowed; then wisdom, honour, plea-
> sure.
> When almost all was out, God made a stay,
> Perceiving that, alone of all his treasure,
>   *Rest* in the bottom lay.
>
> "For if I should," said he,
> "Bestow this jewel also on my creature,
> He would adore my gifts instead of me,
> And rest in nature, not the God of nature:
>   So both should losers be.
>
> "Yet let him keep the rest—
> But keep them with repining restlessness:
> Let him be rich and weary, that, at least,
> If goodness lead him not, yet weariness
>   May toss him to my breast."

Is it not the story of the world written with the point of a diamond?

There can hardly be a doubt that his tendency to unnatural forms was encouraged by the increase of respect to symbol and ceremony shown at this period by some of the external powers of the church—Bishop Laud in particular. Had all, however, who delight in symbols, a power, like George Herbert's, of setting even within the hornlanterns of the more arbitrary of them, such a light of poetry and devotion that their dull sides vanish in its piercing shine, and we forget the symbol utterly in the truth which it cannot obscure, then indeed our part would be to take and be thankful. But there never has been even a living true symbol which the dulness of those who will see the truth only in the symbol has not degraded into the very cockatrice-egg of sectarianism. The symbol is by such always more or less idolized, and the light within more or less patronized. If the truth, for the sake of which all symbols exist, were indeed the delight of those who claim it, the sectarianism of the church would vanish. But men on all sides call that *the truth* which is but its form or outward sign—material or verbal, true or arbitrary, it matters not which—and hence come strifes and divisions.

Although George Herbert, however, could thus illumine all with his divine inspiration, we cannot help wondering whether, if he had betaken himself yet more to vital and less to half artificial symbols, the change would not have been a breaking of the pitcher and an outshining of the lamp. For a symbol may remind us of the truth, and at the same time obscure it—present it, and dull its effect. It is the temple of nature and not the temple of the church, the things made by the hands of God and not the things made by the hands of man, that afford the truest symbols of truth. (pp. 174-87)

Of Nature's symbols George Herbert has made large use; but he would have been yet a greater poet if he had made a larger use of them still. Then at least we might have got rid of such oddities as the stanzas for steps up to the church-door, the first at the bottom of the page; of the lines shaped into ugly altar-form; and of the absurd Easter wings, made of ever lengthening lines. This would not have been much, I confess, nor the gain by their loss great; but not to mention the larger supply of images graceful with the grace of God, who when he had made them said they were good, it would have led to the further purification of his taste, perhaps even to the casting out of all that could untimely move our mirth; until possibly (for illustration), instead of this lovely stanza, he would have given us even a lovelier:

> Listen, sweet dove, unto my song,
> And spread thy golden wings on me;
> Hatching my tender heart so long,
> Till it get wing, and fly away with thee.

The stanza is indeed lovely, and true and tender and clever as well; yet who can help smiling at the notion of the incubation of the heart-egg, although what the poet means is so good that the smile almost vanishes in a sigh?

There is no doubt that the works of man's hands will also afford many true symbols; but I do think that, in proportion as a man gives himself to those instead of studying Truth's wardrobe of forms in nature, so will he decline from the high calling of the poet. George Herbert was too great to be himself much injured by the narrowness of the field whence he gathered his symbols; but his song will be the worse for it in the ears of all but those who, having lost sight of or having never beheld the oneness of the God whose creation exists in virtue of his redemption, feel safer in a low-browed crypt than under "the high embowed roof."

When the desire after system or order degenerates from a need into a passion, or ruling idea, it closes, as may be seen in many women who are especial housekeepers, like an unyielding skin over the mind, to the death of all development from impulse and aspiration. The same thing holds in the church: anxiety about order and system will kill the life. This did not go near to being the result with George Herbert: his life was hid with Christ in God; but the influence of his *profession*, as distinguished from his work, was hurtful to his calling as a poet. He of all men would scorn to claim social rank for spiritual service; he of all men would not commit the blunder of supposing that prayer and praise are that service of God: they are *prayer* and *praise*, not *service*; he knew that God can be

served only through loving ministration to his sons and daughters, all needy of commonest human help: but, as the most devout of clergymen will be the readiest to confess, there is even a danger to their souls in the unvarying recurrence of the outward obligations of their service; and, in like manner, the poet will fare ill if the conventions from which the holiest system is not free send him soaring with sealed eyes. George Herbert's were but a little blinded thus; yet something, we must allow, his poetry was injured by his profession. All that I say on this point, however, so far from diminishing his praise, adds thereto, setting forth only that he was such a poet as might have been greater yet, had the divine gift had free course. But again I rebuke myself and say, "Thank God for George Herbert."

To rid our spiritual palates of the clinging flavour of criticism, let me choose another song from his precious legacy—one less read, I presume, than many. It shows his tendency to asceticism—the fancy of forsaking God's world in order to serve him; it has besides many of the faults of the age, even to that of punning; yet it is a lovely bit of art as well as a rich embodiment of tenderness.

THE THANKSGIVING.

> Oh King of grief!   a title strange yet true,
>   To thee of all kings only due!
> Oh King of wounds! how shall I grieve for thee,
>   Who in all grief preventest me?
> Shall I weep blood? Why, thou hast wept such store,
>   That all thy body was one gore.
> Shall I be scourgéd, flouted, boxéd, sold?
>   'Tis but to tell the tale is told.
> *My God, my God, why dost thou part from me?*
>   Was such a grief as cannot be.
> Shall I then sing, skipping thy doleful story,
>   And side with thy triumphant glory?
> Shall thy strokes be my stroking? thorns my flower?
>   Thy rod, my posy? cross, my bower?
> But how then shall I imitate thee, and
>   Copy thy fair, though bloody hand?
> Surely I will revenge me on thy love,
>   And try who shall victorious prove.
> If thou dost give me wealth, I will restore
>   All back unto thee by the poor.
> If thou dost give me honour, men shall see
>   The honour doth belong to thee.
> I will not marry; or if she be mine,
>   She and her children shall be thine.
> My bosom-friend, if he blaspheme thy name,
>   I will tear thence his love and fame.
> One half of me being gone, the rest I give
>   Unto some chapel—die or live.
> As for my Passion—But of that anon,
>   When with the other I have done.
> For thy Predestination, I'll contrive
>   That, three years hence, if I survive,
> I'll build a spital, or mend common ways,
>   But mend my own without delays.
> Then I will use the works of thy creation,
>   As if I used them but for fashion.
> The world and I will quarrel; and the year
>   Shall not perceive that I am here.
> My music shall find thee, and every string
>   Shall have his attribute to sing,

That all together may accord in thee,
    And prove one God, one harmony.
If thou shalt give me wit, it shall appear;
    If thou hast given it me, 'tis here.
Nay, I will read thy book, and never move
    Till I have found therein thy love—
Thy art of love, which I'll turn back on thee:
    O my dear Saviour, Victory!
Then for my Passion—I will do for that—
    Alas, my God! I know not what.

With the preceding must be taken the following, which comes immediately after it.

THE REPRISAL.

    I have considered it, and find
There is no dealing with thy mighty Passion;
For though I die for thee, I am behind:
    My sins deserve the condemnation.

    O make me innocent, that I
May give a disentangled state and free;
And yet thy wounds still my attempts defy,
    For by thy death I die for thee.

    Ah! was it not enough that thou
By thy eternal glory didst outgo me?
Couldst thou not grief's sad conquest me allow,
    But in all victories overthrow me?

    Yet by confession will I come
Into the conquest: though I can do nought
Against thee, in thee I will overcome
    The man who once against thee fought.

Even embracing the feet of Jesus, Mary Magdalene or George Herbert must rise and go forth to do his will.

It will be observed how much George Herbert goes beyond all that have preceded him, in the expression of feeling as it flows from individual conditions, in the analysis of his own moods, in the logic of worship, if I may say so. His utterance is not merely of personal love and grief, but of the peculiar love and grief in the heart of George Herbert. There may be disease in such a mind; but, if there be, it is a disease that will burn itself out. Such disease is, for men constituted like him, the only path to health. By health I mean that simple regard to the truth, to the will of God, which will turn away a man's eyes from his own conditions, and leave God free to work his perfection in him—free, that is, of the interference of the man's self-consciousness and anxiety. To this perfection St. Paul had come when he no longer cried out against the body of his death, no more judged his own self, but left all to the Father, caring only to do his will. It was enough to him then that God should judge him, for his will is the one good thing securing all good things. Amongst the keener delights of the life which is at the door, I look for the face of George Herbert, with whom to talk humbly would be in bliss a higher bliss. (pp. 187-93)

George MacDonald, "George Herbert," in his
England's Antiphon, *Macmillan & Co., 1868, pp. 174-93.*

George Saintsbury (essay date 1887)

[*Saintsbury was a late-nineteenth—and early-twentieth-century English literary historian and critic. Extremely prolific, he composed histories of English and European literature as well as numerous critical works on individual authors, styles, and periods. In the following excerpt from his* A History of Elizabethan Literature *(written in 1887 and published in 1891), Saintsbury maintains that although Herbert expresses "the everyday emotions of the Christian, just sublimated sufficiently to make them attractive," he is not a great religious poet.*]

George Herbert . . . was born at Montgomery Castle in 1593, of the great house now represented in the English peerage by the holders of the titles of Pembroke, Carnarvon, and Powis. George was the younger brother of the equally well-known Lord Herbert of Cherbury; and after being for some years public orator at Cambridge, turned, it is said, on some despite or disappointment, from secular to worldly business, accepted the living of Bemerton, and after holding it for a short time, died in 1633. Walton's *Life* was hardly needed to fix Herbert in the popular mind, for his famous volume of sacred poems, **The Temple**, would have done so, and has done so far more firmly. It was not his only book by any means; he had displayed much wit as quite a boy in counter-lampooning Andrew Melville's ponderous and impudent Anti-Tami-Cami-Categoria, an attack on the English universities; and afterwards he composed both in Greek, Latin, and English, both in prose and verse. Nothing, however, but **The Temple** has held popular estimation, and that has held it firmly, being much helped no doubt by the Tractarian movement of fifty years ago. It may be confessed without shame and without innuendo that Herbert has been on the whole a greater favourite with readers than with critics, and the reason is obvious. He is not prodigal of the finest strokes of poetry. To take only his own contemporaries, and undoubtedly pupils, his gentle moralising and devotion are tame and cold beside the burning glow of Crashaw, commonplace and popular beside the intellectual subtlety and, now and then, the inspired touch of Vaughan. But he never drops into the flatness and the extravagance of both these writers, and his beauties, assuredly not mean in themselves, and very constantly present, are both in kind and in arrangement admirably suited to the average comprehension. He is quaint and conceited; but his quaintnesses and conceits are never beyond the reach of any tolerably intelligent understanding. He is devout, but his devotion does not transgress into the more fantastic regions of piety. He is a mystic, but of the more exoteric school of mysticism. Thus he is among sacred poets very much (though relatively he occupies a higher place) what the late Mr. Longfellow was among profane poets. He expresses common needs, common thoughts, the everyday emotions of the Christian, just sublimated sufficiently to make them attractive. The fashion and his own taste gave him a pleasing quaintness, which his good sense kept from being ever obscure or offensive or extravagant. The famous "Sweet day so cool, so calm, so bright," and many short passages which are known to every one, express Herbert perfectly. The thought is obvious, usual, in no sense far fetched. The morality is plain and simple. The expression, with a sufficient touch of the daintiness of the time, has nothing that is extraordinarily or ravishingly felicitous whether in phrasing or versing. He is, in short, a poet whom all must respect; whom those that are in sympathy with his vein of thought cannot but revere; who did England an inestimable service, by giving to the highest and purest thoughts that familiar and abiding poetic garb which contributes so much to fix any thoughts in the mind, and of which, to tell the truth, poetry has been much more prodigal to other departments of thought by no means so well deserving. But it is impossible to call him a great poet even in his own difficult class. The early Latin hymn writers are there to show what a great religious poet must be like. Crashaw, if his genius had been less irregular and jocular, might have been such. Herbert is not, and could not have been. (pp. 372-73)

> *George Saintsbury, "Caroline Poetry," in his* A History of Elizabethan Literature, *Macmillan and Co., 1887, pp. 354-93.*

Herbert J. C. Grierson (essay date 1921)

[*Grierson was a Scottish scholar and critic who was considered a leading authority on seventeenth-century English poetry. In the following excerpt, he discusses Herbert as an accomplished, "if not greatly imaginative," artist and compares him to the religious poet Henry Vaughan.*]

The poet in whom the English Church of Hooker and Laud, the Church of the *via media* in doctrine and ritual, found a voice of its own, was George Herbert, the son of Donne's friend Magdalen Herbert, and the younger brother of Lord Herbert of Cherbury. His volume **The Temple, Sacred Poems and Private Ejaculations, By Mr. George Herbert**, was printed at Cambridge in the year that a disorderly collection of the amorous, satirical, courtly and pious poems of the famous Dean of St. Paul's, who died in 1631, was shot from the press in London as *Poems, by J. D., with Elegies on the Author's Death.* As J. D. [John Donne] the author continued to figure on the title-page of each successive edition till that of 1669; nor were the additions made from time to time of a kind to diminish the complex, ambiguous impression which the volume must have produced on the minds of the admirers of the ascetic and eloquent Dean. There is no such record of a complex character and troubled progress in the poetry of Herbert. It was not, indeed, altogether without a struggle that Herbert bowed his neck to the collar, abandoned the ambitions and vanities of youth to become the pious rector of Bemerton. He knew, like Donne, in what light the ministry was regarded by the young courtiers whose days were spent

> In dressing, mistressing and compliment.

His ambitions had been courtly. He loved fine clothes. As Orator at Cambridge he showed himself an adept in learned and elegant flattery, and he hoped 'that, as his predecessors, he might in time attain the place of a Secretary of State'. When he resolved, after the death of 'his most obliging and powerful friends', to take Orders, he 'did acquaint a court-friend' with his resolution, 'who persuaded

him to alter it, as too mean an employment, and too much below his birth, and the excellent abilities and endowments of his mind'. All this is clearly enough reflected in Herbert's poems, and I have endeavoured . . . to emphasize the note of conflict, of personal experience, which troubles and gives life to poetry that might otherwise be too entirely doctrinal and didactic. But there is no evidence in Herbert's most agitated verses of the deeper scars, the profounder remorse which gives such a passionate, anguished *timbre* to the harsh but resonant harmonies of his older friend's *Divine Poems*:

> Despair behind, and death before doth cast
> Such terror, and my feeble flesh doth waste
> By sin in it, which it t'wards hell doth weigh.

Herbert knows the feeling of alienation from God; but he knows also that of reconcilement, the joy and peace of religion:

> You must sit down, says Love, and taste my
>   meat:
>   So I did sit and eat.

Herbert is too in full harmony with the Church of his country, could say, with Sir Thomas Browne, 'There is no Church whose every part so squares unto my Conscience; whose Articles, Constitutions and Customs, seem so consonant unto reason, and as it were framed to my particular Devotion, as this whereof I hold my Belief, the Church of England':

> Beauty in thee takes up her place,
> And dates her letters from thy face,
>   When she doth write.
>
> A fine aspect in fit array,
> Neither too mean, nor yet too gay,
>   Shows who is best. . . .
>
> But, dearest Mother, (what those misse)
> The mean, thy praise and glory is,
>   And long may be.
>
> Blessed be God, whose love it was
> To double moat thee with his grace,
>   And none but thee.

It was from Donne that Herbert learned the 'metaphysical' manner. He has none of Donne's daring applications of scholastic doctrines. Herbert's interest in theology is not metaphysical but practical and devotional, the doctrines of his Church—the Incarnation, Passion, Resurrection, Trinity, Baptism—as these are reflected in the festivals, fabric, and order of the Church and are capable of appeal to the heart. But Herbert's central theme is the psychology of his religious experiences. He transferred to religious poetry the subtler analysis and record of moods which had been Donne's great contribution to love poetry. The metaphysical taste in conceit, too, ingenious, erudite, and indiscriminate, not confining itself to the conventionally picturesque and poetic, appealed to his acute, if not profound mind, and to the Christian temper which rejected nothing as common and unclean. He would speak of sacred things in the simplest language and with the aid of the homeliest comparisons:

> Both heav'n and earth

Paid me my wages in a world of mirth.

Prayer is:

> Heaven in ordinary, man well drest,
> The milky way, the bird of Paradise.

Divine grace in the Sacramental Elements:

> Knoweth the ready way,
>   And hath the privy key
> Op'ning the soul's most subtle rooms;
> While those, to spirits refin'd, at door attend
>   Dispatches from their friend.

Night is God's 'ebony box' in which:

> Thou dost inclose us till the day
> Put our amendment in our way,
> And give new wheels to our disorder'd clocks.

> Christ left his grave-clothes that we might, when
>   grief
> Draws tears or blood, not want an handkerchief.

These are the 'mean' similes which in Dr. Johnson's view were fatal to poetic effect even in Shakespeare. We have learned not to be so fastidious, yet when they are not purified by the passionate heat of the poet's dramatic imagination the effect is a little stuffy, for the analogies and symbols are more fanciful or traditional than natural and imaginative. Herbert's nature is generally 'metaphysical',—'the busy orange-tree', the rose that purges, the 'sweet spring' which is 'a box where sweets compacted lie'. It is at rare moments that feeling and natural image are imaginatively and completely merged in one another:

> And now in age I bud again,
> After so many deaths I live and write;
>   I once more smell the dew and rain,
> And relish versing: O my only light,
>   It cannot be
>   That I am he
> On whom thy tempests fell all night.

But if not a greatly imaginative, Herbert is a sincere and sensitive poet, and an accomplished artist elaborating his argumentative strain or little allegories and conceits with felicitous completeness, and managing his variously patterned stanzas—even the symbolic wings and altars and priestly bells, the three or seven-lined stanzas of his poems on the Trinity and Sunday—with a finished and delicate harmony. *The Temple* breathes the spirit of the Anglican Church at its best, primitive and modest; and also of one troubled and delicate soul seeking and finding peace.

Herbert's influence is discernible in the religious verse of all the minor Anglican poets of the century. . . . Henry Vaughan had written verses of the fashionable kind . . . before the influence of Herbert converted his pen to the service of Heaven; but all his *poetry* is religious. In *Silex Scintillans* he often imitates his predecessor in name and choice of theme, but his best work is of another kind. The difference between Herbert and Vaughan, at his best, is the difference on which Coleridge and Wordsworth dilated between fancy and imagination, between the sensitive and happy discovery of analogies and the imaginative apprehension of emotional identity in diverse experiences, which is the poet's counterpart to the scientific discovery of a common law controlling the most divergent phenomena. Herbert's 'sweet day, so cool, so calm, so bright' is a delightful play of tender fancy. Vaughan's greatest verses reveal a profounder intuition, as when Night is:

> God's silent, searching flight;
> When my Lord's head is fill'd with dew, and all
> His locks are wet with the clear drops of night;
>   His still, soft call;
> His knocking-time; the soul's dumb watch
> When spirits their fair kindred catch.

Vaughan is a less effective preacher, a far less neat and finished artist than Herbert. His temper is more that of the mystic. The sense of guilt which troubles Donne, of sin which is the great alienator of man's soul from God in Herbert's poems, is less acute with Vaughan, or is merged in a wider consciousness of separation, a veil between the human soul and that Heaven which is its true home. His soul is ever questing, back to the days of his own youth, or to the youth of the world, or to the days of Christ's sojourn on earth, when God and man were in more intimate contact:

> In Abraham's tent the winged guests
> —O how familiar then was heaven!—
> Eat, drink, discourse, sit down and rest,
>   Until the cool and shady even;

or else he yearns for the final reconciliation beyond the grave:

> Where no rude shade or night
> Shall dare approach us; we shall there no more
>   Watch stars or pore
> Through melancholy clouds, and say,
>   'Would it were Day!'
> One everlasting Sabbath there shall run
> Without succession, and without a sun.

To this mystical mood Nature reveals herself, not as a museum of spiritual analogies, a garden of religious simples, but as a creature simpler than man, yet, in virtue of its simplicity and innocence, in closer harmony with God. 'Etenim res creatae exserto capite observantes exspectant revelationem filiorum Dei.' At brief moments Vaughan writes of nature and childhood as Wordsworth and Blake were to write, but generally with the addition of some little pietistic tag which betrays his century. It is indeed only in short passages that Vaughan achieves adequate imaginative vision and utterance, but the spirit of these passages is diffused through his religious verse, more quietistic, less practical, in spirit than Herbert's. (pp. xl-xlvi)

> *Herbert J. C. Grierson, in an introduction* to
> Metaphysical Lyrics & Poems of the Seven-
> teenth Century: Donne to Butler, *edited by
> Herbert J. C. Grierson, 1921. Reprint by Ox-
> ford University Press, 1959, pp. xiii-lviii.*

T. S. Eliot (essay date 1944)

[*Perhaps the most influential poet and critic to write in the English language during the first half of the twentieth century, Eliot is closely identified with the Modernist movement. His works are noted for their formal complexity, artistic and intellectual eclecticism, and experi-*

mentation. He introduced a number of terms and concepts that strongly affected critical thought in his lifetime, among them the idea that poets must be conscious of the living tradition of literature in order for their work to have artistic and spiritual validity. Eliot was one of the key revivifiers of modern critical interest in metaphysical poetry, thanks largely to his seminal essay "The Metaphysical Poets," originally published in 1921. In the following excerpt from his 1944 essay "What Is Minor Poetry?" Eliot compares Herbert to Robert Herrick and Thomas Campion, asserting that Herbert is by contrast a "major poet."]

If we have difficulty in separating the writers of long poems into major and minor poets, we have no easier decision with writers of short poems. One very interesting case is George Herbert. We all know a few of his poems, which appear again and again in anthologies; but when we read through his collected poems, we are surprised to find how many of the poems strike us as just as good as those we have met within anthologies. But *The Temple* is something more than a number of religious poems by one author: it was, as the title is meant to imply, a book constructed according to a plan; and as we get to know Herbert's poems better, we come to find that there is something we get from the whole book, which is more than a sum of its parts. What has at first the appearance of a succession of beautiful but separate lyrics, comes to reveal itself as a continued religious meditation with an intellectual framework; and the book as a whole discloses to us the Anglican devotional spirit of the first half of the seventeenth century. What is more, we get to understand Herbert better, and feel rewarded for the trouble, if we know something about the English theological writers of his time; if we know something about the English mystical writers of the fourteenth century; and if we know something of certain other poets his contemporaries—Donne, Vaughan and Traherne, and come to perceive something in common between them in their Welsh origin and background; and finally, we learn something about Herbert by comparing the typical Anglican devotion which he expresses, with the more continental, and Roman, religious feeling of his contemporary Richard Crashaw. So in the end, I, for one, cannot admit that Herbert can be called a 'minor' poet: for it is not of a few favourite poems that I am reminded when I think of him, but of the whole work.

Now compare Herbert with two other poets, one a little senior to him, and one of the previous generation, but both very distinguished writers of lyrics. From the poems of Robert Herrick, also an Anglican parson, but a man of very different temperament, we also get the feeling of a unifying personality, and we get to know this personality better by reading all of his poems, and for having read all of his poems we enjoy still better the ones we like best. But first, there is no such continuous conscious purpose about Herrick's poems; he is more the purely natural and unselfconscious man, writing his poems as the fancy seizes him; and second, the personality expressed in them is less unusual—in fact, it is its honest ordinariness which gives the charm. Relatively, we get much more of him from one poem than we do of Herbert from one poem: still, there is something more in the whole than in the parts. Next,

consider Thomas Campion, the Elizabethan writer of songs. I should say that within his limits there was no more accomplished craftsman in the whole of English poetry than Campion. I admit that to understand his poems fully there are some things one should know: Campion was a musician, and he wrote his songs to be sung. We appreciate his poems better if we have some acquaintance with Tudor music and with the instruments for which it was written; we like them better if we like this music; and we want not merely to read them, but to hear some of them sung, and sung to Campion's own setting. But we do not so much need to know any of the things that, in the case of George Herbert, help us to understand him better and enjoy him more; we need not concern ourselves with what he thought, or with what books he had read, or with his racial background or his personality. All we need is the Elizabethan setting. What we get, when we proceed from those of his poems which we read in anthologies, to read his entire collection, is a repeated pleasure, the enjoyment of new beauties and new technical variations, but no such total impression. We cannot say, with him, that the whole is more than the sum of its parts.

I do not say that even this test—which, in any case, everyone must apply for himself, with various results—of whether the whole is more than the sum of its parts, is in itself a satisfactory criterion for distinguishing between a major and a minor poet. Nothing is so simple as that: and although we do not feel, after reading Campion, that we know the man Campion, as we do feel after reading Herrick, yet on other grounds, because he is so much the more remarkable craftsman, I should myself rate Campion as a more important poet than Herrick, though very much below Herbert. All I have affirmed is, that a work which consists of a number of short poems, even of poems which, taken individually, may appear rather slight, may, if it has a unity of underlying pattern, be the equivalent of a first-rate long poem in establishing an author's claim to be a 'major' poet. (pp. 42-44)

T. S. Eliot, "What Is Minor Poetry," in his On Poetry and Poets, *Farrar, Straus and Cudahy, 1957, pp. 34-51.*

Coleridge praises the religious force of Herbert's poetry:

To feel the full force of the Christian religion it is perhaps necessary, for many tempers, that they should first be made to feel, experimentally, the hollowness of human friendship, the presumptuous emptiness of human hopes. I find more substantial comfort now in pious George Herbert's *Temple,* which I used to read to amuse myself with his quaintness, in short, only to laugh at, than in all the poetry since the poems of Milton.

Samuel Taylor Coleridge in Coleridge's Miscellaneous Criticism, *edited by Thomas Middleton Raysor, The Folcroft Press, 1936.*

William Empson (essay date 1947)

[*Empson was an English critic, poet, and editor. He is best known for* Seven Types of Ambiguity *(1930; revised 1947), a seminal contribution to the formalist school of New Criticism. Much of Empson's work reflects the influence of I. A. Richards and the intellectual milieu of Cambridge University in the 1920s. Empson's critical theory is based on the assumption that all great poetry is ambiguous and that this ambiguity can often be traced to the multiple meanings of words. He therefore analyzed texts by enumerating and discussing these various meanings and examining how they fit together to communicate ideas and emotions. While Empson is widely respected for his intelligence and ingenuity, he has been faulted for the limitations of his approach. In the following excerpt from* Seven Types of Ambiguity, *he examines stylistic and religious elements in Herbert's poem "The Sacrifice."*]

In 'The Sacrifice,' with a magnificence [Herbert] never excelled, the various sets of conflicts in the Christian doctrine of the Sacrifice are stated with an assured and easy simplicity, a reliable and unassuming grandeur, extraordinary in any material, but unique as achieved by successive fireworks of contradiction, and a mind jumping like a flea. Herbert's poems are usually more 'personal' and renaissance than this one, in which the theological system is accepted so completely that the poet is only its mouthpiece. Perhaps this, as a releasing and reassuring condition, is necessary if so high a degree of ambiguity is to seem normal. For, to this extent, the poem is outside the 'conflict' theory of poetry; it assumes, as does its theology, the existence of conflicts, but its business is to state a generalised solution of them. Here, then, the speaker is Jesus, the subject doctrinal, and the method that strange monotony of accent, simplicity of purpose, and rarefied intensity of feeling, which belong to a scholastic abstraction, come to life on the stage of a miracle play.

> They did accuse me of great villainy
> That I did thrust into the Deitie;
> Who never thought that any robberie;
>   Was ever grief like mine?
>
> Some said that I the temple to the floore
> In three days razed, and raised as before.
> Why, he that built the world can do much more.
>   Was ever grief like mine?

He is speaking with pathetic simplicity, an innocent surprise that people should treat him so, and a complete failure to understand the case against him; thus *who* in the third line quoted and *he* in the seventh make their point by applying equally to *I* and the *Deitie*. But before thinking the situation as simple as the speaker one must consider the use of the word *rased* to apply to the two opposite operations concerned; and that the quotation from Jeremiah which makes the refrain refers in the original not to the Saviour but to the wicked city of Jerusalem, abandoned by God, and in the hands of her enemies for her sins.

> Then they condemn me all, with that same
>   breath
> Which I do give them daily, unto death;
> Thus Adam my first breathing rendereth:
>   Was ever grief like mine?

> Hark how they cry aloud still Crucify,
> He is not fit to live a day, they cry;
> Who cannot live less than eternally.
>   Was ever grief like mine?

Me all, 'they all condemn me, they condemn the whole of me (I am Jerusalem and include them), they condemn me unto the total death of which I am not capable, they condemn me and thus call down their own destruction, I give them breath daily till their death, and unto death finally shall I give them'; so that *rendereth* includes 'repay me for my goodness' and 'give up the ghost,' both at their eventual death and in their now killing *me*. The same fusion of the love of Christ and the vindictive terrors of the sacrificial idea turns up in his advice to his dear friends not to weep for him, for *because* he has wept for both, when in his agony they abandoned him, they will need their tears for themselves.

> Weep not dear friends, since I for both have
>   wept
> When all my tears were blood, the while you
>   slept,
> Your tears for your own fortunes should be kept.
>   Was ever grief like mine?

In each case, of course, the stress of the main meaning is on the loving-kindness of Jesus; it is only because this presentment of the sacrificial idea is so powerfully and beautifully imagined that all its impulses are involved.

> Now heal thyself, Physician, now come down;
> Alas, I did so, when I left my crown
> And father's smile for you, to feel his frown.
>   Was ever grief like mine?

The secondary meaning ('to make you feel') is a later refinement, and the Williams manuscript reads 'to feel for you.'

The last verse of all contains as strong and simple a double meaning:

> But now I die; Now, all is finished.
> My woe, man's weal; and now I bow my head:
> Only let others say, when I am dead,
>   Never was grief like mine.

English has no clear form for the Oratio Obliqua. He may wish that his own grief may never be exceeded among the humanity he pities, 'After the death of Christ, may there never be a grief like Christ's'; he may, incidentally, wish that they may *say* this, that he may be sure of recognition, and of a church that will be a sounding-board to his agony; or he may mean *mine* as a quotation from the *others*, 'Only let there be a retribution, only let my torturers say never was grief like theirs, in the day when my agony shall be exceeded.' (Better were it for that man if he had never been born.)

I am not sure how far people would be willing to accept this double meaning; I am only sure that after you have once apprehended it, after you have felt this last clash as a sound, you will never be able to read the poem without remembering that it is a possibility. For the resultant meaning of this apparently complete contradiction, one must consider the way it is used as a religious doctrine; 'Christ has made all safe, a weight is off our shoulders, and it is for that very reason far more urgent that we should be careful. Salvation is by Faith, and this gives an intolerable importance to Works. O death, where is thy sting; because the second death is infinitely terrible.' You may say the pious Herbert could not have intended such a contradiction, because he would have thought it blasphemous, and because he took a 'sunny' view of his religion. Certainly it is hard to say whether a poet is conscious of a particular implication in his work, he has so many other things to think of; but for the first objection, it is merely orthodox to make Christ to insist on the damnation of the wicked (though it might be blasphemous, because disproportionate, to make him insist on it here without insisting more firmly at the same time on its opposite); and for the second objection, it is true George Herbert is a cricket in the sunshine, but one is accustomed to be shocked on discovering the habits of such creatures; they are more savage than they seem.

A memory of the revengeful power of Jehovah gives resonance to the voice of the merciful power of Jesus, even when verbal effects so pretty as these last cannot be found:

> Herod in judgment sits, while I do stand;
> Examines me with a censorious hand.
> I him obey, who all things else command.
>   Was ever grief like mine?

Even in so quiet a line as the second, *me* is made to ring out with a triumphant and scornful arrogance—'the absurdity of the thing'—and there is a further echo from the former dispensation in that his attitude of deference before Herod is one would give full play to his right hand and his stretched-out arm; that he will be far more furious in his *judgment* than his judges; that one would *stand* to exert, as well as to suffer, power.

> Why, Caesar is their only king, not I.
> He clave the stony rock when they were dry;
> But surely not their hearts, as I well try.
>   Was ever grief like mine?

It is by its concentration that this is so powerful. The first line is part of his defence to his judges: 'I am not a political agitator.' In the bitterness of this apology, that his kingdom is not of this world, he identifies Caesar with Moses as the chosen leader of Israel ('Oh no, it was Caesar who gave them the water of life; I am only an honest subject'), and by this irony both the earthly power of the conqueror and the legal rationalism of the Pharisees are opposed both to the profounder mercy of the Christ and to the profounder searchings of heart that he causes; I may *cleave their hearts* with my tenderness or with their despair:

> Ah, how they scourge me! yet my tenderness
> Doubles each lash; and yet their bitterness
> Winds up my grief to a mysteriousness.
>   Was ever grief like mine?

Doubles, because I feel pain so easily, because I feel it painful that they should be so cruel, because I feel it painful they should be so unjust, because my tenderness enrages them, because my tenderness (being in fact power) will return equally each stroke upon them, because I take upon myself those pains also. *Mysteriousness*, because the bitterness in them or (for various reasons) due to them produces

grief no one can fathom, or because it dramatises that grief into a form that can show itself (as in initiation to the Mysteries) to a crowd (as the scourgers also are a crowd), wound up like a string to give out music, and echoing in the mind, repeatable, as a type of suffering.

> Behold they spit on me in scornful wise
> Who with my spittle gave the blind man eyes,
> Leaving his blindness to mine enemies.
>   Was ever grief like mine?

Leaving his blindness wilfully, the conceit implies, as a cruel judgment upon my enemies, that they should in consequence spit upon me and so commit sin. (Father, forgive them, for they know not what they do.) These two events are contrasted, but that they should spit upon me is itself a healing; by it they distinguish me as scapegoat, and assure my triumph and their redemption; and spitting, in both cases, was to mark my unity with man. Only the speed, isolation, and compactness of Herbert's method could handle in this way impulses of such reach and complexity.

> Then on my head a crown of thorns I wear,
> For these are all the grapes Zion doth bear,
> Though I my vine planted and watered there.
>   Was ever grief like mine?

> So sits the earth's great curse in Adam's fall
> Upon my head, so I remove it all
> From the earth on to my brows, and bear the
>   thrall.
>   Was ever grief like mine?

The *thorns* of the curse upon Adam, the wild *grapes* of the wicked city against which Isaiah thundered destruction, and the crown of *vine*-leaves of the Dionysiac revellers (and their descendants the tragedians), all this is lifted on to the head of the Christ from a round world, similar to it, in the middle distance; the world, no longer at the centre of man's vision, of Copernican astronomy. The achievement here is not merely that all these references are brought together, but that they are kept in their frame, of monotonous and rather naive pathos, of fixity of doctrinal outlook, of heartrending and straightforward grandeur.

> They bow their knees to me, and cry, Hail, King!
> Whatever scoffs or scornfulness can bring
> I am the floor, the sink, where they it fling.
>   Was ever grief like mine?

> Yet since man's sceptres are as frail as reeds,
> And thorny all their crowns, bloody their deeds,
> I, who am Truth, turn into truth their deeds.
>   Was ever grief like mine?

I, out of my mercy making their sins as few as possible, reflect that I am indeed a king, and so worthy of mockery; because all kings are as inferior (weak, outcast, or hated) as this; because I am king of kings, and all kings are inferior to me; or because from my outcast kingship of mockery all real kingship takes its strength (the divine right of kings, for instance, and the relief of popular irritation under lords of misrule). He has united Herod and Pilate, 'whose friendship is his enmity,' and his scarlet robe of princes shows that only his blood 'can repair man's decay.'

> Oh all ye who pass by, behold and see;

> Man stole the fruit, but I must climb the tree,
> The tree of life, to all but only me.
>   Was ever grief like mine?

The first line now at last, with an effect of apotheosis, gives the complete quotation from Jeremiah. He climbs the tree to repay what was stolen, as if he was putting the apple back; but the phrase in itself implies rather that he is doing the stealing, that so far from sinless he is Prometheus and the criminal. Either he stole on behalf of man (it is he who appeared to be sinful, and was caught up the tree) or he is climbing upwards, like Jack on the Beanstalk, and taking his people with him back to Heaven. The phrase has an odd humility which makes us see him as the son of the house; possibly Herbert is drawing on the medieval tradition that the Cross was made of the wood of the forbidden trees. Jesus seems a child in this metaphor, because he is the Son of God, because he can take the apples without actually stealing (though there is some doubt about this), because of the practical and domestic associations of such a necessity, and because he is evidently smaller than Man, or at any rate than Eve, who could pluck the fruit without climbing. This gives a pathetic humour and innocence (except ye receive the Kingdom of Heaven as a little child, ye shall in no wise enter therein); on the other hand, the son stealing from his father's orchard is a symbol of incest; in the person of the Christ the supreme act of sin is combined with the supreme act of virtue. Thus in two ways, one behind the other, the Christ becomes guilty; and we reach the final contradiction:

> Lo here I hang, charged with a world of sin
> The greater world of the two . . .

as the complete Christ; scapegoat and tragic hero; loved because hated; hated because godlike; freeing from torture because tortured; torturing his torturers because all-merciful; source of all strength to men because by accepting he exaggerates their weakness; and, because outcast, creating the possibility of society.

> Between two theeves I spend my utmost breath,
> As he that for some robberie suffereth.
> Alas! what have I stolen from you? Death:
>   Was ever grief like mine?

Herbert deals in this poem, on the scale and by the methods necessary to it, with the most complicated and deeply-rooted notion of the human mind. (pp. 226-33)

> *William Empson, "Chapter VII," in his* Seven Types of Ambiguity, *second edition, 1947. Reprint by New Directions, 1966, pp. 192-233.*

Joan Bennett (essay date 1957)

[*Bennett was an English educator who wrote studies on the works of Virginia Woolf (1945) and George Eliot (1948). She is also the author of* Four Metaphysical Poets: Donne, Herbert, Vaughan, Crashaw *(1934; revised 1957). In the following excerpt from that work, she assesses the influence of John Donne on Herbert's style and maintains that all of Herbert's poetry is spiritual autobiography.*]

Herbert's mother, Magdalene Herbert, was the addressee of several of Donne's poems and letters. When she died he made for her a magnificent funeral oration; he must often have visited that house which he describes as 'a court in the conversation of the best' and George Herbert must have been early acquainted with manuscripts of his poetry. The influence of the elder poet on the younger was strong and permanent. Herbert's imagery, like Donne's, works through the mind rather than the senses and the structure of his poems is logical. But, for various reasons, his poetry is simpler than Donne's. The range of his experience was narrower. Donne expresses hate, disgust, jealousy, lust, love, reverence, security and mistrust. He traverses every variety of mood, both as a lover and as a worshipper; and at any given moment the experiences he has already passed through are still present to him. Each poem represents a complex state of mind and a subtle adjustment of impulses. Herbert's narrower experience not only limits his choice of subject-matter, but simplifies the texture of his poems.

At an early age Herbert decided that the emotional peace and satisfaction he sought was not to be found in the love of women. He shut himself off from the whole field of experience in which Donne's *Songs and Sonets* found their origin. His mother was the only woman to whom he ever addressed a poem. When he was only four years old his father died and Magdalene Herbert was free to give all her devotion and shaping influence to her children. She moved with little George to Oxford, where Edward was then studying, and remained there for four years, with both her sons under her eye, George working with tutors and Edward reading for his degree. Afterward she moved with George to London and he went as a day-boy to Westminster College. Not till 1609, the year in which he entered the university, did his mother marry again; so that, throughout his childhood and adolescence, and right up to the threshold of manhood, he had been closely and lovingly watched over by a mother who, as we know, was no ordinary woman. Izaak Walton speaks of her 'great and harmlesse wit, her cheerful gravity and obliging behaviour', but Donne, in his funeral sermon, draws a stronger portrait. He tells us of her 'inclination and conversation, naturally cheerful, and merry, and loving facetiousness, and sharpnesse of wit . . .', and, with impassioned eloquence, he tells of her generosity to the plague-stricken: 'of which, myself, who, at that time, had the favour to be admitted into that family, can, and must testify this, that when the late heavy visitation fell hotly upon this towne, when every doore was shut up, and, lest Death should enter into the house, every house was made a sepulchre of them that were in it, then, then, in that time of infection, diverse persons visited with that infection, had their releefe, and releefe applicable to that very infection, from this house.' And, finally, he tells us how 'In the doctrine, and discipline, of that Church, in which God sealed her to himselfe in Baptisme, shee brought up her children, she assisted her family, she dedicated her soule to God in her life and surrendered it to him in her death; and in that forme of Common Prayer, which is ordained by that Church, and to which she accustomed herself, with her family, twice every day, she joined with that company, which was about her death bed'. We are left with the picture of a woman of quick intelligence, unusual courage, firmness of will and strong religious zeal, who coveted her son's devotion, not for herself, but for the Church. She had always intended George for the Church; soldiering was the family profession, but for this he had not the physique and he resigned himself, at first reluctantly, to an academic career which was to end in a country parsonage. For New Year's day 1610 he sent to his mother his first two poems. The theme of both was the inadequacy of earthly loves. In an accompanying letter he declared that he did not need the help of the muses 'to reprove the vanity of those many love poems that are daily writ, and consecrated to Venus; nor to bewail that so few are writ that look towards God and heaven. For my own part, my meaning (dear mother) is, in these sonnets, to declare my resolution to be, that my poor abilities in poetry, shall be all and ever consecrated to God's glory.' The sonnets show the influence of Donne; the first begins with a question, the second with a statement, each perfectly reproducing the accent of the spoken word:

> My God, where is that ancient heat towards
> thee,
> Wherewith whole showls of *Martyrs* once did
> burn,
> Besides their other flames? Doth Poetry
> Wear *Venus* Livery? only serve her turn?
> Why are not *Sonnets* made of thee? and layes
> Upon thine Altar burnt? Cannot thy love
> Heighten a spirit to sound out thy praise
> As well as any she? Cannot thy *Dove*
> Out-strip their *Cupid* easily in flight?

The macabre jest about the flames is in the metaphysical tradition, as is the conceit with which the second sonnet closes:

> Open the bones, and you shall nothing find
> In the best *face* but *filth*, when, Lord, in thee
> The *beauty* lies in the *discovery*.

Herbert never wavered in his resolution to devote his poetic gifts exclusively to the service of God. In a poem called **"Dulnesse,"** we find him again drawing a parallel between his own theme and that of the love poet:

> The wanton lover in a curious strain
> Can praise his fairest fair;
> And with quaint metaphors her curled hair
> Curl o're again.
> Thou art my lovelinesse, my life, my light,
> Beautie alone to me:
> Thy bloudy death and undeserv'd, makes thee
> Pure red and white.

And the same conscious choice of the love of God as alternative to the love of women prompts **"A Parodie,"** in which Herbert follows the pattern of a song once thought to have been by Donne,

> Soules joy, now I am gone,
> And you alone,
> (Which cannot be,
> Since I must leave myselfe with thee,
> And carry thee with me)
> Yet when unto our eyes
> Absence denyes
> Each others sight,
> And makes to us a constant night,

> When others change to light
> *O give no way to griefe,*
> *But let beliefe*
> *Of mutuall love,*
> *This wonder to the vulgar prove*
> *Our Bodyes, not wee move.*

For Herbert it is God, not an earthly lover, whose absence is inconceivable:

> Souls joy, when thou art gone,
> And I alone,
> Which cannot be,
> Because thou dost abide with me,
> And I depend on thee;

Herbert married Jane Danvers in 1629; he was thirty-six years old and in failing health. It was a childless though, we are told, a happy marriage. Herbert died four years later. A year after his marriage he accepted the living of Bemerton. The two events were not unconnected. Marriage was a carefully considered step in his consecration to God's service. In the prose treatise called **The Country Parson** we learn what he thought about a married priesthood:

> The Country Parson considering that virginity is a higher state then Matrimony, and that the Ministry requires the best and highest things, is rather unmarryed, then marryed. But yet as the temper of his body may be, or as the temper of his Parish may be, where he may have occasion to converse with women, and that among suspicious men, . . . he is rather married then unmarried.

And of the choice of a wife he writes:

> If he be married, the choyce of his wife was made rather by his eare, then by his eye; his judgement, not his affection found out a fit wife for him, whose humble, and liberall disposition he preferred before beauty, riches, or honour.

Thus circumspectly, in strong contrast to the headlong impetuosity of John Donne, Herbert probably chose his own wife.

But it must not be supposed that Herbert was of a placid or equable temperament. Lord Herbert of Cherbury tells us in his autobiography that 'my brother George was not exempt from passion and choler (being infirmities to which all our race is subject)'. And Herbert, in his autobiographical poems **"Affliction,"** speaks of his 'fierce and sudden' youth; the poems often describe his servitude to God as a bondage against which he vainly rebels.

> I struck the board, and cry'd, No more.
> I will abroad.
> What? shall I ever sigh and pine?
> My lines and life are free; free as the rode,
> Loose as the winde, as large as store.
> Shall I be still in suit?
> Have I no harvest but a thorn
> To let me bloud, and not restore
> What I have lost with cordiall fruit?
> Sure there was wine
> Before my sighs did drie it: there was corn
> Before my tears did drown it.
> Is the yeare onely lost to me?

> Have I no bayes to crown it?
> No flowers, no garlands gay? all blasted?
> All wasted?

"The Collar," which is this poem's title, is an emblem of servitude. The poem moves through rebellion against his Master to the sudden recognition that the freedom he is claiming is freedom from God's love:

> But as I rav'd and grew more fierce and wilde
> At every word,
> Me thoughts I heard one calling, *Child!*
> And I reply'd, *My Lord.*

His poetry is not the record of quiet saintliness, but of continual wrestling and continual submission; the collar is not easily worn:

> I know the wayes of Pleasure, the sweet strains,
> The lullings and the relishes of it;
> The propositions of hot bloud and brains;
> What mirth and musick mean; what love and wit
> Have done these twentie hundred yeares, and
> more:
> I know the projects of unbridled store:
> My stuffe is flesh, not brasse; my senses live,
> And grumble oft, that they have more in me
> Then he that curbs them, being but one to five:
> Yet I love thee.

No human love competed with the love of God for Herbert; but the fuller life of worldly intercourse and the sweets of ambition allured him: he complains in "**Affliction (1)**":

> Whereas my birth and spirit rather took
> The way that takes the town;
> Thou didst betray me to a lingring book,
> And wrap me in a gown.

Charles Cotton speaks of him as

> He whose education
> Manners and parts, by high applauses blown,
> Was deeply tainted by Ambition,
> And fitted for a court, . . .

which is in keeping with Herbert's confession in "**Affliction (1)**," that:

> Thou often didst with Academick praise
> Melt and dissolve my rage.

and in *The Country Parson* he describes ambition as one of the commonest and most insidious temptations with which men of his calling can be afflicted:

> Ambition, or untimely desire of promotion to an
> higher state or place, under colour of accommo-
> dation or necessary provision, is a common
> temptation to men of any eminency. . . .

This was the temptation that Herbert resisted, though not without rebellion and remonstrance:

> Were it not better to bestow
> Some place and power on me?
> Then should thy praises with me grow,
> And share in my degree.

he urges in "**Submission,**"

> But when I thus dispute and grieve,
> I do resume my sight,
> And pilfring what I once did give,
> Disseize thee of thy right.

To reject God, for Herbert, would be to prefer the prizes and praises of the world to the act of loving, for God has no rival in his heart. That is why he suffers so acutely under the ebb and flow of his own zeal:

> How should I praise thee, Lord! how should my
> rymes
> Gladly engrave thy love in steel,
> If what my soul doth feel sometimes,
> My soul might ever feel!

No theme occurs more frequently, or is more poignantly expressed, than this distress at the dying away of emotion:

> Whither away delight?
> Thou cam'st but now; wilt thou so soon depart,
> And give me up to night?

His over-mastering desire is to be allowed to love God; the need expressed in the passionate paradox with which "**Affliction (1)**" closes. He has toyed with the thought of seeking some other service and suddenly he turns back to his first and only love with the despairing cry:

> Ah my deare God! though I am clean forgot,
> Let me not love thee, if I love thee not.

Herbert's poetry is the expression of an ardent temperament with a single emotional outlet.

With the exception of a few didactic poems interpreting the doctrine or ritual of the Church, all his poetry is spiritual autobiography. The devotional poet, perhaps even more than the love poet, is exposed to the danger of confiding in his public instead of writing poems. His problem is to build a structure that will stand alone, independently of either the reader's or the poet's private concerns. It is here that the 'Donne tradition' is salutary. Within that tradition the structure of a poem is normally dialectic. Herbert states his premises with precision, usually by means of an image, in the tone of a prose argument. The reader is never befogged; the words represent clear-cut ideas which are the medium through which the poet's emotion is conveyed as well as, often, the cause of that emotion. Herbert knows and states what he thinks, as well as what he feels, about, for example, death and immortality or the relation between God and the soul. This does not mean that his poems are arguments designed to persuade the reader. Herbert takes the reader's intellectual assent for granted. He writes for his fellow-Christian. The substance of each poem is emotional, but the emotion is rooted in thought. As the reader absorbs the poem he becomes aware of that fusion between thought and feeling which constitutes the poet's belief. Suspension of his own irrelevant incredulities is easier than it is with poetry whose intellectual structure is less self-sufficient. A comparison will make the difference clearer. Herbert in a poem called "**Death**" and Tennyson in stanza CXXIX of "In Memoriam," each assert a belief in immortality. Tennyson addresses the spirit of his dead friend:

> Thy voice is on the rolling air;

I hear thee where the waters run;
　Thou standest in the rising sun,
And in the setting thou art fair.

What art thou then? I cannot guess;
　But tho' I seem in star and flower
　To feel thee some diffusive power,
I do not therefore love thee less:

My love involves the love before;
　My love is vaster passion now;
　Tho' mix'd with God and Nature thou,
I seem to love thee more and more.

Far off thou art, but ever nigh;
　I have thee still, and I rejoice;
　I prosper, circled with thy voice;
I shall not lose thee tho' I die.

A statement in the first stanza is followed in the second by a question to which no answer is forthcoming:

What art thou then? I cannot guess;

and in the third and fourth stanzas there are further statements again, but they are intentionally vague. The words 'I seem' dominate the stanza, the total impression left with the reader is that Tennyson perhaps knew what he felt, but certainly not what he thought. Herbert's poem "**Death**" is based on the premise that the death of Christ is the pledge of our resurrection; that he assumes this is made plain in the poem by the juxtaposition of two contrasted pictures representing the pre-Christian and the Christian view of death:

Death, thou wast once an uncouth hideous
　　thing,
　　　　Nothing but bones,
　　　The sad effect of sadder grones:
Thy mouth was open, but thou couldst not sing.

For we consider'd thee as at some six
　　　　Or ten yeares hence,
　　　After the losse of life and sense,
Flesh being turn'd do dust, and bones to sticks.

We lookt on this side of thee, shooting short;
　　　　Where we did finde
　　　The shells of fledge souls left behinde,
Dry dust, which sheds no tears, but may extort.

But since our Saviours death did put some bloud
　　　　Into thy face;
　　　Thou art grown fair and full of grace,
Much in request, much sought for as a good.

For we do now behold thee gay and glad,
　　　　As at dooms-day;
　　　When souls shall wear their new aray,
And all thy bones with beautie shall be clad.

Therefore we can go die as sleep, and trust
　　　　Half that we have
　　　Unto an honest faithfull grave;
Making our pillows either down, or dust.

The plot of the poem is clear and simple, three stanzas to describe death as it seemed before the resurrection, culminating in the lucid and lovely image of bodies that were but

The shells of fledge souls left behinde,

which (with its suggestion of spring and birth) leads on to three stanzas describing death as it seems since the resurrection. The concrete imagery builds up two clearly contrasted pictures, each impregnated with its appropriate feeling, the horror of death the skeleton:

Thy mouth was open, but thou couldst not sing.

and the peace of death:

　　　　As at dooms-day;
　　　When souls shall wear their new aray,
And all thy bones with beautie shall be clad.

A modern reader may be in closer sympathy with Tennyson's indecision, but his stanza remains unsatisfactory as poetry, because he does not say what he means, nor quite mean what he says. Herbert, like Donne, was capable of clear thought in conjunction with vehement feeling. The two kinds of activity abetted each other, so that the logical plotting of a lyric suited his genius. But he modified Donne's style in other respects. His experiences were less complex, less varied, so that he could convey them more simply. He used words more widely current and more often selected his illustrations from every day life. In two poems called "**Jordan**," Herbert describes his stylistic aims, setting them out in conscious distinction both from the elaborateness of the Petrarchists and from the intellectual subtlety of Donne:

Is it no verse, except enchanted groves
And sudden arbours shadow course-spunne
　　lines?
Must purling streams refresh a lovers loves?
Must all be vail'd, while he that reades, divines,
　Catching the sense at two removes?

Shepherds are honest people; let them sing:
Riddle who list, for me, and pull for Prime:
I envie no mans nightingale or spring;
Nor let them punish me with loss of rime,
　Who plainly say, *My God, My King.*

Herbert will not have pastoral affectations, neither will he have the intellectual curiosities of Donne.

When first my lines of heav'nly joyes made mention,
Such was their lustre, they did so excell,
That I sought out quaint words, and trim invention;
My thoughts began to burnish, sprout, and swell,
Curling with metaphors a plain intention,
Decking the sense, as if it were to sell.

Thousands of notions in my brain did runne,
Off'ring their service, if I were not sped:
I often blotted what I had begunne;
This was not quick enough, and that was dead.
Nothing could seem too rich to clothe the sunne,
Much lesse those joyes which trample on his head.

As flames do work and winde, when they ascend,
So I did weave my self into the sense.
But while I bustled, I might heare a friend
Whisper, *How wide is all this long pretence!*
There is in love a sweetnesse readie penn'd:
Copie out onely that, and save expense.

The two poems not only describe the kind of simplicity Herbert intends, they also illustrate the simplicity he achieves. It is the result of concrete imagery, familiar diction and a sound pattern close to the rhythm of speech. He chooses words that recall the affairs of every day. His lines are 'course-spunne' and his imagery of the market place. He creates for us, in the second poem, the picture of a bustling salesman, fidgeting about his wares, 'decking the sense, as if it were to sell', until he is advised to 'save expense'. This is the kind of image he always prefers, an image which associates his experience with the daily traffic of men of affairs or with ordinary household business. When, in **"Church-lock and key,"** he wants to describe his flagging zeal, he likens himself to a cold man impatiently bullying an insufficient fire:

> But as cold hands are angrie with the fire,
>   And mend it still;
> So I do lay the want of my desire,
> Not on my sinnes, or coldnesse, but thy will.

In **"Confession"** grief tortures a man as a carpenter tortures wood or an illness the body:

> No scrue, no piercer can
> Into a piece of timber work and winde,
>   As Gods afflictions into man,
>   When he a torture hath design'd.
> They are too subtill for the sub'tllest hearts;
> And fall, like rheumes, upon the tendrest parts.

He gains his effects from the short, strong, familiar words of daily usage:

> My throat, my soul is hoarse;
> My heart is wither'd like a ground
>   Which thou dost curse.
>   My thoughts turn round,
> And make me giddie; Lord, I fall,
>   Yet call.

Herbert often invented rhyme schemes or metrical patterns to illustrate the experience conveyed in the poem. In **"Longing,"** for instance, each stanza comes to rest in a two-foot line, which reflects the moment of exhaustion after stress:

> Look on my sorrows round!
> Mark well my furnace! O what flames,
>   What heats abound!
>   What griefs, what shames!
> Consider, Lord; Lord, bow thine eare,
>   And heare!

The strong contrasts of crescendo and diminuendo are a favourite device with him. This and other emblematic uses of metre are effective for Herbert because he recreates regular patterns of feeling. Despite his use of logic, his poems rarely progress (as Donne's do) to an unforeseen conclusion. When they seem to do that (as in **"The Collar"**) the surprise is reserved for the last lines. The steps towards the resolution of an emotional problem, in Herbert's poems, are as similar to one another as are the stanza-forms that communicate them. They advance, retreat, tread firmly, haltingly, or whatever it may be, in regular sequences. In **"Deniall"** Herbert invents a metre and rhyme scheme to reflect the broken relationship between God and the soul:

> When my devotions could not pierce
>   Thy silent eares;
> Then was my heart broken, as was my verse:
>   My breast was full of fears
>   And disorder:

Each stanza ends with a short unrhymed line until the last, where the rhyme is completed to suggest the renewed harmonious relation with God that the poet desires.

> O cheer and tune my heartless breast,
>   Deferre no time;
> That so thy favours granting my request,
>   They and my minde may chime,
>   And mend my ryme.

Poets of more complex moods cannot deal so simply with the problem of relating sound to sense, their pattern cannot be predetermined with the same completeness. But what Herbert had to say was usually simple and the kind of device he invented was often admirable for his purpose. At times he went so far as to arrange a pattern for the eye as well as for the ear; in **"The Altar"** and in **"Easter-wings"** the subject is represented by the shape of the print upon the page.

It is a nave device but adequate to the simple mood in which it was conceived. The effect of **"Easter-wings"** is less jejune than is sometimes supposed, for Herbert was sufficiently master of his instrument to make a double use of the pattern. The shape of the wings on the page may have meant more when Emblem Books were popular, the diminuendo and crescendo that bring it about are expressive both of the rise and fall of the lark's song and flight (Herbert's image) and also of the fall of man and his resurrection in Christ (the subject that the image represents).

> Lord, who createdst man in wealth and store,
>   Though foolishly he lost the same,
>   Decaying more and more,
>   Till he became
>   Most poore:
>   With thee
>   O let me rise
>   As larks, harmoniously,
>   And sing this day thy victories:
> Then shall the fall further the flight in me.
>
> My tender age in sorrow did beginne:
>   And still with sicknesses and shame
>   Thou didst so punish sinne,
>   That I became
>   Most thinne.
>   With thee
>   Let me combine
>   And feel this day thy victorie:
>   For, if I imp my wing on thine,
> Affliction shall advance the fight in me.

Herbert's poetry, despite his aristocratic birth and breeding and his considerable learning, leaves the impression of an unsophisticated mind. In certain ways the appeal of his verse is similar to the appeal of John Bunyan's prose. Like Bunyan, though for other reasons, he drew his language and imagery from daily affairs or from his religion. To understand him demands no culture that is not shared by all his co-religionists, and by the many more who are acquainted with the Bible and the teaching of the English church. But besides its simplicity in this sense, Herbert's poetry, like Bunyan's prose, exhibits certain childlike qualities of mind—the playfulness of some of his metrical effects is a case in point; a trick, for instance, like that of **"Trinitie Sunday"** in which three three-lined stanzas with triple rhymes represent the subject:

> Lord, who hast form'd me out of mud,
> 　And hast redeem'd me through thy bloud,
> 　And sanctifi'd me to do good;
>
> Purge all my sinnes done heretofore:
> 　For I confesse my heavie score,
> 　And I will strive to sinne no more.
>
> Enrich my heart, mouth, hands in me,
> 　With faith, with hope, with charitie;
> 　That I may runne, rise, rest with thee.

Such devices convey a child-like quality of mind, native to Herbert perhaps, or else acquired in obedience to the injunction 'except ye become as one of these little ones'. Patterns akin to the acrostic appealed to Herbert, he liked word games. In the poem **"Paradise"** for instance, cutting off the initial letter of the rhyme word represents God pruning his tree:

> I blesse thee, Lord, because I GROW
> Among thy trees, which in a ROW
> To thee both fruit and order OW,

and so on for five stanzas. Such playful effects as these, though exceptional in Herbert's work, indicate a fundamental difference between his mind and Donne's which accounts for other modifications he made in the metaphysical style.

Herbert profited from every aspect of Donne's style, but he always adapted it to his own temperament. He simplified the inner logical pattern, following as a rule a single train of argument; he changed the metrical pattern into something less flexible, though still studying to relate sound to sense; he narrowed the range of diction and imagery, while preserving their actuality. Similarly he adapted Donne's manner of accenting the line so as to reproduce the tone of the spoken word:

> I, like an usurp'd towne, to'another due,
> Labour to'admit you, but Oh, to no end,

writes Donne. This is the rhythm of speech, but only such as men speak under the stress of excitement. There is a suggestion of breathlessness, when we read the line we pant with the effort it describes. This was seldom the effect Herbert required, he preferred the tone of men exchanging news in the market place:

> Having been tenant long to a rich Lord,
> 　Not thriving, I resolved to be bold,

It is on this level that Herbert's poems open, our attention is held, but our expectation is low pitched:

> My God, I heard this day,
> 　That none doth build a stately habitation
> But he that means to dwell therein.

The relation between such an accent and the openings of Donne's poems is clear; Herbert like his master avoids the poetical, the words seem to fall into the natural prose order and to conform without effort to the metrical mould. But the climate of emotion is different:

> For Godsake hold your tongue and let me love!

writes Donne, or

> What if this present were the worlds last night?

No poet can afford to start at such a pitch unless he can sustain it or increase the tension. Herbert must start in low tones if we are to get the full impact of his climax, which consists often in a subtle change of feeling or attitude. His most characteristic gift is the power of controlling the movement of feeling in his poems. The emotional pattern is managed with exquisite tact. The attitudes he handles are subtle and delicate, over emphasis or emphasis in the wrong place, over haste or too much delay, would destroy their effect; but in such matters Herbert is a master. The opening lines of his poems are usually quiet, they place the reader at the heart of the subject just as Donne does, but, unlike Donne, Herbert maintains a demeanour of calm and restraint, and this is so even when, like Donne, he opens with an exclamation or question:

> Oh that I could a sinne once see!
>
> It cannot be. Where is that mightie joy
> 　Which just now took up all my heart?
>
> Oh, what a thing is man! How farre from power,
> 　From setled peace and rest!

The mood is collected, it is the preparation for a discussion of the theme. A similar difference is noticeable between the closing lines of Herbert's poems and those of Donne or of Hopkins. Herbert constantly achieves his effect by relaxing the tension at the end of a poem. The struggle is over and all is peace. **"The Thanksgiving,"** for instance, is a discussion with God, in which the poet tries to offer an equivalent for all that has been given:

> If thou shalt give me wit, it shall appeare,
> 　If thou hast giv'n it me, 'tis here.
> Nay, I will reade thy book, and never move
> 　Till I have found therein thy love,
> Thy art of love, which I'le turn back on thee:
> 　O my deare Saviour, Victorie!

and then the poet falters and the culminating point of the poem suggests a lowering of the voice almost to a whisper:

> Then for thy passion—I will do for that—
> 　Alas, my God, I know not what.

Such a dying away in the last line is Herbert's way of suggesting to his reader that the resources of language have been overpast, what remains to be said can only be stated with the utmost simplicity, as in the last line of **"Dialogue"** when he has enumerated and attempted to compete with all the sufferings of the Saviour:

> Ah no more: Thou break'st my heart,

or the last line of **"Miserie"** in which he has described the folly and wickedness of man and ends with

> My God, I mean myself.

The first two words of the line are not an exclamation but a vocative; it is in an entirely different key from the last line of Hopkins' "**Carrion Comfort**":

> That night, that year
> Of now done darkness I wretch lay wrestling
> with (my God!)
> my God.

If Hopkins had written the last line of Herbert's "**Miserie**" (if the fantasy may be allowed) it would have been an exclamation of agonized discovery:

> (My God!)—I mean myself,

instead of as at present a quiet, humiliated recognition of the fact. In poem no. 45 (in Robert Bridges' edition) Hopkins considers the subject of Herbert's poem "**Miserie**," the abject nature of mankind and therefore of himself: he closes his poem when the horror is at its height:

> I am gall, I am heartburn. God's most deep
> decree
> Bitter would have me taste: my taste was me;
> Bones built in me, flesh filled, blood brimmed
> the curse,
> Selfyeast of spirit a dull dough sours. I see
> The lost are like this, and their scourge to be
> As I am mine, their swetting selves; but worse.

Hopkins' sonnets are a crescendo of emotion, the strongest expression is reserved for the last line. Herbert, on the contrary, comes to rest on a note of quiet acceptance, some sentence that would be mere matter of fact, were it not for what has preceded. Yet the influence of Donne is conceivably present in either case; so differently can poets of different temperament make use of a common tradition. The best known and perhaps the most perfect of Herbert's poems, "**Love (III),**" will illustrate the measure of that difference.

> Love bade me welcome: yet my soul drew back,
> Guiltie of dust and sinne.
> But quick-ey'd Love, observing me grow slack
> From my first entrance in,
> Drew nearer to me, sweetly questioning,
> If I lack'd any thing.
>
> A guest, I answer'd, worthy to be here:
> Love said, You shall be he.
> I the unkinde, ungratefull? Ah my deare,
> I cannot look on thee.
> Love took my hand, and smiling did reply,
> Who made the eyes but I?
>
> Truth Lord, but I have marr'd them: let my
> shame
> Go where it doth deserve.
> And know you not, sayes Love, who bore the
> blame?
> My deare, then I will serve.
> You must sit down, sayes Love, and taste my
> meat:
> So I did sit and eat.

No poem better represents the way in which Herbert assimilated and modified Donne's style. As so often with Donne, the plot of the poem is an argument, in this case a simple discussion between two protagonists. The relation between the soul and God is symbolized by a commonplace human situation, a travel-worn and shamefaced guest receiving hospitality. But Herbert, unlike Donne, develops his single situation at leisure and governs his reader's emotion almost entirely by his management of the tension. Starting at a low pitch he reaches the emotional climax in the middle of the poem:

> I the unkinde, ungratefull? Ah my deare,
> I cannot look on thee.

and can then afford to relax gradually, completing his picture, but without emphasis; when the end is reached the emotion has become so poignant that the simple monosyllables in their prose order,

> So I did sit and eat.

convey more than the most impassioned rhetoric. All the feeling, that Herbert has so gradually and unostentatiously accumulated, rests upon the phrase. A graph might be made of the emotional plan of the poem in the shape of a pyramid; the two statements, 'Love bade me welcome; yet my soul drew back', and 'so I did sit and eat.' are the bases upon which it rests; at the apex is the cry of self-disgust.

When he settled in the parsonage at Bemerton, Herbert did not cease to be the exquisite courtier whom Walton so vividly describes. The same qualities of mind and temper found their outlet in poetry. In its sensitive modulations of tone we discern the master of social behaviour of whom Walton wrote that: 'if during his lifetime he expressed any error, it was, that he kept himself at too great a distance with all his inferiors; and his clothes seemed to prove that he put too great a value on his parts and parentage'; and again, 'the love of a court conversation, mixed with a laudable ambition to be something more than he was, drew him often to attend the king wheresoever the court was . . . he enjoyed his genteel humour for clothes, and court-like company, and seldom looked towards Cambridge unless the king were there, but then he never failed'. The element of vanity in such a temperament, or of social snobbery he overcame (witness the anecdotes at the end of Walton's life as well as the evidence of the poetry itself); but the picture sorts well with some of the most characteristic qualities of the poems. His perfect tact and delicate rendering of the changes of feeling or attitude, and above all his easy command of the right tone, without bluster, without self-consciousness: all this may well owe something to his breeding and his early intercourse. (pp. 49-70)

Joan Bennett, "George Herbert, 1593-1633," in her Four Metaphysical Poets: Donne, Herbert, Vaughan, Crashaw, *second edition, 1953. Reprint by Cambridge at the University Press, 1957, pp. 49-70.*

A. Alvarez (essay date 1961)

[*Alvarez is an English poet, novelist, and critic. "Apparent in his fiction as well as in his criticism and his poetry," Sibyl L. Severance has written, "is Alvarez's belief that the artist must face 'the full range of experience' with his full intelligence." In the following excerpt, Alvarez explores the influence of Donne on Herbert, maintaining that while Donne was the first poet to express forcefully the tension of religious conflict, Herbert created a "common language for religious verse" which directly influenced such poets as Vaughan, Traherne, and Crashaw.*]

Donne's influence has been so firmly associated with a certain intellectual bravura that the wider effects of his realism have scarcely been noticed. The only poet to use Donne's discoveries for wholly original ends was George Herbert; and his ends were so far from the conventional witty detachment that his reputation has suffered.

He has never really escaped the nineteenth-century rôle of the simple, quaint and 'pious rector of Bemerton', for whom even Grierson [in the Introduction to his *Metaphysical Lyrics and Poems of The Seventeenth Century*, 1921] could only say: "if not greatly imaginative, Herbert is a sincere and sensitive poet, and an accomplished artist elaborating his argumentative strain or little allegories and conceits with felicitous completeness, and managing his variously patterned stanzas . . . with a finished and delicate harmony. *The Temple* breathes the spirit of the Anglican Church at its best, primitive and modest; and also of one troubled and delicate soul seeking and finding peace." This is the best that could be said for him. It is not much. Even when the Metaphysicals once more became the fashion, Herbert received relatively little of the attention. Granted L. C. Knights and William Empson have written better on Herbert than on any other poet; but there is little else of importance. If Herbert has had any status in the revival of the School of Donne, that is more because he was Metaphysical than because he was an original artist in his own right. Now that the Metaphysicals are once more falling out of fashion there is a new movement to get Herbert's poetry back wholly into the Church; the latest studies of his poetry have emphasized their pattern of meditation, their ecclesiastical symbolism and emblems, their relation to the liturgy—in short, their piety, in a new and more technical form than before. In this, he is now said to have been influenced as much by Robert Southwell and Sir Philip Sidney as by Donne. Herbert has never really been acquitted of Grierson's regretful charge: "the effect is a little stuffy".

He has, in fact, been consistently unlucky, even in his own time. Although he was twenty years younger than Donne, he died within two years of him and their poems were both first published posthumously in the same year. Inevitably, Herbert's were overshadowed. His poetic reputation, even then, depended more on his piety than his originality.

He owes, of course, a good deal to Donne, but his debt is nowhere as specific as that of the other Metaphysicals. Like all of them, he borrows from time to time, but that is not important. What matters more is that he rises occasionally to Donne's peculiar intensity, which is a question less of phraseology than of movement. When, for example, Herbert writes:

> I have consider'd it, and finde
> There is no dealing with thy mighty passion:
> For though I die for thee, I am behinde;

> My sinnes deserve the condemnation.
> ('The Reprisall')

What he is saying is his own, but that particularly powerful manner of saying would not have been possible without the example of Donne's *Holy Sonnets*:

> Oh, to vex me, contraryes meet in one . . .

Before Donne there had been in English powerful liturgical poetry; the greatest theological poetry, Milton's, was still to come; but devotional poetry that was not concerned with the 'public' occasions of religion had never risen above relatively formal rhetorical conventions. Donne was the first to write with a rhythmic tightness and force which could express the peculiarly tense, energetic and slightly intellectual despair of religious conflict. The same realism which made his love poems different from any that had gone before created, when used for other ends, a new mode: a poetry of religious experience.

It was Herbert, however, who from this initial impulse of Donne's produced a common language for religious verse. The line runs directly from him rather than from Donne. Vaughan owes Herbert an enormous debt; so, though less obviously, does Traherne; Crashaw called his volume *Steps to the Temple*, in deference to Herbert's *The Temple*; other minor seventeenth—century poets invoked him or his book in the same way. And the great religious poet of the nineteenth century, Hopkins, acknowledged Herbert as one of his masters. The difference in surfaces—Hopkins's elaborate complexity and Herbert's equally elaborate simplicity—is endless; but they are both alike in their underlying determination to plot the stresses of religious conflicts as they are rather than as they should be. And occasionally, when Hopkins's overbearing isolation was his theme rather than a force acting obliquely on his poetic technique, they sound alike:

> Thou art indeed just, Lord, if I contend
> With thee; but, sir, so what I plead is just.

The tone and movement are very close to "I.have consider'd it, and finde" . . .

Herbert's influence, however, is something more plottable than 'tone and movement'. The critics agree that his strength lies in what Coleridge called his "pure, manly, and unaffected diction". His editor, Dr Hutchinson, added that he learned this easy, conversational language from Donne. But Herbert does not write simply because he restricts himself to simple subjects and simple statements about them; because, as the legend goes, the essence of his poetry is an unquestioning piety which is occasionally put off centre by his taste for the quaint. On the contrary, his simplicity is the outcome of a great deal of concentration. Instead of cutting down the stuff of his poetry to suit his style, Herbert writes with a clarity that includes the discordant elements and transcends them. His simplicity is not the measure by which he fell short of Donne, but of the distance he went beyond him. It is also the measure of Herbert's influence on the devotional poets who followed him. For Donne's realism was controlled by a sensibility that was so instinctively dialectical and learned that it was too easily taken to be something rather specialized. Metaphysical poetry, in fact, declined because Donne's style was used merely as a formula for self-conscious wit-writing. Herbert, on the other hand, disciplined abilities almost as great as Donne's to less striking ends. The result was he created an idiom which could be used by poets who, in terms of dialectic and learning, may have been less gifted but were not a jot less concerned with the sharpness and force of their religious conflicts.

There are four ways of showing that Herbert's simplicity was a quality complex in itself and attained with great difficulty. First, he wrote about it more or less explicitly; second, he controlled it by deflecting his wit into skills which would enhance rather than ruffle the clear surface of his work; third, he set his specialized learning against a larger background of belief; finally, he based this simplicity on a whole style of behaviour; on manners, that is, rather than on a literary manner.

In his important essay [in *Explorations,* 1946] Professor Knights called Herbert's two **'Jordan'** poems his "literary manifesto". They are his farewell to poetical fashions: to allegory, pastoral, verbal obliquity and complication. But with a difference; his method itself is oblique:

> Who sayes that fictions onely and false hair
> Become a verse? Is there in truth no beautie?
> Is all good structure in a winding stair?
> May no lines passe, except they do their dutie
>   Not to a true, but painted chair? . . .
>
> Shepherds are honest people; let them sing:
> Riddle who list, for me, and pull for Prime:
> I envie no mans nightingale or spring;
> Nor let them punish me with losse of rime,
>   Who plainly say, *My God, My King.*

The poem has puzzled the critics, more or less mildly, ever since Herbert's first detailed commentator, George Ryley, wrote about it in 1714, in his long, dull, unpublished, but determinedly analytical book: *Mr Herbert's Temple/& Church Militant/Explained & Improved/By/A Discourse upon Each Poem/Critical/&/Practical:*

> There is some Difficulty in Reconciling the Titles with ye subject matt^e of ye Poems. Each Poem is an Invective ag^st Dark Poetry; w^ch, by figures, etc, rend^e ye Sence of ye Poem, & ye Drift of ye Author obscure; & to Common Ears Unintelligible. I am ready to say the Author has, in these, Lash'd himself; by prefixing a title y^t either is, or, att Least, is to me very obscure. . . . .Here are 9 or 10 exp^esions y^t may want opening enough to make so short a poem fall und^e ye charge, it draw up ag^st others . . .

The charge is, simply, that Herbert's defence of plainness is also one of the most obscure poems he wrote. There is, of course, an excuse: perhaps Herbert was attacking the vice by parodying it. Yet the elaborations are built up so easily, so convincingly, that Herbert seems less to be criticizing witty elaboration than using the occasion to indulge in it. He has, in short, a natural sophistication and a natural penchant for complexity which he was at pains to discipline into simplicity. I repeat *into*, for he did not get rid of these qualities; he used them in another way.

How and why he did so are the subject of **'The Forerun-**ners', a poem, in its way, almost as finely dramatic as anything of Donne's:

> The harbingers are come. See, see their mark;
> White is their colour, and behold my head.
> But must they have my brain? must they dispark
> Those sparkling notions, which therein were
>   bred?
>   Must dulnesse turn me to a clod?
> Yet they have left me, *Thou art still my God.*
>
> Good men ye be, to leave me my best room,
> E'en all my heart, and what is lodged there:
> I pass not, I, what of the rest become,
> So, *Thou art still my God*, be out of fear.
>   He will be pleased with that ditty;
> And if I please him, I write fine and witty.
>
> Farewell sweet phrases, lovely metaphors.
> But will ye leave me thus? when ye before
> Of stews and brothels onely knew the doores,
> Then did I wash you with my tears, and more,
>   Brought you to Church well drest and clad:
> My God must have my best, ev'n all I had.
>
> Lovely enchanting language, sugarcane,
> Honey of roses, whither wilt thou fly?
> Hath some fond lover 'ticed thee to thy bane?
> And wilt thou leave the Church, and love a sty?
>   Fy, thou wilt soil thy broider'd coat,
> And hurt thyself, and him that sings the
>   note. . . .
>
> Yet, if you go, I passe not; take your way:
> For, *Thou art still my God*, is all that ye
> Perhaps with more embellishment can say.
> Go birds of spring: let winter have his fee;
>   Let a bleake palenesse chalke the doore,
> So all within be livelier than before.

The difference between this and the **'Jordan'** poems is a matter of its point in time. In **'Jordan'** Herbert wrote of the simple style as though it were a willed deprivation, a kind of penance for inventiveness. The choice was either religion *or* wit, devotion *or* invention; either he said "My God, My King" *or* he riddled in sweet phrases. This clash of styles echoed the clash between his secular ambition and his piety. If there is at times something rather self-conscious or over-deliberate in Herbert's earlier simplicity, that is perhaps because the habits of his career died hard.

He was, of course, far from being a simple country parson, however saintlike his later years may have been. He came from a talented and distinguished family. He became Public Orator of Cambridge when he was twenty-six and because of 'his great abilities' was, his biographer Walton says, "very high in the King's favour, and not meanly valued and loved by the most eminent and most powerful of the Court Nobility". Donne, Henry Wotton, Lancelot Andrewes and Bacon were his friends. He helped translate *The Advancement of Learning* into a 'masculine' style of Latin; in return Bacon dedicated to him his *Translation of Certaine Psalmes into English Verse* (1625).

Naturally enough with these talents he appears, from what his biographers say, to have been extremely ambitious, as Donne had been. And like Donne, he took Holy

Orders only after a period of intense personal suffering which came on him when the massive progress of his secular career faltered. It was perhaps the clash between his ambition and his piety that created the analytical tension out of which most of his best poems were written. Herbert himself suggested as much when, as he was dying, he sent the manuscript book of his poems to Nicholas Ferrar, saying that "he shall find there in it a picture of the many spiritual Conflicts that have past betwixt God and my Soul, before I could subject mine to the will of Jesus my Master, in whose service I have now found perfect freedom". But the repose of a fulfilled and reconciled simplicity seems to have come relatively late. He had not, I think, achieved it when he wrote the two **'Jordan'** poems. On the contrary, their disproportionately stylish complexity makes sense only as Herbert's way of showing that he was as much a master of the riddling, embellished manner he had renounced as any elegant and successful courtier. But by the time he wrote **'The Forerunners'** he had made his peace with form and content:

> Let a bleak palenesse chalk the doore,
> So all within be livelier than before.

The new simplicity of his style was the outer form of a new richness of life. It is very much to the point that **'The Forerunners'** is both about writing poetry and growing old. His simplicity is a spiritual quality, the measure of his maturity as a poet.

There is a difference, however, between simplicity and deprivation. Herbert's work may be lucid, controlled, precise, but it is far from being stripped down to its bare essentials. The wit remains, though in a rather transmuted form. His poetry has none of Donne's occasionally ostentatious dialectical brilliance nor of the courtier-poet's elegant super-sophistication. Herbert's wit and ingenuity went, instead, into his verse-forms. He invented an enormous number of them and rarely bothered to repeat a discovery. Perhaps he was helped to this fecundity by his well-known skill in music. But there is a kind of ingenious stylishness in his metres that seems to me to depend as much on sharpness of mind as of ear:

> Come dearest Lord, passe not this holy season,
> My flesh and bones and joynts do pray:
> And e'vn my verse, when by the ryme and reason
> The word is, *Stay,* sayes ever, *Come.*

That is from a poem called **'Home'**. So by transposing the rhyme word Herbert not merely puts a sudden stress on his plea, he also makes the plea itself bring back the subject of the poem: 'Come' rhymes with 'Home'. The metrical forms, in short, bear the weight of a good deal of the wit which would not otherwise have been proper to his subject.

As with his wit, so with his learning. Herbert's career and his reputation among his contemporaries show that in plain ability he was probably not so very much behind Donne, although the uses he put his talents to were rather less spectacular. In that beautiful poem **'The Pearl'**, he drew up his personal credit, fully and without false modesty, in order to dignify his love of God by his renunciation of mere worldly abilities. The list begins:

> I know the wayes of Learning; both the head
> And pipes that feed the presse, and make it runne;
> What reason hath from nature borrowed,
> Or of it self, like a good huswife, spunne
> In laws and policie; what the starres conspire,
> What willing nature speaks, what forc'd by fire;
> Both th'old discoveries, and the new-found seas,
> The stock and surplus, cause and historie:
> All these stand open, or I have the keyes:
>   Yet I love thee.

The list is presumably as inclusive as Donne's would have been; yet though Herbert deploys his learning skilfully throughout his work, it nowhere assumes the central importance of Donne's. For example, in *Les doctrines médiévales chez Donne* Miss M. P. Ramsay decided that Donne was a mediaeval thinker; her evidence was his modes of thinking and his use of the scholastic philosophers. One could prove nothing of the kind of Herbert, despite a command of argument no less accurate and something of the same ease in making his way among the authorities. For to call a Jacobean poet 'mediaeval' is to impute to him a kind of specialization—which was precisely what happened to Donne. But Herbert's poetry is not specialized in this way, although he may have been a product of no less specialized a training. The reason is that the general and dominant framework of his work is not his University learning but, quite simply, the Bible. And the Bible, like the Church liturgy which he also used, was easily and readily available to any devout reader. Even Mr George Ryley managed to make adequate, if uninspired sense of the poems merely by pointing out the Biblical references.

This framework helped Herbert to his simplicity in a number of ways. First, it took away all strain from the references; to understand Herbert was not necessarily a token of the reader's wit. Second, it gave his conceits, although they may owe something to the emblem writers, a homelier directness than Donne's; their force is like that of the parables or, as Professor Knights suggested, of popular pulpit oratory. (It may be that this kind of directness was something of a mixed blessing for Herbert. His failures are nearly all of the homely and hortatory kind. When the cast of a poem is purely that of the teacher, benign and clearcut, a certain didactic monotony intrudes. The work becomes tiresome whenever the poet seems insistently to be writing at less than full pitch.) The third benefit Herbert's poetry gained from the Bible was its air of finality. At his best—in, say, the first **'Affliction'**—Herbert's self-examination and psychological analysis was no less than Donne's, but it was presented within the context of an answer. Donne was continually arguing out his position with God in such a way as to make one believe that there was a good deal to be said on both sides. Herbert, on the other hand, presented his emotional conflicts from the vantage point of their outcome; that is, with a certain finality. It is this that makes the turn-abouts at the end of **'Affliction I'** and **'The Pulley'** inevitable, given the poet's kind of mature and critical humility. But to this, of course, the Bible is only ancillary; the controlling power is Herbert's depth of understanding of his own experience.

These, then, are the technical or semi-technical inducements to simplicity; but its essence lies elsewhere: in Herbert's power of implication. In this his learning and intellectual complexities were less important than what Professor Knights, in a peculiarly suggestive paragraph, called 'the well-bred ease of manner of "the gentleman' ". Herbert mentioned it himself in 'The Pearl':

> I know the wayes of Honour, what maintains
> The quick returns of courtesie and wit . . .

The fullness of Herbert's poetry depends finally, I think, on his constant assumption of manners as a way of expressing not forms and formalities but an implicit fullness of life, a quickness of response and sensitivity. He can leave so much unsaid because his tone implies it all for him:

> Love bade me welcome: yet my soul drew back,
>   Guiltie of dust and sinne.
> But quick-ey'd Love, observing me grow slack
>   From my first entrance in,
> Drew nearer to me, sweetly questioning,
>   If I lack'd any thing.
>
> A guest, I answer'd, worthy to be here:
>   Love said, You shall be he:
> I the unkinde, ungratefull? Ah my deare,
>   I cannot look on thee.
> Love took my hand, and smiling did reply,
>   Who made the eyes but I?
>
> Truth Lord, but I have marr'd them: let my shame
>   Go where it doth deserve.
> And know you not, sayes Love, who bore the blame?
>   My deare, then I will serve.
> You must sit down, sayes Love, and taste my meat:
>   So I did sit and eat.

This is the last poem in *The Temple* and it treats the book's most important subject: the final acceptance of the love of God. But it does so in terms of, in the best sense, manners. The relationship of the poet to his God is that of a guest to his host. On this metaphor the whole poem is based. Love, without being made to seem any less divine or personal, is given social graces and made to use polite formulae: "Love bade me welcome . . ."; "quick-ey'd Love . . . Drew nearer to me, sweetly questioning,/If I lack'd any thing"; "Love took my hand, and smiling did reply . . . (with, incidentally, an elegant-serious pun); "You must sit down, sayes Love, and taste my meat". The poet, too, reacts as a guest, according to the code: he is not clean enough to sit at table, being "Guiltie of *dust* and sinne"; he refuses because he senses a certain rude inadequacy in himself, but accepts directly his refusal itself begins to seem impolite. The balance is delicate and I describe it badly. The essence of the poem is a kind of understood tenderness. The social metaphor in no way makes the poem stiff, unreal or debilitatingly formal; it is, instead, a means of implying a great deal without ever overstating. Certainly, it does not stop the poet speaking out:

> "I the unkinde, ungratefull? Ah my deare,
>   I cannot look on thee."

The intensity of this depends on the control that both precedes and follows it. It has, I think, the same force as that scene at the end of James's *The Awkward Age* when Nanda, after a whole volume of understatement, breaks down for a moment and weeps, so that one realizes suddenly the depth of feeling the polite formulas have, all the time, been covering. Herbert's simplicity, then, is deep and complex because it is born not of bareness but of tact. He knows how to judge to the last degree the feeling implicit in simple, even conventional, phrases.

The difference between this and earlier religious poetry is obvious when one compares Herbert's 'Love (III)' with the passage from Robert Southwell's *S. Peters Complaint* on which it may be based:

> At sorrowes dore I knockt, they crau'd my
>   name;
> I aunswered one, vnworthy to be knowne;
> What one, say they? one worthiest of blame.
> But who? a wretch, not Gods, nor yet his
>   owne.
> A man? O no, a beast; much worse: what
>   creature?
> A rocke: how cald? the rocke of scandale,
>   Peter.

Compared with the beautifully balanced give and take of Herbert's poem Southwell's is crude and his self-degradation rhetorical. The more it grows, the more inhuman and unreal it becomes:

> A man? O no, a beast; much worse: what crea-
>   ture?
> A rocke. . . .

With the instrument of rhetoric, the stronger the religious emotion, the farther it retires from the world of common feelings into the world of allegory, formal and apart. Herbert, on the other hand, even at his worst retires no farther than parable, the simple, more or less vivid tale with an immediate application to the life around him.

I suggested that the power Donne exerted was towards realism and away from the formally poetical. But Donne's realism was of the professional classes, the lawyers, diplomats and the rest, who were intellectual, learned, active and sharp. Herbert translated this to fit his milder, more reposedly devotional sensibility and the easier, more courtly-polite background in which he lived out much of his life. The result was a realism on slightly different terms: a realism based on manners rather than dialectic.

But just as Donne's realism transcended mere logic and intellectualism, so Herbert's went beyond its allegiances to a code of manners, to the Bible, to parables and pulpit oratory. Both of them wrote, in an age of theology, a poetry of direct religious experience:

> And now in age I bud again,
> After so many deaths I live and write;
> I once more smell the dew and ran,
> And relish versing: O my onely light,
>   It cannot be
>   That I am he
> On whom thy tempests fell all night.

This is, I suppose, the most perfect and most vivid stanza in the whole of Herbert's work. But it is, in every sense, so natural that its originality is easily missed. To speak of the love of God as a *whole* delight, of the senses as much as of the spirit, had to my knowledge never been done before. To do it there was needed a combination of realism and personal tact that was Herbert's special gift. His contribution to religious poetry is large and his own. But the ground in which it could flower had been cleared by Donne. (pp. 67-83)

A. Alvarez, "The Poetry of Religious Experience," in his The School of Donne, *Chatto and Windus, 1961, pp. 67-90.*

Arnold Stein (essay date 1968)

[*In the following essay, originally published in 1968, Stein argues that as a religious poet addressing God directly, Herbert mastered the rhetoric of sincerity and developed an art of plainness.*]

As a religious poet Herbert addresses God directly or writes with the intention of being overheard by Him. For traditional and for contemporary reasons, both religious and secular in origin, he aspires to an art of plainness that can achieve absolute sincerity. He is impatient with art but must practice patience. He distrusts rhetoric—as who does not?—but in order to speak sincerely he must master the rhetoric of sincerity.

Some of his more severe claims, assertions, and rejections lend themselves, a little too easily, to the purposes of critical definition. But we do not need to take him at his word in poems like the two sonnets which, according to Walton, were addressed to his mother, or in the pair of sonnets entitled **"Love" (I and II)**. In these poems the contest between human and divine love is presented as if it were a moral scandal, to be treated only in terms of extreme contrasts and a single range of emotion. Everything is externalized, as if a safe imaginative distance were the only proper course. If plainness has anything to do with forthrightness and with the manner attributed to plain dealers, then we must acknowledge a kind of plainness in these poems, though they lack something in art. The case against their sincerity would have to point out that the attitude assumed by the author, and eloquently expressed, does not cost him very much. The desire to believe lends energy, vividness, sharpness, but not precision, depth, or fineness to the expression. When we speak of the rhetoric of sincerity, it is not with such poems in mind.

Let us turn to a poem which does not offer a stiff rejection but raises questions, and in a very mild and casual manner seems to present a radical solution. The poem is **"A true Hymne,"** which begins:

> My joy, my life, my crown!
> My heart was meaning all the day,
> Somewhat it fain would say:
> And still it runneth mutt'ring up and down
> With onely this, *My joy, my life, my crown.*

Herbert then goes on to defend these words, which "may

take part/Among the best in art" if they are "truly said." We may suspect that the navety is in part cultivated; it is plainly meant, however, and comes from a refinement of knowledge rather than a lack of knowledge. These words are symbols; they represent precious wisdom, the soul of living truth which the speaker may pronounce without possessing. It is hard to say them "truly"; the heart was "meaning" them all the day, but even the heart is uncertain—"Somewhat it fain would say," and it runs "mutt'ring up and down." The value of these words, whether in private thought or in art, depends on understanding what they mean and saying them truly.

Herbert ends the second stanza with a firm declaration:

> The finenesse which a hymne or psalme affords,
> Is, when the soul unto the lines accords.

This, though it has an admirable ring and expresses one clear concept of poetic sincerity, does not quite face the problems that have been raised. The accordance of the soul may assume that the heart has understood and that the words have been "truly said," but we are not told how these vital steps are taken, or even that they have been taken. Instead, we have been given a partial definition, which is then extended by a charming example of negative illustration—a whole stanza that shows how not to do it:

> He who craves all the minde,
> And all the soul, and strength, and time,
> If the words onely ryme,
> Justly complains, that somewhat is behinde
> To make his verse, or write a hymne in kinde.

The amused incoherence of the stanza parodies the ambitious poet who starts with high resolution and finds himself hung up, forcing rhyme, splicing syntax, and barely staggering through. After the brave opening, the only words that ring true are "Justly complains." Furthermore, the grounds have been shifted, and we have not followed up the problem of how the words are to be "truly said" or how that accordance of the soul is to be achieved.

The last stanza presents a solution that is indirectly relevant to the problems of literary expression but directly relevant to the heart seeking to address God:

> Whereas if th' heart be moved,
> Although the verse be somewhat scant,
> God doth supplie the want.
> As when th' heart sayes (sighing to be approved)
> *O, could I love!* and stops: God writeth, *Loved.*

We come to see that the writing of poetry has not been at the center of the poem after all. Instead, Herbert has used art as a metaphor to express an experience of religious life. In life, if not in art, the "somewhat scant" expression of the sincere heart may be amended and completed by God. When God writes "Loved," the desire to articulate and the desire to love are at once fulfilled. Their ends are achieved without the ordinary steps of a humanly conducted process. By authoritative acknowledgment virtual expression becomes actual.

If we look at the poem from one point of view, a miracle has taken place: but from another point of view we need recognize only an inspired compression—always possible in dialogue if the correspondent understands the intention, approves it, and fully reciprocates. We may observe, therefore, that Herbert is not simply invoking a miracle, for the ends of expression may often be realized without the full use of normal means. What we cannot do, however, is take the metaphorical analogy of writing poetry as if it were literal. Sincere feelings do not of themselves produce good poems. Herbert surely knew this as well as we do. But he must also have believed that whenever he felt a poem of his to be successful, God's hand had guided his in the composition; and if he felt a poem to be successful that feeling was the sure sense that the expression had realized its end, that God had blessed the end and given him the feeling by reflection. The humility of the man of God and the humility of the artist might both acknowledge that a fumbling, "muttering" intention had by some unexpected swiftness been clarified, and that the awkward wrongness of initial and intermediate stages had somehow been transformed into the triumphantly graceful and right. In retrospect, even the labor of composition—like some fictional by-product of the creative process—might seem to be compressed into a decisive instant of time. (Poets are notoriously inaccurate in reporting on these matters and prefer to believe that their perfect poems were "dictated": which is what we prefer to believe when the evidence to the contrary does not interfere.)

There are at least two ways, then, of looking at the issues raised by this poem. I have been emphasizing the "normal" conditions of the creative process because I am primarily interested in the poet Herbert; and because I am convinced that the religious lyric, though it must fulfill special conditions, must also, and does, answer all the questions we ask of other lyrics. From a literary standpoint the central metaphor of the poem can be interpreted as analogous to the ways in which inspiration figures in the writing of poems. Inspiration is of course the kind of concept that easily crosses a line between the secular and the sacred, and for Herbert so too does the act, or the metaphor, of writing poems. In this poem we are free to interpret the analogy, so long as we recognize that it is a metaphor and is not to be taken literally. But we must also recognize that, for Herbert, though the metaphor may apply to the writing of poetry it has been superseded, as it were, by the higher form of expression to which it refers. The wisdom descending from God crowns, not with understanding but with love, an apparently clumsy human effort to understand and express. We do not expect Herbert to be dissatisfied with the attainment of such an end simply because the means do not seem to justify it. But we do not therefore think Herbert believed that this was the way to write poems, and that the individual details of thought and expression might safely be ignored because they would leap intervening stages if only "th' heart be moved." Herbert knew better, both as poet and as man of God. That he hoped, humbly, for the easier path of inspiration—one does not need to be either poetic or religious to feel the attraction of that course.

But Herbert's metaphors are capable of moving in more than two directions. The central fiction of writing poetry, which may refer to the real writing of poetry and to something real in the experience of religious life, may have still

a third reference. In presenting the fictional account Herbert is at the same time confessing his own unworthiness, his own desire, and intimating the authentic joy which he would feel if what he is describing should happen to him. In other words, the narrative is also a concealed prayer, composed by one of the modern masters of that difficult decorum and rhetoric by means of which one may properly address God and suggest to Him certain courses for human affairs.

And so the cultivated clumsiness of the poem, the shifting of grounds, the apparent navety, and what may have seemed to be a radical solution to the problems of writing poetry, when taken together are something else, or several things else. But if we are at all right about the poem it cannot be taken as a simple assertion about poetry; what seems to be assertion is ultimately part of a complex and tactful statement. Yet we cannot stop here, at the satisfying literary position. We must remember that, for Herbert, the metaphor of writing is in the poem superseded by the fulfillment of the end of expression—here a confirming act which writes and rhymes as poetry but means as metaphor. If he himself believes in the fiction of his poem, then he will find its conclusion a happier one than most of his poems provide, and toward the slower, labored uncertainties of most composition he will feel some understandable impatience.

At this point, if there were time, I should want to comment on the kind of plain style we find in "**The Church-Porch**," and to look at some poems in which Herbert accepts, or even flaunts, a division between truth and beauty. But these poems do not finally say anything distinctive or resonant. The gestures of sincerity by which art is used to expose art can at best make but limited points. A better and more characteristic performance is "**The Forerunners**." Whatever else he is saying in the poem, Herbert is also bidding a fictional farewell to poetry, to the "sweet phrases, lovely metaphors," which he has rescued from the poetic "brothels" in order to bring into the church, repentant and renewed: "My God must have my best, ev'n all I had." The excitement and affection of his address could serve as well for arrival as for departure: "Lovely enchanting language, sugar-cane,/Honey of roses," he exclaims, as preface to imagining the unfortunate relapse of poetry returns to its old ways. He argues against what he knows will happen, and in doing so marks both a separateness of truth and beauty and the bridge of normal relations that leads to their unity:

> Let follie speak in her own native tongue.
> True beautie dwells on high: ours is a flame
>   But borrow'd thence to light us thither.
> Beautie and beauteous words should go
>   together.

Here Platonic solution is emphasized, rather than Platonic division. The statement is handsome and, as well as we can judge from the context and from other poems, heartfelt—a major poetic belief, but not therefore the guiding inspiration of every lyrical utterance.

"Yet if you go," he adds, meaning, when you go, as the poet prepares to settle down for a final accounting:

> Yet if you go, I passe not; take your way:
> For, *Thou art still my God*, is all that ye
> Perhaps with more embellishment can say.

And so a significant division appears, if not between truth and beauty, at least between "true beauty" and what can be said in words. That words are treated as no more than a conventionally detachable garment of style may seem a little disappointing, but Herbert does at least say "perhaps." Besides, in the context of the poem "Thou art still my God" *is* an ultimate expression, one that can be and is developed in other poems but cannot be here. Its meaning cannot be improved upon, and the man preparing to give up everything will not need anything else. The expression is complete, syntactically and otherwise, as the plain saying of "My God, my King" and "My joy, my life, my crown" are not. Nor does the poet's own attitude toward poetic language remotely resemble the stiff certitude with which he elsewhere rejects the misguided efforts of misguided poets. He is not rejecting here but parting, and with fine reluctance and such sweet sorrow.

In "**The Forerunners**" the act of writing poetry stands for the means, made visible and audible, of communing with God; it is a human invention motivated by a borrowed flame "to light us thither," a means of returning to the source of beauty. The house of the church, the house of poetry, and the house of life, the "best room" of which is the heart, are in the poem all reduced to an essential state. As the visible church stands truly, beautifully, but imperfectly for the invisible church, so do the "sweet phrases, lovely metaphors" express imperfectly the "True beautie" on high. In its plainness the essential expression, "Thou art still my God," will fulfill the end of expression, "And if I please him, I write fine and wittie." The essentiality of the expression, when one contemplates its meaning, by itself and in the context of the poem, would seem to be better established than the poet's assurance of writing "fine and wittie." That claim one may perhaps regard as a little assertive, markedly different from the persuasive tact with which art demonstrates the limitations of art in the argument of the poem.

The distinction is a fine one but it needs to be made. I mentioned earlier that if Herbert felt a poem to be successful he would need to believe that the expression had realized its end of pleasing God, and that God had given him his feeling by reflection. But he does not practice the art of silence or the art of discovering only the essential expression, which he can then merely "mutter." He writes poems, even when their aim is to express, or transcend, the inadequacy of poetic expression. We may perhaps regard "Thou art still my God" as a symbolic plainness, an ideal to which his poetic art of plainness may aspire, but it is not itself an expression of that art.

I think we can put matters in the right perspective by drawing a distinction between the symbolic plainness of an ultimate expression and the plainness of a complete poetic action. The latter may (and in Herbert often does) move toward a clarification that resembles the symbolic plainness. But if the poetic action is complete its conclusion will be the result of a process of expression. Though the "true beauty" of "Thou art still my God" may be traced to the compressed inner meaning the expression holds for Herbert, nevertheless that statement does appear three times in the poem, and it works both with and against other statements. In "**The Flower**" Herbert makes another absolute statement: "Thy word is all, if we could spell." Some of his poems are advanced spelling lessons. If "**The Forerunners**" were, say, a poem like "**Aaron**," its process might have included some parsing of the implicit relations between "thou" and "my," or between "art" and "still."

Herbert is acutely aware, as poet and as Christian, of deception, evasiveness, and inadequacy within himself— and, for these, traditional attitudes toward language and art provide useful and established symbols. Besides, many of his more assertive poems take up positions that he does not intend to carry through uncritically. A paradox that furnishes much of his poetic material may help explain why the single attitude is often countered within its own poem and opposed by other poems. The "grosser world," toward the beauty and importance of which the poet feels conflicting emotions, is, in spite of his feelings, a fixed and orderly world regulated by the "word and art" of God. It is the "diviner world of grace" which suddenly alters, and of which God is every day "a new Creatour."

What Herbert writes in "**Superliminare**" may be applied to all instances when he engages himself to "Copie out onely" this or that. He will admit

> Nothing but holy, pure, and cleare,
> Or that which groneth to be so.

That is a program which leaves room for and grants validity to the hopes of individual effort, without regard to cost and efficiency. Herbert's most important subject is the mystery of God's art with man, a subject he confronts with patience and imagination, both passionately involved and scrupulously detached. That God's art with man reveals God's nature he takes for granted, and he assumes that the mysteries which God has concealed in man encourage the study of things human as an authorized reflection of things divine.

We may put these observations together by saying that Herbert does not give us a single, consistent attitude toward expression, that his art of plainness does not bear a single stamp, and that his arguments with God are conducted with great freedom and inventiveness. Whenever as critics we take a single example as our model to copy, we become aware of statements on the other side and of stylistic demonstrations that force us to widen our definitions. From one point of view we may be satisfied to locate the essential Herbert in the ringing declarations of "**H. Baptisme (II)**": "Let me be soft and supple to thy will. . . . My soul bid nothing. . . . Childhood is health." But softness must be "tempered" and suppleness must exert itself in order to be what it is. We do not know enough when we know that the goal expressed so simply is a difficult one to achieve, and that the verbal summation stands for detailed, strenuous efforts by an individual conscious that millions of human beings have in effect said the same thing and have both failed and succeeded. Our general knowledge must also "descend to particulars," for exactness lies not in any general statement but in the clarified order which poetry may achieve when particular expressions work with and against each other. In Herbert's poetry the soul has other lessons to learn, not all of them compatible with what is here presented as the sum of wisdom. For the soul that bids nothing may hear nothing; nor is that spiritual state exempt from posing and artful presumption. Childhood is not health at all in "**Mortification**," but is only one of several stages in the art of dying. That art would seem to be more valuable than spiritual health itself; for the art of knowing possesses more fully whatever it desires and gains, and Herbert never deviates long from this old principle, which represents the uneasy, but enduring and fruitful, marriage of Athens and Jerusalem. Childhood generally symbolizes the will in his poems, but the education of the will is the patient task of intelligence, and Herbert, to his honor, seldom trusts for long any of the attractive substitutes for intelligence. Even that most famous conversion of "**The Collar**"—"Me thoughts I heard one calling, *Child*!/And I reply'd *My Lord*"—rests on the demonstration of an argument that has ruined itself.

As for his plainness, which is not all of one kind, it is above all a rhetoric of sincerity, an art by which he may tell the truth to himself and God. The major devices are not traditional figures but psychological gestures and movements. The excesses of cheerful confidence and the defections of faith decked out as humility are given their full human voice, not as exotic monsters of thought and feeling, but as common faults "whose natures are most stealing, and beginnings uncertaine," faults which are most tenacious when they are not allowed to expose themselves by speaking in their "own native tongue." Belief in the divine desire for human desire grants the human feelings an essential dignity, even in error, and encourages a vigorous freedom of expression. That freedom comes under the general laws of art, and is enlarged, not restricted, by the necessities of religious tact and discipline—as it is enlarged by realizing the complex demands of poetic form.

I propose now to offer more than a token and less than a complete demonstration of his art of plainness by drawing upon three poems: "**The Temper (I)**", "**The Pearl**," and "**Death**."

"**The Temper (I)**" begins with a declaration:

> How should I praise thee, Lord! how should
> my rymes
> Gladly engrave thy love in steel,
> If what my soul doth feel sometimes,
> My soul might ever feel!

And ends with a declaration:

> Whether I flie with angels, fall with dust,
> Thy hands made both, and I am there:
> Thy power and love, my love and trust
> Make one place ev'ry where.

The "plain intention" of the poem is to transform its initial attitude into its concluding one. Our best approach, I think, is from the lines in "**Love (II)**" where God is asked:

> And kindle in our hearts such true desires,
> As may consume our lusts, and make thee way.

Most of "**The Temper**" is devoted to the consuming of false love, but the kindling of true desire coincides with the opening lines of the poem, which speak in the high hortatory voice of love convinced that it is sincere and deserves to have its way. The "how should" and the "if" mark the fiction that represents real desire and invokes the conventions of literary and religious praise. Although the power and sweep of the language obscure the personal motive, which is not in the conventions of praise an illegitimate one, Herbert's characteristic exercise of religious propriety never allows personal desire to speak for the whole man without some discriminating process of clarification. "Gladly engrave thy love in steel" rings beautifully, but pretends to forget that the only standard is God's approval of the offering. The poet's desire is not absurd, but he knows that its expression is, and he compensates in the second stanza by acting out his pretentiousness. If there are forty heavens, or more, when things are right with him he can "peere" over them all. At other times "I hardly reach a score." And sometimes there is a general minus, without arithmetic: "to hell I fall." The kindling and consuming are most intense in the next three stanzas, which clarify the issues and stand apart from the first and last two stanzas. In these middle three stanzas the excesses of pride and humility strive against each other in images of expansion and contraction, and in the movements up and down of actual and psychological space:

> O rack me not to such a vast extent;
> Those distances belong to thee:
> The world's too little for thy tent,
> A grave too big for me.

> Wilt thou meet arms with man, that thou dost
> stretch
> A crumme of dust from heav'n to hell?
> Will great God measure with a wretch?
> Shall he thy stature spell?

> O let me, when thy roof my soul hath hid,
> O let me roost and nestle there:
> Then of a sinner thou art rid,
> And I of hope and fear.

This last stanza (the fifth) is like the first in advancing personal desire while paying tribute to God. We may note that the eloquence of humility is no less moving, no less an expression of real desire, and no less wrong, than the eloquence of pride. By now the two extremes have exhausted each other, and some *tertium quid* must be called on to make peace. The sixth stanza explains the emblematic title, declares acceptance of the divine will, and advances the metaphor of music as a solution to the problem of praise:

> Yet take thy way; for sure thy way is best:
> Stretch or contract me, thy poore debter:
> This is but tuning of my breast,
> To make the musick better.

And so the stanza completes the action of consuming false love by translating the experiences of the poem into terms of acceptance which draw a moral. The metaphor of music discovers a retroactive purpose in the contradictions, a purpose which may also govern present and future action. But Herbert does not stop here, for the kindling and consuming have served "to make thee way," and the seventh stanza is the demonstration of what can happen when way has been made for God:

> Whether I flie with angels, fall with dust,
> 　Thy hands made both, and I am there:
> Thy power and love, my love and trust
> 　Make one place ev'ry where.

One may perhaps describe the metaphor of music as a rational discovery which orders in a quiet, reasonable way the passionate contradictions which have been expressed. But the final stanza establishes, without reference to music, a concord that is more comprehensive. In the language of religion the difference resembles that between intellectual acceptance and entire resignation. Herbert himself might well have thought that the old, restrictive terms were consumed in order to make way for the new, and that he was himself, in a minor, personal way, copying the process by which truth had once come to light—in Augustine's summary statement: "the New Testament reveals what was concealed in the Old." In **"The Quip"** Herbert refuses the arguments of his opponents for he has a single answer ready penned; here the arguments come from his own soul and he must work through them to reach his answer. The simple perfection of that answer cannot be anticipated but comes suddenly, and after a slight pause.

Although the final stanza may be said to express and to demonstrate religious resignation, we may approach it from the traditions of rhetoric. First, we may draw on Aristotle's point that of the three "modes of persuasion furnished by the spoken word" the most important, by and large, is "the personal goodness revealed by the speaker";

in fact, "his character may almost be called the most effective means of persuasion he possesses." Christian rhetoric accepts the point and advances it; where the unity of eloquence and wisdom occurs we may assume the effective presence of inspiration as a proof of character. The chief goal of eloquence is to move, and Christian high style could be thought of as assimilating all the characteristics of the plain style, deriving its elevation primarily from the personal fervor with which the saving truth was expressed.

The last stanza will not fit into a rhetorical category of style. It is adorned and elevated, but the dominant effect is that of plainness and simplicity. The graces of art are subtle though not inscrutable; and we could point to devices not in the handbooks of rhetoric (as Augustine is pleased to note of a passage from the Book of Amos), and perhaps not even in the annals of microlinguistics. But we may spare that demonstration for now. The issues of the poem are resolved in a final expression that unites beauty and truth, eloquence and wisdom. There is no point of leverage for distinguishing between what is said and the authoritative gift of being able to say it: inspiration is the proof of character. An expression as complete and as final in its way as "Thou art still my God" has emerged from a developing pattern of conflict; and although that expression can stand alone, it was created in the act of completing the poem, and it answers all the immediacies of conflict and form. It can stand alone but does not insist on its privilege, as a few ready-penned expressions make some show of doing. We may perhaps apply Herbert's metaphor of wisdom descending from above, the silk twist let down; though in **"The Pearl"** inspiration must precede and direct the poem in order to be present for the final confirma-

Ruins of Herbert's birthplace at Eyton, Shropshire, as depicted in an 1816 issue of the Gentleman's Magazine.

tion. Or we may say that in "**The Temper**" when the poet stopped God wrote "loved" and spelled it out in a whole stanza.

Our next example is "**The Pearl**," a poem with a simpler argument and a basic plot—that of rejecting the ways of the world, the flesh, and the devil, each in a stanza. A final stanza explains why, clarifies the issues, confirms the character of the speaker, and in a simple statement organizes the procedures of the poem into their completed form. We find no acting out of inspiration at the end, but instead a quietly effective definition of the ways of love and understanding. In the penultimate stanza, for the sake of an ultimate plainness the poet unexpectedly elevates the plain style that has been serving him with perfect ease and variety.

The plot is basic and the formula for human temptation is the standard one, but Herbert's conception and performance are markedly fresh and individual. The temptation of the devil, as intellectual pride, he puts first. It is not a temptation at all but little more than an inventory, and not even an explicit rejection. By putting intellectual pride first but not treating it as pride, and by his casual manner and racy diction, he exhibits a surprising and witty indifference to the traditional power of that temptation. Indeed, if we do not recognize the historical issue, the first appearance of the refrain, "Yet I love thee," may seem a little forced and overemphatic. As the poem develops, and as we collect our bearings in motion, we are supposed to recognize that pride is not being located in the intellect alone but is distributed throughout all decisions involving a choice between the love of self and the love of God. In the second stanza the temptations of the world are rejected, without the dignity of a formal recognition but in the course of drawing up an inventory of the ways of honor. The casual raciness becomes intensified, and the tone advances to open mockery:

> I know the wayes of Honour, what maintains
> The quick returns of courtesie and wit:
> In vies of favours whether partie gains,
> When glorie swells the heart, and moldeth it
> To all expressions both of hand and eye,
> Which on the world a true-love-knot may tie,
> And bear the bundle, wheresoe're it goes:
> How many drammes of spirit there must be
> To sell my life unto my friends or foes:
>   Yet I love thee.

Then the third and climactic stanza presents the temptation of the flesh, the ways of pleasure. One does not expect to meet sensitively intelligent Christians who are confident that they are untempted by intellectual pride and the subtle allurements of the world; one expects even less to learn that so rare a person is frankly responsive to the appeals of pleasure:

> I know the wayes of Pleasure, the sweet strains,
> The lullings and the relishes of it;
> The propositions of hot bloud and brains;
> What mirth and musick mean; what love and wit
> Have done these twentie hundred yeares, and
>   more:
> I know the projects of unbridled store:
> My stuffe is flesh, not brasse; my senses live,

> And grumble oft, that they have more in me
> Then he that curbs them, being but one to five:
>   Yet I love thee

These are not, to be sure, the common temptations of the flesh but reflect a refined, more philosophical, concept of pleasure—as if Herbert were revising Socrates' fable in the *Phaedrus* and attributing rebelliousness to the spirited horse of the psychic team. A twentieth-century reader might resent the antique novelty of assigning the products of culture to the ways of pleasure, but he might find some compensation in the formal emphasis on knowledge that echoes through the stanza: "mirth and musick *mean*," and the introductory expression, "I know," is used a second time only in this stanza. What is most distinctive, however, is the passionate immediacy, the full identification of the poet with the feelings expressed. The nonchalance of witty indifference abruptly disappears; and the stanza excludes, for the moment, those quantitative images of profit and loss which partly reflect the amused detachment and superiority of the speaker—the "stock and surplus," "quick returns," "gains," and "drammes of spirit." The controls of knowledge and love are not broken down, but they remain external and neither repress the feelings nor enter into their expression. As for the temptation itself, it is not considered in a formal way, but its presence and force are amply represented by the language of the speaker.

As a measure of Herbert's boldness and candor it is useful to quote an authoritative diagnosis of the symptoms and etiology of imaginative self-temptation. When, according to Augustine, the soul slackens in its powers of determination, the body will try to advance its own interests. Delighted by "corporeal forms and movements," the soul then "becomes entangled with their images which it has fixed in its memory, and is foully defiled by the fornications of the phantasy." When the soul places the end of its own good in the sensuous, it "snatches the deceptive images of corporeal things from within and combines them together by empty thought, so that nothing combines to it to be divine unless it be of such a kind as this." Augustine's diagnosis, with its adaptation of Platonic and Stoic features, may describe the rebellious imagination as we see it, for instance, in "**The Collar**," and it may help identify an occasional lapse in Herbert's spiritual nerve, but it is remarkably irrelevant to the "corporeal forms and movements" of his third stanza. The feelings expressed there have dignity; they are immediate and real, without defilement and resulting self-hatred, and without confusions of the divine. In fact, only the ways of honor come directly under Augustine's analysis, for they are the artificial products of illusive symbolizing, the "deceptive images" patched together with "empty thought."

The first and second stanzas, we noted, resemble each other in their amused detachment. Their plain style is that of argument, which demonstrates indirectly, by witty analysis, that the major temptations do not tempt at all. The greater intensity of the second stanza by moving toward mockery increases the imaginative distance between the objects discussed and the speaker. The plain style of the last stanza will reverse that direction. It is argument, and intellectual, but not detached. Everything is drawn together, and toward the poet at the center of his experience. But the decisive change is initiated by the third stanza with its personal fervor and elevated style.

Let us compare in their relations these last two stanzas and the last two stanzas of **"The Temper (I)"**. In that poem the penultimate stanza ("Yet take thy way; for sure thy way is best") presents an intellectual acceptance which is rather dry and detached but provides the necessary bridge to the comprehensive solution of the last stanza, which is highly charged with feeling but registers as an inspired clarification. In **"The Pearl"** the general procedure is the same but the parts are reversed. The conflict does not take shape until the penultimate stanza, where the climax also occurs; that stanza brings about the shift in direction from analytical distance to synthetic immediacy, as the necessary bridge to the comprehensive solution of the last stanza. In **"The Pearl"** it is the penultimate stanza which is elevated in style and charged with feeling. But its expression is, though intense and candid, consciously limited by the external controls of the context; it cannot speak for the whole man in the poem. Though eloquent and moving, the voice of the stanza cannot possibly bring eloquence and wisdom into the unison of a single speech. The last stanza names inspired wisdom as a presence which has governed the whole action of the poem, but which does not, as in **"The Temper (I)"**, make a personal appearance. The clarification of love and understanding is quietly intellectual, not passionate, and includes the humble disclaimer that whatever has been accomplished by the poem was merely by following instructions:

> Yet through these labyrinths, not my groveling
>   wit,
> But thy silk twist let down from heav'n to me,
> Did both conduct and teach me, how by it
>   To climbe to thee.

In this poem there is no pause inviting God to write the last stanza; an affirming act of the intellect builds on a moment of passion, rather than the reverse. But the proof of character lies in the integration and in the poet's being at one with what he says. There has been no spectacular inspiration, but everything has been drawn together, and the silk twist which has led him through the labyrinths has brought him to the expressive center of what he concludes.

Our final example is the poem **"Death,"** which acknowledges no conflict. The fictional pretext is a slight and transparent one: the difference between the way we used to look at death and the way we look at it now. The plot is not likely to surprise, and since there is no formal conflict the poet's own feelings do not directly participate in the action. Coming to the poem after **"The Temper (I)"** and **"The Pearl,"** one is at first perhaps more conscious of the differences, but the similarities are more significant.

As in many poems that are relatively straightforward and simple in statement, Herbert invents fine devices on which the materials turn, move, and develop—as if they were proceeding by means of the more visible structures of argument, dramatic conflict, or narrative plot. Each stanza of **"Death"** is a kind of self-contained scene, into which the last line brings an unexpected effect. The reader is not likely to be aware that an argument is also being produced,

until he encounters the open "Therefore" at the beginning of the sixth and last stanza. There are three parts of the argument, arranged in a formal diminution of 3:2:1. The first three stanzas give us the old wrong views of death, the next two corrected present views, and the conclusion is drawn in a single stanza. Let us begin with the first three:

> Death, thou wast once an uncouth hideous
>   thing,
>   Nothing but bones,
>   The sad effect of sadder grones:
> Thy mouth was open, but thou couldst not sing.
>
> For we consider'd thee as at some six
>   Or ten years hence,
>   After the losse of life and sense,
> Flesh being turn'd to dust, and bones to sticks.
>
> We lookt on this side of thee, shooting short;
>   Where we did finde
>   The shells of fledge souls left behinde,
> Dry dust, which sheds no tears, but may extort.

The mementos of death are handled with remarkable verve and gaiety. Of **"The Temper (I)"** we could say that the intention of the poem was to transform its initial declaration into its concluding one. Here we have attitudes rather than declarations; and that strange, bluff greeting to death, though startling, original, and arbitrary, does not register at once as a "wrong" attitude asking for correction. Nevertheless, the tone is the exaggerated one of an extreme which the development of the poem will transform. If we borrow an observation from our study of **"The Pearl,"** we may describe the speaker's opening attitude as detached and superior, as if enjoying his analytical distance from the object of his attention. In the fifth stanza the tone will be countered by an opposite extreme of immediacy and identification. Then the argument, expression, and tone of the last stanza will transform the extremes of psychic distance and immediacy into a final attitude.

The second and third stanzas drop the concentrated focus on skull, bones, and grinning jaws, and drop the harsh, summary definition of life as a music of groans, and death as the arrested image of that music. The reason now given for that hideousness is not concentrated and shocking but leisurely and general, as befits an intellectual speculation prefaced by "For we consider'd." The error in human understanding is caused by our faulty sense of time. We think in spans of six or ten years from now and judge death by its appearances then. The detachment is quietly intellectual but does not therefore eliminate some tension of divided attitude. The reader will not find that the studied casualness of rhythm, tone, and detail prevents him from considering any thought of his own death, "some six / Or ten years hence." Furthermore, the ironic turn in the last line of each stanza reintroduces the opportunity for personal concern and relation: "Flesh being turn'd to dust, and bones to sticks. . . . Dry dust, which sheds no tears, but may extort." And that beautiful euphemism for skeletal remains, "The shells of fledge souls left behinde," is a little too successful; we admire the imaginative act and in so doing are reminded of the natural state of the material thus translated.

In addition to these psychological movements which endue a sense of developing conflict, we may note the presence of significant attitudes toward time. The first stanza greets death as it was, not once upon a time but "once," as it was in time past. But the imaginative time of that stanza is the feeling-present, which the shock of the image produces, in spite of the summary intellectualizing of the cause in the immediate past and the assertion that all of this visible effect is not what it seems to be but is what it was "once." The assertion is left dangling as a challenge that is to be made good, but not in the formal time of the second and third stanzas, which does not go all the way back to the "once." The feeling-present returns, though less emphatically, in the suggestions of personal death and in the reference to the dust "which sheds no tears, but may extort." Still more elusively, the sense of future time enters these stanzas. There is an ambiguity in the "six / Or ten years hence"—depending on whether we were considering the case of stanza one, or were considering some case, perhaps our own, from a point in the past identical with our consideration and extending six to ten years into the future. But since the point in the past is not located firmly, the sense of future time is at best weak. Similarly, the flesh and bones "being turn'd" to dust and sticks presents us with a free composition of past, present, and future; any single dimension of time can dominate in that formula, depending on the formal perspective. Finally, the "fledge souls" do evoke the future in a definite but small way; the transaction itself points ahead, and the habits of metaphorical thought on this familiar subject move naturally from the place "left behind" to the far future.

Everything we have considered thus far will reappear, with changes, in the next step of the argument, which begins in the fourth stanza:

> But since our Saviours death did put some bloud
> Into thy face;
> Thou art grown fair and full of grace,
> Much in request, much sought for as a good.

The verve and gaiety continue, but now the mementos of death are looked at from the perspective of life after death. Out of the conventions of that perspective Herbert draws details that emphasize the imaginative nature of his presentation. The hideousness of the skull in the first stanza was the product of its appearance, our perspective, and the grotesque associations brought to bear. In the fourth stanza the perspective and associations are changed; a show of appearance is made, but the literal, physical terms are dominated by their symbolic and metaphorical meanings. The language is matter-of-fact. "But since our Saviours death did put some bloud / Into thy face," and more comforting than "Thy mouth was open, but thou couldst not sing"; but both statements are self-consciously imaginative, two opposing ways of looking at death, each an exaggeration based upon a different view of the truth. The stanza continues to emphasize its imaginative play as it moves further from the possibility of literal presentation. Both the face which is now "fair and full of grace" and the beholder's eye are altered, and the newness of the relationship is underlined by the pleasantry of "grace." The last line of the stanza draws back a little, with a kind of wry humor far gentler than the irony in each of the preceding

last lines. Death is "Much in request"—as if by a change in fashion. That death is "much sought for as a good" moves the significance further from its physical base and advances the dignity of its attractiveness by the deliberate introduction language that has philosophical associations.

The "But since" which opens the fourth stanza is the sign both of argument and of time. Though the dominant time-sense is present it is derived from the Savior's act in the past and lightly suggests the future in "sought for as a good." The sense of the present, however, is not *felt* as in the first stanza but serves mostly as a kind of intellectual transition to the strong present of the fifth stanza. Finally, to touch again on the point of imaginative distance: the fourth stanza maintains a distinctive kind of detachment, because of its intellectualized emphasis on the metaphorical and the witty.

The fifth stanza completes the corrected view of death, bringing the poem to a sudden climax:

> For we do now behold thee gay and glad,
> As at dooms-day;
> When souls shall wear their new aray,
> And all thy bones with beautie shall be clad.

Each of the first three stanzas presents a thesis abruptly at the beginning and then makes additional points to tighten and complicate the scene. In the fourth and fifth stanzas the thought requires the whole four lines for its development, and in the fifth stanza rises to a declarative climax in the last line, reversing the established ironic twist of the first three stanzas and the mildly humorous withdrawal of the fourth. More important, all of the motions of detachment, all of the varieties of analytical distance in the poem are reversed in the sudden rush of imaginative immediacy.

The developing attitudes toward time are also brought to a climax, but the details are more involved and cannot be seen without analysis. Let me summarize briefly. In the first three stanzas the formal time was past, the finished past of "once" in the first stanza and a less definite, recent past in the second and third stanzas. But in the first a sense of the feeling-present dominates; in the second and third present and future both enter, but elusively. In the fourth stanza a similar blend occurs, though the formal time is present. But when we come to the fifth stanza, suddenly there is no sense of the past. The present dominates but draws its intensity from a prophetic vision of the future. That future comes into the poem strongly and positively at this one point, and fully answers the finished past of stanza one. Since that future is imagined as intensely present, the effect is a formal reply to the feeling-present of stanza one.

These answers composed of the oppositions of time and the oppositions of psychic direction are not conclusive. A quiet "Therefore" converts their striking emphasis into mere transition, as if the real answer has been waiting for the commotion to subside:

> Therefore we can go die as sleep, and trust
> Half that we have
> Unto an honest faithfull grave;
> Making our pillows either down, or dust.

Now the time is wholly present: it is the unique product of imagined past and future, but emerging also from the varying stresses on the present which have been drawn like a thread through the labyrinth to this open place. As for either analytical detachment from death or imaginative identification—the final attitude rejects the terms of the contradiction, but draws an essential indifference from detachment and an essential acceptance from identification. The human present of the last stanza copies the calm of eternity, into which no agitations of past or future intrude. Death is not an alien object exciting mixed emotions, nor a lover to be sought and embraced. The imagination of the poem has made death familiar and neutral; it can have no place even in dreams when it has been made subject to a common, everyday idiom which says, "we can go die."

The activity of the mind is less prominent than in the conclusion of "**The Pearl**," but as in that poem an affirming act of the intellect quietly builds on a moment of passion, and the mind that dismisses itself has demonstrated the power and clarity of its self-possession. There is no pause, as in "**The Temper (I)**", inviting God to write the last stanza. The spectacular inspiration comes in the prophetic vision of doomsday, which is followed by the rarest kind of personal clarity, casual and laconic, as if inspiration were part of the everyday order and could be taken for granted. The final state of simplicity is not one of reduced but of alert, refined consciousness. One sign is the attitude toward the body, which is no less than "Half that we have." And even more remarkable than calling the grave "honest" and "faithfull" is doing so with the air of not saying anything unusual. As in "**The Pearl**," the excited elevation of style in the penultimate stanza is followed by an authoritative descent to the plain style. In "**Death**" it is an assimilative plain style, confidently challenging comparison with the height of the preceding stanza. The power of that plain style lies in the passion excluded, in the resistance mastered, and in the deliberate grace of saying difficult things with ease. The grandeur and force of the high style are achieved while talking in an off-hand, humble manner in the common imagery of going to bed. An enlightened rhetorician would observe that this plain style does not austerely reject ornament, which may persuade but must first provide esthetic pleasure. He would add, I am sure, that these graces of style are so natural and fine as to seem in the very grain. The last line, "Making our pillows either down, or dust," awakens a delicate echo of the earlier ironies, as a farewell touch of recognition. And the order of "die as sleep" is beautifully reversed and balanced by "down, or dust."

I shall end by introducing another viewpoint for a moment. In reading Donne Coleridge described the delight of "tracing the leading thought thro'out the whole," by means of which "you merge yourself in the author, you *become He*." Herbert he declares to be "a true poet, but a poet *sui generis*, the merits of whose poems will never be felt without a sympathy with the mind and character of the man." A true poet who requires a conscious act of sympathy would seem to have a different and lesser merit than the poet who compels you to "*become He*." Coleridge justly admires Herbert's diction, "than which nothing can be more pure, manly, and unaffected." But some of the

thoughts are "quaint," and he does not try to follow a leading thought throughout. Identifying oneself with the author would seem to be a modern extension of the most important mode of rhetorical persuasion, "the personal goodness revealed by the speaker" in ancient rhetoric, or the inspired unity of wisdom and eloquence in Christian rhetoric. The merits of identifying oneself with the poet are debatable. But we can draw two firm points from Coleridge's remarks. First, it is clear that Herbert is a master who draws a leading thought through authentic obstacles which both test and refine the ultimate expression of that thought. Secondly, the rhetorical proof of character lies in the poet's convincing demonstrations that *he* becomes what he says, that the flow and shape of his words lead to a unity of eloquence and wisdom, and that he is at the expressive center of what he concludes.

It is tempting to end here, adding only that there are many true poets but few masters of this art of plainness. But it may be well to back up and remember that Herbert's art of plainness is an art and not a summary feature. If we have touched on the essential quality, good; but we can no more do without a full apparatus for understanding his art than he could write poems by plainly saying "Thou art still my God." (pp. 160-80)

Arnold Stein, "George Herbert: The Art of Plainness," in Essential Articles for the Study of George Herbert's Poetry, *edited by John R. Roberts, Archon Books, 1979, pp. 160-80.*

Coleridge on Herbert's *The Temple* :

G. Herbert is a true poet, but a poet *sui generis*, the merits of whose poems will never be felt without a sympathy with the mind and character of the man. To appreciate this volume, it is not enough that the reader possesses a cultivated judgment, classical taste, or even poetic sensibility, unless he be likewise a *Christian*, and both a zealous and an orthodox, both a devout and a *devotional* Christian. But even this will not quite suffice. He must be an affectionate and dutiful child of the Church, and from habit, conviction, and a constitutional predisposition to ceremoniousness, in piety as in manners, find her forms and ordinances aids of religion, not sources of formality; for religion is the element in which he lives, and the region in which he moves.

Samuel Taylor Coleridge in Coleridge's Miscellaneous criticism, *edited by Thomas Middleton Raysor, The Folcroft Press, 1936.*

Stanley Fish (essay date 1972)

[*Fish is an American scholar and critic who has written extensively on seventeenth-century English literature. In the following excerpt, he argues that many of Herbert's poems depict a tension between the independence of the individual and the omnipresence of God.*]

In the third stanza of "**The Flower**," George Herbert gives voice to an article of faith which is itself a description of the action taking place in many of his poems:

> We say amisse,
> This or that is:
> Thy word is all, if we could spell.
>
> (19-21)

The point of doctrine is, of course, a seventeenth-century commonplace: the distinctions—of times, places, objects, persons—we customarily make as we move about in the world are the illusory creations of a limited perspective; if our visions were sufficiently enlarged, we would see that all things visible were not only framed by (Hebrews 11:3) but are informed by (are manifestations of) the word that is God: "Thy word is all."

Herbert's poems characteristically ask us to experience the full force of this admission in all its humiliating implications. If God is all, the claims of other entities to a separate existence, including the claims of the speakers and readers of these poems, must be relinquished. That is, the insight that God's word is all is *self*-destructive, since acquiring it involves abandoning the perceptual and conceptual categories within which the self moves and by means of which it separately exists. To stop saying amiss is not only to stop distinguishing "this" from "that," but to stop distinguishing oneself from God, and finally to stop, to cease to be. Learning to "spell" in these terms is a self-diminishing action in the course of which the individual lets go, one by one, of all the ways of thinking, seeing, and saying that sustain the illusion of his independence, until finally he is absorbed into the deity whose omnipresence he has acknowledged (thy word is *all*).

There is nothing easy about the "letting go" this poetry requires of us. We are, after all, being asked to acquiesce in the discarding of those very habits of thought and mind that preserve our dignity by implying our independence. Naturally (the word is double edged) we resist, and our resistance is often mirrored in the obstinate questionings and remonstrations of the first-person voice. The result is a poetics of tension, reflecting a continuing dialectic between an egocentric vision which believes in, and is sustained by, the distinctions it creates, and the relentless pressure of a *re*solving and *dis*solving insight. That dialectic takes many forms, but its basic contours remain recognizable: the surface argument or plot of a poem proceeds in the context of the everyday world of time and space, where objects and persons are discrete and independent; but at the same time and within the same linguistic space, there is felt the pressure of a larger context which lays claim to that world and everything in it, including speaker, reader, and the poem itself:

> *Lord, my first fruits present themselves to thee;*
> *Yet not mine neither: for from thee they came,*
> *And must return.* (**"The Dedication"**)

The return of these fruits and of everything else to the God of whose substance they are is the self-consuming business of these poems, which can be viewed as a graduated series of "undoings" and "letting go's": (I) the undoing of the perceptual framework in which we live and move and have our (separate) beings. This involves the denying of the usual distinctions between "this" and "that"—a *"making of one place everywhere"*—and the affirmation of a universe where God is all. An inevitable consequence of

this undoing is the gradual narrowing (to nothing) of the distance between the individual consciousness (of both speaker and reader) and God; that is, (2) the undoing of the self as an independent entity, a *"making of no thine and mine"* by making it all thine, a surrender not only of a way of seeing, but of initiative, will, and finally of being (to say "I am" is to say amiss). To the extent that this surrender is also the poet's, it requires the silencing of his voice and the relinquishing of the claims of authorship, and therefore (3) an undoing of the poem as the product of a mind distinct from the mind of God. This undoing, or letting go, is an instance of what it means, in Herbert's own words, to *"make the action fine"* (by making it not mine). And finally, and inevitably, Herbert's poems are undone in still another sense when (4) the insight they yield ("thy word is all") renders superfluous the mode of discourse and knowing of which they themselves are examples. These poems, as they ask their readers to acknowledge their complete dependence, act out that acknowledgment by calling attention to what they are not doing, and indeed could not do. In their final radical modesty, they perform what they require of us, for as they undermine our reliance on discursive forms of thought, and urge us to rest in the immediate apprehension of God's all-effective omnipresence, they become the vehicles of their own abandonment. "God only is," writes Thomas Browne, "all others . . . are something but by a distinction." To read Herbert's poems is to experience the dissolution of the distinctions by which all other things are.

The preceding is a summary statement that raises as many questions as it answers. If the insight of God's omnipresence is violated by the very act of predication ("This or that is"), how does a poet who is committed to that insight practice his craft? How does one avoid saying amiss if language is itself a vehicle for the making of invidious distinctions? How can God's prerogatives be preserved if one produces sentences which automatically arrange persons and objects in hierarchical relationships of cause and effect? Answering these questions will be the burden of this chapter, but we can begin by noting that Herbert baptizes language by making it subversive of its usual functions. In his poetry words tend to lose their referential fixity, and syntactical patterns often obscure the relationships they pretend to establish. In short, Herbert avoids saying amiss in an ultimate context by deliberately saying amiss in the context of a perspective he would have us transcend.

The peculiar force of a Herbert poem, then, often depends on our awareness that the terms in which we are being encouraged to formulate a concept are inadequate to it. In some poems, this awareness is only a momentary thing, the (by) product of a single phrase:

> Subject to ev'ry mounter's bended knee.
> (**"The Holy Scriptures, I,"** 1.14)

To read this line is to experience the insufficiency of its mode of discourse. It is a miniature exercise in epistemology. "Mounter's" involves the reader in the most conventional of homiletic practices, the figuring forth of a spiritual distinction by a spatial image; but "bended" undermines the simple formula (up-good, down-evil) on which the analogy depends, forcing the reader to let go of the image and of the way of thinking that has generated it, and calling into question the very possibility of comprehending spiritual matters in spatial forms. It is called into question in a more substantive way in "**The Temper I**":

> How should I praise thee, Lord!   how should
>   my rymes
> Gladly engrave thy love in steel,
> If what my soul doth feel sometimes,
>   My soul might ever feel!
>
> Although there were some fourtie heav'ns, or
>   more,
> Sometimes I peere above them all;
> Sometimes I hardly reach a score,
>   Sometimes to hell I fall.

If, as Arnold Stein has argued [in *George Herbert's Lyrics*, 1968], the " 'plain intention' " of this poem is "to transform its initial attitude into its concluding one," that transformation is the result of exchanging one way of looking at the world for another. The "initial attitude" is one of complaint: Herbert's inability to praise God as he would like to is a condition, he maintains, of his inability to sustain the occasional moment of perfect joy ("Sometimes I peere above them all"); and that, in turn, is a condition of God's fitful presence. The stated wish to praise God, then, is a thinly disguised accusation of him. Were he more faithful, more constantly in attendance, the poet's lines and rhymes would flow easily and everlastingly. (God here has the role assigned to inspiration in the laments of secular poets). Of course this (hidden) argument holds only if one limits God to times and places, and that is exactly what Herbert is doing in the extended image of the second stanza. Presumably God resides in that fortieth heaven to which the poet occasionally ascends; lower levels receive proportional shares of his emanations and in hell there is (literally) no trace of him at all.

But while this localization of God's presence is consistent with certain Neoplatonic systems and even with the three-tiered universe of popular tradition, it will hardly do for the deity of whom Augustine speaks when he says "He came to a place where He was already". This statement (if it is a statement) illustrates the Christian solution to the problem of thinking and talking about God in terms whose frame of reference he transcends. One uses the terms (no others are available), but simultaneously acknowledges their insufficiency, as Herbert does in the concluding and, in view of his earlier complaint, triumphant, stanza of this poem:

> Whether I flie with angels, fall with dust
>   Thy hands made both, and I am there:
> Thy power and love, my love and trust
>   Make one place ev'ry where.
>
>   (25-28)

The speaker's dilemma, both as would-be praiser and God-seeking man, exists only in his formulation of it, and its solution is effected when that formulation is abandoned or let go. The process of letting go is set in motion in the first line: the pointing of the "whether-or" construction (one supplies the "or") suggests that Herbert is still committed to the divided worlds of the opening stanzas, but at the same time the alliteration of "flie" and "fall" is pull-

ing us in a different direction, toward the dissolving of the distinctions—between angels and dust, heaven and hell—the syntax is supporting. By the end of the following line, "ev'ry where" has been made one place through the agency of the precisely ambiguous "there," which refers neither to the earth ("dust") nor to the ("fourtie") heavens, but to God's hands, the framers, supporters, and therefore, in a real sense, the location, of both. The point of doctrine is, as always, a commonplace—since all things were made by God (John, 1:3) and by him all things consist (Colossians, 1:17), everywhere in his "there"—but the peculiar value of its appearance here resides in the process through which Herbert makes his readers approach it. The reader who negotiates the distance between "Whether" and "there" passes from a (syntactical) world where everything is in its time and place to a world where specification of either is impossible, to a *uni*verse. This same movement is compressed into an even smaller space in the final line, where "one place" actually does become "ev'ry where" in the twinkling of a reading eye. And, of course, the ease with which we take in the paradox is a direct result of the experience of the preceding lines.

As is often the case in a Herbert poem, the resolution of the spiritual or psychological problem also effects the resolution of the poetic problem. For when the speaker is able to say "Yet take thy way; for sure thy way is best (21)" he removes the obstacle to his singing of God's praises; that obstacle is not his uneven spiritual experience, but his too easy interpretation of that experience as a sign of God's desertion. Once he gives up that reading of his situation, he is free to see in it a more beneficent purpose:

> This is but tuning of my breast,
> To make the musick better.
>
>   (23-24)

Thus the very condition the speaker laments finally yields the praise he thought himself debarred from making, and itself becomes the occasion for, because it has been the stimulus to, praise. That is, the sense of heaven's desertion leads to the mental exertions which produce the poem which generates the intuition that God's way is best. What begins as a complaint against God ends with the realization that the supposed basis of the complaint, when properly seen, is something to be thankful for. The poem's movement in effect anticipates the counsel of Sir Thomas Browne, who advises us "so to dispute and argue the proceedings of God as to distinguish even his judgements into mercies (*Religio Medici*, I, 53)."

Just how great a mercy God affords Herbert here can be seen in the poem's penultimate line:

> Thy power and love, my love and trust.
>
>   (27)

What this does is give the poet a part in the action of the concluding line—making one place everywhere ("make" has a multiple subject). God's power and love, His continuing presence in the world, are of course the final cause of this effect, but the poet's love and trust in that other love are necessary for its perception since the perceiving consciousness he was born with suggests something else altogether (that "this" or "that" is).

Making one place everywhere, in contradiction to the appearance (or illusion) of a multiplicity of places, is also the action and the experience of "**Even-Song.**" As in "**The Temper I**," the opening lines suggest a distinction, in some part spatial, which does not survive the reading experience:

> Blest be the God of love,
> Who gave me eyes, and light, and power this
> day,
> Both to be busie, and to play.
> But much more blest be God above,
> Who gave me sight alone.
> (1-5)

Apparently the poet prays to two Gods, the "God of love," and that more powerful and more to be thanked "God above," the God, presumably, of the higher regions. This halving of the world's empire is immediately suspect and is already being challenged by the unifying force of the rhyme "love-above." By the time the reader takes in the pun in line 8—"But I have got his sonne, and he hath none"—the two deities have become one, or, what is in effect the same thing, two coequal and coidentical members of a trinity, and for the remainder of the poem the speaker addresses his remarks unambiguously to a second person singular.

The dividing and distinguishing tendencies of the human consciousness, however, are irrepressible, and they reassert themselves toward the end of the poem:

> I muse, which shows more love,
> The day or night.
> (25-26)

The answer is implicit in what has gone before; since they are both God's they show equally his love; and moreover as manifestations of that love they lose their separate identities, which is exactly what happens to them in this stanza:

> I muse, which shows more love,
> The day or night: that is the gale, this th' harbour;
> That is the walk, and this the arbour;
> Or that the garden, this the grove.
> (25-28)

The speaker muses in the (submerged) context of a familiar proverb: "as different as day and night." At first this sense of difference is reinforced; the "gale and harbour" image is made up of easily separable components, distinct in time and place; the gale *brings* one to the harbour. The distinctness of "walk" and "arbour" however is less immediately striking; either they are adjacent or one encloses the other. The third pair of substitute coordinates actually works against the argument it is supposedly supporting; for while "garden" and "grove" are distinguishable, distinguishing between them requires more of an effort than the heavily alliterative verse ("gale," "garden," "grove"; "harbour," "arbour," "garden") encourages. In the very process of (supposedly) expanding an opposition, Herbert has led us surreptitiously and by degrees to a sense of sameness, and it is this experience that gives force to the triumphant assertion of the following line:

> My God, thou art all love.
> (29)

Here the poet admits that the question he had posed three lines earlier was based on assumptions (that "this" day, or "that" night, is) that are found to be invalid when our perspective on "things" is sufficiently enlarged, as it has been in the course of the poem. Of course, that invalidated perspective is the one we must live with (or in), even after its insufficiency has been demonstrated or experienced, and the speaker returns to it, and to the logical language which is an extension of it, in the final lines:

> My God, thou art all love.
> Not one poore minute scapes thy breast
> But brings a favour from above;
> And in this love, more then in bed, I rest.
> (29-32)

Once again God is "above" (the rhyme of the opening stanza reappears) and man "below," but this formulation is now less dangerously distorting than it might have been at the beginning of the poem because we know now (what we always knew, but less self-consciously) that this way of thinking and verbalizing is an accommodation. That is, we know, even as we read line 32, that resting in bed or anywhere else, we are always resting in God's love which makes one (any) place everywhere.

Examples of this kind could be multiplied indefinitely, but the point, I think, has been made: to read many of Herbert's poems is to experience the dissolution of the lines of demarcation we are accustomed to think of as real. Perhaps the most spectacular of the poems in this mode is "**Church Monuments**," which has been brilliantly analyzed by Joseph Summers [in *George Herbert*, 1954]:

> The dissolution of the body and the monuments
> is paralleled by the dissolution of the sentences
> and stanzas.
>
> The movement and sound of the poem suggest
> the "falls" of the flesh and the monuments and
> the dust in the glass. The fall is not precipitous;
> it is as slow as the gradual fall of the monuments,
> as the crumbling of the glass, as the descent of
> the flesh from Adam to dust. . . . With the
> cluster of consonants, it is impossible to read the
> poem rapidly. The related rhymes, with their internal echoes and repetitions, both give phonetic
> continuity to the poem and suggest the process
> of dissolution. . . . The sentences sift down
> through the rhyme scheme skeleton of the stanzas like the sand through the glass and the glass
> itself has already begun to crumble.

To this obviously authoritative description of what is happening in the poem I would add a description of what is happening in (and to) the reader; for the dissolution of sentences and stanzas and of the objects within them produces a corresponding dissolution, or falling away of, the perceptual framework a reader brings with him to the poem and indeed to life. Thus, in the opening lines the firm sense of time and place, which at first allows us to distance ourselves from objects and processes, is progressively eroded:

> While that my soul repairs to her devotion,

Here I intombe my flesh that it betimes
May take acquaintance of this heap of dust;
To which the blast of deaths incessant motion,
Fed with the exhalation of our crimes,
Drives all at last. Therefore I gladly trust.

(1-6)

The first three lines are replete with distinctions, distinctions of times, persons, objects, spaces, and actions. The body is distinguished from the soul and both from the heaps of dust with which they are bid take acquaintance. The words on which the syntax pivots are "While" and "Here," time and place markers respectively. Even less essential words, like "repairs" and "betimes," contribute to the strong impression of local identities, separable objects, discrete and specifiable moments. Yet no sooner have these demarcations been established and assumed a kind of reality in the reader's mind, than the process of undermining them begins. If it is "impossible to read the poem rapidly" it is also impossible to read the poem in stages because it affords us no natural resting places. Units of meaning that seem complete in themselves are unexpectedly revealed to be only the introductory clauses in a larger utterance, an utterance whose scope finally expands to include the whole poem. It is, in Herbert's own words an "incessant motion," and it proceeds by blurring the distinctions it momentarily establishes. This process begins with "To which (4)," a transition that forces the reader to keep one eye on the three preceding lines at the same time that he is a witness to, and to some extent the agent of, the melting into one another of the objects that fill those lines. Initially, the referent of "which" is assumed to be "dust," but as the "blast" of the verse's "incessant motion" drives us toward the full stop in line 6, the possibilities widen to include, first, "this heap of dust" and then, when we reach the climactic "all," that other "heap of dust," "my flesh." That is to say, the word "all" operates retroactively to make earlier words and phrases mean differently. As the poem opens, "intombe my flesh" seems merely a fancifully witty way of referring to the speaker's immobility while at prayer. Now we see that the witticism is a tautology: his flesh *is* its own tombe, one more heap of dust, exactly like those that are the objects of its contemplation. To take acquaintance of *this* heap of dust is to follow (with a vengeance) the Socratean injunction, "know thyself." It is an injunction to which we too must respond for the simple "our" of line 5 does not allow us, as readers, to exempt ourselves from the statement the poem is making. In the first two lines we are insulated from this shock of recognition by the objects that literally stand between us and "this heap of dust"—the church, its monuments, and the speaker—but by the end of line 6 (which, of course, ends nothing), these have all become one ("at last") and that oneness has been extended outward to embrace us too.

Thus when Herbert declares "Therefore I gladly trust," we await the identification of the object of his trust with more than a syntactical interest, and for a moment we are surprised by what we find:

My bodie to this school, that it may learn
To spell his elements, and finde his birth
Written in dustie heraldrie and lines;
Which dissolution sure doth best discern,

Comparing dust with dust, and earth with earth.
These laugh at Jeat and Marble put for signes.

(7-12)

The body would seem to be a questionable repository of trust given the prediction in the first stanza of its imminent dissolution; and, of course, as the line continues the sense changes, forcing us to replace "my bodie" with "this school" as the object of "trust," a grammatical adjustment which mirrors perfectly the life adjustment the poem is urging us to make. In the school to which both the reader and the body are sent the lessons are strangely self-defeating. One *spells* correctly when one *discerns* the indecipherability of the text; discerning is "sure" only when the object of discernment dissolves; "signes" signify properly only when they become indistinguishable from their surroundings (a word that itself has little meaning at this point); "comparing" becomes an exercise in tautology, "comparing dust with dust." The words I have emphasized all receive both a metrical and a sense stress and together, that is, in isolation, they strongly suggest a process by which some measure of phenomenal clarity can be achieved; but between them and surrounding them are other words, which finally mock the pretensions of this clarifying vocabulary. Consider, for example, lines 9 and 10: The stressed words taken by themselves piece out a strong declarative statement "Written . . . lines/Which . . . sure . . . discern." But for a reader, the firmness of the past participle "written" is severely qualified by the adjective "dustie" which in its forward movement makes it impossible to take the word "lines" literally; in addition, the noun itself has so many possible referents—the lines of body, the genealogical lines of the body's heraldry, the lines of the epitaph (no longer there), the lines of the poem (which are themselves becoming progressively more "dustie")—that "which" is more a question than a pronoun. The question becomes academic with the next word "dissolution." Whatever "which" was, it is no more, having dissolved; only that dissolution is "sure" and, as the line ends, the verb "discern" completes an irony of which it itself is a victim.

The syntactical structures of this poem are no more successful at discerning or distinguishing than are the monuments they so unclearly present. Indeed, the forms of both (syntax and monuments) collapse simultaneously before the reader's eye, and with them collapses the illusion they together perpetuate, the illusion that the world of time and space—where "this or that is"—to which they have reference is permanent or even real. That is to say, discursive linguistic forms, no less then jeat and marble, are extensions of an earthbound consciousness, and, like jeat and marble, they become true (accurate) hieroglyphs only when their pretensions are exposed. Thus in lines 14-16 the imminent failure of the monuments to point out (isolate, individuate) the heaps they have in "trust" (what an irony in *that* word) is imitated in the failure of the syntax to keep separate (point out) its own components:

What shall point out them,
When they shall bow, and kneel, and fall down
flat
To kisse those heaps, which now they have in
trust?

The fact that Hutchinson feels compelled to provide a full gloss of these lines—"What shall distinguish tomb and bodies, when all are, sooner or later, commingled in one heap of dust (499)?"—is a nice comment on the success of Herbert's strategy. Where his editor obligingly provides the distinguishing specificity of "tombs" and "bodies," the poet gives us only an obfuscating series of pronouns and demonstratives—"what," "them," "they," "those," "they"—with the result that the larger structure of the utterance is progressively undermined. "Them," "they," and "those" become one, not in the future of Herbert's "shall," but in the present of his question. And that question is as much the object of irony as are the markers whose dissolution it predicts; for the very basis for asking a question—for rational predication in general—is taken away when the phenomena to which the question would direct our attention will not stay put and are, in fact, in the process of disintegrating. In other words, this self-consuming question convinces us not only of the insubstantiality of monuments, but of the final irrelevance and insufficiency of the way of thinking (spatially and temporally) the act of questioning assumes.

The same use of language—not to specify, but to make specification impossible—is on display in the final lines, where to monuments and bodies and sentences and questions is joined time, as one more earthly mold whose form dissolves in the context of a more inclusive vision:

> That flesh is but the glasse, which holds the dust
> That measures all our time; which also shall
> Be crumbled into dust. Mark here below.
>
> (20-22)

As before, the referents of the relatives expand so that for the second "which" the reader understands not only "time," but "glasse," "flesh" (one hears an echo of the biblical "all flesh is grass") and even "measures," all of which have been crumbled into dust. With this in mind, the final gesture of the first-person voice is more than a little suspect:

> Mark here below.

Mark where? and with what? and in what? "Mark" follows immediately upon "dust" (the heavy stresses of the Lydgatian, or "humpbacked," line pushes them up against each other) and the juxtaposition of the two words undermines the pointing motion of the imperative, leaving the reader to look at one more example of "dustie heraldrie." In this context, the final distich—"How tame these ashes are, how free from lust, / That thou mayst fit thy self against thy fall"—can hardly be taken as seriously as its alliterative neatness would suggest. There is finally something facile about the stance of the speaker, who lectures his body as if he were not implicated in either its pride or its fall. The poem laughs not only at the pretensions of jeat and marble, but at its own pretensions, and also at the facility of those readers who thought to escape from it with an easy and pious conclusion. Summers tells us that the hieroglyphic form of "**Church Monuments**" serves "to reinforce the message," but that message itself crumbles just as we are about to carry it away.

Isabel MacCaffrey has written of Milton [in *Paradise Lost*

As "Myth", 1959] that his "worlds all fit exactly inside each other," an observation that also fits Herbert. In fact it might be a description of the action of "**Church Monuments**," where a succession of worlds or containers, at first separate and discrete, are discovered finally to be perfectly congruent, not only fitting inside each other, but filled with the same substance, dust. Yet in some important respects, this is not a representative poem. More typically the vessels and boxes (a favorite word) of Herbert's poetic landscape, when opened, are found to contain not dust, but Christ. This is uniquely true of the poem "**Sepulchure**," whose ostensible plot is the search for a lodging suitable to hold Christ's body:

> O Blessed bodie! Whither art thou thrown?
> No lodging for thee, but a cold hard stone?
> So many hearts on earth, and yet not one
>   Receive thee?
>
> (1-4)

The speaker's questions depend on two assumptions that do not survive the experience of the poem: (1) that stone and heart are separate and opposed entities, and (2) that the initiative in this situation rests with the heart. The first assumption is challenged even as it is taking form; for while the argument of the stanza distinguishes between heart and stone, their juxtaposition cannot help but bring to mind the biblical characterization of the heart as hard and stony. The second assumption will be overturned when we realize that Christ's entry into the heart is not conditional on its disposition to receive him, and that, in fact, he is already in residence. That realization, however, is still several stanzas away, and for a time we continue to move within the context of the speaker's complaint:

> Sure there is room within our hearts good store;
> For they can lodge transgressions by the score:
> Thousands of toyes dwell there, yet out of doore
>   They leave thee.
> But that which shews them large, shews them
>   unfit.
> What ever sinne did this pure rock commit,
> Which holds thee now? Who hath indited it
>   Of murder?
>
> (5-12)

These lines apparently confirm and extend the opposition of heart and stone: not only is the latter more hospitable than the former ("out of doore/They leave thee"), but it is the more fitting receptacle. Again, however, the two objects are brought closer together, even as they are distinguished: both are now regarded as sepulchures, one for the body of Christ, the other for the body of sin, and, more significantly, both are drawn into the complex of associations evoked by the charged phrase, "this pure rock":

> for they drank of that spiritual Rock
> that followed them: and that Rock was
> Christ.
>
> (I Corinthians 10:4)

> Behold I lay in Sion a chief corner
> stone, elect, precious: and he that
> believeth on him shall not be confounded.
>
> (I Peter 2:6)

In the context of these allusions (and they are hardly recondite), the stanza receives a double reading. The rock of line 10 is simultaneously the stone that holds Christ's body and Christ himself, the sinless rock on which his church (another rock) and all its members ultimately rest. As in "**Church Monuments**," the components of the poem's scene are beginning to collapse into one another and, as they do, the sense made by the syntax becomes problematical. Literally, "Which holds thee now" is a relative clause, but in the multiple perspectives now available to the reader, it becomes a question. Which sepulchre holds thee now, now that supporter and supported, container and contained, have become one? "Oh blessed body! Whither art thou thrown?"

The answer to these questions is given in the penultimate stanza:

> And as of old the Law by heav'nly art
> Was writ in stone; so thou, which also art
> The letter of the word, find'st no fit heart
>   To hold thee.
>   (17-20)

Every reader will recognize this as a near paraphrase of II Corinthians 3:2-3: "Ye are our epistle written in our hearts . . . not with ink, but with the Spirit of the living God; not in tables of stone, but in fleshly tables of the heart." Once more, however, the allusion works against the literal sense of the argument, undermining its urgency; for while in the surface rhetoric the problem remains the finding of a fit heart, II Corinthians tells us that the heart has been made fit by the very person who occupies it. That is to say, "this pure rock" has already made pure the rock which holds it *now*, not the actual stone sepulchre, which, after all, is empty—"And they entered in, and found not the body"—but the sepulchre of our once stony hearts, softened so by the Word inscribed upon them that they are able to produce laments and self-accusing poems.

Reading "**Sepulchre**," then, is like the experience of reading the Scriptures—"This verse marks that, and both do make a motion/Unto a third, that ten leaves off doth lie"—and with each expansive motion, the lines of demarcation with which we began seem less and less real. The answer to the question "O Blessed bodie! Whither art thou thrown?" is finally discovered to be "everywhere" (now made one place), but especially in the inhospitable heart which by virtue of its occupation has become what it is so often termed in another galaxy of biblical allusions—the temple of God. The solution of the problem that was the poem's occasion ("No lodging for thee?") coincides with the dissolution of its phenomenal distinctions, and both solution and dissolution are confirmed in the final stanza:

> Yet do we still persist as we began,
> And so should perish, but that nothing can,
> Though it be cold, hard, foul, from loving man
>   Withhold thee.
>   (21-24)

In these lines the poem's two arguments finally converge, one asserting plainly what the other has all the while been suggesting: the active force in this situation, as in every other, is not the heart but Christ. Paradoxically, this plain point is underlined by the ambiguity of the concluding line

and one-half. Is it that nothing (either stone or heart or stony heart) cold, hard, and foul can keep Christ from loving (adjective) man? or that nothing cold, hard, and foul can keep Christ from loving (participle) man? The pressure to resolve the ambiguity is minimal, because the distinctions that would make one reading better than the other—between loved and loving man, between the heart as agent and Christ as agent, between letting in and forcing entry—are no longer operative. In a world where Christ occupies every position and initiates every action, ambiguity—of place, of person, of agency—is the true literalism. His word is all. (pp. 156-73)

> *Stanley E. Fish, "Letting Go: The Dialectic of the Self in Herbert's Poetry," in his* Self-Consuming Artifacts: The Experience of Seventeenth-Century Literature, *University of California Press, 1972, pp. 156-223.*

W. H. Auden (essay date 1973)

[*Often considered the poetic successor of W. B. Yeats and T. S. Eliot, Auden is also highly regarded for his literary criticism. He was strongly influenced by the ideas of Karl Marx and Sigmund Freud, and as a committed follower of Christianity, he considered it necessary to view art in the context of moral and theological absolutes. Thus, he regarded art as a "secondary world" which should serve a definite purpose within the "primary world" of human history. This purpose is the creation of aesthetic beauty and moral order, qualities that exist only in imperfect form in the primary world but are intrinsic to the secondary world of art. Consequently, it is both morally and aesthetically wrong for an artist to employ evil and suffering as subject matter. While he has been criticized for significant inconsistencies in his thought throughout his career, Auden is generally regarded as a perceptive critic. In the following essay, he provides an overview of Herbert's life and artistic stature, arguing that "of all the so-called 'metaphysical' poets he has the subtlest ear."*]

Reading a poet whose work I admire, it is only very seldom that I find myself wishing: 'Oh, how I would like to have been an intimate friend of his!' There are some, like Byron, whom I would like to have met once, but most, I feel, would either, like Dante and Goethe, have been too intimidating, or, like Wordsworth, too disagreeable. The two English poets, neither of them, perhaps, major poets, whom I would most like to have known well are William Barnes and George Herbert.

Even if Isaak Walton had never written his life, I think that any reader of his poetry will conclude that George Herbert must have been an exceptionally good man, and exceptionally nice as well.

He was born in Montgomery Castle on 3 April 1593, the fifth son of Sir Richard Herbert and Lady Magdalen Herbert, to whom Donne dedicated his elegy 'Autumnal Beauty', and his uncle was Lord Herbert of Cherbury. By birth, that is to say, he enjoyed a secure social position. In addition Nature had endowed him with the gifts of intelligence and personal charm. Educated at Westminster School and Trinity College, Cambridge, he became a Fellow of the latter in 1616, and was appointed Public Orator to the University in 1620. He was not only an excellent Greek and Latin scholar, but also fluent in Italian, Spanish and French, and an accomplished amateur musician who played the lute and composed songs.

For a young man of his breeding and talents one would have prophesied a great future in the world. He soon attracted the attention of two powerful and influential figures, the Duke of Richmond and the Marquess of Hamilton and, when they met, King James I took great fancy to him.

His own ambition was as great as his opportunities. He seems to have dreamed of one day becoming a Secretary of State and this led him somewhat to neglect his duties as Public Orator in order to attend the Court. The Academic Life, evidently, was not altogether to his taste. Walton tells us:

> . . . he had often designed to leave the university, and decline all study, which he thought did impair his health; for he had a body apt to a consumption, and to fevers, and other infirmities, which he judged were increased by his studies . . . But his mother would by no means allow him to leave the university or to travel; and though he inclined very much to both, yet he would by no means satisfy his own desires at so dear a rate as to prove an undutiful son to so affectionate a mother.

This is confirmed in the poem **'Affliction'**.

> Whereas my birth and spirit rather took
>   The way that takes the town;
> Thou didst betray me to a lingring book,
>   And wrap me in a gown.
> I was entangled in the world of strife,
> Before I had the power to change my life.
> Yet, for I threatned oft the siege to raise,
>   Not simpring all mine age,
> Thou often didst with Academick praise
>   Melt and dissolve my rage.
> I took thy sweetned pill, till I came where
> I could not go away, nor persevere.

Though he writes in another poem, **'The Pearl'**:

> I know the wayes of Pleasure, the sweet strains,
> The lullings and the relishes of it;
> The propositions of hot bloud and brains;

one does not get the impression from his work that the temptations of the flesh were a serious spiritual menace to him, as they were to Donne. Nor did he suffer from religious doubts: in the seventeenth century very few people did. His struggle was with worldliness, the desire to move in high circles, to enjoy fame and power, and to such temptations he might very well have succumbed, had not his two aristocratic patrons and then, in 1625, King James, all died, thus dashing his hopes of immediate preferment.

For the first time he began to consider seriously the possibility of taking Holy Orders, a course which his mother had always prayed for. Most of his friends disagreed, thinking the priesthood too mean an employment, too

much below his birth and natural abilities. To one such counsellor, he replied:

> It hath been formerly adjudged that the domestic servants of the King of heaven should be of the noblest families on earth; and though the iniquity of the late times have made clergymen meanly valued, and the sacred name of priest contemptible, yet I will labour to make it honorable by consecrating all my learning, and all my poor abilities, to advance the glory of that God that gave them.

These words show that Herbert was under no illusion as to the sacrifice he would have to make, and to come to a definite decision was clearly a struggle, for he was not ordained a priest until 1630 when he was made Rector of Bemerton, a tiny rural parish on Salisbury Plain. In the previous year he had married Jane Danvers after a courtship of only three days, and the marriage turned out to be a very happy one. In 1633 he died of consumption at the age of only forty.

Since none of his poems were published during his lifetime, we cannot say for certain when any of them were written, but one suspects that it was from the two and a half years of indecision that many of them, particularly those which deal with temptations and feelings of rebellion, must date.

Since all of Herbert's poems are concerned with the religious life, they cannot be judged by aesthetic standards alone. His poetry is the counterpart of Jeremy Taylor's prose: together they are the finest expressions we have of Anglican piety at its best. Donne, though an Anglican, is, both in his poems and his sermons, much too much of a *prima donna* to be typical.

Comparing the Anglican Church with the Roman Catholic Church on the one hand and the Calvinist on the other, Herbert writes:

> A fine aspect in fit aray,
> Neither too mean, nor yet too gay,
>   Shows who is best.
>
> Outlandish looks may not compare:
> For all they either painted are,
>   Or else undrest.
>
> She on the hills, which wantonly
> Allureth all in hope to be
>   By her preferr'd,
>
> Hath kiss'd so long her painted shrines,
> That ev'n her face by kissing shines,
>   For her reward.
>
> She in the valley is so shie
> Of dressing, that her hair doth lie
>   About her eares:
>
> While she avoids her neighbours pride,
> She wholly goes on th' other side,
>   And nothing wears.

Herbert, it will be noticed, says nothing about differences in theological dogma. The Anglican Church has always avoided strict dogmatic definitions. The Thirty-Nine Articles, for example, can be interpreted either in a Calvinist or a non-Calvinist sense, and her Office of Holy Communion can be accepted both by Zwinglians who regard it as a service of Commemoration only, and by those who believe in the Real Presence. Herbert is concerned with liturgical manners and styles of piety. In his day, Catholic piety was typically baroque, both in architecture and in poets like Crashaw. This was too unrestrained for his taste. On the other hand, he found the style of worship practised by the Reformed Churches too severe, too 'inward'. He would have agreed with Launcelot Andrewes who said: 'If we worship God with our hearts only and not also with our hats, something is lacking.' The Reformers, for instance, disapproved of all religious images, but Herbert thought that, on occasions, a stained-glass window could be of more spiritual help than a sermon.

> Doctrine and life, colours and light, in one
> When they combine and mingle, bring
> A strong regard and aw; but speech alone
> 　　Doth vanish like a flaring thing,
> 　　And in the eare, not conscience ring.

Walton tells us that he took enormous pains to explain to his parishioners, most of whom were probably illiterate, the significance of every ritual act in the liturgy, and to instruct them in the meaning of the Church Calendar. He was not a mystic like Vaughan: few Anglicans have been. One might almost say that Anglican piety at its best, as represented by Herbert, is the piety of a gentleman, which means, of course, that at its second best it becomes merely genteel.

As a Christian, he realized that his own style of poetry had its spiritual dangers:

> . . . Is there in truth no beautie?
> Is all good structure in a winding stair?

But as a poet he knew that he must be true to his sensibility, that all he could do was to wash his sweet phrases and lovely metaphors with his tears and bring them

> to church well drest and clad:
> My God must have my best, even all I had.

He is capable of writing lines of a Dante-esque directness. For example:

> Man stole the fruit, but I must climb the tree,
> The Tree of Life to all but only Me.

But as a rule he is more ingenious, though never, I think, obscure.

> 　　Each thing is fully of dutie:
> Waters united are our navigation;
> 　　Distinguished, our habitation;
> 　　Below, our drink; above, our meat;
> Both are our cleanlinesse. Hath one such beau-
> 　tie?
> 　　Then how are all things neat?

He is capable of clever antitheses which remind one of Pope, as when, speaking of a woman's love of pearls for which some diver has risked his life, he says:

> 　　Who with excessive pride
> Her own destruction and his danger wears.

And in a most remarkable sonnet, 'Prayer', he seems to foreshadow Mallarmé.

> Church-bels beyond the starres heard, the souls
> 　bloud,
> 　The land of spices; something understood.

Wit he had in abundance. Take, for example, 'The Church-Porch'. Its subject matter is a series of moral maxims about social behaviour. One expects to be utterly bored but, thanks to Herbert's wit, one is entertained. Thus, he takes the commonplace maxim, 'Don't monopolize the conversation', and turns it into:

> If thou be-Master-gunner, spend not all
> That thou canst speak, at once; but husband it,
> And give men turns of speech: do not forestall
> By lavishnesse thine own, and others wit,
> 　　As if thou mad'st thy will. A civil guest
> 　　Will no more talk all, then eat all the feast.

A good example of his technical skill is the poem 'Denial'. He was, as we know, a skilled musician, and I am sure he got the idea for the structure of this poem from his musical experience of discords and resolving them. The first five stanzas consist of a quatrain, rhymed abab, followed by a line which comes as a shock because it does not rhyme:

> O that thou shouldst give dust a tongue
> 　　　　To crie to thee,
> And then not heare it crying! all day long
> 　　My heart was in my knee,
> 　　But no hearing.

But in the final stanza the discord is resolved with a rhyme.

> O cheer and tune my heartlesse breast,
> 　　Deferre no time;
> That so thy favours granting my request,
> 　　They and my minde may chime,
> 　　And mend my ryme.

This poem and many others also show Herbert's gift for securing musical effects by varying the length of the lines in a stanza. Of all the so-called 'metaphysical' poets he has the subtlest ear. As George Macdonald said of him:

> The music of a poem is its meaning in sound as distinguished from word . . . The sound of a verse is the harbinger of the truth contained in it . . . Herein Herbert excels. It will be found impossible to separate the music of his words from the music of the thought which takes shape in their sound.

And this was Coleridge's estimate:

> George Herbert is a true poet, but a poet *sui generis,* the merits of whose poems will never be felt without a sympathy with the mind and character of the man.

My own sympathy is unbounded. (pp. 7-13)

> *W. H. Auden, in an introduction to* George Herbert, *edited by W. H. Auden, Penguin Books, 1973, pp. 7-13.*

Helen Vendler (essay date 1975)

[*In the following excerpt, Vendler analyzes allegorical and emblematic elements in Herbert's lyrics, noting that he employs them "not [as] the fixed result of inquiry, but rather the fluid means to discovery."*]

Many of Herbert's lyrics use emblematic and allegorical materials, and these poems, considered together, define one aspect of his attachment to traditional materials, on the one hand, and one the other, his inventive departures from those traditions. I see no useful reason, in speaking of Herbert, not to use the two adjectives emblematic and allegorical almost interchangeably, since by his time the impetus to write long narrative allegories was on the wane, and the allegorical method, learned from those works, had become detachable from narrative proper. Rosemond Tuve connected allegory to emblem in *Allegorical Imagery*:

> That [mediaeval Catholic devotional figures] were fully comprehended [in the seventeenth century] is one observation to be made, and that they were deemed worthy of keeping and transmitting is another . . . It may be that we should recognize certain reasonable affinities responsible for the likenesses, drop our preoccupation with chronology and the baroque tensions, and observe how the methods and the subjects of religious allegory—and the traces left by exegetical theory pushing figures beyond didacticism to mystical truth—produce *at any time* imagery with the qualities we had thought were those of the seventeenth century. The phenomenon may be literary instead of psychological.

Among Herbert's lyrics are "allegorical" poems of a strict sort (for example, **"The British Church"** and **"Humilitie"**), some containing narrative material, some not; there are as well poems in which a subject (usually abstract, such as Love or Sin or Hope) is presented "allegorically," that is, engaged in certain actions which define its character; in other poems Herbert uses visual material statically presented in emblematic form (a man in agony, a scale), which is then "read" or "interpreted" allegorically; he also takes pleasure in finding hidden "meanings" in common words or initials, or even in his own poems (**"Coloss. 3.3"**); and finally, he retells spiritual experience as parable (**"Love unknown"** and **"Redemption"**). In each of these cases, the "fiction" of the poem points beyond its own scope, and such a form, whether we call it "allegorical" or not, is clearly rich in possibilities for the poetic generalization of experience. Yet the more we read Herbert's allegorical or emblematic poems, the more we realize how elusively he uses the form, how willing he is to embrace it or drop it at will (especially in the later poems), and how inventively he modifies it in the direction of personal inner experience.

The most famous example of Herbert's verse allegory is **"Love (III),"** the beautiful concluding poem of *The Temple*:

> Love bade me welcome: yet my soul drew back,
> Guiltie of dust and sinne.
> But quick-ey'd Love, observing me grow slack
> From my first entrance in,

> Drew nearer to me, sweetly questioning,
> If I lack'd anything.

> A guest, I answer'd, worthy to be here:
> Love said, You shall be he.
> I the unkind, ungratefull? Ah my deare,
> I cannot look on thee.
> Love took my hand, and smiling did reply,
> Who made the eyes but I?

> Truth Lord, but I have marr'd them: let my shame
> Go where it doth deserve.
> And know you not, sayes Love, who bore the blame?
> My deare, then I will serve.
> You must sit down, sayes Love, and taste my meat:
> So I did sit and eat.

These are two "stories" here. In the first, a "secular" story, a guest arrives at a feast but feels himself unworthy to sup with his host because he is dusty from the road. Pressed to enter, he remains reluctant, then finally consents on condition that he be allowed to serve at table rather than sitting and being served. His host gently refuses this condition, and vanquished by courtesy, the unworthy guest sits and eats. This story sounds rather like one of Jesus' parables, and we would expect it to have some kind of preface or postlude, like "Who is my neighbor?" or "I am the living Bread." But in Herbert's poem we are given neither. Instead, mixed with the secular story is another story in process. In this story, the soul arrives at heaven and is greeted by its Lord; the soul, guilty of sin, draws back in shame. Pressed to enter, he avows his unkindness and ungratefulness, saying he cannot look on his God and live. God reminds him that he made those eyes; the soul retorts that what God made he has marred. His Lord responds that he has borne the blame for that sin. The soul, still overcome with shame, says that in heaven he will take a subservient place. God refuses, and insists that the soul participate fully in the pleasures of heaven. The soul acquiesces and joins his Lord.

We might think that by conflating these two stories, we could arrive at Herbert's poem. But even that is not true. A parabolic poet would have told the first story, and let us guess the application; an emblematic poet would have told the first story, and added the second by way of a gloss to his text. But Herbert, neither parabolic nor allegorical in any "pure" way, has mixed text and gloss, and has added as well a third and perhaps even a fourth element. The third element, part neither of the host-guest-dust story nor of the Lord-soul-sin story, appears in scattered words throughout the poem: "*Love* bade me welcome," "*quick-eyed Love*," "*sweetly* questioning," "Ah *my deare*," "*smiling* did reply," "*my deare*." Something in these words is extrinsic both to a story of Lord-soul-sin and to a story of host-guest-dust. The other incongruous ingredient, which may be thought of as a fourth element, is the rhetoric of debate, of gentle irony, and of competition pervading the poem, making it one of those contests of "gentilesse" typical of medieval literature. Though this "contest in courtesy" may in some sense seem to belong to the host-guest story, normally the parabolic form would exclude such gentle frivolity on God's part, since in a gospel parable God may be a neutral, a stern, or a generous figure, but never a witty one. Therefore, when we read the poem **"Love,"** we slide, so to speak, from genre to genre, from love poem to allegory to homily to *débat*. Herbert is cavalier with his allegory: no writer who wanted to maintain an illusion of allegory would feel free to "give away" his "sentence" as Herbert does in "guiltie of dust and *sinne*." The two attributes, dust and sin, would be kept on two different planes, and the one (dust) would "stand for" the other (sin). In Herbert's consciousness, however, they are simultaneous and coterminous, so that we can scarcely decide where the locus of "reality" lies in the poem.

Even in a far more sustained "parable," **"Redemption,"** Herbert immediately gives his "meaning" away (italics mine):

> Having been tenant long to a rich Lord,
> 　Not thriving, I resolved to be bold,
> 　And make a suit unto him, to afford
> A new small-rented lease, and cancell th'old.
> 　In *heaven* at his manour I him sought.

There was no need to let vehicle give way to tenor in this fashion unless Herbert wanted that effect: the title itself gives the key to the parable, and we scarcely need another clue to the identity of the "rich Lord," especially since we are to see him dying at the end. We can only conclude that Herbert meant what he said in **"Jordan (I)"** when he criticized poets whom one reads "catching the sense at two removes." Mystification is no part of Herbert's allegories; like many other allegories, they exist to be deciphered easily, but they are not concerned to keep up a consistent fictional existence. Even structural figures are, as soon as established, abolished. In the **"Superliminare,"** for which the central image is the instrument used for sprinkling holy water, Herbert addresses his reader:

> Thou, whom the former precepts have
> Sprinkled and taught, how to behave
> Thy self in church; approach, and taste
> The churches mysticall repast.

"Sprinkled and taught" is like "dust and sinne" in joining two orders of significance, and a shadowy version of the same intermingling appears in the invitation to "taste" a "mysticall" repast. It begins to be idle to speak of the literal level and the figurative level, since they coexist so visibly on the same plane in Herbert.

In fact, Herbert is often plaintively explicit in elucidating his figures, not once but often. In **"The Altar,"** he considerately explains his metaphor to God:

> A broken Altar, Lord, thy servant reares,
> Made of a heart, and cemented with teares:
> 　Whose parts are as thy hand did frame;
> 　No workmans tool hath touch'd the same.
> 　　A Heart alone
> 　　Is such a stone,
> 　　As nothing but
> 　　Thy pow'r doth cut.
> 　　Wherefore each part
> 　　Of my hard heart
> 　　Meets in this frame
> 　　To praise thy Name:

> That, if I chance to hold my peace,
> These stones to praise thee may not cease.
> O let thy blessed Sacrifice be mine,
> And sanctifie this Altar to be thine.

Though this is not, I think, one of Herbert's better poems, it is immediately recognizable as his by its peculiar mixture of apparent naiveté with genuine obscurity. The "allegory" seems too simple at first glance, as Herbert takes such pains to elucidate it: the altar is a heart, the cement is tears, God is the stonemason, the altar is a place for sacrifice. But as soon as we begin to examine the terms in their interrelations, mysteries arise. A hard heart is one not likely to spend its time praising God; neither is a hard heart one normally associated with tears. We decide that perhaps the heart *used* to be hard: after all, it is now "broken," presumably by God's "cutting," and God has used the tools of suffering, provoking tears, to re-establish the heart, not in its natural heart-shape, but in the shape of an altar. The heart, we then conclude, has been converted. But Herbert tells us in a paradoxical quatrain that even though it is in pieces, his heart is *still* hard (italics mine):

> Wherefore each part
> Of my *hard* heart
> Meets in this frame,
> To praise thy Name.

The praise seems to be almost involuntary. Has Herbert, God's "servant," reared this altar, or has God forcibly rearranged the pieces of Herbert's heart into a shape which by itself alone praises its creator? The most peculiar dissociation of self takes place in the distinction between "I" and "my heart" ("These stones"), as if to say, "If I am silent, at least these stones will praise thee." (In "Sailing to Byzantium," Yeats makes a similar dissociation: "Consume *my heart* away . . . / and gather *me* / Into the artifice of eternity.") The tears in Herbert's poem, then, seem to be tears of suffering, not tears of contrition, since he is still capable of holding his peace and not praising God. But is it truly possible to have one's heart converted into an altar by God and still remain hostile to him? There is one final step, apparently, which God, having constructed the altar out of the recalcitrant heart, has yet to take: he has to sacrifice something (and that something will be himself) on the altar, put it to use. For this he needs a priest, to repeat on the altar his own original sacrifice in offering himself on the Cross. Only by becoming that priest will Herbert "activate" the hard heart, make it functional, let it do more than utter praises by its mere shape. So Herbert prays that God's sacrifice may be his, and that the altar may finally be sanctified to God's use. The unification of the previously "split" personality into the harmonious image of the priest at the altar provides appropriate closure for the poem.

Nevertheless, something is wrong with this schema. No "hard heart" spoke the first two lines of this poem, the most touching of the whole (perhaps the only touching ones in the poem):

> A broken Altar, Lord, thy servant reares,
> Made of a heart, and cemented with teares.

No one can read these lines without being reminded of the Psalmist (51:17): "A broken and a contrite heart, O God, thou wilt not despise." The conceits, and even some of the phrases, of the poem were determined by Herbert's Biblical sources (Exod. 20:25 and Luke 19:40), and though normally Herbert took sparks from Scripture and fanned them into a flame rather more idiosyncratic than traditional, here the Biblical references acted to constrict rather than to stimulate poetry. From a genuine metaphorical insight (God's quarrying the heart by suffering to make an instrument of his praise) and from an affecting echo of the Psalms, Herbert passes into elaborations that confuse his original intent. A true allegorist would have attached himself more closely to his emblem and allowed himself fewer distractions. Herbert's essential indifference to the strict maintenance of emblematic or allegorical fictions is once again manifest even in so brief a poem. The self is far more genuinely unified in the opening lines than it is by the closing conceit of sacrifice; no coherent personal development can be conjectured to underlie the progress of the poem. Like **"Antiphon (II),"** though for different reasons, **"The Altar"** is a piece of "false wit."

Quite different is the case of **"Hope,"** a poem often anthologized but rarely commented on except by Herbert's editors. It is almost disarmingly simple, consisting of three bare exchanges and one brief comment:

> I gave to Hope a watch of mine: but he
>   An anchor gave to me.
> Then an old prayer-book I did present:
>   And he an optick sent.
> With that I gave a viall full of tears:
>   But he a few green eares.
> Ah Loyterer! I'le no more, no more I'le bring:
>   I did expect a ring.

Herbert's editors have been anxious to define the emblematic meaning of his nouns. Canon Hutchinson is scrupulous on the subject: "The *watch* given to Hope suggests the giver's notion that the time for fulfilment of hopes is nearly due, but the *anchor*, given in return, shows that the soul will need to hold on for some time yet; the *old prayer-book* tells of prayers long used, but the *optick*, or telescope, shows that their fulfilment can only be described afar off; *tears* receive in return only *a few green eares*, which will need time to ripen for harvest; and then the donor's patience gives out." While all these significances are plausible, and the anchor has scriptural authority as well, Herbert takes no care to ensure their coherence (*Q*: "What is it that owns an anchor, a telescope, and ears of corn?" *A*: "Hope") nor to attach explanatory verses. Instead, the poem depends on the oddness of the story it tells.

The poet gives a love-token, the watch—and receives in return, absurdly, something much too large to be given house-room, an anchor. He tries once more, again with a treasured private possession and plausible gift; this time he gets back an impersonal scientific instrument, also too large to be conceived of as a trinket. Finally, he sends the most intimate and smallest gift, a vial of tears (but analogous to a vial of perfume or unguent); he receives back the green ears, uncooked and inedible as well as impersonal (a strange variety of bouquet). Until the last couplet, Hope has been discussed in his presumed absence; now, by a sudden vocative, we are made aware that he has been present all the time. We expect a reproof to this ungentle giver

of preposterous gifts, but we hear instead a bantering reproach: not "Why do you give me such ridiculous and unsuitable tokens?" but "Why do you so delay in giving me what I have been wanting, a ring?" The "marriage" emblem is not consistent with the earlier exchanges (a girl, expecting a ring, would be unlikely to send love-tokens of a watch, an old prayer-book, and a vial full of tears); only the literal meaning has coherence (I expected commitment, and all I kept receiving was postponement). Even when the speaker rebels at the end of the poem, after having navely continued to send gifts in the confidence that Hope would finally yield the expected ring, he "turns" in familiar raillery (with a lilting prosody and mock-serious repetition), assuring us that the rupture with the gently-named "Loyterer" is more apparent than real. Tomorrow he will be presenting yet one more token, and hoping again that the Loiterer will speed his betrothal ("I'll no more, no more I'll bring" is hardly a serious vow). The rueful self-knowledge in the close takes the poem out of the realm of the emblematic and puts it into the realm of introspective lyric; though emblemata remain its forms, they are not its substance.

The most heavy-handed of Herbert's allegorical poems are surely **"The British Church"** and **"Humilitie"**. Three female figures form the emblematic subject of **"The British Church"**; they represent the Church of England, the Church of Rome, and the Church of Geneva, and the poem exists to praise, by contrast with the other churches, the Church of England. There is scarcely a redeeming line in the entire poem, except for the Herbertian version of the golden mean:

> A fine aspect in fit array,
> Neither too mean, not yet too gay,
>   Shows who is best.

The air of gallantry in the metrical verve and alliteration of this generalization shows that the subject of the mean is an attractive one, as we might expect, to Herbert: it suits well with his native delight in neatness and order. So we may conclude that the subject of the poem is itself suitable to Herbert, since his affection for the British Church, as the entire *Temple* shows, was deep, confident, and exclusive. What then could have played him so false in this poem? The poem, in its description of the two rejected damsels, is both simplistic and grotesque—and not with an imitative grotesquerie, but with simple ineptness:

> She on the hills, which wantonly
> Allureth all in hope to be
>   By her preferred,
> Hath kissed so long her painted shrines,
> That ev'n her face by kissing shines,
>   For her reward.
>
> She in the valley is so shy
> Of dressing, that her hair doth lie
>   About her ears:
> While she avoids her neighbour's pride,
> She wholly goes on th'other side,
>   And nothing wears.

The British Church by contrast is said to have "perfect lineaments and hue / Both sweet and bright," but this is not in itself a compelling description. What is wrong with these allegorical figures, poetically speaking? Several answers might be hazarded, all of them with some claim to truth. Herbert perhaps does not understand fully here the difference between visual and verbal emblems. Although visual figures are often identified iconographically by one or two significant features (wanton stance, shiny face=Rome; naked body, hair uncoiffed=Geneva), we expect more from personages suggesting powerful abstractions—at least since Spenser we do. The simple conventional emblem (anchor=Hope) has pure iconographical significance and stands in a closed relation with its signification. In the visual arts, personifications are often similarly rendered in minimal ways, but in the verbal arts they are normally (if successful) far more vividly presented, either by decorative ornament or by developed narrative function. These poor figures are relatively unadorned and are given nothing much to do; they are almost painfully underdeveloped, considering the powerful entities they represent. No true verbal allegorist would let pass such skimpy figures; he would be more interested in their adequate representation. Herbert is concerned here with a schematic opposition after the manner of the emblem books rather than with a full representation in the Spenserian manner.

A second conjecture about the weakness of the poem may come closer to the truth. Herbert's kind of poetry was not particularly well suited to describing damsels: he did not have the relish in delineating female figures, whether good or bad, that is such a characteristic feature in Spenser. It appears that Herbert never really "saw" his allegorical personages in any sense, nor felt compelled to make his readers perceive them first as visual objects and only later as emblems. In fact, Herbert's poetry lacks any well-developed descriptive sense of the outside world. All his descriptive powers seem to have been turned inward and focused on the fluctuations of the soul.

A third speculation about this poetic lapse requires reconsidering the subject of the poem: three rival churches. While it is true that Herbert loved the British Church, he loved it, as *The Temple* shows, in its rituals, its calendar, its sacramental consolations, and its Scripture. He shows no particular interest in it as a corporate body. A solitary soul himself, he rose, in a way we still find humanly moving, to the communal duties of the priesthood; but nothing in *The Country Parson* betrays a true congeniality to the pastoral office in its social and corporate aspects. Herbert found in the Church a daily means of mediation between himself and his God, but he shrank from ecclesiastical rivalries and theological controversies. So he could not, apparently, vivify the corporate churches, rivalrously different, in a series of emblems: the damsels were not real enough to him to enliven the churches, and the churches were not real enough to enliven the damsels.

"Humilitie" is another explicitly "allegorical" poem, and like **"The British Church,"** it is so schematic and algebraic in its story (in which four virtues receive from four submissive beasts tokens representing the beasts' vices) that its predictable end (in which all the virtues except Humility fall to wrangling over the token of Pride, a peacock's plume), though scarcely continuing the virtuousness of

the virtues, at least shows that pride can undo them all, and only humility is a final safeguard. One thing that distinguishes this poem is the Aesopian irony that enlivens the action:

> At length the Crow bringing the Peacocks
>   plume,
> (For he would not) as they beheld the grace
> Of that brave gift, each one began to fume,
> And challenge it as proper to his place,
> Till they fell out: which when the beasts espied,
>   They leapt upon the throne.

The other, more Herbertian aspect is the self-abnegating presence of Humility:

> Humilitie, who held the plume, at this
> Did weep so fast, that the tears trickling down
> Spoil'd all the train: then saying *Here it is*
> *For which ye wrangle*, made them turn their
>   frown
>   Against the beasts.

But the simple conduct of the foreordained narrative, with a beginning, middle, and end, has a complacency of recounting foreign to Herbert's temperament (the same problem is visible in a comparable poem, **"The World"**). Ordinary narrative was usually not a suitable medium for Herbert simply because of its internal, ongoing placidity; he liked doubling-back, self-correction, revision, repentance, enlightenment, complication. If he were to use emblems, they had to be emblems capable of these eddies of avowal and recognition, repudiation and enlargement, and could not be such external and static representations as those of the three churches, nor such simple fabular constructions as those in **"Humilitie."**

Two more successful emblem-poems which may at first seem to occupy a middle ground between the memorable and the unimpressive, and which almost demand comparison with each other, are **"Love-joy"** and Jesu. Devotees of Herbert will remember these poems because they are so indubitably his, but they are not likely to make their way into anthologies as among his greater triumphs. In them, Herbert resorts to a congenial form of emblem—the verbal riddle or puzzle ("Ana- ${MARY \atop ARMY}$ -gram" and **"Coloss. 3.3"** are other instances of the type in Herbert). There are other similarities: in both **"Love-joy"** and **"Jesu,"** one word means two things; a "secular" identity for Jesus is proposed; and the name of Jesus is shown to hide another significance. In each, nature and divinity coincide; in each, it is shown that by linguistic manipulation (pronouncing sounds in one case, interpreting initials in the other) the speaker may come to wisdom. It becomes a challenge, given these correspondences, to attempt to discriminate between the two so-comparable uses of written emblems.

"Jesu"

> Jesu is in my heart, his sacred name
> Is deeply carved there: but th'other week
> A great affliction broke the little frame,
> Ev'n all to pieces: which I went to seek:
> And first I found the corner, where was *J*,
> After, where *E S*, and next where *U* was graved.
> When I had got these parcels, instantly
> I sat me down to spell them, and perceived

That to my broken heart he was *I ease you,*
And to my whole is JESU.

"Love-joy"

As on a window late I cast mine eye,
I saw a vine drop grapes with J and C
Anneal'd on every bunch. One standing by
Ask'd what it meant. I, who am never loth
To spend my judgment, said, It seem'd to me
To be the bodie and the letters both
Of *Joy* and *Charitie.* Sir, you have not miss'd,
The man reply'd; It figures JESUS CHRIST.

It is hard to say which is the more bizarre of the situations imagined in these two poems. Not that each does not begin calmly enough: a broken heart is conventional material, and looking at a stained-glass window is a rational starting-point for a meditation of some sort. It is what happens after the tranquil openings that strikes us as so peculiar to Herbert. In **"Love-joy"** he inscribes initials on things that are normally not written on (grapes); and in the other instance, though a name carved on a heart is quite common in poetry, the idea that a broken heart would also have a broken name—rather like a broken tombstone—seems original with Herbert. Although both poems record intellectual discoveries ("I perceived," "It seemed to me"), the manner in which these discoveries are made is strange. **"Love-joy"** is the simpler of the two poems, though Herbert's simplicity is here, as elsewhere, deceptive. The essential intellectual discovery in **"Love-joy"** is that moral virtue is only a mask, or a veil, hiding divine grace, that behind every exercise of joy or charity stands the figure making those virtues possible, the figure of Jesus. There is a faint hint of the Pharisee in the man who is "never loth to spend [his] judgement," and who can declare so confidently that of course wine-giving grapes stand for joy (in private consumption) and charity (in wedding feasts and such). It is, or could be, a purely naturalistic answer, and the speaker is somewhat complacently satisfied to have found two such suitable words to answer the "riddle" of the meaning of *J* and *C* inscribed on grapes. A secular pleasure in emblems is evident. The speaker's "answer" responds to the picture (the "bodie") and to the letters, too: his answer is quick to point out his knowledge that any "solving" of such an emblem has to make sense of both the picture and the inscription. The "man standing by" gives another interpretation of the emblem: he says, "It figures JESUS CHRIST."

Now with two interprctations on the board, so to speak, the poem ought to enunciate the impasse between them with something like, "Sir, you are wrong, the man reply'd." The "one standing by," like those other "friends" in Herbert, is Jesus himself, and he, more than any other, should have the right to correct mortal perception (as indeed he does in other poems). But here he is the courteous host in his own house. "Sir, you have not miss'd," he replies with gentle irony, concession concealing indulgence; and in defining the figure, he defines the religious life, where virtues like joy and charity have meaning only through participation in Jesus' redemptive grace. This may seem an unduly sectarian poem, but it really takes up once again Herbert's unceasing interest in the proper function of symbolism. The speaker here is, in the words of **"The Elixir,"** looking on glass, and on it staying his eye, seeking an explanation within the natural realm for the symbolism he sees ("Joy" and "Charity," though both can have theological meaning, begin as ordinary English words). If the bystander had said, "Sir, you are wrong," he would have been opposing the divine to the natural, and thus would have opened a chasm between them. By saying, "Sir, you have not miss'd," he implies that continuity by which one can espy heaven through the glass. The natural object (grapes), its pictorial representation in art (the window), its "moral" meaning (Joy and Charity), and its divine import (Jesus Christ) inhabit a continuum. Even if we insist on the theological interpretation of the two abstract nouns (they form the first two nouns in St. Paul's list of the fruits of the Spirit in Galatians 5:6), they appear as "fruits" of the holy life rather than as its source when so named. Their final meaning, Herbert would still have us understand, resides in their divine origin in Jesus Christ.

So what makes this poem "untrivial" is not the simple *presence* of a traditional Christian emblem, as Tuve seems to suggest. It is untrivial by its correction of a mistaken point of view about emblems, and by its irony directed at the complacent interpreter. It is poetic not by its employment of a Christian symbol, nor even by its enunciation of an intellectual discovery, but rather by its chastised selfhood and its perfect final alignment of its four orders of being—natural, aesthetic, moral, and divine.

A portion of the charm of **"Love-joy"** comes from its self-revelation; in **"Jesu,"** the self-revelation is more prolonged, and therefore even more charming. The voice that artlessly narrates the story of his broken heart reminds us, in its "I went to seek," of those other talkative speakers in **"Redemption"** and **"Love unknown."** "Th'other week," this voice tells us plaintively, "A great affliction broke the little frame, / Ev'n all to pieces." This faintly querulous worrying care for his fragile heart reveals the speaker as no hero, but rather as a weak vessel. Stoicism, we think, might be what he needs. Or else a little self-blame, attributing that "great affliction" to some failing of his own (Herbert's characteristic response, more often than not, to affliction). But this is to be a poem about God's tempering the wind to the shorn lamb. The lamb, even in affliction, cooperates proleptically with God's oracular intent by going out to seek the pieces of his broken heart. With exemplary realism, Herbert takes us through the tiny search ("First I found the corner with *J* written on it, next, the piece inscribed *E S*, and last the one with *U*"). What we then expect is that he will rearrange the pieces in the right order and somehow glue them together: the line should read, "When I had got these parcels, instantly / I sat me down to unite them." But this childlike creature, alive to the possibility of sermons in stones, wants to see if there is sense in fragments (a broken heart) as well as in wholeness. The function of a whole heart is to utter praises ("My joy, my life, my crown," "My God and King," "Jesu"—those "private ejaculations" mentioned in the title of the 1633 **Temple**), and to the whole heart Jesus is *Jesu*, the vocative of those ejaculations. What is he to the broken heart? The frail searcher takes his primer and spells out, "I ease you." The vertical upward motion of prayer voiced by the heart in times of wholeness is replaced by the care and solace descending to the broken heart from Jesus. It is a great relief to perceive that one has a right to be comforted. Stoicism, fortitude, heroism are not expected of this shattered soul; he can sit and be consoled. If, however, he had not sat down to spell out the parcels of his broken heart, he would not have perceived the sacred message; the poem is a guide to the perplexed and suggests that brokenness has its own messages, consoling ones, to convey.

But moral advice, however virtuous, does not make a poem, any more than religious symbols do. Even the witty charade (my parts, my whole) does not of itself suffice. It is the winning sweetness of the speaking self, however nave, that enhances the lines into poetry. Even in the suffering of a broken heart, the speaker sets himself staunchly to gather up the pieces, and all his appeal lies in his own adverb, "instantly." Which of us, holding the pieces of our broken heart in our arms, would not sit down to lament our condition? But such is the speaker's confidence in the absolute presence of meaning in all events, that he trustingly sits down not to weep but to spell out the new intelligibility of his state—he rearranges his psyche, and begins a new lesson. His faith is rewarded: the lesson, after all his sturdy and enterprising responses to disaster, is unexpectedly sweet. No exhortation to bear up; no reminders about the value of tears; only kindness—"I ease you." This solace restores the broken heart and enables the poem to end heart-whole, saying "Jesu" again as it did before its "great affliction." The speaker sees, in significant tenses, "That to my broken heart he *was* I ease you, / And to my whole *is* J E S U." These natural motions of the heart, together with the psychological truth of the great relief in abandoning stoicism, combine with the wit in tone and action to make this poem, too, far from trivial. It asserts a fluctuating, but entire, intelligibility in human experience, whether of joy or of crisis. Such small means to such great ends appear in Herbert's most loving uses of emblematic language, and it is no accident that these two successful emblematic poems, together with **"Coloss. 3.3,"** rest on a foundation of the intellectual manipulation of language, and, in the case of **"Love-joy,"** of linguistic signs.

If we look for instances of Herbert's emblematic presentation of visual spectacle, **"The Agonie"** and **"Justice (II)"** come to mind. There are not enough examples of this kind of poetry in Herbert to offer secure generalizations about his practice, but these poems do resemble each other in interesting ways. **"The Agonie"** declares that philosophers, instead of measuring natural things, like seas and fountains, should measure "two vast, spacious things" sounded by few—Sin and Love. The second and third stanzas of the poem give an emblem for each of these vast abstractions. Since no two concepts could seem less alike, we expect a horrifying picture for Sin, and a beautiful picture for Love. For Sin, we might be given a picture approximating the one suggested in **"Sinne (II),"** an earlier poem. There, Herbert says that "we paint the devil foul, yet he / Hath some good in him, all agree" (since he has being); but sin, "flat opposite to th' Almighty" and lacking all being, is more horrible even than the devil:

> If apparitions make us sad,
> By sight of sinne we should grow mad.

> Yet as in sleep we see foul death, and live:
> So devils are our sinnes in perspective.

So, for the emblem for Sin in **"The Agonie,"** we might choose a horned devil. And what for Love? Perhaps the Incarnation, perhaps the Resurrection—in any case, something appropriate to that seraphic word. However, Herbert has advanced considerably in subtlety since the crude approximations of **"Sinne (II)."** For Sin and Love he gives two pictures, one in each stanza, but they are *identical*. Each picture shows Christ shedding blood under torture. One, granted, is the agony in the garden of Mount Olivet; the other is the agony on the cross at Calvary; yet the details are comparable. The beholder can point to either and say, with equal truth, "This is Sin" or "This is Love." As Jesus is made to say of his passion in **"The Sacrifice"**:

> Ah! how they scourge me! yet my tendernesse
> Doubles each lash: and yet their bitternesse
> Windes up my grief to a mysteriousnesse.

The reciprocity of Sin and Love (the paradox of the fortunate fault) winds in Herbert's mind "to a mysteriousnesse" of which these identical emblems are the sign:

> Who would know Sinne, let him repair
> Unto Mount Olivet; there shall he see
> A man so wrung with pains, that all his hair,
>   His skinne, his garments bloudie be.
> Sinne is that presse and vice, which forceth pain
> To hunt his cruell food through ev'ry vein.

> Who knows not Love, let him assay
> And taste that juice, which on the crosse a pike
> Did set again abroach; then let him say
>   If ever he did taste the like.
> Love is that liquour sweet and most divine,
> Which my God feels as bloud; but I, as wine.

It is necessary to recognize that the *visual* portions of the emblems carry the identity: a picture of a man with blood being wrung out of him; a picture of a man with blood being "broached" out of him. The distinctions between the two pictures are made in the mind, not in the pictorial elements. Two distinct meditations are possible when one looks at a picture of Christ's passion: first, how Sin has caused this event; second, how Love has caused this event. Interestingly, only the first of Herbert's "two" emblems follows the emblematic manner, by first presenting the picture, then the explanation—"Sinne is that presse and vice." The second of the two stanzas introduces the "picture" almost casually, between two pauses ("which on the crosse a pike / Did set again abroach"), and the whole intent of the stanza is not to paint a scene, and then draw a moral, but rather to pass immediately beyond the pictorial, beyond even the intellectual definition ("Sin is X"), to the experiential: "Who knows not Love, let him assay / And taste that juice." The motivating moral reason to read an emblem is here given precedence, as it was in the earlier stanza, over the mere pictorial and intellectual pleasure of deciphering emblems; but where the first stanza said, "let him repair / Unto Mount Olivet; there shall he *see*," the second says, "let him assay / And taste . . . / then let him *say*." The involvement in the second emblem is participatory, while the relation to the first was visual (naturally Herbert does not want his bystander to "know" Sin experientially, as he "knows" Love). The second fashion is a more wholehearted way of entering into an emblem and silently corrects the first way, the way of the bystander.

In the second emblem, a double circulatory system is suggested, by which the same "liquour" that flows through the veins of Jesus flows also through the veins of Herbert. Herbert feels from it the elevation and well-being one feels after drinking wine, because being loved confers that same sensation of headiness; but as the "liquour" flows in Jesus, Jesus senses it as his own blood. Is there a common name (instead of the two names *wine* and *blood*) that we can give to this elixir? Herbert answers that in both cases it may properly be called "Love," the word *love* having the convenient property of being both active and passive, since he who loves is said to feel love, and he who is loved is said to experience love. "What do I feel?" asks Jesus, and the answer is "Love" (for man); "What do I feel?" asks Herbert, and the answer is again "Love" (from God). However, though this analysis is logically true, the poem emphasizes not the shared name but the different experience. We do not read, for example:

> What my God feels as blood, but I as wine,
> Is Love, that liquour sweet and most divine.

Because Herbert knows Sin and Love not from God's perspective but from a mortal one, he distinguishes between the divine and the human way of feeling love. The modes of perception differ, but the ontological reality is one. In short, the second emblem in **"The Agonie"** offers far more both for meditation and for participation than the first, which seems almost like a medieval woodcut in its factual exemplifying of every detail. The second emblem, as we would expect from Herbert, embodies a new, more mental and moral aspect of what began as a visual and spatial ("wide and spacious") conceit.

"Justice (II)," like **"The Agonie,"** consists of two emblems—in one sense similar, in another opposed. It draws on imagery representing the Old Law and the New:

> O dreadfull Justice, what a fright and terrour
> Wast thou of old,
> When sinne and errour
> Did show and shape thy looks to me,
> And through their glasse discolour thee!
> He that did but look up, was proud and bold.
>
> The dishes of thy ballance seem'd to gape,
> Like two great pits;
> The beam and scape
> Did like some torturing engine show;
> Thy hand above did burn and glow,
> Danting the stoutest hearts, the proudest wits.
>
> But now that Christs pure vail presents the sight,
> I see no fears:
> Thy hand is white,
> Thy scales like buckets, which attend
> And interchangeably descend,
> Lifting to heaven from this well of tears.
>
> For where before thou still didst call on me,
> Now I still touch
> And harp on thee.

> Gods promises have made thee mine;
> Why should I justice now decline?
> Against me there is none, but for me much.

Once more, through its two emblems, this poem takes up Herbert's concern with epistemology. It presupposes a few axioms: that although God (and his attributes) cannot change, God seems to us to change; and while the "God of justice" of the Old Law seems to become the "God of mercy" in the New Law, since God is unchanging, it is actually our "angle of vision" that makes us see now one aspect, now another. Though the poem employs religious imagery, it is not for that reason any less in touch with what we might call "reality." Since allegory and emblems by their nature generalize, a disagreement (two emblems purporting to represent the same "reality") is unnerving. Which is the "true" picture and which the "false"? Or is there some sense in which these two contradictory emblems, each one bearing the label "Justice," can be reconciled with each other?

The poet has a number of choices in the presentation of his dilemma: the conflicting emblems may be simultaneously present (the most difficult case); the poet may experience first one, then the other; or he may only experience one, but know of the existence of the other. Herbert chooses the second way, less immediate and less problematic than the first, but more convincing than the third. Had he followed the third choice, the poem would have been a poem of the New Law contrasted with the Old (as in **"Decay"**) and would have read, "Of old, Justice was terrifying; men saw it as a frightful balance. But now since Jesus has intervened, we (I) can see Justice as a force lifting us to heaven." Had Herbert taken up the first option, the poem would have been like **"The Temper (I),"** oscillating on "sometimes"—"Sometimes I see Justice as terrifying; sometimes I see it as intercessory." But Herbert avoided both these options and wrote a strange poem of the second choice: "Once I saw Justice thus; now I see it differently." The underlying text is St. Paul's: "For now we see through a glass, darkly; but then face to face." Herbert "rewrites" it to read: "For then I saw through a glass, darkly; but now through a pure veil fearlessly." **"Justice"** seems thus a conversion poem, telling how once Herbert saw Justice misshaped and discolored through the glass of sin and error, but how he now sees it fearlessly through "Christ's pure veil." Hutchinson cites St. Paul (Heb. 10:17-20) who, after invoking God's promise, "And their sins and iniquities will I remember no more," concludes that we may now "enter into the holiest by the blood of Jesus, by a new and living way, which he hath consecrated for us, through the veil, that is to say, his flesh." The passage from the Old Law to the New seems to parallel the individual passage from sin to grace. But though Herbert attributes his dark vision to his own sin and error, he does not count himself the cause of his conversion, or tell of a change of *heart*. He is, perhaps, as full of sin and error as before, but he now chooses to look not on his deserts (who should 'scape whipping?) but rather on God's love. Everything personal has therefore remained the same: Herbert is a sinner, God is just. The true moral import of the poem is that self-regard yields a mistaken perception of reality. When Herbert saw himself at the center of his vision and pondered his own sin and error, the universe (to him, as later to Carlyle) seemed a torture-house. When, however, he ceased looking at his own soul and looked instead at Christ, he saw through Christ another vision of the universe, where, from this well of tears, one could be lifted to heaven. Once again, it is a case of a man looking on a glass (here sin and error) and there staying his eye, or else choosing to look beyond it (here, to the figure of Christ) and then espying the heavens. The process of change from one vision to another is described by Herbert in **"Faith"**:

> That which before was darkned clean
> With bushie groves, pricking the lookers eie,
> Vanisht away, when Faith did change the scene:
> And then appear'd a glorious skie.

The "falsehood" of the first vision in **"Justice"** is shown by a number of locutions: the "looks" of Justice were shown and shaped by a "discolored" glass; the dishes of the balance "seem'd" to gape; the beam and scape "did *show like*" a torturing engine. There is, however, no uncertainty about the present vision. God's hand "is" white, and while a simile appears, its conflation with its tenor (so that one cannot tell whether it is the scales or the buckets which are attending and descending and lifting to heaven) precludes its giving cause for skepticism. By its two emblems, the poem denies the value of a self-centered view of "reality" and chooses rather an upward glance, that very glance forbidden (line 6) by the false humility of self-regard. The final recapitulation of "before" and "now" comes with extraordinary firmness of structure (italics mine):

> For where *before thou still* didst call on *me*
> Now *I still* touch
> And harp on *thee*.
> Gods promises have made *thee mine*;
> Why should *I justice* now decline?
> *Against* me there is *none*, but *for* me *much*.

The perfect reversal of relation exemplified in the first three lines prepares us for the compatibility of Herbert with justice in "thee [Justice] mine" and "I justice," making himself and justice verbal Siamese twins. The temptation with which the poem began—to decline justice—is a plausible response under the Old Law, as we know from the Psalmist: "If thou, Lord, shouldest mark iniquities, O Lord, who shall stand?" (130:3). That response is no longer needed under the New Law, and there is a confident ring to Herbert's "Why should I justice now decline? / Against me there is none, but for me much." Blake would say of this poem, "The eye altering alters all," but Herbert would prefer to say that the medium altering alters all, since vision face-to-face is not to be expected in this world. However, by presenting two versions of a vision-through-a-glass—one self-regarding and the other God-directed—Herbert implies a third state, in which the medium will be dissolved and one will see without mediation. In that state, no names will be needed for attributes like "justice" and "mercy," since those names are only human inventions, each one partial, for aspects of divinity, as Herbert says in **"The Glance"**:

> If thy first glance so powerfull be,
> A mirth but open'd and seal'd up again;

> What wonders shall we feel, when we shall see
> Thy full-ey'd love!

I make so much of the epistemological self-correction in both **"The Agonie"** and **"Justice"** because the correction of the point of view in the latter and the enlargement of the possibilities of emblem-writing in the former seem to be the *raison d'être* of these poems. **"The Agonie"** and **"Justice"** do not exist simply to incarnate Christian symbols in verse. It is true, as Rosemond Tuve remarked with eloquence, that poems employing traditional Biblical, patristic, or liturgical symbols cannot be understood if the reader does not "speak" that language; but to take in the meaning of the building-blocks (to give them a name no nobler than that) is not necessarily to take in the meaning of the poem or Herbert's reason for writing it. Tuve usually stops after explaining the significance of the imagery in Christian terms, but the poems require an additional explanation in personal terms, and an additional scrutiny of poetic (not religious) means.

Herbert's best poems in the emblematic mode repay such triple scrutiny. Two of them, besides **"Love (III),"** stand among his most beautiful and accomplished verses—**"The Windows"** and **"The Rose,"** neither of them in the Williams manuscript. The first is notable in being one of the few poems in *The Temple* having an "unhappy" ending. Herbert is gloomy on the subject of "speech alone," speech not validated by a way of life, and this poetic, so uncompromisingly intertwining life and art, has made some of Herbert's critics uncomfortable. It is a poetic that might not succeed for a poet of lesser genius: "If I please [God]," says Herbert, "I write fine and wittie" (**"The Forerunners"**). For Herbert, pleasing God meant not playing himself false, and Herbert must have noticed that his best poems were the result of his more stringent moments with himself, those times in which he asked himself for the greatest clarity and the most unflinching self-examination. That honesty, so pleasing to God, seemed as well pleasing to the Muse; it is no wonder that Herbert thought the two one.

It is probable that Herbert set himself the same standards (or higher ones) for the composition of sermons as for the writing of poems—an intimidating standard for the preacher, as **"The Windows"** suggests. The poem presents three emblems. The first is the emblem for natural man: he is "a brittle crazie glasse." The second is the emblem for the preacher who has not lived his life in the imitation of Christ: his pale glass lets God's light through, but it shows "watrish, bleak, & thin." The third emblem represents the preacher in whom shines the life of Christ: he is a stained-glass window with Christ's "storie" "annealed" in it, which causes the "light and glorie" to grow yet "more rev'rend." All three appear in the first two stanzas, but the last lines desert the emblem:

> Lord, how can man preach thy eternall word?
>   He is a brittle crazie glasse:
> Yet in thy temple thou dost him afford
>   This glorious and transcendent place,
>   To be a window, through thy grace.

> But when thou dost anneal in glasse thy storie,
>   Making thy life to shine within

The holy Preachers; then the light and glorie
  More rev'rend grows, & more doth win:
  Which else shows watrish, bleak, & thin.

Doctrine and life, colours and light, in one
  When they combine and mingle, bring
A strong regard and aw: but speech alone
  Doth vanish like a flaring thing,
  And in the eare, not conscience ring.

The poem is concerned with the glittering power of rhetoric used to delight the ear but not to awaken the conscience; such sermons "ring" in the ear, but not in the heart. The temptation—familiar to one who had been Orator to Cambridge University—to use the "flowers of rhetoric" of known effect, those means of persuasion so artfully documented in manuals of oratory, would have been considerable, especially since the temptation would have presented itself as a means for serving God: why deny to his service those persuasive means that work so well to convince multitudes in secular life? But Herbert knew:

  The fineness which a hymne or psalme affords,
  Is, when the soul unto the lines accords.

What is true of a hymn or psalm is also true of a sermon. Herbert begins **"The Windows"** in a tone of despondency at his own double unfitness to be a preacher: his temptation to use "speech alone" because of his gifts in that "ringing" speech, and his natural unsuitableness as a "brittle crazie" thing. The support for this conjecture about his state of mind comes chiefly from the "unhappy" ending of the poem but also from the decline into depression at the end of the second stanza. It is not clear in the poem what part in the redemption of the preacher can be played by the preacher himself, and what part must be played by God: from this confusion, the self-doubt and worry of the poem arise.

The first feeling of unworthiness, however, is briskly countered: though man, of himself, is no fit vessel for the Lord's "eternall word," still God, *through his grace*, has afforded man a place in the temple. This seems none of man's doing. Similarly, it is all God's doing when he chooses to "anneal in glasse" his "storie," "making [his] life to shine within / The holy Preachers." Holiness seems here a state caused by God, who makes his light/life shine in those preachers who move hearts and consciences. The third expression of the desirable state of the preacher, however, is not put as an act of intervention on God's part, as the previous two were; it is put impersonally:

  Doctrine and life, colours and light, in one
    When they combine and mingle, bring
  A strong regard and aw.

What causes doctrine and life to combine and mingle? Herbert does not say. In this formula, God would seem to contribute doctrine and light, the preacher life and colors. But how is a preacher who feels, as Herbert does when he writes this poem, "watrish, bleak, and thin" to bring his necessary offering of life and colors? The whole ethos of the poem, voiced in its consistent doublets, predicates a cooperative venture between God and man, or to put it in terms of selfhood, a better possibility than self-sufficient stoicism. Alone, man is brittle and formless ("crazie"), but

God gives him a place both glorious and transcendent; God's light and glory grows, through the holy preacher, more reverend and winning. Doctrine joins with life, colors join with light, both combine and mingle, the result in the congregation is regard and awe. This parade of conjoined things going hand in hand to heaven is broken only by the sullen triad "watrish, bleak, & thin," the first intimation of what may happen if God does not anneal his story. In the second such intimation, all the conjunctions are disbanded into one feared disjunction, that speech should ring in the ear but not in the soul. The "alone" defining fraudulent speech intensifies its separation from the desirable combinings throughout the poem, and is set off by a contrastive rhyme with the mingled unity of "one." The poem, like so many of Herbert's best, is a photographic double-exposure, where we see the brittle, crazy, waterish, bleak, thin, flashy self of the unaided soul on one plane and superimposed on it the glorious, transcendent, holy, reverend, winning, awe-inspiring self of the shining soul. Herbert's soul "knows not what it is," and his qualms of conscience over preaching religion without exemplifying it, and over the question of his responsibility in the matter, cause the oscillations in the poem between glory and ignominy.

Herbert's care for his emblems causes the final, and at first unsettling, abandonment of the imagery of light and windows. The best life has the colored glow of stained glass; less good is the pale and waterish light from uncolored glass; even less good is the brittle crazed glass of natural man; but least good, and most hellish, is the false flare of hypocrisy, which flashes up in rhetoric, then "vanishes" like some spectacular firework, leaving the temple in total darkness. The implied image of the darkened temple is the final argument against trusting to rhetoric alone, and the terrible power of the unholy preacher—that he becomes opaque to God's light and therefore deprives his congregation in the temple of any light but his own *ignis fatuus*— haunts the poem. The sense of the poet's own unworthiness is matched by a yearning apprehension of the beauty and consistency in the life of preachers (and by extension poets) who have become transparent vehicles of God's light and selves colored with "his storie." In that sense, the poet is "wishing [himself] like to one more rich in hope / Featured like him . . . / Desiring this man's art and that man's scope." Like so many of Herbert's poems, this one hides its personal origin in generalized language, speaking of "man" and "holy Preachers," but as Herbert said in another poem about "man," "My God, I mean myself." The use of emblems to show contrary states of the soul is not new, but Herbert's use of these emblems to show two possibilities (or, counting the flare in the darkness, three) in his own evolution contributes that internalization of traditional materials which we have come to expect in *The Temple*, and adds another comment on his own poetics of sincerity.

In the most sophisticated of all his emblem poems, **"The Rose,"** Herbert triumphantly but silently make claims for language over seeing, for sustained experience over fleeting initial response. The quintessential emblem of the world's sweetness is a rose, but the rose has also been used emblematically to show the world's deceptiveness. As an emblem, it first appears innocently, and we need the entire poem to tell us what it is to mean, how we are to "read" it:

> Presse me not to take more pleasure
>   In this world of sugred lies,
> And to use a larger measure
>   Then my strict, yet welcome size.
>
> First, there is no pleasure here:
>   Colour'd griefs indeed there are,
> Blushing woes, that look as cleare
>   As if they could beautie spare.
>
> Or if such deceits there be,
>   Such delights I meant to say;
> There are no such things to me,
>   Who have pass'd my right away.
>
> But I will not much oppose
>   Unto what you now advise:
> Onely take this gentle rose,
>   And therein my answer lies.
>
> What is fairer then a rose?
>   What is sweeter? yet it purgeth,
> Purgings enmitie disclose,
>   Enmitie forbearance urgeth.
>
> If then all that worldlings prize
>   Be contracted to a rose;
> Sweetly there indeed it lies,
>   But it biteth in the close.
>
> So this flower doth judge and sentence
>   Worldly joyes to be a scourge:
> For they all produce repentance,
>   And repentance is a purge.
>
> But I health, not physick choose:
>   Onely though I you oppose,
> Say that fairly I refuse,
>   For my answer is a rose.

Although this is one of those poems in which Herbert set a stanzaic task for himself that not even he could fulfill (since he no doubt intended every stanza following the appearance of the rose to have a rhyme in *-ose*), the effect of the poem lies less in its softly insistent rhyme scheme (which includes, besides the rhymes in *-ose*, four stanzas with rhymes in *-ze*, as in "lies," "prize," "choose") than in its wordless gesture, to which the whole poem is accompaniment. The person to whom the poem is addressed (who could be any worldly tempter) has proffered, as a symbol of worldly joy, a rose, and the poem accompanies Herbert's gift back of the same rose. Herbert's first descriptions of the world represented by the rose are intensely severe. In each of them the reality (given by the noun) is wholly undesirable, and only the appearance (given by the deceiving adjective) is enticing: we have in the world, he says, sugared *lies*, colored *griefs*, and blushing *woes*. These may "look as cleare / As if they could beautie spare," but in reality there is no pleasure in them. The harshness of Herbert's initial perception of the world is betrayed in his "Freudian slip": intending courtesy and meaning to say, "If such delights there be," he lets fall the mask of politeness and instead says, "If such deceits there be." Though he corrects himself instantly, his *contemptus mundi* is evident. It is not clear, however, why he refuses

to embrace worldly delights. First he says that he does take some pleasure in the world, but wishes it kept to his "strict, yet welcome size." Later he says that he does not take advantage of the deceits/delights because he has "pass'd [his] right away." Is he, then, a natural ascetic, or has he taken vows of asceticism? And do such tendencies, whether natural or religious, forbid *all* pleasure in the world or only an inordinate amount of pleasure?

The poem takes a new direction with the presentation of the rose. Though the rose had presumably supplied the imagery of colored griefs and blushing woes, it makes its first actual appearance in Herbert's ostensible refraining from argument. He will, he says, not "much" oppose to his seducer, only a "gentle rose." For the first time in the poem, something worldly has been given both an attractive noun and an attractive adjective: can the world, then, be good after all? Was Herbert's first vehemence, expressing itself in the rhetoric about sugared lies, only a response to his tempter's "pressing," a natural pressure of irritation in return? It seems so, because Herbert gives full appreciation to the beauty and sweetness of the gentle rose:

> What is fairer than a rose?
>   What is sweeter?

For this and the next two stanzas, he counters the indisputable gentleness, fairness, and sweetness of the rose with its inevitable result when used as a purgative. The archaic notion that anything which acts as a purge does so out of natural "enmitie" to its host is essential to the poem, but there is also a suggestion, when Herbert says that the rose "biteth in the close," of the thorns which may prick the unwary grasper. Looked at, the rose is gentle, fair, and sweet; grasped and consumed, it bites and purges.

A new description of the world now surfaces in the poem; Herbert concedes that there are such things as "worldly *joyes*" (where "joy" is the noun-reality, "worldly" the accidental modifier)—an outright reversal of his original argument that any appearance of attractiveness in the world was a deceitful adjectival overlay upon a disappointing reality. There are, then, worldly joys, and they are real joys, and we joy in having them; but the aftermath makes us think twice. These joys contain their own medicine, as a surfeit of eating does, but still Herbert prefers to forego both the joy and the result, choosing health, not indulgence-plus-medicine. It is a reasonable argument, even if we choose to disagree with it, and Herbert cannot be accused of denying the appeal of the world, since he gives his mild answer in full view of the rose than which nothing is fairer or sweeter. His accents in praise of the rose show conviction. But with his more-than-delicate conscience, he perhaps knew what pangs of remorse indulgence would bring him. Even to a sturdier soul, the aftermath of joy can be daunting (Shakespeare's Sonnet CXXIX is a case in point), but the tempter here pretends that there is nothing to be had from roses except pure pleasure. He, of all people, should know better. Herbert nevertheless found it easier to reject the rose than would a poet more visual and more dependent on a daily submersion in natural beauty. **"The Rose"** deserves comparison with Hopkins' more anguished response to the vexed question of "mortal beauty":

> To what serves mortal beauty—dangerous, does
>   set danc-
> ing blood—the O-seal-that-so feature, flung
>   prouder form
> Than Purcell tune lets tread to? See: it does this:
>   keeps warm
> Men's wits to the things that are, what good
>   means—where a glance
> Master more may than gaze, gaze out of counte-
>   nance.

Hopkins is genuinely tempted by the mortal beauty of everything from stallions to ploughmen; Herbert's mind, we sense, is not under any such immediate assault. Emblems, in any case, do not arise under pressure; Herbert has reflected on the rose, its beauty and its properties, and has chosen it as the emblem fitting his notion of worldly delights. He has it to hand when the tempter appears, and the appeal of the poem lies not in any masterful effort to say "Retro me, Satanas," but rather in the imposition of elegance (there is no more elegant poem in **The Temple** than **"The Rose"**) on a situation more likely to provoke defensive expostulation. Not for Herbert the wrestling with the devil of the more primitive saints; a courtly bow and a rose is what the advocate of worldliness receives when he comes to call. The recovery of self-possession (after the initial quick temper) and the giving of the world its due (after the initial denial of its attractions) make the poem a small effort in the equilibrium of virtue; providing a stance is steadfastly held, there is no need to be violent in proclaiming it. Opposition and refusal can be as graceful as accommodation, given the right emblem and its right title; Satan is silenced by the presented rose.

Some of Herbert's allegorical narratives (**"Humilitie"** and **"The World"** among them) seem composed by formula, allegorically predictable and therefore uninteresting (though with incidental charm); but other comparable poems are undeniably successful. We have Coleridge's word for the appeal of **"Love unknown"**; and **"The Pilgrimage,"** like **"Love unknown"** not in the Williams manuscript and therefore among the later poems, is one of Herbert's most mysteriously powerful lyrics. It is impossible to paraphrase in full the unflagging particularity of **"Love unknown,"** but it is certain that the intense interest generated in the incidents and outcome of this "tale long and sad" springs from that particularity. "I well remember all," says the speaker, and indeed he does. One of his most endearing characteristics is the assumption that his listener is as eager to hear as he is to tell: "But you shall heare," "do you understand?" The assumption is natural, since his friend knows him, he says, as well as he knows himself. The passion for accuracy that informs the storyteller's language can be seen in the opening of his tale, full of qualifications and specifications (italics mine):

>   A Lord I had,
> *And have*, of whom some grounds, *which may*
>   *improve*,
> I hold for two lives, *and both lives in me*.
> To him I brought a dish *of fruit* one day,
> And *in the middle* plac'd my heart.

The lord casts a glance at his servant, who seizes the heart and throws it "in a font, wherein did fall / A stream of

bloud, which issu'd from the side / Of a great rock." The poor heart was there "dipt and dy'd, / And washt, and wrung"; later, as a result of that treatment, the heart characteristically became "well, / And clean and fair." For this narrator, one word will never do where three or four can serve. When he finds his heart callous, he describes the remedy at length and with zest:

> But with a richer drug than scalding water
> I bath'd it often, ev'n with holy bloud,
> Which at a board, while many drunk bare wine,
> A friend did steal into my cup for good,
> Ev'n taken inwardly, and most divine
> To supple hardness.

Such a passage is the equivalent of a recipe. In it, as in **"Redemption"** and **"Love (III),"** Herbert shows his willingness to let text and gloss intermingle. "A richer drug" is interpreted at once as "holy bloud," and later in the poem the speaker is allowed a *lapsus linguae* that betrays his full knowledge of allegorical equivalency:

> I found that some had stuff'd the bed with
>   thoughts,
> I would say *thorns*.

Besides the speaker's loquaciousness (though his tale is said to be sad, there is an exuberance in the narration that belies the adjective) and his perfect acquaintance with both "levels" of his allegorical narrative, we also notice his undaunted purpose. He always has an end in view; and the frustration of each of his ends provides the lurking comedy of the poem, and its perpetual irony. He has in mind to bring, in placation, some fruit to his Lord—and what happens? His poor heart, in the middle of the fruit, gets thrown into a bloody font and washed and wrung. He wishes to present a sheep from his fold, "Thinking with that, which I did thus present, / To warm his love, which I did fear grew cold." Outraged, he narrates the sequel, with a pun on "tender" that also displays some outrageousness:

> But as my heart did tender it, the man,
> Who was to take it from me, slipt his hand,
> And threw my heart into the scalding pan;
> My heart, that brought it (do you understand?)
> The offerers heart.

That purpose frustrated, he goes home with another purpose in mind:

>   Where to repair the strength
> Which I had lost, I hasted to my bed.
> But when I thought to sleep out all these faults
>   (I sigh to speak)
> I found that some had stuff'd the bed with
>   thoughts,
> I would say thorns.

He cannot even go to bed without a purpose—to repair lost strength, to sleep out faults. The poem exists to show that man proposes, but God disposes, and the narrator's little plans—involving a dish of fruit here, a sheep there, a good night's sleep elsewhere—are bound to fail. The equableness of the narration, in spite of the putatively horrible experiences it retells (being wrung and scalded and pricked with thorns), gives a melodiousness to the poem that belies its claims of suffering. This might seem to be a fault, and in fact did seem so to Coleridge, who said that the poem illustrated "the characteristic fault of our elder poets," namely, "conveying the most fantastic thoughts in the most correct and natural language." Judged by Romantic expressive criteria, the poem entirely lacks fright and terror, imitative dislocation of speech, and evocative language. But the very notion of allegory is that what is being told *did not happen.* Nobody's heart was actually thrown into scalding water or washed in blood. A physical reaction to the physical events would be indecorous.

Again, it is characteristic of Herbert to recount his spiritual struggles in the past tense; they almost always are represented as having happened yesterday, so that the poem is giving today's view, a view tempered by knowledge of the purpose and result of each affliction. In this poem, the superior knowledge is not directly attributed in the first instance to the indignant speaker. Rather, his "friend" gently draws the moral: "Your heart was foul, I fear . . . Your heart was hard, I fear . . . Your heart was dull, I fear." To each suggestion, the poor speaker replies with willing admission: "Indeed it's true . . . Indeed it's true . . . Indeed a slack and sleepie state of minde / Did oft possesse me." It is as though the speaker already knows the truth and only needs the friend's reminder to voice it. This degree of self-knowledge explains the quasi-apologetic tone that mingles with the indignation of the narrative, and it prevents the speaker from adopting a tone of active suffering. In point of fact, the narrator has been healed, as the conclusion points out:

> *Truly, Friend,*
> *For ought I heare, your Master shows to you*
> *More favour then you wot of. Mark the end.*
> *The Font did onely, what was old, renew:*
> *The Caldron suppled, what was grown too hard:*
> *The Thorns did quicken, what was grown too*
>   *dull:*
> *All did but strive to mend, what you had marr'd.*
> *Wherefore be cheer'd, and praise him to the full*
> *Each day, each houre, each moment of the week,*
> *Who fain would have you be new, tender, quick.*

The poem may be seen as an internal colloquy, or dialogue of the mind with itself. In that colloquy, the reader is led to ratify the voice of the kind explanatory friend over the garrulous self-important voice of the narrator, at least when the speaker is at his most circumstantial and easily impressed:

> As I one even-tide
>   (I sigh to tell)
> Walkt by my self abroad, I saw a large
> And spacious fornace flaming, and thereon
> A boyling caldron, round about whose verge
> Was in great letters set AFFLICTION.
> The greatness shew'd the owner.

The friend's voice is the voice of reflection, the speaker's the voice of immersion, and they must of necessity differ. Yet without the shamed admissions of the speaker, reflection could not arise. In spite of his disclaimer at the beginning ("In my faintings I presume your love / Will more complie then help"), the speaker needs the help of his

"deare friend," nowhere more than at the end of his troubles, when his cry is heartfelt:

> Deare, could my heart not break,
>   When with my pleasures ev'n my rest was gone?

The "compliance" he expects at the beginning from his "deare friend" is sympathy for his troubles: some remark affirming the worth of his own self-consciously worthy nature (all those dishes of fruit and sheep), and rebuking the impolite responses of his Lord (who ignored those gifts and practiced violence on his tenant). Instead, the friend courteously, but steadily, takes the Lord's part. The tentative ("I fear") and brief interpolations of the friend resemble nothing so much as the tentative interpretations proffered by an analyst: the sufferer is free to reject the interpretations, but is more likely to accept them, if only because he is struck by their hidden truth. We may, in the interests of historical accuracy, substitute "spiritual director" or "confessor" for analyst, but the result is much the same. And the wished-for end is also much the same—that one should be "new, tender, quick," responding not with clichés and old patterns of resentment, but with a fresher, quickened self.

In spite of the appealing realism of the narrator's voice and the healing gravity of the "friend's" replies, we must ask why, so late in his career, Herbert found this way of expressing affliction and redemption an attractive one, what it offered him that other modes (such as the ones found in the several **"Affliction"** poems) could not. I think that for Herbert the appeal of this kind of poem lay in distancing himself from himself. In effect, in poems like **"Love unknown"** Herbert is allegorizing not only his experiences but also himself. To allegorize oneself is different from writing about Everyman: it means to take one's own personality, exaggerate it, broaden it, delete its more eccentric specificities while retaining its individual character. In the latter aspect it differs from caricature, which is at pains to emphasize particular eccentricities. A self-allegory is recognizable as an individual person, yet not as wholly identical with the author. Many characteristics of the narrator in **"Love unknown"** remind us of Herbert: the liking for colloquy, the tendency to complain, the naveté, the childlike speech, the forthrightness, the attacks of misery. All of these are represented in various Herbert lyrics by a genuine authorial "I." But in the first-person poems, Herbert is at the center of the stage; even in the impersonally phrased poems like **"Prayer (I)"** he often clearly "means himself." By inventing a genuine persona in **"Love unknown"** (as he also does, but less sustainedly, in **"Redemption"**), he achieves a detachment from self that we admire because it avoids a miserable concentration on the trivial events in one small life. We may regret the almost inevitable comic perspective that the entrance of a dramatized persona brings with it, and we may criticize a form which allows mildness of apprehension to coexist with images of boiling caldrons. But the allegorical narrative of **"Love unknown"** is an attempt and an approach which remains strangely winning and memorable, if not so immediately moving as the nonallegorical first-person lyrics. The greatest poem in *The Temple*, after all, depends on just such a dramatized persona, the self-conscious guest in **"Love (III)."** Even in that delicate poem there is a comic perspective. Herbert was never above humor at his own expense, and it is deeply characteristic of his self-irony that he, a person who so loved neatness and order, should invent a final banquet in which the guests must sit down just as they are, dusty and in travel garments. "I did expect a ring," says the narrator in **"Hope"**; the pilgrim in **"Love (III)"** "did expect" a final banquet where everyone would have a new white wedding garment; the speaker in **"Love unknown"** "did expect" that God would be pleased with his fruits and his sheep. These comic personae carry the burden of Herbert's ironies. We may prefer his miseries, or his joys, to his humor, but in his best poetry, as in **"Love (III),"** all three are found combined.

A sadder self-allegory appears in **"The Pilgrimage"**:

> I travell'd on, seeing the hill, where lay
>   My expectation.
>   A long it was and weary way.
>   The gloomy cave of Desperation
> I left on th' one, and on the other side
>   The rock of Pride.
>
> And so I came to Fancies medow strow'd
>   With many a flower:
>   Fain would I here have made abode,
>   But I was quicken'd by my houre.
> So to Cares cops I came, and there got through
>   With much ado.
>
> That led me to the wilde of Passion, which
>   Some call the wold;
>   A wasted place, but sometimes rich.
>   Here I was robb'd of all my gold,
> Save one good Angell, which a friend had ti'd
>   Close to my side.
>
> At length I got unto the gladsome hill,
>   Where lay my hope,
>   Where lay my heart; and climbing still,
>   When I had gain'd the brow and top,
> A lake of brackish waters on the ground
>   Was all I found.
>
> With that abash'd and struck with many a sting
>   Of swarming fears,
>   I fell, and cry'd, Alas my King!
>   Can both the way and end be tears?
> Yet taking heart I rose, and then perceiv'd
>   I was deceiv'd:
>
> My hill was further: so I flung away,
>   Yet heard a crie
>   Just as I went, *None goes that way*
>   *And lives*: If that be all, said I,
> After so foul a journey death is fair,
>   And but a chair.

Joseph Summers [in his *George Herbert: His Religion and Art*, 1954] described the presence in this poem of both the conventional (the pilgrimage) and the unconventional (the avoiding of the envisaged happy end); Ryley [George Ryley in his *Mr. Herbert's Temple and Church Militant Explained and Improved by a Discourse upon Each Poem Critical and Practical*, 1715] pointed out its unusual beginning *in medias res*. Beyond these larger observations, some inquiry is necessary concerning the success of the poem, achieved in unusual and unexpected ways. There are many things apparently "wrong" from an allegorical point of view about the way the poem is written. The first "wrongness" is the flouting of allegorical expectation described, but not explained, by Summers. "Is this the promised end?" we ask when we find first the brackish waters, next the inaccessible "further" hill, and finally the taunt of death. This is a grisly set of "dissolves," made more so by the perspective thus cast on the whole preceding "plot." This sequence of experiences has been, says Herbert, "so foul a journey." Such revulsion at the total Christian pilgrimage is, so far as I know, unheard-of outside this poem. The true wayfaring Christian may have his trials and his sloughs of despond, but it is unthinkable that Piers Plowman or Christian should fling out in anger, "After so foul a journey, death is fair." There is some global indictment of life here that a stricter "allegory" would forbid, because the trials of the pilgrim would, in a more traditional poem, fall under the generally approved rubric of Christian purification by suffering. But no good end is unambiguously attached to the afflictions in this poem; the journey is simply foul, in itself and in its result. It neither strengthens resolve, braces the soul, cleanses the heart, nor has any other moral effect. It only causes nausea, a revulsion which makes even that "uncouth hideous thing," death, seem fair: how much more hideous, then, is the life described as this "foul journey." In this access of felt truth, lyric response subdues allegorical expectation; what began as a pilgrimage (a noun that can scarcely take "foul" as a modifying adjective) ends as a journey, and a foul one at that. Whether the two perspectives—"the Christian pilgrimage" and "this foul journey"—can be reconciled, I am not sure. The poem attempts the rhetoric of pilgrimage, but abandons entirely the ascending tone of increasing faith which normally makes allegory close with Piers becoming Christ or trumpets sounding on the other side.

It is scarcely possible to read this poem and not think of Vaughan's **"Regeneration,"** a poem following Herbert in the extreme simplicity of pilgrim narrative ("I came, I perceived, I entered, I said," and so forth) but which, in its descriptive fullness, causes Herbert's poem to seem a skeleton. The initial gestures toward description in Herbert (a gloomy cave, a meadow with "many a flower") are fatigued; the phases of the journey are labeled before we even have a chance to experience them. "The gloomy cave of Desperation," "the rock of Pride," "Fancies meadow," "Cares cops," "the wilde of Passion"—Herbert cannot wait to gloss his allegory, which he does more baldly and retrospectively here than anywhere else in *The Temple*. We can hardly imagine an allegory more perfunctory. The poem is like a game board, with areas staked out and labeled "Cares cops," "the rock of Pride," and so on. Flatlanders live here. Why, if he wanted to use it so blankly, did Herbert choose an emblematic landscape?

The answer must be sought, paradoxically, in Herbert's subsequent forsaking of labels in the second half of the poem. The gladsome hill, the lake of brackish waters, and the swarming fears remain allegorically unidentified, and by that very fact rebuke the earlier categories. The early stages are mapped out for the pilgrim, Herbert implies, by others. Any Christian knows that the straight and narrow path lies between presumption (or Pride) on the one hand

and despair (or Desperation) on the other. The early "milk and sweetnesses" of "Fancie" are classically followed by periods of "Care." The fulcrum of the change from the general to the personal is the stanza on Passion, with its first clouding of the schema through the riddling paradox, "A wasted place, but sometimes rich." Nothing comparably mysterious inhered in the former cave, rock, meadow, or copse. The second mystery allowed into the poem is the mystery of deception. "At length *I got* unto the gladsome hill," says Herbert, and in a poem such as this, told in the past tense, we must take such a statement as true (otherwise it would read, "At length I got unto what I thought was the gladsome hill"). The simple form Herbert uses permits us, along with him, to be deceived, but it raises the query of the validity of this presumed "past" tense. All of Herbert's recapitulatory poems (of which **"The Collar"** is the most famous) purport to retell yesterday's events, but in fact seem rather to transport us back into yesterday as a present experience, tenses notwithstanding. The formulation of experience into lyric is always at war with the lyric recreation of the experience. The surest way to "break" a past tense and transform it into the present is to insert direct discourse, which by its nature is forever "present." In **"The Pilgrimage,"** the immediacy of the poem is at its highest in the last three stanzas, which begin with an echo of the opening line of the poem (italics mine):

> I travell'd on, *seeing* the *hill, where lay*
> *My expectation . . .*

> At length I got unto the gladsome *hill*,
> *Where lay my hope,*
> *Where lay my heart*; and *climbing* still . . .
> A lake of brackish waters on the ground
> Was all I found.

The unexpected entrance of the present participle, absent from the poem since the first line, draws us into the action as we were not drawn in during the passage of the named stations. At the same time, the poignant displacement of the echo one metrical foot back in the line (an effect Herbert would have intended) exerts its own disappointment:

> . . . the hill, where lay
> My expectation.
> . . . the hill
> Where lay my hope.

The other variations—the note of achieved joy in the adjective "gladsome" added to "hill"; the admission of emotion in the increasingly more passionate series "my expectation," "my hope," "my heart"—quicken the previous schematic weariness of the poem into feeling. Again, lyric impulse takes precedence over allegory, and bursts wholly out in the central line of the poem, a line entirely "present" and not at all "remembered":

> Can both the way and end be tears?

Unanswered, Herbert rises bravely and then perceives he was deceived; but at the very moment of deception he makes his strongest claim—"the hill where" becomes "my hill." His hill it is, and he will have it yet. But the contest is a draw. The anonymous cry, "None goes that way and lives" (which may be taken either as taunt or warning), provokes Herbert into a piece of notable, if desperate bra-

vado: "I cannot be worse treated than I have been; if that be your only threat, it is an empty one; after such a foul journey death seems fair." The horror of death is put aside here with quick *sprezzatura*, chiefly because death is not the real subject of this poem, whose theme is rather the foul journey, whose insight is the despairing one that both the way and end are tears.

The conquering of allegorical narrative by lyric dialogue, the transformation of past-tense recapitulation into present speech, the abandonment of manned stations in favor of anonymous encounter, all make this poem a very peculiar example of "allegory." In **"Peace,"** however, to cite a comparable poem, Herbert's allegory is tranquil. He seeks Peace in solitude, in the cosmos, and in nature, only to find, through the discourse of "a rev'rend good old man," that peace is to be found in the bread made of Christ's body. The didactic intent cohabits peacefully with the allegorical quest, and Herbert's first role as naïf seeker yields easily to his second, and silent, role as docile audience. **"Peace"** does not, in short, dispute its form in the way that **"The Pilgrimage"** does. If **"The Pilgrimage"** had continued as it began through its first half (excepting the paradoxical line about Passion), it would have been a wholly unremarkable poem. Vaughan learned from its mid-way change of styles to adopt its second form of unnamed experiences for the second half of his **"Regeneration,"** giving us by an unexpected restitutive kindness of literary history, the "successful" pilgrimage poem that the more saddened Herbert could not write. Without Herbert's example we could not have had Vaughan's heavenly grove and second spring:

> The unthrift Sunne shot vitall gold
> A thousand peeces,
> And heaven its azure did unfold
> Checqur'd with snowie fleeces,
> The aire was all in spice
> And every bush
> A garland wore; Thus fed my Eyes
> But all the Eare lay hush.

Vaughan's fountain, cistern, stones, and wind descend from Herbert's hill and lake and angel; if we prefer in some moments Vaughan's bank of flowers to Herbert's lake of brackish waters, we must at least acknowledge its lineage.

Herbert's exhausted language as the poem begins, his tired sense of the twice-told tale, his scrupulous but dry concessives ("but sometimes rich"), are phrased in an eternity of endurance. "I travell'd on . . . and so I came . . . so I came and there got through . . . that led me to . . . at length I got . . . when I had gain'd . . . I fell . . . yet taking heart I rose . . . and then perceived . . . so I flung away . . . yet heard a cry"—such a narrative form is unstoppable except by a declaration or a defiance, differing in that aspect from its vaguely felt model, the Passion of Christ, which also contained a fall at the top of a hill and a cry of abandonment. In this poem, Herbert re-examines the *Imitatio Christi*: the crucifixion is less painful finally, says Herbert, than the *via dolorosa*. Hopkins, perhaps learning from Herbert, said in "The Wreck of the Deutschland" that it is not the single extremity that prompts the heart to ask for ease; rather, it is "the jading and jar of the cart, time's tasking."

In **"The Pilgrimage,"** then, Herbert passes beyond his original allegorical schema (which may in itself have been initially a way to contain intractable emotion) and allows his emotion finally to overflow its vessels. A poem like **"The Pilgrimage"** constrains us to acknowledge the perseverance of Herbert's mind. Suspecting that both the way and end are tears, he not only does not bury and deny his intuition, but rather invents a table to embody it, and draws the tale out to its intolerable conclusion. As Stevens would say, he brings the storm to bear.

There are two conclusions to be drawn from Herbert's habitual resorting to allegorical and emblematic forms. The first affirms how much such forms pleased Herbert: he is perfectly at home in them, beginning, "I travell'd on" or "Having been tenant long," offering "this gentle rose," or musing, "As on a window late I cast mine eye." He launches with extreme ease and habituation into the genre, relishing the figurative possibility of emblematic description or allegorical narrative. But—and this must be the second conclusion—in almost every case he causes something odd to happen in the poem, bringing the form into question. In **"The Windows,"** a simple emblem (preachers are like stained glass) is bifurcated, trifurcated, and quadrifurcated, so to speak, into crazed glass, wat'rish glass, annealed glass, and no glass; in **"Love-joy,"** "misinterpretation" and "true interpretation" of a single emblem vie and are reconciled; in **"Jesu,"** emblems are rearrangeable in whole or broken forms; in **"Humilitie"** and **"The Pilgrimage,"** an "unhappy ending" is affixed to an allegorical form which normally would presuppose a cheerful resolution; in **"Justice (II),"** emblems are shown to be created according to one's angle of vision; in **"The Agonie,"** one emblem is shown to yield two "true" readings; in **"Love (III),"** text and gloss are strangely intermingled both with each other and with added elements; **"Hope,"** while maintaining the allegorical fiction of an exchange of gifts, takes no care that those gifts should be literally plausible; **"The Rose"** contains two entirely opposed emblematic truths in the same object; and **"Love unknown"** uses the mildest of tones to recount what, fictively speaking, are horrific sufferings. In short, any allegorical or emblematic form, in Herbert's hands, is undergoing a constant critique of its own possibilities comparable with, but not identical to, the continuing critique of his own feelings so pervasively conducted in the lyrics. The possible stodginess and complacency of these figurative forms, once they have been shorn of their narrative fullness, on the one hand, or their visual accompaniment, on the other, are skirted by Herbert with his customary penetration and grace. For him, figures and schemes are not the fixed result of inquiry, but rather the fluid means to discovery. (pp. 57-99)

Helen Vendler, in her The Poetry of George Herbert, *Cambridge, Mass.: Harvard University Press, 1975, 303 p.*

Barbara Kiefer Lewalski   (essay date 1979)

[*In the following excerpt, Lewalski analyzes Herbert's Protestant poetics, concluding that the poet "undertakes nothing less than the task of becoming a Christian psalmist."*]

If we find in Donne's poems a selective and progressive employment of several features important to the new Protestant aesthetics, George Herbert's volume of religious verse, **The Temple**, develops this aesthetics fully and harmoniously, as the very foundation of his poetry. How much Herbert may have been influenced by Donne is impossible to determine, but certainly there would have been some association through Donne's close friendship with Herbert's mother, Magdalen Herbert. And Donne himself testified to the relationship by sending Herbert one of his emblem rings, together with a personal verse letter in Latin. Moreover, the poetics implicit in the sermons of so distinguished a preacher as Donne could hardly have failed to impress his younger contemporary.

But Herbert, not Donne, was the poet praised and imitated by contemporaries as the creator of a new movement and a new model for religious poetry. Vaughan identified Herbert as "The first, that with any effectual success attempted a *diversion* of this foul and overflowing *stream*" of lascivious poetry to sacred uses, and he located himself among the "many pious *Converts*" gained by Herbert's "holy *life* and *verse*." Richard Crashaw entitled his collection of religious lyrics *Steps to the Temple* in tribute to Herbert; Christopher Harvey conceived his book of lyrics, *The Synagogue*, as a "shadow of **The Temple**"; Robert Herrick's *Noble Numbers* contain many echoes of Herbert; Samuel Speed imitated Herbert closely in several of his *Prison-Pietie* poems; Edward Taylor constantly looked to Herbert's example; his impress is everywhere on the minor religious verse of the period. I suggest that Herbert's art is in large measure founded upon the elements of Protestant poetics . . . —biblical genre theory, biblical tropes, Protestant ways with emblem, metaphor, and typology, and Protestant theory regarding the uses of art in religious subjects—and that this poetics affords a necessary corrective to approaches to Herbert through medieval iconography, Salesian meditation, the plain style, or the so-called Augustinian abrogation of art. These approaches, and also the perceptive close readings of several Herbert poems which Arnold Stein [in his *George Herbert's Lyrics*, 1968] and, more recently, Helen Vendler [in her The Poetry of George Herbert, 1975] have given us, have illuminated several aspects of Herbert's art—which is of course finally the product of his unique poetic sensibility. However, we need to recognize how that sensibility responded creatively to several elements in the new Protestant aesthetics in order to take more adequate measure of Herbert's superb art and artfulness.

To begin with, it is clear that the conception of the Christian life rendered in Herbert's prose and poetry conforms in large outline to Protestant-Pauline theology. Herbert's manual for ministers, **A Priest to the Temple, or The Country Parson**, unequivocally asserts the centrality of the scriptures for the religious life of the parson and his congregation: " . . . the chief and top of his knowledge consists in the book of books, the storehouse and magazene of life and comfort, the holy Scriptures. There he sucks, and lives." His only extant theological commentary, the "BRIEFE NOTES relating to the dubious and offensive places in the following CONSIDERATIONS" by Juán de Valdés (Valdesso), a Spanish Catholic biblical scholar and reformer in the Erasmian tradition, registers his delight that "... God in the midst of Popery should open the eyes of one to understand and expresse so cleare-ly and excellently the intent of the Gospell in the accepta-tion of Christs righteousnesse ... a thing strangely bur-ied, and darkned by the Adversaries, and their great stum-bling-block." In one place he paraphrases Valdés approv-ingly on the matter, against the papists: "He meaneth (I suppose) that a man presume not to merit, that is, to oblige God, or justify himselfe before God, by any acts or exer-cises of Religion." Nevertheless he finds Valdés too much the papist in his attitude toward scripture. He complains repeatedly that Valdés "slights the Scripture too much," as when he seems to put it on a par with images or pictures of Christ, or speaks of it as "but childrens meat." And he declares that Valdés' "opinion of the Scripture is unsuffer-able" when he regards it (as Augustine did) as a means which might be dispensed with by those illuminated by the Spirit.

The first poem of *The Temple*, "The Church-porch," is about the externals of the Christian life, the moral virtues and social manners appropriate to a Christian profession. The poem is concerned with the natural order, but it does not treat nature as directly propaedeutic to grace in the scholastic or Hookerian sense. Interestingly enough, sev-eral of the topics considered in that poem—the avoidance of covetousness, luxury, drunkenness, gaming, swearing, and especially idleness; the importance of educating chil-dren properly, governing one's household, and finding and following a suitable calling; the value of cleanliness, decen-cy, and order in the person, the household, and in God's house—are also emphasized in Herbert's *The Country Parson* as traits characterizing the good minister and as qualities he should seek to promote in his parish. Indeed the catalogue of positive virtues urged in the manual—"The Countrey Parson is exceeding exact in his Life, being holy, just, prudent, temperate, bold, grave in all his wayes"—would provide a useful index for the topics of the poem. Since this is so, we cannot describe "The Church-porch" simply in terms of the natural and moral reforma-tion to be undertaken prior to spiritual growth.

Rather, the prescribed behavior is set forth as the interface between the Church and the world (as the church porch is in architectural terms). The poem is concerned with the external reformation of life in its visible manifestations—the turning away from evil promised at baptism; in Protes-tant terms, such behavior may or may not be accompanied by the action of grace in the heart which alone regenerates. Herbert's structure builds directly upon that perception: as the "Superliminare" engraved above the portal of the Church makes clear, these are matters of behavior only; the essence of true religion is within "The Church"—"Thou, whom the former precepts have / Sprinkled and taught, how to behave / Thy self in church; approach, and taste / The churches mysticall repast."

The collection of shorter lyrics entitled "The Church" traces the internal spiritual life of the speaker, who is a particular individual recounting personal experience but who also exhibits through that experience the Protestant-Pauline paradigm of salvation. According to Izaak Wal-

ton's hagiographic biography, Herbert described his book as "a picture of the many spiritual Conflicts that have past betwixt God and my Soul, before I could subject mine to the will of Jesus my Master"; Walton also records that on his deathbed Herbert sent his manuscript of poems to his good friend Nicholas Ferrar with instructions to publish it if he thought it would "turn to the advantage of any de-jected poor Soul" and otherwise to burn it. Whether or not these statements incorporate some Walton embellish-ments, the assumption behind them—that a particular spiritual life may epitomize and present common religious experience—is entirely consonant with Herbert's recorded views. In *The Country Parson* he urges the minister to preach to others out of the "Library" of his own life, be-cause, "though the temptations may be diverse in divers Christians, yet the victory is alike in all, being by the self-same Spirit. Neither is this true only in the military state of a Christian life [the temptations], but even in the peace-able also; when the servant of God ... in a quiet sweet-nesse seeks how to please his God." Moreover, the individ-ual-typical speaker of "The Church" is a Calvinist in the-ology. In regard to the much-controverted question of whether the Christian can lay claim to anything whatsoev-er of human merit or of initiative in good actions he is taught in "The Holdfast" that he must absolutely repudi-ate any such claim:

> I Threatned to observe the strict decree
> Of my deare God with all my power &
> might.
> But I was told by one, it could not be;
> Yet I might trust in God to be my light.
> Then will I trust, said I, in him alone.
> Nay, ev'n to trust in him, was also his:
> We must confesse that nothing is our own.
> Then I confesse that he my succour is:
> But to have nought is ours, not to confesse
> That we have nought. I stood amaz'd at
> this,
> Much troubled, till I heard a friend ex-
> presse,
> That all things were more ours by being his.
> What Adam had, and forfeited for all,
> Christ keepeth now, who cannot fail or fall.

And in "The Water-course" he affirms the Calvinist dou-ble predestination, attributing it to the simple dictate of God's will,

> Who gives to man, as he sees fit, { Salvation.
> { Damnation."
> (ll 9-10)

We do not, however, find in Herbert the agonized outcries by which Donne dramatized the early stages of the process of regeneration—the fears of God's rejection and the ter-rors of conscience attendant upon the conviction of sin. Rather, though Herbert's speaker often laments his sins and his spiritual barrenness, and often complains of God's withdrawal of favors, he does not agonize about his elec-tion. On the "Superliminare" above the portal of entry to the Church is also written, "Nothing but holy, pure, and cleare, / Or that which groneth to be so, / May at his perill further go" (ll. 6-8). He sees himself as one whose groans and longings give presumptive evidence of his own calling to enter the Church. Within "The Church" the first group of poems, beginning with "The Altar" and culminating with the two adjacent poems **"Repentance"** and **"Faith,"** explores the speaker's conversion in terms of his struggle to understand, accept, and make the appropriate response (repentance and faith) to the fundamental ground of salvation, justification through Christ's sacrifice. The second and much the largest group of poems, from **"Prayer (I)"** to (perhaps) **"The Crosse,"** presents the alternating afflictions and comforts, temptations and joys, judgments and graces, victories and backslidings, and the emotional states attendant upon these vacillations, which characterize the long, slow process of sanctification in the Protestant paradigm. The final group of poems, from **"The Flower"** to **"Love (III),"** presents the mature Christian's attainment of a plateau of joy, confidence, assurance, and anticipation of heaven; in these poems the major conflicts, including his anxieties about his poetic praises, are eased for Herbert's speaker.

The context afforded by Protestant poetics also sheds light upon the vexed question of unity in *The Temple*—the relation of the long prefatory poem, **"The Church-porch"** and the long epilogue, **"The Church Militant,"** to the central body of lyrics, **"The Church,"** as well as the question of what thematic and structural coherence is manifested in the collection as a whole. The poems were not of course written in their present sequence, and the precise chronology of their composition is not known. **"The Church Militant"** is presumed to predate the rest of the work; it appears among the sixty-nine (out of one hundred sixty-eight poems of *The Temple*) contained in the Dr. Williams manuscript. The Williams poems, comprising many of those on Church feasts, liturgy, and architecture, were evidently written some time before Herbert's ordination in 1630, and many of them were extensively revised in the later Bodleian manuscript and the 1633 first edition. However, as Amy Charles demonstrates, the poems added to the later collection do not substantially alter, but further develop, the fundamental scheme of the soul's uneven progress already evident in the Williams manuscript. It seems clear from this that the conception of the volume and the basic order of poems carry the poet's authority and have significance. That significance develops in part from the metaphor of Herbert's title, *The Temple*: contemporary Protestant formulations of the temple trope and of the typology of the Old Testament Temple provide the terms for Herbert's unifying motif, the temple in the heart of man.

Herbert critics have pointed to the traditional typological significance of the three parts of the Old Testament Temple—the Porch or Outer Court typifying the external and visible aspect of the Church from which none are exclud-

Painting of Herbert at Bemerton.

ed, the Holy Place typifying the communion of the invisible Church on earth, and the Holy of Holies, typifying the highest heaven of the saints—and have often tried to fit Herbert's structure to these terms as to a Procrustean bed. It seems obvious that Herbert made some use of these conventional associations in the first two sections of his work, though his application is rather to the Christian individual than to the ecclesiastical body. Joseph Hall provides an analogue for this emphasis: "In every renewed man, the individuall temple of God; the outward parts are allowed common to God and the world; the inwardest and secretest, which is the heart, is reserved onely for the God that made it. . . . Onely the true Christian hath intire and private conversation with the holy One of Israel." This perception was also strikingly rendered by the Protestant emblematist Zacharias Heyns, portraying the risen Christ inhabiting a large human heart with the Old Testament Temple in the background and the motto, *"Templum Christi cor hominis."*

In Herbert's volume, **"The Church-porch"** relates to the Porch or Outer Court of the Old Testament Temple. Here the speaker sets forth a series of dry, didactic prescriptions regarding the externals of the Christian life and the behavior fitting a Christian profession which constantly echo classical and Hebraic moral principles. These precepts have a relation both to the Church and to the world, even as a church porch itself does; moreover, Herbert's **"Church-porch"** as an architectural metaphor has affinities with the entrances both to the Old Testament Temple and to classical temples, since both kinds have contributed directly to the definition of the external moral behavior appropriate to the Christian life, although both are but shadowy types of the Christian temple in the heart. The lyrics of **"The Church"** define the Christian temple as the inner essence of the Christian experience, the relationship and dialogue between Christ and the individual soul together with the distresses and joys attendant upon that communion.

But the equation does not hold for the third term: Herbert's **"Church Militant"** cannot be made to relate to the Holy of Holies in the Old Testament Temple, or to its commonly designated antitype, the heavenly kingdom. Indeed, Herbert suggests the soul's movement into that third realm at the end of **"The Church,"** in a series of poems on the last things—**"Death," "Dooms-day," "Judgement," "Heaven"**—followed by the final, exquisite lyric, **"Love (III),"** which intimates the soul's gracious reception at the heavenly banquet. This is entirely consonant with the typological terms Herbert has established. At Christ's crucifixion the veil of the Temple separating the Holy of Holies from the Holy Place was rent from top to bottom (Matt. 27:15) so that Christians, exercising the new priesthood of all believers, find no sharp distinction in their spiritual experience between the regenerate life on earth and in heaven, "Having . . . boldnesse to enter into the Holiest by the blood of Jesus, / By a new and living way which hee hath consecrated for us, through the veile, that is to say, His flesh" (Heb. 10:19-20). There is not, then, and ought not to be, an "architectural" counterpoint in Herbert's scheme to the Temple Holy of Holies; rather, **"The Church Militant"** shifts from a spatial to a temporal

scheme to present a third dimension of the Christian Church on earth—its public, visible form. For **"The Church Militant"** the significant terms are set forth by the extended opening passage about the Ark—both Noah's Ark and more importantly the Ark of the Covenant—and also by allusions throughout the poem to the fleeing woman of the Apocalypse. All these were recognized types of the Church Militant in its relation to the world, and emphasized as such in contemporary Protestant literature. Robert Cawdrey indicates the basis for this typology in his *Treasurie . . . of Similies,* "As the Arke was carried from place to place, and never rested in one certaine place: So likewise the militant Church here on earth, hath no certaine place, but is posted from piller to post." And Daniel Featley's comment on the images he identifies as "The Embleme of the Church Militant" seems almost a précis of Herbert's poem: "If the Spouse of Christ be a pilgrime, and flieth from place to place, from Citie to Citie, from Kingdome to Kingdom . . . the portable Arke in the Old Testament, and the flying woman in the New, are images of the militant Church in this world." Herbert's **"The Church Militant"** develops just such a vision of the Church traveling ever westward as Sin dogs her heels, destroying and taking over one by one the civilizations she has established, until at length the Lord comes to judge both the Church and the world.

Herbert's governing conception is that the Old Testament Temple, with its intimations of permanence, has its true antitype only in the hearts of the elect who look forward to individual salvation, but that the wandering Ark is the nearest type for the corporate body of the Church, which has no security here and is (as Augustine also thought) in constant conflict with the world. Herbert's overarching typological symbol, the Temple, is then an appropriate ground of unity for his entire work, foreshadowing in different ways three dimensions of the New Covenant Church. The prefatory poem, **"The Church-porch"** explores the external behavior proper to the Christian in his interaction with the world. The dominant central section, **"The Church"** presents the intimate spiritual experience of the regenerate heart. And the epilogue, **"The Church Militant"** is again concerned with an external dimension, the constant tribulations of the visible church in this world, typified by the wandering Ark which is itself a foreshadowing of the more permanent Temple.

Herbert's conceptual plan for *The Temple* in regard to the genres employed and the stances of the speaker owes something also to the analogy sometimes drawn between the three parts of the Old Testament Temple and the three books of Solomon. Beza compares the Book of Proverbs to "the utter common court for the people"; he finds that Ecclesiastes serves as an avenue into the Holy Place—"The Church is as it were lead to enter into the Holy Place by the *booke of Ecclesiastes, called the Preacher"*; and he relates Canticles to the movement of the Church through the Holy Place, bringing it "even to the entery of the Sanctuary, or Holy of Holies." These equations are reflected in Herbert's volume: **"The Church-porch"** is a Christian revision and fusion of Proverbs and Ecclesiastes (teaching moral precepts pertaining to external behavior and preparing for entry into the Church); and **"The Church"** adumbrates at least some aspects of Canticles, treating the encounters of Christ and the soul throughout life, and leading the soul to the point of entry into the Holy of Holies, or Heaven.

As we have seen, many sixteenth- and seventeenth-century exegetes linked Proverbs and Ecclesiastes closely, as sharing a common didactic mode and a common subject matter—precepts for moral, political, and domestic behavior pertaining primarily to the duties of man to man, though including as well certain sacred duties of piety toward God. Proverbs, addressed to the young or to new beginners in the Christian life as if by a father or teacher, were either brief, pithy, pointed sentences enunciating truths or precepts of behavior (maxim, adage, aphorism), or else "figurative and darke kinde of speeches" (especially similitude and enigma). Herbert's sustained interest in the first of these kinds is indicated by his collection and translation of a large number of *Outlandish Proverbs*, chiefly from French, Italian, and Spanish sources. In the book of Ecclesiastes Solomon as a preacher set forth moral commonplaces in the same kinds of figures, but now woven into a continuous and eloquent poetic sermon on the central topic of moral philosophy, the highest good or human happiness. Herbert's **"The Church-porch"** seems intended as a Christian version of these books. The speaker adopts the role of father-teacher-preacher setting forth rules of conduct and behavior in a verse sermon ("A verse may finde him, who a sermon flies," l. 5) assumed to be delivered as from the Church Porch to one still outside the Church itself. The audience, "Thou, whose sweet youth and early hopes inhance / Thy rate and price, and mark thee for a treasure" (ll. 1-2), is specified (like the audience of Proverbs) as a typical young beginner in the Christian life but one giving strong evidence of election. And as **"Superliminare"** makes clear, these precepts are understood to bring the youth from the Common Court to the door of the Holy Place, from the Church Porch to the Church.

The topics of **"The Church-porch"** are those associated with Proverbs and Ecclesiastes—precepts of morality and manners. Herbert's apparently haphazard organization of topics admits of rationalization according to several Christian schemes—the Ten Commandments; the seven deadly sins and their opposing virtues; the four cardinal virtues; duties to self, to neighbor, and to God. In its exploration of these various topics, the sermon also resembles an examination of conscience, usually conducted according to one or another of these formulas. Herbert's governing plan of organization seems to be the last-mentioned one—duties to self, neighbor, and God—with the other patterns complexly related to it, and the whole formulated with special reference to the well-born, socially active youth imagined as audience. Personal moral duties are especially related to the cardinal virtues: upholding temperance, the speaker warns against lust, drunkenness, blasphemy (presented as an abuse of the lips), lies, idleness (involving failures in the duties of one's station in life as magistrate, scholar, estate-holder, father of a family), and finally gluttony. Justice—giving to each his due—is explored in terms of proper thrift in the use of money, that is, avoiding both covetousness and excessive spending on clothes or gaming. Fortitude dictates an appropriate

boldness, best evidenced in self-command and the eschewing of duels. Prudence is to be manifested in the proper use of mirth and wit, and a carriage toward the great not marred by pride, servility, or envy. Duties to others are examined in terms of several kinds of relationships: the claims and limitations of friendship; the dictates of civility in discourse; magnanimity in giving and receiving benefits; cleanliness; charity. Duties to God are defined in terms of proper behavior at public sermons and prayers, and proper regard for God's preachers. However, this governing scheme is not easily identifiable; it seems to have been deliberately camouflaged by an apparently haphazard shifting from topic to topic in imitation of the disjunctive form of Proverbs and Ecclesiastes, with their constant shifts in subject matter and their frequent doubling back and repetition of topics.

Like Ecclesiastes, this long stanzaic poem is conceived formally as a loosely ordered poetic sermon, and its precepts are often presented as grounded upon personal experience: "Shall I, to please anothers wine-sprung minde, / Lose all mine own? God hath giv'n me a measure / Short of his canne and bodie" (ll. 37-39); "Were I an *Epicure*, I could bate swearing" (l. 60). Moreover, the rhetorical figures employed are precisely those usually associated with the Book of Proverbs. The stanzas often begin with brief moral imperatives—"Abstain wholly, or wed" (l. 13); "Drink not the third glasse" (l. 25); "Flie idlenesse" (l. 79); "Be thriftie, but not covetous" (l. 151); "Play not for gain, but sport" (l. 193); "Be sweet to all" (l. 211); "Laugh not too much" (l. 229)—and then develop such topics through maxims, aphorisms, similitudes, antitheses and enigmas. Maxims or aphorisms are often found in the couplet conclusion to a stanza: "Stay at the third glasse: if thou lose thy hold, / Then thou are modest, and the wine grows bold" (ll. 41-42); "He pares his apple, that will cleanly feed" (l. 64); "Who breaks his own bond, forfeiteth himself: / What nature made a ship, he makes a shelf " (ll. 119-120); "Who cannot rest till hee good-fellows finde, / He breaks up house, turns out of doores his minde" (ll. 149-150). Antitheses are frequent, though Herbert's stanzaic form precludes the constant use we find in Proverbs: "Some till their ground, but let weeds choke their sonne: / Some mark a partridge, never their childes fashion" (ll. 98-99); "Who fears to do ill, sets himself to task: / Who fears to do well, sure should wear a mask" (ll. 125-126); "Thy clothes being fast, but thy soul loose about thee" (l. 414). Similitude or metaphor is very frequent: "Game is a civil gunpowder, in peace / Blowing up houses with their whole increase" (ll. 203-204); "Man is Gods image; but a poore man is / Christs stamp to boot" (ll. 379-380); "Man is a shop of rules, a well truss'd pack / Whose every parcell under-writes a law" (ll. 141-142); "Christ purg'd his temple; so must thou thy heart" (l. 423); "As gunnes destroy, so may a little sling" (l. 352). And, as in Proverbs, some figures are enigmas, characterized by obscurity and brevity: "God made me one man; love makes me no more, / Till labour come, and make my weaknesse score" (ll. 287-288); "The Jews refused thunder; and we, folly" (l. 449).

"The Church" is in some respects a new version of the Song of Songs, understood in its Protestant signification as an allegorical treatment of the relationship between

Christ and every elect soul, rather than in the mystical or ecstatic terms which often characterized Roman Catholic treatments of its central marriage-betrothal situation. So read, Canticles offered Herbert a model for tracing the development of a loving, personal relationship between Christ and the speaker (who incorporates many roles and moods and associations). Herbert, however, transposes the Bridegroom-Bride relationship into an association of loving friends, which also helps to define several other relations between Christ (or the Godhead) and the speaker—of king and subject, lord and servant, Savior and redeemed one, loving father and child. All these relationships are suggested early in the sequence and are explored and transformed as it proceeds. Moreover, Canticles, understood as a collection of love songs or ballads or as an epithalamium with a strong dramatic or dialogic aspect, also provided a model for Herbert's use of motifs and models from love poetry, as well as of various kinds of dialogue.

The opening poems present the beginnings of a love relationship with the principals as yet distant, separated. In **"The Altar"** the speaker states the fundamental basis of the relationship correctly enough but without much personal warmth, using the lord-servant metaphor—"A broken ALTAR, Lord, thy servant reares"; the speaker's hard heart is the altar which can only be hewed and sanctified by the Lord's power; and the speaker-servant's duty is praise, voluntary or involuntary, resulting from the Lord's action upon him. In **"The Sacrifice,"** the longest poem of the collection, Christ is the speaker, recounting his suffering and grief in irony-laden terms, and indicting mankind for callousness and ingratitude. Christ here woos the soul, confronting it with his love act, his sacrifice, to determine "If stonie hearts will melt with gentle love" (l. 90). The speaker now understands that he has been faced with a love challenge by the author of a new *Ars Amatoria* and his first response (in **"The Thanksgiving"**) is the natural one of attempting to match or even to outdo the lover:

> But how then shall I imitate thee, and
> 　　Copie thy fair, though bloudie hand?
> Surely I will revenge me on thy love,
> 　　And trie who shall victorious
> 　　　prove. . . .
> Nay, I will read thy book, and never move
> 　　Till I have found therein thy love,
> Thy art of love, which I'le turn back on thee:
> 　　O my deare Saviour, Victorie!
> 　　　　　　　　　　　(ll. 15-18, 45-48)

Of course he finds to his chagrin that he cannot in any measure imitate or accommodate Christ's passion, and so must perforce accept a love relationship based upon radical inequality, recognizing Christ both as the initiator of the relationship and the enabler of his own response. The speaker's only love victory can be to share in Christ's conquest over him (**"The Reprisall"**). Working from this new understanding of love, the association between Christ and the speaker develops in terms of a variety of relationships, associated by means of the pervasive love language with the Bridegroom and Bride of Canticles. However, Herbert makes little direct use of that formulation, and when he does, avoids its erotic and mystical connotations. Instead,

the love language proclaims God's love as the ground for all the relationships between God and the speaker.

As has been noted above, the speaker's painfully attained realization in these opening poems of the utter inequality which must characterize his love relationship with Christ also functions as a critique of Catholic meditation on the Passion. The speaker is forced to give over his foolish and presumptuous (Catholic) efforts to achieve an imaginative identification with the crucified Christ and to participate in his sacrifice by imitation, turning instead to a proper Protestant concern with the meaning of Christ's sacrifice for his own redemption and his spiritual life. In this interest he explores the relationship which is the theological ground of all the others—Christ as Savior and the speaker as his redeemed. **"The Agonie,"** the poem following immediately upon the challenge-and-response poems just discussed, provides the very definition of love by reference to Christ's role as Savior: "Who knows not Love, let him assay / And taste that juice, which on the crosse a pike / Did set again abroach. . . . / Love is that liquor sweet and most divine, / Which my God feels as bloud; but I, as wine" (ll. 13-15, 17-18).

This Savior-redeemed relation is adumbrated in numerous poems, and it is at times central. In **"Easter"** the Lord takes the speaker "by the hand" to rise with him (ll. 3-4); in **"Grace"** the speaker begs for the Savior's "suppling grace" to counter the effects of sin in a hard heart "void of love" (ll. 18-19); in **"Even-song"** the speaker's opening apostrophe, "Blest be the God of love," grounds that title upon God's gift of his Son and his constant favors; **"Prayer (II)"** lauds Christ's "unmeasurable love" in taking "our flesh and curse" (ll. 13-15). **"Dialogue"** harks back to the problem explored in the first love-challenge poems—the infinite distance between the Savior and his redeemed—but now the speaker pridefully attempts to resign completely from the relationship, based as it must be upon his lack of merit: "I disclaim the whole designe" (l. 23). Christ, however, shames the speaker by appealing to his own willing resignation of *"glorie and desert"* to assume the role of Savior (l. 30). Finally, in **"The Holdfast"** the speaker learns at last, in dialogic exchange with a "friend," that he loses nothing by the total resignation he must make of all claims to merit and even to personal responsibility for his faith and trust, since "all things were more ours by being his. / What Adam had, and forfeited for all, / Christ keepeth now, who cannot fail or fall" (ll. 12-14).

The speaker is related to Christ also as servant to lord, or sometimes subject to king, and the terms of this relationship also are transmuted by love. **"Redemption"** places the speaker in the relation of a tenant to a "rich Lord," seeking that lord in places of power and wealth to beg for a revision of his lease (a new covenant); then with fine self-irony he discovers his suit already granted as his lord dies amidst "a ragged noise and mirth / Of theeves and murderers" (ll. 12-13). **"Affliction (I)"** also brings the speaker to ironic self-realization in terms of these roles. He entered the service of a king attracted by and expecting to share in his "glorious houshold stuffe" (l. 9)—his joys and pleasures—but finds instead groans and sorrows, sickness and disappointment. He threatens rebellion but then perceives that the greatest loss would be a loss of the love upon which the relationship is based:

> Well, I will change the service, and go seek
> Some other master out.
> Ah my deare God! though I am clean forgot,
> Let me not love thee, if I love thee not.
>
> (ll. 63-66)

In **"Obedience"** he undertakes formally, by writing, to convey lordship over himself, but then perceives that he cannot do this by way of gift or donation; the right is already God's "by way of purchase" (l. 35). In **"Love unknown"** he complains vehemently to a "Friend" about his lord's apparently arbitrary rejection of the various gifts he offered in testimony of his service, seizing instead upon his heart and subjecting it to various afflictions. He is advised however that *"your Master shows to you / More favour than you wot of,"* in seeking thus to make his heart *"new, tender, quick"* (ll. 62-63, 70). In **"Artillerie"** God, as "Dread Lord," chides his servant for disobedience to the good motions sent him, and he responds by begging for some attention to his own "artillery" of tears and prayers. He concludes, however, that he must perforce accept God's terms: "Yet if thou shunnest, I am thine: / I must be so, if I am mine. / There is no articling with thee" (ll. 29-31). At length in **"The Odour. 2 Cor. 2.15"** he associates the language of sweetness and spices reminiscent of Canticles with the terms *Master* and *Servant*: Exclaiming "How sweetly doth *My Master* sound!" he finds in these words "an orientall fragrancie" (l. 5), and begs that the words *"My servant"* might "creep & grow / To some degree of spicinesse" to God (ll. 14-15), projecting thereby a developing commerce in such sweet breathings.

Closely related to the lord-subject or master-servant relation is that of father and child. In **"H. Baptisme (II)"** he understands the ideal spiritual situation to be that of a child—"let me still / Write thee great God, and me a childe: / Let me be soft and supple to thy will" (ll. 6-8)—though he does not yet invoke God as Father. In the familiar poem of rebellion, **"The Collar,"** the resolution is attained precisely through the transmutation of the former relationship into the latter. The speaker rebels because he perceives himself in servitude, in bondage, his collar an emblem of that condition, his life defined by duties and demands and renunciations dictated by fear. Interrupting these wild rebellious thoughts comes the Lord's call *"Child!"* which reminds the speaker of Paul's assurance that he is not a bond-slave to God but a son, heir to the promises and the kingdom. Recalling that other relationship, he can then accept the master-servant association also: "Me thoughts I heard one calling, *Child!* / And I reply'd, *My Lord*" (ll. 35-36). Later, in **"The Crosse"** he finds full resolution of his woes and agonies through a most profound understanding of the father-child relationship, identifying his crosses and his filial acceptance of them in terms of the paradigm established by God's Son, Christ: "these thy contradictions / Are properly a crosse felt by thy Sonne, / With but foure words, my words, *Thy will be done*" (ll. 34-36).

But the primary relation explored through these poems is that of loving friends, not fixed in the Canticles' relation of Bride and Bridegroom but exchanging the roles of lover and beloved; this relation is explored by transmuting and universalizing the love language from Canticles and from contemporary love poetry. In **"Good Friday"** and **"Jesu,"** Christ is imagined to write upon, or to have his name engraved upon, the speaker's heart in love-emblem fashion. **"Love (I)"** perceives God as "Immortall Love" and seeks a way to restore to him the love songs now addressed to mortal loves in praise of "a skarf or glove" (l. 13). **"Love (II)"** petitions God as "Immortall Heat" to kindle true desires in the speaker's heart: "Then shall our hearts pant thee" (l. 6), and send back the fire in true hymns. **"Mattens"** imagines God as wooer, expending all his art of love upon the speaker—"My God, what is a heart, / That thou shouldst it so eye, and wooe, / Powring upon it all thy art / . . . Teach me thy love to know" (ll. 9-11, 16). Other poems portray the speaker in various conditions common to lovers and to the Bride of Canticles: In **"Frailtie"** he confesses his fickleness and his attraction to worldly joys, by which he affronts "those joyes, wherewith thou didst endow / And long since wed / My poore soul, ev'n sick of love" (ll. 19-21). In **"The Pearl. Matth. 13.45"** he feels but overcomes the attraction of other loves (learning, honor, pleasure), depending upon God for a silk-twist (such as Ariadne gave to Theseus) to lead him safely through the world's labyrinth. In **"Deniall"** he suffers bitterly from apparent rejection: "When my devotions could not pierce / Thy silent eares; / Then was my heart broken, as was my verse: / . . . Therefore my soul lay out of sight, / Untun'd, unstrung" (ll. 1-3, 21-22). In **"The Search"** he laments the loved one's departure—"Whither, O, whither art thou fled, / My Lord, my Love?"—and, describing his constant sighs and searches, he begs for a reunion. In **"Longing"** he is a grieving, broken-hearted lover begging for an audience: "With sick and famisht eyes, / With doubling knees and weary bones, / To thee my cries, / To thee my grones, / To thee my sighs, my tears ascend: / . . . Bowels of pitie, heare! / Lord of my soul, love of my minde, / . . . My love, my sweetnesse, heare!" (ll. 1-5, 19-20, 79).

In **"Dulnesse"** he undertakes a blazon of Christ (who is much fitter than any Petrarchan lady to be the object of his serenades, his "window-songs"):

> Thou art my lovelinesse, my life, my light,
> Beautie alone to me;
> Thy bloudy death and undeserv'd, makes thee
> Pure red and white.
>
> (ll. 9-12)

But here he aspires to "*Look* onely"—even angels are not fit to love Christ. He does find a way to return love in one of the late poems, **"Bitter-sweet"**; as his Lord both loves and strikes, so he can answer this duality, "And all my sowre-sweet dayes, / I will lament, and love" (ll. 7-9). In **"The Glance,"** which follows immediately, he proclaims himself able to endure absences by recalling God's first loving glance vouchsafed him—"I felt a sugred strange delight, / Passing all cordials made by any art, / Bedew, embalme, and overrunne my heart" (ll. 5-7); on the strength of that remembered love-glance, he looks forward to the time, "when we shall see / Thy full-ey'd love!" (ll. 19-20).

In **"Unkindnesse,"** friendship is designated as the standard for the speaker's evaluation of his responses to Christ's overtures: "But when thy grace / Sues for my heart, I thee displace, / Nor would I use a friend, as I use Thee" (ll. 18-20). And when he weighs by the same standard Christ's sacrifice performed *"Onely to purchase my goodwill"* (l. 24), he recognizes that it far surpasses the deed of any friend.

The poem **"Clasping of Hands"** explores and resolves the paradox of lovers' self-possession through possession of and by each other, by appealing to the quality commonly understood to characterize true friendship, the obliteration of *meum* and *tuum*: "O be mine still! still make me thine! / Or rather make no Thine and Mine!" (ll. 19-20). Finally, in **"A Parodie"** he is able to transpose a secular Petrarchan love poem into the terms of this special love relationship: the tenor of the secular lament for absence is radically altered by the speaker's parenthetical recognition that Christ is not really, but only apparently, absent from him, and that when he half-believes such lies, "Thou com'st and dost relieve" (l. 30).

In this regard, the dialogic-dramatic character usually ascribed to Canticles, whereby certain passages were ascribed to the Bride and others to the Bridegroom, have an analogue in Herbert's presentation of the love relationship he is tracing. His lyrics present an interplay of voices which combine more intimately as the relationship develops. At the outset the voice of Christ (or of the Godhead) and that of the speaker are quite separate, contained within separate poems. Christ delivers his love-challenge in **"The Sacrifice"** and in the following poems the speaker attempts, unsuccessfully, to respond to that challenge in his own personal terms, with his individual voice (**"The Thanksgiving," "The Agonie"**). But then he comes to realize that only when his voice is joined with and responsive to Christ's voice will he be able to love or to praise. At times the divine voice is present directly, as an interlocutor or commentator whose part is quoted verbatim by the speaker, as when, in **"Redemption,"** the tenant-speaker hears and quotes his lord's words establishing the desired New Covenant at his death—*"Your suit is granted"* (l. 14). In **"The Bag"** he quotes at some length Christ's somewhat bizarre offer of the spear-rent in his side as a mail pouch for petitions to the Father; in **"The Pulley"** he personates the Creator explaining why he withheld the gift of rest from man; and in **"The Crosse"** he is recalled from desperation over his griefs and miseries by appropriating Christ's words in accepting his own crosses—*"Thy will be done"* (l. 35). In other poems a "friend" or messenger—or a better self—takes the divine part in directing or rebuking or aiding the speaker, providing thereby an analogue to the catechising which Herbert urged so forcefully as central to the duties of the country parson. In **"Artillerie"** a seeming shooting star rebukes the speaker for expelling good motions from his heart. In **"Jordan (II)"** a "friend" provides a directive to the would-be Christian poet struggling to divest his praises of artifice and self-display, to "Copie out" the sweetness love has already penned (ll. 17-18). In **"Love unknown"** a "Friend" interprets the apparently cruel and arbitrary behavior of the lord toward the speaker and his gifts by pronouncing the interpretive motto for

each emblematic episode: *"Your heart was foul, I fear"*; *"Your heart was hard, I fear"*; *"Your heart was dull, I fear"* (ll. 18, 37, 55).

In still other poems, especially those directly concerned with the making of poetry, the speaker often finds the divine voice providing a resolution of his poetic problems through the medium of scripture: a few words of a scripture text are quoted in the poem as a means of relating God's voice and God's art to the poet's own art. In **"Jordan (I)"** he finds a model for his own plainness in a near-quotation of Psalm 145:1, *"My God, My King"* (l. 15). In **"A true Hymne"** he tries unsuccessfully to make up a hymn of praise from certain scriptural epithets—"My joy, my life, my crown"—but he cannot get beyond these beginnings; in such a case he can depend upon God to supply the substance of the praises even as he supplies the substance of the love relationship—"As when th'heart sayes (sighing to be approved) / O, *could I love*! and stops: God writeth, *Loved*" (ll. 19-20). And in "The Posie" he adopts as the content of his own posie or motto the phrase, *"Lesse then the least / Of all thy mercies,"* echoing Jacob's words upon returning home a rich man after his exile with Laban.

In a few poems the interaction of the divine and human voices is explored more profoundly. **"Deniall"** presents a temporary disruption of the relationship: complaining that in God's absence both his heart and verse are broken, the speaker begs for God's return to "cheer and tune my heartlesse breast" (l. 26), and the final lines enact that return through the restoration of rhyme and form to the verses. The poem **"Dialogue"** exhibits another occasion of apparent collapse of the relationship, as the speaker and Christ engage in a debate in alternating stanzas, the speaker attempting to resign from the divine plan for his salvation grounded as it is upon his utter worthlessness, and Christ pointing to his own resignation of "glorie and desert" in assuming man's guilt. The relationship is restored as the speaker gives over the argument—"Ah! no more: thou break'st my heart" (l. 32). In the penultimate poem of **"The Church,"** **"Heaven,"** Echo supplies authoritative "divine" answers to the speaker's catechism of questions about eternity by repeating the speaker's own words; Echo's admitted origin in the "holy leaves" (of scripture) indicates the basis for the speaker's power to supply the answers to his own questions and to complete his poetic verses through the "divine" echo of his own voice. Here, through dialogic interchange, the human poet and his divine echo collaborate most intimately in the creation of a poem.

Finally, in **"Love (III)"** the relationship between Christ and the speaker attains full fruition. The speaker is still painfully conscious of his unworthiness and is ready to draw back, but now Christ, identified simply as "Love," assumes the role of perfect host offering a banquet with utmost courtesy to the speaker as an honored guest. He thereby evokes from the guest-speaker a matching courtesy, a willing and graceful acceptance of the host's generosity and his own unworthiness. This banquet of course alludes to the Church's communion banquet and also to the heavenly repast, climaxing the sacramental imagery and motifs developed in several lyrics—**"The H. Communion," "The Collar," "Peace," "The Banquet,"** and many more. But the sacramental motif is not the subsuming theme of the volume; rather it contributes to the complex pattern of relationships between Christ and the soul which we have been tracing, and which are so triumphantly resolved in this final poem. This poem also exhibits a perfect interplay of voices in the Christian poet's praises. We do not find here (as Stanley Fish's version of Herbert's aesthetics might lead us to expect) the Divine Voice subsuming the voice of the human poet and leaving him engaged in silent, ecstatic perception of divine truth. Nor, I think, will most readers find, with Fish [in his *Self-Consuming Artifact*, 1972] that this exquisite, ritualized colloquy is a rather harsh, brow-beating defeat of the speaker by Christ. Instead, this final poem is also a dialogue with the parts of the two speakers clearly defined, though now intimately blended, in the spirit and tone of courteous exchange appropriate to the occasion, into a poem of the most exquisite harmony and delightfulness. Such divine perfecting of human art is the goal of Herbert's aesthetics and of his speaker's quest as Christian poet.

An even more important generic resource for the lyrics of **"The Church"** is the Book of Psalms. In fact, Herbert seems to have conceived his book of lyrics as a book of Christian psalms, and his speaker as a new David, a Christian Psalmist. For one thing, Herbert's lyrics clearly exhibit what many patristic commentators and contemporary Protestants understood to be the inner essence of the Psalms, the analysis of the full range of spiritual emotions at their most intense—joy and grief, exaltation and desolation, misery and contentment, sorrow and consolation, fear and hope, rebellion and love of God—representing thereby to man the anatomy of his own soul. Many of Herbert's titles and opening lines indicate his presentation of just such a range of feeling: **"Affliction," "Love," "Sighs and Grones," "Miserie," "Dulnesse"** ("Why do I languish thus, drooping and dull"), **"The Bunch of Grapes"** ("Joy, I did lock thee up"), **"Longing"** ("With sick and famisht eyes"), **"The Collar"** ("I struck the board, and cry'd, No more"), **"The Flower"** ("How fresh, O Lord, how sweet and clean / Are thy returns!"), **"The Temper (II)"** ("It cannot be. Where is that mightie joy, / Which just now took up all my heart?").

In addition, Herbert's lyrics seem to relate themselves to one or another of the three fundamental categories of biblical lyric which commentators found represented in the Book of Psalms—psalms, hymns, and spiritual songs. Psalms were defined by Wither and others as sonnet-like, argumentative, meditative, or prayer-like poems on diverse subjects—a description which encompasses the largest category of Herbert's poems. Hymns were by definition joyful praises of God or thanksgivings to him: in Herbert this category covers the broad range from the elegant simplicity of the hymn portion of **"Easter"** to the lofty eloquence of **"Providence."** Spiritual songs were taken to be artful lyric pieces specifically intended for singing: in Herbert there are several song-like poems which were given contemporary musical settings, for instance, **"Christmas," "Antiphon (II)," "The Starre," "Vertue," "The Dawning."** Also, the numerous lesser kinds which Wither, Wil-

let, Beza, Donne, Gataker, and others found in the Psalms are very fully represented in Herbert. There are some fifteen sonnets (e.g., **"Redemption," "The H. Scriptures (I)"**); meditations and soliloquies (such as, **"Life," "Employment (II)," "The Discharge"**); many complaints (**"Affliction I-V," "Josephs coat"**); laments for tribulations (**"Deniall," "Grief," "The Crosse"**); prayers for benefits (**"The Call," "Grace"**); petitions against adversities (**"Sighs and Grones"**); poems of instruction (**"Constancie," "Humilitie," "Charms and Knots"**); consolations (**"The Flower," "The Forerunners"**); rejoicings (**"Man," "Church-musick," "Even-song," "Mattens"**); praises of God for his glories (**"Easter," "Antiphon (I)"**); thanksgivings for God's benefits (**"Providence," "Praise (II)"**); artful acrostic poems (**"Coloss. 3:3,"** and in a related kind, **"Paradise," "The Altar," "Easter-wings"**); ballads (Herbert's **"The 23d Psalme"** is in ballad measure); love songs (**"A Parodie," "Dulnesse," "Love (I)"**); dramatic poems (**"Dialogue," "Death"**). I do not suggest that Herbert set out to write in each of the lyric kinds contemporary theorists associated with the Psalms, but it seems likely that this theory, together with the example set by the Sidney-Countess of Pembroke psalms, sanctioned and encouraged his incorporation of such a rich variety of forms and kinds in his book of religious lyric. Recognition of this range should counter the critical assumption that Herbert's poems all aspire to the condition of the personal meditation, and the concomitant disposition to rate them according to the complexity with which they render the play of mind and feeling. We ought rather to applaud the rich generic diversity Herbert has achieved in his attempt to provide (even as the Book of Psalms was thought to do) a compendium of religious lyric kinds in his "Church."

Moreover, Herbert's speaker as Christian poet is set forth as a *figura* of the biblical Psalmist. We have noted how readily Protestants from Luther and Calvin to Perkins and Donne presented themselves as correlative types or antitypes to David, recapitulating his spiritual experiences, afflictions, and conflicts in their own lives. We have noted also how constantly David is identified in the sixteenth and seventeenth centuries as the appropriate model for the Christian poet, affording examples of the most magnificent poetic texture and figurative language, but also raising with special force the aesthetic problem of the poet's stance in relation to the divine truth of his subject matter and the necessary divine participation in his poetic creation. Herbert's speaker manifests his role as New Covenant *figura* of David the Psalmist in various ways. His several poems of affliction, complaint, and lamentation recall the Penitential Psalms. And even as David, forbidden to build the Temple of Jerusalem, prepared his Psalms as a songbook for that Temple and as a type of the New Testament Church located in the broken and contrite heart, so Herbert built a ***Temple*** which is also a volume of lyrics. Moreover, Herbert's pervasive concern with the problem of creating fit praises for God recalls the designation of David's Psalms as *Sephir Tehillim*, the Book of Praises. Also, as the Psalmist was understood to speak sometimes in his own person, at other times to personate the whole company of the faithful, and at still other times to speak for Christ or God himself, so Herbert's speaker renders his personal conflicts in such a way that they represent those of any faithful Christian, and he also often personates the Divine Voice. Finally, as David's Psalms were understood to be of his own penning and yet in another sense wholly inspired by the Spirit, so Herbert wrestles constantly with the paradox of his responsibility to create poems of praise, yet his inability to do so unless God will enable him and participate with him in those praises.

Several poems throughout the collection show Herbert's speaker, in quasi-typological terms, taking on the role of New Covenant psalmist as he appropriates and turns to his own uses the Psalmist's words and forms. The first poem of **"The Church," "The Altar,"** is in some respects a New Testament version of Psalm 51, perhaps the most frequently paraphrased and most fully annotated of all David's psalms (at least by Protestants), and widely recognized as a paradigm for Christian conversion and repentance. Herbert's imagery of the "broken ALTAR . . . / Made of a heart, and cemented with teares" alludes to Psalm 51:17, "The sacrifices of God are a broken spirit: a broken and a contrite heart, O God, thou wilt not despise"—thereby associating the speaker's heart with David's, which is the type of the Christian altar and Church. Moreover, the speaker's prayer that the stones of his heart hewed by God's action may generate praises even without his own volition points up the paradox that in some sense the praises are not his own but God's; David's perception in Psalm 51 that his praises are directly dependent upon the action of God—"O Lord open thou my lips, and my mouth shall shew foorth thy praise" (v. 15)—provides a model for the resolution of that paradox. In **"Sion"** the speaker again recalls the Psalmist's groans and the praises emerging from his broken and contrite heart (as well as his roles as musician to King Saul and author of the Church's book of prayers and praises). He thereby identifies his own art with the Davidic type of the New Covenant church in the heart which contrasts so markedly with the gorgeous material splendors of Solomon's physical temple: "All Solomons sea of brasse and world of stone / Is not so deare to thee as one good grone /. . . . The note is sad, yet musick for a King" (ll. 17-18, 24).

The speaker also appropriates the Psalmist's words and forms to confront the problem of praise and to afford models or starting points for his own praises. As we have seen, **"Easter"** is a New Covenant version of Psalm 57:7-11, involving the interaction of the risen (restored) heart, the struggles of the poetic lute to resound in harmony with Christ's cross, and the corrections and completions afforded by God's Spirit. In this exquisite lyric the Psalmist's emphasis upon his own early awakening is recapitulated and revised by the New Covenant psalmist who recognizes that Christ's rising will ever precede, and be the precondition for, his own spiritual and poetic resurrections. Elsewhere, in **"Jordan (I),"** the speaker explains his renunciation of the "fictions . . . and false hair" (l. 1) of secular love poetry by echoing a phrase from the Psalms, *"My God, My King."* The poem **"Providence,"** in which the speaker presents himself as the world's high priest articulating praises for all creation, is in some portions a very free descant upon several verses of Psalm 104 wherein God's bounty to all living creatures is enumerated and celebrated. Similarly, **"Praise (II)"** seems closely related to

Psalm 116 in its argument of love and praise, and in the speaker's direct and fitting response to God's merciful hearing, sparing, and saving him. As his counterpart to David's promise to offer "the sacrifice of thanksgiving" in the courts of the Lord's house, Herbert's speaker promises his artful praises: "Wherefore with my utmost art / I will sing thee, / And the cream of all my heart / I will bring thee" (ll. 9-12). And in the later, very moving poem **"The Forerunners,"** the poet confronts and then resolves the problem of age and waning poetic powers by repeating as a refrain Psalm 31:14 as his only necessary poetic statement—"Thou art [still] my God"—in final, full understanding that God's power, not his own, is the source of the praises produced by the New Covenant temple built in the heart, even as it is of that Temple itself.

Herbert's **"23d Psalme"** is his only complete psalm version; it appears near the end of his collection, marking a moment in which Herbert has been able to merge his voice completely with that of the Psalmist. Rendering each of the six psalm verses by one quatrain, and following closely the general argument and imagery of the original, Herbert nonetheless makes the poem wholly his own in diction, tone, and texture. For one thing, he heightens the effect of simplicity and directness by using ballad measure and almost wholly monosyllabic diction. For another, certain formulations unwarranted by the text of the psalm emphasize specifically Herbertian concerns—mutuality ("While he is mine, and I am his, / What can I want or need," ll. 3-4); the question of merit ("And all this not for my desert, / But for his holy name," ll. 11-12); and, most obviously, the poem's concluding focus, not present in the psalm, upon the problem of fit praise:

> Surely thy sweet and wondrous love
> Shall measure all my dayes;
> And as it never shall remove,
> So neither shall my praise.
>
> (ll. 21-24)

In **"Love (III)"** the speaker perfects his role as new psalmist. The dramatic situation rendered in the poem recalls Psalm 23:5, "Thou preparest a table before me, in the presence of mine enemies: thou annointest my head with oyle, my cuppe runneth over," and also Luke 12:37, "The Lord when he commeth . . . shall girde himselfe, and make them to sit downe to meate, and will come foorth and serve them." Though these Old and New Testament texts reverberate profoundly in the poem, Herbert's speaker has here devised his own formulation of the sweetness of divine love and care in terms of the courteous dialogue of host and guest. In so doing, he has moved beyond quotation or paraphrase or imitation of David and even beyond creative variations upon the Psalms, to voice his own intensely personal yet universal, simple yet exquisitely artful, New Covenant psalm of praise.

"The Church Militant" is modeled in some respects upon the Book of Revelation—conceived not as a series of ecstatic prophetic visions but as a poetic treatise on church history, in accordance with the exegetical emphasis of such contemporary Protestant commentators as Henry Bullinger, who described the book as an "ecclesiastical history of the troubles and persecutions of the Church."

The central symbol of the Apocalypse was taken to be the Woman clothed with the Sun and fleeing into the Wilderness (Rev. 12), universally identified as a figure of the Church Militant oppressed by her enemies: as Daniel Featley observed, this "embleme" of the Church Militant shows that "The Spouse of Christ . . . [is] a pilgrime, and flieth from place to place, from Citie to Citie, from Kingdome to Kingdome." Moreover, several commentators, notably Paraeus, analyzed the structure of the work as a series of acts presenting "diverse, or rather (as we shall see) the same things touching the Church," separated by choric songs and hymns. Herbert's poem transposes some of these elements into a poetic account of Church history, past and to come. He uses the imagery of Revelation: the Church is the pilgrim-Spouse of Christ, likened to the sun in that she traverses the world in an ever-westward direction. In the course of this journey she establishes various centers of civilization and then is forced to flee from each as Sin takes over in turn the communities she has established. At length both complete the course and arrive at their starting point in the East, where "Judgement may meet them both & search them round" (l. 269). Also, the structure discerned in Revelation of acts separated by choric passages has its analogue in **"The Church Militant,"** in which five episodes or stages in the history of the Church, recounted in heroic couplets, are set off from each other by a repeated lyric refrain combining Psalm verses 139:17 and 89:6, *"How deare to me, O God, thy counsels are! / Who may with thee compare?"* The speaker in this poem adopts the public stance and universal perspective of the church historian (a role the commentators often assigned to John of Patmos) and this persona is at a far remove from the intimate, personal voice speaking the lyrics of **"The Church."**

In these respects, **"The Church Militant"** may be seen as Herbert's Book of Revelation, rendering his own all-encompassing account of the providential course laid down for the visible Church throughout history. That generic association, together with the speaker's joyful embracing of this providential course (circular and distressing as it is shown to be within the bounds of earthly history) makes this work a fitting completion for the three-part structure which is Herbert's *Temple*.

Herbert's use of imagery and metaphor also repays scrutiny in terms of artistic precepts and models derived from scripture. His language requires, and has received from such critics as Vendler, Fish, and Stein, a close poem-by-poem analysis to reveal its artful perfection. But one aspect of Herbert's art deserving of much more attention is his elaboration of certain biblical metaphors into pervasive patterns of imagery which unify the volume and further define the Christian speaker. As we have seen, **"H. Scriptures (II)"** provides a key both to Herbert's understanding of metaphorical patterns in scripture, and to his use of such patterns in his own poetry. The process involves recognizing the subtle connections between disparate texts—"This verse marks that, and both do make a motion / Unto a third, that ten leaves off doth lie:"—and recognizing also how these related texts interpret, and are interpreted by, a Christian's life. This poem indicates that Herbert's fundamental biblical metaphors, activated by biblical allusions and echoes, will not be present in every poem and often not in consecutive poems, but that the patterns will emerge as the images in disparate poems connect with and reflect upon each other. Moreover, as we have seen above, many of Herbert's specific images, and especially the dominant patterns portraying the Christian as God's husbandry and the temple in the heart, are reinforced by visual emblems familiar in contemporary religious emblem books.

One pervasive metaphorical pattern portrays sin (and the grief it causes) as a sickness, afflicting the soul with manifold pains. The speaker complains of such maladies in many poems: "Lord, how I am all ague"; "The growth of flesh is but a blister; / Childhood is health"; "If thou shalt let this venome lurk / And in suggestions fume and work, / My soul will turn to bubbles straight"; "My thoughts are all a case of knives, / Wounding my heart / With scatter'd smart, / . . . Nothing their furie can controll, / While they do wound and pink my soul"; "How shall infection / Presume on thy perfection?"; "My head doth burn, my heart is sick, / While thou dost ever, ever stay"; "My throat, my soul is hoarse; / My heart is wither'd like a ground / Which thou dost curse"; "One ague dwelleth in my bones, / Another in my soul . . . / I am in all a weak, disabled thing." In Herbert's usage the familiar image of God as divine physician is not often a part of this metaphorical pattern, though in several poems God is identified as the source of the cure so badly needed by the soul. In **"Affliction (I)"** the speaker complains of his physical and spiritual ills with great bitterness: "My flesh began unto my soul in pain, / Sicknesses cleave my bones; / Consuming agues dwell in ev'ry vein, / And tune my breath to grones. / Sorrow was all my soul; I scarce beleeved. / Till grief did tell me roundly, that I lived" (ll. 25-30); moreover, the speaker here accuses God of playing the role of deceiving physician, offering him the "sweetned pill" (l. 47) of academic praises to bind him to the clerical life, and then, lest he achieve contentment, bringing him further sicknesses. In **"Repentance"** he identifies God's rebuke for sin as the cause of spiritual sickness: "Bitternesse fills our bowels; all our hearts / Pine, and decay, / And drop away, / And carrie with them th'other parts" (ll. 27-30). But he also finds in God the certain cure:

> But thou wilt sinne and grief destroy;
> That so the broken bones may joy,
> And tune together in a well-set song,
> Full of his praises,
> Who dead men raises.
> Fractures well cur'd make us more strong.
>
> (ll. 31-36)

Later, Christ's blood is identified as the balsam "which doth both cleanse and close / All sorts of wounds" afflicting the sinner's heart (**"An Offering,"** ll. 19-21).

Closely associated with this metaphorical pattern is that of God the chastiser, deliberately inflicting torment and anguish upon the guilty soul. Poems developing this metaphor usually conclude that the torment is somehow beneficial. The speaker finds his soul stretched as on a rack when God extends and then seems to withdraw his love: "O rack me not to such a vast extent; / . . . Wilt thou meet arms with man, that thou dost stretch / A crumme of dust from heav'n to hell?" Elsewhere he cries out: "Kill me not ev'ry day, / Thou Lord of life"; or recognizes that "No scrue, nor piercer can / Into a piece of timber work and winde, / As Gods afflictions into man, / When he a torture hath design'd"; or imagines God using his "dart" upon the heart—with allusion to the emblematic darts Divine Love infixed in Anima's heart in several emblems. Two poems focus centrally upon the figure of God the chastiser and tormenter, with the speaker begging to be spared the deserved punishment. In **"Sighs and Grones"** the speaker begs God not to bruise, scourge, blind, grind, or kill him, or wreak upon him the apocalyptic vengeance: "O do not fill me / With the turn'd viall of thy bitter wrath!" (ll. 19-20), but rather as Savior to reprieve and relieve him. Toward the end of the collection, in **"Discipline,"** the speaker identifies the bow of the God of vengeance described in Exodus with that of the Divine Cupid, thereby arguing that God may achieve the chastisement of the heart through love:

> Then let wrath remove;
> Love will do the deed:
>   For with love
> Stonie hearts will bleed.
>
> Love is swift of foot;
> Love's a man of warre,
>   And can shoot,
> And can hit from farre.
>
> Who can scape his bow?
>
>   (ll. 17-25)

An even more important metaphorical pattern presents God as gardener and the speaker as plant or tree, expected to flower or to bring forth fruits and be ever responsive to the rains, dews, sunshine, or tempests sent from heaven as well as to the cultivation of the divine gardener. This metaphor-cluster is developed from allusions to God who planted a Garden in Eden with Adam and Eve in it (Gen. 2:8-10); to Christ who cursed the barren fig tree and declared that his followers should be known by their fruits (Luke 13:6-9, Matt. 7:15-20); and to God as husbandman pruning branches from or grafting branches into the true vine, Christ (John 15:1-8). As we have seen, this metaphor was given visual embodiment in emblems by Camerarius, Wither, Mannich, Peacham, Hulsius, and others. Herbert's speaker in "Employment (I)" begs to be a flower in God's garland, but he fears that he will be "nipt in the bud" by frosts (l. 4). **"Employment (II)"** contrasts man's cycle of growth, in which the winter of age arrives before fruition, with the orange tree's ideal condition, bearing blossoms and fruits at once:

> Oh that I were an Orenge-tree,
>   That busie plant!
> Then should I ever laden be,
>   And never want
> Some fruit for him that dressed me.
>
>   (ll. 21-25)

Elsewhere, the speaker sees himself as a dead stock calling for dews of grace from above, or finds that he, "Like a nipt blossome, hung / Discontented." He is sometimes a tree bearing fruit and at other times a "rotten tree." He knows that he was once, but is no more, "a garden in a Paradise,"

and his sense of barrenness in his vocation is such that he now feels himself "ev'n in Paradise to be a weed."

In the latter half of the collection, several poems use the gardening metaphor centrally and more positively. In **"Life"** the speaker imagines himself making a posy and watching it quickly wither, deriving there-from a lesson regarding the sweetness and usefulness even of a short life, for the flower that he himself is: "Since if my sent be good, / I care not if / It be as short as yours" (ll. 17-18). **"Paradise"** presents the speaker as a tree in the paradise of the Church, becoming fruitful through the divine gardener's protection and pruning; the poem is formally an emblem, representing by the artful pruning of the verses (letters are lopped off from the rhyme words in each succeeding line of the triplet stanzas) the necessary pruning of the speaker by God so he may produce better fruit:

> I Blesse thee Lord, because I GROW
> Among thy trees, which in a ROW
> To thee both fruit and order OW.
>
> What open force, or hidden CHARM
> Can blast my fruit, or bring me HARM,
> Since the inclosure is thine ARM?
>
> Inclose me still for fear I START.
> Be to me rather sharp and TART,
> Then let me want thy hand & ART.
>
> When thou dost greater judgements SPARE,
> And with thy knife but prune and PARE,
> Ev'n fruitfull trees more fruitfull ARE.
>
> Such sharpnes shows the sweetest FREND:
> Such cuttings rather heal then REND:
> And such beginnings touch their END.

"The Flower" might almost serve as an emblem poem beneath the Wither emblem depicting flowers alternately scorched by the sun of afflictions and temptations and revived by the rain and dew of God's grace. The speaker sees himself as a flower experiencing the return of spring showers after winter frosts: he can hardly believe that "my shrivel'd heart / Could have recover'd greennesse" or remember "That I am he / On whom thy tempests fell all night" (ll. 8-9, 41-42). He longs for Paradise "where no flower can wither," but rejoices that "now in age I bud again, / . . . I once more smell the dew and rain, / And relish versing" (ll. 23, 36, 38-39). The poem's conclusion makes the flower-gardener metaphor fully explicit and brings the metaphorical pattern to happy resolution:

> These are thy wonders, Lord of love,
> To make us see we are but flowers that glide:
>   Which when we once can finde and
>   prove,
> Thou hast a garden for us, where to bide.
>
>   (ll. 43-46)

Herbert's dominant metaphor is that of the temple in the heart of man, developed from a variety of texts which identify the Christian as the temple of the Holy Spirit, as a lively stone in God's temple, or as God's building (1 Cor. 3:9, 16; 1 Pet. 2:5), and which contrast Solomon's Old Testament Temple with this new temple not made with hands (Acts 7:47-48). Assimilated to the metaphorical pattern are other texts presenting the heart as synecdoche for the

Christian himself and so as the site of this temple: the Psalmist's claim that the Lord desires "a broken and a contrite heart" rather than burnt offerings (Psalm 51:16-17), God's promise to write the Law not in stone tablets but in the fleshy tables of the heart (Jer. 31:33), God's promise to take away our stony hearts and give us new hearts of flesh (Ezek. 36:26). As we have seen, the School of the Heart emblem books drew upon the same range of biblical imagery, and Herbert's poems often recall such visual representations. Herbert's sequence presents a version of this metaphorical pattern akin to that in several of the Protestant heart emblems and most notably in the heart-book of Cramer; in these emblems the hands of God work externally and powerfully upon the heart to soften, cure, shape, and build it into a fitting temple or dwelling place. Herbert begins to develop the pattern in these terms in **"The Altar,"** which presents the speaker's heart as antitype of the Old Testament altars of unhewn stone, in that it must be shaped by God's hand, not man's, into a fitting altar of praise. Like David's heart this heart-altar is broken and contrite, but it is still a "hard heart" made of stones. In **"Nature"** the heart is seen to be stony, requiring the engraving of God's law upon it, or better still, the substitution of the promised new heart of flesh:

> O smooth my rugged heart, and there
> Engrave thy rev'rend Law and fear;
> Or make a new one, since the old
>   Is saplesse grown,
>   And a much fitter stone
> To hide my dust, then thee to hold.
>
> (ll. 13-18)

"The Church-floore" begins the construction within the heart—"Blest be the *Architect*, whose art / Could build so strong in a weak heart" (ll. 19-20)—and **"Sion"** directly contrasts Solomon's glorious but inferior Temple at Jerusalem with this new temple now building: "And now thy Architecture meets with sinne; / For all thy frame and fabrick is within. / There thou art struggling with a peevish heart" (ll. 11-13). Other poems point to specific actions of God upon the heart: the speaker is amazed that God treats the heart as if it were "Silver, or gold, or precious stone / . . . Powring upon it all thy art"; the name "Jesu" is "deeply carved" in the heart but the letters are scattered since the heart is broken; the heart is "cut" by the crossed ropes of contradiction and frustration. **"Love unknown"** develops an emblem-book sequence (strongly reminiscent of certain plates in Cramer and Mannich) in which a "Lord" acts arbitrarily and apparently strangely toward the speaker's heart, casting it first into a font where it is bathed with blood from a rock, then into a huge blazing furnace labelled "AFFLICTION," and finally onto a bed of thorns to cure (respectively) its foulness, hardness, dullness. Later poems emphasize especially God's soothing and curative actions upon the heart: in **"An Offering"** a balsam or blood from heaven cleanses and cures its "many holes" (l. 4), and in **"The Glance"** the speaker feels "a sugred strange delight, / Passing all cordials made by any art, / Bedew, embalme, and overrunne my heart" (ll. 5-7).

Less prominent than the formulation just traced are two other ways of imaging the divine action on the heart which have affinities to the Jesuit Heart Books of Haeften, Bivero

and the *Vis Amoris*; Herbert's occasional use of these formulations softens somewhat the emotional effect of the Protestant version of the metaphor, with its overwhelming emphasis upon God's activity and man's helplessness. In a few poems, Herbert presents the heart as an active character. Sometimes the speaker engages by dispute or remonstrance with its recalcitrance: he urges his "greedie heart" to be content, to "sit down" and "Grasp not at much." Again, he complains that it is a "Busie, enquiring heart," which is seen to "prie, / And turn, and leer" in its seeking after the future. Elsewhere the heart, as synecdoche for the speaker, undertakes various pious actions: it prays and "lies all the yeare" at Christ's feet; weeping for Christ's absence it picks up crumbs of hope, and knocks at Christ's door desiring his return. The effect of this is to show the heart galvanized to some activity though not to much accomplishment—an altogether different effect from that achieved in Haeften' emblems of Anima and Divine Love together accomplishing all the stages in the purification of the heart. Some other Herbert poems recall Jesuit emblems of the Divine Cupid or the Dove inhabiting the heart, but in these poems the Christ figure is more like the adult, resurrected Christ of Heyns' emblem, occupying a heart presented as antitype of the Old Testament Temple. In Herbert's poems Christ's occupancy of the heart is uneasy and incomplete: he is constantly disturbed by "loud complaints and puling fears," and he is restricted to "some one corner of a feeble heart," pinched and straitened by Sin and Satan. Also, the Spirit's residency is not a present fact but a future hope: in "Whitsunday" the speaker prays that the Spirit may come to "spread thy golden wings in me; / Hatching my tender heart" (ll. 2-3). The effect is to suggest that the divine occupancy is just beginning, since the temple of the heart is still under construction.

Herbert also makes constant use of the biblical symbolic mode, typology, to characterize the speaker and to explore the nature of the spiritual life. This symbolism is important not only to *The Temple* as a whole (as we have seen), but also to the argument of many individual lyrics. Herbert's use of typology is characteristically Protestant in its focus upon the individual Christian as referent for the types, but the emphasis is uniquely his own. He characteristically presents within the compass of a single poem the speaker's progress from an identification with and recapitulation of various Old Testament types, to a comprehension within himself of the Christic fulfillment of those types. The first poem in **"The Church"** sets forth the terms for this progress from type to antitype with reference to the various aspects most important to the speaker's self-definition—as a Christian everyman, as priest, and as poet. The emblematic poem **"The Altar"** presents the speaker's heart as recapitulation of that altar of unhewn stones divinely prescribed in the Old Testament ("thou shalt not build it of hewen stone: for if thou lift up thy toole upon it, thou hast polluted it," Exod. 20:25):

> A broken ALTAR, Lord, thy servant reares,
> Made of a heart, and cemented with teares:
>   Whose parts are as thy hand did frame;
>   No workmans tool hath touch'd the same.
>   A HEART alone

Is such a stone,
As nothing but
Thy pow'r doth cut.
Wherefore each part
Of my hard heart
Meets in this frame,
To praise thy Name:
That, if I chance to hold my peace,
These stones to praise thee may not cease.
O let thy blessed SACRIFICE be mine,
And sanctifie this ALTAR to be thine.

But since the new altar is not simply stone, but a heart, it is also the antitype to the Old Testament altar—pointed to in that medley of biblical texts promising the exchange of a heart of flesh for the stony heart (Ezek. 11:19); or a new covenant inscribed in the heart, "I will put my law in their inward parts, and write it in their hearts" (Jer. 31:33); or a new dwelling place for God not in houses built by men's hands but with the man "that is poore and of a contrite spirit" (Isa. 66:1-2). The fundamental situation of the speaker as Christian everyman is thus posed in typological terms in this first poem: the need for his Old Testament stony altar-heart to be hewn by God's power and wholly transformed into its New Testament antitype, a heart of flesh, a temple not built with hands.

The speaker's progress from type to antitype is perhaps most clearly traced in **"The Bunch of Grapes,"** which also affords the most explicit statement of Herbert's conception of typology as God's symbolism. As Rosemond Tuve has noted, the poem depends for its meaning upon our recognition of the traditional typological relationship between the grapes hanging from the pole carried by the spies and Christ on the cross, the true vine pressed in the winepress of the Passion (Isa. 63:3) to become the wine of the New Covenant. What is most significant and characteristic, however, is the location of the entire typological relationship in the heart of the speaker. The poem is about the speaker's loss of spiritual joy and contentment; as he explores that loss he first sees himself recapitulating the wanderings of the Israelites in the desert, as a correlative type with them:

For as the Jews of old by Gods command
        Travell'd, and saw no town;
So now each Christian hath his journeys
    spann'd:
        Their storie pennes and sets us down.
        A single deed is small renown.
Gods works are wide, and let in future times;
His ancient justice overflows our crimes.
                                        (ll. 8-14)

Unlike the Israelites, however, he is given no cluster of grapes, no tangible earnest or assurance of the Promised Land. The resolution comes as the speaker recognizes the antitype, Christ's redemptive sacrifice, as a yet more basic part of his spiritual experience: "But can he want the grape, who hath the wine?" (l. 22). Tracing a progress within himself from type to antitype, he can finally affirm that this earnest of Christ's sacrifice affords him a less tangible but far more certain and all-embracing guarantee of spiritual joy. More complexly, **"Josephs coat"** traces the same typological paradigm within the speaker.

Joseph's coat of many colors (gift of his loving father but cause of his sufferings and imprisonment) is the type of the humanity of Christ, of which he was denuded at the crucifixion. The speaker, rendering in song his many griefs and sorrows—"Wounded I sing, tormented I endite"—seems to possess a "Joseph's coat" of many colors in the variety of joys and pains in his life. He is brought to this condition because God has given to anguish "One of Joyes coats" (the flesh of Christ), and thereby has provided "relief / To linger in me" (ll. 11-12). Accordingly, he is himself a new Joseph, possessed of a new coat of many colors, in that he can now see his variegated life of joys and sorrows as evidence of his Father's special love: "I live to shew his power, who once did bring / My *joyes* to *weep*, and now my *griefs* to *sing*" (ll. 13-14).

The emphasis in **"The Altar"** upon the speaker's desire to praise, and his prayer that the stones of his heart might themselves send forth praises if his intended praises fail, point also to the speaker's role as priest: as New Covenant priest he has special responsibility to offer the sacrifice of praise, which is the antitype of the Old Testament bloody sacrifice. Subsequent poems also explore in typological terms this aspect of the speaker's self-definition as priest. **"The Collar"** at first presents him in fierce rebellion, regarding his clerical collar as an emblem of slavery, and complaining especially that the eucharistic elements afford him no sense of joy and fruition: "Sure there was wine / Before my sighs did drie it: there was corn / Before my tears did drown it" (ll. 10-12). His problem is that he experiences the spiritual life entirely in terms of duties, obligations, and Old Testament legal servitude. This problem is resolved as the Lord's call, *"Child!"* reminds him that his New Covenant status (Gal. 4:3-7) is not that of a bondslave, but that of a child and son, heir to the promises and the kingdom. The same pattern obtains in **"Aaron,"** but in this poem the New Covenant resolution is more fully possessed. The speaker begins by recognizing his need as priest to clothe himself with Aaron's Old Testament priestly garments and ornaments, yet his utter inability to put on the holiness they symbolize—and demand. He then comes to understand that this responsibility is now not his, that Christ is now his head, breast, music, dress. At length, he perceives that as a priest of the New Covenant he is himself (through Christ) the antitype and fulfillment of the Old Testament Aaron:

        So holy in my head,
    Perfect and light in my deare breast,
My doctrine tun'd by Christ, (who is not dead,
    But lives in me while I do rest)
        Come people; Aaron's drest.
                                        (ll. 21-25)

The focus on praise in **"The Altar"** also inaugurates the theme of the special responsibility of the Christian poet to find fit ways to praise, relating that theme also to the typological paradigm of the Old Testament altar of stone, and New Covenant temple in the heart. The Jordan poems continue this motif. In **"Jordan (I),"** the title invokes the typological relationship of the Israelites' crossing Jordan into the Promised Land to Christian baptism, to announce the baptism of the speaker's verse to the service of God; the poem proclaims his renunciation of "old" poetic styles for a new, plain, devotional and biblical mode. **"Jordan (II)"** explores the matter more profoundly, and in more personal terms. The speaker finds that he himself began by adhering to a "law of works" in poetry, seeking out "quaint words, and trim invention" (l. 3) and curling his plain intention with metaphors, on the assumption that such embellishments are appropriate to divine praise. But he then discovers that such "works" have no merit, because of his corruption—"so did I weave myself into the sense" (l. 14). Finally he recognizes that worthy praises, like the renovation of the heart, must be essentially God's doing, and adopts a proper New Covenant poetic—to copy out the sweetness that is *"in love . . . [al]- readie penn'd"* (l. 17), i.e., in God's Word. He has hereby crossed Jordan again and situated his verse more securely in the Promised Land. **"Sion"** brings this motif to a kind of resolution: the speaker now fully understands that Solomon's Temple with its glorious embellishments was not the mode of praise God most desires: "All Solomons sea of brasse and world of stone / Is not so deare to thee as one good grone" (ll. 17-18). Such "grones," which find their type in the Psalmist and their antitype in the speaker, are now perceived as the true New Covenant mode of praise, and the truest music. In these hymns, produced by the humble and contrite heart, "the note is sad, yet musick for a King" (l. 24).

Again, **"Love (III)"** brings these typological themes to their period. The stone altar has become a banquet table of intimate communion, and the communion table is itself type of the heavenly feast, when God "shall girde himselfe, and make them sit downe to meate, and will come foorth and serve them" (Luke 12:37). The speaker as Christian everyman thus experiences the complete transformation of his stony heart, the speaker as priest participates in the sacrament of thanks-giving, and the speaker as poet has created an exquisite hymn of New Covenant praises, based now not on groans but upon perfected joys.

From all this it is evident that these diverse, artful, and exquisitely crafted poems are founded upon a far more sophisticated poetics than is sometimes inferred from those Herbertian lines which seem to renounce art as inappropriate to religious subject matter, to embrace "plainness," and to affirm utter dependence upon God. Rather, such passages ask interpretation in terms of various biblical contexts, even as contemporary sermon theory defined sermonic art according to a scriptural standard. As we have seen, Herbert constructs a biblical frame of reference for his poems: they receive generic definition by reference to certain poetic books of the Bible, they utilize dominant biblical metaphors as unifying image patterns, and they employ typological symbolism in characteristically Protestant ways to explore the spiritual development of the speaker and to serve as an organizing principle of the entire volume. The art Herbert eschews involves the conventional poetic devices and ornament of secular poetry; and the plainness he embraces is consonant with that "sweet art" embodied in the scriptures.

Moreover, Herbert explores the role of the Christian poet by setting his speaker in quasi-typological relation to the great biblical poets, so that his poems become in some re-

spects responses to and creative versions of their works. At various times his speaker assumes a persona like that of the Solomon of Proverbs and Ecclesiastes, the Beloved in Canticles, the prophet-historian of Revelation, and especially the Psalmist. And even as the biblical poets were perceived to create their own poems but withal to serve as agents for the Holy Spirit who is the primary author of everything in the scriptures, so Herbert recognized and dramatized the divine agency by incorporating the Divine Voice in several of his poems, and showing it in dialogic tension with that of the human speaker. Like so many of his predecessors and contemporaries in the creation of Christian poetry, Herbert in the lyrics of **"The Church"** modeled himself most directly upon David the Psalmist, manifesting in himself David's spiritual agonies and states of soul, and echoing and reworking Davidic themes, images, and entire psalms in his own verses. But his poetry constitutes an impressive new achievement in this kind, in that it moves beyond an imitative and derivative to a genuinely creative conception and use of biblical poetics. Herbert undertakes nothing less than the task of becoming a Christian psalmist, transposing (as he indicates in **"Easter"**) the elements of biblical art upon a Christian lute resounding in harmony with Christ's cross. The undertaking results in the creation of religious lyrics of surpassing beauty, biblically-derived yet original, simple yet of great variety and complexity, "plain" yet exhibiting "Utmost art." (pp. 283-316)

> *Barbara Kiefer Lewalski, "George Herbert: Artful Psalms from the Temple in the Heart,"* in her Protestant Poetics and the Seventeenth-Century Religious Lyric, *Princeton University Press, 1979, pp. 283-316.*

Paul Elmer More on Herbert's temperament:

There was, in fact, something of Hamlet in his mental disposition, and the subtleties of the imagination overbalanced the will to act. It was his nature to hesitate and dally until some impulse from without stimulated him, and then his movement was curiously abrupt. So it was that, in 1629, he suddenly married Jane Danvers, a relative of the Earl of Danby with whom he had become acquainted through his mother's second husband. Tradition would have it that this event occurred only three days after his first interview with the lady, and such haste would suit well enough with his temper.

Paul Elmer More in his Shelburne Essays (4th series), *1911.*

A. D. Nuttall   (essay date 1980)

[*In the following excerpt, Nuttall examines Herbert's attitudes towards poetry and Protestant theology in* The Temple.]

Imagine—if you can—God reading this poem:

"Dialogue"

Sweetest Saviour, if my soul
 Were but worth the having,
Quickly should I then controll
 Any thought of waving.
But when all my care and pains
Cannot give the name of gains
To thy wretch so full of stains,
What delight or hope remains?

What, Child, is the ballance thine,
 Thine the poise and measure?
If I say, Thou shalt be mine;
 Finger not my treasure.
What the gains in having thee
Do amount to, onely he,
Who for man was sold, can see;
That transferr'd th' accounts to me.

But as I can see no merit,
 Leading to this favour:
So the way to fit me for it
 Is beyond my savour.
As the reason then is thine;
So the way is none of mine:
I disclaim the whole designe:
Sinne disclaims and I resigne.

That is all, if that I could
 Get without repining;
And my clay, my creature, would
 Follow my resigning:
That as I did freely part
With my glorie and desert,
Left all joyes to feel all smart— —
 Ah! no more: thou break'st my heart.

Is God pleased with what he reads? The question put thus to a twentieth-century reader sounds almost idiotically bald, but few people of the seventeenth century would have regarded it as improper. There is of course a certain theological discomfort in the notion of *reading* (with its implication of consecutive apprehension) applied to one whose understanding is total and instantaneous, but this we can easily correct. As we do so, our phrase at once takes on a more seventeenth-century flavour: is this poem pleasing to God?

Our first answer is likely to be some sort of 'yes'. God cannot fail to be gratified to see his creature, George Herbert, so submissive to his will, so sensible of the sacrifice performed on his behalf. The Christian humility of the poem is perfect, except perhaps for one thing (and here we must press a little harder on our unimaginable image, God watching the growth of the poem from over Herbert's shoulder). The humility of the first stanza is of course deliberately presented by the poet as wrong-headed. Accordingly, it at once invites a loving correction from God. But before God can, so to speak, clear his throat to answer, lo, the creature Herbert is scribbling away at the second stanza and God's part is there, written out neatly for him. Herbert in the poem does not simply submit himself to the will of God; he personally supplies the divine correction.

The first literary effect of this is to turn the 'George Herbert' who offers the first stanza into a dramatic character. The George Herbert who blushes and fidgets in the first stanza cannot be the same person as the George Herbert whose comprehensive (too comprehensive) piety produces the whole poem. Had the second stanza continued in the same mode and voice as the first, giving us in place of the divine response a change of attitude—say an expression of grateful acceptance—on *Herbert's* part, the split between author and speaker would never have become obvious. More importantly, the expression on the face of the divine eavesdropper might have remained benevolently unironic. As things are, a certain sense of incongruity is inescapable. Herbert, the character *within* the poem, displays the inept incomprehension of mere humanity, but Herbert the author undertakes to supply on God's behalf the answers only God can give.

The pattern in which Herbert's merely human conception of God is externally corrected recurs in his poetry. The voice ranting in his skull is silenced by another voice, half-heard, more distant and at the same time more intimate than the first, but fundamentally Other:

 Methoughts I heard one calling Child.

Thus Herbert's poems dramatize one of the most important requirements of the religious temper, which is quite simply that God should be other than oneself. But by that very act of dramatizing (which is a kind of usurpation) they blaspheme it.

To suppose the immediate attention of God himself directed to all this fictive ingenuity is no wild assumption. On the contrary, it is a necessary implication of Christian doctrine. Moreover, as I have hinted, to imagine God so can prove instructive even for the modern, unbelieving student of literature. One immediate consequence of this rather odd exercise of the spiritual imagination is vastly to increase the difference between the poetry of Donne and the poetry of Herbert. The passing twinge of shame we feel on Herbert's behalf (akin to the social embarrassment we may feel on behalf of a precociously intelligent child) rarely if ever visits the reader of Donne. Donne the suppliant and Donne the poet remain one, truly humble flesh.

The logical knot of Herbert's poetry can be drawn still tighter, until presumption becomes something like sheer contradiction. Herbert, a mere man, explains on God's behalf the things which man is incapable of seeing for himself; but since it is a man who does this explaining, it cannot after all be true that man is thus incapable. Philosophers will easily recognize the salient features of this battle-scarred terrain. They may think of Sartre, who sought to explain in words the inefficacy of language, or of the logical positivists, who offered the proposition (itself neither analytical nor based on sense-perception) that all meaningful propositions are either analytic or based on sense-perception. But is the devotional poetry of Herbert really self-destructive in this way? There seems to be a case (at the very least) for saying, 'No, it is not'.

The best and most nearly complete answer is that which refers us to Revelation and tradition. Herbert, in putting words into the mouth of God, is not attempting some grotesque act of up-staging; he is merely doing what Christians, as part of a dynamic religious tradition, have always done, that is, rephrase and re-point the eternal truths of the faith. The faith of Islam confines its adherents to the petrified text of the Koran. This has never been the Christian way. What else does the parish priest do each Sunday but speak on behalf of God in his interpretation of Scripture? Seen in this light, Herbert's poetic practices may no longer appear as an idiosyncratic aberration but rather a natural extension of his ordinary duties as Rector of Bemerton.

Does this, then, abolish our difficulty? It is likely that most practising priests would answer that it does not. Even in the pulpit the special embarrassment of the modest man entrusted with a most immodest task is common, for all that the speaker is physically exalted and sustained above the heads of his congregation, is softly fenced in with the symbols of his traditional office. In the terms of current criticism, the church, the vestments, the pulpit provide a supportive semasiological apparatus, one function of which is to impersonalize the speaker's words. Yet even so the better sort of priest will tell you that he can hardly recall his own sermons without a kind of shame. It is therefore hardly surprising that in the personal mode of a devotional lyric (in which an immediate intercourse between God and the subject is proposed) this feeling of shame is instantly exacerbated. Herbert, quite clearly, felt it. Moreover, in the case of the devotional poetry there are strong theological grounds for this disquiet. To be sure, the Protestant answer to the parson's modest doubts has always been that they are or should be merely irrelevant. It is not the man who speaks but God who speaks in him, and behind this lies the austere Augustinian doctrine that all the good we do is really done by God working in us. But notice that this answer is more applicable to the pronouncements of the priest to his flock than it is to that strange activity called prayer, in which the subject habitually finds himself drawn to *supply* harsh answers from his unseen, inaudible interlocutor.

Let us consider an artificial example:

> Lord, give me a thousand pounds. Ah, Lord, but
> now I see that to ask for a thousand pounds may
> be mere greed. Be it then according to thy will.

Notice that in this fairly typical prayer, there are, so to speak, two selves. There is the baser self, which asks, and there is the higher self, which cancels the request. The relation of the baser self to God is unreflective. The higher self, on the other hand, rationalizes its relation to God. It is consciously theological. The consequence of this increased consciousness is an immediate loss of that innocence in which alone petitionary prayer is morally possible. Once the thought has occurred that God both knows what ought to be done and will in any case do what ought to be done, one is hard put to it to avoid a second thought: petitionary prayer is otiose. The fact that God might have responded to an innocent petition, artlessly offered, is now irrelevant. Indeed, it could be said that the language of the phrase 'petitionary prayer is otiose' is redundant: prayer *is* petition, *is* a kind of asking. Prayer itself, therefore, becomes otiose, and is replaced by a lordly gesture of assent. And if human petition is otiose, human approval of God's freedom of action, or human permission to God to exercise his will is still more plainly otiose. It might be supposed that the pattern of thought in this particular specimen of self-cancelling prayer is so clear that a few repeti-

tions would convince the subject that it might be discontinued forthwith. Yet it appears that many Christians persevere with it throughout their lives, embarking each night upon a petition which they must know will be withdrawn before the sentence is completed. Many of Herbert's poems are in this sense not prayers so much as modest refusals to pray. The better self in my specimen ended by saying, 'Be it then according to thy will'. Clearly, this with no great violence could be re-expressed as 'But thou wilt say to me, "These things are not for men to describe".' Now we have a formal example of speaking on behalf of God, or ascribing words to God. Protestantism has two ways of construing this better self. One is to call it 'conscience', the other is to invoke the notion of grace.

It seems plain that the first of these, 'conscience' will be of small service to us in our present difficulty. If we say that conscience may properly supply the presumable answers of God we give our assent to what must now be seen as a venial fiction. God has not in fact spoken by a direct and miraculous intervention; rather, conscience has supplied the better thought. It soon becomes apparent that this scheme is not adequate to contain the spiritual drama of Herbert's poetry. Herbert repeatedly shows us in his poems how the merely human is broken in upon by something which is not human, is not natural at all, is God himself. Take these lines (from **"Love III"**):

> Love bade me welcome: yet my soul drew back,
>   Guiltie of dust and sinne.
> But quick-ey'd Love, observing me grow slack
>   From my first entrance in,
> Drew nearer to me, sweetly questioning,
>   If I lack'd any thing.
>
> A guest, I answer'd, worthy to be here:
>   Love said, You shall be he.
> I the unkinde, ungratefull? Ah my deare,
>   I cannot look on thee.
> Love took my hand, and smiling did reply
>   Who made the eyes but I?

If (forgetting style and metre for a moment) we substitute 'Conscience reminds us that God would say' for 'love said' in the second stanza, the effect of a subjective universe shattered from without is virtually lost.

If anyone here answers, 'But the voice of conscience is *simpliciter* the voice of God', I might begin by querying that *simpliciter*. Certainly in **"Love III"** we cannot substitute 'conscience' for 'Love' without some very odd results:

> Conscience took my hand, and smiling did reply
>   Who made the eyes but I?

But of course the basic suggestion that to the Protestant mind God is present in the movements of conscience is perfectly sound. If we stress this aspect of conscience we shall find that we have really already moved to the second major explanation of 'the better self', namely *grace*.

The doctrine of grace at once confronts us with an almost frighteningly complete solution of our problem. For to say that grace produces the utterances of the better self is to say that these utterances are not in fact the work of a *self* at all, but the work of God. And this in blunt terms means that while George Herbert may be said to have written the first and third stanzas of **"Dialogue,"** God actually wrote the second and fourth stanzas. Thus the poem is not a dramatization of the relation between God and man but is an actual example of it. It is not a mimetic performance but is a recorded conversation which once took place between Herbert and God. One is tempted to add that the very authorship of *The Temple* now becomes a dual affair. Herbert wrote most of it, but God wrote quite a lot. Moreover, we now lose our distinction between Herbert the dramatic character who frets in the first stanza and Herbert the poet whose comprehensive theological understanding supplies the rest. Herbert the man collapses back into Herbert the character. Such is the radical interpretation.

A more moderate application of Protestant theology might allow to Herbert the poet, as distinct from Herbert the dramatic character, the role of versifying the communications of grace and of incorporating them into an artistic whole. This, it will be noticed, has an immediate ring of sanity. The 'joint-authorship' account is simply incredible, and this is no less true, I fancy, for the seventeenth-century mind than it is for the twentieth-century mind. But that Herbert might have believed himself to be modifying and re-phrasing impulses vouchsafed to him by God seems entirely possible.

The only trouble with the moderate account is that it readmits the demon we have been labouring to expel. For, clearly, the George Herbert who wrote the whole poem has his own moral and artistic purposes in phrasing God's communication as he does. The 'better self' is with us once more and is in a manner 'using' the good insights granted by God. This 'using' is partly aesthetic. God's communications are given a high finish and a certain metrical form in order that they may harmonize with the rest. The distinction I assume here between a supposedly simple Godly insight and the 'worked up' poetic version may seem a little forced. A reading of the **"Jordan"** poems, however, should soon convince the reader that the distinction was perfectly real to Herbert.

> *What, Child, is the ballance thine*
> *Thine the poise and measure?*
> *If I say, Thou shalt be mine;*
> *Finger not my treasure.*
> *What the gains in having thee*
> *Do amount to, onely be,*
> *Who for man was sold, can see;*
> *That transferr'd th' accounts to me.*

These words are God's but at the same time they are very evidently Herbert's. If we read as historians of ideas we may well miss the crucial point here. To the alert literary critic it is surely inescapable. The elegantly chiastic repetition of 'thine', the hushed meiosis of 'transferr'd th' accounts to me' are especially Herbertian. Thus these divine yet Herbertian stanzas work in the moral economy of the poem (in the teeth of all Calvinist disclaimers of human merit) to establish a kind of moral credit for Herbert. How else, after all, did he earn his reputation for sanctity and virtue? By a paradox familiar to readers of Protestant literature the disclaiming of merit is somehow felt to be itself meritorious. There is a sense that Herbert has, after all, got in first with the right sentiment.

Yet none of this will quite do. Again we need to imagine God ruefully smiling to find his words anticipated. Or perhaps not smiling. It is hard to believe that Herbert did not foresee that these stanzas would enhance his reputation for piety. The insinuation of sanctity by disclaiming sanctity is horribly close (in an intelligent poet) to bad faith. And Herbert was very intelligent.

I have argued that a sense of impropriety, of some degree of personal usurpation in Herbert's divine speeches persists, after the various theological excuses have been exhausted. This thesis, however, is open to an objection of quite a different kind. All our difficulties, it might be said, spring from an elementary confusion. What we have been treating as prayers in poetic form are really poems which imitate or represent prayer. They are from first to last dramatic fictions, with (as commonly) a fictional addressee within the poem—God—and a real addressee outside the poem—the reader. The thought of God eavesdropping on their composition holds no terrors, since he will most certainly understand them for what they are, pictures of the way a man might pray.

Now in the world of fiction it is commonly assumed that the mode of expression need not be realistically compatible with that which is expressed. For example, a Shakespearean character may affirm in excellent blank verse that he has no ear for poetry. To conclude that he is a liar or a fool, to tax him with his perfect cadences, is *logically* absurd. The 'I' of much love poetry is obviously fictional in a similar way. The lover in the poem may cry out that he is in every way exhausted, while the author may betray in the vigour of his writing a state of abounding imaginative health. The conventions of fiction easily permit all this. So with the poetry of Herbert: there need be nothing disingenuous or contradictory in the fact that the George Herbert who prays *within* the poem misconstrues his faith while George Herbert the author stage-manages the misconstruction, since the Herbert who exists within the poem is himself merely a fictional construct. The language given to God likewise exists on a plane of pure fiction. Remember the words of Aristotle: history tells us 'what Alcibiades did' but tragedy tells us 'what would happen' (*Poetics*, 1451b). Herbert's poetry does not pretend to give us what God said, it gives us through the well-known and accepted conventions of fiction what God *would* say. As soon as we see this, it could be said, the supposed offence of Herbert in answering for God is much reduced. To say what God would say, to explore the hypothetical, is after all very close to the professional duty of the priest discussed earlier. Thus, it may be thought, the heat is off. Herbert is not shouldering God aside in the very act of prayer, correcting his own human inadequacy with a blasphemous anticipation of the divine response; he is rather projecting upon the screen of English literature a representation in profile of the ways in which God's love meets, frustrates and exalts the praying human subject.

Now even if this account were true we must once again insist that while it may indeed reduce the urgency of our problem it certainly does not remove it altogether. Even if Herbert were giving us not prayers, but pictures of prayers, some mimetic fidelity to the real conditions of prayer must presumably be required. It would be an insult to the faithful to offer them a representation of prayer which confessed no obligation to notice what prayer is actually like. There is indeed a sense in which our original hesitation over the propriety of providing answers for God is actually underlined when fictional status is assigned to them. Within the poem we are told that the one element which can save the praying subject from a hopeless subjectivism is the voice from outside. But now we are assured that the words of God are a fiction. The one element which could mitigate our human isolation and disclose the divine substance (the one element which, incidentally, is absent from ordinary prayer) is feigned by the poet.

There is a curious analogy here with the novels of Virginia Woolf. There, because of the chosen mode of writing, the reader is confined to a single stream of subjective consciousness. Moreover, there seems to be implicit in this choice of mode a certain philosophical claim, that really the world is like this. Not surprisingly, the reader soon finds himself a prey to solipsistic unease. But this unease is magically dispelled by Virginia Woolf's employment of a plurality of consciousnesses. As we step from the mind of Lily Briscoe into the mind of Mrs Ramsay, the world of the novel reassumes its proper solidity. A thing which can be seen from more than one side must be three-dimensional; the perceptions of Paul can after all be corrected externally—by the perceptions of Charles. And so, we may suppose, all is well again. But this power of passing from mind to mind, which alone can confer reality on things, is possible only in fiction. This generates the absurd conclusion that fiction can give us real substance while reality cannot.

Of course there are some writers who emphasize the spurious licence of fiction to heal and cure in order to make a sardonic point about the real sickness of things. Such, in the view of some critics, was Fielding's purpose when, by an ostentatiously improbable exertion of comic vicissitude, he repeatedly saved Tom Jones from the likely consequences of his thoughtlessness. He was thus a better moralist than Sir John Hawkins or Dr Johnson took him for, since, so far from exalting natural impulse and letting the rest go hang, his very comic extravagance, rightly understood, implies strong support for an ethic of considerate and responsible action: those who rely so heavily upon the saving intervention of the comic spirit *ex machina* are surely not to be themselves relied upon in ordinary life, where the Comic Spirit has no power to save. That Fielding may have worked to this end is perhaps just credible. But that Herbert should have sought by the incongruously obtrusive availability of God in his poems to appraise his readers of the real unavailability of God is simply incredible.

The argument I have stated can be blurred in various ways. That the voice of God, coming from outside the natural order, can alone illumine the benighted condition of merely natural man—all this is perfectly fair as an account of the state of affairs proposed in the poetry of Herbert. But the notion of God's external voice is really ambiguous. In my argument it was suggested that the one sufficient remedy was an actual, audible reply. Thus the *fact* of a

reply, it was implied, is in a way more crucial than the *content* of the reply. But this audible reply (it was pointed out) is precisely what does *not* occur in real prayer (outside the special experiences of mystics). This antithesis between fact and content is, however, misleading. The very nature of Christ's teaching proclaims it Other than the world, and this *fact about content* supplies an adequate external corrective to the merely human. This would mean that the fiction whereby Herbert has God speak at the end of the poem becomes after all a venial fiction, since it is no longer on the *fact* of a *heard* reply that the very existence of an external correction depends.

Yet it is somehow exceedingly difficult to get rid utterly of the sense that Herbert has - for whatever excellent purpose—'taken over' the speech of God. Take **"The Quip"**:

> The merrie world did on a day
> With his train-bands and mates agree
> To meet together, where I lay,
> And all in sport to geere at me.
>
> First, Beautie crept into a rose,
> Which when I pluckt not, Sir, said she,
> Tell me, I pray, Whose hands are those?
> *But thou shalt answer, Lord, for me.*
>
> Then Money came, and chinking still,
> What tune is this, poore man? said he:
> I heard in Musick you had skill.
> *But thou shalt answer, Lord, for me.*
>
> Then came brave Glorie puffing by
> In silks that whistled, who but he?
> He scarce allow'd me half an eie.
> *But thou shalt answer, Lord, for me.*
>
> Then came quick Wit and Conversation,
> And he would needs a comfort be,
> And, to be short, make an Oration.
> *But thou shalt answer, Lord, for me.*
>
> Yet when the houre of thy designe
> To answer these fine things shall come;
> Speak not at large; say, I am thine:
> And then they have their answer home.

Here if ever Herbert is in fine form. The swift allegorical sketches—sly Beauty, creeping into her rose, provoking Money, jangling his coins, Glory in his 'whistling' silks and that darting allusion to the 'and to be brief, Gentlemen' employed by all really prolix speakers—these have something of the vigour of the droll mediaeval figures in the *Ancrene Wisse* together with the added grace and wit of one who has moved—and enjoyed moving—in courtly circles. Herbert the artist is in high good humour. But what does the poem say? It says that it would be wrong for Herbert to give God's answer and then, instead of lapsing into a devout silence, actually *tells* God what to say! To be sure, the phrase God is asked to pronounce proclaims his ownership of Herbert, but, if that is so, why cannot he be allowed to say so for himself—especially as the poem has told the reader four times that is what must happen? The whole poem takes its tone from the bad company it ostensibly rejects. It is *bumptious*. Herbert loves to present himself as the helpless child of God. Here the child, cuckoo-like, has somehow outgrown his nourisher and seems to nudge his exhausted protector into the required behaviour.

Note that with this poem we cannot say that Herbert the character defers to God, while Herbert the author supplies the conventional divine reply. Within the fiction of the poem it is the same George Herbert which defers to and instructs his creator.

Thus, even if we take the poems as radical fictions, difficulties persist. But in truth they are not fictions. We are not dealing with an Ovidian or a Cavalier, but with the author of the **"Jordan"** poems. Herbert was a strict Protestant and he did not hold with playing games. Indeed the **"Jordan"** poems are the final test of the 'games' view of Herbert.

"Jordan I"

Who sayes that fictions onely and false hair
Become a verse?   Is there in truth no beautie?
Is all good structure in a winding stair?
May no lines passe, except they do their dutie
    Not to a true, but painted chair?

Is it no verse, except enchanted groves
And sudden arbours shadow course-spunne
    lines?
Must purling streams refresh a lovers loves?
Must all be vail'd, while he that reades, divines,
    Catching the sense at two removes?

Shepherds are honest people; let them sing:
Riddle who list, for me, and pull for Prime:
I envie no mans nightingale or spring;
Nor let them punish me with losse of rime,
    Who plainly say, *My God, My King.*

"Jordan II"

When first my lines of heav'nly joyes made mention,
Such was their lustre, they did so excell,
That I sought out quaint words, and trim invention;
My thoughts began to burnish, sprout, and swell,
Curling with metaphors a plain intention,
Decking the sense, as if it were to sell.

Thousands of notions in my brain did runne,
Off 'ring their service, if I were not sped:
I often blotted what I had begunne;
This was not quick enough, and that was dead.
Nothing could seem too rich to clothe the sunne,
Much lesse those joyes which trample on his head.

As flames do work and winde, when they ascend,
So did I weave my self into the sense.
But while I bustled, I might heare a friend
Whisper, *How wide is all this long pretence!
There is in love a sweetnesse readie penn'd:
Copie out onely that, and save expense.*

Modern readers of Herbert, faced with these poems, show an extraordinary tendency to flee to inessentials. Thus it is customary to draw laborious distinctions between them: in **"Jordan I"** Herbert is happy to let the rest write pretty poems and merely expresses a personal preference for another mode, but in **"Jordan II"** he is simply telling the story of his own development from an ornate to a plain style - and so forth. It is surely better to face the matter squarely. The **"Jordan"** poems have the same title because they are at bottom the same poem. In these poems Herbert is not saying that some sorts of poetry are nicer than others; he is saying that poetry itself must at last be burned away by truth. Why are the poems called **"Jordan"**? Because the poet is crossing the river beyond which nothing less than the most perfect simplicity is tolerated. As Stanley Fish [in his *Self-consuming Artifacts: The Experience of Seventeenth-Century Literature*, 1972] has admirably insisted, Herbert learns in the **"Jordan"** poems that there is nothing for *him* to write at all: a 'plain style' is not the solution, but is rather, 'the last infirmity of the noble poetic mind'.

And, of course, this mid-river poetry is crucified by inconsistency. It is, necessarily, poetically parasitic upon the devices it so austerely renounces. I say 'necessarily' because that which is renounced is finally poetry, *simpliciter*. The poem tells us that all we need to say is 'My God, My King', but *that* is not a poem, and Herbert the artist must needs leave us more (even while telling us that in God's eye this 'more' is really 'less'). To read the **"Jordan"** poems in succession is to experience the contradiction all the more poignantly. For even the pretext of a valediction, a last venial farewell to poetry, can scarcely be sustained when the exercise is *repeated*. To misquote Heraclitus, no man passes twice over the same Jordan. Herbert cannot let go.

But in any case the inconsistency is inescapable within the confines of a single **"Jordan"** poem. If Herbert really means it when he says that 'My God, My King' is enough, why did he not cancel all that went before? The answer is not, 'Well then, he does not really mean it.' He does mean it and he is riven. We insult him if we pretend otherwise.

Nevertheless my imagined opponent may still fight back. That Herbert should in a poem explicitly renounce poetry will scarcely surprise the educated reader. The renunciation of art in favour of nature is after all one of the older tropes of the conscious artist. Style is an infinitely elastic medium. It expands to embrace the very rejection of style until that rejection is at last—a style. In **"Jordan II"** as if it were to sell' may be read by one reader as an idiosyncratic flicker of Puritan contempt, but another, more knowing reader will see in it a *literary* echo—'I will not praise that purpose not to sell'. Further examples are easily found: *Ingenium nobis ipsa puella facit*; 'Foole, said my Muse to me, looke in thy heart and write'; 'Sans sans, I pray you'. The game is an old one; why should not Herbert be playing like the rest?

There is perhaps a sense in which Herbert may be drawn by what may be termed the purely literary impulse of his writing into this game. But at the same time he resists with a resistance which is partly extra-literary. For, after all, Herbert really was a Protestant parson. Certain radical elements in Protestant thought really did imply the rejection of poetry. Even in the eighteenth century Dr Johnson could still feel that religious poetry was infected with a kind of duplicity [in his "Life of Waller"], and of course this duplicity approaches most nearly to mendacity in those poets who profess a severely Protestant approach. T. S. Eliot once observed that complete atheists are incapable of genuine blasphemy [in his "Baudelaire," *Selected Essays*, 1951] *Credo quia absurdum*. It is *because* Herbert lies and blasphemes that we know he is a great religious poet. The player-poet, on the other hand, is safe, for he 'nothing affirmeth'.

In saying this I deliberately break a circle which we have all been taught, first by the New Critics and after them by the structuralists, to regard as sacred. This is the principle by which any work of art is permitted to propose its own inviolable limits of reference. In real life opinions catch and rub on one another; continuities are demanded and inconsistencies condemned. But, if, say, "Sailing to Byzantium" commends the inhuman and "The Circus Animals' Desertion" commends the human, it is gauche (we are told) to speak of a conflict, or even a change of mind. They are merely different poems. Attempts have been made, indeed, to extend the principle further. After Wittgenstein many philosophers proposed that what had previously been thought of as inconsistencies should be not so much solved as dissolved, conjured away. We were to do this by referring the seemingly discordant elements to separate, encapsulated 'language games'. This book is written in a contrary spirit. Instead, it proposes a world of warm connection and violent collision and a literature everywhere rent and energized by commerce with that world.

The polite assumption that all systems are separate and closed has had its effect not only on literary criticism but also on the history of ideas. Philosophical or ideological theories are treated as cultural phenomena rather than as propositions which may be true or false. The effect is to emasculate critical enquiry. For example, it is somehow bad form to describe a given body of thought in any other terms than would be accepted by the original proponent. To say 'Calvinism is antinomianism' is to be met with the pained rejoinder, 'No, no, antinomian is a term of abuse; you cannot have read Calvin'. The possibility that Calvin may have flinched from or failed to perceive the real implications of his thought is set aside as illogical; the thought and his version of the thought are one and the same. Reasoning is thus flattened, made two-dimensional. The third dimension, the dimension of implication and consequence, the proper arena of criticism, at once apparent to any one who reads his Calvin with the question 'Is this true?' in his mind - this is utterly abolished. In what follows I propose to ignore this taboo and to reassert our ancient liberties.

Certainly the old poets never thought themselves confined to a uniformly fictitious realm. They themselves break the sacred circle again and again. Herbert does so, quite clearly, in **"The Dedication"** (itself a poem) prefixed to *The Temple*:

"The Dedication"

Lord, my first fruits present themselves to thee;
Yet not mine neither: for from thee they came,
And must return.   Accept of them and me,

And make us strive, who shall sing best thy name.
Turn their eyes hither, who shall make a gain:
Theirs, who shall hurt themselves or me, re-
frain.

The fatal interaction of real and fictional universes is here implicit in the very form. Dedications are necessarily done not by the characters within poems but by authors. Thus, at the very beginning of *The Temple* the relation between Herbert the poet and Herbert the worshipper is insistently problematic. The poems are themselves offered to God. This at once confounds our neat resolution of difficulties whereby God was allowed to be the addressee within the poem while outside it was the reader who was addressed. A dedication, merely by being a dedication, refers to the poems as poems and therefore stands outside their fictional preserve. Yet even in the dedication Herbert addresses God, and does so in verse which is very like what follows in the main body of the text. Of course, he knows that *The Temple* consists of poems which will be read by people, and in a sense the poems are written for these people—or at least for those of them who may obtain spiritual profit. Again one is reminded of the village priest, who prays to God indeed, but with one eye, so to speak, on his congregation. He must adjust his language to their needs and all his persuasion of God must at the same time persuade his human listeners. In such a situation, one might say, rhetoric which cannot properly be directed at God has nevertheless an acceptable function. The rhetoric is for the congregation. But in fact it is rarely possible for a man placed in such a situation to remain so artificially clear-headed. And, even if he did, the spectacle might not be entirely pleasing. If we insist that the dedication is just a poem like the rest and so preserve the fictional closure, the sentiments expressed in it become an ingenious, illusionist joke, an amusing reference to a state of affairs which would exist if real prayer were going on. But Herbert's dedication is not a joke, and has never been taken so by generations of qualified readers, that is, by poetry-loving Christians.

In fact the 'games' view of Herbert is under attack from two sides at once. It is fought, with deadly seriousness, in the poems and it is virtually outlawed, or at least threatened, by the Protestant theology which Herbert the man accepted. I do not argue either that Protestantism or Herbert was consistently and at all times committed to the extreme Puritan rejection of fiction. But I do argue that the extreme Puritan position was, at the very least, felt by him to be relevant and formidable. The one reply he would never have made is, 'Oh, but that wasn't me speaking; it was a fictional *persona*; it is only a poem, you see.' Even if we suppose that Herbert's Protestantism may have allowed him the occasional trope or metaphor, there is one trope which he could never use with an easy consciousness of fiction, and that is the trope of pretended simplicity. That Herbert should have offered as a sophisticated joke something which corresponds in every particular with a treasured belief is, once more, simply incredible. The situation has its ironies. The New Critics and the structuralists are ideologically committed to preserving the separate autonomy of fiction; Herbert as poet falls naturally within this field. But Herbert also, three centuries and more before the first of the New Critics reared his head, belongs to a faction which is identifiably opposed to theirs. Thus in engaging with Herbert they are dealing with a poet whose very concept of composition is on their terms impermissible. F. R. Leavis, on the other hand, falls (by this broadest of classifications) on Herbert's side. Incorrigibly Leavis connected literature with reality and had the scars to prove it. The word (it is not quite un-usable) which links Herbert and Leavis is of course 'Puritan'.

The hard thing having been said, it is now necessary to say the softer things. Herbert's attitude to fiction is not always so unkind. He can offer God 'a *wreathed* garland of deserved praise' (**"A Wreath"**) and in **"A True Hymne"** he affirms that the simple words, 'My joy, my life, my Crown' are 'among the best *in art*', so reconciling art and truth. In the second Latin poem addressed to his mother Herbert praises both her piety and her style (*scriptio*) and grants that while the greatest beauty lay in the kernel, some was to be found in the shell:

Bellum putamen, nucleus bellissimus

Again, it is well known and may indeed be relevant that Anglicans of Herbert's stamp allowed the propriety of beautiful church furnishing (the Lutheran Church, says Herbert, is 'shie of dressing'). Herbert's friend, Nicholas Ferrar, in *The Winding Sheet* frankly grants that flourishes of style are 'gracefull when they fall in naturally of themselves' and certainly makes free use of them in his own writing. But such Anglican softening to external beauty is constantly thwarted and opposed by a fiercer asceticism. 'Roses and lilies speak of God', says Herbert, significantly enough in one of the two sonnets addressed to his mother, but in **"The Quip"** the rose is seen as something sinister, an emblem of seduction, and in the poem which is actually called **"The Rose"** this theme recurs. The reflex of feeling is typical. 'My joy, my life, my Crown' may be called for a moment 'among the best in art' but we all know that these words alone do not compose a poem and are in this regard exactly parallel to 'My God, My King' in **"Jordan I."** Nicholas Ferrar, immediately after the words we quoted a moment ago, adds that really a plain style is best and before he died made a great bonfire of all his books of literature, 'many Hundreths in all kind of Languages, which he had in all places gotten with great search, and some cost. . . . Comedies, Tragedies, Love-Hymns, Heroicall Poems, and such like.' So great was the smoke that men came running from the fields, 'and within a few dayes, it was by rumour spread at Market Townes all the country over, that Mr. Nic: Ferrar lay a dying, but could not dye till he had burned all his Conjuring-Bookes. . . .' As he lay, waiting for death, he wrote, 'The having an Orlando in the house, is sufficient ground to have it burnt down over their heads, that truly feare God'. The hold of Augustine and of Calvin had hardly begun to weaken. *Quid Athenae Hierosolymis?*

The *Short Title Catalogue* (1475-1640) lists no fewer than 96 editions of Calvin's writings and 50 of Beza. These easily head the list (Luther and Bullinger come next with 38 each). Each of the years between 1548 and 1634 saw the publication of one work or more by Calvin. Between 1578 and 1581 there were six to eight every year. Calvin's record of publications in English was not overtaken until the

early seventeeth century, and then it was by William Perkins and Henry Smith, both Calvinists. The influence of Calvin on the Thirty-nine Articles is crushingly evident. Article ix affirms that all men naturally deserve damnation and adds that this infection of nature persists even in the regenerate. Article x asserts the spiritual and moral impotence of man: 'We have no power to good works . . . without the grace of God' and Article xi adds that we are accounted righteous before God only by the merit of Christ. Article xii explains that good works, so called, can in no way endure the severity of God's judgement and are pleasing to him only because they are a sign of faith. Works done *before* grace, meanwhile, are 'not pleasing to God and have the nature of Sin' (Article xiii). This doctrine was anathematized by the Council of Trent at its sixth session, in January 1547. The germ of Calvinism lies, as W. H. Halewood observes [in his *The Poetry of Grace: Reformation Themes and Structures in English Seventeenth-century Poetry*, 1970] not so much in Augustine as in Paul's Epistle to the Galatians. Christ is the only possible agent of salvation; to hope for salvation under the law is to put faith in the saving power of human effort, which in Paul's view is a ridiculous blasphemy. The contrast is thus made absolute between, on the one hand, God, spirit, faith and salvation and, on the other, Man, flesh, law and damnation.

But there Augustine enters. The doctrine of *Galatians* might almost have been deduced independently from Augustine's Platonizing insistence that God is not just good; he is good-*ness*. Whenever our actions are good, they have goodness in them, and where there is goodness, there is God, and where there is God, there are not we. It is characteristic of the Reformation not to soften the edges of these doctrines but rather to harden them. The Thirty-nine Articles tell us that 'good works' before grace are not pleasing to God, but Luther goes further. He suggests that a sinful nature might be a positive recommendation in the eyes of God: 'If I am unfit for prayer because of my sins, well and good. I do not want to become more fit. For, alas, to God I am more than fit for prayer because I am an exceedingly great sinner. Sin alone permits the triumphant operation of grace. Luther asks, 'What connection could there be between abundant mercy and human holiness?' In his commentary on *Galatians* he reaffirms that 'Christ was given, not . . . for small sins, but for great and huge sins' and adds a moment later that really monstrous sins, so far from placing us in the Devil's power, are really our best armour against him. Well might Satan feel confused. Luther joyously concludes with the words which were to fire the controversy between Major and Amsdorf, 'My righteousness does me no good but rather puts me at a disadvantage before God.' Such language must strike us as seriously unbalanced. Yet when we encounter similar sentiments in Augustine it is fairly easy to see a kind of splendour in them, partly because we sense that Augustine is grappling with the appalling complacency of late Roman stoicism, 'the rational man armed in his virtue' and the like, and partly because Augustine's thought it always more dialectical, less brutally simple than Luther's. Yet Luther was no crank, but a revered and highly effective figure.

Nevertheless, the special violence of Luther's intelligence can never have been general. There can be no doubt that the ordinary religion of Protestant England was never so paradoxical as this. But Luther's extravagance is always rational, which is as much as to say that the inferences he makes *might* at any point be made by others, for they follow of themselves. His most extreme conclusions really are latent in the common theology. As a guide to ordinary assumptions he is indeed uncertain; as a guide to the occasional, half-suppressed terrors of the intelligent he may be very good indeed.

Calvin, whose style is altogether quieter, is more radical still. God the Father, he explains, really hates us:

> Because oure minde can neither desirously enoughe take holde of life in the mercie of God, nor receive it with suche thankfulnesse as we ought, but when it is before striken and throwne downe wyth the feare of the wrath of God and drede of eternal death, we are so taught by holy Scripture, that *wythout Christe wee maye see God in manner wrathfully bent againste us, and his hande armed to our destruction*: that wee maye embrace hys goodwyll and fatherly kindnesse no otherwere, but in Christe.

The italics are mine. It would appear that we have only one friend in the Trinity. The Father is our enemy. Blake's Urizen is no harsh caricature of Calvin's God-the-Father, but is if anything a more sympathetic figure than the original.

Thus Calvin begins to build for us the character of God, compounded, it would seem, of a hostile (and omnipotent) Father, a loving (and omnipotent) Son and an (omnipotent) Spirit. So far, so disquieting. As we read on, the picture, so far from lightening, grows darker. Calvin proceeds to clarify this obscure, troubling personality, not by explaining away the hatred (which he considers manifestly just) but by weakening the love:

> For God whyche is the hyghest ryghteousnesse, can not love wickednesse whiche he seeth in us all. Therefore we al have in us that, which is worthy of the hatred of God.

And at once he explains that God's only motive for loving us at all, in the person of Christ, is that he 'wyll not lose that which ys his in us'.

One's first response to the proposition that the Father hates us while the Son loves is to conclude that the Father is no Christian. For him, justice is not transcended by love; for that mystery we must turn to the Son. Bizarre as the notion must appear, there is a certain symmetry in the idea that of the persons of the Trinity it is Christ who is the Christian. But this makeshift comfort proves short-lived. Christ, after all, loves us only as one loves his property; he trembles for us only as one trembles for an endangered investment. The grim doctrine of Article ix is easily recognized: 'We are all . . . borne to damnation of hell.' All that is good is God's; the rest is uniformly black, with no gradations. It might be objected that to argue thus is to imply that there is no moral difference between man and Satan. Calvin does not shrink from this conclusion, but eagerly embraces it. He quotes with pure approval the

following words from Augustine's commentary on the Gospel of John (XLIL.xl.8):

> Let no man flatter himself; *of himself he is Satan.* His blessing comes from God alone. For what do you have of your own but sin?

I have given the passage in the modern translation of Ford Lewis Battles. The sixteenth-century translator, Thomas Norton, may have found it hard to stomach, for he flinches from the frontal specificity of 'Satan' and writes instead 'hee is a devill'. The doctrine is indeed stark. In so far as man exists separately from God, he sins. *Esse est peccare.* 'Of oure selves wee are nothing but evell.'

It may be thought that in one respect we must have overstated the case: that, while every *moral* act of man is thus tainted, there exists a considerable territory—the operations, say, of pure reason—which may be thought of as morally neutral. Here perhaps is space to lick our wounds? Not so. Calvin will have none of this. His thought is fiercely binary and tends always to the elimination of middle terms. *Everything* we do is wicked; certainly our reasoning is thus:

> Therefore mans reason neither approcheth, nor goeth towarde, nor ones directeth syghte unto this trueth. . . . But bicause we being dronke with a false persuasion of oure owne deepe insight, do very hardely suffer oure selves to be persuaded, that in matters of god [sic] it is utterly blynde and dull.

Here the good reader's ears should twitch. We have been here before. If our insight is thus depraved, our reasoning is vain, and, if our reasoning is vain, our theology is vain. What then of the *Institutes*—a work of reason from beginning to end? The Calvinist answer is distressingly simple. The *Institutes* was not written by Calvin; it was written by God. This answer, so far from being extravagant, would be accepted, with downcast eyes and a modest smile, by Calvin himself. Remember the divine stanzas in Herbert. We asked, did Herbert write this material, or did God? Already that question should seem less wild.

The doctrine grows, then, from Paul and Augustine, especially from that in Augustine which was anti-Pelagian. It is difficult for the modern reader to understand the consistency and intensity of Protestant opposition to Pelagius. The man himself (especially if one has just been reading Calvin) seems luminously sane. Certainly the opposition hardened at the Reformation. Earlier Roman Catholic censure had been moderate, qualified at many points by respect for that in Pelagius which is pellucidly just (the proceedings of the Synod of Arles are highly informative). Pelagius held that men are capable of good, that spiritual effort was therefore necessary and desert possible. Like Dostoevsky's Grand Inquisitor, he thought that for God to ask more of man than man could perform was monstrous, but unlike the Inquisitor he drew the conclusion that God must have given man the necessary strength and discernment. This is the doctrine which Protestant writers, almost to a man, treat as a grotesque superstition. As Patrick Grant has written [in his *The Transformation of Sin*, 1974], the Thirty-nine Articles, the Augsberg Confession, the Statements of Carnesecchi all tell the same, anti-

Pelagian tale. The contempt is automatic yet ferocious and (this must be said) unintelligible to the author of this book. Augustine remorselessly opposed Pelagius's view that man might be capable of good. Yet, to Calvin, Augustine was not anti-Pelagian enough. Luther's bizarre contention that God wants us to sin is mirrored in Calvin in a form which is clearly anti-Pelagian:

> And there was no necessitie to compell God to geve him any other than a meane will and a fraile will, that of mans fall he myghte gather matter for his owne glory.

It may be thought that we could hardly be further from the loving, other-directed God of Herbert.

Certainly Herbert could never state the doctrine in its full Calvinist clarity. He remains sure that, although God hates sin, he loves the sinner, and the strangely bleak triumph over evil we find in Calvin becomes in Herbert an altogether more mysterious victory of love over hate *within* the mind of God: 'Notwithstanding his infinite hate of sinne, his love overcame that hate, and with an exceeding great victory. Yet even Herbert's God can, for example, revel in the exercise of naked, capricious power in order to subject and terrify his creatures:

> God delights to have men feel, and acknowledg, and reverence his power, and therefore he often overturnes things when they are thought past danger; that is his time of interposing. As when a Merchant hath a ship come home after many a storme which it hath escaped, he destroyes it sometimes in the very Haven. . . . If a farmer should depend upon God all the yeer, and being ready to put hand to sickle, shall then secure himself, and think all cock-sure; then God sends such weather as lays the corn, and destroys it: or if he depend upon God further, even till he imbarn his corn, and then think all sure; God sends a fire, and consumes all that he hath.

All this is done that men may 'fear continually'. Meanwhile it is evident from Herbert's poetry that he adheres to the view that all virtue lies with God, but of course the poems show us the doctrine only as it applies to Herbert himself, where it might be thought that personal modesty might influence theology. In fact, however, Herbert's notes on the *One Hundred and Ten Considerations* of Juan de Valdes make two things clear: first that Herbert fully accepted the Protestant doctrine of divine grace and, second, that he was nevertheless obscurely troubled by it. De Valdes (1500-41) was a Spaniard and (of course) a Roman Catholic, but was strongly drawn to stress the importance of faith as against works in the economy of salvation. He exercised a crucial influence on Carnesecchi (who was to be both beheaded and burned for his Lutheran heresies). The *One Hundred and Ten Considerations* was itself suppressed by the Spanish Inquisition. In his 'Sixth Consideration' de Valdes drew a distinction between natural and acquired depravity and asserted that man might by his own powers free himself from the latter. Evidently he had moved only part of the way towards Calvin's position. Herbert in response is flustered, and generates a whole series of hasty distinctions. Certainly, he says, both 'actual' sins and 'original' sins can be removed only by grace; in-

deed, there may be another category of behaviour consisting of habits, and this in turn may be subdivided into 'habits opposed to the theological virtues' and 'habits opposed to the moral virtues'; the first (once more) can be cleared only by grace and, as for the other sort, while it is true that Pagans before the birth of Christ succeeded in suppressing such ill habits, they were able to do so 'only by the general Providence of God'. 'Generall Providence', it would appear, is equivalent to Calvin's 'common grace', which would seem to leave man with precisely nothing which he can do 'of himself'. On other occasions, de Valdes is almost too strong a Protestant for Herbert, but in such places Herbert gives a sort of troubled assent. For example, de Valdes urges that God's will operates both directly and indirectly through human agents: 'Neither Pharaoh nor Judas, nor those who are *vessels of wrath* could cease to be such.' Herbert comments, 'This doctrine however true in substance, yet needeth discreet, and wary explaining.' But the prior doctrine, that we can do nothing good, commands his ready assent: if the priest is thanked for his charity, he must direct those that thank him to glorify God, 'so that the thanks may go the right way, and thither onely, where they are onely due'.

These, then, are the extremes of Protestantism. Man's nature is totally depraved and he can never deserve salvation. Any good we may seem to do is really God's work, not ours. *Sponte enim peccamus*, says Calvin in his commentary on Paul's Epistle to the Romans, *quia peccatum non esset, nisi voluntarium*, 'We sin of our own accord, for, if the sin were not voluntary, it would be no sin.' *Certum enim est*, says Calvin in his homily on I Samuel 2, *hominem non posse libero suo arbitrio sese ad virtutem erigere ac componere*, 'It is certain that man cannot of his own free will raise himself up and dispose himself to virtue'. We are free to sin but not to do good, and so we are not really free at all. And, of course, we are predestined to eternal damnation. At this most dreadful of doctrines Calvin himself paused in his Latin with the famous shudder—*Decretum quidem horribile fateor*, 'It is a terrible decree, I grant'. Its basis is the old one; all is done for the sake of victory; grace alone can lift damnation; in damning all God provides himself with material on which his own grace may act. This grace is given only to some and never by desert.

In this theology we who are not Calvinists may detect one ray of light. As the face of God, the perfect, the all-glorious, grows steadily darker, the face of man grows—against the intention of the writer—slowly lighter. For Calvin can love this dreadful God. Someone in the universe can love someone other than himself and even love (remember the words of Christ) his enemy. Of course we can only make this point by ignoring one element in Calvinism, namely that which teaches us that, if Calvin's love of God is really good, it was God not Calvin who moved Calvin's will to love, so that the love of Calvin for God is in truth only another instance of the divine self-love—and the darkness drops again. But, as we shall see, the argument is rarely maintained with so much pertinacity; the sense persists that the universe is an arena in which God wins all the contests except one. The contest God loses is the moral contest, in which man, the humiliated, triumphs, as generosity morally transcends self-glorification. This, to be sure, is never openly confessed, but it is perceptible in the *Institutes* and grows clearer in the poetry of Herbert.

I have so far contented myself with giving the extremes (which are also the fundamentals) of Calvin's theology. This seemed the fairest course, since it is part of my thesis that Herbert's theology contains a powerful Calvinist element and I would not be thought guilty of evading the challenge implicit in such an assertion: can the sweet-natured country parson really have anything in him of the most terrible of theologians? If I were to confine myself to the periphery of Calvinism considered as a distinctive theology, if I were never to venture outside the platitudes of common Christianity and were to make *them* the basis of my link between Calvin and Herbert, I should have demonstrated nothing. But if the hard doctrines can be shown to be common to both, something will have been achieved. (pp. 1-29)

A. D. Nuttall, "The Temple," in his Over-heard by God: Fiction and Prayer in Herbert, Milton, Dante, and St. John, *Methuen, 1980, pp. 1-82.*

J. A. W. Bennett   (essay date 1982)

[*In the following excerpt, Bennett explores the medieval background to Herbert's Passion poetry.*]

George Herbert's Passion poetry . . . has a medieval ancestry. In his **'Sacrifice'** 'compacted lie' all the figural features that from the time of Prudentius till the printings of the so-called *Biblia Pauperum* in the fifteenth century had come to cluster round the theme of the Passion. It is the summation of all the poetry that the Easter *Improperia* had generated, and its position at the forefront of *The Temple*, as well as its length, testifies to the prominence in Herbert's mind of Christ as the Man of Sorrows. We find no trace of *Christus miles* here. But we do find a more liberal extension of the text 'Popule meus, quid tibi feci?' (Micah 6:3) than any medieval vernacular poem affords. The closest analogue is a fourteenth-century refrain poem on the same text, which happens to be by another Herbert, the friar William who wrote the *Quis est iste qui venit de Edom?* . . . and a dozen other religious poems or translations. He is at least as good a poet as Richard Rolle: witness his version of *Popule meus*, which begins:

> My volk, what habbe y do the?
> Other in what thing tened the?
>   Gyn nouthe and ons…¹ere thou me:
> Vor vrom Egypte ich ladde the,
> Thou me ledest to rode tre.
>   My volk, what habbe y do the?¢
> Thorou wyldernesse ich ladde the,
> And vourty yer bihedde the,
> And aungeles bred ich yaf to the,
> And in-to reste ich broughte the.
>   My volk, what habbe y do the?

Neither the friar's poem nor George Herbert's corresponds completely with the Reproaches as now sung on Good Friday, though some Latin text of the services for Holy Week was undoubtedly the basis of **'The Sacrifice.'**

The Good Friday service is one of the few texts in the Roman Liturgy that is deliberately given dramatic form: the celebrant reciting 'Popule meus, quid tibi feci?', the deacon and subdeacon repeating it in response to each verse. The Reproaches had easily been incorporated into the Towneley Crucifixion play: no sooner has the Cross and its burden been lifted into the *mortice* (the same term is used in Dunbar's 'Passion'), so that it stands up 'like a mast', than Jesus breaks out into alliterative rhyming stanzas suggested by the biblical 'Is it nothing to you, all ye that pass by?' (Lam. 1:12). They take little else from Scripture save the concluding five lines, which expand 'Father, forgive them', and an unexpected application of the text 'The foxes have holes':

> All creatures that Kynde may kest
> Beestys, byrdys, all have thay rest
>   When thay ar wo begon
> But Godys son, that shuld be best,
> Hase not where apon his hede to rest
>   Bot on his shulder bon

—a posture doubtless suggested by contemporary miniatures of the Crucifixion.

In the play the appeal is first addressed to 'my folk', but soon to 'sinful man', in the singular, as in earlier appeals that render 'respice in faciem Christi' as 'Loke, man, to Jesu Crist', 'man and wyman, loket to me'. The verse of the play is not memorable in itself, yet the visual impact of the scene must have been great. The actual hoisting of the Cross with its living burden, a 'business' taking several minutes, would attract all eyes, and produce a sudden silence after the frenzied shouting and cursing. And Christ's appeal to the executioners as his brethren would be the more poignant because it was scorned:

> 'Yis: what we do full well we knaw.
>   Yee, that shall he find within a thraw.'

The monologue of Herbert's 'Sacrifice', by contrast, lacks dramatic or even liturgical context. But behind it, as the late Rosemond Tuve forcefully demonstrated, lie centuries of typological exegesis, which had taken final shape in the illustrations to the so-called *Biblia Pauperum* [in her *A Reading of George Herbert*, 1952], one of the most influential of early printed books. And we can still profit from a glance at earlier versions of the Reproaches.

From the oldest extant Middle English rendering I have quoted above. It begins with 'Ego te de Egypto eduxi':

> Vor vrom Egypte ich ladde the,
> Thou me ledest to rode tre,

and goes on to the striking of the rock and the Kings of Canaan. Herbert radically rearranges and extends these typological allusions, intercalating in ordered sequences incidents of the Passion—as in the verse:

> Then they accuse me of great blasphemie,
> That I did thrust into the Deitie,
> Who never thought it any robberie

—a phrase deriving from Phil. 2:6: 'Who thought it not

robbery to be equal with God', part of the Epistle for Palm Sunday. But more notable is a new and pervasive ironical bitterness of tone, as in: 'I, who am Truth, turn into truth their deeds', or:

> Why, Caesar is their onely King, not I:
> He clave the stonie rock, when they were drie;
> But surely not their hearts, as I well trie.

The Jews had cried, 'We have no King but Caesar' (John 19:15)—as if it had been Caesar who had saved their fathers by giving them water from the rock in the wilderness. In the Latin text the juxtaposition is: 'Ego te potavi aqua salutis de petra; et tu me potasti felle et aceto'. St. Paul himself had said 'that rock was Christ' (1 Cor. 10:4); and accordingly it is depicted as a type of Christ's wounded side in the *Biblia Pauperum* and Books of Hours. But for Herbert *rock* also signified stony-hearted hearers of the word (Luke 8:6), impervious to pity; a figure that in **'The Sinner'** he applies to himself:

> And though my hard heart scarce to thee can
>   grone,
> Remember that thou once didst write in stone.

The 'fel et acetum' come later in **'The Sacrifice'** and their bitterness is now more than physical:

> They give me vineger mingled with gall,
> But more with malice: yet, when they did call,
> With Manna, Angels food, I fed them all.

The 'aungeles mete' figures in the medieval texts, but not in contrast to the gall, though one medieval poem gives, more poignantly, love-position as counterpart to gall:

> A luf drink I ask of the
> Ayzell and gall thai gaf to me.

Herbert's tone does not change even when Christ prophesies that evil will turn to good:

> Nay, after death their spite shall further go;
> For they will pierce my side, I full well know;
> That as sinne came, so Sacraments might flow.

Sin came first through Eve, taken from man's side; so Eve figures opposite the pierced side in Books of Hours, the *Bible Moralisée*, the *Biblia Pauperum*. The Sacraments in question are Baptism and the Eucharist, the water and the blood which flowed from the riven side: that liquor, as Herbert describes it elsewhere, 'sweet and most divine, / Which my God feels as bloud; but I, as wine'. The pattern of the last line of the verse follows St. Paul: 'Where sin abounded, grace doth much more abound' (Rom. 5:20). Yet there is strangely little of grace in this poem. The sense of grief, by being extended too far, has, for once, overmastered it.

Christ as a man acquainted with grief is presented more than once in medieval verse:

> Of all the payne that I suffer sare
> Within my herte it greves me mare
> The unkyndenes that I fynd in the:

so run the central lines of *Homo, vide*. But nowhere before Herbert does this grief approach vindictiveness. There is no room in **'The Sacrifice'** for the traditional colloquy be-

tween Justice and Mercy. Here Christ seems to anticipate the Final Judgement. So, to be sure, he does when he descends into hell in *Piers Plowman*. But there, as in Dunbar's 'Resurrection', the note of mercy is struck repeatedly: 'to be merciable to man then, my kynd it asketh . . . and my mercy shall be shewed to many of my brethren' (*P.Pl.* B xviii. 371, 390). Whereas here Christ spends his last breath in a self-regarding reproach, 'As he that for some robberie suffereth':

> Alas! what have I stollen from you? *Death*.

So even the redemptive work of the Cross takes on a sombre colour that permeates every verse, and not least the last, when Christ answers his own question:

> Onely let others say, when I am dead,
>   Never was grief like mine.

The ironies and double meanings that abound in **'The Sacrifice'** made it inevitable that the poem should attract the attention of the author of *Seven Types of Ambiguity* [William Empson]. But they are mostly traditional ironies, as old as St. Bernard. That the tree of life is the Cross (l. 203) we know from the *Vision of a Rood*; and the Cross was early represented as a tree stripped of its branches, being shown thus in the Winchester Psalter and on the Bury Cross. That the Crucifixion was conceived of as an ascent of the Cross (l. 202), *salire in ligno*, we know from the *Passio* of St. Andrew and the medieval Meditations. And that Christ himself was both the new fruit of the tree ('tam nova poma', as Fortunatus has it in the hymn *Crux benedicta nitet*) and the climber who in the terms of the Canticles 'ascendam in palmam et apprehendam fructus eius'— this we know from passages collected in, or rather scattered throughout, Miss Tuve's study; to which we may add the *Responsio Crucis* in Kennedy's *Passioun*, where the Cross says:

> I lay full low, but now I stand on fute,
> Fresche flurisand in the fruite of sic a kyn,
> Quhilk to ded men is werray medicyne

—this in reply to the Virgin's claim that its fruit was of her body, free from the sin of Adam, who 'staw the frute'. Herbert has it thus:

> Man stole the fruit, but I must climbe the tree;
> The tree of life to all, but onely me:
>   Was ever grief like mine?

But he goes no further to suggest that Christ is the 'new fruit' than the opening words of the next stanza: 'Lo, here I *hang* . . .'. The dominant implication is that to steal fruit is easy but to climb this bitter tree is a fatal undertaking; and Empson's insistence that the image is of a child trying to put back apples seems perverse. Yet he was surely right in seeing more in this poem than the survival and continuation of a traditional mode. Its tone is harsher and more ironic than that of any medieval antecedent, or of any contemporary presentation: contrast Francis Quarles's summary use of the figure:

> He did but climb the cross, and then came down
> To the gates of hell; triumph'd, and fetch'd a
>   crown.

The visual aspect too has altered. The appeal is no longer 'Behold my pain, behold my wounds', but 'Look, how *they* runne . . . *See, they* lay hold on me'. The dimension is now triangular; the speaker, the spectators, the actors in the drama.

Actors in the drama: the phrase reminds us of the strictly theatrical terms in which another Caroline poet, Robert Herrick, presents the Crucifixion. His 'Good Friday: *Rex Tragicus*, or Christ going to His Cross', compels us to question the general view of Herrick as a pagan parson, a cheerful bucolic. For one thing it is tinged with contempt for

> the base, the dull, the rude,
> Th'inconstant, and unpurged multitude

who make up the bored audience who wait for the chief actor to appear and

> *Yawn* for thy coming: some ere this time cry
> 'How he defers, how loath he is to die.'
> Amongst this *scum*, the soldier with his spear
> And that sour fellow, with his vinegar,
> His spunge and stick, do ask why Thou dost
>   stay?

Surely this scene is the more vivid because the poet has lived through the execution of the saintly Laud and the martyred Charles, whose emblematic frontispiece to *Eikon Basilike* bore the distich:

> With joie I take this Crown of Thorn,
> Though sharp, yet easie to be borne.

The next lines likewise recall the King and his bearing on the memorable scene:

> Not as a thief, shalt thou ascend the Mount,
> But like a person of some high account;
> The Cross shall be thy stage; and thou shalt
>   there
> The spacious field have for thy theatre.
> Thou art that Roscius and that marked-out man
> That must this day act the tragedian
> To wonder and affrightment: Thou art he
> Whom all the flux of nations comes to see:
> Not those poor thieves that act their parts with
>   thee:
> Those act without regard, when once a King
> And God, as Thou art, comes to suffering.
> No, no, the scene from Thee takes life and sense
> And soul and spirit, plot, and excellence.
> Why then begin, great King! ascend thy throne
> And thence proceed, to act thy Passion
> To such a height, to such a period raised,
> As Hell, and Earth, and Heaven may stand
>   amazed. . . .

There is more than rhetoric here; there is a strength and dignity and a full articulation of theme that neither Donne nor Herbert surpassed. The true place of the poem is alongside Marvell's Horatian Ode, in which the 'Royal Actor' is taken from Carisbrooke so that he

> The Tragick Scaffold might adorn
> While round the armed bands
> Did *clap* their bloody hands.

Marvell's 'scene' is the classical *scena*, the stage or plat-

form of the Greek or Roman theatre; and Herrick's 'Roscius' shows that he too is thinking of the classical theatre rather than of mystery plays. But he can reckon also on all the associations that the Renaissance had brought to the image of the world as a Divine theatre: 'The great theatre of the world', in Calderón's phrase. There is something of a specifically theatrical, scenic quality in Rembrandt's great etchings of the Passion. Yet even this conception can be found adumbrated in Christian writing of far earlier date. Honorius 'of Autun', in his *Gemma Animae* (c. 1100), writes:

> It is known that those who recited tragedies in theatres presented the actions of opponents by gestures before the people. In the same way *tragicus noster* [viz. the priest celebrating mass] represents by his gestures in the theatre of the Church (*in theatro ecclesiae*), the struggle of Christ and teaches them the victory of His redemption.

Though several of Herbert's poems are dramatic in tone, none picture the Passion in Herrick's terms. For a counterpoise to **'The Sacrifice'** we must turn to his sonnet **'Redemption'**, one of a cluster of poems full of allusions to the Crucifixion, though unique in its parabolic quality. The title is as near as it brings us to overtly scriptural language or theme; and even the title is ambiguous. A hint of the legal sense of 'redemption' (strong in St. Anselm's soteriology) is present in the first quatrain, with its leasehold image (found also in **'A Friend Unknown'**):

> Having been tenant long to a rich Lord,
> Not thriving, I resolved to be bold,
> And make a suit unto him, to afford
> A new small-rented lease, and cancell th'old.

The stance here is not unlike that taken at the opening of Herbert's more famous **'The Collar'** (which must be read as 'yoke', Christ's 'easy' yoke of Matt. 11:30). The suppliant seeks this lord at his manor, only to be told that he has gone to take possession of some *dear-bought* land:

> I straight return'd, and knowing his great birth,
> Sought him accordingly in great resorts;
> In cities, theatres, gardens, parks, and courts:
> At length I hard a ragged noise and mirth
> Of theeves and murderers: there I him espied,
> Who straight, *Your suit is granted*, said, and
>   died.

This is Herbert at his finest: dense in suggestion, and mounting quickly in the sestet to a pregnant climax. Only the last couplet hints at the parable of the vineyard in the Synoptic Gospels from which the whole develops. In the parable, after the householder's husbandmen had beaten, stoned, and killed his servant, he sends his son, saying: 'They will reverence my son'. Instead they take him and slay him. Told, in Luke 20, on the eve of the Passion, the story must early have found a place in Holy Week devotions, and it still has a place in the *Improperia*, where 'Quid ultra debui facere tibi?' is followed immediately by 'Ego quidem plantavi te vineam meam', an allusion amplified in the tract for Holy Saturday from Isaiah 5:1, 2: 'Vinea facta est delecto in cornu' etc. The identity of reference is confirmed by the illustrated *Speculum Humanae*

Salvationis, where the same opening shows Christ carrying the Cross, the sacrifice of Isaac, the murder of the son in this parable of the vineyard, and the grapes brought from Canaan. No other parable acquires the status of a historical antitype, which this collocation implies.

By the same token, the central passage of **'The Agonie'**, a poem that comes shortly before **'Redemption'** in *The Temple*, owes much of its force to traditional typology. Much—but not all: as so often, Herbert here achieves his effect by beginning with an almost banal line ('Philosophers have measur'd mountains') and concluding with a seemingly simple and colloquial phrase ('If ever he did taste the like'). But in between comes the stanza:

> Who would know Sinne, let him repair
> Unto Mount Olivet; there shall he see
> A man so *wrung* with pains, that all his hair,
> His skinne, his garments bloudie be.
> Sinne is that presse and vice, which forceth pain
> To hunt his cruell food through ev'ry vein.

Knowing the medieval poem in which a champion is asked

> Why thoenne ys thy shroud red wyth blod al
>   ymeind,
> As troddares in wrynge wyth most al bys-
>   preynd?

we know that this man pressed by sin is he who cometh from Edom. The *Golden Legend* cites from Pseudo-Dionysius' *Celestial Hierarchy* a passage in which the Angels at the Ascension ask Christ, 'Why is thy clothing red and thy vestments as trodden or fulled in a press?' To which the answer is, in the words of Isaiah 63: *Torcular calcavi*, 'the press I have turned and fouled [sic] all alone': the press being the Cross, with which the body was pressed 'in such wise that the blood sprang out. And after that He opened the tavern of heaven and poured out the wine of the Holy Ghost' (iii. 100: Caxton's translation). So in the last couplet of **'The Agonie'**,

> Love is that liquour sweet and most divine,
> Which my God feels as bloud; but I, as wine,

liquor is used in a specific sense found (for example) in Numbers 6:3: 'Neither shall he drink any liquor of grapes'. Christ had indeed felt it as life-blood welling from him; the Christian, tasting the Eucharistic wine, receives it as life-giving blood. Thus in **'The Invitation'** Herbert says:

> Weep what ye have drunk amisse,
>   And drink this,
> Which before ye drink is bloud.

The actual figure of a winepress appears in late medieval miniatures: for example, in the *Hours* of Catherine of Cleves (c.1440) now in the Pierpont Morgan Library, New York: beneath a bloodstained figure of Christ standing victorious, and alone, on a reclining cross is a smaller representation of the same figure, holding whip and scourge, crouched beneath a press. Hopkins, in a verse thronged with scriptural images of the Passion, will apply the figure to the wine of the Eucharist:

> For us the Vine was fenced with thorn,
> Five ways the precious branches torn;
> Terrible fruit was on the tree

> In the acre of Gethsemane;
> For us by Calvary's distress
> The wine was rackèd from the press;
> Now in our altar-vessels stored
> Is the sweet Vintage of our Lord.
> ('Barnfloor and Winepress')

The title of Herbert's poem, some modern readers may need to be reminded, alludes to the Agony in the Garden of Gethsemane: hence it comes first in his Passion sequence, which jumps almost at once to the still more allusive **'Good Friday'**, of which this verse is typical:

> Since bloud is fittest, Lord to write
> Thy sorrows in, and bloudie fight;
> My heart hath store, write there, where in
> One box doth lie both ink and sinne.

The figure here seems to be transferred from that of Christ's charter or chirograph, as Friar William Herbert (amongst many others) had applied it:

> Sith he my robe tok
> Also ich find in bok
>   He ys to me ybounde
> And helpe he wol, ich wot,
> Vor love the chartre wrot,
>   The enke orn of hys wounde.

Another fourteenth-century poem approaches still closer to Herbert, for it includes the metaphor that we have already met in **'The Sacrifice'**:

> For thogh my hert be hard as stone,
> Yit maist thou gostly write theron
> With naill and with spere kene
> And so shullen the lettres be sene. . .
> Write upon my hert boke
> Thy faire and swete lovely loke. . . .

A final instance of Herbert's medieval affinities comes, fittingly, from his **'Easter'**:

> Awake, my lute, and struggle for thy part
>   With all thy art.
> The crosse taught all wood to resound his name,
>   Who bore the same.
> His stretchèd sinews taught all strings, what key
> Is best to celebrate this most high day.

No less a critic than C. S. Lewis has cited this seemingly bizarre conceit as an instance of deliberate Metaphysical shock, *discors concordia*, coupling the sacred Cross with profane 'fiddle-strings'. In fact Herbert was simply rewording a patristic commonplace, derived from a Messianic exegesis of Psalm 57, the Easter psalm, of which verses 8-9 run: 'Paratum cor meum, Deus; exsurge gloria mea, exsurge psalterium et cithara' (My heart is fixed, O God; awake, my glory, awake psaltery and harp'), with which was always coupled Psalm 81:2: 'Sumite psalmum et date tympanum, psalterium jucundum, cum cithara' (Take pipe and tabor, pleasant psaltery and harp). The harp, according to Augustine, signifies Christ as man in His suffering: 'caro humanus patiens' (*Enarrationes in Psalmos, PL* 36. 671-2). Cassiodorus had extended this: 'the harp means the glorious passion which with stretched sinews and counted bones (*tensis nervis . . . dinumeratisque ossibus*—cf. Ps. 22:17) sounded forth his bitter suffering as in a spiritual song (*carmen intellectuale*)': *PL* 70.

404. Sedulius had put this into verse in his *Carmen Paschalé*. The conceit reappears in Bede and in the *Vitis Mystica* (see n. 6 to Ch. VII) and, as F. P. Pickering has pointed out [in his *Literature and Art in the Middle Ages*, 1970], it is the reason why David's ten-stringed harp is presented as a type of Christ in a twelfth-century miniature from south-east Germany. A nameless German poet developed it, affirming that as soon as Christ was stretched on the Cross the sweet sound of the harp resounded through all the world and down into hell (as if Christ were a divine Orpheus?). A German *Passional* says that God the Father spanned the strings on the harp of the Cross and played till the strings broke. The insistence in the Bonaventuran *Meditationes* and the mystery plays (as in Dunbar's 'Passion') on the stretching of the arms on the Cross because the nail-holes had been bored too far apart, and on ropes to pull down the feet, kept this image of the tautened body vividly present. It is found in a fifteenth-century vernacular sermon from Worcester:

> But who harpid ther? Truliche Crist himsilf and
> non other. What was [his] harpe? Nothyng ell
> but his owne precius bodi. This harpe was wrafte
> so hie whan it was nailed o the rode tre that al
> the strengis o the harpe, ye, al the synwes and
> al the veynes [in] Cristes bodi al to-rayssched
> and to-brak at tones. . . . whan musyk was first
> vownde ther wer but fowr strengis e the
> harpe. . . . Had Crist thes fowr strengis in his
> harpe? Ye vorsotha a had—the virst streng in his
> rith arm, the secunde in his left arm, the third
> streng in his rith leg, and te vowrthe in his left
> leg. Wyth this strengis Crist, for a wulde be vyr
> herd, wente up on to an hy hil, on to the hil o
> Calverye, and ter tempred his harpe and song so
> hie therto that a was herd bothe to hevene and
> to helle and te al the world over.

A little earlier Robert Mannyng of Bourne had claimed that the great Grosseteste justified his delight in minstrelsy by saying that 'to the croys by gode skille [with good reason]/Ys the harpe lykened wele' (*Handlyng Synne*, 4755-6). Lydgate compares the Cross to David's harp ('A Seying of the Nightingale', 307) and later in the fifteenth century, in the *Epistle of Othea*, Christ is strained as a harp to make the music of love.

Herbert, then, can properly match the wooden frame of his lute with the Cross and its strings with the stretched sinews of Christ's body: the lute here symbolizing his art, his verse, which must be stretched to the limit in praise and adoration on 'this most high day'.

It remains to take note—for neither Rosemond Tuve nor Louis Martz did so—of Herbert's most formal and deliberate treatment of the Passion, in the twenty-one sets of Latin verses, the ***Passio Discerpta***, which merit more than the perfunctory attention that Grosart and Canon Hutchinson gave to them. These epigrams are of a distinctly late Renaissance, almost baroque cast; yet their themes are precisely those of late-medieval devotion: the bloody sweat, the crown of thorns, the purple robe, the *alapes* or striking on the face, the flagellation, the penitent thief, the casting of lots ('against custom, your garments are given to your enemies; but you give us yourself'), the nails, the

bowed head, the sun darkened, the opened graves, the earthquake, the rent veils, the sympathy of Nature with its Lord—this last an adaptation of an ancient theme:

> Agnoscitque tuam Machina tota Crucem.
> Hunc ponas animam mundi, Plato: vel tua
>   mundum
> Ne nimium vexet quaestio, pone meam:

a cryptic allusion, which we may render: 'So you may lay aside your world soul, Plato; or, lest that question vex the world too much, lay aside mine.' Donne makes the same Platonic reference at the end of his 'Resurrection': ' . . . this body'a soule, / If not of any man, yet of the whole [world]'. More important than an exact rendering is the final phrase: *pone meam*. We should not be dazzled by the wit and metrical facility of the Public Orator of Cambridge into thinking that these accomplished verses are mere exercises. This is not to say that all are equally successful. But it is to remind ourselves that like earlier aureate poems by Dunbar and others they were designed as a form of worship; and the choice of subject itself testifies to Herbert's Christocentric theology. His Country Parson, we remember, 'knows nothing but the Crosse of Christ, his mind being defixed on it with those nailes wherewith his Master was'. (pp. 153-67)

> *J. A. W. Bennett, "Donne, Herbert, Herrick,"
> in his* Poetry of the Passion: Studies in Twelve
> Centuries of English Verse, *Oxford at the
> Clarendon Press, 1982, pp. 145-67.*

FURTHER READING

Bibliography

Roberts, John R. *George Herbert: An Annotated Bibliography of Modern Criticism, 1905-1974*. Columbia & London: University of Missouri Press, 1978, 280 p.

  Annotated bibliography of secondary sources that includes critic, subject, and title indexes.

Biography

Charles, Amy M. *A Life of George Herbert*. Ithaca, N. Y.: Cornell University Press, 1977, 242 p.

  Extensively researched biography.

Walton, Izaak. "The Life of Mr. George Herbert." *In his The Lives of John Donne, Sir Henry Wotton, Richard Hooker, George Herbert, and Robert Sanderson*, pp. 251-339. 1927. Reprint. London: Oxford University Press, 1962, 426 p.

  Reprint of the 1675 revised edition of Walton's biographical essay on Herbert.

Criticism

Blunden, Edmund. "George Herbert's Latin Poems." In *Essays and Studies by Members of The English Association*, Vol. XIX, collected by D. Nichol Smith, pp. 29-39. Oxford: Clarendon Press, 1934.

  Discusses the general decline of interest in the Latin poetry of various English authors and provides translations of and brief commentary on several of Herbert's poems.

Ellrodt, Robert. "George Herbert and the Religious Lyric." In *English Poetry and Prose, 1540-1674*, edited by Christopher Ricks, pp. 173-205. History of Literature in the English Language, Vol. 2. London: Barrie & Jenkins, 1970.

Discusses the contributions of Herbert and other metaphysical poets to the development of religious poetry.

Fish, Stanley. *The Living Temple: George Herbert and Catechizing*. Berkeley: University of California Press, 1978, 201 p.

Examines the formal structure and rhetorical strategies of *The Temple* in relation to Reformation catechism.

George Herbert Journal 1– (1977–).

Scholarly journal devoted to the study of Herbert. Publishes biographical and critical essays on Herbert as well as notes, book reviews, and essays on the literary and social climate of the seventeenth century.

Linkin, Harriet Kramer. "Herbert's Reciprocal Writing: Poetry as Sacred Pun." In *Traditions and Innovations: Essays on British Literature of the Middle Ages and Renaissance*, edited by David G. Allen and Robert A. White, pp. 214-22. Newark: University of Delaware Press, 1990.

Views Herbert's use of puns as an attempt "to devise a language of transcendence that will gain God's hearing."

Lull, Janis. *The Poem in Time: Reading George Herbert's Revisions of "The Church."* Newark: University of Delaware Press, 1990, 167 p.

Textual criticism and interpretation of poems in "The Church" section of Herbert's *The Temple*.

Miller, Edmund, and DiYanni, Robert, eds. *Like Season'd Timber: New Essays on George Herbert*. Seventeenth-Century Texts and Studies, edited by Anthony Low, Vol. 1. New York: Peter Lang, 1987, 396 p.

Collects biographical and critical studies by various scholars. Subdivided into five major sections, the essays in this volume "explore a series of interrelated contexts focusing on Herbert's biography, the relationship of the fine arts to Herbert's poetry, the world of Herbert's less familiar works, Renaissance contemporaries of Herbert, and the influence of Herbert on later writers."

Patrides, C. A., ed. *George Herbert: The Critical Heritage*. The Critical Heritage Series, edited by B. C. Southam. London: Routledge & Kegan Paul, 1983, 390 p.

Reprints critical excerpts from seventy-four essays, books, and poems published between 1615 and 1936. The editor provides an introductory essay on Herbert's critical reputation from the seventeenth century to the present.

Sherwood, Terry G. *Herbert's Prayerful Art*. Toronto: University of Toronto Press, 1989, 190 p.

Focuses on Herbert's spirituality as expressed in *The Temple*.

Stewart, Stanley. *George Herbert*. Boston: Twayne Publishers, 1986, 182 p.

Overview of Herbert's life and career.

Additional coverage of Herbert's life and career is contained in the following sources published by Gale Research: *Concise Dictionary of British Literary Biography, Before 1660*; *Dictionary of Literary Biography*, Vol. 121; and *Poetry Criticism*, Vol. 4.

Richard Lovelace

1618-1657?

English poet and dramatist.

INTRODUCTION

Lovelace has the paradoxical reputation of a minor poet whose best works are regarded as classics of English poetry. His poems "To Lucasta, Going to the Warres" and "To Althea, From Prison," which contains the famous lines "Stone Walls doe not a Prison Make, / Nor I'ron bars a Cage," are often quoted and anthologized as examples of extraordinary poetic achievement. Yet critics have also dismissed Lovelace as a sophisticated dilettante given to mere moments of inspiration. Sometimes considered a Cavalier poet, despite the fact that his attitude toward the royal cause is difficult to define, Lovelace is recognized as an important figure in seventeenth-century English literature and as an artist deeply dedicated to his metier.

Lovelace's life was essentially tragic. A writer, translator, connoisseur of music and painting, courtier, and soldier, he embodied the Renaissance ideal of the universal man; however, due to the vicissitudes of the political struggles in seventeenth-century England, this brilliant courtier ended his life a victim of political persecution and poverty. A scion of a prominent Kentish family, Lovelace was born in 1618, probably in the Netherlands, where his father died as a soldier. He was educated at Charterhouse School and at Oxford, where he became known for his wit and social charm. In his first year at Oxford, Lovelace wrote a comedy, *The Scholar*, which was favorably received. He obtained a degree early, in his second or third year of studies, upon the insistence of one of the queen's ladies following a royal visit to the university in 1636. After graduation, as his biographer Anthony à Wood wrote, Lovelace "retired in great splendour" to the Court, where he won the admiration of all owing to his "innate modesty, virtue and courtly deportment." Eager to serve his king, Lovelace participated in Charles I's two military campaigns against Scotland, the Bishops' Wars of 1639 and 1640, during which time he wrote the tragedy *The Soldier*, which was subsequently lost. In 1642, the poet joined in the intense political struggle between Charles and Parliament, presenting a royalist petition to a hostile House of Commons. Arrested and imprisoned, Lovelace was released on bail after seven weeks, upon petitioning Parliament for clemency.

Although a declared supporter of the king, Lovelace did not take part in the English Civil War; he may have provided financial assistance to fellow-royalists, but the extent of his generosity is difficult to determine. It is known that he lived on the Continent sometime between 1642 and 1646, mostly in the Netherlands. In 1646, he was seriously wounded at Dunkirk, fighting for the French in their war

against Spain. He returned to England the following year, though still viewed as an enemy by Parliament. Lovelace was arrested in 1648, and during his ten-month imprisonment he prepared *Lucasta* for publication. When he regained his freedom in April 1649, the king had been executed, the monarchy abolished, and Oliver Cromwell had ascended to power. Lovelace spent his remaining years living in obscurity and writing poetry.

Lovelace's literary oeuvre consists of two collections of poetry—*Lucasta* and *Lucasta: Posthume Poems*. Included in the posthumous volume are several translated epigrams by Catullus and other translations of lesser-known Latin and French poetry. As exemplified by his best-known works, the principal themes of Lovelace's poetry are individual honor and dignity, dedication to a political and human ideal, belief in the redemptive power of love, and imprisonment—both in a literal sense and as a metaphor of the human condition. Also prominent in Lovelace's poetry is the figure of Lucasta (or *Lux casta*, Latin for "pure light"). Early biographers identified Lucasta as the object of Lovelace's love and devotion, but later scholars have tended to interpret Lucasta as a symbol for the poet's ideals. Commentators have noted that the poet's idealism, especially in the political realm, seems haunted by skepticism, puzzlement, and hesitation. For instance, in "To Lucasta, From Prison," even his devotion to the king remains open to doubt. This uncertainty, critics have argued, is what definitely sets Lovelace apart from those among his peers who are often described as Cavalier poets—principally Thomas Carew, Robert Herrick, and Sir John Suckling. In Lovelace's posthumous volume, the melancholy tone of his earlier works yields to a kind of ironic resignation. This mood is clearly expressed in "A Fly Caught in a Cobweb," in which Lovelace meditates about "Small type of great ones, that do hum, / Within this Whole World's narrow Room." Yet Lovelace seems to find solace in his poetry; removed from the turmoil of political life, he remained faithful to his vocation.

Highly, sometimes even extravagantly, praised by his contemporaries, Lovelace was almost forgotten in the eighteenth century. In the nineteenth century most critics maintained that, apart from a few extraordinary poems, Lovelace's poetry deserved no attention. Commentators accused him of obscurity and poor craftsmanship—an attitude typified by Edmund Gosse, who deemed Lovelace the epitome of slovenliness. However, as the Italian scholar Alfredo Rizzardi has noted, the critical perception of Lovelace started changing in 1921, when H. J. C. Grierson included him in his collection *Metaphysical Lyrics and Poems of the Seventeenth Century.* Almost immediately, scholars turned their attention to the hitherto-ignored intellectual, philosophical quality of Lovelace's poetry. For example, in his introduction to a 1921 edition of Lovelace's poem, William Lyon Phelps, while characterizing much of Lovelace's work as disappointing and perplexing, observed that "those who love originality in thought and expression will find much to admire." According to Phelps, "Lovelace was not only a Cavalier poet, he was a 'metaphysical' poet, a true son of Donne, inspired by the great master." As research on Lovelace progressed, scholars have challenged various critical dogmas attached to perceptions of his poetry. In 1945, Willa McClung Evans questioned the belief that Lovelace was careless in preparing his poems for publication. She examined manuscripts of poems that were set to music, noting that Lovelace's corrections, which reflected the poet's keen interest in the relation of word to tone, hardly indicate laxity. Furthermore, as critics tackled the complex and multi-layered symbolism of Lovelace's poetic language, they came to recognize a decipherable, and significant, poetic message. Commenting on the deceptive imagery of "To my Worthy Friend Mr *Peter Lilly*: on that excellent Picture of his Majesty, and the Duke of York, drawne by him at *Hampton-Court*," Gerald Hammond argued that the famous image of "Clouded Majesty" admirably serves the purpose of the poem. "Majesty," asserted Hammond, "can be obscured, but it uses such obscurity to emerge all the greater—whether those clouds and mists be the confinements which it is subjected to or the tears through which it must look. . . . Eyes are the key to the poem, and Lovelace looks carefully at the eyes of both sitters, seeing the younger take lustre from his father's eyes. At this point in the poem we see the triumphant image of a pair of royal eagles, so that the clouds and mists which began the poem now turn out only to have been those which hide the mountain top from our eyes, but through which the eagle himself can see clearly. The obscurity is ours, not his."

A man of many talents and interests, Lovelace was above all a poet, struggling to grasp and to express poetically the human condition. Perhaps lacking the intuition of a genius, he is regarded as an important poet attuned to the immense complexities of emotions and ideas. Furthermore, critics have praised his ability to attain universality by developing his themes in various contexts. In George Profitt's words, "In 'Lucasta, Going beyond the Seas' the desire for peace is in an erotic context; in 'To Althea, From Prison' the context is philosophical, reminiscent of Boethius; in 'The Grass-hopper' it is political. But in each the desire for a 'paradise within' and the articulation is generalized, reflective, with limited dramatization and limited self-analysis." Lovelace, concludes this critic, places "his own experiences within the general categories of behaviour."

PRINCIPAL WORKS

Lucasta: Epodes, Odes, Sonnets, Songs, & c. To Which Is Added Aramantha, A Pastorall　(poetry)　1649
Lucasta: Posthume Poems of Richard Lovelace, Esq.　(poetry)　1659-60
The Poems of Richard Lovelace. 2 vols.　(poetry)　1925
Selected Poems　(poetry)　1987

CRITICISM

John Tatham　(poem date 1645?)

[*Tatham was a Caroline poet and playwright whose best-known work is* The Fancies Theater *(1640), a poetry collection. Here, in a poem written sometime before or during September 1645, he exhorts Lovelace to return to England from the Netherlands. The critic's reference to "Althea" indicates that Lovelace's poem "To Althea, from Prison" was known at least several years before its publication in 1649.*]

Come A*donis*, come again,
　　what distast could drive thee hence,
Where so much *delight* did reign,
　　sateing ev'n the *soul* of *sense?*
And though thou *unkind* hast prov'd,
　　never *Youth was* more belov'd.
　　　　Then lov'd *Adonis* come away,
　　　　For *Venus* brooks not thy delay.

Wert thou sated with the S*poil*
　　of so many *Virgins Hearts*,
And therefore didst *change* thy Soil,
　　to seek *fresh* in other parts:
D*angers* wait on *forreigne Game*,
　　we have D*eer* more *sound* and *tame.*
　　　　Then lov'd *Adonis*, &c.

Phillis, fed with thy *delights*,

in thy *absence pines* away;
And *Love* too hath lost his *Rites*:
  not one *Lasse* keeps *Holi-day*.
They have chang'd their *Mirth* for *Cares*,
  and do onely *sigh* thy *A*irs.
    Then lov'd *Adonis*, &c.

Elpine, in whose Sager Looks
  thou wert wont to *take* D*e*light,
Hath forsook his D*rink* and *Books*,
  'cause he cann't enjoy thy *sight*.
He hath laid his L*earning* by,
  'cause his *Wit* wants *Company*.
    Then lov'd A*donis* come away,
    For F*riendship* brooks not thy D*elay*.

All the S*wains* that one did use
  to converse with *Love* and *thee*,
In the *language* of thy *Muse*,
  have forgot *Loves Deity*:
They deny to *write* a line,
  and do onely talk of *thine*.
    Then lov'd A*donis* come away,
    For F*riendship* brooks not thy D*elay*.

By thy sweet A*lthea's* voice
  we conjure thee to return;
Orwe'l rob thee of that *choice*
  in whose *Flames* each Heart would *burn*:
That inspir'd by *her* and *sack*,
  such Company we will not lack.
    That *Poets* in the Age to come,
    Shall write of our *Elizium*.

                    (pp. xliii-xliv)

John Tatham, in a poem from The Poems of
Richard Lovelace, *edited by C. H. Wilkinson,
1925. Reprint by Oxford at the Clarendon
Press, 1930, pp. xliii-xliv.*

Andrew Marvell   (poem date 1649)

[*One of the foremost Metaphysical poets, Marvell is primarily known for his lyrical poems, in particular "The Garden" and "To His Coy Mistress," and for his verse satires, which include "The Last Instructions to a Painter." Neglected for more than two centuries, Marvell's poetry won high praise from T. S. Eliot and other twentieth-century writers, who appreciated the intellectual intricacy of his poems. Below, in a poem originally published in 1649, he offers a poetic tribute to Lovelace.*]

Sɪʀ,

Our times are much degenerate from those
Which your sweet Muse which your fair Fortune chose,
And as complexions alter with the Climes,
Our wits have drawne th' infection of our times.
That candid Age no other way could tell
To be ingenious, but by speaking well.
Who best could prayse, had then the greatest prayse,
Twas more esteemed to give, then weare the Bayes:
Modest ambition studi'd only then,
To honour not her selfe, but worthy men.
These vertues now are banisht out of Towne,
Our Civill Wars have lost the Civicke crowne.

He highest builds, who with most Art destroys,
And against others Fame his owne employs.
I see the envious Caterpillar sit
On the faire blossome of each growing wit.
  The Ayre's already tainted with the swarms
Of Insects which against you rise in arms.
Word-peckers, Paper-rats, Book-scorpions,
Of wit corrupted, the unfashion'd Sons.
The barbed Censurers begin to looke
Like the grim consistory on thy Booke;
And on each line cast a reforming eye,
Severer then the young Presbytery.
Till when in vaine they have thee all perus'd,
You shall for being faultlesse be accus'd.
You wrong'd in her the Houses Priviledge.
Some that you under sequestration are,
Because you write when going to the Warre,
And one the Book prohibits, because *Kent*
Their first Petition by the Authour sent.
  But when the beauteous Ladies came to know
That their deare *Lovelace* was endanger'd so:
Lovelace that thaw'd the most congealed brest,
He who lov'd best and them defended best.
Whose hand so rudely grasps the steely brand,
Whose hand so gently melts the Ladies hand.
They all in mutiny though yet undrest
Sally'd and would in his defence contest.
And one the loveliest that was yet e're seen,
Thinking that I too of the rout had been,
Mine eyes invaded with a female spight
(She knew what pain 'twould be to lose that
  sight.)
O no, mistake not, I reply'd, for I
In your defence, or in his cause would dy.
But he secure of glory and of time
Above their envy, or mind aid doth clime.
Him, valianst men, and fairest Nymphys approve,
His Booke in them finds Judgement, with you
  Love.

                    (pp. 151-52)

Andrew Marvell, in a poem in his The Poems
of Andrew Marvell, *edited by James Reeves
and Martin Seymour-Smith, Barnes & Noble,
Inc. 1969, pp. 151-52.*

Francis Lenton   (poem date 1649)

[*Lenton was a poet and anagrammatist whose writings include* The Young Gallants Whirligigg: or Youths Reakes *(1629). In the following poem, originally published in 1649, he extols Lovelace as a poet in whose works the spirit of classical Greek and Latin poetry lives.*]

Poets, and Painters have some near relation,
Compar'd with Fancy and Imagination;
The one paints shadowed persons (in pure kind,)
The other points the Pictures of the Mind
In purer Verse.   And as rare *Zeuxes* fame
Shin'd till *Apelles* Art eclips'd the same
By a more exquisite, and curious line
Than *Zeuxefes* (with pensill far more fine,)
So have our modern Poets, late done well
Till thine appear'd (which scarce have paralel.)
  They like to *Zeuxes* Grapes beguile the sense,
But thine do ravish the Intelligence;

Like the rare banquet of *Apelles*, drawn,
And covered over with most curious Lawn.
   Thus if thy careles draughts are cal'd the best,
What would thy lines have beene, had'st thou
    profest
That faculty (infus'd) of Poetry,
Which adds such honour unto thy Chivalry?
Doubtles thy verse had all as far transcended
As *Sydneyes* Prose, who Poets once defended.
   For when I read thy much renowned Pen,
My Fancy there finds out another *Ben*
In thy brave language, judgement, wit, & art,
Of every piece of thine, in every part:
Where thy seraphique *Sydneyan* fire is raised
   high,
In Valour, Vertue, Love, and Loyalty:
   Virgil was styl'd the loftiest of All,
Ovid the smoothest, and most naturall,
Martiall concise, and witty, quaint, and pure,
Iuvenall grave and learned, (though obscure:)
   But all these rare ones, which I heere reherse,
Do live againe in Thee, and in thy Verse:
Although not in the language of their time,
Yet in a speech as copious and sublime:
   The rare *Apelles*, in thy picture wee
Perceive, and in thy soule *Apollo* see.
Wel may each grace, & muse then crown thy
   praise
With Mars his Banner, and *Minerva's* Bayes.

                          (pp. 11-12)

> *Francis Lenton, in a poem from* The Poems of
> Richard Lovelace, *edited by C. H. Wilkinson,
> 1925. Reprint by Oxford at the Clarendon
> Press, 1930, pp. 11-12.*

John Hall (poem date 1649)

[*Hall was an English essayist and poet whose works include* Horae Vacivae; or, Essays, Poems, Satyre against
Presbytery *(1648) and* An Humble Motion to the Parliament of England concerning the Advancement of
Learning and Reformation of the Universities *(1649).
In the following poem, he admires Lovelace's "double
glory" as a poet and a man of action.*]

If the desire of Glory speak a mind
More nobly operative, & more refin'd,
What vast soule moves thee? Or what Hero's
   spirit
(Kept in'ts traduction pure) dost thou inherit,
That not contented with one single Fame,
Dost to a double glory spread thy Name?
And on thy happy temples safely set
Both th' *Delphick* wreath and *Civic* Coronet?
   Wast not enough for us to know how far
Thou couldst in season suffer, act, and dare?
But we must also witnesse with what height
And what *Ionick* sweetnesse thou canst write?
And melt those eager passions that are
Stubborn enough t'enrage the God of war,
Into a noble Love, which may aspire
In an illustrious Pyramid of Fire,
Which having gained his due station may
Fix there, and everlasting flames display.
This is the braver path, time soone can smother
The dear-bought spoils & tropheis of the other.
How many fiery Heroes have there been,

Whose triumphs were as soone forgot, as seen?
Because they wanted some diviner one
To rescue the from night and make the known.
   Such art thou to thy selfe: while others dream
Strong flatt'ries on a fain'd or borrow'd theam,
Thou shalt remaine in thine owne lustre bright,
And adde unto't *LUCASTA'S* chaster light.
   For none so fit to sing great things as He
That can act o're all lights of Poetry.
Thus had *Achilles* his owne Gests design'd,
He had his Genius *Homer* far outshin'd.

                          (pp. 9-10)

> *John Hall, in a poem from* The Poems of
> Richard Lovelace, *edited by C. H. Wilkinson,
> 1925. Reprint by Oxford at the Clarendon
> Press, 1930, pp. 9-10.*

Thomas Rawlins (poem date 1649)

[*Rawlins was a poet and a playwright whose works include the tragedy* The Rebellion *(1640), the poetry collection* Calanthe *(1648), and the comedy* Tom Essence
*(1676). In the poem below, originally published in 1649,
he describes Lovelace's poetry as a timeless offering to
love.*]

Chast as Creation meant us, and more bright
Then the first day in's uneclipsed light,
Is thy *Lucasta,* and thou offerest heere
Lines to her *Name* as undefil'd and cleere:
Such as the first indeed more happy dayes,
(When Vertue, Wit, and Learning, wore the
   bayes;
Now Vice assumes) would to *her memory* give
A *Vestall Flame,* that should for ever live
Plac't in a Christal Temple, rear'd to be
The Embleme of her thoughts integrity;
And on the Porch thy *Name* insculpt, my
   Friend,
Whose Love like to the flame can know no end:
The Marble steps that to the Alter brings
The hallowed *Priests* with their cleane Offerings
Shall hold their *Names,* that humbly crave to be
Votaries to' th' shrine, and grateful *Friends* to
   thee:
So shal we live (although our Offrings prove
Meane to the World) for ever by thy *Love.*

                          (pp. 12-13)

> *Thomas Rawlins, in a poem from* The Poems
> of Richard Lovelace, *edited by C. H. Wilkin-
> son, 1925. Reprint by Oxford at the Clarendon
> Press, 1930, pp. 12-13.*

Eldred Revett (poem date 1657)

[*In the following excerpt, originally published in his*
Poems *(1657), Revett lauds Lovelace's poetry as powerful and inspiring.*]

As in the presence of some Prince, not one,
But rates his bliss, as he is next the throne,
To which he adds not but himself applies
To boast the Kings to him indulgencies:
Thus Sir (as one you suffer) I appear
Not to give to your fame, but to be near.

How must I then approach? how my self
  shew,
So just, as that I can be, just to you!
Thou great dispenser of that all we be
Who giv'st us else enough, but to thanke thee
Thou hast our cheaper gratitude out-went
And mak'st us sin in being excellent.
   How from thy first chaste flames thou didst
    inspire
That earth we fashion'd with *Promethean* fire?
And thine rise no less bright for what they lent
From the Communicative Element:
But the insinuating Rayes derive
Something from us that was not primitive:
Though pure in their own essences they dwell
Not to be mixt with our corruptible;
And should we in our courser matter die
Would rise to their own immortalitie.
But at a kingdomes second birth though ne'r
So much devout to the already heire,
A Nation throngs, and doth (suspended) pay
Duty howe're unto the newer day,
Thus from ador'd *Lucasta* we come on
But to bring hither our devotion:
And though we crowd with a tumultuous pace,
We have like *Janus* a respective face:
Thou that immortal wer't enough before,
Dost now but ever live, and all this ore;
And art above the Eagle that assumes
(By casting the now aged off) new plumes,
Who dost thy first as vigorous not shed,
But when thou would'st renew thy pomp dost
   spread.
   Vast *Heroe* that will not alone not die,
But lay'st steps to thine immortalitie,
Who dost in thy applausive, Giant-wars
From thine own blest ascent invade the Stars;
Thou hast throughout divided the cleft mount,
And to thine aid with its own spire dost crown't,
Though as thou grow'st near heav'n it hangs the
   while
As in a dear expectance of the pile,
That swells no sacrilegious hight to gain
But doth the weighty machine there sustain.
   There then advance thy glory till our sight
Conceive thee some new·disputable light;
That we cannot define from whence it streams
Although we find thee by thy warmth and
   beams.
                                      (pp. lx-lxi)

Eldred Revett, in a poem from The Poems of
Richard Lovelace, *edited by C. H. Wilkinson,
1925. Reprint by Oxford at the Clarendon
Press, 1930, pp. lx-lxi.*

Charles Cotton   (poem date 1660)

[*Cotton was an English poet and translator whose works
include a translation of Montaigne's* Essays. *In the
poem below, he lauds Lovelace as a paragon of virtue,
fortitude, and modesty.*]

To pay my Love to thee, and pay it so,
As Honest men should what they justly owe;
Were to write better of thy Life then can
The assured'st Pen of the most worthy man:
Such was thy composition, such thy mind

Improv'd to vertue, and from vice refin'd,
Thy Youth an abstract of the Worlds best parts,
Invr'd to Arms and exercis'd in Arts;
Which with the Vigour of a man, became
Thine and thy Countries Piramids of Flame;
Two glorious Lights to guide our hopeful Youth,
Into the paths of Honour and of Truth.
   These parts (so rarely met) made up in thee
What man should in his full perfection be;
So sweet a Temper into every sence
And each affection breath'd an Influence
As smooth'd them to a Calme, which still with-
   stood
The ruffling passions of untamed Blood,
Without a Wrinckle in thy face, to show
Thy stable brest could no disturbance know.
In Fortune humble, constant in mischance,
Expert in both, and both serv'd to advance
Thy Name by various Trialls of thy Spirit,
And give the Testimony of thy merit;
Valiant to envy of the bravest men
And learned to an undisputed Pen,
Good as the best in Both, and great, but Yet
No dangerous *Courage* nor offensive *Wit*:
These ever serv'd, the one for to defend,
The other Nobly to advance thy friend,
Under which title I have found my name
Fix'd in the living Chronicle of Fame,
To times succeeding; Yet I hence must go
Displeas'd, I cannot celebrate thee so;
But what respect, acknowledgement and love,
What these together, when improv'd improve;
Call it by any Name (so it express
Ought like a Tribute to thy Worthyness,
And may my bounden gratitude become)
LOVELACE I offer at thy Honour'd Tomb.
   And though thy Vertues many friends have
      bred
To love thee liveing, and lament thee Dead
In Characters far better couch'd then these,
Mine will not blott thy Fame nor theirs encrease,
'Twas by thine own great merits rais'd so high,
That Maugre time, and Fate, it shall not dye.
                                      (pp. 223-24)

Charles Cotton, in a poem from The Poems of
Richard Lovelace, *edited by C. H. Wilkinson,
1925. Reprint by Oxford at the Clarendon
Press, 1930, pp. 223-24.*

Samuel Holland   (poem date 1660)

[*In the poem below, originally published in 1660, Holland praises Lovelace's works—particularly his* Lucasta:
Posthume Poems—*as poetry worthy of comparison with
the great classics.*]

Me thinks when Kings, Prophets, and Poets dye,
We should not bid men weep, nor ask them why,
But the great loss should by instinct impair
The Nations like a pestilential ayr,
And in a moment men should feel the Cramp
Of grief, like persons poyson'd with a damp;
All things in nature should their death deplore,
And the Sun look less lovely than before,
The fixed Stars should change their constant
   spaces,
And Comets cast abroad their flagrant faces;

Yet still we see Princes and Poets fall
Without their proper pomp of funerall,
Men look about as if they nere had known
The Poets Lawrell, or the Princes Crown;
Lovelace hath long been dead, and we can be
Oblig'd to no man for an Elegie.
Are you all turn'd to silence, or did he
Retain the only sap of Poesie,
That kept all branches living, must his fall
Set an eternal period upon all?
So when a Spring-tide doth begin to fly
From the green shoar, each neighbouring creek
    grows dry.
But why do I so pettishly detract
An age that is so perfect, so exact,
In all things excellent, it is a Fame,
Or glory to deceased *Lovelace* Name;
For he is weak in wit who doth deprave
Anothers worth to make his own seem brave;
And this was not his aim, nor is it mine,
I now concieve the scope of their designe,
Which is with one consent to bring, and burn
Contributary Incence on his Urn,
Where each mans Love and Fancy shall be try'd,
As when great *Johnson* or brave *Shakspear* dy'd.
Wits must unite, for Ignorance we see,
Hath got a great train of Artillerie,
Yet neither shall, nor can it blast the Fame
And honour of deceased *Lovelace* Name,
Whose own *Lucasta* can support his credit
Amongst all such who knowingly have read it:
But who that Praise can by desert discusse
Due to those Poems that are Posthumous;
And if the last conceptions are the best,
Those by degrees do much transcend the rest,
So full, so fluent, that they richly sute
With *Orpheus* Lire or with *Anacreons* Lute,
And he shall melt his wing that shall aspire
To reach a Fancy or one accent higher.
Holland and *France* have known his nobler
    parts,
And found him excellent in Arms, and Arts.
To sum up all, few Men of Fame but know
He was *tam Marti, quam Mercurio.*

(pp. 229-31)

Samuel Holland, in a poem from The Poems
of Richard Lovelace, *edited by C. H. Wilkinson, 1925. Reprint by Oxford at the Clarendon
Press, 1930, pp. 229-31.*

Alexander Brome   (poem date 1661)

[*Brome was a Caroline poet and playwright whose plays
include* The Cunning Lovers (1654) *and* Fancy's Festivals (1657). *In the following poem, first published in
1661, he praises Lovelace as a refined poet whose art is
misunderstood by the unpoetical culture of Cromwell's
England.*]

So through the *Chaos* crept the first born ray,
That was not yet grown up to be a day,
And form'd the *World*; as do your powerful
    rythmes [rhymes?]
Through the thick darkness of these verseless
    times,
These *antigenius* dayes, this boystrous age,
Where there dwells nought of Poetry but rage:

Just so crept learning forth the rav'nous fire
Of the Schismatick *Goths,* and *Vandals* ire:
As do in these more barbarous dayes our times,
VVhen what was meant for ruine, but refines.
Why mayn't we hope for *Restauration,* when
As ancient *Poets* Townes, the new rais'd men,
The tale of *Orpheus* and *Amphion* be
Both solid truths with this *Mythology*?
For though you make not stones & trees to
    move,
Yet men more senceless you provoke to love.
I can't but think, spite of the filth that's hurl'd
Over this small *Ench'ridion of the World,*
A *day* will break, when we again may see
Wits like themselves, club in an harmony.
Though *Pulpiteers* can't do it, yet 'tis fit
Poets have more *success,* because more *wit.*
Their *Prose* unhing'd the State; why mayn't your
    verse
Polish those souls, that were fil'd rough by
    theirs?
Go on, and prosper; though I want your skill,
In weighty matters tis enough to will.
And novv the *Reader* looks I should help rear
Your glories *Trophy,* else what make I here?
'Tis not to praise you; for one may as well
Go tell *Committees* that there is an hell,
Or tell the World there is a *Sun,* as praise
Your amorous fancy, which it self cant raise
'Bove *Envies* reach or flatteries; Ladies love
To kiss those accents; who dares disapprove
What they stile good? our lines, our lives, and
    all;
[By their *opinions* either rise or fall:]
Therefore the cause why these are fixed here,
Is livery-like to shew some great man's near;
    Let them stand bare, and usher, not com-
        mend;
    They are not for *Encomiums,* but t'attend.
                    (pp. lxxxvi-lxxxvii)

Alexander Brome, in a poem from The Poems
of Richard Lovelace, *edited by C. H. Wilkinson, 1925. Reprint by Oxford at the Clarendon
Press, 1930, pp. lxxxvi-lxxxvii.*

James Russell Lowell   (essay date 1864)

[*Lowell was a celebrated American poet and essayist,
and an editor of two leading journals, the* Atlantic
Monthly *and the* North American Review. *He is noted
for his satirical and critical writings, including* A Fable
for Critics (1848), *a book-length poem featuring critical
portraits of his contemporaries. Commentators generally
agree that Lowell possessed a judicious critical sense, despite the fact that he sometimes relied upon mere impressions rather than critical precepts in his writings.
Most literary historians rank him with the major nineteenth-century American critics. In the following excerpt
from an originally unsigned review, Lowell praises Lovelace's well-known poems but dismisses his other works
as hopelessly obscure and dull.*]

Three short pieces of Lovelace's have lived, and deserved
to live: **"To Lucasta from Prison," "To Lucasta on going
to the Wars,"** and **"The Grasshopper."** They are graceful,
airy, and nicely finished. The last especially is a charming

poem, delicate in expression, and full of quaint fancy, which only in the latter half is strained to conceit. As the verses of a gentleman they are among the best, though not of a very high order as poetry. He is to be classed with the *lucky* authors who, without great powers, have written one or two pieces so facile in thought and fortunate in phrase as to be carried lightly in the memory, poems in which analysis finds little, but which are charming in their frail completeness. This faculty of hitting on the precise *lilt* of thought and measure that shall catch the universal ear and sing themselves in everybody's memory, is a rare gift. (p. 310)

All that Lovelace wrote beside these three poems is utterly worthless, mere chaff from the threshing of his wits . . . The poems are obscure, without anything in them to reward perseverance, dull without being moral, and full of conceits so far-fetched that we could wish the author no worse fate than to carry them back to where they came from. We are no enemies to what are commonly called conceits, but authors bear them, as heralds say, with a difference. And a terrible difference it is! With men like Earle, Donne, Fuller, Butler, Marvell, and even Quarles, conceit means wit; they would carve the merest cherry-stone of thought in the quaintest and delicatest fashion. But with duller and more painful writers, such as Gascoyne, Marston, Felltham, and a score of others, even with cleverer ones like Waller, Crashawe, and Suckling, where they insisted on being fine, their wit is conceit. Difficulty without success is perhaps the least tolerable kind of writing. (p. 311)

> *James Russell Lowell, in an originally unsigned review of "Lucasta: The Poems of Richard Lovelace, Esq.," in* The North American Review, *Vol. XCIX, No. CCIV, July 1864, pp. 310-17.*

Bliss Carman (poem date 1890)

[*A Canadian poet and essayist, Carman wrote* Songs from Vagabondia *(1894), followed by two sequels, with the American poet Richard Hovey. His other books include* Sappho *(1905),* Sanctuary *(1929), volumes of poetry, and theoretical works such as* The Poetry of Life *(1905). In the poem reprinted below, Carman meditates on Lovelace's poetic legacy.*]

> Ah, Lovelace, what desires have sway
>   In the white shadow of your heart,
> Which no more measures day by day,
>   Nor sets the years apart?
>
> How many seasons for your sake
>   Have taught men over, age by age,
> "Stone walls do not a prison make,
>   Nor iron bars a cage!"—
>
> Since that first April when you fared
>   Into the Gatehouse, well content,
> Caring for nothing so you cared
>   For honour and for Kent.
> How many, since the April rain
>   Beat drear and blossomless and hoar
> Through London, when you left Shoe Lane,
>   A-marching to no war!

> Till now, with April on the sea,
>   And Sunshine in the woven year,
> The rain-winds loose from reverie
>   A lyric and a cheer.

> *Bliss Carman, in a poem in* The Athenaeum, *Vol. 1, No. 3259, April 12, 1890, p. 468.*

Louise Imogen Guiney (essay date 1890)

[*In the following excerpt, Guiney describes Lovelace's versification and phraseology as generally faulty, but praises the tenderness and lyricism of his best-known poems.*]

Like all good men and true of his day. Lovelace embroidered his Saxon speech with conceits and filigrees. Rash as are his pretty strophes on "**Amaranthe's Shining Hair,**" on "**Lucasta Paying her Obsequies,**" and on "**Gratiana Dancing,**" who will abide this agricultural apostrophe of a lady's glove:

> Thou snowy farm with thy five tenements!

whose figure is carried on in cold blood through rents, tillage, and ejections? His versification is generally hasty and heedless. Some allowance for the lack of smoothness may be made here, as well as for Suckling, since neither lived to supervise his printed book. Lovelace's phraseology is frequently nave to the last degree. "Reverend lady-cows" are in his pastures; and his apostatizing acquaintances are "as the divel not half so trewe!" He rendered literally the diverting old French sophism, *Si Jacques le Roy du Scavoir*:

> If James, the king of wit,
> To see me found not fit,
>   Sure this the cause hath been:
> That, ravished with my merit,
> He thought I was all spirit,
>   And so not to be seen!

"**The Falcon,**" "**The Snail,**" and "**Female Glory**" afford a good study of Lovelace's wonted manner. His two noblest lyrics are simply incomparable.

We owe to the Parliamentarians, and to their propensity for caging the King's singing-birds, Lovelace's romantic and spirited prison-songs to Lucasta and to Althea. The second is generally known by the initial line of the closing stanza, "Stone walls do not a prison make." It is too long for insertion here, and too precious to divide into sections; but every reader will rate it as a masterpiece. (pp. 954-55)

It might surprise Lovelace, who had but a modest opinion of himself, despite the popular adoration, to know how many bosoms have throbbed over his farewell "**To Lucasta on Going to the Wars.**" Its high tenderness is very characteristic of his genius. This song is like the "Dear and Only Love" of that other rapid writer, Montrose, inasmuch as no painstaking could have made either more shapely and strong; and they rank together as two "beautiful old rhymes," more chivalrous in thought and expression than any of their kindred in English literature. (p. 955)

> *Louise Imogen Guiney, "English Lyrics Under*

the First Charles," in Harper's New Monthly Magazine, *Vol. LXXX, No. CCCCLXXX, May 1890, pp. 946-59.*

F. W. Moorman   (essay date 1911)

[*In the following excerpt, Moorman describes Lovelace as a minor poet who nevertheless wrote some of the most memorable poems in English literature.*]

Lovelace's standing among English poets is peculiar. He has left us two or three songs which are included in almost every anthology of English verse, and which deserve enduring fame; in addition to these, he wrote a considerable number of lyric, descriptive and complimentary poems, of which it may, without rancour, be said that it would have been better if they had remained in manuscript and perished with his two plays. For, in them, he exhibits most, if not all, of the faults of taste found in Elizabethan sonneteers, together with the fantastic extravagances of the seventeenth century school of lyrists. His love-lyrics to Lucasta are as frigidly rhetorical as the worst poems in Cowley's *Mistress*, while his "**Pastoral: to Amarantha**" abounds in the otiose conceits of what Ruskin has taught us to call "the pathetic fallacy." To what excesses a labouring fancy, unrestrained by good taste, may run is well illustrated by such poems as "**Ellinda's Glove**" or "**Lucasta's Muff**," by the verses entitled "**A Loose Saraband**," in which he declares that love has made a whipping-top of his bleeding heart, or by the opening stanza of the song, "**Lucasta Weeping**":

> Lucasta wept, and still the bright
> Enamoured god of day,
> With his soft handkerchief of light,
> Kissed the wet pearls away.

Judged by the bulk of his poems, Lovelace has more in common with Habington than with the typical cavalier lyrists, Suckling and Carew; and, although his addresses entitled "**The Grasshopper**" and "**The Snail**" faintly recall the Anacreontic "**Ode to the Cicada**," he cannot well be called a neo-classic or a follower of Jonson.

When compared with his other poems, Lovelace's two songs "**To Althea from Prison**" and "**Going to the Wars**" seem nothing less than miracles of art. In them, there is no trace of the pedantry or prolixity, the frigid conceit and the tortured phrase, of his other poems; in their simplicity, their chivalrous feeling and their nobility of thought, they touch perfection. And scarcely inferior to them, though not so well known, is his song, "**To Lucasta going beyond the Seas**," the third stanza of which deserves to rank with the most memorable things in English lyric poetry:

> Though seas and land betwixt us both,
> Our faith and troth,
> Like separated souls,
> All time and space controls:
> Above the highest sphere we meet,
> Unseen, unknown, and greet as angels greet.

Had Lovelace always written like this, the comparison which the seventeenth century biographer, William Win-

stanley, drew between him and Sir Philip Sidney might win our glad approval. (pp. 28-9)

> *F. W. Moorman, "Cavalier Lyrists," in* The Cambridge History of English Literature: Cavalier and Puritan, Vol. VII, *edited by A. W. Ward and A. R. Waller, G. P. Putnam's Sons, 1911, pp. 1-29.*

Alexander C. Judson   (essay date 1925)

[*An American scholar and editor, Judson is the author of* The Life of Edmund Spenser *(1945) and* Notes on the Life of Edmund Spenser *(1949). In the following excerpt, he argues that Lucasta does not refer to Lovelace's beloved, but rather symbolizes the poet's idea of truth.*]

When Lovelace issued his slender volume of poems in 1649, he called it **Lucasta: Epodes, Odes, Sonnets, Songs, etc.** It contains, besides commendatory verses, fifty-five poems. Of these, seventeen are addressed to Lucasta, or at least refer in some way to her. There are also four poems to Ellinda, and one each to Gratiana, Chloe, and Althea. Ten years later, after Lovelace's death, his brother collected and published another volume of his poems, which he entitled **Lucasta: Posthume Poems of Richard Lovelace, Esq.** In this second volume, Lucasta's name still appears most frequently: Lucasta figures in ten poems, Laura in two, and Chloris in one. Since most writers on Lovelace have been content to repeat Anthony à Wood's casual identification of Lucasta as Lucy Sacheverel, with little or no search for corroboration in the poetry concerned, it may not be amiss to give further study to the question of Lucasta's identity.

Before turning, however, to this problem, let us consider briefly an idea about Lucasta and Lovelace which has been several times advanced, but which may, I think, be safely dismissed as sentimental conjecture. We are asked to picture Lovelace pining away because his betrothed had married another man, and finally dying miserably in London of a broken heart. Thus Rev. J. H. B. Masterman, in his *Age of Milton*, says: "According to tradition, his death was due to despair, caused by the unfaithfulness of the lady addressed as Lucasta, who married under the impression that he was dead." (p. 77)

I have been able to discover no evidence whatever for the idea here advanced. Of his early biographers neither Aubrey nor Winstanley throws any light on his love affair, and Wood, who is the chief source of our knowledge of Lovelace, distinctly says that he pined away, not because of disappointment in love, but because of poverty [see Further Reading]. "After the murther of King Charles I," writes Wood, "Lovelace was set at liberty, and having by that time consumed all his estate, grew very melancholy (which brought him at length into a consumption)," etc. Wood certainly did not attribute any of Lovelace's melancholy to the loss of Lucasta.

And yet I can think of nothing except an inattentive reading of Wood that could have occasioned these statements. In the preceding paragraph, Wood describes Lovelace's departure to France in 1646 to fight under Louis XIV, his being wounded at Dunkirk, and his return to England in 1648. Upon his return he was imprisoned, says Wood, in Lord Petre's house in Aldersgate Street, and there, to quote again, "he framed his poems for the press, entitled *Lucasta* . . . . *etc.* . . . . The reason why he gave that title was because, some time before, he had made his amours to a gentlewoman of great beauty and fortune, named Lucy Sacheverel, whom he usually called Lux casta; but she upon a strong report that Lovelace was dead of his wound received at Dunkirk, soon after married." He lost his betrothed. He died of melancholy. What more natural than to connect the two facts? Very likely someone's careless reading of Wood is responsible for the tradition to which Mr. Masterman refers.

Certainly the contents of the poems to Lucasta could not have given rise to such a tradition. In none is there any hint of the loss of Lucasta, or of despair arising from this or any other cause; nor in the eight elegies on Lovelace written by his friends within two years of his death is there a single reference to Lucasta's faithlessness. We may, then, I think, free Lucy Sacheverel from any responsibility—even unintentional—for Lovelace's pitiful end.

But the main problem already proposed remains, namely, whether the Lucasta of the poems really does represent the woman to whom, according to Wood, Lovelace made his amours. Thomas Seccombe in his article on Lovelace in the *Dictionary of National Biography* remarks that Lucasta was possibly an imaginary personage, after whom, in accordance with the familiar practice of the time, he called his poems. My own examination of the poems to Lucasta has, in spite of Wood's statement, convinced me that this supposition is not merely possible, but in the highest degree probable. I do not believe that these poems can have been written about any woman whom Lovelace loved and sought in marriage.

The reasons that have led me to this conclusion are as follows:

1. With two or three exceptions the poems that concern Lucasta read like frigid exercises, not genuine love poems. It is of course a commonplace that much Elizabethan and Caroline love poetry is conventional; yet even beside the conventional poetry of that day, the love poems to Lucasta seem curiously lacking in feeling. They are almost completely devoid of ardor and tenderness, and are remarkable only for the utter lack of restraint shown in their conceits. One exception is **"To Lucasta: Going beyond the Seas,"** which contains the fine passage:

> Above the highest sphere we meet
> Unseen, unknown, and greet as angels greet.

This poem, however, seems to be reminiscent of Donne's famous "Valediction Forbidding Mourning," a fact that makes at least questionable whether the apparent feeling as well as the matter may not be owing to Donne. A second exception is **"To Lucasta: Going to the Wars."** There is a distinct note of tenderness here; yet the primary devotion shown in this poem is of course to the king and to the king's cause. The third and last exception that I find is a poem entitled **"Calling Lucasta from Her Retirement."** In this poem Lovelace represents himself, seconded by trees,

waters, air, and fire, as summoning her from the "dire monument" of her "black room." At the end he declares she comes, and that her coming makes him forget even the tragedy of civil war:

> See! she obeys! By all obeyed thus
> No storms, heats, colds, no souls contentious,
> Nor civil war is found; I mean, to us.

Most of the poem is labored and obscure, and leaves the reader with the suspicion that Lucasta may here be no more than a symbol for the clear light of truth. Is it not odd that Lovelace, even assuming he felt no tenderness, could not have simulated it more successfully in his love poems?

It may be objected that he was one of those men not gifted with the power of expressing their feelings in verse. Yet how genuinely his lines on Charles glow when in **"To Althea: From Prison"** he sings of the sweetness, mercy, and majesty of his king. So, too, in his little-known poem **"To Lucasta: From Prison,"** there throbs a splendid devotion to Charles. In this poem Lovelace turns over in his mind the various things he might love, such as Peace, War, Religion, Parliament, Liberty, Property, etc. But he finds some impediment to his loving any of these. He ends his poem thus:

> Since, then, none of these can be
> Fit objects for my love and me;
> What then remains but th' only spring
> Of all our loves and joys, the King?
>
> He who being the whole ball
> Of day on earth, lends it to all;
> When seeking to eclipse his right
> Blinded we stand in our own light.
>
> And now an universal mist
> Of error is spread o'er each breast,
> With such a fury edged as is
> Not found in th' inwards of th' abyss.
>
> Oh, from thy glorious starry wain
> Dispense on me one sacred beam
> To light me where I soon may see
> How to serve you, and you trust me!

The "starry wain" mentioned in the last stanza is Charlemagne's Wain, or Wagon, the seven stars forming the Great Dipper, which during the seventeenth century was associated with the name of Charles I. The poem was pretty evidently written during Lovelace's second imprisonment, at a time when events were hurrying Charles toward his execution. It is addressed to Lucasta, but there is no real love in the poem for anyone but Charles. So also in certain of his occasional verses—especially in **"The Grasshopper, To My Noble Friend, Mr. Charles Cotton," "The Lady A. L., My Asylum in a Great Extremity,"** and **"To His Dear Brother, Colonel F. L."**—a clear flame of affection warms and illumines the halting, obscure lines. Lovelace was certainly not a man devoid of feeling, nor incapable of conveying that feeling into his poetry, facts that make the frigidity of his love poetry all the more noteworthy.

2. The poems to Lucasta contain no individualizing descriptive touches such as the thought of an actual woman

would naturally give rise to. We do not learn whether she was fair or dark, tall or short, responsive, reserved, or proud. We do not know where she lived, for I think we may quickly dismiss as of no significance the reference to Tunbridge in the poem **"Lucasta, Taking the Waters at Tunbridge."** . . . We do, to be sure, meet some conventional praise of her charms: her eyes rival the sun in brightness; and when she steps into a pool of water, it is purified by the touch of her body. But not one simple detail, such even as Herrick gives us of his probably imaginary Julia, or Carew of his enigmatical Celia, do we find in these poems. If ever a woman was less than a shadow, that woman is Lucasta.

3. The seventeen commendatory poems in English, Latin, and Greek, written for Lovelace's 1649 volume, and the eight elegies, collected and published in 1660 by his brother, Dudley Posthumus Lovelace, and reprinted by Hazlitt, furnish no indication that their authors supposed Lucasta had any identity. In one of the commendatory poems in particular, that of Colonel John Pinchbacke, the thought seems strongly to invite a reference to Lucasta, for the Celia (most likely of Carew) and the Sacharissa of Waller are both mentioned; but there is no word of Lucasta.

4. One poem among those in the first volume of *Lucasta* argues strongly against identifying Lucasta with any real woman. It has exactly the cynicism of Donne's early poems in which he insists on variety in love. The opening phrase, "The beauteous star to which I first did bow," must surely refer to Lucasta, who again and again, in playful allusion to her name, is addressed as one of the heavenly bodies. The most significant lines of this poem (entitled **"A Paradox"**) are as follows:

> 'Tis true the beauteous star
>   To which I first did bow
> Burnt quicker, brighter far
>   Than that which leads me now; . . . .
>
> So from the glorious sun
>   Who to his height hath got,
> With what delight we run
>   To some black cave or grot! . . . .
>
> The god that constant keeps
>   Unto his deities
> Is poor in joys, and sleeps
>   Imprisoned in the skies.
>   This knew the wisest, who
>   From Juno stole, below
>   To love a bear or cow.

Can it be that Lovelace would have written in this way about a real woman whom he had loved or courted?

5. In composing witty love verses with no particular woman in mind, he would have been doing what many other poets of the age did. Cowley, for example, admits that his volume of love poems called *The Mistress* was written merely because "poets are scarce thought freemen of their company without paying some duties . . . . to Love." So Vaughan, alluding in his poems to Amoret, assures us in the Preface that "the fire at highest is but Platonic." Recent critics feel pretty confident that classic models rather than real women inspired most of Herrick's poems to his "many dainty mistresses." There is no reason

why Lovelace also should not have wished to prove himself a freeman of the company of poets by paying some duties to Love.

Perhaps no one of the arguments I have adduced would by itself be convincing. Taken together they lead me to a conclusion not indeed at variance with what Wood actually says, but at variance with the natural implication of his statement. Lovelace may have courted Lucy Sacheverel. He may have loved her. He may even have named his book after her. But that he should have consistently identified her in his own mind with the person addressed as Lucasta in his poems seems to me, in view of the poems themselves, incredible. (pp. 78-82)

Alexander C. Judson, "Who Was Lucasta?" in Modern Philology, *Vol. XXIII, No. 1, August 1925, pp. 77-82.*

The Times Literary Supplement   (essay date 1926)

[*In the following excerpt, the anonymous critic argues that Lovelace cannot be called a true Cavalier poet because his work displays many traits of Renaissance poetry.*]

Lovelace . . . was a Cavalier. He was a country gentleman, with that devotion to the existing state of things to which country gentlemen are prone because of their devotion to the very soil of their England. . . . Poet, painter, and, in his own estimation, first of all soldier (according to Prince Rupert's, not Cromwell's, notion of a soldier), he would live his life in key with the Renaissance idea of life as an art, not a duty. In this the Cavaliers were the cousins of "Il Cortegiano" and of Philip Sidney; and it was their misfortune that life could not be lived in their time and their country as an art, because an aggressive faith in other ideals was blocking the way. . . . The Cavalier drew upon his reason more than did the Roundhead. The wise Puritan lived by faith in what God would make of man, did man do His will. The Cavalier, looking about him, saw, not a "mess," but an established order, expressing, as he believed, the will of God. It was an order which, if left to take its course, would give him and his fellows scope for living the life to which they had been called. To break it up in the hope of something better was unreasonable. . . . One of the most interesting of Lovelace's poems is that which he wrote **"To Lucasta from Prison"** in 1648, when he knew that the King's cause was practically lost. Since he may not love Lucasta he would turn to the love of peace, war, religion, Parliament, liberty, property, public faith, any part of the established order. He finds all of them debauched, and even reformation changed from a cleansing of the wheels of State into an unskilful "disjointing" of a watch:—

> Since then none of these can be
>   Fit objects for my Love and me;
> What then remaines, but th' only spring
>   Of all our loves and joyes? The King.
>
> He who being the whole Ball
>   Of Day on Earth, lends it to all;
> When seeking to ecclipse his right,
>   Blinded, we stand in our owne light.

        And now an universall mist
            Of Error is spread or'e each breast,
        With such a fury edg'd, as is
            Not found in th' inwards of th' Abysse.

        Oh from thy glorious Starry Waine
            Dispense on me one sacred Beame
        To light me where I soone may see
            How to serve you, and you trust me.

The order is broken; but he can still look up to the idea of the order, asking nothing for himself. He "suggests what 'Cavalier' came to mean when glorified by defeat."

To some extent, then, Lovelace is the true Cavalier. Had he been all Cavalier, his poetry would be less interesting than it is. The signs of his period are written plain upon his poetry. He comes after Donne and after Jonson. He shares the fashionable liking for the Anacreontea and for Horace; **"The Grasse-hopper"** is a quaint mixture of the two; **"The Ant"** shows traces of both; and **"The Snayl"** is a very odd and ingenious perversion of Anacreontics by "metaphysical" second thoughts. He is learned and far-fetched. . . . He has learned from Jonson not a little about lyrical form. But he is a gentleman, a courtier, a soldier (in that sense, a Cavalier); and it is not so much beneath his dignity as outside his conception of life as an art to la-bour at his verses like a mere poet (still more, to take an interest in his proofs). If he labours, it is usually at the fashionable elaboration of learned allusion and indirect statement, not with the file. And, therefore, he can write worse than any other poet in English who can write as well as he:—

        Then prest she *Narde* in ev'ry veine
            Which from her kisses trilled;
        And with the balme heald all it's paine
            That from her hand distilled.

There is as much of that doggerel in Lovelace as there is of verse like this:—

        Thou strange inverted *Aeson*, that leap'st ore,
        From thy first Infancy into fourscore,
        That to thine own self hast the Midwife play'd,
        And from thy brain spring'st forth the heav'nly
            maid! . . .
        Thou Rod of *Aaron* with one motion hurl'd,
        Bud'st a perfume of Flowers through the World.
        Thou strange calcined Seeds within a glass,
        Each Species *Idaea* spring'st as 't was . . .

Let us add that in his **"Bella Bona Roba,"** his **"Faire Beg-ger,"** and so forth, and in his very jolly drinking songs, he can ruffle it with the loudest; and, what with the good and the bad in him, he may seem to be a complete Cavalier.

And yet to read in him steadily, taking the bad with the good, is to be haunted by a feeling that, after all, he is not a true Cavalier poet. Something else, some other spirit, keeps breaking through. It may be seen in his very faults. He is not content to make, by insufficient labour, faults out of the poetic manner of his own time, which Donne and Crashaw could use to great ends. He must lapse (as he does in **"Lucasta at the Bath,"** and in his first **"Loose Sar-aband,"** from which a doggerel stanza has been quoted) into the old faults of the previous age. Against **"Gratiana dauncing and singing,"** which needs no praise to-day, set

the next poem in the book—the almost equally well-known **"Scrutinie."** It leaves one uneasy. Suckling did this sort of thing perfectly; and it must be done with no trace of effort. There is effort in Lovelace's declaration of incon-stancy. It is very clever; but it shows that, though he can dash, he is not really dashing. And now for something very different:—

        Into the Garden is she come,
        Love and Delights *Elisium*;
        If ever Earth show'd all her store,
        View her discoloured budding Floore;
        Here her glad Eye she largely feedes,
        And stands 'mongst them, as they 'mong weeds;
        The flowers in their best aray,
        As to their Queen their Tribute pay,
        And freely to her Lap proscribe
        A Daughter out of ev'ry Tribe:
        Thus as she moves, they all bequeath
        At once the Incense of their Breath.

That—and, indeed, nearly all of **"Amarantha: a Pastor-all"**—is not Cavalier: it is Elizabethan out of due time. It prepares us for the truth about greater things.

        If to be absent were to be
                Away from thee;
            Or that when I am gone,
                You or I were alone;
        Then my *Lucasta* might I crave
        Pity from blustring winde, or swallowing
            wave. . . .

There is no need to quote more. Obviously the author of that had read his Donne, with "Fools have no way to meet But by their feet," and knew all about the fashionable "Platonicks." But no less obviously, in spite of a "foaming blew-god," the-mind of the author of that poem is much simpler, graver, and sweeter a mind than that which is commonly regarded as Cavalier The interest of reading Lovelace through, with all the difficulties of bad writing and bad printing, is the interest of disentangling the dispo-sition of the poet from the fashions of his age. Much may be learned from poems like the song **"To Amarantha, that she would dishevell her haire,"** and the ode **"The Rose"** and **"The Answer to Sir Thomas Wortley's Sonnet"**; so that we may come to understand why it is that Lovelace seems to set us thinking not of Suckling or Carew or Stan-ley, as we should expect, but of Wyatt or Ralegh or Sid-ney. And when we come to his few great lyrics, their per-fection seems a little less accidental, or miraculous, than it did. **"To Althea, from Prison"** has much more of the pe-riod in it than those disputed gods that wanton in the air. . . . It has the benefit of all that Campion and Jonson had taught about lyric form. But in making it, and in mak-ing **"To Lucasta, Going to the Warres,"** Lovelace took no more from the fashion than he needed for the perfect shap-ing of his own spirit. That spirit belonged to a past age. For all his clever mind, able to twist itself in thoughts and pick up analogies from many kinds of desultory learning, able, too, to scoff and defy and show off, his spirit was sim-ple, devout, passionate; fit for a world in which the tide of life and beauty was flowing, not for a time in which the ebb was dragging out over rocks and weeds and mud. For the most part, his mind was at war with his spirit, and in poetry he followed his mind. When he spoke from the depths, he spoke simply, at first intention, in the old way.

"Richard Lovelace," in The Times Literary Supplement, *No. 1253, January 21, 1926, p. 41.*

Mario Praz (essay date 1926)

[*Praz was an Italian scholar and critic whose writings include the widely acclaimed* La Carne, la morte e il diavolo nella letterature romantica *(1930,* The Romantic Agony, *1935). In the following excerpt, he discusses Lovelace's poetry in the context of seventeenth-century European literature.*]

The study of a minor poet can hardly be an aim in itself. Lovelace's contribution to poetry is slender and, as [C. H. Wilkinson] reminds us, accessible in most of the anthologies of English verse. But our picture of the moods, predilections, customs of the seventeenth century would hardly be complete without an acquaintance with the entire work of Lovelace: he is one of the most striking of the minor figures, though shining mostly with a reflected light.

The main source of this light is, obviously, Donne. A Donneish flavour can easily be detected throughout the whole of Lovelace's work, nowhere better than in such poems as **'The Apostacy of one, and but one Lady'** and **'The Ant.'** Arguments, conceits, intonations, all recall almost irresistibly the greater poet: who, for instance, can read the beginning of the fourth stanza of **'The Ant,'** 'Austere and Cynick!' without being reminded of 'Rebel and Atheist too' of Donne's *Loves Deity?* Everything in Lovelace recalls the greater poet's style without, unfortunately, the earnest passion and intellectual flame which redeem much that is far-fetched and even preposterous in that style. Behind Donne's conceits we always see a profound and restless mind in the act of inventing new ways of expression for his new modes of thought; behind Lovelace's conceits we too often find—emptiness. When the lava has been discharged by the volcano, the Neapolitan craftsman collects it hard and cold, and carves it into pipe-bowls and objects of vertu. Lovelace, with most of the minor metaphysical poets, like the Neapolitan craftsman is merely picking up cold lava on the slopes of a volcano. And he often contrives to shape pretty things with it, studded and glittering with quaint bits of information, with *Aurum fulminans,* fair Paulinas, crowned Venices, not to speak of the Romantick Phoenixes and the jellies left by the fallen stars: a curio-hunter who is occasionally also a poet.

A poet he doubtless is in the best known among his lyrics, as in the popular song **'To Althea, From Prison,'** in which he makes a spirited poem out of a commonplace. Voiture, an author with whom Lovelace was acquainted, as appears from his lines prefixed to John Davies' translation of Voiture's Letters, has a *rondeau* written in a similar strain. . . .

Dans la prison qui vous va renfermant
Votre grande âme agit incessamment,
Et ce divin esprit que rien n'enserre
Vole partout, sans erreur toujours erre,
S'étend, s'élève et va plus aisément.

Vous parcourez l'un et l'autre élément,
Vous pénétrez jusques au firmament,
Et visitez le ciel, l'onde et la terre
  Dans la prison.

Vous ne gênez votre coeur vainement;
Vous connoissez et voyez sainement
Tout ce qui brille et qui n'est que de verre;
Vous possédez la paix durant la guerre:
C'est être heureux et libre entièrement
  Dans la prison.

Indeed, most of the subjects of his poems Lovelace shares with contemporary poets, not only English, but also foreign. . . . Lovelace evidently was well read in contemporary literature, as were most of the poets of his age . . . from Théophile, Saint-Amant, Tristan, Voiture, the Jesuit Casimire, Marino and his Italian imitators they drew constant inspiration. Without such poems as A. G. Brignole Sale's on whipped courtesans . . . giving the lead, Lovelace's song on **'A Guiltlesse Lady imprisoned, after penanced'** would probably never have been written; while **'The Faire Begger'** is ultimately to be traced to Achillini's *Bellissima Mendica.* . . . This poem of Achillini has been often imitated, for instance in the following sonnet by Alessandro Adimari (Tersicore, Firenze, 1637):

Bella Stracciata.

Altri vagheggi pur gli ostri di Tiro,
E di seriche pompe il corpo ammanti,
Ch' io, mendica mia bella, i tuoi sembianti
Più ricchi in questi stracci amo, & ammiro.

O Sol, che fra le nubi, e fra 'l zaffiro
D' uno squarciato Cielo apri i tuoi vanti,
Posson per tutto i desiosi Amanti
Ferirti con lo sguardo, e col sospiro.

Tu, qual vago Giardin, mostri di fuori
Per i cancelli tuoi, ch' aperti stanno,
E del fianco, e del sen le rose, e i fiori.

Così gli Atleti al campo Eleo sen vanno
(Abito, che s' adatta anco a gli Amori)
Ricchi di palme, e poveri di panno.

I have quoted this sonnet only in order to show how the *motifs* of many of Lovelace's poems lose the unusual flavour they may have for a modern reader when considered in connexion with the rest of contemporary literature. What seems quaint to-day was fashionable then; only the great poets never appear quaint to us, because they are much above the fashions of their own day. If any author ever did stick to fashion, this was doubtless Richard Lovelace, the accomplished gentleman dear 'tam Marti quam Mercurio.' He was a little of a cosmopolitan; in his lines to Lily he poses as (and evidently was) a connoisseur of paintings, quotes Vasari and Vermander, and declares his intention of showing to the indifferent Englishmen 'what due renown to thy fair Art they owe': he was, in a word, an ideal representative of the last of English generations to be brought up under the influence of the Italian Renaissance: the Cavaliers—a generation closely modelled on Baldassar Castiglione's Complete Gentleman. . . . Poetry was but one of the many accomplishments of the Gentleman: it served only to confer additional honour on the Courtier, in the case of Lovelace, on the priest, in the case of Crashaw: 'subservient recreation for vacant hours, not the great business of the soul,' as Crashaw's editor puts it. Such poets are often at their best when achieving some unheard-of feat: Crashaw's *Bulla, Musicks Duell* are more than clever; here cleverness merges into real poetry. Lovelace's **'Toad and Spyder'** is little more than a mere article of vertu, or a counterpart of those odd nightmarish inventions of the Dutch painters, which were so much in vogue at the time; but, in a narrow range, it is somewhat of a masterpiece for clever perversity of humour. It is to be regretted that the writers of the seventeenth century were only seldom aware of the possibilities of fun latent in their artificial style and command of words, and too often succeeded in producing things only unintentionally humorous, and therefore ridiculous. (pp. 320-22)

> *Mario Praz, in a review of "The Poems of Richard Lovelace," in* The Modern Language Review, *Vol. XXI, No. 3, July 1926, pp. 319-22.*

Willa McClung Evans   (essay date 1947)

[*An American literary scholar, Evans frequently wrote on the relation between music and poetry. In the excerpt below, she reconstructs the historical circumstances surrounding the composition of Lovelace's poem "The Vintage to the Dungeon," calling it the work of a remarkably conscientious and serious poet.*]

From the fact that Lovelace was committed to the Gatehouse in 1642, critics have inferred that **"The Vintage to the Dungeon"** reflected the poet's experiences in jail. The inference has not been without a certain appeal—an appeal which has served to perpetuate the tradition that Lovelace's lyrics were the poet's hasty, careless, and spontaneously penned reactions to his immediate environment or experience. Elsewhere, I have discussed evidences that Lovelace was not the irresponsible versifier that his critics have dubbed him; many of the irregularities of his metrical patterns were not the result of haste and carelessness but of the deliberate preparation of a text that could be set to music; and several of Lovelace's songs were revised before being sent to the printer. . . . Lovelace drew upon literary source material for theme and imagery and . . . the apparent freshness and spontaneity of his verse was thus the result of artful calculation. More specifically, the concept of prison life mirrored in **"The Vintage to the Dungeon,"** was not the poet's unconsidered reaction to his immediate environment, but the adaptation of certain scenes and ideas set forth in [in William Cartwright's play] *The Royall Slaue.*

"The Vintage to the Dungeon" is a dramatic lyric, the singer purporting to be a prisoner offering advice and encouragement to his fettered companions. The theme of the song is the cavalier sentiment: freedom of the body is not essential to the freedom of the spirit. The word "Dungeon"—defined by Webster as "A close dark prison or vault, commonly underground, like the lower rooms in the donjon or keep of a castle"—in the title of the song, suggests the nature of the singer's background. The companions to whom the words are addressed are "pent Soules," "sadde" in mind, wretched in body. Their arms are "pin-

ion'd," their limbs shackled. If Lovelace wrote this lyric as a result of his own prison experiences, the implication is that he looked about in the dungeon, observed the plight of his fellow captives, took up his pen and wrote a lyrical invitation to the prisoners to drink away their cares, and triumph over their miseries by dancing to the clank of their chains.

Such an interpretation of the poem is not in keeping with what is known of Lovelace's confinement in the Gatehouse. Seventeenth-century prisons were "carried on as private profit-making concerns of the gaolers," and those committed were allowed to live outside the walls if they could pay to keep guards in attendance. Or if the prisoners preferred to remain inside, they could bribe "the gaoler" to give them private suites or apartments, and have their own servants bring in food, lights, fires, furniture and whatever else was needed. In 1642 Lovelace was still in possession of his estates, was accustomed to living in luxury and to spending money freely; and it is thus unlikely that he experienced the physical misery suffered by the prisoners described in **"The Vintage to the Dungeon."** Even if the poet did not avail himself of the comforts money could have obtained for him, but accepted the accommodations assigned to the poorest and meanest of the inmates, he was not apt to have been bound in chains and thrown into a dungeon along with several other manacled wretches—as the song suggests. According to John Taylor, the Gatehouse provided "Good Lodgeing roomes, and diet." It was, moreover, a small prison, customarily used to detain a few prisoners at a time, and these but for short periods before or after trial. The political nature of Lovelace's misdemeanor and his release on bail after but seven weeks of imprisonment, argue that the poet was not regarded as dangerous and deserving of severe punishment. The chances thus that Lovelace obtained the conception of prison life portrayed in **"The Vintage to the Dungeon"** from his own experience in the Gatehouse are not very strong.

Yet the "sadde" fellows Lovelace invited to drink and to dance were not mere figments of the poet's imagination. He had seen their dungeon and watched them dance to the clank of their shackles in Cartwright's *The Royall Slaue* performed before the King and Queen at Oxford in 1636.

The play opened presenting a "City in the front, and a Prison on the side," with four prisoners singing from within a dungeon. The theme of their song expressed the same philosophic sentiment that Lovelace exhorted the prisoners in **"The Vintage to the Dungeon"** to accept: liberty is not dependent upon the freedom of the body. Cartwright's prisoners likewise exhorted one another to drink away their cares, and to keep time to their singing by rattling their chains. (pp. 62-5)

From what can be deduced regarding Lovelace's environment in the Gatehouse and from what is known of the prison life portrayed in The Royall Slaue it would appear that the play rather than the jail provided the conception of the prisoners' lot in **"The Vintage to the Dungeon."** Furthermore, there is evidence that in 1636 there was a demand for such a song. (p. 66)

The success of the first performance of *The Royall Slaue* increased rather than diminished the demand for such a song as **"The Vintage to the Dungeon."** Their Majesties enjoyed the play so much that the Queen requested another performance as part of the Christmas festivity at Hampton Court. Thus if Lovelace did not prepare his song for the first presentation of the play, he may well have written it for the Court performance, when several changes were introduced in the staging. Even after the latter performance of the play, there were still occasions when **"The Vintage to the Dungeon"** might have been sung. For the court was accustomed to continuity in its entertainments, and liked to be reminded of past pleasures. Thus Lovelace's song would have been welcomed at informal court gatherings when some reminder of *The Royall Slaue* was in order. And the fact that the popular court composer and singer, William Lawes, set to music both Cartwright's prisoners' song and **"The Vintage to the Dungeon"** strengthens the idea that the two songs were composed for performance before the court, either upon the same or closely related occasions.

While it would thus seem logical that the author of **"The Vintage to the Dungeon"** wrote the stanzas in 1636 when the court was in a mood to appreciate the song, it is possible that he waited to pen the lines until he was a prisoner in the Gatehouse in 1642. The specific date of composition is irrelevant. The significance of the evidence here presented is that *before* Lovelace became a prisoner, he and the potential listeners to his song were familiar with the prison philosophy, the images pertaining to jail life, and the general concept of prison environment that appear in **"The Vintage to the Dungeon."** Whether the date of composition was 1636, 1642, or that of some intervening year, the process of writing the poem was the work of a conscious artist who was able to select from the sources at his disposal details pertaining to prison life which his audience would understand when sung. (pp. 67-8)

> *Willa McClung Evans, "Lovelace's Concept of Prison Life in 'The Vintage to the Dungeon',"* in Philological Quarterly, *Vol. XXVI, No. 1, January 1947, pp. 62-8.*

William Empson (essay date 1947)

[*Empson was a distinguished English critic and poet whose writings include* Some Versions of the Pastoral *(1935),* The Structure of Complex Words *(1951),* Milton's God *(1961), and the acclaimed* Seven Types of Ambiguity. *In the following excerpt from the last-named work, originally published in 1930, he examines the semantic complexities of Lovelace's "To Althea."*]

An example of [a] type of ambiguity . . . , the most ambiguous that can be conceived, occurs when the two meanings of the word, the two values of the ambiguity, are the two opposite meanings defined by the context, so that the total effect is to show a fundamental division in the writer's mind. You might think that such a case could never occur and, if it occurred, could not be poetry, but as a matter of fact it is, in one sense or another, very frequent, and admits of many degrees. (p. 192)

Evidently the simplest way for the two opposites defined by the context to be suggested to the reader is by some disorder in the action of the negative; as by its being easily passed over or too much insisted upon. Thus in the Keats *Ode to Melancholy*

> No, no; go not to Lethe; neither twist

tells you that somebody, or some force in the poet's mind, must have wanted to go to Lethe very much, if it took four negatives in the first line to stop them. (p. 205)

Shakespeare sometimes throws in a 'not' apparently to suggest extra subtlety:

> LENOX.   And the right valiant Banquo walked too late,
> Whom you may say (if 't please you) Fleans kill'd,
> For Fleans fled: Men must not walke too late.
> Who cannot want the thought, how monstrous
> It was for Malcolme, and Donalbaine
> To kill their gracious Father?
>   (*Macbeth*, III. vi.)

Who *can* avoid thinking, is the meaning; but the *not* breaks through the irony into 'Who must not feel that they have not done anything monstrous at all?' 'Who must not avoid thinking altogether about so touchy a state matter?' This is not heard as the meaning, however, the normal construction is too strong, and the negative acts as a sly touch of disorder. (p. 209)

It is not so much that 'not' was said lightly and might easily be ignored as that it implied a conflict (or why should you be saying one of the innumerable things the subject was *not*, instead of the one thing it *was*?), and it was upon this conflict, rather than upon the value of the passage as information, that the reader's sympathy devolved.

> Stone walls do not a prison make,
>   Nor iron bars a cage;
> Minds innocent and quiet take
>   That for a hermitage.
>
>   ('To Althea')

The point of [Lovelace's **'To Althea, From Prison'**] is to describe those services that are freedom; constancy to a mistress, loyalty to a political party, obedience to God, and the limited coziness of good company; thus to focus its mood, to discover what shade of interpretation Lovelace is putting on the blank cheque of a paradox, is in a sense to define the meaning of *not* in the first two lines. This is done to some extent by the grammar of the verse itself.

That may be 'the fact that they do not make a prison,' and we are then told that this notion withdraws the mind, as if to a *hermitage*, from the anxieties of the world. But on the face of it, *that* is the *cage* or *prison* itself, and by being singular, so that it will not apply to *walls* or *bars*, it admits that they do, in fact, make even for quiet minds a *prison* and a *cage*. It is curious to read 'those' instead of *that,* and see how the air of wit evaporates and generous carelessness becomes a preacher's settled desire to convince. If you read 'them' there is a further shift because the metre becomes prose; the sentiment might be by Bunyan, and one wonders if it is at all true.

However, this experiment has hardly a fair chance, as there is another ambiguity which gives the verse recklessness, with an air both of paradox and of reserve. *Take* is a verb active in feeling though presumably here passive in sense; thus though it mainly says, 'such minds accept prison for their principles and can turn it into a hermitage,' there is some implication that 'such minds imprison themselves, escape from life, perhaps escape from their mistress, into jail, and cannot manage without their martyrdom.' It is the proximity of *quiet* which hushes this meaning, and keeps it from spoiling the proportions of the poem as a whole; 'such persons, madam, were aware of the advantages of retiring from the world, and are accepting their misfortune with some philosophy.' There is another shade of meaning which is almost 'mistake,' as in 'cry you mercy, I took you for a joint-stool'; 'such minds may be so innocent that they know no difference between a prison and a hermitage'; for this they may be mocked or revered, but it is with irony that the poet includes himself among them; or 'so quiet that they pretend not to know the difference,' with a saintly impertinence that would have pleased George Herbert.

All these meanings are no more than slight overtones or gracenotes; the main meaning is sufficiently brave and is conveyed with enough fervour to stand alone; thus, looking back to *that,* it may after all refer to *walls* and *bars,* and be attracted into the singular by the neighbouring *hermitage.* (pp. 209-11)

> *William Empson, in a chapter in his* Seven Types of Ambiguity, *revised edition, New Directions, 1947, pp. 192-233.*

Mark Van Doren   (essay date 1951)

[*One of the most versatile men of letters in twentieth-century American literature, Van Doren wrote poetry (for which he won the Pulitzer Prize in 1939), novels, biographies, short stories, drama, criticism, and social commentary. His scholarly works include* American and British Literature Since 1890 *(1930), which he wrote with his brother, Carl Van Doren. Below, Van Doren offers a minute semantic and formal analysis of* "To Lucasta, Going to the Warres."]

Perhaps no poet has said more in twelve short lines than Lovelace says in [**"To Lucasta, Going to the Warres,"** a] farewell to his mistress as he leaves her on his way to war—to honorable war, whose claims rival in his feeling, since he is a Cavalier, the claims of love. Once more we have a love poem whose subject is separation; indeed, this is the best subject love has if it will be talking; but Lovelace is not lamenting his necessity to leave. He is justifying it, even exulting in it, and he is counting on Lucasta to understand. She may have called him unkind to go, as the first line suggests; but that is only his cue to speak with all the authority verse can give his voice. The authority sounds in the imperative sentence with which the poem begins.

That it is the authority of intelligence, however, is manifest in the completeness with which the next two lines

comprehend the sweetness of the person he is leaving. There may have been gentleness in the fourth word uttered at all, the "Sweet" set off with commas as if a bow or a kiss accompanied it, but lines 2 and 3 can leave no doubt in Lucasta's mind that her lover values the quality in her most opposite to the quality of the experience he now seeks. She is faithful and good, and her spirit is serene. But listen to the verse as it says this.

> That from the nunnery—

the line looks shorter than it is. The ballad stanza of which it is the second line requires that it have three iambic feet, and that it rhyme with the fourth line. It does both things, but only if we stretch out the word "nunnery" as we speak it, and give its last light syllable a fuller emphasis than it normally receives. When we do that—and the stanza makes us do it—we perceive how reluctant the lover is to leave the nest of his happiness. He lingers over the word, which again, since the sense runs on from it into the next line, hangs in the air an instant as if it were unwilling to go the way of other words.

Its essence passes, in fact, into the next line. Without pause and yet without hurry, slowly and most reverently, we hear:

> That from the nunnery
> Of thy chaste breast and quiet mind—

from all that, what? This remains to be seen, but meanwhile the third line has made it clear why "nunnery" was used, and why it was no exaggeration. It is a slow line, mostly monosyllables; and each monosyllable must be deliberately pronounced. Only the "of" and the "and" are unimportant. "Thy chaste breast"—the reader will be aware that he is being forced to say "thy" as if its reference were gravely important, and to say "chaste breast" as if much time had been lovingly allotted to it. Indeed it is physically impossible to say "chaste breast" fast. Both words end in sounds that are unintelligible in English unless they are painstakingly articulated, and the sameness of the sound here makes this doubly true. Another sort of sameness appears in "quiet" and "mind," two words that open themselves slowly on the long *i* and remain open, poised there as "nunnery" was poised at the end of the line before. There is a recollection in them also of "unkind" that closed line one on the same sound. They answer the accusation in that word, suggesting by the very vowel they use, and use so seriously, that if the lover is unkind it is because he has to be, and that he has counted the cost. He knows what he is leaving, he knows whom he is being unfaithful to. She is a lady perfect in virtue and serenity, whose chaste breast and quiet mind are a whole world, removed from every other world, in which he would stay if he could.

The poem, poised then once more on "mind," flies swiftly to the ground for the conclusion of its opening stanza.

> To war and arms I fly—

there is the long *i* again, but between it and the sounds it recalls, and for the first time in the poem thus far, there is the heavier note of "war and arms." Heavier, not merely because war and arms are in themselves alarming terms, but also—and Lovelace knows this well—because their vowel is hard and alien. The nunnery is no more, the chaste breast and quiet mind are already put far behind as the lover goes racing away—almost literally flying—as if to a new mistress who will make him forget this one who watches him go. There indeed he goes, saying the rest of the poem as it were over his shoulder, firmly, and without any further attempt to recapture the tone of lines 2 and 3. They have done their work, but he must now do his.

"True, a new mistress now I chase"—he makes the confession at once, and proceeds to describe her. The stanza in which he does so is the cleverest of the three, and for that reason the poorest, though it is only relatively poor. Cleverness is a fine thing even if it is not the finest. In this case it consists in saying that the mistress is a man—"the first foe in the field." She is the enemy. And this enemy has a forceful front: all three of the key words in line 6 begin with the same letter, the stout letter *f*. "True"—the beginning word, suggestive of logic and argument, was itself a sign that the speaker intended to make his point by any means available. These are the means; and repetition is another, for the second pair of lines in this stanza says the same thing over: with a still stronger faith than had been proved in lines 2 and 3 of the poem, his embraces are now to be bestowed on a sword, a horse, a shield—impossible things to embrace, particularly the horse, but the exaggeration is consistent with the cleverness. An idea is working now, not a feeling; which again is consistent with the tone of persuasion, that undertakes paradox if it must.

The third stanza returns to the deeper level of the first, though now there is a mixture of feeling and thought. For one thing, Lucasta is addressed again: in the third line another epithet is set off between commas—"Dear," to balance the "Sweet" with which the song began. "Thou too" and "thee"—it is clear that the poet's discourse is once more in the second person. So is it clear that Lovelace is asking Lucasta to think with him and understand him. Her quiet mind is to take in one last paradox. Such a mind is above being interested in cleverness for its own sake, so he will be very serious; still, the statement is one that must be understood by the intellect, and therefore, though with consummate tenderness, he makes it with the last breath he uses.

Yet you too, he says, must adore the inconstancy my second stanza has confessed. Only you, as a matter of fact, *could* adore it. For you are truly extraordinary in being able to comprehend that I could not love you as much as I do if I did not love something else still more than that. I love it more, and you have helped me to do so, because *you* love it as much as you do. One of the reasons I love you—indeed it is the controlling reason—is that distinction in you, that capacity to worship Honor, which has educated me. The qualities of persons are even more important than the persons themselves. Your faithfulness and quietness are still more beautiful than you, being permanent, abstract things. We compliment persons, but we praise qualities; and praise is the greater act, deserved only by the greatest persons. The greatest Person of all we never compliment—how absurd is the very thought. We praise God, and for His qualities of strength and goodness.

So with you, for there is in you something still more important and lovable than yourself. It is Honor, which now I am giving every evidence that I love. Therefore you must consent, as I know you do.

The last two lines of the poem say all of that, and as much more as verse is capable of saying when a master uses it. The longest prose paraphrase would still not capture the whole meaning of these justly famous lines. They are famous precisely because they cannot *be* paraphrased.

> I could not love thee, Dear, so much,
> Loved I not Honor more.

There they are, and the statement is complete. So is the poem—one of the briefest masterpieces in the world, and one of the best proofs that poetry can say what nothing else can. A good line of poetry, like any line well and straightly drawn, is the shortest distance between two points. And the two present points are worlds apart: the nunnery, the battlefield. (pp. 22-6)

> *Mark Van Doren, " 'To Lucasta, on Going to the Wars', Richard Lovelace," in his* Introduction to Poetry, *The Dryden Press, 1951, pp. 21-6.*

Cleanth Brooks   (lecture date 1959)

[*Brooks is a distinguished American critic best known as one of the pioneers of New Criticism, an approach that focuses on the internal tensions of a literary work regardless of its psychological or social contexts. His writings include* Yoknapatawpha Country *(1963),* A Shaping Joy: Studies in the Writer's Craft *(1972), and* Historical Evidence and the Reading of Seventeenth Century Poetry *(1991). In the following excerpt from a 1959 lecture, Brooks provides an erudite and penetrating analysis of Lovelace's philosophical poem "The Grasse-Hopper," paying particular attention to the poet's dexterous use of complex symbolism, literary allusions, and verbal ambiguity.*]

[One could well illustrate the relation of poetic structure to politics and morality from Lovelace's poem **"The Grasshopper."**] The first part of Lovelace's poem derives from the Anacreontic poem "The Grasshopper." (I use Abraham Cowley's translation.)

> Happy *Insect* what can be
> In happiness compar'd to thee?
> Fed with nourishment divine,
> The dewy *Mornings* gentle *Wine!*
> *Nature* waits upon thee still,
> And thy verdant Cup does fill;
> 'Tis fill'd where ever thou does tread,
> *Natures* selfe's thy Ganimed.
> Thou does drink, and dance, and sing;
> Happier than the happiest King! . . .

Lovelace evidently began his poem as a free translation of the Greek poem; but he went on to develop out of it a thoroughly different poem—different in theme and different in tone. The little Anacreontic poem becomes merely a starting point of the poem that Lovelace actually writes. Whereas the Greek poet contents himself with giving a charming account of the insect's life, Lovelace uses the account of the grasshopper's life to set up the contrast between the spurious summer of nature and the genuine summer to which men have access. If we are interested in the way in which the poem was composed, we shall certainly want to know what sources Lovelace used, and there may be a special delight in seeing how he has reshaped his sources to his own purpose. But a mere roundup of the sources will never in itself tell us what the poet has done with them. A bad poem may assimilate Anacreon as well as a good poem. The value of a poem as a work of art is not to be determined by an account of its sources.

In the same way, the history of ideas might tell us a great deal about this poem. The historian can trace the development of such concepts as that of the actual considered to be a dim and limited reflection of the ideal—specifically, the summer of the grasshopper in the natural world of the seasons viewed as a mere shadow of the genuine summer which transcends the seasonal world of nature. The historians of ideas can trace for us the development of the concept of richness based not upon the possession of goods but upon one's freedom from wants—that is, the notion of richness as completeness. The ideas that Lovelace is using here are familiar to most readers and can be taken for granted; but I concede that the reader who is not familiar with these concepts might have serious trouble with the poem. Even so, criticism has to be distinguished from the scholarship of the history of ideas, for the obvious reason that the historian of ideas may find just as much to explain in a poor and unsuccessful poem as in a good poem.

It is the critic of moralistic bias . . . who is most likely to object sharply to modern critical procedure. The serious moralist finds it hard not to become impatient with a critic who seems to ignore the moral problems, and to concern himself merely with "form" and technique. Nor will he necessarily be satisfied with the critic's concession that wisdom is certainly to be found in poetry. Lovelace's poem, for example, says, among other things, that happiness is not dependent upon external circumstances but is an inward quality. But the moralist argues that this is surely the doctrine that ought to be emphasized in any critical account of the poem. For it may appear to him that it is this moral truth that gives the poem its value.

But the sternest moralist will have to concede that many poems that contain admirable doctrine—Longfellow's "Psalm of Life," for example—are very poor poems. Furthermore, if one tries to save the case by stipulating that the doctrine must not only be true, but must be rendered clearly, acceptably, and persuasively, he will have come perilously close to reducing the poet's art to that of the mere rhetorician.

Moralists as diverse as Marxists and the later Van Wyck Brooks are all for making the Muse a rewrite girl. But the Muse is willful and stubborn: a thesis presented eloquently and persuasively is not necessarily the same thing as a poem. **"The Grasshopper"** is, among other things, a document in the personal history of Lovelace, testifying to his relation with Charles Cotton. It is an instance of Lovelace's regard for the classics; it incorporates an amalgam of ideas inherited from the Christian-classical tradition of Western thought; it is an admonition to find happiness

within oneself. The point is that it could be all of these things and yet be a very poor poem. It could be all of these things and not be a poem at all. It could be, for example, a letter from Lovelace to Charles Cotton, or an entry in Lovelace's commonplace book.

It happens to be a poem and a rather fine one. But defense of this judgment, if it were questioned, would involve an examination of the structure of the poem as poem. And with this kind of examination the so-called "new criticism" is concerned. I should be happy to drop the adjective "new" and simply say: with this kind of judgment, literary criticism is concerned.

Lovelace's poem is a little masterpiece in the management of tone. Lovelace makes the life of the insect thoroughly Lucullan. The grasshopper is "drunk ev'ry night": Lovelace provides him with a carved bed in which to sleep off his debauch. But actually the grasshopper is up with the dawn, for his tipple is a natural distillation, the free gift of heaven. The joys to which he abandons himself are all innocent and natural, and his merrymaking makes men merry too.

The grasshopper's life, then, though described in terms that hint at the human world, is not used to symbolize a type of human experience to be avoided. We have here no fable of the ant and the grasshopper. Lovelace would not reform the little wastrel, but delights in him, so joyously and thoughtlessly at home in his world.

Stanzas V and VI define very delicately and precisely this attitude, one of humor and amusement, touched with the merest trace of pity. The grasshopper is happy because he cannot possibly foresee the harvest or the biting blasts of winter. "But ah the Sickle! Golden Eares are Cropt." Everything in the line conspires to place the emphasis upon the word *golden*, a word rich in every sort of association: wealth, ripeness, luxury, the Saturnian age of gold. But the full force of *golden* is perhaps not realized until we come to line 13: "Poore verdant foole! and now green Ice!" The clash of gold and green absorbs and carries within it the whole plight of the grasshopper. Green suggests not only the little insect's color but all that is growing, immature, unripe, and innocently simple. The oaten ears on which the grasshopper loves to swing change, by natural process, from green to gold; the grasshopper cannot change with them. The mature oaten ears may resemble the precious metal—one remembers Milton's "vegetable gold"—but greenness turned to something hard and stiff and cold—the sliver of green ice—is a pathetic absurdity.

I should not press the contrast so hard, had Lovelace not insisted on the color, and emphasized its connection with springing verdure by his phrase "Poore verdant foole!" And here it becomes proper to acknowledge the critic's debt to the lexicographer and to concede that my suggestion that verdant here means *gullible* has no specific dictionary warrant. The Oxford Dictionary's first entry for this sense of *verdant* is as late as 1824; the same dictionary, however, does indicate that *green* could carry these connotations as early as 1548. In the context of this poem, verdant, followed by the phrase "green ice," and associated as it is with "fool," must surely carry the meaning of inexperienced, thoughtless innocence.

The gentle and amused irony that suffuses "Poore verdant foole" continues through the lines that follow: the grasshopper's joys are measured by the instability of the insect's precarious perch—"Large and as lasting, as thy Peirch of Grasse." But the speaker soon turns from his contemplation of these ephemeral joys to man's perdurable joys—from the specious summer of nature to the genuine summer which he and his noble friend can create, each in the other's breast.

The poem pivots sharply in the fifth stanza, and the management of tone is so dexterous that we may be tempted to pass over the last half of the poem too easily. But these latter stanzas have their difficulties and if we want to understand the poem I think we shall want to find precisely what goes on. Moreover, these stanzas present their problem of tone also. The poem must not seem smug and sanctimonious; man's happiness must not seem too easily achieved. For if man rises superior to the animal kingdom, he is not, for all of that, a disembodied spirit. He is animal too, and he has to reckon with the "frost-stretch'd winges" of the North Wind and with the blackness of the winter night. Moreover, as man, he has his peculiar bugbears of a sort that the grasshopper does not have to contend with. There is at least a hint of this in the reference to "untempted kings."

As a general comment, suffice it to say that in this poem the flesh is given its due: the warm hearth, the lighted casements, and showers of old Greek wine fortify the friends against the winter night and give a sense of real gaiety and mirth. If there is high thinking, the living is not so plain as to be unconvincing. And the sentiment on which the poem closes is none the less serious because it comes out of festivity and has been warmed by wine. He who "wants himselfe"—who owns things but has not mastered himself—is poor indeed. It is this full possession of himself, this lack of dependence upon things, which makes him richer than "untempted Kings."

The last phrase, however, is curious. In this context, Lovelace ought to be writing to his friend: "since we are untempted by material possessions, we are actually richer than kings." The force of the contrast depends upon the fact that kings are more than most men tempted by material possessions. Why then *untempted* kings? The solution is probably to be sought in the source of the poem. In the Anacreontic "Grasshopper" the insect is referred to as a king—the Greek text has BasileXs—and Abraham Cowley, Lovelace's contemporary, uses the word king in his translation. Lovelace, then, for his fit audience who knew the Greek poem, is saying: we are like the grasshopper, that rare specimen, an untempted king; but we are richer than he, since our joys do not end with the natural summer, but last on through the genuine (and unending) summer of the heart.

But it is Stanzas VIII and IX that cause the real trouble. As C. H. Hartmann remarks: "Lovelace himself could on occasion become so involved as to be utterly incomprehensible even without the assistance of an eccentric printer."

To deal first with Stanza IX: the drift of the argument is plain enough, but Lovelace's editor, Wilkinson, also confesses to difficulties here: the friends will whip night away from their casements. But what are we to make of the phrase "as clear Hesper"? Wilkinson writes "The meaning would seem to be that 'just as Hesperus shines clearer as the day draws to a close, so will our tapers whip night from the lighted casements of the room where we amuse ourselves.'. . . " But I fail to see the relevance of his argument that Hesper shines the brighter as the skies darken. Why not simply read "as clear Hesper" as an ellipsis for "as clear Hesper does"? Our tapers will whip away night as clear Hesper whips it away. Moreover, the poet chooses as the dispeller of gloom the modest light of the star just because it is modest. He is not claiming that he and his friend can abolish winter. "Dropping *December*" *shall* come weeping in. The friendly association with Cotton will not do away with the wintry night. What the human being can do is to rid the night of its horror—exorcise the hag—maintain a small circle of light amid the enveloping darkness. This is precisely what the evening star, clear Hesper, does, and all that he and his friend with their gleaming tapers propose to do. As with light, so with heat. Their hearth will be an Aetna, but an Aetna is epitome—a tiny volcano of heat. The poet is very careful not to claim too much.

Stanza VIII contains the most difficult passage in the poem, and Lovelace's editors have not supplied a note. "Dropping *December*" means *dripping*, or *rainy* December. But why will December lament the usurping of his reign? Does the warm fire and pleasant company maintained by the two friends constitute the usurpation against which he will protest? We may at first be inclined to think so, but the lines that follow make it plain that December is not crying out against, but rejoicing in, the two friends' festivities. Seeing them at their wine, December exclaims that he has "his Crowne againe." But what is December's crown? One looks for it throughout Greek and Roman mythology in vain.

We have here, I am convinced, a topical allusion. The crown of December is evidently the Christmas festivities, festivities actually more ancient than Christianity—the age-old feast of the winter solstice of which the Roman Saturnalia is an instance. December's crown is indeed a venerable one. And who has stolen December's crown—who has usurped his reign? The Puritans, by abolishing the celebration of Christmas. We remember that it is a Cavalier poet writing, and I suspect, if we care to venture at dating the poem, we shall have to put it at some time between the Puritan abolition of Christmas in 1642 and the publication of Lovelace's volume, *Lucasta*, in 1649. Line 23, then, "And spite of this cold Time and frosen Fate," is seen to refer to more than the mere winter season. It must allude to the Puritan domination—for Lovelace, a cold time and frozen fate indeed. I would not press the historical allusion. The poem is certainly not primarily an anti-Puritan poem. The basic contrast is made between animal life and the higher and more enduring joys to which man can attain. But a casual allusion to the troubled state of England would be a thoroughly natural one for the poet of **"To Althea from Prison"** to have written, and nowhere more appropriately than here, in a poem to a close friend. (pp. 106-12)

Cleanth Brooks, "Literary Criticism: Poet, Poem, and Reader," in Varieties of Literary Experience: Eighteen Essays in World Literature, edited by Stanley Burnshaw, New York University Press, 1962, pp. 95-114.

George Fenwick Jones   (essay date 1959)

[*Jones is an American educator and critic who has written extensively on medieval German and French literature. His books include* Honor in German Literature *(1959),* The Ethos of the Song of Roland *(1963), and* Walter von der Vogelweide *(1968). In the following excerpt, he traces the history of the term "honor," which is a key motif in Lovelace's "To Lucasta, Going to the Warres."*]

[My purpose] is to ascertain what Richard Lovelace meant by the word "honour" in the much-quoted couplet: "I could not love thee, dear, so much / Lov'd I not honour more." Although the *New English Dictionary* cites the passage as an early example of honor in its modern meaning of noble sentiment or character, . . . Lovelace probably used the word in its older sense of reputation or good name.

The difficulty of ascertaining his intent lies in the fact that English, like most other European languages, now uses a single noun "honor" to express two different ideas. (p. 131)

When we say, "He is a man of honor," honor means an inner quality of soul or character, a nice sense of right and wrong. On the other hand, when we say, "He is a scoundrel; yet he enjoys great honor because of his wealth," the word honor refers to an exterior possession, namely the respect, admiration, or opinion of other people. Since public esteem need not be merited, it is obvious that honor in the first sense is quite unlike honor in the second sense. "Subjective" and "objective" honor are different concepts, even if they can be expressed by a single vocable.

In order to discover what Lovelace meant by honor in his couplet, we must observe that he was writing in accord with an ancient, yet ever modern, literary tradition, that of the struggle between love and honor, in which the word "honor" was conventionally used to designate reputation or good name. (p. 132)

[In] literary conflicts between love and honor, honor was conventionally an external value. Although the word had, by Lovelace's day, acquired a secondary meaning of inner integrity, it is most unlikely that he used it in this sense in his famous couplet. From the twelfth century onwards the concept of true honor, at least among churchmen and didactic writers, had begun to show the influence of Stoic tradition, in which the word *honestum* was used to mean not only what is honored but also what should be honored, namely, that which is morally right. This new subjective meaning was transmitted by Cicero's *De Officiis,* a popular work throughout the Middle Ages. Cicero, who seems to have been the first to use the word *honestum* in this trans-

ferred sense, did so only in translating the Greek Stoics; elsewhere he used the word in its customary objective sense. From the *De Officiis* the new use of the word went into various medieval Latin textbooks and was reflected in many didactic and clerical works. But the new meaning did not displace the basic meaning of the word, even though *honestum,* in the sense of respectedness, did presuppose respectable behavior as well as wealth or social position. It is also to be noted that the new meaning first attached itself to the adjective *honestus* and its derivatives *honnête* and *honest,* and only much later to the nouns. In the King James Bible, published some forty years before the **Lucasta,** the noun *honor* appears only in an objective sense, while honest and honestly are used in the New Testament to refer to good (i.e., respectable) behavior and therefore may be said to have moral overtones. [As C. L. Barber wrote in his The Idea of Honour in the English Drama (1591-1700)], the word *honor,* as used in English dramas during the seventeenth century, most often had objective meaning, particularly in the dramas written for the cavaliers.

In thirteenth-century Germany the word *êre* was used to render not only *honos* but also *honestum*; and thus, among scholars, it acquired moral content as *honestum* acquired it. . . . As the words for virtue (*tugent*) and glory (*êre*) began to acquire moral meaning, the old commonplace began to change its meaning in German literature, not only among the clerics but even among the secular court poets. . . . Just as the ancient Germanic warriors had to win fame to be worthy of their loves, their late-mediaeval descendants had, at least in the eyes of the didactic writers, to live respectably in order to win theirs. It could be argued that Lovelace expressed a similar thought when, in his epitaph for Mrs. Tilmer, he referred to virgins whose beauty led the young world to honor. More probably, however, he meant that their beauty led young men to maintain their good names. Many clerics and bourgeois intellectuals, excluded from the honor code of the ruling classes, accepted the Stoic idea that true honor was inner integrity rather than public acclaim. But, in spite of centuries of sermonizing, they could never weaken the aristocracy's primary concern for an untarnished reputation, as the long-lived custom of dueling proved.

As C. H. Hartmann has shown, Lovelace was a true cavalier. As a cavalier he was the heir of an unbroken military tradition derived, via the Saxons and Normans, from ancient Germanic times—a military tradition, with its pagan code of honor sharpened by classical tradition and hardly affected by Christian teaching. And one would expect that he would show the idea of honor that belongs to that tradition. In any case, there is no evidence that Lovelace intended any new or ethical value in his use of the word "honour" in his famous couplet. And there is linguistic reason to doubt that he had any such intention, since the word "honour" and its derivatives appear elsewhere in **Lucasta** only with objective meaning. Naturally the verb "to honour" and the plural form of the noun "honours" can only be objective. Likewise, "honest" and "honourable" must be objective when applied to inanimate objects such as a ring or plate. The same is true of the word in the title **"The Right Hon. My Lady Anne Lovelace,"** since respect is due to her marital status rather than to her own or even her husband's personal merit. In the expression "each honest Englishman" there is no implication of trustworthiness, all Englishmen of birth and substance being included. Lovelace sometimes uses the word "honour" to mean "splendor," as in "the honour of that brow" or in the "honours" of a breast. We have seen that he believed that virgins' beauty makes men strive for honor and that desire for honor causes men to do good deeds. Similarly, pride and "honour" cause a little bee to fly to Lucasta's face. Since thirst for honor leads to virtue, it is not surprising that he lists "honour" and "vertue" in the same series, just as Geoffrey of Monmouth had done seven centuries earlier. We should remember, however, that Geoffrey had included "fame" in the same series; and we should note that Lovelace later includes "glory."

No new or moral meaning is called for by the word "honour" in our couplet, since Lovelace was writing in the well-established tradition of the warrior's choice between love and action, between shame and glory. The fact that he was consciously following literary tradition rather than expressing personal experience is suggested by his conventional language—he carries a shield like a knight of old, although cavalrymen of his day generally wore a casque and cuirass and often carried a carbine or a horse pistol. His reference to constancy also harks back to chivalric tradition, in which *constantia* (German *stœte*) was one of the cardinal virtues of a knight.

It is apparent that Lovelace, who was well-versed in the classics, was clearly aware of the tradition of the warrior's choice. Many artists of his and earlier times depicted the warrior torn between a beautiful woman and the call to glory; and Corneille had revived all the old motifs of this tradition in his *Cid*, which appeared only some twelve years before **"To Lucasta."** All Lovelace wished to say was that no man of honor could be worthy or capable of true love unless he were even more concerned about his good name; and that Lucasta, like other courtly ladyloves, should adore an inconstancy caused by thirst for fame and honor. (pp. 139-43)

> *George Fenwick Jones, "Lov'd I Not Honour More: The Durability of a Literary Motif," in* Comparative Literature, *Vol. XI, No. 2, Spring 1959, pp. 131-43.*

Geoffrey Walton   (essay date 1962)

[*In the following excerpt, Walton describes Lovelace as an uneven poet and a dilettante whose technical shortcomings are redeemed by his refined sensibility.*]

[Lovelace] is a very uneven poet and often seems both careless and amateurish. His finer sensibility, however, redeems the clumsiness of his syntax, and he is a poet of very varied interest. His famous lyrics to Lucasta and Althea, **'A Mock Song'** and, with them, Montrose's 'My dear and only love . . . ' voice the Cavalier attitude at its best to life and to the war. We find here the surviving code of chivalry and the public values of the seventeenth-century country gentleman expressed with great clarity and with intellectual ingenuity and sophistication of tone. Lovelace

is not on Marvell's level of intelligence, but he is not a simpleton—he is a courtier and a soldier of European culture; beside his work, the revolutionary and nationalist ardours of the Romantics of his class seem crude. One sees the more private interests of the Kentish squire, and once again the rural roots of the Cavaliers, in another interesting group of poems, **'The Ant,' 'The Snail,' 'The Toad and the Spider,' 'The Falcon,'** and **'The Grasshopper.'** These combine first-hand observations of nature with superstition, and traditional knowledge of field sports with literary allusion and inoffensive moralizing in a manner very characteristic of the early seventeenth century. The following examples must suffice:

> Look up, then, miserable Ant, and spie
>   Thy fatal foes, for breaking of her law,
> Hov'ring above thee, Madam, *Margaret Pie*,
>   And her fierce servant, Meagre—Sir *John Daw*;
> Thy Self and Storehouse now they do store up,
> And thy whole Harvest too within their Crop.
>
> Thus we unthrifty thrive within Earths Tomb
>   For some more rav'nous and ambitious Jaw:
> The *Grain* in th' *Ants*, the *Ants* in the *Pie's* womb,
>   The *Pie* in th' *Hawk's*, the *Hawk's* i' th' *Eagle's* maw:
> So scattering to hord 'gainst a long Day,
> Thinking to save all, we cast all away.

and the deservedly famous

> O thou that swing'st upon the waving haire
>   Of some well-filled Oated Beard,
> Drunke ev'ry night on a delicious teare,
>   Dropt thee from Heav'n where now thou art rear'd. . . .

It must not, incidentally, be forgotten that **'The Grasshopper'** is an invitation to conviviality of which the insect is supposed to set an example. **'A Loose Saraband'** is even more bacchanalian:

> Lord!   What is man and sober?

Poetry of this quality on themes of all these kinds would seem to end with Lovelace and his friends, such as Charles Cotton. Charles II's 'mob of gentlemen' are inferior even in drinking songs.

Lovelace's love poetry has similar qualities—freshness and exuberance, a delicacy and strength of fancy, and a courtly tone. He is not often vulgar like Suckling, but sometimes has a deeper cynicism that surprises one. **'The Scrutinie'** is tough and detached in the manner of Donne's *Communitie*. He has some brilliant contracted conceits, such as:

> Like the Sun in's early ray,
> But shake your head and scatter day.
> To *Amarantha*

or:

> Not yet look back, not yet; must we
> Run then like spoakes in wheeles eternally,
> And never overtake?

from **'A Forsaken Lady to her False Servant'** a fine dramatic monologue in couplets. **'Ellinda's Glove'** is equally brilliant at greater length:

> Thou snowy Farm with thy five Tenements!
>   Tell thy white Mistris here was one
>   That call'd to pay his dayly rents;
> But she a-gathering Flowers and Hearts is gone,
> And thou left void to rude Possession. . . .

'Gratiana Dancing and Singing,' another large-scale conceit, is at once ingenious, rhythmically subtle, and also a little clumsy:

> See! with what constant Motion,
> Even and glorious as the Sun,
>   *Gratiana* steers that Noble Frame,
> Soft as her breast, sweet as her voyce
> That gave each winding law and poiz,
>   And swifter than the wings of Fame.
> She beat the happy Pavement
> By such a Starre made Firmament,
>   Which now no more the Roofe envies,
> But swells up high with *Atlas* ev'n,
> Bearing the brighter, nobler Heav'n,
>   And, in her, all the Deities. . . .

Lovelace was never a 'Son of Ben', and there seems to be a lack of his disciplining influence over the suns and flowers that burst forth a little too brightly in this poetry. The gentle, courtly tone is Lovelace's own contribution, and owes nothing directly to others. But this sometimes lapses badly; the vital elements of irony and humour fall into abeyance and exaggeration effects get out of control. I think that this is the defect, rather than mere indecency as Dr Johnson and the nineteenth-century critics thought, of such things as:

> Heere wee'll strippe and cool our fire
> In Creame below, in milke-baths higher;
>   And when all Wells are drawne dry,
> I'll drink a teare out of thine eye.

or **'Lucasta taking the Waters at Tunbridge'** or **'Love made in the First Age'**; there is also the 'reverend lady cow' in **'Amarantha.'** If Suckling foreshadows the tone of Charles II's Court, Lovelace by these flaws in the quality of his wit gives an indication that the Donne-Jonson aristocratic synthesis was breaking up with the Court that had cherished it. (pp. 161-64)

> *Geoffrey Walton, "The Cavalier Poets," in*
> From Donne to Marvell: A Guide to English
> Literature, Vol. 3, *edited by Boris Ford, revised edition, Cassell & Company Ltd., 1962, pp. 152-64.*

Douglas Bush (essay date 1962)

[*Bush was an educator, literary historian, and critic whose writings include* Mythology and the Renaissance Tradition in English Poetry *(1932) and* Science and English Poetry *(1950). In the following excerpt, he describes Lovelace as a gentleman amateur whose fame rests on a handful of exceptional poems.*]

As soldier, courtier, lover, poet, scholar, musician, and connoisseur of painting, the 'extraordinary handsome' Lovelace exemplified the tradition of Sidney and Casti-

glione. His poems display the extreme unevenness of a gentleman amateur, and fame has rightly fixed upon the few lyrics in which he struck a simple, sincere, and perfect attitude; in these, with pure and exalted idealism, he enshrined the cavalier trinity, beauty, love, and loyal honour. **'To Lucasta, Going to the Wars'**, which states a chivalric theme far older than its century, is Jonsonian in its logical brevity and completeness; we may remember, by the way, that Lovelace was the first literal translator of the terse Catullus (to use Herrick's epithet). **'To Althea, from Prison'** (which perhaps owes a hint to Voiture's 'Dans la prison', though 'prison philosophy' was a cavalier convention) might almost be called a royalist broadside, refined and ennobled but retaining the air of masculine spontaneity. The cavalier spirit and the quiet hermitage of the mind receive a more complex and more moving celebration in **'The Grasshopper'**; here, starting from Anacreon and taking in Horace (especially *Epode* xiii), Lovelace depicts the winter of royalists bereft of their king and the inward, eternal summer they can create for themselves. Plainer and more directly topical is **'To Lucasta, from Prison'**, in which, with sober and selfless dignity, Lovelace views the disruption of the established order. In the bulk of his verse, he represents courtly lyricism, modern continental fashions, and the influence of Donne. He has a wider range of theme and tone and image than Carew and Suckling; as a craftsman he is nearer the former than the latter, though his art, like Carew's, is not always rewarding. He has energy and originality, but, along with some other poets of his time (including his kinsman Stanley), he often illustrates the pernicious anaemia of the secular metaphysical muse, the dwindling from cosmic audacities into laboured and eccentric artifice. The radiant Elizabethan vision of Gratiana dancing hovers between inspired *naveté* and fantastic sophistication. With much that is simply dull, Lovelace offers some miscellaneous and incidental attractions, but his achievement remains a handful of poems. (pp. 122-23)

> *Douglas Bush, "Jonson, Donne, and Their Successors," in his* English Literature in the Earlier Seventeenth Century: 1600-1660, *revised edition, Oxford at the Clarendon Press, 1962, pp. 107-79.*

Norman N. Holland (essay date 1964)

[*Holland is an American authority on the psychology of literature. His books include* Psychoanalysis and Shakespeare *(1966) and* The Dynamics of Literary Response *(1968). In the following excerpt, he examines two poems, "The Scrutinie" and "To Lucasta, Going to the Warres," applying the insights of Freudian psychology.*]

[Lovelace's poem **"The Scrutinie,"** in which a philanderer, tired of his newest conquest, praises the virtues of infidelity, essentially] puts forward as fair a rather dirty deal—at least for the girl. And this paradox of a just injustice leads to a variety of ambiguities and paradoxes. The most obvious one is the title, **"The Scrutinie,"** which in 1649 meant not a careful looking-at something, so much as an investigation, a critical or judicial inquiry. The poem, in effect, uses this meaning two ways: the first two stanzas are a "scrutinie" or judicial inquiry into the rights and wrongs of jilting the "Lady"; the second two stanzas suggest a judicial inquiry, a scrutiny, into the merits of other women.

The paradox of a just injustice gives rise to the style of the poem: the tension between the conventional euphemisms ("Beauties," "imbrace," "joy") and the sordidness of what the poet is up to; the tension between the rigid form of the poem and its conversational, argumentative, even flippant, quality. The images move slickly from stanza to stanza: from morning and night in the first stanza to the twelve hours of loving in the second; from the face at the end of the second to the "brown hair" at the beginning of the third; from the "ground" at the end of the third to the "round" that begins the fourth. That rhyme itself is part of the poem's slick pretense of fairness: Lovelace is using a very strict rhyme-scheme, only six rhyme-sounds in twenty lines. Furthermore, the rhymes work out his idea at the end of stanza four that he will return to the lady by picking up the -ee rhyme which was used in the first stanza: "sated with variety," "thine I vow'd to be," "I swore to thee" "That fond impossibility."

The poem, then, moves away and comes back. It comes round again to the lady with whom the poem started. The last line, "Ev'n sated with Varietie," I take it, means 'sated with variety—even as I am this morning,' bringing the poet not only back to the lady, but back to her in the same condition that he is in after this somewhat exhausting night. Or, perhaps, 'sated with Varietie—and longing for one love.' In either case, the going away and coming back completes the paradoxes of the poem, that to break his vow is reasonable and right, that a short affair is a "long" and "tedious" one, that to wrong the "Lady" is to do right by all other beauties.

The most striking feature of the poem, of course, is the third stanza with its grandly Freudian images of searching in her hair and probing for treasure in unplowed ground. No one who has read much seventeenth-century poetry would assume that this symbolism was unconscious. What may be unconscious are the implications of Lovelace's phrasing. In effect, Lovelace is comparing the finding of joy in a woman to the finding of treasure in earth—dirt. The image is hardly a very complimentary one to the fair sex, and indeed he refers in the fourth stanza to the ladies he contemplates seducing as "meaner Beauties." His images treat love as possession, and in the fourth stanza "spoyles," a military term, introduces the idea of triumphing over the woman. In effect, Lovelace sees love as taking or possessing—and this is where he began in the first stanza:

> Why should you think I am forsworn,
> Since *thine* I vow'd to be?

The poem is saying that Lovelace will not be possessed by the lady of the poem—rather, he will seek to possess, briefly, "all other Beauties." In this context, notice Lovelace's use of the word "must." He uses it twice, in the second and third stanzas. The first time he uses it to inhibit himself, to say that were he faithful, he "*must* all other beauties wrong." In the third stanza, he uses it to describe a drive: "I *must* search the black and fair." He is describing a compulsion in the middle stanzas, whereas both the first and

last stanzas are conditional, argumentative, paradoxical. The first and last stanzas describe a man free to choose, unpossessed by any woman; the middle stanzas describe a man possessed by an insatiable drive.

In a second sense, then, the poem goes away and comes back, just as the poet promises to do with the lady of the poem: he proclaims his freedom at the outset; he admits his captivity to "all other Beauties" in the middle; he announces his freedom again at the end. We could sum this all up by saying that the poem is, in essence, about detachment and involvement, freedom and captivity: a man free from any one woman, but held captive by the idea of woman. (pp. 44-6)

The poem is working out a well-known set of attitudes, those of the Don Juan. The poem shows quite explicitly two of the four elements that Freud suggests as defining this kind of behavior: the tendency to run through an endless series of women; the tendency to think of these women as low or debased. Freud suggests that the quest for an endless series represents a quest for something we fear to have directly; the series is "endless for the reason that every surrogate . . . fails to provide the desired satisfaction." For the Don Juan, the woman he really desires is the mother, and it is, as the poem says, a "fond impossibility" to be the "thine" of that first love. Notice, in this context, the primitive terms in which the poet's courtship is carried on: swearing and forswearing, "dot [ing] upon thy face," and then, finally, "sated." These are oral terms from the first and most primitive love. The poet runs away from the lady as from a devouring mouth that wishes to make him forever hers, to incorporate him. He presents his running away, not as a fear of being possessed by someone it is dangerous to be possessed by, but under the guise of logic and fairness; having loved the lady, the poet would be unfair to her and to all other beauties not to love as many other ladies as possible. And, of course, in a psychological sense, he is being logical: since the lady gave in, she cannot be the ultimate love he is looking for, a quite explicit working-out of the Don Juan idea that the woman who has given in is low and unsatisfactory. And, though the poem does not say so, we can guess that the masculine logic and justice the poem invokes conceal another threatening figure, the father, fear of whom drives him away.

At the same time, however, the poem shows a second Don-Juan trait; it treats women rather harshly. We have already noted that women are described as "un-plow'd-up ground"; later he speaks of the women he will sleep with as "meaner beauties." The title itself contains a hidden pun: Lovelace wrote enough Latin poetry to know that "scrutiny" comes from Latin *scruta* meaning trash or garbage, and this scrutiny, whether we consider it an investigation of the rights and wrongs of his leaving this lady or the scrutiny of other ladies, ultimately is a picking over of trash. Love in this poem is aggression and debasement; emotions are turned into things. Embraces are something you can be robbed of, like an object; joy is something you can "find"; sexual satisfaction is treasure to be dug up out of the dirt. The lover triumphs over the lady he conquers, bringing home the "spoyles" of victory. In short, the poem presents us with the basic conflict in the Don Juan: the failure to bring together the affectionate and sensual currents in love.

But there is a still deeper conflict beneath this ambivalence at the phallic level. Were the poet really to love the "Lady," he would be "thine." In effect, he would lose his self which he "must" assert by playing the Don Juan and treating emotional relations as things. It is as though Lovelace saw only two alternatives: proving his separate existence by phallically degrading women; accepting loss of identity by falling "sated," back to his first love and being "thine." Not unsurprisingly in this poem which treats genital love in terms of vowing, tasting, forswearing, and verbal argument, we are finding an oral conflict: the problem of establishing a self separate from an all-supplying Lady. To love in a real sense is to be engulfed; to achieve a separate self, one "must search the black and faire," totally and dispassionately in control "Like skilfull Minerallist's" probing dirt. In effect, or so the poem seems to say, it is *only* by separating the affectionate and sensual currents in love that the speaker can retain an identity.

The poem, however, pretends to resolve this conflict. The poet having "lov'd [his] round," the lyric, too, comes round to its conclusion, closes itself off with the rhymes with which it began. The lover, conditionally, at least, returns to his lady, sated as he was at the beginning of the poem. But this is merely a verbal resolution; there is no mastery of the real underlying conflict that created the poem. The last line makes this failure all too clear. The final stanza has achieved its sense of coming round again to the beginning by the fourth line: "I laden will returne to thee." But the line following, the last line of the poem, "Ev'n sated with Varietie," is totally anticlimactic as well as ambiguous. There is a sense of superfluity in the final couplet, as though the poet did not choose as a developed personality to return, but (perhaps driven by his rhyme-scheme) simply lapsed back, sated sensually, but still in an emotional sense unsatisfied. . . . [Though] presumptuous, it is not too difficult to see how to improve the final stanza:

> Then, if when I have lov'd my round
> Thou prove the pleasant'st she
> With spoyles of meaner Beauties crown'd
> I laden will return to thee,
> Be thine, as thine I vow'd to be.

Such a last line suggests, as Lovelace's does, coming round to the beginning, but such a conclusion would also suggest rational and responsible choice instead of a child's exhaustion.

The poem, as it stands, neither finally asserts the poet's self nor finally brings together the sensual and emotional currents of love nor finally separates them. Instead the poem tries to deal with emotions in terms of being "sated," "dot[ing] upon thy Face" or finding "all joy in thy browne haire." Genital love is displaced upward. The poem fails to get at its underlying conflict and instead translates it into a mere verbal—oral—paradox. I think this is why, as we read the poem, we sense that it has no real feeling in it, that it degenerates into childish ingenuity and cuteness and, finally, nastiness.

Freud suggests that the failure to bring together the affectionate current in love and the sensual is universal among civilized and educated people, at least in some degree. And certainly, we have all gone through the very early oral crisis of discovering our selves as separate from our mothers. From the point of view of psychoanalytic evaluation, then, we can say that Lovelace's **"Scrutinie"** introduces two universal disturbing experiences to which, I think, we can all respond; but the poem fails to offer any mastery of those disturbances except on a merely verbal level. The poem, then, is somewhat less than totally satisfactory as a form of play. Someone reading it for the first time would be justified in predicting that this poem is not of the quality that "can please many and please long," in short, that it is not a very good poem.

By way of contrast, consider another poem by Lovelace [**"To Lucasta, Going to the Warres"**], which, psychologically, is very similar. . . . (pp. 48-50)

This poem, like the other, talks one girl into letting the poet leave for others (at least metaphorically), but the whole thing has been pitched to a higher plane. In her name and the first stanza, Lovelace stresses Lucasta's chastity, the fact that the world she creates is a "Nunnerie." As in the other poem, he visualizes himself as possessed, almost held a passive captive by Lucasta in that nunnery. He must escape, "flie," and in the second stanza, he no longer addresses Lucasta; he is in the world of the active lover, chasing, embracing. Where in the other poem he uses images of aggression for love, in this poem, Lovelace uses images of love to describe aggression. He is unpossessed by the new mistress; he is the one doing the chasing and embracing. He is outside the new mistress, where in the first stanza he had to fly from within the nunnery. As in **"The Scrutinie,"** Lovelace sees being in love (the first stanza) as a dangerous passivity, while phallic aggression (second stanza) establishes a man's identity. The second stanza thus provides a basis for the poet's shift from, in the first stanza, rather passively restating Lucasta's complaint to actively asserting his own point of view in the third. (p. 51)

We can guess . . . that (as in **"The Scrutinie"**) there is an element of fear in the poet's flying the two-person world of love and the "Nunnerie" for the many-personed world connoted by "Honour." In this context, the poem as a whole becomes a reversal in which the social world of fearless, masculine honor serves as, if not itself a nunnery, at least a monastic retreat from the love of the first stanza, felt as dangerous and engulfing. This element of fear, perhaps not so strangely, shows most clearly in the celebrated last lines: we can read them, I could not love thee (Deare) so much, Had I not the defense of loving Honour more. We can also think of these lines as a reversal (in the manner of dreams) of the real thought underneath: I could not love Honour so much, Loved I not thee, Deare, more—or, perhaps, feared I not thee, Deare, more.

The second stanza accomplishes this flight and reveals in its phrasing the unconscious context. The lines alternate or hover between the conventional terms of heterosexual love, "Mistresse," "Faith," "imbrace" (lines 1 and 3) and the terms of all-male combat, "Foe," "Sword," "Shield." In effect, there is a strong homosexual component to the poet's noble renunciation: he turns away from heterosexual love to "chase" and "imbrace" a masculine "Foe." The abrupt bumping back and forth line by line, from love to fighting, itself suggests the to-and-fro not only of battle but also of the sexual act. Thus, stanza two merges in form as well as content male aggression and love between a man and a woman. This defensive maneuver, translating heterosexual love into homosexual competition or aggression represents, strange as it may seem, a sublimation widely accepted and even encouraged in our culture as well as Lovelace's—think, for example, of the usual schoolroom reading of *Antony and Cleopatra*: that Antony ought to leave off effeminate loving so he can engage in the cruel cold-blooded conquests that represent the masculine "high Roman fashion."

In one sense, then, we can say that this poem does not resolve the psychological conflict underlying it any more successfully than does **"The Scrutinie."** What it does do is work out a sublimation of the poet's Don-Juan-impulse into the world of war. The poet enjoys and accepts an honor which includes Lucasta's chastity, the very thing that demands the sublimation he embraces. "Where natural resistances to satisfaction have not been sufficient," says Freud, "men have at all times erected conventional ones so as to be able to enjoy love." "The very incapacity of the sexual instinct to yield complete satisfaction as soon as it submits to the first demands of civilization becomes the source . . . of the noblest cultural achievements which are brought into being by ever more extensive sublimation of its instinctual components."

We have, then, two poems very similar in intellectual and psychological content and style, but one of which *feels* very much the better poem. In terms of play, the first poem does not master the conflict between affectionate and sensual love but regresses to a more primitive, more childish psychological level; the poet becomes "sated with variety" and like a fed infant falls back into his mother's bosom. The first poem raises a well-nigh universal conflict, but fails to resolve it, resorting instead to a merely verbal—or oral—paradox. The second poem raises the same universal conflict and also uses a merely verbal resolution—but it offers something more. As one critic points out, the word "Deare" in the next-to-the-last line connotes a far higher level of value and respect than the first stanza does; it would be a flaw had the poet used the first line's oral, primitive "sweet," suggesting mere enjoyment, in place of "dear" suggesting esteem: I could not love thee, sweet, so much. Loved I not Honour more. The second poem raises the same universal conflict as the first and also fails to master it, but in place of a true resolution offers as mastery a sublimation in the direction of "civilized" behavior which is itself well-nigh universal. It seems fair to conclude that the second poem is more likely to "please many and please long," because it makes us re-enact both a disturbing influence and a defense we have all in our different ways made.

We could put that a different way. Against real, emotional, heterosexual love, felt as confining and restricting, the first poem offers male promiscuity as a defense; the second offers as a defense homosexual aggression. This homosexual aggression is itself something deeply charged and the poem offers a second line of defense—sublimation into "honor." The second poem thus provides both a deeper, more intense disturbance than the first and a more complex mastery. Again, it would be sensible to guess that, for most readers, the second poem will offer more satisfaction as "play" than the first. (pp. 52-4)

> *Norman N. Holland, "Literary Value: A Psychoanalytic Approach," in* Literature and Psychology, *Vol. XIV, No. 2, Spring 1964, pp. 43-55.*

Bruce King (essay date 1965)

[*In the following excerpt, King argues that Lovelace's allegorical poems, although ostensibly mourning the Cavalier defeat, actually express the poet's despair at the human condition.*]

One purpose of rhetoric is to lie. Poetic affirmations should be regarded with suspicion, especially if the poet is not religious or mystical. Consider **"To Althea, From Prison."** Every school child knows the poem, and knows that it represents the gay, confident, debonair Cavalier spirit. But does it? Isn't our concept of the Cavalier spirit partly Restoration propaganda and partly a nineteenth-century romanticization derived from Scott? For that matter is Lovelace's tone really so confident? "Stone walls doe not a Prison make, / Nor I'ron bars a Cage." This might sound like a confident affirmation to someone with an ear for Victorian music; by Caroline standards it sounds a little strained. **"Althea"** is not about chivalry or public virtues, it is about states of mind ("And in my soule am free"). Its idealism might be considered as a strategy for denying the effect of physical surroundings upon the mind. The poem's affirmation is really a turning inward, a process that is common to many of Lovelace's poems. **"The Vintage to the Dungeon"** might be a blueprint for the strategy of **"Althea"**:

I

Sing out pent Soules, sing cheerefully!
Care Shackles you in Liberty,
Mirth frees you in Captivity:
    Would you double fetters adde?
      Else why so sadde?
        Chorus
Besides your pinion'd armes you'l finde
Griefe too can manakell the minde.

II

Live then Pris'ners uncontrol'd;
Drinke oth' strong, the Rich, the Old,
Till wine too hath your Wits in hold;
    Then if still your Jollitie,
      And Throats are free;
        Chorus
Tryumph in your Bonds and Paines,
And daunce to th' Musick of your Chaines.

"The Vintage" is not a simple drinking song; as in **"Althea"** the theme is deceptive. It says sing, affirm, drink, do anything to fight off the effects of imprisonment upon the mind.

Lovelace's power derives not from a simple chivalric code but from a complex awareness that his ideals offer protection against reality. The best poems acknowledge the actual world, while trying out idealistic postures in reply. The ideals offered in **"Althea," "The Grasse-hopper,"** and **"To Lucasta, Going to the Warres"** might be described as defensive masks. The lesser poems are more completely disillusioned and do not offer any protection, or do so crudely. In **"To Lucasta from Prison, An Epode"** Lovelace lists his grievances against life. Here, and also in **"Mock Song,"** the awkward wit is more painful than relieving. Tensions accumulate and are not discharged. How, Lovelace asks, can peace love him, if it despises the earth. "War is lov'd so ev'ry where." Parliament is "beheaded," property is insecure; and ever since Parliament began borrowing money on it "Publick Faith" has become a mockery: "For she that couzens all, must me." A religious reform might be desirable,

> But not a Reformation so,
>   As to reforme were to ore'throw;
> Likes Watches by unskilfull men
>   Disjoynted, and set ill againe.

Here is Lovelace's image of his time:

> And now an universall mist
>   Of Error is spread or'e each breast,
> With such a fury edg'd, as is
>   Not found in th' inwards of th' Abysse.

With the world out of joint Lovelace's defense against total demoralization is a purposefully blind trust in monarchy and honor. He appears to have been aware that while ideals are without power in the world, they may be psychologically necessary. The snail is one of his favorite images: "Wise Emblem of our Politick World, / Sage Snayl, within thine own self curl'd." The snail's self-containment is an example of how to keep one's values during times of evil and disorder:

> But banish't, I admire his fate
> Since neither Ostracisme of State,
> Nor a perpetual exile,
> Can force this Virtue change his Soyl;
> And wheresoever he doth go,
> He wanders with his Country too.

Lovelace's poems often record a feeling of exile.

When reality makes demands upon people, vague public values are often used to cover resulting conflicts. The famous song **"To Lucasta, Going to the Warres"** mocks while affirming soldierly values. The surprising wit of its middle stanza represents a discharge of psychic tension. The rhetoric of courtship provides pivotal words ("chase," "imbrace," "mistresse") upon which to introduce, and then by mockery to master, the pressures of reality:

> True; a new Mistress now I chase,
>   The first Foe in the Field;
> And with a stronger Faith imbrace
>   A Sword, a Horse, a Shield.

Lovelace's confidence is a not very consistently worn mask, the purpose of which is to ward off reality. Honor represents a tension of will, the snail's ability to remain true to itself in exile; but demoralization lies behind the affirmations, waiting for a relaxation of will, a moment of slackness.

While his values may seem quixotic and arbitrarily imposed upon disintegrating forms of society, without such a blind affirmation of honor Lovelace's sentiments become crude. In a **"Saraband"** ("Nay, prethee Dear") there is a coarsening of touch:

> See all the World how't staggers,
>   More ugly drunk then we,
> As if far gone in daggers,
>   And blood it seem'd to be.

The carefree Cavalier attitude suddenly appears as a desperate reaction to brutal reality. The withdrawal and the turning to drink become gross sensuality:

> Now, is there such a Trifle
>   As Honour, the fools Gyant?
> What is there left to rifle,
>   When Wine makes all parts plyant?
> Let others Glory follow,
> In their false riches wallow,
> And with their grief be merry;
> Leave me but Love and Sherry.

If the subject of **"Saraband"** bears obvious similarities to other Cavalier libertine poems, the tone is coarser and more aggressive. Carew's libertinism has a strategic value in the battle of the sexes; but Lovelace's libertinism lacks balance and suggests a total disillusionment with experience. It has none of the allure of libertinism that Milton warns against in *Comus*. It is a libertinism that results rather from hatred of life than love of the senses.

The pressure of reality must have been very great upon Lovelace. It comes into his poems unexpectedly, often breaking their mood, but creating the necessary tension that raises his best work above that of most Caroline lyricists. It is not surprising that many poems in the posthumous edition of 1659 are distrustful, violent, even paranoiac in reaction to society. The natural world becomes filled with emblems of a distasteful reality. **"A Fly caught in a Cobweb"** is described as "Small type of great ones, that do hum, / Within this whole World's narrow Room." The snail becomes a "Wise Emblem of our Politick World." The Ant represents the new order ("For thy example is become our Law"), which is seen as uselessly striving against devouring fate. The law of the animal world is also the law of man. Because life is insecure, deferment of pleasure is pointless:

> Thue we unthrifty thrive within Earths
>   Tomb,
>   For some more rav'nous and ambitious
>   Jaw:
> The *Grain* in th' *Ants*, the *Ants* in the
>   *Pies* womb,
>   The *Pie* in th' *Hawks*, the *Hawks* ith'
>   *Eagles* maw:
> So scattering to hord 'gainst a long Day,
> Thinking to save all, we cast all away.
>
>   (**"The Ant"**)

This is a truth about Lovelace which is often missed: he is not untouched by the skeptical or cynical; indeed, his more affirmative poems are examples of a disillusioned mind trying to hang on to something, anything, in a world where it can find no resting place, no secure perch. Nor is the cynicism merely political. The disillusioned streak in Lovelace's poetry is not a matter of party or commitment. The distrust is deeper, and it affects the antennae of his sensibility, changing the way he feels the world. References to imprisonment and images of dungeons are common to his poetry, often occurring in such unexpected places as the opening lines of **"The Triumphs of Philamore and Amoret,"** and of **"Night,"** an otherwise innocent poem ("Night! loathed Jaylor of the lock'd up Sun"). (pp. 511-13)

[In her *Poetry and Politics Under the Stuarts*, C. V.] Wedgwood suggests that after the death of Charles I the Cavalier poets lost their spirit of gallantry and that disintegration set in. She speaks of a rotting away of the cause. Lovelace's **"Advice"** to his brother illustrates a deeper insecurity, however, than merely having been vanquished. The insecurity is spiritual and physical as well as political. There is a generalized distrust of the world. The poem begins with Lovelace warning his brother to avoid sea voyages; all activity leads to disaster:

> . . . dream, dream still,
> Lull'd in *Dione's* cradle, dream, untill
> Horrour awake your sense, and you now
>   find
> Your self a bubled pastime for the Wind,
> And in loose *Thetis* blankets torn and
>   tost;
> Frank to undo thy self why art at cost.

If the sea is dangerous, land is no better; inactivity also leads to disaster. The image for this insecurity is metaphysical in the best sense; it finds a correspondence between a particular idea and the nature of the world:

> Nor be too confident, fix'd on the shore,
> For even that too borrows from the store
> Of her rich Neighbour, since, now wisest know,
> (And this to *Galileo's* judgment ow)
> The palsie Earth it self is every jot
> As frail, inconstant, waveing as that blot
> We lay upon the Deep; . . .

The poem is an uneven, confused, but surprising performance. Its skepticism is intense. All things on earth will be "Turn'd to that Antick confus'd state they were." There is no way out of such a condition. The "golden mean" has "wrongs entail'd upon't." Stoic indifference should be a means to neutralize pain: "A breast of proof defies all Shocks of Fate, / Fears in the best, hopes in the worser state!" but the poem's conclusion suggests Lovelace's inability to anaesthetize the turmoil of reality:

> Draw all your Sails in quickly, though no storm
> Threaten your ruine with a sad alarm;
> For tell me how they differ, tell me pray,
> A cloudly tempest, and a too fair day.

This is distrust of optimism with a vengeance.

If we were to compare Lovelace's **"Advice"** to his brother with Dryden's poem to his *Honor'd Kinsman*, we would see two radically different reactions by Royalists to revolu-tion. Whereas Dryden speaks of retirement as a means of achieving happiness "Unvex'd with anxious cares, and void of strife," Lovelace advocates a desperate withdrawal from reality. Whereas Dryden's poem is a prescription for happiness and future reward, Lovelace's poem is meant to neutralize hope. Dryden's aim is to praise a constructive, decent style of life, Lovelace's is to avoid harm. But, amazingly, Lovelace's poem is *meant* to be optimistic. Its tone is occasionally even jaunty, and it contains several passages to the effect that life cannot always be so bad as it is now; but no sooner does Lovelace say this than he warns against hope. Even the fairest day may lead to ruin. The poet's theme of cautionary balance is strongly in conflict with his insecure and fearful attitude.

With **"Going to the Warres"** and **"Althea," "The Grasse-hopper"** is central to any interpretation of Lovelace. But it is a poem in which the poet's attitude and the conventions of his theme need to be separated. **"The Grasse-hopper"** belongs to the mid-seventeenth-century tradition of poetry of solitude and retirement: a tradition usually associated with disappointed Royalists, but which might well include Marvell and others who, though perhaps not Royalists, found rural retreat a comfort, whether in fact or symbolically, from the confusions of the Civil War and the resulting chaos. I think Professor D. C. Allen is right when he writes of the grasshopper as Cavalier and poet. Lovelace's mind does seem to channel political pressures into traditional images; **"The Ant," "The Grasse-hopper's"** companion piece, is an image of husbandry and puritanism: "thy example is become our Law." Singing insects are poets of whom the Ant is an enemy:

> And thou almighty foe, lay by thy sting,
> Whilst thy unpay'd Musicians, Crickets, sing.

"The Grasse-hopper" is not, however, limited to despair at the Royalist defeat. Rather than political events it is nature as revealed in images of time and seasons that is the destroyer of man's happiness. The moral is almost medieval. The material world is subject to change and decay; all things are mutable. Earthly joys are insecure.

I do not think that Lovelace is using traditional images of mutability to express a change in the political climate. The images are metaphors of something fundamental rather than topical. They express a similar insecurity before the temporal world to that expressed in Lovelace's **"Advice"** to his brother. Lovelace does not complain. He has already adopted a psychological attitude to defend himself against reality. Man is a fool not to have expected the worst:

> But ah the Sickle!   Golden Eares are Cropt;
>   *Ceres* and *Bacchus* bid good night;
> Sharpe frosty fingers all your Flowr's have topt,
>   And what sithes spar'd, Winds shave off quite.
> Poore verdant foole! and now green Ice! thy Joys
>   Large and as lasting, as thy Peirch of Grasse,
> Bid us lay in 'gainst Winter, Raine, and poize
>   Their flouds, with an o'reflowing glasse.

These images are recalled at the end of the poem where the unpleasantness of the actual world, as represented by the political situation and the winter season, will be ignored and replaced by a subjective reality.

The conclusion of "**The Grasse-hopper**" involves a strategy for dealing with reality. The poem has long since stopped being about insects. But what is the central subject of the poem and what is Lovelace's solution to the problem it raises? If the poem has primarily been about defeated Royalists then its conclusion affirms the primacy of personal relationships during a period of public confusion. The structure of the poem, however, argues against such an interpretation. After the two movements describing the joys and fate of the grass-hopper we are seemingly offered drink and friendship as consolations for life. However, to see conviviality as Lovelace's reply to reality would be to miss the point. It would replace one set of external props with another, and would make nonsense of the poem's final stanza:

> Thus richer then untempted Kings are we,
>   That asking nothing, nothing need:
> Though Lord of all what Seas imbrace; yet he
>   That wants himselfe, is poore indeed.

The prominence given to friendship in the final stanzas is deceptive. Lovelace, like Marvell and other mid-seventeenth-century poets, tends to give more prominence to examples and less to development of theme than we usually expect. It is almost the style of the period, and it is sometimes confusing. Perhaps that is why Geoffrey Walton claims " 'The Grasshopper' is an invitation to conviviality of which the insect is supposed to set an example;" if Professor Walton were right, the fate of the insect would be sufficient argument against accepting the invitation. While the grass-hopper is normally a symbol of light-heartedness, it is used here as an example of the false joys of the external world and therefore of the vanity of human wishes. The poem's theme is neither politics nor conviviality, but attitudes of mind; its final defense against reality is rather stoical fortitude and lack of desire than friendship. To be "untempted" by any hope is to ask nothing and is one way to cope with a mutable world. The attitudes that Lovelace creates are striking, but they are, finally, defenses against demoralization. (pp. 513-15)

> Bruce King, "Green Ice and a Breast of Proof," in College English, Vol. 26, No. 7, April 1965, pp. 511-15.

Randolf L. Wadsworth, Jr. (essay date 1970)

[*Wadsworth is an American literary scholar who has written on seventeenth-century English literature. Below, he analyzes the symbolism of Lovelace's poem "The Snayl," defining it as an allegorical expression of the poet's political views. Wadsworth also comments on the ancient textual and emblematic motifs Lovelace used to develop his allegory of the snail.*]

"**The Snayl**" by Richard Lovelace is obscure in both image and theme. Its mode—ethical and political allegory derived from emblems and riddles—was going out of fashion even at its writing; its argument appears to want logical continuity; and its wit involves plays on meanings no longer idiomatic. A limited explication and some appropriately old-fashioned commentary may nevertheless offer modern readers an interpretation of this poem consistent with its sources and setting, revealing it as an ingenious exercise in subversive propaganda, further illustrating the ways in which poets even as late as Lovelace could spin allegory from venerable commonplace lore, and furnishing evidence that the poet's stoical faith is from a store larger and richer than we had thought it.

A topsy-turvy Interregnum world is the setting of several Lovelace poems. In the corrosive "**Mock-Song**" all order and degree are toppled because 'our Dragon hath vanquish'd the St George'. "**The Grasse-hopper**" laments the death of Charles I and the suppression of ancient ceremony. "**Another,**" the companion poem to "**The Snayl,**" is wholly preoccupied with exile, bespeaking the Cavaliers' fear of proscription and banishment. We may therefore suspect that when Lovelace calls the snail 'Wise Emblem of our Politick World' and 'Deep Riddle of Mysterious State' he intends another ruefully ironic comment on conditions under the Commonwealth. A contemporary reader would surely have seen in these attributions a challenge to augment his appreciation of "**The Snayl**" by relating popular snail lore to the situation in England. Recreating this process of enrichment, let us track the snail in such commonplace surroundings as classical literature, the more familiar Renaissance collections of emblems and riddles, and the Bible.

Prudence is the commonest attribute of snails in popular literature, so we might as well begin with it; upon returning to our text we shall see presently that Lovelace departs from the same point. Æsop tells how the original, cautious snail sought permission from Jove to carry its dwelling with it, explaining, 'I would rather always carry a heavy burden than, if I were free, be unable to avoid a bad neighbourhood'. The snail's proverbial tardiness is likewise connected with circumspection. A character in Plautus's *Poenulus* complains of two citizens that they would rush to dine at his villa, but that called to court as his witnesses they drag their feet and surpass the snail for sluggishness. The citizens retort that there is no reason to rush into a dangerous task for which they are ill paid, for there is none so poor that he has nothing to lose. The snail is more wise than wilful.

Similar doctrines underlie two emblems in [*Symbolorum et Emblematum Centuriae Quatuor,*] the popular sixteenth-century collection of Joachim Camerarius. Emblem IV, XCVII offers the snail as an *exemplum* to all who would live to old age safe at home. Its motto, 'Bene qui latuit', comes from an epistle of Ovid in which the exiled poet urges upon a young friend in Rome a life of deliberate prudence and politic retreat. Camerarius amplifies this in a commentary built on two other familiar texts, Claudian's epigram on the Old Man of Verona and Horace, *Epistulae*, I, X. Encouragement of Falstaff's formula for valour is tempered by references to the ethical mean and by the assertion of Seneca that the ideal life includes both action and discreet withdrawal at times appropriate to each. Under a notice that the snail seeks nothing outside itself, the succeeding emblem adds more practical advice. An engraving of a snail speared to the ground and its caption remind us that those who rush forth fearlessly risk death. The supporting text is built on quotations, attributed to Plautus and Polybius, demonstrating the superiority of those who profit from the experience of others so as to reach similar goals without danger to themselves. Camerarius would have us understand that the snail's habit of retreating into its shell when threatened is wisdom, not cowardice.

The first couplet of "**The Snayl**" echoes these earlier treatments. Lovelace at once implies desire for surcease, envy of the snail's independence, and counsel to withdraw like the snail from the complex and potentially threatening world of affairs. Yet the opening quatrain in its entirety is a series of witty ambiguities suggesting less innocuous intentions. 'Wise Emblem' does not merely compliment the sagacity of the snail; that is done by 'Sage Snayl' in the second line. It suggests as well the existence of traditional lore about snails and remarks the discernment of the poet who makes it germane. 'Our Politick World' is more equivocal still. 'Politick' is of course an older form of 'political', so that the phrase means 'the world of human (or even English) politics'. The lesson of the snail, then, is simply that disengagement is more comfortable than involvement, a notion endorsed by the many Royalists who willingly left England after the execution of Charles I. But 'Politick' is also just an older spelling of 'politic', which in Lovelace's time as today meant 'prudent', 'artful', 'expedient', or even 'devious'. Thus 'Our Politick World' might signify the upside-down world of Interregnum England, where guile and subterfuge rule the day; the moral in this case would be to shun the frontal assault and achieve one's aims by indirection. The second couplet is equally capable of at least two interpretations, both of which reinforce the less innocent reading of the first. 'Softly' may modify either 'instruct' or 'to make hast', just as 'feet' may belong either to the poem or to its author. Asking for instruction, Lovelace specifies both its form and content: obliquely, both through the poem and by its own example, the snail is to teach the fine art of accomplishing much while appearing to do little.

A connexion between the snail and such crafty tactics was unquestionably current in Renaissance England. The anonymous *A Herrings Tale* (London, 1598), an early example of the mock-epic, has as its hero a snail named Avernishon, Sir Lymazon, who is determined to scale the highest tower of Tintagel Castle. After convincing himself that the achievement is worth the hardships and risks that it will entail, he finally embarks—but only by a devious route:

> This while Sir Lymazon the upmost storie wan,
> And with soft haste to mount the middle spire
>   began,
> Step after step he slides, and length steals from
>   his way,
> Yet length he seemes to adde, swarving, but not
>   astray:
> For not direct he climes, climing direct, may
>   breede
> More speede then ease, and more hazard of fall
>   then speede.
> Like as the Gerfaulcon, a point of height to win,
> Upon the wagling winged Heron, doth not begin
> His stairie mount upright, but elsewhere soareth
>   out,

> And turning tayle, a winding compasse sets
>   about . . .
> So our Deawes-sonne sometimes an hold most
>   circle makes,
> Now lines in angles sharpe, now in obtuse he
>   brakes:
> There true love knots he twines, here paints
>   flowres or tree,
> Uncouth the shapes, but bootfull to his bent they
>   bee.

After reaching the top of the spire the snail challenges the resident weather-cock for sole possession of the height. Sir Lymazon is then likened to a leopard, a castle, a knight in armour, a tiger, and several other exemplars of prowess and invulnerability. But the author returns at length to the familiar theme of slow, steady, and devious progress:

> Slow-pac'd was Lymazon, but where he list he
>   goes,
> And for him nature did in lesse assize contrive,
> He causde supplying art to follow, not to strive
> With nature, whiles not forth direct his march
>   he takes,
> But a wide winding circuit of his way he
>   makes . . .
> His eye did guide his pace, his judgement led his
>   eye.

In the end the weather-cock is taken by surprise. Success attends a policy deliberate, determined, and deceptive.

Lines 5-12 of "**The Snayl**" evoke the association of the snail with politic indirection. Ostensibly the passage is mere scene-painting, but like the beguiling depiction with which Lovelace begins "**The Grasse-hopper**" it hints at a larger intention. According to the N.E.D., the epithets 'compendious' and 'strickt' had several contemporary meanings. 'Compendious' as 'economical' and 'strickt' as 'stern in matters of conscience and virtue' or 'holding a rigorous and austere standard of living' are appropriate only later in the poem, but other meanings add depth to this passage. Something compendious, besides having all its substance in small scope, may be expeditious ('slowly fast') or profitable. 'Strickt' may apply to one who is confined, but it also characterizes one as admitting no abatement in a course of action. If the 'compendious' snail is 'Large *Euclids* strickt epitome' primarily because it embodies all geometry in a confined space, the charming fantasy which follows also recalls the snail's reputation for politic indirection and for unflagging progress by a roundabout course which masks intentions and avoids risks. Lovelace's imagery is remarkably like that of *A Herrings Tale*. The figures which this snail describes in its meandering but encyclopedic progress through Euclid are 'bootfull to his bent', for neither its whereabouts nor its motives can easily be deduced from them. In this whole passage Lovelace is in fact expanding the implications of 'softly to make hast', making both the snail and the poem go 'slowly fast' to mark for the Cavalier audience a route to take after their defeat at arms. Determined subversion has often won where other means have failed.

Snails do not succeed through guile alone, however; they have long been models of perseverance as well. Another good Renaissance instance beside Sir Lymazon is the snail of Camerarius, IV, XCIX, struggling up a hill and admonishing us between breaths to learn early from its example of virtue and industry if we hope to be thought truly worthy. Camerarius explains in his text that little by little and with prudent delay the snail undertakes the trying journey to the highest pass, which by ingenuity and through indefatigable striving it finally achieves. Speed is not essential in matters of virtue; anything salutary is timely. *Felix gloria* compensates for any delay in the accomplishment of virtuous tasks, so onward and upward. Camerarius flatly contradicts an older Continental tradition which makes the snail a symbol of ignavia or sloth and argues from its slow pace that it is obviously pursuing the Good—with all due caution, yet with unflagging determination.

Lovelace in developing his argument follows the sequence of Camerarius. From the snail's discretion and superior intelligence he moves directly to its embodiment of industry and perseverance. Lines 13-20 begin with the play on 'Preventing Rival of the Day' and end by providing a night shift for the assiduous snail through an old association with the moon. 'Strickt' indeed, this snail admits no abatement in a course of action, but makes up in application whatever it might have lost through tardiness in execution. There are in addition specific Royalist overtones in the couplet 'And thou from thin own liquid Bed – New *Phoebus* heav'st thy pleasant Head'. As 'Phoebus' had long been a common poetic appellation for English monarchs, it might well have reminded a contemporary reader of a Stuart King in the Isle of Wight or in France and foreshadowed his return from exile across the 'liquid Bed' of the Solent or the English Channel. Those who work unremittingly may after all hope to see their labours requited.

The snail, though, has other attributes deserving of even greater rewards. Its prudence extends to its economy, its portable house containing nothing superfluous. For why make heavier than need be the burden which makes possible its mobility? Plutarch treats as a commonplace the modesty and even penury of the snail's menage and later catalogues the sorts of good which accompany the rejection of specious wealth and a reliance on other resources. [According to "On the Love of Wealth," in his *Moralia*, wealth] is nothing; piety, the pursuit of wisdom, mastery of self are all, and they alone can sustain the soul without external trappings or applause. The snail benefits from the meanness of its lot. Poor in material goods, it is rich in spiritual excellence. A similar implication adds ethical weight to a riddle of Symposius:

> Porto domum mecum, semper migrare parata,
> Mutatoque solo non sum miserabilis exsul,
> Sed mihi consilium de caelo nascitur.

No self-contained creature which takes its counsel from heaven can be wretched in mere earthly exile.

The assumptions behind these two citations are explicit in Camerarius. Extending the homily of Emblem iv, xcix on the attainment of virtue through perseverance, Emblem iv, c recapitulates the Stoic definition of the Good. Above an engraving of two crawling snails is the motto 'Fert omnia Secum', below it a caption extolling those who carry all their possessions with them, living free from the power of Fortune. The commentary begins with a story by the Stoic philosopher Stilpo of Megara. When his native town of Priene had been invested and others fleeing with all their worldly goods asked the Sage Bias why he was not likewise encumbered, this worthy replied that indeed he had all his possessions with him. The house-bearing snail also carries its *penates* and all its substance; no matter where it wanders, it never needs an inn: 'Omnia mea mecum'. Since virtue has everything in itself and all goods attend one in the possession of virtue, Camerarius reasons that the snail, which appears to be wholly self-sufficient, must be like the Good Man of the Stoics both virtuous and wise. Only virtue and truth—*virtus et doctrina*—triumph over Fortune. Camerarius substantiates his emblem's caption by defining its *omnia* as *virtus et doctrina*. He ends with a maxim of Carneades, 'Omnis fortuna in sensu habitat sapientis'. The understanding of Carneades's Wise Man comprises all Fortune in her double guise, both chance and possessions. The snail is an exemplar of Stoic and Christian virtues, its lesson the consolation of Philosophy.

This last emblem furnishes strong presumptive evidence that Lovelace knew the work of Camerarius. The snail of Emblem IV, C never needs an inn (*diversorium*), and in **"Another"** Lovelace says, 'Then when the Sun the South doth Winne, – He baits him hot at his own Inne'. Admittedly, this similitude is obvious and its repetition perhaps only coincidental, but a second similarity is less likely to be fortuitous. **"Another"** closes with this passage, which might also owe something to the riddle of Symposius:

> But banisht, I admire his fate
> Since neither Ostracisme of State,
> Nor a perpetual exile,
> Can force this Virtue change his Soyl;
> For wheresoever he doth go,
> He wanders with his Country too.

Camerarius is unique among the popular emblematists in his identification of the snail with *virtus*. In these lines, at once rueful and jocular, Lovelace makes the same equation as Camerarius: the snail is a Virtue ('penes est virtus') and lives beyond the reach of ostracism or exile ('fortuna . . . liber ab arbitrio') because its soil or substance ('omnia') is always with it.

Lovelace follows much the same reasoning from line 37 of **"The Snayl,"** beginning like Camerarius with 'Oeconomick Virtues' and ending with the exaltation of the snail as the embodiment of spiritual excellence. The change to these new motifs has been foreshadowed by 'compendious' and 'strickt', as well as by the example of the snail's wisdom and determination. One wonders, though, why Lovelace calls the snail 'analys'd King'. This may reflect the riddle of Symposius, the point being that both snails and Stuart kings take their counsel directly from heaven. It is just conceivable that Lovelace intends a grim quibble on 'analys'd' to recall the late King Charles, now alas resolved into his constituent parts. But surely the succeeding lines evoke a wry comparison between the snail and the late King, who perhaps did not discipline what was his and who, on his final progress to the Isle of Wight, could not remove his men and city too. The scattering of the 'Silver Train' in line 46 may suggest in addition the dispersion of the Court after the flight of young Charles abroad. Yet here, as in **"The Grasse-hopper,"** there is a playful manipulation of myth so that what was a reproach becomes a sign of hope. Although the improvident grasshopper perishes when 'Golden Eares are Cropt', the legend of its translation to Elysium sustains the faith of Lovelace and Cotton that they can 'poize . . . with an o'erflowing glasse' the floods and cold of winter, achieving for themselves 'A Genuine Summer' and 'everlasting Day'. The snail that reminds one of past defeat and instant penury seems also like the snail of Camerarius to promise replenishment from inexhaustible resources; for 'Then after a sad Dearth and Rain – Thou scatterest thy Silver Train' is also an image of regeneration, and there is the further promise of a new 'Cloth of Gold' drawn from the 'rich Mines within'. The delicate tracery of the snail, which earlier in the poem represented a politic course, now calls to mind the splendour of regal vestments and becomes a reminder to Royalists that their burden, too, is tolerable. They know from the example of the snail that virtue sustains and renews itself: the righteousness of the King's cause gives its adherents patience under their suffering and promises a happy issue out of all their afflictions.

All this prepares for the poem's Camerarian end, where Lovelace combines economy and moral uprightness in a snail made monk and saint. But before examining the close of **"The Snayl"** we must consider one more theme from traditional sources and its appearance earlier in the text.

The nineteenth 'Hieroglyphicke' of George Wither's *A Collection of Emblemes* (1635) gives an interesting twist to a familiar snail motif. Around an engraving of a snail negotiating a twig high above a stream is the motto 'Lente sed attente' above is the paraphrase 'When thou a *Dangerous-Way* dost goe, – Walke *surely*, though thy pace be *slowe*'. The accompanying poem admonishes procrastinators, the over bold, and those

> . . . who so much wrong
> Gods *Gratiousnesse*, as if their thinkings were,
> That (seeing he deferres his *Iudgements* long)
> His *Vengeance*, he, for ever, would forbeare.

The snail teaches 'that *Continuance* perfects many things, – Which seeme, at first, unlikely to be done' and warns 'that some *Affaires* require – More *Heed* then *Haste*'.

> And, in a *Mysticke-sense*, it seemes to preach
> *Repentance* and *Amendment*, unto those
> Who live, as if they liv'd beyond *Gods* reach;
> Because, he long deferres deserved Blowes:
> For, though *Iust-Vengeance* moveth like a
>   *Snaile*,
> And slowly comes; her comming will not faile.

The old saw 'slowly but surely' is neatly reversed. Through the intellectual habit of universal analogy the snail becomes more than a model of determination and prudence. It is a synecdoche for the Apocalypse.

In the fifty-eighth psalm, the sole Biblical snail also figures divine retribution. After vividly describing the wicked, the psalmist calls down upon them a series of curses which ends, 'As a snail which melteth, let every one of them pass away'. God will punish them in His wrath, and 'The righ-

teous shall rejoice when he seeth the vengeance: he shall wash his feet in the blood of the wicked. So that a man shall say, Verily, there is a reward for the righteous: verily he is a God that judgeth in the Earth.'

A perceptive Roundhead might have found ominous even the first twenty lines of **"The Snayl"**: no ruling faction regards with equanimity a 'Politick' and determined opposition whose stubborn striving is embodied in a 'New *Phoebus*'. Lines 21-6 go even farther by associating the snail with awesome destructive forces and by suggesting that the enmity of the snail (or of what it represents) is to be feared. Although the lines by themselves are obscure, there is a significant clue in the specific correlation 'Bold Nature . . . Of thee, as Earth-quakes, is affraid'. In the Bible earthquakes warn and punish the wicked, encourage and liberate the oppressed, and accompany the Apocalypse. In Lovelace's time earthquakes were commonly feared as premonitions of God's judgement, figuring the visitation of His wrath upon the ungodly. Lovelace's snail is cousin to those of Wither and the psalmist; and after learning in lines 37-56 that it is also related to the snails of Plutarch and Camerarius, one suspects that behind the poem is a dialectical formula: The snail and those who follow its example are good and will be saved; those who ignore or oppose it are evil and will be damned if they persist. The logic would have seemed straightforward to a contemporary because the eventual overthrow of Commonwealth usurpers and the restoration of God's anointed ruler were, in the orthodox and conservative Anglican view, mere earthly analogues of the eternal processes of judgement and vindication.

This last theme appears again in the final section of **"The Snayl,"** where it mingles with echoes of others and unites the closing cadences with the earlier mention of earthquakes. We have already remarked that the snail is here made a monk and saint. The analogy with cloistral regimen is obvious, and the image of the saint prepares for the intimations of exaltation in the last couplet. The poem appears to end as it began, in somewhat envious contemplation of the snail's peaceful isolation, but there are here as at the outset hints of other meanings. 'Strickt' recurs in line 55. 'Resolve' and 'dissolve' in the final quatrain are in fact synonymous with 'analyze', perhaps recalling the treatment of 'Oeconomick Virtues' and self-sufficiency. The 'shot Star' is likewise a rich image. A meteor was thought to purify the upper air by its passage and then to be refined itself at last into primordial jelly. But exaltation and peaceful dissolution do not exhaust the possibilities: 'Like a snail which melteth, let every one of them pass away' is also a curse. Meteors were linked with earthquakes in the popular imagination. The two had a common birth in the phenomenon of dry exhalation and were alike regarded as premonitions of the Last Judgment. Lovelace implies in this final image the dialectical synthesis we have presupposed, simultaneously heartening Cavaliers and admonishing regicides. The 'shot Star' could well bode the triumph of the 'New *Phoebus*' now in exile and foretell the fall of tyrants nearer home. As the interpretation of a prodigy depends largely upon the attitude of the beholder, Lovelace rightly lets the reader judge according

Engraving of Lucasta in Lovelace's first collection of verse.

to his party whether such an eventuality were welcome or abhorrent.

Lovelace, then, turns traditional snail lore to the task of topical commentary. The time was ripe for the disengagement and caution enjoined by Camerarius and others. A man within his own self curled need be no more truly defeated than the persevering snail, which by a slow, prudent, and politic course prevails at last in a worthy cause. 'Softly to make hast' and 'slowly fast' recall Camerarius and *A Herrings Tale*. Both tradition and Lovelace exploit the full richness of 'Politick', 'Compendious', and 'Strickt'. Evocations of the ethical mean might suggest to the Courtly High-Church party their own *via media*, a way in civil war as in religion. Like Symposius and Camerarius, Lovelace offers comfort to exiles and hope to those who struggle against great odds for righteous ends. The snail is firmly identified with virtue, which doubly sustains its agents: 'omnia adsunt bona quem penes est virtus.' Finally, the poem is a menacing affront to the ruling faction, for Lovelace practises deception, preaches subversion, and imaginatively restates the imprecation of Psalm 58 and the dire warnings of Wither's emblem. Roundheads seeking to rebut or suppress the poem would have run an even greater risk than usually attends the refutation of satirical obliquity: to acknowledge that the shoe fit would also be to own that the foot trod the nearest way to perdition.

Lovelace meant **"The Snayl"** to move and enlighten readers who shared his plight, his intellectual habits, and his store of commonplace learning. One cannot hope through scholarship to recreate ideal conditions for its appreciation. Commentary and analysis help to clarify the poem's allegory and its logic, but cannot restore the pleasure and satisfaction felt upon discovering new and timely applications for familiar lore. Yet to dismiss the piece out of hand is unfair to Lovelace, however deficient his limited intention appears to rigorous modern criticism. **"The Snayl"** is at least one of the more ingenious examples of Royalist propaganda. Moreover, it avoids the strident tone and frenzied rhetoric of so many poems with the same ends, and like **"The Grasse-hopper"** it hides beneath a sometimes playful surface a quiet, dignified, and even affecting affirmation of faith in an eternal order only temporarily deranged. (pp. 751-60)

Randolph L. Wadsworth, Jr., "On 'The Snayl' by Richard Lovelace," in The Modern Language Review, *Vol. 65, No. 4, October 1970, pp. 750-60.*

Joseph H. Summers   (essay date 1970)

[*Summers is an American literary scholar and editor whose books include* George Herbert: His Religion and Art *(1954) and* The Muse's Method: An Introduction to "Paradise Lost" *(1962). In the excerpt below, he describes Lovelace as a technically inferior poet but observes, nonetheless, that he is "a small master of mixed metaphor."*]

The aesthetic problem (for the reader if not the poets) of how the new style gentleman could write of love without marring his effects with the sordid and brutal was [an issue throughout the seventeenth] century. Lovelace, who is sometimes contrasted with Suckling to Suckling's disadvantage did not find any real solution. When he was not striking noble and self-congratulatory poses in his few 'Cavalier' poems which have been so extraordinarily popular in the past hundred years or so . . . , Lovelace could be more shocking than Suckling, particularly when his elevated and low passages were crudely juxtaposed. Very few poets in the seventeenth century who wrote as much as Lovelace displayed such incompetence. One wonders sometimes whether he meant to say what he did, or even whether he always knew what he said. According to all reports, he was extremely handsome and a great favourite with the ladies, and he wrote some brilliant phrases and lines ('Poor verdant fool! and now green ice!' of **"The Grasshopper,"** 'Shake your head and scatter day' of **"To Amarantha,"** or the opening of **"La Bella Bona Roba"**: 'I cannot tell who loves the skeleton / Of a poor marmoset, naught but bone, bone. / Give me a nakedness with her clothes on.') But he has little sense of structure and his syntax is sometimes shaky or hopelessly wrenched. He is also a small master of mixed metaphor; **"To Lucasta. The Rose,"** perhaps his outstanding achievement in that direction, seems clearly constructed with the expectation that if the images are pretty, the sense will take care of itself. And few poets in any age have attained the sheer mindlessness of a couplet from **"The Snail"**:

> Strict, and locked up, th'art hood o'er
> And ne'er eliminat'st thy door.

(pp. 48-9)

Joseph H. Summers, "Gentlemen of the Court and of Art: Suckling, Herrick, and Carew," in his The Heirs of Donne and Jonson, Chatto & Windus, *1970, pp. 41-75.*

Manfred Weidhorn   (essay date 1970)

[*Weidhorn is an Austrian-born American scholar whose books include* Dreams in Seventeenth-Century English Literature *(1970). In the following excerpt, he discusses the principal themes and motifs of Lovelace's poetry, shedding light on the poetic relevance of Lovelace's interest in the art and music of his time.*]

Lovelace was a minor poet in an age of giants. Though he produced a few gems, his verse is limited in themes or ideas. The difference between Lovelace and his greater contemporaries is partly accounted for by natural endowments—the others were talented individuals, if not outright geniuses, whereas Lovelace was simply a sensitive, well-trained gentleman with a touch of the poet—and partly by manner of life. The code of the gentleman included proficiency in love, or at least in composing love poetry. Lovelace wrote poetry, much of it concerned with love, because doing so, like graceful fencing and dancing, was good form. If he tossed off an excellent lyric, so much the better, but he was not committed day and night to a quest for literary immortality. This sketch of Lovelace's aspiration is, however, only an inference. We have no statement by him of his intentions. As with many seventeenth-century literary figures, none of his personal writings—diary, letters, family papers—is extant. Careful perusal of the poetry discovers only conventional remarks; even his tastes in the literature of his time are deduced with difficulty. (p. 31)

In several places, Lovelace conjoins poetry and music. In the seventeenth century, as in ancient Greece, the two existed symbiotically; poetry was written for singer, instrument, auditors. Many of Lovelace's own poems were set to music and so circulated long before they saw print, or were written for a popular tune, **"A la Chabot," "A la Bourbon," "Courante Monsieur."** Music itself was actively participated in by many persons, was thought to be effective in treating the emotions and health, and, in the cosmological thinking, was part of the harmony of the heavenly bodies. The distinct and joint powers of word and note are celebrated in the charming **"Dialogue"** between a lute and a voice. The two, admiring each other, delineate the peculiar powers which enable each one to move heaven and hell:

> LUTE.   Sing, Laura, sing, whilst silent are the
> spheres,
> And all the eyes of heaven are turn'd
> to ears.
> VOICE.   Touch thy dead wood, and make each

living tree
Unchain its feet, take arms, and follow thee.

The paradox is that dead wood—the instrument—animates the living tree; the dead wood gives life to the forest it sprang from. This allusion to the supernatural musical powers of Orpheus and Amphion also evokes the basic mystery of music itself, the mystery adumbrated by Benedict's half-scornful remark [in Shakespeare's *Much Ado About Nothing*], "Is it not strange that sheep's guts should hale souls out of men's bodies?"

In the second stanza, the poet punningly fuses "chords" and "heart (cordium) string," so that "tremble" and "shake" refer on one level to the sympathetic vibration of strings, as though the heart literally contained strings, on another level to the emotional response to the music and, last, to the ornaments of seventeenth-century lute playing:

> VOICE.   Touch the divinity of thy chords, and
> make
> Each heartstring tremble, and each
> sinew shake.
> LUTE.   Whilst with your voice you rarefy the
> air,
> None but an host of angels hover here.

In the third stanza, Lovelace describes the traditional powers of music and song to captivate the non-human world—beasts, angels, demons:

> VOICE.   Touch thy soft lute, and in each gentle
> thread
> The lion and the panther captive lead.
> LUTE.   Sing, and in heav'n enthrone deposed
> Love,
> Whilst angels dance, and fiends in
> order move.

By being played, the strings of the lute in effect become the leashes of the wild beasts they tame.

In such poems and especially in his references to the music of the spheres, Lovelace is generally looking back to older modes of thought. But on the third of the major arts, painting, Lovelace has some well-defined, forward-looking ideas. He himself was among the few Englishmen responding to the new art of the Renaissance. His poetry exhibits a connoisseur's awareness of the work of recent masters, as well as of their biographers, Giorgio Vasari and Carel Vermander.

Two poems addressed to Lely define the new outlook. **"To my worthy Friend . . . "** praises Lely for turning away from antiquated procedures:

> Not as of old, when a rough hand did speak
> A strong aspect, and a fair face a weak;
> When only a black beard cri'd villain, and
> By hieroglyphics we could understand;
> When crystal typifi'd in a white spot,
> And the bright ruby was but one red spot.

Lovelace refers to the inheritance of medieval iconology, of a nonrealistic technique in which figurative and moral considerations were of greater import than duplication of physical reality. The visual image was often a personification, a rendering visible, of an abstract idea. Truth would be represented as a naked woman not because anything erotic was intended but because the truth is by essence without adornment or dress. This series of symbolic conventions, which he calls "hieroglyphics," Lovelace rejects in favor of the finer touches of representational realism:

> Thou dost the things orientally the same,
> Not only paint'st its colour, but its flame:
> Thou sorrow canst design without a tear,
> And with the man his very hope or fear;
> So that th' amazed world shall henceforth find
> None but my Lely ever drew a mind.

In [*Lucasta. Posthume Poems*] appeared another panegyric to Lely, **"Painture,"** a broad-ranging commentary on the state of the arts. As Keats was to observe of the Grecian urn, Lovelace notes the power of painting to eternize the transient, to overcome time:

> When Beauty once thy virtuous paint hath on,
> Age needs not call her to vermilion;
> Her beams ne'er shed or change like th' hair of
>   day,
>   . . . . .
> Whilst we wipe off the num'rous score of years,
> And do behold our grandsires as our peers;
> With the first father of our house compare
> We do the features of our new-born heir;
> For though each copied a son, they all
> Meet in thy first and true original.

Painting not only imitates reality but is actually a form of creation:

> What princess not
> But comes to you to have herself begot?
>   . . . . .
> So by your art you spring up in two moons
> What could not else be form'd by fifteen suns;
>   . . . . .
> O sacred painture; that dost fairly draw
> What but in mists deep inward poets saw;
>   . . . . .
> Thou that in frames eternity doest bind,
> And art a written and a bodi'd mind;
>   . . . . .
> That contemplation into matter brought,
> Bodi'd ideas, and could form a thought.

Like music, painting leads us beyond ourselves and our imperfect world. **"Amyntor's Grove"** tells of works by

> Titian, Raphael, Giorgione,
> Whose art ev'n Nature hath outdone;
> For if weak Nature only can
> Intend, not perfect, what is man,
> These certainly we must prefer,
> Who mended what she wrought and her.

Lovelace's responsiveness to music and painting is equalled by his interest in certain small creatures, and this observation of nature constitutes one of his contributions to seventeenth-century English poetry, although writing about small creatures was not unusual. "Let other poets write of dogs, / Some sing of fleas, or fighting frogs," proclaims James Shirley as he begins a poem on birds. The old belief in the system of correspondences caused the writer to take joy in the small representative thing which mirrored the larger world, the microcosm in which he could study the macrocosm. As Jonson put it, "In small proportions we just beauty see." Lovelace is less concerned with the cosmological import of the creatures he describes, however, than with the curiosity, amusement, and teasing humor which they stimulate. He contemplates their fate with geniality and affection.

These poems fall into two groups: those dealing with a variety of insects (ant, bee, grasshopper, spider, fly), and those with birds and small beasts (falcon, heron, toad, snail). The minute creatures enter some of the amatory poems as part of lavish compliments to the lady, but Lovelace's personal touch really appears in a series of poems describing the creatures for their own sake. In **"The Snail,"** after touching on the moral overtones—"Wise emblem of our politic world, / Sage snail, within thine own self curl'd, / Instruct me softly to make haste, / Whilst these my feet go slowly fast"—the poet concentrates with good humor on its strange movements:

> Compendious snail! thou seem'st to me
> Large Euclid's strict epitome;
> And, in each diagram, dost fling
> Thee from the point unto the ring.
> A figure now triangular,
> An oval now, and now a square;
> And then a serpentine dost crawl,
> Now a straight line, now crook'd, now all . . .

Lovelace nicely brings out the touch of absurdity in the snail's ways: "Thou thine own daughter, then, and sire, / That son and mother art entire." With mock solemnity, the poet sings of the snail's thrift and religious virtues, its self-containedness. In another poem on the same subject, Lovelace returns to the ridiculousness of the creature with a mock-heroic invocation:

> The centaur, siren, I forgo,
> Those have been sung, and loudly too;
> Nor of the mixed sphinx I'll write,
> Nor the renown'd hermaphrodite:
> Behold, this huddle doth appear
> Of horses, coach, and charioteer;
> That moveth him by traverse law,
> And doth himself both drive and draw;
> Then, when the sun the south doth win,
> He baits him hot in his own inn.

Even more stimulating than the snail was the ant, which elicited from Lovelace one of the best of these poems. **"The Ant"** begins with an indulgent, teasing address to the hardworking creature:

> Forbear, thou great good husband, little ant;
>   A little respite from thy flood of sweat!
> Thou, thine own horse and cart, under this plant
>   Thy spacious tent, fan thy prodigious heat;
> Down with thy double load of that one grain!
> It is a granary for all thy train.

The figurative significance is underlined, "Cease, large example of wise thrift, a while, / (For thy example is become our law)"; the aim is not to convert us to the ant's austerity but to teach the ant—and ourselves—the value of relaxation:

> And teach thy frowns a seasonable smile:
> So Cato sometimes the nak'd Florals saw.

. . . . .
Austere and cynic! not one hour t' allow,
    To lose with pleasure what thou got'st with
        pain,
But drive on sacred festivals thy plough,
    Tearing highways with thy o'ercharged wain.
Not all thy lifetime one poor minute live,
And thy o'erlabour'd bulk with mirth relieve?

The ant is reminded of its natural enemies waiting to destroy it and the fruit of its hard work:

Look up, then, miserable ant, and spy
    Thy fatal foes, for breaking of her law,
Hov'ring above thee: Madam—Margaret Pie,
    And her fierce servant, Meagre—Sir John
        Daw;
Thyself and storehouse now they do store up,
And thy whole harvest too within their crop.

In the last stanza, the poet enlarges the scope of the discussion by including all human endeavor. He had done the same at the outset of **"The Snail"**; here, however, having been cozened into enjoying a charming description of quaint nature, we are suddenly confronted with the truth of our mortality, in an unexpected place:

Thus we unthrifty thrive within earth's tomb
    For some more rav'nous and ambitious jaw:
The grain in th' ant's, the ant's in the pie's
        womb,
    The pie in th' hawk's, the hawk's in th' eagle's
        maw:
So scattering to hoard 'gainst a long day,
Thinking to save all, we cast all away.

This conclusion recalls Aesop's fables and Hamlet's reflections in the graveyard as well as his remarks to Claudius on the king's progress through the guts of a worm, and it looks ahead to Burns's moral in "To a Mouse" and to Tennyson's unease at the tableau of "Nature red in tooth and claw." The vanity of human endeavors; the return of dust to dust; the analogy between the ant's predicament and ours ("as flies to wanton boys are we to the gods"); the bitter war of nature—these great themes are sounded genially and in an unfaltering voice.

The ant's industrious life, touched on by the Proverbs of Solomon and by Horace (Satire I, i), was often juxtaposed, in fable, with the grasshopper's insouciance. Popularized in the Middle Ages, dialogues between the two insects recurred in French literature down to La Fontaine. Lovelace himself presented the somewhat different fate of the happy grasshopper: it is overtaken by the cycle of the seasons. The poem on this subject is even more fraught with moral application, but the discussion of its full philosophic scope belongs in the next chapter. It suffices to note now its similarity in tone to Lovelace's other insect and beast lyrics:

O thou that swing'st upon the waving hair
    Of some well-filled oaten beard,
Drunk ev'ry night with a delicious tear
    Dropt thee from heav'n, where now th' art
        rear'd:

The joys of earth and air are thine entire,
    That with thy feet and wings dost hop and fly;
And when thy poppy works thou dost retire

To thy carv'd acorn-bed to lie.

The poet's joys are at one with the insect's, but then the horizon becomes overcast:

But ah the sickle! golden ears are cropt;
    Ceres and Bacchus bid good night;
Sharp frosty fingers all your flow'rs have topt,
    And what scythes spar'd, winds shave off
        quite.

Poor verdant fool, and now green ice!

Despite the grasshopper's cheerful character, its doom is like the ant's; and both reflect the human experience: "Thy joys, / . . . Bid us lay in 'gainst winter rain."

A more frequently observed disaster overtakes the common housefly—entrapment. Lovelace refers to this state a half-dozen times, as when describing the plight of the unrequited low-born lover, "This heard, sir, play still in her eyes, / And be a-dying lives, like flies / Caught by their angle-legs and whom / The torch laughs piecemeal to consume." Another "Song" turns the analogy around and uses it in a negative sense: the mistress does not behave like a fly: "Strive not, vain lover, to be fine, / . . . You lessen to a fly your mistress' thought, / To think it may be in a cobweb caught."

An insect is ingeniously worked into another sort of love poem, **"A Black Patch on Lucasta's Face."** In order to turn a graceful compliment, the poet forwards a fanciful explanation of the presence of this fashionable beauty mark: "Dull as I was, to think that a court fly / Presum'd so near her eye, / When 'twas th' industrious bee / Mistook her glorious face for Paradise." The bee settles near her eyes, and soon

Acts the romantic phoenix' fate:

. . . . .
Chaf'd he's set on fire,
And in these holy flames doth glad expire;
And that black marble tablet there,
    So near her either sphere,
Was plac'd: nor foil, nor ornament,
But the sweet little bee's large monument.

The entrapment of the fly or the death of the bee delineates the plight of the lover. The image is developed at length in a different manner in **"A Fly about a Glass of Burnt Claret."** This concoction of paradoxes toys with the idea of alcoholic beverage as a potent "fire water." Again the poet addresses the insect in the voice of a friendly, experienced counselor: "Forbear this liquid fire, fly, / It is more fatal than the dry, / That singly, but embracing, wounds, / And this at once both burns and drowns." To drive his point home, he amusingly catalogues the wines' effects on all sorts of unlikely people:

'Tis this makes Venus' altars shine,
This kindles frosty Hymen's pine;
When the Boy grows old in his desires,
This flambeau doth new light his fires.

. . . . .
The Vestal drinking this doth burn.

The fly disregards the kindly warning:

Dost thou the fatal liquor sup,

One drop, alas! thy bark blows up.

. . . . .

And now th' art fall'n magnanimous fly,
In, where thine ocean doth fry,
Like the Sun's son who blush'd the flood
To a complexion of blood.

The poet compassionately comes to the rescue: "Yet see! my glad auricular (=small finger) / Redeems thee (though dissolv'd) a star; / . . . / See! in the hospital of my hand / Already cur'd, thou fierce dost stand." The poem concludes with a surprising turn, for the fly, not learning from its debacle, returns for more: "Burnt insect! dost thou reaspire / The moist-hot glass and liquid fire? / I see! 'tis such a pleasing pain, / Thou wouldst be scorched and drown'd again." The fly confronting the large glass of the burning liquid—and love is often described as a fire—is all too human: its shock and relapse are ours.

Lovelace's interest in the helpless insect prompted him to translate two of Martial's epigrams on the subject: VI, xv, on an ant embedded in amber; and IV, xxxii, on a bee in honey. The creatures' last moments are marked by desperate struggles. The gnat or bee "who, trapp'd in her (spider's) prepared toil, / To their destruction keep a coil." In fact, such a predicament becomes the subject of **"A Fly Caught in a Cobweb."** Like the poems on the snail and the ant, this poem is moralizing, genial, playful. The human import is brought out in the first lines:

Small type of great ones, that do hum
Within this whole world's narrow room,
That with a busy hollow noise
Catch at the people's vainer voice,

. . . . .

Poor fly caught in an airy net.

The fly's peculiar disaster depicts nicely enough man's predicament, one wrought by his aspiring nature: "Thy wings have fetter'd now thy feet." The fly had managed well so far to escape a common doom of insects, the flame, only to be overtaken by another, the spider. The fly's desperate motions—again detailed by Lovelace—hardly move the confident, lordly spider:

Where, like a lion in a toil,
Howe'er, thou keep'st a noble coil,
And beat'st thy gen'rous breast, that o'er
The plains thy fatal buzzes roar,
Till thy all-belli'd foe, round elf,
Hath quarter'd thee within himself.

The fly suffers a death that is not only ignominious in itself but also, because of its consequences, hideous and diverting:

But now devour'd art like to be
A net spun for thy family,
And, straight expanded in the air,
Hang'st for thy issue too a snare.
Strange witty death, and cruel ill,
That killing thee, thou thine dost kill!

. . . . .

Thou art thine en'my's sepulchre,
And in thee buriest too thine heir.

The analogy between insect and man breaks down here be-cause there is nothing in human endeavors that quite corresponds to this horrible fate; the poet has moved beyond the human significance of the fly's death to the amusing, ironic aspects of the incident itself. The poetic naturalist has taken over from the moralist. Something is nevertheless salvaged from the fly's disaster:

Yet Fates a glory have reserv'd
For one so highly hath deserv'd;
As the rhinoceros doth die
Under his castle-enemy,
As through the crane's trunk throat doth speed
The asp doth on his feeder feed;
Fall yet triumphant in thy woe,
Bound with the entrail of thy foe.

The fly's death amid its enemy's entrails (the cobweb) is so close to the epic description of the dying warrior's piercing his opponent's belly and dying in the other's entrails—dying on his foe, "going down swinging"—as to allow the poet to dignify by means of sophistry the fly's fate.

We note here Lovelace's keen sense of the natural enmities in the world order. Not only the fly and the spider but also the rhinoceros and the elephant, the crane and the asp, and, earlier, the ant and the magpie or daw, the magpie and the hawk, the hawk and the eagle—all are figures locked in mortal combat. A lengthy poem is devoted entirely to describing another duel involving a spider, **"The Toad and Spider."** The poet sides with the insect: "First from his den rolls forth that load / Of spite and hate, the speckl'd toad." In the manner of the epic hero, Arachne prays to Athene for help. The request is granted. The battle begins as, dodging the toad's breath, "On the toad's blue-chequer'd skull / The spider gluttons herself full, / And vomiting her Stygian seeds, / Her poison." The toad shakes her off, rushes to a curative herb for relief, and "then with repeated strength, and scars / That, smarting, fire him to new wars, / Deals blows." Avoiding a shot of the toad's spume, the spider makes some headway: "One eye she hath spit out / . . . / And one eye wittily spar'd, that he / Might but behold his misery." The swelling toad again totters to his curative herb; but, through the intercession of Athena and the spider's "lar" or household god, the plant has been removed. "The all-confounded toad doth see / His life fled with his remedy." He dies with a "dismal horrid yell," and the spider celebrates a triumph. Thus ends a counterpart, according to Mario Praz, of the nightmarish inventions of contemporary Dutch painters and, in its way, a curio of dark humor.

An equally ferocious battle, this time between a falcon and a heron, is described in **"The Falcon."** The invocation laments man's earthbound state:

Fair princess of the spacious air,
That hast vouchsaf'd acquaintance here,
With us [who] are quarter'd below stairs,
That can reach heav'n with naught but pray'rs;
Who, when our activ'st wings we try,
Advance a foot into the sky.

The battle is initiated as, exiled by dogs, "The heron mounted doth appear/On his own Peg'sus a lancier." Each prepares himself with his peculiar tactics:

And now he takes the open air,
Draws up his wings with tactic care,
Whilst th' expert falcon swift doth climb
In subtle mazes serpentine.

The falcon takes the offensive; the heron, "resolv'd to fall / His and his en'my's funeral," counterattacks lethally but is in turn mortally wounded: "Whilst her [falcon's] own bells in the sad fall/Ring out the double funeral." Siding with the aristocratic bird, Lovelace describes its funeral as attended by the varieties of hawk and proclaims its immortality. (pp. 32-44)

The writing of these poems is to be attributed . . . to an interest in conflict. Wherever exists amplitude of life, in meadow, forest, jungle, there obtains destructive competition, struggle, suffering. Man is deeply, perhaps morbidly, fascinated by such struggle; and Lovelace in effect presents in his animal poetry a detached, esthetic picture of conflict, viewed amorally, as a basic law of brutal Nature. Perhaps for that reason he confines himself to beasts; in human affairs, the gratuitous, universal lust for combat is usually masked with alleged issues, principles, ideals.

These duel poems also grow out of Lovelace's general interest in animal nature. Though no "nature" poet, he expressed a sympathy for animals that was rare in those days. Geoffrey Walton speaks of Lovelace as being, in these poems, "Something of a naturalist as well as a chivalrous Kentish squire" who blends his gentleman's private interest in animals, field sports, and heraldry with poetic tradition and expresses the rural roots of the Cavalier. There exists, in fact, a tradition of poetry about small animals: Aesop's fables, Virgil's "Gnat," poems in the *Greek Anthology*, the medieval Renard tales, Chaucer's "Nun's Priest's Tale" and "Parliament of Fowls," and, later, the fables of La Fontaine ("The Grasshopper and the Ant"). In such works, however, the emphasis is often satiric or allegorical; the human characteristics the animals represent usually predominate over their lifelike animal traits. Lovelace remains, on the other hand, close to observed facts, so that sometimes, as in the **"Snail"** or **"Fly Caught,"** the creature's plight is examined even when it ceases to parallel human affairs.

Although . . . Lovelace sometimes lapses into exaggeration, didacticism and bombast, he masters the challenge of limited form presented by such a subject matter. For Robin Skelton, Lovelace approximates Suckling and Carew by using a mock-heroic tone which implies amusement at the solemnities of conventional verse, awareness of the discrepancy between fine words and their artificiality, and duplicity in moralizing while at the same time poking fun at his audience's earnestness. Hugh Kenner best states Lovelace's contribution: "Men would be the poorer had they nothing to say about the doom of flies, and Lovelace's real subject is the human glory of his own loquacious wit, neither teaching nor moving but simply, on each amenable occasion, distinguishing by speech men from the brutes."

At the same time, we must not overemphasize the cheerfulness of tone. The small creatures are constantly dueling, overtaken by adversity, trapped. The image of the trapped insect is related to Lovelace's obsession with prison and confinement. . . . Lovelace presents a natural world filled with images of distasteful reality: the fly is emblematic of prominent personages; the snail, of the politic world; the ant, of puritanical austerity now become "our Law." The law of animal life in this insecure world is the law of man: "Us small ants."

Lovelace is clearly no innovator in this manner of writing; he merely handles it better than virtually anyone else. The possible influences on him are varied: the Dutch still-life paintings he saw during his travel years; the late Renaissance emblem books by such as Alciati and Camerarius, and the Latin anthologies by Gruter and Dornavius; the animal verses of the Pléiades poets (Joachim Du Bellay, Remy Belleau, and, notably, Pierre de Ronsard); the epitaphs, elegies, descriptions, narratives, and emblems written by various poets in what a student of the subject has called "the golden age of animal poetry in England"; and, always before these works, the *Greek Anthology* lyrics on locust and cicada, on the strange death of animals, on the contest of raven and scorpion, poems whose tone Lovelace caught and improved.

Nothing in the seventeenth century—not quite Drayton's or Herrick's "fairy-land" poems, certainly not Donne's ratiocinative seduction poem, "The Flea"—is similar. In the eighteenth century, not Blake's cryptic "The Fly" but Burns's seriocomic addresses to a louse and a mouse and Cowper's animal poems are analogous. Not until the poems of Marianne Moore and especially Robert Frost do we come upon a like tone of voice—the humorous, whimsical, observant, teasing, casual tone of Frost's "Fireflies in the Garden," "The White-Tailed Hornet," "To a Moth Seen in Winter," "Departmental," "The Considerable Speck." . . . The two poets are clearly kindred spirits, though Frost possesses a sense of humor, an ingenuity, a rhetoric, above all a sense of relevance, a perceptiveness, a realism about both animal behavior and human feelings that Lovelace could but reach for. (pp. 44-6)

· · · · ·

Although a staunch defender of king and established church, Lovelace wrote no devotional poems and little that touches on Christianity. In this respect he is nearly alone in an age when even such secular-minded men as Jonson, Herrick, Carew, and Marvell composed in verse an occasional prayer or confessional. If we may judge from his poetry, Lovelace was the sort of Royalist who regards religion as an institution of practical importance for the maintenance of the fabric of society but allows it as little as possible to impinge on his own way of life.

In the occasional poems written for the death of acquaintance or friend, some Christian consolation appears, of course, as it would in the works of all but defiant atheists. Yet these references, as in the elegy on the Princess Katherine, lack depth of conviction or insight; Lovelace introduces the religious imagery in order to continue the tissue of paradoxes that is the core of the poem. The elegy on the death of Cassandra Cotton is the only other poem with any Christian overtones: "Remove this earth / To its last death and first victorious birth." The fifty-year-old lady who died a virgin is presented as a saintly example to all young virgins:

> Dare but live like her:
> Dare to live virgins.
>
> . . . . .
>
> Whilst not a blemish or least stain is seen
> On your white robe 'twixt fifty and fifteen;
> But as it in your swathing-bands was given,
> Bring't in your winding-sheet unsoil'd to heav'n.

In effective lines, the poet paints a picture of the Christian life as lived, say, at Little Gidding and as celebrated by George Herbert:

> Dare to affect a serious holy sorrow,
> To which delights of palaces are narrow,
> And lasting as their smiles, dig you a room
> Where practise the probation of your tomb,
> With ever-bended knees and piercing pray'r
> Smooth the rough pass through craggy earth to
>   air.

He concludes with the basic Christian paradox of life: "You are more dead and buried than she."

When one of Lovelace's brothers was killed in action, the poet addressed lines of consolation to another brother, Francis, **"Immoderately Mourning My Brother's Untimely Death."** In these, dealing with so personal a grief, eschewing paradox or compliment, Lovelace makes use of no Christian consolation whatever. The poem is instead wholly Stoic in outlook. Indeed, secular philosophy seems to have meant more to Lovelace than Christianity as a way of meeting the difficulties of life, for his casual Christian references pale before the greater intensity found in numerous poems with a marked Stoic or Epicurean outlook. That Stoicism interested Lovelace is indicated as well by his translating from Seneca's Latin some lines of the Greek Stoic, Cleanthes.

The poem to Francis attempts to assuage with Stoic control their grief over brother William's death. It is a paraphrase of a Latin elegy by Sarbiewski which was imitated and translated by many others in the seventeenth and eighteenth centuries. Lovelace's version is curt, well turned. Its burden is that weeping merely swells grief and that the wise man should accede to fate's decrees:

> If tears could wash the ill away,
> A pearl for each wet bead I'd pay;
> But as dew'd corn the fuller grows,
> So water'd eyes but swell our woes.
>
> . . . . .
>
> Iron decrees of Destiny
> Are ne'er wip'd out with a wet eye.
> But this way you may gain the field,
> Oppose but sorrow, and 'twill yield;
> One gallant thorough-made resolve
> Doth starry influence dissolve.

The references to Fate, the Iron decrees of Destiny, the starry influence; the emphasis on resolve, firmness, opposition to grief—all these are an elaboration of the line from Cleanthes, "Fates lead the willing, but unwilling draw."

A different sort of adversity confronts the persona of **"A Forsaken Lady."** She addresses a young man whom she loves but who has been pursuing another lady to no avail. Though weeping over him, she enjoys seeing him trapped in the same unrequited love that tortures her. But then she changes her tone—her emotions are freezing up; she hardens, masters herself: "But I am chang'd! Bright reason / . . . / Hath reach'd me pow'r to scorn as well as thee: / Hail, holy cold! chaste temper, hail!" She has achieved the Stoic apathy, which is here fused with the image of the Petrarchan cold, haughty lady.

The Stoic posture is evoked in Lovelace's description of a portrait by Lely of Charles I and his son, who were painted at Hampton Court in the midst of the rising political turmoil and who therefore had much to be resigned to:

> See!   what a clouded majesty, and eyes
> Whose glory through their mist doth brighter
>   rise!
> See!   what an humble bravery doth shine,
> And grief triumphant breaking through each
>   line!
> How it commands the face!   so sweet a scorn
> Never did happy misery adorn!

It might be said that king and son are trying to cheer each other, or that Lely—and Lovelace in turn—is trying to cheer them all, everyone working hard at the proverbial "stiff upper lip," at pose instead of poise. (pp. 47-9)

Lovelace is a poet, not a philosopher; and his "philosophic" positions are instinctual responses, not reasoned choices. A Lovelace poem may be Stoic or Epicurean in the sense that a man who never read a book of philosophy may be Stoic if he says, "I must finish the work before I take the vacation," or an Epicurean if he says, "To hell with the work: I'm going on vacation now!" If we judge by the number of poems, Lovelace was attracted more to the Epicurean position, to the drink imbibed with a flourish of insouciance; but he also had his Stoic moments. Most writers, in any case, are not all one or the other but have moods in which either attitude dominates.

Thus, when about to present himself to the hardened London theater audience as a playwright for the first time, Lovelace stoically steels himself for probable rejection. Satisfied with what he has written and content to have it understood by "the few, the worthy," he seeks no other gain or pleasure: "Profit he knows none, / Unless that of your approbation." On the other hand, when someone else's aspirations come into play, it is easier to strike a contented Epicurean note. Thus the hardworking, dutiful ant is urged to turn from duty to pleasure; or the poet's brother Francis is exhorted, on the occasion of a trip abroad, to think of comfort in lieu of ambition:

> Frank, wilt live handsomely?   trust not too far
> Thyself to waving seas;
>
> . . . . .
>
> Yet settle here your rest, and take your state,
>
> . . . . .
>
>   Nay, steadfast stand,
> As if discover'd were a New-found-land.

The sea is treacherous and dangerous; even the seemingly settled earth, we now know, moves wildly; and its movement is symbolic of the giddy whirl of human life and society. The solution is not for man to place himself at the mercies of the even more uncertain seas but to look within, to contract his desires and needs, to settle for the moderate:

> To rear an edifice by art so high
> That envy should not reach it with her eye,
> Nay, with a thought come near it—wouldst thou know
> How such a structure should be rais'd?   build low.

With proper resolution, he can withstand all: "A breast of proof defies all shocks of fate."

The idea of the golden mean here expressed is central to Horace's fusion of Aristotelian ethics with Epicurean retirement and mild pleasure-seeking. The poem is indeed deeply influenced by Horace; and Katherine McEuen, a student of Classical influences on English poetry, finds it an excellent paraphrase typical of the vein of Classicism in Lovelace's work. He follows the Latin closely, except when interpolating a thought (like the reference to the earth's movement) which applies Horace to the modern situation.

Unabashed Epicurean, even hedonistic, expressions abound in Lovelace's work, notably in the dozen or so poems celebrating drink. Man has always responded ambivalently to alcoholic beverages; at once boon and bane, they liberate him while also unmanning him in several ways. The ambivalence is reflected in the way most people boast of their intoxication, whether rare or frequent, and in the large number of slang and colloquial expressions for drunkenness. Hence a half-smirking allusive tone properly characterizes the poem **"The Fly About a Glass of Burnt Claret."** The fiery quality of the liquid is attributable not only to its being burnt claret but also to its taste and effects. The fly's debacle in falling into it is our debacle: "I see! 'tis such a pleasing pain, / Thou wouldst be scorch'd and drown'd again." The paradoxes in the poem—"liquid fire," "scorch'd and drown'd," "pleasing pain"—are so many jokes on inebriation and ambivalence.

The positive, restorative qualities of wine are celebrated in the bacchanalian "A Loose Saraband (1659)." . . . Influenced ultimately by Anacreon's joint praises of wine and love, the poem renders somewhat more unto Bacchus than unto Venus:

> Here is a double fire,
>   A dry one and a wet.
> True lasting heavenly fuel
> Puts out the vestal jewel,
> When once we twining marry
> Mad love with wild canary.

The drunk, like the lover, projects onto the world his feelings:

> See all the world, how 't staggers,
>   More ugly drunk than we,
> As if far gone in daggers
>   And blood it seem'd to be:
> We drink our glass of roses,
> Which naught but sweets discloses,
> Then, in our loyal chamber,
> Refresh us with love's amber.
>
>   . . . . .
> What of Elysium's missing?
> Still drinking and still kissing.

The paean comes to a memorable climax with the question, "Lord! what is man and sober?" The two entities "man" and "sobriety" are mutually exclusive. Lovelace takes the usual definition of man as a rational creature and mischievously suggests that the reverse is true, that only drunken reasonlessness brings out true manliness.

The poem is rounded off with a carefree, glowing conclusion:

> Now is there such a trifle
>   As honour, the fool's giant?
> What is there left to rifle,
>   When wine makes all parts pliant?
> Let others glory follow,
> In their false riches wallow,
> And with their grief be merry:
> Leave me but love and sherry.

The ridicule of honor and glory is reminiscent of similar sallies by Falstaff or by the persona of Donne's lyrics and anticipates such poems as Burns's "Jolly Beggars." Such ridicule, together with the hedonistic abandonment to wine and to the love that follows, expresses a side of Lovelace less known than his Cavalier steadfastness in **"To Althea"** and his devotion to honor in **"To . . . Wars."**

Drink is equally important in the soldier's life. The capacity to ingest it deeply is, in such a milieu, as much a touchstone of masculinity as swordplay or sexual prowess. (pp. 50-3)

Drink is also a stimulant of friendly intercourse and witticisms, a cement of friendship. It is therefore prominent in a visit to the country house of an old friend; after arrival and sightseeing, Lovelace relaxes with his host: "We bound our loose hair with the vine, / The poppy and the eglantine; / One swell'd an oriental bowl / . . . / So drench'd we our oppressing cares." A similar quiet communion with a friend takes place under less auspicious circumstances in **"The Grasshopper."** Lovelace addresses Charles Cotton as the winter of political discontent and turmoil settles over the land—gone are the bluster, camaraderie and gregarious abandonment of the military toast, the loosening of inhibitions in an erotic situation, or the effusive joys of a country visit. The grasshopper's happy but transient existence bears a lesson for the two friends:

> Poor verdant fool, and now green ice! thy joys,
>   Large and as lasting as thy perch of grass,
> Bid us lay in 'gainst winter rain, and poise
>   Their floods with an o'erflowing glass.

Wine is a balance against the floods of rain; friendship and continent private pleasure, against public disaster. Like the grasshopper, which was "drunk ev'ry night with a delicious tear,"

> Thou best of men and friends!   we will create
> A genuine Summer in each other's breast.
>   . . . . .
> Dropping December shall come weeping in,
>   Bewail th' usurping of his reign;
> But when in show'rs of old Greek we begin,
>   Shall cry he hath his crown again.

In this bleak time the poet chooses neither Stoic repression of desires nor adherence to duty in the face of difficulties but withdrawal, endurance through friendship, drink, modest pleasures:

> Night as clear Hesper shall our tapers whip
> From the light casements where we play,
> And the dark hag from her black mantle strip,
> And stick there everlasting day.

The grasshopper sets for the Cavaliers, which it symbolizes, an example of conviviality. This image has a venerable history, going all the way back to Homer, Hesiod, Plato, Philostratus, Meleager. Among the Greeks, the grasshopper was associated with musicianship and poetry, with noblemen and insouciance, with men in political disfavor—all of which recalls the character and plight of Lovelace and the Cavaliers. In Renaissance emblem books, the grasshopper symbolized content, hope, fragility. The poem, in effect, sounds the mid-seventeenth-century Royalist retreat from affairs of state, society, and war. (pp. 53-5)

This turn to Epicureanism rather than Stoicism in the face of public disaster is also characteristic of poems dealing with a personal disaster, physical confinement. We readily associate Lovelace with jail because he was twice imprisoned and because his single most famous poem deals with the subject. As a matter of fact, images of incarceration, like those of trapped insects, haunted his imagination and appear in even innocent-looking poems.

The extreme is no doubt the "witty" torture used in Spanish prisons, one involving confinement within confinement (in **"The Toad and Spider"**):

> Heretics' bare heads are arm'd
> In a close helm, and in it charm'd
> An overgrown and meagre rat,
> That piecemeal nibbles himself fat.

More is revealed of prison life by a simile in **"Aramantha,"**

> Now, as a prisoner new cast,
> Who sleeps in chains that night his last,
> Next morn is wak'd with a reprieve,
> And from his trance not dream bid live,
> Wonders (his sense not having scope)
> Who speaks, his friend or his false hope.

Such a happy experience Lovelace probably knew first-hand; in **"The Triumphs,"** he inserted six clearly autobiographical lines:

> What fate was mine, when in mine obscure cave
> (Shut up almost close prisoner in a grave)
> Your beams could reach me through this vault
>   of night,
> And canton the dark dungeon with light!
> Whence me, as gen'rous spahis, you unbound,
> Whilst I now know myself both free and
>   crown'd.

The exact interpretation of these lines is uncertain; whatever the aid given him, Lovelace must have awakened one day to better conditions in jail and not been able to believe his luck.

But confinement may be spiritual instead of, or as well as, physical: **"A Guiltless Lady Imprison'd"** contains a series of complimentary paradoxes addressed to a pretty whore:

> See! that which chains you you chain here;
>   The prison is thy prisoner;
> How much thy jailor's keeper art!
>   He binds your hands, but you his heart.

The lover is bound, or possessed . . . , he is akin to a misguided bee or trapped fly. Night to him is the

> Loathed jailor of the lock'd-up sun,
>   And tyrant-turnkey on committed day,
> Bright eyes lie fetter'd in thy dungeon,
>   And heaven itself doth thy dark wards obey,

and equally constricting is another fact of daily life, clothing:

> Love's martyrs of the town,
> All day imprison'd in a gown,
> Who, rack'd in silk 'stead of a dress,
> Are clothed in a frame or press,
> And with that liberty and room
> The dead expatiate in a tomb.

Amarantha is urged to let her hair fly "unconfin'd," even as in the golden age the young lovers were "unconfined." But now "Will I fling all at her feet I have, / My life, my love, my very soul a slave? / Tie my free spirit only unto her, / And yield up my affection prisoner?" Hence the persona of **"To Lucasta. From Prison"** is shackled in two ways, to Lucasta as well as to the jail walls. Thrown back upon his resources, he must reconsider his values in a dissolving world. After all the other political institutions fail to pass muster, he consecrates himself anew to the king.

This sober scrutiny of self and body politic is quite different from the two remaining poems on prison life: **"The Vintage to the Dungeon"** and **"To Althea. From Prison."** In them, Stoic sentiments are complemented, if not displaced, by Epicurean ones, as the theme of drinking fuses with the theme of prison to produce two of Lovelace's most characteristic and well-known creations. The **"Vintage to the Dungeon"** is brief and simple:

> Sing out, pent souls, sing cheerfully!
> Care shackles you in liberty,
> Mirth frees you in captivity:
>   Would you double fetters add?
>   Else why so sad?
>
> Chorus: Besides your pinion'd arms you'll
>   find
>   Grief too can manacle the mind.
>
> Live then pris'ners uncontroll'd;
> Drink o' th' strong, the rich, the old,
> Till wine too hath your wits in hold;
>   Then if still your jollity
>   And throats are free—
>
> Chorus: Triumph in your bonds and pains,
>   And dance to th' music of your
>   chains.

This lyric is a rousing assertion of the human capacity to overcome adversity. The paradox of triumphing within man's bonds and pains is rendered vividly concrete in the image of dancing to the chains' music—man turning to good use the very thing that curtails his happiness, making his music where he finds it, letting himself go in the worst of circumstances. The sounds of the chain are transformed by the imagination from a reminder of sorrow into an accompaniment of joy; the very thing which confines man's body liberates his soul. By dancing grief away, the prisoner also effaces the chains; they are not chains if not regarded as such. The impediments are transcended. Thus this simple, lovely couplet best celebrates the power of the imagination.

If, as Willa Evans conjectured in "Lovelace's Concept of Prison Life," **"The Vintage to the Dungeon"** did not grow out of the poet's prison experiences, the same may hold true of **"To Althea. From Prison,"** which the unreliable Wood associated with Lovelace's 1642 incarceration in Gatehouse.

> When Love with unconfined wings
>   Hovers within my gates,
> And my divine Althea brings
>   To whisper at the grates;
> When I lie tangled in her hair,
>   And fetter'd to her eye,
> The gods, that wanton in the air,
>   Know no such liberty.
>
> When flowing cups run swiftly round
>   With no allaying Thames,
> Our careless heads with roses bound,
>   Our hearts with loyal flames;
> When thirsty grief in wine we steep,
>   When healths and draughts go free,
> Fishes, that tipple in the deep,
>   Know no such liberty.
>
> When, like committed linnets, I
>   With shriller throat shall sing
> The sweetness, mercy, majesty,
>   And glories of my king;
> When I shall voice aloud how good
>   He is, how great should be;
> Enlarged winds, that curl the flood,
>   Know no such liberty.
>
> Stone walls do not a prison make,
>   Nor iron bars a cage;
> Minds innocent and quiet take
>   That for an hermitage;
> If I have freedom in my love,
>   And in my soul am free,
> Angels alone, that soar above,
>   Enjoy such liberty.

The greatest of prison poems, **"To Althea. From Prison"** defies analysis. As with all great art, its essence is simplicity, seeming artlessness obtained from polish and care. Built on a Cavalier antithesis of bodily confinement and spiritual liberty, it comes to express "the triumph of mind over matter" in words "simple and profound, limpid and musical." The first three stanzas examine the theme in three different ways, each one concluding with the paradox that the imprisoned man has greater liberty than have the free creatures and forces of nature. "Know no such liberty" is the refrain. The three prison pastimes, the means to spiritual freedom and happiness, are the standard ones—women, wine, song—celebrated by hedonists from Anacreon through Goliard and Burns to the latest "Beat" poet; and we recall Frans Hals's "Laughing Cavalier" painting as a perfect analogue to this lyric.

The stanzas are carefully constructed. Each consists of two quatrains, the "b" rhyme (*ee*) of the second quatrain remaining the same throughout the poem. Each of the first three stanzas begins with "when"; the seventh line of each compares the prisoner's state with another creature—gods, fishes, winds, and angels. The joys of the first three fall short of his joys; only angels can match his freedom, for he has become angel-like, a free spirit.

In the first stanza, ideas of freedom and confinement are manipulated paradoxically. The poet lies in jail "*tangled* in her hair" and "*fettered* to her eye" yet thereby is made free by love's "unconfined" wings. The stanza describing, in the manner of **"Vintage to the Dungeon,"** the abandonment to drink is tied to the first and third by its references to the heart "bound" with "loyal flames"—loyal to his mistress Althea and to his king (stanza three), whose praise he will sing. The basic Cavalier themes of love and honor are thus counterpointed with hedonistic delights and with the elusive, protean idea of freedom: man may be "free to" even while not being "free from." The climactic stanza draws the conclusion with memorable generalization, powerful aphoristic lines which round out this brief depiction of the elements of true freedom—constancy to mistress, loyalty to political party, the coziness of good company and potation in jail.

The idea that the mind, not external circumstances, determines man's happiness has found expression in all places and ages. (pp. 56-61)

The idea is, in fact, a major theme of Lovelace's poetry. In **"Another"** [on the snail]," he gives a twist to Horace's remark that wherever man flees to, the heavens are the same:

> But, banished, I admire his fate,
> Since neither ostracism of state,
> Nor a perpetual exile
> Can force this virtue change his soil:
> For wheresoever he doth go,
> He wanders with his country too.

These lines contain a personal reference; for the defeated, hounded Royalist envies the snail and its self-sufficiency, its repose, its capacity to remain true to itself; its "prison" is its home. In **"A Guiltless Lady Imprisoned,"** the beautiful charmer is less confined than she seems since she actually imprisons her jailor's heart. The first lines of **"To Lucasta. From Prison"** request, as we have seen, freedom from the lady, not from the prison walls. To "dance to the music of your chains" is to deny confidently the ultimate reality of prison; for "Care shackles you in liberty, / Mirth frees you in captivity." The poet builds his own world with his values even as the friends in **"The Grasshopper"** created "everlasting day" and inner summer amid the pervasive night and winter.

The great adversity, throughout Lovelace's work, is entrapment, whether in prison amid political defeat or to a lady. And the problem is whether to deal with it by physical flight; or by ascent to something higher through self-discipline; or by dying like the trapped insect. In **"To Althea,"** the testing by imprisonment of his loyalty and endurance elicits these proud assertions of his devotion to the king. Prison is the acid test of values, loyalty, integrity; it is, to use current expressions, "the moment of truth," the occasion for revealing "grace under pressure." (pp. 62-3)

Though a Royalist broadside, **"To Althea"** is ennobled with an air of masculine spontaneity, with a rare note of idealism any reader can respond to. Speaking with the stance, the gestures, peculiar to the poet's time and place—the Cavalier's buoyant flourish of loyalty in the gloom of 1640-60—the poem transcends its historical setting and achieves immortality by capturing the essence of its age, by extracting the universal from the temporal, by making the values of a bygone civilization at its finest come alive.

Though **"To Althea"** expresses something of the Stoic creed that "Fates lead the willing, but unwilling draw," the sanguine turning from adversity and confinement to joy and inner freedom is helped by wine and the image of the beloved—a situation that smacks not a little of Epicurean values. As Hartmann states in *The Cavalier Spirit*, the idea that jail is no jail if conscience is clear is part of the Cavalier's Epicurean philosophy which found pleasure in any experience not without nobility. Is this uncertainty as to proper labels not evidence of how difficult it sometimes is to distinguish between the two philosophies in lyric poetry? In any case, questions of whether **"To Althea"** is Stoic or Epicurean vanish before this bold celebration of man's proved ability to confront his adversity, ignore his environment, and master his destiny. (p. 63)

Manfred Weidhorn, in his Richard Lovelace, *Twayne Publishers, Inc., 1970, 185 p.*

Raymond A. Anselment (essay date 1971)

[*In the following excerpt, Anselment interprets Lovelace's poem "The Falcon" as an allegorical homage to the Cavalier cause.*]

[The] defeat of the Royalist cause had great impact on Lovelace. While the poems collected in the 1659 posthumous edition of *Lucasta* make no direct references to the dead king or the defeated Royalists, a subdued and disillusioned tone more frequently replaces the "Cavalier spirit" associated with the *Lucasta* of 1649. But it would be misleading to conclude, as one provocative critic suggests, that many of the poems "are distrustful, violent, even paranoiac in reaction to society." At times pessimistic yet never defeatist, Richard Lovelace confronted the bleak period of the fifties with more than the Cavalier escapism of wine or women. This is apparent in the one poem he wrote in tribute to Charles I and the Cavalier ideals, **"The Falcon."**

As in **"The Grasshopper,"** a more famous counterpart in the 1649 edition, the implications of **"The Falcon"** are much more complex than the simple title might suggest. Ostensibly concerned with falconry, the opening of the lengthy and uneven poem addresses a falcon perched on a lady's wrist. The initial focus on the silver-chained bird, remarkably similar to the opening image of Lovelace's **"A Lady with a Falcon on her fist,"** shifts in the sixth stanza

to the falcon's fate when she is set on a heron. The next eight stanzas describe in military terminology the encounter and the deaths of both birds; then the lament in the final three stanzas fulfills a promised epicedium. Unlike **"A Lady with a Falcon on her fist,"** which transforms the falcon into a complimentary symbol of feminine power, **"The Falcon"** contains no direct equation with a larger meaning; the poem could be grouped with **"The Toad and Spyder"** in illustration of Lovelace's ability to depict confrontations in nature as miniature military campaigns. But the final stanza implies that the poem is much more complicated:

> But thy eternal name shall live
> Whilst Quills from Ashes fame reprieve,
> Whilst open stands Renown's wide dore,
> And Wings are left on which to soar;
> Doctor *Robbin*, the Prelate *Pye*,
> And the poetick *Swan* shall dye,
> Only to sing thy Elegie.

The poet, who introduces the duel between the falcon and the heron with the awkward transition "now a quill from thine own Wing / I pluck, thy lofty fate to sing," has left the world of aristocratic falconers and self-conscious poets; now the poetic swan, he deliberately evokes the world of the bestiary fable and thereby invites the reader to find another level of meaning for Doctor Robbin, Prelate Pye, and the various other birds in previous stanzas who mourn the falcon's death. More important, he implies that the falcon, the heron, and their battle have hidden, even allegorical dimension.

The key to the poem's ultimate significance is found in the opening stanzas. Using the same technique employed in his allegorical poem **"The Ant,"** Lovelace begins the poem with an apostrophe—this time to a falcon. Again the object of the poem is first characterized, and then the section culminates in a comparison with a lady. In **"The Falcon,"** however, the contrast is achieved more naturally. Lovelace does not need to forcefully intrude a Lucasta as he does into the world of the ant, for the slight shift to the woman completes the opening image of the mounted falcon:

> Free beauteous Slave, thy happy feet
> In silver Fetters vervails meet,
> And trample on that noble Wrist
> The Gods have kneel'd in vain t' have kist:
> But gaze not, bold deceivèd Spye,
> Too much oth' lustre of her Eye;
> The Sun, thou dost out-stare, alas!
> Winks at the glory of her Face.

An additional stanza, favorably contrasting the falcon's captive state with the fabled existence of the phoenix, pursues the extravagant compliment still further; but the falcon is never displaced, for the direction and verve of the first section derive from Lovelace's description of the falcon.

Addressed in the first words of the poem as "Fair Princesse of the spacious Air," the falcon has deigned to make man's acquaintance and

> With us are quarter'd below stairs,
> That can reach Heav'n with nought but Pray'rs;

Who when our activ'st wings we try,
Advance a foot into the Sky.

The inversion, effectively conveyed in the contrast between the beautiful mistress of undefinable realms and her servile captors "quarter'd below stairs," forcefully and paradoxically stresses the gentle falcon's regal and indomitable spirit. While man vainly struggles against his limitations, his captive falcon, the next stanzas vividly reveal, freely mounts the air, shoots "Heav'ns Ark," or swoops "so swift unto our Sence, / As thou wert sent Intelligence." In her power, swiftness, and grace, the falcon is more than a hawking bird; she seems to achieve mythic proportions. Able even to outgaze the sun, she is

> Bright Heir t' th' Bird Imperial,
> From whose avenging penons fall
> Thunder and Lightning twisted Spun;
> Brave Cousin-german to the Sun. . . .

The deliberate contrast between earthbound man and the noble falcon evokes a number of traditional associations which have particular meaning for the poet. Throughout both editions of **Lucasta**, and increasingly in the later, more somber, poems, Lovelace is preoccupied with space. In the various prison poems physical constraint can be endured and "Angels alone that sore above, / Injoy such Liberty" if the mind and spirit remain unbroken. When Lovelace does not turn to the solace of wine, friendship, or honor, a bleak epode like **"To Lucasta. From Prison"** can still offer the sustaining ideals of love and loyalty. After the cause was doomed and Charles was killed, the poems increasingly turn to the self-containment emblematized in the snail; but Lovelace never ceases to idealize the heroic spirit. If **"A Fly caught in a Cobweb"** expresses the disillusionment of a poet who has come to believe the plight of the fly is "Small type of great ones, that do hum, / Within this whole World's narrow Room," yet he is still able to assert:

> Was it not better once to play
> I' th' light of a Majestick Ray?
> Where though too neer and bold, the fire
> Might sindge thy upper down attire,
> And thou ith' storm to loose an Eye,
> A Wing, or a self-trapping Thigh;
> Yet hadst thou faln like him, whose Coil
> Made Fishes in the Sea to broyl.

The falcon, although a captive in a similar world of man, embodies these ideals. A solitary figure whose will cannot be broken, the soaring falcon symbolizes in seventeenth-century literature the idealistic aspirations of the meditative soul and mind. In the context of **"The Falcon"** the bird readily becomes the liberated and undaunted spirit whose courage, independence, and loyalty are a source of inspiration and exhilaration. The boldness and power of her flight, which [Symon Latham, a seventeenth-century writer on falconry,] likens to a "Conqueror in the contry, keeping in awe and subiection the most part of all the Fowle that flie," suggest the heroic values found in the martial realm. Also traditionally a symbol of royal bearing and an emblem of great renown, in her magnificent splendor this bird represents grandeur and nobility. In short, for Lovelace the falcon embodies the intangible ideals that comprise the Cavalier spirit.

But the falcon's close relationship with both the "Bird Imperial" and the sun suggests another possible significance. Whether specifically alluding to the mythological eagle of Jove or just generally to the eagle, Lovelace enhances the falcon's stature and emphasizes her likeness to the eagle. Similarly the suggestion that the falcon is related to the sun and has the extraordinary ability to gaze into its brightness, although not without some basis in Greek mythology, is traditionally reserved only for the eagle. In the seventeenth century, when the falcon was considered a member of the eagle family, Lovelace's allusion would have been readily understood, and no difficulty encountered in accepting the falcon as "heir" to the eagle. Nevertheless the slight alteration of a potential symbol places the falcon in a context imbued with further symbolic ramifications.

The association with the eagle and the sun, even more obvious symbols of royalty than the falcon, inevitably suggests Charles I. Lovelace uses both as symbols of the king in **"To my Worthy Friend Mr. Peter Lilly,"** and they are commonplace in the poetry written about Charles I. Thus the suggestion that the falcon is heir to the bird of lightning and thunder is remarkably similar to George Wither's earlier characterization of "the Most Illustrious King, Charles": "You, Sir, who beare *Ioves* Thunders in your Fist, / And, (shake this *Islands* Empire, when you list)." But among the poems using similar descriptions, the most interesting and significant is "The Parliament of Birds" in John Ogilby's *The Fables of Aesop Paraphras'd in Verse, and adorn'd with Sculpture*. Published in 1651, the fortieth fable in this collection retells the famous debate among the birds. Although Ogilby twice goes out of his way to remind the reader that this parliament takes place in "The Silver Age," it is obvious that the republic of birds created after "Civill War turn'd Kingdoms into States" is a thinly disguised allegory of contemporary English history. In the course of debating the new direction of government now that the eagles and lions have been vanquished, the grave parrot declares,

> Great things for us, Sir, Providence hath done,
> And we have through a world of dangers run,
> The *Eagle,* and the gentle *Falcon* are
> Destroyd or Sequester'd by happy War;
> The *Kitish* Peers, and *Bussard* Lords are flown,
> Who sate with us till we could sit alone.

Used here and later as interchangeable symbols of monarchy, the eagle and the gentle falcon provide Lovelace with an obvious allegorical precedent. When the falcon is linked with the sun, as Lovelace does in **"The Falcon,"** a symbolic reading is more probable, for contemporary poets refer to Charles even more often as the sun. In fact, the few poems published after the execution of the king continually see Charles in terms of the sun, and the sun eclipsed by the dog-star is virtually a poetic cliché.

The difficulty, of course, is determining the extent to which **"The Falcon"** develops this or any other hidden meaning. Since the poem ends in the allegorical realm of the beast fable, the elaborately described battle between the falcon and the heron could contain an allegorical potential similar, for example, to the battle of the birds in

Ogilby's "The Parliament of Birds." In fact Lovelace, re-calling Ogilby's description of the eventual confrontation of the "Eagles and Hauks" with the militant "All Monarch-hating *Storks* and *Cranes,* who march, / Like Sons of thunder, through Heavens Christall Arch," might have consciously fashioned his own version of the internecine struggle for England's future. If this is true, the detailed and technical description of the duel with the heron might represent a particular military campaign or actual event in English history. Unfortunately any extended allegorical reading confronts the same obstacle found in Andrew Marvell's "The Nymph complaining for the death of her Faun": the poem verges on allegory yet is not consistently allegorical. Charles I's death was a momentous event mourned by many, but he did not die in battle, as a strictly allegorical reading of **"The Falcon"** would have to conclude.

The crux of the poetic interpretation then is the poetic mode; here Lovelace's other "bestiary" poems suggest a possible solution. Four other poems in the 1659 edition find political relevance in the world of lesser creatures; two poems describe the snail as a "Wise Emblem of our Politick World," **"A Fly caught in a Cobweb"** is "Small type of great ones," and **"The Ant"** is "large example of wise thrift . . . [that has] become our Law." Since the reader is invited to find analogies to his own situation in each of the poems, allegorical interpretations are not ruled out; but Lovelace is essentially an emblematic poet. Following the common practice of this form of literature, he explores the significance of the emblems as means to a didactic conclusion. The tenuous boundaries between literal or figurative and symbolic or allegorical, which tend at any rate to disintegrate in emblem poetry, are not pressing concerns, for Lovelace's primary intention is to expose the various facets of relevance. In the case of **"The Ant,"** the most allegorical of the four poems, the ant is certainly the stereotyped Puritan, and actual historical events are suggested in such lines as "drive on sacred Festivals, thy Plow; / Tearing high-ways with thy ore charged Wain." But when the whimsical tone changes and the poem warns the ant that "Madam, *Margaret Pie,* / And her fierce Servant, Meagre, Sir *John Daw*" will eat both him and his storehouse, the historical allegory is broken. No counterpart to either the magpie or the daw is intended in the specific events and characters of English history, and at best the poem's conclusion represents both birds as some nebulous force characteristic of man's precarious existence. In blending different levels of allegory, Lovelace transforms an emblem commonly found in the popular seventeenth-century editions of illustrated Aesop's fables into a multifaceted vehicle which describes discontinuously both a political situation and the universal nature of man. This same multiplicity is found in the emblematic nature of **"The Falcon."**

When Lovelace moves from his description of the falcon to the lengthy account of her death, he makes essentially the same shift as he does in **"The Ant."** Margaret Pie and Sir John Daw have no specifically allegorical significance in the fate of the ant, and the heron similarly contains a less localized meaning. In narrating the hunt for the heron, the poem describes an encounter familiar to seven-

teenth-century falconers. The bold falcon closes in on her prey, and the desperate heron is driven to a frantic counterattack:

When now he turns his last to wreak
The palizadoes of his Beak;
The raging foe impatient
Wrack'd with revenge, and fury rent,
Swift as the Thunderbolt he strikes,
Too sure upon the stand of Pikes,
There she his naked breast doth hit
And on the case of Rapiers's split.

But ev'n in her expiring pangs
The *Heron's* pounc'd within her Phangs,
And so above she stoops to rise
A Trophee and a Sacrifice;
Whilst her own Bells in the sad fall
Ring out the double Funerall.

The poetic account is not purely imaginative, for it was popularly believed [as Samuel Wesley wrote in his 1685 work *Maggots*] "The Custom of the Hearn when she sees the Hawk, stooping at her, and no way of escape, is to turn her Long Bill upwards, upon which the Hawk not being able to stop, runs itself through, and so both often drop down dead together." In Lovelace's version this natural occurrence is viewed from a military perspective, but the diction is apparently quite neutral. While the heron is likened to a lancer and a halberdier and the falcon a general, neither these characterizations nor the military imagery in their battle could be construed with absolute certainty as direct allusions to the English civil war; and the military metaphor may be merely an attempt to ennoble the fight between natural enemies. Still the imagery cannot be entirely dismissed, and the narrative seems to contain some further intention, because the battle has an important emblematic dimension.

A famous collection of emblems by Joachim Camerarius published in 1596 reveals that the encounter with the heron, among falconers "the most noblest and stately flight that is," also has a moral connotation. Under the title "EXITVS IN DVBIO EST" Camerarius reproduces the emblem of a falcon attacking a heron. The emblem, which could accompany Lovelace's poem as well, then draws the moral "Sunt dubii eventus incertaque praelia Martis: / Vincitur haud raro, qui prope victor erat." The falcon and the heron are made an explicit emblem of military battle, and the tacitly anticipated defeat of the falcon illustrates the uncertain nature of war. Establishing for the seventeenth century a specific interpretation of the falcon's death struggle, this emblematic association gives greater significance to **"The Falcon"**—a similar emblem described in military terms.

Lovelace's description of the falcon's "lofty fate" is still further complicated because the poet does not maintain a detached objectivity. As the deadly duel unfolds, the heron on the moor is first a "proper Halberdier"; then as he is caught between the advancing spaniels and the circling falcon he is a "hedg'd-in *Heron*," a "wary *Heron*," and finally a "desp'rate *Heron*." The falcon, on the other hand, is the "expert *Falcon*" and the "bold Gen'ral" who never loses the initiative. Even when she misses her first attack she quickly regains control; and at all times the falcon is the active force of magnificent power. Reduced to passivity, the heron can only retreat before this onslaught; when he asserts himself his action is a suicidal last resort:

> Noble he is resolv'd to fall
> His, and his En'mies funerall,
> And (to be rid of her) to dy
> A publick Martyr of the Sky.

The heron, fulfilling his resolution to die nobly, achieves his victory; but the mortally wounded falcon overshadows this triumph. In a final exertion of courageous spirit the falcon seizes her enemy and struggles to raise "A Trophee and a Sacrifice." Refusing to see death as defeat, Lovelace reverses the emblematic tradition and gives the falcon the greater victory. The victory, however, is qualified:

> Ah Victory, unhap'ly wonne!
> Weeping and Red is set the Sun,
> Whilst the whole Field floats in one tear,
> And all the Air doth mourning wear.

More than unrelieved sadness, the total effect of the falcon's death is closer to bittersweet sorrow: the regal bird is triumphant in her death, yet the loss of this noble life remains a disturbing waste. The heron, an opponent of lesser strength and daring, should ordinarily never have killed the magnificent bird; and in the mortal confrontation the falcon's heroic superiority is evident. Yet Lovelace also understands the desperation that leads the heron to his final action. Although the poem never loses its partisanship, this greater perspective further redefines an elegiac grief whose complexity can only be fully grasped with a more precise understanding of the falcon's significance.

The nature of the lament in the poem's specifically allegorical conclusion reinforces the probability that the falcon is actually complexly symbolic. Nature's extraordinary response to the death, a grief-stricken reaction that engulfs the earth, the air, and the sun, would hardly be appropriate if the falcon were an ordinary bird. Similarly the poet's fervent assertion that her "eternal name shall live" as long as men value and aspire to greatness is distressingly hyperbolic unless the falcon is symbolic. Moreover, the mourning birds who grieve for the gentle falcon are all more than coincidentally related. Led by the "various *Herald-Jay*," the hobby, musket, lanner, goshawk, and tercel—all lesser falcons—file by in procession. Together with the poetic swan, Lovelace adds, "Doctor *Robbin*" and "Prelate *Pye*" will also sing the falcon's elegy. "Doctor" and "prelate" are commonly used in the seventeenth century to identify the Anglican clergy; the procession of hawks led by heralds suggests, of course, the court or nobility. By consciously identifying the clerical birds and deliberately linking them with the noble hawks, Lovelace strongly implies that the extreme sorrow is for the loss of something dear to the Royalist cause.

Indeed the falcon may symbolize the cause itself, and the poem may ultimately be about the Cavalier defeat in the English civil war and the passing of an era. The symbolic potential of the falcon, the emblematic and bestiary precedents, and the strong military overtones in the fight between the two adversaries all point to this conclusion. Intending no specific battle but using the struggle between

the falcon and the heron as a kind of symbolic epitome of the entire conflict, Lovelace could be coming to terms with the bitter wisdom implied in the emblem "EXITVS IN DVBIO EST." A Royalist deeply committed to the losing side, he would understandably believe that his Cavalier cause was superior; he might also share the contemporary attitude that the revolutionists were fanatic zealots. This would account for the outcome of the battle and the curious depiction of the heron as "A publick Martyr of the Sky." The poetic rationalization of a defeated Royalist, **"The Falcon"** then further implies that the very nature of the Cavalier spirit contributed to its own defeat. Against an enemy that values above all else the destruction of its foe, gallant courage and heroic pride—like the hurtling falcon's strike—can ironically become fatal virtues. Yet this same spirit, the symbolic poem strikingly asserts, also realizes a paradoxical victory. Like **"A Fly caught in a Cobweb,"** **"The Falcon"** ultimately finds solace in a defeat in which the vanquished "Fall yet triumphant in thy woe."

But in this poem victory does not depend upon the negative consolation that in being destroyed the defeated also destroys; nor does it rely only on the belief that mitigating circumstances led to defeat. In transposing the Cavalier defeat into the world of nature, Lovelace creates a more neutral context analogous to the impersonal and inexorable course of history. This wider and more objective perspective enables the poet to view the two enemies as opposing forces caught up in the larger sweep of events. Because he understands their individual situations, he can see their deaths as a "double Funerall." At the same time this vision, a form of tolerant detachment which implies a mature acceptance of the falcon's death, concomitantly redefines defeat. Refusing to accept the emblematic moral "Vincitur haud raro, qui prope victor erat," the poem unmistakably stresses the falcon's victory. As part of the onrushing course of history, the cause or individual may be unable to change its destiny; yet paradoxically the gallant spirit, as Lovelace repeatedly asserts in his other poetry, "Doth *Starry Influence* dissolve." Appealing to a form of stoic idealism which makes physical defeat secondary, **"The Falcon"** contradicts the emblematic association and finds victory in the manner in which the heroic uncompromisingly meet death. The doomed Royalists, like the falcon struggling to regain her "spacious Air," must inevitably fall; yet in meeting this destined fate they too manifest and ultimately vindicate the essence of the Cavalier spirit.

In providing an idealistic consolation this elegiac resolution also indirectly suggests the personification of the Cavalier spirit, Charles I. Like the falcon, the king proudly and regally defied any attempts to curb his sovereignty; furthermore his spirit and very nature, becoming his own heroic undoing, inevitably led to his death. And in death, as Marvell's famous account reveals, "*He* nothing common did or mean / Upon that memorable Scene." In the 1650's, even without *Eikon Basilike* and the growing reverence for the executed monarch, the correlation between **"The Falcon"** and the king triumphant in death would have been unavoidable.

In any case the poem's symbolic nature, which permitted

Lovelace to circumvent rigid censorship laws prohibiting pro-Royalist sympathies, effectively reinforces the elegiac resolution. The falcon, in Lovelace's interpretation an exemplum of ennobling heroism, is also in emblem literature an illustration of "The virtuous mind, and truely noble spright." Together with the eagle, closely linked in the poem with the falcon, both birds are emblematic illustrations of unconquerable will; and their proud, indomitable spirits commonly inspire seventeenth-century emblem writers to moralize, "Though *Fortune* may, his person grind; / She, cannot harme him, in his *Minde.*" The falcon in death becomes then an even more appropriate and affirmative symbolization of Charles on the scaffold and the Royalists in defeat.

In reconciling himself to great loss, Lovelace achieves in **"The Falcon"** paradoxical forms of "griefe triumphant" and "victorious sorrow." Rejecting the bitter conclusion of **"The Ant"** and the negative satisfaction of **"A Fly caught in a Cobweb,"** he returns to the more positive view found in **"To my Worthy Friend Mr. Peter Lilly."** First published in the 1649 edition of *Lucasta*, this poem praises Lely's ability to draw the minds and not just the outward features of Charles I and his son the Duke of York. In admiring the portrait painted during the troubled period of civil war, Lovelace marvels at the royal composure captured on canvas:

> See!   what a *clouded Majesty!* and eyes
> Whose glory through their mist doth brighter
>   rise!
> See!   what an humble bravery doth shine,
> And griefe triumphant breaking through each
>   line;
> How it commands the face!   so sweet a scorne
> Never did *happy misery* adorne!
> So sacred a contempt!   that others show
> To this, (oth' height of all the wheele) below.

The son, inspired by his father's example, also bears his sadness lightly; and "both doe grieve the same victorious sorrow." Their stoic self-containment, an ideal that Lovelace never ceases to admire, affords them the inner security described in the later emblematic snail poems or the verbose **"Advice to my best Brother. Coll: Francis Lovelace."** However, their inviolable tranquility is more directly and unreservedly praised as a triumph over adversity; there is, for example, none of the limitation found in the almost tedious, Polonius-like advice to his brother that "A breast of proof defies all Shocks of Fate, / Fears in the best, hopes in the worser state." The "breast of proof" exemplified in the king and his son eschews all fear. Refusing to retreat from life, they understand its dangers yet scornfully surmount them with a courage tempered by suffering. This heroism, which Lovelace found in the painting at Hampton Court, was dramatized at Charles's death; again in a poem which elegizes both this event and the loss of the Cavalier cause, the note of victory is unmistakably present.

In commemorating a "Victory, unhap'ly wonne," **"The Falcon"** optimistically reasserts an idealistic vision. Although the price of triumph modulates the enthusiasm into the elegiac strain that dominates the poem's conclusion, a complex blend of admiration and inspiration over-balances the tone of sadness. Throughout the poem, and even in her death, the focus remains on the greatness of the falcon; and this involved significance paradoxically both increases and lessens the emptiness of sorrow. The natural inclination to lament a loss of this dimension is apparent, but the poem does not offset this with an insincere consolation or a forced attempt to stave off demoralization. The ideals symbolized in the falcon will endure, the poem concludes, only as long as they inspire men. And **"The Falcon"** is a tribute to their endurance. Richard Lovelace, whatever dire economic and social misfortunes befell him in the fifties, could still respond to the flight of the falcon. (pp. 404-17)

Raymond A. Anselment," 'Griefe Triumphant' and 'Victorious Sorrow': A Reading of Richard Lovelace's 'The Falcon'," in The Journal of English and Germanic Philology, *Vol. LXX, No. 3, July 1971, pp. 404-17.*

Thomas Clayton   (essay date 1974)

[*Clayton is an American scholar whose works include* The Booke of Thomas Moore: Some Aids to Scholarly and Critical Shakespearean Studies *(1969),* The Non-Dramatic Works of John Suckling *(1971), and* Cavalier Poets *(1978). In the following excerpt, he expresses admiration for Lovelace's original handling of mythological themes in "Cupid Far Gone," characterizing the poem as polymorphously perverse and "a mythopoetical jeu d'esprit."*]

In ["**Cupid Fargone**," Lovelace's] mythopoetical *jeu d'esprit*, Cupid becomes "polymorphous perverse" and runs amuck, ending his un-Senecan ramble in a comically half-demonic and perhaps playfully blasphemous as well as classical-Herculean harrowing of hell—hence the double sense of the title's "Far Gone." The overall "drift" and most of the points are clear enough, but the sense of lines 28-30 is confused, owing either to an authorial slip or to interference with the text by the publishers of *Lucasta.* **Posthume Poems** (William Godbid for Clement Darby, 1659) or by Dudley Posthumus Lovelace, the poet's brother, who arranged for the publication of the book. The trouble is with "Argos," which should certainly be "Argo"; that is, the ship used by the Argonauts in their quest for the Golden Fleece and the counterpart of Charon's ferryboat; and, in another element, the constellation, Argo Navis, which, as the largest of the fifteen constellations south of the ecliptic identified in Ptolemy's *Almagest,* Lovelace would certainly have known about. (Professor Rhodes Dunlap of the University of Iowa called my attention to the constellation in this connection.) So much seems assured by the use of the nautical term, "rigg'd." But the error, which has gone uncorrected in modern editions, is of special interest in suggesting what appears to have been a complex of ideas in genesis and intention, and becomes an analogous complex in effect.

The confusion in the text of *Lucasta. Posthume Poems* is in effect between Argos Panoptes, the herdsman with eyes all over his body who was appointed by Hera as guard over Io; Odysseus' dog, which recognized its master upon his return to Ithaca after twenty years' absence (*Odyssey,*

XXII, 292); the craftsman in the *Argonautica* who built the ship, Argo; Argo, the ship itself; and Argo Navis, the constellation. The close proximity of "Argo(s)" and "Cerberus" suggests a process of association linked by dogs as well as by infernal presences and fittings ("rigg'd" and "leash'd"), and it seems quite possible—though a matter of mere speculation—that resonances of "Argo[s]" suggested "Cerberus" to Lovelace, since neither the three-headed dog itself nor the hunting is by any means inevitable in this poem, although Cerberus complements Charon in keeping in hell what Charon ferries in. That Charon shall have "Argo(s) rigg'd with stars," which involves the promise of celestial translation, almost certainly owes something to the image of Argo the herdsman, through the immemorially traditional association between eyes and stars, as well as to the constellation. Given the vagaries of Renaissance spelling and the commonplace confusion between "Pluto" and "Plutus," for example, it is in fact quite possible that Lovelace *wrote* "Argos," but "Argo" is what he certainly must have "intended."

The prospect of Cerberus' being leashed to Cupid himself and going "a hunting" with him is a stroke of minor but jovial genius. Hades is traditionally associated with horses, but the metamorphosis of Cerberus to a hunting dog is the contribution of Lovelace the poet and country gentleman. It has the pleasantly "erotic" effect of more or less uniting Charon, here to be promoted to golden-fleecing, with Cerberus and Cupid, nether-dog and deity, in the hearty sport of *venery*—a tacit syllepsis of which the frequently punning Lovelace can hardly have been unaware.

Thomas Clayton, "Lovelace's 'Cupid Far Gone'," in The Explicator, *Vol. 33, No. 4, December 1974, Item 32.*

Gerald Hammond　(lecture date 1985)

[*In the following excerpt from a paper read in 1985 before the British Academy, Hammond argues that obscure imagery and symbolism in Lovelace's work is poetically justified, thus challenging the traditional critical view that Lovelace's obscurity is due to a lack of poetic inspiration.*]

I want to give a reconsideration to the life of Richard Lovelace and question the degree to which his poetry has been obscured by the label *cavalier*, used either as a noun or an adjective. I know that subjecting cavalier poetry to the rigours of criticism is sometimes held to be a breach of decorum, at best; but I hold a counter view about the achievements of those poets who wrote in the 1640s and 50s. This is that during the twenty years at the center of the seventeenth century, the novel not yet in existence and the theatres being closed down, any imaginative response to those trans-shifting times was likely to take the form of a lyric poem. Richard Lovelace's life and poetry provide a useful test-case, to tell how limited our responses to these poets have so far been. Any fresh approach must begin with our principal source of knowledge about Lovelace's life, Anthony Wood's biography in his *Athenæ Oxoniensis*.

When Wood came to write his account he seems to have been fascinated by the resplendent figure this poet cut. He repeatedly returns to the image of the glittering cavalier:

> . . . the most amiable and beautiful person that ever eye beheld, a person also of innate modesty, virtue and courtly deportment . . . much admired and adored by the female sex . . . [and then] he became as much admired by the male, as before by the female, sex . . . After he had left the University he retired in great splendor to the Court . . . when he was in his glory he wore Cloth of gold and silver . . . his common discourse was not only significant and witty, but incomparably graceful . . .

All the contemporary evidence bears out Wood's account. The Dulwich Gallery portrait shows us the flowing locks, soulful eyes, sensuous mouth, and shining armour of this Philip Sidney of the 1640s, soldier and poet in one—*tam Marti quam Mercurio* as one of his elegists put it, echoing the motto which that flamboyant figure of a previous generation, Walter Ralegh, had taken as his own. The poems which greeted Lovelace's first volume, *Lucasta*, in 1649, describe a forward youth who had contrived to continue with books and armour; and not surprisingly they add to their warrior poet figure the image of the great lover. This tradition went back at least five years. A poem by John Tatham, written sometime before September 1645, and titled 'Upon my Noble friend, *Richard Lovelace* Esquire . . . ', salutes him with the refrain 'Then lov'd *Adonis* come away, / For *Venus* brooks not thy delay'.

The name, of course, presents a temptation impossible to resist—not only a *love-lace*, some reminder of intimacy worn on the body, but, if we think of Richard the unrequited lover, then Richard *Loveless*; or Richard the requited, *Lovelass*; or the poet warbling his love-lays. Indeed, the name was attractive enough for one of his friends to christen his daughter *Lovelice*; and two of the commendatory poems to *Lucasta* contrive to come to a resounding end on the word love (one of these is Andrew Marvell's). *Lovelace* is the first name to come to mind when we think of Pope's mob of elegant gentlemen or hear the phrase *cavalier poet*, with all its overtones of the amorous and the amateurish.

Lucasta seems designed to consolidate the image. After the congratulations of friends and kinsmen, it opens with two lyrics which are quintessentially cavalier, 'To Lucasta, Going beyond the Seas' and 'To Lucasta, Going to the Warres'. Those who have considered the matter have concluded that *Lucasta*, as a volume, has no reason to the ordering of its poems beyond the very understandable one of putting the most attractive at the front, thereby luring the casual browser into a firm sale. These are the Lovelace poems remembered by every one, his contribution to English poetry, that in an age of great lyricists, he gave us some of the purest lyrics of all—lines whose clarity has fixed them upon our cultural consciousness as definitive renditions of the cavalier experience.

But the third poem in the volume, directly following the two farewells to Lucasta, points towards another Lovelace, a figure of dirt and obscurity, who developed as a poet through his whole life, rather than burning his talent out in the most flashy lyrics of *Lucasta*. Its title is **'A Para-dox'**, and its plot is one familiar to any reader of seven-teenth-century poetry, a defence of inconstancy. Love-lace's defence is not one of the most familiar ones, such as, 'I love others in order to appreciate you all the more'. Rather, he argues that he forsakes 'the beauteous Starre' to which he 'first did bow', despite his knowledge that this star 'Burnt quicker, brighter far / Then that which leads me now', simply because the new one is fouler:

> Through foule, we follow faire
> For had the World one face
> And Earth been bright as Ayre,
> We had knowne neither place.

'Faire' will stay only a memory, while 'foule' is pursued eternally, all in the name of freedom:

> The God that constant keepes
> Unto his Deities,
> Is poore in Joyes, and sleepes
> Imprison'd in the skies:
> This knew the wisest, who
> From *Juno* stole, below
> To love a Beare, or Cow.

The word 'imprisoned' in this stanza is, despite the poem's earliness in the volume, by no means Lovelace's first glance at confinement. He is, after all, even more than Ra-legh or Wilde, our chief prison poet, and **'To Lucasta, Going beyond the Seas'** had already introduced the pros-pect of an 'after-fate' where the two lovers 'Can speake like spirits unconfin'd / In Heav'n'; and **'To Lucasta, Going to the Warres'** had seen Lovelace running from 'the Nun-nerie / Of thy chaste breast, and quiet minde'. The rest of the volume is shot through with images of imprisonment and hiding away, not only in those poems which claim ac-tually to derive from Lovelace's two spells of incarcera-tion, but in poems which probably antedate the civil war, such as **'The Vintage to the Dungeon'**, and poems on quite other topics. When Lovelace looks at a glove [in **"Elinda's Glove"**] he describes it as an '*Ermin* Cabinet', whose only tenants are Ellinda's fingers: any others will find it impos-sible to 'fit / The slender turnings of thy narrow Roome'. And, on another tack [in **'An Elegie. On the Death of Mrs. Cassandra Cotton'**], he observes the burial service of Cas-sandra Cotton as taking place in a dismal chancel with the corpse surrounded by a stifling ring of black-veiled mourners. Even a poem in praise of movement, **'Gratiana dauncing and singing'**, has its central image in the idea of the lover's thoughts and hopes being 'chain'd to her brave feet'. Best known is **'The Grasse-hopper'**, which opposes to that insect's thoughtless openness to the entire joys of earth and heaven the image of Richard Lovelace and Charles Cotton confined to one house in the middle of dark December, finding consolation in wine, poetry, and their blazing hearth.

We have come to see this last form of confinement as the cavalier winter, so well described by Earl Miner [in *The Cavalier Mode from Jonson to Cotton* (1971)], as the peri-od of waiting out the horror of the external world turned upside down, with a trusted friend and the salvageable consolations of civic culture in a rural retreat: a retreat into obscurity made necessary not only by the understand-

able desire to save oneself by keeping as low a profile as possible, but also by a refusal to be contaminated by the values of the Commonwealth. And we no longer think, as C. V. Wedgwood wrote about the cavalier poets in 1946 [in *Velvet Studies*], that while 'their experience of life was vivid, harsh and dangerous, anxious and despairing . . . hardly a breath of it reaches their verse', for we have now come to see that in many of those apparently mindless, or at least thoughtless, lyrics of the 1640s the political and cultural anxieties are only thinly disguised. But we need also to recognize that they are less simply defined than the division of England into cavalier and puritan would lead us to believe. Lovelace, our quintessential cavalier, is a good example of a man for whom the external pressures, powerful as they were, seem only to have reinforced strong interior needs for self-concealment.

Chief among the pressures were the two periods of impris-onment he endured in the 1640s. (pp. 203-06)

The eleventh edition of the *Encyclopedia Britannica* sum-marized his achievement like this:

> The world has done no injustice to Lovelace in neglecting all but a few of his modest offerings to literature. But critics often do him injustice in dismissing him as a gay cavalier, who dashed off his verses hastily and cared little what became of them. It is a mistake to class him with Suck-ling: he has neither Suckling's easy grace nor his reckless spontaneity . . . In many places it takes time to decipher his meaning. The expression is often elliptical, the syntax inverted and tortuous, the train of thought intricate and discontinuous.

And the writer goes on to explain that these faults are 'not the first thoughts of an improvisatore, but thoughts ten or twenty stages removed from the first'. This represented an improvement in critical response to Lovelace. Previously the general complaint had been that in all but the few faultless lyrics, Lovelace's poetry was slapdash and there-fore obscure. Now it was claimed that the obscurity was a consequence of trying to say too much. We have prog-ressed very little beyond this. (pp. 207-08)

[The general belief among modern critics seems to be] that, the few priceless lyrics apart, Lovelace's poetry is un-interesting, amateurish, and above all obscure, either through his having taken too little or too much care with it. And even friendly critics have found it useful to pre-serve this view. Randolph Wadsworth begins his essay on **'The Snayl'** with the bald sentence ' "The Snayl" by Rich-ard Lovelace is obscure in both image and theme'; and after many pages of careful explication, he closes with the faint praise that 'to dismiss the piece out of hand is unfair to Lovelace, however deficient his limited intention ap-pears to rigorous modern criticism'. It is strange to com-pare . . . modern complaints at Lovelace's obscurity with his contemporaries' broad and generous praise—unexpectedly generous, for it came from both sides, from men like John Hall and Andrew Marvell, and, a little later, from Milton's nephew Edward Phillips, whose as-sessment of Lovelace as a potential epic poet might very possibly reflect his uncle's favourable opinion.

. . . . .

Really, there are fewer obscurities in Lovelace's verse than the modern criticism implies, and where they occur they repay consideration rather than automatic dismissal, for they show places where Lovelace has put his poetry under great personal and cultural pressure. A case in point is the opening of his poem addressed to his brother Francis, who was, as the title has it, 'immoderately mourning my Brothers untimely death at *Carmarthen*'. The poem is a translation of one of the great lyrics of the period, Casimir Sarbiewski's Latin ode against tears. Sarbiewski opens by saying that if tears were an adequate means of mourning, then he would buy them with his richest jewels. Here is how one seventeenth-century English poet rendered the first four lines of Sarbiewski's poem:

> If mournfull eyes could but prevent
> The evils they so much lament
> Sidonian Pearles, or Gems more rare,
> Would be too cheap for ev'ry teare.

And here is another version of the lines, this time by Henry Vaughan:

> If *Weeping Eyes* could wash away
> Those *Evills* they mourn for *night and day*,
> Then gladly I to *cure* my *fears*
> With my best *Jewells* would buy *tears*.

Lovelace, in contrast, compresses the four lines into two, and while he keeps the image of buying tears with jewels, he does something which radically obscures it:

> If teares could wash the Ill away,
> A Pearle for each wet bead I'd pay.

Tear . . . pearl . . . bead, because they all mean the same thing, muddy what should be the clear distance between tenor and vehicle. Whatever way you read it, the image becomes self-defeating. Either one pays jewels for jewels, or tears for tears, or there is no difference between jewels and tears. This is deliberate and powerful. A poem which opposes immoderate mourning for one's younger brother dead in the civil war must, equally, say that any mourning, no matter how immoderate, is insufficient. As the poem goes on to say, 'I'ron decrees of Destinie / Are ner'e wipe't out with a wet Eye'. But what does wipe them out? An act of will perhaps—'One gallant thorough-made Resolve'—for in another poem Lovelace raises the possibility of wiping out iron:

> Stone Walls doe not a Prison make,
>   Nor I'ron bars a Cage;
> Mindes innocent and quiet take
>   That for an Hermitage.

The word *that*, used there indeterminately to refer back to stone walls, prison, iron bars, and cage, might well be taken by the kind of criticism I have quoted from as another example of Lovelace's sloppiness, had not William Empson shown how craftily it obscures the apparent clarity of the first two lines of the stanza: '*that* is the *cage* or *prison* itself, and by being singular, so that it will not apply to *walls* or *bars*, it admits that they do, in fact, make even for quiet minds a *prison* and a *cage*'. Often the obscurity of Lovelace's metaphors derives from his perception that there are no distinctions between things; that everything is, essentially, the same as everything else.

Formally, Lovelace's obscurity is a part of his apparent facility, the verse being so lyrical that syntactic and metaphorical imprecisions are masked. Take the opening stanza of '**To Lucasta. From Prison**'. It sounds simple, but stop to think about it and there is a puzzle:

> Long in thy Shackels, liberty,
> I ask not from these walls, but thee;
> Left for a while anothers Bride
> To fancy all the world beside.

Lovelace's editor, Colonel Wilkinson, recognized the reader's problem here, and unusually for this generally unhelpful edition, provided a paraphrase:

> The meaning is 'I do not ask liberty from my prison but of thee, Lucasta, whose prisoner I have long been, in order that leaving thee for awhile I may be able to turn my fancy to anything else.

Lovelace has packed together his actual physical constraint in prison, his being shackled to Lucasta, his wish for freedom from her, but his need to stay within the prison walls: outside them he will think only of her and ignore the world; inside the prison he sees the possibility of thinking about the outside world rather than her. This is all crammed into twenty-five words—hence the knottiness—but it introduces a poem whose progress from this point is carefully languid, as Lovelace ranges before his fancy all the new possible objects of his love, searching for something to which he can 'confine' his 'free Soule'. Having cast off Lucasta, he ranges through virtually all the institutions which go to make up the mid-seventeenth-century experience—peace, war, religion, Parliament, liberty, property, a Reformation, and the Public Faith. All, like Lucasta, are found wanting, not because they possess him too much, as she does, but because they have either chosen to reject him or have failed to satisfy him. He ends with only one possible confinement left—the king, 'th'only spring / Of all our loves and joyes'—but the stability of even this image is threatened as Lovelace sees the clouds obscuring the divine light of majesty:

> He who being the whole Ball
>   Of Day on Earth, lends it to all;
> When seeking to ecclipse his right,
>   Blinded, we stand in our owne light.
>
> And now an universall mist
>   Of Error is spread or'e each breast,
> With such a fury edg'd, as is
>   Not found in th' inwards of th' Abysse.
>
> Oh from thy glorious Starry Waine
>   Dispense on me one sacred Beame
> To light me where I soone may see
>   How to serve you, and you trust me.

The images are Marvellian. . . . Not the least value of a more serious estimation of Lovelace's poetry is that it will throw more light on Marvell, for we have not sufficiently realized that for Marvell Lovelace was the most influential of contemporary poets. This is not only a matter of words and images, but of the way Lovelace approaches his subjects too. It is characteristic of him to make his way to the king through a devious route which begins with Lucasta and then traverses everything else of importance in the country. A consequence is that the import of the final stanza . . . is hard to determine.

In Marvell's poetry we would be tempted to call this kind of approach to the subject oblique or indirect, but in Lovelace's case obscure seems the more fitting word, not sneeringly, but because of its connotations of darkness and hiding away. At the point of greatest clarity **'To Lucasta. From Prison'** refuses to deliver its expected cavalier sentiment. Now, for a cavalier, Lovelace is unusually reticent. There is nothing in his corpus which proclaims the openly Royalist sympathies found in such works and poems as Stanley's *Psalterium Carolinum*, Herrick's 'To the King Upon his Welcome to Hampton-Court', Vaughan's 'The Proffer', Cowley's *The Civil War*, Cartwright's 'November', Suckling's 'On New Year's Day 1640: to the King' or Cleveland's 'Upon the King's Return from Scotland'. The absence of such explicit praise for Charles has led us to read it as implicit in a number of poems. For example, it has become taken for granted that the 'Golden Eares' which are cropped by the sickle in 'The Grasse-hopper' signify the execution of Charles I. The best-known critical discussion of the poem opens with the assertion that the poem was written 'sometime after the collapse of the royal cause and the execution of King Charles'. This may be so, but it needs to be explained just how the poem came to be inserted into a volume which was ready for the press many months before Charles's execution. The ears, I am sure, are Charles's, but Lovelace is actually making a grim and bitter joke against him, for *crop-eared* was a common term of contempt in the 1640s for the puritans. This has some bearing, too, upon **'To Lucasta. From Prison'**. It still seems to be the common belief that this poem's dating should be during the time of Lovelace's second imprisonment. [Hugh Maclean, editor of *Ben Jonson and the Cavalier Poets* (1974),] notes that 'this poem was presumably composed while Lovelace was confined in Peterhouse Prison, from June, 1648, until April, 1649'. But a good few years ago H. M. Margoliouth threw severe doubt upon that dating. He chose to do so in a review, rather than an article, so it has been generally unnoticed, but its logic seems persuasive to me. For a start, just as with **'The Grasse-hopper'**, how do we explain the 'addition of new matter to books after they had been licensed . . . there must be a prima facie assumption against any poem being later than the date of licensing'. To this negative point Margoliouth added the positive one that, in essence, this poem is a restatement of the Kentish petition, for the delivering of which Lovelace suffered his first imprisonment; and he offers the clinching point that the *Public Faith*, made much of in stanza ten, was 'pledged by Parliament on June 10th 1642, when Lovelace was still in prison'.

Those who sustain the image of the cavalier Lovelace will find it comforting to date the poem some six or seven years after the petition, to show the unwavering constancy of the man. I want to propose a different Lovelace: a man who developed politically from an instinctive cavalier into one who shares with Andrew Marvell the claim to be the great poet of the most wide-ranging political belief of the 1640s and early 1650s. If we accept Margoliouth's early date for **'To Lucasta. From Prison'**, then we can see, in its final stanzas, the beginnings of Lovelace's movement towards what Ronald Hutton, in his [*The Royalist War Effort 1642-1646* (1982)], has called 'militant neutralism'.

In those stanzas Lovelace sees that 'an universall mist / Of Error is spread or'e each breast'. The inclusiveness is important. The condition of the country spreads to all, from Parliament and the Public Faith right down to the imprisoned poet. Prison begins the poem as more a metaphor than a reality: the literal *these walls* being dwarfed by the figurative *shackles* in which Lucasta has confined him. But at the poem's end we are in the real darkness of a prison—a double obscurity, for the prisoner who has no light to see by, and for others who can not see him and do not know of him. In the poem's strange final lines Lovelace calls for one sacred beam 'To light me where I soone may see / How to serve you, and you trust me'. One might reply that to have suffered incarceration for the courageous act of presenting a loyal petition ought to have been sufficient for the poet to be sure of the king's trust. . . . I suspect that the doubt conveyed here signals the beginnings of Lovelace's abandonment of the king. To understand why, we need to consider the humiliating experience of the Kentish petition: the climacteric moment of Lovelace's life, when he realized the futility not merely of the grand gesture, but of the whole Royal Cause. (pp. 209-16)

By appreciating Lovelace's growing neutralism, we can begin to see how passionately analytical is his perception of the country's condition. **'The Grasse-hopper'** is only a Royalist poem if one approaches it with cavalier assumptions—which, of course, a number of Lovelace's readers had. But others would have been attuned to the irony of Charles's cropped ears—history's retribution for the barbarities inflicted upon Prynne perhaps—and to the criticism in the final stanza of a king who, although he had everything, could not rest untempted. 'Lord of all what Seas imbrace' might well recall Ship money: it certainly comes uncomfortably close to the name of the great ship launched just before the civil war, which Charles took so much pride in, because its title was so apposite to his position, the *Sovereign of the Seas*. Likewise, **'The Snayl'** analyses Charles, but not from [a] committed Royalist position. . . . It opens with the sun, and closes with the hermit, a satiric evocation of a career which moved from courtly luxury to the austerity of salads. Its companion poem, **'Another'** on the snail, aims at his son, in permanent exile on the continent, whose self-absorption denies him the wit to appreciate that his country can exist without him:

> Yet the Authentick do beleeve,
> Who keep their Judgement in their Sleeve,
> That he is his own Double man,
> And sick, still carries his Sedan:
> Or that like Dames i' th' Land of Luyck,
> He wears his everlasting Huyck:
> But banisht, I admire his fate
> Since neither Ostracisme of State,
> Nor a perpetual exile,
> Can force this Virtue change his Soyl;
> For wheresoever he doth go,
> He wanders with his Country too.

The poem which shows how shrewdly Lovelace analyzed the movement of men's minds in the 1640s is one which initially promises to be his most explicitly Royalist piece. Its title is '**To my Worthy Friend Mr** *Peter Lilly*: **on that excellent Picture of his Majesty, and the Duke of Yorke, drawne by him at** *Hampton-Court*'. Lely's portrait belongs to the period when Charles was held at Hampton Court, and it depicts one of the occasional visits which his son was allowed to pay him. The first half of the poem seems uncannily prophetic of the *Eikon Basilike*, as it develops a series of rapturous paradoxes very much in the manner of a Counter Reformation poet praising a martyr. Its opening image of a clouded majesty recalls the closing image of '**To Lucasta. From Prison**':

> See!   what a *clouded Majesty*!   and eyes
> Whose glory through their mist doth brighter
>   rise!
> See!   what an humble bravery doth shine,
> And griefe triumphant breaking through each
>   line;
> How it commands the face!   so sweet a scorne
> Never did *happy misery* adorne!
> So sacred a contempt!   that others show
> To this, (oth' height of all the wheele) below;
> That mightiest Monarchs by this shaded booke
> May coppy out their proudest, richest looke.
>
> Whilst the true *Eaglet* this quick luster spies,
> And by his *Sun*'s enlightens his owne eyes;
> He cares his cares, his burthen feeles, then
>   streight
> Joyes that so lightly he can beare such weight;
> Whilst either eithers passion doth borrow,
> And both doe grieve the same victorious sorrow.

The picture has come to be known as 'Clouded Majesty' after Lovelace's poem, and it fits its apparent purpose well. Majesty can be obscured, but it uses such obscurity to emerge all the greater—whether those clouds and mists be the confinements which it is subjected to or the tears through which it must look (tears, of course, for its suffering people). Eyes are the key to the poem, and Lovelace looks carefully at the eyes of both sitters, seeing the younger take lustre from his father's eyes. At this point in the poem we see the triumphant image of a pair of royal eagles, so that the clouds and mists which began the poem now turn out only to have been those which hide the mountain top from our eyes, but through which the eagle himself can see clearly. The obscurity is ours, not his. All this is reinforced by a Crashaw-like series of baroque paradoxes, of which *clouded majesty* is the first, followed by *humble bravery, grief triumphant, happy misery,* and *sacred contempt.*

Structurally this poem is very like '**The Grasse-hopper**'. Both take up their first half in describing an image of the king. Then, exactly half-way through, they turn in direct address to a friend, a manœuvre which asks us to revise our allegiances. These are the next four lines of the Lely poem:

> These my best *Lilly* with so bold a spirit
> And soft a grace, as if thou didst inherit
> For that time all their greatnesse, and didst draw
> With those brave eyes your *Royall Sitters* saw.

Here the syntax is doubly elliptical, the kind of thing which those who want Lovelace to be merely a cavalier dilettante might label slipshod. But these are revealing obscurities because here the Royalist vision comes under pressure as our scrutiny turns from the *basileus* to the *ikon*. For a start, the sentence turns out to be no sentence at all, 'These my best *Lilly*' being neither the subject nor object of a verb. Then there is the compression of 'those brave eyes your *Royall Sitters* saw'. I guess that the principal sense requires us to insert something like *through which* between *brave eyes* and *your Royal sitters*, reinforcing the idea that Lely, during the time he painted this picture, put on much of his subjects' greatness. But this is, itself, a shrewd appreciation of the whole curious phenomenon of having such a picture painted at such a time. The one thing we know about Charles's strategy in the last years of his life is that his overriding concern was to preserve the image of majesty which he embodied: he carried it through his trial, right down to the two shirts he wore at his execution. He became, as this poem puts it, a pattern for princes to 'coppy out their proudest, richest looke'.

This is how Lely's sitters intended to be seen and, were they artists, how they would have portrayed themselves. That Lely should see through their eyes is Lovelace's recognition of the total work of art which Charles's life had become. But Lovelace, it turns out, is more interested in Lely's art than in Charles's suffering, and a more straightforward interpretation of that piece of syntax makes the eyes Lely's, not Charles's, requiring only *which* to be inserted between *brave eyes* and *your Royal sitters*. In her 1983 Chatterton lecture Elizabeth Cook showed what protean words *brave* and *bravery* were in the Renaissance, ranging in meaning and connotation from a virtually meaningless cliché of admiration to a specific artistic sense of 'crafty, well made, technically fine'. Something like that transference of meaning happens here as the bravery shifts from the royal couple's eyes to the artist's. As those sitters came under Lely's scrutiny they saw how bravely he saw them—artists are eagles as much as monarchs are, because of the keenness of their sight, and also because they can so fearlessly look on suffering monarchs.

We might now see how, through all the apparent excesses of the first half of the poem, Lovelace's eyes are actually fixed on the artistic process through which the suffering monarch has been portrayed. *Clouded majesty* is literally true, for the whole right half of the double portrait is dominated by its backcloth of thick, dark clouds, behind the Duke of York's head, mirroring his taller father's expression on the left half. The ecstasy of suffering in *grief triumphant* is tempered by the phrase *breaking through each line*, for *line*, like other words in the first half of the poem—*show, shaded, copy out, lustre, borrow*—carries a technical, artistic sense too. The lines on Charles's face are the lines of art, no less than Cromwell's warts would prove to be. *How it commands the face!*—grief, of course, but the grief the artist has, to take a word from later in the poem, *designed*. This is, after all, a very technically absorbed poem, and it should not surprise us that its use of the word *sitter*, in the sense of one who sits for a portrait, is the first recorded in English. The remainder of the poem concentrates on the details of the craft:

> Not as of old, when a rough hand did speake
> A strong Aspect, and a faire face, a weake;

When only a black beard cried *Villaine*, and
By *Hieroglyphicks* we could understand;
When *Chrystall* typified in a white spot,
And the bright *Ruby* was but one red blot;
Thou dost the things *Orientally* the same,
Not only paintst its colour, but its *Flame*:
Thou sorrow canst designe without a teare,
And with the Man his very *Hope* or *Feare*;
So that th' amazed world shall henceforth finde
None but my *Lilly* ever drew a *Minde*.

There are implications here, I suspect, that the days of such ikons as Charles and his son are numbered; but, in any case, the striking thing is how, by the end of the poem, the intensity of their suffering has given way to a panegyric on the power of the new realism in art, in which Charles is diminished to the shadows of *the man* and *a mind*. The artist himself is not affected by what he is supposed to see: 'Thou sorrow canst designe without a teare' refers principally to Lely's ability to penetrate the stoical appearance of his royal sitters, but it also describes the artist's necessary detachment, that he paints their sorrow without himself feeling it.

One of Lely's critics [R. M. Beckett], defending him against the charge that he was a turncoat who first painted for one side and then the other . . . writes [in his *Lely* (1951)] that 'as a professional painter from abroad, Lely was a neutral observer of the domestic struggle . . . his only personal interest would be in the possible extension of patronage which a return of the court might bring'. Lovelace had no qualms about Lely's shift of allegiance. In the 1650s he wrote a second poem addressed to him, in which the praise and fellow feeling of the first Lely poem is no exception. It reflects a response which Lovelace frequently makes to the characters and events of the civil war. In **'The Falcon'**, a poem which allegorizes the war into a beast fable, the battle in which both sides kill each other he beholds 'with mingled pleasure and affright'. This is the heart of his vision of Lely's painting. What he admires in Lely he desires for himself, because it should be obvious that everything I have said about the technique of the painter refers to the technique of the poet too—right down to the same vocabulary of *line, shaded book, copy out*, and *design*—that is, a perspective which can give him the detached realism of the Dutch artists he so admired. But he could not share Lely's obvious claim to be neutral, for he was irreparably tainted by his association with the Royalist cause. After the second imprisonment the camera obscura needed to be one which he actually inhabited.

. . . . .

I want to extend the interest in design and composition which the Lely poem shows to the whole of ***Lucasta***. I do not subscribe to the view that it is a miscellany, with no principle to its ordering of poems other than putting the best first. Without attempting to justify the placing of every poem in it, let me at least compare the way the volume opens and closes. It opens with **'To Lucasta, Going beyond the Seas'** and **'To Lucasta, Going to the Warres'**. The sentiments are cavalier, but the situation is not so easily described. If we take these poems as being addressed to an audience in the year the volume appeared, the situation matches the sentiment. The truest cavalier response to total defeat was to carry on the fight from the Continent. But if these poems are meant to recall, as they surely do for most readers, the opening of the civil war and the early 1640s, then they come closer to a confession than a boast. For whatever complex reason, while a civil war was being waged in England, involving all his family and many of his friends, Lovelace had fought in a side-show in France—a strange honour to have embraced in preference to the nunnery of Lucasta's chaste breast. The next poem . . . is **'A Paradox'**, where he describes his destiny as the pursuit of foulness.

Lucasta, I have no doubt, was a real enough person, but she stands for much more. She embodies not only the female identity which Lovelace must abandon, in order to embrace the mistress of war, but the whole country of England too—in a later poem he describes her as 'that bright Northerne star'. At a time when the forward youth must appear in armour, Lovelace proposes that to fight honourably now can only be done beyond the seas. The two poems repeat themselves, both abandoning the various identities of Lucasta. I say various, because the third element in her complex identity is the one which Marvell's youth also has to abandon, that is the muse. More than anything else, she is the image of Lovelace's art.

The final poems in the volume are also concerned with Lucasta (incidentally, only fourteen of the poems in the volume are either addressed to her or feature her as a character). One is the last poem of the volume proper, called, significantly, **'Calling Lucasta from her Retirement'**; the other is Lovelace's most ambitious poem, the long pastoral added to the end of the volume, and separately advertised on the title-page, **'Aramantha'**.

'Calling Lucasta from her Retirement' is the climax to a series of poems which gradually proclaim female ascendancy. Its immediate predecessor, **'A Lady with a Falcon on her fist'** ends with complete male submission to the lady and her female bird of prey. Then a volume which began by wishing farewell to Lucasta, and virtually consigning her to a nunnery, ends by welcoming her—and what we now see is a Lucasta profoundly changed. At the volume's opening she was all passivity; now she has a total transforming influence:

Arise and climbe our whitest highest Hill,
There your sad thoughts with joy and wonder
fill,
And see Seas calme as Earth, Earth as your Will.

In contrast to those opening poems, this is a poem of peace—or, at least, a poem which asserts the resolve to live in peace. It ends like this:

Awake from the dead Vault in which you dwell,
All's Loyall here, except your thoughts rebell,
Which so let loose, often their Gen'rall quell.

See! She obeys! by all obeyed thus;
No storms, heats, Colds, no soules contentious,
Nor Civill War is found—I meane, to us.

Lovers and Angels, though in Heav'n they show
And see the Woes and Discords here below,
What they not feele, must not be said to know.

It is a resolve to live obscurely too, for to live like a lover or angel is to remove yourself from the common experience: in the words of that final stanza, to show and see, but not to feel (rather like Lely painting Charles, or Lovelace observing Lely's portrait). The implications of this idea are worked out in the long pastoral poem added at the end of the volume, '**Aramantha**'.

In this poem Lovelace, having encountered the rural nymph Aramantha, is lectured by her on the self-defeating behaviour which he, like all other men, has exhibited:

> Fond man thus to a precipice
> Aspires, till at the top his eyes
> Have lost the safety of the plain,
> Then begs of Fate the vales againe.

Perplexed by this charge that to his own precipice he goes, he tells her that she is cruel, and that Lucasta would have consoled him for the sorrow he feels, rather than have offered him criticism. Aramantha replies with a taunt that between Lucasta and her are no odds, apart from Lucasta's prouder livery. Stung by this, he makes to kill her: and at this point of male violence imposed upon the innocent countryside, the poem turns to the imagery of civil war. This is the moment when eyes are opened and obscurities stripped away:

> Now as in warre intestine, where
> Ith' mist of a black Battell, each
> Layes at his next, then makes a breach
> Through th' entrayles of another whom
> He sees nor knows when he did come
> Guided alone by Rage and th' Drumme,
> But stripping and impatient wild,
> He finds too soon his onely child.
> So our expiring desp'rate Lover
> Far'd, when amaz'd he did discover
> *Lucasta* in this Nymph, his sinne
> Darts the accursed Javelin
> 'Gainst his own breast, which she puts by
> With a soft Lip and gentle Eye . . .

Aramantha is Lucasta. This carefully wrought personal allegory still has more than sixty lines to run as Lovelace explores his own reconciliation with those elements of himself which Lucasta represents. These lines are explicitly political too, for in her narrative of how she came to be where she is, Lucasta tells him how she was hounded by *Hydraphil* and *Philanact*. *Hydraphil* is, as commentators have pointed out, the lover of the many-headed multitude, i.e. Parliament. *Philanact* seems to have foxed them, but its derivation is fairly obvious; from the Homeric αναξ, ανακτοδ, it signifies the *lover of the prince*, the Royalist cause. These two, she says,

> . . . whilst they for the same things fight,
> As BARDS Decrees, and DRUIDS rite,
> For safeguards of their proper joyes,
> And Shepheardes freedome, each destroyes
> The glory of this Sicilie;
> Since seeking thus the remedie,
> They fancy (building on false ground)
> The means must them and it confound,
> Yet are resolv'd to stand or fall,
> And win a little or lose all.
> From this sad storm of fire and blood

> She fled to this yet living Wood;
> Where she 'mongst savage beasts doth find
> Her self more safe then humane kind.

Lovelace's response is to hang his own arms up, break his sword, fold his ensigns, and betake him to the shepherd's life with Lucasta.

'**Aramantha**' is an ideal, pastoral summation of Lovelace's neutrality. But how to live it in reality? This is the topic of most of the best poems in Lovelace's second volume, ***Lucasta: Posthume Poems***, and our reading of them gains much when we set them in the context of the life which he lived in the 1650s, until his death in 1657. (pp. 218-27)

Where *Lucasta* had traced Lovelace's experiences through the 1640s, the ***Posthume Poems*** volume explores those obscure and dirty places which he inhabited in the 1650s. Its first two poems reintroduce the complex figure of Lucasta, whose 'Reserved looks' in the first poem convey the 'sad indifference' of the national and poetic muse which 'both kills, and doth reprieve'; and who, in the second, '**Lucasta laughing**', 'laughs again / at our ridiculous pain; / And at our merry misery / She laughs until she cry'. In this volume Lovelace repeatedly looks through glittering outsides to the self-absorptions which they hide:

> Strive not, vain Lover, to be fine,
> Thy silk's the Silk-worms, and not thine.

'**Love made in the first Age**' parodies all Edenic visions, to show their ultimately crude origins. The target is both the rural idyll of the cavalier retreat and the primitivism of sects like the Adamites and Levellers. All are exposed as solipsistic, ultimately masturbatory. Female masturbation is the object of '**Her Muffe**': only hinted at in the Ostrich fan poem in *Lucasta*, here it makes a wider satirical point—that when we see the fine lady with her hands in her muff, what we see are hands in the hidden muff. The curious snail, that '**Deep Riddle of Mysterious State**', is also sexually self-sufficient: 'That big still with thy self dost go, / And liv'st an aged Embrio'. If sexual self-absorption is one necessary ingredient of obscurity, the other is dirt. . . . In '**Lucasta at the Bath**' sex and dirt are combined, Lovelace's chaste heroine sharing the waters with bathers covered with venereal suppurations. The poem is an interestingly soiled companion piece to '**Lucasta, taking the waters at Tunbridge**' in the first volume—but then I think that in many of this volume's poems Lovelace is rewriting his earlier verse. The change is the one signalled in the closing lines of '**Her Muffe**':

> But I, in my Invention tough,
> Rate not this outward bliss enough,
> But still contemplate must the hidden Muffe.

In '**A Loose Saraband**' his tough invention matches the cheapness of his whore to the sordid state of the whole nation:

> Love never was Well-willer
> Unto my Nag or mee,
> Ne'r watter'd us ith' Cellar,
> But the cheap Buttery:
> At th' head of his own Barrells,
> Where broach'd are all his Quarrels,
> Should a true noble Master

Still make his Guest his Taster.

See all the World how't staggers,
    More ugly drunk then we,
As if far gone in daggers,
    And blood it seem'd to be.

Dirt is the condition of man's public honours as well as his private enjoyments. **'A Mock Charon'** has the devils in hell welcoming an English statesman with trepidation because they sense his power to infect them:

Welcome to Rape, to Theft, to Perjury,
    To all the ills thou wert, we cannot hope to be;
Oh pitty us condemn'd!   Oh cease to wooe,
    And softly, softly breath, least you infect us too.

This volume's insect poems also explore obscure, dirty places. **'A Fly caught in a Cobweb'** opens by making its political allegory explicit:

Small type of great ones, that do hum,
    Within this whole World's narrow Room . . .

At the heart of the poem, worked out in careful detail, is the process by which the fly is digested by the spider and then transformed into the material from which the web is made to catch his own children: an image not without strong political overtones for supporters of the royal cause. Even dirtier are the mock-heroics of **'The Toad and Spyder'**. Lovelace had already treated the futility of warfare in the mutual destruction of the falcon and the heron in the poem called **'The Falcon'**; but that poem left some room for heroism. This one only piles filth on filth, as when the spider feeds on the toad's 'blew-checquer'd' Scull':

And Vomiting her *Stygian* Seeds,
    Her poyson, on his poyson, feeds

or when the toad, having the spider at her mercy,

fainting, sick and yellow, pale,
    She baths him with her sulph'rous Stale.

The cavalier response to defeat and Charles's execution was often to retreat into cynicism, nostalgia, regret, heroic idealism, or religious truth. There is little of any of this in Lovelace—he was the one poet of the interregnum who did not try his hand at a religious poem. Instead he developed a form of satire rooted not in the accepted moral consensus, for he saw none he could share, but in the special form of his own obscurity. This was not the pseudo-obscurity of a cavalier retirement into a country retreat, or the Continent, but the genuine obscurity of one hidden away in the dirtiest corner of London, from where he could look out at the new England of the 1650s. The recurrent idea behind these *Posthume Poems* is that out of his own degradation comes the sense that he is, more than anything else, a poet. Hunger, want, and dirt sharpen the vocation: peace, contentment, and ease merely dull it. Something like this is the tenor of **'Advice to my best Brother. Coll: Francis Lovelace'**, which begins as if it were to recommend, in the convention of all the other cavalier poems of this type, the advantages of a rural retreat; but which confounds the whole genre by suddenly dissolving its image of peace and security into the horrified knowledge that man has no control over his state:

Yet settle here your rest, and take your state,
And in calm *Halcyon's* nest ev'n build your Fate;
Prethee lye down securely, *Frank*, and keep
With as much no noyse the inconstant Deep
As its Inhabitants; nay stedfast stand,
As if discover'd were a New-found-land
Fit for Plantation here; dream, dream still,
Lull'd in *Dione's* cradle, dream, untill
Horrour awake your sense, and you now find
Your self a bubled pastime for the Wind,
And in loose *Thetis* blankets torn and tost;
Frank to undo thy self why art at cost?

But Lovelace's response to the horror was to control it through poetry. The poem which shows how far he had travelled from the bright amateur of Charles I's court is one of the lightest in the volume. In **'To a Lady with child that ask'd an Old Shirt'** he uses the custom of sending linen to ladies about to give birth to make the connection between his poverty—I guess he only has the one shirt—and the kind of poetry he now writes:

And why an honour'd ragged Shirt, that shows,
Like tatter'd Ensigns, all its Bodies blows?
Should it be swathed in a vest so dire,
It were enough to set the Child on fire;
Dishevell'd Queens should strip them of their
    hair,
And in it mantle the new rising Heir:
Nor do I know ought worth to wrap it in,
Except my parchment upper-coat of Skin:
And then expect no end of its chast Tears,
That first was rowl'd in Down, now Furs of
    Bears.
    But since to Ladies 't hath a Custome been
Linnen to send, that travail and lye in;
To the nine Sempstresses, my former friends,
I su'd, but they had nought but shreds and ends.
At last, the jolli'st of the three times three,
Rent th' apron from her smock, and gave it me,
'Twas soft and gentle, subt'ly spun no doubt;
Pardon my boldness, Madam; *Here's the clout.*

It is striking to see how easily and lightly Lovelace can manage so personal a poem, one which celebrates his neglect, obscurity, and degradation. Out of these elements has come a new language for poetry—*Here's the clout,* which might well stand as the motto for the final poem in the volume, **'On *Sanazar's* being honoured with six hundred Duckets by the *Clarissimi of Venice*, for composing an *Eligiack Hexastick of* The City. A Satyre'**. Its position makes it analogous to the pastoral **'Aramantha'** in the first volume, and it, too, is a taking stock of what has gone before; but now the passive ideal of living in quiet cultivation of the rural muse has given way to a vision of an embattled poet looking out from Grub Street at the city around him. Unlike Sannazar's poem, this is no elegiac treatment of urban life. The poet here is forced to beg for wine in December—an ironic echo of **'The Grasse-hopper'** this—and has for his normal daily fare a fortified toast. The concern throughout is the uses of poetry: not its ideal, therapeutic uses, as in **'Aramantha'**, but its actual uses in the real world—beginning with a recollection of the last play to be performed at Court, nearly twenty years earlier, Fletcher's *The Scornful Lady*, and one of its central characters, a young rake who promised his servants satin clothes if his schemes prospered. The character's name was *Loveless*, spelt *Lovelace* in the poem, and raising his ghost gives Lovelace an opportunity for self-mockery, contrasting the dandy he once was with his present lice-ridden state—indeed, there is a bizarrely proleptic echo of Wood's description of him in his glory, wearing cloth of gold and silver—but the point is that now, in the late 1650s, a new set of poetic dandies should take the advice of Richard Lovelace on how best to prostitute themselves:

> You that do suck for thirst your black quil's
>   blood,
> And chaw your labour'd papers for your food,
> I will inform you how and what to praise,
> Then skin y' in Satin as young *Lovelace* plaies.
> Beware, as you would your fierce guests, your
>   lice,
> To strip the cloath of Gold from cherish'd vice;
> Rather stand off with awe and reverend fear,
> Hang a poetick pendant in her Ear.
> Court her as her Adorers do their glass,
> Though that as much of a true Substance has,
> Whilst all the gall from your wild ink you drain,
> The beauteous Sweets of Vertues Cheeks to
>   stain;
> And in your Livery let her be known,
> As poor and tattered as in her own.
> Nor write, nor speak you more of sacred writ,
> But what shall force up your arrested wit.
> Be chast Religion, and her Priests your scorn,
> Whilst the vain Fanes of Idiots you adorn.
> It is a mortal errour you must know,
> Of any to speak good, if he be so.
> Rayl till your edged breath flea your raw throat,
> And burn all marks on all of gen'rous note;
> Each verse be an inditement, be not free
> Sanctity 't self from thy Scurrility.
> *Libel* your Father, and your Dam *Buffoon*,
> The Noblest Matrons of the Isle *Lampoon*,
> Whilst *Aretine* and 's bodies you dispute,
> And in your sheets your Sister prostitute.

All 267 lines of the poem are fixed on the state of poetry. Even the civil war has found its ultimate futility in an absurd war between the poets. And Lovelace finally turns on the abiding female principle of his earlier work and cuts this to ribbons too. The whole enterprise of writing poems to a mistress is mocked, followed by an ironic recapitulation of all those triumphant women at the end of **Lucasta** in the figures of the new tribe of women writers:

> Each snatches the male quill from his faint hand
> And must both nobler write and understand,
> He to her fury the soft plume doth bow,
> O Pen, nere truely justly slit till now!

Like that image of the slit pen, the poem as a whole is graceless and offensive. 'His common discourse', wrote Wood, 'was not only significant and witty, but incomparably graceful, which drew respect from all Men and Women'. That was the courtier Lovelace. Obscurity taught him the values of plain speaking, to pursue what he called in this satire 'nak'd poesie'. It made him, what we have so far been unwilling to grant, a true precursor of Rochester, Dryden, and Pope, as in this description of the poet operating like any other hustler on the streets of London:

> There is not in my mind one sullen Fate
> Of old, but is concentred in our state.
> Vandall ore-runners, Goths in Literature,
> Ploughmen that would *Parnassus* new manure;
> Ringers of Verse that All-in All-in chime
> And toll the changes upon every Rhime.
> A Mercer now by th' yard does measure ore
> An Ode which was but by the foot before;
> Deals you an Ell of Epigram, and swears
> It is the strongest and the finest Wears.
> No wonder if a Drawer Verses Rack,
> If 'tis not his 't may be the Spir't of Sack;
> Whilst the Fair Bar-maid stroaks the Muses
>   teat,
> For milk to make the Posset up compleat.

The streets of London are a good place to end. Lovelace travelled the short distance from the Court to Gunpowder Alley, off Shoe Lane, and his poetry went with him. There is a street vigour in the rhythm and language of this poem, not least typified by his use of *barmaid* here antedating the *OED's* first recorded use of the word by some 120 years. Lovelace chose the streets of London rather than Kent, the Court in exile, or any of the significant number of cavalier retreats. Within a year of this poem he was dead. (pp. 228-34)

> *Gerald Hammond, "Richard Lovelace and the*
> *Uses of Obscurity," in* Proceedings of the Brit-
> *ish Academy,* Vol. LXXI, *1986, pp. 203-34.*

George Parfitt   (essay date 1985)

[*Parfitt is a Trinidadian-born English literary scholar and editor whose writings include* Ben Jonson: Public Poet and Private Man *(1976),* Fiction of the First World War *(1987), and* English Poetry of the First World War *(1988). In the following excerpt, he comments on the general characteristics of Lovelace's poetry, praising the poet's seriousness, objectivity, and noble conception of love.*]

Carew died in 1639, before the outset of the Civil War; Suckling seems to have poisoned himself in Paris, probably in 1641; Lovelace, who was imprisoned for his support of the King, lived until 1658, by which time the crown had been offered to Cromwell. He is thus the only one of the three who, as a royalist, had to work out a way of coping with the establishment of a regime with which he could have had no sympathy.

A glance at Lovelace as he is usually represented in anthologies might suggest that he coped with life by adopting a careless, libertine manner:

> Why should you sweare I am forsworn
>   Since thine I vow'd to be?
> Lady it is already Morn,
>   And 'twas last night I swore to thee
> That fond impossibility.
>   ("The Scrutinie")

Elsewhere his carelessness is technical:

> This knew the wisest, who
> From Juno stole, below
> To love a Beare, or Cow.
>   ("A Paradox")

But Lovelace is seldom convincing when he follows Suckling, and he cannot get near Carew for eroticism. Often, in fact, he seems more like Sidney than anyone else, in poems like **"Love Conquer'd"** and **"A Loose saraband,"** and he shows more awareness of major Donne that Suckling does:

> Though Seas and Land betwixt us both,
> Our Faith and Troth
> Like separated soules,
> All time and space controule:
> Above the highest sphere we meet
> Unseen, unknowne, and greet as Angels greet.
> **("Song. To Lucasta, Going beyond the Seas")**

This stanza provides a clue to one of the emphases which make it inadequate to speak of Lovelace as 'Cavalier', for his concern with 'soul' is not shared by Carew or Suckling. The love he writes of in his famous **"To Lucasta, Going to the Warres"** involves 'the Nunneries of thy chaste breast, and quiet minde', while the equally famous **"To Althea, From Prison"** also associates love with innocence and quiet:

> Stone Walls doe not a Prison make,
> Nor I'ron bars a Cage;
> Mindes innocent and quiet take
> That for an Hermitage;
> If I have freedome in my Love,
> And in my soule am free;
> Angels alone that sore above
> Injoy such Liberty.

'Nunnerie', 'chaste', 'quiet', 'innocent', 'Hermitage'—the words together describe ideals very different from the conventional views of the cavalier. Whereas Suckling tears at love as if to find freedom in nihilism, Lovelace looks to love for quasi-religious serenity.

In fact, although Lovelace is often technically sloppy, he is a serious poet in his awareness of values other than those of sexual love. He makes efforts, albeit rather naively at times, to compare love's value with other values, and to that extent is not a complacent representative of a smug court. His attractive bird and insect poems show this in their mixture of amusement with sober considerations of lessons to be learned from other species. And it is this awareness of, and sympathy with, things beyond the courtly that enables Lovelace to write **"The Grasse-hopper."** Here there is identification with the insect's hedonistic freedom—'The Joyes of Earth and Ayre are thine intire'—but also with the melancholy of transience—'But ah the Sickle! Golden Eares are Cropt'. The grasshopper teaches humankind, and so the poet addresses his friend, Charles Cotton:

> Thou best of Men and Friends! We will create
> A genuine Summer in each others breast.

and can build to this conclusion:

> Though Lord of all what Seas imbrace; yet he
> That wants himself, is poore indeed.

The dignity and stress upon self-knowledge and friendship are Jonsonian, but they are Lovelace's own. **"The Grasse-hopper"** is a poem of what can be saved from defeat, but it is also a commentary upon what had led to that defeat.

Charles's court had, pre-war, too often mistaken seeming peace for real and flattery for love: Lovelace had come to understand something of this.

The idea of making a 'Genuine Summer' is clearly consistent with the language of nunnery and hermitage in the poems to Althea and Lucasta quoted above. In **"To Lucasta, Going beyond the Seas"** the desire for peace is in an erotic context; in **"To Althea, From Prison"** the context is philosophical, reminiscent of Boethius; in **"The Grasse-hopper"** it is political. But in each the desire is for a 'paradise within' and the articulation is generalized, reflective, with limited dramatization and limited individual self-analysis. Lovelace seems concerned to place his own experiences within general categories of behaviour. (pp. 32-4)

George Parfitt, "The Lyric," in his English Poetry of the Seventeenth Century, *Longman, 1985, pp. 18-57.*

Parry on Lovelace as an embodiment of the Cavalier spirit:

The poet who most tellingly registered the effects of political division and war on the leisured and refined society of Stuart England was Richard Lovelace. His mistresses—Lucasta, Aramantha, Ellinda, Althea—were perfections of their kind, and he observed their graces and their gestures, their slightest allurements, with an eye as sharp and appreciative as Herrick's: Aramantha's dishevelling her hair, Lucasta's breathtaking manipulation of her fan, her tantalizing descent to the bath, these are moments of Cavalier rapture; yet there are poems too when the honours due to love are set aside in favour of the imperatives of war, and when love becomes a memory which serves to counteract the misery of political imprisonment. The song 'To Lucasta, going to the Wars' perfectly catches the crisis of the times as the courtier, so long inured to peace, prepares to meet the challenge of war in a spirit of Cavalier gallantry, while 'To Althea from Prison' rises above misfortune to express the poet's royalist sympathies with a conviction that makes a victory of defeat.

Graham Parry, in his The Seventeenth Century: The Intellectual and Cultural Context of English Literature, 1603-1700, *Longman, 1989.*

Gerald Hammond (essay date 1987)

[*In the following excerpt, Hammond traces the development of Lovelace's poetic style, defining his oeuvre as multifaceted and observing that he was able to write both charmingly elegant pieces and powerful satirical poems.*]

Andrew Marvell wrote only two poems in commendation of the work of fellow poets. One was for *Paradise Lost*. The other, some twenty years earlier, was for Richard Lovelace's first volume of poems, *Lucasta,* in 1649. They were both, in their way, as much political as artistic statements. The old, blind poet hailed in the later poem had narrowly avoided the wrath of the restored Stuart monarchy. The cavalier whom Marvell defends so vigorously in the first was in prison, with his property sequestered by a parliament which saw him as a political enemy. Marvell's is the only one of the commendatory poems to *Lucasta* which addresses the matter of the authorities' refusal to allow the volume to be published: the Stationer's Register records that it was licensed on 4 February 1648, but it was not actually published until 14 May 1649. After lamenting the degeneration of the times to the point that he now sees 'the envious caterpillar sit / On the fair blossom of each growing wit', Marvell expands the insect image to describe the siege which the imprisoned Lovelace is undergoing:

> The air's already tainted with the swarms
> Of insects which against you rise in arms.
> Word-peckers, paper-rats, book-scorpions,
> Of wit corrupted, the unfashioned sons.
> The barbed censurers begin to look
> Like the grim consistory on thy book;
> And on each line cast a reforming eye,
> Severer than the young Presbytery.
>
> Till when in vain they have thee all perused,
> You shall for being faultless be accused.
> Some reading your *Lucasta,* will allege
> You wronged in her the House's privilege.
> Some that you under sequestration are,
> Because you write when going to the war,
> And one the book prohibits, because Kent
> Their first petition by the author sent.

In the couplet which rounds off this list of speculations about the authorities' motives, Marvell has gone back seven years, to the very beginnings of the civil war. S.R. Gardner, whose history of those times is still authoritative, thought that if there were one specific act which led to the outbreak of war, then it was the attempt by Kentish supporters of Charles I to present a loyal petition to parliament, and parliament's suppression of it, having it publicly burned and its organizers imprisoned. These men, led by Sir Edward Dering, were moderate statesmen. With them out of the way their place was filled by younger members of the gentry, who saw this as the opportunity to mobilize the county and march on London, to present the petition in a form and manner which parliament could not resist. At their head was the twenty-four-year-old Richard Lovelace.

In spite of his youth Lovelace had already made a name for himself at court. He had achieved things: an honorary degree from Oxford, a comedy called *The Scholars* which had been presented at Salisbury Court, and military service with Goring's regiment during the two Bishops' wars of 1639-40. But more significant than all of these was the splendid public image which he had created. Anthony Wood, a man not given to excessive hyperbole, had this to say about the young Lovelace:

> . . . the most amiable and beautiful person that ever eye beheld, a person also of innate modesty, virtue and courtly deportment, which made him then, but especially after, when he retired to the great city, much admired and adored by the female sex.

But while such images could be cultivated in the 1630s,

the next decade put them under a brutal examination. The courtier poets were among the chief casualties. Sir John Suckling took a regiment north in the Bishops' war, all of them decked out in scarlet coats and white doublets. Three years later he committed suicide to avoid his imminent poverty. Edmund Waller tried to put his poetic royalism into practical action by organizing a plot to capture London for the King in 1643. The whole thing went disastrously wrong, and Waller was forced into making the most public and grovelling of apologies to parliament, his name becoming a byword for cowardice. Lovelace's story was not quite so extreme as Suckling's or Waller's, but it bears comparison. Marching at the head of several thousand Kentish men to Blackheath common, he and his fellow leader, Sir William Boteler, were first out-manœuvred and then put out of commission. Boteler ended up in the Fleet prison, Lovelace in the Gatehouse. The remaining Kentish hotheads were told to go home and behave better in future. By the time Lovelace's petition for release was allowed, in June 1642, the civil war had begun.

Up to this point everything seems to fit Lovelace into the pattern of the archetypal cavalier poet. During this first spell in prison it is quite likely that he had begun to write those definitive accounts of the cavalier experience, whether as a loyal prisoner—'Stone walls do not a prison make, / Nor iron bars a cage'—or leaving his mistress for the battlefield: 'I could not love thee (dear) so much, / Loved I not honour more.' References to him in the 1640s reinforce our view of him as the ideal poet-lover-soldier which the word *cavalier* epitomizes. John Tatham wrote a poem to him describing him as 'loved Adonis', for whose return Venus can scarcely bear to wait. One of the commendatory poems to *Lucasta* is addressed 'To the Honourable, Valiant, and Ingenious Colonel Richard Lovelace'; and another, by John Hall, asks how so proficient a soldier can be so fine a lover too:

> Was't not enough for us to know how far
> Thou couldst in season suffer, act, and dare?
> But we must also witness with what height
> And what Ionic sweetness thou canst write?
> And melt those eager passions that are
> Stubborn enough t'enrage the god of war,
> Into a noble love . . .

And Marvell's poem moves from its image of the besieged Lovelace, to his rescue by a cavalry charge of ladies, intent on the rescue of their darling:

> But when the beauteous ladies came to know
> That their dear Lovelace was endangered so:
> Lovelace that thawed the most congealed breast,
> He who loved best, and them defended best,
> Whose hand so rudely grasps the steely brand,
> Whose hand so gently melts the ladies' hand,
> They all in mutiny though yet undrest
> Sallied, and would in his defence contest.

The cavalier image was strong enough for the authorities to put Lovelace back in gaol in 1648. While the army was preparing the ground for Charles's execution, there were the beginnings of popular discontent in Kent; and by imprisoning him they were ensuring that at least one of the possible leaders of a revolt was out of action. During this period, late 1648 to early 1649, the publication of *Lucasta* was held up, and Marvell's poem was written. By the time of his second release, Charles was dead and Cromwell's rule assured.

What are we to make of Marvell's defence of Lovelace? After all, within a very short period he would be writing in powerful praise of the Commonwealth—and he is the only major Metaphysical poet who had puritan sympathies. Does the Lovelace poem mark a final stage in his Royalism before the almost exact Charles-Cromwell balance of the 'Horatian Ode'? Or is it an honourable payment of a debt of friendship to a fellow poet now down on his luck? The answer belongs more to a life of Marvell than to an introduction to Lovelace's poems, but the question is worth raising here if only to emphasize the strong links between the two. Marvell is much the more important figure in our view of the seventeenth century and its poetry: critical writing on him outnumbers that on Lovelace by fifty to one. But Lovelace, older by just three years, was a strong influence on Marvell, and not the other way round.

To take the most significant example, there is the long pastoral poem **'Aramantha'** which brings *Lucasta* to a close. Critics of Marvell's 'Upon Appleton House' only occasionally glance at it, and when they do their purpose is to show how the one poet got it wrong while the other triumphed. James Turner, in *The Politics of Landscape*, compares the two poems, judging that 'despite a considerable resemblance on the surface', Lovelace's poem lacks the control of Marvell's. All very well, but that recognition of a considerable resemblance ought to be tempered by some acknowledgement of **'Aramantha's'** priority. For the reader who has not checked the dates there is no indication of which came first, and no sense that it must have been Marvell's reading of **'Aramantha'** in 1649 which introduced him to the idea of a political pastoral, written in octosyllabic couplets, in which the local landscape comes to represent the whole of England, its flora and fauna emerging as types of the factions which fought out the civil war, and which is presided over by an heroine who gradually develops from a vision of arcadian innocence into a complex figure of national and personal salvation. Lovelace does not manage it as subtly as Marvell, but the huge ambition behind this attempt to relate personal to national destiny still makes it one of the most haunting of the mid-century's poems.

When Aramantha tells Alexis that fond (i.e. foolish) man

> to a precipice
> Aspires, till at the top his eyes
> Have lost the safety of the plain,
> Then begs of Fate the vales again

she is summarizing Lovelace's own experiences in the 1640s, and the national experience too. Like many of the poems in this and Lovelace's second volume, **'Aramantha'** stands as an imaginative attempt to find ways of comprehending what had happened to turn the world upside down. Its near complete neglect by critics merely demonstrates how partial our view of the century's poetry still is.

I do not recommend that the reader begin with **'Ara-**

mantha', but reading it between the *Lucasta* poems . . . and the *Lucasta Posthume Poems* volume will reinforce the suspicions which should have begun to form around the earlier lyrics, that Lovelace is a more complete poet than the label *cavalier* would imply, and will help point towards his concern with the nature of his art in the later poems. Its plot is very simple. A rural nymph, Aramantha, encounters a weeping man, Alexis. Alexis, we know from other poems, is Lovelace's name for himself. He is weeping for his supposedly dead Lucasta. Aramantha, after taunting him for his unreasonableness, eventually reveals herself to be Lucasta, and Alexis, overcome with joy, destroys his weapons and retires with her to her pastoral idyll.

In her account of how she came to be exiled into the country Lucasta describes England during the civil war as a state in which both sides, in the name of freedom, destroy

> The glory of this Sicily;
> Since seeking thus the remedy,
> They fancy (building on false ground)
> The means must them and it confound,
> Yet are resolved to stand or fall,
> And win a little or lose all.

This is cruder in statement, but a parallel vision to Marvell's 'Horatian Ode' and 'Appleton House'. The influence Lovelace had upon him was not merely a matter of words and phrases (although it is not difficult to trace these) but one of a lesson in how to be neutral amid 'this sad storm of fire and blood'. Lucasta was doubtless a real person, but she stands for much more than one individual personality—for England itself, and for the poet's muse. **'Aramantha'** shows that the way for Lovelace to recover these things is to stand apart from faction: scarcely an attitude which we would expect a true cavalier to take.

Perhaps Lovelace never was the kind of cavalier which Suckling and Waller tried to be, not after the Kentish petition anyway. The second poem in *Lucasta* is **'To Lucasta, Going to the Wars'**, and it contains the celebrated cavalier preference for the battlefield over his mistress:

> Tell me not (Sweet) I am unkind,
>   That from the nunnery
> Of thy chaste breast, and quiet mind,
>   To war and arms I fly.

This is the Lovelace which everyone responds to: the effortlessly lyrical statement of elegantly heroic behaviour. It is clever too. Notice how the word *arms* clinches the preference—not her arms, which he runs from, but the soldier's arms, which he runs to. A masculine embrace is superimposed upon a feminine one. But this poem follows directly after **'To Lucasta, Going beyond the Seas'**, and the ordering of these poems ought to give us pause. They are autobiographically correct. Lovelace did not, as his co-petitioner William Boteler did, stay in England and fight for the King. Instead he went to France and fought in the service of the French king at the siege of Dunkirk. He never, so far as we know, took any part in the civil war, although all of his brothers did. Again, the word *cavalier* seems an odd one to attach to him.

This is not to say that Lovelace never writes cavalier poetry, but he almost never writes the kind of crude and explicit propaganda which other poets of the 1630s and 1640s did. And a poem like **'To Lucasta. From Prison'** becomes a more subtle composition if we cease to regard it as the product of an unthinking and instinctive Royalist. There Lovelace, after having surveyed the whole country and the degeneration of its institutions, fixes on the king as 'th' only spring / Of all our loves and joys'. But the poem does not end here, and its final three stanzas retreat a little from this certainty of monarchical radiance to a puzzlement at its occlusion, both nationally and in the experience of the man locked away in the prison cell.

> He who being the whole ball
>   Of day on Earth, lends it to all;
> When seeking to eclipse his right,
>   Blinded, we stand in our own light.
>
> And now an universal mist
>   Of error is spread o'er each breast,
> With such a fury edged, as is
>   Not found in th' inwards of th' abyss.
>
> Oh from thy glorious starry wain
>   Dispense on me one sacred beam
> To light me where I soon may see
>   How to serve you, and you trust me.

This is not a mindless panegyric on Charles, but a sombre attempt to understand how it is possible to serve him properly. What kind of action, or inaction, is now needed? And its inclusiveness is characteristic of Lovelace: the 'we' who 'stand in our own light' are not a 'we' opposed to 'them', but the whole nation. Set it against real cavalier poetry, such as these lines by Thomas Carew [from "A New-Year's Gift. To the King"], and it becomes clear that Lovelace's is a poetry of a different order.

> Then as a father let him be
> With numerous issue blest, and see
> The fair and godlike offspring grown
> From budding stars to suns full blown.
> Circle with peaceful olive boughs,
> And conquering bays, his regal brows.
> Let his strong virtue overcome,
> And bring him bloodless trophies home:
> Strew all the pavements, where he treads
> With loyal hearts, or rebels' heads.

All this is not to argue that Lovelace is primarily a political poet—rather, that his poetry includes politics in its general grasp of the mid-century experience. There is, in essence, a coherent poetic personality behind a poem as apparently bizarre and apolitical as **'Lucasta's Fan, With a Looking Glass in it'**, which begins with an apostrophe to an ostrich, and one as obviously political as **'A Fly Caught in a Cobweb'**, which opens with an explicit parallel between the insect and the world's politicians. Between the two stands **'The Grasshopper'** which poises the political and the apolitical. This is, everyone agrees, a poem about friendship, monarchy, the civil war, the good life, the good man, survival in hard times—it is about grasshoppers too, so that we register both tenor and vehicle when we see the insect who sang through summer reduced to 'green ice' in one of those bitter winters which marked the seventeenth century. In a similar way, the poem about Lucasta's fan encourages us to pay attention to the literal

object—and Lovelace writes at his best when he focuses on the impedimenta of polite or impolite life, that is, objects like muffs, shirts, gloves, and glasses of burnt claret—but the perspectives he takes up encourage us to move beyond realism, to the surreal and the symbolic. Here it is relevant to stress his documented interest in the latest achievements of Dutch painting, a super realism which worked in a similar way, making a fly on a cow's flank bigger than a church steeple in the background.

So Lucasta, with her ostrich feather fan winging her side, becomes, for a zany moment, an ostrich herself as she makes her way across the floor

> Sometime they wing her side, then strive to
>   drown
>   The day's eye's-piercing beams, whose
>   am'rous heat
> Solicits still, till with this shield of down
>   From her brave face, his glowing fires are
>   beat.

Such perspectives are typical of Marvell's poetry too, and it is hard to believe that the many odd ways of looking at things which recur throughout *Lucasta* did not encourage him to think of poems as vehicles for visual experimentation. The altered perspectives always have a purpose. A society full of ostriches is one of this poem's concerns, and its final stanza, focusing on the broken fan with its smashed mirror, contains a line of subdued but powerful political comment: 'Now fall'n the brittle favourite lies, and burst'.

We can argue that it is all an accident—that the last thing Lovelace intended us to think of was a character like the Duke of Buckingham when he used the phrase 'brittle favourite'. This is certainly how most critics have treated his poetry, but it wilfully ignores the sheer persistence of his oblique approaches to political matters. Consider another poem from early in *Lucasta*, titled simply **'Sonnet'**. . . . It is simply another reworking of a hackneyed seventeenth-century theme, that it will do no more harm for the lady he courts to share her favours with him than for her to let someone else wear a piece of her jewellery. This is its first stanza:

> Depose your finger of that ring,
>   And crown mine with't awhile;
> Now I restore't—pray does it bring
>   Back with it more of soil?
> Or shines it not as innocent,
>   As honest, as before 'twas lent?

This is undistinguished stuff, and probably quite early. However, it is set quite deliberately in a prominent place in a volume of poems which was licensed at the time when Charles I was under the arrest of his own subjects, and which was published not long after his execution. And there its first three lines wear, with no hint of embarrassment, words which armies had fought over, and would probably do so again: *depose, crown, restore*.

Lovelace's second volume, *Lucasta, Posthume Poems*, contains those poems he probably wrote in the 1650s. As its title indicates, it appeared after his death, under the auspices of his brother Dudley. We do not know exactly when he died, but if Anthony Wood's account is to be believed, his experience through the last few years of his life was one of increasing degradation and despair. The contrast with the dazzling young man who was described as the handsomest man in England in the late 1630s, and who marched on London at the head of the young Kentish gentry could hardly be greater.

> After the murder of King Charles I Lovelace was set at liberty, and having by time consumed all his estate, grew very melancholy, (which brought him at length into a consumption) became very poor in body and purse, was the object of charity, went in ragged clothes (whereas when he was in his glory he wore cloth of gold and silver) and mostly lodged in obscure and dirty places, more befitting the worst of beggars, than poorest of servants . . . He died in a very mean lodging in Gunpowder Alley near Shoe Lane . . .

C.H. Wilkinson, the editor of the Oxford edition of Lovelace's poetry, poured scorn on this account, and he is generally held to have debunked it sufficiently for it to be considered little better than a piece of fiction. But there is no real reason to distrust Wood. Scholars who have tested his other biographies have found him to be astonishingly reliable, and himself a supporter of the royal cause, there seems little reason for him to have exaggerated Lovelace's misfortunes when members of this loyal family were still alive and helping him by answering his enquiries.

Furthermore, to read the poems of this volume is to move from *Lucasta's* generally court-centred view of English life to a Gunpowder Alley centered one—the buttery rather than the wine cellar, as **'A Loose Saraband'** has it, where shirts are as tattered as their wearers, and where political struggles are seen in terms of flies trapped in cobwebs. The striking thing is that while Lovelace's poetry grows increasingly personal, it does not become self-indulgent. **'A Fly About a Glass of Burnt Claret'** is a good example. Watching a fly struggle in the fiery liquor, Lovelace is encouraged to meditate upon his own experience. The fly is a noble lover, hurling himself at a heart of fire which will consume him, and an heroic soldier, sacrificing himself to save his country. He is also entirely insignificant and insanely suicidal. Rescued by the little finger of providence, his instinct is to hurl himself again into the 'moist-hot-glass and liquid fire'. It is all a wonderfully controlled way for Lovelace to look at his own destiny, as victim of the lover-soldier image he had carried into the 1640s.

Lover and soldier, but poet too. The third element makes his *Posthume Poems* so important in the development of seventeenth-century poetry (even if we have so far failed to appreciate this). These poems increasingly emphasize the claim that, more than anything else, he is a professional poet, and that his destiny is bound up with his choice of profession. At times the effect is Yeats-like, as in **'To a Lady with child that asked an Old Shirt'**, where the ragged shirt, all he has to offer, turns out to be the apron from the muse's smock. Of more direct significance is the sense that he stands right at the beginning of Restoration and Augustan satire, with its strong concern with the poet's role. This he explores in a number of poems, and

most ambitiously in the final poem in the volume—its equivalent to 'Aramantha'—the splendidly titled **'On Sannazar's being honoured with six hundred ducats by the Clarissimi of Venice, for composing an Elegiac Hexastich of the City. A Satire'**. Here tone, diction and imagery are authentically Dryden's and Pope's. Here is *MacFlecknoe* a generation earlier, in this portrait of the hungry poet eagerly looking forward to a commission to write a poem in celebration of a marriage:

> With what a fury have I known you feed,
> Upon a contract, and the hopes 't might speed;
> Not the fair bride, impatient of delay,
> Doth wish like you the beauties of that day;
> Hotter than all the roasted cooks you sat
> To dress the fricace of your alphabet,
> Which sometimes would be drawn dough ana-
>   gram,
> Sometimes acrostic parched in the flame;
> Then posies stewed with sippets, mottoes by,
> Of minced verse a miserable pie.

And here is the *Dunciad*, still three generations away, in this picture of the hacks who are beginning to create the Grub Street fraternity:

> A mercer now by th' yard does measure o'er
> An ode which was but by the foot before;
> Deals you an ell of epigram, and swears
> It is the strongest and the finest wares.
> No wonder if a drawer verses rack,
> If 'tis not his 't may be the spir't of sack;
> Whilst the fair bar-maid strokes the Muse's teat,
> For milk to make the posset up complete.

To have come to this sardonic view of poetry as commodity from lines like 'I could not love thee (dear) so much / Loved I not honour more' shows how far Lovelace had travelled through these two turbulent decades. He lost a lot: his health and property, and any memorial beyond the poems themselves. He died obscurely and his grave has disappeared. But the later poems show no diminution in his achievement, and although Wood's account of his having grown 'into a melancholy' which led to his ill health and death may be reflected in the mordancy of some of his satire, other poems show the same light elegance which marked the early poems of *Lucasta*—only now they have an edge of irony to make them even more valuable. Thus the trifle which he wrote to commend a guide to chess playing sums up the fate of princes, and all other forms of power—court, clergy, commons—in the simulated perplexity of its couplet: 'Strange, serious wantoning, all that they / Blustered, and cluttered for, *you play*.' So that's what it all meant: a tongue-in-cheek reflection upon Charles, Strafford, Laud, Pym, and Cromwell, suitably fitting for the friend and mentor of Andrew Marvell. (pp. 7-19)

Gerald Hammond, in an introduction to Richard Lovelace: Selected Poems, *edited by Gerald Hammond, Fyfield Books, 1987, pp. 7-19.*

FURTHER READING

Allen, Dom Cameron. "An Explication of Lovelace's 'The Grasse-Hopper'." *Modern Language Quarterly* 18, No. 1 (March 1957): 25-42.

Examines the literary and historical symbolism in Lovelace's allegorical and philosophical poem, with particular reference to classical sources. Allen suggests that the poem adumbrates "a private world of the poet's own heart where all is warm light and the grasshopper lives in a kingdom made eternal by his song."

Courthope, W. J. "Cavalier and Roundhead." In his *A History of English Poetry*, Vol. VIII, pp. 285-333. London: Macmillan, 1924.

Includes a brief overview of Lovelace's life and poetry.

Evans, Willa McClung. "Richard Lovelace's 'Mock-Song'." *Philological Quarterly* XXIV, No. 4 (October 1945): pp. 317-28.

An analysis of a manuscript version of "A Mock Song," which was set to music by John Cave. Evans maintains that the textual corrections implicitly refute the belief, held by some critics, that Lovelace was careless in preparing his manuscripts for publication.

Hartmann, Cyril Hughes. *The Cavalier Spirit and Its Influence on the Life and Work of Richard Lovelace*. London: G. Routledge & Sons, 1925, 150 p.

A detailed survey of Lovelace's life within the context of the political conflict between Charles I and Parliament.

Howarth, R. G. Introduction to *Minor Poets of the Seventeenth Century*, edited by R. G. Howarth, pp. vii-xxviii. London: J. M. Dent & Sons, 1931.

Describes Lovelace as an uneven poet whose essence was a " 'mind innocent and quiet,' which turbulent times deprived of the opportunity to flower in a congenial environment."

King, Bruce. "Civil War and Interregnum Literature." In his *Seventeenth-Century English Literature*, pp. 127-55. London: Macmillan, 1982.

Includes a brief overview of Lovelace's life and a commentary on his best-known poems.

Lindsay, Philip. "Richard Lovelace." In his *For King and Parliament*, pp. 170-202. London: Evans Brothers, 1949.

An account of Lovelace's life, focusing on his involvement in the political struggles of his times.

Margoliuth, H. M. "The Poems of Richard Lovelace." *The Review of English Studies* III, No. 9 (January 1927): 89-95.

A review of C. H. Wilkinson's 1925 edition of Lovelace's works, with commentary on the poet's literary achievement.

Palmer, Paulina. "Lovelace: Some Unnoticed Allusions to Carew." *Notes and Queries* n.s. 14, No. 13 (March 1967): 96-8.

Traces the poetic borrowings of Lovelace from Thomas Carew, showing how he transformed Carew's metaphors and phraseology.

Parry, Graham. "Cultural Life During the Civil War and the Commonwealth, 1642-1659." In his *The Seventeenth Century: The Intellectual and Cultural Context of English Literature, 1603-1700*, pp. 83-106. London: Longman, 1989.

Includes a concise discussion of Lovelace.

Pattison, Bruce. "Divergences." In his *Music and Poetry of the English Renaissance*, pp. 191-202. London: Methuen, 1970.

Includes a brief commentary on Lovelace's appreciation of music.

Pearson, Norman Holmes. "Lovelace's 'To Lucasta, Going to the Warres'." *The Explicator* VII, No. 7 (June 1949): 58.

Interprets Lovelace's celebrated poem as a successful resolution of the paradox created by the opposing claims of love and honor.

Rizzardi, Alfredo. *La poesia dei Cavalieri*. Bologna: Cappelli, 1969, 335 p.

A chronological survey of the critical reception of Lovelace's poetry. This work is available only in Italian.

Rogers, Robert. "Literary Value and the Clinical Fallacy." *Literature and Psychology* XIV, Nos. 3-4 (Summer-Fall 1964): 116-21.

Comments on Norman H. Holland's psychoanalytic interpretation of Lovelace's poems. Rogers criticizes the fallacy of ascribing aesthetical relevance to objective clinical judgments.

Turner, James. "The Happy State." In his *The Politics of Landscape*, pp. 85-115. Cambridge: Harvard University Press, 1979.

Includes a discussion of Lovelace's use of landscape as a poetic device.

Waite, Arthur E. "Richard Lovelace." *Gentleman's Magazine* CCLVII (November 1884): 459-77.

A short biography of Lovelace.

Wilkinson, C. H. Introduction to *The Poems of Richard Lovelace*, by Richard Lovelace, edited by C. H. Wilkinson, pp. xiii-lxxxvii. Oxford: Clarendon Press, 1930.

A detailed discussion of Lovelace's life and poetic career, including comments on the minor literary figures who were part of his social milieu.

Wood, Anthony à. *Athenae Oxonienses*. 2 vols. London: Thomas Bennet, 1691-92.

Contains an often-quoted account of Lovelace's later years.

Metaphysical Poets

INTRODUCTION

The term Metaphysical poets designates a group of seventeenth-century writers that includes as its principal figures John Donne, George Herbert, Richard Crashaw, Andrew Marvell, Henry Vaughan, and Thomas Traherne, together with lesser figures like Thomas Carew, John Cleveland, Richard Lovelace, Abraham Cowley and Edward, Lord Herbert of Cherbury. The term was first used in connection with Donne by John Dryden, in his *Discourse Concerning the Original and Progress of Satire* (1693), wherein he stated, "Donne affects the metaphysics not only in his satires but in his amorous verses...; and [he] perplexes the mind of the fair sex with nice speculations of philosophy." Samuel Johnson, foremost critic of the Augustan Age, was the first to classify the Metaphysical poets as a distinct group distinguished by their use of elaborate argumentation, abstruse comparisons, and disdain for emotionalism. Thus in his famous essay "The Life of Cowley," included in *Lives of the English Poets* (1779-81), Johnson forwarded the idea that "the metaphysical poets were men of learning, and to shew their learning was their whole endeavour." The use of the label "Metaphysical poets" is widely disputed by modern critics, who question the assumption that the poets thus designated were seriously interested in the philosophical exploration of the ultimate nature of reality; indeed, many commentators argue that the so-called Metaphysical poets have in reality almost nothing in common. Nonetheless, the majority of critics agree that in the overall body of Metaphysical poetry, certain stylistic tendencies seem prevalent—including the use of dialectical reasoning, logical contradiction, incongruous images, harsh, inelegant rhythms, and most importantly, the use of the "Metaphysical conceit," a paradoxical metaphor that unites disparate associations or experiences in a unified thought.

A major figure in seventeenth-century English poetry in his own right, John Donne is also considered the originator of the Metaphysical school. His career is divided into secular and religious phases. His earliest years were those of a scholar and adventurer; he participated in naval expeditions of the Earl of Essex against Spain, and later served as secretary to Sir Thomas Egerton, a high-ranking minister, until he lost favor at court by secretly marrying Egerton's niece. Donne's satires, elegies, and love lyrics were mostly completed before the death of Elizabeth I in 1603. In contrast to the more classicizing verse of his contemporaries, Donne's lyric poetry reveals the influence of contemporary dramatic poets, with the realistic imagery and intellectual sophistication characteristic of Shakespearean metaphor. Donne's later religious poetry evidences the same vigor and stylistic individuality of his early secular works. In both phases, his lyrics are distinctive in their use of dialogue and incident to develop a particular theme; in the earlier phase, dialogue with his mistress or his wife; in the latter, dialogue with God articulating spiritual torment, a prominent theme of the two *Anniversaries*.

George Herbert, younger brother of the poet and philosopher Edward, Lord Herbert of Cherbury, was a favorite at the court of James I. He retired from court affairs in 1625 to pursue a career in the Anglican church. Herbert's most important work appeared posthumously as *The Temple: Sacred Poems and Private Ejaculations*, a collection that reflects his deeply religious nature and commitment to Anglican Christianity. Herbert's poems epitomize the Metaphysical mode—direct, unassuming language united with keen philosophical insight, sensuous imagery, and aristocratic refinement, but his work is considered more restrained than that of Donne, who utilized metaphysical imagery to express intense subjective emotion. Richard Crashaw is unique among the devotional poets of the Metaphysical school in that he converted to Roman Catholicism in 1645 and subsequently moved to Italy, where he held a number of minor ecclesiastical positions. His *Steps to the Temple*, a collection of religious poems, was influenced by the Baroque verse of Giambattista Marino, who favored extravagant imagery, excessive ornamentation, and verbal conceits. *Sacred Poems, with Other Delights of the Muses*, composed of secular lyrics, was incorporated with *Steps to the Temple* as a companion volume; both are considered remarkable for their "anti-English" qualities—purity of style, lavish imagery, and mellifluous cadences. Unlike Donne, Herbert, and Crashaw, whose careers were ultimately defined by religious interests, Andrew Marvell led the life of a worldly politician, working in various capacities both under Oliver Cromwell's regime and the restored monarchy of Charles II. Marvell's audacious wit, fusing intellectual subtlety with sensuous verve, is typical of the school of Donne. His most famous work, *The First Anniversary of the Government under His Highness the Lord Protector*, written after the death of Charles I, assumes the form of an Horatian Ode, wherein Cromwell is compared to Julius Caesar. Marvell's republican sympathies notwithstanding, the poem's most famous lines are a tribute to Charles's noble deportment on the scaffold.

Henry Vaughan, a Welsh poet, is generally aligned with the Metaphysical school. However, critics agree that two qualities set him apart—a fascination with the naive consciousness of childhood, and an extraordinary responsiveness to natural surroundings in the manner of William Wordsworth. The work upon which his present-day reputation is based, *Silex Scintillans; or, Sacred Poems and Private Ejaculations*, explores the contrasting themes of man's alienation from God and the lyrical beauty of nature. Thomas Traherne, considered an important figure but of lesser stature than Vaughan, became an Anglican clergyman after leaving Oxford University. His poems, not discovered until the end of the nineteenth century, were at first assumed to be the work of Vaughan, owing to their similar thematic focus on childhood innocence and Platonic conception of nature. Traherne's poetry underscores a profound conviction of the Platonic interdependence of sense perception and the spirit, each intensifying the experience of the other. From a stylistic viewpoint, Traherne's versification is considered plainer, more repetitive, and in general less distinguished than Vaughan's.

The careers of the lesser Metaphysical poets—Lord Herbert, Carew, Cleveland, Lovelace, and Cowley—are viewed somewhat differently from their predecessors in so far as their poetry is less cohesive stylistically, revealing a more classical emphasis that would become more pronounced after 1660. Lord Herbert was one of the few poets of his age who was also a serious scholar of religious and metaphysical thought. His poetry reflects these concerns, exploring the relation of appearance to reality and the nature of the soul. His lyrical aptitude—as well as his intellectual depth—are demonstrated in poems like "Elegy over a Tomb" and "An Ode upon a Question Moved, Whether Love Should Continue for Ever," the latter a dramatized meditation that bears comparison to Donne's "The Extasie." The remaining figures, Carew, Cleveland, Lovelace, and Cowley, were all associated with the circle of Charles I, and their style reflects the sophistication and artificiality of court life. Carew, for example, borrowed heavily from the classical poetry of Ben Jonson, though his *Elegy* on Donne reveals that he was also influenced by the latter poet. Cleveland's epigrammatical verse is considered even more academic in style. His "The Hecatomb to His Mistresse," for example, is noted for its elaborate development of metaphysical conceits that string together as many disparate images as possible in a kind of comical game. Lovelace, a prominent member of the Cavalier poets, obeyed classical notions of decorum yet tended to adopt a complex point of view, as in "The Grasse-Hopper," an allegory on the plight of the Cavaliers after the death of Charles I, or in "To Aramantha; That She Would Dishevell Her Hair," which addresses the limits of love in a fleeting world. Often said to be the last of the Metaphysicals, Cowley was an eclectic writer capable of working in a wide range of styles. His most important poem in the Metaphysical manner, *The Mistress; or, Several Copies of Love-Verses*, was a direct imitation of Donne's *Songs and Sonnets*. Comprised of some one hundred individual poems, the cycle covers a wide thematic range, from pastoral life to unrequited love. Cowley's use of elaborate metaphors that derive their intellectual force from cleverly structured paradox led Johnson to criticize the poet as the creator of "discordia concors"—in effect the Metaphysical style—in his "The Life of Cowley."

The reputation of the Metaphysical poets was first established in the eighteenth century by Dryden, Johnson, and Alexander Pope, though none of these critics approved of their eccentricity. The neoclassical taste for simplicity and disregard for figurative language resulted in a decline in the Metaphysicals' critical stature in the late eighteenth century, while nineteenth-century critics, influenced by the movements of Romanticism and Historicism, had even less interest. The Metaphysicals' revival occurred

after the First World War, during the rewriting of English literary history by modernist critics who valued them for their complexity and bold experimentation. The two most important moments in this reevaluation were H. J. C. Grierson's introduction to his *Metaphysical Lyrics and Poems of the Seventeenth Century* (1921) and T. S. Eliot's essay "Metaphysical Poets," which first appeared in 1921 as a response to Grierson. Eliot asserted that the Metaphysical poets were successful because they had the inherent advantage of writing in a period when thought and feeling were closely fused, as opposed to the "dissociation of sensibility" that began with Milton. Eliot's modernist reassessment has influenced most twentieth-century critics; however, recent scholars, including Rosemond Tuve, have explored historicist interpretations, for example classifying the Metaphysical poets as a branch of the European Baroque.

REPRESENTATIVE WORKS

Carew, Thomas
  Poems by Thomas Carew, Esquire, One of the Gentlemen of the Privie-Chamber, and Sewer in Ordinary to His Majesty   1640; revised editions, 1642, 1651
Cowley, Abraham
  The Mistress; or, Several Copies of Love-Verses   1647
  Poems   1656
Crashaw, Richard
  Epigrammatum Sacrorum Liber   1634
  Steps to the Temple; Sacred Poems, with Other Delights of the Muses   1646; revised edition 1648
  Carmen Deo Nostro   1652
  Steps to the Temple, The Delights of the Muses, and Carmen Deo Nostro   1670
Donne, John
  The First Anniversarie. An Anatomie of the World. Wherein By Occasion of the untimely death of Mistris Elizabeth Drury, the frailtie and decay of this whole World is represented   1611
  The Second Anniversarie. Of the Progres of the Soule. Wherein, By Occasion Of the Religious death of Mistris Elizabeth Drury, the incommodities of the Soule in this life, and her exaltation in the next, are Contemplated   1612
  Devotions upon Emergent Occasions, and Severall steps in my sickness   1624
  Poems   1633
Herbert, George
  The Temple: Sacred Poems and Private Ejaculations   1633
Lovelace, Richard
  Lucasta: Epodes, Odes, Sonnets, Songs &c. To Which Is Added Aramantha, A Pastorall   1649
  Lucasta. Posthume Poems of Richard Lovelace, Esq.   1659-60
Marvell, Andrew
  The First Anniversary of the Government under His Highness the Lord Protector   1655
  Miscellaneous Poems   1681
Traherne, Thomas

Poetical Works   1903
Poems of Felicity   1910
Vaughan, Henry
   *Silex Scintillans; or Sacred Poems and Private Ejacula-
      tions*   1650; revised edition, 1655

*Dates given indicate first publication; Traherne's works remained
in manuscript until the early twentieth century.

EARLY DEFINITIONS

John Dryden

[*Regarded by many scholars as the father of modern
English poetry and criticism, Dryden was also a prolific
and accomplished Restoration dramatist. In the following excerpt from* A Discourse Concerning the Original
and Progress of Satire *(1693), Dryden stresses the philosophical or "metaphysical" character of John Donne's
and Abraham Cowley's verse, thus initiating the critical
provenance of the term "metaphysical poetry."*]

[Donne] affects the metaphysics, not only in his satires,
but in his amorous verses, where nature only should reign;
and perplexes the minds of the fair sex with nice speculations of philosophy, when he should engage their hearts,
and entertain them with the softnesses of love. In this (if
I may be pardoned for so bold a truth) Mr. Cowley has
copied him to a fault; so great a one, in my opinion, that
it throws his *Mistress* infinitely below his Pindarics and his
latter compositions, which are undoubtedly the best of his
poems, and the most correct. . . .

Would not Donne's *Satires*, which abound with so much
wit, appear more charming, if he had taken care of his
words, and of his numbers?

> *John Dryden, extract from "A Discourse Con-
> cerning the Original and Progress of Satire,"
> in* The Metaphysical Poets: Key Essays on
> Metaphysical Poetry and the Major Meta-
> physical Poets, *edited by Frank Kermode,
> Fawcett World Library, 1969, p. 121.*

Samuel Johnson

[*Johnson is one of the outstanding figures in English literature and a leader in the history of textual and aesthetic criticism. In the following excerpt from "The Life
of Cowley" (1779) in his influential critical biography,*
Lives of the English Poets *(10 vols., 1779-81; reissued
in 1783 as* The Lives of the Most Eminent English
Poets*), Johnson critiques the stylistic canon of the metaphysical poets from a neoclassical viewpoint, emphasizing their general disregard for the proprieties of Augustan verse.*]

Wit, like all other things subject by their nature to the
choice of man, has its changes and fashions, and at differ-

ent times takes different forms. About the beginning of the
seventeenth century appeared a race of writers that may
be termed the metaphysical poets; of whom, in a criticism
on the works of Cowley, it is not improper to give some
account.

The metaphysical poets were men of learning, and to shew
their learning was their whole endeavour; but, unluckily
resolving to shew it in rhyme, instead of writing poetry,
they only wrote verses, and very often such verses as stood
the trial of the finger better than of the ear; for the modulation was so imperfect, that they were only found to be
verses by counting the syllables.

If the father of criticism has rightly denominated poetry
$\tau \epsilon \chi \nu \pi \ \mu \iota \mu \eta \tau \iota \kappa \eta$, an imitative art, these writers will,
without great wrong, lose their right to the name of poets;
for they cannot be said to have imitated any thing; they
neither copied nature nor life; neither painted the forms
of matter, nor represented the operations of the intellect.

Those, however, who deny them to be poets, allow them
to be wits. Dryden confesses of himself and his contemporaries, that they fall below Donne in wit, but maintains
that they surpass him in poetry.

If Wit be well described by Pope, as being "that which has
been often thought, but was never before so well expressed," they certainly never attained, nor ever sought it;
for they endeavoured to be singular in their thoughts, and
were careless of their diction. But Pope's account of wit
is undoubtedly erroneous: he depresses it below its natural
dignity, and reduces it from strength of thought to happiness of language.

If by a more noble and more adequate conception that be
considered as Wit, which is at once natural and new, that
which, though not obvious, is, upon its first production,
acknowledged to be just; if it be that, which he that never
found it, wonders how he missed; to wit of this kind the
metaphysical poets have seldom risen. Their thoughts are
often new, but seldom natural; they are not obvious, but
neither are they just; and the reader, far from wondering
that he missed them, wonders more frequently by what
perverseness of industry they were ever found.

But Wit, abstracted from its effects upon the hearer, may
be more rigorously and philosophically considered as a
kind of *discordia concors*; a combination of dissimilar images, or discovery of occult resemblances in things apparently unlike. Of wit, thus defined, they have more than
enough. The most heterogeneous ideas are yoked by violence together; nature and art are ransacked for illustrations, comparisons, and allusions; their learning instructs,
and their subtilty surprises; but the reader commonly
thinks his improvement dearly bought, and, though he
sometimes admires, is seldom pleased.

From this account of their compositions it will be readily
inferred, that they were not successful in representing or
moving the affections. As they were wholly employed on
something unexpected and surprising, they had no regard
to that uniformity of sentiment which enables us to conceive and to excite the pains and the pleasure of other
minds: they never enquired what, on any occasion, they

should have said or done; but wrote rather as beholders than partakers of human nature; as Beings looking upon good and evil, impassive and at leisure; as Epicurean deities making remarks on the actions of men, and the vicissitudes of life, without interest and without emotion. Their courtship was void of fondness, and their lamentation of sorrow. Their wish was only to say what they hoped had never been said before.

Nor was the sublime more within their reach than the pathetick; for they never attempted that comprehension and expanse of thought which at once fills the whole mind, and of which the first effect is sudden astonishment, and the second rational admiration. Sublimity is produced by aggregation, and littleness by dispersion. Great thoughts are always general, and consist in positions not limited by exceptions, and in descriptions not descending to minuteness. It is with great propriety that Subtility, which in its original import means exility of particles, is taken in its metaphorical means for nicety of distinction. Those writers who lay on the watch for novelty could have little hope of greatness; for great things cannot have escaped former observation. Their attempts were always analytick; they broke every image into fragments; and could no more represent, by their slender conceits and laboured particularities, the prospects of nature, or the scenes of life, than he, who dissects a sun-beam with a prism, can exhibit the wide effulgence of a summer noon.

What they wanted however of the sublime, they endeavoured to supply by hyperbole; their amplification had no limits; they left not only reason but fancy behind them; and produced combinations of confused magnificence, that not only could not be credited, but could not be imagined.

Yet great labour, directed by great abilities, is never wholly lost: if they frequently threw away their wit upon false conceits, they likewise sometimes struck out unexpected truth: if their conceits were farfetched, they were often worth the carriage. To write on their plan, it was at least necessary to read and think. No man could be born a metaphysical poet, nor assume the dignity of a writer, by descriptions copied from descriptions, by imitations borrowed from imitations, by traditional imagery, and hereditary similes, by readiness of rhyme, and volubility of syllables.

In perusing the works of this race of authors, the mind is exercised either by recollection or inquiry; either something already learned is to be retrieved, or something new is to be examined. If their greatness seldom elevates, their acuteness often surprises; if the imagination is not always gratified, at least the powers of reflection and comparison are employed; and in the mass of materials which ingenious absurdity has thrown together, genuine wit and useful knowledge may be sometimes found, buried perhaps in grossness of expression, but useful to those who know their value; and such as, when they are expanded to perspicuity, and polished to elegance, may give lustre to works which have more propriety though less copiousness of sentiment.

This kind of writing, which was, I believe, borrowed from

Marini and his followers, had been recommended by the example of Donne, a man of very extensive and various knowledge; and by Jonson, whose manner resembled that of Donne more in the ruggedness of his lines than in the cast of his sentiments.

When their reputation was high, they had undoubtedly more imitators than time has left behind. Their immediate successors, of whom any remembrance can be said to remain, were Suckling, Waller, Denham, Cowley, Cleveland, and Milton. Denham and Waller sought another way to fame, by improving the harmony of our numbers. Milton tried the metaphysick style only in his lines upon Hobson the Carrier. Cowley adopted it, and excelled his predecessors, having as much sentiment, and more musick. Suckling neither improved versification, nor abounded in conceits. The fashionable style remained chiefly with Cowley; Suckling could not reach it, and Milton disdained it. (pp. 122-25)

Samuel Johnson, "Metaphysical Wit," in The Metaphysical Poets: Key Essays on Metaphysical Poetry and the Major Metaphysical Poets, *edited by Frank Kermode, Fawcett World Library, 1969, pp. 122-25.*

Dryden on the style of Cleveland and Donne:

We cannot read a verse of Cleveland's without making a face at it, as if every word were a pill to swallow: he gives us many times a hard nut to break our teeth, without a kernel for our pains. So that there is this difference betwixt his *Satires* and doctor Donne's; that the one gives us deep thoughts in common language, though rough cadence; the other gives us common thoughts in abstruse words.

John Dryden in his Essay of Dramatic Poesy, *1668.*

T. S. Eliot

[*Perhaps the most influential poet and critic to write in the English language during the first half of the twentieth century, Eliot is closely identified with many of the qualities denoted by the term Modernism: experimentation, formal complexity, artistic and intellectual eclecticism, and a classicist's view of the artist working at an emotional distance from his or her creation. In the following essay, Eliot essentially rejects Samuel Johnson's criticisms of metaphysical poetry, arguing that "the poets of the seventeenth century . . . were the direct and normal development of the precedent age."*]

By collecting these poems [*Metaphysical Lyrics and Poems of the Seventeenth Century: Donne to Butler*] from the work of a generation more often named than read, and more often read than profitably studied, Professor Grierson has rendered a service of some importance. Certainly the reader will meet with many poems already preserved in other anthologies, at the same time that he discovers poems such as those of Aurelian Townshend or Lord Herbert of Cherbury here included. But the function of such an anthology as this is neither that of Professor Saintsbury's admirable edition of Caroline poets nor that of the *Oxford Book of English Verse*. Mr. Grierson's book is in itself a piece of criticism, and a provocation of criticism; and we think that he was right in including so many poems of Donne, elsewhere (though not in many editions) accessible, as documents in the case of "metaphysical poetry." The phrase has long done duty as a term of abuse, or as the label of a quaint and pleasant taste. The question is to what extent the so-called metaphysicals formed a school (in our own time we should say a "movement"), and how far this so-called school or movement is a digression from the main current.

Not only is it extremely difficult to define metaphysical poetry, but difficult to decide what poets practise it and in which of their verses. The poetry of Donne (to whom Marvell and Bishop King are sometimes nearer than any of the other authors) is late Elizabethan, its feeling often very close to that of Chapman. The "courtly" poetry is derivative from Jonson, who borrowed liberally from the Latin; it expires in the next century with the sentiment and witticism of Prior. There is finally the devotional verse of Herbert, Vaughan, and Crashaw (echoed long after by Christina Rossetti and Francis Thompson); Crashaw, sometimes more profound and less sectarian than the others, has a quality which returns through the Elizabethan period to the early Italians. It is difficult to find any precise use of metaphor, simile, or other conceit, which is common to all the poets and at the same time important enough as an element of style to isolate these poets as a group. Donne, and often Cowley, employ a device which is sometimes considered characteristically "metaphysical"; the elaboration (contrasted with the condensation) of a figure of speech to the farthest stage to which ingenuity can carry it. Thus Cowley develops the commonplace comparison of the world to a chessboard through long stanzas ("To Destiny"), and Donne, with more grace, in "A Valediction," the comparison of two lovers to a pair of compasses. But elsewhere we find, instead of the mere explication of the content of a comparison, a development by rapid association of thought which requires considerable agility on the part of the reader.

> On a round ball
> A workeman that hath copies by, can lay
> An Europe, Afrique, and an Asia,
> And quickly make that, which was nothing, *All*,
> So doth each teare,
> Which thee doth weare,
> A globe, yea world by that impression grow,
> Till thy tears mixt with mine doe overflow
> This world, by waters sent from thee, my heaven
> dissolved so.

Here we find at least two connexions which are not implicit in the first figure, but are forced upon it by the poet: from the geographer's globe to the tear, and the tear to the deluge. On the other hand, some of Donne's most successful and characteristic effects are secured by brief words and sudden contrasts—

> A bracelet of bright hair about the bone,

where the most powerful effect is produced by the sudden contrast of associations of "bright hair" and of "bone." This telescoping of images and multiplied association is characteristic of the phrase of some of the dramatists of the period which Donne knew: not to mention Shakespeare, it is frequent in Middleton, Webster, and Tourneur, and is one of the sources of the vitality of their language.

Johnson, who employed the term "metaphysical poets," apparently having Donne, Cleveland, and Cowley chiefly in mind, remarks of them that "the most heterogeneous ideas are yoked by violence together." The force of this impeachment lies in the failure of the conjunction, the fact that often the ideas are yoked but not united; and if we are to judge of styles of poetry by their abuse, enough examples may be found in Cleveland to justify Johnson's condemnation. But a degree of heterogeneity of material compelled into unity by the operation of the poet's mind is omnipresent in poetry. We need not select for illustration such a line as—

> Notre âme est un trois-mâts cherchant son Icarie;

we may find it in some of the best lines of Johnson himself ("The Vanity of Human Wishes"):—

> His fate was destined to a barren strand,
> A petty fortress, and a dubious hand;
> He left a name at which the world grew pale,
> To point a moral, or adorn a tale,

where the effect is due to a contrast of ideas, different in degree but the same in principle, as that which Johnson mildly reprehended. And in one of the finest poems of the age (a poem which could not have been written in any other age), the "Exequy" of Bishop King, the extended comparison is used with perfect success: the idea and the simile become one, in the passage in which the Bishop illustrates his impatience to see his dead wife, under the figure of a journey:—

> Stay for me there; I will not faile
> To meet thee in that hollow Vale.
> And think not much of my delay;
> I am already on the way,
> And follow thee with all the speed
> Desire can make, or sorrows breed.
> Each minute is a short degree,
> And ev'ry houre a step towards thee.
> At night when I betake to rest,
> Next morn I rise nearer my West
> Of life, almost by eight houres sail,
> Than when sleep breath'd his drowsy
> gale. . . .
> But heark! My Pulse, like a soft Drum
> Beats my approach, tells *Thee* I come;
> And slow howere my marches be,
> I shall at last sit down by *Thee*.

(In the last few lines there is that effect of terror which is several times attained by one of Bishop King's admirers, Edgar Poe.) Again, we may justly take these quatrains from Lord Herbert's Ode, stanzas which would, we think, be immediately pronounced to be of the metaphysical school:—

> So when from hence we shall be gone,

And be no more, nor you, nor I,
    As one another's mystery,
Each shall be both, yet both but one.

This said, in her up-lifted face,
    Her eyes, which did that beauty crown,
    Were like two starrs, that having faln down,
Look up again to find their place:

While such a moveless silent peace
    Did seize on their becalmed sense,
    One would have thought some influence
Their ravished spirits did possess.

There is nothing in these lines (with the possible exception of the stars, a simile not at once grasped, but lovely and justified) which fits Johnson's general observations on the metaphysical poets in his essay on Cowley. A good deal resides in the richness of association which is at the same time borrowed from and given to the word "becalmed"; but the meaning is clear, the language simple and elegant. It is to be observed that the language of these poets is as a rule simple and pure; in the verse of George Herbert this simplicity is carried as far as it can go—a simplicity emulated without success by numerous modern poets. The *structure* of the sentences, on the other hand, is sometimes far from simple, but this is not a vice; it is a fidelity to thought and feeling. The effect, at its best, is far less artificial than that of an ode by Gray. And as this fidelity induces variety of thought and feeling, so it induces variety of music. We doubt whether, in the eighteenth century, could be found two poems in nominally the same metre, so dissimilar as Marvell's "Coy Mistress" and Crashaw's "Saint Teresa"; the one producing an effect of great speed by the use of short syllables, and the other an ecclesiastical solemnity by the use of long ones:—

Love, thou art absolute sole lord
Of life and death.

If so shrewd and sensitive (though so limited) a critic as Johnson failed to define metaphysical poetry by its faults, it is worth while to inquire whether we may not have more success by adopting the opposite method: by assuming that the poets of the seventeenth century (up to the Revolution) were the direct and normal development of the precedent age; and, without prejudicing their case by the adjective "metaphysical," consider whether their virtue was not something permanently valuable, which subsequently disappeared, but ought not to have disappeared. Johnson has hit, perhaps by accident, on one of their peculiarities, when he observes that "their attempts were always analytic"; he would not agree that, after the dissociation, they put the material together again in a new unity.

It is certain that the dramatic verse of the later Elizabethan and early Jacobean poets expresses a degree of development of sensibility which is not found in any of the prose, good as it often is. If we except Marlowe, a man of prodigious intelligence, these dramatists were directly or indirectly (it is at least a tenable theory) affected by Montaigne. Even if we except also Jonson and Chapman, these two were notably erudite, and were notably men who incorporated their erudition into their sensibility: their mode of feeling was directly and freshly altered by their reading and thought. In Chapman especially there is a di-

rect sensuous apprehension of thought, or a recreation of thought into feeling, which is exactly what we find in Donne:—

in this one thing, all the discipline
Of manners and of manhood is contained;
A man to join himself with th' Universe
In his main sway, and make in all things fit
One with that All, and go on, round as it;
Not plucking from the whole his wretched part,
And into straits, or into nought revert,
Wishing the complete Universe might be
Subject to such a rag of it as he;
But to consider great Necessity.

We compare this with some modern passage:—

No, when the fight begins within himself,
A man's worth something. God stoops o'er his
    head,
Satan looks up between his feet—both tug—
He's left, himself, i' the middle; the soul wakes
And grows. Prolong that battle through his life!

It is perhaps somewhat less fair, though very tempting (as both poets are concerned with the perpetuation of love by offspring), to compare with the stanzas already quoted from Lord Herbert's Ode the following from Tennyson:—

One walked between his wife and child,
With measured footfall firm and mild,
And now and then he gravely smiled.
    The prudent partner of his blood
    Leaned on him, faithful, gentle, good,
    Wearing the rose of womanhood.
And in their double love secure,
The little maiden walked demure,
Pacing with downward eyelids pure.
    These three made unity so sweet,
    My frozen heart began to beat,
    Remembering its ancient heat.

The difference is not a simple difference of degree between poets. It is something which had happened to the mind of England between the time of Donne or Lord Herbert of Cherbury and the time of Tennyson and Browning; it is the difference between the intellectual poet and the reflective poet. Tennyson and Browning are poets, and they think; but they do not feel their thought as immediately as the odour of a rose. A thought to Donne was an experience; it modified his sensibility. When a poet's mind is perfectly equipped for its work, it is constantly amalgamating disparate experience; the ordinary man's experience is chaotic, irregular, fragmentary. The latter falls in love, or reads Spinoza, and these two experiences have nothing to do with each other, or with the noise of the typewriter or the smell of cooking; in the mind of the poet these experiences are always forming new wholes.

We may express the difference by the following theory:— The poets of the seventeenth century, the successors of the dramatists of the sixteenth, possessed a mechanism of sensibility which could devour any kind of experience. They are simple, artificial, difficult, or fantastic, as their predecessors were; no less nor more than Dante, Guido Cavalcanti, Guinizelli, or Cino. In the seventeenth century a dissociation of sensibility set in, from which we have never recovered; and this dissociation, as is natural, was due to the influence of the two most powerful poets of the century, Milton and Dryden. Each of these men performed certain poetic functions so magnificently well that the magnitude of the effect concealed the absence of others. The language went on and in some respects improved; the best verse of Collins, Gray, Johnson, and even Goldsmith satisfies some of our fastidious demands better than that of Donne or Marvell or King. But while the language became more refined, the feeling became more crude. The feeling, the sensibility, expressed in the "Country Churchyard" (to say nothing of Tennyson and Browning) is cruder than that in the "Coy Mistress."

The second effect of the influence of Milton and Dryden followed from the first, and was therefore slow in manifestation. The sentimental age began early in the eighteenth century, and continued. The poets revolted against the ratiocinative, the descriptive; they thought and felt by fits, unbalanced; they reflected. In one or two passages of Shelley's "Triumph of Life," in the second *Hyperion*, there are traces of a struggle toward unification of sensibility. But Keats and Shelley died, and Tennyson and Browning ruminated.

After this brief exposition of a theory—too brief, perhaps, to carry conviction—we may ask, what would have been the fate of the "metaphysical" had the current of poetry descended in a direct line from them, as it descended in a direct line to them? They would not, certainly, be classified as metaphysical. The possible interests of a poet are unlimited; the more intelligent he is the better; the more intelligent he is the more likely that he will have interests: our only condition is that he turn them into poetry, and not merely meditate on them poetically. A philosophical theory which has entered into poetry is established, for its truth or falsity in one sense ceases to matter, and its truth in another sense is proved. The poets in question have, like other poets, various faults. But they were, at best, engaged in the task of trying to find the verbal equivalent for states of mind and feeling. And this means both that they are more mature, and that they wear better, than later poets of certainly not less literary ability.

It is not a permanent necessity that poets should be interested in philosophy, or in any other subject. We can only say that it appears likely that poets in our civilization, as it exists at present, must be *difficult*. Our civilization comprehends great variety and complexity, and this variety and complexity, playing upon a refined sensibility, must produce various and complex results. The poet must become more and more comprehensive, more allusive, more indirect, in order to force, to dislocate if necessary, language into his meaning. (A brilliant and extreme statement of this view, with which it is not requisite to associate oneself, is that of M. Jean Epstein, "La Poésie d'aujourd-hui.") Hence we get something which looks very much like the conceit—we get, in fact, a method curiously similar to that of the "metaphysical poets," similar also in its use of obscure words and of simple phrasing.

> Ô géraniums diaphanes, guerroyeurs sortilèges,
> Sacrilèges monomanes!
> Emballages, dévergondages, douches!   Ô pres-
>   soirs

> Des vendanges des grands soirs!
> Layettes aux abois,
> Thyrses au fond des bois!
> Transfusions, représailles,
> Relevailles, compresses et l'éternel potion,
> Angélus! n'en pouvoir plus
> De débâcles nuptiales! de débâcles nuptiales!

The same poet could write also simply:—

> Elle est bien loin, elle pleure,
> Le grand vent se lamente aussi . . .

Jules Laforgue, and Tristan Corbière in many of his poems, are nearer to the "school of Donne" than any modern English poet. But poets more classical than they have the same essential quality of transmuting ideas into sensations, of transforming an observation into a state of mind.

> Pour l'enfant, amoureux de cartes et d'estampes,
> L'univers est égal à son vaste appétit.
> Ah, que le monde est grand à la clarté des
>   lampes!
> Aux yeux du souvenir que le monde est petit!

In French literature the great master of the seventeenth century—Racine—and the great master of the nineteenth—Baudelaire—are more like each other than they are like anyone else. The greatest two masters of diction are also the greatest two psychologists, the most curious explorers of the soul. It is interesting to speculate whether it is not a misfortune that two of the greatest masters of diction in our language, Milton and Dryden, triumph with a dazzling disregard of the soul. If we continued to produce Miltons and Drydens it might not so much matter, but as things are it is a pity that English poetry has remained so incomplete. Those who object to the "artificiality" of Milton or Dryden sometimes tell us to "look into our hearts and write." But that is not looking deep enough; Racine or Donne looked into a good deal more than the heart. One must look into the cerebral cortex, the nervous system, and the digestive tracts.

May we not conclude, then, that Donne, Crashaw, Vaughan, Herbert and Lord Herbert, Marvell, King, Cowley at his best, are in the direct current of English poetry, and that their faults should be reprimanded by this standard rather than coddled by antiquarian affection? They have been enough praised in terms which are implicit limitations because they are "metaphysical" or "witty," "quaint" or "obscure," though at their best they have not these attributes more than other serious poets. On the other hand, we must not reject the criticism of Johnson (a dangerous person to disagree with) without having mastered it, without having assimilated the Johnsonian canons of taste. In reading the celebrated passage in his essay on Cowley we must remember that by wit he clearly means something more serious than we usually mean today; in his criticism of their versification we must remember in what a narrow discipline he was trained, but also how well trained; we must remember that Johnson tortures chiefly the chief offenders, Cowley and Cleveland. It would be a fruitful work, and one requiring a substantial book, to break up the classification of Johnson (for there has been none since) and exhibit these poets in all their difference of kind and of degree, from the massive music of

Donne to the faint, pleasing tinkle of Aurelian Townshend—whose "Dialogue between a Pilgrim and Time" is one of the few regrettable omissions from this excellent anthology. (pp. 212-23)

> *T. S. Eliot, "The Metaphysical Poets," in his* Homage to John Dryden: Three Essays on Poetry of the Seventeenth Century, *L. and Virginia Woolf, 1924, pp. 212-23.*

John Crowe Ransom

[*An American critic, poet, and editor, Ransom is considered one of the most influential literary theorists of the twentieth century. As a critic, Ransom is regarded as a pioneer in the New Criticism movement. In* The New Criticism *(1941), his most important work, Ransom proposed a close reading of poetic texts and insisted that criticism should be based on a study of the structure and text of a given poem, not its content. In the following excerpt from that work, Ransom offers a counter-critique of T. S. Eliot's essay "The Metaphysical Poets," purporting that poets of the metaphysical school "offer us an art which has a very formal mode of composition, but in it the texture dominates the structure and all but threatens its life."*]

One essay of Eliot's is the most famous and valuable, and probably at the same time the most difficult, of them all. It is "The Metaphysical Poets," written in 1921 in review of Grierson's new anthology of metaphysical verse. This school of poetry is either very brilliant or else very pretentious; a critical talent is heavily tried to say which, and then to say why. The critical observations which Eliot makes in this essay are quoted more than any others of his, or so at least in my own critical circles. Its public effect has been to have just about upset the old comparative valuations of the great cycles of English poetic history: reducing the 19th Century heavily and the Restoration and 18th Century a little less, elevating the 16th and early 17th Centuries to supreme importance as the locus of the poetic tradition operating at its full. Yet there is difficulty in following Eliot's argument precisely; and it does not contain much real analysis of metaphysical poetry proper.

Eliot considers the usual way of defining metaphysical poetry in terms of its conceits, or metaphors, but rejects it; the historical body of this poetry is too various to admit so simple an explanation. Page 241 (of the *Selected Essays*):

> Not only is it difficult to define metaphysical poetry, but difficult to decide what poets practice it, and in which of their verses. The poetry of Donne (to whom Marvell and Bishop King are sometimes nearer than any of the other authors) is late Elizabethan, its feeling often very close to that of Chapman. The "courtly" poetry is derivative from Jonson, who borrowed liberally from the Latin; it expires in the next century with the sentiment and witticism of Prior. There is finally the devotional verse of Herbert, Vaughan, and Crashaw (echoed long after by Christina Rossetti and Francis Thompson); Crashaw, sometimes more profound and less sectarian than the others, has a quality which returns through the

Elizabethan period to the early Italians. It is difficult to find any precise use of metaphor, simile, or other conceit, which is common to all the poets and at the same time important enough as an element of style to isolate these poets as a group. Donne, and often Cowley, employ a device which is sometimes considered characteristically "metaphysical"; the elaboration (contrasted with the condensation) of a figure of speech to the farthest stage to which ingenuity can carry it. Thus Cowley develops the commonplace comparison of the world to a chessboard through long stanzas ("To Destiny"), and Donne, with more grace, in "A Valediction," the comparison of two lovers to a pair of compasses.

But generally there are complications. He cites an example from Donne of the "telescoping" of images, or the passing from one metaphor into a second which depends on it, a procedure that cannot possibly be the same as the farthest possible elaboration of the one metaphor. He quotes Johnson's unfavorable saying (based chiefly on Cleveland and Cowley) that in metaphysical poetry "the most heterogeneous ideas are yoked by violence together." But a degree of heterogeneity of material is always present in poetry (we could almost say it is the differentia of poetry as compared with prose), and Eliot can cite Johnson's own verse to this effect. And if the "violence" that Johnson objected to refers to some outrageous forcing of the sense, Eliot can say that

> in one of the finest poems of the age (a poem which could not have been written in any other age), the "Exequy" of Bishop King, the extended comparison is used with perfect success: the idea and the simile become one, in the passage in which the Bishop illustrates his impatience to see his dead wife, under the figure of a journey:
>
> Stay for me there; I will not faile
> To meet thee in that hollow Vale.
> And think not much of my delay;
> I am already on the way,
> And follow thee with all the speed
> Desire can make, or sorrows breed.
> Each minute is a short degree,
> And ev'ry hour a step towards thee.
> At night when I betake to rest,
> Next morn I rise nearer my West
> Of life, almost by eight hours sail,
> Than when sleep breath'd his drowsy
>   gale. . . .
> But heark!   My Pulse, like a soft Drum
> Beats my approach, tells Thee I come;
> And slow howere my marches be,
> I shall at last sit down by Thee.

That is the only full-bodied and extended passage of metaphysical poetry that Eliot quotes. And presently he is saying that the language of the metaphysical poets is usually "simple and pure"; but that the grammatical *structure* (his italics) may be "far from simple."

Eliot then proceeds to his own thesis. Metaphysical poetry cannot be defined as some tricky habit of metaphor. It should be defined as a very various poetry of the 17th Century which was "the direct and normal development of the precedent age." That would make it a highly inclusive poetry. But Eliot spends almost the rest of the essay on a very wide speculation as to how this class of poetry differs from later poetry, with regret that its virtue was allowed to lapse. The virtue which lapsed was not something peculiar to Donne and other metaphysical poets, but something entirely common in poets of Donne's time and even before him:

> It is certain that the dramatic verse of the later Elizabethan and early Jacobean poets expresses a degree of development of sensibility which is not found in any of the prose, good as it often is. If we except Marlowe, a man of prodigious intelligence, these dramatists were directly or indirectly (it is at least a tenable theory) affected by Montaigne. Even if we except also Jonson and Chapman, these two were notably erudite, and were notably men who incorporated their erudition into their sensibility: their mode of feeling was directly and freshly altered by their reading and thought. In Chapman especially there is a direct sensuous apprehension of thought, or a recreation of thought into feeling, which is exactly what we find in Donne:

> > in this one thing, all the discipline
> > Of manners and of manhood is contained;
> > A man to join himself with th' Universe
> > In his main sway, and make in all things fit
> > One with that All, and go on, round as it;
> > Not plucking from the whole his wretched part,
> > And into straits, or into nought revert,
> > Wishing the complete Universe might be
> > Subject to such a rag of it as he;
> > But to consider great Necessity.

> We compare this with some modern passage:

> > No, when the fight begins within himself,
> > A man's worth something. God stoops o'er his head,
> > Satan looks up between his feet—both tug—
> > He's left, himself, i' the middle; the soul wakes
> > And grows. Prolong that battle through his life!

I skip a passage in which the antithesis between the old and the modern is illustrated by another pairing, Lord Herbert and Tennyson, and resume:

> The difference is not a simple difference of degree between poets. It is something which had happened to the mind of England between the time of Donne or Lord Herbert of Cherbury and the time of Tennyson and Browning; it is the difference between the intellectual poet and the reflective poet. Tennyson and Browning are poets, and they think; but they do not feel their thought as immediately as the odour of a rose. A thought to Donne was an experience; it modified his sensibility. When a poet's mind is perfectly equipped for its work, it is constantly amalgamating disparate experience; the ordinary man's experience is chaotic, irregular, fragmentary. The latter falls in love, or reads Spinoza, and these two experiences have nothing to do with each other, or with the noise of the typewriter or the smell of cooking; in the mind of the poet these experiences are always forming new wholes.

We may express the difference by the following theory: The poets of the seventeenth century, the successors of the dramatists of the sixteenth, possessed a mechanism of sensibility which could devour any kind of experience. They are simple, artificial, difficult, or fantastic, as their predecessors were; no less nor more than Dante, Guido Cavalcante, Guinizelli, or Cino. In the seventeenth century a dissociation of sensibility set in, from which we have never recovered; and this dissociation, as is natural, was aggravated by the influence of the two most powerful poets of the century, Milton and Dryden. Each of these men performed certain poetic functions so magnificently well that the magnitude of the effect concealed the absence of others. The language went on and in some respects improved, the best verse of Collins, Gray, Johnson, and even Goldsmith, satisfies some of our fastidious demands better than that of Donne or Marvell or King. But while the language became more refined, the feeling became more crude. The feeling, the sensibility, expressed in the "Country Churchyard" (to say nothing of Tennyson and Browning) is cruder than that in the "Coy Mistress."

The second effect of the influence of Milton and Dryden followed from the first, and was therefore slow in manifestation. The sentimental age began early in the eighteenth century, and continued. The poets revolted against the ratiocinative, the descriptive; they thought and felt by fits, unbalanced; they reflected. In one or two passages of Shelley's "Triumph of Life," in the second *Hyperion*, there are traces of a struggle toward unification of sensibility. But Keats and Shelley died, and Tennyson and Browning ruminated.

It is a brief exposition, worth far more attention than we shall have time for. With the fall of the metaphysical poets the direct line of tradition was broken; it happened rather suddenly. The metaphysical poets were the last in the old line, but the first we meet as we go back, therefore tending to look the more odd to us. Eliot argues that if the tradition had been carried on, they would not have come to look odd, and would not even have been specially designated as "metaphysical" poets. For

> they were, at best, engaged in the task of trying to find the verbal equivalent for states of mind and feeling. And this means both that they are more mature, and that they wear better, than later poets of certainly not less literary ability.

This is about the sum of Eliot's remarks. Now feeling is distinguished by the critic from thought; but Eliot seems to say that the older poets did not make this distinction, and were superior to the modern poets in being able to do without it. Modern poets think a while, and then decide to work in some feelings; but they should be able to assimilate thinking into feeling, as once the poets did. These could "feel their thought"; they had a sensibility "which could devour any kind of experience"; they wrote no poetry that was merely "reflective" or consisted in thought not immediately felt. Lamenting the modern dualism of thought and feeling, Eliot thinks he finds it bridged in the older order of English poetry, though the technique by which it was accomplished was let go, and has never been rediscovered.

I confess that I know very little about that; and I must add that, having worked to the best of my ability to find the thing Eliot refers to in the 17th Century poets, and failed, I incline to think there was nothing of the kind there. I have often tried—as what critic has not—to find some description of poetry which would regard it as a single unified experience, and exempt it from the dilemma of logic; but we must not like some philosophers become the fools of the shining but impractical ideal of "unity" or of "fusion." The aspiration here is for some sort of fusion of two experiences that ordinarily repel one another: the abstracted exercise of reason in hard fact and calculation; and the inclusive experience of literally everything at once. But we cannot have our theory magical and intelligible at the same time. For it would seem that from that precise moment when the race discovers that what has seemed to be an undifferentiated unity is really a complex of specialized functions, there can be no undifferentiated unity again; no return. We do not quite know how to feel a thought. The best we can do is to conduct a thought without denying all the innocent or irrelevant feelings in the process. The dualism remains. But a poem is an experience in time; and after we have had it once we can have it again, and better, by reading it a second time. We think through it at more leisure this time, and leisurely or even sprawling thinking, thinking that is in something less than entire bondage to the animal or scientific will, is the only poetic formula that I, at any rate, can find.

Such a formula indicates that we can realize the *structure*, which is the logical thought, without sacrificing the *texture*, which is the free detail—or, if anybody insists, which is the feelings that engage with the free detail. For, again, Eliot's talk is psychologistic, or affective, but we may easily translate it into objective or cognitive terms. We recall his big emotion as attaching to the main thought, and translate that simply as the logical structure of the poem; then we recall the little feelings attaching to the play of the words, and translate them as its local texture. "Sensibility," the term which Eliot has presented to the new critics, is the organ which excretes the feelings, as he would say, or the detailed perceptions, as we would say. But I think we must waive the psychological magic involved in the act of feeling our thought in honor of something much tamer and more credible: the procedure of suspending the course of the main thought while we explore the private character of the detail items. We stop following the main thought, and take off in a different direction, as we follow the private history of an item; then we come back to the main thought.

That may be only a formula which will do for most poems. And what is different and new about a metaphysical poem? Most of the new critics still prefer to take metaphysical as describing a poetical effect which is not in Chapman and the Elizabethan dramatists unless very slightly; nor in the French Symbolists, of whom Eliot in his essay takes a notice I have not mentioned; and consists apparently in the structural device of making the whole poem, or some whole passage of it, out of the single unit metaphor. There are many such poems in Donne and other poets, and they seem distinct enough structurally from other poems. Henry King's poem is the example Eliot cites.

I should not regard Chapman's passage about the Universe as "metaphysical"; nor deny on the other hand that it is very fine poetry and does not have to be metaphysical. We have an explicit thought-structure, and it is attended even by an explicit moral valuation; it would not be entirely ineligible for the discourse of a modern Hegelian, like Josiah Royce. It is what we should call "reflective" or philosophical verse. But it is not without a local texture, and this gets in very cunningly though without recourse to magic; it is slight and unobtrusive but positive and sharp; it is perhaps most visible in the phonetic dimension contributed to the object everywhere by the excellent metric; but beyond that it is in a few local items such as a man's *main sway*, the idea of his going on with the Universe in the *round*, the witty aside which corrects *into straits* to *into nought*, and the calling of the man a *rag* of the Universe. This is not what we think of as metaphysical poetry, and it is not for being metaphysical that we prefer it to Browning's passage, which is entirely comparable. Browning's structure consists in saying: "When a man's fight begins within himself, his soul wakes and grows." It too is explicitly stated. The principal piece of texture is in the parenthetic remark—a violent interpolation—which stops to give a sort of rough-neck picture of the man's fight within himself: it is a tugging match between God and Satan. Eliot may very well talk about the modern crudeness of Browning's "feeling" though he could talk as easily about the crudeness of Browning's imagination or perception.

And now for Bishop King's poem. The passage here is one long unitary metaphor. Its fact-structure or thought-structure is not given away (it is almost given away once, inadvertently); we have to infer it from the metaphor. The language is simple and logical enough; if we could remove sleep's drowsy gale and the military-voyage business about the drum, the language might be said not to have a texture. (In some of Herbert's metaphysical poems, Eliot says, the language is perfectly plain; it has no texture.) In that case we seem to have in a metaphysical poem one without either a visible structure or a local texture; we shall discuss that in a moment. But the structure which we require for the understanding of the poem is not hard to supply. His wife has died, and what he says to her in the poem is in lieu of something like this:

> You are in Heaven, and I am eager to join you. I think of each passing minute and hour as bringing me that much nearer, and I wake each morning thinking I have gained by eight hours nearer. Can you not hear my pulse, ticking away the moments which separate us?

But all that, however accurately we imagine we render it, has disappeared—if it ever existed—or has been "assimilated" into the image of an impatient 17th-century explorer-traveler, following across land and sea a lady who has made an incomprehensible journey to an ocean paradise in the West; a very secular transformation.

We think normally of metaphor as developing from a detail of the poem and making an item of local texture, centrifugal or tangential with respect to the central structure; "importing" something foreign into it, as Richards has it. But King's poem without its metaphor would have no structure, and no being. Mr. Cleanth Brooks has written about the importance of the "functional" or structural metaphors: they are all "vehicle," to quote Richards again, with no tenor. Little local metaphors of this sort are common, I believe, as when Hamlet speaks of his "sea" of troubles. The metaphysical conceit is a variety of the functional or structural metaphor, where the central structure, and not merely a casual detail, has no explicit tenor but only a "vehicle" covering it. And the issue is, I think, whether this sort of metaphor is structure or texture. The answer would be that, to whatever degree, it must serve both purposes. The all-vehicle metaphor must be transparent enough to discover its tenor, and that tenor will have to be an experience rather generalized and of little distinctness, such as love, death, valediction, and conventional religious experience. As for texture, there is not necessarily within the vehicle any "local excitement," any detail which does more than function within the discourse of the vehicle in a commonplace manner. It seems at first sight then that a metaphysical poem has no texture. On the contrary, we must figure texture with respect to tenor, and we conclude that any detail which is functional for the vehicle but foreign for the tenor is texture. There would be a great deal of this.

The consequence is that the tenor of a metaphysical poem is conventional and generalized, while its texture is thick and odd; the texture can easily be grotesque, and raise considerations of propriety. The tenor or fact-structure is forced into an alien form; in being particularized it is distorted. In the Bishop's poem the Drum image comes out of the exuberance with which he plays the game of the traveler, but it may seem jaunty for the actual occasion, or even wrenched; where is the actual pulse-aspect in the old Bishop which is like this Admiral Drake's drum?

The example of metaphysical poetry most commonly mentioned (by Johnson, by Eliot, by everybody) is the passage from Donne's "Valediction" about the compasses. The poet is leaving his mistress but their souls are still joined:

> If they be two, they are two so
> As stiff twin compasses are two;
> Thy soul, the fixed foot, makes no show
> To move, but doth if the other do.
>
> And though it in the center sit,
> Yet when the other far doth roam,
> It leans, and hearkens after it,
> And grows erect as that comes home.
>
> Such wilt thou be to me, who must,
> Like the other foot, obliquely run;
> Thy firmness makes my circle just,
> And makes me end where I begun.

The compasses as a mathematical instrument may be for

Donne's age a symbol of great Necessity, and the activities they throw back upon the lovers' souls identified with them may be dignified, but they are awkward. He must run obliquely, in a circle, instead of going straight to his errand and dispatching it; she must lean towards him most when he is most distant, and grow erect instead of running to meet him as he returns; and, returned, what activity remains for this pair? These are strange little patterns of behavior for lovers, but the all-vehicle or metaphysical figure insists upon them, allows no other; it particularizes the lovers, and tries to endear them to us, by making them slightly—in spite of the compasses—eccentric. The Restoration and 18th Century felt that such poetic representations were irresponsible though interesting. We today are grown again more susceptible to their brilliance as sharply-textured representations. They offer us an art which has a very formal mode of composition, but in it the texture dominates the structure and all but threatens its life.

The formula of the metaphysical conceit is dangerously close to that of satire: where the general behavior of the victim is so particularized, or identified with some well-known analogous behavior so exclusively, as to become ridiculous. This poetry runs a great risk.

We must concede the sharp texture. And it gives us confidence in this manner of reasoning to reflect that Donne, and such poets as use the metaphysical conceits, are gifted with a passion for the sharp textures; always, and in common figures as well as in metaphysical ones. Donne has many poems ordinary enough in their principle of structure, not in the metaphysical method, which still in the vigor of their detail differentiate him from the 19th Century; and from Chapman too. One, for example, is "On His Mistris"; the one in which the poet forbids his secret bride to attend him abroad in the disguise of a page. For men will spy out her womanhood:

> Men of France, changeable Camelions,
> Spittles of diseases, shops of fashions,
> Loves fuellers, and the rightest company
> Of Players, which upon the worlds stage be,
> Will quickly know thee, and no lesse, alas,
> Th' indifferent Italian, as we passe
> His warme land, well content to thinke thee
>   Page,
> Will hunt thee with such lust, and hideous rage,
> As *Lots* faire guests were vext.   But none of
>   these
> Nor spungy hydroptique Dutch shall thee dis-
>   please,
>
> If thou stay here.

Spittles of course are hospitals; as we might say, walking hospitals. The passage has rhetorical generalizations in it; it is almost Miltonic, but inserts the spungy hydroptic Dutch carefully as an afterthought, not a member of the cordinate series as Milton would have had it; and altogether has sharper detail than Milton fancies. The poem concludes:

> Nor let thy lookes our long hid love confesse,
> Nor praise, nor dispraise me, nor blesse nor
>   curse
> Openly loves force, nor in bed fright thy Nurse

With midnights startings, crying out, oh, oh
Nurse, o my love is slaine, I saw him goe
Oer the white Alpes alone; I saw him I,
Assail'd, fight, taken, stabb'd, bleed, fall, and
    die.
Augure me better chance, except dread *Jove*
Thinke it enough for me to have had thy love.

The detail in the dream is not metaphorical at all; but at least it is imaginative. We say such detail is fresh, sharp, energetic, and lively or vivid; but surely one term is better than another for the critic. In ontological language we might say that Donne enforces the particularity of his object. In our present terms we say that his texture is unusually distinct; that is, it distinguishes itself more than usually from the train of the prose structure.

It has proved hard for critics to define the metaphysical conceit in any terms. Mine may not seem, for the purpose, perspicuous. But I submit that definition in Eliot's usual terms, a matter of an emotion with some local feelings, would have been next to impossible. (pp. 175-92)

> *John Crowe Ransom, "T. S. Eliot: The Historical Critic," in his* The New Criticism, *New Directions, 1941, pp. 135-208.*

SURVEYS AND OVERVIEWS

Herbert J. C. Grierson

[*Grierson was a Scottish educator and scholar who was considered in his time a leading authority on John Milton, John Donne, and Walter Scott. In the following excerpt, Grierson assesses the historical progression of metaphysical poetry from John Donne and his successors to Abraham Cowley, asserting that their work is distinguished by "above all the peculiar blend of passion and thought."*]

I

Metaphysical Poetry, in the full sense of the term, is a poetry which, like that of the *Divina Commedia*, the *De Natura Rerum*, perhaps Goethe's *Faust*, has been inspired by a philosophical conception of the universe and the rôle assigned to the human spirit in the great drama of existence. These poems were written because a definite interpretation of the riddle, the atoms of Epicurus rushing through infinite empty space, the theology of the schoolmen as elaborated in the catechetical disquisitions of St. Thomas, Spinoza's vision of life *sub specie aeternitatis*, beyond good and evil, laid hold on the mind and the imagination of a great poet, unified and illumined his comprehension of life, intensified and heightened his personal consciousness of joy and sorrow, of hope and fear, by broadening their significance, revealing to him in the history of his own soul a brief abstract of the drama of human destiny. 'Poetry is the first and last of all knowledge—it is as immortal as the heart of man.' Its themes are the simplest experiences of the surface of life, sorrow and joy, love and battle, the peace of the country, the bustle and stir of towns, but equally the boldest conceptions, the profoundest intuitions, the subtlest and most complex classifications and 'discourse of reason', if into these too the poet can 'carry sensation', make of them passionate experiences communicable in vivid and moving imagery, in rich and varied harmonies.

It is no such great metaphysical poetry as that of Lucretius and Dante that the present essay deals with. . . . Of the poets from whom it culls, Donne is familiar with the definitions and distinctions of Mediaeval Scholasticism; Cowley's bright and alert, if not profound mind, is attracted by the achievements of science and the systematic materialism of Hobbes. Donne, moreover, is metaphysical not only in virtue of his scholasticism, but by his deep reflective interest in the experiences of which his poetry is the expression, the new psychological curiosity with which he writes of love and religion. The divine poets who follow Donne have each the inherited metaphysic, if one may so call it, of the Church to which he is attached, Catholic or Anglican. But none of the poets has for his main theme a metaphysic like that of Epicurus or St. Thomas passionately apprehended and imaginatively expounded. Donne, the most thoughtful and imaginative of them all, is more aware of disintegration than of comprehensive harmony, of the clash between the older physics and metaphysics on the one hand and the new science of Copernicus and Galileo and Vesalius and Bacon on the other:

A seventeenth-century view of Oxford, with two scholars in debate.

The new philosophy calls all in doubt,
The element of fire is quite put out;
The sun is lost and the earth, and no man's wit
Can well direct him where to look for it.
And freely men confess that this world's spent,
When in the planets and the firmament
They seek so many new; they see that this
Is crumbled out again to his atomies.

   Have not all souls thought
For many ages that our body is wrought
Of air and fire and other elements?
And now they think of new ingredients;
And one soul thinks one, and another way
Another thinks, and 'tis an even lay.

The greatest English poet, indeed, of the century was, or believed himself to be, a philosophical or theological poet of the same order as Dante. *Paradise Lost* was written to be a justification of 'the ways of God to men', resting on a theological system as definite and almost as carefully articulated in the *De Doctrina Christiana* as that which Dante had accepted from the *Summa* of Aquinas. And the poet embodied his argument in a dramatic poem as vividly and intensely conceived, as magnificently and harmoniously set forth, as the *Divina Commedia*. But in truth Milton was no philosopher. The subtleties of theological definition and inference eluded his rationalistic, practical, though idealistic, mind. He proved nothing. The definitely stated argument of the poem is an obvious begging of the question. What he did was to create, or give a new definiteness and sensible power to, a great myth which, through his poem, continued for a century or more to dominate the mind and imagination of pious protestants without many of them suspecting the heresies which lurked beneath the imposing and dazzling poem in which was retold the Bible story of the fall and redemption of man.

Metaphysical in this large way, Donne and his followers to Cowley are not, yet the word describes better what is the peculiar quality of their poetry than any other, e.g. fantastic, for poetry may be fantastic in so many different ways, witness Skelton and the Elizabethans, and Hood and Browning. It lays stress on the right things—the survival, one might say the reaccentuation, of the metaphysical strain, the *concetti metafisici ed ideali* as Testi calls them in contrast to the simpler imagery of classical poetry, of mediaeval Italian poetry; the more intellectual, less verbal, character of their wit compared with the conceits of the Elizabethans; the finer psychology of which their conceits are often the expression; their learned imagery; the argumentative, subtle evolution of their lyrics; above all the peculiar blend of passion and thought, feeling and ratiocination which is their greatest achievement. Passionate thinking is always apt to become metaphysical, probing and investigating the experience from which it takes its rise. All these qualities are in the poetry of Donne, and Donne is the great master of English poetry in the seventeenth century.

The Italian influence which Wyatt and Surrey brought into English poetry at the Renaissance gave it a more serious, a more thoughtful colour. They caught, especially Wyatt in some of the finest of his sonnets and songs, that spirit of 'high seriousness' which Chaucer with all his ad-miration of Italian poetry had failed to apprehend. English mediaeval poetry is often gravely pious, haunted by the fear of death and the judgement, melancholy over the 'Falls of Princes'; it is never serious and thoughtful in the introspective, reflective, dignified manner which it became in Wyatt and Sackville, and our 'sage and serious' Spenser, and in the songs of the first group of Elizabethan courtly poets, Sidney and Raleigh and Dyer. One has but to recall 'My lute, awake! perform the last', 'Forget not yet the tried intent', 'My mind to me a kingdom is', and to contrast them in mind with the songs which Henry VIII and Cornish were still composing and singing when Wyatt began to write, in order to realize what Italy and the Renaissance did to deepen the strain of English lyric poetry as that had flowed under French influence from the thirteenth to the sixteenth centuries. But French influence, the influence of Ronsard and his fellows, renewed itself in the seventies, and the great body of Elizabethan song is as gay and careless and impersonal as the earlier lyric had been, though richer in colour and more varied in rhythm. Then came Donne and Jonson (the schoolman and the classical scholar, one might say, emphasizing for the moment single aspects of their work), and new qualities of spirit and form were given to lyrical poetry, and not to lyrical poetry alone.

In dealing with poets who lived and wrote before the eighteenth century we are always confronted with the difficulty of recovering the personal, the biographical element, which, if sometimes disturbing and disconcerting, is yet essential to a complete understanding of their work. Men were not different from what they are now, and if there be hardly a lyric of Goethe's or Shelley's that does not owe something to the accidents of their lives, one may feel sure it was in varying degrees the same with poets three hundred years ago. Poems are not written by influences or movements or sources, but come from the living hearts of men. Fortunately, in the case of Donne, one of the most individual of poets, it is possible to some extent to reproduce the circumstances, the inner experiences from which his intensely personal poetry flowed.

He was in the first place a Catholic. Our history text-books make so little of the English Catholics that one is apt to forget they existed and were, for themselves at any rate, not a political problem, but real and suffering individuals. 'I had my first breeding and conversation', says Donne, 'with men of a suppressed and afflicted religion, accustomed to the despite of death and hungry of an imagined martyrdom.' In these circumstances, we gather, he was carefully and religiously educated, and after some years at Oxford and Cambridge was taken or sent abroad, perhaps with a view to entering foreign service, more probably with a view to the priesthood, and visited Italy and Spain. And then, one conjectures, a reaction took place, the rebellion of a full-blooded, highly intellectual temperament against a superimposed bent. He entered the Inns of Court in 1592, at the age of nineteen, and flung himself into the life of a student and the life of a young man about town, Jack Donne, 'not dissolute but very neat, a great visitor of ladies, a great frequenter of plays, a great writer of conceited verses'. 'Neither was it possible that a vulgar soul should dwell in such promising features.' He joined the band of reckless and raffish young men who sailed with Essex to Cadiz and the Islands. He was taken into the service of Sir Thomas Egerton. Ambition began to vie with the love of pleasure, when a hasty marriage closed a promising career, and left him bound in shallows and in miseries, to spend years in the suitorship of the great, and to find at last, not altogether willingly, a haven in the Anglican priesthood, and reveal himself as the first great orator that Church produced.

The record of these early years is contained in Donne's satires—harsh, witty, lucid, full of a young man's scorn of fools and low callings, and a young thinker's consciousness of the problems of religion in an age of divided faiths, and of justice in a corrupt world—and in his Love Songs and Sonnets and Elegies. The satires were more generally known; the love poems the more influential in courtly and literary circles.

Donne's genius, temperament, and learning gave to his love poems certain qualities which immediately arrested attention and have given them ever since a power at once fascinating and disconcerting despite the faults of phrasing and harmony which, for a century after Dryden, obscured, and to some still outweigh, their poetic worth. The first of these is a depth and range of feeling unknown to the majority of Elizabethan sonneteers and song-writers. Over all the Elizabethan sonnets, in greater or less measure, hangs the suggestion of translation or imitation. Watson, Sidney, Daniel, Spenser, Drayton, Lodge, all of them, with rarer or more frequent touches of individuality, are pipers of Petrarch's woes, sighing in the strain of Ronsard or more often of Desportes. Shakespeare, indeed, in his great sequence, and Drayton in at any rate one sonnet, sounded a deeper note, revealed a fuller sense of the complexities and contradictions of passionate devotion. But Donne's treatment of love is entirely unconventional except when he chooses to dally half ironically with the convention of Petrarchian adoration. His songs are the expression in unconventional, witty language of all the moods of a lover that experience and imagination have taught him to understand—sensuality aerated by a brilliant wit; fascination and scornful anger inextricably blended:

> When by thy scorn, O murdress, I am dead
> And that thou think'st thee free
> From all solicitations from me,
> Then shall my ghost come to thy bed;

the passionate joy of mutual and contented love:

> All other things to their destruction draw,
>   Only our love hath no decay;
> This no to-morrow hath nor yesterday,
>   Running it never runs from us away,
> But truly keeps his first, last, everlasting day;

the sorrow of parting which is the shadow of such joy; the gentler pathos of temporary separation in married life:

> Let not thy divining heart
>   Forethink me any ill,
> Destiny may take thy part,
>   And may thy fears fulfil;
>   But think that we
> Are but turn'd aside to sleep;

> They who one another keep
>   Alive ne'er parted be;

the mystical heights and the mystical depths of love:

> Study me then you who shall lovers be
> At the next world, that is, at the next Spring:
> For I am every dead thing
> In whom love wrought new Alchemy.

If Donne had expressed this wide range of intense feeling as perfectly as he has done at times poignantly and startlingly; if he had given to his poems the same impression of entire artistic sincerity that Shakespeare conveys in the greater of his sonnets and Drayton once achieved; if to his many other gifts had been added a deeper and more controlling sense of beauty, he would have been, as he nearly is, the greatest of love poets. But there is a second quality of his poetry which made it the fashion of an age, but has been inimical to its general acceptance ever since, and that is its metaphysical wit. 'He affects the metaphysics', says Dryden, 'not only in his satires but in his amorous verses where nature only should reign; and perplexes the minds of the fair sex with nice speculations of philosophy when he should engage their hearts and entertain them with the softnesses of love.' 'Amorous verses', 'the fair sex', and 'the softnesses of love' are the vulgarities of a less poetic and passionate age than Donne's, but metaphysics he does affect. But a metaphysical strand, *concetti metafisici ed ideali*, had run through the mediaeval love-poetry of which the Elizabethan sonnets are a descendant. It had attained its fullest development in the poems of Dante and his school, had been subordinated to rhetoric and subtleties of expression rather than thought in Petrarch, and had lost itself in the pseudo-metaphysical extravagances of Tebaldeo, Cariteo, and Serafino. Donne was no conscious reviver of the metaphysics of Dante, but to the game of elaborating fantastic conceits and hyperboles which was the fashion throughout Europe, he brought not only a full-blooded temperament and acute mind, but a vast and growing store of the same scholastic learning, the same Catholic theology, as controlled Dante's thought, jostling already with the new learning of Copernicus and Paracelsus. The result is startling and disconcerting,—the comparison of parted lovers to the legs of a pair of compasses, the deification of his mistress by the discovery that she is only to be defined by negatives or that she can read the thoughts of his heart, a thing 'beyond an angel's art'; and a thousand other subtleties of quintessences and nothingness, the mixture of souls and the significance of numbers, to say nothing of the aerial bodies of angels, the phoenix and the mandrake's root, Alchemy and Astrology, legal contracts and *non obstantes*, 'late school-boys and sour prentices', 'the king's real and his stamped face'. But the effect aimed at and secured is not entirely fantastic and erudite. The motive inspiring Donne's images is in part the same as that which led Shakespeare from the picturesque, natural and mythological, images of *A Midsummer-Night's Dream* and *The Merchant of Venice* to the homely but startling phrases and metaphors of *Hamlet* and *Macbeth*, the 'blanket of the dark', the

> fat weed
> That rots itself in ease on Lethe wharf,

'the rank sweat of an enseamed bed'. It is the same desire for vivid and dramatic expression. The great master at a later period of dramatic as well as erudite pulpit oratory coins in his poems many a startling, jarring, arresting phrase:

> For God's sake hold your tongue and let me
>   love:
> Who ever comes to shroud me do not harm
>   Nor question much
> That subtle wreath of hair, which crowns my
>   arm:
> I taught my silks their rustling to forbear
> Even my opprest shoes dumb and silent were.
> I long to talk with some old lover's ghost
> Who died before the God of love was born;
>
> Twice or thrice had I loved thee
> Before I knew thy face or name,
> So in a voice, so in a shapeless flame,
> Angels affect us oft and worshipped be;
>
> And whilst our souls negotiate there
>   We like sepulchral statues lay;
> All day the same our postures were
>   And we said nothing all the day.
>
> My face and brest of haircloth, and my head
> With care's harsh, sudden hoariness o'er-spread.

These vivid, simple, realistic touches are too quickly merged in learned and fantastic elaborations, and the final effect of every poem of Donne's is a bizarre and blended one; but if the greatest poetry rises clear of the bizarre, the fantastic, yet very great poetry may be bizarre if it be the expression of a strangely blended temperament, an intense emotion, a vivid imagination.

What is true of Donne's imagery is true of the other disconcerting element in his poetry, its harsh and rugged verse. It is an outcome of the same double motive, the desire to startle and the desire to approximate poetic to direct, unconventional, colloquial speech. Poetry is always a balance, sometimes a compromise, between what has to be said and the prescribed pattern to which the saying of it is adjusted. In poetry such as Spenser's, the musical flow, the melody and harmony of line and stanza, is dominant, and the meaning is adjusted to it at the not infrequent cost of diffuseness—if a delightful diffuseness—and even some weakness of phrasing logically and rhetorically considered. In Shakespeare's tragedies the thought and feeling tend to break through the prescribed pattern till blank verse becomes almost rhythmical prose, the rapid overflow of the lines admitting hardly the semblance of pause. This is the kind of effect Donne is always aiming at, alike in his satires and lyrics, bending and cracking the metrical pattern to the rhetoric of direct and vehement utterance. The result is often, and to eighteenth-century ears attuned to the clear and defined, if limited, harmony of Waller and Dryden and Pope was, rugged and harsh. But here again, to those who have ears that care to hear, the effect is not finally inharmonious. Donne's verse has a powerful and haunting harmony of its own. For Donne is not simply, no poet could be, willing to force his accent, to strain and crack a prescribed pattern; he is striving to find a rhythm that will express the passionate fullness of his mind, the fluxes and refluxes of his moods; and the felicities of verse are as frequent and startling as those of phrasing. He is one of the first masters, perhaps *the* first, of the elaborate stanza or paragraph in which the discords of individual lines or phrases are resolved in the complex and rhetorically effective harmony of the whole group of lines:

> If yet I have not all thy love,
> Deare, I shall never have it all,
> I cannot breathe one other sigh, to move,
> Nor can entreat one other tear to fall,
> And all my treasure, which should purchase
>   thee,
> Sighs, tears, and oaths, and letters I have spent.
> Yet no more can be due to me,
> Than at the bargain made was meant,
> If then thy gift of love was partial,
> That some to me, some shuld to others fall,
>   Deare, I shall never have thee all.
>
> But I am none; nor will my sunne renew.
> You lovers for whose sake the lesser sunne
>   At this time to the Goat is run
>   To fetch new lust and give it you,
>   Enjoy your summer all;
> Since she enjoys her long night's festival,
> Let me prepare towards her, and let me call
> This hour her Vigil and her Eve, since this

> Both the years / and the days / deep mid / night is.

The wrenching of accent which Jonson complained of is not entirely due to carelessness or indifference. It has often both a rhetorical and a harmonious justification. Donne plays with rhythmical effects as with conceits and words and often in much the same way. Mr. Fletcher Melton's interesting analysis of his verse has not, I think, established his main thesis, which like so many 'research' scholars he over-emphasizes, that the whole mystery of Donne's art lies in his use of the same sound now in *arsis*, now in *thesis*; but his examples show that this is one of many devices by which Donne secures two effects, the troubling of the regular fall of the verse stresses by the intrusion of rhetorical stress on syllables which the metrical pattern leaves unstressed, and, secondly, an echoing and re-echoing of similar sounds parallel to his fondness for resemblances in thoughts and things apparently the most remote from one another. There is, that is to say, in his verse the same blend as in his diction of the colloquial and the bizarre. He writes as one who *will* say what he has to say without regard to conventions of poetic diction or smooth verse, but what he has to say is subtle and surprising, and so are the metrical effects with which it is presented. There is nothing of unconscious or merely careless harshness in such an effect as this:

> Poor soul, in this thy flesh what dost thou know?
> Thou know'st thyself so little that thou knowst
>   not
> How thou didst die, nor how thou wast begot.
> Thou neither know'st how thou at first camest
>   in,
> Nor how thou took'st the poison of man's sin;
> Nor dost thou though thou know'st that thou art
>   so

By what way thou art made immortal know.

In Donne's pronunciation, as in southern English to-day, 'thou', 'how', 'soul', 'know', 'though', and 'so' were not far removed from each other in sound and the reiterated notes ring through the lines like a tolling bell. Mr. Melton has collected, and any careful reader may discover for himself, many similar subtleties of poetical rhetoric; for Donne is perhaps our first great master of poetic rhetoric, of poetry used, as Dryden and Pope were to use it, for effects of oratory rather than of song, and the advance which Dryden achieved was secured by subordinating to oratory the more passionate and imaginative qualities which troubled the balance and movement of Donne's packed but imaginative rhetoric.

It was not indeed in lyrical verse that Dryden followed and developed Donne, but in his eulogistic, elegiac, satirical, and epistolary verse. The progress of Dryden's eulogistic style is traceable from his earliest metaphysical extravagances through lines such as those addressed to the Duchess of York, where Waller is his model, to the verses on the death of Oldham in which a more natural and classical strain has entirely superseded his earlier extravagances and elegancies. In truth Donne's metaphysical eulogies and elegies and epistles are a hard nut to crack for his most sympathetic admirers. And yet they have undeniable qualities. The metaphysics are developed in a more serious, a less paradoxical, strain than in some of the songs and elegies. In his letters he is an excellent, if far from a perfect, talker in verse; and the personality which they reveal is a singularly charming one, grave, loyal, melancholy, witty. If some of the elegiac pieces are packed with tasteless and extravagant hyperboles, the *Anniversaries* (especially the second) remains, despite all its faults, one of the greatest poems on death in the language, the fullest record in our literature of the disintegrating collision in a sensitive mind of the old tradition and the new learning. Some of the invocational passages in *Of the Progresse of the Soule* are among the finest examples of his subtle and passionate thinking as well as of his most elaborate verse rhetoric.

But the most intense and personal of Donne's poems, after the love songs and elegies, are his later religious sonnets and songs; and their influence on subsequent poetry was even more obvious and potent. They are as personal and as tormented as his earlier 'love-song weeds', for his spiritual Aeneid was a troubled one. To date his conversion to Anglicanism is not easy. In his satires there is a veiled Roman tone. By 1602 he disclaims to Egerton 'all love of a corrupt religion', but in the autumn of the previous year he had been meditating a satire on Queen Elizabeth as one of the world's great heretics. His was not a conversion but a reconciliation, an acquiescence in the faith of his country, the established religion of his legal sovereign, and the act cost him some pangs. 'A convert from Popery to Protestantism,' said Dr. Johnson, 'gives up so much of what he has held as sacred as anything that he retains, there is so much laceration of mind in such a conversion, that it can hardly be sincere and lasting.' Something of that laceration of mind is discernible in Donne's religious verse:

Show me dear Christ that spouse so bright and
    clear.

But the conflict between the old and the reformed faiths was not the only, nor perhaps the principal trouble for Donne's enlightened mind ready to recognize in all the Churches 'virtual beams of one sun', 'connatural pieces of one circle'. A harder fight was that between the secular, the 'man of the world' temper of his mind and the claims of a pious and ascetic calling. It was not the errors of his youth, as the good Walton supposed, which constituted the great stumbling block, though he never ignores these:

O might those sighs and tears return again
Into my breast and eyes, which I have spent,
That I might in this holy discontent
Mourn with some fruit, as I have mourned in
    vain.

It was rather the temperament of one who, at a time when a public career was more open to unassisted talent, might have proved an active and useful, if ambitious, civil servant, or professional man, at war with the claims of a religious life which his upbringing had taught him was incompatible with worldly ambition. George Herbert, a much more contented Anglican than Donne ever became, knew something of the same struggle before he bent his neck to the collar.

The two notes then of Donne's religious poems are the Catholic and the personal. He is the first of our Anglo-Catholic poets, and he is our first intensely personal religious poet, expressing always not the mind simply of the Christian as such, but the conflicts and longings of one troubled soul, one subtle and fantastic mind. For Donne's technique—his phrasing and conceits, the metaphysics of mediaeval Christianity, his packed verse with its bold, irregular fingering and echoing vowel sounds—remains what it had been from the outset. The echoing sounds in lines such as these cannot be quite casual:

O might those *sighs* and tears return again
Into my breast and *eyes*, which *I* have spent,
That *I* might in this holy discontent
Mourn with some fruit, as *I* have mourned in
    vain;
In mine *Idolat'ry* what showers of rain
Mine eyes did waste?   What griefs *my* heart did
    rent?
That sufferance was *my* sin; now *I* repent
Cause *I* did suffer *I* must suffer pain.

In the remaining six lines the same sound never recurs.

A metaphysical, a philosophical poet, to the degree to which even his contemporary Fulke Greville might be called such, Donne was not. The thought in his poetry is not his primary concern but the feeling. No scheme of thought, no interpretation of life became for him a complete and illuminating experience. The central theme of his poetry is ever his own intense personal moods, as a lover, a friend, an analyst of his own experiences worldly and religious. His philosophy cannot unify these experiences. It represents the reaction of his restless and acute mind on the intense experience of the moment, a reading of it in the light now of one, now of another philosophical or theological dogma or thesis caught from his multifarious reading, developed with audacious paradox or more serious intention, as an expression, an illumination of that mood to himself and to his reader. Whether one choose to call him a metaphysical or a fantastic poet, the stress must be laid on the word 'poet'. Whether verse or prose be his medium, Donne is always a poet, a creature of feeling and imagination, seeking expression in vivid phrase and complex harmonies, whose acute and subtle intellect was the servant, if sometimes the unruly servant, of passion and imagination.

II

Donne's influence was felt in his own day by two strangely different classes of men, both attached by close ties to the Court. For the Court, the corrupt, ambitious, intriguing, dissolute but picturesque and dazzling court of the old pagan Elizabeth, the pedantic and drunken James, the dignified and melancholy and politically blinded Charles, was the centre round which all Donne's secular interests revolved. He can speak of it as bitterly and sardonically as Shakespeare in *Hamlet*:

> Here's no more newes, then vertue, I may as well
> Tell you Cales or St. Michael's tale for newes, as
>   tell
> That vice doth here habitually dwell. . . .
> But now 'tis incongruity to smile,
> Therefore I end; and bid farewell a while,
> *At Court*, though *From Court* were the better
>   style.

He knows its corruptions as well as Milton and commends Lady Bedford as Milton might have commended Alice Egerton. All the same, to be shut out from the Court, in the city or the country, is to inhabit a desert, or sepulchre, for *there*:

> The Princes favour is defused o'er all,
> From which all Fortunes, Names, and Natures
>   fall.
> And all is warmth and light and good desire.

It was among the younger generation of Courtiers that Donne found the warmest admirers of his paradoxical and sensual audacities as a love-poet, as it was the divines who looked to Laud and the Court for Anglican doctrine and discipline who revered his memory, enshrined by the pious Izaak Walton, as of a divine poet and preacher. The 'metaphysicals' were all on the King's side. Even Andrew Marvell was neither Puritan nor Republican. 'Men ought to have trusted God', was his final judgement on the Rebellion, 'they ought to have trusted the King with the whole matter'. They were on the side of the King, for they were on the side of the humanities; and the Puritan rebellion, whatever the indirect constitutional results, was in itself and at the moment a fanatical upheaval, successful because it also threw up the John Zizka of his age; its triumph was the triumph of Cromwell's sword.

> And for the last effect
> Still keep the sword erect.

> Besides the force it has to fright
> The spirits of the shady night,
>   The same arts that did gain
>   A power must it maintain.

To call these poets the 'school of Donne' or 'metaphysical' poets may easily mislead if one takes either phrase in too full a sense. It is not only that they show little of Donne's subtlety of mind or 'hydroptic, immoderate thirst of human learning', but they want, what gives its interest to this subtle and fantastic misapplication of learning,—the complexity of mood, the range of personal feeling which lends such fullness of life to Donne's strange and troubled poetry. His followers, amorous and courtly, or pious and ecclesiastical, move in a more rarefied atmosphere; their poetry is much more truly 'abstract' than Donne's, the witty and fantastic elaboration of one or two common moods, of compliment, passion, devotion, penitence. It is very rarely that one can detect a deep personal note in the delightful love-songs with which the whole period abounds from Carew to Dryden. The collected work of none of them would give such an impression of a real history behind it, a history of many experiences and moods, as Donne's Songs and Sonnets and the Elegies, and, as one must still believe, the sonnets of Shakespeare record. Like the Elizabethan sonneteers they all dress and redress the same theme in much the same manner, though the manner is not quite the Elizabethan, nor the theme. Song has superseded the sonnet, and the passion of which they sing has lost most of the Petrarchian, chivalrous strain, and become in a very definite meaning of the words, 'simple and sensuous'. And if the religious poets are rather more individual and personal, the personal note is less intense, troubled and complex than in Donne's Divine Poems; the individual is more merged in the Christian, Catholic or Anglican.

Donne and Jonson are probably in the main responsible for the unconventional purity and naturalness of their diction, for these had both 'shaken hands with' Spenserian archaism and strangeness, with the 'rhetoric' of the sonneteers and poems like *Venus and Adonis*; and their style is untouched by any foreshadowing of Miltonic diction or the jargon of a later poetic vocabulary. The metaphysicals are the masters of the 'neutral style', of a diction equally appropriate, according as it may be used, to prose and verse. If purity and naturalness of style is a grace, they deserved well of the English language, for few poets have used it with a more complete acceptance of the established tradition of diction and idiom. There are no poets till we come perhaps to Cowper, and he has not quite escaped from jargon, or Shelley, and his imagination operates in a more ethereal atmosphere, whose style is so entirely that of an English gentleman of the best type, natural, simple, occasionally careless, but never diverging into vulgar colloquialism, as after the Restoration, or into conventional, tawdry splendour, as in the century of Akenside and Erasmus Darwin. Set a poem by George Herbert beside Gray at his best, e.g.

> Sweet day so cool, so calm, so bright,
> The bridal of the earth and sky,
> The dew shall weep thy fall to-night,
>   For thou must die; &c.

set that beside even a good verse from Gray, and one realizes the charm of simplicity, of perfect purity of diction:

> Still is the toiling hand of Care;

> The panting herds repose:
> Yet hark how through the peopled air
>   The busy murmur glows!
> The insect-youth are on the wing,
> Eager to taste the honied spring,
> And float amid the liquid noon:
> Some lightly o'er the current skim,
> Some show their gaily-gilded trim
>   Quick-glancing to the sun.

'The language of the age is never the language of poetry', Gray declares, and certainly some of our great poets have created for themselves a diction which was never current, but it is equally true that some of the best English poetry has been written in a style which differs from the best spoken language only as the language of feeling will naturally diverge from the language of our less exalted moods. It was in the seventeenth-century poets that Wordsworth found the best corrective to the jargon of the later eighteenth-century poetry, descriptive and reflective, which he admired in his youth and imitated in his early poems; for as Coleridge pointed out, the style of the 'metaphysicals' 'is the reverse of that which distinguishes too many of our most recent versifiers; the one conveying the most fantastic thoughts in the most correct language, the other in the most fantastic language conveying the most trivial thoughts'.

But even the fantastic thoughts, the conceits of these courtly love poets and devout singers are not to be dismissed so lightly as a later, and still audible, criticism imagined. They played with thoughts, Sir Walter Scott complained, as the Elizabethans had played with words. But to play with thoughts it is necessary to think. 'To write on their plan', says Dr. Johnson, 'it was at least necessary to read and think. No man could be born a metaphysical poet, nor assume the dignity of a writer, by descriptions copied from descriptions, by imitations borrowed from imitations, by traditional imagery and hereditary similes, by readiness of rhyme and volubility of syllables.' Consider a poem, *The Repulse*, by a comparatively minor poet, Thomas Stanley. That is not a mere conceit. It is a new and felicitous rendering of a real and thrilling experience, the discovery that you might have fared worse in love than not to be loved, you might have been loved and then abandoned. Carew's *Ask me no more* is a coruscation of hyperboles, but

> Now you have freely given me leave to love,
>   What will you do?

is a fresh and effective appeal to the heart of a woman. And this is what the metaphysicals are often doing in their unwearied play with conceits, delightfully naughty, extravagant, fantastic, frigid—they succeed in stumbling upon some conceit which reveals a fresh intuition into the heart, or states an old plea with new and prevailing force. And the divine poets express with the same blend of argument and imagination the deep and complex currents of religious feeling which were flowing in England throughout the century, institutional, theological, mystical, while in the metaphysical subtleties of conceit they found something that is more than conceit, symbols in which to express or adumbrate their apprehensions of the infinite.

The direct indebtedness of the courtly poets to Ben Jonson is probably, as Professor Gregory Smith has recently argued, small. But not only Herrick, metaphysical poets like Carew and Stanley and others owe much both of their turn of conceit and their care for form to Jonson's own models, the Latin lyrists, Anacreon, the Greek Anthology, neo-Latin or Humanist poetry so rich in neat and pretty conceits. Some of them, as Crashaw and Stanley, and not only these, were familiar with Italian and Spanish poetry, Marino and Garcilasso and their elegantly elaborated confections. But their great master is Donne. If he taught them many heresies, he instilled into them at any rate the pure doctrine of the need of passion for a lover and a poet. What the young courtiers and university wits admired and reproduced in different degrees and fashions were his sensual audacity and the peculiar type of evolution which his poems accentuated, the strain of passionate paradoxical reasoning which knits the first line to the last and is perhaps a more intimate characteristic than even the far-fetched, fantastic comparisons. This intellectual, argumentative evolution had been of course a feature of the sonnet which might fancifully be called, with its double quatrain and sestet, the poetical analogy of the syllogism. But the movement of the sonnet is slow and meditative, a single thought expanded and articulated through the triple division, and the longer, decasyllabic line is the appropriate medium:

> Then hate me when thou wilt; if ever, now;
> Now while the world is bent my deeds to cross,
> Join with the spite of Fortune, make me bow,
> And do not drop in for an after-loss;
> Ah, do not when my heart hath scaped this sorrow,
> Come in the rearward of a conquer'd woe,
> Give not a windy night a rainy morrow,
> To linger out a purpos'd overthrow.
> If thou wilt leave me, do not leave me last
> When other petty griefs have done their spite,
> But in the onset come; so shall I taste
> At first the very worst of Fortune's might;
> And other strains of woe which now seem woe,
> Compared with loss of thee will not seem so.

What Donne had done was to quicken this movement, to intensify the strain of passionate ratiocination, passionate, paradoxical argument, and to carry it over from the sonnet to the song with its shorter lines, more winged and soaring movement, although the deeper strain of feeling which Donne shares with Shakespeare, and with Drayton at his best, made him partial to the longer line, at least as an element in his stanzas, and to longer and more intricate stanzas. Lightening both the feeling and the thought, the courtly poets simplified the verse, attaining some of their most wonderful effects in the common ballad measure [4, 3] or the longer [4, 4] measure in couplets or alternate rhymes. But the form and content are intimately associated. It is the elaboration of the paradoxical argument, the weight which the rhetoric lays on those syllables which fall under the metrical stress, that gives to these verses, or seems to give, their peculiar *élan*:

> My love is of a birth as rare
>   As 'tis for object strange and high;
> It was begotten by Despair

Upon Impossibility.

The audacious hyperboles and paradoxical turns of thought give breath to and take wings from the soaring rhythm.

It is needless here to dwell at length on the several poets from whom I have selected examples of love-song and complimentary verses. Their range is not wide—love, compliment, elegy, occasionally devotion. Herrick had to leave the court to learn the delights of nature and country superstitions. Lord Herbert of Cherbury, philosopher and coxcomb, was just the person to dilate on the Platonic theme of soul and body in the realm of love on which Donne occasionally descanted in half ironical fashion, Habington with tedious thin-blooded seriousness, Cleveland and others with naughty irreverence. But Lord Herbert's *Ode*, which has been, like most of his poems, very badly edited, seems to me the finest thing inspired by Donne's *Ecstasy* and more characteristic of the romantic taste of the court of Charles. But the poetic ornament of that Court is Thomas Carew. This young careless liver was a careful artist with a deeper vein of thought and feeling in his temperament than a first reading suggests. His masque reveals the influence of Bruno. In Carew's poems and Vandyke's pictures the artistic taste of Charles's court is vividly reflected, a dignified voluptuousness, an exquisite elegance, if in some of the higher qualities of man and artist Carew is as inferior to Wyatt or Spenser as Vandyke is to Holbein. His *Ecstasy* is the most daring and poetically the happiest of the imitations of Donne's clever if outrageous elegies; Cartwright's *Song of Dalliance* its nearest rival. His letter to Aurelian Townshend on the death of the King of Sweden breathes the very enchanted air of Charles's court while the storm was brewing as yet unsuspected. The text of Richard Lovelace's *Lucasta* (1649) is frequently corrupt, and the majority of the poems are careless and extravagant, but the few good things are the finest expression of honour and chivalry in all the Cavalier poetry of the century, the only poems which suggest what 'Cavalier' came to mean when glorified by defeat. His *Grasshopper* has suffered a hard fate by textual corruption and from dismemberment in recent anthologies. Only the fantastic touch about 'green ice' ranks it as 'metaphysical', for it is in fact an experiment in the manner of the Horatian ode, not the heroic ode, but the lighter Epicurean, meditative strain of 'Solvitur acris hiems' and 'Vides ut alta stet nive candidum', description yielding abruptly to reflection. A slightly better text or a little more care on the poet's part would have made it perfect. The gayest of the group is Sir John Suckling, the writer of what should be called *vers de société*, a more careless but more fanciful Prior. . . . Thomas Stanley, classical scholar, philosopher, translator, seems to me one of the happiest of recent recoveries, elegant, graceful, felicitous, and if at times a little flat and colourless, not always flat like the Catholic puritan William Habington.

But the strongest personality of all is Andrew Marvell. Apart from Milton he is the most interesting personality between Donne and Dryden, and at his very best a finer poet than either. Most of his descriptive poems lie a little outside my beat, though I have claimed *The Garden* as metaphysical,

Annihilating all that's made
To a green thought in a green shade.

. . . [His] few love poems and his few devotional pieces are perfect exponents of all the 'metaphysical' qualities—passionate, paradoxical argument, touched with humour and learned imagery:

As lines, so loves oblique, may well
   Themselves in every angle greet:
But ours so truly parallel,
   Though infinite, can never meet;

and above all the sudden soar of passion in bold and felicitous image, in clangorous lines:

But at my back I always hear
Time's wingèd chariot hurrying near,
And yonder all before us lie
Deserts of vast eternity.
Thy beauty shall no more be found;
Nor in thy marble vault shall sound
My echoing song: then worms shall try
That long preserv'd virginity;
And your quaint honour turn to dust;
And into ashes all my lust.
The grave's a fine and private place,
But none I think do there embrace.

These lines seem to me the very roof and crown of the metaphysical love lyric, at once fantastic and passionate. Donne is weightier, more complex, more suggestive of subtle and profound reaches of feeling, but he has not one single passage of the same length that combines all the distinctive qualities of the kind, in thought, in phrasing, in feeling, in music; and Rochester's most passionate lines are essentially simpler, less metaphysical.

When wearied with a world of woe,

might have been written by Burns with some differences. The best things of Donne and Marvell could only have been composed—except, as an imitative *tour de force*, like Watson's

Bid me no more to other eyes—

in the seventeenth century. But in that century there were so many poets who could sing, at least occasionally, in the same strain. Of all those whom Professor Saintsbury's ardent and catholic but discriminating taste has collected there is none who has not written too much indifferent verse, but none who has not written one or two songs showing the same fine blend of passion and paradox and music. The 'metaphysicals' of the seventeenth century combined two things, both soon to pass away, the fantastic dialectics of mediaeval love poetry and the 'simple, sensuous' strain which they caught from the classics—soul and body lightly yoked and glad to run and soar together in the winged chariot of Pegasus. Modern love poetry has too often sacrificed both to sentiment.

III

English religious poetry after the Reformation was a long time in revealing a distinctive note of its own. Here as elsewhere, Protestant poetry took the shape mainly of Biblical paraphrases or dull moralizings less impressive and sombre than the *Poema Morale* of an earlier century. Sylvester's translation of Du Bartas's *Weeks and Days* eclipsed all previous efforts and appealed to Elizabethan taste by its conceits and aureate diction. Catholic poets, on the other hand, like Robert Southwell, learned from the Italians to write on religious themes in the antithetic, 'conceited', 'passionating' style of the love poets of the day. His *Tears of St. Peter*, if it is not demonstrably indebted to Tansillo's *Le Lagrime di San Pietro*, is composed in the same hectic strain and with a superabundance of the conceits and antitheses of that and other Italian religious poems of the sixteenth century:

> Launch forth, my soul, into a main of tears,
>   Full-fraught with grief, the traffic of thy mind,
> Torn sails will serve, thoughts rent with guilty
>   fears,
>   Give care the stern, use sighs in lieu of wind:
> Remorse thy pilot; thy misdeeds thy card;
> Torment thy haven, shipwreck thy best reward.

His best poem, *The Burning Babe*, to have written which Jonson 'would have been content to destroy many of his', has the warmth and glow which we shall find again in the poetry of a Roman convert like Crashaw. It is in Donne's poems, *The Crosse, The Annuntiation and Passion, The Litanie*, that the Catholic tradition which survived in the Anglican Church becomes articulate in poetry; and in his sonnets and hymns that English religious poetry becomes for the first time intensely personal, the record of the experiences and aspirations, not of the Christian as such merely, but of one troubled and tormented soul. But the Catholic tradition in Donne was Roman rather than Anglican, or Anglican with something of a conscious effort; and Donne's passionate outpourings of penitence and longing lack one note of religious poetry which is audible in the songs of many less complex souls and less great poets, the note of attainment, of joy and peace. The waters have gone over him, the waters of fear and anguish, and it is only in his last hymns that he seems to descry across the agitation of the waves by which he is overwhelmed a light of hope and confidence:

> Swear by thyself that at my death thy Son
>   Shall shine as he shines now and heretofore;
> And having done that thou hast done,
>   I fear no more.

The poet in whom the English Church of Hooker and Laud, the Church of the *via media* in doctrine and ritual, found a voice of its own, was George Herbert, the son of Donne's friend Magdalen Herbert, and the younger brother of Lord Herbert of Cherbury. His volume *The Temple, Sacred Poems and Private Ejaculations, By Mr. George Herbert*, was printed at Cambridge in the year that a disorderly collection of the amorous, satirical, courtly and pious poems of the famous Dean of St. Paul's, who died in 1631, was shot from the press in London as *Poems, by J. D., with Elegies on the Author's Death*. As J. D. the author continued to figure on the title-page of each successive edition till that of 1669; nor were the additions made from time to time of a kind to diminish the complex, ambiguous impression which the volume must have produced on the minds of the admirers of the ascetic and eloquent Dean. There is no such record of a complex character and troubled progress in the poetry of Herbert. It was

not, indeed, altogether without a struggle that Herbert bowed his neck to the collar, abandoned the ambitions and vanities of youth to become the pious rector of Bemerton. He knew, like Donne, in what light the ministry was regarded by the young courtiers whose days were spent

> In dressing, mistressing and compliment.

His ambitions had been courtly. He loved fine clothes. As Orator at Cambridge he showed himself an adept in learned and elegant flattery, and he hoped 'that, as his predecessors, he might in time attain the place of a Secretary of State'. When he resolved, after the death of 'his most obliging and powerful friends', to take Orders, he 'did acquaint a court-friend' with his resolution, 'who persuaded him to alter it, as too mean an employment, and too much below his birth, and the excellent abilities and endowments of his mind'. All this is clearly enough reflected in Herbert's poems, . . . [including] the note of conflict, of personal experience, which troubles and gives life to poetry that might otherwise be too entirely doctrinal and didactic. But there is no evidence in Herbert's most agitated verses of the deeper scars, the profounder remorse which gives such a passionate, anguished *timbre* to the harsh but resonant harmonies of his older friend's *Divine Poems*:

> Despair behind, and death before doth cast
> Such terror, and my feeble flesh doth waste
> By sin in it, which it t'wards hell doth weigh.

Herbert knows the feeling of alienation from God; but he knows also that of reconcilement, the joy and peace of religion:

> You must sit down, says Love, and taste my
>   meat:
>   So I did sit and eat.

Herbert is too in full harmony with the Church of his country, could say, with Sir Thomas Browne, 'There is no Church whose every part so squares unto my Conscience; whose Articles, Constitutions and Customs, seem so consonant unto reason, and as it were framed to my particular Devotion, as this whereof I hold my Belief, the Church of England':

> Beauty in thee takes up her place,
> And dates her letters from thy face,
>   When she doth write.
>
> A fine aspect in fit array,
> Neither too mean, nor yet too gay,
>   Shows who is best. . . .
>
> But, dearest Mother, (what those misse)
> The mean, thy praise and glory is,
>   And long may be.
>
> Blessed be God, whose love it was
> To double moat thee with his grace,
>   And none but thee.

It was from Donne that Herbert learned the 'metaphysical' manner. He has none of Donne's daring applications of scholastic doctrines. Herbert's interest in theology is not metaphysical but practical and devotional, the doctrines of his Church—the Incarnation, Passion, Resurrection, Trinity, Baptism—as these are reflected in the festivals, fabric, and order of the Church and are capable of appeal to the heart. But Herbert's central theme is the psychology of his religious experiences. He transferred to religious poetry the subtler analysis and record of moods which had been Donne's great contribution to love poetry. The metaphysical taste in conceit, too, ingenious, erudite, and indiscriminate, not confining itself to the conventionally picturesque and poetic, appealed to his acute, if not profound mind, and to the Christian temper which rejected nothing as common and unclean. He would speak of sacred things in the simplest language and with the aid of the homeliest comparisons:

> Both heav'n and earth
> Paid me my wages in a world of mirth.

Prayer is:

> Heaven in ordinary, man well drest,
> The milky way, the bird of Paradise.

Divine grace in the Sacramental Elements:

> Knoweth the ready way,
> And hath the privy key
> Op'ning the soul's most subtle rooms;
> While those, to spirits refin'd, at door attend
> Dispatches from their friend.

Night is God's 'ebony box' in which:

> Thou dost inclose us till the day
> Put our amendment in our way,
> And give new wheels to our disorder'd clocks.
> Christ left his grave-clothes that we might, when grief
> Draws tears or blood, not want an handkerchief.

These are the 'mean' similes which in Dr. Johnson's view were fatal to poetic effect even in Shakespeare. We have learned not to be so fastidious, yet when they are not purified by the passionate heat of the poet's dramatic imagination the effect is a little stuffy, for the analogies and symbols are more fanciful or traditional than natural and imaginative. Herbert's nature is generally

'metaphysical',—'the busy orange-tree', the rose that purges, the 'sweet spring' which is 'a box where sweets compacted lie'. It is at rare moments that feeling and natural image are imaginatively and completely merged in one another:

> And now in age I bud again,
> After so many deaths I live and write;
> I once more smell the dew and rain,
> And relish versing: O my only light,
> It cannot be
> That I am he
> On whom thy tempests fell all night.

But if not a greatly imaginative, Herbert is a sincere and sensitive poet, and an accomplished artist elaborating his argumentative strain or little allegories and conceits with felicitous completeness, and managing his variously patterned stanzas—even the symbolic wings and altars and priestly bells, the three or seven-lined stanzas of his poems on the Trinity and Sunday—with a finished and delicate harmony. *The Temple* breathes the spirit of the Anglican Church at its best, primitive and modest; and also of one

troubled and delicate soul seeking and finding peace. Herbert's influence is discernible in the religious verse of all the minor Anglican poets of the century, but his two greatest followers were poets of a temper different from his own. Henry Vaughan had written verses of the fashionable kind . . . before the influence of Herbert converted his pen to the service of Heaven; but all his *poetry* is religious. In *Silex Scintillans* he often imitates his predecessor in name and choice of theme, but his best work is of another kind. The difference between Herbert and Vaughan, at his best, is the difference on which Coleridge and Wordsworth dilated between fancy and imagination, between the sensitive and happy discovery of analogies and the imaginative apprehension of emotional identity in diverse experiences, which is the poet's counterpart to the scientific discovery of a common law controlling the most divergent phenomena. Herbert's 'sweet day, so cool, so calm, so bright' is a delightful play of tender fancy. Vaughan's greatest verses reveal a profounder intuition, as when Night is:

> God's silent, searching flight;
> When my Lord's head is fill'd with dew, and all
> His locks are wet with the clear drops of night;
> His still, soft call;
> His knocking-time; the soul's dumb watch
> When spirits their fair kindred catch.

Vaughan is a less effective preacher, a far less neat and finished artist than Herbert. His temper is more that of the mystic. The sense of guilt which troubles Donne, of sin which is the great alienator of man's soul from God in Herbert's poems, is less acute with Vaughan, or is merged in a wider consciousness of separation, a veil between the human soul and that Heaven which is its true home. His soul is ever questing, back to the days of his own youth, or to the youth of the world, or to the days of Christ's sojourn on earth, when God and man were in more intimate contact:

> In Abraham's tent the winged guests
> —O how familiar then was heaven!—
> Eat, drink, discourse, sit down and rest,
> Until the cool and shady even;

or else he yearns for the final reconciliation beyond the grave:

> Where no rude shade or night
> Shall dare approach us; we shall there no more
> Watch stars or pore
> Through melancholy clouds, and say,
> 'Would it were Day!'
> One everlasting Sabbath there shall run
> Without succession, and without a sun.

To this mystical mood Nature reveals herself, not as a museum of spiritual analogies, a garden of religious simples, but as a creature simpler than man, yet, in virtue of its simplicity and innocence, in closer harmony with God. 'Etenim res creatae exserto capite observantes exspectant revelationem filiorum Dei.' At brief moments Vaughan writes of nature and childhood as Wordsworth and Blake were to write, but generally with the addition of some little pietistic tag which betrays his century. It is indeed only in short passages that Vaughan achieves adequate imaginative vision and utterance, but the spirit of these passages is diffused through his religious verse, more quietistic, less practical, in spirit than Herbert's.

Vaughan's quietist and mystical, Herbert's restrained and ordered, temper and poetry are equally remote from the radiant spirit of Richard Crashaw. Herbert's conceits are quaint or homely analogies, Vaughan's are the blots of a fashion on a style naturally pure and simple. Crashaw's long odes give the impression at first reading of soaring rockets scattering balls of coloured fire, the 'happy fireworks' to which he compares St. Teresa's writings. His conceits are more after the confectionery manner of the Italians than the scholastic or homely manner of the followers of Donne. Neither spiritual conflict controlled and directed by Christian inhibitions and aspirations, nor mystical yearning for a closer communion with the divine, is the burden of his religious song, but love, tenderness, and joy. In Crashaw's poetry, as in the later poetry of the Dutch Vondel, a note is heard which is struck for the first time in the seventeenth century, the accent of the convert to Romanism, the joy of the troubled soul who has found rest and a full expansion of heart in the rediscovery of a faith and ritual and order which give entire satisfaction to the imagination and affections. And that is not quite all. The Catholic poet is set free from the painful diagnosis of his own emotions and spiritual condition which so preoccupies the Anglican Herbert:

> How should I praise thee, Lord!　how should
> 　my rhymes
> Gladly engrave thy name in steel,
> If what my soul doth feel sometimes
> 　My soul might ever feel!
>
> Although there were some forty heav'ns or
> 　more,
> Sometimes I peer above them all;
> Sometimes I hardly reach a score,
> 　Sometimes to hell I fall.

The Catholic poet loses this anxious sense of his own moods in the consciousness of the *opus operatum* calling on him only for faith and thankfulness and adoration. It is this *opus operatum* in one or other of its aspects or symbols, the Cross, the name of Christ, the Incarnation, the Eucharist, the life of the saint or death of the martyr, which is the theme of all Crashaw's ardent and coloured, sensuous and conceited odes, composed in irregular rhythms which rise and fall like a sparkling fountain. All other moods are merged in faith and love:

> 　　Faith can believe
> As fast as love new laws can give.
> Faith is my force.　Faith strength affords
> To keep pace with those powerful words.
> And words more sure, more sweet than they
> Love could not think, truth could not say.

Crashaw's poetry has a limited compass of moods, but it has two of the supreme qualities of great lyric poetry, poetry such as that of Shelley and Swinburne, ardour and music. (pp. xiii-xlvii)

IV

When Dryden and his generation passed judgement, not merely on the conceits, but on the form of the earlier poet-ry, what they had in view was especially their use of the decasyllabic couplet in eulogistic, elegiac, and satiric and narrative verses. 'All of them were thus far of Eugenius his opinion that the sweetness of English verse was never understood or practised by our fathers . . . and every one was willing to acknowledge how much our poesy is improved by the happiness of some writers yet living, who first taught us to mould our thoughts into easy and significant words, to retrench the superfluities of expression, and to make our rhyme so properly a part of the verse, that it should never mislead the sense, but itself be led and governed by it.' 'Donne alone', Dryden tells the Earl of Dorset, 'of all our countrymen had your talent: but was not happy enough to arrive at your versification; and were he translated into numbers and English, he would yet be wanting in the dignity of expression.' Sweetness and strength of versification, dignity of expression—these were the qualities which Dryden and his generation believed they had conferred upon English poetry. 'There was before the time of Dryden no poetical diction, no system of words at once refined from the grossness of domestic use, and free from the harshness of terms appropriated to particular arts. . . . Those happy combinations of words which distinguish poetry from prose had been rarely attempted; we had few elegances or flowers of speech, the roses had not yet been plucked from the brambles, or different colours had not been joined to enliven one another.' Johnson is amplifying and emphasizing Dryden's 'dignity of expression', and it is well to remember that Scott at the beginning of the next century is still of the same opinion. It is also worth remembering, in order to see a critical period of our poetical history in a true perspective, that Milton fully shared Dryden's opinion of the poetry of his time, though he had a different conception of how poetic diction and verse should be reformed. He, too, one may gather from his practice and from occasional references, disapproved the want of selection in the 'metaphysicals'' diction, and created for himself a poetic idiom far removed from current speech. His fine and highly trained ear disliked the frequent harshness of their versification, their indifference to the well-ordered melody of vowel and consonant, the grating, 'scrannel pipe' concatenations which he notes so scornfully in the verse of Bishop Hall:

> Teach each hollow grove to sound his love
> Wearying echo with one changeless word.

And so he well might, and all his auditory besides, with his "teach each" ' (*An Apology for Smectymnuus*). But the flowers which Milton cultivated are not those of Dryden, nor was his ear satisfied with the ring of the couplet. He must have disliked as much as Dryden the breathless, headlong overflow of *Pharonnida* (if he ever read it), the harsh and abrupt crossing of the rhythmical by the rhetorical pattern of Donne's *Satires*, but he knew that the secret of harmonious verse lay in this subtle crossing and blending of the patterns, 'apt numbers, fit quantity of syllables, and the sense variously drawn out from one verse into another'. Spenser was Milton's poetic father, and his poetic diction and elaborately varied harmony are a development of Spenser's art by one who has absorbed more completely the spirit, understood more perfectly the art, of Virgil and the Greeks, who has taken Virgil and Homer for his teachers rather than Ariosto and Tasso. Dryden's reform was due to no such adherence to an older and more purely poetic tradition though he knew and admired the ancients. His development was on the line of Donne and the metaphysicals, their assimilation of poetic idiom and rhythm to that of the spoken language, but the talk of which Dryden's poetry is an idealization is more choice and select, less natural and fanciful, and rises more frequently to the level of oratory. Like other reforms, Dryden's was in great measure a change of fashion. Men's minds and ears were disposed to welcome a new tone and tune, a new accent, neither that of high song,

> passionate thoughts
>   To their own music chanted,

nor of easy, careless, but often delightful talk and song blended, which is the tone of the metaphysical lyric, but the accent of the orator, the political orator of a constitutional country.

It was in satire, the Satires of Hall, Marston, and Donne—especially the last—that the 'unscrewing' of the decasyllabic couplet began, in part as a deliberate effort to reproduce the colloquial ease of Horace's, the harshness of Persius's satiric style and verse. The fashion quickly spread to narrative, eulogistic, elegiac, and reflective poetry, and like other fashions—*vers libre* for example—was welcomed by many who found in it an easier *gradus ad Parnassum*, a useful discovery when every one had at times to pen a compliment to friend or patron.

After Spenser Elizabethan narrative poetry suffered almost without exception from the 'uncontented care to write better than one could', the sacrifice of story and character to the elaboration of sentimental and descriptive rhetoric. Shakespeare's *Venus and Adonis* and *Rape of Lucrece* are no exception to this failure to secure that perfect balance of narrative, dramatic and poetic interest, which makes Chaucer's tales unsurpassed models in their kind. The 'metaphysical' fashion changed merely the character of the rhetoric, shifting the weight from diction and verse to wit, to dinoia One can study the result in Davenant's *Gondibert* and Cowley's *Davideis*, where the dramatic thread of story is almost lost to sight in the embroidery of comment and 'witty' simile:

> Oswald in wars was worthily renowned;
>   Though gay in Courts, coarsely in Camps
>   could live;
> Judg'd danger soon, and first was in it found;
>   Could toil to gain what he with ease did give.
>
> Yet toils and dangers through ambition lov'd;
>   Which does in war the name of Virtue own;
> But quits that name when from the war remov'd,
>   As Rivers theirs when from their Channels
>   gone.

The most readable—if with somewhat of a wrestle—is Chamberlayne's *Pharonnida*. The story is compounded of the tedious elements of Greek romance—shepherds and courts and loves and rapes and wars—and no one can take the smallest interest in the characters. The verse is breathless and the style obscure, as that of Mr. Doughty is, because the writer uses the English language as if he had found it lying about and was free of it without regard to any tradition of idiom or structure. Still Chamberlayne does realize the scenes which he describes and decorates with all the arabesques of a fantastic and bewildering yet poetic wit:

> The Spring did, when
> The princess first did with her pleasure grace
> This house of pleasure, with soft arms embrace
> The Earth—his lovely mistress—clad in all
> The painted robes the morning's dew let fall
> Upon her virgin bosom; the soft breath
> Of Zephyrus sung calm anthems at the death
> Of palsy-shaken Winter, whose large grave,
> The earth, whilst they in fruitful tears did lave,
> Their pious grief turned into smiles, they throw
> Over the hearse a veil of flowers; the low
> And pregnant valleys swelled with fruit, whilst
>   Heaven
> Smiled on each blessing its fair hand had given.

But the peculiar territory of the metaphysical poets, outside love-song and devout verse, was eulogy and elegy. They were pedants but also courtiers abounding in compliments to royal and noble patrons and friends and fellow poets. Here again Donne is the great exemplar of erudite and transcendental, subtle and seraphic compliments to noble and benevolent countesses. One may doubt whether the thing ought to be done at all but there can be no doubt that Donne does it well, and no one was better aware of the fact than Dryden, whose eulogies, whether in verse or in prose, as the dedication of the *State of Innocence* to Mary of Modena, are in the same seraphic vein and indeed contain lines that are boldly 'lifted' from Donne. They are not vivid by the accumulation of concrete details, though there are some not easily to be surpassed, as Ben Jonson's favourite lines:

> No need of lanterns, and in one place lay
> Feathers and dust, to-day and yesterday.

But the most vivid impressions are secured not by objective detail, but by the suggestion of their effect upon the mind. The nervous effect of storm and calm is conveyed by Donne's conceits and hyperboles in a way that is not only vivid but intense.

One cannot say much for the metaphysical eulogies of Donne's imitators. Even Professor Saintsbury has omitted many of them from his collection of the other poems by their authors, as Godolphin's lines on Donne and on Sandys's version of the Psalms, which are by no means the worst of their kind. He has, on the other hand, included one, Cleveland's on Edward King, some lines of which might be quoted to illustrate the extravagances of the fashion:

> I like not tears in tune, nor do I prize
> His artificial grief who scans his eyes.
> Mine weep down pious beads, but why should
>   I
> Confine them to the Muses' rosary?
> I am no poet here; my pen's the spout
> Where the rain-water of mine eyes run out
> In pity of that name, whose fate we see
> Thus copied out in grief's hydrography.
> The Muses are not mermaids, though upon

His death the ocean might turn Helicon. . . .
When we have filled the roundlets of our eyes
We'll issue 't forth and vent such elegies
As that our tears shall seem the Irish Seas,
We floating islands, living Hebrides.

The last word recalls the great poem which appeared
along with it:

Where ere thy bones are hurl'd,
Whether beyond the stormy Hebrides,
Where thou perhaps under the whelming tide
Visit'st the bottom of the monstrous world.

Cleveland is not much worse than Joseph Beaumont on
the same subject, and neither is quite so offensive as Francis Beaumont in his lines on the death of Mrs. Markham:

As unthrifts grieve in straw for their pawned
beds,
As women weep for their lost maidenheads
(When both are without hope of remedy),
Such an untimely grief have I for thee.

It would be difficult to imagine anything in worse taste,
yet, from the frequency with which the poem recurs in
manuscript collections, it was apparently admired as a
flight of 'wit'. There are better elegies than these, as Herrick's and Earle's and Stanley's on Beaumont and Fletcher, Cleveland's (if it be his) on Jonson, Carew's noble lines
on Donne, but in proportion as they become readable they
cease to be metaphysical. Donne's *a priori* transcendentalism few or none were able to recapture. Their attempts to
rise meet the fate of Icarus. The lesser metaphysical poets
are most happy and most poetical when their theme is not
this or that individual but death in general. Love and
death are the foci round which they moved in eccentric cycles and epicycles. Their mood is not the sombre mediaeval horror of 'Earth upon earth', nor the blended horror
and fascination of Donne's elegies, or the more magnificent prose of his sermons. They dwell less in the Charnel
House. Their strain is one of pensive reflection on the fleet-
ingness of life, relieved by Christian resignation and hope:

Like as the damask rose you see,
Or like the blossom on the tree,
Or like the dainty flower in May,
Or like the morning of the day,
Or like the sun, or like the shade,
Or like the gourd which Jonas had—
Even such is man: whose thread is spun,
Drawn out and cut and so is done.

If none can scape Death's dreadful dart,
If rich and poor his beck obey,
If strong, if wise, if all do smart,
Then I to scape shall have no way.
  O grant me grace, O God, that I
  My life may mend since I must die.

In Abraham Cowley 'metaphysical' poetry produced its
last considerable representative, and a careful study of his
poetry reveals clearly what was the fate which overtook
it. His wit is far less bizarre and extravagant than much
in Donne, to say nothing of Cleveland and Benlowes. But
the central heat has died down. Less extravagant, his wit
is also less passionate and imaginative. The long wrestle
between reason and the imagination has ended in the vic-

tory of reason, good sense. The subtleties of the schoolmen
have for Cowley none of the significance and interest they
possessed for Donne:

So did this noble Empire wast,
Sunk by degrees from glories past,
And in the School-men's hands it perished quite
at last.
Then nought but words it grew,
And those all barbarous too.
It perish't and it vanisht there,
The life and soul breath'd out, became but
empty air.

The influence of the new philosophy simplified with such
dogmatic simplicity by Hobbes has touched him,—atoms
and determinism, witness the ode *To Mr. Hobbes* and the
half-playful, charming *Destinie*; and though that philosophy might appeal to the imagination, the intellectual
imagination, by its apparent simplicity and coherency, it
could make no such appeal to the spiritual nature as the
older, which had its roots in the heart and conscience,
which had endeavoured to construct a view of things
which should include, which indeed made central, the requirements and values of the human soul. Cowley is not
wanting in feeling any more than in fancy, witness his
poem *On the Death of Mr. William Hervey*, and he was a
Christian, but neither his affections nor his devotion expressed themselves imaginatively as these feelings did in

Map of Cambridge in 1574.

Donne's most sombre or bizarre verses or those of his spiritual followers; his wit is not the reflection of a sombre or bizarre, a passionately coloured or mystically tinted conception of life and love and death. The fashion of 'metaphysical' wit remains in Cowley's poems when the spirit that gave it colour and music is gone. Yet Cowley's poetry is not merely frigid and fantastic. The mind and temper which his delightful essays, and the poems which accompany them, express has its own real charm—a mind of shy sensitiveness and clear good sense. It was by a natural affinity that Cowley's poetry appealed to Cowper. But wit which is not passionate and imaginative must appeal in some other way, and in Dryden it began to do so by growing eloquent. The interest shifted from thought to form, the expression not the novelty of the thought, wit polished and refined as an instrument of satire and compliment and declamation on themes of common interest. Dryden and Pope brought our witty poetry to a brilliant close. They are the last great poets of an age of intense intellectual activity and controversy, theological, metaphysical, political. 'The present age is a little too warlike', Atterbury thought, for blank verse and a great poem. With the peace of the Augustans the mood changed, and poetry, ceasing to be witty, became sentimental; but great poetry is always metaphysical, born of men's passionate thinking about life and love and death. (pp. xlix-lviii)

> *Herbert J. C. Grierson, in an introduction to* Metaphysical Lyrics & Poems of the Seventeenth Century: Donne to Butler, *edited by Herbert J. C. Grierson, Oxford at the Clarendon Press, 1921, pp. xiii-lviii.*

Helen Gardner

[*Gardner is a leading English critic and scholar of seventeenth-century English verse. In the following excerpt, Gardner gives a general overview of metaphysical poetry and its stylistic provenance.*]

The term 'metaphysical poets' came into being long after the poets to whom we apply it were dead. Samuel Johnson, who coined it, did so with the consciousness that it was a piece of literary slang, that he was giving a kind of nickname. When he wrote in his *Life of Cowley* that 'about the beginning of the seventeenth century appeared a race of writers that may be termed the metaphysical poets', his 'may be termed' indicates that he did not consider that these poets had the right to be called 'metaphysical' in the true sense. He was adapting a witty sally from Dryden who, writing in 1693, said of Donne:

> He affects the metaphysics, not only in his satires, but in his amorous verses, where nature only should reign; and perplexes the minds of the fair sex with nice speculations of philosophy, when he should engage their hearts, and entertain them with the softnesses of love. In this . . . Mr Cowley has copied him to a fault.

Between Dryden and Johnson comes Pope, who is reported by Spence to have remarked that 'Cowley, as well as Davenant, borrowed his metaphysical style from Donne'. But the only writer I know of before Dryden who spoke

as if there were a 'metaphysical school' is Drummond of Hawthornden (1585-1649) who, in an unfortunately undated letter, speaks of poets who make use of 'Metaphysical *Ideas* and *Scholastical Quiddities*'.

What we call metaphysical poetry was referred to by contemporaries as 'strong lines', a term which calls attention to other elements in metaphysical poetry than its fondness for indulging in 'nice speculations of philosophy' in unusual contexts. The term is used in connexion with prose as well as with verse—indeed the earliest use I know of is by a prose writer—and so invites us to look at metaphysical poetry in a wider context. Like the later term 'metaphysical', the term 'strong-lined' is a term of disapproval. It too is a kind of slang, a phrase which would seem to have been coined by those who disliked this way of writing. Thus Burton, in the preface to *The Anatomy of Melancholy* (1621), contrasts his own 'loose free style' with 'neat composition, strong lines, hyperboles, allegories', and later speaks disparagingly of the 'affectation of big words, fustian phrases, jingling termes, strong lines, that like *Acastes* arrows caught fire as they flew'; and Quarles, in the preface to *Argalus and Parthenia* (1629), declares:

> I have not affected to set thy understanding on the Rack, by the tyranny of *strong lines*, which (as they fabulously report of *China* dishes) are made for the third *Generation* to make use of, and are the meere itch of wit; under the colour of which, many have ventured (trusting to the *Oedipean* conceit of their ingenious Reader) to write *non-sense*, and felloniously father the created expositions of other men; not unlike some painters, who first make the picture, then, from the opinions of better judgements, conclude whom it resembles.

These are complaints against an established manner in prose and verse. It is a manner which developed in the last decade of the sixteenth century with the cry everywhere for 'More matter and less words'. In prose, Cicero, the model for the sixteenth century, was dethroned in favour of the Silver Latin writers, Seneca and Tacitus. Recommending Sir Henry Savile's translation of Tacitus in 1591, Antony Bacon commends Tacitus because he 'hath written the most matter with the best conceit in the fewest words of any Historiographer', and adds 'But he is hard. *Difficilia quae pulchra*; the second reading will please thee more than the first, and the third than the second.' The same conception that difficulty is a merit is applied to poetry in Chapman's preface to *Ovid's Banquet of the Sense* (1595), where he declares that poetry, unlike oratory, should not aim at clarity: 'That Poetry should be as pervial as oratory and plainness her special ornament, were the plain way to barbarism.' Poetry, like prose, should be close-packed and dense with meaning, something to be 'chewed and digested', which will not give up its secrets on a first reading. In the 1590's also formal satire first appeared in English, and the satirists took as their model Persius, the most obscure of Roman satirists, and declared that satire should be 'hard of conceit and harsh of style'. The same period sees the vogue of the epigram and the great popularity of Martial.

What came to be called by its denigrators the 'strong-lined' style had its origins in this general desire at the close of Elizabeth's reign for concise expression, achieved by an elliptical syntax, and accompanied by a staccato rhythm in prose and a certain deliberate roughness in versification in poetry. Along with this went admiration for difficulty in the thought. Difficulty is indeed the main demerit in this way of writing for those who dislike it, and the constant complaint of its critics is that it confuses the pleasures of poetry with the pleasures of puzzles. It is one of its merits for those who approve it. Jasper Mayne, in his elegy on Donne, put his finger on one of the delights of reading 'strong-lined' verse when he said

> Wee are thought wits, when 'tis understood.

It makes demands upon the reader and challenges him to make it out. It does not attempt to attract the lazy, and its lovers have always a certain sense of being a privileged class, able to enjoy what is beyond the reach of vulgar wits. The great majority of the poets included in this book did not write to be read by all and sundry. Few of them published their poems. They were 'Chamber poets', as Drayton, with the jealousy of the professional for the amateur, complains. Their poems passed from hand to hand in manuscript. This is a source of both weakness and strength. At times the writing has the smell of a coterie, the writer performing with a self-conscious eye on his clever readers. But at its best it has the ease and artistic sincerity which comes from being able to take for granted the understanding of the audience for whom one writes.

The first characteristic that I shall isolate in trying to discuss the admittedly vague and, it is often thought, unsatisfactory term 'metaphysical poetry' is its concentration. The reader is held to an idea or a line of argument. He is not invited to pause upon a passage, 'wander with it, and muse upon it, and reflect upon it, and bring home to it, and prophesy upon it, and dream upon it' as a 'starting-post towards all the "two-and-thirty Palaces" '. Keats's advice can be followed profitably with much poetry, particularly with Elizabethan and Romantic poetry; but metaphysical poetry demands that we pay attention and read on. . . . It is, of course, possible and pleasurable to linger over passages of striking beauty and originality, but, on the whole, I think that to do so is to miss the special pleasure that metaphysical poetry has to give. It does not aim at providing, to quote Keats again, 'a little Region to wander in', where lovers of poetry 'may pick and choose, and in which images are so numerous that many are forgotten and found new in a second Reading'. A metaphysical poem tends to be brief, and is always closely woven. Marvell, under the metaphor of a garland, characterizes his own art finely in 'The Coronet' when he speaks of a 'curious frame' in which the flowers are 'set with Skill and chosen out with Care'. And Donne in a sermon, speaking of the Psalms as especially dear to him in that they were poems, stresses the same elements of deliberate art (curiosity), and economy of language, when he defines psalms as

> Such a form as is both curious, and requires diligence in the making, and then when it is made, can have nothing, no syllable taken from it, nor added to it.

Concentration and a sinewy strength of style is the mark

of Ben Jonson as well as of Donne, and such adjectives as 'strenuous' and 'masculine' applied to him by his admirers point to a sense in which he too was in some degree a 'strong-lined' man, and explain why so many younger writers were able to regard both him and Donne as equally their masters. Behind both, as behind much of the poetry of their followers, lies the classical epigram, and there is some truth in saying that a metaphysical poem is an expanded epigram. Almost all the poets in this collection exercised their skill in the writing of epigrams. Their efforts make on the whole very dreary reading; but the vogue of the epigram helped to form the taste for witty poetry. The desire for concentration and concision marks also the verse forms characteristic of seventeenth-century lyric. It appears in the fondness for a line of eight syllables rather than a line of ten, and in the use of stanzas employing lines of varying length into which the sense seems packed, or of stanzas built on very short lines. A stanza of Donne or Herbert is not, like rhyme royal or a Spenserian stanza, an ideal mould, as it were, into which the words have flowed. It is more like a limiting frame in which words and thoughts are compressed, a 'box where sweets compacted lie'. The metaphysical poets favoured either very simple verse forms, octosyllabic couplets or quatrains, or else stanzas created for the particular poem, in which length of line and rhyme scheme artfully enforced the sense. In . . . 'The Triple Foole', Donne suggests, in passing, this conception of the function of rhyme and metre:

> I thought, if I could draw my paines,
> Through Rimes vexation, I should them allay,
> Griefe brought to numbers cannot be so fierce,
> For, he tames it, that fetters it in verse.

The second characteristic of metaphysical poetry, its most immediately striking feature, is its fondness for conceits, and here, of course, Jonson and Donne part company. A conceit is a comparison whose ingenuity is more striking than its justness, or, at least, is more immediately striking. All comparisons discover likeness in things unlike: a comparison becomes a conceit when we are made to concede likeness while being strongly conscious of unlikeness. A brief comparison can be a conceit if two things patently unlike, or which we should never think of together, are shown to be alike in such a way, or in such a context, that we feel their incongruity. Here a conceit is like a spark made by striking two stones together. After the flash the stones are just two stones. Metaphysical poetry abounds in such flashes, as when Cartwright in his New Year's poem, promising to be a new man, declares that he will not be new as the year is new when it begins again its former cycle, and then thinks of two images of motion without progression, the circulation of the blood and a mill:

> Motion as in a Mill
> Is busie standing still.

The wit of this depends on our being willing to suppress our memory of other features of mills, and particularly on our not allowing ourselves to think that mills are very usefully employed grinding corn while 'standing still'. Normally metaphor and simile allow and invite the mind to stray beyond the immediate point of resemblance, and in extended or epic simile, which is the diametrical opposite of the conceit, the poet himself expatiates freely, making the point of comparison a point of departure. In an extended conceit, on the other hand, the poet forces fresh points of likeness upon us. Here the conceit is a kind of 'hammering out' by which a difficult join is made. I borrow the phrase from Shakespeare's poet-king Richard II, who occupies himself in prison composing a conceited poem:

> I have been studying how I may compare
> This prison where I live unto the world:
> And for because the world is populous,
> And here is not a creature but myself,
> I cannot do it; yet I'll hammer it out.
> My brain I'll prove the female to my soul. . . .

Longer conceits set themselves to 'prove' likeness. They may, as here, start from a comparison which the speaker owns is far from obvious and then proceeds to establish. Or they may start from one that is immediately acceptable generally and then make us accept further resemblances in detail after detail. Thus nobody, I imagine, would think Lady Macbeth is being particularly ingenious when she compares the troubled face of her husband to a book in which men may 'read strange matters'. She leaves our imaginations to give further content to this comparison of finding meaning in a book and meaning in a face and to the deliberately imprecise words 'strange matters'. But when Lady Capulet takes up the same comparison to urge Juliet to wed Count Paris she expands the comparison for us in detail after detail so that it becomes a conceit, and most people would add a very tasteless and ineffective one.

> Read o'er the volume of young Paris' face
> And find delight writ there with beauty's pen;
> Examine every married lineament,
> And see how one another lends content;
> And what obscur'd in this fair volume lies
> Find written in the margent of his eyes.
> This precious book of love, this unbound lover,
> To beautify him, only lacks a cover. . . .
> That book in many eyes doth share the glory
> That in gold clasp locks in the golden story:
> So shall you share all that he doth possess,
> By having him making yourself no less.

Elizabethan poetry, dramatic and lyric, abounds in conceits. They are used both as ornaments and as the basis of songs and sonnets. What differentiates the conceits of the metaphysicals is not the fact that they very frequently employ curious learning in their comparisons. Many of the poets whom we call metaphysical, Herbert for instance, do not. It is the use which they make of the conceit and the rigorous nature of their conceits, springing from the use to which they are put, which is more important than their frequently learned content. A metaphysical conceit, unlike Richard II's comparison of his prison to the world, is not indulged in for its own sake. It is used, as Lady Capulet uses hers, to persuade, or it is used to define, or to prove a point. Ralegh's beautiful comparison of man's life to a play is a good example of a poem which seems to me to hover on the verge of becoming a metaphysical poem. Its concision and completeness and the ironic, colloquially made point at the end—'Onely we dye in earnest, that's no Jest'—bring it very near, but it remains in the region

of the conceited epigram and does not cross the border. On the other hand, Lady Capulet's conceit fails to be metaphysical in another way. She does not force us to concede the justness of her initial comparison by developing it, she merely argues from various arbitrarily chosen points of comparison between a book and a bachelor. In a metaphysical poem the conceits are instruments of definition in an argument or instruments to persuade. The poem has something to say which the conceit explicates or something to urge which the conceit helps to forward. It can only do this if it is used with an appearance of logical rigour, the analogy being shown to hold by a process not unlike Euclid's superimposition of triangles. I have said that the first impression a conceit makes is of ingenuity rather than of justice: the metaphysical conceit aims at making us concede justness while admiring ingenuity. Thus, in one of the most famous of all metaphysical conceits, the comparison of the union in absence of two lovers with the relation between the two legs of a compass, Donne sustains the comparison through the whole process of drawing a circle, because he is attempting to give a 'proof by analogy' of their union, by which he can finally persuade his mistress not to mourn. In another of his unfortunately rare asides on the art of poetry, Donne, again speaking of the Psalms, said:

> In all Metricall compositions . . . the force of
> the whole piece is for the most part left to the
> shutting up; the whole frame of the Poem is a
> beating out of a piece of gold, but the last clause
> is as the impression of the stamp, and that is it
> that makes it currant.

We might expand this by saying that the brilliant abrupt openings for which metaphysical poetry is famous, are like the lump of gold flung down on the table to be worked; the conceits are part of the beating out by which the metal is shaped to receive its final stamp, which is the point towards which the whole has moved.

Argument and persuasion, and the use of the conceit as their instrument, are the elements or body of a metaphysical poem. Its quintessence or soul is the vivid imagining of a moment of experience or of a situation out of which the need to argue, or persuade; or define arises. Metaphysical poetry is famous for its abrupt, personal openings in which a man speaks to his mistress, or addresses his God, or sets a scene, or calls us to mark this or see that. A great many of the poems in this collection are inspired by actual occasions either of personal, or, less often, public interest. The great majority postulate an occasion. We may not accept that Donne's 'Good Friday' was, actually 'made as I was riding westward that day', as a heading in some manuscripts tells us, but we must accept as we read the poem that he is riding westward and thinking as he rides. Marvell calls us to look at little T. C. in her garden. The child of one of Marvell's friends, Theophila Cornewall, bore the same beautiful name as her elder sister who had died two days after her baptism, a name which has a foreboding ring since the proverb says that the 'Darlings of the Gods' die young. This lovely poem would seem to have arisen from thoughts suggested by the name and family history of a friend's child. Whether Marvell actually caught sight of her in a garden we have no means of knowing. But he does not convey to us his sense of the transience of spring and the dangerous fragility of childhood through general reflections on human life. He calls us to watch with him a child 'in a Prospect of Flowers'. Equally, when his subject belongs to the ideal world of pastoral, not the world of daily life, his nymph is set before us complaining for her fawn while the little beast's life-blood is ebbing away. She tells of her betrayal in love as the tears are running down her cheeks in mourning for the creature who consoled her for that betrayal. Even poems of generalized reflection are given the flavour of spontaneous thought, as when Herbert opens his poem 'Man' with 'My God, I heard this day . . .', and thus gives the poem the air of having sprung from the casual overhearing of a chance remark.

The manner of metaphysical poetry originates in developments in prose and verse in the 1590s. The greatest glory of that decade is that it saw the flowering of the drama. Metaphysical poetry is the poetry of the great age of our drama. Its master John Donne was, we are told, 'a great frequenter of plays' in his youth. As an ambitious young man of social standing he would not have considered writing for the players, and his work is too personal, wilful, and idiosyncratic for us to imagine him doing so with any success. But his strong dramatic imagination of particular situations transforms the lyric and makes a metaphysical poem more than an epigram expanded by conceits. I have begun this volume a little before Donne with poems which in some ways anticipate the metaphysical manner: Ralegh's fine passionate conceit of a pilgrimage, written when he was under sentence of death, some specimens of Fulke Greville's 'close, mysterious and sentencious way of writing', Southwell's meditations, Shakespeare's strange celebration of married chastity in the most 'strong-lined' of all poems, if 'strong lines' are riddles, Alabaster's attempts at the concise expression of theological paradox, Wotton's laconic comment on the greatest scandal of the age. But the minute the reader reaches Donne, he will have the same sense of having arrived as when, in a collection of pre-Shakespearian plays, we hear the voice of Marlowe. Ralegh is too discursive, Greville too heavy and general, Southwell too dogged in his conceits and in his verse, one line padding at the same pace after another, Shakespeare too remote, and too symbolic, creating a static world where Love and Constancy are deified. The vehement, colloquial tone of the Satire 'Of Religion' creates the sense of an actual historical situation in which urgent choices present themselves. In the three splendid Elegies a man is speaking to a woman at a moment when all the faculties are heightened, as in drama, by the thought of what impends. He is about to go to the wars—what will she say to him when he returns, perhaps mutilated? He has to travel and she wants to come with him as his page—he is horrified at the thought of such romantic folly and implores her to be his true mistress and 'home of love'. With the tide of passion rising in him, impatient for the moment when she will be his, he watches her undressing for bed. The sense of the moment gives Donne's wit its brilliance and verve, the aptness and incongruity of the comparisons being created by their contexts. Without this, as in some of his complimentary pieces, he labours to be witty and never becomes 'air-borne'. The fading of this desire to

make poems out of particular moments, made imaginatively present rather than remembered, and played over by wit rather than reflected upon, is apparent towards the end of this volume. The metaphysical style peters out, to be replaced by the descriptive and reflective poetry of the eighteenth century, a century which sees the rise of the novel and has virtually no drama.

The strong sense of actual and often very ordinary situations which the metaphysical poets convey makes me agree with Grierson in thinking that words such as 'conceited' or 'fantastic' do not sum up their quality at all. A reader may at times exclaim 'Who would ever think such a thought in such a situation?' He will not exclaim 'Who can imagine himself in such a situation?' Dryden praised Donne for expressing deep thoughts in common language. He is equally remarkable for having extraordinary thoughts in ordinary situations. The situations which recur in seventeenth-century lyric are the reverse of fantastic, and often the reverse of ideal or romantic situations. Thus, a very favourite topic is the pleasure of hearing a beautiful woman sing or play. This domestic subject is, of course, a favourite on the Continent, and not merely with the poets, but with the painters. Such poems usually go beyond compliment to create a sense of the occasion; as Waller, in praising Lady Isabella Rich, whom Dorothy Osborne described as 'Lady Isabella that speaks and looks and plays and sings and all so prettily', expresses exactly the delight which we receive during an actual performance from artistry:

> Such moving sounds from such a careless touch,
> So unconcern'd her selfe, and we so much!

Again there are a great many poems which arise out of the common but unromantic situation of love between persons of very different ages. A mature man may rather ruefully complain to 'a very young Lady'

> That time should mee so far remove
> From that which I was borne to love.

This Horatian theme of the charm of young girls to older men is given various twists. The situation is reversed when Cartwright persuades his Chloe not to mind being older than he is; and at the end of the period Rochester gives us a fresh variation on the theme that age and youth are not so incompatible as the romantics claim by writing a song for 'A Young Lady to her Ancient Lover'.

The most serious and impassioned love poetry of the century argues, or assumes as a base for argument, that love is a relation between two persons loving—'It cannot *be* love till I love her that loves me'. The poems which Donne wrote on the experience of loving where love is returned, poems in which 'Thou' and 'I' are merged into 'We', are his most original and profound contributions to the poetry of human love. It is not possible to find models for such poems as 'The Good-Morrow', 'The Anniversarie', 'The Canonization', and, less perfect but still wonderful, 'The Extasie'. These poems have the right to the title metaphysical in its true sense, since they raise, even when they do not explicitly discuss, the great metaphysical question of the relation of the spirit and the senses. They raise it not as an abstract problem, but in the effort to make the experience of the union of human powers in love, and the union of two human beings in love, apprehensible. We never lose our sense of a 'little roome' which love has made 'an every where'. In the lighter verses of Donne's followers this theme that love is the union of two human beings, not the service of a votarist to a goddess, is handled with a mixture of gallantry, sensibility and good sense that has a peculiar charm:

> 'Tis not how witty, nor how free,
> Nor yet how beautifull she be,
> But how much kinde and true to me.

This is a very characteristic note. There are plenty of high and chivalrous fancies, and the Platonic ideal of love as the union of souls casts its spell; but the tone of the bargain scene in *The Way of the World* is anticipated in many lyrics in which the speaker sets forward the terms on which he is willing to make the 'world without end bargain' of love. The question 'What shall I do if she does not love me?' is often handled and usually with a glance at the old chivalric answer. Suckling's impudent 'The devil take her' is flat blasphemy against the religion of love. King's exquisite 'Tell me no more how fair she is' is chivalrous enough, as is Waller's 'It is not that I love you less'; but earlier servants of love would not, I think, have shown so stoical an acceptance of the fact that their love was hopeless, nor been so sensible in resolving not to keep their wounds green by hearing the lady's praises or by haunting her company. In one of his beautifully tempered songs of love unreturned, Godolphin seriously considers what creates the obligation to constancy. Parting for the wars, or parting to go abroad, or the final parting of death, actual or anticipated, are also favourite subjects. They too inspire poems which are metaphysical in both senses, as lovers ponder such questions as 'Can love subsist without the things that elemented it?' and 'Shall we meet in another world, and, if so, shall we know each other?'

The seventeenth century was, as Cowley said, 'a warlike, various and tragical age'. A glance at the biographical notes will show how many of the poets included in this book at one time or another 'trailed a pike', or 'raised a troop of horse', or went on missions abroad, or played a part in public affairs. They were for the most part men of the world who knew its ways. Their wit, high-flown and extravagant though it is, goes with a strong sense of the realities of daily life, the common concerns of men and women. And in spite of Johnson's accusation of pedantry, it has the flavour of the wit of conversation between friends who urge each other on to further flights. Donne perhaps meant what he said when, in the stanza of 'The Will' in which he restores gifts to those from whom he had received them, he leaves

> To Nature, all that I in Ryme have writ;
> And to my company my wit.

'I know the world and believe in God' wrote Fulke Greville, a Calvinist who was well acquainted with the winding stair of politics. Donne might have said the same, and Herbert has no need to tell us that he knows the ways of Learning, Honour, and Pleasure; it is apparent in all his poetry that he was not unworldly because of lack of knowledge of the world. The strength of the religious poetry of the metaphysical poets is that they bring to their praise and prayer and meditation so much experience that is not in itself religious. Here too the poems create for us particular situations out of which prayer or meditation arises: Donne riding westward, or stretched out upon his deathbed; Herbert praying all day long 'but no hearing', or noting his own whitening hair, or finding, after a night of heaviness, joy in the morning; Vaughan walking to spend his hour, or sitting solitary at midnight thinking of departed friends. Even with Crashaw, where this sense of the poet's own situation is unimportant, how vividly he dramatizes, rather than narrates, the story of St Teresa, and invokes the weeping Magdalen; and how vigorously he urges the hesitant Countess of Denbigh against delay.

Much stress has been laid recently upon the strongly traditional element in the conceits of metaphysical religious poetry. A good deal that seems to us remote, and idiosyncratic, the paradoxes and the twistings of Scripture to yield symbolic meanings, reaches back through the liturgy and through commentaries on Scripture to the Fathers and can be paralleled in medieval poetry. It is also true that the metaphysical manner of setting a subject, 'hammering it out', and then 'shutting it up' is closely allied to the method of religious meditation and that many metaphysical poems are poetical meditations. And yet, as strongly—or even more strongly—as in reading the secular poetry, the more we suggest common qualities and the more we set the poets in a tradition, the more strongly we are aware of their intensely individual treatment of common themes. How individually, for instance, Herbert treats the old theme of the stages of human life and the traditional lesson of the *Ars Moriendi* in 'Mortification'. Who else but Herbert would, with compassionate irony in place of the usual gloom of the moralist, show man as unconsciously amassing at each stage what he needs for his burial? And how tenderly and sympathetically he epitomizes each stage of our strange eventful pilgrimage, catching its very essence: the dreamless sleep of boyhood, the retraction of energies and interests in middle age, and the pathos of old age, unable to speak for rheum. The comparison of sleep to death, and of a bed to a grave, is stock enough. It is transformed by the further haunting image

> Successive nights, like rolling waves,
> Convey them quickly, who are bound for death.

The poem concludes with an old moral for its 'shutting up'; but the moral is made new by the time we reach it, because Herbert has so expanded our understanding of our dying life. The metaphysical style heightens and liberates personality. It is essentially a style in which individuality is expressed. The best pupils in the school of Donne learned from their master how to speak their own minds in their own voices. (pp. xix-xxxiii)

> *Helen Gardner, in an introduction to* The Metaphysical Poets, *edited by Helen Gardner, Oxford University Press, London, 1967, pp. xix-xxxiv.*

Robert Lathrop Sharp

[*In the following excerpt, Sharp reviews the principal*

stylistic elements of metaphysical poetry, noting that "revolt, obscurity, and harshness" are the hallmarks of its aesthetic.]

Of Course, the metaphysicals are not a hard and fast group. It is impossible to say that certain poets and not others deserve the adjective as it is usually applied. Certain poets, however, are outstanding, and it is of them that we usually think first. John Donne (1572-1631) is the most original and the best known. According to the usual custom, his poems circulated in manuscript before their publication in 1633 and were widely imitated. Edward, Lord Herbert of Cherbury (1583-1648); George Herbert (1593-1633), his younger brother; Henry King (1592-1669), Bishop of Chichester; Richard Crashaw (1612?-1649); John Cleveland (1613-1658); Abraham Cowley (1618-1667); Andrew Marvell (1621-1678); and Henry Vaughan (1622-1695) are other eminent figures. George Herbert, Crashaw, and Vaughan differ from the others in that their best poetry is religious; but because Donne, after taking holy orders, repented the secular and profane verses of his youth and turned to sacred poetry, this difference presents no difficulty. In fact it accounts for the appearance in the metaphysical tradition of two strains: first, sceptical naturalism, with its libertine and cynical spirit; and second, deep religious feeling. Most of the seventeenth-century poets wrote religious lines at some time during their lives, and those who were metaphysical in one kind were usually so in the other.

But I would emphasize not that the foregoing names represent the best metaphysical poetry, secular and religious, but rather that other poets, their contemporaries, show much in common with them and give reason for a loose grouping. Thomas Carew, Sir John Suckling, and Richard Lovelace, poets of the court, have more than occasional moments in which they prove themselves the compeers of the metaphysicals. And a horde of writers who are now not even names, such as Thomas Philipott (*Poems*, 1646) and Eldred Revett (*Poems*, 1657), as well as others more or less well known and reprinted in Saintsbury's *Minor Poets of the Caroline Period*, show that in many respects they, too, are metaphysicals. If characteristics are considered more important than traditional classification, the boundaries of the metaphysical group will remain flexible. Moreover, because poets do not always write in the same vein, a seventeenth-century poet may show surprising versatility. He may at one moment write in a couplet which with its precision and click foreshadows the meter of Pope, and at another in the loosest of lines. Likewise he may not be consistent in tone and manner. The spirit of neoclassicism, as it developed gradually throughout the century, was, to be sure, repugnant to the metaphysicals, just as the metaphysical manner was repugnant to it. Yet this may best be said of neoclassicism at its primmest and of the metaphysical spirit at it wildest. The extremes clashed, but in between were all degrees of compromise. It was unusual for a writer to commit himself to one style or to choose consciously between what were common contemporary styles.

There is good reason for refusing to call the metaphysicals a school. They were unorganized and without a common purpose. Some evidence of connection exists, of course: personal acquaintance, their imitation of one another, and their common admiration for Donne's wit. Donne was close to Henry King and both the Herberts. He greatly influenced George Herbert, as the latter in turn influenced Crashaw and Vaughan, and as Cowley influenced Marvell. Echoes of Donne's lines appear often enough throughout the middle part of the century to indicate that his elegists had truly prophesied his popularity. Cleveland, in his day, was largely imitated. But, more important, many prefaces and poems indicate that some of the metaphysicals had much the same attitude toward poetry, believed more or less alike in regard to diction, harmony, ordonnance, and the function of wit.

Differences are also to be met with: in the matter of genius, for instance, for Donne towers above the rest; in the degree of realism, for some of the metaphysicals, especially Crashaw, are elaborately ornamented and baroque; in their degree of piety, for the scurrilous flavor of the irreligious poets seems incompatible with the chaste ardor of George Herbert. Some are passionately serious; others are cerebral fops, cocksure and jaunty. Yet the truth is that, Donne excepted, these divergencies are more inevitable than the similarities; they are explained by the poet's native ability. One expects poets to be individual and different, perhaps unique. It is the metaphysical esthetic, agreed to by a group of poets, that is significant here. The poetry of John Donne shows certain outstanding traits which later poets imitated either directly or indirectly and which form the basis of an esthetic never fully formulated, perhaps, but understood by the metaphysicals and followed according to some sort of tacit agreement. At the center of this esthetic was wit.

In the Elizabethan period the term "wit" usually meant intellect, though it accumulated new meanings rapidly thereafter. Hobbes's attack on the identification of fancy and wit shows the stage which the word had reached by 1650. But long before that date, in the plays of Jonson and Chapman, there are some signs that wit indicated ingenuity or facility of invention. That for Bacon wit meant intellect was due to his use of the conservative phraseology of dignified prose; the poets and playwrights were not shackled to his definitions. As early as 1593 Gabriel Harvey wrote in *Pierce's Supererogation*:

> Arte may giue out precepts and directoryes in *communi forma*; but it is superexcellent witt that is the mother pearle of precious Inuention, and the goulden mine of gorgeous Elocution. Na, it is a certaine pregnant and liuely thing without name, but a queint mistery of mounting conceit, as it were a knacke of dexterity, or the nippitaty of the nappiest grape, that infinitly surpasseth all the Inuention and Elocution in the world.

A significant passage. Sensing the inadequacy of the old definition of wit, Harvey attempted a new one and succeeded remarkably; his phrases describe even the temper of the new wit. Already, then, a "certaine pregnant and liuely thing" has become the source of poetic invention.

Since poetry was assigned to the province of the imagination, or fancy, which, as Bacon said, was not tied down to the laws of matter, wit and fancy thus became more or less identical in function. The creative imagination, in the Aristotelian sense, was not yet fully defined in England. Digging in a "mine of rich and pregnant fancy," the metaphysicals followed the vein of their own wit. Their farfetched metaphors and similes were in perfect accord with their own theories, which emphasized the intellectual delight of new combinations. For, as Edward Benlowes wrote in the preface of his *Theophila* (1652), "Vivacity of *Fancie* in a florid Style disposeth Light and Life to a Poem, wherein the Masculine and refined Pleasures of the *Understanding* transcend the feminine and sensual of the *Eye*." That poetry should be written for the understanding rather than the eye is a belief which occurs with equal clearness in Carew's elegy on Donne.

It is an easy step from this conception of the poetic faculty to the *discordia concors* in which Dr. Johnson found the essence of metaphysical wit. The theory as well as the practice of the seventeenth century justifies his perception. T. S. Eliot, on the other hand, finds most significant not the yoking of dissimilar things but the "sensuous apprehension of thought," a tendency to feel metaphysical thought or to turn thought into feeling, a poetic process best indicated, perhaps, by its opposite, the tendency of the nineteenth-century romantics to turn feeling into thought. But while Mr. Eliot's phrase is true of Donne, it is less true of the other metaphysicals, who were not nearly so much concerned with feeling. Wit as an intellectual faculty became of more importance to them, and poetry less a matter of experience than a "knacke of dexterity." Their esthetic allowed this substitution. Superficial virtuosity replaced real feeling and served to conceal the lack of genuine inventive power. Consequently, wit assumed the importance of an end rather than a means; it became the whole poetic process. In occasional poetry it found an opportunity for the originality which it prized; in paradox and cynicism it found a chance to subvert the accepted values, staled by tradition and repetition. Even some of the religious poems seem tours de force in which wit has the upper hand over feeling.

The titles of occasional poems well illustrate what a premium was placed upon novelty and liveliness of fancy. Robert Heath's *Clarastella* (1650) contains verses with the heading, "On a dust got in Clarastella's eie"; and in *Poesis Rediviva* (1656), by John Collop, is a poem entitled "On Pentepicta: A Lady with enamell'd Teeth, black, white, and yellow." It is not strange to find that the poet tried to make up for the triviality of his subject by being original and clever.

> Can I with patience this my rival see
> Courting those flames so long ador'd by mee?
> Forcing her shut her eies from me, and thaw
> A tear, which all my sighes ne'r thence could
>   draw?
> Canst thou small crum of earth eclips my Sun,
> And make it set in clouds e'r day be done?
> Could ought but Atomes to this Orb aspire?

Coleridge claimed that the metaphysicals tried to make the common appear uncommon, unfortunately suggesting that, like Wordsworth, they started from the simple situations of "nature." Rather, they often started from highly artificial situations; so often, in fact, that Coleridge's state-

ment might be changed to read that they tried to give interest and significance to what was of little consequence in connection with human nature.

The early metaphysicals, especially Donne, did try to make the common appear uncommon. Donne succeeded in stirring the old associations at the root of emotions, in evoking new moods from old situations. But the rapidity with which metaphysical wit became a poetic method gave the lesser poets of the middle of the century a means of approach which took the place of the poetic experience. Even for a genius such as Cowley it was necessary that wit be carefully nurtured as a productive force in itself. It was insulated against the agitation of neighboring emotions, as Cowley testifies in the preface of his *Works* (1656): "The truth is, for a man to write well, it is necessary to be in good humor; neither is *Wit* less eclipsed with the unquietness of *Mind*, then *Beauty* with the *Indisposition of Body*."

Peace of mind has seldom been considered requisite to the production of good poetry. Coleridge thought the exact opposite, for he stated in special reference to one of Cowley's Pindaric odes: "It is therefore a species of *wit*, a pure work of the *will*, and implies a leisure and self-possession both of thought and of feeling, incompatible with the steady fervour of a mind possessed and filled with the grandeur of its subject." And earlier, in *The Guardian*, Steele had declared that if the poet "be not truly moved, he must at least work up his imagination as near as possible to resemble reality": "Deep reflections are made by a head undisturbed; and points of wit and fancy are the work of a heart at ease."

Many metaphysicals, if not Donne, would have agreed with Cowley. A wit demanding sedulous attention and the sacrifice of much else to it distinguished them from other poets. It was the duty of this wit to seek not only the unusual but also the rare and abstract, to go beyond earthly things into the realm of metaphysics. Sir Aston Cockain expressed clearly his recognition of what was expected of him:

> Stifle therefore (my Muse) at their first birth
> All thoughts that may reflect upon the earth:
> Be metaphysical, disdaining to
> Fix upon any thing that is below.

The poets were not consistent enough always to deserve to be called metaphysical in the literal sense, nor did they establish any system. But their work is full of metaphysical implications, lighting up unexpectedly the distant reaches of the universe.

Yet—and here I believe Dr. Johnson's acuteness is proved—the true metaphysical strain in the poetry of the time has the farfetched image as its companion, for it was by means of this that subtle analysis and rarefied speculation found expression. Sometimes concrete, sometimes as abstract as the thought behind it, the imagery of the metaphysicals is characterized by the extravagant metaphor. It might be said of their poetry, as of a seventeenth-century Clarinda,

> Her ex'lence Metaphysicall,
> Partakes not of old Natures stamps,
> For she is supernaturall,

Her Luminaries, Heavens Lamps.

Donne's best poetry had used wit effectively; that is, most of his conceits have power and depth. His followers, however, were neither so successful as poets nor so fortunate in coming at the beginning of the fashion. As the century wore on, their excesses became more extravagant, conspicuous, and grotesque. The feeling and sincerity of Donne were replaced by a spectacular wit. Christopher Harvey's *Synagogue*, Nicholas Hookes's *Amanda*, Edward Benlowes' *Theophila*, and John Cleveland's *Poems* are exhibitions of cleverness. In Cleveland we see a style which cannot last long because it is incapable of growth. It is a temporary thing, demanding that the reader's taste be as specially developed and, therefore, as temporary.

> Nature's confectioner, the bee
> (Whose suckets are moist alchemy,
> The still of his refining mould
> Minting the garden into gold),
> Having rifled all the fields
> Of what dainties Flora yields,
> Ambitious now to take excise
> Of a more fragrant paradise,
> At my Fuscara's sleeve arrived
> Where all delicious sweets are hived.
> The airy freebooter distrains
> First on the violets of her veins,
> Whose tincture, could it be more pure,
> His ravenous kiss had made it bluer.
> Here did he sit and essence quaff
> Till her coy pulse had beat him off;
> That pulse which he that feels may know
> Whether the world's long-lived or no.
> The next he preys on is her palm,
> That alm'ner of transpiring balm;
> So soft, 'tis air but once removed;
> Tender as 'twere a jelly gloved.
> Here, while his canting drone-pipe scanned
> The mystic figures of her hand,
> He tipples palmistry and dines
> On all her fortune-telling lines.

After this sort of thing the genuine feeling in the poetry of Marvell and Vaughan could not save the metaphysical fashion from extinction.

Besides wit, to which I shall refer as "extravagance," the metaphysicals continued the obscurity and the harshness of Donne. Both of these traits demand comment here.

The obscurity of Donne and other early metaphysicals, such as Lord Herbert, is different from that of the later metaphysicals, whose thought was less subtle and involved but whose expression was artfully complicated. The difficulty of the poetry of the early metaphysicals is due particularly to their learning, subtlety, and subjectivity; the poetry of many of the later metaphysicals, however, is knotty and perplexing because of their jumbled syntax, their dread of simple statement, their elliptical and crowded lines. I do not wish to emphasize this distinction, for it is not always in evidence. King and Marvell were later metaphysicals; yet their style remains fairly close to Donne's. The point is that such writers as Cleveland, Benlowes, and Eldred Revett recognized obscurity as a trait of their colleagues and attained it themselves not by thinking deeply but, rather, by writing unnaturally.

Lord Herbert, who is as metaphysical in the literal sense as any except Donne, is also one of the most obscure. Some of his conceits have that beauty and fitness which touch early seventeenth-century poetry with magic:

> This said, in her up-lifted face,
>   Her eyes which did that beauty crown,
>   Were like two starrs, that having faln down,
> Look up again to find their place.

But the opening stanza of *A Vision*,

> Within an *open curled Sea of Gold*
> A *Bark of Ivory*, one day, I saw,
>   Which striking with his *Oars* did seem to draw
> Tow'rds a fair *Coast*, wch I then did behold,

introduces a poem which completely mystifies the reader until he makes use of the marginal notes. Their presence shows that the obscurity was intentional; the poem was designed as a puzzle, as a test of wit.

Moreover, many of Lord Herbert's poems, with their talk of "souls," "influences," and "motions," are filled with Platonic philosophy and with cosmological learning. As in Donne's verse, philosophy, science, and theology form a solid background for his allusions and figures. Passages once rich and modern have become cold and obscure. Yet such a passage as this was never immediately intelligible:

> Black beamy hairs, which so seem to arise
>   From the extraction of those eyes,
> That into you she destin-like doth spin
> The beams she spares, what time her soul retires,
>   And by those hallow'd fires,
>   Keeps house all night within.

Herbert's poems offer little illustration of the obscurity arising from confused syntax, ellipsis, and crowded lines. Of these three fruitful sources of obscurity Benlowes' *Theophila* is full. It is distinguished both by its complete lack of the normal phrases of prose and by its eccentric diction. Benlowes packed his ideas so tightly in his short stanza that the style is highly elliptical; phrases are telescoped and transitional phrases omitted. Of the place to which his soul is to retire he writes:

> There sweet Religion strings, and tunes, and
>   skrues
>   The *Souls Theorb*', and doth infuse
> Grave *Dorick Epods* in th' *Enthusiastick* Muse.

He says in an introductory poem that he is to "Enucle'ate *Mysteries* to th' Ear," but earthly beauty is not driven from his mind without being described:

> Fly, Fancie, Beauties arched *Brow*,
> Darts, wing'd with Fire, thence sparkling flow.
> From Flash of Lightning *Eye-balls* turn;
> Contracted Beams of Chrystal burn.
> Wave *Curls*, which Wit *Gold-tresses* calls,
> That golden Fleece to Tinsel falls.

In the height of fashion, *Theophila* was greatly admired by some readers, although Samuel Butler was not one of them; therefore Benlowes scarcely needed to defend the style and manner of his poem. Yet if required to do so, he would not have been at a loss. A remark in his preface indicates one point, at least, that he would have made and gives us a partial statement of the metaphysical esthetic. For Benlowes was referring to this esthetic when he drew his distinction between the "Masculine and refined

Pleasures of the *Understanding*" and the "feminine and sensual of the *Eye*." All of Benlowes' colleagues would have agreed with this opinion; it was really a tenet of theirs and was responsible for the intellectual flavor of their poetry. Wit should result in obscurity; the more it did so, the more obvious was its excellence.

The poems of the Duchess of Newcastle are mentioned here only because they are prefaced by a statement not unlike that of Benlowes. Evidently it was intended to forestall criticism. At the beginning of one of the three sections of the volume, a section highly poetic in the metaphysical sense, she requests the reader to go slow in order to comprehend her wit:

> I must entreat my *Noble Reader*, to read this part of my *Book* very slow, and to observe very strictly every word they read; because in most of these *Poems*, every word is a *Fancy*. Wherefore if they loose, by not marking, or skip by too hasty reading, they will intangle the *Sense* of the whole *Copy*.

Part of the obscurity of metaphysical poetry was due to diction. Two observations may be made on Coleridge's remark that the metaphysicals wrote in the middle style, that is, a style fit for either prose or verse. He was thinking (1) of the directness and concreteness of their phraseology as compared to later, neoclassical circumlocution; (2) of the best work of Donne, George Herbert, and Vaughan, which is marked, now and then, by almost monosyllabic simplicity:

> A bracelet of bright haire about the bone.

> Sweet day, so cool, so calm, so bright.

The vocabulary of the metaphysicals was larger and more difficult than that of Waller and Denham. Though Donne's coinages are not numerous, one finds sesquisuperlative and omni-praegnant, as well as polysyllabic and difficult words such as esloygne, interinanimates, mastix, interbring, extrinsique, methridate, ostracisme, electrum, and precontract. The verbal eccentricities of the other metaphysicals are remarkable. In the first canto of Benlowes' *Theophila* are angelance, courtisms, breams, chamleted, enlabyrinth'd, coruscant, fuco'd cheeks; odes are called Lust's paperplots. Cowley used compound epithets and polysyllables—"Th' *Antiperistasis of Age*"—as well as words from physics, chemistry, astronomy, and medicine. Thomas Stanley also used antiperistasis. Chamberlayne has panpharmacon in his *Pharonnida*. Nathaniel Whiting's *Albino and Bellama* and many of Cleveland's poems contain unusual words. As late as 1683, in a metaphysical elegy on Dr. John Owen, appeared the hybrid Theo-Christo-Pneumatology, but the height of invention in diction had already been reached by John Hall in the word aldiboronifuscophonio.

In their use of perverse diction the metaphysicals were, doubtless, often playful. But certainly they took delight in their coinages, and their habit encouraged other poets of

the century to coin words freely. Thus the clarity of English poetry was threatened. Henry More, for instance, was influenced alike by the Spenserian and metaphysical strains, both of which can be traced in his poetry. In the first canto of his *Psychozoia* are two groups of unusual words, one archaic, the other hard and eccentric. In the first group, obviously derived from Spenser, are ywrapt, ne, wot, wained (weaned), ybrent; and in the second group are fulvid, plicatures, immutations, and such phrases as riving tortures spight, lamping shewes, grisell gray, crudled clouds, coppell'd hat. Poetry made up of similar phrases belongs at least on the border line of the metaphysical tradition:

> But 'mongst these glaring glittering rows of light,
> And flaming Circles, and the grisell gray,
> And crudled clouds, with silver tippings dight,
> And many other deckings wondrous gay,
> As *Iris* and the *Halo*; there doth play
> Still-pac'd *Euphrona* in her Conique tire;
> By stealth her steeple-cap she doth assay
> To whelm on th' earth: So School-boyes do aspire
> With coppell'd hat to quelme the Bee all arm'd with ire.

Although verbal license was not so essential to the metaphysicals as were their dizzy twists and turns of thought, it became one cause of the revolt. Later Waller was praised for being scrupulously nice about his diction; he was a model for the "choice of tuneful Words t'express our Thought."

The metaphysicals also got much of their effect from the extended meaning and ambiguity of words. Sometimes words were forced slightly beyond their proper use in order to take on an extra suggestiveness. In his *English Poetry and the English Language* (1934), where he discusses this point, Mr. F. W. Bateson cites the inexactness of Herrick's use of "Infanta" as a typically metaphysical device:

> Aske me why I send you here
> This sweet Infanta of the yeere.

These poets experimented with the meanings of words, aware of how much they depended upon extra-denotative associations. Their phrases were shaped to arouse a succession of responses which would be lost if precision replaced ambiguity.

More examples, particularly from Donne's poetry, may be found in Mr. William Empson's *Seven Types of Ambiguity*. Though the ambiguity which Mr. Empson analyzes is a part of all poetry, not alone that written by the metaphysicals, his quotations from the early seventeenth century are numerous. The metaphysicals not only continued to use the Elizabethan pun (one type of ambiguity), as in George Herbert's "Having been tenant long to a rich Lord," or Donne's "When thou hast done, thou hast not done," but perfected a highly complex syntactical ambiguity. The phrases are put together in such a way that they work either forwards or backwards. Mr. Empson's commentary on Donne's *Valediction: of weeping* is highly illuminating but much too lengthy to reproduce here: it takes up more than seven pages. A much simpler example is the last stanza of John Hall's *Epicurean Ode*:

> Since man's but pasted up of Earth,
> And ne're was cradled in the skies,
> What *Terra Lemnia* gave thee birth?
> What Diamond eyes?
> Or thou alone
> To tell what others were, came down?

Here the fourth line is ambiguous in construction and has a double value: Diamond is a noun parallel to *Terra Lemnia* and also an adjective.

Ambiguity is likewise responsible for the apparent confusion of this stanza from Lovelace's *Grasse-hopper*:

> Night as cleare *Hesper* shall our Tapers whip
> From the light Casements where we play,
> And the darke Hagge from her black mantle strip,
> And sticke there everlasting Day.

Several of these words have more than one sense to contribute to the entire meaning: "cleare," "whip," and "sticke," for instance, serve to enrich the stanza with their various possibilities.

But such genius for multiple associations was lost upon the Augustans, who demanded precision as a quality of language. Ambiguity is one kind of vagueness, and vagueness of any kind was obscure and unsatisfactory to a generation that transferred poetic effect from connotative to denotative language. Even the puns of Dryden and Pope depended upon a relative clearness of outline. Hazy analogies that defied logical connection were disliked, as is amusingly illustrated by Dr. Johnson's remarks on Gray's *Cat*:

> Selima, the cat, is called a nymph, with some violence both to language and sense; but there is good use made of it when it is done; for of the two lines—
>
> What female heart can gold despise?
> What cat's averse to fish?
>
> the first refers merely to the nymph, and the second only to the cat.

The other metaphysicals could imitate Donne's harshness but not its psychological fitness. They came to regard it as a desirable quality in some kinds of poetry and referred to it, together with the condensed and elliptical thought which generally accompanied it, as "masculinity" or as "strength." The strong line was consistently opposed to the feminine smoothness of the weak line and represented force and concentration as distinct from the long-drawn-out thought of the Spenserians.

In praising Donne's genius Carew wrote in his elegy that

> whatsoever wrong
> By ours was done the Greeke, or Latine tongue,
> Thou hast redeem'd, and open'd Us a Mine
> Of rich and pregnant phansie; drawne a line
> Of masculine expression,

and added that Donne's imagination was too strong for Spenserian lines:

> Yet thou maist claime
> From so great disadvantage greater fame,
> Since to the awe of thy imperious wit
> Our stubborne language bends, made only fit
> With her tough-thick-rib'd hoopes to gird about
> Thy Giant phansie, which had prov'd too stout
> For their soft melting Phrases.

Bishop Sprat had the same distinction in mind when he undertook to defend Cowley against those "who upbraid some of his pieces with roughness, and with more contractions than they are willing to allow."

> But these Admirers of gentlenesse without sinews should know that different Arguments must have different Colours of Speech: that there is a kind of variety of Sexes in Poetry as well as in Mankind: that as the peculiar excellence of the Feminine Kind is smoothnesse and beauty, so strength is the chief praise of the Masculine.

So, too, early and late references to Cleveland's style mention masculinity, which is practically identified with the metaphysical manner. Fuller, for instance, said in his *Worthies*, "Such who have *Clevelandized*, endeavouring to imitate his masculine style, could never go beyond the hermaphrodite, still betraying the weaker sex in their deficient conceits." And as late as 1687 a commendatory poem in an edition of Cleveland contained the lines,

> Each Word of thine swells pregnant with a Page,
> Then why do some Mens nicer Ears complain
> Of the uneven Harshness of thy Strain?
> Preferring to the Vigour of thy Muse,
> Some smooth, weak Rhymer, that so gently flows,
> That Ladies may his easie Strains admire
> And melt like Wax before the softning Fire.
> Let such to Women write, you write to Men;
> We study Thee, when we but play with Them.

To see what they were attempting to do, it is necessary to remember that the metaphysicals were skillful prosodists. The profusion of stanzaic forms which their poetry shows is a sufficient indication of their interest in metrics and their technical skill. They would not have been content to use a metrical form only once, as George Herbert famously did, if they had racked their brains to invent it. They would have clung to a dearly purchased thing. They regarded form as neither an end in itself nor of equal importance with what they had to say. But they were capable of working with it freely and bending it to their need. Likewise they could, when they chose to do so, write harmoniously and sweetly. Their lyric grace contributed much to the enviable reputation of the seventeenth century for harmony. In no period have lyric and song been sweeter. The Elizabethan talent for phrases that sing themselves existed in the metaphysicals along with their admiration of strong lines: Donne, Lord Herbert, Crashaw, Carew, Marvell—most of them show it brilliantly. However, it is as if that talent was thought less of because it was inherited and was not their own creation. Perhaps it put them too much in mind of their debt to their predecessors. Their strong lines were their own contribution to English poetry, a contribution which their own generation sufficiently recognized. Unless the modern reader appreciates this attitude, he is likely to overlook or explain away their harshness and thus misunderstand their esthetic.

The metaphysicals allowed themselves metrical license in certain types of poetry where they thought strong lines were appropriate. We can identify these types through statements by Cowley, Bishop Sprat, and Henry Reynolds.

Cowley's irregular odes were written, as he said, in imitation of Pindar's style and manner. That the reader might know what he meant by those words, he paraphrased two of Pindar's odes, avoiding literal translation for several reasons, among which is the following:

> And lastly, (which were enough alone for my purpose) we must consider that our Ears are strangers to the Musick of his *Numbers*, which sometimes (especially in *Songs* and *Odes*) almost without any thing else, makes an excellent *Poet*; for though the *Grammarians* and *Criticks* have laboured to reduce his Verses into regular feet and measures . . . yet in effect they are little better than *Prose* to our Ears.

Cowley assumed that the English ear would be displeased by the harshness which a literal translator would be bound to reproduce, since there was a tradition of smoothness and harmony in the writing of songs and odes. It is significant that Cowley does not mention other types. In them, we may infer, the English reader had become accustomed to harshness because of the practice of the metaphysicals.

An edition of Cowley's works was published in 1668. For it Bishop Sprat, Cowley's intimate friend, wrote a biographical sketch, wherein he protected Cowley from detraction.

> If his Verses in some places seem not as soft and flowing as some would have them, it was his choice, not his fault. He knew that in diverting mens minds there should be the same variety observ'd as in the prospects of their Eyes, where a Rock, a Precipice, or a rising Wave is often more delightful than a smooth, even ground or a calm Sea. Where the matter required it, he was as gentle as any man. But where higher Virtues were chiefly to be regarded, an exact numerosity was not then his main care.

Three points, clearly evident in Sprat's apology, are helpful to our purpose: (1) Cowley was harsh by choice; (2) his harshness depended on his subject matter; (3) "an exact numerosity" was not considered one of the higher virtues of poetry.

Finally, in his preface to *Mythomystes* (ca. 1633) Henry Reynolds wrote that he would not discuss things of lesser importance, such as "where the strong line (as they call it), where the gentle, sortes best." Thus the evidence leads to a division of types according to the metaphysical esthetic, and a corresponding approval of harshness where it was appropriate.

The work of the metaphysicals as a whole supports this evidence. Though probably not attempting a new prosody, they thought that harshness had its advantages in satire— so far they were conventional—and in elegiac, expository,

and occasional poetry. The example set by Donne was, of course, at the root of the whole matter, and since he did not define types we cannot be positive in our conclusions. The verse letter, for instance, we cannot be sure of, although it is likely that freedom was allowed here too. Bishop Sprat thought that some of Cowley's verse letters were smooth, but Donne's are as harsh as anything he wrote. In any case, we may confidently say of metaphysical poetry that the less lyrical it is, the more likely it is to show the unmistakable combination of harshness and wit.

These three qualities that caused the revolt, extravagance, obscurity, and harshness, are more than stylistic. They include a habit of looking at experience, a way of seeing things. Harshness is apparently only a matter of style; yet it tells something about the mind that created it. And obscurity and the idiom of which conceits are a part are closely related to thought. In considering a poem as a whole it is impossible to separate the way a poet thinks from what he thinks. The thought process is present in the structure of the verse, and the style is significant of much beyond itself. Particularly is this true of Donne, whose idiom is so tightly woven with his thought. As I have indicated, he departed from tradition in the way he saw things as well as in his expression of them. His cynicism, his fondness for paradox, his capacity for revealing hidden and unexpected connections between different parts of life, the patterns of his logic—all these show an individual apprehension of experience. Although the other metaphysicals did not see and feel life exactly as did Donne, they imitated his esthetic. Consequently their poetry, like his, has often a similar way of looking at experience, of emphasizing certain things and omitting others.

Like that of the Elizabethans, the outlook of the metaphysicals was imaginative and sensitive. But the world which they experienced was, in general, more subjective. Subjective truth was to them more interesting than external fact. A corner of the heart was even more important than the physical world to which science was trying to find the key. The metaphysicals had no interest in general truths. Much of their charm comes from their habit of combining what is small and insignificant with the large, of seeing much in little. Marvell's *On a Drop of Dew* is an example.

> See how the Orient Dew,
> Shed from the Bosom of the Morn
>   Into the blowing Roses,
> Yet careless of its Mansion new;
> For the clear Region where 'twas born
>   Round in its self incloses:
> And in its little Globes Extent,
> Frames as it can its native Element.
>   How it the purple flow'r does slight,
>   Scarce touching where it lyes,
>   But gazing back upon the Skies,
>   Shines with a mournful Light;
>   Like its own Tear,
> Because so long divided from the Sphear.

Thus they laid themselves open to the charge that they distorted nature and violated probability. Instead of maintaining the relationships and proportions in external nature, they had only their imagination as a standard of

Abraham Cowley by Sir Peter Lely.

truth. They used physical symbols, but only as a means of communicating highly individualized states of mind. Almost every stanza in Crashaw's *Sainte Mary Magdalene or The Weeper* illustrates this.

> Vpwards thou dost weep.
> Heaun's bosome drinks the gentle
>   stream.
> Where th' milky riuers creep,
> Thine floates aboue; & is the cream.
> Waters aboue th' Heauns, what they be
> We' are taught best by thy TEARES & thee.

In their religious verse the distortion of reality often became simply a neglect of reality. Their attention was turned to the celestial world in search of confirmation of faith.

> When I survey the bright
>   Coelestiall spheare:
> So rich with jewels hung, that night
> Doth like an Æthiop bride appeare.
>   My soule her wings doth spread
>   And heaven-ward flies,
> Th' Almighty's Mysteries to read
> In the large volumes of the skies.

The religious minded could seek heavenly knowledge, but of what vital worth was it to a century rapidly shifting its intellectual emphasis to science?

The partiality of the metaphysicals for abstractions also became displeasing to a scientific age. They seemed to avoid tangible things and to seek to express that which had no real existence. I have already quoted Donne's phrases, "A quintessence even from nothingnesse" and "I am rebegot of absence, darknesse, death; things which are not." Marvell's *Definition of Love* begins in a similarly abstract way:

> My Love is of a birth as rare
> As 'tis for object strange and high:
> It was begotten by despair
> Upon Impossibility.

One of the triumphs of the metaphysicals is what they achieved in their flashes of insight. When their conceits come off successfully, they reveal a depth of poetry which modern poets envy. Marvell's

> But at my back I alwaies hear
> Times winged Charriot hurrying near,

and Vaughan's

> I saw Eternity the other night
> Like a great Ring of pure and endless light,

are eminently successful. But we must allow even here for a change in taste; it is possible that the generation after the metaphysicals saw exaggeration where we see only splendid success. It is significant, I think, that Cleveland's couplet which Dryden liked so well,

> For beauty, like white powder, makes no noise
> And yet the silent hypocrite destroys,

is satirical. Dryden admired its thrusting quality; exaggeration served a purpose in satire. We recognize that insight, depth, and imaginative daring seem to go together, that the first two often come as a result of the third. But there is inevitably a quality of extravagance in the daring, and from one point of view a kind of distortion.

The metaphysical tradition encouraged eccentricity, and in the hands of lesser poets it resulted in a poetry which could not grow further. It ended in the blind alley of its own extravagance. Brilliantly promising at first, it had run counter to the conservative forces in poetry, and these, it so happened, became dominant as the years of the century went by. A poet of great influence might have extended the fashion beyond its natural life, but the change in intellectual climate did not permit such a poet to appear. From Donne the tradition got its life blood, which had to nourish more than it could. With the growth of an imitative poetry the tradition lost its vitality even as it developed. Not even Cowley could add much life to it, though another limb put out through him and he was imitated by Marvell. Cowley's conceits are on the surface; the intensity and depth of Donne's poetry are absent. Marvell appears to be a conspicuous exception. His imagination was more genuinely metaphysical than Cowley's, and his best poetry combines delicacy, imagination, and power. To most modern readers *To his Coy Mistress* is one of the great metaphysical lyrics. His success, however, lay in recapturing an older idiom, and those poems which we now admire seem to have had little influence in his own time.

Of the poets of the latter part of the century Dryden alone had the necessary creative genius for a sustained and vigorous poetry. But he was of a different breed from the metaphysicals; his taste was not shaped as theirs had been. In fact his greatness lies in his responding to new circumstances and creating the kind of poetry that matched the spirit of the age.

Many of the metaphysicals died before 1660—Donne, the Herberts, Carew, Crashaw, Suckling, Lovelace, John Hall, and Cleveland. And those who lived later had done either all their work or their best work before 1660. Cowley produced little English poetry between 1660 and his death in 1667. Henry King's *Poems* appeared in 1657, and the verse included in later editions was actually written earlier. Edward Benlowes' only considerable English poem, *Theophila*, was published in 1652. Thomas Stanley's poems were the work of his youth and had all appeared by 1656. Marvell lived until 1678, but except for the satires and *On Paradise Lost* his poems were written before 1660. And Henry Vaughan, though he did not die until 1695, wrote little during the last forty years of his life. His *Thalia Rediviva*, not published until 1678, contains many undated poems, but it is likely that for the most part they were written before 1655.

Of course the tradition was still alive after 1660, though its vigor had departed. Dryden's early poetry is metaphysical in its reliance on points of wit. And at this time some of the lesser poets brought out poems connected with the tradition. Alexander Brome published his *Songs and other Poems* in 1661, and Katherine Philips' *Poems* came out in 1667, three years after her death. Editions of the other metaphysicals also appeared at this time. Cleveland and Cowley, for instance, were popular. But it is significant that the edition of Donne's poems in 1669 was the last during the seventeenth century.

There are interesting traces of the metaphysical style in four poets whose work is difficult to date—Traherne, Cotton, Flatman, and Ayres. The evidence that their poetry might give us for the extended life of the metaphysical fashion is lacking because so little is known about when it was actually written. Some of it very likely belongs to the 1670's and 1680's. Flatman's poems came out originally in 1674 and appeared with additions during his lifetime, for he lived until 1688. And Philip Ayres published his *Lyric Poems* in 1687, twenty-five years before his death. Since Traherne, however, died in 1674, his poems belong somewhat earlier. I think that the same thing may be said of most of the pieces in Cotton's *Poems on Several Occasions* (1689), for when the author was still "Charles Cotton the Younger" he was praised for his poetic skill by Sir Aston Cockain in terms which indicate that he had written a considerable amount of verse by 1658. Although we cannot be certain, I think that we may safely place Flatman and Ayres last. Thus the curve of metaphysical inspiration continues to descend, for both Traherne and Cotton have more power in their metaphysical lines than does either Flatman or Ayres. Traherne is in the tradition of the religious poets and writes with their glow and fervor, if not with their success. In spirit Cotton is closely allied with Lovelace and Suckling, and his poems reveal unexpected flashes of metaphysical wit which are not much dimmed by comparison with theirs. Flatman and Ayres are much

feebler, the latter in a double sense, perhaps, since his poems are translations from Petrarch and others. In their lines the tradition dies unimpressively.

In the work of these four poets, then, the qualities that we associate with the metaphysical tradition make their last appearance. After the 1680's, at the latest, they have ceased to influence the creative poetic imagination of their age and of the neoclassical period, except as Dryden or Pope, looking back, marveled at the lustre of the wit set in such an undisciplined poetry. (pp. 34-60)

> *Robert Lathrop Sharp, "The Course of Metaphysical Poetry," in his* From Donne to Dryden: The Revolt Against Metaphysical Poetry, *1940. Reprint by Archon Press, 1965, pp. 34-61.*

CULTURAL AND SOCIAL INFLUENCES

L. C. Knights

[*Knights was a renowned English Shakespearean scholar and critic. In the following essay, Knights delineates the cultural and social frame that influenced the genesis of metaphysical poetry in the early seventeenth century.*]

It seems appropriate to begin a paper of this kind with the simple reminder that works of literature, once they have left their authors' hands, are only kept alive by being recreated and possessed by individuals, and that it is only in terms of their active recreation in the fresh individual context of my experience and your experience that the main function of literature can be defined. In other words, literature is important because it *means* something to you and me and to everyone who is willing to accept its creative discipline; because it takes its place in the developing experience of our lives. It can, of course, serve other interests, such as the one I intend to pursue here—an interest in the meaning of 'culture' and in the relations of culture with economic and social activities; but it can only serve them at all fruitfully when they stem from that vivid personal apprehension and enjoyment that is the basis of all good criticism, as it is the main end of all reading.

It is in the light of these simple truths that we should consider T. S. Eliot's remark [in *The Use of Poetry and the Use of Criticism*] about 'sociological criticism, which has to suppress so much of the data, and which is ignorant of so much of the rest'. The question is, What *are* the data of 'sociological criticism'? My own answer would be that the relevant evidence is of very varied kinds, but that the primary and indispensable evidence is that offered by literary criticism, by the co-ordinated sensitiveness, powers of analysis, tact and sense of values of the individual playing upon literature itself. Divorced from *taste* sociological criticism becomes the barren exercise it so often is. Taste alone will not of course provide all the evidence—the data—needed for an enquiry of this kind. But it is only a developed feeling for literature, a responsiveness to the varied uses of language, that will tell us *what we are enquiring about*. When we have some idea of that we can usefully pursue our researches outside literature.

What we are enquiring is, in the first place, I suppose, to what extent the interests, perceptions and modes of judgment, embodied in the fresh original creation of a work of art, are fostered and stabilized by day-to-day living in the society within which the artist works. We want to know, therefore, something about such things as these: (i) The nature of the predominate forms of work—of getting a living—in any period, with special emphasis on the varied other-than-economic satisfactions involved; (ii) the forms of personal and wider social relations (beginning with the smaller units of family and neighbourhood), and the relations between different social groups; (iii) the traditions active in different groups and in the nation as a whole—religious, educational, 'cultural', and political traditions, traditions of personal behaviour and responsibility, and so on. We want to know a good many other things too, ranging from what may be called the practical organization of culture (the channels of demand and supply in literature and the other arts, and so on), to the current feeling for Nature and the natural processes. So the programme I have sketched is not one that can be carried out by any one person: it is essentially a matter for co-operative enquiry. But if we are agreed that the culture of a period depends on the kind and quality of the interests and modes of being fostered in ways such as I have indicated, and that these in turn are only present for discussion when the investigator has a sensitiveness to specific values similar in kind to that of the good critic, then we have some hope of making sociological criticism something other than an academic *substitute* for literary criticism, and of making it useful. If you ask me what the use is, I should say that, apart from strengthening our hold on literature that we like, it has the use of all historical and sociological study that is permeated by a sense of human values; that it deepens our insight into the intimate dependence of individual growth on factors outside the individual, and makes more vivid and specific the truth that civilization is essentially co-operative, involving co-operation with the living and the dead. In these ways it offers us principles that can guide our thinking about some of the more fundamental problems of the present. Since these are often distorted or obscured in the abstract terms of politics, sociological criticism (as I intend it) has the additional advantage of bringing us back from abstractions to the realities of personal satisfactions and personal fulfilment in certain specific circumstances.

* * * *

After this beginning to a paper with a rather grand title ["On the Social Background of Metaphysical Poetry"], what I actually have to offer will probably appear extremely slight. I shall be concerned with only a very few of the ways in which it is possible to work out *from* literature—from Metaphysical poetry—to 'the life of the time' in the early seventeenth century; and even within the narrow limits I have chosen I can do little more than suggest what seem to me to be interesting possibilities. Perhaps the demands of a war-time routine will be accepted as an excuse

for offering what is little more than a draft programme of work to be done.

I.

The observation to start from is that Metaphysical poetry touches life at many points. I am not referring to subject-matter (though that is varied), but to the range of interest and awareness that is brought to bear on any 'subject'. We come from the poetry with a renewed sense of the multiple nature of man, of the possibility—actualized in the best of the poems—of living simultaneously at many levels. In Donne's love poetry, for example, man—the actual experiencing individual—is felt as intimately enmeshed in the world of sense and instinct; and sense and passion are vividly expressed in their fresh immediacy. But in Donne there is always present the need to become *fully* aware of the immediate emotion, and the effort to apprehend—to grasp and realize—leads inevitably to the quickening of faculties so often only dimly present in the expression of sensation and feeling. In the best of his love poems there is active not only passion or affection but a ranging and enquiring mind and a spirit capable of perceiving values. Conversely, the most ecstatic experience is felt in terms 'which sense may reach and apprehend'. This is only another way of saying that in Donne thought, feeling and bodily sensation are intimately blended. And with this dimension of depth is a dimension of breadth: 'the most heterogeneous ideas' are brought to a focus. The range of Donne's intellectual and worldly interests is a commonplace of criticism; and it is because these interests are so vividly *there*—whether introduced directly or by way of simile and metaphor—that the greater poems of passion seem so solidly grounded.

> And though each spring do add to love new
>   heat,
> As princes do in times of action get
> New taxes, and remit them not in peace,
> No winter shall abate the spring's increase.

The triumphant assurance of this—the conclusion of *Love's Growth*—does not depend on any exclusion of the world of which the lovers form a part. Throughout *Songs and Sonnets* the love themes are defined in terms of the poet's interest in an eager, active world of merchants and astronomers, princes and their favourites, schoolboys and prentices:

> Soldiers find wars, and lawyers find out still
>   Litigious men, which quarrels move,
>   Though she and I do love.

And besides the range of interests there is also a range of feeling. Thus the love expressed in the greater poems, intensely personal though it is, is not felt simply as an individual personal possession; it is felt in terms of more-than-personal life and growth:

> A single violet transplant,
>   The strength, the colour, and the size,
> (All which before was poor and scant,)
>   Redoubles still and multiplies.
> When love, with one another so
>   Interinanimates two souls . . .
>
> And yet no greater, but more eminent,

> Love by the Spring is grown;
> As in the firmament,
> Stars by the Sun are not enlarg'd, but shown.
> Gentle love deeds, as blossoms on a bough,
> From love's awakened root do bud out now.

These examples come from poems containing highly intellectual argument, but they suggest that Donne shares something of the feeling for *natural* growth—as wholesome and right for man—that informs Shakespeare's plays:

> For his bounty,
> There was no winter in it, an autumn 'twas
> That grew the more by reaping.
>
> She that herself will sliver and disbranch
> From her material sap, perforce must wither
> And come to deadly use.

Without overlooking the important differences from Donne, we can say something similar of Herbert. Whereas Donne illuminates passion by play of mind, Herbert brings to the expression of his religious experience the familiar world of everyday things. But his homely imagery is not simply a form of expression; it is an index of habitual modes of thought and feeling in which the different aspects and different levels of his personal experience are brought into intimate relation to each other. An additional observation is that the stream of his personal experience—more clearly than Donne's—is fed from sources apparently remote in the social topography of the period. His poetry, with its intellectual cast and its tone of courtesy, is plainly the work of one who moves easily in the cultivated circles of his time: 'I know the ways of learning . . . honour . . . pleasure'; and the contemporary learning that he assimilates takes its place in a solid traditional education that respects, without being overawed by, the new science. Thus scientific achievement and a certain complacence in the scientist are focussed simultaneously in the first *Vanity* poem.

> The fleet Astronomer can bore,
> And thred the spheres with his quick-piercing mind:
> He views their stations, walks from door to door,
> Surveys, *as if he had design'd*
> *To make a purchase there*: he sees their dances,
> And knoweth long before
> Both their full-ey'd aspects, and secret glances . . .
>
> The subtle Chymic can devest
> And strip the creature naked, till he finde
> The callow principles within their nest:
> *There he imparts to them his mind,*
> Admitted to their bed-chamber, before
> They appear trim and drest
> To ordinary suitors at the door.

But if Herbert is courtly and Metaphysical he is also popular. He has an instinctive feeling for common speech—pithy, sententious and shrewd, summing up character in a concrete image:

> Then came brave Glory puffing by
> In silks that whistled, who but he?

And as with Donne his interests and the modes of his sensibility are integrated in a uniquely personal idiom.

What I am trying to do is to put into terms more immediately useful for my purpose the familiar conception of the Metaphysicals as possessing 'a mechanism of sensibility that could devour any kind of experience'. The later generation of these poets, apart from Marvell, had not the force of Donne or Herbert, but almost all the poets represented in Professor Grierson's well-known anthology express a vivid play of various interests that are felt as having an intimate bearing on each other: the sensibility is not compartmentalized. That is why the greater poems make such a disturbing, reverberating impact on the mind of the reader, and even the poems that appear slight on a first reading are found to have behind them a range and weight of experience: in almost all there is 'the recognition, implicit in the expression of every experience, of other kinds of experience that are possible'.

Now the assumption on which I am working is that a positive distinctive quality common to half-a-dozen good poets and a number of competent and interesting ones, all writing within the same half-century, is not likely to be the result of a purely literary relationship to the founder of the 'school' whose individual genius can be regarded as the sole source of his followers' idiom. It is much more likely that the distinctive note of Metaphysical poetry—the implicit recognition of the many-sidedness of man's nature—is in some ways socially supported; that—to borrow some phrases from a suggestive passage in Yeats's criticism—'unity of being' has some relation to a certain 'unity of culture'. Professor Grierson remarks [in his introduction to *The Poems of John Donne*], 'It was only the force of Donne's personality that could achieve even an approximate harmony of elements so divergent as are united in his love-verses'. When we recognize the truth in this, as we must, we need to keep in mind also the complementary truth tersely expressed by Ben Jonson: 'Rare Poems ask rare friends'.

II.

The tag from Jonson suggests where we should begin our enquiries. We need to know who the Metaphysical poets expected to be interested in their verses, who they met and at what levels, what were the functions, interests and traditions of those who composed their immediate circle. All these questions represent work still to be done. We can say in a general way, however, that the social milieu of the Metaphysical poets was aristocratic in tone, connecting in one direction (partly but certainly not exclusively through patronage) with the inner circles of the Court, in another with the universities and with the middle and upper ranks of the ecclesiastical, administrative and legal hierarchies, and in yet another with the prosperous merchant class represented by Izaak Walton and the Ferrars. A short study of the life of Sir Henry Wotton, a representative member of Donne's circle, may serve to point some provisional conclusions concerning the over-lapping aristocratic groups from which the 'rare friends' were drawn.

Henry Wotton was born in 1568. He came of a Kentish family that had provided the state with soldiers, administrators and diplomats throughout the Tudor period. Mr. Logan Pearsall Smith, from whose admirable *Life* of Wotton I take my information, tells us that, 'High public service, love of learning and of Italy and of poetry, were among the influences inherited from the past' (*Life and Letters*, I). Educated at Winchester and Oxford, where he formed a lifelong friendship with John Donne, he went abroad to study law and languages. After five years in the German states, Austria, Italy and Switzerland (where he spent fourteen months in the house of the scholar Casaubon) he returned to England and became one of the secretaries of the Earl of Essex. He accompanied Essex on the Cadiz expedition of 1596 and the Islands Voyage of 1597 (again in company with Donne), and on the disastrous Irish expedition of 1599. There followed a further adventurous period on the Continent, in which he was of service to the future James I, and early in the new reign he was knighted and sent as ambassador to the Venetian Republic. Wotton served three terms as ambassador in Venice, from 1604 to 1610, from 1616 to 1619, and again from 1621 to 1623. Between the first two of these he was engaged in various diplomatic missions, and sat in the Addled Parliament of 1614. For a short period in 1612 he was in disgrace because of some unexpected consequences of his 'definition of an Ambassador': 'An Ambassador is an honest man sent to lie abroad for the good of his country'. Between the second and the third embassies to Venice Wotton was employed in James I's fruitless negotiations with the Emperor for a European peace. When he finally returned to settle in England in 1623 he was given the Provostship of Eton, and in 1626 he entered deacon's orders. At Eton, with occasional visits to London, Oxford and his old home in Kent, he passed the tranquil remainder of his life, reading, writing, fishing, and taking a lively interest in the boys of the school. In 1638, the year before his death, he was visited by Milton, and in reply to a subsequent letter and a gift copy of *Comus* wrote his well-known commendation of that poem.

Robert Boyle, the famous chemist, who as a boy spent some time directly under Wotton's charge in the Provost's house at Eton, described him as 'a person that was not only a fine gentleman himself, but very well skilled in the art of making others so'. To consider Wotton's activities, interests and attainments is to form an idea of the qualities that the age considered proper to a fine gentleman. A large part of Wotton's adult life was spent in the service of the state, and he has of course a place in the political and diplomatic history of the time. But he was far from being merely a public figure. 'A wit and courtier, with the self-possession of a man of action, ready for any adventure and disguise, he was yet by nature and inclination a scholar and student; and beneath his cosmopolitan experience, and the taste and culture of Italy, he had preserved something of the simplicity and piety of the old Wottons, and an untouched devotion to the religion of his country'. A scholar and a friend of scholars, he 'was deeply read in history and moral philosophy and civil law'. As a minor poet he is still remembered for his poem on Elizabeth of Bohemia and the *Character of a Happy Life*, written during his period of disgrace in 1612. His prose writings include *The State of Christendom*, a fragmentary *Survey of Education*, and *The Elements of Architecture*, which is said to show

the Palladian taste that reached England towards the end of the reign of James I. He was also—to borrow a word from the later seventeenth century, whose tastes he in some ways anticipated—something of a *virtuoso*. He had an amateur interest in the 'superior novelties' of science; he sent to King James a copy of Galileo's *Siderius Nuncius* (1610), which describes the discoveries made through the newly invented telescope—commenting that these would involve some radical changes in judicial astrology; he visited Kepler in 1620 and described the latter's *camera obscura* in a letter to Bacon, remarking, 'I owe your Lordship even by promise . . . some trouble this way; I mean by the commerce of philosophical experiments, which surely, of all other, is the most ingenuous traffic' (*Life and Letters*, II). He liked to visit the glass factories near Venice, and he collected and sent home from Italy cuttings of flowers and fruit trees. He was also one of the first English connoisseurs of Italian art. His will may be cited here as suggesting the variety of his interests. It mentions, besides books, manuscripts and Italian pictures: 'my great Loadstone; and a piece of Amber of both kinds naturally united, and only differing in degree of concoction, which is thought somewhat rare'; 'a piece of Crystal Sexangular (as they all grow) grasping divers several things within it, which I bought among the Rhaetian Alps, in the very place where it grew'; 'my *Viol di Gamba*, which hath been twice in Italy'; and 'my chest, or Cabinet of Instruments and Engines of all kinds of uses: in the lower box whereof, are some fit to be bequeathed to none but so entire an honest man' as the legatee.

What emerges very clearly from Mr. Logan Pearsall Smith's biography is that Wotton's scholarly, artistic and quasi-scientific interests were by no means private hobbies, carefully kept apart from his public interests; they were shared with a large and varied circle of friends, and they permeated his ordinary social living. Mr. Smith describes Wotton's habitual mode of life at Venice:

> Being prohibited by his position from any association with the nobles of Venice, he was largely dependent for society on the members of his own household. But these young men, his own nephews, sons of Kentish squires, or scholars fresh from Oxford or Cambridge, formed just the kind of society in which he delighted. Together they made what Wotton called a "domestic college" of young Englishmen in their Venetian palace. They had their chaplain and their religious services; they read aloud the classics, or some new book of weight at stated hours, and dined together, toasting by name their friends in England. They occupied themselves sometimes with music, (the ambassador himself playing on the viol de gamba), sometimes with chemical experiments, or again with philosophical speculations, attempting, as Wotton put it, to mend the world in the speculative part, since they despaired of putting it right in the practical and moral . . . "In summa we live happily, merrily, and honestly", one of his household writes; "let State businesses go as they will, we follow our studies hard and love one another".

We do not really know how far upwards in the social scale the kinds of interest that we find in Wotton permeated.

James I was bookish, and Charles I was a cultivated man, but it is quite likely that the tone of the inner court circle was set by men whose interests in the arts did not go very far beyond the opportunities for display that they afforded. The fact remains, however, that Wotton's circle was on a comparatively intimate footing with the greater social figures, and that it formed an integral part of the contemporary aristocracy.

In so far as Wotton was representative of a class—and he was certainly not unrepresentative—two points of some importance for our understanding of the seventeenth century emerge. The first is that the aristocracy from whom so many of the friends and patrons of the Metaphysical poets was drawn was a functional aristocracy. The general significance of this was indicated by D. W. Harding in two articles in the *Musical Times* (May and June, 1938) on 'The Social Background of Taste in Music':

> Common experience suggests that the people who really influence public taste (at the moment chiefly by sanctioning its low level) are those who remain in close touch with industry and commerce and public affairs—what may conveniently be called the upper business class. The leisured are of less account. They or their ancestors were influential while they made their money, but once elevated to the ranks of the leisured they receive deference without possessing influence. They are respected for having secured their translation from the real world, but what they choose to do after metamorphosis is of no moment to those in "active" life. The ideals which make some mark on general opinion are those of men like Lord Nuffield, who, besides being public-spirited, are also responsible industrialists, still in direct touch with business. And at present men of this sort may encourage public interest in the welfare of the unemployed or the usefulness of universities to business life, but they rarely stand effectively committed to a belief in the value of the arts.

> Presumably (though here the evidence of the historian is required) the older traditions of respecting significant music grew up when the patrons of the arts were people of "practical" importance—rulers, statesmen, ambassadors, men of power in the Church, merchant princes, lords in direct control of their estates. And their taste for music and the other arts was not an idiosyncrasy to be shut away in their private lives: it was an integral part of their public personality. To have had business dealings with them while remaining a confessed philistine must have been like meeting modern business men without knowing anything of golf courses, restaurants, the motor show, air travel, or foreign resorts; possible no doubt, but a trifle embarrassing on both sides.

The second point, which has a more direct bearing on the particular qualities of Metaphysical poetry, is that in this milieu there was not only 'a current of ideas', but a current fed from varied sources. Consider for a moment Ben Jonson. Jonson wrote masques for the Court and lyric poems that helped to set the tone of much court poetry in Charles's reign. He was a scholar, moving easily in the circle of ideas represented by such men as Camden, Casaubon and Selden. He was also a writer for the popular stage, with an eager interest in the everyday life of London and an ingrained feeling for that native vigour expressed in the colloquial English of his day. Wherever we look we find that the channels of interest form a criss-cross pattern. In Jonson's or Donne's or Wotton's circle, politics and public affairs, scholarship and 'the new philosophy', literature and the arts, meet and cross: they are not compartmentalized. In other words, the milieu offers a variety of interests; it offers a positive incentive to flexibility of mind, and so does something to prepare the ground for that maturity of judgment that comes when varied fields of experience are seen in relation to each other.

In another way too Wotton can be instanced as representative. 'Izaak Walton rightly insists', says Mr. Logan Pearsall Smith, 'on the importance of Bocton [the family home in Kent] in the history of Sir Henry Wotton's life. It was indeed the memories and traditions centred about this ancient house that played a predominant part in the formation of his character. From his family and ancestors he inherited that peculiar combination of culture and old-fashioned piety, of worldly wisdom and ingenuousness of nature, "the simplicity", as he called it, "of a plain Kentish man", which gave in after years a certain graceful singularity to his conduct, difficult for the courtiers among whom he moved to understand. He loved everything that savoured of Kent, all the local ways and phrases, and when ambassador abroad he surrounded himself with the sons of Kentish neighbours. Bocton he always regarded as his home, finding even the air about it better and more wholesome than other air; to the end of his life he returned thither when he could, although as a younger son he possessed no claim on the place save that of affection' (*Life and Letters*, I). I am very doubtful of Wotton's 'singularity' in this respect. At all events the country house in this period had an importance not merely social but cultural. Few of the greater places can have maintained such a vigorous intellectual life as contemporaries admired at Tew, where Lucius Cary, Viscount Falkland, gathered his friends and made what Clarendon called 'a University bound in a lesser volume'. But the tradition of 'housekeeping' inherited by a good many noblemen and gentlemen of the early seventeenth century seems to have included the duty of maintaining, in various capacities and for longer or shorter periods, scholars and men of letters. And because the great houses were an integral part of English rural life—not just holiday resorts for hunting and shooting—their owners were genuinely in touch with the activities and traditions of the countryside. Ben Jonson was a shrewd and realistic observer of the life about him, and this is how he described Penshurst, the seat of the Sidney family in Kent:

> The blushing apricot and wooly peach
> Hang on thy walls, that every child may reach.
> And though thy walls be of the country stone,
> They are reared with no man's ruin, no man's
>   groan;
> There's none that dwell about them wish them
>   down,
> But all come in, the farmer and the clown,
> And no one empty handed, to salute

> Thy lord and lady, though they have no suit.
> Some bring a capon, some a rural cake,
> Some nuts, some apples; some that think they
>   make
> The better cheeses bring 'em, or else send
> By their ripe daughters whom they would com-
>   mend
> This way to husbands, and whose baskets bear
> An emblem of themselves in plum or pear . . .

This is an idealized but not, I think, a misleading picture, and it gives a fair impression of what 'housekeeping' meant for many great families of the time. It meant hospitality, and it meant sharing in the community life of the village in a fairly intimate fashion. It meant something altogether different from a condescending interest in 'the villagers'. In the same poem Jonson tells how King James paid a surprise visit to Penshurst when the mistress of the house was away:

> What great I will not say, but sudden cheer
> Didst thou then make 'em!   and what praise
>   was heaped
> On thy good lady then!   who therein reaped
> The just reward of her high huswifery;
> To have her linen, plate, and all things nigh
> When she was far, and not a room but dressed
> As if it had expected such a guest.

The 'good lady' who is praised for her 'high huswifery' is Lady Lisle, and it is significant that Jonson can use these homely terms in her praise.

I do not want to idealize the life of the aristocratic households in town and country in which the poets and men of letters had a footing. But it does seem true to say that they were places where a variety of living interests were taken for granted, and where men of different bents and occupations could find some common ground. And since the country houses were still functional units in the rural economy of the time, I think they helped to foster that intimate feeling for natural growth and the natural order—something so very different from the modern 'appreciation of nature'—that almost disappears from English poetry after Marvell.

III.

The question of the traditions active in the social groups from which the Metaphysical poets were drawn is far too large for me to venture on any inclusive generalizations. I will only note one or two features of the religious tradition that have a direct bearing on my present theme.

We have recently been reminded that Donne and his generation were the inheritors of the mediaeval view of man that saw him as half way between the beasts and the angels, and as sharing something of the nature of both. According to this view man shares sense and instinct with the animals. But, like the angels, he is capable of intellectual knowledge, though whereas the angels know at once, intuitively, man can only attain knowledge of a limited kind by the exercise of reason. Wretched and worthless through sin, he is capable of salvation through grace. The mediaeval view of man's central place in the universe was undermined by the discoveries and new intellectual currents of the Renaissance. Donne and his contemporaries were forced to question the old assumptions: 'The new philoso-

phy puts all in doubt'. But all the same they were still conscious of the old tradition which sanctioned the view of man as a being existing at many levels—not just a rational being as the eighteenth century tended to see him, not just an economic unit as a powerful trend of thought in the nineteenth century was content to assume. Now 'the idea of man' implicit or explicit in the religious tradition has its own importance. But there is something more important, though more difficult to formulate: I mean the fact that religion in the early seventeenth century is not set over against life; it still in some way *grows out* of the life that it sets itself to foster. George Herbert is close enough to the central Anglican tradition to be instanced as representative. That Herbert's religion is not lacking in elements of imaginative grandeur may be seen from the powerful dramatic play of his poem, *The Sacrifice,* and no one who knows his poems of personal exploration and self-discovery will think of him in terms of a nave piety. But to understand Herbert we need to know not only his greater poems—poems that appeal to men of very different faiths—but also his more pedestrian verses where he states very simply the bases of his faith and outlook. There is, for example, *The Church-Porch,* where the precepts of good neighbourliness are tempered and refined by Herbert's personal courtesy and feeling for other people as individuals. And behind this feeling for the direct contact of men in small social units is a pervasive sense of the wider order of nature in which the parish or neighbourhood has its setting and to which it belongs. We see something of this in *Providence*:

> Sheep eat the grass, and dung the ground for
>   more:
> Trees after bearing drop their leaves for soil.

It is the fact that Herbert does not need to insist (for the assumption is that everybody knows) that makes this significant. It is not an accident that in the greater poems of personal experience—in *Vertue, Life* and *The Flower,* for example—the defining is done in terms of imagery drawn from the world of seasonal growth, decay and renewal. The bearing of this aspect of the religious tradition is clear when we consider the implications of the very different idiom of the later seventeenth century. There is no need to question the sincerity of Dryden's religious beliefs, either in *Religio Laici* or *The Hind and the Panther*; but those beliefs—except when they draw on Dryden's powerful conception of social order—seem to have very little to do with his most vital mundane interests.

> Rest then, my soul, from endless anguish freed:
> Nor sciences thy guide, nor sense thy creed.
> Faith is the best insurer of thy bliss;
> The bank above must fail before the venture
>   miss.

A religion that can be expressed in such terms has plainly lost connexion with the deeper sources of vitality and spiritual health; and for this reason it cannot enrich human living with a sense of significance in all its parts as the tradition active in Herbert's—and in Shakespeare's—day enriched it.

IV.

The conditions I have described could not last. In Carew's

poem, *In Answer of an Elegiacal Letter, upon the Death of the King of Sweden* . . . (1632), the poet praises the 'halcyon days of Charles I.

> But let us, that in myrtle bowers sit
> Under secure shades, use the benefit
> Of peace and plenty, which the blessed hand
> Of our good king gives this obdurate land;
> Let us of revels sing . . .
> . . . What though the German drum
> Bellow for freedom and revenge, the noise
> Concerns not us, nor should divert our joys;
> Nor ought the thunder of their carabines
> Drown the sweet airs of our tuned violins.

Even here there is a suggestion of a culture self-conscious and on the defensive. In Marvell the older tradition is still active. But Marvell's greatest poem is concerned with the clash of irreconcilable forces long latent in society.

> Though Justice against Fate complain,
> And plead the ancient rights in vain:
>   But those do hold or break
>   As Men are strong or weak.
> Nature that hateth emptiness,
> Allows of penetration less:
>   And therefore must make room
>   Where greater spirits come.

A glance at the background of literature in the period immediately following the mid-century break may serve to bring out by contrast what is meant by saying that Metaphysical poetry touches life at many points, and that its implicit recognition of the many-sidedness of man's nature was socially supported. To start with, of course, the mediaeval traditions—questioned and undermined but still active in Donne's day—do not survive the Civil War. The new intellectual current is rationalist and materialist, pointing forward to the Enlightenment of the eighteenth century. Restoration assumptions concerning man's nature are narrower than those previously accepted. Whereas man had been recognized as a complex being, rooted in instinct, swayed by passions, and at the same time an intellectual and spiritual being, he is now something much simpler. He is a reasonable creature, in the limited way in which the new age understood 'Reason': he is in fact something much more like a mechanism than a mystery; for, says Hobbes, 'What is the Heart, but a Spring; and the Nerves, but so many Strings; and the Joints but so many Wheels, giving motion to the whole Body, such as was intended by the Artificer?' Partly in consequence of these changes in the intellectual climate literature tends to stress the rational and social elements in man to the exclusion of other qualities. Dryden is a great poet, but, as I have already suggested, there are wide ranges of human potentiality and human experience that he is quite unaware of.

The changes in social organization were equally marked. At the Restoration the Court was the centre of polite letters. But Charles II's courtiers, though some of them were interested in the Royal Society, were far from being the intellectual centre of a national culture. Wotton would have been sadly out of place at that Court, not only on account of his piety. Cultivated women such as the Countess of Bedford or Mrs. Herbert disappear from the social scene.

Country housekeeping in the old sense—though still a factor in the national life—is rapidly giving way before the attractions of a life in town. And what 'the Town' thought of the country is amply demonstrated in the comedies of the period. When one reads Professor Pinto's *Life* of Rochester, probably the most gifted of the mob of gentlemen who wrote with ease, one is conscious of a rather chilly wind of emptiness. It is symptomatic that in Rochester, 'wit', canalized into satire, is completely divorced from 'feeling'. And in the best of his love poems the feeling is both simple—a momentary tenderness—and quite unrelated to that fuller life so actively present in Donne's poems even when he is most absorbed by his passion.

* * * *

Those aspects of the background of poetry in the early Stuart period that I have indicated need to be explored in detail before we can reach any certain conclusions about the influence of social life on poetry. And a fuller exploration would certainly make distinctions where I have generalized. (One obvious distinction would be between the first two decades of the seventeenth century, still partly Elizabethan, and the two or three decades that followed, when taste was certainly changing). But it does seem to me that further knowledge of the facts of social life in the first half of the seventeenth century is likely to substantiate the conclusions to which literary criticism points. They are: (i) that the social milieu of the Metaphysical poets was one in which there was an *active* culture: there was 'a current of ideas in the highest degree animating and nourishing to the creative power'; (ii) that through this milieu the poets whose work brings so much of the 'the whole soul of man into activity' touched life at many points. Tradition and the actual social organization alike fostered a range of contacts with contemporary life that is, to say the least, rare in the later history of English poetry. (pp. 37-52)

> *L. C. Knights, "On the Social Background of Metaphysical Poetry," in* Scrutiny, *Vol. XIII, No. 1, Spring, 1945, pp. 37-52.*

Mary Cole Sloane

[In the following excerpt, Sloane considers the impact of seventeenth-century British empiricist philosophy on forming the world view of the metaphysical poets.]

Although we are aware of important differences among them, we customarily have placed five poets—John Donne, George Herbert, Henry Vaughan, Richard Crashaw, and Thomas Traherne—in one literary classification. Following Dryden's lead, we have applied a common term, "metaphysical," to their poetic output. The name has stuck despite a tendency to associate some of these poets with "mannerism," a category drawn from art history, and despite Louis L. Martz's perceptive suggestion that the common denominator in their poetry is the religious meditation. But, regardless of how we categorize them in broad and general terms, the five poets have eluded classification when it comes to the particulars of their poetic styles. This is especially true of definitions of the metaphysical conceit which, if tailored to fit the metaphors of Donne and Herbert, are somehow inappropriate when applied to the metaphors of Vaughan or Traherne.

What has only recently begun to be recognized is the impact on the metaphysical poets of the deep epistemological upheaval that occurred during the seventeenth century. Modern recognition of the significance of epistemology is becoming increasingly pertinent to our understanding of the intellectual milieu in which the metaphysical poets wrote.

Looking at metaphysical poetry in the light of how its creators felt they acquired knowledge raises the question of their relationship to the medieval concept of world order with which they, from the beginning of the twentieth century's revival of

interest in them, often have been associated. If the metaphysical poets were indeed questioning accepted ways of knowing, it is unreasonable to assume that they, either consciously or unconsciously, could leave unchallenged the concept of a universe in which everything corresponded perfectly to everything else. It is even less reasonable to assume that, writing after the Ptolemaic picture of world order had received so many threatening blows, they could let that picture find its way into their poetry unadulterated. There would, in this context, appear to be an inconsistency in the traditional appraisal of the metaphysical poets' place in the history of thought. The inconsistency becomes overwhelmingly apparent if we concentrate our attention on precisely how each of the metaphysical poets regarded the visual world from which he obtained his metaphors.

To arouse our suspicions that metaphysical poetry was indeed responsive to an epistemological upheaval, we need only compare the attitude toward the senses of its first and last representatives, Donne and Traherne. On Easter Sunday, 1628, John Donne told the congregation that had gathered in the old Gothic Cathedral of St. Paul's in London that "sight is so much the Noblest of all the senses, as that it is all the senses." His ultimate purpose in thus elevating the sense of sight, as he explicated his Biblical text, was to debase it in order to impress upon the minds of his listeners that man saw through a glass darkly. Earlier, reading from the book of nature rather than the Book of scripture, he had noted that

> Sight is the noblest sense of any one,
> Yet sight hath only colour to feed on,
> And colour is decai'd: summers robe growes
> Duskie, and like an oft dyed garment showes.
> (*The first Anniversary*, lines 353-356)

Donne's wistful distrust of what he sees is a far cry from Traherne's joyous exaltation later in the century in what his senses enable him to experience:

> For *Sight* inherits Beauty, *Hearing* Sounds,
> The *Nostril* Sweet Perfumes,
> All *Tastes* have hidden Rooms
> Within the *Tongue*; and *Feeling Feeling* Wounds
> With Pleasure and Delight; but I
> Forgot the rest, and was all Sight, or Ey.
> Unbodied and Devoid of Care,
> Just as in Heavn the Holy Angels are.
> For Simple Sence

Is Lord of all Created Excellence.
(*The Preparative*, lines 31-40)

The juxtaposition of the two passages suggests that in regard to the validity of knowledge obtained through the senses a change has most certainly occurred. This could be expected, for the lives of the metaphysical poets spanned that period in intellectual history immediately preceding John Locke's refutation of the concept of the innate idea.

The seventeenth century, writes K. G. Hamilton [in his *Two Harmonies: Poetry and Prose in the Seventeenth Century*], saw the shift of the center of philosophical interest "from metaphysics to epistemology; from a concern with the nature and verbalization of truth to a primary interest in the way in which truth can become known." The epistemological theories of the early church fathers and their heirs had been concerned basically with man's knowledge of God; how man came to know his immediate terrestrial environment was always subsidiary to that larger question. The philosophers who most influenced the mainstream of Medieval or Renaissance thought had not struggled with the sticky problem of sensory experience for it's own sake. Indeed, it would have been blasphemy to do so. Thus a certain measure of cautious skepticism had been almost mandatory, since it was precisely the search for knowledge that had been the original sin responsible for the fall of man and the consequent corruption not only of man, but also of the physical world itself. Man's presumption in the face of forbidden knowledge had brought upon him the wrath of God. Typically, the late sixteenth-century poet, Sir John Davies, asks in his philosophical verse-essay about the soul,

> What is this *knowledge*? but the Skie-stolne fire,
> For which the *Thiefe* still chaind in Ice doth sit?
> (*Nosce Teipsum*, lines 41-42)

His Prometheus is accompanied by such other guilty human beings as Ixion, Phaeton, and Icarus. Approximately a half-century earlier, the emblematist Andreas Alciati had drawn examples from the same list for his *Emblematum Liber* of 1531. Sir Francis Bacon found it necessary, in *The Advancement of Learning*, published in 1605, to raise learning from the lowly position to which he felt it had fallen. His solution was one that frequently would be reverted to by men who found themselves in the guilt-producing dilemma between God and science. There was to Bacon a forbidden knowledge, a knowledge of God, that man could not arrive at through the use of his senses. But there also was a legitimate human knowledge—that of man's observable surroundings. It was, of course, this latter kind of knowledge that would be emphasized throughout the succeeding centuries.

When interest was moving during the Renaissance toward the latter kind of knowledge, those thinkers who were either directly or indirectly concerned had at their disposal two basic epistemological concepts which had been absorbed by the medieval philosophers into various theories concerning man's knowledge of God. From Plato had come the concept that everything that was available to the senses was in a state of flux and therefore could not present man with a knowledge of the real. Aristotle contributed the concept that the active intellect abstracted forms from images that existed materially in nature. Associated with Plato was the assumption that man was born with a faint memory of the ideal, while associated with Aristotle was the assumption that all knowledge was acquired through sensory experience. But the implications inherent in Aristotle's emphasis on the senses were not used to challenge the popular medieval concept of world order that persisted well into the Renaissance.

One need only to cite Donne's extensive use of microcosm-macrocosm imagery to illustrate that he, born in the early 1570's, must have absorbed the primarily Platonic belief in a universe made up of terrestrial-celestial correspondences—that emblematic concept of the universe that has been shown by E.M.W. Tillyard to be so much a part of Elizabethan poetry. The seventeenth century would end, however, with an emphasis on the physical universe itself. This new emphasis was consistent with the materialism propounded by Thomas Hobbes in his *Leviathan* of 1651 and with the death-blow given to the Platonic concept of the innate idea by Locke when, in his *An Essay Concerning Humane Understanding* of 1691, he declared that the human mind at birth was a *tabula rasa*. Locke, in effect, provided a conscious epistemological rationale that could justify the Renaissance concept of art as the imitation of nature and that could provide the Augustan writers with a secure epistemological base on which to construct their various mimetic theories. Placed thus between a period that emphasized the Platonic approach to epistemology and a period that followed a more Aristotelian approach, the metaphysical poets were in a unique position to respond to any suspicions concerning the old concept and also to consider any cultural glimmerings suggesting the new. Their predicament calls to mind a phrase that Roy Daniells used in regard to the metaphysical poets and the concept of mannerism. He wrote [in his *Milton, Mannerism and Baroque*] that with the concept available, the style of the metaphysical poets no longer seemed like an aberration "but rather as the logical development from Spenserian or Sidneyan smoothness and the necessary bridge from this island of stability to the Baroque *terra firma* on which the larger works of Milton are erected." Because the metaphysical poets wrote on the eve of an epistemological revolution, it also might be possible to see their poetry as suggestive of a journey from the stable island of medieval epistemology to the *terra firma* of the *tabula rasa*. For in the seventeenth century it was quite possible for a poet seeking images to swing inconsistently back and forth between what were considered either primarily Aristotelian or primarily Platonic conceptions of knowledge obtained through the senses. The metaphysical poets seemed to have been uncommonly aware of this possibility; there is evidence that the epistemological problem surfaced with more directness than was really necessary for the creation of poetic imagery. They were, with the exception of Crashaw, highly suspicious of the concept of universal analogy. That this is so ultimately can be established through an analysis of their visual imagery. Although only Traherne consciously formulated an epistemological theory, the metaphoric challenge to the concept of universal analogy can be established at the outset. The new resolu-

tions had not yet been articulated; but the old most certainly were found wanting.

That metaphoric challenge is evident in Donne's fondness for indiscriminately ransacking not only nature and art, but also diverse philosophic and scientific concepts for vehicles wherein to contain his wit. One ransacking is most pertinent here, for it shows his attitude toward epistemology. In his "Ecclogue" of 1613, he playfully carried an aspect of medieval epistemology to the point of absurdity. His Idios, trying to explain to Allophanes why he was not at the court for the wedding of the Earl of Sommerset, argues that he did not need to be there because

> Kings (as their patterne, God) are liberall
> Not onely in fulnesse, but capacitie,
>   Enlarging narrow men, to feele and see,
> And comprehend the blessings they bestow.
> So, reclus'd hermits often times do know
> More of heavens glory, then a worldling can.
>   (*Ecclogue,* lines 44-49)

Idios, of course, is basing his argument on the assumption that man's mind is a microcosmic representation of the macrocosm:

> As man is of the world, the heart of man,
>   Is an epitome of Gods great booke.
>   (*Ibid.*, lines 51-52)

But Allophanes chides Idios for being so naively accepting:

>   Dreamer, thou art.
>   Think'st thou, fantastique that thou hast a
>   part
> In the East-Indian fleet, because thou hast
>   A little spice, or Amber in thy taste?
>   (*Ibid.*, lines 55-58)

Although the real reason behind Allophanes' challenge is that it gives him the opportunity to make laudatory statements about king and court, the challenge shows that Donne was aware of several epistemological possibilities and could subject to doubt, whether seriously or not, the generally accepted assumptions of his time.

The imagery used by Donne in the *Anniversary* poems is undoubtedly more seriously meant and thus more potentially significant than Allophanes' challenge of Idios' epistemology. When Donne wrote the poems to commemorate the death of the young Elizabeth Drury, he could not have anticipated the extent to which the problem of her identity would concern scholars in a more literal age. The "rich Soule which to her heaven is gone" has been variously identified. Therefore Frank Manley suggests that perhaps Elizabeth Drury as a symbol may be capable of too many associations to be pinned down to a single and specific one. But Manley raises the possibility that the imagery is related to various Renaissance concepts of wisdom, and Hiram Haydn has interpreted the death of Elizabeth Drury as the repeal of natural law. Both of these have epistemological implications, and an epistemological interpretation might indeed be valid. This is not to suggest, though, that other interpretations can be negated. But Donne's awareness of the epistemological upheaval of the seventeenth century is decidedly apparent when the *Anni-*

versary poems are compared to Sir John Davies' *Nosce Teipsum*.

While Donne presents us with a crumbling and disordered universe and Davies emphasizes harmony, neither challenges the assumptions that the fall of man clouded man's mind and that only death would bring man perfect knowledge. In *The second Anniversary*, which can be regarded as the fideistic answer to *The first Anniversary*, Donne writes:

> Thinke then, my soule, that death is but a
>   Groome,
> Which brings a Taper to the outward roome,
> Whence thou spiest first a little glimmering
>   light,
> And after brings it nearer to thy sight:
> For such approaches doth heaven make in
>   death.
>
>   (lines 85-89)

Similarly, near the end of *Nosce Teipsum*, Davies warns his soul:

> Know that thou canst know nothing perfectly,
> While thou art Clouded with this flesh of mine.
>   (lines 1915-1916)

Like Donne, Davies could refer to human speculation as resulting in confusion:

> One thinks the *Soule* is *Aire*, another Fire,
>   Another *Blood*, defus'd about the hart;
> Another saith, the *Elements* conspire,
>   And to her *Essence* each doth give a part.
>   (*Nosce Teipsum*, lines 209-212)

But Davies sets out to resolve that confusion while Donne takes quite a different path:

> Have not all soules thought
>   For many ages, that our body' is wrought
> Of Ayre, and Fire, and other Elements?
>   And now they thinke of new ingredients,
> And one Soule thinkes one, and another way
> Another thinkes, and 'tis an even lay.
>   (*The second Anniversary*, lines 263-268)

Ultimately, Davies optimistically claims that

> . . . in *mans minde* we finde an appetite
> To *learne*, and *know the truth* of everie thing;
> Which is connaturall, and borne with it
> And from the *Essence* of the *Soule* doth spring.
>   (*Nosce Teipsum*, lines 1305-1308)

For Davies, with a security of which Donne would not have been remotely capable, can write of man's appetite for learning:

> With this *desire* she hath a native *might*
>   To finde out everie truth, if she had time,
> Th' innumerable effectes to sort aright,
>   And by degrees, from cause to cause to clime.
>   (*Ibid*, lines 1309-1312)

Davies, answering the challenge of atheism that became crucial toward the end of the sixteenth century, polished every possible conceptual weapon with which his culture provided him in order to defeat Christianity's adversaries. R.L. Colie [in the *Philological Quarterly*, 1964] has sug-

gested that whereas "Davies had asserted that it was possible for the soul to know, and organized his theory of knowledge around the soul, Donne denied the soul knowledge even of itself." Accepting on faith that the soul was immortal, Donne would not have presumed, as Davies did, to set up arguments to prove his point. Instead, he declares unqualifiedly that such knowledge is beyond man's capacity:

> Thou neither know'st, how thou first cam'st in,
> Nor how thou took'st the poyson of mans sinne.
> Nor dost thou, (though thou know'st, that thou
>   art so)
> By what way thou art immortall, know.
>   (*The second Anniversary*, lines 257-260)

Against the whole *nosce teipsum* theme he could imply a most devastating warning:

> Thou art too narrow, wretch, to comprehend
> Even thy selfe.
>   (*Ibid.*, lines 261-262)

In contrast, Davies, accepting traditional faculty psychology, claimed:

> That *Powre* which gave my eyes, the world to
>   view;
> To view my selfe enfus'd an *inward light*;
> Whereby my *Soule*, as by a Mirror true,
> Of her owne forme may take a perfect sight.
>   (*Nosce Teipsum*, lines 193-196)

Although Donne's negation of man's potentiality for self knowledge can be interpreted as a witty argument in support of his eventual fideistic resolution, it nevertheless also supports what becomes an epistemological theme in the *Anniversary* poems. Charles Monroe Coffin has shown that Donne successfully but without commitment could select imagery from both the Ptolemaic and Copernican theories of the universe. In the *Anniversary* poems, Donne successfully draws from various aspects of the epistemological theories available to him and appraises them as useless.

He suggests his epistemological orientation very early in *The first Anniversary* by mourning the disappearance of the Platonic innate idea when he complains that "memory" as well as sense (line 28) has been lost. In *The second Anniversary* (lines 291-292), he claims that it is pedantic for man to depend on fantasy, that faculty of the soul responsible in scholastic philosophy for mental apprehension. Furthermore, his departed Elizabeth is presented as one who "first tried indifferent desires/By vertue . . . " (*Ibid*, lines 75-76) in a prince and court metaphor that recalls Davies' description of the soul's "prince," who reigns over the passions (*Nosce Teipsum*, lines 1209-1216). But Donne's most devastating metaphor of the loss of man's mental capacity is his passage that concerns not function, but quality:

> But this were light, did our lesse volume hold
> All the old Text; or had wee chang'd to gold
> Their silver; or dispos'd into lesse glasse
> Spirits of vertue, which then scatter'd was.
> But 'tis not so; w'are not retir'd, but dampt;
> And as our bodies, so our mindes are crampt:
> 'Tis shrinking, not close weaving that hath thus,

In minde, and body both bedwarfed us.
                    (*The first Anniversary*, lines 147-154)

Looking inward, then, Donne finds no security whatever
in the traditional approaches to knowledge. For, as Colie
has put it, Donne was quite aware that "a crooked mind
cannot measure a crooked world; man's ways of knowing
are as skewed as the world they seek to know." That
"crooked world" itself, whose dominating images of decay
and ugliness have been traced by Victor Harris to similar
images in sources propounding the theory that man's fall
initiated the world's progressive physical deterioration,
complicates the epistemological problem and presents a
related esthetic one. Davies not only had found the mind
adequate for its terrestrial purposes, but also had found
the earth of sufficient value to account for man's delight
in the visual arts (*Nosce Teipsum*, lines 997-1000). Donne,
on the other hand, uses his emphasis on the sense of sight
to negate the world's visual potentialities for either knowledge or beauty by eliminating all possibility of Aristotelian
abstraction. One could, from a world that was a wan
ghost, an ugly monster, a dry cinder, or even a dead and
rotten carcass, perhaps still arrive at some kind of ideal abstraction. But the Donne who mourns the loss of a Platonic standard when he calls Elizabeth's death the loss of "the
best, the first originall/of all faire copies" (*The first Anniversary*, lines 227-228), also sums up the distorted visual
remains of a once perfect world as "fragmentary Rub-
bidge" (*The second Anniversary*, line 82) and thus utterly
worthless. Looking outward, the eyes do not encounter
anything of value,

> For the worlds beauty is decai'd, or gone,
> Beauty, that's colour, and proportion.
>   (*The first Anniversary*, lines 249-250)

Thus, to Donne, the traditional ways whereby man has
known are of little or no avail for either religious or esthetic purposes. And we can in this light regard, at least in
part, the lines that conclude Donne's famous passage
claiming that the "new Philosophy calls all in doubt":

> Prince, Subject, Father, Sonne, are things forgot,
> For every man alone thinkes he hath got
> To be a Phoenix, and that then can bee
> None of that kinde, of which he is, but hee.
>   (*The first Anniversary*, lines 215-218)

Haydn has suggested that the passage reflects Montaigne's
emphasis on man as individual rather than as type. Regarded in the light of the *Anniversary* poems' negative references to epistemology, Donne's would-be phoenix becomes, certainly, an individual who has suffered the loss
of the means of arriving at universals by whatever method.
Donne's skepticism regarding man's ability to know himself is balanced by his skepticism regarding man's potential knowledge of the universe. Both would affect metaphorical manifestations of the visual.

Whether he liked it or not, Donne became his own phoenix in regard to esthetics. The door of classicism, from
whatever direction he approached it, was closed to him.
The techniques and content of classicism were available,
but he had to use those techniques and reorder that content without reference to classical guidelines. He concludes *The first Anniversary* by recalling the Renaissance

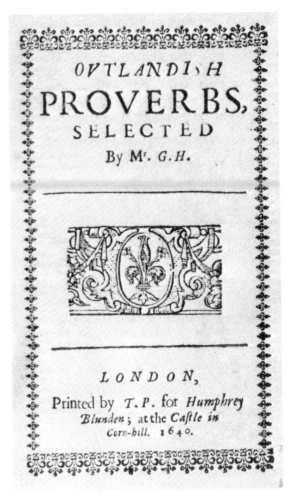

Title page to Outlandish Proverbs *by George Herbert.*

concept that the work of art has something that could preserve the universal:

> Verse hath a middle nature: heaven keepes
>   Soules,
> The Grave keepes bodies, Verse the Fame en-
>   roules.
>   (lines 473-474)

But he endorses this concept hesitantly:

> Nor could incomprehensiblenesse deterre
> Mee, from thus trying to emprison her,
> Which when I saw that a strict grave could doe,
> I saw not why verse might not do so too.
>   (*Ibid.*, lines 469-472)

Elsewhere he could take issue altogether with the prevailing Renaissance belief that the way to deal with man's
mortality was to immortalize him in art. Writing of his
own verses, he says:

> Mine are short-liv'd; the tincture of your name
>   Creates in them, but dissipates as fast,
> New spirits: for, strong agents with the same
>   Force that doth warme and cherish, us doe
>   wast;
> Kept hot with strong extracts, no bodies last:

So, my verse built of your just praise, might want
   Reason and likelihood, the firmest Base,
   And made of miracle, now faith is scant,
Will vanish soone, and so possesse no place,
   And you, and it, too much grace might dis-
     grace.
     (*To the Countesse of Bedford. On New-yeares
       day*, lines 16-25)

Donne saw not only the mind being deprived of its correspondence to the macrocosm but also saw man's mind emptied of any endowment that would enable him to perceive correspondences if they had existed. Thus he was presented with esthetic problems similar to those that Erwin Panofsky found had beset the mannerist painters who earlier had veered away from the esthetic security of the High Renaissance. That security, Panofsky writes [in his *Idea, a Concept in Art Theory*], had been challenged by the question of whether the beautiful was an actual possibility; in their search for an answer the mannerist theorists, because of their emphasis on the individual artistic personality, became conscious of the gap between the subject or mind and object. Donne, who used the phoenix in *The first Anniversary* to pejoratively exemplify man's need to be a unique individual, also was aware of that gap. He gives his reasons:

For fluid vertue cannot be look'd on,
Nor can endure a contemplation.
As bodies change, and as I do not weare
Those spirits, humors, blood I did last yeare,
And, as if on a streame I fixe mine eye,
That drop, which I looked on, is presently
Pusht with more waters from my sight, and
   gone,
So in this sea of vertues, can no one
Bee insisted on.
   (*Obsequies to the Lord Harrington, brother to
   the Lady Lucy, Countesse of Bedford,*
       lines 43-51)

Donne underscores this cognizance of a gap between mind and object by claiming that trying to crystallize an object for eternity, an attempt which would imply the acceptance of an absolute standard, was ultimately doomed to failure.

This loss of security would, of course, have a profound effect on the makers of visual images, as it did on the mannerist painters. For, combined with the fact that to Western man the epistemological emphasis had always been a visual one, was the confounding suspicion that the particular was losing its absolute relationship to the abstract. Thus, in Donne's poetry—and to various degrees and with various manifestations in the poetry of the other metaphysical poets—the visual image was no longer able to carry the full meaning it had carried for the poets of the sixteenth century. In many instances, it had no significance except that which man was willing to assign it. It could still represent man's ideas, but there was no assurance that the representations—except when they were of traditional religious symbols—contained either intrinsic or cosmic significance. New discoveries had upset the old relationships between mind and object. Or, as Helen Gardner observed in another context, the division between man and God is overwhelmingly evident in Donne's sacred poetry.

A similar division, although perhaps not so passionately expostulated, exists in the poetry of Herbert. In fact, in his short poem "The Foil," he laments most emphatically the wideness of the chasm between heaven and earth:

         If we could see below
The sphere of vertue, and each shining grace
     As plainly as that above doth show;
This were the better skie, the brighter place.

God hath made the starres the foil
To set off vertues; griefs to set off sinning:
     Yet in this wretched world we toil,
As if grief were not foul, nor vertue winning.

Virtue here is as elusive a quality as it had been to Donne, who could complain that "fluid virtue," in the Platonic sense, gave him nothing positive to work with. But Herbert not only expresses bewilderment that earth reflects so little of the virtue of heaven, he also observes that man is quite apt to misinterpret that which is available to him. Although according to Herbert, the stars, placed at some midpoint between heaven and earth, should give man some indication of virtue as grief should give him some knowledge of sin, man misinterprets the signs; he is capable, in fact, of giving them the opposite meaning from that which had been intended.

Traditionally, of course, Herbert has been regarded as a simple, uncomplicated follower of the word of God, as a man who humbly and unquestioningly pursued the life of a parish priest. But he also is a man who had the Platonic theory of forms sufficiently uppermost in his mind to enable him, in rejecting the secular poetic traditions of the Renaissance, to ask:

May no lines passe, except they do their dutie
   Not to a true, but painted chair?
            (*Jordan* I, lines 4-5)

His skepticism regarding man's ability to arrive at universals as well as his frustration in failing to find concrete forms with which to express his abstract concepts comes out in such passages as,

O that I could a sinne once see!
We paint the devil foul, yet he
Hath some good in him, all agree.
Sinne is flat opposite to th'Almighty, seeing
It wants the good of *vertue*, and of *being*.
           (*Sinne* II, lines 1-5)

Laurence Howard Jacobs has shown [in his dissertation, "Knowledge in the Poetry of George Herbert"] that the poem "poses epistemological problems by noting the inability of man to know what sin is, and by connecting sin to the major means of human knowledge, sight." Jacobs has, in fact, found the problem of knowledge to be a "central and recurrent theme of Herbert's poetry." Herbert's skepticism, Jacobs points out, is evident in such passages as the following from "The Flower."

We say amisse,
This or that is:
Thy word is all, if we could spell.

            (lines 19-21)

His analysis shows that there also is a direct epistemological emphasis, for example, in "Dulnesse," "Divinitie," and "Vanitie" and definite reference to epistemological problems in "The Foil," "Artillerie," "Providence," "The Elixir," and "The Agonie". His detailed study of Herbert's epistemological doubts places Herbert decidedly on the roster of those metaphysical poets who were aware of the seventeenth-century's epistemological confusion. Jacobs writes that Herbert's "persistent but unemphatic interest in epistemological problems coincides with the basic insights of Renaissance Pyrrhonism, of Montaigne's skepticism, of Baconian empiricism, and most importantly, with the skeptical faith of Sir Thomas Browne and John Donne." He sees in Herbert's work not only a distrust of the senses, but also an awareness of the inadequacy of language and concludes that to Herbert poetry ultimately "looks forward to the moment when poems cease and God will be seen no longer in the darkened glass of human knowledge, but understood directly."

Thus there is in the poetry of both Donne and Herbert a skepticism toward man's ways of knowing that goes beyond that which was a frequent precursor of religious faith. That their poetry reveals a sure knowledge of the older world view and its epistemological assumptions is obvious. But they were aware also that there *was* an epistemological problem. Crashaw, on the other hand, may not have been; at least there is no significant evidence that would indicate an awareness. However, he may have been responding to, rather than articulating what was occurring. For there is an undercurrent of epistemological confusion in his

> O these wakefull wounds of thine!
>   Are they Mouthes?   or are they eyes?
> Be they Mouthes, or be they eyne,
>   Each bleeding part some one supplies.
> *(On the wounds of our crucified Lord,*
>   lines 1 - 4)

The conscious recognition of the problems of epistemology did not stop with Donne and Herbert. Crashaw's younger contemporary, Vaughan, expressed his doubt about man's ways of knowing precisely in terms that had been associated with the emblematic view of the universe. To find answers to the questions of man's relation to himself, God, and the universe, the poet eschews his study in favor of nature itself:

> I summon'd nature: peirc'd through all her
>   store,
> Broke up some seales, which none had touch'd
>   before,
>   Her wombe, her bosome, and her head
>   Where all her secrets lay a bed
> I rifled quite, and having past
> Through all the Creatures, came at last
> To search my selfe.
>   *(Vanity of Spirit,* lines 9 - 15)

Although, in other poems, Vaughan finds spiritual comfort in observation of such natural phenomena as light and waterfalls, here he judges nature incapable of giving him meaningful answers. Having found nature inadequate, he resorts to the *nosce teipsum* solution that had been the basis of Davies' poem on the soul. But whereas Davies observed therein a comfortingly traditional kind of order,

Vaughan found what he calls "traces, and sounds of a strange kind." Thus he struggles with the problem of subject-object relationship:

> Here of this mighty spring, I found some drills,
> With Ecchoes beaten from th'eternall hills;
>   Weake beames, and fires flash'd to my sight,
>   Like a young East, or Moone-shine night,
>   Which shew'd me in a nook cast by
>   A peece of much antiquity,
>   With Hyeroglyphicks quite dismembred,
>   And broken letters scarce remembred.
>   *(Ibid.,* lines 17 - 24)

To examine nature, and even to seek sealed knowledge that had not been previously revealed, was nothing out of the ordinary. Nor was the return to oneself. For, although man's senses were dull and his mind lacking in perfection, knowledge was still possible, as Davies so confidently tells us. Traditional concepts enabled one to fit everything together, if not into a complete whole at least into a satisfying approximation. But in this poem Vaughan finds that this is no longer possible. At first he, too, is hopeful that hieroglyphics might contain within themselves, albeit enigmatically, the secrets of the universe:

> I tooke them up, and (much Joy'd) went about
> T'unite those peeces, hoping to find out
>   The mystery.
>   *(Ibid.,* lines 25 - 27)

Spenser, in surveying that which he saw around him, had found security in the belief that when

> . . . this worlds great workmaister did cast
> To make al things such as we now behold,
> It seemes that he before his eyes had plast
> A goodly paterne, to whose perfect mould
> He fashioned them as comely as he could,
> That now so faire and seemely they appeare,
> As nought may be amended any wheare.
> *(An Hymne in Honour of Beautie,* lines 29 -
>   35)

Vaughan, however, does not find an eternal pattern. He even suspects the validity of the very symbols that would enable him to infer that an eternal pattern existed. At his disposal are neither the Neoplatonic concept, found in Spenser's *Fowre Hymnes,* that earthly beauty is an intimation of eternal perfection nor the Hermetic concept that the objects of this earth partially reveal eternal mysteries. Vaughan finds that he cannot bring the hieroglyphics into any meaningful order and that

>   . . . this neer done,
> That little light I had was gone:
> It grieved me much.
>   *(Vanity of Spirit,* lines 27 - 29)

It is not only what he says, but also Vaughan's selection of imagery that is important, for during the Renaissance "hieroglyphs" were regarded as enigmatic earthly manifestations of the secrets of the universe. Thus he indicates his awareness that there was an epistemological problem that had not been resolved.

While Vaughan could dismiss the problem with a wistful acknowledgment of the traditional answer—that on earth man's means of knowing were necessarily limited—Traherne found its resolution crucial. One of the major questions with which Traherne struggled was that of how the finite mind could know the infinity of God. His answer, which glances forward to the eighteenth century as well as backward toward the sixteenth, suggests that one could expect his visual imagery to be strikingly different from the conceited imagery of the earlier metaphysical poets. He opens his *Centuries* with an inward look:

> An Empty Book is like an Infants Soul, in which
>   any Thing may
>   be Written. It is Capable of all Things, but
>   containeth Nothing.
> I hav a Mind to fill this with Profitable Wonders.

The "Profitable Wonders" with which he ultimately attempts to fill the infant soul are emphatically drawn from observation:

> A Wide Magnificent and Spacious Skie,
> So rich tis Worthy of the Deitie,
> Clouds here and there like Winged Charets fly-
>   ing,
> Flowers ever flourishing, yet always Dying,
> A Day of Glory where I all things see,
> As twere enriched with Beams of Light for me.
>   (*Nature,* lines 53 - 58)

If we regard Traherne's lines in the light of the visual images created by Donne, Herbert, and Crashaw—or even occasionally by Vaughan—what strikes us immediately is that it is the natural world itself to which Traherne turns in his struggles to understand his relation to the universe. It is precisely by observing the glory of God's creation and emphasizing the knowledge obtained through such sensory experience that Traherne develops his theory of the soul's relation to infinity. This is much closer to Locke's corollary to the concept of the *tabula rasa* than anything the other metaphysical poets conceived. Locke claimed that "the visible marks of extraordinary wisdom and power appear so plainly in all the works of creation" that the seriously reflecting man could not miss "the discovery of a deity" simply by looking around him.

Traherne was not even considering the broken hieroglyphs of which Vaughan complained. Yet the overall world view that those hieroglyphs represented was something with which Traherne most certainly had to come to grips. As has been generally agreed, a strong element of the Platonic runs through all of Traherne's writings. It was, of course, the inward look that ultimately became meaningful to Traherne. For, in spite of his assertion that the infant soul was an empty book, his delight in the sensuous appeal of the exterior world led to the conclusion:

> Of it I am th'inclusive Sphere,
>   It doth entire in me appear
> As well as I in it: It givs me Room,
>   Yet lies within my Womb.
>   (*Misapprehension,* lines 62 - 65)

Traherne's involvement with "th'inclusive Sphere" provides not only the means whereby he declares his philosophical precociousness, but also the epistemological orientation from which he creates imagery so very different from that of the earlier metaphysical poets. As Marjorie

Nicolson has shown [in her *Breaking of the Circle*], seventeenth-century literature provides a wealth of images that express either a conscious retiring into an inward world or an expanding outward to an exterior world—what she distinguishes as claustrophobia or agoraphobia respectively. Donne, whom one would normally categorize as belonging to the agoraphobics, could, as Toshihiko Kawasaki has shown [in *Seventeenth-Century Imagery: Essays on the uses of Figurative Language from Donne to Farquhar*], wittily challenge a commonplace by depicting the world as the copy of man. His purpose in the following was to present a theory of the expansiveness of man's mind:

> Inlarge this Meditation upon this *great world*,
> Man so farr, as to consider the immesitie of the
> creatures this world produces; our *creatures* are
> our *thoughts, creatures* that are borne Gyants:
> that reach from East to West, from *earth* to
> *Heaven*, that doe not onley bestride all the *Sea*
> and *Land*, but span the Sunn and Firmament at
> once; My thoughts reach all, comprehend all.

This would at first glance seem quite consistent with the line of thinking that prompted Traherne to write:

> The Thoughts of Men appear
> Freely to mov within a Sphere
>   Of endless Reach; and run,
> Tho in the Soul, beyond the Sun.
> The Ground on which they acted be
> Is unobserv'd Infinity.
>   (*Consummation,* lines 1 - 6)

But, as Nicolson suggested, Traherne, ultimately seeks infinity. Donne's thought, on the other hand, springs back upon itself. The mind may be bigger than the world, but like the world it produces "Serpents and vipers" and "diseases and sickness of all sorts." The mind is bigger than the world because of the enormous depravity that it contains. Donne comments:

> And can the other world name so many *veni-*
> *mous*, so many consuming, so many monstrous
> creatures, as we can diseases, of all these kindes.
> O miserable abundance.

He eventually makes the point that as the diseases of the microcosmic body require a physician, so do the diseases of the soul. He discusses the expansiveness of man's mind for the sole purpose of drawing an analogy. The passage is quite in keeping with the use he makes of most images: it serves as a means whereby he can analyze, in an emblematic way, quite another set of thoughts. However, to Traherne, man's thoughts, moving freely toward the "endless Reach," like infinity itself, seem limitless:

> Extended throu the Sky,
> Tho here, beyond it far they fly:
>   Abiding in the Mind
> An endless Liberty they find:
> Throu-out all Spaces can extend,
> Nor ever meet or know an End.
>   (*Consummation,* lines 7 - 11)

The comparison points out a difference in the basic epistemological orientations of the two poets. There is nothing in Donne's words that would on the surface challenge the emblematic world into which he was born. Although acceptance of the older world view is not typical of his writing as a whole, his use of the analogy—even in this reversed form—would appear to be consistent with a correspondence theory of the universe. The same, though, cannot be said about the above passage by Traherne, whose mental wanderings into the infinite are not terminated but, as Stanley Stewart has found, tend to eliminate boundaries. Furthermore, Richard Douglas Jordan has shown that Traherne's comparison of the "Infant Soul" to an "Empty Book" has far-reaching implications. According to Jordan [in his *Temple of Eternity: Thomas Traherne's Philosophy of Time*], it was not Traherne's intention that man should either seek infinity through a return to childhood or look for a mystic identification with eternity. To Traherne, he writes, the soul, was endowed with an inner feeling regarding infinity, but was empty at birth, and it was man's prerogative to develop his own faculties to a point at which they, themselves, could become divine. Thus Traherne's epistemological theory, Jordan suggests, is one in which it is experience obtained through the senses alone that enables man to perceive God in the world around him and in history, both secular and Biblical: it is with thoughts gained through sensory experience that he participates in the spiritual "now" of eternity. What becomes really important as far as Traherne's visual imagery is concerned is that he seeks no hidden meanings, analogies or correspondences. The very fact that he fought so assiduously to reconcile Platonism with the concept of a mind that was blank at birth would necessitate his taking a different and more contemporary attitude toward the image. Indeed, there runs throughout Traherne's poetry an exaltation of the senses as a new discovery. In spite of the fact that he could sometimes write of the body as vile, he more frequently lauds

> The spacious Room
>> Which thou hast hidden in mine Eye,
> The Chambers for Sounds
>> Which thou hast prepar'd in mine Ear,
> The Receptacles for Smells
>> Concealed in my Nose;
> The feeling of my Hands,
>> The taste of my Tongue.
>> *(Thanksgivings for the Body,* lines 92 - 99)

Thus the physical senses have become to Traherne a much more secure means of knowing than they had been to any of the other metaphysical poets. This becomes particularly important in light of the fact that while all but Crashaw were consciously aware of epistemological problems, Traherne, one of the latest in time, was the only one to resolve those problems into what apparently became for him a satisfactory and complete theory.

More important than any specific theory, though, is what can be concluded from subjecting the metaphysical poets to a scrutiny of epistemological concerns: their awareness of epistemological problems placed them in a position to react to changing concepts of the subject-object relationship. They responded in two ways, both inextricably involved with the metaphysical conceit. The first is that they challenged the medieval concept of an emblematic universe of correspondences; the second is that in doing so they created imagery that was individual and peculiar. Since Samuel Johnson described the metaphysical conceit as a poetic aberration in which the most heterogenous ideas are yoked together by violence, the salient characteristics of the metaphysical conceit have been variously accounted for. Two of the many explanations which are especially pertinent here are Mario Praz's theory that the metaphysical conceit was consistent with the Renaissance emblem and Joseph A. Mazzeo's observation that the metaphysical conceit was based on a "poetic of correspondences." These are not mutually exclusive, for both emblematist and metaphysical poets were heirs—as were all men of the Renaissance—of the medieval belief that everything that existed was linked by universal analogy. What sets the metaphysical poets apart from other poets is the fact that, in consciously or unconsciously responding to the epistemological concerns of their century, they also were responding to the shattering skepticism regarding the concept of universal analogy. They reacted as individuals, but an analysis of their reactions reveals a progression toward a final rejection of that concept by Traherne. Donne and Herbert were already showing signs of unrest by tending to use the psychological remnants of an emblematic universe as a stylistic technique of exploration rather than as an underlying affirmative principle. Vaughan, in keeping with his disappointment in the symbolic hieroglyphs, sometimes even anticipated the next age by drawing his spiritual conclusions directly from observation of nature. Even Crashaw, whose poetry is atypically lacking in epistemological concern, responded to the changing concepts through his intense, almost overstated, appeal to all of the senses.

Certainly, the tendency to try to make their images meaningful in ways that were far from traditional is one of the distinguishing characteristics of the metaphysical poets. But this was not, on their part, the result of conscious calculation; it was their response to the *Zeitgeist*, which had presented them with an almost insoluble epistemological dilemma. For most of them, the skepticism regarding knowledge obtained through the senses, combined with an almost desperate need to visualize, posed a problem that was basic to their creative struggles. Whether the metaphysical poets made direct statements regarding epistemology or not, what appeared to Neoclassic critics as affected intellectualizing was at least partially the result of an epistemological confusion. Presented with a creative problem that was peculiar to the seventeenth century, they solved that problem creatively and peculiarly. For whether or not a creative artist is aware he is doing so, he must operate under epistemological assumptions. He need not be able to articulate an epistemological theory precisely, or even consciously, for those assumptions to play a strong part in the way he presents knowledge to the outside world. (pp. 1-23)

Mary Cole Sloane, "The Noblest Sense and the Book of Nature," in her The Visual in Metaphysical Poetry, *Humanities Press, 1981, pp. 1-23.*

STYLISTIC AND THEMATIC VARIATIONS

Helen C. White

[*In the following excerpt, White examines the poetic canon of John Donne, whom she upholds as "the enkindling influence, the seminal force, for the entire group" of metaphysical poets.*]

In Metaphysical poetry the religious lyrists of the seventeenth century found ready to their hand an instrument of expression that was to prove peculiarly stimulating to their capacities and adaptable to their purpose. And, it should be added, like every other artistic instrument that fits the hand of the user, it was to prove compliant with their weakness as well as their strength. It was a singularly ductile instrument, becoming a very different thing in the hands of Crashaw from what it was in the hands of Herbert, and in Vaughan's something still different, as individual genius discovered and developed fresh possibilities and applied them to new ends. Indeed, so striking is this variety and individuality that English metaphysical poetry from Donne to Traherne is better viewed as a movement than as a type, and a movement in the English rather than in the Continental sense, with the emphasis on diversity and general and casual influence rather than on self-conscious co-operation to clearly envisaged ends. But, in spite of this diversity and individualism, it still remains true that all these major religious lyrists are metaphysicals, with certain clearly discernible likenesses in objective and operation.

Of recent years there has been a good deal of interest in metaphysical poetry, and not a little excellent work has been done in the definition and elucidation of the type. While for the most part discriminating, this study has been thoroughly sympathetic. For most of the recent critics have been keenly aware of the likenesses between the world in which these men lived and the world in which we live, and of the light to be shed on our problems by the contemplation of theirs. Even so objective and historically minded a study as the recent one of Mr. J. B. Leishman [*The Metaphysical Poets*, 1934] owes no small part of its momentum to its author's appreciation of these values, an appreciation very seldom expressed but implicit in the selection of issues for discussion and the careful focussing of conclusions. So, too, for a man like Mr. T. S. Eliot who, both as critic and creative artist, is so widely involved in the ethical and esthetic discussion of the present time, the study of the metaphysicals affords a veritable arsenal of instructive parallels and possible correctives. The criticism of metaphysical poetry is, therefore, a very live issue of contemporary criticism, and a good deal more than disengaged curiosity or sympathetic antiquarianism enters into its discussion.

Whatever their theories as to the origin or value of metaphysical poetry, all critics from Dr. Johnson to Miss Joan Bennet are agreed that the distinctive characteristic of the genre is its intellectual emphasis, an emphasis apparent both in the preoccupations of the poet and in his procedure. All critics would agree, too, that the metaphysical poets sometimes overdid this intellectual emphasis, but

there is very wide disagreement as to the extent of this excess, its seriousness, and its artistic and human consequences. For Dr. Johnson, the fact that they overemphasized the intellectual element is the definitive element in their claims to literary immortality in poetry. For Mr. T. S. Eliot the fact that they sometimes overdid it does not appear so much of a fault when you consider how the romantics, for instance, underdid it. The devil you know may be less of a risk, but he is certainly more of a burden than the one you do not happen to have on your hands. At the same time, as Mr. T. S. Eliot well knows, it is easy to exaggerate the heinousness of the sins one is not tempted to fall into at the expense of those one is. Since our immediate problem is neither the direction of contemporary criticism nor the absolute value of metaphysical poetry, but an understanding of its possibilities and implications as an instrument for the religious lyrists of the time, it is well for us to begin at least with an inquiry as to what exactly it was that the metaphysical poets had to work with in this instrument of expression.

Probably the most satisfactory brief definition of the type is Professor Grierson's [in his *Background of English Literature and other collected Essays and Addresses*, 1925], "Metaphysical Poetry, in the full sense of the term, is a poetry which, like that of the *Divina Commedia*, the *De Natura Rerum*, perhaps Goethe's *Faust*, has been inspired by a philosophical conception of the universe and of the rôle assigned to the human spirit in the great drama of existence." That definition is especially valuable, because it reminds us that metaphysical poetry is no isolated phenomenon peculiar to the seventeenth century, but a recurrent aspect of universal poetry. It also sets up as a starting point the ideal of a full and complete development of what we find only in part and to a degree in the seventeenth-century lyric. Mr. Grierson then proceeds to give us a working clue to the partial and the embryonic, "The distinctive note of 'metaphysical' poetry is the blend of passionate feeling and paradoxical ratiocination." That definition, however, takes us out of the general field and into the poetry of one individual, John Donne.

The question of how far the course of any movement like this may be attributed to the work of one individual artist is a large one, not likely ever to be definitely settled. But even the most thoroughgoing opponents of the heroic theory of history would grant that a movement may be illuminatingly studied in the work of one man, if he can be fairly regarded as central and typical. All students of the English metaphysical poets would agree that Donne is the central figure in the group. Certainly not because Donne is typical, for it would be a very rash man indeed who would claim that Donne was typical of anybody but himself, but all students agree that he is the most metaphysical of the English metaphysicals in the sense of having perhaps more of the distinctively metaphysical qualities than any other poet of his time. Moreover, he was, it is generally agreed, the enkindling influence, the seminal force, for the entire group.

The beginnings of John Donne's poetry are distinctly secular, not to say profane, and they are highly personal, but they are significant for the whole development of English metaphysical poetry. For here in these early love poems meet two elements of crucial importance, a change in the movement of the spirit of the time, and a man who in temperament and experience was fitted to seize upon the emergent elements in the life about him.

When John Donne began to write his love poems, Elizabethan literature was in the heyday of its splendor. The first burst of pure song had, it is true, pretty much spent itself, but the emotional and imaginative brilliance of the Elizabethan genius was beginning to enjoy more than compensating self-expression in the drama. There was still the lavish and unconscious outpouring of energy characteristic of any great period of creative art. This does not mean that there were not shadows on that poetry as there were on the life of the time, but there was a reckless abandon, a confidence of energy that showered its forces upon the slightest undertaking without any fear that the life-giving waters would ever cease to flow. The result we all know, an almost unparalleled brilliance and passion and abundance of beauty and life. Every success in this imperfect world seems to bring its own defects in its train. Lack of coherence, lack of plan, lack of economy, all these are different names for what was to prove the great deficiency of Elizabethan literature, lack of control. The results are to be seen in the formlessness and the extravagance and the often grotesque incongruity of even the greatest of Elizabethan geniuses. But in Donne's first poems these liabilities are still redeemed by the beauty and vitality of youth.

It is that last word that gives us the clue to the problem. For the extravagance of youth so easily slips over into fantasy, and with the passing of the years fantasy hardens into the eccentricity of maturity. That in itself is a factor in the development of some of the less happy aspects of metaphysical poetry that has not received so much attention as it deserves. But Miss Kathleen Lea has suggested that just as the Elizabethan conceit is heavily indebted to the Italian conceit through the habit of the Elizabethan of skimming over Italian poetry and taking up the figures and ideas which attracted him without reference to the context, so the much-puzzled-over metaphysical comparison is really a development of Elizabethan exuberance in the use of the simile. Certainly, extravagance and forcing of relations between images and ideas is not to be considered a Jacobean invention.

On the other hand, there does seem to have been some flagging of imaginative energy at the end of the sixteenth century. What happened then may simply be just another example of the way in which the human mind and imagination become used to strong fare, so that that which at first offered all necessary stimulus has presently by familiarity become commonplace, and the overstimulated nerves are craving something stronger than what has ceased to satiate their appetite. The large element of ingenuity in Elizabethan poetry may also have contributed its share to the passion for novelty that is one of the characteristics of an oversophisticated time. But there is another factor that has not as yet received much consideration that may well account for not a little of this change in temper. For when the general passion of the seventeenth century for tightening man's grip on his world is considered, it

would be surprising if it did not affect the poetry of the time. Certainly something self-conscious and deliberate comes into the art of the new century, and something of the old spacious freedom and casualness of less rigorous times is lost. And as the swirl of conflicting forces latent in the movements of the age deepens, this effort to control the exuberance of the energies of the time, wise and inevitable at it may seem, in itself intensifies the intellectualism of Renaissance poetry.

Something should be said, too, of the development of Elizabethan literature in the direction of the ideal and the formal. So living, so fresh, is the first lyric outburst of the Elizabethan genius that it is tempting to forget how derivative and how ideal much of it was. The throbbing of English hearts through the symbols of ancient mythology and the breathing of the winds of English life and nature into the figures of ancient poesy are too much of a reality for it to be easy for us to remember how conventional much of Elizabethan love poetry was even in its heyday. But with the passing of time, some of those figures were bound to wear a little thin, and the voice of poetic enthusiasm to grow a little sharper, while artistic skill, maturing, would more and more translate the first happy borrowings of youthful emulation into the studied elegance of conscious imitation.

It is, it must never be forgotten, a little society in which these things are happening. It is a society which enjoys a central position in its day, enriched with the converging of all the streams of the life of the time upon its walls. But it is a section only of the society of its time, this of London, pretty much confined to the ranks of greatness and fashion. It has its

own standards, its own pretensions, its own vanities, even. One of them is a taste for some of the elegances of learning without the labors. To the common human weakness for the striking and the dramatic it adds the taste of all small societies for the topical and the timely. So while it shows little ardor for pursuing the business of learning to any heights or depths, it makes a good deal of effort to "keep up." It has no monopoly on genius or even talent, but holding as it does the sources of wealth and power, it can very effectively pull toward itself whatever of aspiring talent there is outside its charmed circles. And it knows how, very effectively, because quite tacitly, to impose its own standards, its taste for display, its passion for self-aggrandizement and prestige, its faith in its own sphere of power and action rather than of contemplation, on the art it patronizes and sustains. Chapman, we know, wearied of the pretensions of this society and addressed himself to more strenuous and highly trained understandings, with an assumption of obscurity that is familiar to us, for much the same reasons, in a good deal of the high-brow literature of our own day. What Donne really thought of the various noble ladies he courted for patronage we have little way of knowing, but there is an extraordinary difference in tone and value between what he implies in his various letters and dedications to his female patronesses and what he says of their sex in sermon and satire. It would look as if he compensated for the attendance he danced on their by no means unexacting and uncritical presences by a very low view of their sex in general (though, it should be added in fairness, pretty much the prevailing view of his day), particularly as regards judgment and intellect. Be that as it may, there is no question that the great bulk of Donne's verse was written with an eye to the smart world in which he aspired to play a conspicuous part.

The metaphysical poetry of Donne is, then, what might reasonably be expected at such a juncture from such a man. Donne flouts but does not entirely sweep aside the conventions of his day in the most conventional field of all, love poetry. Some of his lyrics are pure Petrarchanism, with all the burnings and humble aspirations to the "inexpressive she" that any lovesick young man about Elizabeth's London could desire. But a large number are of the other type that has made him famous. They are a revolt against a literary convention, one of the most brilliant rebellions known to English literature, a revolt against what was restrictive and artificial and hackneyed and stale in that convention, it is true, but also a revolt against what was ideal and graceful in it.

One can fancy the young Donne saying to himself, "Love is all that you have been saying about it all these years, but it is also this—hate, and contempt, and hunger, and revulsion, and curiosity, and vanity, and wild ecstasy, all in one." One can fancy him saying that his fellow poets had done justice to love and the heart and the fancy and the adoring eyes, but that love was also an affair of the nerves and the curious hands and the restless brain. One can fancy him saying, too, that enough had been said of love in gardens and on balconies; he was going to sing of love in the crowded and whispering houses and lanes of London, and the camps and the inns he knew.

Donne has an eye for the life about him. It is very easy to lose sight of that fact in the contemplation of his curious and often remote learning, just as so many readers of his sermons have been so much impressed by the magnificent passages on man's mortality and the fear of death that they have failed to note the countless flashes of the world of the time in which some contemporary attitude or mood is suggested in a line or two, or some aspect of the day-to-day scene is etched unforgettably in a moral example or a psychological illustration. Many of the types of the time, the middle-class merchant, the returned traveller with his tobacco and his fantastic costume, the Puritan, the young man about town, the soldier from foreign parts, the peddler with his chaffering, jostle their way through his pages. The various crafts of the day, the coinage, the sports, the games, the small inventions, some hardly above the level of gadgets, the petty formalities of the law, the mysteries of navigation, the physic of the time, the whipping of madmen, the ruined abbeys, the hangings in the queen's palace, all these yield their tribute of comparison and allusion. So do the day-to-day happenings of London, the Russian merchants, the plague bill, news from Virginia, the popular sympathy for Essex after his death, the various minor officials, pursuivants and informers, that battened on the misfortunes of the Recusants, to name only a few, come into the verses, grave and grimly gay, of the young John Donne. There is much to justify the words of Edmund Gosse [in his *Jacobean Poets*, 1894], "Donne

was . . . by far the most modern and contemporaneous of the writers of his time." And with hardly an exception, this stream of contemporaneity is urban, almost exclusively of London.

Moreover, much of this daily material is handled with that candor, that absence of any impulse to idealism, that emphasis on the component physical detail, the literal and uncontexted sense reaction, that is in our day described as realism. And in Donne's case, as in ours, the detail so presented ranges anywhere from the dull and sluggish to the nauseous and the hideous, and the reaction anywhere from contempt to loathing. That effect which, in speaking of the sermons, Signor Praz [in his *Secetismo è Marinismo in Inghilterra*, 1925] has so eloquently described as "a livid subterranean stream of macabre realism," is no less characteristic of the poems. This does not mean that grace and charm do not come within the purview of Donne's roving eye. They do, and they may easily be taken for granted or disregarded by the student who is interested in the more novel and sensational aspect of Donne's work. After all, the creator of Juliet and Imogen noticed that Marion's nose was red and raw. It is simply that the reader who has been living with the more chivalric and delicate sonneteers of Donne's generation cannot fail to be struck by this aspect of Donne's genius and may well be pardoned if, as so often happens, he takes this "realism" for the characteristic note of the poet.

But this realistic element, striking as it is, is only one element in the imaginative effect of Donne's verses. There is, also, that element of passionate awareness of implications larger than those of the moment with which realism is so often obsessed and a mingling of beauty with ugliness, and light with darkness, in passages such as those which Signor Praz has in mind. Indeed, it is precisely this mingling of the homely, not to say commonplace, and even at times hardly decent, with some of the largest and sublimest movements of the imagination of the race, that gives that curious effect which most readers have vaguely described as mystical. In such passages there is at once something very startling and very impressive, something of wonder or awe and very often something of blasphemy, something of beauty and not a little of horror, but all intensely and immediately present to the nerves and the emotions. There is something of the fascination of primitive art in such passages, for near and far are suddenly brought together without any attempt at perspective, with a sensuous immediacy that brings out startlingly and inescapably all the latent possibilities of the theme. Nothing better illustrates this aspect of Donne's genius and better reveals one facet of the metaphysical mystery than the first stanza of "The Relique":

> When my grave is broke up againe
> 　　Some second ghest to entertaine,
> 　(For graves have learn'd that woman-head
> 　　To be to more then one a Bed)
> 　　　And he that digs it, spies
> A bracelet of bright haire about the bone,
> 　　　Will he not let'us alone,
> And thinke that there a loving couple lies,
> Who thought that this device might be some way
> To make their soules, at the last busie day,

Meet at this grave, and make a little stay?

But this is only one aspect of the metaphysical effect, and not the one that has caught the attention of most readers. That which has aroused the widest interest is the large part which more purely intellectual elements play in this poetry. It was these elements that took the eye of Dr. Johnson—"The metaphysical poets were men of learning, and to shew their learning, was their whole endeavour." In general, contemporary criticism has rebutted that verdict. It is not that the present generation of critics have a higher opinion of the humility of the metaphysicals than did the great eighteenth-century judge, but that most critics of the present have recognized that the elements that suggest display are very differently motivated from what he thought. For a man like Chapman, as for Dr. Johnson, the difference between the educated and the uneducated was a real one. For a man like Donne it may be asked if it was. Certainly, it played no part in his thought or feeling. For in Donne, though there was much of the dramatizing, there was very little of the dramatic. It is not a moral egotism but an intellectual that confines his consciousness to the type of person he is himself. Perhaps the best example of this taking-for-granted is to be seen in the various complimentary verses he addresses to the influential and high-placed ladies who befriended him. The Countess of Bedford and Magdalen Herbert were unquestionably women of intelligence and general culture, but there is no reason to believe that they had the background in theology, scholastic or contemporary, to enjoy a good many of the comparisons and allusions which Donne inflicts on them. The making of such allusions would be understandable, if Donne held ideals of women's intellectual capacity like those which Sir Thomas More held, but, as we have seen, he most emphatically did not. It is simply that even when Donne paid a compliment, he in no way departed from his own sphere, because no other was present to his consciousness.

Donne was a man of large and varied learning. He had read the great scholastic writers, the Fathers of the Church, the great masters of pagan learning and ancient wisdom. And he was to an extraordinary degree conversant with the movements of his own time in religious controversy, in political thinking, in science in all its branches, in the reports of discovery, and in all those borderland branches of human curiosity where fantasy jostles fact as in alchemy and Hermetism. To judge from the use he made of this learning in the citation of authorities in his prose writings and his sermons, he must have taken careful notes on his reading. And to judge from the allusions in his verse, he must have read with a very lively attention to everything picturesque and striking as well as to the main arguments of his authors. But the most interesting thing about this learning was that much of it was acquired in the days of his youth and his early manhood when nothing was farther from his thoughts than the career of learning and piety to which he was destined. It was acquired, partly from a desire to work out his own intellectual problems (he read heavily in the controversy between Canterbury and Rome, for instance), partly out of a fashion of learning, for learning was in those days a grace of society and an embellishment of the statecraft and courtiership to

which Donne aspired, but most, we may be sure, out of that wide-ranging curiosity that is one of the dominating traits of his mind, that thirst for knowledge that is one of the manifestations of his great and basic thirst for life.

In that fascinating portrait of the young Donne which Professor Grierson has prefixed to his edition of Donne's verse, there are two things that look out of the alert gravity of the face, a deep sense of himself, a consciousness of the life surging within his own identity, and a hunger and thirst, that might almost be called a greed, for life. Much has been made in a somewhat levelling modernity, of the dichotomy between learning and life, between books and living. Like all of the idols of the marketplace, it has some justification in partial human fact. There are unquestionably a good many men, students even, for whom the stream of life swerves aside around the walls of the library, and they will never believe that such an academic ox-bow is not a universal experience. But there are other men for whom the waters of life flow through all areas of their consciousness, for whom there are no walls between the various types of experience. Such a one was the young Donne, who plunged into the speculations of Plato or Paracelsus or Pico with the same zest with which he plunged into the varieties of amatory experience which sixteenth-century London offered to the young man about town. The discriminations of scholasticism served to define the shades of romantic experience in his youth, as in his maturity the memory of youthful sensuality and passion illuminated the oscillations of religious aspiration and defeat. Everything alike was a part of that experience which he craved with a thirst even more immoderate and "hydroptique" than that which he attributed to Pico della Mirandola.

This enviable unity of consciousness was due in part, or perhaps rather, was possible, because Donne was still living in the era of universal knowledge. As Mr. Basil Willey has reminded us [in *The Seventeenth Century Background*, 1934], "The major interests of life had not as yet been mechanically apportioned to specialists, so that one must dedicate oneself wholly to fact, or wholly to value." The result was that a roving imagination could draw upon a wide variety of fields of learning and experience alike without being troubled by any difference in kind of its grasp upon them, and so make use of their common relevances and their total implications. But quite as important as this freedom of appropriation was the way in which it was carried out, not merely a matter of intellectual attitude but also of emotional reaction. The essence of the matter is to be found in the fact that to Donne what he read, what he thought, had the same kind of immediate potency of stimulus and energy that sense experience had. As Mr. T. S. Eliot has said [in his *Homage to John Dryden*, 1924]: "A thought to Donne was an experience; it modified his sensibility. When a poet's mind is perfectly equipped for its work, it is constantly amalgamating disparate experience; the ordinary man's experience is chaotic, irregular, fragmentary. . . . The poets of the seventeenth century, the successors of the dramatists of the sixteenth, possessed a mechanism of sensibility which could devour any kind of experience."

Obviously in minds such as these the reflective elements

in experience play a larger part than they do in most minds, as Mr. Eliot very well suggests in the essay from which the passage above is taken. There is warmth in the response of such men to ideas that leave the ordinary man puzzled or cold. The result is that surprising reality with which unexpected feeling invests abstractions that usually remain unassimilably outside the day-to-day range of experience. The familiarity with which Donne so often embraces eternity, that final extension of time, the least tangible of the familiar dimensions of experience, is one evidence. The result is that combination of the expansion of wonder with the tension of apprehension that Mr. Herbert Read has so well summed up in his phrase, "the emotional apprehension of thought." But this emotional element in Donne's apprehension of thought does not, as emotion so often does, blurr or deflect the operations of the mind. As Mr. Leishman has pointed out so comprehensively: "He (Donne) does not idealize his experiences or transform them by association into splendid visions; he grapples with them, carefully analyzes them, and often tries to interpret them by means of intellectual conceptions. But though a philosophic or metaphysical poet, he is still a poet, because he always tries to communicate the concrete experience itself, and not merely the results of his reflection upon it."

It is that emotional blending of analysis and realistic illustration, in which satire jostles wonder and whimsy awe, that gives us the fascination of a passage like the following:

> Eternall God, (for whom who ever dare
> Seeke new expressions, doe the Circle square,
> And thrust into strait corners of poore wit
> Thee, who art cornerlesse and infinite)
> I would but blesse thy Name, not name thee
>   now.

In such a passage not the least astonishing of its qualities is this emotional versatility. It is reminiscent of that mingling of emotions that is one of the distinguishing qualities of sophisticated and decadent art in any age. One thinks of the mingling of magnificence and pain in a brocade-bedizened cross-bearing Christ of the Spanish Golden Age, like that of Montanes at Seville, or of the scream of torture breaking the rapture of youthful beauty and delight in the opera *Aphrodite*. But the emotional complexity of Donne's work is really a very different affair with more of the baroque than the Gongoristic or decadent in it. It is not just a mingling of emotion, one feeling suddenly shot through with another, for the elements of Donne's experience tend to preserve at once their identity and their interpenetrability. It is rather the swift setting of emotion against emotion with the same defiance of perspective that we have seen already in the handling of imagery. Ordinary human feeling moves much less quickly, clings more tenaciously to the purchase it has already won, retreats before a new emotional onslaught more slowly. It is sluggish in its rich diffusion, and when it is finally threatened by a shift in direction, it does not move with such clean completeness as does the emotion of Donne. Yet at the same time there is nothing trivial or mercurial in this mobility of feeling.

The explanation is, of course, that in Donne feeling like imagination is submissive to the operations of the logical

faculty. It is the expression of thought that is the center of his purpose, with the stress on the relation of separate identities, and not the rich diversity of the creative fancy. It is one of the forward-looking and anticipatory elements in Donne's genius, this tight clutch of the mind on its own operations. It is not of that Elizabethan world to which the abundance of his imagination still belongs, but it looks forward rather to the age of prose and reason. So often one feels in a particularly rich passage of Elizabethan poetry that the author has simply plunged into a pool of imagination and feeling in which he is thrashing about, trusting that sooner or later he will touch shore. But the Jacobean will leave nothing to chance. He is not disposed to stay in calm waters; he has the same taste for the high seas that his Elizabethan brother has, but one feels in his case that an objective is in his eye and that however broken the rhythm of his progress, he is heading steadily toward it. True, as yet, rationalism is impeded by the richness of its materials, so that often the effect is ingenious and the operation of the mind tortuous, but the direction is discernible.

This does not mean that Donne is immune to the seductions of the casual and incidental comparison. No Elizabethan is more sensitive to the allurements of the particular detail, the chance-caught analogy, the fine-spun association than Donne, but always he pushes through to the complete adumbration of the thought on which he started. It is at this point that the metaphysical conceit is most liable to alienate at some time or other its hardiest admirer. For the very absorption in the unravelling of the intricate logical relations behind the metaphor distracts a little that complete surrender that most of us find necessary for the appreciation of emotion. Yet as Mr. T. S. Eliot has warned us again and again, we must not set our level of poetic enjoyment so low that the delight of thinking is interdicted. For ecstasy is the transcending and not the remission of thought. As Mr. Herbert Read puts it [in "The Nature of Metaphysical Poetry," *Criterion*, vol. I] "Metaphysical poetry is determined logically: its emotion is a joy that comes with the triumph of the reason, and is not a simple instinctive ecstasy."

Joy and delight, however, are highly relative terms, and nowhere more so than where the equilibrium between thought and feeling is in question. There are very few readers of poetry who would not at some time or other recognize the delight of seeing a complicated matter reduced to simplicity, a mass of discordant elements brought to unity. This purely intellectual satisfaction is to be had again and again in Donne as in all his followers. But there is another type of intellectual operation of which the delight is less certain, from the point of view, at least, of poetry. One of the main features of the development of seventeenth-century thought is the imposition of mathematical pattern upon the multiplicity of reality. More and more, experience is reduced to a diagram, a process, a development, the logical conclusion of which we have seen in our own day in some of the mechanistic conceptions of human nature in which all the mysteries of perception and will are subsumed under formulae of automatic stimulus and response. As Mr. Willey has suggested, such a process is attempted and carried through because it answers some need or predisposition of the human mind. That reaching for a clear notion, an outline from which the accidents of the particular are sloughed off in the piling up of cases and illustrations, is to be seen at work in Donne more than has usually been realized. One striking example is the fascination which the map figure seems to have had for his imagination. The solemn and lovely "Hymne to God my God, in my sicknesse," with which, according to Walton, Donne comforted himself on his death bed, affords perhaps the most brilliant instance of his employment of that figure with which he had played even since the youthful "The good-morrow," and which now at the gates of death could yet hold once more his roving thoughts:

> Whilst my Physitians by their love are growne
> Cosmographers, and I their Mapp, who lie
> Flat on this bed, that by them may be showne
> That this is my South-west discoverie
> *Per fretum febris*, by these streights to die,
> I joy, that in these straits, I see my West;
> For, though theire currants yeeld returne to
> none,
> What shall my West hurt me? As West and East
> In all flatt Maps (and I am one) are one,
> So death doth touch the Resurrection.

Metaphysical poetry after Donne was used for all sorts of purposes, from a trifle like John Cleveland's "Fuscara, or the Bee Errant" to Edward Benlowes' "Theophila." It may be said at once that its full possibilities for English poetry were probably never fairly tested or exploited in the one genre that would do full justice to them, a full-dress philosophic poem. But many of them were developed to a very distinguished result in the more fragmentary lyric forms of Donne's successors in the school of devotional poetry, Herbert, Crashaw, Vaughan, and Traherne. It would be a mistake to attribute all or even a majority of the characteristic effects of these poets to either the example of Donne or the type of verse he so brilliantly adumbrated. But there were unquestionably peculiar advantages in the metaphysical idiom for the expression of religious experience.

In the first place, the very fact of the existence of a highly intellectual and yet enkindling poetry was of great importance to an age that more than most was basically intellectual in its approach to religion. That absorption in controversy that so many of the most thoughtful of the religious leaders of the time deplored was in itself, in spite of its too frequent aridity, a witness to the seriousness with which these men took the necessity of thinking through their religious convictions. The precise definition of belief, the exegesis of the implications of belief, the defence of one's own belief against the various assaults of other points of view, all these intellectual aspects of the matter held the center in the religious activity of the time. Consequently, however much the devotional poets might deplore the doctrinal over-emphasis of the time and however much they might seek in their own experience for something more inward and more varied, the intellectual aspects of religion were bound to play a very considerable part in their writing. The intellectual element is not, of course, of the same importance in the work of all of Donne's successors. Herbert and Vaughan, for instance, vary a good deal in philosophic interest and philosophic capacity. But for all, the problem

of expressing religious ideas in verse is a real one. Consequently, an example so striking as Donne's and a technique so firm were bound to prove of great service in the solution of this problem. And, it should be added in view of the lush crop of weeds that was to spring up in this field, the faults of Donne were not minimized in the use his followers made of his example. That loss of context and blindness to the involvement of more than one party in poetic communication that are responsible for some of Donne's aridities and failures of taste were not to be redeemed, for instance, in Crashaw. For good and for ill, then, Donne's intellectualism was to affect his successors.

The same is true of his contribution to the solution of another of the major problems of seventeenth-century religious poetry, the problem of mediation between religious feeling and those instruments of sense and imagination that, under the conditions of human communication, are indispensable for the expression of thought and feeling in any field. The elaborate medieval apparatus that had so well served Dante and the other religious poets of the Middle Ages had been rejected by the Reformation. The familiar symbols of the world after death, the human intermediation of the saints, expressed in a thousand legends of this world and the next, the symbolism and pageantry of church rite and festival, with all the accumulated imaginative and emotional values that had gathered about them for fifteen hundred years, these things had for the most part been rejected. The figure of Mary the Virgin and Mother, though not entirely excluded from the thought of the time, was under suspicion. Iconoclasm with its fear of idolatry and its resolution against superstition was at the door of the Protestant consciousness, and much of what had given food to the Christian imagination for centuries was shut without. Even the human life of Christ had lost some of its direct imaginative appeal in the prevailing theological preoccupations. The Old Testament held its own fairly well in parallel and illustration, and those portions of the New dealing with the organization and customs of the early Church were in the center of contemporary controversy. Moreover, the large part played by the Psalms in the literary life of the time must never be forgotten. But, again, it is the revelatory and authoritarian aspects of the Bible rather than its imaginative richness and suggestiveness that dominate the general consciousness. It is tempting to wonder what would have happened if the invention of printing had become generally effective in the thirteenth century or been delayed until the eighteenth. Certainly, the history of the Reformation period would have been very different, but it is idle to speculate whether or not the emphasis of Protestant religious experience would have been more imaginative and less intellectual, and the instruments of its first expression less verbal and more symbolic. The fact remains that the general state of mind furnished a very considerable problem for the religious poet.

It was a problem to which there was more than one solution, of course. One, Milton was to find, and though his solution presupposed a more spacious attitude toward the questions of symbol and allegory than the average Puritan of his time would have been able to compass, it remains a very satisfactory one. But even so, it was probably better suited to epic than to lyric poetry. Another is suggested by the intellectual objective which (in the words of Mr. Willey) the Platonist, John Smith, set up as the goal of the enlightened believer, "to think of God without allowing the busy imagination to stain his white radiance with its phantasms." That is a very lofty view of religious purpose, but one better suited to the capacities and the objectives of the mystic and the philosopher than of the poet. On the contrary, Donne's use of scholastic philosophy, of contemporary science, of the daily life of London, opened up rich possibilities for the sensuous coinage which religious values need for imaginatively effective communication. One of the great dangers of religious symbolism is that it may become remote, too well-worn, too specialized in its connotations for the wider stimulus needful for religious life. Of these evils there was little danger in the wide range of imaginative material that, as we have seen, Donne invoked.

Fortunately, no one of his successors tried to follow his example literally in the precise constituents of his imagery. In some ways Herbert comes closest, but there is a domestic tinge to the homeliness of Herbert's day-to-day imagery that Donne's lacks, and that makes it Herbert's own. Then, too, the pageantry of the ecclesiastical year, not as it is splendidly realized in cathedrals but as quietly observed in a parish church, comes to enrich his material of figure and allusion. Vaughan, likewise, extends the field of metaphysical imagery. For the urban Donne, nature, with the exception of a very few gorgeous descriptions of natural phenomena viewed pictorially, meant the "book of the creatures," ensconced and confined within the theological hierarchy. Vaughan opens up a whole new field of sense impression and of imaginative implication when he enriches that traditional conception with the discoveries of his own very individual sensitiveness to the beauty and wonder of the natural world. Traherne, in his turn, carries the awareness of nature as a treasure house of the revealing of God in some ways farther, while in other directions he adds new realms to the self-consciousness of Donne in his reminiscences of the childish self Donne seems to have forgotten. Crashaw returns to sources which Donne had rejected, and carries that blend of sense and divinity to which Donne had given credit to heights and in some ways to extremes beyond Donne's reach. But in varying degrees and in different directions all of these poets profited by the freshening and widening of the imagery of religious poetry which Donne had accomplished.

The same is true of what Donne achieved in the more purely musical aspects of his verse. Later Elizabethan secular poetry had been growing sweeter, smoother, more elegant, in its less happy moments, more facile. There is hardly any strength in art but which carries in its very realization the seeds of its own exaggeration, its own corruption. The early seventeenth century in England was an age when piety was taken for granted in large sections of society and yet, in some ways, insulated from large sections of the common life by a greater strenuousness of application. It is not surprising that under such conditions piety was relatively voluble and self-expressive, and yet religious feeling was to some degree stultified by over-definition and controversy. In such an age the religious

poet needs to have a special care for freshness and variety of expression, for that accent and discrimination that constitute distinction of style. This is the more necessary because, as we have seen, religious poetry is a mixed genre, where two standards have jurisdiction and one may be accepted, mistakenly, as satisfaction for the other. So generous is the passion for edification in its acceptances that too often piety is allowed to cloak shallowness and banality of expression.

The very sharpness and precision of the working of Donne's mind and imagination are reflected in the felicity of his diction, a felicity in which precision is never sacrificed to grace and very seldom even to the sensational effect dear to Donne's heart. That precision goes to the length at times of a coinage or an adaptation, but, as a rule, Donne's command of the general vocabulary, enriched, of course, by the special terms of science and philosophy, is wide enough and pliant enough for his purposes. The same is true of his syntax. A transferred epithet, a compression of idiom, an inversion or a transposition for emphasis, these elements of surprise and of novelty are often to be found, but again, for the most part, Donne follows the movement of talk. It is, to be sure, that glorified and pregnant talk that was the ideal of Matthew Arnold, but often there is no sign that the poet is emulous of anything but conversational directness and energy until the moment comes when suddenly he soars quite out of his plane. Yet even after these flashes of splendor he can be counted upon to return to that middle ground on which he habitually moves.

This is one reason for the freshness and trenchancy of his music. But it is not the only one. Like practically all Elizabethans, Donne experimented with variety of form in line and stanza pattern. Like almost all of these masters of singing he bent each pattern to his own ends. A notable example is to be found in the "Holy Sonnets." True, they have fourteen lines and a sonnet rhyme scheme. But within the line Donne certainly makes the most of that liberty of variation that is the one sure note of English prosody. The following is a somewhat extreme example but valuable for the evidence of how far Donne could go in a thoroughly serious, not to say solemn poem:

> And can that tongue adjudge thee unto hell,
> Which pray'd forgivenesse for his foes fierce
>   spight?
> No, no; but as in my idolatrie
> I said to all my profane mistresses,
> Beauty, of pitty, foulnesse onely is
> A signe of rigour: so I say to thee,
> To wicked spirits are horrid shapes assign'd,
> This beauteous forme assures a pitious minde.

Much more typical of the usual Donne effect is that of the opening lines of the tenth of these sonnets:

> Death be not proud, though some have called
>   thee
> Mighty and dreadfull, for, thou art not soe,
> For, those, whom thou think'st, thou dost over-
>   throw,
> Die not, poore death, nor yet canst thou kill mee.

Indeed, here is the perfect musical counterpart of that

emotional effect found so often in Donne where the imagination seems to fly out into infinity only to be caught swiftly and noiselessly back. Anyone who has ever been in Venice on St. Mark's feast day will remember how the lion of the Evangelist floats on silken standards before the great church. As the April winds from the sea swell and fling out their shining folds, that exquisite heraldry fills the whole radiant scene, and then as the breeze fails, they swing crumpling back to the literal banners, tethered to their unyielding standards. So it is with the music of John Donne.

For always there is to be felt the grip of an unseen and implicit principle of control, and that is the argument, the closely articulated, persistently held thread of the comparison, or the exposition, or the analysis, or the proof, that here, as in the realms of feeling and imagination, is, for Donne, ultimately supreme. The shortcomings of the resulting music are obvious. Not its dissonances, not its deliberate cacophonies, not even its broken chords, with their sudden jets and starts of melody, are its most teasing deficiency, but this truncation of splendor, this sudden thwarting of starbound beauty. But even the defects of Donne's music have their value for devotional poetry. The unimpeded pursuit of the infinite has its predestined repulses, and he who hopes to compress the ineffable into words had best take care of facility or the intoxication of his own rapture. For both the music of Donne is tonic.

The genius of Herbert was for the smoother, more limpid modes, and that of Crashaw for the higher and the more sustained flights of feeling. At his best finer and freer than Donne, Vaughan yet could not hold his music on the higher ranges which Donne deliberately rejected, and Traherne's gifts were nowhere less those of poetry than in this matter of singing. Yet all of them owe much of their best strength and distinction, even in their own peculiar achievements, to the astringent freshness, the vigorous reality, of Donne's music. (pp. 73-94)

Helen C. White, in her The Metaphysical Poets, *1936. Reprint by Collier Books, 1962, 414 p.*

Louis L. Martz

[*Martz is an American critic and scholar who has written extensively on the subject of seventeenth-century and metaphysical poetry. In the following essay, Martz explores metaphysical themes in English devotional poetry from the early seventeenth century, focusing on the works of John Donne and his immediate successors.*]

The basic principle of devotional poetry in the seventeenth century is prefigured in a poem by Robert Southwell entitled 'Looke home', written sometime around 1590:

> Retyred thoughts enjoy their owne delights,
> As beawtie doth in selfe beholding eye:
> Mans mind a myrrour is of heavenly sights,
> A breefe wherein all marvailes summed lye.
> Of fayrest formes, and sweetest shapes the store,
> Most gracefull all, yet thought may grace them
>   more.

> The mind a creature is, yet can create,
> To natures paterns adding higher skill:
> Of finest workes wit better could the state,
> If force of wit had equall power of will.
> Devise of man in working hath no end,
> What thought can thinke another thought can
>   mend.

It is no accident that these lines from an Elizabethan poet should prefigure the famous stanza in Marvell's 'Garden' which speaks of how 'the Mind . . . Withdraws into its happiness':

> The Mind, that Ocean where each kind
> Does streight its own resemblance find;
> Yet it creates, transcending these,
> Far other Worlds, and other Seas;

while at the same time four other lines from Southwell's 'Looke home' seem to foreshadow certain lines in the middle of Marvell's 'On a Drop of Dew':

> Mans soule of endles beauties image is,
> Drawne by the worke of endlesse skill and
>   might:
> This skilfull might gave many sparkes of blisse,
> And to discerne this blisse a native light.
>   So the Soul, that Drop, that Ray
> Of the clear Fountain of Eternal Day,
> Could it within the humane flow'r be seen,
>   Remembring still its former height,
>   Shuns the sweat leaves and blossoms green;
>   And, recollecting its own Light,
> Does, in its pure and circling thoughts, express
> The greater Heaven in an Heaven less.

In these passages by Southwell and Marvell we find enclosed the central image of the place where the basic religious action of the period was performed: the mind, the soul, where the images received through the senses could be transformed by means of an inner light, the light of human 'wit', that is, the intellect, the understanding, the power of reason. In Southwell's poem, as in Marvell's, the emphasis falls upon the action of thought, upon the creative power of human reason, 're-collecting' its light by remembrance, and also by collecting together its own interior faculties.

It is the same action that another Elizabethan poet, William Alabaster, described in one of his holy sonnets written in the very last years of the sixteenth century, where he says:

> soe moves my love about the heavenlie spheare
> and draweth thence with an attractive fire
> the purest argument witt can desire,
> whereby devotion after may arise;
> and theis conceiptes, digest by thoughts retire,
> are turned into aprill showers of teares.
>
>   (Sonnet 15)

Here is a definition of the meaning of the phrase 'devotional poetry'. 'Devotion,' says Alabaster, is a state of mind that arises after love of the divine has searched out in heavenly things certain topics upon which the power of wit may operate. And these 'conceits', that is, these conceptions, are then digested by the retirement of thought into a state of concentrated attention in which fervent emotions are generated and thoughts are converted into tears—or into joy or into other devout manifestations.

'Devotion', then, is an active, creative state of mind, a 'poetical' condition, we might say, in which the mind works at high intensity. Thus François de Sales declares that 'devotion is no other thing than a spiritual nimbleness and vivacity, by means of which charity [i.e. the love of God] works in us, or we by her, readily and heartily.' Charity and devotion, he declares, 'differ no more, the one from the other, than the flame from the fire; in as much as charity, being a spiritual fire, when it breaks out into flame, is called devotion: so that devotion adds nothing to the fire of charity, save the flame which makes charity ready, active and diligent, not only in observing the commandments of God, but in practising the heavenly counsels and inspirations.'

The phrase 'devotional poetry' should not, then, be taken to indicate verse of rather limited range, 'merely pious' pieces without much poetic energy. Devotion is for these poets a state of mind created by the 'powers of the soul' in an intense, dramatic action, focused upon one central issue. Thus, for example, Alabaster concentrates upon the image of the Cross:

> Now I have found thee, I will ever more
> embrace this standerd where thou sitest above:
> feed greedy eyes, and from hence never rove,
> sucke hungrye Soule of this eternall store.
> Issue my hearte from thy two leaved dore
> and lett my lipps from kissinge not remove.
> O that I were transformed into Love
> and as a plante might springe upp in his flowre,
> like wandring ivy, or sweete hony suckle,
> how would I with my twine aboute it buckle!
> and kiss his feete with my ambitiouse bowes
> and clime alonge uppon his sacred brest
> and make a garland for his wounded browes!
> Lord, soe I am if here my thoughtes might
> rest.
>
> (34)

Here again we have the emphasis upon the power of thoughts, with a highly emotional and dramatic concentration of the senses upon the image of the crucified Christ.

In another of his sonnets Alabaster gives an explicit account of how these thoughts operate upon images:

> The sunne begins upon my heart to shine:
> now lett a cloude of thoughts in order traine
> as dewy spangles wonte, and entertaine
> in many drops his Passione Divine,
> that on them, as a rainbow, may recline
> the white of innocence, the black of paine,
> the blew of stripes, the yellow of disdaine,
> and purple which his blood doth weell designe.
>
> (70)

That is, purple which well signifies or represents Christ's blood. This poem is entitled in one manuscript 'A Morninge Meditation', and, of course, the sun that begins to shine upon the speaker's heart is at first the physical sun. But we become gradually aware that it is ultimately the Son of God whom the speaker is contemplating and that this Son is warming his heart. This is no random thinking,

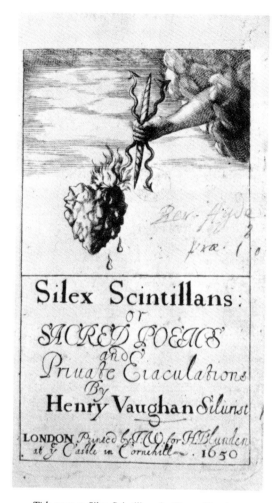

Title page to Silex Scintillans *by Henry Vaughan.*

but rather 'thoughts in order': a process of 'passionate paradoxical reasoning which knits the first line to the last'—to use Grierson's old description of the metaphysical style [*Metaphysical Lyrics and Poems of the Seventeenth Century*, 1921]. The poem concludes with a passage that represents the search for unity in multiplicity, which is the true nature of a metaphysical action, in the strict sense of that word 'metaphysical.'

> And lett those thousand thoughts powre on
>   mine eyes
> a thousand tears, as glasses to beehould him,
> and thousand tears, thousand sweete words de-
>   vise
> uppon my lipps, as pictures to unfold him.
> Soe shall reflect three rainbowes from one sunne:
> thoughts, tears, and words, all end in Actione.

'In Actione'—that is, devout, unified, concentrated action: a nimble, vigorous state of mind perhaps better represented in the alternative ending that one manuscript gives for this sonnet: 'yet actinge all in one'.

Finally, to take one more example from this interesting precursor of the seventeenth-century line of religious poets, Alabaster sums up in a brilliant little drama the action that he has here been describing:

> When without tears I looke on Christ, I see
> only a story of some passion
> which any common eye may wonder on,
> butt if I look through tears Christ smiles on mee,
> yea there I see my selfe: and from that tree
> he bendeth downe to my devotione . . .
>
> (71)

Here again the word 'devotion' occurs as the outcome of a vigorous internal drama: through the power of the speaker's mental action he sees Christ smile on him and bend down to assist the activity of the human soul.

By combining the techniques of devotion with the techniques of the Elizabethan sonnet, Alabaster has here produced poetry of a strongly 'metaphysical' cast. His sonnets thus suggest that we should be extremely cautious in estimating the influence of Donne upon the course of devotional poetry in the seventeenth century. And indeed, the more we ponder the peculiar quality of Donne's religious consciousness, the more we realize that his Hymns and Holy Sonnets do not lend themselves to imitation.

Let me explain and illustrate what I mean by the inimitable peculiarity of Donne's religious consciousness. Two Holy Sonnets will perhaps serve to make my point. First, Holy Sonnet 9, which develops a remarkably intricate series of dramatic postures. The poem is at first spoken furtively to the self as if God were not present and would not hear the blasphemous thoughts that the speaker is uttering, as he tries to evade his human responsibilities:

> If poysonous mineralls, and if that tree,
> Whose fruit threw death on else immortall us,
> If lecherous goats, if serpents envious
> Cannot be damn'd; Alas; why should I bee?

It is the *tree's* fault that death came upon us; and we can see a further bit of hypocrisy and wilful misunderstanding in the word 'serpents', because we know very well that one 'serpent' has been damned to eternity. And that cry, 'Alas; why should I bee?' is implicitly answered in the very next line, as though an answer had occurred to the self-deluding speaker between the lines, for he goes on to ask:

> Why should intent or reason, borne in mee,
> Make sinnes, else equall, in mee, more heinous?

He knows perfectly well the traditional answer: it is the power of reason that makes man damnable when 'mineralls' or trees cannot be damned. But 'borne in mee' turns the blame towards the Creator; and he has a further complaint which he goes on to express in his querulous way:

> And mercy being easie, and glorious
> To God, in his sterne wrath, why threatens hee?

It is as though the mention of the name of God reminds the speaker that he is, however he may pretend, speaking in the presence of his God. Suddenly his whole resistance breaks down in anguish and fear:

> But who am I, that dare dispute with thee?
> O God, Oh! of thine onely worthy blood,
> And my teares, make a heavenly Lethean flood,
> And drowne in it my sinnes blacke memorie.

> That thou remember them, some claime as debt,
> I thinke it mercy, if thou wilt forget.

In that last line the speaker seems to be saying that perhaps the best he can hope for is that he will be utterly forgotten and wiped out of God's mind, although he would prefer to have only his sins forgotten. The poem stands on the edge of despair, but never quite falls into the pit. What is most striking here is the continuously shifting nature of the argument, the way in which the speaker's mind seems to be racing ahead of itself, answering questions implicitly even while they are being asked. It is this constantly shifting nature of the speaker's stance within a given poem that makes Donne's poems basically inimitable. His search for the One moves along the edge of a quicksand, with a feeling that the steps of reason are always on the verge of disaster; yet reason never does collapse; in fact, it emerges triumphant in the sestet of this sonnet, with an exact command of the theology of redemption, in spite of all the evasions and curious questions raised en route.

We can see a similar shifting of the mind in a sonnet that is not often analysed, though frequently mentioned, Holy Sonnet 17, written after the death of Donne's wife. Here again, one is struck by the fact that the opening posture, in this case, one of serenity, is utterly deceptive:

> Since she whome I lovd, hath payd her last debt
> To Nature, and to hers, and my good is dead,
> And her soule early into heaven ravished,
> Wholy in heavenly things my mind is sett.
> Here the admyring her my mind did whett
> To seeke thee God; so streames do shew the
>   head . . .

Thus far the speaker's state of mind seems secure and even placid, strangely serene for Donne. But it is all illusory, for the next two lines tell us that this speaker is, as always, dissatisfied:

> But though I have found thee, and thou my
>   thirst hast fed,
> A holy thirsty dropsy melts mee yett.

He longs for the satisfaction of his love for God, and so another and a more perplexing question follows with a repetition of the word 'but':

> But why should I begg more love, when as thou
> Dost wooe my soule for hers; offring all thine:

This is Grierson's reading, based on the Westmoreland manuscript, and it is indeed a perplexing one. As it stands it seems to say that God is wooing the speaker's soul in order to rejoin it with the soul of his beloved lady; God's love brings to perfection the true love of two human beings. Yet Miss Gardner's emendation [in her *Divine Poems*] is attractive, which makes the question read thus:

> But why should I begg more love, when as thou
> Dost wooe my soule, for hers offring all thine:

As Miss Gardner explains, the speaker is then asking why he needs to beg for more love when God is offering God's love in place of his lady's love. From one standpoint this meaning leads better into the next two lines:

> And dost not only feare least I allow

My love to saints and Angels, things divine, . . .

Donne may be alluding to his lady here under the traditional Petrarchan category of saints and angels. On the
other hand, there seems to be a clear allusion to the theological problems raised by Catholic devotion to saints and
angels, a practice of course forbidden, or severely restricted, by the Protestants. In either case (and we may take
both interpretations simultaneously) the last four lines of
the poem flow together to produce a curious sense of latent
threat to the opening security:

> And dost not only feare least I allow
> My love to saints and Angels, things divine,
> But in thy tender jealosy dost doubt
> Least the World, fleshe, yea Devill putt thee out.

Donne seems to be saying here that God may very well
have some reason to fear that the speaker will love saints
and angels, things divine, but it is an excess of tender jealousy for God to fear that, at this stage of his life, the world,
the flesh, or the devil could ever put God out of the speaker's heart. And yet the very mention of the world, the
flesh, and the devil at the end indicates the speaker's
awareness that this is a danger, this is a just fear. As in
many of Donne's poems, the ending is a most precarious
resolution and leaves the reader with no sense that the
ever-recurrent instability of this speaker's mind has really
been overcome.

The contrast between Donne's instability and Herbert's
deeply achieved security makes the poetry of these two
men vastly different. I think we do not do Herbert's poetry
a favour when we seek to emphasize its restlessness. What
we have in his poetry as presented in the whole *Temple* is
the *memory* of states of restlessness now securely overcome and retrospectively viewed as dangers overpassed.
As Herbert's *Temple* now exists it is an edifice in which
the praise of God is securely rendered, from a vantage
point of victory. It is probably only an accident of the
modern temper that we should regard a state of continuous instability as more interesting than a state of achieved
security. Certainly the seventeenth century did not regard
Donne as a greater religious poet than Herbert. Vaughan,
as we know, revered Herbert as a 'Saint' and imitated his
poetry almost as though it were holy writ.

Herbert's poetry at its best is represented in that well-
known poem 'Vertue', which will show clearly the enormous difference between the basic state of mind and consequently the basic poetical techniques of Donne and Herbert:

> Sweet day, so cool, so calm, so bright,
> The bridall of the earth and skie:
> The dew shall weep thy fall to night;
>   For thou must die.
>
> Sweet rose, whose hue angrie and brave
> Bids the rash gazer wipe his eye:
> Thy root is ever in its grave,
>   And thou must die.
>
> Sweet spring, full of sweet dayes and roses,
> A box where sweets compacted lie;
> My musick shows ye have your closes,
>   And all must die.

> Onely a sweet and vertuous soul,
> Like season'd timber, never gives;
> But though the whole world turn to coal,
>   Then chiefly lives.

The poem creates that sense of deliberate architectural
building, block by block, which marks the Herbertian
technique, and which he shares with Ben Jonson and the
Sons of Ben. As in the design of a classical building, one
seems to see at once how it is put together, why it produces
this effect of total serenity and full command. The parallel-
ism in the opening phrases of the first three stanzas is explicit, all being neatly bound together in the middle of the
poem, in the ninth line. Then all the repetitions of 'sweet'
are bound together once again in the opening line of the
final stanza. On the other side of the stanzas, the rhymes
are carefully built. The second and fourth lines of the first
three stanzas contain the same rhyme, meeting on the
word 'die', three times repeated; thus a melancholy oscil-
lation is produced between 'Sweet' and 'die' at beginning
and end of these three stanzas. Then, in the last stanza, the
shift in the position of 'sweet', and the change in rhyme,
mark a change towards a positive, optimistic mood.

Meanwhile, underneath all this carefully built symmetry
there is a rich and fluent sub-structure of association developing out of the repetitions of that word 'sweet', used
with many implications. Consider all that the word 'sweet'
may imply as recorded in the *OED*, in addition to indicating a pleasant flavour. As applied to smell it means: having
a pleasant odour, fragrant. As applied to hearing it means:
having a pleasant sound, being musical, harmonious. As
applied to sight it means: lovely, charming. Or, to give the
richest of the *OED* definitions, the word means: 'free from
offensive or disagreeable taste or smell; not corrupt, pu-
trid, sour, or stale; free from taint or noxious matter; in
a sound or wholesome condition.' Furthermore, as in
'sweetheart', it may of course mean: beloved, precious,
dear—as in Lovelace's poem: 'Tell me not (Sweet) I am
unkind.' All these meanings are compacted in the five repetitions of the word 'sweet', along with the central and
summary use of the noun 'sweets', meaning perfumes or
fragrant flowers, not chocolates. Then at the very close the
poem takes a double turn, for although the 'sweet and vertuous soul' is like 'season'd timber' in its strength, it is unlike timber in a final regard, because even seasoned timber
will turn to ashes, after a long time: but the 'sweet and vertuous soul' will live. As in the design of a classical building, what seems at first so clear and obvious grows from
a very subtle convergence of lines and perspectives. Such
art as this is founded upon security, can arise only from
security. It lies at the farthest remove from the vehement,
rushing, questioning and often querulous action of Donne.

We should note, too, that Herbert's technique of repetition pervades the entire *Temple*. A similar repetition of the
word 'sweet', for instance, binds 'Vertue' and 'The Odour'
together, though they are separated by some eighty pages
in the standard edition; and of course the word 'sweet' occurs dozens of times in the intervening poems and elsewhere. There are many other words which stretch their
tentacular affiliations throughout the full range of Herbert's book, sometimes dominating single poems, at other
times linking many poems: words such as 'grief', 'blood',

'heart', 'love', 'dust', 'musick', along with kindred terms, and many other repeated words which every reader will wish to emphasize for himself. Thus, after 'The Sacrifice' has presented the words of Christ from the Cross: 'Was ever grief like mine', the next poem, 'The Thanksgiving', picks up the word 'grief' and savours its various meanings: suffering, sorrow, injury, pain, 'the grief of a wound':

> Oh King of grief! (a title strange, yet true,
>   To thee of all kings onely due)
> Oh King of wounds! how shall I grieve for thee,
>   Who in all grief preventest me?
> Shall I weep bloud? why, thou hast wept such
>   store
>   That all thy body was one doore.

Then, in 'The Agonie' three key words, 'love', 'sweet', and 'bloud', are brought together in the final lines:

> Love is that liquour sweet and most divine,
> Which my God feels as bloud; but I, as wine.

Upon the fabric established by these repetitions, Herbert weaves an astonishing variety of designs, including some of the boldest familiarity with God found anywhere in literature. I think, for example, of 'The Bag', which opens with a firm rejection of 'despair', by alluding to the occasion when Jesus calmed the waves of the sea (*Matthew* 8. 24-7):

> Away despair! my gracious Lord doth heare.
>   Though windes and waves assault my keel,
>   He doth preserve it: he doth steer,
>   Ev'n when the boat seems most to reel.
> Storms are the triumph of his art:
> Well may he close his eyes, but not his heart.

Within this context of security Herbert then proceeds to tell 'a strange storie' about the Incarnation and the Crucifixion, all done in the most intimate fashion:

> But as he was returning, there came one
>   That ran upon him with a spear.
>   He, who came hither all alone,
>   Bringing nor man, nor arms, nor fear,
>   Receiv'd the blow upon his side,
> And straight he turn'd, and to his brethren
>   cry'd,
>
> If ye have any thing to send or write,
>   I have no bag, but here is room:
>   Unto my Fathers hands and sight,
>   Beleeve me, it shall safely come.
>   That I shall minde, what you impart,
> Look, you may put it very neare my heart.
>
> Or if hereafter any of my friends
>   Will use me in this kinde, the doore
>   Shall still be open; what he sends
>   I will present, and somewhat more,
>   Not to his hurt. Sighs will convey
> Any thing to me. Harke, Despair away.

The letter-bag, we see, turns out to be Christ's own side, with allusion to the *Gospel of John*, 10.9: 'I am the door: by me if any man enter in, he shall be saved, and shall go in and out, and find pasture.' At the same time, when we look at the shaping of these stanzas, turning them on the side, it appears as though each stanza represents the shape of a bag. This effect is quite in line with the sort of visual wit that Herbert works in other poems. But my point is the way in which this witty intimacy lives within the state of security and could not otherwise exist.

The same is true of 'Conscience', where the speaker intimately addresses his conscience as though it were a troublesome, foolish babbler, or a child causing difficulty by its chattering:

> Peace pratler, do not lowre:
> Not a fair look, but thou dost call it foul:
> Not a sweet dish, but thou dost call it sowre:
>   Musick to thee doth howl.
> By listning to thy chatting fears
> I have both lost mine eyes and eares.

He proceeds in the next stanza to state the ideal which he seeks and within which his poems work:

> Pratler, no more, I say:
> My thoughts must work, but like a noiselesse
>   sphere;
> Harmonious peace must rock them all the day:
>   No room for pratlers there.
> If thou persistest, I will tell thee,
> That I have physick to expell thee.

Then, picking up the word 'physick', he develops it into a theological metaphor, that the medical prescription will be the blood of Christ tasted at his table:

> And the receit shall be
> My Saviours bloud: when ever at his board
> I do but taste it, straight it cleanseth me,
>   And leaves thee not a word;
>   No, not a tooth or nail to scratch,
>   And at my actions carp, or catch.
>
> Yet if thou talkest still,
> Besides my physick, know there's some for thee:
> Some wood and nails to make a staffe or bill
>   For those that trouble me:
>   The bloudie crosse of my deare Lord
>   Is both my physick and my sword.

Notice how the troublesome conscience is treated as a dramatic character quite distinct from the speaker's whole self. The blood of Christ is not only the speaker's own cure, but it also provides a tough weapon against conscience itself. The curiously bantering tone of the poem could only be successful within the familiar confidence that Herbert has achieved in speaking in the presence of his God.

Henry Vaughan, in his creative, deliberate imitation of George Herbert's poetry, has frequently attempted to achieve the intimacy in which Herbert so securely lives. But Vaughan's consciousness lives in a different universe, an unstable and insecure state of mind, in which the speaker attempts to maintain the memory of certain moments of illumination: especially that moment represented in the engraved title-page and prefatory poem to *Silex Scintillans* (1650), when the power of God struck him and his rocky heart flashed with the fire of love. Vaughan's mystic consciousness lives in the effort to recover that event, the beginning of his spiritual life. Thus, instability and a groping movement seem to be essential to the action of Vaughan's poetry, even when he is most closely imitating Herbert. One poem, filled with echoes of Herbert, will illustrate the difference: 'The Resolve'. The title is, of course, reminiscent of Herbert's way of entitling many of his poems, such as 'The Reprisall', from which Vaughan takes his opening line, echoing word by word the first line of Herbert's poem:

> I have consider'd it; and find . . .

But each poet is considering quite a different thing. Herbert is considering how he may repay the love of God, as described in the preceding poem, 'The Thanksgiving', where he honours Christ as the King of Grief in the passage quoted previously; how he might deal with Christ's 'mighty passion'. He goes on to explain that he will solve this problem 'by confession' in which he 'will overcome/The man, who once against thee fought.' Significantly, Vaughan is not considering the Passion; his poetry, unlike Herbert's, is not centred on the Cross. What Vaughan's centre is, the poem gradually and gropingly reveals:

> I have consider'd it; and find
>   A longer stay
> Is but excus'd neglect.   To mind
>   One path, and stray
> Into another, or to none,
>   Cannot be love;
> When shal that traveller come home,
>   That will not move?
> If thou wouldst thither, linger not,
>   Catch at the place. . . .

The last phrase, 'Catch at the place', is an echo of the phrase in Herbert's poem 'Affliction (I)', where Herbert says his 'sudden soul caught at the place' (line 17), that is to say, the place in the ministry of the Church into which God has 'enticed' him. In Herbert's poem we know exactly where the 'place' is, for he has spoken of the joys in the service of God which he has hoped to find. But in Vaughan's poem, characteristically, we do not know what place the speaker is seeking, we do not know what path he 'minds', intends to follow. And Vaughan continues with his exhortations for many lines, without telling us the ultimate goal.

> Tell youth, and beauty they must rot,
>   They'r but a *Case*;
> Loose, parcell'd hearts wil freeze: The Sun
>   With scatter'd locks
> Scarce warms, but by contraction
>   Can heat rocks;
> Call in thy *Powers*; run, and reach
>   Home with the light,
> Be there, before the shadows stretch,
>   And *Span* up night;
> Follow th *Cry* no more.

Clearly, the speaker is urging a concentration of the powers of his soul upon some ultimate aim, and he is going to escape from the way of the world, 'the *Cry*' (with a reference not only to the general opinion of the world but perhaps also to the cry of a pack of hounds). Another explicit echo of Herbert's poem 'Affliction (I)', lines 19-22:

> At first thou gav'st me milk and sweetnesses;

>   I had my wish and way:
> My dayes were straw'd with flow'rs and happinesse;
>   There was no moneth but
> May.

is added as Vaughan continues thus:

> there is
> An ancient way
> All strewed with flowres, and happiness
> And fresh as *May*;

In Herbert's poem this sense of happiness is an illusion indicating the speaker's misunderstanding of the way of Christ; but here in Vaughan the imagery of nature and springtime indicates a true and ultimate goal, as the poem concludes:

> There turn, and turn no more; Let wits,
>   Smile at fair eies,
> Or lips; But who there weeping sits,
>   Hath got the *Prize*.

In the very last word, italicized by Vaughan, we understand the goal. It is that expressed by St. Paul in his *Epistle to the Philippians* (3. 14): 'I press for the mark for the prize of the high calling of God in Christ Jesus.'

What has Vaughan learned then from Herbert's poetry? He has learned how to use familiar conversation in colloquy with the self; he has learned how to use familiar allusions in the presence of God. But the structure of Vaughan's poetry lacks the kind of architectural neatness which we find in Herbert at his best. As in 'The Resolve', Vaughan's best poems move tentatively with a roving action, seeking the ancient way which Vaughan at his best frequently symbolizes in imagery from nature, from the pastoral scenes of the Bible, or from the memory of the innocence of those 'early days' of his own childhood.

A more elaborate indication of these aspects of Vaughan's poetry may be found in the longer poem 'Ascension-day', in which all the finest aspects of Vaughan's art are brought together. Here is a poem in which he uses many of the traditional modes of religious meditation. The opening 'aspirations' are followed by the use of all the senses to apprehend vividly ('as though one were present') the action in the scene:

> I greet thy Sepulchre, salute thy Grave,
> That blest inclosure, where the Angels gave
> The first glad tidings of thy early light,
> And resurrection from the earth and night.
> I see that morning in thy Converts tears,
> Fresh as the dew, which but this dawning wears!
> I smell her spices, and her ointment yields,
> As rich a scent as the now Primros'd-fields:
> The Day-star smiles, and light with thee deceast,
> Now shines in all the Chambers of the East.
> What stirs, what posting intercourse and mirth
> Of Saints and Angels glorifie the earth?
> What sighs, what whispers, busie stops and
>   stays:
> Private and holy talk fill all the ways?
> They pass as at the last great day, and run
> In their white robes to seek the risen Sun;
> I see them, hear them, mark their haste, and
>   move

Amongst them, with them, wing'd with faith
  and love.

In this 'composition of place', directed towards this scene of light, Vaughan is able to bring to bear the ancient technique of using the senses in a spiritual exercise, a technique which he has been unable to use effectively in other poems where he has attempted to meditate upon Eucharistic scenes. He cannot, for example, grasp the Passion of Christ visually, although he tries to do so in his very weak poem entitled 'The Passion', a poem cast in the past tense, unable to achieve the presence of God. But here the sense of presence is achieved as the speaker proceeds to associate the scene of the Ascension with the early days of *Genesis* and the beauties of nature as Vaughan himself could visualize them. Three areas of action then are brought together here: the fields of Bethany on the Ascension day, the scene in Eden in the days before the Fall, and the vestiges of that original beauty which still can be seen in nature at present:

> I walk the fields of *Bethani* which shine
> All now as fresh as *Eden*, and as fine.
> Such was the bright world, on the first seventh
>   day,
> Before man brought forth sin, and sin decay;
> When like a Virgin clad in *Flowers* and *green*
> The pure earth sat, and the fair woods had seen
> No frost, but flourish'd in that youthful vest,
> With which their great Creator had them drest:
> When Heav'n above them shin'd like molten
>   glass,
> While all the Planets did unclouded pass;
> And Springs, like dissolv'd Pearls their Streams
>   did pour
> Ne'r marr'd with floods, nor anger'd with a
>   showre.

In this setting, bright with natural beauty and with memories of the Bible, Vaughan is able to fulfil the quest that he began in the first part of *Silex Scintillans* in his poem 'The Search', where he roved through the traditional places of Christ's residence, and was unable to find his Lord. But now

> With these fair thoughts I move in this fair
>   place,
> And the last steps of my milde Master trace;
> I see him leading out his chosen Train,
> All sad with tears, which like warm Summer-
>   rain
> In silent drops steal from their holy eyes,
> Fix'd lately on the Cross, now on the skies.
> And now (eternal Jesus!) thou dost heave
> Thy blessed hands to bless, these thou dost leave;
> The cloud doth now receive thee, and their sight
> Having lost thee, behold two men in white!
> Two and no more: *what two attest, is true*,
> Was thine own answer to the stubborn Jew.
> Come then thou faithful witness! come dear
>   Lord
> Upon the Clouds again to judge this world!

Thus the poem concludes with two precise biblical allusions; first to the scene of the Ascension itself (*Acts* 1.9-11), and secondly to the verse of the *Gospel of John* (8.17), where Jesus answers the Pharisees by saying, 'It is also written in your Law, that the testimony of two men is true.' In a way characteristic of Vaughan's best work, this poem then ends abruptly with a brief prayer.

This poem is very little indebted to George Herbert and not at all to John Donne. Its roving action is an original achievement by Vaughan, working within a mode of versification characteristic of the Sons of Ben Jonson, where the development of couplet-rhetoric was moving towards its Augustan culmination.

Meanwhile, in exile on the continent, Richard Crashaw was bringing to conclusion his efforts to achieve ecstatic expression in the continental mode of the baroque. One poem must serve here as an example of the way in which Crashaw was departing from the central modes of English poetry, adapting the phraseology of Herbert, the couplet-rhetoric of Ben Jonson, the techniques of the Elizabethan love-song, and bringing all these modes into an idiom that was essentially foreign to the English tradition. Crashaw's poetry remains an anomaly in English literature, an example of a continental importation which never struck a firm hold upon the English scene, and in the end had to seek its proper nourishment in exile. I choose his poem on the Assumption of the Virgin Mary, a poem that may have been written before Crashaw left England in the early sixteen forties, since it was published in part in the first edition of *Steps to the Temple* (1646). Here, however, a passage of sixteen lines (19-34) is lacking, which appeared in the edition of 1648 where we find the longest version of the poem; the posthumous edition of 1652 omits ten other lines (47-56), whether on Crashaw's authorization or not, we shall never know. I take the version of 1648 to be the best as well as the longest, and it is on this that I base my comments.

The poem opens in the manner of a formal meditation with a composition of the scene of the Virgin Mary's Assumption:

> Hark!   she is call'd, the parting houre is come.
> Take thy farewell, poore world!   Heav'n must
>   goe home.
> A peece of Heav'nly Earth, purer and brighter
> Than the chast stars, whose choice lamps come
>   to light her,
> While through the Christall orbes, clearer than
>   they,
> She climbs; and makes a farre more milky way.

Now the speaker, being present at the scene, hears the song of Christ, as in the *Song of Solomon* (2. 10-13), calling his beloved, while the poem modulates gracefully from pentameter couplets into a song of neatly balanced tetrameter couplets:

> She's call'd. Harke how the deare immortall
>   Dove
> Sighes to his silver mate. *Rise up my Love*,
>   *Rise up my faire, my spotlesse one*,
>   *The winters past, the Rain is gone*:
>   *The spring is come, the Flowers appeare*,
>   *No sweets but thou are wanting here*.

Then, picking up the biblical 'come away', Crashaw transmutes the measure into the verse form of an Elizabethan song, echoing the invitation found in many Elizabethan song-books, as in Campion's lyric:

Come away, arm'd with loves delights,
Thy sprightfull graces bring with thee;

or in Dowland's lyric:

Come away, come sweet Love,
The golden morning breakes:
All the earth, all the ayre
Of love and pleasure speaks;

or in Ben Jonson's song:

Come away, come away,
We grow jealous of your stay.

In this popular mode Crashaw then presents his sacred parody in a madrigal of Christ:

Come away my love,
Come away my dove,
Cast off delay:
The Court of Heav'n is come,
To waite upon thee home;
Come, come away.

Then, in the long passage missing in 1646, the speaker subtly effects a shifting of voices suggested by the fact that the above madrigal is not italicized as the voice of Christ alone, but is rather presented as a song in which the human speaker may also be singing. But now the voice clearly shifts to that of the human speaker, developing the imagery of the *Song of Solomon* into his own fallen landscape, as he longs for the presence of the Virgin who can help to heal all mortal sorrow:

The Flowers appeare,
Or quickly would, were thou once here.
The spring is come; Or if it stay,
'Tis to keepe time with thy delay.
The raine is gone, Except as much as wee,
Detain in needfull *Teares*, to weep the want of
      thee.
            The winters past,
            Or if he make lesse haste,
      His answer is, Why, she doth so;
If summer come not, how can winter go?
            Come away, come away,
The shrill winds chide, the waters weep thy stay,
The fountaines murmure; and each loftiest Tree,
Bowes lowest his leavy top, to looke for thee.

But now the madrigal of Christ is heard again:

Come away my love,
Come away my dove, &c.

Thus the speaker finds that Mary must indeed now leave this earth, and he accepts the loss, finding his consolation in her praise:

She's call'd again; And will she goe?
When Heav'n bids come, who can say No?
Heav'n calls her, and she must away,
Heav'n will not, and she cannot stay.
Goe then, goe (*glorious*) on the golden wings
Of the bright youth of Heav'n that sings
Under so sweet a burden, *Goe*,
Since thy dread *Son* will have it so.
And while thou goest, our Song and wee,
Will as wee may reach after thee.
      Haile, holy Queen, of humble Hearts!

We in thy praise wil have our parts . . .

Though our poore joyes are parted so,
Yet shall our lips never let goe
Thy gracious name, but to the last
Our loving song shall hold it fast.

In this determination the speaker now creates his own earthly madrigal, in an intricate pattern of trimeter, tetrameter, and dimeter, concluding with a firm tetrameter couplet:

Thy precious Name shall bee
Thy self to us, and wee
With holy care will keep it by us.
      Wee to the last
      Will hold it fast;
And no Assumption shall deny us.
      All the sweetest showers
      Of our fairest flowers,
Will wee strow upon it;
      Though our sweets cannot make
      It sweeter, they can take
Themselves new sweetnesse from it.
      Maria, Men and Angels sing,
      Maria, Mother of our King.

Thus the celebration has achieved its climax. After a short pause, the poem then quietly modulates into its final movement, where, with full serenity, the speaker expresses his faith that Heaven and Earth are still united in the praise and presence of Mary, despite her bodily removal to Heaven. First, the poet speaks in stately, elegant pentameters, and lastly, in direct and simple four-foot lines, with an effect of intellectual poise and control:

Live, Rosie Princesse, live, and may the bright
Crowne of a most incomparable light
Embrace thy radiant browes: O may the best
Of everlasting joyes bath thy white brest.
      Live our chaste love, the holy mirth
      Of heav'n, the Humble pride of Earth.
      Live, crowne of women, Queen of men;
      Live Mistrisse of our Song; And when
      Our weake desires have done their best,
      Sweet Angels come, and sing the Rest.

The poem represents Crashaw's art of baroque celebration at its best, with its subtly shifting voices, varied repetitions, multiple perspectives, and modulating verse forms, all its variety held together under the artful control of the human speaker, whose simple language opens and concludes his hymn.

Crashaw died at Loreto in 1649, and Vaughan's inspiration ebbed away in the second part of *Silex Scintillans* in 1655; the great era of English devotional poetry thus ended with the coming of the Puritan Commonwealth. Devotional poetry flourished in England during a period of some fifty years, while the established church provided a way of resolving the religious issues of the time. It was a brief era in which all the currents of religious life, both continental and English, could meet and make a little stay. But the inner tensions of the time could not for long be tempered to the spirit of devotion. John Milton found that he could not complete his poem on the Passion, but had to wait until his strenuous, indomitable genius could find the larger forms in which his voice could master the war-ring issues of his day. (pp. 101-21)

Louis L. Martz, "The Action of the Self: Devotional Poetry in the Seventeenth Century," in Metaphysical Poetry, *Edward Arnold, 1970, pp. 101-122.*

A. J. Smith

[*In the following excerpt, Smith studies the prominent thematic motifs of Caroline love poetry written after 1631.*]

> We step and do not step into the same rivers; we are and are not.
>
> Heraclitus of Ephesus, Fragment 81

> Desire, and Love, are the same thing; save that by Desire, we always signifie the Absence of the Object; by Love, most commonly the Presence of the same. So also by Aversion, we signifie the Absence; and by Hate, the Presence of the Object . . . And because the constitution of a mans Body, is in continuall mutation; it is impossible that all the same things should always cause in him the same Appetites, and Aversions: much lesse can all men consent, in the Desire of almost any one and the same Object.

> But whatsoever is the object of any mans Appetite or Desire; that is it, which he for his part calleth *Good*: And the object of his Hate, and Aversion, *Evill*; And of his Contempt, *Vile* and *Inconsiderable*. For these words of Good, Evill, and Contemptible, are ever used with relation to the person that useth them: There being nothing simply and absolutely so; nor any common Rule of Good and Evil, to be taken from the nature of the objects themselves; but from the Person of the man
>
> Hobbes, *Leviathan* 1, 6

The love poetry written in England after Donne's death confirms the decadence of a long European tradition of lyric verse which did not outlast the seventeenth century. It is easy to picture the Caroline love poets cooing wittily round Court and Town while the serious issues of the day were contested elsewhere, whether in Westminster and the shires, or at Horton, Bemerton, and Little Gidding. Carew and Stanley may seem pitifully small fry as the heirs of Cavalcanti and Tasso, or as revellers in the wake of mighty causes. Yet this Stuart love poetry is not negligible. It has its own voice and character, and something quite distinctive to say; and its appraisal of love is shrewd enough to illustrate its times and a small area of general experience. No other European poets use their wit to pose the predicament of beings who see that their love is an appetite of nature, and yet yearn to find spiritual value in it.

By the 1640s European rhetoricians who had never heard of Donne were analysing wit and classifying witty poetry. A historian of ideas, had there been one, might have traced a long preoccupation with wit in the Italian Courts and Academies. Donne extended the scope of wit in a way which has no parallel outside Britain. An incidental interest of the British poets who wrote of love after 1633 is that they show us what he really stood for in his own time and place.

The mark of Caroline lyric poetry is its vividly articulated dramatic syntax:

> Go search the valleys; pluck up every rose,
> You'll find a scent, a blush of her in those;
> Fish, fish for pearl or coral, there you'll see
> How oriental all her colours be;
> Go, call the echoes to your aid, and cry
> Chloris! Chloris! for that's her name for
>   whom I die.
>
> Anon., 'Tell me, you wandering
>   spirits of the air'

The fluent immediacy with which the slight witty hyperbole is urged to excited life makes the rhetoric of Tudor song seem stately, as if earlier writers were more concerned to heighten the ceremonial blazon than to simulate impassioned thinking:

> Hark! did ye ever hear so sweet a singing?
>   They sing young Love to waken.
> The nymphs unto the woods their Queen are
>   bringing.
>   There was a note well taken!
> O good! O most divinely dittied!
> A Queen and song most excellently fitted.
>   I never saw a fairer,
>   I never heard a rarer.
> Then sung the nymphs and shepherds of Diana:
>   Long live fair Oriana.
>
> Thomas Hunt, 1601

Caroline love poetry does not move like this. Its particular impulse calls for subtlety in the formal management of quite complex syntactical units:

> What though I spend my hapless days
>   In finding entertainments out,
>   Careless of what I go about,
> Or seek my peace in skilful ways,
> Applying to my eyes new rays
> Of beauty, and another flame
> Unto my heart, my heart is still the same.
>
> Godolphin, 'To Chloris'

We feel the virtuosity of these taut dramatic modulations, which are yet so suavely subdued to the easy flow that gives the stanza the excitement of spontaneous self-discovery.

The unpredictable mental life of such writing as this shows us how far lyric poets have moved on from a rhetoric of celebration and lament. Donne and Jonson brought about a general advance in intellectual control, which even the poetic minnows display in their lucid exactness and restraint, and their resolved grasp of quite intricate ideas:

> Though poorer in desert I make
>   My selfe whilst I admyre,
> The fuell which from hope I take
>   I give to my desire.
>
> Godolphin, 'Song: Noe more unto my
>   thoughts appeare'

Often a lyric civilly flaunts its lineage in nice metaphysical discriminations:

Love, like that angel that shall call
　　Our bodies from the silent grave,
Unto one age doth raise us all,
　　None too much, none too little, have;
Nay, that the difference may be none,
He makes two, not alike, but one.
　　　　　Cartwright, 'To Chloe, who wished
　　　　　　　herself young enough for me'

The ironic play of wit gives the best of these Caroline poets an intellectual vitality which is quite unlike the ingenious hyperbolising of a Serafino d'Aquila, or a Gongora, in the way it tempers ardour with intelligence. Their wit keeps them wary of the prescribed professions of love, so that passion is always guarded by an awareness of the frailty of our commitments and our lives:

Celia: Then thus my willing armes I winde
　　　　About thee, and am so
　　Thy pris'ner; for my selfe I bind,
　　　　Untill I let thee goe.
Cleon: Happy that slave, whom the faire foe
　　　　Tyes in so soft a chaine.
Celia: Farre happier I, but that I know
　　　　Thou wilt breake loose againe.
Cleon: By thy immortall beauties never.
Celia: 　　Fraile as thy love's thine oath.
Cleon: Though beauties fade, my faith lasts ever.
Celia: 　　Time will destroy them both.
　　　　　Carew, 'A Pastorall Dialogue'

The writing gets its life from the way it challenges the accepted categories of love, as well as love poetry. A quite minor poet, such as Stanley, persistently undercuts his own praises on precise philosophical grounds:

Though when I lov'd thee thou wert fair,
　　Thou art no longer so;
Those glories all the pride they wear
　　Unto opinion owe
　　　　　　　'The Deposition'

The touch of a sceptical logic keeps poetic exuberance cool:

Beauties, like stars, in borrow'd lustre shine;
And 'twas my love that gave thee thine.

With quiet reasonableness the conceited argument turns back upon itself the old hyperbole that a woman is a star, proposing a more accurate relation between the terms of the comparison which draws the mind on to ponder the relativeness of beauty. There is a pungent economy of wit in the way a qualifying aside will transform the sense:

The flames that dwelt within thine eye
Do now, with mine, expire

The slight parenthesis demolishes the old troubadour account of the way love moves us, and gives poignancy to the lovers' assumption that their love is wholly relative to their state of desire. Stanley's diction frequently arrests us so, persuading us that a mind is coolly at work in the heat of the passion, and had better be attended to:

Since by thy scorn thou dost restore
The wealth my love bestow'd

That unexpected 'wealth' confirms the paradox, quietly

suggesting a more basic sense in which a lover's desire lends his mistress her attractive power.

Stanley's poems move by a riddling logic, and with contentious independence. 'The Idolater' draws support from a familiar strictness when it proposes that the worship of a mistress is idolatry; but then it leaves this old bogy behind in favour of the subtler argument that the true idolatry is to worship disdain in the shrine of love, which is what a man does when he continues to love a woman who rejects him. The petrarchan manner is ironically assumed, for the poem mocks the familiar complaint against a mistress's unkindness in a patronising display of solicitude, which shows the lover his fate and warns him off it by dethroning the lady:

Since thou (Love's votary before
Whilst he was kind) dost him no more,
But, in his shrine, Disdain adore,
Nor will this fire (the gods prepare
To punish scorn) that cruel Fair,
(Though now from flames exempted) spare

Stanley's analytic manner may be cultivated, but it is not all sham. His qualifications do sharpen the ironies, they have place in a structure of argument as well as witty spirit. The elaborate syntax controls a tense syllogistic movement, so delicately articulating the stages of consecutive reasoning that the pattern of the stanza itself points the wit.

The point of Stanley's logic is another matter. In this poem the logical processes are always subordinate to the smooth resolution of the syntax, which his elaborate discriminations do not threaten to disturb. The wit may be sceptical but it scarcely makes Donne's impact. It moves with elegant point and neat antithesis, and Stanley's cavilling relativism does not finally challenge the conventions of love. Donne looks outward to the way people actually behave, and his wit quite radically sifts the world about it; Stanley's poem simply re-orders the conventions of a game of love, inviting us to admire the neat dexterity of the performance.

Yet these Caroline love lyrics are more than mere jewels whose beauty is sufficient to itself. They resonate with the impulses of an imaginative engagement that goes beyond the play of conceit. A simple setting from natural life will quite disturbingly involve the senses in the spirit of the scene:

The Lark now leaves his watry Nest
　　And climbing, shakes his dewy Wings . . .
Awake, awake, the Morn will never rise,
　　Till she can dress her Beauty at your Eies.
　　　　　　　Davenant, 'Song'

Such devices persistently invite us to relate the promptings of desire to the vitality and decay of nature. In Habington's 'To Roses in the bosome of Castara' the lover supposes that his mistress's breasts are a nunnery, in which the flowers she places between them are virgin nuns, who will prosper there in saintly sweetness, exempt from the world's contagion, until they at last fade into a hallowed demise and find an appropriate monument in that marble place:

> In those white cloysters live secure
> From the rude blasts of wanton breath,
> Each houre more innocent and pure,
> Till you shall wither into death.

The slight conceited compliment, so delicately turned, plays out a drama of innocence and corruption in which the lover's part is uneasily ambiguous. Caught between desire and admiration, he fosters the mortal contagion which rages everywhere in the world while celebrating the one condition which can avert it. Her virgin innocence is sacred to him because it sustains the natural life which his own heat would blast; she hallows the flowers only while she remains impervious to her lover's persuasions. The lover's dilemma nicely brings out a self-frustrating contrariness in love itself as we experience it now. Herbert's 'Life' might be a response to such a use of natural innocence, turning on the frailty of gathered flowers as so many of these mid-century lyric poems do - 'they/By noone most cunningly did steal away/And withered in my hand'. The affinity here of two such different vocations at least shows us how deeply their own involvement in natural processes disturbed the seventeenth-century poets.

Townshend finds a different way of setting amorous desire against innocence when he makes his mistress's breasts at once a saving distraction, such as might have averted the Fall, and a temptation which would have served Satan's purpose better than the apple:

> Yett had hee ledd mee to thy brest,
> 　　That waye was best
> To have seduct mee from thy lipp.
> Those apples tempt mee most; They bee
> 　　Fruit of that Tree,
> 　　That made our first forefathers slipp.
> I dare not touch them least I dye
> The death thou threatnest with thyne Eye.
> 　　　　　　　　　　'Pure Simple Love'

In Caroline love poetry the Garden of Eden tends to replace the Golden Age and the state of nature as the condition of a sexual well-being we have lost. Lovelace's version of original innocence teasingly echoes Tasso's 'bell'età dell'oro':

> When cursed No stained no maid's bliss
> And all discourse was summed in Yes.
> 　　And naught forbad, but to forbid.
> Love, then unstinted, love did sip,
> And cherries plucked fresh from the lip,
> 　　On cheeks and roses free he fed;
> Lasses like autumn plums did drop,
> And lads indifferently did crop
> 　　A flower and a maidenhead.
> 　　　　　　　'Love made in the first age'

Carew's Elysium is simply a place where the frustrations of lovers are appeased, and our restrictive codes of sexual conduct do not hold:

> All things are lawfull there, that may delight
> Nature, or unrestrained Appetite.
> 　　　　　　　　'A Rapture,' 111-12

The Court love poets, are always ironically aware of their dilemma when they propose that unassuaged desire is at once the cause and the measure of our distance from bliss.

These slight love lyrics keep coming back to the frailty of our desires and our lives. Stanley's 'On a Violet in her Breast' involves the lover's senses in the dropping and revival of a flower, as if he feels that his own virility is subject to the same processes of revival and decay. The terms in which he praises the lady are understandably plaintive, assuming as they do that beauty must wilfully squander itself in the moment of its proud fruition:

> this violet, which before
> Hung sullenly her drooping head,
> As angry at the ground that bore
> The purple treasure which she spread

The examples of Herbert and Vaughan are there to remind us that there may be more than conceit in the discovery of moral tendencies in the processes of nature. 'She swells with pride . . . Yet weeps that dew which kissed her last.' The involvement of human lovers in the moral vitality of a flower gives peculiar irony to that imitative 'swell and turn' of the stanza which Saintsbury noted [in his *Minor Poets of the Caroline Period*], whose effect is a sudden rearing up from a dropping cadence:

> Doth smilingly erected grow,
> Transplanted to those hills of snow.

The prospect of that delicious transplantation finally and fatally distinguishes flower and lover. The purity which gives new life to the plant arouses his blasting lust.

Stanley's little poem is true to its time and place, not least because it has more in it than courtly hyperbole. Its particular character comes out if we put it by Marino's 'Fiori, stelle d'Aprile', which Praz says [in the *Modern Language Review*, 1925] 'supplied both motif and conceits for "On a Violet in her Breast" ':

> Fiori, stelle d'Aprile,
> Che'l vostro ciel terreno
> Cangiaste col bel seno,
> Or cangerete e qualitate e stile.
> Tra le nevi viveste,
> Di quel petto celeste.
> Non so giá se vivrete entro l'ardore
> Di questo acceso core.

Marino's elegant antithesis between the sustaining snows of her breast and the destructive fire of his ardent heart says something quite different about love, and simply belongs to another world.

Their concern for the processes of organic life leads seventeenth-century love poets to try human passions in a prospect of universal flux, and to disturb the intimacies of lovers with the witness of lust turned to dust by its own heat:

> *Castara*, see that dust, the sportive wind
> So wantons with.　'Tis happ'ly all you'le finde
> Left of some beauty: and how still it flies,
> To trouble, as it did in life, our eyes.
> 　　　　Habington, 'To *Castara*: Upon Beautie'

Carew sets off a woman's beauty against a whole cosmos in constant evanescence, which he depicts in vivid touches as a pageant of momentary splendours forever vanishing; and he typically discovers the universal condition in particular yearnings of sense:

Ask me no more whether doth stray,
The golden Atomes of the day

'A Song'

The fervent repetitions insistently question our standing in the universe, and the fixity of the universal order itself; as if the stars 'That downwarde fall in dead of night' are resplendent chiefly in their dying interruption of the dark. The haunting cosmic image, so casually thrown off, delicately hints that when she has accumulated all these transitory glories she herself will prove only another such beauty of a moment. Yet the recognition that beauty is an effect of transitoriness no more provokes metaphysical distress than it allows us to rest easy with a hyperbole of praise; nor does it open the old invitation to use our youth while we have it - 'Gather the rose of love.' Carew's exquisitely balanced phrasing finely weighs the loss with the glory:

Ask me no more where Jove bestowes,
When June is past, the fading rose:
For in your beauties orient deepe,
These flowers as in their causes, sleepe.

The parenthetical falling cadence isolates and lingers out that last main verb, as if to surprise us with the promise of so fine a dissolution; dying itself becomes not so much an end as a quiet turning back to the source of vitality and beauty, even a fresh recruitment of life.

A powerful myth of death and resurrection is conceitedly entertained without losing all its power to console. Carew wrote when Donne's celebration of dead innocence might well have been taken for literal truth. Yet in this poem we feel the poise of a mind that responds to quite opposite qualities in a woman's beauty, and keeps them both in play behind the rich lyric celebration, constantly trying the effect of the powers it appraises. The poem holds a fine balance between conflicting impulses, celebrating this life the more keenly for the impermanence of all our attachments of sense, and yet giving scope to the yearning for some absolute quality in the splendours we admire.

These poets understand what they take on when they commit themselves to love in a universe which may have no stability, and no meaning. Hall's 'An Epicurean Ode' lightly tries the assurance of a lover against the prospect of a chance world of flux, questioning love's absoluteness without subsiding into hedonism or despair:

Since that this thing we call the world
By chance on Atomes is begot,
Which though in dayly motions hurld
    Yet weary not,
    How doth it prove
Thou art so fair and I in Love?

The honour paid to beauty and love does not at all gainsay the possibility that we are 'but pasted up of Earth', and not cradled in the skies; indeed Hall is true to the Caroline mode in celebrating his love while questioning the very point and dignity of our existence, and nicely holding such opposite dispositions in balance.

The seventeenth-century English poets are certainly not alone in finding a metaphysical dilemma in love. Dante and the Florentine neoplatonists were at least as much

concerned as any later writers to discover some final value in a human attachment. Yet these Caroline songsters are haunted by a fear that the sexual impulse itself may negate or threaten love, as if lovers bring on change and death when they re-enact the concupiscence of Adam and Eve. They take love to be an affection of nature, which is subject to all the uncertainties of sense in a universe that does not favour us. The insecurity of lovers may be heightened by the alarms of the times, as it seems to be in Jordan's 'A Cavalier's Lullaby for his Mistress', which might serve for the Audenism of the 1640s:

Sweet!   sleep; lie still, my dear!
    Dangers be strangers
For ever, unto thy eye or ear

Invoking love's peace in the midst of war, the poet only localises the imperative attempt to find stability in a universe of unrest. The urgency of such writing is well accounted for by Hall's vision of a fugitive liaison, which his plea seeks to stabilise:

Romira, stay,
And run not thus like a young Roe away

'The Call'

In this poem too the lovers' first need is to find an assured place for their love in the midst of wars, and the perturbations wars arouse:

No enemie
Pursues thee (foolish girle) tis onely I,
    I'le keep off harms,
If thou'l be pleas'd to garrison mine arms;
    What dost thou fear
I'le turn a Traitour?

But their attempt only confirms the incongruity of love with our lapsed condition:

Here on this plain
Wee'l talk *Narcissus* to a flour again

Lying down on the grass to spin legends of 'Love Martyrs' they try all human beings may do to arrest their fate, while beyond them the sinking sun marks the hostility of time to lovers.

These poets buy at a price the imaginative detachment that allows them to invest with a strange beauty even a sense of our inability to master such accidents as love and death:

Pilgrime: Whose soile is this that such sweet Pasture yields?
            Or who art thou whose Foot
                stand never still?
            Or where am I?
Time: In love.
Pilgrime: His Lordship lies above.
Time: Yes and below, and round about
            Where in all sorts of flow'rs are
                growing
        Which as the early Spring puts out,
            Time fals as fast a mowing.
        Townshend, 'A Dialogue betwixt Time
                        and a Pilgrime'

Quite disturbingly evocative so far; yet all Townshend can

find to ease his dreamlike bewilderment at last is a trite choral praise of growing old together, which leaves us with the thought that they are happy whose threads Fate entwines as one 'and yet draws hers the longer'. This is a typical let-down, for few of these poems make much of the big questions they pose. Some Caroline love poets, caught between delight and unease, show no wish to do more with their conflicting urges than to hold them in nice equipoise, mellowing exhilaration with wistfulness as Herrick does, or striking a low-keyed witty poignancy which may have its own beauty:

> Go lovely Rose,
> Tell her that wastes her time and me
> Waller

Repeatedly some deeply felt self-frustration will be betrayed by a trivial resolution, or the plain evidence that the poet does not know what to make of his own insight. Stanley can manage no more with his revitalised violet than a conceited praise of the lady's breasts, as feeble in wit as in erotic vigour, whose snipsnap antithesis quite belies the rich suggestiveness of his earlier contemplation of the flower:

> Since thou from them dost borrow scent,
> And they to thee lend ornament.

Hall's peremptory summons to Romira leaves the lovers with nothing but a platitude to affirm when they have made their truce with time:

> Nay, thou maist prove
> That mans most Noble Passion is to Love.

Sentience dwindles to ingenuity, conceit remains conceit. Carew proposes no effective way in which a lady's eyes really might have the power to preserve the light of fallen stars, or her voice might incubate the song of the wintering nightingale; and he winds up his poem with the elaborate fancy that the phoenix itself flies to the lady's fragrant bosom to die. For all their promises, these poems finish up cleverly toying with love. Vaughan's early songs to his Amoret make a striking case in point. They are full of the hermetic ideas which would inform the myth of *Silex Scintillans* but here just work as conceits, limply sustaining the routine moves of the game:

> If Creatures then that have no sence,
> But the loose tye of influence,
> (Though fate, and time each day remove
> Those things that element their love)
> At such vast distance can agree,
> Why, Amoret, why should not wee.
> 'To Amoret gone from him'

We might ask how far these Caroline love poems show purposeful intelligence, or genuinely reason anything out at all. Few of them even seek to sustain an argument through the poem; frequently the sense is complete in the first stanza, and can only be elaborated or varied thereafter. The test case must be Stanley, a poet who repeatedly leaves us feeling that the poem has somehow slipped through our fingers and left no trace. He disputes, qualifies, sharply distinguishes; but little of substance emerges:

> Waters, plants, and stones know this:

> That they love; not what Love is.
> 'The Magnet'

There is a real distinction made here, but nothing in the poem turns on it and it leads nowhere; Stanley simply tips his cap to Donne. Repeatedly we catch the poet slipping away from a real revision of ideas about love to seize some adventitious excitement, which may be quite at odds with his argument:

> Let us twine like amorous trees,
> And like rivers melt in one.

The anatomising of passion quite abruptly gives way to a straight invitation to embrace; Stanley is imagining erotic play at this point, rather than resolving anything about love or marriage. He leaves us wondering if his movement of proof is really more than a clever gloss upon the persuasion to love, or whether the apparatus of his logic itself may be simply too mechanical to hold what he really wants to say. 'The Tomb' quite starkly shows up the world of difference between Stanley's wit and Donne's:

> When, cruel fair one, I am slain
> By thy disdain,
> And, as a trophy of thy scorn
> To some old tomb am borne

The forceful speech-rhythms of 'The Apparition' are a long way from this. Donne's savage mockery has been dissipated in a chattering lyric neatness, a trite diction, and a mechanical chime. Where Donne cuts deep in his searching of erotic life, Stanley's verse slips easily along without resisting the mind because it is not effectively engaged with sexual behaviour at all.

The show of intellectual bravura may be challenging but it is really an effect of art, a clever deployment of the processes of logic rather than purposeful thinking. Stanley

Portrait of Andrew Marvell.

would have scorned comparison with Cleveland, whose verse gets its life from a knock-about ingenuity:

> Since 'tis my Doom, Love's under-Shreive,
>   Why this Repreive?
> Why doth my She-Advowson flie
>   Incumbency?

Yet the two poets only play different versions of the old game of conceited wit, which leads nowhere and says nothing new of love. Stanley studiously maintains his witty argument at the level of an urbane performance, cultivating a civilised anonymity and an impersonal intellectual grace. He may well have felt a need to do more than this, for his writing often displays a quality of mind and force of imagination such as have little scope in these neat witty movements. We might judge him to be reducing vital issues to the small compass of his art rather than simply playing with the common counters of petrarchism, as his Italian counterparts do. Nonetheless the outcome is a highly refined feat of poetic equilibrium, which preserves its fine composure by determinedly fencing out such forces of life as it cannot easily assimilate or order. It seems a trivial art by definition.

Not all mid-seventeenth-century love poets so resolutely set themselves to perfect an art of wit, and to admit only as much of living experience as might be controlled and impersonalised within its terms. Yet the writing of even the best of them often stirs with disquiets which seem to find no adequate focus in the categories of amorous poetry. Vaughan was only one poet who came to think that a commitment to sexual love is enough in itself to insulate poets from the truth of their condition. Nevertheless Dante, Petrarch, and Michelangelo had admitted all the universe to their love poetry, and even made love a way to final reality. After Donne the love of another human being turns back upon itself, and the poets who write of love are caught up in a different kind of activity from that of the poets who struggle to bring home to themselves their own desperate need of grace, or solitarily face up to a degenerating creation. In mid-seventeenth-century Britain sexual love had become categorically distinct from the love that moves the sun and the other stars. A choice now compelled itself between a fashionable amorousness and the imperative search for truth.

If Caroline poetry was a backwater, that need not be because the poets were reactionaries who followed the King in wanting to do without politics altogether, as Miss C. V. Wedgwood argued. It seems that sexual love no longer offered a proving-ground for the issues which really confronted people. The roll-call of poets who had some part in the civic events of the 1640s is impressive enough: Lovelace, Montrose, Newcastle, Godolphin, Davenant, Waller. Yet their work seems curiously remote from their public career. No doubt some of them were not much more than 'gentlemen who wrote with ease' [Alexander Pope, *The First Epistle of the Second Book of Horace Imitated*]. Love was the courtly fashion, as ever; and there are Caroline wits enough who stand at the fag end of the long tradition of court jongleurs, still plying the old prescriptions of lyric love long after they were played out.

Yet Carew, and Suckling, and Rochester later, are not like their courtly forebears in England or in Europe. The special character of their work reflects a distinctive understanding of our nature; and the distance between them and the Tudor songwriters may be a real index of change. The best of these Stuart love poets show us that something quite drastic was happening to society and sexual manners in seventeenth-century England. Their feeling for the life of their own time and place is sharp enough to make the comparison with earlier love poetry illuminating. They mark a decisive shift in attitudes to love over the century that followed Queen Elizabeth's death, and the shift partly defines us too.

Their poetry witnesses the temper of its own society vividly enough. It seeks strong erotic excitements, celebrating a lady's beauty by figuring the poet's wish to undress her as she walks before him (Suckling, 'Upon my Lady Carlile's walking in Hampton Court Garden'), and finding a dozen ingeniously indirect ways of fancying a mistress's pudenda, or relishing acts of penetration. We are invited to savour the special allure of a lady not yet enjoyed by her husband, of a mistress who is being bled by the surgeons, of plump beauty, of beauty in rags or in chains:

> But if too rough, too hard they presse,
> Oh they but closely, closely kisse.
>   Lovelace, 'A Guiltlesse Lady imprisoned;
>   after penanced'

Carew makes no bones about the motives of lovers when he resolves the argument for singleness in love with the image of a wolf which starves because it cannot decide between two sheep before it ('Incommunicabilitie of Love'). But if these poets assume that love is a concentrating of appetite they well understand how social life must inhibit the predator's scope; and much of their art goes in refining erotic provocation, or tricking out desire:

> and with amorous Charmes
> Mixt with thie flood of Frozen snowe
> In Crimson streames Ile force the redd Sea
>   flowe.
>   Carew, 'On the Green Sickness'

The focus of such displays of a decadent sensibility is not in question. This image of the penetration of a virgin occurs in a celebration of England as a new Paphos where 'Whatever pleaseth lawfull is' (Carew, 'To the Queene'), and Henrietta Maria queens it over a Court of Love. 'S'egli piace è lice', as Tasso wrote, but the indulgent law holds here only for that improved Golden Age which is the Queen's decorous economy of love. The new style of Court hyperbole extols the Queen's power to order the wild lusts unleashed by the King's godlike virility; and the new version of chivalry values a woman's capacity to hold a man by concentrating his errant fancies:

> He, only can wilde lust provoke,
> Thou, those impurer flames canst choke;
> And where he scatters looser fires,
> Thou turn'st them into chast desires . . .
> Which makes the rude Male satisfied
> With one faire Female by his side
>   Carew, 'To the Queene'

Just such a civilising harmony of sexual powers is figured in Carew's Court masque *Coelum Britannicum*, which elaborately enlarges chivalric ceremony into a universal play of virile energies, so that knightly valour becomes sexual puissance, and beauty is the power to satisfy it:

> Pace forth thou mighty British Hercules,
> With thy choyce band, for onely thou, and these,
> May revell here, in Loves Hesperides.

So nice a fusion of Tasso and Donne, with its Jonsonian refinement of texture, suggests that Carew does not feel called upon to innovate in such work. The writing is distinguished from earlier love poetry, as from the classical poems Carew reworked, by the way it expresses a particular society. Charles's Court was not like the great Renaissance Courts. It had its own myth of state and its own style, which the Queen's school of love helped to confirm. In particular it seems to have settled for a naturalistic understanding of sexual behaviour which Donne had worked out privately in his verse, as though Donne's example lent authority to that newly congenial way of understanding our own nature. No doubt Donne spoke for his time, and people fastened on him because he showed them to themselves. Certainly there could have been no place for a Spenser or a Sidney in a court whose elaborate rituals of love are styled by their celebrants platonic, though they proceed on assumptions as ironically remote from Plato's as from the transcendentalism of Dante and Ficino. This Caroline love poetry has more of the spirit of Horner than Diotima in it. Times have moved on when a quiet country parson can turn Jonson's sensuous mythologising to cheerful erotic fantasy—

> I dream'd this mortal part of mine
> Was Metamorphoz'd to a Vine;
> Which crawling one and every way
> Enthrall'd my dainty Lucia
>
> Herrick, 'The Vine'

-or when the distinguished translator of a prime text of neoplatonic love emerges in his own poetry as a thoroughgoing relativist, who locates a woman's beauty in her power to arouse male desire.

The new understanding of love gets such coherence as it has from its realisation of the manners of a close social circle, in which an ethic of honour and style makes a brilliant ritual of the natural urge to satisfy desire. The favoured conceits of this court coterie tend to set in play a few basic motives which may be checked in their scope by each other, but are chiefly regulated by the fact that they cannot be realised outside civilised society; so that sexual prowess must be reconciled with the requirements of good manners, and the satisfactions which civil life itself offers. None of these motives operates simply, for the assumption that our nature is common to our kind, and that human beings are alike in their desires and appetites, undercuts both social rank and the conventions that prescribe women's conduct. The rivalry between women and men becomes at bottom a struggle for advantage in which both parties desire like ends, and either sex has a power the other envies. A woman's attractions and fame only mirror men's desire for her, which they seek to satisfy when they celebrate her. Carew candidly undertakes to praise a lady on condition that she give herself to him for their mutual pleasure; he will spend his treasure if she will unlock hers - 'so we each other blesse' ('To a lady that desired I would love her'). Waller's 'The Story of Phoebus and Daphne, Applied' is a mythic embroidering of this bargaining game, which falls so flaccidly at last because it finds an easy way out:

> He catched at love, and filled his arms with bays.

In this poem the struggle between lover and mistress comes down to a simple trial between desire and chastity; and the fame that accrues to both of them is just the unlooked-for product of the lover's poetical pursuit, which he contemplates with equal self-satisfaction.

Carew's poetry in particular mythologises a civil order which is founded in the mutual accommodation of natural drives:

> Plant in their Martiall hands, Warr's seat,
>   Your peacefull pledges of warme snow,
> And, if a speaking touch, repeat
>   In Loves knowne language, tales of woe;
> Say, in soft whispers of the Palme,
>   As Eyes shoot darts, so Lips shed Balme.
> For though you seeme like Captives, led
>   In triumph by the Foe away,
> Yet on the Conqu'rers necke you tread,
>   And the fierce Victor proves your prey.
> What heart is then secure from you,
> That can, though vanquish'd, yet subdue?
>
> *Coelum Britannicum*, 1036-47

Such a nice equipoise of conflicting impulses is precariously regulated by wit, which is all that may give men and women mastery over themselves or the civic jungle. The drastic naturalism of a Donne and a Jonson impels the moves of a coterie game.

In the 1630s this was the Court game of love. The writings of Carew, and Suckling, and Lovelace, always keep us aware of their close society and the strains it imposes, which are outwardly domesticated in urbane manners. 'If it pleases it is lawful' pulls against 'If it is lawful then it will please.' The draconian regimen of a Virgin Queen has long been left behind. A highly guarded ritual of bargaining for advantage follows out the presumption that we are all moved by like natural impulses, which require at once outlet and regulation. A woman's celebrity now depends upon her power to excite, and accrues to her as the reward of her skill in exploiting a man's desire without denying it.

The refined preoccupations of a self-centred Court limit poetic art to a witty image of the manners of a coterie, whose first concern is to bring its more disruptive urges into urbane control. Style is one way by which a man may assert his self-possession, as we see by the common affectation of elegant rakishness, and the deriding of impassioned servitude in favour of a cool detachment. Yet style will not resolve a real clash of interests. Carew is a superior artist because he admits contrary impulses to his poems and holds them in tense balance, when his associates are happy to fall back upon cliches of sentiment or party loyalties.

Carew's best lyrics invoke familiar attitudes only to confound them totally:

> Then shalt thou weepe, entreat, complaine
> To Love, as I did once to thee
>   'Song: To my inconstant Mistris.'

'To my inconstant Mistris' promises a revenge, not because the suitor has been spurned in his attempt upon invincible chastity, but because his mistress has been unfaithful to her established lover. The poem assumes that she was once obdurate, yielded, swore oaths of fidelity to her lover, and then betrayed him; so that it is he who now rejects her for the promise of a surer bliss with another mistress, 'Which my strong faith shall purchase me'. The confrontation of lover and mistress is no trial of high principles but a comedy of social intrigue, in which faithful sentiment counters errant appetite.

Carew's wit is sharp and subtle, but it cuts nothing like so deep as Donne's. Carew is sceptical and relative only far enough to quicken the spirit of a song, for his poems do not commit the lover to the jungle they evoke, in which momentary appetites masquerade under the styles of morality. They find an accommodation with contrarious circumstance, and their measured coolness tempers the clashing motives into mannerly composure. 'Ingratefull beauty threatned' redresses old odds by trying the real balance of power between a lover and his mistress, weighing her pride against his capacity to give her beauty its fame, and urging that her fatal attractions are nothing without her lover's response to them:

> That killing power is none of thine,
>   I gave it to thy voyce, and eyes:
> Thy sweets, thy graces, all are mine

The manner of amused condescension is beautifully created; and the point has substance. To argue that her attractions would not have any power but for the fame which he has given her is to do a little more than wittily play for advantage, or deny the mystery of love:

> Thou art my starre, shin'st in my skies

The suave possessive pronoun marks the distance between Carew and those idealising poets for whom the lady is truly a star - 'Un'alta stella di nova bellezza/che del sol ci to' l'ombra la sua luce' (Dino Frescobaldi, c. 1300). It suggests that the beauty we attribute to a woman is partly a projection of our own desire for her, and partly a reflection of the celebrity we give her; she is distinguished not by her inherent beauty of spirit but by the heat she kindles in her lovers.

Carew devastatingly puts down presumptuous beauty by reminding her that what really distinguishes her from the common herd is not her inherent quality at all:

> Thou hadst, in the forgotten crowd
>   Of common beauties, liv'd unknowne

His unruffled sanity mocks the excesses of lovers with its insistence that love is no more than an accommodation of our sexual urges to the needs of civil life. We feel his intelligence in his exact discrimination of words and phrasing, his nice articulation of a quite complex vision of civil manners, the deflating play of his scepticism upon any extreme claim. If his poems do not move with Donne's unpredictable force they nonetheless create their own poise, offering

the civilised pleasure of disharmony resolved, disproportion redressed. The precise patterning of 'To my inconstant Mistris' has moral symmetry in itself in the way it works out opposite fates from contrary causes; though the activity of mind is of a different order from the suddenness which startles us in 'Womans Constancy'. Carew's elegant mode of wit does not call for shock or richly charged diction; he aims for coolheaded lucidity, and the balanced articulation of his reasoning realises an order in which justice is exactly achieved:

> If the quick spirits in your eye
> Now languish, and anon must dye;
> If every sweet, and every grace,
> Must fly from that forsaken face:
>   Then (Celia) let us reape our joyes,
>   E're time such goodly fruit destroyes.
>
> Or, if that golden fleece must grow
> For ever, free from aged snow;
> If those bright Suns must know no shade,
> Nor your fresh beauties ever fade:
> Then feare not (Celia) to bestow,
> What still being gather'd, still must grow.
>   Thus, either Time his Sickle brings
>   In vaine, or else in vaine his wings.
>   'Song: Perswasions to enjoy'

His lyrics typically advance by producing a like sanction from opposite causes, or by challenging some orthodox pose of love and then sharply drawing out the consequences either way, so as to open his adversary to the exact finishing stroke. This power to make a drama of a complicated chain of argument does give his stanzas the feel of spontaneous reasoning; though they move to complete a pattern rather than to search out shocking truth.

Carew's wit realises itself through his mastery of a rhetoric, that elegant yet subtle modulation of the sense across the elaborate stanza pattern. We feel the fine temper of his mind in his infinitely delicate counterposing of ideas, nice control of tone and nuance, subtle varying of the tension between syntax and formal pattern so as to point, edge, inflect. Such finished artistry plainly did not flow; much of the 'trouble and pain' Suckling twitted him with in 'A Session of the Poets' must have gone to suggest an intelligence in tight self-control, so that each stanza seems to unfold the resolved order of a complex thought which is held whole and taut in the mind. There is a civilising spirit akin to Marvell's at work in the cool suppleness of the poise, the weighing of opposite possibilities, the colloquial ease which yet preserves the ardour of song.

Suckling himself was a hedonist who scorned such artistic pains, yet saw as clearly as Rochester what scope love now offered its more drastic devotees. His poetry endorses a life centred in a style, which tempers the zeal for pleasure with a lively scepticism. Love is a flame, which rarely burns just at the right height but 'would die, Held down or up too high' ('Song: No, no, fair heretic'); or it is a clock that strikes 'Strange blisses/And what you like best' at quite unpredictable moments ('That none beguiled be'). The precariousness of these blisses only confirms the arbitrariness of attachments which are founded in the need to satisfy involuntary appetite, or fancy:

> I am confirm'd a woman can
> Love this, or that, or any other man
> > 'Verses'

In Suckling's poetry love always disappoints, for the reality never can come up to the imagined expectation. Women may keep their hold on men only by holding off fulfilment:

> Fruition adds no new wealth, but destroys,
> And while it pleaseth much the palate, cloys
> 'Against Fruition'

A man will free himself of his bondage to women just by putting down rebellious flesh:

> A quick corse, methinks, I spy
> In ev'ry woman . . .
> They mortify, not heighten me
> > 'Farewell to Love'

Lovers operate in an area of total uncertainty where will is at the mercy of chance and occasion, as well as vanity pretending to be scruple - 'I hate a fool that starves her love/Only to feed her pride' (''Tis now, since I sate down before'). They are fools of their own appetites:

> For thou and I, like clocks, are wound
> Up to the height, and must move round
> > 'To His Rival'

The writing quite pointedly suggests that the hazards of love only instance the uncertainties of our lives altogether in the arbitrary universe we inhabit.

Love in Suckling's poetry, as it never becomes in Donne's, is a predatory sport which we indulge because we can find no better way of fulfilling our nature. But he is no mere cynical seducer. His poems define a social activity, and their self-mocking manner prescribes men's attitudes to women in polite society, unsentimentally intimating the kind of bargains they must make with themselves as well as their desirable adversaries - 'I offer'd forty crowns/To lie with her a night or so . . . ' ('Proffer'd Love Rejected'). While Milton was meditating the apotheosis of artificial style, 'natural easy Suckling' sought a way of refining in lyric verse the casual civility of coffee house and salon:

> I prithee spare me, gentle boy,
> Press me no more for that slight toy,
> That foolish trifle of an heart

Suckling's affectation of negligent indifference to love, his bland mockery of his former follies, proclaim that he is his own man and not the humiliated slave of a woman or his importunate senses:

> Then hang me, ladies, at your door,
> If e'er I dote upon you more.
> > 'Verses: I am confirm'd a woman can'

Love must be kept in its place among the affairs of a man of the world and the Town:

> When I am hungry, I do eat,
> And cut no fingers 'stead of meat . . .
> I visit, talk, do business, play,
> And for a need laugh out a day
> > 'The Careless Lover'

The studied elegance serves to distinguish a gentleman

from 'th'unhallow'd sort of men' ('Against Fruition'), however little difference there may be in their sexual natures, and their fallen condition. This Caroline mode makes a gentlemanly ritual of conviviality, coupling love with tippling as if we show our mettle in the style of our pleasures.

A witty style at least gave an opening to intelligence, as Johnson observed of the metaphysical poets; and in Charles's court the wit that served to heighten erotic excitements soon turned to question its own ends. Lovelace was a bold poetical voluptuary, who nonetheless sought in poetry a way of posing choices which seemed to confront loyal gentlemen in the 1630s and 1640s. He wittily sets against each other the claims on a man's devotion, settling the conflict of loyalties with a flourish which cannot be gainsaid:

> I could not love thee (Deare) so much,
> Lov'd I not Honour more.
> > 'Song: To Lucasta, Going to the Warres'

Love or arms, the boudoir or the camp? The old dilemma is quite succinctly pointed, even if the appeal to honour seems little more than a generous vaunt. Lovelace does not show how his honour may genuinely reconcile the rival modes of manliness; he simply makes a profession which will placate both sides, flaunts the talisman that all must approve.

Lovelace's liveliest love poems characteristically invite us to ponder a wittily posed debate between conflicting loyalties. 'To Althea, From Prison' ('When Love, with unconfined wings') paradoxically opts for physical captivity rather than the bondage of love, because confinement in a just interest is the only freedom worth having:

> When flowing cups run swiftly round
> > With no allaying Thames,
> Our careless heads with roses bound,
> > Our hearts with loyal flames;
> When thirsty grief in wine we steep,
> > When healths and draughts go free,
> Fishes, that tipple in the deep,
> > Know no such liberty.

But then honourable love itself becomes a liberating constraint when it confirms a man's allegiance to a cause which is distinguished by its gallant style. Love, loyal pledges, devotion to the King, freedom, are the unimpeachable articles of Lovelace's chivalric creed, and he can do little more than declaim them with spirit while keeping up the show of proving them, as if our intelligence really might have something to work upon. All the poem really yields us is a lively image of its times, albeit warmed by that generous assurance of devotion.

The brittleness of a faith founded in loyal enthusiasm shows up in a poem which does try to face hard circumstances, 'To Lucasta, From Prison'. This time Lovelace soon slips aside from his witty play upon the several modes of bondage to ask himself seriously what freedom of soul is now possible. He uses the momentary liberty imprisonment gives him to try his loving allegiance around the various causes which offered for it in the late 1640s, rejecting each claimant in turn as unworthy, or no longer accessible in the circumstances: peace, war, religion, Parliament, liberty, property, political reform, the public faith. At last he falls back on the one absolute loyalty:

> What then remains but th'only spring
> Of all our loves and joyes? The KING

Yet he celebrates the King's power and right very forlornly when he sees that 'now an universall mist/Of Error is spread or'e each breast'; and the poem finishes with a bewildered plea to the King—or it might be God - for light to see 'How to serve you, and you trust me'. The cavalier temper at the limit of its resource looks to personal loyalty in a way which gives weight to Miss Wedgwood's claim that the political irrelevance of these poets shows us why the King's cause was bound to fail. With the King gone too, the mist would soon envelop Lovelace and his kind.

Lovelace miserably endured the ruin of his cause, and his poems offer evidence enough of the way the Court culture crumbled under the stress of civil war. Carew died just before war broke out; and Suckling fled to France in 1641 after failing to rescue Strafford, only to die by his own hand, or by horrible accident, a year later. Vaughan's abandonment of his Amoret in pursuit of lost innocence and countries beyond the stars, his sudden persuasion that a man could do no more in the impending cataclysm than seek to save himself, measures the shock Royalists sustained by the events of 1648-9; and we see how little love poetry mattered to them then.

When the Cavalier voice makes itself heard again there is a difference:

> I have been in love, and in debt, and in drink,
> This many and many a year

Booze, women, and debt: this is Brome, comically hitting off a character (he calls the poem 'The Mad Lover'), in which vein he is readily represented as the voice of a fagged out Royalism. Rochester confirms the altered style:

> While each brave *Greek* embrac'd his Punk,
> Lull'd her asleep, and then grew drunk.
>   'Grecian Kindness: A Song'

The heroic struggle for Troy finishes up in the common human solaces, cynically coarsened by the diction.

Brome in one way, as Rochester in another, does reveal the poverty of love poets as the seventeenth century wore on. On the continent love dwindles to a clever-pretty arcadianism; in England people are still desperately trying to say something real, and saying something desperate. To write of love at all was to search for something stable to hold on to, some vestige of the humane culture of the Renaissance Courts. Christopher Hill argues that the Stuarts precipitated a flight of Court gentry to their country estates. For this or whatever reason, the poetry often looks to country patrons and rural activities. Ben Jonson's celebrations of the great country houses propose a version of civil culture, just as Fanshawe's famous ode of 1630 glorifies the attempt to order English society about the great country properties:

> Beleeve me Ladies you will finde
> In that sweet life, more solid joyes,

> More true contentment to the minde,
> Than all Town-toyes.
> *An Ode Upon . . . His Majesties Proclamation . . .*
> *Commanding the Gentry to reside upon their*
>   *Estates in the Country*

This is the contentment of innocence, which shows up the guilty discontents of political life:

> 'Tis innocence in the sweet blood
> Of Cherryes, Apricocks and Plummes
>   To be imbru'd.

Here, while fortune lasted, was a prospect of Eden to hold on to. The choice between country retirement and an involvement in affairs became a moral dilemma. The love poets who wrote after the war suggest, however exaggeratedly, that there was a social crisis here too in the dwindling of the satisfactions of civil life to the point where sex and style preoccupied their art. They seek in sexual pleasure something that will give life a savour when the order which sustained poetic love is dissolving about them. Love poetry no longer rehearses a metaphysical quest, or a moral trial, but dwindles to the chronicle of a coterie pursuit, a ritual of search and momentary satisfactions centred on St James, Covent Garden, and 'the Fields of Lincolns Inn'.

The love poetry that follows the Restoration offers a changed style of love. Etherege, Sedley, and Buckhurst are not so much urbane as knowing, not detached but eagerly ribald. The fine composure is lost, and there seems nothing but the chase and its outcome to order men's manners:

> Cuffley! whose beauty warms the age,
> And fills our youth with love and rage,
> Who like fierce wolves pursue the game,
> While secretly the lecherous dame
> With some choice gallant takes her flight
> And in a corner fucks all night.
>   Etherege, 'Mr Etherege's Answer'

These lyrics and verse letters of the Restoration rakes shift the focus of fashionable fellowship to the Town, ousting Court manners in favour of sexual adventury in the Holborn streets. They are witty chiefly in the way they temper a lively engagement in the sport with sharp self-appraisal, and a devastating candour about sexual motives:

> Against the Charmes our *Ballocks* have,
> How weak all humane skill is?
> Since they can make a *Man* a *Slave*,
> To such a *Bitch* as *Phillis*.
>   Rochester, 'Song'

The put down could scarcely be deadlier, or funnier. Love, already made contingent upon whim by the conceit that beauty is the lover's gift, comes down at last to the genital urge which draws us to a woman in spite of ourselves and her sheer disagreeableness. Far from preserving our independence, the new naturalism makes us abject slaves of our own cravings.

In these poems the wanton vagaries of our common nature mock social rank:

> Thus she who Princes had deny'd,
> With all their Pomp and Train,

> Was, in the lucky Minute try'd,
>   And yielded to a Swain.
>   Rochester, 'A Song: As *Cloris*
>   full of harmless thoughts'

Fidelity is a sin against nature:

> 'Tis not that I'm weary grown
> Of being yours, and yours alone:
> But with what Face can I incline,
> To damn you to be only mine?
>   Rochester, 'Upon his Leaving his Mistress'

The actuality of women's desires demolishes courtly myth:

> That much she fears, (but more she loves,)
>   Her Vassal should undo her.
>   Rochester, 'To Corinna: A Song'

Pastoral idyll comes down to the sexual feats of Strephon, Phillis and Coridon under a tattered blanket in Lincoln's Inn Fields (Rochester, 'Song'), or to the undoing of Cloris in a pigsty:

> Now pierced is her Virgin Zone
>   She feels the Foe within it;
> She hears a broken amorous Groan,
> The panting Lover's fainting moan,
>   Just in the happy Minute.
>   Rochester, 'A Song: To Chloris'

A casual scepticism, following out Donne to the candid limit, collapses the entire metaphysic of beauty:

> This shows Love's chiefest magic lies
> In women's cunts, not in their eyes
>   Etherege, 'Mr Etherege's Answer'

Such verses spiritedly and derisively define their little world. They ritualise the manners of a coterie, and are themselves coterie performances, like tippling, which keep up the fellowship of the game. Drinking, drabbing, and gaming, so wittily turned into art of a kind, impose their own terms on poets who seek no other recourse than stylish wit to give them some mastery over chance and their own nature.

When the local style of young English aristocrats sets the poetic mode, and the pastimes of moneyed youth come to determine the moral temper of art, then nobility itself has shifted its value. 'Al cor gentil ripara sempre amore.' The noble idealism of a Guinizelli or a Sidney is no longer in sight, and the sport of the Town becomes a faith. Love poets no more expect the attachments of sex to carry their minds beyond the world of sense than they search a woman's beauty for a ray of the Divine Essence, or take women themselves for miracle-working stars. The very idea that the lover may progress up a scale of qualities towards a realm of pure spirit loses its meaning in a universe ordered by quantitative laws, in which love is a mere glow upon the blind biological urge.

Neoplatonism has gone out of the window with pseudo-Dionysius, and taken with it the assumption that sense and spirit pull in opposite directions. The metaphysical pretensions of love poetry have quietly lost their credit, and Rochester, Etherege, Sedley, Buckhurst and their peers are left to seek such assurance as they may find in

sexual prowess carried off with verve, the dregs of chivalric errantry. If the young bloods and rakes now take over love poetry this is no mere modish annexation but a mark of what love has come to mean, and perhaps even a portent of what life no longer means. When we next encounter a considerable body of love poetry in English it will be more notable for feeling than for intellectual grasp.

The Restoration wits decisively brought love down to earth when they made a way of life of the hunt for sexual satisfaction, and allowed men only the release of a dwindling into sentiment and marriage. They found no need to look beyond nature for the cause of a woman's power over men, and saw a jungle of natural appetites at work behind the artificial manners of polite society. Their cult of witty virility left them little but a ritual of manhood to hold on to when the chase lost its zest, and appetite palled. In their verses love itself becomes nothing more than a dulling debility of taste:

> Love a Women! you're an Ass
>   'Tis a most insipid Passion;
>   Rochester, 'Song'

Rochester took the ingenious pursuit of pleasure further than his fellows, and asked more of it. He is always struggling to wring a faith from our errant devotions:

> Lest once more wand'ring from that Heav'n,
>   I fall on some base heart unblest;
> Faithless to thee, False, unforgiv'n
>   And lose my Everlasting rest.
>   'A Song: Absent from thee I languish still'

> Let the Porter, and the Groom,
>   Things design'd for dirty Slaves,
> Drudge in fair Aurelia's Womb,
>   To get Supplies for Age and Graves.
>   'Song'

It is characteristic of him to imply a search for a saving grace when he turns in distaste from pleasures which so unbecomingly level gentleman with drudge, and prefers witty talk over a bottle instead.

Rochester's poetry shows an extreme determination to make love a mere puppet of sexual pleasure; yet it also expresses the anguish of an existence which is devoid of metaphysical sense, and racked by arbitrary discontents. Rochester confirms the proven shortcomings of our experience by his awareness of what life might be:

> How blest was the Created State
>   Of Man and Woman, e're they fell,
> Compar'd to our unhappy Fate,
>   We need not fear another hell!

'The Fall: A Song' follows Donne in ironically measuring our distance from the innocent state by our loss of sexual pleasure, and inadequate sexual performance:

> Naked, beneath cool Shades, they lay,
>   Enjoyment waited on Desire:
> Each Member did their Wills obey,
>   Nor could a Wish set Pleasure higher.

Our sad decline from this blissful condition becomes a symptom of a present existence in which the descendants of Adam and Eve are no more than 'poor Slaves to Hope and Fear', who can never have a secure hold on their joys:

> They lessen still as they draw near,
>   And none but dull Delights endure.

'The Fall' runs true to its age in its easy way of entertaining universal inquietudes. Yet Rochester's throwaway close is no mere drollery of wit:

> Then, Cloris, while I Duty pay,
>   The Nobler Tribute of my Heart,
> Be not You so severe to say,
>   You love me for a frailer Part.

The irony is disturbing as well as frank. She is to keep up the pretence of a sentimental loyalty, though they both know that the reality is frailer, because their illusion of satisfaction and permanence is all they may have to console them.

Rochester finds in sexual life a telling instance of the precariousness of our condition. He shares with his associates a dedication to the momentary bliss of union, but he will not profess their brave relish for the brevity of our attachments. His 'Love and Life' is no such offspring of Donne's naturalism as Suckling's 'No such constant Lover' or Etherege's 'To a Lady, Asking Him How Long He Would Love Her'. With the past already lost, and the future not yet his, then 'The present Moment's all my Lot', which he dedicates 'as fast as it is got' to his mistress. This fragile reassurance is as much as we may give or expect:

> Then talk not of Inconstancy,
>   False Hearts, and broken Vows:
> If I, by Miracle can be
> This live-long Minute true to thee,
>   'Tis all that Heav'n allows.

It scarcely seems ironic that an article of a rake's creed should so readily become a judgment of life, and even threaten our sense of identity and permanence. The poet must be taking his scepticism seriously when he discerns behind the relativeness of our assurances a universal condition which gives us no hold on our fleeting experience, or our own being. Like other poems of the day, 'Love and Life' brings home to us through love the little time we have, and the vanity of our striving for permanence. As earlier European lyrics, the song takes love to epitomise the life of sense, pointing the insecurity of our condition. What makes it distinctive and disturbing is Rochester's profession of a faith which has been won by miracle out of a chaos of change and delusion, yet still may never be sure of itself for more than the present moment. The poem quite poignantly sets off sceptical self-candour with yearning, and catches the dilemma of beings who cannot reconcile their rage for the immutable with the actuality of their state. There seems to be more in question than a tradition of love poetry when the present rapport becomes our only certitude, and frail sense governs our lives. The slight love lyric intimates that not only poetic love but a mind has come to the end of its resource.

Rochester writes of love as we find it now, at this stage of our degeneration from an original state of bliss. Yet he takes no account of sin or grace. The Fall he laments is no more than the loss of a golden age of love, which comes

home to a man most intimately in the untimely decline of his member, that humiliating evidence of the way our powers come short of our appetite and will. The part sex played in Adam's ruin gives him some warrant for this ribald limiting of the consequences of the Fall to the inadequacy of our sexual powers. But the paradox of Rochester's poetry is that it restricts life to secular experience, and even to present sensation, while sharpening our sense of the way in which we fall ever further short of what we might be. Rochester still looks to a falling away from that right state to account for the way life fails us, and to show us why our affairs never go as they might. Whether he is gambling with despair or simply seeking a faith he poses the dilemma of all these seventeenth-century love poets, who so often fail their own insights because love itself can no longer sustain what they want to make of it. In the compacts they make with their frail fellow-creatures they find neither coherence nor certitude. They never get beyond the self-frustrating sense that their own desire at once brings home to them and accounts for the way life disappoints us, offering us splendours which fade and fail, and promises which always fall short.

Seventeenth-century love poets differ from their predecessors in that they no longer find in love a choice between sense and spirit, or a proof that sense is inherently depraved and the sensible world a delusion. They assume that our degeneration from the created state will be made good not when we renounce or transcend our human capacities, but when we recover them and realise them fully. A yearning for lost innocence resonates through seventeenth-century lyric poetry, expressing itself most poignantly in praises of young girls, whose natural charms stir wistful guilt in the worldly admirer. Comparing girls with shortlived flowers is one way of confronting innocence with blasting lust; another way is to recall a harmless affection which has disturbingly matured into desire:

> Ah! Chloris! that I now could sit
>   As unconcerned as when
> Your infant beauty could beget
>   No pleasure, nor no pain.
>   Sedley, 'To Chloris'

Versions of the intimacies between a young girl and her older admirer range from the delicate to the perverse, from Bold's warnings of the power innocent beauty has over men ('Chloris, forbear a while') to Rochester's 'A Song of a Young Lady to her Ancient Lover'. They mingle celebration with regret in a curious manner of elegiac poignancy, as if our very hankering after innocence sadly confirms the fatal ambiguity of our state, reminding us that we cannot now love innocently.

The disjuncture of love which undoes Milton's Adam comes to seem too simply represented as a separation of sense from innocence. Seventeenth-century love poets do not even find themselves torn between their devotion to a woman and the love they owe to God; rather, they are caught in the fatal ambiguity of a condition which perverts their very yearning for the condition of the first lovers into impulses of corruption and death. Love offers scant moral choice to lovers who cannot alter their own condition, or disregard their own nature. For them, sexual love simply brings out the contradictoriness of the world and our present being when it leaves us so vulnerable to the opposite impulses we find in ourselves. To be conscious of that divided heart which Marvell spoke of ('A Dialogue between the Soul and Body') is to balance against each other the extreme claims the world makes upon us. The man who wishes to get on reasonable terms with life in the world has no alternative but to reach an accommodation with himself and his fellows, so that he may gain what he can without relinquishing too much:

> Mirabell: Well, have I liberty to offer conditions
> - that when you are dwindled into a wife, I may
> not be beyond measure enlarged into a husband?
> Congreve, *The Way of the World*,
> IV, 5, 206-8

In the seventeenth century few poets act in the faith that the love of another human being might have absolute spiritual worth, and fewer still take sexual love to be anything other than a natural affection, which shares the decay of nature since the Fall. Love quite intimately brings home to us our present condition at this stage of man's decline from the first state of nature, though it does not offer us a way of bettering it. Love poetry ceases to stage a moral drama and turns to lyric reflection, plangently drawing out the way things are with us, and pointing the irony of a craving which so disturbingly accompanies its expectations with the certainty of disillusion. It is a haunted art, because it sets off the promise of fulfilment against the sad actuality, and holds both states in prospect by way of making us more disquietingly aware how far love is prey to time.

The election that confronted these poets was nonetheless imperative. Their very awareness of what it means to be a creature of time, and need to understand what sin has wrought upon us as time runs on, effectively turned them away from the idealism they sometimes professed and committed them to sense. They looked to organic processes to show them how our circumstances distinguish us from the created life around us, tacitly acknowledging that all natural existence is subject to the same laws. Such differences as we may pose between sensible being and spiritual being are in any case less critical than the contrast between fallen and unfallen nature; and other creatures may not have wholly shared our own lapse. Reading the creation aright we may still glimpse the original state in the present decay. In the seventeenth century the effort to see things as they really are readily became a search for the condition of the Eden we have lost.

The question that oppressed categorical spirits was how men who acknowledge their distance from the just state may yet remain part of a corrupt social order at all. For them, the one choice which mattered was that between some sort of accommodation with the degenerating world, and abandonment of it, whether a man should make such terms as he might with his unregenerate self and his fellows, or commit himself wholly in the one cause that really matters. The heroic motive in seventeenth-century poetry was the lonely resolve to master our fallen condi-

tion so that a man might remake himself nearer the first state. After Donne, sexual love offered no way of furthering such a radical end as that. (pp. 221-53)

*A. J. Smith, " 'Among the Wastes of Time':
Seventeenth-Century Love Poetry, and the
Failure of Love," in his* The Metaphysics of
Love: Studies in Renaissance Love Poetry
from Dante to Milton, *Cambridge University
Press, 1985, pp. 221-53.*

Frances Austin

[*In the following essay, Austin provides a formal, stylistic analysis of metaphysical poetry by John Donne and Henry Vaughan.*]

Donne's best-known lyrics have been much analysed. His *Verse Letters* are less known and a passage from one of them has therefore been chosen for examination here. Between 1608 and her death in 1627 Donne wrote at least eight Verse Letters to Lucy, Countess of Bedford, patroness and friend to many of the best poets of the day. Most of these belong to the years 1609-14. The first five stanzas of 'To the Countess of Bedford at New Year's Tide' show many of the characteristics of Donne's writing. They combine the intimate and formal, as befits a poet addressing his patron:

> This twilight of two yeares, not past nor next,
>   Some embleme is of mee, or I of this,
> Who Meteor-like, of stuffe and forme perplext,
>   Whose *what*, and *where*, in disputation is,
>   If I should call mee *any thing*, should
>   misse.
>
> I summe the yeares, and mee, and finde mee not
>   Debtor to th'old, nor Creditor to th'new,
> That cannot say, My thankes I have forgot,
>   Nor trust I this with hopes, and yet
>   scarce true
>   This bravery is, since these times shew'd
>   mee you.
>
> In recompence I would show future times
>   What you were, and teach them to'urge
>   towards such,
> Verse embalmes vertue; and Tombs, or Thrones
>   of rimes,
>   Preserve fraile transitory fame, as much
>   As spice doth bodies from corrupt aires
>   touch.
>
> Mine are short-liv'd; the tincture of your name
>   Creates in them, but dissipates as fast
> New spirits; for, strong agents with the same
>   Force that doth warme and cherish, us
>   doe wast;
>   Kept hot with strong extracts, no bodies
>   last:
>
> So, my verse built of your just praise, might want
>   Reason and likelihood, the firmest Base,
> And made of miracle, now faith is scant,
>   Will vanish soone, and so possesse no
>   place,
>   And you, and it, too much grace might
>   disgrace.

Donne's syntax is at its most compressed and elliptical.

The vocabulary presents little difficulty although, because of the semiformal style of address (the formal pronoun *you* takes the place of the intimate *thou*, which Donne normally uses for lovers in *Songs and Sonets*), there is a sprinkling of words of Latin and French origin. Even so, native words outnumber them by about five to one and there are, as usual in Donne, whose lines of monosyllabic words.

The poet begins by drawing attention to himself as he stands poised between the 'two yeares'. This uncertainty about position is expressed by the typical Donne interrogatives: *what* and *where* in line 4. These come in a simile drawn from astronomy, a subject of topical interest. The simile is introduced by a compressed compound: *Meteor-like*. This links the two objects compared, the meteor and the poet, more closely than is usual in simile. In the second stanza the poet decides that he owes nothing to the past and can expect nothing of the future. A swift reversal is then introduced with the double conjunction *and yet*. In the final line and a half of the stanza he disclaims his assessment of the past year and shifts the focus from himself to the addressee: *since these times shew'd mee you*. The apparent awkwardness of two juxtaposed pronouns at the end of the line is typical of Donne. Not only does it foreground *you* by its end position and stress but also places poet and patroness in dramatic relationship.

The next stanzas consider the commemorative value of verse. A second simile, drawn from the custom of embalming, is followed by another of topical interest from alchemy. This contains the most detailed and extended analogy of the three similes and, like the others, it uses Romance and specifically Latin vocabulary. The fourth stanza says that the essence of his patroness's being is so strong that it may ultimately destroy the verse in which the poet seeks to preserve it, just as alchemical agents, if too powerful, burn and destroy the substance which they initially sustain. Hence, his verse, based on the miraculous in alchemy may, in this time of scepticism, vanish and so 'disgrace' the very graciousness that he is commemorating. The extract ends with this typical paradox, conveyed through the rhetorical figure of *polyptoton*, with the juxtaposition of *grace* and *disgrace*.

Obscurity rises from Donne's use of grammatical words, especially pro-forms. The grammatical words, usually thought 'empty', are essential to meaning in Donne's dialectic and give it its distinctive energy.

As is usual, personal pronouns do not function as pro-forms in most places. Initially first person singular pronouns dominate as the poet concentrates on his own condition. The subject form *I* is slightly less prominent (not numerically less) than the oblique *me*, because the grammatical subject is of less significance than the semantic subject indicated sometimes by *I* but more often by *me*. *Me* receives full stress twice, once in line 2 and again in line 6. Both instances come at mid-line before the caesura. *I* is stressed clearly only once in line 2 where it is chiastically balanced with *me*. The second person *you* is fully stressed at the end of the second stanza on its first appearance. This indicates the shift of focus. On its second occurrence, in line 12, it is unstressed, the emphasis here being on the essential nature of the Countess, which is conveyed

in the verb form *were*. The stressed position of the pronoun in the last line of the extract closes this transitional passage by drawing attention once more to the subject of the poem. An absolute use of the possessive pronoun *Mine* occurs in line 16 and there is an instance of *it* in the final line. Both pronouns refer deictically to the poet's verse, although *it* refers unambiguously to the word *verse* itself and *Mine* refers strictly to *Tombs, or Thrones of rimes* at the end of line 13, since it is followed by the plural verb *are*. *Verse* occurs at the beginning of the same line and is included in the meaning. In these two instances the personal pronouns are pro-forms and as such they add to the elliptical quality of the extract. Their reference is not immediately clear because they are in both cases some distance away from the noun for which they substitute.

Demonstrative pronouns functioning as pro-forms add further to the compression and difficulty of unravelling meaning. At the end of the second line the referent of *this* is not altogether clear. It could be 'This twilight of two years' and, indeed, that seems at first to make most sense, but the other possibility: 'Some embleme', is probably intended because of the chiastic construction of the line. In line 8 the initial *That* substitutes for *th'old*, itself an ellipsis for 'the old year'. *This* in the following line, meaning *the new*, similarly represents 'the new year'. Here adjectives unusually take on the function of pro-forms and this increases the range of Donne's elliptical forms. A similar usage comes in the first line, in which *past* and *next* also imply an entire nominal group. *Such* sometimes functions like a demonstrative. An instance occurs at the end of line 12. This is a good example of the pro-form *such* not used as part of a simile as so often it is. It refers back directly to the clause 'What you were'. All these instances of demonstrative pro-forms as well as *such* are in stressed positions. The resulting ellipses and the need to search back through the poem to find referents add to the semantic difficulty.

Little importance attaches to verbs functioning as pro-forms in this extract. Nor does it to lexically full forms of primary auxiliaries. Forms of the verb *be* are used sparingly. *Is* occurs twice in a stressed position but neither time does it greatly affect the meaning of the poem. The first instance, at the end of line 4, is further emphasized by inversion of the adverbial adjunct and verb. This, related to the notion of the poet's 'being', which he is questioning, has more significance than the second instance in line 10, although this also receives stress. *Were* in line 12 is more integrated into the meaning. It confirms the 'essential being' of the poet's patroness, the 'essence' with which he is concerned. Even though attention is further drawn to the verb by the reference of *such* at the end of the line, however, the emphasis is not as striking as it sometimes is in Donne's poems. Perhaps this is because the subject is not picked up in the stanzas immediately following. Only one auxiliary functioning as a pro-form occurs in this passage. At line 15 *doth* substitutes for the full verbal group 'doth preserve'. This is easily understood and is not stressed. In passing we may note the lexically empty *do* in *doe wast* in line 19. This is not an instance of emphatic *do* and is the one truly 'lexically empty' word in the extract.

The syntax of this extract includes both the normal English S V C order of statements that is typical of *Songs and Sonets* and the more complex clause structure of some of Donne's longer poems. Complexity in the first and last stanzas, with inversion, embedding and subordination, results in both cases in a clause complex that takes up the entire stanza. The fourth stanza, which is closely linked to the fifth by the conjunction *so*, also has some inversion and embedding. The other stanzas (two and three) have short co-ordinate clauses and are much simpler. Occasionally there is no conjunction and clauses are simply juxtaposed. There is no syntactic link between lines 10 and 11 after the change of direction in the final clause of the second stanza. The break is only syntactic, however: semantically the clause follows on with the initial phrase 'In recompense', a typical example of Donne's pursuing a train of thought through juxtaposed statements.

As might be expected, all three similes involve slightly longer and more complex clauses. The first, in the first stanza, is preceded by a resumptive *who*, which introduces a relative clause. This is then suspended until after the simile and a short embedded conditional clause. The stanza also includes much inversion and also chiasmus in the extremely compressed second line. *I of this* is elliptical not only by reason of the pro-form *this* but because the verb is omitted and has to be 'understood' from the preceding clause. The final stanza is complicated more by embedding than inversion. The main co-ordinate clauses run: 'So my verse . . . might want / Reason and likelihood . . . And . . . will vanish soon . . . And you, and it, too much grace might disgrace'. The only inversion comes in this final clause and complicates an otherwise straightforward but highly contrived rhetorical statement. In this clause the two conjoined complements *you* and *it* are thematic, and Donne thereby foregrounds his 'verse', the focus of the three preceding stanzas, as well as his patroness, the subject of the whole poem towards whom he will shortly direct the reader's attention.

Through alternation of complex and simple clause structure the syntax mirrors the various moods of the passage. The note of uncertainty in two of the stanzas is conveyed by inverted and embedded clauses, as well as by rhetorical figures. The statement 'now faith is scant' is indicative of the times in which Donne was writing. We might compare the confident assertion of Shakespeare when engaged on a similar exercise:

> Not marble nor the gilded monuments
> Of princes shall outlive this powerful rhyme,
> But you shall shine more bright in these contents
> Than unswept stone besmeared with sluttish
>   time.
> > (Sonnet 55, 1-4)

or:

> So long as men can breathe or eyes can see,
> So long lives this, and this gives life to thee.
> > (Sonnet 18, 13-14)

Shakespeare had no doubt about the durability of his verse—a theme common in classical poetry. Donne lived in an age when questioning had begun to take the place of assertion. This uncertainty shows in the texture of his

verse, which, like the image of the meteor, is almost always 'of stuff and form perplexed'. The ways in which Donne conveys his meaning through language are hallmarks of the metaphysical mode of writing.

The language of Vaughan's 'Unprofitablenes' differs in kind from that used in the extract from Donne. In contrast the meaning is immediately clear, even though it is conveyed throughout by metaphor:

> How rich, O Lord! how fresh thy visits are!
> 'Twas but Just now my bleak leaves hopeles
>   hung.
> > Sullyed with dust and mud;
> Each snarling blast shot through me, and did
>   share
> Their Youth, and beauty, Cold showres nipt,
>   and wrung
> > Their spiciness, and bloud;
> But since thou didst in one sweet glance survey
> Their sad decays, I flourish, and once more
> > Breath all perfumes, and spice;
> I smell a dew like *Myrrh*, and all the day
> Wear in my bosome a full Sun; such store
> > Hath one beame from thy Eys.
> But, ah, my God! what fruit hast thou of this?
> What one poor leaf did ever I yet fall
> > To wait upon thy wreath?
> Thus thou all day a thankless weed doest dress,
> And when th'hast done, a stench, or fog is all
> > The odour I bequeath.

The poem is in three parts: the speaker's condition before the intervention of God; his revival as a result of God's regenerative power; and finally his ultimate failure to yield any return to his Creator. The theme is typical of Vaughan. The final state, in which man fails to make a due return to his Creator, haunted his imagination. He asked for the following words to be engraved on his tombstone: *Servus inutilis: peccator maximus hic iaceo* ('A useless servant: here I, the greatest sinner, lie').

The metaphor of the plant—at times it seems to be a tree but at the end it is specifically called a 'weed'—is implicit rather than overt. Typically it is taken from the natural world. By extension through the whole poem it becomes a miniature allegory. It also has an emblematic quality, although it is not a static emblem such as would have been found in the preceding century. There is, too, an emblematic-type image: 'all the day / [I] Wear in my bosome a full Sun'. Without knowledge of the emblem tradition this seems a strange concept, incapable of apprehension or of being visualized. The extended metaphor of the plant makes for a consistency of texture and evenness that is often lacking in Vaughan's longer poems. Although this poem does not reach the heights of some of Vaughan's poetry, it never flags.

The syntax is straightforward. Typically, the poem opens with exclamations, although these are neither forceful nor abrupt. The movement of the verse is conversational, as often in Vaughan. The opening statement occupies the second and third lines. The pentameter followed by a three-stressed line creates a conversational tone, which makes initially for a leisurely pace. This is the longest clause in the poem. Subsequent clauses, although shorter, often run over lines and thus, with intervening short lines, reinforce the impression of speech.

In this poem it is vocabulary that enriches and deepens the meaning. Groups of words reflect Vaughan's main preoccupations. There are biblical echoes throughout. More obvious, however, are words taken from alchemy and hermeticism. Those which represent the divine spark or essence are *spice* and the derivative noun extended from the adjectival form, *spiciness*. Another is *dew* and, importantly, *Sun*, the source of life itself. *Glance* is also associated with the engendering essence and, by association, *beame* would seem to be drawn into the group. *Blood* is also associated with hermetic vocabulary. That these words cluster in the stanza in which the speaker experiences a revitalization is no accident.

Of greater semantic significance are the words drawn from nature. Vaughan uses three types of nature vocabulary, which he both conflates and juxtaposes. A combination of words may give a clear indication of which type predominates in any one place. In this poem two are used alternately and reflect the alteration in the speaker's condition. When he is in a state of original sin, the vocabulary is that of the ordinary natural world: *dust*; *mud*; *leaves*; *showers* and the evocation of wind in *snarling blast*. Once God has embraced man in his 'glance', however, the vocabulary changes. Nature words from the Bible appear: *perfumes*; *spice* and *Myrrh*, recalling the language of the *Song of Songs*. The mood changes again in the last six lines as the speaker contemplates once more his natural and unworthy state. The vocabulary, therefore, returns to that of the natural world of the opening. *Weed*; *stench* and *fog* are the only 'odour'—juxtaposition of the biblical-type word is deliberate—that he believes he can ultimately yield his Maker.

The types of word that are of most significance for the meaning of the poem, apart from the nouns already mentioned, are adjectives and verbs. Adjectives give the verse an immediate lift. In the first line both *rich* and *fresh* are heavily stressed. Adjectives, as has been pointed out, are relatively unusual in metaphysical poetry. Here, the use of *fresh* is particularly happy. The word itself is commonplace but its unusual placing in this context evokes, even if only half-consciously, all the associations of fresh air and an outdoor world. The spring-like quality of God is contrasted to the experience of man. *Bleak* in collocation with *leaves* in the following line is not only unforeseen but destroys the positive associations of *rich* and *fresh*. *Snarling* in line 4 follows up the wintry side of nature with an aggressive adjective that is vivid in its evocation of sight and sound. After this the adjectives diminish and are unremarkable. Their incidence at the outset, however, has already done its work.

The verbs also change in the different sections of the poem. At the beginning, the activity of the natural agents, wind and rain, is conveyed by the monosyllabic verbs *shot* and *nipt*. Both have short vowels and end with the voiceless plosive /t/. These sounds reinforce the meaning of *share*, an older variant of *shear* in the sense 'cut off'. It is monosyllabic and, by reason of the initial voiceless fricative, slightly onomatopoeic. It conjures up the sound of tearing

or ripping. The final verb *wrung* is mimetic rather than onomatopaeic, the sound reflecting the movement. Other verbs connected with twisting movements, such as *wriggle* and *writhe*, begin with the orthographic combination *wr*, now pronounced simply /r/. *Wrung* also has a short vowel. The dynamic and predominantly staccato verbs of this first part indicate the brutal force of nature in its malign or destructive aspect. In the middle section, as the nature words change, so too do the verbs. They attach to the speaker rather than to the natural objects and although mainly dynamic, differ in kind from the earlier ones. They are durative rather than momentary or punctual. *Flourish* is only marginally dynamic, being midway between a state and an action. *Breathe* also, although classed as a dynamic verb, is an involuntary process and not strongly active. *Smell* is classified as a stative verb of inert perception. Finally, *wear* does not denote activity and in this context is not even the result of deliberate choice on the part of the subject but the result of God's regenerative powers. It is virtually drawn, therefore, into the midway category of 'stance' verbs, like *flourish*. Throughout this section the speaker is being worked on and the verbs, although not passives, more or less reflect this passivity. *Flourish* has two syllables and *breathe* a long vowel. Their final fricative consonants further lengthen the sound and help to create a sense of space. In this they are quite unlike the shorter verbs of the first part of the poem, which mainly end in voiceless stops. They are, like the earlier verbs, partly onomatopoeic.

The various strands of the vocabulary and the way in which they are deployed are the principal means by which Vaughan enriches his meaning and they give this poem its particular emphasis. The sound of the words, especially the verbs, underlines the sense the poet seeks to convey.

For Vaughan, sound is often of the first importance and can strike the reader before the meaning becomes clear. To end this examination of some details in the poetry, I will look at this feature in a short extract from one of the best-known poems, 'The Morning Watch':

> In what Rings,
> And *Hymning Circulations* the quick world
> Awakes, and sings;
> The rising winds,
> And falling springs,
> Birds, beasts, all things
> Adore him in their kinds.
> Thus all is hurl'd
> In sacred *Hymnes*, and *Order*, The great *Chime*
> And *Symphony* of nature.
>
> (ll.9-18)

These lines contain extended examples of assonance and 'consonantal chime'. The most frequently repeated vowel is /ɪ/, often followed by a nasal /n/ or /ŋ/. The diphthongs /eɪ/ and /aɪ/ also occur several times. These sounds establish a pattern in the reader's mind. They reach a climax with the word *Chime*, and this carries through into the first part of the following line with the word *Symphony*. The rhyme for *Chime* is outside the unit of meaning and almost beyond the range of the inner ear, since it comes six lines further on. Nevertheless, *Chime* reverberates on the ear because of the previous insistence on two of its three sounds, so that on a first reading the fact that it does not rhyme with a preceding word is likely to pass unnoticed. The reader experiences a sense of fulfilment and satisfaction. The word does indeed 'chime' in the mind as it draws the dominant sounds of the passage together in one word, like a chord that brings to a close a passage of music. Further assonance can be traced in the passage, especially in the repeated /3:/ of *Circulations*; *world*; *Birds*; *hurl'd* and *world* again. The lines are a web of interweaving sounds that harmonize the disparate parts of the world they are intended to signify. Thus meaning and sound are at one in a way which is peculiar to Vaughan and which makes up a considerable part of the overall appeal of his poetry, even when it is not as clearly demonstrable as it is in this extract. (pp. 155-65)

Frances Austin, "Analysis of Passages," in her The Language of the Metaphysical Poets, *The Macmillan Press Ltd., 1992, pp. 155-65.*

FURTHER READING

Beer, Patricia. *An Introduction to the Metaphysical Poets.* 1972. Reprint. London: The MacMillan Press, 1980, 115 p.
    Survey intended for the general student.

Bennett, Joan. *Five Metaphysical Poets: Donne, Herbert, Vaughan, Crashaw, Marvell.* 1934. Reprint. Cambridge: Cambridge University Press, 1964, 151 p.
    Reviews the principal contributors to the Metaphysical poetry movement.

Bloom, Harold, ed. *John Donne and the Seventeenth-Century Metaphysical Poets: Modern Critical Views.* New York: Chelsea House Publishers, 1986, 274 p.
    Compiles "a representative selection of the best criticism available upon the principal seventeenth-century English poets, with the exception of John Milton."

Bush, Douglas. *English Literature in the Earlier Seventeenth Century, 1600-1660.* Oxford: Clarendon Press, 1945, 621 p.
    Extensive discussion of the poetry of Jonson, Donne, and their Metaphysical successors.

Evans, Gillian. *The Age of the Metaphysicals.* Authors in Their Age. London: Blackie & Son, 1978, 140 p.
    Biographical and critical resume of the major Metaphysical poets.

Hammond, Gerald, ed. *The Metaphysical Poets: A Casebook.* London: The Macmillan Press, 1974, 254 p.
    Reviews Metaphysical poetry criticism from the earliest seventeenth-century commentary to recent studies.

Hunter, Jim. *The Metaphysical Poets.* 1965. Reprint. London: Evans Brothers, 1972, 160 p.
    Critical and historical introduction to the subject.

Kermode, Frank, ed. *The Metaphysical Poets: Key Essays on Metaphysical Poetry and the Major Metaphysical Poets.* Greenwich, Conn.: Fawcett Publications, 1969, 351 p.
    Highly regarded critical and historical overview.

Leishman, J. B. *The Metaphysical Poets: Donne, Herbert, Vaughan, Traherne.* 1934. Reprint. New York: Russell & Russell, 1963, 232 p.
    Contextualist study of the movement's major figures.

Mackenzie, Donald. *The Metaphysical Poets.* London: Macmillan Education, 1990, 128 p.
    Traces "the development of the distinctive Metaphysical style from Donne to Marvell."

Martz, Louis L. *The Poetry of Meditation: A Study in English Religious Literature of the Seventeenth Century.* 1954. Reprint. New Haven, Conn.: Yale University Press, 1962, 375 p.
    Examines the genre of the meditative poem from Donne to Herbert.

McCarron, William and Shenk, Robert. *Lesser Metaphysical Poets: A Bibliography, 1961-1980.* San Antonio, Tex.: Trinity University Press, 1983, 52 p.
    Selective bibliography of the lesser figures of the Metaphysical movement.

Miner, Earl. *The Metaphysical Mode from Donne to Cowley.* Princeton, N.J.: Princeton University Press, 1969, 291 p.
    Study of the Metaphysical style that aims "to differentiate between the kinds of Metaphysical poetry written by the various major writers of that race."

Seelig, Sharon Cadman. *The Shadow of Eternity: Belief and Structure in Herbert, Vaughan and Traherne.* Lexington: The University Press of Kentucky, 1981, 194 p.
    Study of Herbert, Vaughan, and Traherne that aims "not to deduce biography from poetry but to examine the way in which the poetry itself creates a universe of assent with its own particular laws and limits."

Skulsky, Harold. *Language Recreated: Seventeenth-Century Metaphorists and the Act of Metaphor.* Athens: University of Georgia Press, 1992, 294 p.
    Considers how "figurative language behaves in a major tradition of English poetry: seventeenth-century lyric."

Smith, A. J. *Metaphysical Wit.* Cambridge: Cambridge University Press, 1991, 270 p.
    Defines the parameters of Metaphysical wit, asserting that it "focuses an interest in the rendering of our ambiguous state when sensation and idea interfuse in...language."

Tuve, Rosemond. *Elizabethan and Metaphysical Imagery: Renaissance Poetic and Twentieth-Century Critics.* Chicago: The University of Chicago Press, 1947, 442 p.
    Highly regarded study of images in English sixteenth- and seventeenth-century verse.

Wallerstein, Ruth. *Studies in Seventeenth-Century Poetic.* Madison: The University of Wisconsin Press, 1965, 421 p.
    Explores seventeenth-century poetic esthetics, focusing in particular on the work of Marvell.

Wanamaker, Melissa C. *Discordia Concors: The Wit of Metaphysical Poetry.* Port Washington, N.Y.: Kennikat Press, 1975, 166 p.
    Thematic analysis of the dominant figures of Metaphysical poetry.

Williamson, George. *Six Metaphysical Poets.* New York: The Noonday Press, 1967, 274 p.

Determines the character of Metaphysical poetry and reviews the movement's key figures.

Literature Criticism from 1400 to 1800

Cumulative Indexes

How to Use This Index

The main references

Calvino, Italo
  1923-1985.....CLC **5, 8, 11, 22, 33, 39,**
                                73; SSC 3

---

list all author entries in the following Gale Literary Criticism series:

CLC = *Contemporary Literary Criticism*
CLR = *Children's Literature Review*
CMLC = *Classical and Medieval Literature Criticism*
DC = *Drama Criticism*
LC = *Literature Criticism from 1400 to 1800*
NCLC = *Nineteenth-Century Literature Criticism*
PC = *Poetry Criticism*
SSC = *Short Story Criticism*
TCLC = *Twentieth-Century Literary Criticism*

The cross-references

See also CANR 23; CA 85-88;
  obituary CA 116

---

list all author entries in the following Gale biographical and literary sources:

AAYA = *Authors & Artists for Young Adults*
AITN = *Authors in the News*
BLC = *Black Literature Criticism*
BW = *Black Writers*
CA = *Contemporary Authors*
CAAS = *Contemporary Authors Autobiography Series*
CABS = *Contemporary Authors Bibliographical Series*
CANR = *Contemporary Authors New Revision Series*
CAP = *Contemporary Authors Permanent Series*
CDALB = *Concise Dictionary of American Literary Biography*
CDBLB = *Concise Dictionary of British Literary Biography*
DA = *DISCovering Authors*
DLB = *Dictionary of Literary Biography*
DLBD = *Dictionary of Literary Biography Documentary Series*
DLBY = *Dictionary of Literary Biography Yearbook*
HW = *Hispanic Writers*
JRDA = *Junior DISCovering Authors*
MAICYA = *Major Authors and Illustrators for Children and Young Adults*
MTCW = *Major 20th-Century Writers*
SAAS = *Something about the Author Autobiography Series*
SATA = *Something about the Author*
WLC = *World Literature Criticism, 1500 to the Present*
YABC = *Yesterday's Authors of Books for Children*

Literary Criticism Series
Cumulative Author Index

Anthony, Piers 1934- . . . . **CLC 35**
See also CA 21-24R; CANR 28; DLB 8;
MTCW

Antoine, Marc
See Proust, (Valentin-Louis-George-Eugene-)
Marcel

Antoninus, Brother
See Everson, William (Oliver)

Antonioni, Michelangelo 1912- . . . . . **CLC 20**
See also CA 73-76

Antschel, Paul 1920-1970. . . . . . **CLC 10, 19**
See also Celan, Paul
See also CA 85-88; CANR 33; MTCW

Anwar, Chairil 1922-1949 . . . . **TCLC 22**
See also CA 121

Apollinaire, Guillaume . . **TCLC 3, 8, 51; PC 7**
See also Kostrowitzki, Wilhelm Apollinaris
de

Appelfeld, Aharon 1932- . . . . **CLC 23, 47**
See also CA 112; 133

Apple, Max (Isaac) 1941-. . . . . **CLC 9, 33**
See also CA 81-84; CANR 19; DLB 130

Appleman, Philip (Dean) 1926- . . . . . **CLC 51**
See also CA 13-16R; CAAS 18; CANR 6,
29

Appleton, Lawrence
See Lovecraft, H(oward) P(hillips)

Apteryx
See Eliot, T(homas) S(tearns)

Apuleius, (Lucius Madaurensis)
125(?)-175(?) . . . . **CMLC 1**

Aquin, Hubert 1929-1977. . . . . **CLC 15**
See also CA 105; DLB 53

Aragon, Louis 1897-1982. . . . . . . **CLC 3, 22**
See also CA 69-72; 108; CANR 28;
DLB 72; MTCW

Arany, Janos 1817-1882. . . . . **NCLC 34**

Arbuthnot, John 1667-1735 . . . . **LC 1**
See also DLB 101

Archer, Herbert Winslow
See Mencken, H(enry) L(ouis)

Archer, Jeffrey (Howard) 1940- . . . . **CLC 28**
See also BEST 89:3; CA 77-80; CANR 22

Archer, Jules 1915- . . . . **CLC 12**
See also CA 9-12R; CANR 6; SAAS 5;
SATA 4

Archer, Lee
See Ellison, Harlan

Arden, John 1930- . . . . **CLC 6, 13, 15**
See also CA 13-16R; CAAS 4; CANR 31;
DLB 13; MTCW

Arenas, Reinaldo 1943-1990 . . . . **CLC 41**
See also CA 124; 128; 133; HW

Arendt, Hannah 1906-1975 . . . . **CLC 66**
See also CA 17-20R; 61-64; CANR 26;
MTCW

Aretino, Pietro 1492-1556 . . . . **LC 12**

Arghezi, Tudor 1880-1967 . . . . **CLC 80**
See also Theodorescu, Ion N.

Arguedas, Jose Maria
1911-1969 . . . . **CLC 10, 18**
See also CA 89-92; DLB 113; HW

Argueta, Manlio 1936-. . . . . **CLC 31**
See also CA 131; HW

Ariosto, Ludovico 1474-1533. . . . . **LC 6**

Aristides
See Epstein, Joseph

Aristophanes
450B.C.-385B.C. . . . . **CMLC 4; DC 2**
See also DA

Arlt, Roberto (Godofredo Christophersen)
1900-1942 . . . . **TCLC 29**
See also CA 123; 131; HW

Armah, Ayi Kwei 1939-. . . . . **CLC 5, 33**
See also BLC 1; BW; CA 61-64; CANR 21;
DLB 117; MTCW

Armatrading, Joan 1950-. . . . . **CLC 17**
See also CA 114

Arnette, Robert
See Silverberg, Robert

Arnim, Achim von (Ludwig Joachim von
Arnim) 1781-1831 . . . . **NCLC 5**
See also DLB 90

Arnim, Bettina von 1785-1859. . . . **NCLC 38**
See also DLB 90

Arnold, Matthew
1822-1888 . . . . **NCLC 6, 29; PC 5**
See also CDBLB 1832-1890; DA; DLB 32,
57; WLC

Arnold, Thomas 1795-1842 . . . . . **NCLC 18**
See also DLB 55

Arnow, Harriette (Louisa) Simpson
1908-1986 . . . . **CLC 2, 7, 18**
See also CA 9-12R; 118; CANR 14; DLB 6;
MTCW; SATA 42, 47

Arp, Hans
See Arp, Jean

Arp, Jean 1887-1966. . . . . **CLC 5**
See also CA 81-84; 25-28R; CANR 42

Arrabal
See Arrabal, Fernando

Arrabal, Fernando 1932- . . . **CLC 2, 9, 18, 58**
See also CA 9-12R; CANR 15

Arrick, Fran. **CLC 30**

Artaud, Antonin 1896-1948 . . . . . **TCLC 3, 36**
See also CA 104

Arthur, Ruth M(abel) 1905-1979. . . . **CLC 12**
See also CA 9-12R; 85-88; CANR 4;
SATA 7, 26

Artsybashev, Mikhail (Petrovich)
1878-1927 . . . . **TCLC 31**

Arundel, Honor (Morfydd)
1919-1973 . . . . **CLC 17**
See also CA 21-22; 41-44R; CAP 2;
SATA 4, 24

Asch, Sholem 1880-1957 . . . . **TCLC 3**
See also CA 105

Ash, Shalom
See Asch, Sholem

Ashbery, John (Lawrence)
1927- . . . . . . **CLC 2, 3, 4, 6, 9, 13, 15, 25,**
41, 77
See also CA 5-8R; CANR 9, 37; DLB 5;
DLBY 81; MTCW

Ashdown, Clifford
See Freeman, R(ichard) Austin

Ashe, Gordon
See Creasey, John

Ashton-Warner, Sylvia (Constance)
1908-1984 . . . . **CLC 19**
See also CA 69-72; 112; CANR 29; MTCW

Asimov, Isaac
1920-1992 . . . . . . **CLC 1, 3, 9, 19, 26, 76**
See also BEST 90:2; CA 1-4R; 137;
CANR 2, 19, 36; CLR 12; DLB 8;
DLBY 92; JRDA; MAICYA; MTCW;
SATA 1, 26, 74

Astley, Thea (Beatrice May)
1925- . . . . **CLC 41**
See also CA 65-68; CANR 11, 43

Aston, James
See White, T(erence) H(anbury)

Asturias, Miguel Angel
1899-1974 . . . . **CLC 3, 8, 13**
See also CA 25-28; 49-52; CANR 32;
CAP 2; DLB 113; HW; MTCW

Atares, Carlos Saura
See Saura (Atares), Carlos

Atheling, William
See Pound, Ezra (Weston Loomis)

Atheling, William, Jr.
See Blish, James (Benjamin)

Atherton, Gertrude (Franklin Horn)
1857-1948 . . . . **TCLC 2**
See also CA 104; DLB 9, 78

Atherton, Lucius
See Masters, Edgar Lee

Atkins, Jack
See Harris, Mark

Atticus
See Fleming, Ian (Lancaster)

Atwood, Margaret (Eleanor)
1939- . . . . . **CLC 2, 3, 4, 8, 13, 15, 25, 44;**
SSC 2
See also BEST 89:2; CA 49-52; CANR 3,
24, 33; DA; DLB 53; MTCW; SATA 50;
WLC

Aubigny, Pierre d'
See Mencken, H(enry) L(ouis)

Aubin, Penelope 1685-1731(?). . . . . **LC 9**
See also DLB 39

Auchincloss, Louis (Stanton)
1917- . . . . **CLC 4, 6, 9, 18, 45**
See also CA 1-4R; CANR 6, 29; DLB 2;
DLBY 80; MTCW

Auden, W(ystan) H(ugh)
1907-1973 . . . . . . **CLC 1, 2, 3, 4, 6, 9, 11,**
14, 43; PC 1
See also CA 9-12R; 45-48; CANR 5;
CDBLB 1914-1945; DA; DLB 10, 20;
MTCW; WLC

Audiberti, Jacques 1900-1965 . . . . . . **CLC 38**
See also CA 25-28R

Auel, Jean M(arie) 1936-. . . . . **CLC 31**
See also AAYA 7; BEST 90:4; CA 103;
CANR 21

Auerbach, Erich 1892-1957 . . . . **TCLC 43**
See also CA 118

Augier, Emile 1820-1889 . . . . **NCLC 31**

August, John
See De Voto, Bernard (Augustine)

Baron, David
See Pinter, Harold

Baron Corvo
See Rolfe, Frederick (William Serafino Austin Lewis Mary)

Barondess, Sue K(aufman)
1926-1977 . . . . **CLC 8**
See also Kaufman, Sue
See also CA 1-4R; 69-72; CANR 1

Baron de Teive
See Pessoa, Fernando (Antonio Nogueira)

Barres, Maurice 1862-1923 . . . . . . **TCLC 47**
See also DLB 123

Barreto, Afonso Henrique de Lima
See Lima Barreto, Afonso Henrique de

Barrett, (Roger) Syd 1946- . . . . **CLC 35**
See also Pink Floyd

Barrett, William (Christopher)
1913-1992 . . . . **CLC 27**
See also CA 13-16R; 139; CANR 11

Barrie, J(ames) M(atthew)
1860-1937 . . . . **TCLC 2**
See also CA 104; 136; CDBLB 1890-1914;
CLR 16; DLB 10; MAICYA; YABC 1

Barrington, Michael
See Moorcock, Michael (John)

Barrol, Grady
See Bograd, Larry

Barry, Mike
See Malzberg, Barry N(athaniel)

Barry, Philip 1896-1949. . . . . **TCLC 11**
See also CA 109; DLB 7

Bart, Andre Schwarz
See Schwarz-Bart, Andre

Barth, John (Simmons)
1930- . . . . . . **CLC 1, 2, 3, 5, 7, 9, 10, 14,
27, 51; SSC 10**
See also AITN 1, 2; CA 1-4R; CABS 1;
CANR 5, 23; DLB 2; MTCW

Barthelme, Donald
1931-1989 . . . . . . **CLC 1, 2, 3, 5, 6, 8, 13,
23, 46, 59; SSC 2**
See also CA 21-24R; 129; CANR 20;
DLB 2; DLBY 80, 89; MTCW; SATA 7,
62

Barthelme, Frederick 1943- . . . . **CLC 36**
See also CA 114; 122; DLBY 85

Barthes, Roland (Gerard)
1915-1980 . . . . **CLC 24**
See also CA 130; 97-100; MTCW

Barzun, Jacques (Martin) 1907- . . . . **CLC 51**
See also CA 61-64; CANR 22

Bashevis, Isaac
See Singer, Isaac Bashevis

Bashkirtseff, Marie 1859-1884 . . . **NCLC 27**

Basho
See Matsuo Basho

Bass, Kingsley B., Jr.
See Bullins, Ed

Bass, Rick 1958- . . . . **CLC 79**
See also CA 126

Bassani, Giorgio 1916- . . . . **CLC 9**
See also CA 65-68; CANR 33; DLB 128;
MTCW

Bastos, Augusto (Antonio) Roa
See Roa Bastos, Augusto (Antonio)

Bataille, Georges 1897-1962 . . . . **CLC 29**
See also CA 101; 89-92

Bates, H(erbert) E(rnest)
1905-1974 . . . . **CLC 46; SSC 10**
See also CA 93-96; 45-48; CANR 34;
MTCW

Bauchart
See Camus, Albert

Baudelaire, Charles
1821-1867 . . . . **NCLC 6, 29; PC 1**
See also DA; WLC

Baudrillard, Jean 1929- . . . . **CLC 60**

Baum, L(yman) Frank 1856-1919 . . . **TCLC 7**
See also CA 108; 133; CLR 15; DLB 22;
JRDA; MAICYA; MTCW; SATA 18

Baum, Louis F.
See Baum, L(yman) Frank

Baumbach, Jonathan 1933- . . . . . . **CLC 6, 23**
See also CA 13-16R; CAAS 5; CANR 12;
DLBY 80; MTCW

Bausch, Richard (Carl) 1945- . . . . . . **CLC 51**
See also CA 101; CAAS 14; CANR 43;
DLB 130

Baxter, Charles 1947-. . . . . **CLC 45, 78**
See also CA 57-60; CANR 40; DLB 130

Baxter, George Owen
See Faust, Frederick (Schiller)

Baxter, James K(eir) 1926-1972 . . . . **CLC 14**
See also CA 77-80

Baxter, John
See Hunt, E(verette) Howard, Jr.

Bayer, Sylvia
See Glassco, John

Beagle, Peter S(oyer) 1939-. . . . . **CLC 7**
See also CA 9-12R; CANR 4; DLBY 80;
SATA 60

Bean, Normal
See Burroughs, Edgar Rice

Beard, Charles A(ustin)
1874-1948 . . . . **TCLC 15**
See also CA 115; DLB 17; SATA 18

Beardsley, Aubrey 1872-1898 . . . . . **NCLC 6**

Beattie, Ann
1947- . . . . **CLC 8, 13, 18, 40, 63; SSC 11**
See also BEST 90:2; CA 81-84; DLBY 82;
MTCW

Beattie, James 1735-1803 . . . . **NCLC 25**
See also DLB 109

Beauchamp, Kathleen Mansfield 1888-1923
See Mansfield, Katherine
See also CA 104; 134; DA

**Beauvoir, Simone (Lucie Ernestine Marie
Bertrand) de**
1908-1986 . . . . **CLC 1, 2, 4, 8, 14, 31, 44,
50, 71**
See also CA 9-12R; 118; CANR 28; DA;
DLB 72; DLBY 86; MTCW; WLC

Becker, Jurek 1937-. . . . . **CLC 7, 19**
See also CA 85-88; DLB 75

Becker, Walter 1950-. . . . . **CLC 26**

Beckett, Samuel (Barclay)
1906-1989 . . . . . **CLC 1, 2, 3, 4, 6, 9, 10,
11, 14, 18, 29, 57, 59**
See also CA 5-8R; 130; CANR 33;
CDBLB 1945-1960; DA; DLB 13, 15;
DLBY 90; MTCW; WLC

Beckford, William 1760-1844 . . . . **NCLC 16**
See also DLB 39

Beckman, Gunnel 1910-. . . . . **CLC 26**
See also CA 33-36R; CANR 15; CLR 25;
MAICYA; SAAS 9; SATA 6

Becque, Henri 1837-1899. . . . . **NCLC 3**

Beddoes, Thomas Lovell
1803-1849 . . . . **NCLC 3**
See also DLB 96

Bedford, Donald F.
See Fearing, Kenneth (Flexner)

Beecher, Catharine Esther
1800-1878 . . . . **NCLC 30**
See also DLB 1

Beecher, John 1904-1980. . . . . **CLC 6**
See also AITN 1; CA 5-8R; 105; CANR 8

Beer, Johann 1655-1700. . . . . **LC 5**

Beer, Patricia 1924-. . . . . **CLC 58**
See also CA 61-64; CANR 13; DLB 40

Beerbohm, Henry Maximilian
1872-1956 . . . . **TCLC 1, 24**
See also CA 104; DLB 34, 100

Begiebing, Robert J(ohn) 1946-. . . . . **CLC 70**
See also CA 122; CANR 40

Behan, Brendan
1923-1964 . . . . **CLC 1, 8, 11, 15, 79**
See also CA 73-76; CANR 33;
CDBLB 1945-1960; DLB 13; MTCW

Behn, Aphra 1640(?)-1689 . . . . **LC 1**
See also DA; DLB 39, 80, 131; WLC

Behrman, S(amuel) N(athaniel)
1893-1973 . . . . **CLC 40**
See also CA 13-16; 45-48; CAP 1; DLB 7,
44

Belasco, David 1853-1931 . . . . **TCLC 3**
See also CA 104; DLB 7

Belcheva, Elisaveta 1893- . . . . **CLC 10**

Beldone, Phil "Cheech"
See Ellison, Harlan

Beleno
See Azuela, Mariano

Belinski, Vissarion Grigoryevich
1811-1848 . . . . **NCLC 5**

Belitt, Ben 1911-. . . . . **CLC 22**
See also CA 13-16R; CAAS 4; CANR 7;
DLB 5

Bell, James Madison 1826-1902 . . . **TCLC 43**
See also BLC 1; BW; CA 122; 124; DLB 50

Bell, Madison (Smartt) 1957- . . . . . . **CLC 41**
See also CA 111; CANR 28

Bell, Marvin (Hartley) 1937-. . . . . **CLC 8, 31**
See also CA 21-24R; CAAS 14; DLB 5;
MTCW

Bell, W. L. D.
See Mencken, H(enry) L(ouis)

Bellamy, Atwood C.
See Mencken, H(enry) L(ouis)

Bidart, Frank 1939- . . . . **CLC 33**
See also CA 140

Bienek, Horst 1930- . . . . **CLC 7, 11**
See also CA 73-76; DLB 75

Bierce, Ambrose (Gwinett)
1842-1914(?) . . . . . **TCLC 1, 7, 44; SSC 9**
See also CA 104; 139; CDALB 1865-1917;
DA; DLB 11, 12, 23, 71, 74; WLC

Billings, Josh
See Shaw, Henry Wheeler

Billington, Rachel 1942- . . . . **CLC 43**
See also AITN 2; CA 33-36R

Binyon, T(imothy) J(ohn) 1936- . . . . **CLC 34**
See also CA 111; CANR 28

Bioy Casares, Adolfo 1914- . . . . **CLC 4, 8, 13**
See also CA 29-32R; CANR 19, 43;
DLB 113; HW; MTCW

Bird, C.
See Ellison, Harlan

Bird, Cordwainer
See Ellison, Harlan

Bird, Robert Montgomery
1806-1854 . . . . **NCLC 1**

Birney, (Alfred) Earle
1904- . . . . **CLC 1, 4, 6, 11**
See also CA 1-4R; CANR 5, 20; DLB 88;
MTCW

Bishop, Elizabeth
1911-1979 . . . . . . **CLC 1, 4, 9, 13, 15, 32;**
PC 3
See also CA 5-8R; 89-92; CABS 2;
CANR 26; CDALB 1968-1988; DA;
DLB 5; MTCW; SATA 24

Bishop, John 1935- . . . . **CLC 10**
See also CA 105

Bissett, Bill 1939- . . . . **CLC 18**
See also CA 69-72; CANR 15; DLB 53;
MTCW

Bitov, Andrei (Georgievich) 1937- . . . **CLC 57**
See also CA 142

Biyidi, Alexandre 1932-
See Beti, Mongo
See also BW; CA 114; 124; MTCW

Bjarme, Brynjolf
See Ibsen, Henrik (Johan)

Bjornson, Bjornstjerne (Martinius)
1832-1910 . . . . **TCLC 7, 37**
See also CA 104

Black, Robert
See Holdstock, Robert P.

Blackburn, Paul 1926-1971 . . . . . . **CLC 9, 43**
See also CA 81-84; 33-36R; CANR 34;
DLB 16; DLBY 81

Black Elk 1863-1950 . . . . **TCLC 33**

Black Hobart
See Sanders, (James) Ed(ward)

Blacklin, Malcolm
See Chambers, Aidan

Blackmore, R(ichard) D(oddridge)
1825-1900 . . . . **TCLC 27**
See also CA 120; DLB 18

Blackmur, R(ichard) P(almer)
1904-1965 . . . . **CLC 2, 24**
See also CA 11-12; 25-28R; CAP 1; DLB 63

Black Tarantula, The
See Acker, Kathy

Blackwood, Algernon (Henry)
1869-1951 . . . . **TCLC 5**
See also CA 105

Blackwood, Caroline 1931- . . . . **CLC 6, 9**
See also CA 85-88; CANR 32; DLB 14;
MTCW

Blade, Alexander
See Hamilton, Edmond; Silverberg, Robert

Blaga, Lucian 1895-1961 . . . . **CLC 75**

Blair, Eric (Arthur) 1903-1950
See Orwell, George
See also CA 104; 132; DA; MTCW;
SATA 29

Blais, Marie-Claire
1939- . . . . **CLC 2, 4, 6, 13, 22**
See also CA 21-24R; CAAS 4; CANR 38;
DLB 53; MTCW

Blaise, Clark 1940- . . . . **CLC 29**
See also AITN 2; CA 53-56; CAAS 3;
CANR 5; DLB 53

Blake, Nicholas
See Day Lewis, C(ecil)
See also DLB 77

Blake, William 1757-1827 . . . . . . **NCLC 13**
See also CDBLB 1789-1832; DA; DLB 93;
MAICYA; SATA 30; WLC

Blasco Ibanez, Vicente
1867-1928 . . . . **TCLC 12**
See also CA 110; 131; HW; MTCW

Blatty, William Peter 1928- . . . . **CLC 2**
See also CA 5-8R; CANR 9

Bleeck, Oliver
See Thomas, Ross (Elmore)

Blessing, Lee 1949- . . . . **CLC 54**

Blish, James (Benjamin)
1921-1975 . . . . **CLC 14**
See also CA 1-4R; 57-60; CANR 3; DLB 8;
MTCW; SATA 66

Bliss, Reginald
See Wells, H(erbert) G(eorge)

Blixen, Karen (Christentze Dinesen)
1885-1962
See Dinesen, Isak
See also CA 25-28; CANR 22; CAP 2;
MTCW; SATA 44

Bloch, Robert (Albert) 1917- . . . . **CLC 33**
See also CA 5-8R; CANR 5; DLB 44;
SATA 12

Blok, Alexander (Alexandrovich)
1880-1921 . . . . **TCLC 5**
See also CA 104

Blom, Jan
See Breytenbach, Breyten

Bloom, Harold 1930- . . . . **CLC 24**
See also CA 13-16R; CANR 39; DLB 67

Bloomfield, Aurelius
See Bourne, Randolph S(illiman)

Blount, Roy (Alton), Jr. 1941- . . . . . **CLC 38**
See also CA 53-56; CANR 10, 28; MTCW

Bloy, Leon 1846-1917 . . . . **TCLC 22**
See also CA 121; DLB 123

Blume, Judy (Sussman) 1938- . . . **CLC 12, 30**
See also AAYA 3; CA 29-32R; CANR 13,
37; CLR 2, 15; DLB 52; JRDA;
MAICYA; MTCW; SATA 2, 31

Blunden, Edmund (Charles)
1896-1974 . . . . **CLC 2, 56**
See also CA 17-18; 45-48; CAP 2; DLB 20,
100; MTCW

Bly, Robert (Elwood)
1926- . . . . **CLC 1, 2, 5, 10, 15, 38**
See also CA 5-8R; CANR 41; DLB 5;
MTCW

Bobette
See Simenon, Georges (Jacques Christian)

Boccaccio, Giovanni 1313-1375
See also SSC 10

Bochco, Steven 1943- . . . . **CLC 35**
See also CA 124; 138

Bodenheim, Maxwell 1892-1954 . . . **TCLC 44**
See also CA 110; DLB 9, 45

Bodker, Cecil 1927- . . . . **CLC 21**
See also CA 73-76; CANR 13; CLR 23;
MAICYA; SATA 14

Boell, Heinrich (Theodor) 1917-1985
See Boll, Heinrich (Theodor)
See also CA 21-24R; 116; CANR 24; DA;
DLB 69; DLBY 85; MTCW

Boerne, Alfred
See Doeblin, Alfred

Bogan, Louise 1897-1970 . . . . . **CLC 4, 39, 46**
See also CA 73-76; 25-28R; CANR 33;
DLB 45; MTCW

Bogarde, Dirk . . . . **CLC 19**
See also Van Den Bogarde, Derek Jules
Gaspard Ulric Niven
See also DLB 14

Bogosian, Eric 1953- . . . . **CLC 45**
See also CA 138

Bograd, Larry 1953- . . . . **CLC 35**
See also CA 93-96; SATA 33

Boiardo, Matteo Maria 1441-1494 . . . . **LC 6**

Boileau-Despreaux, Nicolas
1636-1711 . . . . **LC 3**

Boland, Eavan 1944- . . . . **CLC 40, 67**
See also DLB 40

Boll, Heinrich (Theodor)
1917-1985 . . . . **CLC 2, 3, 6, 9, 11, 15, 27,**
39, 72
See also Boell, Heinrich (Theodor)
See also DLB 69; DLBY 85; WLC

Bolt, Lee
See Faust, Frederick (Schiller)

Bolt, Robert (Oxton) 1924- . . . . **CLC 14**
See also CA 17-20R; CANR 35; DLB 13;
MTCW

Bomkauf
See Kaufman, Bob (Garnell)

Bonaventura . . . . **NCLC 35**
See also DLB 90

Bond, Edward 1934- . . . . **CLC 4, 6, 13, 23**
See also CA 25-28R; CANR 38; DLB 13;
MTCW

Bonham, Frank 1914-1989........ **CLC 12**
See also AAYA 1; CA 9-12R; CANR 4, 36;
JRDA; MAICYA; SAAS 3; SATA 1, 49,
62

Bonnefoy, Yves 1923-........ **CLC 9, 15, 58**
See also CA 85-88; CANR 33; MTCW

Bontemps, Arna(ud Wendell)
1902-1973 .... **CLC 1, 18**
See also BLC 1; BW; CA 1-4R; 41-44R;
CANR 4, 35; CLR 6; DLB 48, 51; JRDA;
MAICYA; MTCW; SATA 2, 24, 44

Booth, Martin 1944-............. **CLC 13**
See also CA 93-96; CAAS 2

Booth, Philip 1925-............. **CLC 23**
See also CA 5-8R; CANR 5; DLBY 82

Booth, Wayne C(layson) 1921- ..... **CLC 24**
See also CA 1-4R; CAAS 5; CANR 3, 43;
DLB 67

Borchert, Wolfgang 1921-1947 ..... **TCLC 5**
See also CA 104; DLB 69, 124

Borel, Petrus 1809-1859........ **NCLC 41**

Borges, Jorge Luis
1899-1986 ... **CLC 1, 2, 3, 4, 6, 8, 9, 10,
13, 19, 44, 48; SSC 4**
See also CA 21-24R; CANR 19, 33; DA;
DLB 113; DLBY 86; HW; MTCW; WLC

Borowski, Tadeusz 1922-1951 ...... **TCLC 9**
See also CA 106

Borrow, George (Henry)
1803-1881 .... **NCLC 9**
See also DLB 21, 55

Bosman, Herman Charles
1905-1951 .... **TCLC 49**

Bosschere, Jean de 1878(?)-1953... **TCLC 19**
See also CA 115

Boswell, James 1740-1795.......... **LC 4**
See also CDBLB 1660-1789; DA; DLB 104;
WLC

Bottoms, David 1949-............. **CLC 53**
See also CA 105; CANR 22; DLB 120;
DLBY 83

Boucicault, Dion 1820-1890...... **NCLC 41**

Boucolon, Maryse 1937-
See Conde, Maryse
See also CA 110; CANR 30

Bourget, Paul (Charles Joseph)
1852-1935 .... **TCLC 12**
See also CA 107; DLB 123

Bourjaily, Vance (Nye) 1922- .... **CLC 8, 62**
See also CA 1-4R; CAAS 1; CANR 2;
DLB 2

Bourne, Randolph S(illiman)
1886-1918 .... **TCLC 16**
See also CA 117; DLB 63

Bova, Ben(jamin William) 1932-.... **CLC 45**
See also CA 5-8R; CAAS 18; CANR 11;
CLR 3; DLBY 81; MAICYA; MTCW;
SATA 6, 68

Bowen, Elizabeth (Dorothea Cole)
1899-1973 ...... **CLC 1, 3, 6, 11, 15, 22;
SSC 3**
See also CA 17-18; 41-44R; CANR 35;
CAP 2; CDBLB 1945-1960; DLB 15;
MTCW

Bowering, George 1935-........ **CLC 15, 47**
See also CA 21-24R; CAAS 16; CANR 10;
DLB 53

Bowering, Marilyn R(uthe) 1949-... **CLC 32**
See also CA 101

Bowers, Edgar 1924- .... **CLC 9**
See also CA 5-8R; CANR 24; DLB 5

Bowie, David .... **CLC 17**
See also Jones, David Robert

Bowles, Jane (Sydney)
1917-1973 .... **CLC 3, 68**
See also CA 19-20; 41-44R; CAP 2

Bowles, Paul (Frederick)
1910- .... **CLC 1, 2, 19, 53; SSC 3**
See also CA 1-4R; CAAS 1; CANR 1, 19;
DLB 5, 6; MTCW

Box, Edgar
See Vidal, Gore

Boyd, Nancy
See Millay, Edna St. Vincent

Boyd, William 1952-........ **CLC 28, 53, 70**
See also CA 114; 120

Boyle, Kay
1902-1992 ..... **CLC 1, 5, 19, 58; SSC 5**
See also CA 13-16R; 140; CAAS 1;
CANR 29; DLB 4, 9, 48, 86; MTCW

Boyle, Mark
See Kienzle, William X(avier)

Boyle, Patrick 1905-1982.......... **CLC 19**
See also CA 127

Boyle, T. Coraghessan 1948-.... **CLC 36, 55**
See also BEST 90:4; CA 120; DLBY 86

Boz
See Dickens, Charles (John Huffam)

Brackenridge, Hugh Henry
1748-1816 .... **NCLC 7**
See also DLB 11, 37

Bradbury, Edward P.
See Moorcock, Michael (John)

Bradbury, Malcolm (Stanley)
1932- .... **CLC 32, 61**
See also CA 1-4R; CANR 1, 33; DLB 14;
MTCW

Bradbury, Ray (Douglas)
1920- .... **CLC 1, 3, 10, 15, 42**
See also AITN 1, 2; CA 1-4R; CANR 2, 30;
CDALB 1968-1988; DA; DLB 2, 8;
MTCW; SATA 11, 64; WLC

Bradford, Gamaliel 1863-1932..... **TCLC 36**
See also DLB 17

Bradley, David (Henry, Jr.) 1950- .. **CLC 23**
See also BLC 1; BW; CA 104; CANR 26;
DLB 33

Bradley, John Ed 1959-........... **CLC 55**

Bradley, Marion Zimmer 1930-..... **CLC 30**
See also AAYA 9; CA 57-60; CAAS 10;
CANR 7, 31; DLB 8; MTCW

Bradstreet, Anne 1612(?)-1672 .... **LC 4**
See also CDALB 1640-1865; DA; DLB 24

Bragg, Melvyn 1939- .... **CLC 10**
See also BEST 89:3; CA 57-60; CANR 10;
DLB 14

Braine, John (Gerard)
1922-1986 .... **CLC 1, 3, 41**
See also CA 1-4R; 120; CANR 1, 33;
CDBLB 1945-1960; DLB 15; DLBY 86;
MTCW

Brammer, William 1930(?)-1978 .... **CLC 31**
See also CA 77-80

Brancati, Vitaliano 1907-1954..... **TCLC 12**
See also CA 109

Brancato, Robin F(idler) 1936- ..... **CLC 35**
See also AAYA 9; CA 69-72; CANR 11;
CLR 32; JRDA; SAAS 9; SATA 23

Brand, Max
See Faust, Frederick (Schiller)

Brand, Millen 1906-1980........... **CLC 7**
See also CA 21-24R; 97-100

Branden, Barbara .... **CLC 44**

Brandes, Georg (Morris Cohen)
1842-1927 .... **TCLC 10**
See also CA 105

Brandys, Kazimierz 1916-........ **CLC 62**

Branley, Franklyn M(ansfield)
1915- .... **CLC 21**
See also CA 33-36R; CANR 14, 39;
CLR 13; MAICYA; SAAS 16; SATA 4,
68

Brathwaite, Edward (Kamau)
1930- .... **CLC 11**
See also BW; CA 25-28R; CANR 11, 26;
DLB 125

Brautigan, Richard (Gary)
1935-1984 .... **CLC 1, 3, 5, 9, 12, 34, 42**
See also CA 53-56; 113; CANR 34; DLB 2,
5; DLBY 80, 84; MTCW; SATA 56

Braverman, Kate 1950- .... **CLC 67**
See also CA 89-92

Brecht, Bertolt
1898-1956 ..... **TCLC 1, 6, 13, 35; DC 3**
See also CA 104; 133; DA; DLB 56, 124;
MTCW; WLC

Brecht, Eugen Berthold Friedrich
See Brecht, Bertolt

Bremer, Fredrika 1801-1865 ..... **NCLC 11**

Brennan, Christopher John
1870-1932 .... **TCLC 17**
See also CA 117

Brennan, Maeve 1917-............. **CLC 5**
See also CA 81-84

Brentano, Clemens (Maria)
1778-1842 .... **NCLC 1**

Brent of Bin Bin
See Franklin, (Stella Maraia Sarah) Miles

Brenton, Howard 1942-........... **CLC 31**
See also CA 69-72; CANR 33; DLB 13;
MTCW

Breslin, James 1930-
See Breslin, Jimmy
See also CA 73-76; CANR 31; MTCW

Breslin, Jimmy .... **CLC 4, 43**
See also Breslin, James
See also AITN 1

Bresson, Robert 1907- .... **CLC 16**
See also CA 110

Buchwald, Art(hur) 1925-......... **CLC 33**
See also AITN 1; CA 5-8R; CANR 21;
MTCW; SATA 10

Buck, Pearl S(ydenstricker)
1892-1973 .... **CLC 7, 11, 18**
See also AITN 1; CA 1-4R; 41-44R;
CANR 1, 34; DA; DLB 9, 102; MTCW;
SATA 1, 25

Buckler, Ernest 1908-1984........ **CLC 13**
See also CA 11-12; 114; CAP 1; DLB 68;
SATA 47

Buckley, Vincent (Thomas)
1925-1988 .... **CLC 57**
See also CA 101

Buckley, William F(rank), Jr.
1925- .... **CLC 7, 18, 37**
See also AITN 1; CA 1-4R; CANR 1, 24;
DLBY 80; MTCW

Buechner, (Carl) Frederick
1926- .... **CLC 2, 4, 6, 9**
See also CA 13-16R; CANR 11, 39;
DLBY 80; MTCW

Buell, John (Edward) 1927-........ **CLC 10**
See also CA 1-4R; DLB 53

Buero Vallejo, Antonio 1916- ... **CLC 15, 46**
See also CA 106; CANR 24; HW; MTCW

Bufalino, Gesualdo 1920(?)-........ **CLC 74**

Bugayev, Boris Nikolayevich 1880-1934
See Bely, Andrey
See also CA 104

Bukowski, Charles 1920-.... **CLC 2, 5, 9, 41**
See also CA 17-20R; CANR 40; DLB 5,
130; MTCW

Bulgakov, Mikhail (Afanas'evich)
1891-1940 .... **TCLC 2, 16**
See also CA 105

Bullins, Ed 1935- .... **CLC 1, 5, 7**
See also BLC 1; BW; CA 49-52; CAAS 16;
CANR 24; DLB 7, 38; MTCW

Bulwer-Lytton, Edward (George Earle Lytton)
1803-1873 .... **NCLC 1**
See also DLB 21

Bunin, Ivan Alexeyevich
1870-1953 .... **TCLC 6; SSC 5**
See also CA 104

Bunting, Basil 1900-1985.... **CLC 10, 39, 47**
See also CA 53-56; 115; CANR 7; DLB 20

Bunuel, Luis 1900-1983 .... **CLC 16, 80**
See also CA 101; 110; CANR 32; HW

Bunyan, John 1628-1688 .... **LC 4**
See also CDBLB 1660-1789; DA; DLB 39;
WLC

Burford, Eleanor
See Hibbert, Eleanor Alice Burford

Burgess, Anthony
1917- ..... **CLC 1, 2, 4, 5, 8, 10, 13, 15,
22, 40, 62**
See also Wilson, John (Anthony) Burgess
See also AITN 1; CDBLB 1960 to Present;
DLB 14

Burke, Edmund 1729(?)-1797........ **LC 7**
See also DA; DLB 104; WLC

Burke, Kenneth (Duva) 1897-.... **CLC 2, 24**
See also CA 5-8R; CANR 39; DLB 45, 63;
MTCW

Burke, Leda
See Garnett, David

Burke, Ralph
See Silverberg, Robert

Burney, Fanny 1752-1840 .... **NCLC 12**
See also DLB 39

Burns, Robert 1759-1796....... **LC 3; PC 6**
See also CDBLB 1789-1832; DA; DLB 109;
WLC

Burns, Tex
See L'Amour, Louis (Dearborn)

Burnshaw, Stanley 1906-..... **CLC 3, 13, 44**
See also CA 9-12R; DLB 48

Burr, Anne 1937- .... **CLC 6**
See also CA 25-28R

Burroughs, Edgar Rice
1875-1950 .... **TCLC 2, 32**
See also CA 104; 132; DLB 8; MTCW;
SATA 41

Burroughs, William S(eward)
1914- .... **CLC 1, 2, 5, 15, 22, 42, 75**
See also AITN 2; CA 9-12R; CANR 20;
DA; DLB 2, 8, 16; DLBY 81; MTCW;
WLC

Burton, Richard F. 1821-1890.... **NCLC 42**
See also DLB 55

Busch, Frederick 1941- ... **CLC 7, 10, 18, 47**
See also CA 33-36R; CAAS 1; DLB 6

Bush, Ronald 1946- .... **CLC 34**
See also CA 136

Bustos, F(rancisco)
See Borges, Jorge Luis

Bustos Domecq, H(onorio)
See Bioy Casares, Adolfo; Borges, Jorge
Luis

Butler, Octavia E(stelle) 1947- ..... **CLC 38**
See also BW; CA 73-76; CANR 12, 24, 38;
DLB 33; MTCW

Butler, Samuel 1612-1680 .... **LC 16**
See also DLB 101, 126

Butler, Samuel 1835-1902 ...... **TCLC 1, 33**
See also CA 104; CDBLB 1890-1914; DA;
DLB 18, 57; WLC

Butler, Walter C.
See Faust, Frederick (Schiller)

Butor, Michel (Marie Francois)
1926- .... **CLC 1, 3, 8, 11, 15**
See also CA 9-12R; CANR 33; DLB 83;
MTCW

Buzo, Alexander (John) 1944-...... **CLC 61**
See also CA 97-100; CANR 17, 39

Buzzati, Dino 1906-1972 .... **CLC 36**
See also CA 33-36R

Byars, Betsy (Cromer) 1928-....... **CLC 35**
See also CA 33-36R; CANR 18, 36; CLR 1,
16; DLB 52; JRDA; MAICYA; MTCW;
SAAS 1; SATA 4, 46

Byatt, A(ntonia) S(usan Drabble)
1936- .... **CLC 19, 65**
See also CA 13-16R; CANR 13, 33;
DLB 14; MTCW

Byrne, David 1952-............. **CLC 26**
See also CA 127

Byrne, John Keyes 1926-......... **CLC 19**
See also Leonard, Hugh
See also CA 102

Byron, George Gordon (Noel)
1788-1824 .... **NCLC 2, 12**
See also CDBLB 1789-1832; DA; DLB 96,
110; WLC

C.3.3.
See Wilde, Oscar (Fingal O'Flahertie Wills)

Caballero, Fernan 1796-1877..... **NCLC 10**

Cabell, James Branch 1879-1958 ... **TCLC 6**
See also CA 105; DLB 9, 78

Cable, George Washington
1844-1925 .... **TCLC 4; SSC 4**
See also CA 104; DLB 12, 74

Cabral de Melo Neto, Joao 1920-... **CLC 76**

Cabrera Infante, G(uillermo)
1929- .... **CLC 5, 25, 45**
See also CA 85-88; CANR 29; DLB 113;
HW; MTCW

Cade, Toni
See Bambara, Toni Cade

Cadmus
See Buchan, John

Caedmon fl. 658-680............. **CMLC 7**

Caeiro, Alberto
See Pessoa, Fernando (Antonio Nogueira)

Cage, John (Milton, Jr.) 1912-..... **CLC 41**
See also CA 13-16R; CANR 9

Cain, G.
See Cabrera Infante, G(uillermo)

Cain, Guillermo
See Cabrera Infante, G(uillermo)

Cain, James M(allahan)
1892-1977 .... **CLC 3, 11, 28**
See also AITN 1; CA 17-20R; 73-76;
CANR 8, 34; MTCW

Caine, Mark
See Raphael, Frederic (Michael)

Calderon de la Barca, Pedro
1600-1681 .... **LC 23; DC 3**

Caldwell, Erskine (Preston)
1903-1987 .... **CLC 1, 8, 14, 50, 60**
See also AITN 1; CA 1-4R; 121; CAAS 1;
CANR 2, 33; DLB 9, 86; MTCW

Caldwell, (Janet Miriam) Taylor (Holland)
1900-1985 .... **CLC 2, 28, 39**
See also CA 5-8R; 116; CANR 5

Calhoun, John Caldwell
1782-1850 .... **NCLC 15**
See also DLB 3

Calisher, Hortense 1911-.... **CLC 2, 4, 8, 38**
See also CA 1-4R; CANR 1, 22; DLB 2;
MTCW

Callaghan, Morley Edward
1903-1990 ....**CLC 3, 14, 41, 65**
See also CA 9-12R; 132; CANR 33;
DLB 68; MTCW

Calvino, Italo
1923-1985 ..... **CLC 5, 8, 11, 22, 33, 39,
73; SSC 3**
See also CA 85-88; 116; CANR 23; MTCW

Cameron, Carey 1952-............ **CLC 59**
See also CA 135

Cameron, Peter 1959-. . . . . **CLC 44**
See also CA 125

Campana, Dino 1885-1932. . . . . . . **TCLC 20**
See also CA 117; DLB 114

Campbell, John W(ood, Jr.)
1910-1971 . . . . **CLC 32**
See also CA 21-22; 29-32R; CANR 34;
CAP 2; DLB 8; MTCW

Campbell, Joseph 1904-1987 . . . . **CLC 69**
See also AAYA 3; BEST 89:2; CA 1-4R;
124; CANR 3, 28; MTCW

Campbell, (John) Ramsey 1946- . . . . **CLC 42**
See also CA 57-60; CANR 7

Campbell, (Ignatius) Roy (Dunnachie)
1901-1957 . . . . **TCLC 5**
See also CA 104; DLB 20

Campbell, Thomas 1777-1844 . . . . **NCLC 19**
See also DLB 93

Campbell, Wilfred. . . . . **TCLC 9**
See also Campbell, William

Campbell, William 1858(?)-1918
See Campbell, Wilfred
See also CA 106; DLB 92

Campos, Alvaro de
See Pessoa, Fernando (Antonio Nogueira)

Camus, Albert
1913-1960 . . . . **CLC 1, 2, 4, 9, 11, 14, 32,
63, 69; DC 2; SSC 9**
See also CA 89-92; DA; DLB 72; MTCW;
WLC

Canby, Vincent 1924-. . . . . **CLC 13**
See also CA 81-84

Cancale
See Desnos, Robert

Canetti, Elias 1905- . . . . . . **CLC 3, 14, 25, 75**
See also CA 21-24R; CANR 23; DLB 85,
124; MTCW

Canin, Ethan 1960-. . . . . **CLC 55**
See also CA 131; 135

Cannon, Curt
See Hunter, Evan

Cape, Judith
See Page, P(atricia) K(athleen)

Capek, Karel
1890-1938 . . . . **TCLC 6, 37; DC 1**
See also CA 104; 140; DA; WLC

Capote, Truman
1924-1984 . . . . . . **CLC 1, 3, 8, 13, 19, 34,
38, 58; SSC 2**
See also CA 5-8R; 113; CANR 18;
CDALB 1941-1968; DA; DLB 2;
DLBY 80, 84; MTCW; WLC

Capra, Frank 1897-1991. . . . . **CLC 16**
See also CA 61-64; 135

Caputo, Philip 1941-. . . . . **CLC 32**
See also CA 73-76; CANR 40

Card, Orson Scott 1951- . . . . **CLC 44, 47, 50**
See also CA 102; CANR 27; MTCW

Cardenal (Martinez), Ernesto
1925- . . . . **CLC 31**
See also CA 49-52; CANR 2, 32; HW;
MTCW

Carducci, Giosue 1835-1907. . . . . . . **TCLC 32**

Carew, Thomas 1595(?)-1640. . . . . . . **LC 13**
See also DLB 126

Carey, Ernestine Gilbreth 1908- . . . . **CLC 17**
See also CA 5-8R; SATA 2

Carey, Peter 1943-. . . . . **CLC 40, 55**
See also CA 123; 127; MTCW

Carleton, William 1794-1869. . . . . **NCLC 3**

Carlisle, Henry (Coffin) 1926-. . . . . . **CLC 33**
See also CA 13-16R; CANR 15

Carlsen, Chris
See Holdstock, Robert P.

Carlson, Ron(ald F.) 1947-. . . . . **CLC 54**
See also CA 105; CANR 27

Carlyle, Thomas 1795-1881. . . . . . **NCLC 22**
See also CDBLB 1789-1832; DA; DLB 55

Carman, (William) Bliss
1861-1929 . . . . **TCLC 7**
See also CA 104; DLB 92

Carossa, Hans 1878-1956. . . . . **TCLC 48**
See also DLB 66

Carpenter, Don(ald Richard)
1931- . . . . **CLC 41**
See also CA 45-48; CANR 1

Carpentier (y Valmont), Alejo
1904-1980 . . . . **CLC 8, 11, 38**
See also CA 65-68; 97-100; CANR 11;
DLB 113; HW

Carr, Emily 1871-1945. . . . . **TCLC 32**
See also DLB 68

Carr, John Dickson 1906-1977 . . . . . . **CLC 3**
See also CA 49-52; 69-72; CANR 3, 33;
MTCW

Carr, Philippa
See Hibbert, Eleanor Alice Burford

Carr, Virginia Spencer 1929-. . . . . . . **CLC 34**
See also CA 61-64; DLB 111

Carrier, Roch 1937-. . . . . **CLC 13, 78**
See also CA 130; DLB 53

Carroll, James P. 1943(?)-. . . . . **CLC 38**
See also CA 81-84

Carroll, Jim 1951- . . . . **CLC 35**
See also CA 45-48; CANR 42

Carroll, Lewis . . . . **NCLC 2**
See also Dodgson, Charles Lutwidge
See also CDBLB 1832-1890; CLR 2, 18;
DLB 18; JRDA; WLC

Carroll, Paul Vincent 1900-1968. . . . **CLC 10**
See also CA 9-12R; 25-28R; DLB 10

Carruth, Hayden 1921- . . . . **CLC 4, 7, 10, 18**
See also CA 9-12R; CANR 4, 38; DLB 5;
MTCW; SATA 47

Carson, Rachel Louise 1907-1964. . . **CLC 71**
See also CA 77-80; CANR 35; MTCW;
SATA 23

Carter, Angela (Olive)
1940-1992 . . . . . . **CLC 5, 41, 76; SSC 13**
See also CA 53-56; 136; CANR 12, 36;
DLB 14; MTCW; SATA 66;
SATA-Obit 70

Carter, Nick
See Smith, Martin Cruz

Carver, Raymond
1938-1988 . . . **CLC 22, 36, 53, 55; SSC 8**
See also CA 33-36R; 126; CANR 17, 34;
DLB 130; DLBY 84, 88; MTCW

Cary, (Arthur) Joyce (Lunel)
1888-1957 . . . . **TCLC 1, 29**
See also CA 104; CDBLB 1914-1945;
DLB 15, 100

Casanova de Seingalt, Giovanni Jacopo
1725-1798 . . . . **LC 13**

Casares, Adolfo Bioy
See Bioy Casares, Adolfo

Casely-Hayford, J(oseph) E(phraim)
1866-1930 . . . . **TCLC 24**
See also BLC 1; CA 123

Casey, John (Dudley) 1939-. . . . . **CLC 59**
See also BEST 90:2; CA 69-72; CANR 23

Casey, Michael 1947-. . . . . **CLC 2**
See also CA 65-68; DLB 5

Casey, Patrick
See Thurman, Wallace (Henry)

Casey, Warren (Peter) 1935-1988 . . . **CLC 12**
See also CA 101; 127

Casona, Alejandro. . . . . **CLC 49**
See also Alvarez, Alejandro Rodriguez

Cassavetes, John 1929-1989. . . . . . . **CLC 20**
See also CA 85-88; 127

Cassill, R(onald) V(erlin) 1919-. . . **CLC 4, 23**
See also CA 9-12R; CAAS 1; CANR 7;
DLB 6

Cassity, (Allen) Turner 1929- . . . . **CLC 6, 42**
See also CA 17-20R; CAAS 8; CANR 11;
DLB 105

Castaneda, Carlos 1931(?)-. . . . . **CLC 12**
See also CA 25-28R; CANR 32; HW;
MTCW

Castedo, Elena 1937-. . . . . **CLC 65**
See also CA 132

Castedo-Ellerman, Elena
See Castedo, Elena

Castellanos, Rosario 1925-1974. . . . . **CLC 66**
See also CA 131; 53-56; DLB 113; HW

Castelvetro, Lodovico 1505-1571. . . . . **LC 12**

Castiglione, Baldassare 1478-1529 . . . **LC 12**

Castle, Robert
See Hamilton, Edmond

Castro, Guillen de 1569-1631. . . . . . . **LC 19**

Castro, Rosalia de 1837-1885 . . . . . **NCLC 3**

Cather, Willa
See Cather, Willa Sibert

Cather, Willa Sibert
1873-1947 . . . . . . **TCLC 1, 11, 31; SSC 2**
See also CA 104; 128; CDALB 1865-1917;
DA; DLB 9, 54, 78; DLBD 1; MTCW;
SATA 30; WLC

Catton, (Charles) Bruce
1899-1978 . . . . **CLC 35**
See also AITN 1; CA 5-8R; 81-84;
CANR 7; DLB 17; SATA 2, 24

Cauldwell, Frank
See King, Francis (Henry)

Caunitz, William J. 1933- . . . . **CLC 34**
See also BEST 89:3; CA 125; 130

Causley, Charles (Stanley) 1917-..... **CLC 7**
See also CA 9-12R; CANR 5, 35; CLR 30;
DLB 27; MTCW; SATA 3, 66

Caute, David 1936-.............. **CLC 29**
See also CA 1-4R; CAAS 4; CANR 1, 33;
DLB 14

Cavafy, C(onstantine) P(eter)...... **TCLC 2, 7**
See also Kavafis, Konstantinos Petrou

Cavallo, Evelyn
See Spark, Muriel (Sarah)

Cavanna, Betty .... **CLC 12**
See also Harrison, Elizabeth Cavanna
See also JRDA; MAICYA; SAAS 4;
SATA 1, 30

Caxton, William 1421(?)-1491(?)..... **LC 17**

Cayrol, Jean 1911-.................. **CLC 11**
See also CA 89-92; DLB 83

Cela, Camilo Jose 1916-...... **CLC 4, 13, 59**
See also BEST 90:2; CA 21-24R; CAAS 10;
CANR 21, 32; DLBY 89; HW; MTCW

Celan, Paul .... **CLC 53**
See also Antschel, Paul
See also DLB 69

Celine, Louis-Ferdinand
.... **CLC 1, 3, 4, 7, 9, 15, 47**
See also Destouches, Louis-Ferdinand
See also DLB 72

Cellini, Benvenuto 1500-1571 .... **LC 7**

Cendrars, Blaise
See Sauser-Hall, Frederic

Cernuda (y Bidon), Luis
1902-1963 .... **CLC 54**
See also CA 131; 89-92; DLB 134; HW

Cervantes (Saavedra), Miguel de
1547-1616 .... **LC 6, 23; SSC 12**
See also DA; WLC

Cesaire, Aime (Fernand) 1913-.. **CLC 19, 32**
See also BLC 1; BW; CA 65-68; CANR 24,
43; MTCW

Chabon, Michael 1965(?)- .... **CLC 55**
See also CA 139

Chabrol, Claude 1930-............. **CLC 16**
See also CA 110

Challans, Mary 1905-1983
See Renault, Mary
See also CA 81-84; 111; SATA 23, 36

Challis, George
See Faust, Frederick (Schiller)

Chambers, Aidan 1934-.......... **CLC 35**
See also CA 25-28R; CANR 12, 31; JRDA;
MAICYA; SAAS 12; SATA 1, 69

Chambers, James 1948-
See Cliff, Jimmy
See also CA 124

Chambers, Jessie
See Lawrence, D(avid) H(erbert Richards)

Chambers, Robert W. 1865-1933... **TCLC 41**

Chandler, Raymond (Thornton)
1888-1959 .... **TCLC 1, 7**
See also CA 104; 129; CDALB 1929-1941;
DLBD 6; MTCW

Chang, Jung 1952-............... **CLC 71**
See also CA 142

Channing, William Ellery
1780-1842 .... **NCLC 17**
See also DLB 1, 59

Chaplin, Charles Spencer
1889-1977 .... **CLC 16**
See also Chaplin, Charlie
See also CA 81-84; 73-76

Chaplin, Charlie
See Chaplin, Charles Spencer
See also DLB 44

Chapman, George 1559(?)-1634...... **LC 22**
See also DLB 62, 121

Chapman, Graham 1941-1989 ..... **CLC 21**
See also Monty Python
See also CA 116; 129; CANR 35

Chapman, John Jay 1862-1933 ..... **TCLC 7**
See also CA 104

Chapman, Walker
See Silverberg, Robert

Chappell, Fred (Davis) 1936-.... **CLC 40, 78**
See also CA 5-8R; CAAS 4; CANR 8, 33;
DLB 6, 105

Char, Rene(-Emile)
1907-1988 .... **CLC 9, 11, 14, 55**
See also CA 13-16R; 124; CANR 32;
MTCW

Charby, Jay
See Ellison, Harlan

Chardin, Pierre Teilhard de
See Teilhard de Chardin, (Marie Joseph)
Pierre

Charles I 1600-1649 .... **LC 13**

Charyn, Jerome 1937- .... **CLC 5, 8, 18**
See also CA 5-8R; CAAS 1; CANR 7;
DLBY 83; MTCW

Chase, Mary (Coyle) 1907-1981 ...... **DC 1**
See also CA 77-80; 105; SATA 17, 29

Chase, Mary Ellen 1887-1973....... **CLC 2**
See also CA 13-16; 41-44R; CAP 1;
SATA 10

Chase, Nicholas
See Hyde, Anthony

Chateaubriand, Francois Rene de
1768-1848 .... **NCLC 3**
See also DLB 119

Chatterje, Sarat Chandra 1876-1936(?)
See Chatterji, Saratchandra
See also CA 109

Chatterji, Bankim Chandra
1838-1894 .... **NCLC 19**

Chatterji, Saratchandra .... **TCLC 13**
See also Chatterje, Sarat Chandra

Chatterton, Thomas 1752-1770 .... **LC 3**
See also DLB 109

Chatwin, (Charles) Bruce
1940-1989 .... **CLC 28, 57, 59**
See also AAYA 4; BEST 90:1; CA 85-88;
127

Chaucer, Daniel
See Ford, Ford Madox

Chaucer, Geoffrey 1340(?)-1400 ..... **LC 17**
See also CDBLB Before 1660; DA

Chaviaras, Strates 1935-
See Haviaras, Stratis
See also CA 105

Chayefsky, Paddy .... **CLC 23**
See also Chayefsky, Sidney
See also DLB 7, 44; DLBY 81

Chayefsky, Sidney 1923-1981
See Chayefsky, Paddy
See also CA 9-12R; 104; CANR 18

Chedid, Andree 1920-............ **CLC 47**

Cheever, John
1912-1982 ...... **CLC 3, 7, 8, 11, 15, 25,
64; SSC 1**
See also CA 5-8R; 106; CABS 1; CANR 5,
27; CDALB 1941-1968; DA; DLB 2, 102;
DLBY 80, 82; MTCW; WLC

Cheever, Susan 1943-.......... **CLC 18, 48**
See also CA 103; CANR 27; DLBY 82

Chekhonte, Antosha
See Chekhov, Anton (Pavlovich)

Chekhov, Anton (Pavlovich)
1860-1904 ...... **TCLC 3, 10, 31; SSC 2**
See also CA 104; 124; DA; WLC

Chernyshevsky, Nikolay Gavrilovich
1828-1889 .... **NCLC 1**

Cherry, Carolyn Janice 1942-
See Cherryh, C. J.
See also CA 65-68; CANR 10

Cherryh, C. J. .... **CLC 35**
See also Cherry, Carolyn Janice
See also DLBY 80

Chesnutt, Charles W(addell)
1858-1932 .... **TCLC 5, 39; SSC 7**
See also BLC 1; BW; CA 106; 125; DLB 12,
50, 78; MTCW

Chester, Alfred 1929(?)-1971....... **CLC 49**
See also CA 33-36R; DLB 130

Chesterton, G(ilbert) K(eith)
1874-1936 .... **TCLC 1, 6; SSC 1**
See also CA 104; 132; CDBLB 1914-1945;
DLB 10, 19, 34, 70, 98; MTCW;
SATA 27

Chiang Pin-chin 1904-1986
See Ding Ling
See also CA 118

Ch'ien Chung-shu 1910-.......... **CLC 22**
See also CA 130; MTCW

Child, L. Maria
See Child, Lydia Maria

Child, Lydia Maria 1802-1880 .... **NCLC 6**
See also DLB 1, 74; SATA 67

Child, Mrs.
See Child, Lydia Maria

Child, Philip 1898-1978 .... **CLC 19, 68**
See also CA 13-14; CAP 1; SATA 47

Childress, Alice 1920-.......... **CLC 12, 15**
See also AAYA 8; BLC 1; BW; CA 45-48;
CANR 3, 27; CLR 14; DLB 7, 38; JRDA;
MAICYA; MTCW; SATA 7, 48

Chislett, (Margaret) Anne 1943-.... **CLC 34**

Chitty, Thomas Willes 1926-....... **CLC 11**
See also Hinde, Thomas
See also CA 5-8R

Chomette, Rene Lucien 1898-1981 . . **CLC 20**
 See also Clair, Rene
 See also CA 103

Chopin, Kate . . . . **TCLC 5, 14; SSC 8**
 See also Chopin, Katherine
 See also CDALB 1865-1917; DA; DLB 12,
 78

Chopin, Katherine 1851-1904
 See Chopin, Kate
 See also CA 104; 122

Chretien de Troyes
 c. 12th cent. - . . . . **CMLC 10**

Christie
 See Ichikawa, Kon

Christie, Agatha (Mary Clarissa)
 1890-1976 . . . . . . **CLC 1, 6, 8, 12, 39, 48**
 See also AAYA 9; AITN 1, 2; CA 17-20R;
 61-64; CANR 10, 37; CDBLB 1914-1945;
 DLB 13, 77; MTCW; SATA 36

Christie, (Ann) Philippa
 See Pearce, Philippa
 See also CA 5-8R; CANR 4

Christine de Pizan 1365(?)-1431(?) . . . . **LC 9**

Chubb, Elmer
 See Masters, Edgar Lee

Chulkov, Mikhail Dmitrievich
 1743-1792 . . . . **LC 2**

Churchill, Caryl 1938- . . . . **CLC 31, 55**
 See also CA 102; CANR 22; DLB 13;
 MTCW

Churchill, Charles 1731-1764. . . . . **LC 3**
 See also DLB 109

Chute, Carolyn 1947- . . . . **CLC 39**
 See also CA 123

Ciardi, John (Anthony)
 1916-1986 . . . . **CLC 10, 40, 44**
 See also CA 5-8R; 118; CAAS 2; CANR 5,
 33; CLR 19; DLB 5; DLBY 86;
 MAICYA; MTCW; SATA 1, 46, 65

Cicero, Marcus Tullius
 106B.C.-43B.C. . . . . **CMLC 3**

Cimino, Michael 1943- . . . . **CLC 16**
 See also CA 105

Cioran, E(mil) M. 1911- . . . . **CLC 64**
 See also CA 25-28R

Cisneros, Sandra 1954- . . . . **CLC 69**
 See also AAYA 9; CA 131; DLB 122; HW

Clair, Rene. . . . . **CLC 20**
 See also Chomette, Rene Lucien

Clampitt, Amy 1920- . . . . **CLC 32**
 See also CA 110; CANR 29; DLB 105

Clancy, Thomas L., Jr. 1947-
 See Clancy, Tom
 See also CA 125; 131; MTCW

Clancy, Tom. **CLC 45**
 See also Clancy, Thomas L., Jr.
 See also AAYA 9; BEST 89:1, 90:1

Clare, John 1793-1864 . . . . **NCLC 9**
 See also DLB 55, 96

Clarin
 See Alas (y Urena), Leopoldo (Enrique
 Garcia)

Clark, Al C.
 See Goines, Donald

Clark, (Robert) Brian 1932- . . . . **CLC 29**
 See also CA 41-44R

Clark, Eleanor 1913- . . . . **CLC 5, 19**
 See also CA 9-12R; CANR 41; DLB 6

Clark, J. P.
 See Clark, John Pepper
 See also DLB 117

Clark, John Pepper 1935- . . . . **CLC 38**
 See also Clark, J. P.
 See also BLC 1; BW; CA 65-68; CANR 16

Clark, M. R.
 See Clark, Mavis Thorpe

Clark, Mavis Thorpe 1909- . . . . **CLC 12**
 See also CA 57-60; CANR 8, 37; CLR 30;
 MAICYA; SAAS 5; SATA 8, 74

Clark, Walter Van Tilburg
 1909-1971 . . . . **CLC 28**
 See also CA 9-12R; 33-36R; DLB 9;
 SATA 8

Clarke, Arthur C(harles)
 1917- . . . . . . **CLC 1, 4, 13, 18, 35; SSC 3**
 See also AAYA 4; CA 1-4R; CANR 2, 28;
 JRDA; MAICYA; MTCW; SATA 13, 70

Clarke, Austin 1896-1974. . . . . **CLC 6, 9**
 See also CA 29-32; 49-52; CAP 2; DLB 10,
 20

Clarke, Austin C(hesterfield)
 1934- . . . . **CLC 8, 53**
 See also BLC 1; BW; CA 25-28R;
 CAAS 16; CANR 14, 32; DLB 53, 125

Clarke, Gillian 1937- . . . . **CLC 61**
 See also CA 106; DLB 40

Clarke, Marcus (Andrew Hislop)
 1846-1881 . . . . **NCLC 19**

Clarke, Shirley 1925- . . . . **CLC 16**

Clash, The . . . . **CLC 30**
 See also Headon, (Nicky) Topper; Jones,
 Mick; Simonon, Paul; Strummer, Joe

Claudel, Paul (Louis Charles Marie)
 1868-1955 . . . . **TCLC 2, 10**
 See also CA 104

Clavell, James (duMaresq)
 1925- . . . . **CLC 6, 25**
 See also CA 25-28R; CANR 26; MTCW

Cleaver, (Leroy) Eldridge 1935- . . . . **CLC 30**
 See also BLC 1; BW; CA 21-24R;
 CANR 16

Cleese, John (Marwood) 1939- . . . . . **CLC 21**
 See also Monty Python
 See also CA 112; 116; CANR 35; MTCW

Cleishbotham, Jebediah
 See Scott, Walter

Cleland, John 1710-1789 . . . . **LC 2**
 See also DLB 39

Clemens, Samuel Langhorne 1835-1910
 See Twain, Mark
 See also CA 104; 135; CDALB 1865-1917;
 DA; DLB 11, 12, 23, 64, 74; JRDA;
 MAICYA; YABC 2

Cleophil
 See Congreve, William

Clerihew, E.
 See Bentley, E(dmund) C(lerihew)

Clerk, N. W.
 See Lewis, C(live) S(taples)

Cliff, Jimmy. **CLC 21**
 See also Chambers, James

Clifton, (Thelma) Lucille
 1936- . . . . **CLC 19, 66**
 See also BLC 1; BW; CA 49-52; CANR 2,
 24, 42; CLR 5; DLB 5, 41; MAICYA;
 MTCW; SATA 20, 69

Clinton, Dirk
 See Silverberg, Robert

Clough, Arthur Hugh 1819-1861. . **NCLC 27**
 See also DLB 32

Clutha, Janet Paterson Frame 1924-
 See Frame, Janet
 See also CA 1-4R; CANR 2, 36; MTCW

Clyne, Terence
 See Blatty, William Peter

Cobalt, Martin
 See Mayne, William (James Carter)

Coburn, D(onald) L(ee) 1938- . . . . . . **CLC 10**
 See also CA 89-92

Cocteau, Jean (Maurice Eugene Clement)
 1889-1963 . . . . **CLC 1, 8, 15, 16, 43**
 See also CA 25-28; CANR 40; CAP 2; DA;
 DLB 65; MTCW; WLC

Codrescu, Andrei 1946- . . . . **CLC 46**
 See also CA 33-36R; CANR 13, 34

Coe, Max
 See Bourne, Randolph S(illiman)

Coe, Tucker
 See Westlake, Donald E(dwin)

Coetzee, J(ohn) M(ichael)
 1940- . . . . **CLC 23, 33, 66**
 See also CA 77-80; CANR 41; MTCW

Coffey, Brian
 See Koontz, Dean R(ay)

Cohen, Arthur A(llen)
 1928-1986 . . . . **CLC 7, 31**
 See also CA 1-4R; 120; CANR 1, 17, 42;
 DLB 28

Cohen, Leonard (Norman)
 1934- . . . . **CLC 3, 38**
 See also CA 21-24R; CANR 14; DLB 53;
 MTCW

Cohen, Matt 1942- . . . . **CLC 19**
 See also CA 61-64; CAAS 18; CANR 40;
 DLB 53

Cohen-Solal, Annie 19(?)- . . . . **CLC 50**

Colegate, Isabel 1931- . . . . **CLC 36**
 See also CA 17-20R; CANR 8, 22; DLB 14;
 MTCW

Coleman, Emmett
 See Reed, Ishmael

Coleridge, Samuel Taylor
 1772-1834 . . . . **NCLC 9**
 See also CDBLB 1789-1832; DA; DLB 93,
 107; WLC

Coleridge, Sara 1802-1852. . . . . . . **NCLC 31**

Coles, Don 1928- . . . . **CLC 46**
 See also CA 115; CANR 38

Colette, (Sidonie-Gabrielle)
 1873-1954 . . . . . . **TCLC 1, 5, 16; SSC 10**
 See also CA 104; 131; DLB 65; MTCW

Collett, (Jacobine) Camilla (Wergeland)
 1813-1895 . . . . **NCLC 22**

Cowley, Malcolm   1898-1989 . . . .   **CLC 39**
See also CA 5-8R; 128; CANR 3; DLB 4,
48; DLBY 81, 89; MTCW

Cowper, William   1731-1800. . . . . . .   **NCLC 8**
See also DLB 104, 109

Cox, William Trevor   1928- . .   **CLC 9, 14, 71**
See also Trevor, William
See also CA 9-12R; CANR 4, 37; DLB 14;
MTCW

Cozzens, James Gould
1903-1978 . . . .   **CLC 1, 4, 11**
See also CA 9-12R; 81-84; CANR 19;
CDALB 1941-1968; DLB 9; DLBD 2;
DLBY 84; MTCW

Crabbe, George   1754-1832. . . . . .   **NCLC 26**
See also DLB 93

Craig, A. A.
See Anderson, Poul (William)

Craik, Dinah Maria (Mulock)
1826-1887 . . . .   **NCLC 38**
See also DLB 35; MAICYA; SATA 34

Cram, Ralph Adams   1863-1942. . . .   **TCLC 45**

Crane, (Harold) Hart
1899-1932 . . . .   **TCLC 2, 5; PC 3**
See also CA 104; 127; CDALB 1917-1929;
DA; DLB 4, 48; MTCW; WLC

Crane, R(onald) S(almon)
1886-1967 . . . .   **CLC 27**
See also CA 85-88; DLB 63

Crane, Stephen (Townley)
1871-1900 . . . . .   **TCLC 11, 17, 32; SSC 7**
See also CA 109; 140; CDALB 1865-1917;
DA; DLB 12, 54, 78; WLC; YABC 2

Crase, Douglas   1944- . . . .   **CLC 58**
See also CA 106

Crashaw, Richard   1612(?)-1649. . . . . .   **LC 24**
See also DLB 126

Craven, Margaret   1901-1980. . . . . . .   **CLC 17**
See also CA 103

Crawford, F(rancis) Marion
1854-1909 . . . .   **TCLC 10**
See also CA 107; DLB 71

Crawford, Isabella Valancy
1850-1887 . . . .   **NCLC 12**
See also DLB 92

Crayon, Geoffrey
See Irving, Washington

Creasey, John   1908-1973. . . . .   **CLC 11**
See also CA 5-8R; 41-44R; CANR 8;
DLB 77; MTCW

Crebillon, Claude Prosper Jolyot de (fils)
1707-1777 . . . .   **LC 1**

Credo
See Creasey, John

Creeley, Robert (White)
1926- . . . . .   **CLC 1, 2, 4, 8, 11, 15, 36, 78**
See also CA 1-4R; CAAS 10; CANR 23, 43;
DLB 5, 16; MTCW

Crews, Harry (Eugene)
1935- . . . .   **CLC 6, 23, 49**
See also AITN 1; CA 25-28R; CANR 20;
DLB 6; MTCW

Crichton, (John) Michael
1942- . . . .   **CLC 2, 6, 54**
See also AAYA 10; AITN 2; CA 25-28R;
CANR 13, 40; DLBY 81; JRDA;
MTCW; SATA 9

Crispin, Edmund . . . .   **CLC 22**
See also Montgomery, (Robert) Bruce
See also DLB 87

Cristofer, Michael   1945(?)- . . . .   **CLC 28**
See also CA 110; DLB 7

Croce, Benedetto   1866-1952 . . . . . .   **TCLC 37**
See also CA 120

Crockett, David   1786-1836 . . . .   **NCLC 8**
See also DLB 3, 11

Crockett, Davy
See Crockett, David

Croker, John Wilson   1780-1857 . .   **NCLC 10**
See also DLB 110

Crommelynck, Fernand   1885-1970 . .   **CLC 75**
See also CA 89-92

Cronin, A(rchibald) J(oseph)
1896-1981 . . . .   **CLC 32**
See also CA 1-4R; 102; CANR 5; SATA 25,
47

Cross, Amanda
See Heilbrun, Carolyn G(old)

Crothers, Rachel   1878(?)-1958. . . . .   **TCLC 19**
See also CA 113; DLB 7

Croves, Hal
See Traven, B.

Crowfield, Christopher
See Stowe, Harriet (Elizabeth) Beecher

Crowley, Aleister. . . . .   **TCLC 7**
See also Crowley, Edward Alexander

Crowley, Edward Alexander   1875-1947
See Crowley, Aleister
See also CA 104

Crowley, John   1942-. . . . .   **CLC 57**
See also CA 61-64; CANR 43; DLBY 82;
SATA 65

Crud
See Crumb, R(obert)

Crumarums
See Crumb, R(obert)

Crumb, R(obert)   1943-. . . . .   **CLC 17**
See also CA 106

Crumbum
See Crumb, R(obert)

Crumski
See Crumb, R(obert)

Crum the Bum
See Crumb, R(obert)

Crunk
See Crumb, R(obert)

Crustt
See Crumb, R(obert)

Cryer, Gretchen (Kiger)   1935-. . . . . .   **CLC 21**
See also CA 114; 123

Csath, Geza   1887-1919. . . . .   **TCLC 13**
See also CA 111

Cudlip, David   1933- . . . .   **CLC 34**

Cullen, Countee   1903-1946 . . . . .   **TCLC 4, 37**
See also BLC 1; BW; CA 108; 124;
CDALB 1917-1929; DA; DLB 4, 48, 51;
MTCW; SATA 18

Cum, R.
See Crumb, R(obert)

Cummings, Bruce F(rederick)   1889-1919
See Barbellion, W. N. P.
See also CA 123

Cummings, E(dward) E(stlin)
1894-1962 . . . . . .   **CLC 1, 3, 8, 12, 15, 68;
PC 5**
See also CA 73-76; CANR 31;
CDALB 1929-1941; DA; DLB 4, 48;
MTCW; WLC 2

Cunha, Euclides (Rodrigues Pimenta) da
1866-1909 . . . .   **TCLC 24**
See also CA 123

Cunningham, E. V.
See Fast, Howard (Melvin)

Cunningham, J(ames) V(incent)
1911-1985 . . . .   **CLC 3, 31**
See also CA 1-4R; 115; CANR 1; DLB 5

Cunningham, Julia (Woolfolk)
1916- . . . .   **CLC 12**
See also CA 9-12R; CANR 4, 19, 36;
JRDA; MAICYA; SAAS 2; SATA 1, 26

Cunningham, Michael   1952- . . . .   **CLC 34**
See also CA 136

Cunninghame Graham, R(obert) B(ontine)
1852-1936 . . . .   **TCLC 19**
See also Graham, R(obert) B(ontine)
Cunninghame
See also CA 119; DLB 98

Currie, Ellen   19(?)-. . . . .   **CLC 44**

Curtin, Philip
See Lowndes, Marie Adelaide (Belloc)

Curtis, Price
See Ellison, Harlan

Cutrate, Joe
See Spiegelman, Art

Czaczkes, Shmuel Yosef
See Agnon, S(hmuel) Y(osef Halevi)

D. P.
See Wells, H(erbert) G(eorge)

Dabrowska, Maria (Szumska)
1889-1965 . . . .   **CLC 15**
See also CA 106

Dabydeen, David   1955- . . . .   **CLC 34**
See also BW; CA 125

Dacey, Philip   1939- . . . .   **CLC 51**
See also CA 37-40R; CAAS 17; CANR 14,
32; DLB 105

Dagerman, Stig (Halvard)
1923-1954 . . . .   **TCLC 17**
See also CA 117

Dahl, Roald   1916-1990. . . . .   **CLC 1, 6, 18, 79**
See also CA 1-4R; 133; CANR 6, 32, 37;
CLR 1, 7; JRDA; MAICYA; MTCW;
SATA 1, 26, 73; SATA-Obit 65

Dahlberg, Edward   1900-1977. . .   **CLC 1, 7, 14**
See also CA 9-12R; 69-72; CANR 31;
DLB 48; MTCW

Dale, Colin. . . . .   **TCLC 18**
See also Lawrence, T(homas) E(dward)

Dale, George E.
See Asimov, Isaac

Daly, Elizabeth 1878-1967........ **CLC 52**
See also CA 23-24; 25-28R; CAP 2

Daly, Maureen 1921-............ **CLC 17**
See also AAYA 5; CANR 37; JRDA;
MAICYA; SAAS 1; SATA 2

Daniel, Samuel 1562(?)-1619....... **LC 24**
See also DLB 62

Daniels, Brett
See Adler, Renata

Dannay, Frederic 1905-1982....... **CLC 11**
See also Queen, Ellery
See also CA 1-4R; 107; CANR 1, 39;
MTCW

D'Annunzio, Gabriele
1863-1938 .... **TCLC 6, 40**
See also CA 104

d'Antibes, Germain
See Simenon, Georges (Jacques Christian)

Danvers, Dennis 1947-............ **CLC 70**

Danziger, Paula 1944-............ **CLC 21**
See also AAYA 4; CA 112; 115; CANR 37;
CLR 20; JRDA; MAICYA; SATA 30,
36, 63

Dario, Ruben 1867-1916.......... **TCLC 4**
See also CA 131; HW; MTCW

Darley, George 1795-1846........ **NCLC 2**
See also DLB 96

Daryush, Elizabeth 1887-1977.... **CLC 6, 19**
See also CA 49-52; CANR 3; DLB 20

Daudet, (Louis Marie) Alphonse
1840-1897 .... **NCLC 1**
See also DLB 123

Daumal, Rene 1908-1944........ **TCLC 14**
See also CA 114

Davenport, Guy (Mattison, Jr.)
1927-................... **CLC 6, 14, 38**
See also CA 33-36R; CANR 23; DLB 130

Davidson, Avram 1923-
See Queen, Ellery
See also CA 101; CANR 26; DLB 8

Davidson, Donald (Grady)
1893-1968 .... **CLC 2, 13, 19**
See also CA 5-8R; 25-28R; CANR 4;
DLB 45

Davidson, Hugh
See Hamilton, Edmond

Davidson, John 1857-1909....... **TCLC 24**
See also CA 118; DLB 19

Davidson, Sara 1943-............ **CLC 9**
See also CA 81-84

Davie, Donald (Alfred)
1922-............... **CLC 5, 8, 10, 31**
See also CA 1-4R; CAAS 3; CANR 1;
DLB 27; MTCW

Davies, Ray(mond Douglas) 1944-.. **CLC 21**
See also CA 116

Davies, Rhys 1903-1978.......... **CLC 23**
See also CA 9-12R; 81-84; CANR 4

Davies, (William) Robertson
1913-........ **CLC 2, 7, 13, 25, 42, 75**
See also BEST 89:2; CA 33-36R; CANR 17,
42; DA; DLB 68; MTCW; WLC

Davies, W(illiam) H(enry)
1871-1940 .... **TCLC 5**
See also CA 104; DLB 19

Davies, Walter C.
See Kornbluth, C(yril) M.

Davis, Angela (Yvonne) 1944-...... **CLC 77**
See also BW; CA 57-60; CANR 10

Davis, B. Lynch
See Bioy Casares, Adolfo; Borges, Jorge
Luis

Davis, Gordon
See Hunt, E(verette) Howard, Jr.

Davis, Harold Lenoir 1896-1960.... **CLC 49**
See also CA 89-92; DLB 9

Davis, Rebecca (Blaine) Harding
1831-1910 .... **TCLC 6**
See also CA 104; DLB 74

Davis, Richard Harding
1864-1916 .... **TCLC 24**
See also CA 114; DLB 12, 23, 78, 79

Davison, Frank Dalby 1893-1970... **CLC 15**
See also CA 116

Davison, Lawrence H.
See Lawrence, D(avid) H(erbert Richards)

Davison, Peter (Hubert) 1928-..... **CLC 28**
See also CA 9-12R; CAAS 4; CANR 3, 43;
DLB 5

Davys, Mary 1674-1732............ **LC 1**
See also DLB 39

Dawson, Fielding 1930-........... **CLC 6**
See also CA 85-88; DLB 130

Dawson, Peter
See Faust, Frederick (Schiller)

Day, Clarence (Shepard, Jr.)
1874-1935 .... **TCLC 25**
See also CA 108; DLB 11

Day, Thomas 1748-1789............ **LC 1**
See also DLB 39; YABC 1

Day Lewis, C(ecil)
1904-1972 .... **CLC 1, 6, 10**
See also Blake, Nicholas
See also CA 13-16; 33-36R; CANR 34;
CAP 1; DLB 15, 20; MTCW

Dazai, Osamu .... **TCLC 11**
See also Tsushima, Shuji

de Andrade, Carlos Drummond
See Drummond de Andrade, Carlos

Deane, Norman
See Creasey, John

de Beauvoir, Simone (Lucie Ernestine Marie
Bertrand)
See Beauvoir, Simone (Lucie Ernestine
Marie Bertrand) de

de Brissac, Malcolm
See Dickinson, Peter (Malcolm)

de Chardin, Pierre Teilhard
See Teilhard de Chardin, (Marie Joseph)
Pierre

Dee, John 1527-1608 .... **LC 20**

Deer, Sandra 1940-.............. **CLC 45**

De Ferrari, Gabriella .... **CLC 65**

Defoe, Daniel 1660(?)-1731......... **LC 1**
See also CDBLB 1660-1789; DA; DLB 39,
95, 101; JRDA; MAICYA; SATA 22;
WLC

de Gourmont, Remy
See Gourmont, Remy de

de Hartog, Jan 1914-............. **CLC 19**
See also CA 1-4R; CANR 1

de Hostos, E. M.
See Hostos (y Bonilla), Eugenio Maria de

de Hostos, Eugenio M.
See Hostos (y Bonilla), Eugenio Maria de

Deighton, Len .... **CLC 4, 7, 22, 46**
See also Deighton, Leonard Cyril
See also AAYA 6; BEST 89:2;
CDBLB 1960 to Present; DLB 87

Deighton, Leonard Cyril 1929-
See Deighton, Len
See also CA 9-12R; CANR 19, 33; MTCW

Dekker, Thomas 1572(?)-1632...... **LC 22**
See also CDBLB Before 1660; DLB 62

de la Mare, Walter (John)
1873-1956 .... **TCLC 4, 52**
See also CDBLB 1914-1945; CLR 23;
DLB 19; SATA 16; WLC

Delaney, Franey
See O'Hara, John (Henry)

Delaney, Shelagh 1939-........... **CLC 29**
See also CA 17-20R; CANR 30;
CDBLB 1960 to Present; DLB 13;
MTCW

Delany, Mary (Granville Pendarves)
1700-1788 .... **LC 12**

Delany, Samuel R(ay, Jr.)
1942-.................... **CLC 8, 14, 38**
See also BLC 1; BW; CA 81-84; CANR 27,
43; DLB 8, 33; MTCW

Delaporte, Theophile
See Green, Julian (Hartridge)

De La Ramee, (Marie) Louise 1839-1908
See Ouida
See also SATA 20

de la Roche, Mazo 1879-1961...... **CLC 14**
See also CA 85-88; CANR 30; DLB 68;
SATA 64

Delbanco, Nicholas (Franklin)
1942-.................... **CLC 6, 13**
See also CA 17-20R; CAAS 2; CANR 29;
DLB 6

del Castillo, Michel 1933-......... **CLC 38**
See also CA 109

Deledda, Grazia (Cosima)
1875(?)-1936 .... **TCLC 23**
See also CA 123

Delibes, Miguel .... **CLC 8, 18**
See also Delibes Setien, Miguel

Delibes Setien, Miguel 1920-
See Delibes, Miguel
See also CA 45-48; CANR 1, 32; HW;
MTCW

DeLillo, Don
1936-..... **CLC 8, 10, 13, 27, 39, 54, 76**
See also BEST 89:1; CA 81-84; CANR 21;
DLB 6; MTCW

de Lisser, H. G.
See De Lisser, Herbert George
See also DLB 117

De Lisser, Herbert George
1878-1944 . . . . **TCLC 12**
See also de Lisser, H. G.
See also CA 109

Deloria, Vine (Victor), Jr. 1933-. . . . **CLC 21**
See also CA 53-56; CANR 5, 20; MTCW;
SATA 21

Del Vecchio, John M(ichael)
1947- . . . . **CLC 29**
See also CA 110; DLBD 9

de Man, Paul (Adolph Michel)
1919-1983 . . . . **CLC 55**
See also CA 128; 111; DLB 67; MTCW

De Marinis, Rick 1934-. . . . . **CLC 54**
See also CA 57-60; CANR 9, 25

Demby, William 1922-. . . . . **CLC 53**
See also BLC 1; BW; CA 81-84; DLB 33

Demijohn, Thom
See Disch, Thomas M(ichael)

de Montherlant, Henry (Milon)
See Montherlant, Henry (Milon) de

de Natale, Francine
See Malzberg, Barry N(athaniel)

Denby, Edwin (Orr) 1903-1983 . . . . . **CLC 48**
See also CA 138; 110

Denis, Julio
See Cortazar, Julio

Denmark, Harrison
See Zelazny, Roger (Joseph)

Dennis, John 1658-1734. . . . . **LC 11**
See also DLB 101

Dennis, Nigel (Forbes) 1912-1989. . . . **CLC 8**
See also CA 25-28R; 129; DLB 13, 15;
MTCW

De Palma, Brian (Russell) 1940-. . . . **CLC 20**
See also CA 109

De Quincey, Thomas 1785-1859 . . . **NCLC 4**
See also CDBLB 1789-1832; DLB 110

Deren, Eleanora 1908(?)-1961
See Deren, Maya
See also CA 111

Deren, Maya . . . . **CLC 16**
See also Deren, Eleanora

Derleth, August (William)
1909-1971 . . . . **CLC 31**
See also CA 1-4R; 29-32R; CANR 4;
DLB 9; SATA 5

de Routisie, Albert
See Aragon, Louis

Derrida, Jacques 1930-. . . . . **CLC 24**
See also CA 124; 127

Derry Down Derry
See Lear, Edward

Dersonnes, Jacques
See Simenon, Georges (Jacques Christian)

Desai, Anita 1937-. . . . . **CLC 19, 37**
See also CA 81-84; CANR 33; MTCW;
SATA 63

de Saint-Luc, Jean
See Glassco, John

de Saint Roman, Arnaud
See Aragon, Louis

Descartes, Rene 1596-1650 . . . . **LC 20**

De Sica, Vittorio 1901(?)-1974 . . . . . **CLC 20**
See also CA 117

Desnos, Robert 1900-1945. . . . . . . **TCLC 22**
See also CA 121

Destouches, Louis-Ferdinand
1894-1961 . . . . **CLC 9, 15**
See also Celine, Louis-Ferdinand
See also CA 85-88; CANR 28; MTCW

Deutsch, Babette 1895-1982 . . . . **CLC 18**
See also CA 1-4R; 108; CANR 4; DLB 45;
SATA 1, 33

Devenant, William 1606-1649 . . . . . . **LC 13**

Devkota, Laxmiprasad
1909-1959 . . . . **TCLC 23**
See also CA 123

De Voto, Bernard (Augustine)
1897-1955 . . . . **TCLC 29**
See also CA 113; DLB 9

De Vries, Peter
1910-1993 . . . . **CLC 1, 2, 3, 7, 10, 28, 46**
See also CA 17-20R; 142; CANR 41;
DLB 6; DLBY 82; MTCW

Dexter, Martin
See Faust, Frederick (Schiller)

Dexter, Pete 1943-. . . . . **CLC 34, 55**
See also BEST 89:2; CA 127; 131; MTCW

Diamano, Silmang
See Senghor, Leopold Sedar

Diamond, Neil 1941- . . . . **CLC 30**
See also CA 108

di Bassetto, Corno
See Shaw, George Bernard

Dick, Philip K(indred)
1928-1982 . . . . **CLC 10, 30, 72**
See also CA 49-52; 106; CANR 2, 16;
DLB 8; MTCW

Dickens, Charles (John Huffam)
1812-1870 . . . . **NCLC 3, 8, 18, 26**
See also CDBLB 1832-1890; DA; DLB 21,
55, 70; JRDA; MAICYA; SATA 15

Dickey, James (Lafayette)
1923- . . . . **CLC 1, 2, 4, 7, 10, 15, 47**
See also AITN 1, 2; CA 9-12R; CABS 2;
CANR 10; CDALB 1968-1988; DLB 5;
DLBD 7; DLBY 82; MTCW

Dickey, William 1928-. . . . . **CLC 3, 28**
See also CA 9-12R; CANR 24; DLB 5

Dickinson, Charles 1951-. . . . . **CLC 49**
See also CA 128

Dickinson, Emily (Elizabeth)
1830-1886 . . . . **NCLC 21; PC 1**
See also CDALB 1865-1917; DA; DLB 1;
SATA 29; WLC

Dickinson, Peter (Malcolm)
1927-. . . . . **CLC 12, 35**
See also AAYA 9; CA 41-44R; CANR 31;
CLR 29; DLB 87; JRDA; MAICYA;
SATA 5, 62

Dickson, Carr
See Carr, John Dickson

Dickson, Carter
See Carr, John Dickson

Didion, Joan 1934-. . . . . **CLC 1, 3, 8, 14, 32**
See also AITN 1; CA 5-8R; CANR 14;
CDALB 1968-1988; DLB 2; DLBY 81,
86; MTCW

Dietrich, Robert
See Hunt, E(verette) Howard, Jr.

Dillard, Annie 1945-. . . . . **CLC 9, 60**
See also AAYA 6; CA 49-52; CANR 3, 43;
DLBY 80; MTCW; SATA 10

Dillard, R(ichard) H(enry) W(ilde)
1937- . . . . **CLC 5**
See also CA 21-24R; CAAS 7; CANR 10;
DLB 5

Dillon, Eilis 1920-. . . . . **CLC 17**
See also CA 9-12R; CAAS 3; CANR 4, 38;
CLR 26; MAICYA; SATA 2, 74

Dimont, Penelope
See Mortimer, Penelope (Ruth)

Dinesen, Isak. . . . . **CLC 10, 29; SSC 7**
See also Blixen, Karen (Christentze
Dinesen)

Ding Ling. . . . . **CLC 68**
See also Chiang Pin-chin

Disch, Thomas M(ichael) 1940-. . . **CLC 7, 36**
See also CA 21-24R; CAAS 4; CANR 17,
36; CLR 18; DLB 8; MAICYA; MTCW;
SAAS 15; SATA 54

Disch, Tom
See Disch, Thomas M(ichael)

d'Isly, Georges
See Simenon, Georges (Jacques Christian)

Disraeli, Benjamin 1804-1881 . . **NCLC 2, 39**
See also DLB 21, 55

Ditcum, Steve
See Crumb, R(obert)

Dixon, Paige
See Corcoran, Barbara

Dixon, Stephen 1936-. . . . . **CLC 52**
See also CA 89-92; CANR 17, 40; DLB 130

Doblin, Alfred . . . . **TCLC 13**
See also Doeblin, Alfred

Dobrolyubov, Nikolai Alexandrovich
1836-1861 . . . . **NCLC 5**

Dobyns, Stephen 1941-. . . . . **CLC 37**
See also CA 45-48; CANR 2, 18

Doctorow, E(dgar) L(aurence)
1931- . . . . . **CLC 6, 11, 15, 18, 37, 44, 65**
See also AITN 2; BEST 89:3; CA 45-48;
CANR 2, 33; CDALB 1968-1988; DLB 2,
28; DLBY 80; MTCW

Dodgson, Charles Lutwidge 1832-1898
See Carroll, Lewis
See also CLR 2; DA; MAICYA; YABC 2

Dodson, Owen (Vincent)
1914-1983 . . . . **CLC 79**
See also BLC 1; BW; CA 65-68; 110;
CANR 24; DLB 76

Doeblin, Alfred 1878-1957. . . . . . . **TCLC 13**
See also Doblin, Alfred
See also CA 110; 141; DLB 66

Doerr, Harriet 1910- . . . . **CLC 34**
See also CA 117; 122

Domecq, H(onorio) Bustos
See Bioy Casares, Adolfo; Borges, Jorge
Luis

Domini, Rey
See Lorde, Audre (Geraldine)

Dominique
See Proust, (Valentin-Louis-George-Eugene-) Marcel

Don, A
See Stephen, Leslie

Donaldson, Stephen R. 1947-...... **CLC 46**
See also CA 89-92; CANR 13

Donleavy, J(ames) P(atrick)
1926- .... **CLC 1, 4, 6, 10, 45**
See also AITN 2; CA 9-12R; CANR 24;
DLB 6; MTCW

Donne, John 1572-1631 .... **LC 10, 24; PC 1**
See also CDBLB Before 1660; DA;
DLB 121

Donnell, David 1939(?)- .... **CLC 34**

Donoso (Yanez), Jose
1924- .... **CLC 4, 8, 11, 32**
See also CA 81-84; CANR 32; DLB 113;
HW; MTCW

Donovan, John 1928-1992 .... **CLC 35**
See also CA 97-100; 137; CLR 3;
MAICYA; SATA 29

Don Roberto
See Cunninghame Graham, R(obert)
B(ontine)

Doolittle, Hilda
1886-1961 ..... **CLC 3, 8, 14, 31, 34, 73;
PC 5**
See also H. D.
See also CA 97-100; CANR 35; DA;
DLB 4, 45; MTCW; WLC

Dorfman, Ariel 1942- .... **CLC 48, 77**
See also CA 124; 130; HW

Dorn, Edward (Merton) 1929-... **CLC 10, 18**
See also CA 93-96; CANR 42; DLB 5

Dorsan, Luc
See Simenon, Georges (Jacques Christian)

Dorsange, Jean
See Simenon, Georges (Jacques Christian)

Dos Passos, John (Roderigo)
1896-1970 ... **CLC 1, 4, 8, 11, 15, 25, 34**
See also CA 1-4R; 29-32R; CANR 3;
CDALB 1929-1941; DA; DLB 4, 9;
DLBD 1; MTCW; WLC

Dossage, Jean
See Simenon, Georges (Jacques Christian)

Dostoevsky, Fedor Mikhailovich
1821-1881 .... **NCLC 2, 7, 21, 33; SSC 2**
See also DA; WLC

Doughty, Charles M(ontagu)
1843-1926 .... **TCLC 27**
See also CA 115; DLB 19, 57

Douglas, Ellen
See Haxton, Josephine Ayres

Douglas, Gavin 1475(?)-1522........ **LC 20**

Douglas, Keith 1920-1944 .... **TCLC 40**
See also DLB 27

Douglas, Leonard
See Bradbury, Ray (Douglas)

Douglas, Michael
See Crichton, (John) Michael

Douglass, Frederick 1817(?)-1895.. **NCLC 7**
See also BLC 1; CDALB 1640-1865; DA;
DLB 1, 43, 50, 79; SATA 29; WLC

Dourado, (Waldomiro Freitas) Autran
1926- .... **CLC 23, 60**
See also CA 25-28R; CANR 34

Dourado, Waldomiro Autran
See Dourado, (Waldomiro Freitas) Autran

Dove, Rita (Frances) 1952- ... **CLC 50; PC 6**
See also BW; CA 109; CANR 27, 42;
DLB 120

Dowell, Coleman 1925-1985........ **CLC 60**
See also CA 25-28R; 117; CANR 10;
DLB 130

Dowson, Ernest Christopher
1867-1900 .... **TCLC 4**
See also CA 105; DLB 19

Doyle, A. Conan
See Doyle, Arthur Conan

Doyle, Arthur Conan
1859-1930 .... **TCLC 7; SSC 12**
See also CA 104; 122; CDBLB 1890-1914;
DA; DLB 18, 70; MTCW; SATA 24;
WLC

Doyle, Conan 1859-1930
See Doyle, Arthur Conan

Doyle, John
See Graves, Robert (von Ranke)

Doyle, Sir A. Conan
See Doyle, Arthur Conan

Doyle, Sir Arthur Conan
See Doyle, Arthur Conan

Dr. A
See Asimov, Isaac; Silverstein, Alvin

Drabble, Margaret
1939- .... **CLC 2, 3, 5, 8, 10, 22, 53**
See also CA 13-16R; CANR 18, 35;
CDBLB 1960 to Present; DLB 14;
MTCW; SATA 48

Drapier, M. B.
See Swift, Jonathan

Drayham, James
See Mencken, H(enry) L(ouis)

Drayton, Michael 1563-1631........ **LC 8**

Dreadstone, Carl
See Campbell, (John) Ramsey

Dreiser, Theodore (Herman Albert)
1871-1945 .... **TCLC 10, 18, 35**
See also CA 106; 132; CDALB 1865-1917;
DA; DLB 9, 12, 102; DLBD 1; MTCW;
WLC

Drexler, Rosalyn 1926- .... **CLC 2, 6**
See also CA 81-84

Dreyer, Carl Theodor 1889-1968.... **CLC 16**
See also CA 116

Drieu la Rochelle, Pierre(-Eugene)
1893-1945 .... **TCLC 21**
See also CA 117; DLB 72

Drop Shot
See Cable, George Washington

Droste-Hulshoff, Annette Freiin von
1797-1848 .... **NCLC 3**
See also DLB 133

Drummond, Walter
See Silverberg, Robert

Drummond, William Henry
1854-1907 .... **TCLC 25**
See also DLB 92

Drummond de Andrade, Carlos
1902-1987 .... **CLC 18**
See also Andrade, Carlos Drummond de
See also CA 132; 123

Drury, Allen (Stuart) 1918-........ **CLC 37**
See also CA 57-60; CANR 18

Dryden, John 1631-1700 .... **LC 3, 21; DC 3**
See also CDBLB 1660-1789; DA; DLB 80,
101, 131; WLC

Duberman, Martin 1930-.......... **CLC 8**
See also CA 1-4R; CANR 2

Dubie, Norman (Evans) 1945-...... **CLC 36**
See also CA 69-72; CANR 12; DLB 120

Du Bois, W(illiam) E(dward) B(urghardt)
1868-1963 .... **CLC 1, 2, 13, 64**
See also BLC 1; BW; CA 85-88; CANR 34;
CDALB 1865-1917; DA; DLB 47, 50, 91;
MTCW; SATA 42; WLC

Dubus, Andre 1936- .... **CLC 13, 36**
See also CA 21-24R; CANR 17; DLB 130

Duca Minimo
See D'Annunzio, Gabriele

Ducharme, Rejean 1941-.......... **CLC 74**
See also DLB 60

Duclos, Charles Pinot 1704-1772 ..... **LC 1**

Dudek, Louis 1918- .... **CLC 11, 19**
See also CA 45-48; CAAS 14; CANR 1;
DLB 88

Duerrenmatt, Friedrich
1921-1990 ...... **CLC 1, 4, 8, 11, 15, 43**
See also Durrenmatt, Friedrich
See also CA 17-20R; CANR 33; DLB 69,
124; MTCW

Duffy, Bruce (?)-................. **CLC 50**

Duffy, Maureen 1933- .... **CLC 37**
See also CA 25-28R; CANR 33; DLB 14;
MTCW

Dugan, Alan 1923- .... **CLC 2, 6**
See also CA 81-84; DLB 5

du Gard, Roger Martin
See Martin du Gard, Roger

Duhamel, Georges 1884-1966 .... **CLC 8**
See also CA 81-84; 25-28R; CANR 35;
DLB 65; MTCW

Dujardin, Edouard (Emile Louis)
1861-1949 .... **TCLC 13**
See also CA 109; DLB 123

Dumas, Alexandre (Davy de la Pailleterie)
1802-1870 .... **NCLC 11**
See also DA; DLB 119; SATA 18; WLC

Dumas, Alexandre
1824-1895 .... **NCLC 9; DC 1**

Dumas, Claudine
See Malzberg, Barry N(athaniel)

Dumas, Henry L. 1934-1968 ..... **CLC 6, 62**
See also BW; CA 85-88; DLB 41

du Maurier, Daphne
  1907-1989 . . . . **CLC 6, 11, 59**
  See also CA 5-8R; 128; CANR 6; MTCW;
  SATA 27, 60

Dunbar, Paul Laurence
  1872-1906 . . . . **TCLC 2, 12; PC 5; SSC 8**
  See also BLC 1; BW; CA 104; 124;
  CDALB 1865-1917; DA; DLB 50, 54, 78;
  SATA 34; WLC

Dunbar, William   1460(?)-1530(?) . . . . **LC 20**

Duncan, Lois   1934- . . . . **CLC 26**
  See also AAYA 4; CA 1-4R; CANR 2, 23,
  36; CLR 29; JRDA; MAICYA; SAAS 2;
  SATA 1, 36, 75

Duncan, Robert (Edward)
  1919-1988 . . . . **CLC 1, 2, 4, 7, 15, 41, 55;**
                                               PC 2
  See also CA 9-12R; 124; CANR 28; DLB 5,
  16; MTCW

Dunlap, William   1766-1839 . . . . **NCLC 2**
  See also DLB 30, 37, 59

Dunn, Douglas (Eaglesham)
  1942- . . . . **CLC 6, 40**
  See also CA 45-48; CANR 2, 33; DLB 40;
  MTCW

Dunn, Katherine (Karen)   1945- . . . . . **CLC 71**
  See also CA 33-36R

Dunn, Stephen   1939- . . . . **CLC 36**
  See also CA 33-36R; CANR 12; DLB 105

Dunne, Finley Peter   1867-1936 . . . . **TCLC 28**
  See also CA 108; DLB 11, 23

Dunne, John Gregory   1932- . . . . **CLC 28**
  See also CA 25-28R; CANR 14; DLBY 80

Dunsany, Edward John Moreton Drax
  Plunkett   1878-1957
  See Dunsany, Lord; Lord Dunsany
  See also CA 104; DLB 10

Dunsany, Lord . . . . **TCLC 2**
  See also Dunsany, Edward John Moreton
  Drax Plunkett
  See also DLB 77

du Perry, Jean
  See Simenon, Georges (Jacques Christian)

Durang, Christopher (Ferdinand)
  1949- . . . . **CLC 27, 38**
  See also CA 105

Duras, Marguerite
  1914- . . . . . . **CLC 3, 6, 11, 20, 34, 40, 68**
  See also CA 25-28R; DLB 83; MTCW

Durban, (Rosa) Pam   1947- . . . . **CLC 39**
  See also CA 123

Durcan, Paul   1944- . . . . **CLC 43, 70**
  See also CA 134

Durrell, Lawrence (George)
  1912-1990 . . . . **CLC 1, 4, 6, 8, 13, 27, 41**
  See also CA 9-12R; 132; CANR 40;
  CDBLB 1945-1960; DLB 15, 27;
  DLBY 90; MTCW

Durrenmatt, Friedrich
  . . . . **CLC 1, 4, 8, 11, 15, 43**
  See also Duerrenmatt, Friedrich
  See also DLB 69, 124

Dutt, Toru   1856-1877 . . . . **NCLC 29**

Dwight, Timothy   1752-1817 . . . . . . **NCLC 13**
  See also DLB 37

Dworkin, Andrea   1946- . . . . **CLC 43**
  See also CA 77-80; CANR 16, 39; MTCW

Dwyer, Deanna
  See Koontz, Dean R(ay)

Dwyer, K. R.
  See Koontz, Dean R(ay)

Dylan, Bob   1941- . . . . . . **CLC 3, 4, 6, 12, 77**
  See also CA 41-44R; DLB 16

Eagleton, Terence (Francis)   1943-
  See Eagleton, Terry
  See also CA 57-60; CANR 7, 23; MTCW

Eagleton, Terry . . . . **CLC 63**
  See also Eagleton, Terence (Francis)

Early, Jack
  See Scoppettone, Sandra

East, Michael
  See West, Morris L(anglo)

Eastaway, Edward
  See Thomas, (Philip) Edward

Eastlake, William (Derry)   1917- . . . . . **CLC 8**
  See also CA 5-8R; CAAS 1; CANR 5;
  DLB 6

Eberhart, Richard (Ghormley)
  1904- . . . . **CLC 3, 11, 19, 56**
  See also CA 1-4R; CANR 2;
  CDALB 1941-1968; DLB 48; MTCW

Eberstadt, Fernanda   1960- . . . . **CLC 39**
  See also CA 136

Echegaray (y Eizaguirre), Jose (Maria Waldo)
  1832-1916 . . . . **TCLC 4**
  See also CA 104; CANR 32; HW; MTCW

Echeverria, (Jose) Esteban (Antonino)
  1805-1851 . . . . **NCLC 18**

Echo
  See Proust, (Valentin-Louis-George-Eugene-)
  Marcel

Eckert, Allan W.   1931- . . . . **CLC 17**
  See also CA 13-16R; CANR 14; SATA 27,
  29

Eckhart, Meister   1260(?)-1328(?) . . **CMLC 9**
  See also DLB 115

Eckmar, F. R.
  See de Hartog, Jan

Eco, Umberto   1932- . . . . **CLC 28, 60**
  See also BEST 90:1; CA 77-80; CANR 12,
  33; MTCW

Eddison, E(ric) R(ucker)
  1882-1945 . . . . **TCLC 15**
  See also CA 109

Edel, (Joseph) Leon   1907- . . . . . . **CLC 29, 34**
  See also CA 1-4R; CANR 1, 22; DLB 103

Eden, Emily   1797-1869 . . . . **NCLC 10**

Edgar, David   1948- . . . . **CLC 42**
  See also CA 57-60; CANR 12; DLB 13;
  MTCW

Edgerton, Clyde (Carlyle)   1944- . . . . **CLC 39**
  See also CA 118; 134

Edgeworth, Maria   1767-1849 . . . . . . **NCLC 1**
  See also DLB 116; SATA 21

Edmonds, Paul
  See Kuttner, Henry

Edmonds, Walter D(umaux)   1903- . . **CLC 35**
  See also CA 5-8R; CANR 2; DLB 9;
  MAICYA; SAAS 4; SATA 1, 27

Edmondson, Wallace
  See Ellison, Harlan

Edson, Russell . . . . **CLC 13**
  See also CA 33-36R

Edwards, G(erald) B(asil)
  1899-1976 . . . . **CLC 25**
  See also CA 110

Edwards, Gus   1939- . . . . **CLC 43**
  See also CA 108

Edwards, Jonathan   1703-1758 . . . . **LC 7**
  See also DA; DLB 24

Efron, Marina Ivanovna Tsvetaeva
  See Tsvetaeva (Efron), Marina (Ivanovna)

Ehle, John (Marsden, Jr.)   1925- . . . . **CLC 27**
  See also CA 9-12R

Ehrenbourg, Ilya (Grigoryevich)
  See Ehrenburg, Ilya (Grigoryevich)

Ehrenburg, Ilya (Grigoryevich)
  1891-1967 . . . . **CLC 18, 34, 62**
  See also CA 102; 25-28R

Ehrenburg, Ilyo (Grigoryevich)
  See Ehrenburg, Ilya (Grigoryevich)

Eich, Guenter   1907-1972 . . . . **CLC 15**
  See also CA 111; 93-96; DLB 69, 124

Eichendorff, Joseph Freiherr von
  1788-1857 . . . . **NCLC 8**
  See also DLB 90

Eigner, Larry . . . . **CLC 9**
  See also Eigner, Laurence (Joel)
  See also DLB 5

Eigner, Laurence (Joel)   1927-
  See Eigner, Larry
  See also CA 9-12R; CANR 6

Eiseley, Loren Corey   1907-1977 . . . . . **CLC 7**
  See also AAYA 5; CA 1-4R; 73-76;
  CANR 6

Eisenstadt, Jill   1963- . . . . **CLC 50**
  See also CA 140

Eisner, Simon
  See Kornbluth, C(yril) M.

Ekeloef, (Bengt) Gunnar
  1907-1968 . . . . **CLC 27**
  See also Ekelof, (Bengt) Gunnar
  See also CA 123; 25-28R

Ekelof, (Bengt) Gunnar . . . . **CLC 27**
  See also Ekeloef, (Bengt) Gunnar

Ekwensi, C. O. D.
  See Ekwensi, Cyprian (Odiatu Duaka)

Ekwensi, Cyprian (Odiatu Duaka)
  1921- . . . . **CLC 4**
  See also BLC 1; BW; CA 29-32R;
  CANR 18, 42; DLB 117; MTCW;
  SATA 66

Elaine . . . . **TCLC 18**
  See also Leverson, Ada

El Crummo
  See Crumb, R(obert)

Elia
  See Lamb, Charles

Eliade, Mircea   1907-1986 . . . . **CLC 19**
  See also CA 65-68; 119; CANR 30; MTCW

Eliot, A. D.
  See Jewett, (Theodora) Sarah Orne

Fainzilberg, Ilya Arnoldovich 1897-1937
See Ilf, Ilya
See also CA 120

Fair, Ronald L. 1932-............. **CLC 18**
See also BW; CA 69-72; CANR 25; DLB 33

Fairbairns, Zoe (Ann) 1948- .... **CLC 32**
See also CA 103; CANR 21

Falco, Gian
See Papini, Giovanni

Falconer, James
See Kirkup, James

Falconer, Kenneth
See Kornbluth, C(yril) M.

Falkland, Samuel
See Heijermans, Herman

Fallaci, Oriana 1930-............. **CLC 11**
See also CA 77-80; CANR 15; MTCW

Faludy, George 1913-............. **CLC 42**
See also CA 21-24R

Faludy, Gyoergy
See Faludy, George

Fanon, Frantz 1925-1961 .... **CLC 74**
See also BLC 2; BW; CA 116; 89-92

Fanshawe, Ann .... **LC 11**

Fante, John (Thomas) 1911-1983 ... **CLC 60**
See also CA 69-72; 109; CANR 23;
DLB 130; DLBY 83

Farah, Nuruddin 1945-............. **CLC 53**
See also BLC 2; CA 106; DLB 125

Fargue, Leon-Paul 1876(?)-1947 ... **TCLC 11**
See also CA 109

Farigoule, Louis
See Romains, Jules

Farina, Richard 1936(?)-1966 .... **CLC 9**
See also CA 81-84; 25-28R

Farley, Walter (Lorimer)
1915-1989 .... **CLC 17**
See also CA 17-20R; CANR 8, 29; DLB 22;
JRDA; MAICYA; SATA 2, 43

Farmer, Philip Jose 1918-....... **CLC 1, 19**
See also CA 1-4R; CANR 4, 35; DLB 8;
MTCW

Farquhar, George 1677-1707 .... **LC 21**
See also DLB 84

Farrell, J(ames) G(ordon)
1935-1979 .... **CLC 6**
See also CA 73-76; 89-92; CANR 36;
DLB 14; MTCW

Farrell, James T(homas)
1904-1979 .... **CLC 1, 4, 8, 11, 66**
See also CA 5-8R; 89-92; CANR 9; DLB 4,
9, 86; DLBD 2; MTCW

Farren, Richard J.
See Betjeman, John

Farren, Richard M.
See Betjeman, John

Fassbinder, Rainer Werner
1946-1982 .... **CLC 20**
See also CA 93-96; 106; CANR 31

Fast, Howard (Melvin) 1914- ...... **CLC 23**
See also CA 1-4R; CAAS 18; CANR 1, 33;
DLB 9; SATA 7

Faulcon, Robert
See Holdstock, Robert P.

Faulkner, William (Cuthbert)
1897-1962 ..... **CLC 1, 3, 6, 8, 9, 11, 14,
18, 28, 52, 68; SSC 1**
See also AAYA 7; CA 81-84; CANR 33;
CDALB 1929-1941; DA; DLB 9, 11, 44,
102; DLBD 2; DLBY 86; MTCW; WLC

Fauset, Jessie Redmon
1884(?)-1961 .... **CLC 19, 54**
See also BLC 2; BW; CA 109; DLB 51

Faust, Frederick (Schiller)
1892-1944(?) .... **TCLC 49**
See also CA 108

Faust, Irvin 1924-................ **CLC 8**
See also CA 33-36R; CANR 28; DLB 2, 28;
DLBY 80

Fawkes, Guy
See Benchley, Robert (Charles)

Fearing, Kenneth (Flexner)
1902-1961 .... **CLC 51**
See also CA 93-96; DLB 9

Fecamps, Elise
See Creasey, John

Federman, Raymond 1928- ...... **CLC 6, 47**
See also CA 17-20R; CAAS 8; CANR 10,
43; DLBY 80

Federspiel, J(uerg) F. 1931-........ **CLC 42**

Feiffer, Jules (Ralph) 1929-.... **CLC 2, 8, 64**
See also AAYA 3; CA 17-20R; CANR 30;
DLB 7, 44; MTCW; SATA 8, 61

Feige, Hermann Albert Otto Maximilian
See Traven, B.

Fei-Kan, Li
See Li Fei-kan

Feinberg, David B. 1956-......... **CLC 59**
See also CA 135

Feinstein, Elaine 1930-............ **CLC 36**
See also CA 69-72; CAAS 1; CANR 31;
DLB 14, 40; MTCW

Feldman, Irving (Mordecai) 1928-.... **CLC 7**
See also CA 1-4R; CANR 1

Fellini, Federico 1920-............ **CLC 16**
See also CA 65-68; CANR 33

Felsen, Henry Gregor 1916- .... **CLC 17**
See also CA 1-4R; CANR 1; SAAS 2;
SATA 1

Fenton, James Martin 1949-....... **CLC 32**
See also CA 102; DLB 40

Ferber, Edna 1887-1968.......... **CLC 18**
See also AITN 1; CA 5-8R; 25-28R; DLB 9,
28, 86; MTCW; SATA 7

Ferguson, Helen
See Kavan, Anna

Ferguson, Samuel 1810-1886 ..... **NCLC 33**
See also DLB 32

Ferling, Lawrence
See Ferlinghetti, Lawrence (Monsanto)

Ferlinghetti, Lawrence (Monsanto)
1919(?)- .... **CLC 2, 6, 10, 27; PC 1**
See also CA 5-8R; CANR 3, 41;
CDALB 1941-1968; DLB 5, 16; MTCW

Fernandez, Vicente Garcia Huidobro
See Huidobro Fernandez, Vicente Garcia

Ferrer, Gabriel (Francisco Victor) Miro
See Miro (Ferrer), Gabriel (Francisco
Victor)

Ferrier, Susan (Edmonstone)
1782-1854 .... **NCLC 8**
See also DLB 116

Ferrigno, Robert 1948(?)-......... **CLC 65**
See also CA 140

Feuchtwanger, Lion 1884-1958 ..... **TCLC 3**
See also CA 104; DLB 66

Feydeau, Georges (Leon Jules Marie)
1862-1921 .... **TCLC 22**
See also CA 113

Ficino, Marsilio 1433-1499 .... **LC 12**

Fiedeler, Hans
See Doeblin, Alfred

Fiedler, Leslie A(aron)
1917-.............. **CLC 4, 13, 24**
See also CA 9-12R; CANR 7; DLB 28, 67;
MTCW

Field, Andrew 1938-.............. **CLC 44**
See also CA 97-100; CANR 25

Field, Eugene 1850-1895 .... **NCLC 3**
See also DLB 23, 42; MAICYA; SATA 16

Field, Gans T.
See Wellman, Manly Wade

Field, Michael .... **TCLC 43**

Field, Peter
See Hobson, Laura Z(ametkin)

Fielding, Henry 1707-1754 .... **LC 1**
See also CDBLB 1660-1789; DA; DLB 39,
84, 101; WLC

Fielding, Sarah 1710-1768 .... **LC 1**
See also DLB 39

Fierstein, Harvey (Forbes) 1954- ... **CLC 33**
See also CA 123; 129

Figes, Eva 1932-................ **CLC 31**
See also CA 53-56; CANR 4; DLB 14

Finch, Robert (Duer Claydon)
1900-..................... **CLC 18**
See also CA 57-60; CANR 9, 24; DLB 88

Findley, Timothy 1930-............ **CLC 27**
See also CA 25-28R; CANR 12, 42;
DLB 53

Fink, William
See Mencken, H(enry) L(ouis)

Firbank, Louis 1942-
See Reed, Lou
See also CA 117

Firbank, (Arthur Annesley) Ronald
1886-1926 .... **TCLC 1**
See also CA 104; DLB 36

Fisher, M(ary) F(rances) K(ennedy)
1908-1992 .... **CLC 76**
See also CA 77-80; 138

Fisher, Roy 1930-................ **CLC 25**
See also CA 81-84; CAAS 10; CANR 16;
DLB 40

Fisher, Rudolph 1897-1934 .... **TCLC 11**
See also BLC 2; BW; CA 107; 124; DLB 51,
102

Fisher, Vardis (Alvero) 1895-1968.... **CLC 7**
See also CA 5-8R; 25-28R; DLB 9

Fiske, Tarleton
See Bloch, Robert (Albert)

Fitch, Clarke
See Sinclair, Upton (Beall)

Fitch, John IV
See Cormier, Robert (Edmund)

Fitgerald, Penelope 1916- .... CLC 61

Fitzgerald, Captain Hugh
See Baum, L(yman) Frank

FitzGerald, Edward 1809-1883 .... NCLC 9
See also DLB 32

Fitzgerald, F(rancis) Scott (Key)
1896-1940 .... TCLC 1, 6, 14, 28; SSC 6
See also AITN 1; CA 110; 123;
CDALB 1917-1929; DA; DLB 4, 9, 86;
DLBD 1; DLBY 81; MTCW; WLC

Fitzgerald, Penelope 1916-...... CLC 19, 51
See also CA 85-88; CAAS 10; DLB 14

Fitzgerald, Robert (Stuart)
1910-1985 .... CLC 39
See also CA 1-4R; 114; CANR 1; DLBY 80

FitzGerald, Robert D(avid)
1902-1987 .... CLC 19
See also CA 17-20R

Fitzgerald, Zelda (Sayre)
1900-1948 .... TCLC 52
See also CA 117; 126; DLBY 84

Flanagan, Thomas (James Bonner)
1923- .... CLC 25, 52
See also CA 108; DLBY 80; MTCW

Flaubert, Gustave
1821-1880 ..... NCLC 2, 10, 19; SSC 11
See also DA; DLB 119; WLC

Flecker, (Herman) James Elroy
1884-1915 .... TCLC 43
See also CA 109; DLB 10, 19

Fleming, Ian (Lancaster)
1908-1964 .... CLC 3, 30
See also CA 5-8R; CDBLB 1945-1960;
DLB 87; MTCW; SATA 9

Fleming, Thomas (James) 1927- .... CLC 37
See also CA 5-8R; CANR 10; SATA 8

Fletcher, John Gould 1886-1950... TCLC 35
See also CA 107; DLB 4, 45

Fleur, Paul
See Pohl, Frederik

Flooglebuckle, Al
See Spiegelman, Art

Flying Officer X
See Bates, H(erbert) E(rnest)

Fo, Dario 1926-................. CLC 32
See also CA 116; 128; MTCW

Fogarty, Jonathan Titulescu Esq.
See Farrell, James T(homas)

Folke, Will
See Bloch, Robert (Albert)

Follett, Ken(neth Martin) 1949- .... CLC 18
See also AAYA 6; BEST 89:4; CA 81-84;
CANR 13, 33; DLB 87; DLBY 81;
MTCW

Fontane, Theodor 1819-1898 ..... NCLC 26
See also DLB 129

Foote, Horton 1916-............. CLC 51
See also CA 73-76; CANR 34; DLB 26

Foote, Shelby 1916- .... CLC 75
See also CA 5-8R; CANR 3; DLB 2, 17

Forbes, Esther 1891-1967......... CLC 12
See also CA 13-14; 25-28R; CAP 1;
CLR 27; DLB 22; JRDA; MAICYA;
SATA 2

Forche, Carolyn (Louise) 1950-..... CLC 25
See also CA 109; 117; DLB 5

Ford, Elbur
See Hibbert, Eleanor Alice Burford

Ford, Ford Madox
1873-1939 .... TCLC 1, 15, 39
See also CA 104; 132; CDBLB 1914-1945;
DLB 34, 98; MTCW

Ford, John 1895-1973............. CLC 16
See also CA 45-48

Ford, Richard 1944-............. CLC 46
See also CA 69-72; CANR 11

Ford, Webster
See Masters, Edgar Lee

Foreman, Richard 1937-.......... CLC 50
See also CA 65-68; CANR 32

Forester, C(ecil) S(cott)
1899-1966 .... CLC 35
See also CA 73-76; 25-28R; SATA 13

Forez
See Mauriac, Francois (Charles)

Forman, James Douglas 1932-...... CLC 21
See also CA 9-12R; CANR 4, 19, 42;
JRDA; MAICYA; SATA 8, 70

Fornes, Maria Irene 1930-...... CLC 39, 61
See also CA 25-28R; CANR 28; DLB 7;
HW; MTCW

Forrest, Leon 1937-.............. CLC 4
See also BW; CA 89-92; CAAS 7;
CANR 25; DLB 33

Forster, E(dward) M(organ)
1879-1970 ..... CLC 1, 2, 3, 4, 9, 10, 13,
15, 22, 45, 77
See also AAYA 2; CA 13-14; 25-28R;
CAP 1; CDBLB 1914-1945; DA; DLB 34,
98; DLBD 10; MTCW; SATA 57; WLC

Forster, John 1812-1876 .... NCLC 11

Forsyth, Frederick 1938-...... CLC 2, 5, 36
See also BEST 89:4; CA 85-88; CANR 38;
DLB 87; MTCW

Forten, Charlotte L. .... TCLC 16
See also Grimke, Charlotte L(ottie) Forten
See also BLC 2; DLB 50

Foscolo, Ugo 1778-1827......... NCLC 8

Fosse, Bob .... CLC 20
See also Fosse, Robert Louis

Fosse, Robert Louis 1927-1987
See Fosse, Bob
See also CA 110; 123

Foster, Stephen Collins
1826-1864 .... NCLC 26

Foucault, Michel
1926-1984 .... CLC 31, 34, 69
See also CA 105; 113; CANR 34; MTCW

Fouque, Friedrich (Heinrich Karl) de la Motte
1777-1843 .... NCLC 2
See also DLB 90

Fournier, Henri Alban 1886-1914
See Alain-Fournier
See also CA 104

Fournier, Pierre 1916-........... CLC 11
See also Gascar, Pierre
See also CA 89-92; CANR 16, 40

Fowles, John
1926- .... CLC 1, 2, 3, 4, 6, 9, 10, 15, 33
See also CA 5-8R; CANR 25; CDBLB 1960
to Present; DLB 14; MTCW; SATA 22

Fox, Paula 1923-............... CLC 2, 8
See also AAYA 3; CA 73-76; CANR 20,
36; CLR 1; DLB 52; JRDA; MAICYA;
MTCW; SATA 17, 60

Fox, William Price (Jr.) 1926- ..... CLC 22
See also CA 17-20R; CANR 11; DLB 2;
DLBY 81

Foxe, John 1516(?)-1587 .... LC 14

Frame, Janet .... CLC 2, 3, 6, 22, 66
See also Clutha, Janet Paterson Frame

France, Anatole .... TCLC 9
See also Thibault, Jacques Anatole Francois
See also DLB 123

Francis, Claude 19(?)- .... CLC 50

Francis, Dick 1920- .... CLC 2, 22, 42
See also AAYA 5; BEST 89:3; CA 5-8R;
CANR 9, 42; CDBLB 1960 to Present;
DLB 87; MTCW

Francis, Robert (Churchill)
1901-1987 .... CLC 15
See also CA 1-4R; 123; CANR 1

Frank, Anne(lies Marie)
1929-1945 .... TCLC 17
See also CA 113; 133; DA; MTCW;
SATA 42; WLC

Frank, Elizabeth 1945-........... CLC 39
See also CA 121; 126

Franklin, Benjamin
See Hasek, Jaroslav (Matej Frantisek)

Franklin, (Stella Maraia Sarah) Miles
1879-1954 .... TCLC 7
See also CA 104

Fraser, Antonia (Pakenham)
1932- .... CLC 32
See also CA 85-88; MTCW; SATA 32

Fraser, George MacDonald 1925-.... CLC 7
See also CA 45-48; CANR 2

Fraser, Sylvia 1935-............. CLC 64
See also CA 45-48; CANR 1, 16

Frayn, Michael 1933-...... CLC 3, 7, 31, 47
See also CA 5-8R; CANR 30; DLB 13, 14;
MTCW

Fraze, Candida (Merrill) 1945- ..... CLC 50
See also CA 126

Frazer, J(ames) G(eorge)
1854-1941 .... TCLC 32
See also CA 118

Frazer, Robert Caine
See Creasey, John

Frazer, Sir James George
See Frazer, J(ames) G(eorge)

Frazier, Ian 1951-............... CLC 46
See also CA 130

Frederic, Harold 1856-1898...... **NCLC 10**
See also DLB 12, 23

Frederick, John
See Faust, Frederick (Schiller)

Frederick the Great 1712-1786...... **LC 14**

Fredro, Aleksander 1793-1876..... **NCLC 8**

Freeling, Nicolas 1927-.......... **CLC 38**
See also CA 49-52; CAAS 12; CANR 1, 17;
DLB 87

Freeman, Douglas Southall
1886-1953 .... **TCLC 11**
See also CA 109; DLB 17

Freeman, Judith 1946-............ **CLC 55**

Freeman, Mary Eleanor Wilkins
1852-1930 .... **TCLC 9; SSC 1**
See also CA 106; DLB 12, 78

Freeman, R(ichard) Austin
1862-1943 .... **TCLC 21**
See also CA 113; DLB 70

French, Marilyn 1929-...... **CLC 10, 18, 60**
See also CA 69-72; CANR 3, 31; MTCW

French, Paul
See Asimov, Isaac

Freneau, Philip Morin 1752-1832 .. **NCLC 1**
See also DLB 37, 43

Freud, Sigmund 1856-1939 .... **TCLC 52**
See also CA 115; 133; MTCW

Friedan, Betty (Naomi) 1921-...... **CLC 74**
See also CA 65-68; CANR 18; MTCW

Friedman, B(ernard) H(arper)
1926-...................... **CLC 7**
See also CA 1-4R; CANR 3

Friedman, Bruce Jay 1930-.... **CLC 3, 5, 56**
See also CA 9-12R; CANR 25; DLB 2, 28

Friel, Brian 1929-.......... **CLC 5, 42, 59**
See also CA 21-24R; CANR 33; DLB 13;
MTCW

Friis-Baastad, Babbis Ellinor
1921-1970 .... **CLC 12**
See also CA 17-20R; 134; SATA 7

Frisch, Max (Rudolf)
1911-1991 ..... **CLC 3, 9, 14, 18, 32, 44**
See also CA 85-88; 134; CANR 32;
DLB 69, 124; MTCW

Fromentin, Eugene (Samuel Auguste)
1820-1876 .... **NCLC 10**
See also DLB 123

Frost, Frederick
See Faust, Frederick (Schiller)

Frost, Robert (Lee)
1874-1963 .... **CLC 1, 3, 4, 9, 10, 13, 15,
26, 34, 44; PC 1**
See also CA 89-92; CANR 33;
CDALB 1917-1929; DA; DLB 54;
DLBD 7; MTCW; SATA 14; WLC

Froy, Herald
See Waterhouse, Keith (Spencer)

Fry, Christopher 1907-...... **CLC 2, 10, 14**
See also CA 17-20R; CANR 9, 30; DLB 13;
MTCW; SATA 66

Frye, (Herman) Northrop
1912-1991 .... **CLC 24, 70**
See also CA 5-8R; 133; CANR 8, 37;
DLB 67, 68; MTCW

Fuchs, Daniel 1909-1993 .... **CLC 8, 22**
See also CA 81-84; 142; CAAS 5;
CANR 40; DLB 9, 26, 28

Fuchs, Daniel 1934-.............. **CLC 34**
See also CA 37-40R; CANR 14

Fuentes, Carlos
1928-...... **CLC 3, 8, 10, 13, 22, 41, 60**
See also AAYA 4; AITN 2; CA 69-72;
CANR 10, 32; DA; DLB 113; HW;
MTCW; WLC

Fuentes, Gregorio Lopez y
See Lopez y Fuentes, Gregorio

Fugard, (Harold) Athol
1932-.... **CLC 5, 9, 14, 25, 40, 80; DC 3**
See also CA 85-88; CANR 32; MTCW

Fugard, Sheila 1932-.............. **CLC 48**
See also CA 125

Fuller, Charles (H., Jr.)
1939-................. **CLC 25; DC 1**
See also BLC 2; BW; CA 108; 112; DLB 38;
MTCW

Fuller, John (Leopold) 1937-....... **CLC 62**
See also CA 21-24R; CANR 9; DLB 40

Fuller, Margaret .... **NCLC 5**
See also Ossoli, Sarah Margaret (Fuller
marchesa d')

Fuller, Roy (Broadbent)
1912-1991 .... **CLC 4, 28**
See also CA 5-8R; 135; CAAS 10; DLB 15,
20

Fulton, Alice 1952-.............. **CLC 52**
See also CA 116

Furphy, Joseph 1843-1912....... **TCLC 25**

Fussell, Paul 1924-.............. **CLC 74**
See also BEST 90:1; CA 17-20R; CANR 8,
21, 35; MTCW

Futabatei, Shimei 1864-1909..... **TCLC 44**

Futrelle, Jacques 1875-1912 ...... **TCLC 19**
See also CA 113

G. B. S.
See Shaw, George Bernard

Gaboriau, Emile 1835-1873 ...... **NCLC 14**

Gadda, Carlo Emilio 1893-1973 .... **CLC 11**
See also CA 89-92

Gaddis, William
1922-........ **CLC 1, 3, 6, 8, 10, 19, 43**
See also CA 17-20R; CANR 21; DLB 2;
MTCW

Gaines, Ernest J(ames)
1933-................. **CLC 3, 11, 18**
See also AITN 1; BLC 2; BW; CA 9-12R;
CANR 6, 24, 42; CDALB 1968-1988;
DLB 2, 33; DLBY 80; MTCW

Gaitskill, Mary 1954-............ **CLC 69**
See also CA 128

Galdos, Benito Perez
See Perez Galdos, Benito

Gale, Zona 1874-1938 .... **TCLC 7**
See also CA 105; DLB 9, 78

Galeano, Eduardo (Hughes) 1940-... **CLC 72**
See also CA 29-32R; CANR 13, 32; HW

Galiano, Juan Valera y Alcala
See Valera y Alcala-Galiano, Juan

Gallagher, Tess 1943-......... **CLC 18, 63**
See also CA 106; DLB 120

Gallant, Mavis
1922-........ **CLC 7, 18, 38; SSC 5**
See also CA 69-72; CANR 29; DLB 53;
MTCW

Gallant, Roy A(rthur) 1924- .... **CLC 17**
See also CA 5-8R; CANR 4, 29; CLR 30;
MAICYA; SATA 4, 68

Gallico, Paul (William) 1897-1976 ... **CLC 2**
See also AITN 1; CA 5-8R; 69-72;
CANR 23; DLB 9; MAICYA; SATA 13

Gallup, Ralph
See Whitemore, Hugh (John)

Galsworthy, John 1867-1933.... **TCLC 1, 45**
See also CA 104; 141; CDBLB 1890-1914;
DA; DLB 10, 34, 98; WLC 2

Galt, John 1779-1839........... **NCLC 1**
See also DLB 99, 116

Galvin, James 1951-.............. **CLC 38**
See also CA 108; CANR 26

Gamboa, Federico 1864-1939..... **TCLC 36**

Gann, Ernest Kellogg 1910-1991.... **CLC 23**
See also AITN 1; CA 1-4R; 136; CANR 1

Garcia, Cristina 1958-............ **CLC 76**
See also CA 141

Garcia Lorca, Federico
1898-1936 .. **TCLC 1, 7, 49; DC 2; PC 3**
See also Lorca, Federico Garcia
See also CA 104; 131; DA; DLB 108; HW;
MTCW; WLC

Garcia Marquez, Gabriel (Jose)
1928- .... **CLC 2, 3, 8, 10, 15, 27, 47, 55;
SSC 8**
See also Marquez, Gabriel (Jose) Garcia
See also AAYA 3; BEST 89:1, 90:4;
CA 33-36R; CANR 10, 28; DA;
DLB 113; HW; MTCW; WLC

Gard, Janice
See Latham, Jean Lee

Gard, Roger Martin du
See Martin du Gard, Roger

Gardam, Jane 1928-.............. **CLC 43**
See also CA 49-52; CANR 2, 18, 33;
CLR 12; DLB 14; MAICYA; MTCW;
SAAS 9; SATA 28, 39

Gardner, Herb.................. **CLC 44**

Gardner, John (Champlin), Jr.
1933-1982 ..... **CLC 2, 3, 5, 7, 8, 10, 18,
28, 34; SSC 7**
See also AITN 1; CA 65-68; 107;
CANR 33; DLB 2; DLBY 82; MTCW;
SATA 31, 40

Gardner, John (Edmund) 1926-..... **CLC 30**
See also CA 103; CANR 15; MTCW

Gardner, Noel
See Kuttner, Henry

Gardons, S. S.
See Snodgrass, W(illiam) D(e Witt)

Garfield, Leon 1921-............. **CLC 12**
See also AAYA 8; CA 17-20R; CANR 38,
41; CLR 21; JRDA; MAICYA; SATA 1,
32

Glasscock, Amnesia
See Steinbeck, John (Ernst)

Glasser, Ronald J. 1940(?)- .... **CLC 37**

Glassman, Joyce
See Johnson, Joyce

Glendinning, Victoria 1937- .... **CLC 50**
See also CA 120; 127

Glissant, Edouard 1928- .... **CLC 10, 68**

Gloag, Julian 1930- .... **CLC 40**
See also AITN 1; CA 65-68; CANR 10

Gluck, Louise (Elisabeth)
1943- .... **CLC 7, 22, 44**
See also Glueck, Louise
See also CA 33-36R; CANR 40; DLB 5

Glueck, Louise .... **CLC 7, 22**
See also Gluck, Louise (Elisabeth)
See also DLB 5

Gobineau, Joseph Arthur (Comte) de
1816-1882 .... **NCLC 17**
See also DLB 123

Godard, Jean-Luc 1930- .... **CLC 20**
See also CA 93-96

Godden, (Margaret) Rumer 1907- ... **CLC 53**
See also AAYA 6; CA 5-8R; CANR 4, 27,
36; CLR 20; MAICYA; SAAS 12;
SATA 3, 36

Godoy Alcayaga, Lucila 1889-1957
See Mistral, Gabriela
See also CA 104; 131; HW; MTCW

Godwin, Gail (Kathleen)
1937- .... **CLC 5, 8, 22, 31, 69**
See also CA 29-32R; CANR 15, 43; DLB 6;
MTCW

Godwin, William 1756-1836...... **NCLC 14**
See also CDBLB 1789-1832; DLB 39, 104

Goethe, Johann Wolfgang von
1749-1832 .... **NCLC 4, 22, 34; PC 5**
See also DA; DLB 94; WLC 3

Gogarty, Oliver St. John
1878-1957 .... **TCLC 15**
See also CA 109; DLB 15, 19

Gogol, Nikolai (Vasilyevich)
1809-1852 ...... **NCLC 5, 15, 31; DC 1;**
SSC 4
See also DA; WLC

Goines, Donald 1937(?)-1974....... **CLC 80**
See also AITN 1; BLC 2; BW; CA 124; 114;
DLB 33

Gold, Herbert 1924- .... **CLC 4, 7, 14, 42**
See also CA 9-12R; CANR 17; DLB 2;
DLBY 81

Goldbarth, Albert 1948- .... **CLC 5, 38**
See also CA 53-56; CANR 6, 40; DLB 120

Goldberg, Anatol 1910-1982 .... **CLC 34**
See also CA 131; 117

Goldemberg, Isaac 1945- .... **CLC 52**
See also CA 69-72; CAAS 12; CANR 11,
32; HW

Golden Silver
See Storm, Hyemeyohsts

Golding, William G(erald)
1911-1993 .... **CLC 1, 2, 3, 8, 10, 17, 27,**
58
See also AAYA 5; CA 5-8R; 141;
CANR 13, 33; CDBLB 1945-1960; DA;
DLB 15, 100; MTCW; WLC

Goldman, Emma 1869-1940 ...... **TCLC 13**
See also CA 110

Goldman, Francisco 1955- .... **CLC 76**

Goldman, William (W.) 1931- .... **CLC 1, 48**
See also CA 9-12R; CANR 29; DLB 44

Goldmann, Lucien 1913-1970 ...... **CLC 24**
See also CA 25-28; CAP 2

Goldoni, Carlo 1707-1793 .... **LC 4**

Goldsberry, Steven 1949- .... **CLC 34**
See also CA 131

Goldsmith, Oliver 1728-1774........ **LC 2**
See also CDBLB 1660-1789; DA; DLB 39,
89, 104, 109; SATA 26; WLC

Goldsmith, Peter
See Priestley, J(ohn) B(oynton)

Gombrowicz, Witold
1904-1969 .... **CLC 4, 7, 11, 49**
See also CA 19-20; 25-28R; CAP 2

Gomez de la Serna, Ramon
1888-1963 .... **CLC 9**
See also CA 116; HW

Goncharov, Ivan Alexandrovich
1812-1891 .... **NCLC 1**

Goncourt, Edmond (Louis Antoine Huot) de
1822-1896 .... **NCLC 7**
See also DLB 123

Goncourt, Jules (Alfred Huot) de
1830-1870 .... **NCLC 7**
See also DLB 123

Gontier, Fernande 19(?)- .... **CLC 50**

Goodman, Paul 1911-1972.... **CLC 1, 2, 4, 7**
See also CA 19-20; 37-40R; CANR 34;
CAP 2; DLB 130; MTCW

Gordimer, Nadine
1923- .... **CLC 3, 5, 7, 10, 18, 33, 51, 70**
See also CA 5-8R; CANR 3, 28; DA;
MTCW

Gordon, Adam Lindsay
1833-1870 .... **NCLC 21**

Gordon, Caroline
1895-1981 .... **CLC 6, 13, 29**
See also CA 11-12; 103; CANR 36; CAP 1;
DLB 4, 9, 102; DLBY 81; MTCW

Gordon, Charles William 1860-1937
See Connor, Ralph
See also CA 109

Gordon, Mary (Catherine)
1949- .... **CLC 13, 22**
See also CA 102; DLB 6; DLBY 81;
MTCW

Gordon, Sol 1923- .... **CLC 26**
See also CA 53-56; CANR 4; SATA 11

Gordone, Charles 1925- .... **CLC 1, 4**
See also BW; CA 93-96; DLB 7; MTCW

Gorenko, Anna Andreevna
See Akhmatova, Anna

Gorky, Maxim................... **TCLC 8**
See also Peshkov, Alexei Maximovich
See also WLC

Goryan, Sirak
See Saroyan, William

Gosse, Edmund (William)
1849-1928 .... **TCLC 28**
See also CA 117; DLB 57

Gotlieb, Phyllis Fay (Bloom)
1926- .... **CLC 18**
See also CA 13-16R; CANR 7; DLB 88

Gottesman, S. D.
See Kornbluth, C(yril) M.; Pohl, Frederik

Gottfried von Strassburg
fl. c. 1210- .... **CMLC 10**

Gottschalk, Laura Riding
See Jackson, Laura (Riding)

Gould, Lois .... **CLC 4, 10**
See also CA 77-80; CANR 29; MTCW

Gourmont, Remy de 1858-1915.... **TCLC 17**
See also CA 109

Govier, Katherine 1948- .... **CLC 51**
See also CA 101; CANR 18, 40

Goyen, (Charles) William
1915-1983 .... **CLC 5, 8, 14, 40**
See also AITN 2; CA 5-8R; 110; CANR 6;
DLB 2; DLBY 83

Goytisolo, Juan 1931- .... **CLC 5, 10, 23**
See also CA 85-88; CANR 32; HW; MTCW

Gozzi, (Conte) Carlo 1720-1806 .. **NCLC 23**

Grabbe, Christian Dietrich
1801-1836 .... **NCLC 2**
See also DLB 133

Grace, Patricia 1937- .... **CLC 56**

Gracian y Morales, Baltasar
1601-1658 .... **LC 15**

Gracq, Julien................. **CLC 11, 48**
See also Poirier, Louis
See also DLB 83

Grade, Chaim 1910-1982 .... **CLC 10**
See also CA 93-96; 107

Graduate of Oxford, A
See Ruskin, John

Graham, John
See Phillips, David Graham

Graham, Jorie 1951- .... **CLC 48**
See also CA 111; DLB 120

Graham, R(obert) B(ontine) Cunninghame
See Cunninghame Graham, R(obert)
B(ontine)
See also DLB 98

Graham, Robert
See Haldeman, Joe (William)

Graham, Tom
See Lewis, (Harry) Sinclair

Graham, W(illiam) S(ydney)
1918-1986 .... **CLC 29**
See also CA 73-76; 118; DLB 20

Graham, Winston (Mawdsley)
1910- .... **CLC 23**
See also CA 49-52; CANR 2, 22; DLB 77

Grant, Skeeter
See Spiegelman, Art

Granville-Barker, Harley
1877-1946 .... **TCLC 2**
See also Barker, Harley Granville
See also CA 104

Grass, Guenter (Wilhelm)
1927- .. **CLC 1, 2, 4, 6, 11, 15, 22, 32, 49**
See also CA 13-16R; CANR 20; DA;
DLB 75, 124; MTCW; WLC

Gratton, Thomas
See Hulme, T(homas) E(rnest)

Grau, Shirley Ann 1929- .... **CLC 4, 9**
See also CA 89-92; CANR 22; DLB 2;
MTCW

Gravel, Fern
See Hall, James Norman

Graver, Elizabeth 1964- .... **CLC 70**
See also CA 135

Graves, Richard Perceval 1945- .... **CLC 44**
See also CA 65-68; CANR 9, 26

Graves, Robert (von Ranke)
1895-1985 ...... **CLC 1, 2, 6, 11, 39, 44,
45; PC 6**
See also CA 5-8R; 117; CANR 5, 36;
CDBLB 1914-1945; DLB 20, 100;
DLBY 85; MTCW; SATA 45

Gray, Alasdair 1934- .... **CLC 41**
See also CA 126; MTCW

Gray, Amlin 1946- .... **CLC 29**
See also CA 138

Gray, Francine du Plessix 1930-.... **CLC 22**
See also BEST 90:3; CA 61-64; CAAS 2;
CANR 11, 33; MTCW

Gray, John (Henry) 1866-1934 .... **TCLC 19**
See also CA 119

Gray, Simon (James Holliday)
1936- .... **CLC 9, 14, 36**
See also AITN 1; CA 21-24R; CAAS 3;
CANR 32; DLB 13; MTCW

Gray, Spalding 1941- .... **CLC 49**
See also CA 128

Gray, Thomas 1716-1771 ...... **LC 4; PC 2**
See also CDBLB 1660-1789; DA; DLB 109;
WLC

Grayson, David
See Baker, Ray Stannard

Grayson, Richard (A.) 1951- .... **CLC 38**
See also CA 85-88; CANR 14, 31

Greeley, Andrew M(oran) 1928- .... **CLC 28**
See also CA 5-8R; CAAS 7; CANR 7, 43;
MTCW

Green, Brian
See Card, Orson Scott

Green, Hannah
See Greenberg, Joanne (Goldenberg)

Green, Hannah .... **CLC 3**
See also CA 73-76

Green, Henry .... **CLC 2, 13**
See also Yorke, Henry Vincent
See also DLB 15

Green, Julian (Hartridge)
1900- .... **CLC 3, 11**
See also Green, Julien
See also CA 21-24R; CANR 33; DLB 4, 72;
MTCW

Green, Julien 1900- .... **CLC 77**
See also Green, Julian (Hartridge)

Green, Paul (Eliot) 1894-1981...... **CLC 25**
See also AITN 1; CA 5-8R; 103; CANR 3;
DLB 7, 9; DLBY 81

Greenberg, Ivan 1908-1973
See Rahv, Philip
See also CA 85-88

Greenberg, Joanne (Goldenberg)
1932- .... **CLC 7, 30**
See also CA 5-8R; CANR 14, 32; SATA 25

Greenberg, Richard 1959(?)- .... **CLC 57**
See also CA 138

Greene, Bette 1934- .... **CLC 30**
See also AAYA 7; CA 53-56; CANR 4;
CLR 2; JRDA; MAICYA; SAAS 16;
SATA 8

Greene, Gael .... **CLC 8**
See also CA 13-16R; CANR 10

Greene, Graham
1904-1991 .... **CLC 1, 3, 6, 9, 14, 18, 27,
37, 70, 72**
See also AITN 2; CA 13-16R; 133;
CANR 35; CDBLB 1945-1960; DA;
DLB 13, 15, 77, 100; DLBY 91; MTCW;
SATA 20; WLC

Greer, Richard
See Silverberg, Robert

Greer, Richard
See Silverberg, Robert

Gregor, Arthur 1923- .... **CLC 9**
See also CA 25-28R; CAAS 10; CANR 11;
SATA 36

Gregor, Lee
See Pohl, Frederik

Gregory, Isabella Augusta (Persse)
1852-1932 .... **TCLC 1**
See also CA 104; DLB 10

Gregory, J. Dennis
See Williams, John A(lfred)

Grendon, Stephen
See Derleth, August (William)

Grenville, Kate 1950- .... **CLC 61**
See also CA 118

Grenville, Pelham
See Wodehouse, P(elham) G(renville)

Greve, Felix Paul (Berthold Friedrich)
1879-1948
See Grove, Frederick Philip
See also CA 104; 141

Grey, Zane 1872-1939 .... **TCLC 6**
See also CA 104; 132; DLB 9; MTCW

Grieg, (Johan) Nordahl (Brun)
1902-1943 .... **TCLC 10**
See also CA 107

Grieve, C(hristopher) M(urray)
1892-1978 .... **CLC 11, 19**
See also MacDiarmid, Hugh
See also CA 5-8R; 85-88; CANR 33;
MTCW

Griffin, Gerald 1803-1840 .... **NCLC 7**

Griffin, John Howard 1920-1980.... **CLC 68**
See also AITN 1; CA 1-4R; 101; CANR 2

Griffin, Peter .... **CLC 39**

Griffiths, Trevor 1935-.......... **CLC 13, 52**
See also CA 97-100; DLB 13

Grigson, Geoffrey (Edward Harvey)
1905-1985 .... **CLC 7, 39**
See also CA 25-28R; 118; CANR 20, 33;
DLB 27; MTCW

Grillparzer, Franz 1791-1872...... **NCLC 1**
See also DLB 133

Grimble, Reverend Charles James
See Eliot, T(homas) S(tearns)

Grimke, Charlotte L(ottie) Forten
1837(?)-1914
See Forten, Charlotte L.
See also BW; CA 117; 124

Grimm, Jacob Ludwig Karl
1785-1863 .... **NCLC 3**
See also DLB 90; MAICYA; SATA 22

Grimm, Wilhelm Karl 1786-1859 .. **NCLC 3**
See also DLB 90; MAICYA; SATA 22

**Grimmelshausen, Johann Jakob Christoffel
von** 1621-1676 .... **LC 6**

Grindel, Eugene 1895-1952
See Eluard, Paul
See also CA 104

Grossman, David 1954- .... **CLC 67**
See also CA 138

Grossman, Vasily (Semenovich)
1905-1964 .... **CLC 41**
See also CA 124; 130; MTCW

Grove, Frederick Philip .... **TCLC 4**
See also Greve, Felix Paul (Berthold
Friedrich)
See also DLB 92

Grubb
See Crumb, R(obert)

Grumbach, Doris (Isaac)
1918- .... **CLC 13, 22, 64**
See also CA 5-8R; CAAS 2; CANR 9, 42

Grundtvig, Nicolai Frederik Severin
1783-1872 .... **NCLC 1**

Grunge
See Crumb, R(obert)

Grunwald, Lisa 1959-............ **CLC 44**
See also CA 120

Guare, John 1938- .... **CLC 8, 14, 29, 67**
See also CA 73-76; CANR 21; DLB 7;
MTCW

Gudjonsson, Halldor Kiljan 1902-
See Laxness, Halldor
See also CA 103

Guenter, Erich
See Eich, Guenter

Guest, Barbara 1920-............. **CLC 34**
See also CA 25-28R; CANR 11; DLB 5

Guest, Judith (Ann) 1936- .... **CLC 8, 30**
See also AAYA 7; CA 77-80; CANR 15;
MTCW

Guild, Nicholas M. 1944-......... **CLC 33**
See also CA 93-96

Guillemin, Jacques
See Sartre, Jean-Paul

Guillen, Jorge 1893-1984.......... **CLC 11**
See also CA 89-92; 112; DLB 108; HW

Guillen (y Batista), Nicolas (Cristobal)
1902-1989 . . . . **CLC 48, 79**
See also BLC 2; BW; CA 116; 125; 129;
HW

Guillevic, (Eugene) 1907- . . . . **CLC 33**
See also CA 93-96

Guillois
See Desnos, Robert

Guiney, Louise Imogen
1861-1920 . . . . **TCLC 41**
See also DLB 54

Guiraldes, Ricardo (Guillermo)
1886-1927 . . . . **TCLC 39**
See also CA 131; HW; MTCW

Gunn, Bill . . . . **CLC 5**
See also Gunn, William Harrison
See also DLB 38

Gunn, Thom(son William)
1929- . . . . **CLC 3, 6, 18, 32**
See also CA 17-20R; CANR 9, 33;
CDBLB 1960 to Present; DLB 27;
MTCW

Gunn, William Harrison 1934(?)-1989
See Gunn, Bill
See also AITN 1; BW; CA 13-16R; 128;
CANR 12, 25

Gunnars, Kristjana 1948- . . . . **CLC 69**
See also CA 113; DLB 60

Gurganus, Allan 1947- . . . . **CLC 70**
See also BEST 90:1; CA 135

Gurney, A(lbert) R(amsdell), Jr.
1930- . . . . **CLC 32, 50, 54**
See also CA 77-80; CANR 32

Gurney, Ivor (Bertie) 1890-1937 . . . **TCLC 33**

Gurney, Peter
See Gurney, A(lbert) R(amsdell), Jr.

Gustafson, Ralph (Barker) 1909- . . . . **CLC 36**
See also CA 21-24R; CANR 8; DLB 88

Gut, Gom
See Simenon, Georges (Jacques Christian)

Guthrie, A(lfred) B(ertram), Jr.
1901-1991 . . . . **CLC 23**
See also CA 57-60; 134; CANR 24; DLB 6;
SATA 62; SATA-Obit 67

Guthrie, Isobel
See Grieve, C(hristopher) M(urray)

Guthrie, Woodrow Wilson 1912-1967
See Guthrie, Woody
See also CA 113; 93-96

Guthrie, Woody . . . . **CLC 35**
See also Guthrie, Woodrow Wilson

Guy, Rosa (Cuthbert) 1928- . . . . **CLC 26**
See also AAYA 4; BW; CA 17-20R;
CANR 14, 34; CLR 13; DLB 33; JRDA;
MAICYA; SATA 14, 62

Gwendolyn
See Bennett, (Enoch) Arnold

H. D. . . . . **CLC 3, 8, 14, 31, 34, 73; PC 5**
See also Doolittle, Hilda

Haavikko, Paavo Juhani
1931- . . . . **CLC 18, 34**
See also CA 106

Habbema, Koos
See Heijermans, Herman

Hacker, Marilyn 1942- . . . . **CLC 5, 9, 23, 72**
See also CA 77-80; DLB 120

Haggard, H(enry) Rider
1856-1925 . . . . **TCLC 11**
See also CA 108; DLB 70; SATA 16

Haig, Fenil
See Ford, Ford Madox

Haig-Brown, Roderick (Langmere)
1908-1976 . . . . **CLC 21**
See also CA 5-8R; 69-72; CANR 4, 38;
CLR 31; DLB 88; MAICYA; SATA 12

Hailey, Arthur 1920- . . . . **CLC 5**
See also AITN 2; BEST 90:3; CA 1-4R;
CANR 2, 36; DLB 88; DLBY 82; MTCW

Hailey, Elizabeth Forsythe 1938- . . . **CLC 40**
See also CA 93-96; CAAS 1; CANR 15

Haines, John (Meade) 1924- . . . . **CLC 58**
See also CA 17-20R; CANR 13, 34; DLB 5

Haldeman, Joe (William) 1943- . . . . . **CLC 61**
See also CA 53-56; CANR 6; DLB 8

Haley, Alex(ander Murray Palmer)
1921-1992 . . . . **CLC 8, 12, 76**
See also BLC 2; BW; CA 77-80; 136; DA;
DLB 38; MTCW

Haliburton, Thomas Chandler
1796-1865 . . . . **NCLC 15**
See also DLB 11, 99

Hall, Donald (Andrew, Jr.)
1928- . . . . **CLC 1, 13, 37, 59**
See also CA 5-8R; CAAS 7; CANR 2;
DLB 5; SATA 23

Hall, Frederic Sauser
See Sauser-Hall, Frederic

Hall, James
See Kuttner, Henry

Hall, James Norman 1887-1951 . . . **TCLC 23**
See also CA 123; SATA 21

Hall, (Marguerite) Radclyffe
1886(?)-1943 . . . . **TCLC 12**
See also CA 110

Hall, Rodney 1935- . . . . **CLC 51**
See also CA 109

Halliday, Michael
See Creasey, John

Halpern, Daniel 1945- . . . . **CLC 14**
See also CA 33-36R

Hamburger, Michael (Peter Leopold)
1924- . . . . **CLC 5, 14**
See also CA 5-8R; CAAS 4; CANR 2;
DLB 27

Hamill, Pete 1935- . . . . **CLC 10**
See also CA 25-28R; CANR 18

Hamilton, Clive
See Lewis, C(live) S(taples)

Hamilton, Edmond 1904-1977 . . . . . . **CLC 1**
See also CA 1-4R; CANR 3; DLB 8

Hamilton, Eugene (Jacob) Lee
See Lee-Hamilton, Eugene (Jacob)

Hamilton, Franklin
See Silverberg, Robert

Hamilton, Gail
See Corcoran, Barbara

Hamilton, Mollie
See Kaye, M(ary) M(argaret)

Hamilton, (Anthony Walter) Patrick
1904-1962 . . . . **CLC 51**
See also CA 113; DLB 10

Hamilton, Virginia 1936- . . . . **CLC 26**
See also AAYA 2; BW; CA 25-28R;
CANR 20, 37; CLR 1, 11; DLB 33, 52;
JRDA; MAICYA; MTCW; SATA 4, 56

Hammett, (Samuel) Dashiell
1894-1961 . . . . **CLC 3, 5, 10, 19, 47**
See also AITN 1; CA 81-84; CANR 42;
CDALB 1929-1941; DLBD 6; MTCW

Hammon, Jupiter 1711(?)-1800(?) . . **NCLC 5**
See also BLC 2; DLB 31, 50

Hammond, Keith
See Kuttner, Henry

Hamner, Earl (Henry), Jr. 1923- . . . **CLC 12**
See also AITN 2; CA 73-76; DLB 6

Hampton, Christopher (James)
1946- . . . . **CLC 4**
See also CA 25-28R; DLB 13; MTCW

Hamsun, Knut . . . . **TCLC 2, 14, 49**
See also Pedersen, Knut

Handke, Peter 1942- . . **CLC 5, 8, 10, 15, 38**
See also CA 77-80; CANR 33; DLB 85,
124; MTCW

Hanley, James 1901-1985 . . . **CLC 3, 5, 8, 13**
See also CA 73-76; 117; CANR 36; MTCW

Hannah, Barry 1942- . . . . **CLC 23, 38**
See also CA 108; 110; CANR 43; DLB 6;
MTCW

Hannon, Ezra
See Hunter, Evan

Hansberry, Lorraine (Vivian)
1930-1965 . . . . **CLC 17, 62; DC 2**
See also BLC 2; BW; CA 109; 25-28R;
CABS 3; CDALB 1941-1968; DA;
DLB 7, 38; MTCW

Hansen, Joseph 1923- . . . . **CLC 38**
See also CA 29-32R; CAAS 17; CANR 16

Hansen, Martin A. 1909-1955 . . . . . **TCLC 32**

Hanson, Kenneth O(stlin) 1922- . . . . **CLC 13**
See also CA 53-56; CANR 7

Hardwick, Elizabeth 1916- . . . . **CLC 13**
See also CA 5-8R; CANR 3, 32; DLB 6;
MTCW

Hardy, Thomas
1840-1928 . . . . . . **TCLC 4, 10, 18, 32, 48;**
SSC 2
See also CA 104; 123; CDBLB 1890-1914;
DA; DLB 18, 19; MTCW; WLC

Hare, David 1947- . . . . **CLC 29, 58**
See also CA 97-100; CANR 39; DLB 13;
MTCW

Harford, Henry
See Hudson, W(illiam) H(enry)

Hargrave, Leonie
See Disch, Thomas M(ichael)

Harlan, Louis R(udolph) 1922- . . . . . **CLC 34**
See also CA 21-24R; CANR 25

Harling, Robert 1951(?)- . . . . **CLC 53**

Harmon, William (Ruth) 1938- . . . . . **CLC 38**
See also CA 33-36R; CANR 14, 32, 35;
SATA 65

Helforth, John
See Doolittle, Hilda

Hellenhofferu, Vojtech Kapristian z
See Hasek, Jaroslav (Matej Frantisek)

Heller, Joseph
1923-　．．．．．．．．**CLC 1, 3, 5, 8, 11, 36, 63**
See also AITN 1; CA 5-8R; CABS 1;
CANR 8, 42; DA; DLB 2, 28; DLBY 80;
MTCW; WLC

Hellman, Lillian (Florence)
1906-1984　．．．．．．**CLC 2, 4, 8, 14, 18, 34,**
　　　　　　　　　　　　　　44, 52; DC 1
See also AITN 1, 2; CA 13-16R; 112;
CANR 33; DLB 7; DLBY 84; MTCW

Helprin, Mark　1947-　．．．．．**CLC 7, 10, 22, 32**
See also CA 81-84; DLBY 85; MTCW

Helyar, Jane Penelope Josephine　1933-
See Poole, Josephine
See also CA 21-24R; CANR 10, 26

Hemans, Felicia　1793-1835　．．．．．．**NCLC 29**
See also DLB 96

Hemingway, Ernest (Miller)
1899-1961　．．．．**CLC 1, 3, 6, 8, 10, 13, 19,**
　　　　　　　　30, 34, 39, 41, 44, 50, 61, 80; SSC 1
See also CA 77-80; CANR 34;
CDALB 1917-1929; DA; DLB 4, 9, 102;
DLBD 1; DLBY 81, 87; MTCW; WLC

Hempel, Amy　1951-　．．．．．．．．．．．．．**CLC 39**
See also CA 118; 137

Henderson, F. C.
See Mencken, H(enry) L(ouis)

Henderson, Sylvia
See Ashton-Warner, Sylvia (Constance)

Henley, Beth　．．．．．．．．．．．．．．．．．．．．**CLC 23**
See also Henley, Elizabeth Becker
See also CABS 3; DLBY 86

Henley, Elizabeth Becker　1952-
See Henley, Beth
See also CA 107; CANR 32; MTCW

Henley, William Ernest
1849-1903　．．．．．．．．．．．．．．．．．．**TCLC 8**
See also CA 105; DLB 19

Hennissart, Martha
See Lathen, Emma
See also CA 85-88

Henry, O.　．．．．．．．．．．．．．**TCLC 1, 19; SSC 5**
See also Porter, William Sydney
See also WLC

Henryson, Robert　1430(?)-1506(?)．．．．**LC 20**

Henry VIII　1491-1547．．．．．．．．．．．．．**LC 10**

Henschke, Alfred
See Klabund

Hentoff, Nat(han Irving)　1925-　．．．．．**CLC 26**
See also AAYA 4; CA 1-4R; CAAS 6;
CANR 5, 25; CLR 1; JRDA; MAICYA;
SATA 27, 42, 69

Heppenstall, (John) Rayner
1911-1981　．．．．．．．．．．．．．．．．．．**CLC 10**
See also CA 1-4R; 103; CANR 29

Herbert, Frank (Patrick)
1920-1986　．．．．．．．．．**CLC 12, 23, 35, 44**
See also CA 53-56; 118; CANR 5, 43;
DLB 8; MTCW; SATA 9, 37, 47

Herbert, George　1593-1633　．．．．**LC 24; PC 4**
See also CDBLB Before 1660; DLB 126

Herbert, Zbigniew　1924-　．．．．．．．．**CLC 9, 43**
See also CA 89-92; CANR 36; MTCW

Herbst, Josephine (Frey)
1897-1969　．．．．．．．．．．．．．．．．．．**CLC 34**
See also CA 5-8R; 25-28R; DLB 9

Hergesheimer, Joseph
1880-1954　．．．．．．．．．．．．．．．．．．**TCLC 11**
See also CA 109; DLB 102, 9

Herlihy, James Leo　1927-　．．．．．．．．．．**CLC 6**
See also CA 1-4R; CANR 2

Hermogenes　fl. c. 175-　．．．．．．．．．．．**CMLC 6**

Hernandez, Jose　1834-1886．．．．．．**NCLC 17**

Herrick, Robert　1591-1674　．．．．．．．．**LC 13**
See also DA; DLB 126

Herring, Guilles
See Somerville, Edith

Herriot, James　1916-．．．．．．．．．．．．．．**CLC 12**
See also Wight, James Alfred
See also AAYA 1; CANR 40

Herrmann, Dorothy　1941-．．．．．．．．．**CLC 44**
See also CA 107

Herrmann, Taffy
See Herrmann, Dorothy

Hersey, John (Richard)
1914-1993　．．．．．．．．．**CLC 1, 2, 7, 9, 40**
See also CA 17-20R; 140; CANR 33;
DLB 6; MTCW; SATA 25

Herzen, Aleksandr Ivanovich
1812-1870　．．．．．．．．．．．．．．．．**NCLC 10**

Herzl, Theodor　1860-1904．．．．．．．**TCLC 36**

Herzog, Werner　1942-．．．．．．．．．．．．**CLC 16**
See also CA 89-92

Hesiod　c. 8th cent. B.C.-　．．．．．．．．．**CMLC 5**

Hesse, Hermann
1877-1962　．．．．**CLC 1, 2, 3, 6, 11, 17, 25,**
　　　　　　　　　　　　　　　69; SSC 9
See also CA 17-18; CAP 2; DA; DLB 66;
MTCW; SATA 50; WLC

Hewes, Cady
See De Voto, Bernard (Augustine)

Heyen, William　1940-　．．．．．．．．**CLC 13, 18**
See also CA 33-36R; CAAS 9; DLB 5

Heyerdahl, Thor　1914-．．．．．．．．．．．．**CLC 26**
See also CA 5-8R; CANR 5, 22; MTCW;
SATA 2, 52

Heym, Georg (Theodor Franz Arthur)
1887-1912　．．．．．．．．．．．．．．．．．．**TCLC 9**
See also CA 106

Heym, Stefan　1913-．．．．．．．．．．．．．．**CLC 41**
See also CA 9-12R; CANR 4; DLB 69

Heyse, Paul (Johann Ludwig von)
1830-1914　．．．．．．．．．．．．．．．．．．**TCLC 8**
See also CA 104; DLB 129

Hibbert, Eleanor Alice Burford
1906-1993　．．．．．．．．．．．．．．．．．．．**CLC 7**
See also BEST 90:4; CA 17-20R; 140;
CANR 9, 28; SATA 2; SATA-Obit 74

Higgins, George V(incent)
1939-　．．．．．．．．．．．．．．．**CLC 4, 7, 10, 18**
See also CA 77-80; CAAS 5; CANR 17;
DLB 2; DLBY 81; MTCW

Higginson, Thomas Wentworth
1823-1911　．．．．．．．．．．．．．．．．．**TCLC 36**
See also DLB 1, 64

Highet, Helen
See MacInnes, Helen (Clark)

Highsmith, (Mary) Patricia
1921-　．．．．．．．．．．．．．．**CLC 2, 4, 14, 42**
See also CA 1-4R; CANR 1, 20; MTCW

Highwater, Jamake (Mamake)
1942(?)-　．．．．．．．．．．．．．．．．．．．**CLC 12**
See also AAYA 7; CA 65-68; CAAS 7;
CANR 10, 34; CLR 17; DLB 52;
DLBY 85; JRDA; MAICYA; SATA 30,
32, 69

Hijuelos, Oscar　1951-　．．．．．．．．．．．．**CLC 65**
See also BEST 90:1; CA 123; HW

Hikmet, Nazim　1902(?)-1963．．．．．．**CLC 40**
See also CA 141; 93-96

Hildesheimer, Wolfgang
1916-1991　．．．．．．．．．．．．．．．．．．**CLC 49**
See also CA 101; 135; DLB 69, 124

Hill, Geoffrey (William)
1932-　．．．．．．．．．．．．．．．．**CLC 5, 8, 18, 45**
See also CA 81-84; CANR 21;
CDBLB 1960 to Present; DLB 40;
MTCW

Hill, George Roy　1921-　．．．．．．．．．．．．**CLC 26**
See also CA 110; 122

Hill, John
See Koontz, Dean R(ay)

Hill, Susan (Elizabeth)　1942-　．．．．．．．**CLC 4**
See also CA 33-36R; CANR 29; DLB 14;
MTCW

Hillerman, Tony　1925-．．．．．．．．．．．．**CLC 62**
See also AAYA 6; BEST 89:1; CA 29-32R;
CANR 21, 42; SATA 6

Hillesum, Etty　1914-1943　．．．．．．．**TCLC 49**
See also CA 137

Hilliard, Noel (Harvey)　1929-．．．．．．**CLC 15**
See also CA 9-12R; CANR 7

Hillis, Rick　1956-．．．．．．．．．．．．．．．．**CLC 66**
See also CA 134

Hilton, James　1900-1954．．．．．．．．**TCLC 21**
See also CA 108; DLB 34, 77; SATA 34

Himes, Chester (Bomar)
1909-1984　．．．．．．．．．**CLC 2, 4, 7, 18, 58**
See also BLC 2; BW; CA 25-28R; 114;
CANR 22; DLB 2, 76; MTCW

Hinde, Thomas　．．．．．．．．．．．．．．．．．**CLC 6, 11**
See also Chitty, Thomas Willes

Hindin, Nathan
See Bloch, Robert (Albert)

Hine, (William) Daryl　1936-．．．．．．．**CLC 15**
See also CA 1-4R; CAAS 15; CANR 1, 20;
DLB 60

Hinkson, Katharine Tynan
See Tynan, Katharine

Hinton, S(usan) E(loise)　1950-　．．．．．**CLC 30**
See also AAYA 2; CA 81-84; CANR 32;
CLR 3, 23; DA; JRDA; MAICYA;
MTCW; SATA 19, 58

Hippius, Zinaida　．．．．．．．．．．．．．．．．．**TCLC 9**
See also Gippius, Zinaida (Nikolayevna)

Hiraoka, Kimitake　1925-1970
See Mishima, Yukio
See also CA 97-100; 29-32R; MTCW

Hirsch, E(ric) D(onald), Jr. 1928-... **CLC 79**
See also CA 25-28R; CANR 27; DLB 67;
MTCW

Hirsch, Edward 1950- .... **CLC 31, 50**
See also CA 104; CANR 20, 42; DLB 120

Hitchcock, Alfred (Joseph)
1899-1980 .... **CLC 16**
See also CA 97-100; SATA 24, 27

Hoagland, Edward 1932- .... **CLC 28**
See also CA 1-4R; CANR 2, 31; DLB 6;
SATA 51

Hoban, Russell (Conwell) 1925- .. **CLC 7, 25**
See also CA 5-8R; CANR 23, 37; CLR 3;
DLB 52; MAICYA; MTCW; SATA 1, 40

Hobbs, Perry
See Blackmur, R(ichard) P(almer)

Hobson, Laura Z(ametkin)
1900-1986 .... **CLC 7, 25**
See also CA 17-20R; 118; DLB 28;
SATA 52

Hochhuth, Rolf 1931-........ **CLC 4, 11, 18**
See also CA 5-8R; CANR 33; DLB 124;
MTCW

Hochman, Sandra 1936-......... **CLC 3, 8**
See also CA 5-8R; DLB 5

Hochwaelder, Fritz 1911-1986...... **CLC 36**
See also Hochwalder, Fritz
See also CA 29-32R; 120; CANR 42;
MTCW

Hochwalder, Fritz.............. **CLC 36**
See also Hochwaelder, Fritz

Hocking, Mary (Eunice) 1921- ..... **CLC 13**
See also CA 101; CANR 18, 40

Hodgins, Jack 1938-............. **CLC 23**
See also CA 93-96; DLB 60

Hodgson, William Hope
1877(?)-1918 .... **TCLC 13**
See also CA 111; DLB 70

Hoffman, Alice 1952-............. **CLC 51**
See also CA 77-80; CANR 34; MTCW

Hoffman, Daniel (Gerard)
1923- .... **CLC 6, 13, 23**
See also CA 1-4R; CANR 4; DLB 5

Hoffman, Stanley 1944-........... **CLC 5**
See also CA 77-80

Hoffman, William M(oses) 1939- ... **CLC 40**
See also CA 57-60; CANR 11

Hoffmann, E(rnst) T(heodor) A(madeus)
1776-1822 .... **NCLC 2; SSC 13**
See also DLB 90; SATA 27

Hofmann, Gert 1931-............. **CLC 54**
See also CA 128

Hofmannsthal, Hugo von
1874-1929 .... **TCLC 11**
See also CA 106; DLB 81, 118

Hogan, Linda 1947-............. **CLC 73**
See also CA 120

Hogarth, Charles
See Creasey, John

Hogg, James 1770-1835.......... **NCLC 4**
See also DLB 93, 116

Holbach, Paul Henri Thiry Baron
1723-1789 .... **LC 14**

Holberg, Ludvig 1684-1754 .... **LC 6**

Holden, Ursula 1921-............. **CLC 18**
See also CA 101; CAAS 8; CANR 22

Holderlin, (Johann Christian) Friedrich
1770-1843 .... **NCLC 16; PC 4**

Holdstock, Robert
See Holdstock, Robert P.

Holdstock, Robert P. 1948-........ **CLC 39**
See also CA 131

Holland, Isabelle 1920- .... **CLC 21**
See also CA 21-24R; CANR 10, 25; JRDA;
MAICYA; SATA 8, 70

Holland, Marcus
See Caldwell, (Janet Miriam) Taylor
(Holland)

Hollander, John 1929-...... **CLC 2, 5, 8, 14**
See also CA 1-4R; CANR 1; DLB 5;
SATA 13

Hollander, Paul
See Silverberg, Robert

Holleran, Andrew 1943(?)-........ **CLC 38**

Hollinghurst, Alan 1954-.......... **CLC 55**
See also CA 114

Hollis, Jim
See Summers, Hollis (Spurgeon, Jr.)

Holmes, John
See Souster, (Holmes) Raymond

Holmes, John Clellon 1926-1988.... **CLC 56**
See also CA 9-12R; 125; CANR 4; DLB 16

Holmes, Oliver Wendell
1809-1894 .... **NCLC 14**
See also CDALB 1640-1865; DLB 1;
SATA 34

Holmes, Raymond
See Souster, (Holmes) Raymond

Holt, Victoria
See Hibbert, Eleanor Alice Burford

Holub, Miroslav 1923-............ **CLC 4**
See also CA 21-24R; CANR 10

Homer c. 8th cent. B.C.- .... **CMLC 1**
See also DA

Honig, Edwin 1919-.............. **CLC 33**
See also CA 5-8R; CAAS 8; CANR 4;
DLB 5

Hood, Hugh (John Blagdon)
1928- .... **CLC 15, 28**
See also CA 49-52; CAAS 17; CANR 1, 33;
DLB 53

Hood, Thomas 1799-1845........ **NCLC 16**
See also DLB 96

Hooker, (Peter) Jeremy 1941-...... **CLC 43**
See also CA 77-80; CANR 22; DLB 40

Hope, A(lec) D(erwent) 1907- .... **CLC 3, 51**
See also CA 21-24R; CANR 33; MTCW

Hope, Brian
See Creasey, John

Hope, Christopher (David Tully)
1944- .... **CLC 52**
See also CA 106; SATA 62

Hopkins, Gerard Manley
1844-1889 .... **NCLC 17**
See also CDBLB 1890-1914; DA; DLB 35,
57; WLC

Hopkins, John (Richard) 1931-...... **CLC 4**
See also CA 85-88

Hopkins, Pauline Elizabeth
1859-1930 .... **TCLC 28**
See also BLC 2; CA 141; DLB 50

Hopley-Woolrich, Cornell George 1903-1968
See Woolrich, Cornell
See also CA 13-14; CAP 1

Horatio
See Proust, (Valentin-Louis-George-Eugene-)
Marcel

Horgan, Paul 1903- .... **CLC 9, 53**
See also CA 13-16R; CANR 9, 35;
DLB 102; DLBY 85; MTCW; SATA 13

Horn, Peter
See Kuttner, Henry

Hornem, Horace Esq.
See Byron, George Gordon (Noel)

Horovitz, Israel 1939-............ **CLC 56**
See also CA 33-36R; DLB 7

Horvath, Odon von
See Horvath, Oedoen von
See also DLB 85, 124

Horvath, Oedoen von 1901-1938... **TCLC 45**
See also Horvath, Odon von
See also CA 118

Horwitz, Julius 1920-1986........ **CLC 14**
See also CA 9-12R; 119; CANR 12

Hospital, Janette Turner 1942-..... **CLC 42**
See also CA 108

Hostos, E. M. de
See Hostos (y Bonilla), Eugenio Maria de

Hostos, Eugenio M. de
See Hostos (y Bonilla), Eugenio Maria de

Hostos, Eugenio Maria
See Hostos (y Bonilla), Eugenio Maria de

Hostos (y Bonilla), Eugenio Maria de
1839-1903 .... **TCLC 24**
See also CA 123; 131; HW

Houdini
See Lovecraft, H(oward) P(hillips)

Hougan, Carolyn 1943- .... **CLC 34**
See also CA 139

Household, Geoffrey (Edward West)
1900-1988 .... **CLC 11**
See also CA 77-80; 126; DLB 87; SATA 14,
59

Housman, A(lfred) E(dward)
1859-1936 .... **TCLC 1, 10; PC 2**
See also CA 104; 125; DA; DLB 19;
MTCW

Housman, Laurence 1865-1959 ..... **TCLC 7**
See also CA 106; DLB 10; SATA 25

Howard, Elizabeth Jane 1923- ... **CLC 7, 29**
See also CA 5-8R; CANR 8

Howard, Maureen 1930- ..... **CLC 5, 14, 46**
See also CA 53-56; CANR 31; DLBY 83;
MTCW

Howard, Richard 1929- ...... **CLC 7, 10, 47**
See also AITN 1; CA 85-88; CANR 25;
DLB 5

Howard, Robert Ervin 1906-1936... **TCLC 8**
See also CA 105

Howard, Warren F.
See Pohl, Frederik

Johnson, Benj. F. of Boo
See Riley, James Whitcomb

Johnson, Benjamin F. of Boo
See Riley, James Whitcomb

Johnson, Charles (Richard)
1948- .... **CLC 7, 51, 65**
See also BLC 2; BW; CA 116; CAAS 18;
CANR 42; DLB 33

Johnson, Denis 1949- .... **CLC 52**
See also CA 117; 121; DLB 120

Johnson, Diane 1934- .... **CLC 5, 13, 48**
See also CA 41-44R; CANR 17, 40;
DLBY 80; MTCW

Johnson, Eyvind (Olof Verner)
1900-1976 .... **CLC 14**
See also CA 73-76; 69-72; CANR 34

Johnson, J. R.
See James, C(yril) L(ionel) R(obert)

Johnson, James Weldon
1871-1938 .... **TCLC 3, 19**
See also BLC 2; BW; CA 104; 125;
CDALB 1917-1929; CLR 32; DLB 51;
MTCW; SATA 31

Johnson, Joyce 1935- .... **CLC 58**
See also CA 125; 129

Johnson, Lionel (Pigot)
1867-1902 .... **TCLC 19**
See also CA 117; DLB 19

Johnson, Mel
See Malzberg, Barry N(athaniel)

Johnson, Pamela Hansford
1912-1981 .... **CLC 1, 7, 27**
See also CA 1-4R; 104; CANR 2, 28;
DLB 15; MTCW

Johnson, Samuel 1709-1784........ **LC 15**
See also CDBLB 1660-1789; DA; DLB 39,
95, 104; WLC

Johnson, Uwe
1934-1984 .... **CLC 5, 10, 15, 40**
See also CA 1-4R; 112; CANR 1, 39;
DLB 75; MTCW

Johnston, George (Benson) 1913- ... **CLC 51**
See also CA 1-4R; CANR 5, 20; DLB 88

Johnston, Jennifer 1930- .... **CLC 7**
See also CA 85-88; DLB 14

Jolley, (Monica) Elizabeth 1923- ... **CLC 46**
See also CA 127; CAAS 13

Jones, Arthur Llewellyn 1863-1947
See Machen, Arthur
See also CA 104

Jones, D(ouglas) G(ordon) 1929-... **CLC 10**
See also CA 29-32R; CANR 13; DLB 53

Jones, David (Michael)
1895-1974 .... **CLC 2, 4, 7, 13, 42**
See also CA 9-12R; 53-56; CANR 28;
CDBLB 1945-1960; DLB 20, 100; MTCW

Jones, David Robert 1947-
See Bowie, David
See also CA 103

Jones, Diana Wynne 1934- .... **CLC 26**
See also CA 49-52; CANR 4, 26; CLR 23;
JRDA; MAICYA; SAAS 7; SATA 9, 70

Jones, Edward P. 1950- .... **CLC 76**
See also CA 142

Jones, Gayl 1949- .... **CLC 6, 9**
See also BLC 2; BW; CA 77-80; CANR 27;
DLB 33; MTCW

Jones, James 1921-1977.... **CLC 1, 3, 10, 39**
See also AITN 1, 2; CA 1-4R; 69-72;
CANR 6; DLB 2; MTCW

Jones, John J.
See Lovecraft, H(oward) P(hillips)

Jones, LeRoi .... **CLC 1, 2, 3, 5, 10, 14**
See also Baraka, Amiri

Jones, Louis B. .... **CLC 65**
See also CA 141

Jones, Madison (Percy, Jr.) 1925-... **CLC 4**
See also CA 13-16R; CAAS 11; CANR 7

Jones, Mervyn 1922- .... **CLC 10, 52**
See also CA 45-48; CAAS 5; CANR 1;
MTCW

Jones, Mick 1956(?)- .... **CLC 30**
See also Clash, The

Jones, Nettie (Pearl) 1941- .... **CLC 34**
See also CA 137

Jones, Preston 1936-1979 .... **CLC 10**
See also CA 73-76; 89-92; DLB 7

Jones, Robert F(rancis) 1934-...... **CLC 7**
See also CA 49-52; CANR 2

Jones, Rod 1953- .... **CLC 50**
See also CA 128

Jones, Terence Graham Parry
1942- .... **CLC 21**
See also Jones, Terry; Monty Python
See also CA 112; 116; CANR 35; SATA 51

Jones, Terry
See Jones, Terence Graham Parry
See also SATA 67

Jong, Erica 1942- .... **CLC 4, 6, 8, 18**
See also AITN 1; BEST 90:2; CA 73-76;
CANR 26; DLB 2, 5, 28; MTCW

Jonson, Ben(jamin) 1572(?)-1637...... **LC 6**
See also CDBLB Before 1660; DA; DLB 62,
121; WLC

Jordan, June 1936-......... **CLC 5, 11, 23**
See also AAYA 2; BW; CA 33-36R;
CANR 25; CLR 10; DLB 38; MAICYA;
MTCW; SATA 4

Jordan, Pat(rick M.) 1941- .... **CLC 37**
See also CA 33-36R

Jorgensen, Ivar
See Ellison, Harlan

Jorgenson, Ivar
See Silverberg, Robert

Josipovici, Gabriel 1940- .... **CLC 6, 43**
See also CA 37-40R; CAAS 8; DLB 14

Joubert, Joseph 1754-1824 .... **NCLC 9**

Jouve, Pierre Jean 1887-1976...... **CLC 47**
See also CA 65-68

Joyce, James (Augustine Aloysius)
1882-1941 .... **TCLC 3, 8, 16, 35; SSC 3**
See also CA 104; 126; CDBLB 1914-1945;
DA; DLB 10, 19, 36; MTCW; WLC

Jozsef, Attila 1905-1937......... **TCLC 22**
See also CA 116

Juana Ines de la Cruz 1651(?)-1695 ... **LC 5**

Judd, Cyril
See Kornbluth, C(yril) M.; Pohl, Frederik

Julian of Norwich 1342(?)-1416(?) .... **LC 6**

Just, Ward (Swift) 1935-........ **CLC 4, 27**
See also CA 25-28R; CANR 32

Justice, Donald (Rodney) 1925- .. **CLC 6, 19**
See also CA 5-8R; CANR 26; DLBY 83

Juvenal c. 55-c. 127 .... **CMLC 8**

Juvenis
See Bourne, Randolph S(illiman)

Kacew, Romain 1914-1980
See Gary, Romain
See also CA 108; 102

Kadare, Ismail 1936- .... **CLC 52**

Kadohata, Cynthia................ **CLC 59**
See also CA 140

Kafka, Franz
1883-1924 .... **TCLC 2, 6, 13, 29, 47;**
SSC 5
See also CA 105; 126; DA; DLB 81;
MTCW; WLC

Kahn, Roger 1927-............... **CLC 30**
See also CA 25-28R; SATA 37

Kain, Saul
See Sassoon, Siegfried (Lorraine)

Kaiser, Georg 1878-1945 .... **TCLC 9**
See also CA 106; DLB 124

Kaletski, Alexander 1946-........ **CLC 39**
See also CA 118

Kalidasa fl. c. 400- .... **CMLC 9**

Kallman, Chester (Simon)
1921-1975 .... **CLC 2**
See also CA 45-48; 53-56; CANR 3

Kaminsky, Melvin 1926-
See Brooks, Mel
See also CA 65-68; CANR 16

Kaminsky, Stuart M(elvin) 1934-... **CLC 59**
See also CA 73-76; CANR 29

Kane, Paul
See Simon, Paul

Kane, Wilson
See Bloch, Robert (Albert)

Kanin, Garson 1912-.............. **CLC 22**
See also AITN 1; CA 5-8R; CANR 7;
DLB 7

Kaniuk, Yoram 1930-............. **CLC 19**
See also CA 134

Kant, Immanuel 1724-1804 ...... **NCLC 27**
See also DLB 94

Kantor, MacKinlay 1904-1977 ...... **CLC 7**
See also CA 61-64; 73-76; DLB 9, 102

Kaplan, David Michael 1946- ...... **CLC 50**

Kaplan, James 1951- .... **CLC 59**
See also CA 135

Karageorge, Michael
See Anderson, Poul (William)

Karamzin, Nikolai Mikhailovich
1766-1826 .... **NCLC 3**

Karapanou, Margarita 1946-....... **CLC 13**
See also CA 101

Karinthy, Frigyes 1887-1938...... **TCLC 47**

Karl, Frederick R(obert) 1927-..... **CLC 34**
See also CA 5-8R; CANR 3

King, Francis (Henry)   1923- . . . . .   **CLC 8, 53**
See also CA 1-4R; CANR 1, 33; DLB 15;
MTCW

King, Stephen (Edwin)
1947- . . . .   **CLC 12, 26, 37, 61**
See also AAYA 1; BEST 90:1; CA 61-64;
CANR 1, 30; DLBY 80; JRDA; MTCW;
SATA 9, 55

King, Steve
See King, Stephen (Edwin)

Kingman, Lee.   **CLC 17**
See also Natti, (Mary) Lee
See also SAAS 3; SATA 1, 67

Kingsley, Charles   1819-1875 . . . . .   **NCLC 35**
See also DLB 21, 32; YABC 2

Kingsley, Sidney   1906- . . . .   **CLC 44**
See also CA 85-88; DLB 7

Kingsolver, Barbara   1955- . . . .   **CLC 55**
See also CA 129; 134

Kingston, Maxine (Ting Ting) Hong
1940- . . . .   **CLC 12, 19, 58**
See also AAYA 8; CA 69-72; CANR 13,
38; DLBY 80; MTCW; SATA 53

Kinnell, Galway
1927- . . . .   **CLC 1, 2, 3, 5, 13, 29**
See also CA 9-12R; CANR 10, 34; DLB 5;
DLBY 87; MTCW

Kinsella, Thomas   1928- . . . .   **CLC 4, 19**
See also CA 17-20R; CANR 15; DLB 27;
MTCW

Kinsella, W(illiam) P(atrick)
1935- . . . .   **CLC 27, 43**
See also AAYA 7; CA 97-100; CAAS 7;
CANR 21, 35; MTCW

Kipling, (Joseph) Rudyard
1865-1936 . . . .   **TCLC 8, 17; PC 3; SSC 5**
See also CA 105; 120; CANR 33;
CDBLB 1890-1914; DA; DLB 19, 34;
MAICYA; MTCW; WLC; YABC 2

Kirkup, James   1918- . . . .   **CLC 1**
See also CA 1-4R; CAAS 4; CANR 2;
DLB 27; SATA 12

Kirkwood, James   1930(?)-1989 . . . . . .   **CLC 9**
See also AITN 2; CA 1-4R; 128; CANR 6,
40

Kis, Danilo   1935-1989 . . . .   **CLC 57**
See also CA 109; 118; 129; MTCW

Kivi, Aleksis   1834-1872 . . . .   **NCLC 30**

Kizer, Carolyn (Ashley)
1925- . . . .   **CLC 15, 39, 80**
See also CA 65-68; CAAS 5; CANR 24;
DLB 5

Klabund   1890-1928 . . . .   **TCLC 44**
See also DLB 66

Klappert, Peter   1942- . . . .   **CLC 57**
See also CA 33-36R; DLB 5

Klein, A(braham) M(oses)
1909-1972 . . . .   **CLC 19**
See also CA 101; 37-40R; DLB 68

Klein, Norma   1938-1989 . . . .   **CLC 30**
See also AAYA 2; CA 41-44R; 128;
CANR 15, 37; CLR 2, 19; JRDA;
MAICYA; SAAS 1; SATA 7, 57

Klein, T(heodore) E(ibon) D(onald)
1947- . . . .   **CLC 34**
See also CA 119

Kleist, Heinrich von   1777-1811 . . . .   **NCLC 2**
See also DLB 90

Klima, Ivan   1931- . . . .   **CLC 56**
See also CA 25-28R; CANR 17

Klimentov, Andrei Platonovich   1899-1951
See Platonov, Andrei
See also CA 108

Klinger, Friedrich Maximilian von
1752-1831 . . . .   **NCLC 1**
See also DLB 94

Klopstock, Friedrich Gottlieb
1724-1803 . . . .   **NCLC 11**
See also DLB 97

Knebel, Fletcher   1911-1993 . . . .   **CLC 14**
See also AITN 1; CA 1-4R; 140; CAAS 3;
CANR 1, 36; SATA 36; SATA-Obit 75

Knickerbocker, Diedrich
See Irving, Washington

Knight, Etheridge   1931-1991 . . . .   **CLC 40**
See also BLC 2; BW; CA 21-24R; 133;
CANR 23; DLB 41

Knight, Sarah Kemble   1666-1727 . . . . .   **LC 7**
See also DLB 24

Knowles, John   1926- . . . . . .   **CLC 1, 4, 10, 26**
See also AAYA 10; CA 17-20R; CANR 40;
CDALB 1968-1988; DA; DLB 6; MTCW;
SATA 8

Knox, Calvin M.
See Silverberg, Robert

Knye, Cassandra
See Disch, Thomas M(ichael)

Koch, C(hristopher) J(ohn)   1932- . . .   **CLC 42**
See also CA 127

Koch, Christopher
See Koch, C(hristopher) J(ohn)

Koch, Kenneth   1925- . . . .   **CLC 5, 8, 44**
See also CA 1-4R; CANR 6, 36; DLB 5;
SATA 65

Kochanowski, Jan   1530-1584 . . . .   **LC 10**

Kock, Charles Paul de
1794-1871 . . . .   **NCLC 16**

Koda Shigeyuki   1867-1947
See Rohan, Koda
See also CA 121

Koestler, Arthur
1905-1983 . . . .   **CLC 1, 3, 6, 8, 15, 33**
See also CA 1-4R; 109; CANR 1, 33;
CDBLB 1945-1960; DLBY 83; MTCW

Kogawa, Joy Nozomi   1935- . . . .   **CLC 78**
See also CA 101; CANR 19

Kohout, Pavel   1928- . . . .   **CLC 13**
See also CA 45-48; CANR 3

Koizumi, Yakumo
See Hearn, (Patricio) Lafcadio (Tessima
Carlos)

Kolmar, Gertrud   1894-1943 . . . .   **TCLC 40**

Konrad, George
See Konrad, Gyoergy

Konrad, Gyoergy   1933- . . . . . .   **CLC 4, 10, 73**
See also CA 85-88

Konwicki, Tadeusz   1926- . . . . .   **CLC 8, 28, 54**
See also CA 101; CAAS 9; CANR 39;
MTCW

Koontz, Dean R(ay)   1945- . . . .   **CLC 78**
See also AAYA 9; BEST 89:3, 90:2;
CA 108; CANR 19, 36; MTCW

Kopit, Arthur (Lee)   1937- . . . .   **CLC 1, 18, 33**
See also AITN 1; CA 81-84; CABS 3;
DLB 7; MTCW

Kops, Bernard   1926- . . . .   **CLC 4**
See also CA 5-8R; DLB 13

Kornbluth, C(yril) M.   1923-1958 . . . .   **TCLC 8**
See also CA 105; DLB 8

Korolenko, V. G.
See Korolenko, Vladimir Galaktionovich

Korolenko, Vladimir
See Korolenko, Vladimir Galaktionovich

Korolenko, Vladimir G.
See Korolenko, Vladimir Galaktionovich

Korolenko, Vladimir Galaktionovich
1853-1921 . . . .   **TCLC 22**
See also CA 121

Kosinski, Jerzy (Nikodem)
1933-1991 . . . .   **CLC 1, 2, 3, 6, 10, 15, 53,
70**
See also CA 17-20R; 134; CANR 9; DLB 2;
DLBY 82; MTCW

Kostelanetz, Richard (Cory)   1940- . .   **CLC 28**
See also CA 13-16R; CAAS 8; CANR 38

Kostrowitzki, Wilhelm Apollinaris de
1880-1918
See Apollinaire, Guillaume
See also CA 104

Kotlowitz, Robert   1924- . . . .   **CLC 4**
See also CA 33-36R; CANR 36

Kotzebue, August (Friedrich Ferdinand) von
1761-1819 . . . .   **NCLC 25**
See also DLB 94

Kotzwinkle, William   1938- . . .   **CLC 5, 14, 35**
See also CA 45-48; CANR 3; CLR 6;
MAICYA; SATA 24, 70

Kozol, Jonathan   1936- . . . .   **CLC 17**
See also CA 61-64; CANR 16

Kozoll, Michael   1940(?)- . . . .   **CLC 35**

Kramer, Kathryn   19(?)- . . . .   **CLC 34**

Kramer, Larry   1935- . . . .   **CLC 42**
See also CA 124; 126

Krasicki, Ignacy   1735-1801 . . . .   **NCLC 8**

Krasinski, Zygmunt   1812-1859 . . . .   **NCLC 4**

Kraus, Karl   1874-1936 . . . .   **TCLC 5**
See also CA 104; DLB 118

Kreve (Mickevicius), Vincas
1882-1954 . . . .   **TCLC 27**

Kristeva, Julia   1941- . . . .   **CLC 77**

Kristofferson, Kris   1936- . . . .   **CLC 26**
See also CA 104

Krizanc, John   1956- . . . .   **CLC 57**

Krleza, Miroslav   1893-1981 . . . .   **CLC 8**
See also CA 97-100; 105

Kroetsch, Robert   1927- . . . . . .   **CLC 5, 23, 57**
See also CA 17-20R; CANR 8, 38; DLB 53;
MTCW

Larson, Charles R(aymond) 1938-... **CLC 31**
  See also CA 53-56; CANR 4

Latham, Jean Lee 1902-.......... **CLC 12**
  See also AITN 1; CA 5-8R; CANR 7;
  MAICYA; SATA 2, 68

Latham, Mavis
  See Clark, Mavis Thorpe

Lathen, Emma.................... **CLC 2**
  See also Hennissart, Martha; Latsis, Mary
  J(ane)

Lathrop, Francis
  See Leiber, Fritz (Reuter, Jr.)

Latsis, Mary J(ane)
  See Lathen, Emma
  See also CA 85-88

Lattimore, Richmond (Alexander)
  1906-1984 .... **CLC 3**
  See also CA 1-4R; 112; CANR 1

Laughlin, James 1914-............ **CLC 49**
  See also CA 21-24R; CANR 9; DLB 48

Laurence, (Jean) Margaret (Wemyss)
  1926-1987 .. **CLC 3, 6, 13, 50, 62; SSC 7**
  See also CA 5-8R; 121; CANR 33; DLB 53;
  MTCW; SATA 50

Laurent, Antoine 1952- .... **CLC 50**

Lauscher, Hermann
  See Hesse, Hermann

Lautreamont, Comte de
  1846-1870 .... **NCLC 12**

Laverty, Donald
  See Blish, James (Benjamin)

Lavin, Mary 1912-...... **CLC 4, 18; SSC 4**
  See also CA 9-12R; CANR 33; DLB 15;
  MTCW

Lavond, Paul Dennis
  See Kornbluth, C(yril) M.; Pohl, Frederik

Lawler, Raymond Evenor 1922- .... **CLC 58**
  See also CA 103

Lawrence, D(avid) H(erbert Richards)
  1885-1930 ...... **TCLC 2, 9, 16, 33, 48;**
                                            SSC 4
  See also CA 104; 121; CDBLB 1914-1945;
  DA; DLB 10, 19, 36, 98; MTCW; WLC

Lawrence, T(homas) E(dward)
  1888-1935 .... **TCLC 18**
  See also Dale, Colin
  See also CA 115

Lawrence of Arabia
  See Lawrence, T(homas) E(dward)

Lawson, Henry (Archibald Hertzberg)
  1867-1922 .... **TCLC 27**
  See also CA 120

Lawton, Dennis
  See Faust, Frederick (Schiller)

Laxness, Halldor................. **CLC 25**
  See also Gudjonsson, Halldor Kiljan

Layamon fl. c. 1200-............ **CMLC 10**

Laye, Camara 1928-1980 .... **CLC 4, 38**
  See also BLC 2; BW; CA 85-88; 97-100;
  CANR 25; MTCW

Layton, Irving (Peter) 1912-..... **CLC 2, 15**
  See also CA 1-4R; CANR 2, 33, 43;
  DLB 88; MTCW

Lazarus, Emma 1849-1887........ **NCLC 8**

Lazarus, Felix
  See Cable, George Washington

Lazarus, Henry
  See Slavitt, David R(ytman)

Lea, Joan
  See Neufeld, John (Arthur)

Leacock, Stephen (Butler)
  1869-1944 .... **TCLC 2**
  See also CA 104; 141; DLB 92

Lear, Edward 1812-1888 .... **NCLC 3**
  See also CLR 1; DLB 32; MAICYA;
  SATA 18

Lear, Norman (Milton) 1922- ...... **CLC 12**
  See also CA 73-76

Leavis, F(rank) R(aymond)
  1895-1978 .... **CLC 24**
  See also CA 21-24R; 77-80; MTCW

Leavitt, David 1961-........ **CLC 34**
  See also CA 116; 122; DLB 130

Leblanc, Maurice (Marie Emile)
  1864-1941 .... **TCLC 49**
  See also CA 110

Lebowitz, Fran(ces Ann)
  1951(?)-................. **CLC 11, 36**
  See also CA 81-84; CANR 14; MTCW

le Carre, John .... **CLC 3, 5, 9, 15, 28**
  See also Cornwell, David (John Moore)
  See also BEST 89:4; CDBLB 1960 to
  Present; DLB 87

Le Clezio, J(ean) M(arie) G(ustave)
  1940-...................... **CLC 31**
  See also CA 116; 128; DLB 83

Leconte de Lisle, Charles-Marie-Rene
  1818-1894 .... **NCLC 29**

Le Coq, Monsieur
  See Simenon, Georges (Jacques Christian)

Leduc, Violette 1907-1972........ **CLC 22**
  See also CA 13-14; 33-36R; CAP 1

Ledwidge, Francis 1887(?)-1917 ... **TCLC 23**
  See also CA 123; DLB 20

Lee, Andrea 1953- .... **CLC 36**
  See also BLC 2; BW; CA 125

Lee, Andrew
  See Auchincloss, Louis (Stanton)

Lee, Don L...................... **CLC 2**
  See also Madhubuti, Haki R.

Lee, George W(ashington)
  1894-1976 .... **CLC 52**
  See also BLC 2; BW; CA 125; DLB 51

Lee, (Nelle) Harper 1926-...... **CLC 12, 60**
  See also CA 13-16R; CDALB 1941-1968;
  DA; DLB 6; MTCW; SATA 11; WLC

Lee, Julian
  See Latham, Jean Lee

Lee, Larry
  See Lee, Lawrence

Lee, Lawrence 1941-1990......... **CLC 34**
  See also CA 131; CANR 43

Lee, Manfred B(ennington)
  1905-1971 .... **CLC 11**
  See also Queen, Ellery
  See also CA 1-4R; 29-32R; CANR 2

Lee, Stan 1922-................. **CLC 17**
  See also AAYA 5; CA 108; 111

Lee, Tanith 1947-............... **CLC 46**
  See also CA 37-40R; SATA 8

Lee, Vernon..................... **TCLC 5**
  See also Paget, Violet
  See also DLB 57

Lee, William
  See Burroughs, William S(eward)

Lee, Willy
  See Burroughs, William S(eward)

Lee-Hamilton, Eugene (Jacob)
  1845-1907 .... **TCLC 22**
  See also CA 117

Leet, Judith 1935- .... **CLC 11**

Le Fanu, Joseph Sheridan
  1814-1873 .... **NCLC 9**
  See also DLB 21, 70

Leffland, Ella 1931- .... **CLC 19**
  See also CA 29-32R; CANR 35; DLBY 84;
  SATA 65

Leger, Alexis
  See Leger, (Marie-Rene Auguste) Alexis
  Saint-Leger

Leger, (Marie-Rene Auguste) Alexis
  Saint-Leger 1887-1975........ **CLC 11**
  See also Perse, St.-John
  See also CA 13-16R; 61-64; CANR 43;
  MTCW

Leger, Saintleger
  See Leger, (Marie-Rene Auguste) Alexis
  Saint-Leger

Le Guin, Ursula K(roeber)
  1929- .... **CLC 8, 13, 22, 45, 71; SSC 12**
  See also AAYA 9; AITN 1; CA 21-24R;
  CANR 9, 32; CDALB 1968-1988; CLR 3,
  28; DLB 8, 52; JRDA; MAICYA;
  MTCW; SATA 4, 52

Lehmann, Rosamond (Nina)
  1901-1990 .... **CLC 5**
  See also CA 77-80; 131; CANR 8; DLB 15

Leiber, Fritz (Reuter, Jr.)
  1910-1992 .... **CLC 25**
  See also CA 45-48; 139; CANR 2, 40;
  DLB 8; MTCW; SATA 45;
  SATA-Obit 73

Leimbach, Martha 1963-
  See Leimbach, Marti
  See also CA 130

Leimbach, Marti .... **CLC 65**
  See also Leimbach, Martha

Leino, Eino .... **TCLC 24**
  See also Loennbohm, Armas Eino Leopold

Leiris, Michel (Julien) 1901-1990... **CLC 61**
  See also CA 119; 128; 132

Leithauser, Brad 1953-........... **CLC 27**
  See also CA 107; CANR 27; DLB 120

Lelchuk, Alan 1938-.............. **CLC 5**
  See also CA 45-48; CANR 1

Lem, Stanislaw 1921-........ **CLC 8, 15, 40**
  See also CA 105; CAAS 1; CANR 32;
  MTCW

Lemann, Nancy 1956-............. **CLC 39**
  See also CA 118; 136

Lemonnier, (Antoine Louis) Camille
  1844-1913 .... **TCLC 22**
  See also CA 121

Lively, Penelope (Margaret)
    1933- .... **CLC 32, 50**
    See also CA 41-44R; CANR 29; CLR 7;
    DLB 14; JRDA; MAICYA; MTCW;
    SATA 7, 60

Livesay, Dorothy (Kathleen)
    1909- .... **CLC 4, 15, 79**
    See also AITN 2; CA 25-28R; CAAS 8;
    CANR 36; DLB 68; MTCW

Livy   c. 59B.C.-c. 17 .... **CMLC 11**

Lizardi, Jose Joaquin Fernandez de
    1776-1827 .... **NCLC 30**

Llewellyn, Richard .... **CLC 7**
    See also Llewellyn Lloyd, Richard Dafydd
    Vivian
    See also DLB 15

Llewellyn Lloyd, Richard Dafydd Vivian
    1906-1983 .... **CLC 80**
    See also Llewellyn, Richard
    See also CA 53-56; 111; CANR 7;
    SATA 11, 37

Llosa, (Jorge) Mario (Pedro) Vargas
    See Vargas Llosa, (Jorge) Mario (Pedro)

Lloyd Webber, Andrew   1948-
    See Webber, Andrew Lloyd
    See also AAYA 1; CA 116; SATA 56

Llull, Ramon   c. 1235-c. 1316..... **CMLC 12**

Locke, Alain (Le Roy)
    1886-1954 .... **TCLC 43**
    See also BW; CA 106; 124; DLB 51

Locke, John   1632-1704 .... **LC 7**
    See also DLB 101

Locke-Elliott, Sumner
    See Elliott, Sumner Locke

Lockhart, John Gibson
    1794-1854 .... **NCLC 6**
    See also DLB 110, 116

Lodge, David (John)   1935-........ **CLC 36**
    See also BEST 90:1; CA 17-20R; CANR 19;
    DLB 14; MTCW

Loennbohm, Armas Eino Leopold   1878-1926
    See Leino, Eino
    See also CA 123

Loewinsohn, Ron(ald William)
    1937- .... **CLC 52**
    See also CA 25-28R

Logan, Jake
    See Smith, Martin Cruz

Logan, John (Burton)   1923-1987..... **CLC 5**
    See also CA 77-80; 124; DLB 5

Lo Kuan-chung   1330(?)-1400(?)...... **LC 12**

Lombard, Nap
    See Johnson, Pamela Hansford

London, Jack........ **TCLC 9, 15, 39; SSC 4**
    See also London, John Griffith
    See also AITN 2; CDALB 1865-1917;
    DLB 8, 12, 78; SATA 18; WLC

London, John Griffith   1876-1916
    See London, Jack
    See also CA 110; 119; DA; JRDA;
    MAICYA; MTCW

Long, Emmett
    See Leonard, Elmore (John, Jr.)

Longbaugh, Harry
    See Goldman, William (W.)

Longfellow, Henry Wadsworth
    1807-1882 .... **NCLC 2**
    See also CDALB 1640-1865; DA; DLB 1,
    59; SATA 19

Longley, Michael   1939-.......... **CLC 29**
    See also CA 102; DLB 40

Longus   fl. c. 2nd cent. - .... **CMLC 7**

Longway, A. Hugh
    See Lang, Andrew

Lopate, Phillip   1943- .... **CLC 29**
    See also CA 97-100; DLBY 80

Lopez Portillo (y Pacheco), Jose
    1920- .... **CLC 46**
    See also CA 129; HW

Lopez y Fuentes, Gregorio
    1897(?)-1966 .... **CLC 32**
    See also CA 131; HW

Lorca, Federico Garcia   1898-1936
    See Garcia Lorca, Federico

Lord, Bette Bao   1938- .... **CLC 23**
    See also BEST 90:3; CA 107; CANR 41;
    SATA 58

Lord Auch
    See Bataille, Georges

Lord Byron
    See Byron, George Gordon (Noel)

Lord Dunsany .... **TCLC 2**
    See also Dunsany, Edward John Moreton
    Drax Plunkett

Lorde, Audre (Geraldine)
    1934-1992 .... **CLC 18, 71**
    See also BLC 2; BW; CA 25-28R; 142;
    CANR 16, 26; DLB 41; MTCW

Lord Jeffrey
    See Jeffrey, Francis

Lorenzo, Heberto Padilla
    See Padilla (Lorenzo), Heberto

Loris
    See Hofmannsthal, Hugo von

Loti, Pierre .... **TCLC 11**
    See also Viaud, (Louis Marie) Julien
    See also DLB 123

Louie, David Wong   1954- .... **CLC 70**
    See also CA 139

Louis, Father M.
    See Merton, Thomas

Lovecraft, H(oward) P(hillips)
    1890-1937 .... **TCLC 4, 22; SSC 3**
    See also CA 104; 133; MTCW

Lovelace, Earl   1935-.............. **CLC 51**
    See also CA 77-80; CANR 41; DLB 125;
    MTCW

Lovelace, Richard   1618-1657........ **LC 24**
    See also DLB 131

Lowell, Amy   1874-1925 .... **TCLC 1, 8**
    See also CA 104; DLB 54

Lowell, James Russell   1819-1891 .. **NCLC 2**
    See also CDALB 1640-1865; DLB 1, 11, 64,
    79

Lowell, Robert (Traill Spence, Jr.)
    1917-1977 ... **CLC 1, 2, 3, 4, 5, 8, 9, 11,
    15, 37; PC 3**
    See also CA 9-12R; 73-76; CABS 2;
    CANR 26; DA; DLB 5; MTCW; WLC

Lowndes, Marie Adelaide (Belloc)
    1868-1947 .... **TCLC 12**
    See also CA 107; DLB 70

Lowry, (Clarence) Malcolm
    1909-1957 .... **TCLC 6, 40**
    See also CA 105; 131; CDBLB 1945-1960;
    DLB 15; MTCW

Lowry, Mina Gertrude   1882-1966
    See Loy, Mina
    See also CA 113

Loxsmith, John
    See Brunner, John (Kilian Houston)

Loy, Mina .... **CLC 28**
    See also Lowry, Mina Gertrude
    See also DLB 4, 54

Loyson-Bridet
    See Schwob, (Mayer Andre) Marcel

Lucas, Craig   1951-.............. **CLC 64**
    See also CA 137

Lucas, George   1944-.............. **CLC 16**
    See also AAYA 1; CA 77-80; CANR 30;
    SATA 56

Lucas, Hans
    See Godard, Jean-Luc

Lucas, Victoria
    See Plath, Sylvia

Ludlam, Charles   1943-1987..... **CLC 46, 50**
    See also CA 85-88; 122

Ludlum, Robert   1927- .... **CLC 22, 43**
    See also AAYA 10; BEST 89:1, 90:3;
    CA 33-36R; CANR 25, 41; DLBY 82;
    MTCW

Ludwig, Ken...................... **CLC 60**

Ludwig, Otto   1813-1865 .... **NCLC 4**
    See also DLB 129

Lugones, Leopoldo   1874-1938 ..... **TCLC 15**
    See also CA 116; 131; HW

Lu Hsun   1881-1936 .... **TCLC 3**

Lukacs, George .... **CLC 24**
    See also Lukacs, Gyorgy (Szegeny von)

Lukacs, Gyorgy (Szegeny von)   1885-1971
    See Lukacs, George
    See also CA 101; 29-32R

Luke, Peter (Ambrose Cyprian)
    1919- .... **CLC 38**
    See also CA 81-84; DLB 13

Lunar, Dennis
    See Mungo, Raymond

Lurie, Alison   1926-........ **CLC 4, 5, 18, 39**
    See also CA 1-4R; CANR 2, 17; DLB 2;
    MTCW; SATA 46

Lustig, Arnost   1926-.............. **CLC 56**
    See also AAYA 3; CA 69-72; SATA 56

Luther, Martin   1483-1546 .... **LC 9**

Luzi, Mario   1914-................. **CLC 13**
    See also CA 61-64; CANR 9; DLB 128

Lynch, B. Suarez
    See Bioy Casares, Adolfo; Borges, Jorge
    Luis

Lynch, David (K.)   1946-........... **CLC 66**
    See also CA 124; 129

Lynch, James
    See Andreyev, Leonid (Nikolaevich)

Malley, Ern
See McAuley, James Phillip

Mallowan, Agatha Christie
See Christie, Agatha (Mary Clarissa)

Maloff, Saul 1922- .... **CLC 5**
See also CA 33-36R

Malone, Louis
See MacNeice, (Frederick) Louis

Malone, Michael (Christopher)
1942- .... **CLC 43**
See also CA 77-80; CANR 14, 32

Malory, (Sir) Thomas
1410(?)-1471(?) .... **LC 11**
See also CDBLB Before 1660; DA;
SATA 33, 59

Malouf, (George Joseph) David
1934- .... **CLC 28**
See also CA 124

Malraux, (Georges-)Andre
1901-1976 ...... **CLC 1, 4, 9, 13, 15, 57**
See also CA 21-22; 69-72; CANR 34;
CAP 2; DLB 72; MTCW

Malzberg, Barry N(athaniel) 1939-... **CLC 7**
See also CA 61-64; CAAS 4; CANR 16;
DLB 8

Mamet, David (Alan)
1947- .... **CLC 9, 15, 34, 46**
See also AAYA 3; CA 81-84; CABS 3;
CANR 15, 41; DLB 7; MTCW

Mamoulian, Rouben (Zachary)
1897-1987 .... **CLC 16**
See also CA 25-28R; 124

Mandelstam, Osip (Emilievich)
1891(?)-1938(?) .... **TCLC 2, 6**
See also CA 104

Mander, (Mary) Jane 1877-1949... **TCLC 31**

Mandiargues, Andre Pieyre de ...... **CLC 41**
See also Pieyre de Mandiargues, Andre
See also DLB 83

Mandrake, Ethel Belle
See Thurman, Wallace (Henry)

Mangan, James Clarence
1803-1849 .... **NCLC 27**

Maniere, J.-E.
See Giraudoux, (Hippolyte) Jean

Manley, (Mary) Delariviere
1672(?)-1724 .... **LC 1**
See also DLB 39, 80

Mann, Abel
See Creasey, John

Mann, (Luiz) Heinrich 1871-1950... **TCLC 9**
See also CA 106; DLB 66

Mann, (Paul) Thomas
1875-1955 .... **TCLC 2, 8, 14, 21, 35, 44;**
SSC 5
See also CA 104; 128; DA; DLB 66;
MTCW; WLC

Manning, David
See Faust, Frederick (Schiller)

Manning, Frederic 1887(?)-1935... **TCLC 25**
See also CA 124

Manning, Olivia 1915-1980 ...... **CLC 5, 19**
See also CA 5-8R; 101; CANR 29; MTCW

Mano, D. Keith 1942- .... **CLC 2, 10**
See also CA 25-28R; CAAS 6; CANR 26;
DLB 6

Mansfield, Katherine ... **TCLC 2, 8, 39; SSC 9**
See also Beauchamp, Kathleen Mansfield
See also WLC

Manso, Peter 1940- .... **CLC 39**
See also CA 29-32R

Mantecon, Juan Jimenez
See Jimenez (Mantecon), Juan Ramon

Manton, Peter
See Creasey, John

Man Without a Spleen, A
See Chekhov, Anton (Pavlovich)

Manzoni, Alessandro 1785-1873.. **NCLC 29**

Mapu, Abraham (ben Jekutiel)
1808-1867 .... **NCLC 18**

Mara, Sally
See Queneau, Raymond

Marat, Jean Paul 1743-1793 .... **LC 10**

Marcel, Gabriel Honore
1889-1973 .... **CLC 15**
See also CA 102; 45-48; MTCW

Marchbanks, Samuel
See Davies, (William) Robertson

Marchi, Giacomo
See Bassani, Giorgio

Margulies, Donald .... **CLC 76**

Marie de France c. 12th cent. -.... **CMLC 8**

Marie de l'Incarnation 1599-1672.... **LC 10**

Mariner, Scott
See Pohl, Frederik

Marinetti, Filippo Tommaso
1876-1944 .... **TCLC 10**
See also CA 107; DLB 114

Marivaux, Pierre Carlet de Chamblain de
1688-1763 .... **LC 4**

Markandaya, Kamala .... **CLC 8, 38**
See also Taylor, Kamala (Purnaiya)

Markfield, Wallace 1926- .... **CLC 8**
See also CA 69-72; CAAS 3; DLB 2, 28

Markham, Edwin 1852-1940 ..... **TCLC 47**
See also DLB 54

Markham, Robert
See Amis, Kingsley (William)

Marks, J
See Highwater, Jamake (Mamake)

Marks-Highwater, J
See Highwater, Jamake (Mamake)

Markson, David M(errill) 1927-.... **CLC 67**
See also CA 49-52; CANR 1

Marley, Bob .... **CLC 17**
See also Marley, Robert Nesta

Marley, Robert Nesta 1945-1981
See Marley, Bob
See also CA 107; 103

Marlowe, Christopher
1564-1593 .... **LC 22; DC 1**
See also CDBLB Before 1660; DA; DLB 62;
WLC

Marmontel, Jean-Francois
1723-1799 .... **LC 2**

Marquand, John P(hillips)
1893-1960 .... **CLC 2, 10**
See also CA 85-88; DLB 9, 102

Marquez, Gabriel (Jose) Garcia ...... **CLC 68**
See also Garcia Marquez, Gabriel (Jose)

Marquis, Don(ald Robert Perry)
1878-1937 .... **TCLC 7**
See also CA 104; DLB 11, 25

Marric, J. J.
See Creasey, John

Marrow, Bernard
See Moore, Brian

Marryat, Frederick 1792-1848 .... **NCLC 3**
See also DLB 21

Marsden, James
See Creasey, John

Marsh, (Edith) Ngaio
1899-1982 .... **CLC 7, 53**
See also CA 9-12R; CANR 6; DLB 77;
MTCW

Marshall, Garry 1934- .... **CLC 17**
See also AAYA 3; CA 111; SATA 60

Marshall, Paule 1929- .. **CLC 27, 72; SSC 3**
See also BLC 3; BW; CA 77-80; CANR 25;
DLB 33; MTCW

Marsten, Richard
See Hunter, Evan

Martha, Henry
See Harris, Mark

Martin, Ken
See Hubbard, L(afayette) Ron(ald)

Martin, Richard
See Creasey, John

Martin, Steve 1945- .... **CLC 30**
See also CA 97-100; CANR 30; MTCW

Martin, Violet Florence
1862-1915 .... **TCLC 51**

Martin, Webber
See Silverberg, Robert

Martindale, Patrick Victor
See White, Patrick (Victor Martindale)

Martin du Gard, Roger
1881-1958 .... **TCLC 24**
See also CA 118; DLB 65

Martineau, Harriet 1802-1876.... **NCLC 26**
See also DLB 21, 55; YABC 2

Martines, Julia
See O'Faolain, Julia

Martinez, Jacinto Benavente y
See Benavente (y Martinez), Jacinto

Martinez Ruiz, Jose 1873-1967
See Azorin; Ruiz, Jose Martinez
See also CA 93-96; HW

Martinez Sierra, Gregorio
1881-1947 .... **TCLC 6**
See also CA 115

Martinez Sierra, Maria (de la O'LeJarraga)
1874-1974 .... **TCLC 6**
See also CA 115

Martinsen, Martin
See Follett, Ken(neth Martin)

Martinson, Harry (Edmund)
1904-1978 .... **CLC 14**
See also CA 77-80; CANR 34

McGinniss, Joe 1942-............. **CLC 32**
See also AITN 2; BEST 89:2; CA 25-28R;
CANR 26

McGivern, Maureen Daly
See Daly, Maureen

McGrath, Patrick 1950-.......... **CLC 55**
See also CA 136

McGrath, Thomas (Matthew)
1916-1990 .... **CLC 28, 59**
See also CA 9-12R; 132; CANR 6, 33;
MTCW; SATA 41; SATA-Obit 66

McGuane, Thomas (Francis III)
1939-............... **CLC 3, 7, 18, 45**
See also AITN 2; CA 49-52; CANR 5, 24;
DLB 2; DLBY 80; MTCW

McGuckian, Medbh 1950-........ **CLC 48**
See also DLB 40

McHale, Tom 1942(?)-1982...... **CLC 3, 5**
See also AITN 1; CA 77-80; 106

McIlvanney, William 1936-....... **CLC 42**
See also CA 25-28R; DLB 14

McIlwraith, Maureen Mollie Hunter
See Hunter, Mollie
See also SATA 2

McInerney, Jay 1955-........... **CLC 34**
See also CA 116; 123

McIntyre, Vonda N(eel) 1948- ..... **CLC 18**
See also CA 81-84; CANR 17, 34; MTCW

McKay, Claude .... **TCLC 7, 41; PC 2**
See also McKay, Festus Claudius
See also BLC 3; DLB 4, 45, 51, 117

McKay, Festus Claudius 1889-1948
See McKay, Claude
See also BW; CA 104; 124; DA; MTCW;
WLC

McKuen, Rod 1933-............ **CLC 1, 3**
See also AITN 1; CA 41-44R; CANR 40

McLoughlin, R. B.
See Mencken, H(enry) L(ouis)

McLuhan, (Herbert) Marshall
1911-1980 .... **CLC 37**
See also CA 9-12R; 102; CANR 12, 34;
DLB 88; MTCW

McMillan, Terry (L.) 1951-..... **CLC 50, 61**
See also CA 140

McMurtry, Larry (Jeff)
1936-......... **CLC 2, 3, 7, 11, 27, 44**
See also AITN 2; BEST 89:2; CA 5-8R;
CANR 19, 43; CDALB 1968-1988;
DLB 2; DLBY 80, 87; MTCW

McNally, Terrence 1939-...... **CLC 4, 7, 41**
See also CA 45-48; CANR 2; DLB 7

McNamer, Deirdre 1950-......... **CLC 70**

McNeile, Herman Cyril 1888-1937
See Sapper
See also DLB 77

McPhee, John (Angus) 1931- ...... **CLC 36**
See also BEST 90:1; CA 65-68; CANR 20;
MTCW

McPherson, James Alan
1943-.................. **CLC 19, 77**
See also BW; CA 25-28R; CAAS 17;
CANR 24; DLB 38; MTCW

McPherson, William (Alexander)
1933-...................... **CLC 34**
See also CA 69-72; CANR 28

McSweeney, Kerry .... **CLC 34**

Mead, Margaret 1901-1978....... **CLC 37**
See also AITN 1; CA 1-4R; 81-84;
CANR 4; MTCW; SATA 20

Meaker, Marijane (Agnes) 1927-
See Kerr, M. E.
See also CA 107; CANR 37; JRDA;
MAICYA; MTCW; SATA 20, 61

Medoff, Mark (Howard) 1940- ... **CLC 6, 23**
See also AITN 1; CA 53-56; CANR 5;
DLB 7

Meged, Aharon
See Megged, Aharon

Meged, Aron
See Megged, Aharon

Megged, Aharon 1920-............. **CLC 9**
See also CA 49-52; CAAS 13; CANR 1

Mehta, Ved (Parkash) 1934-....... **CLC 37**
See also CA 1-4R; CANR 2, 23; MTCW

Melanter
See Blackmore, R(ichard) D(oddridge)

Melikow, Loris
See Hofmannsthal, Hugo von

Melmoth, Sebastian
See Wilde, Oscar (Fingal O'Flahertie Wills)

Meltzer, Milton 1915-............ **CLC 26**
See also AAYA 8; CA 13-16R; CANR 38;
CLR 13; DLB 61; JRDA; MAICYA;
SAAS 1; SATA 1, 50

Melville, Herman
1819-1891 ...... **NCLC 3, 12, 29; SSC 1**
See also CDALB 1640-1865; DA; DLB 3,
74; SATA 59; WLC

Menander
c. 342B.C.-c. 292B.C.... **CMLC 9; DC 3**

Mencken, H(enry) L(ouis)
1880-1956 .... **TCLC 13**
See also CA 105; 125; CDALB 1917-1929;
DLB 11, 29, 63; MTCW

Mercer, David 1928-1980.......... **CLC 5**
See also CA 9-12R; 102; CANR 23;
DLB 13; MTCW

Merchant, Paul
See Ellison, Harlan

Meredith, George 1828-1909... **TCLC 17, 43**
See also CA 117; CDBLB 1832-1890;
DLB 18, 35, 57

Meredith, William (Morris)
1919-.............. **CLC 4, 13, 22, 55**
See also CA 9-12R; CAAS 14; CANR 6, 40;
DLB 5

Merezhkovsky, Dmitry Sergeyevich
1865-1941 .... **TCLC 29**

Merimee, Prosper
1803-1870 .... **NCLC 6; SSC 7**
See also DLB 119

Merkin, Daphne 1954-............ **CLC 44**
See also CA 123

Merlin, Arthur
See Blish, James (Benjamin)

Merrill, James (Ingram)
1926-........ **CLC 2, 3, 6, 8, 13, 18, 34**
See also CA 13-16R; CANR 10; DLB 5;
DLBY 85; MTCW

Merriman, Alex
See Silverberg, Robert

Merritt, E. B.
See Waddington, Miriam

Merton, Thomas
1915-1968 .... **CLC 1, 3, 11, 34**
See also CA 5-8R; 25-28R; CANR 22;
DLB 48; DLBY 81; MTCW

Merwin, W(illiam) S(tanley)
1927-...... **CLC 1, 2, 3, 5, 8, 13, 18, 45**
See also CA 13-16R; CANR 15; DLB 5;
MTCW

Metcalf, John 1938-.............. **CLC 37**
See also CA 113; DLB 60

Metcalf, Suzanne
See Baum, L(yman) Frank

Mew, Charlotte (Mary)
1870-1928 .... **TCLC 8**
See also CA 105; DLB 19

Mewshaw, Michael 1943-.......... **CLC 9**
See also CA 53-56; CANR 7; DLBY 80

Meyer, June
See Jordan, June

Meyer, Lynn
See Slavitt, David R(ytman)

Meyer-Meyrink, Gustav 1868-1932
See Meyrink, Gustav
See also CA 117

Meyers, Jeffrey 1939-............ **CLC 39**
See also CA 73-76; DLB 111

Meynell, Alice (Christina Gertrude Thompson)
1847-1922 .... **TCLC 6**
See also CA 104; DLB 19, 98

Meyrink, Gustav .... **TCLC 21**
See also Meyer-Meyrink, Gustav
See also DLB 81

Michaels, Leonard 1933-...... **CLC 6, 25**
See also CA 61-64; CANR 21; DLB 130;
MTCW

Michaux, Henri 1899-1984 ...... **CLC 8, 19**
See also CA 85-88; 114

Michelangelo 1475-1564............ **LC 12**

Michelet, Jules 1798-1874....... **NCLC 31**

Michener, James A(lbert)
1907(?)-.......... **CLC 1, 5, 11, 29, 60**
See also AITN 1; BEST 90:1; CA 5-8R;
CANR 21; DLB 6; MTCW

Mickiewicz, Adam 1798-1855 ..... **NCLC 3**

Middleton, Christopher 1926-...... **CLC 13**
See also CA 13-16R; CANR 29; DLB 40

Middleton, Stanley 1919-........ **CLC 7, 38**
See also CA 25-28R; CANR 21; DLB 14

Migueis, Jose Rodrigues 1901-..... **CLC 10**

Mikszath, Kalman 1847-1910 ..... **TCLC 31**

Miles, Josephine
1911-1985 .... **CLC 1, 2, 14, 34, 39**
See also CA 1-4R; 116; CANR 2; DLB 48

Militant
See Sandburg, Carl (August)

Moore, Marie Lorena 1957-
See Moore, Lorrie
See also CA 116; CANR 39

Moore, Thomas 1779-1852........ NCLC 6
See also DLB 96

Morand, Paul 1888-1976.......... CLC 41
See also CA 69-72; DLB 65

Morante, Elsa 1918-1985........ CLC 8, 47
See also CA 85-88; 117; CANR 35; MTCW

Moravia, Alberto...... CLC 2, 7, 11, 27, 46
See also Pincherle, Alberto

More, Hannah 1745-1833 .... NCLC 27
See also DLB 107, 109, 116

More, Henry 1614-1687............. LC 9
See also DLB 126

More, Sir Thomas 1478-1535 .... LC 10

Moreas, Jean.................. TCLC 18
See also Papadiamantopoulos, Johannes

Morgan, Berry 1919-............. CLC 6
See also CA 49-52; DLB 6

Morgan, Claire
See Highsmith, (Mary) Patricia

Morgan, Edwin (George) 1920-..... CLC 31
See also CA 5-8R; CANR 3, 43; DLB 27

Morgan, (George) Frederick
1922-..................... CLC 23
See also CA 17-20R; CANR 21

Morgan, Harriet
See Mencken, H(enry) L(ouis)

Morgan, Jane
See Cooper, James Fenimore

Morgan, Janet 1945-............. CLC 39
See also CA 65-68

Morgan, Lady 1776(?)-1859...... NCLC 29
See also DLB 116

Morgan, Robin 1941-............. CLC 2
See also CA 69-72; CANR 29; MTCW

Morgan, Scott
See Kuttner, Henry

Morgan, Seth 1949(?)-1990 .... CLC 65
See also CA 132

Morgenstern, Christian
1871-1914 .... TCLC 8
See also CA 105

Morgenstern, S.
See Goldman, William (W.)

Moricz, Zsigmond 1879-1942 ..... TCLC 33

Morike, Eduard (Friedrich)
1804-1875 .... NCLC 10
See also DLB 133

Mori Ogai .... TCLC 14
See also Mori Rintaro

Mori Rintaro 1862-1922
See Mori Ogai
See also CA 110

Moritz, Karl Philipp 1756-1793 ...... LC 2
See also DLB 94

Morland, Peter Henry
See Faust, Frederick (Schiller)

Morren, Theophil
See Hofmannsthal, Hugo von

Morris, Bill 1952-............... CLC 76

Morris, Julian
See West, Morris L(anglo)

Morris, Steveland Judkins 1950(?)-
See Wonder, Stevie
See also CA 111

Morris, William 1834-1896 ...... NCLC 4
See also CDBLB 1832-1890; DLB 18, 35, 57

Morris, Wright 1910-... CLC 1, 3, 7, 18, 37
See also CA 9-12R; CANR 21; DLB 2;
DLBY 81; MTCW

Morrison, Chloe Anthony Wofford
See Morrison, Toni

Morrison, James Douglas 1943-1971
See Morrison, Jim
See also CA 73-76; CANR 40

Morrison, Jim .... CLC 17
See also Morrison, James Douglas

Morrison, Toni 1931-..... CLC 4, 10, 22, 55
See also AAYA 1; BLC 3; BW; CA 29-32R;
CANR 27, 42; CDALB 1968-1988; DA;
DLB 6, 33; DLBY 81; MTCW; SATA 57

Morrison, Van 1945- .... CLC 21
See also CA 116

Mortimer, John (Clifford)
1923- .... CLC 28, 43
See also CA 13-16R; CANR 21;
CDBLB 1960 to Present; DLB 13;
MTCW

Mortimer, Penelope (Ruth) 1918-.... CLC 5
See also CA 57-60

Morton, Anthony
See Creasey, John

Mosher, Howard Frank 1943-...... CLC 62
See also CA 139

Mosley, Nicholas 1923-........ CLC 43, 70
See also CA 69-72; CANR 41; DLB 14

Moss, Howard
1922-1987 .... CLC 7, 14, 45, 50
See also CA 1-4R; 123; CANR 1; DLB 5

Mossgiel, Rab
See Burns, Robert

Motion, Andrew 1952-............ CLC 47
See also DLB 40

Motley, Willard (Francis)
1912-1965 .... CLC 18
See also BW; CA 117; 106; DLB 76

Mott, Michael (Charles Alston)
1930-.................... CLC 15, 34
See also CA 5-8R; CAAS 7; CANR 7, 29

Mowat, Farley (McGill) 1921- ..... CLC 26
See also AAYA 1; CA 1-4R; CANR 4, 24,
42; CLR 20; DLB 68; JRDA; MAICYA;
MTCW; SATA 3, 55

Moyers, Bill 1934-............... CLC 74
See also AITN 2; CA 61-64; CANR 31

Mphahlele, Es'kia
See Mphahlele, Ezekiel
See also DLB 125

Mphahlele, Ezekiel 1919-......... CLC 25
See also Mphahlele, Es'kia
See also BLC 3; BW; CA 81-84; CANR 26

Mqhayi, S(amuel) E(dward) K(rune Loliwe)
1875-1945 .... TCLC 25
See also BLC 3

Mr. Martin
See Burroughs, William S(eward)

Mrozek, Slawomir 1930-........ CLC 3, 13
See also CA 13-16R; CAAS 10; CANR 29;
MTCW

Mrs. Belloc-Lowndes
See Lowndes, Marie Adelaide (Belloc)

Mtwa, Percy (?)-................. CLC 47

Mueller, Lisel 1924-............. CLC 13, 51
See also CA 93-96; DLB 105

Muir, Edwin 1887-1959 .... TCLC 2
See also CA 104; DLB 20, 100

Muir, John 1838-1914 .... TCLC 28

Mujica Lainez, Manuel
1910-1984 .... CLC 31
See also Lainez, Manuel Mujica
See also CA 81-84; 112; CANR 32; HW

Mukherjee, Bharati 1940- .... CLC 53
See also BEST 89:2; CA 107; DLB 60;
MTCW

Muldoon, Paul 1951-.......... CLC 32, 72
See also CA 113; 129; DLB 40

Mulisch, Harry 1927-............. CLC 42
See also CA 9-12R; CANR 6, 26

Mull, Martin 1943-............... CLC 17
See also CA 105

Mulock, Dinah Maria
See Craik, Dinah Maria (Mulock)

Munford, Robert 1737(?)-1783 .... LC 5
See also DLB 31

Mungo, Raymond 1946-.......... CLC 72
See also CA 49-52; CANR 2

Munro, Alice
1931- .... CLC 6, 10, 19, 50; SSC 3
See also AITN 2; CA 33-36R; CANR 33;
DLB 53; MTCW; SATA 29

Munro, H(ector) H(ugh) 1870-1916
See Saki
See also CA 104; 130; CDBLB 1890-1914;
DA; DLB 34; MTCW; WLC

Murasaki, Lady................. CMLC 1

Murdoch, (Jean) Iris
1919-...... CLC 1, 2, 3, 4, 6, 8, 11, 15,
22, 31, 51
See also CA 13-16R; CANR 8, 43;
CDBLB 1960 to Present; DLB 14;
MTCW

Murphy, Richard 1927-.......... CLC 41
See also CA 29-32R; DLB 40

Murphy, Sylvia 1937-............. CLC 34
See also CA 121

Murphy, Thomas (Bernard) 1935-... CLC 51
See also CA 101

Murray, Albert L. 1916- .... CLC 73
See also BW; CA 49-52; CANR 26; DLB 38

Murray, Les(lie) A(llan) 1938- ..... CLC 40
See also CA 21-24R; CANR 11, 27

Murry, J. Middleton
See Murry, John Middleton

Murry, John Middleton
1889-1957 .... TCLC 16
See also CA 118

Musgrave, Susan 1951- .... CLC 13, 54
See also CA 69-72

Norris, Frank
See Norris, Benjamin Franklin, Jr.
See also CDALB 1865-1917; DLB 12, 71

Norris, Leslie 1921- .... CLC 14
See also CA 11-12; CANR 14; CAP 1;
DLB 27

North, Andrew
See Norton, Andre

North, Anthony
See Koontz, Dean R(ay)

North, Captain George
See Stevenson, Robert Louis (Balfour)

North, Milou
See Erdrich, Louise

Northrup, B. A.
See Hubbard, L(afayette) Ron(ald)

North Staffs
See Hulme, T(homas) E(rnest)

Norton, Alice Mary
See Norton, Andre
See also MAICYA; SATA 1, 43

Norton, Andre 1912- .... CLC 12
See also Norton, Alice Mary
See also CA 1-4R; CANR 2, 31; DLB 8, 52;
JRDA; MTCW

Norway, Nevil Shute 1899-1960
See Shute, Nevil
See also CA 102; 93-96

Norwid, Cyprian Kamil
1821-1883 .... NCLC 17

Nosille, Nabrah
See Ellison, Harlan

Nossack, Hans Erich 1901-1978 ..... CLC 6
See also CA 93-96; 85-88; DLB 69

Nosu, Chuji
See Ozu, Yasujiro

Nova, Craig 1945- .... CLC 7, 31
See also CA 45-48; CANR 2

Novak, Joseph
See Kosinski, Jerzy (Nikodem)

Novalis 1772-1801 .... NCLC 13
See also DLB 90

Nowlan, Alden (Albert) 1933-1983 .. CLC 15
See also CA 9-12R; CANR 5; DLB 53

Noyes, Alfred 1880-1958 .... TCLC 7
See also CA 104; DLB 20

Nunn, Kem 19(?)- .... CLC 34

Nye, Robert 1939- .... CLC 13, 42
See also CA 33-36R; CANR 29; DLB 14;
MTCW; SATA 6

Nyro, Laura 1947- .... CLC 17

Oates, Joyce Carol
1938- ...... CLC 1, 2, 3, 6, 9, 11, 15, 19,
33, 52; SSC 6
See also AITN 1; BEST 89:2; CA 5-8R;
CANR 25; CDALB 1968-1988; DA;
DLB 2, 5, 130; DLBY 81; MTCW; WLC

O'Brien, E. G.
See Clarke, Arthur C(harles)

O'Brien, Edna
1936- ... CLC 3, 5, 8, 13, 36, 65; SSC 10
See also CA 1-4R; CANR 6, 41;
CDBLB 1960 to Present; DLB 14;
MTCW

O'Brien, Fitz-James 1828-1862... NCLC 21
See also DLB 74

O'Brien, Flann .... CLC 1, 4, 5, 7, 10, 47
See also O Nuallain, Brian

O'Brien, Richard 1942- .... CLC 17
See also CA 124

O'Brien, Tim 1946-......... CLC 7, 19, 40
See also CA 85-88; CANR 40; DLBD 9;
DLBY 80

Obstfelder, Sigbjoern 1866-1900... TCLC 23
See also CA 123

O'Casey, Sean
1880-1964 .... CLC 1, 5, 9, 11, 15
See also CA 89-92; CDBLB 1914-1945;
DLB 10; MTCW

O'Cathasaigh, Sean
See O'Casey, Sean

Ochs, Phil 1940-1976............. CLC 17
See also CA 65-68

O'Connor, Edwin (Greene)
1918-1968 .... CLC 14
See also CA 93-96; 25-28R

O'Connor, (Mary) Flannery
1925-1964 .... CLC 1, 2, 3, 6, 10, 13, 15,
21, 66; SSC 1
See also AAYA 7; CA 1-4R; CANR 3, 41;
CDALB 1941-1968; DA; DLB 2;
DLBY 80; MTCW; WLC

O'Connor, Frank .... CLC 23; SSC 5
See also O'Donovan, Michael John

O'Dell, Scott 1898-1989.......... CLC 30
See also AAYA 3; CA 61-64; 129;
CANR 12, 30; CLR 1, 16; DLB 52;
JRDA; MAICYA; SATA 12, 60

Odets, Clifford 1906-1963 .... CLC 2, 28
See also CA 85-88; DLB 7, 26; MTCW

O'Doherty, Brian 1934-.......... CLC 76
See also CA 105

O'Donnell, K. M.
See Malzberg, Barry N(athaniel)

O'Donnell, Lawrence
See Kuttner, Henry

O'Donovan, Michael John
1903-1966 .... CLC 14
See also O'Connor, Frank
See also CA 93-96

Oe, Kenzaburo 1935- .... CLC 10, 36
See also CA 97-100; CANR 36; MTCW

O'Faolain, Julia 1932-....... CLC 6, 19, 47
See also CA 81-84; CAAS 2; CANR 12;
DLB 14; MTCW

O'Faolain, Sean
1900-1991 .... CLC 1, 7, 14, 32, 70;
SSC 13
See also CA 61-64; 134; CANR 12;
DLB 15; MTCW

O'Flaherty, Liam
1896-1984 .... CLC 5, 34; SSC 6
See also CA 101; 113; CANR 35; DLB 36;
DLBY 84; MTCW

Ogilvy, Gavin
See Barrie, J(ames) M(atthew)

O'Grady, Standish James
1846-1928 .... TCLC 5
See also CA 104

O'Grady, Timothy 1951- .... CLC 59
See also CA 138

O'Hara, Frank
1926-1966 .... CLC 2, 5, 13, 78
See also CA 9-12R; 25-28R; CANR 33;
DLB 5, 16; MTCW

O'Hara, John (Henry)
1905-1970 .... CLC 1, 2, 3, 6, 11, 42
See also CA 5-8R; 25-28R; CANR 31;
CDALB 1929-1941; DLB 9, 86; DLBD 2;
MTCW

O Hehir, Diana 1922- .... CLC 41
See also CA 93-96

Okigbo, Christopher (Ifenayichukwu)
1932-1967 .... CLC 25; PC 7
See also BLC 3; BW; CA 77-80; DLB 125;
MTCW

Olds, Sharon 1942-............ CLC 32, 39
See also CA 101; CANR 18, 41; DLB 120

Oldstyle, Jonathan
See Irving, Washington

Olesha, Yuri (Karlovich)
1899-1960 .... CLC 8
See also CA 85-88

Oliphant, Margaret (Oliphant Wilson)
1828-1897 .... NCLC 11
See also DLB 18

Oliver, Mary 1935-............ CLC 19, 34
See also CA 21-24R; CANR 9; DLB 5

Olivier, Laurence (Kerr)
1907-1989 .... CLC 20
See also CA 111; 129

Olsen, Tillie 1913- ..... CLC 4, 13; SSC 11
See also CA 1-4R; CANR 1, 43; DA;
DLB 28; DLBY 80; MTCW

Olson, Charles (John)
1910-1970 ..... CLC 1, 2, 5, 6, 9, 11, 29
See also CA 13-16; 25-28R; CABS 2;
CANR 35; CAP 1; DLB 5, 16; MTCW

Olson, Toby 1937- .... CLC 28
See also CA 65-68; CANR 9, 31

Olyesha, Yuri
See Olesha, Yuri (Karlovich)

Ondaatje, (Philip) Michael
1943- .... CLC 14, 29, 51, 76
See also CA 77-80; CANR 42; DLB 60

Oneal, Elizabeth 1934-
See Oneal, Zibby
See also CA 106; CANR 28; MAICYA;
SATA 30

Oneal, Zibby .... CLC 30
See also Oneal, Elizabeth
See also AAYA 5; CLR 13; JRDA

O'Neill, Eugene (Gladstone)
1888-1953 .... TCLC 1, 6, 27, 49
See also AITN 1; CA 110; 132;
CDALB 1929-1941; DA; DLB 7; MTCW;
WLC

Onetti, Juan Carlos 1909-....... CLC 7, 10
See also CA 85-88; CANR 32; DLB 113;
HW; MTCW

O Nuallain, Brian 1911-1966
See O'Brien, Flann
See also CA 21-22; 25-28R; CAP 2

Paterson, Katherine (Womeldorf)
   1932- .... **CLC 12, 30**
   See also AAYA 1; CA 21-24R; CANR 28;
   CLR 7; DLB 52; JRDA; MAICYA;
   MTCW; SATA 13, 53

Patmore, Coventry Kersey Dighton
   1823-1896 .... **NCLC 9**
   See also DLB 35, 98

Paton, Alan (Stewart)
   1903-1988 .... **CLC 4, 10, 25, 55**
   See also CA 13-16; 125; CANR 22; CAP 1;
   DA; MTCW; SATA 11, 56; WLC

Paton Walsh, Gillian 1937-
   See Walsh, Jill Paton
   See also CANR 38; JRDA; MAICYA;
   SAAS 3; SATA 4, 72

Paulding, James Kirke 1778-1860.. **NCLC 2**
   See also DLB 3, 59, 74

Paulin, Thomas Neilson 1949-
   See Paulin, Tom
   See also CA 123; 128

Paulin, Tom...................... **CLC 37**
   See also Paulin, Thomas Neilson
   See also DLB 40

Paustovsky, Konstantin (Georgievich)
   1892-1968 .... **CLC 40**
   See also CA 93-96; 25-28R

Pavese, Cesare 1908-1950 .... **TCLC 3**
   See also CA 104; DLB 128

Pavic, Milorad 1929- .... **CLC 60**
   See also CA 136

Payne, Alan
   See Jakes, John (William)

Paz, Gil
   See Lugones, Leopoldo

Paz, Octavio
   1914- .... **CLC 3, 4, 6, 10, 19, 51, 65;**
                                PC 1
   See also CA 73-76; CANR 32; DA;
   DLBY 90; HW; MTCW; WLC

Peacock, Molly 1947-............. **CLC 60**
   See also CA 103; DLB 120

Peacock, Thomas Love
   1785-1866 .... **NCLC 22**
   See also DLB 96, 116

Peake, Mervyn 1911-1968....... **CLC 7, 54**
   See also CA 5-8R; 25-28R; CANR 3;
   DLB 15; MTCW; SATA 23

Pearce, Philippa .... **CLC 21**
   See also Christie, (Ann) Philippa
   See also CLR 9; MAICYA; SATA 1, 67

Pearl, Eric
   See Elman, Richard

Pearson, T(homas) R(eid) 1956- .... **CLC 39**
   See also CA 120; 130

Peck, John 1941- .... **CLC 3**
   See also CA 49-52; CANR 3

Peck, Richard (Wayne) 1934- ...... **CLC 21**
   See also AAYA 1; CA 85-88; CANR 19,
   38; JRDA; MAICYA; SAAS 2; SATA 18,
   55

Peck, Robert Newton 1928-....... **CLC 17**
   See also AAYA 3; CA 81-84; CANR 31;
   DA; JRDA; MAICYA; SAAS 1;
   SATA 21, 62

Peckinpah, (David) Sam(uel)
   1925-1984 .... **CLC 20**
   See also CA 109; 114

Pedersen, Knut 1859-1952
   See Hamsun, Knut
   See also CA 104; 119; MTCW

Peeslake, Gaffer
   See Durrell, Lawrence (George)

Peguy, Charles Pierre
   1873-1914 .... **TCLC 10**
   See also CA 107

Pena, Ramon del Valle y
   See Valle-Inclan, Ramon (Maria) del

Pendennis, Arthur Esquir
   See Thackeray, William Makepeace

Pepys, Samuel 1633-1703........... **LC 11**
   See also CDBLB 1660-1789; DA; DLB 101;
   WLC

Percy, Walker
   1916-1990 .... **CLC 2, 3, 6, 8, 14, 18, 47,**
                                 65
   See also CA 1-4R; 131; CANR 1, 23;
   DLB 2; DLBY 80, 90; MTCW

Perec, Georges 1936-1982 .... **CLC 56**
   See also CA 141; DLB 83

Pereda (y Sanchez de Porrua), Jose Maria de
   1833-1906 .... **TCLC 16**
   See also CA 117

Pereda y Porrua, Jose Maria de
   See Pereda (y Sanchez de Porrua), Jose
   Maria de

Peregoy, George Weems
   See Mencken, H(enry) L(ouis)

Perelman, S(idney) J(oseph)
   1904-1979 ... **CLC 3, 5, 9, 15, 23, 44, 49**
   See also AITN 1, 2; CA 73-76; 89-92;
   CANR 18; DLB 11, 44; MTCW

Peret, Benjamin 1899-1959 ...... **TCLC 20**
   See also CA 117

Peretz, Isaac Loeb 1851(?)-1915... **TCLC 16**
   See also CA 109

Peretz, Yitzkhok Leibush
   See Peretz, Isaac Loeb

Perez Galdos, Benito 1843-1920... **TCLC 27**
   See also CA 125; HW

Perrault, Charles 1628-1703 .... **LC 2**
   See also MAICYA; SATA 25

Perry, Brighton
   See Sherwood, Robert E(mmet)

Perse, St.-John .... **CLC 4, 11, 46**
   See also Leger, (Marie-Rene Auguste) Alexis
   Saint-Leger

Peseenz, Tulio F.
   See Lopez y Fuentes, Gregorio

Pesetsky, Bette 1932-............. **CLC 28**
   See also CA 133; DLB 130

Peshkov, Alexei Maximovich 1868-1936
   See Gorky, Maxim
   See also CA 105; 141; DA

Pessoa, Fernando (Antonio Nogueira)
   1888-1935 .... **TCLC 27**
   See also CA 125

Peterkin, Julia Mood 1880-1961.... **CLC 31**
   See also CA 102; DLB 9

Peters, Joan K. 1945-............. **CLC 39**

Peters, Robert L(ouis) 1924-........ **CLC 7**
   See also CA 13-16R; CAAS 8; DLB 105

Petofi, Sandor 1823-1849........ **NCLC 21**

Petrakis, Harry Mark 1923-........ **CLC 3**
   See also CA 9-12R; CANR 4, 30

Petrov, Evgeny .... **TCLC 21**
   See also Kataev, Evgeny Petrovich

Petry, Ann (Lane) 1908- ...... **CLC 1, 7, 18**
   See also BW; CA 5-8R; CAAS 6; CANR 4;
   CLR 12; DLB 76; JRDA; MAICYA;
   MTCW; SATA 5

Petursson, Halligrimur 1614-1674 .... **LC 8**

Philipson, Morris H. 1926-........ **CLC 53**
   See also CA 1-4R; CANR 4

Phillips, David Graham
   1867-1911 .... **TCLC 44**
   See also CA 108; DLB 9, 12

Phillips, Jack
   See Sandburg, Carl (August)

Phillips, Jayne Anne 1952- ..... **CLC 15, 33**
   See also CA 101; CANR 24; DLBY 80;
   MTCW

Phillips, Richard
   See Dick, Philip K(indred)

Phillips, Robert (Schaeffer) 1938-... **CLC 28**
   See also CA 17-20R; CAAS 13; CANR 8;
   DLB 105

Phillips, Ward
   See Lovecraft, H(oward) P(hillips)

Piccolo, Lucio 1901-1969......... **CLC 13**
   See also CA 97-100; DLB 114

Pickthall, Marjorie L(owry) C(hristie)
   1883-1922 .... **TCLC 21**
   See also CA 107; DLB 92

Pico della Mirandola, Giovanni
   1463-1494 .... **LC 15**

Piercy, Marge
   1936- .... **CLC 3, 6, 14, 18, 27, 62**
   See also CA 21-24R; CAAS 1; CANR 13,
   43; DLB 120; MTCW

Piers, Robert
   See Anthony, Piers

Pieyre de Mandiargues, Andre 1909-1991
   See Mandiargues, Andre Pieyre de
   See also CA 103; 136; CANR 22

Pilnyak, Boris .... **TCLC 23**
   See also Vogau, Boris Andreyevich

Pincherle, Alberto 1907-1990 ... **CLC 11, 18**
   See also Moravia, Alberto
   See also CA 25-28R; 132; CANR 33;
   MTCW

Pinckney, Darryl 1953- .... **CLC 76**

Pindar 518B.C.-446B.C......... **CMLC 12**

Pineda, Cecile 1942-.............. **CLC 39**
   See also CA 118

Pinero, Arthur Wing 1855-1934 ... **TCLC 32**
   See also CA 110; DLB 10

Pinero, Miguel (Antonio Gomez)
   1946-1988 .... **CLC 4, 55**
   See also CA 61-64; 125; CANR 29; HW

Pinget, Robert 1919- .... **CLC 7, 13, 37**
   See also CA 85-88; DLB 83

Price, Richard 1949- .... CLC 6, 12
See also CA 49-52; CANR 3; DLBY 81

Prichard, Katharine Susannah
1883-1969 .... CLC 46
See also CA 11-12; CANR 33; CAP 1;
MTCW; SATA 66

Priestley, J(ohn) B(oynton)
1894-1984 .... CLC 2, 5, 9, 34
See also CA 9-12R; 113; CANR 33;
CDBLB 1914-1945; DLB 10, 34, 77, 100;
DLBY 84; MTCW

Prince 1958(?)- .... CLC 35

Prince, F(rank) T(empleton) 1912- .. CLC 22
See also CA 101; CANR 43; DLB 20

Prince Kropotkin
See Kropotkin, Peter (Aleksieevich)

Prior, Matthew 1664-1721 .... LC 4
See also DLB 95

Pritchard, William H(arrison)
1932- .... CLC 34
See also CA 65-68; CANR 23; DLB 111

Pritchett, V(ictor) S(awdon)
1900- .... CLC 5, 13, 15, 41
See also CA 61-64; CANR 31; DLB 15;
MTCW

Private 19022
See Manning, Frederic

Probst, Mark 1925- .... CLC 59
See also CA 130

Prokosch, Frederic 1908-1989.... CLC 4, 48
See also CA 73-76; 128; DLB 48

Prophet, The
See Dreiser, Theodore (Herman Albert)

Prose, Francine 1947-............ CLC 45
See also CA 109; 112

Proudhon
See Cunha, Euclides (Rodrigues Pimenta) da

Proust, (Valentin-Louis-George-Eugene-)
Marcel 1871-1922 .... TCLC 7, 13, 33
See also CA 104; 120; DA; DLB 65;
MTCW; WLC

Prowler, Harley
See Masters, Edgar Lee

Prus, Boleslaw.................. TCLC 48
See also Glowacki, Aleksander

Pryor, Richard (Franklin Lenox Thomas)
1940- .... CLC 26
See also CA 122

Przybyszewski, Stanislaw
1868-1927 .... TCLC 36
See also DLB 66

Pteleon
See Grieve, C(hristopher) M(urray)

Puckett, Lute
See Masters, Edgar Lee

Puig, Manuel
1932-1990 .... CLC 3, 5, 10, 28, 65
See also CA 45-48; CANR 2, 32; DLB 113;
HW; MTCW

Purdy, A(lfred Wellington)
1918- .... CLC 3, 6, 14, 50
See also CA 81-84; CANR 42

Purdy, Al
See Purdy, A(lfred Wellington)
See also CAAS 17; DLB 88

Purdy, James (Amos)
1923- .... CLC 2, 4, 10, 28, 52
See also CA 33-36R; CAAS 1; CANR 19;
DLB 2; MTCW

Pure, Simon
See Swinnerton, Frank Arthur

Pushkin, Alexander (Sergeyevich)
1799-1837 .... NCLC 3, 27
See also DA; SATA 61; WLC

P'u Sung-ling 1640-1715 .... LC 3

Putnam, Arthur Lee
See Alger, Horatio, Jr.

Puzo, Mario 1920- .... CLC 1, 2, 6, 36
See also CA 65-68; CANR 4, 42; DLB 6;
MTCW

Pym, Barbara (Mary Crampton)
1913-1980 .... CLC 13, 19, 37
See also CA 13-14; 97-100; CANR 13, 34;
CAP 1; DLB 14; DLBY 87; MTCW

Pynchon, Thomas (Ruggles, Jr.)
1937- .. CLC 2, 3, 6, 9, 11, 18, 33, 62, 72
See also BEST 90:2; CA 17-20R; CANR 22;
DA; DLB 2; MTCW; WLC

Qian Zhongshu
See Ch'ien Chung-shu

Qroll
See Dagerman, Stig (Halvard)

Quarrington, Paul (Lewis) 1953-.... CLC 65
See also CA 129

Quasimodo, Salvatore 1901-1968 ... CLC 10
See also CA 13-16; 25-28R; CAP 1;
DLB 114; MTCW

Queen, Ellery.................. CLC 3, 11
See also Dannay, Frederic; Davidson,
Avram; Lee, Manfred B(ennington);
Sturgeon, Theodore (Hamilton); Vance,
John Holbrook

Queen, Ellery, Jr.
See Dannay, Frederic; Lee, Manfred
B(ennington)

Queneau, Raymond
1903-1976 .... CLC 2, 5, 10, 42
See also CA 77-80; 69-72; CANR 32;
DLB 72; MTCW

Quevedo, Francisco de 1580-1645.... LC 23

Quin, Ann (Marie) 1936-1973 .... CLC 6
See also CA 9-12R; 45-48; DLB 14

Quinn, Martin
See Smith, Martin Cruz

Quinn, Simon
See Smith, Martin Cruz

Quiroga, Horacio (Sylvestre)
1878-1937 .... TCLC 20
See also CA 117; 131; HW; MTCW

Quoirez, Francoise 1935-........... CLC 9
See also Sagan, Francoise
See also CA 49-52; CANR 6, 39; MTCW

Raabe, Wilhelm 1831-1910 .... TCLC 45
See also DLB 129

Rabe, David (William) 1940-... CLC 4, 8, 33
See also CA 85-88; CABS 3; DLB 7

Rabelais, Francois 1483-1553 .... LC 5
See also DA; WLC

Rabinovitch, Sholem 1859-1916
See Aleichem, Sholom
See also CA 104

Radcliffe, Ann (Ward) 1764-1823 .. NCLC 6
See also DLB 39

Radiguet, Raymond 1903-1923 .... TCLC 29
See also DLB 65

Radnoti, Miklos 1909-1944 .... TCLC 16
See also CA 118

Rado, James 1939-............... CLC 17
See also CA 105

Radvanyi, Netty 1900-1983
See Seghers, Anna
See also CA 85-88; 110

Raeburn, John (Hay) 1941-........ CLC 34
See also CA 57-60

Ragni, Gerome 1942-1991 .... CLC 17
See also CA 105; 134

Rahv, Philip.................... CLC 24
See also Greenberg, Ivan

Raine, Craig 1944-............... CLC 32
See also CA 108; CANR 29; DLB 40

Raine, Kathleen (Jessie) 1908- ... CLC 7, 45
See also CA 85-88; DLB 20; MTCW

Rainis, Janis 1865-1929 .... TCLC 29

Rakosi, Carl.................... CLC 47
See also Rawley, Callman
See also CAAS 5

Raleigh, Richard
See Lovecraft, H(oward) P(hillips)

Rallentando, H. P.
See Sayers, Dorothy L(eigh)

Ramal, Walter
See de la Mare, Walter (John)

Ramon, Juan
See Jimenez (Mantecon), Juan Ramon

Ramos, Graciliano 1892-1953 ..... TCLC 32

Rampersad, Arnold 1941-.......... CLC 44
See also CA 127; 133; DLB 111

Rampling, Anne
See Rice, Anne

Ramuz, Charles-Ferdinand
1878-1947 .... TCLC 33

Rand, Ayn 1905-1982..... CLC 3, 30, 44, 79
See also AAYA 10; CA 13-16R; 105;
CANR 27; DA; MTCW; WLC

Randall, Dudley (Felker) 1914-...... CLC 1
See also BLC 3; BW; CA 25-28R;
CANR 23; DLB 41

Randall, Robert
See Silverberg, Robert

Ranger, Ken
See Creasey, John

Ransom, John Crowe
1888-1974 .... CLC 2, 4, 5, 11, 24
See also CA 5-8R; 49-52; CANR 6, 34;
DLB 45, 63; MTCW

Rao, Raja 1909- .... CLC 25, 56
See also CA 73-76; MTCW

Raphael, Frederic (Michael)
1931- . . . . **CLC 2, 14**
See also CA 1-4R; CANR 1; DLB 14

Ratcliffe, James P.
See Mencken, H(enry) L(ouis)

Rathbone, Julian 1935- . . . . **CLC 41**
See also CA 101; CANR 34

Rattigan, Terence (Mervyn)
1911-1977 . . . . **CLC 7**
See also CA 85-88; 73-76;
CDBLB 1945-1960; DLB 13; MTCW

Ratushinskaya, Irina 1954- . . . . **CLC 54**
See also CA 129

Raven, Simon (Arthur Noel)
1927- . . . . **CLC 14**
See also CA 81-84

Rawley, Callman 1903-
See Rakosi, Carl
See also CA 21-24R; CANR 12, 32

Rawlings, Marjorie Kinnan
1896-1953 . . . . **TCLC 4**
See also CA 104; 137; DLB 9, 22, 102;
JRDA; MAICYA; YABC 1

Ray, Satyajit 1921-1992 . . . . **CLC 16, 76**
See also CA 114; 137

Read, Herbert Edward 1893-1968 . . . . **CLC 4**
See also CA 85-88; 25-28R; DLB 20

Read, Piers Paul 1941- . . . . . . **CLC 4, 10, 25**
See also CA 21-24R; CANR 38; DLB 14;
SATA 21

Reade, Charles 1814-1884 . . . . **NCLC 2**
See also DLB 21

Reade, Hamish
See Gray, Simon (James Holliday)

Reading, Peter 1946- . . . . **CLC 47**
See also CA 103; DLB 40

Reaney, James 1926- . . . . **CLC 13**
See also CA 41-44R; CAAS 15; CANR 42;
DLB 68; SATA 43

Rebreanu, Liviu 1885-1944 . . . . **TCLC 28**

Rechy, John (Francisco)
1934- . . . . **CLC 1, 7, 14, 18**
See also CA 5-8R; CAAS 4; CANR 6, 32;
DLB 122; DLBY 82; HW

Redcam, Tom 1870-1933 . . . . **TCLC 25**

Reddin, Keith . . . . **CLC 67**

Redgrove, Peter (William)
1932- . . . . **CLC 6, 41**
See also CA 1-4R; CANR 3, 39; DLB 40

Redmon, Anne . . . . **CLC 22**
See also Nightingale, Anne Redmon
See also DLBY 86

Reed, Eliot
See Ambler, Eric

Reed, Ishmael
1938- . . . . **CLC 2, 3, 5, 6, 13, 32, 60**
See also BLC 3; BW; CA 21-24R;
CANR 25; DLB 2, 5, 33; DLBD 8;
MTCW

Reed, John (Silas) 1887-1920 . . . . . . **TCLC 9**
See also CA 106

Reed, Lou . . . . **CLC 21**
See also Firbank, Louis

Reeve, Clara 1729-1807 . . . . **NCLC 19**
See also DLB 39

Reid, Christopher (John) 1949- . . . . . **CLC 33**
See also CA 140; DLB 40

Reid, Desmond
See Moorcock, Michael (John)

Reid Banks, Lynne 1929-
See Banks, Lynne Reid
See also CA 1-4R; CANR 6, 22, 38;
CLR 24; JRDA; MAICYA; SATA 22, 75

Reilly, William K.
See Creasey, John

Reiner, Max
See Caldwell, (Janet Miriam) Taylor
(Holland)

Reis, Ricardo
See Pessoa, Fernando (Antonio Nogueira)

Remarque, Erich Maria
1898-1970 . . . . **CLC 21**
See also CA 77-80; 29-32R; DA; DLB 56;
MTCW

Remizov, A.
See Remizov, Aleksei (Mikhailovich)

Remizov, A. M.
See Remizov, Aleksei (Mikhailovich)

Remizov, Aleksei (Mikhailovich)
1877-1957 . . . . **TCLC 27**
See also CA 125; 133

Renan, Joseph Ernest
1823-1892 . . . . **NCLC 26**

Renard, Jules 1864-1910 . . . . **TCLC 17**
See also CA 117

Renault, Mary . . . . **CLC 3, 11, 17**
See also Challans, Mary
See also DLBY 83

Rendell, Ruth (Barbara) 1930- . . **CLC 28, 48**
See also Vine, Barbara
See also CA 109; CANR 32; DLB 87;
MTCW

Renoir, Jean 1894-1979 . . . . **CLC 20**
See also CA 129; 85-88

Resnais, Alain 1922- . . . . **CLC 16**

Reverdy, Pierre 1889-1960 . . . . **CLC 53**
See also CA 97-100; 89-92

Rexroth, Kenneth
1905-1982 . . . . **CLC 1, 2, 6, 11, 22, 49**
See also CA 5-8R; 107; CANR 14, 34;
CDALB 1941-1968; DLB 16, 48;
DLBY 82; MTCW

Reyes, Alfonso 1889-1959 . . . . **TCLC 33**
See also CA 131; HW

Reyes y Basoalto, Ricardo Eliecer Neftali
See Neruda, Pablo

Reymont, Wladyslaw (Stanislaw)
1868(?)-1925 . . . . **TCLC 5**
See also CA 104

Reynolds, Jonathan 1942- . . . . **CLC 6, 38**
See also CA 65-68; CANR 28

Reynolds, Joshua 1723-1792 . . . . **LC 15**
See also DLB 104

Reynolds, Michael Shane 1937- . . . . **CLC 44**
See also CA 65-68; CANR 9

Reznikoff, Charles 1894-1976 . . . . **CLC 9**
See also CA 33-36; 61-64; CAP 2; DLB 28,
45

Rezzori (d'Arezzo), Gregor von
1914- . . . . **CLC 25**
See also CA 122; 136

Rhine, Richard
See Silverstein, Alvin

R'hoone
See Balzac, Honore de

Rhys, Jean
1890(?)-1979 . . . . **CLC 2, 4, 6, 14, 19, 51**
See also CA 25-28R; 85-88; CANR 35;
CDBLB 1945-1960; DLB 36, 117; MTCW

Ribeiro, Darcy 1922- . . . . **CLC 34**
See also CA 33-36R

Ribeiro, Joao Ubaldo (Osorio Pimentel)
1941- . . . . **CLC 10, 67**
See also CA 81-84

Ribman, Ronald (Burt) 1932- . . . . **CLC 7**
See also CA 21-24R

Ricci, Nino 1959- . . . . **CLC 70**
See also CA 137

Rice, Anne 1941- . . . . **CLC 41**
See also AAYA 9; BEST 89:2; CA 65-68;
CANR 12, 36

Rice, Elmer (Leopold)
1892-1967 . . . . **CLC 7, 49**
See also CA 21-22; 25-28R; CAP 2; DLB 4,
7; MTCW

Rice, Tim 1944- . . . . **CLC 21**
See also CA 103

Rich, Adrienne (Cecile)
1929- . . . . **CLC 3, 6, 7, 11, 18, 36, 73, 76;**
PC 5
See also CA 9-12R; CANR 20; DLB 5, 67;
MTCW

Rich, Barbara
See Graves, Robert (von Ranke)

Rich, Robert
See Trumbo, Dalton

Richards, David Adams 1950- . . . . . . **CLC 59**
See also CA 93-96; DLB 53

Richards, I(vor) A(rmstrong)
1893-1979 . . . . **CLC 14, 24**
See also CA 41-44R; 89-92; CANR 34;
DLB 27

Richardson, Anne
See Roiphe, Anne Richardson

Richardson, Dorothy Miller
1873-1957 . . . . **TCLC 3**
See also CA 104; DLB 36

Richardson, Ethel Florence (Lindesay)
1870-1946
See Richardson, Henry Handel
See also CA 105

Richardson, Henry Handel . . . . **TCLC 4**
See also Richardson, Ethel Florence
(Lindesay)

Richardson, Samuel 1689-1761 . . . . **LC 1**
See also CDBLB 1660-1789; DA; DLB 39;
WLC

Richler, Mordecai
1931- .... CLC 3, 5, 9, 13, 18, 46, 70
See also AITN 1; CA 65-68; CANR 31;
CLR 17; DLB 53; MAICYA; MTCW;
SATA 27, 44

Richter, Conrad (Michael)
1890-1968 .... CLC 30
See also CA 5-8R; 25-28R; CANR 23;
DLB 9; MTCW; SATA 3

Riddell, J. H. 1832-1906 .... TCLC 40

Riding, Laura .... CLC 3, 7
See also Jackson, Laura (Riding)

Riefenstahl, Berta Helene Amalia 1902-
See Riefenstahl, Leni
See also CA 108

Riefenstahl, Leni .... CLC 16
See also Riefenstahl, Berta Helene Amalia

Riffe, Ernest
See Bergman, (Ernst) Ingmar

Riley, James Whitcomb
1849-1916 .... TCLC 51
See also CA 118; 137; MAICYA; SATA 17

Riley, Tex
See Creasey, John

Rilke, Rainer Maria
1875-1926 .... TCLC 1, 6, 19; PC 2
See also CA 104; 132; DLB 81; MTCW

Rimbaud, (Jean Nicolas) Arthur
1854-1891 .... NCLC 4, 35; PC 3
See also DA; WLC

Rinehart, Mary Roberts
1876-1958 .... TCLC 52
See also CA 108

Ringmaster, The
See Mencken, H(enry) L(ouis)

Ringwood, Gwen(dolyn Margaret) Pharis
1910-1984 .... CLC 48
See also CA 112; DLB 88

Rio, Michel 19(?)- .... CLC 43

Ritsos, Giannes
See Ritsos, Yannis

Ritsos, Yannis 1909-1990 ..... CLC 6, 13, 31
See also CA 77-80; 133; CANR 39; MTCW

Ritter, Erika 1948(?)- .... CLC 52

Rivera, Jose Eustasio 1889-1928... TCLC 35
See also HW

Rivers, Conrad Kent 1933-1968...... CLC 1
See also BW; CA 85-88; DLB 41

Rivers, Elfrida
See Bradley, Marion Zimmer

Riverside, John
See Heinlein, Robert A(nson)

Rizal, Jose 1861-1896........... NCLC 27

Roa Bastos, Augusto (Antonio)
1917- .... CLC 45
See also CA 131; DLB 113; HW

Robbe-Grillet, Alain
1922- ...... CLC 1, 2, 4, 6, 8, 10, 14, 43
See also CA 9-12R; CANR 33; DLB 83;
MTCW

Robbins, Harold 1916-............. CLC 5
See also CA 73-76; CANR 26; MTCW

Robbins, Thomas Eugene 1936-
See Robbins, Tom
See also CA 81-84; CANR 29; MTCW

Robbins, Tom............... CLC 9, 32, 64
See also Robbins, Thomas Eugene
See also BEST 90:3; DLBY 80

Robbins, Trina 1938- .... CLC 21
See also CA 128

Roberts, Charles G(eorge) D(ouglas)
1860-1943 .... TCLC 8
See also CA 105; DLB 92; SATA 29

Roberts, Kate 1891-1985 .... CLC 15
See also CA 107; 116

Roberts, Keith (John Kingston)
1935- .... CLC 14
See also CA 25-28R

Roberts, Kenneth (Lewis)
1885-1957 .... TCLC 23
See also CA 109; DLB 9

Roberts, Michele (B.) 1949-........ CLC 48
See also CA 115

Robertson, Ellis
See Ellison, Harlan; Silverberg, Robert

Robertson, Thomas William
1829-1871 .... NCLC 35

Robinson, Edwin Arlington
1869-1935 .... TCLC 5; PC 1
See also CA 104; 133; CDALB 1865-1917;
DA; DLB 54; MTCW

Robinson, Henry Crabb
1775-1867 .... NCLC 15
See also DLB 107

Robinson, Jill 1936-.............. CLC 10
See also CA 102

Robinson, Kim Stanley 1952- ...... CLC 34
See also CA 126

Robinson, Lloyd
See Silverberg, Robert

Robinson, Marilynne 1944-........ CLC 25
See also CA 116

Robinson, Smokey................ CLC 21
See also Robinson, William, Jr.

Robinson, William, Jr. 1940-
See Robinson, Smokey
See also CA 116

Robison, Mary 1949- .... CLC 42
See also CA 113; 116; DLB 130

Rod, Edouard 1857-1910 .... TCLC 52

Roddenberry, Eugene Wesley 1921-1991
See Roddenberry, Gene
See also CA 110; 135; CANR 37; SATA 45

Roddenberry, Gene .... CLC 17
See also Roddenberry, Eugene Wesley
See also AAYA 5; SATA-Obit 69

Rodgers, Mary 1931-.............. CLC 12
See also CA 49-52; CANR 8; CLR 20;
JRDA; MAICYA; SATA 8

Rodgers, W(illiam) R(obert)
1909-1969 .... CLC 7
See also CA 85-88; DLB 20

Rodman, Eric
See Silverberg, Robert

Rodman, Howard 1920(?)-1985..... CLC 65
See also CA 118

Rodman, Maia
See Wojciechowska, Maia (Teresa)

Rodriguez, Claudio 1934-......... CLC 10
See also DLB 134

Roelvaag, O(le) E(dvart)
1876-1931 .... TCLC 17
See also CA 117; DLB 9

Roethke, Theodore (Huebner)
1908-1963 ...... CLC 1, 3, 8, 11, 19, 46
See also CA 81-84; CABS 2;
CDALB 1941-1968; DLB 5; MTCW

Rogers, Thomas Hunton 1927- ..... CLC 57
See also CA 89-92

Rogers, Will(iam Penn Adair)
1879-1935 .... TCLC 8
See also CA 105; DLB 11

Rogin, Gilbert 1929-............. CLC 18
See also CA 65-68; CANR 15

Rohan, Koda .... TCLC 22
See also Koda Shigeyuki

Rohmer, Eric.................... CLC 16
See also Scherer, Jean-Marie Maurice

Rohmer, Sax .... TCLC 28
See also Ward, Arthur Henry Sarsfield
See also DLB 70

Roiphe, Anne Richardson 1935- ... CLC 3, 9
See also CA 89-92; DLBY 80

Rojas, Fernando de 1465-1541 ...... LC 23

**Rolfe, Frederick (William Serafino Austin
Lewis Mary)** 1860-1913...... TCLC 12
See also CA 107; DLB 34

Rolland, Romain 1866-1944...... TCLC 23
See also CA 118; DLB 65

Rolvaag, O(le) E(dvart)
See Roelvaag, O(le) E(dvart)

Romain Arnaud, Saint
See Aragon, Louis

Romains, Jules 1885-1972 .... CLC 7
See also CA 85-88; CANR 34; DLB 65;
MTCW

Romero, Jose Ruben 1890-1952 ... TCLC 14
See also CA 114; 131; HW

Ronsard, Pierre de 1524-1585 .... LC 6

Rooke, Leon 1934-............. CLC 25, 34
See also CA 25-28R; CANR 23

Roper, William 1498-1578 .... LC 10

Roquelaure, A. N.
See Rice, Anne

Rosa, Joao Guimaraes 1908-1967... CLC 23
See also CA 89-92; DLB 113

Rosen, Richard (Dean) 1949-....... CLC 39
See also CA 77-80

Rosenberg, Isaac 1890-1918....... TCLC 12
See also CA 107; DLB 20

Rosenblatt, Joe.................... CLC 15
See also Rosenblatt, Joseph

Rosenblatt, Joseph 1933-
See Rosenblatt, Joe
See also CA 89-92

Rosenfeld, Samuel 1896-1963
See Tzara, Tristan
See also CA 89-92

Shange, Ntozake
    1948- . . . . **CLC 8, 25, 38, 74; DC 3**
    See also AAYA 9; BLC 3; BW; CA 85-88;
    CABS 3; CANR 27; DLB 38; MTCW

Shanley, John Patrick   1950- . . . . **CLC 75**
    See also CA 128; 133

Shapcott, Thomas William   1935- . . . **CLC 38**
    See also CA 69-72

Shapiro, Jane. . . . . **CLC 76**

Shapiro, Karl (Jay)   1913- . . **CLC 4, 8, 15, 53**
    See also CA 1-4R; CAAS 6; CANR 1, 36;
    DLB 48; MTCW

Sharp, William   1855-1905 . . . . **TCLC 39**

Sharpe, Thomas Ridley   1928-
    See Sharpe, Tom
    See also CA 114; 122

Sharpe, Tom. **CLC 36**
    See also Sharpe, Thomas Ridley
    See also DLB 14

Shaw, Bernard. . . . . **TCLC 45**
    See also Shaw, George Bernard

Shaw, G. Bernard
    See Shaw, George Bernard

Shaw, George Bernard
    1856-1950 . . . . **TCLC 3, 9, 21**
    See also Shaw, Bernard
    See also CA 104; 128; CDBLB 1914-1945;
    DA; DLB 10, 57; MTCW; WLC

Shaw, Henry Wheeler
    1818-1885 . . . . **NCLC 15**
    See also DLB 11

Shaw, Irwin   1913-1984. . . . . . **CLC 7, 23, 34**
    See also AITN 1; CA 13-16R; 112;
    CANR 21; CDALB 1941-1968; DLB 6,
    102; DLBY 84; MTCW

Shaw, Robert   1927-1978 . . . . **CLC 5**
    See also AITN 1; CA 1-4R; 81-84;
    CANR 4; DLB 13, 14

Shaw, T. E.
    See Lawrence, T(homas) E(dward)

Shawn, Wallace   1943- . . . . **CLC 41**
    See also CA 112

Sheed, Wilfrid (John Joseph)
    1930- . . . . **CLC 2, 4, 10, 53**
    See also CA 65-68; CANR 30; DLB 6;
    MTCW

Sheldon, Alice Hastings Bradley
    1915(?)-1987
    See Tiptree, James, Jr.
    See also CA 108; 122; CANR 34; MTCW

Sheldon, John
    See Bloch, Robert (Albert)

Shelley, Mary Wollstonecraft (Godwin)
    1797-1851 . . . . **NCLC 14**
    See also CDBLB 1789-1832; DA; DLB 110,
    116; SATA 29; WLC

Shelley, Percy Bysshe
    1792-1822 . . . . **NCLC 18**
    See also CDBLB 1789-1832; DA; DLB 96,
    110; WLC

Shepard, Jim   1956-. . . . . **CLC 36**
    See also CA 137

Shepard, Lucius   1947- . . . . **CLC 34**
    See also CA 128; 141

Shepard, Sam
    1943- . . . . **CLC 4, 6, 17, 34, 41, 44**
    See also AAYA 1; CA 69-72; CABS 3;
    CANR 22; DLB 7; MTCW

Shepherd, Michael
    See Ludlum, Robert

Sherburne, Zoa (Morin)   1912-. . . . . . **CLC 30**
    See also CA 1-4R; CANR 3, 37; MAICYA;
    SATA 3

Sheridan, Frances   1724-1766. . . . . **LC 7**
    See also DLB 39, 84

Sheridan, Richard Brinsley
    1751-1816 . . . . **NCLC 5; DC 1**
    See also CDBLB 1660-1789; DA; DLB 89;
    WLC

Sherman, Jonathan Marc . . . . **CLC 55**

Sherman, Martin   1941(?)- . . . . **CLC 19**
    See also CA 116; 123

Sherwin, Judith Johnson   1936-. . . **CLC 7, 15**
    See also CA 25-28R; CANR 34

Sherwood, Robert E(mmet)
    1896-1955 . . . . **TCLC 3**
    See also CA 104; DLB 7, 26

Shiel, M(atthew) P(hipps)
    1865-1947 . . . . **TCLC 8**
    See also CA 106

Shiga, Naoya   1883-1971. . . . . **CLC 33**
    See also CA 101; 33-36R

Shimazaki Haruki   1872-1943
    See Shimazaki Toson
    See also CA 105; 134

Shimazaki Toson . . . . **TCLC 5**
    See also Shimazaki Haruki

Sholokhov, Mikhail (Aleksandrovich)
    1905-1984 . . . . **CLC 7, 15**
    See also CA 101; 112; MTCW; SATA 36

Shone, Patric
    See Hanley, James

Shreve, Susan Richards   1939-. . . . . . **CLC 23**
    See also CA 49-52; CAAS 5; CANR 5, 38;
    MAICYA; SATA 41, 46

Shue, Larry   1946-1985. . . . . **CLC 52**
    See also CA 117

Shu-Jen, Chou   1881-1936
    See Hsun, Lu
    See also CA 104

Shulman, Alix Kates   1932- . . . . . . **CLC 2, 10**
    See also CA 29-32R; CANR 43; SATA 7

Shuster, Joe   1914- . . . . **CLC 21**

Shute, Nevil. **CLC 30**
    See also Norway, Nevil Shute

Shuttle, Penelope (Diane)   1947- . . . . . **CLC 7**
    See also CA 93-96; CANR 39; DLB 14, 40

Sidney, Mary   1561-1621 . . . . **LC 19**

Sidney, Sir Philip   1554-1586. . . . . . . **LC 19**
    See also CDBLB Before 1660; DA

Siegel, Jerome   1914- . . . . **CLC 21**
    See also CA 116

Siegel, Jerry
    See Siegel, Jerome

Sienkiewicz, Henryk (Adam Alexander Pius)
    1846-1916 . . . . **TCLC 3**
    See also CA 104; 134

Sierra, Gregorio Martinez
    See Martinez Sierra, Gregorio

Sierra, Maria (de la O'LeJarraga) Martinez
    See Martinez Sierra, Maria (de la
    O'LeJarraga)

Sigal, Clancy   1926-. . . . . **CLC 7**
    See also CA 1-4R

Sigourney, Lydia Howard (Huntley)
    1791-1865 . . . . **NCLC 21**
    See also DLB 1, 42, 73

Siguenza y Gongora, Carlos de
    1645-1700 . . . . **LC 8**

Sigurjonsson, Johann   1880-1919. . . **TCLC 27**

Sikelianos, Angelos   1884-1951 . . . . **TCLC 39**

Silkin, Jon   1930- . . . . **CLC 2, 6, 43**
    See also CA 5-8R; CAAS 5; DLB 27

Silko, Leslie Marmon   1948- . . . . **CLC 23, 74**
    See also CA 115; 122; DA

Sillanpaa, Frans Eemil   1888-1964. . . **CLC 19**
    See also CA 129; 93-96; MTCW

Sillitoe, Alan
    1928- . . . . **CLC 1, 3, 6, 10, 19, 57**
    See also AITN 1; CA 9-12R; CAAS 2;
    CANR 8, 26; CDBLB 1960 to Present;
    DLB 14; MTCW; SATA 61

Silone, Ignazio   1900-1978 . . . . **CLC 4**
    See also CA 25-28; 81-84; CANR 34;
    CAP 2; MTCW

Silver, Joan Micklin   1935- . . . . **CLC 20**
    See also CA 114; 121

Silver, Nicholas
    See Faust, Frederick (Schiller)

Silverberg, Robert   1935- . . . . **CLC 7**
    See also CA 1-4R; CAAS 3; CANR 1, 20,
    36; DLB 8; MAICYA; MTCW; SATA 13

Silverstein, Alvin   1933- . . . . **CLC 17**
    See also CA 49-52; CANR 2; CLR 25;
    JRDA; MAICYA; SATA 8, 69

Silverstein, Virginia B(arbara Opshelor)
    1937- . . . . **CLC 17**
    See also CA 49-52; CANR 2; CLR 25;
    JRDA; MAICYA; SATA 8, 69

Sim, Georges
    See Simenon, Georges (Jacques Christian)

Simak, Clifford D(onald)
    1904-1988 . . . . **CLC 1, 55**
    See also CA 1-4R; 125; CANR 1, 35;
    DLB 8; MTCW; SATA 56

Simenon, Georges (Jacques Christian)
    1903-1989 . . . . **CLC 1, 2, 3, 8, 18, 47**
    See also CA 85-88; 129; CANR 35;
    DLB 72; DLBY 89; MTCW

Simic, Charles   1938-. . . **CLC 6, 9, 22, 49, 68**
    See also CA 29-32R; CAAS 4; CANR 12,
    33; DLB 105

Simmons, Charles (Paul)   1924-. . . . . **CLC 57**
    See also CA 89-92

Simmons, Dan   1948-. . . . . **CLC 44**
    See also CA 138

Simmons, James (Stewart Alexander)
    1933- . . . . **CLC 43**
    See also CA 105; DLB 40

Simms, William Gilmore
1806-1870 .... **NCLC 3**
See also DLB 3, 30, 59, 73

Simon, Carly 1945-.............. **CLC 26**
See also CA 105

Simon, Claude 1913-...... **CLC 4, 9, 15, 39**
See also CA 89-92; CANR 33; DLB 83;
MTCW

Simon, (Marvin) Neil
1927- .... **CLC 6, 11, 31, 39, 70**
See also AITN 1; CA 21-24R; CANR 26;
DLB 7; MTCW

Simon, Paul 1942(?)- .... **CLC 17**
See also CA 116

Simonon, Paul 1956(?)- .... **CLC 30**
See also Clash, The

Simpson, Harriette
See Arnow, Harriette (Louisa) Simpson

Simpson, Louis (Aston Marantz)
1923-................ **CLC 4, 7, 9, 32**
See also CA 1-4R; CAAS 4; CANR 1;
DLB 5; MTCW

Simpson, Mona (Elizabeth) 1957-... **CLC 44**
See also CA 122; 135

Simpson, N(orman) F(rederick)
1919-................... **CLC 29**
See also CA 13-16R; DLB 13

Sinclair, Andrew (Annandale)
1935-.................... **CLC 2, 14**
See also CA 9-12R; CAAS 5; CANR 14, 38;
DLB 14; MTCW

Sinclair, Emil
See Hesse, Hermann

Sinclair, Iain 1943-.............. **CLC 76**
See also CA 132

Sinclair, Iain MacGregor
See Sinclair, Iain

Sinclair, Mary Amelia St. Clair 1865(?)-1946
See Sinclair, May
See also CA 104

Sinclair, May.................. **TCLC 3, 11**
See also Sinclair, Mary Amelia St. Clair
See also DLB 36

Sinclair, Upton (Beall)
1878-1968 .... **CLC 1, 11, 15, 63**
See also CA 5-8R; 25-28R; CANR 7;
CDALB 1929-1941; DA; DLB 9; MTCW;
SATA 9; WLC

Singer, Isaac
See Singer, Isaac Bashevis

Singer, Isaac Bashevis
1904-1991 .... **CLC 1, 3, 6, 9, 11, 15, 23,
38, 69; SSC 3**
See also AITN 1, 2; CA 1-4R; 134;
CANR 1, 39; CDALB 1941-1968; CLR 1;
DA; DLB 6, 28, 52; DLBY 91; JRDA;
MAICYA; MTCW; SATA 3, 27;
SATA-Obit 68; WLC

Singer, Israel Joshua 1893-1944 ... **TCLC 33**

Singh, Khushwant 1915-.......... **CLC 11**
See also CA 9-12R; CAAS 9; CANR 6

Sinjohn, John
See Galsworthy, John

Sinyavsky, Andrei (Donatevich)
1925- .... **CLC 8**
See also CA 85-88

Sirin, V.
See Nabokov, Vladimir (Vladimirovich)

Sissman, L(ouis) E(dward)
1928-1976 .... **CLC 9, 18**
See also CA 21-24R; 65-68; CANR 13;
DLB 5

Sisson, C(harles) H(ubert) 1914-..... **CLC 8**
See also CA 1-4R; CAAS 3; CANR 3;
DLB 27

Sitwell, Dame Edith
1887-1964 .... **CLC 2, 9, 67; PC 3**
See also CA 9-12R; CANR 35;
CDBLB 1945-1960; DLB 20; MTCW

Sjoewall, Maj 1935-.............. **CLC 7**
See also CA 65-68

Sjowall, Maj
See Sjoewall, Maj

Skelton, Robin 1925-............. **CLC 13**
See also AITN 2; CA 5-8R; CAAS 5;
CANR 28; DLB 27, 53

Skolimowski, Jerzy 1938-......... **CLC 20**
See also CA 128

Skram, Amalie (Bertha)
1847-1905 .... **TCLC 25**

Skvorecky, Josef (Vaclav)
1924-................ **CLC 15, 39, 69**
See also CA 61-64; CAAS 1; CANR 10, 34;
MTCW

Slade, Bernard................. **CLC 11, 46**
See also Newbound, Bernard Slade
See also CAAS 9; DLB 53

Slaughter, Carolyn 1946-.......... **CLC 56**
See also CA 85-88

Slaughter, Frank G(ill) 1908- ...... **CLC 29**
See also AITN 2; CA 5-8R; CANR 5

Slavitt, David R(ytman) 1935-... **CLC 5, 14**
See also CA 21-24R; CAAS 3; CANR 41;
DLB 5, 6

Slesinger, Tess 1905-1945 .... **TCLC 10**
See also CA 107; DLB 102

Slessor, Kenneth 1901-1971....... **CLC 14**
See also CA 102; 89-92

Slowacki, Juliusz 1809-1849 ..... **NCLC 15**

Smart, Christopher 1722-1771....... **LC 3**
See also DLB 109

Smart, Elizabeth 1913-1986........ **CLC 54**
See also CA 81-84; 118; DLB 88

Smiley, Jane (Graves) 1949-.... **CLC 53, 76**
See also CA 104; CANR 30

Smith, A(rthur) J(ames) M(arshall)
1902-1980 .... **CLC 15**
See also CA 1-4R; 102; CANR 4; DLB 88

Smith, Betty (Wehner) 1896-1972... **CLC 19**
See also CA 5-8R; 33-36R; DLBY 82;
SATA 6

Smith, Charlotte (Turner)
1749-1806 .... **NCLC 23**
See also DLB 39, 109

Smith, Clark Ashton 1893-1961 .... **CLC 43**

Smith, Dave................... **CLC 22, 42**
See also Smith, David (Jeddie)
See also CAAS 7; DLB 5

Smith, David (Jeddie) 1942-
See Smith, Dave
See also CA 49-52; CANR 1

Smith, Florence Margaret
1902-1971 .... **CLC 8**
See also Smith, Stevie
See also CA 17-18; 29-32R; CANR 35;
CAP 2; MTCW

Smith, Iain Crichton 1928- .... **CLC 64**
See also CA 21-24R; DLB 40

Smith, John 1580(?)-1631 .... **LC 9**

Smith, Johnston
See Crane, Stephen (Townley)

Smith, Lee 1944-.............. **CLC 25, 73**
See also CA 114; 119; DLBY 83

Smith, Martin
See Smith, Martin Cruz

Smith, Martin Cruz 1942-......... **CLC 25**
See also BEST 89:4; CA 85-88; CANR 6,
23, 43

Smith, Mary-Ann Tirone 1944-..... **CLC 39**
See also CA 118; 136

Smith, Patti 1946- .... **CLC 12**
See also CA 93-96

Smith, Pauline (Urmson)
1882-1959 .... **TCLC 25**

Smith, Rosamond
See Oates, Joyce Carol

Smith, Sheila Kaye
See Kaye-Smith, Sheila

Smith, Stevie............. **CLC 3, 8, 25, 44**
See also Smith, Florence Margaret
See also DLB 20

Smith, Wilbur A(ddison) 1933-..... **CLC 33**
See also CA 13-16R; CANR 7; MTCW

Smith, William Jay 1918- .... **CLC 6**
See also CA 5-8R; DLB 5; MAICYA;
SATA 2, 68

Smith, Woodrow Wilson
See Kuttner, Henry

Smolenskin, Peretz 1842-1885.... **NCLC 30**

Smollett, Tobias (George) 1721-1771 .. **LC 2**
See also CDBLB 1660-1789; DLB 39, 104

Snodgrass, W(illiam) D(e Witt)
1926- .... **CLC 2, 6, 10, 18, 68**
See also CA 1-4R; CANR 6, 36; DLB 5;
MTCW

Snow, C(harles) P(ercy)
1905-1980 .... **CLC 1, 4, 6, 9, 13, 19**
See also CA 5-8R; 101; CANR 28;
CDBLB 1945-1960; DLB 15, 77; MTCW

Snow, Frances Compton
See Adams, Henry (Brooks)

Snyder, Gary (Sherman)
1930- .... **CLC 1, 2, 5, 9, 32**
See also CA 17-20R; CANR 30; DLB 5, 16

Snyder, Zilpha Keatley 1927- ...... **CLC 17**
See also CA 9-12R; CANR 38; CLR 31;
JRDA; MAICYA; SAAS 2; SATA 1, 28,
75

Soares, Bernardo
    See Pessoa, Fernando (Antonio Nogueira)

Sobh, A.
    See Shamlu, Ahmad

Sobol, Joshua . . . . **CLC 60**

Soderberg, Hjalmar 1869-1941 . . . . **TCLC 39**

Sodergran, Edith (Irene)
    See Soedergran, Edith (Irene)

Soedergran, Edith (Irene)
    1892-1923 . . . . **TCLC 31**

Softly, Edgar
    See Lovecraft, H(oward) P(hillips)

Softly, Edward
    See Lovecraft, H(oward) P(hillips)

Sokolov, Raymond 1941- . . . . **CLC 7**
    See also CA 85-88

Solo, Jay
    See Ellison, Harlan

Sologub, Fyodor . . . . **TCLC 9**
    See also Teternikov, Fyodor Kuzmich

Solomons, Ikey Esquir
    See Thackeray, William Makepeace

Solomos, Dionysios 1798-1857 . . . **NCLC 15**

Solwoska, Mara
    See French, Marilyn

Solzhenitsyn, Aleksandr I(sayevich)
    1918- . . . . . . **CLC 1, 2, 4, 7, 9, 10, 18, 26,**
                                                        34, 78
    See also AITN 1; CA 69-72; CANR 40;
        DA; MTCW; WLC

Somers, Jane
    See Lessing, Doris (May)

Somerville, Edith 1858-1949 . . . . . . **TCLC 51**

Somerville & Ross
    See Martin, Violet Florence; Somerville,
        Edith

Sommer, Scott 1951- . . . . **CLC 25**
    See also CA 106

Sondheim, Stephen (Joshua)
    1930- . . . . **CLC 30, 39**
    See also CA 103

Sontag, Susan 1933- . . . **CLC 1, 2, 10, 13, 31**
    See also CA 17-20R; CANR 25; DLB 2, 67;
        MTCW

Sophocles
    496(?)B.C.-406(?)B.C. . . . . **CMLC 2; DC 1**
    See also DA

Sorel, Julia
    See Drexler, Rosalyn

Sorrentino, Gilbert
    1929- . . . . **CLC 3, 7, 14, 22, 40**
    See also CA 77-80; CANR 14, 33; DLB 5;
        DLBY 80

Soto, Gary 1952- . . . . **CLC 32, 80**
    See also AAYA 10; CA 119; 125; DLB 82;
        HW; JRDA

Soupault, Philippe 1897-1990 . . . . . . **CLC 68**
    See also CA 116; 131

Souster, (Holmes) Raymond
    1921- . . . . **CLC 5, 14**
    See also CA 13-16R; CAAS 14; CANR 13,
        29; DLB 88; SATA 63

Southern, Terry 1926- . . . . **CLC 7**
    See also CA 1-4R; CANR 1; DLB 2

Southey, Robert 1774-1843 . . . . . . **NCLC 8**
    See also DLB 93, 107; SATA 54

Southworth, Emma Dorothy Eliza Nevitte
    1819-1899 . . . . **NCLC 26**

Souza, Ernest
    See Scott, Evelyn

Soyinka, Wole
    1934- . . . . **CLC 3, 5, 14, 36, 44; DC 2**
    See also BLC 3; BW; CA 13-16R;
        CANR 27, 39; DA; DLB 125; MTCW;
        WLC

Spackman, W(illiam) M(ode)
    1905-1990 . . . . **CLC 46**
    See also CA 81-84; 132

Spacks, Barry 1931- . . . . **CLC 14**
    See also CA 29-32R; CANR 33; DLB 105

Spanidou, Irini 1946- . . . . **CLC 44**

Spark, Muriel (Sarah)
    1918- . . . . **CLC 2, 3, 5, 8, 13, 18, 40;**
                                                        SSC 10
    See also CA 5-8R; CANR 12, 36;
        CDBLB 1945-1960; DLB 15; MTCW

Spaulding, Douglas
    See Bradbury, Ray (Douglas)

Spaulding, Leonard
    See Bradbury, Ray (Douglas)

Spence, J. A. D.
    See Eliot, T(homas) S(tearns)

Spencer, Elizabeth 1921- . . . . **CLC 22**
    See also CA 13-16R; CANR 32; DLB 6;
        MTCW; SATA 14

Spencer, Leonard G.
    See Silverberg, Robert

Spencer, Scott 1945- . . . . **CLC 30**
    See also CA 113; DLBY 86

Spender, Stephen (Harold)
    1909- . . . . **CLC 1, 2, 5, 10, 41**
    See also CA 9-12R; CANR 31;
        CDBLB 1945-1960; DLB 20; MTCW

Spengler, Oswald (Arnold Gottfried)
    1880-1936 . . . . **TCLC 25**
    See also CA 118

Spenser, Edmund 1552(?)-1599 . . . . **LC 5**
    See also CDBLB Before 1660; DA; WLC

Spicer, Jack 1925-1965 . . . . . . **CLC 8, 18, 72**
    See also CA 85-88; DLB 5, 16

Spiegelman, Art 1948- . . . . **CLC 76**
    See also AAYA 10; CA 125; CANR 41

Spielberg, Peter 1929- . . . . **CLC 6**
    See also CA 5-8R; CANR 4; DLBY 81

Spielberg, Steven 1947- . . . . **CLC 20**
    See also AAYA 8; CA 77-80; CANR 32;
        SATA 32

Spillane, Frank Morrison 1918-
    See Spillane, Mickey
    See also CA 25-28R; CANR 28; MTCW;
        SATA 66

Spillane, Mickey . . . . **CLC 3, 13**
    See also Spillane, Frank Morrison

Spinoza, Benedictus de 1632-1677 . . . . **LC 9**

Spinrad, Norman (Richard) 1940- . . . **CLC 46**
    See also CA 37-40R; CANR 20; DLB 8

Spitteler, Carl (Friedrich Georg)
    1845-1924 . . . . **TCLC 12**
    See also CA 109; DLB 129

Spivack, Kathleen (Romola Drucker)
    1938- . . . . **CLC 6**
    See also CA 49-52

Spoto, Donald 1941- . . . . **CLC 39**
    See also CA 65-68; CANR 11

Springsteen, Bruce (F.) 1949- . . . . . . **CLC 17**
    See also CA 111

Spurling, Hilary 1940- . . . . **CLC 34**
    See also CA 104; CANR 25

Squires, (James) Radcliffe
    1917-1993 . . . . **CLC 51**
    See also CA 1-4R; 140; CANR 6, 21

Srivastava, Dhanpat Rai 1880(?)-1936
    See Premchand
    See also CA 118

Stacy, Donald
    See Pohl, Frederik

Stael, Germaine de
    See Stael-Holstein, Anne Louise Germaine
        Necker Baronn
    See also DLB 119

Stael-Holstein, Anne Louise Germaine Necker
    Baronn 1766-1817 . . . . **NCLC 3**
    See also Stael, Germaine de

Stafford, Jean 1915-1979 . . . **CLC 4, 7, 19, 68**
    See also CA 1-4R; 85-88; CANR 3; DLB 2;
        MTCW; SATA 22

Stafford, William (Edgar)
    1914-1993 . . . . **CLC 4, 7, 29**
    See also CA 5-8R; 142; CAAS 3; CANR 5,
        22; DLB 5

Staines, Trevor
    See Brunner, John (Kilian Houston)

Stairs, Gordon
    See Austin, Mary (Hunter)

Stannard, Martin 1947- . . . . **CLC 44**
    See also CA 142

Stanton, Maura 1946- . . . . **CLC 9**
    See also CA 89-92; CANR 15; DLB 120

Stanton, Schuyler
    See Baum, L(yman) Frank

Stapledon, (William) Olaf
    1886-1950 . . . . **TCLC 22**
    See also CA 111; DLB 15

Starbuck, George (Edwin) 1931- . . . . **CLC 53**
    See also CA 21-24R; CANR 23

Stark, Richard
    See Westlake, Donald E(dwin)

Staunton, Schuyler
    See Baum, L(yman) Frank

Stead, Christina (Ellen)
    1902-1983 . . . . **CLC 2, 5, 8, 32, 80**
    See also CA 13-16R; 109; CANR 33, 40;
        MTCW

Stead, William Thomas
    1849-1912 . . . . **TCLC 48**

Steele, Richard 1672-1729 . . . . **LC 18**
    See also CDBLB 1660-1789; DLB 84, 101

Steele, Timothy (Reid) 1948- . . . . **CLC 45**
    See also CA 93-96; CANR 16; DLB 120

Steffens, (Joseph) Lincoln
1866-1936 . . . . **TCLC 20**
See also CA 117

Stegner, Wallace (Earle)
1909-1993 . . . . **CLC 9, 49**
See also AITN 1; BEST 90:3; CA 1-4R;
141; CAAS 9; CANR 1, 21; DLB 9;
MTCW

Stein, Gertrude
1874-1946 . . . . **TCLC 1, 6, 28, 48**
See also CA 104; 132; CDALB 1917-1929;
DA; DLB 4, 54, 86; MTCW; WLC

Steinbeck, John (Ernst)
1902-1968 . . . . . . **CLC 1, 5, 9, 13, 21, 34,
45, 75; SSC 11**
See also CA 1-4R; 25-28R; CANR 1, 35;
CDALB 1929-1941; DA; DLB 7, 9;
DLBD 2; MTCW; SATA 9; WLC

Steinem, Gloria 1934- . . . . **CLC 63**
See also CA 53-56; CANR 28; MTCW

Steiner, George 1929- . . . . **CLC 24**
See also CA 73-76; CANR 31; DLB 67;
MTCW; SATA 62

Steiner, K. Leslie
See Delany, Samuel R(ay, Jr.)

Steiner, Rudolf 1861-1925 . . . . **TCLC 13**
See also CA 107

Stendhal 1783-1842 . . . . **NCLC 23**
See also DA; DLB 119; WLC

Stephen, Leslie 1832-1904 . . . . **TCLC 23**
See also CA 123; DLB 57

Stephen, Sir Leslie
See Stephen, Leslie

Stephen, Virginia
See Woolf, (Adeline) Virginia

Stephens, James 1882(?)-1950 . . . . . . **TCLC 4**
See also CA 104; DLB 19

Stephens, Reed
See Donaldson, Stephen R.

Steptoe, Lydia
See Barnes, Djuna

Sterchi, Beat 1949- . . . . **CLC 65**

Sterling, Brett
See Bradbury, Ray (Douglas); Hamilton,
Edmond

Sterling, Bruce 1954- . . . . **CLC 72**
See also CA 119

Sterling, George 1869-1926 . . . . **TCLC 20**
See also CA 117; DLB 54

Stern, Gerald 1925- . . . . **CLC 40**
See also CA 81-84; CANR 28; DLB 105

Stern, Richard (Gustave) 1928- . . . **CLC 4, 39**
See also CA 1-4R; CANR 1, 25; DLBY 87

Sternberg, Josef von 1894-1969 . . . . . **CLC 20**
See also CA 81-84

Sterne, Laurence 1713-1768 . . . . **LC 2**
See also CDBLB 1660-1789; DA; DLB 39;
WLC

Sternheim, (William Adolf) Carl
1878-1942 . . . . **TCLC 8**
See also CA 105; DLB 56, 118

Stevens, Mark 1951- . . . . **CLC 34**
See also CA 122

Stevens, Wallace
1879-1955 . . . . **TCLC 3, 12, 45; PC 6**
See also CA 104; 124; CDALB 1929-1941;
DA; DLB 54; MTCW; WLC

Stevenson, Anne (Katharine)
1933- . . . . **CLC 7, 33**
See also CA 17-20R; CAAS 9; CANR 9, 33;
DLB 40; MTCW

Stevenson, Robert Louis (Balfour)
1850-1894 . . . . **NCLC 5, 14; SSC 11**
See also CDBLB 1890-1914; CLR 10, 11;
DA; DLB 18, 57; JRDA; MAICYA;
WLC; YABC 2

Stewart, J(ohn) I(nnes) M(ackintosh)
1906- . . . . **CLC 7, 14, 32**
See also CA 85-88; CAAS 3; MTCW

Stewart, Mary (Florence Elinor)
1916- . . . . **CLC 7, 35**
See also CA 1-4R; CANR 1; SATA 12

Stewart, Mary Rainbow
See Stewart, Mary (Florence Elinor)

Stifter, Adalbert 1805-1868 . . . . . . **NCLC 41**
See also DLB 133

Still, James 1906- . . . . **CLC 49**
See also CA 65-68; CAAS 17; CANR 10,
26; DLB 9; SATA 29

Sting
See Sumner, Gordon Matthew

Stirling, Arthur
See Sinclair, Upton (Beall)

Stitt, Milan 1941- . . . . **CLC 29**
See also CA 69-72

Stockton, Francis Richard 1834-1902
See Stockton, Frank R.
See also CA 108; 137; MAICYA; SATA 44

Stockton, Frank R. . . . . **TCLC 47**
See also Stockton, Francis Richard
See also DLB 42, 74; SATA 32

Stoddard, Charles
See Kuttner, Henry

Stoker, Abraham 1847-1912
See Stoker, Bram
See also CA 105; DA; SATA 29

Stoker, Bram . . . . **TCLC 8**
See also Stoker, Abraham
See also CDBLB 1890-1914; DLB 36, 70;
WLC

Stolz, Mary (Slattery) 1920- . . . . **CLC 12**
See also AAYA 8; AITN 1; CA 5-8R;
CANR 13, 41; JRDA; MAICYA;
SAAS 3; SATA 10, 71

Stone, Irving 1903-1989 . . . . **CLC 7**
See also AITN 1; CA 1-4R; 129; CAAS 3;
CANR 1, 23; MTCW; SATA 3;
SATA-Obit 64

Stone, Oliver 1946- . . . . **CLC 73**
See also CA 110

Stone, Robert (Anthony)
1937- . . . . **CLC 5, 23, 42**
See also CA 85-88; CANR 23; MTCW

Stone, Zachary
See Follett, Ken(neth Martin)

Stoppard, Tom
1937- . . . **CLC 1, 3, 4, 5, 8, 15, 29, 34, 63**
See also CA 81-84; CANR 39;
CDBLB 1960 to Present; DA; DLB 13;
DLBY 85; MTCW; WLC

Storey, David (Malcolm)
1933- . . . . **CLC 2, 4, 5, 8**
See also CA 81-84; CANR 36; DLB 13, 14;
MTCW

Storm, Hyemeyohsts 1935- . . . . **CLC 3**
See also CA 81-84

Storm, (Hans) Theodor (Woldsen)
1817-1888 . . . . **NCLC 1**

Storni, Alfonsina 1892-1938 . . . . **TCLC 5**
See also CA 104; 131; HW

Stout, Rex (Todhunter) 1886-1975 . . . **CLC 3**
See also AITN 2; CA 61-64

Stow, (Julian) Randolph 1935- . . **CLC 23, 48**
See also CA 13-16R; CANR 33; MTCW

Stowe, Harriet (Elizabeth) Beecher
1811-1896 . . . . **NCLC 3**
See also CDALB 1865-1917; DA; DLB 1,
12, 42, 74; JRDA; MAICYA; WLC;
YABC 1

Strachey, (Giles) Lytton
1880-1932 . . . . **TCLC 12**
See also CA 110; DLBD 10

Strand, Mark 1934- . . . . . . **CLC 6, 18, 41, 71**
See also CA 21-24R; CANR 40; DLB 5;
SATA 41

Straub, Peter (Francis) 1943- . . . . . . **CLC 28**
See also BEST 89:1; CA 85-88; CANR 28;
DLBY 84; MTCW

Strauss, Botho 1944- . . . . **CLC 22**
See also DLB 124

Streatfeild, (Mary) Noel
1895(?)-1986 . . . . **CLC 21**
See also CA 81-84; 120; CANR 31;
CLR 17; MAICYA; SATA 20, 48

Stribling, T(homas) S(igismund)
1881-1965 . . . . **CLC 23**
See also CA 107; DLB 9

Strindberg, (Johan) August
1849-1912 . . . . **TCLC 1, 8, 21, 47**
See also CA 104; 135; DA; WLC

Stringer, Arthur 1874-1950 . . . . **TCLC 37**
See also DLB 92

Stringer, David
See Roberts, Keith (John Kingston)

Strugatskii, Arkadii (Natanovich)
1925-1991 . . . . **CLC 27**
See also CA 106; 135

Strugatskii, Boris (Natanovich)
1933- . . . . **CLC 27**
See also CA 106

Strummer, Joe 1953(?)- . . . . **CLC 30**
See also Clash, The

Stuart, Don A.
See Campbell, John W(ood, Jr.)

Stuart, Ian
See MacLean, Alistair (Stuart)

Stuart, Jesse (Hilton)
1906-1984 . . . . . . **CLC 1, 8, 11, 14, 34**
See also CA 5-8R; 112; CANR 31; DLB 9,
48, 102; DLBY 84; SATA 2, 36

Sturgeon, Theodore (Hamilton)
1918-1985 . . . . **CLC 22, 39**
See also Queen, Ellery
See also CA 81-84; 116; CANR 32; DLB 8;
DLBY 85; MTCW

Sturges, Preston 1898-1959 . . . . . . **TCLC 48**
See also CA 114; DLB 26

Styron, William
1925- . . . . **CLC 1, 3, 5, 11, 15, 60**
See also BEST 90:4; CA 5-8R; CANR 6, 33;
CDALB 1968-1988; DLB 2; DLBY 80;
MTCW

Suarez Lynch, B.
See Borges, Jorge Luis

Suarez Lynch, B.
See Bioy Casares, Adolfo; Borges, Jorge
Luis

Su Chien 1884-1918
See Su Man-shu
See also CA 123

Sudermann, Hermann 1857-1928 . . **TCLC 15**
See also CA 107; DLB 118

Sue, Eugene 1804-1857 . . . . **NCLC 1**
See also DLB 119

Sueskind, Patrick 1949- . . . . **CLC 44**

Sukenick, Ronald 1932- . . . . . **CLC 3, 4, 6, 48**
See also CA 25-28R; CAAS 8; CANR 32;
DLBY 81

Suknaski, Andrew 1942- . . . . **CLC 19**
See also CA 101; DLB 53

Sullivan, Vernon
See Vian, Boris

Sully Prudhomme 1839-1907 . . . . . . **TCLC 31**

Su Man-shu . . . . **TCLC 24**
See also Su Chien

Summerforest, Ivy B.
See Kirkup, James

Summers, Andrew James 1942- . . . . . **CLC 26**
See also Police, The

Summers, Andy
See Summers, Andrew James

Summers, Hollis (Spurgeon, Jr.)
1916- . . . . **CLC 10**
See also CA 5-8R; CANR 3; DLB 6

Summers, (Alphonsus Joseph-Mary Augustus)
Montague 1880-1948 . . . . **TCLC 16**
See also CA 118

Sumner, Gordon Matthew 1951- . . . . **CLC 26**
See also Police, The

Surtees, Robert Smith
1803-1864 . . . . **NCLC 14**
See also DLB 21

Susann, Jacqueline 1921-1974 . . . . . . **CLC 3**
See also AITN 1; CA 65-68; 53-56; MTCW

Suskind, Patrick
See Sueskind, Patrick

Sutcliff, Rosemary 1920-1992 . . . . . . **CLC 26**
See also AAYA 10; CA 5-8R; 139;
CANR 37; CLR 1; JRDA; MAICYA;
SATA 6, 44; SATA-Obit 73

Sutro, Alfred 1863-1933 . . . . **TCLC 6**
See also CA 105; DLB 10

Sutton, Henry
See Slavitt, David R(ytman)

Svevo, Italo . . . . **TCLC 2, 35**
See also Schmitz, Aron Hector

Swados, Elizabeth 1951- . . . . **CLC 12**
See also CA 97-100

Swados, Harvey 1920-1972 . . . . **CLC 5**
See also CA 5-8R; 37-40R; CANR 6;
DLB 2

Swan, Gladys 1934- . . . . **CLC 69**
See also CA 101; CANR 17, 39

Swarthout, Glendon (Fred)
1918-1992 . . . . **CLC 35**
See also CA 1-4R; 139; CANR 1; SATA 26

Sweet, Sarah C.
See Jewett, (Theodora) Sarah Orne

Swenson, May 1919-1989 . . . . . **CLC 4, 14, 61**
See also CA 5-8R; 130; CANR 36; DA;
DLB 5; MTCW; SATA 15

Swift, Augustus
See Lovecraft, H(oward) P(hillips)

Swift, Graham 1949- . . . . **CLC 41**
See also CA 117; 122

Swift, Jonathan 1667-1745 . . . . **LC 1**
See also CDBLB 1660-1789; DA; DLB 39,
95, 101; SATA 19; WLC

Swinburne, Algernon Charles
1837-1909 . . . . **TCLC 8, 36**
See also CA 105; 140; CDBLB 1832-1890;
DA; DLB 35, 57; WLC

Swinfen, Ann . . . . **CLC 34**

Swinnerton, Frank Arthur
1884-1982 . . . . **CLC 31**
See also CA 108; DLB 34

Swithen, John
See King, Stephen (Edwin)

Sylvia
See Ashton-Warner, Sylvia (Constance)

Symmes, Robert Edward
See Duncan, Robert (Edward)

Symonds, John Addington
1840-1893 . . . . **NCLC 34**
See also DLB 57

Symons, Arthur 1865-1945 . . . . **TCLC 11**
See also CA 107; DLB 19, 57

Symons, Julian (Gustave)
1912- . . . . **CLC 2, 14, 32**
See also CA 49-52; CAAS 3; CANR 3, 33;
DLB 87; DLBY 92; MTCW

Synge, (Edmund) J(ohn) M(illington)
1871-1909 . . . . **TCLC 6, 37; DC 2**
See also CA 104; 141; CDBLB 1890-1914;
DLB 10, 19

Syruc, J.
See Milosz, Czeslaw

Szirtes, George 1948- . . . . **CLC 46**
See also CA 109; CANR 27

Tabori, George 1914- . . . . **CLC 19**
See also CA 49-52; CANR 4

Tagore, Rabindranath 1861-1941 . . . . **TCLC 3**
See also CA 104; 120; MTCW

Taine, Hippolyte Adolphe
1828-1893 . . . . **NCLC 15**

Talese, Gay 1932- . . . . **CLC 37**
See also AITN 1; CA 1-4R; CANR 9;
MTCW

Tallent, Elizabeth (Ann) 1954- . . . . . **CLC 45**
See also CA 117; DLB 130

Tally, Ted 1952- . . . . **CLC 42**
See also CA 120; 124

Tamayo y Baus, Manuel
1829-1898 . . . . **NCLC 1**

Tammsaare, A(nton) H(ansen)
1878-1940 . . . . **TCLC 27**

Tan, Amy 1952- . . . . **CLC 59**
See also AAYA 9; BEST 89:3; CA 136;
SATA 75

Tandem, Felix
See Spitteler, Carl (Friedrich Georg)

Tanizaki, Jun'ichiro
1886-1965 . . . . **CLC 8, 14, 28**
See also CA 93-96; 25-28R

Tanner, William
See Amis, Kingsley (William)

Tao Lao
See Storni, Alfonsina

Tarassoff, Lev
See Troyat, Henri

Tarbell, Ida M(inerva)
1857-1944 . . . . **TCLC 40**
See also CA 122; DLB 47

Tarkington, (Newton) Booth
1869-1946 . . . . **TCLC 9**
See also CA 110; DLB 9, 102; SATA 17

Tarkovsky, Andrei (Arsenyevich)
1932-1986 . . . . **CLC 75**
See also CA 127

Tartt, Donna 1964(?)- . . . . **CLC 76**
See also CA 142

Tasso, Torquato 1544-1595 . . . . **LC 5**

Tate, (John Orley) Allen
1899-1979 . . . . **CLC 2, 4, 6, 9, 11, 14, 24**
See also CA 5-8R; 85-88; CANR 32;
DLB 4, 45, 63; MTCW

Tate, Ellalice
See Hibbert, Eleanor Alice Burford

Tate, James (Vincent) 1943- . . . **CLC 2, 6, 25**
See also CA 21-24R; CANR 29; DLB 5

Tavel, Ronald 1940- . . . . **CLC 6**
See also CA 21-24R; CANR 33

Taylor, Cecil Philip 1929-1981 . . . . . **CLC 27**
See also CA 25-28R; 105

Taylor, Edward 1642(?)-1729 . . . . **LC 11**
See also DA; DLB 24

Taylor, Eleanor Ross 1920- . . . . **CLC 5**
See also CA 81-84

Taylor, Elizabeth 1912-1975 . . . **CLC 2, 4, 29**
See also CA 13-16R; CANR 9; MTCW;
SATA 13

Taylor, Henry (Splawn) 1942- . . . . . . **CLC 44**
See also CA 33-36R; CAAS 7; CANR 31;
DLB 5

Taylor, Kamala (Purnaiya) 1924-
See Markandaya, Kamala
See also CA 77-80

Taylor, Mildred D. . . . . **CLC 21**
See also AAYA 10; BW; CA 85-88;
CANR 25; CLR 9; DLB 52; JRDA;
MAICYA; SAAS 5; SATA 15, 70

Tolson, Melvin B(eaunorus)
1898(?)-1966 .... **CLC 36**
See also BLC 3; BW; CA 124; 89-92;
DLB 48, 76

Tolstoi, Aleksei Nikolaevich
See Tolstoy, Alexey Nikolaevich

Tolstoy, Alexey Nikolaevich
1882-1945 .... **TCLC 18**
See also CA 107

Tolstoy, Count Leo
See Tolstoy, Leo (Nikolaevich)

Tolstoy, Leo (Nikolaevich)
1828-1910 ..... **TCLC 4, 11, 17, 28, 44;
SSC 9**
See also CA 104; 123; DA; SATA 26; WLC

Tomasi di Lampedusa, Giuseppe 1896-1957
See Lampedusa, Giuseppe (Tomasi) di
See also CA 111

Tomlin, Lily .... **CLC 17**
See also Tomlin, Mary Jean

Tomlin, Mary Jean   1939(?)-
See Tomlin, Lily
See also CA 117

Tomlinson, (Alfred) Charles
1927- .... **CLC 2, 4, 6, 13, 45**
See also CA 5-8R; CANR 33; DLB 40

Tonson, Jacob
See Bennett, (Enoch) Arnold

Toole, John Kennedy
1937-1969 .... **CLC 19, 64**
See also CA 104; DLBY 81

Toomer, Jean
1894-1967 ..... **CLC 1, 4, 13, 22; PC 7;
SSC 1**
See also BLC 3; BW; CA 85-88;
CDALB 1917-1929; DLB 45, 51; MTCW

Torley, Luke
See Blish, James (Benjamin)

Tornimparte, Alessandra
See Ginzburg, Natalia

Torre, Raoul della
See Mencken, H(enry) L(ouis)

Torrey, E(dwin) Fuller   1937- .... **CLC 34**
See also CA 119

Torsvan, Ben Traven
See Traven, B.

Torsvan, Benno Traven
See Traven, B.

Torsvan, Berick Traven
See Traven, B.

Torsvan, Berwick Traven
See Traven, B.

Torsvan, Bruno Traven
See Traven, B.

Torsvan, Traven
See Traven, B.

Tournier, Michel (Edouard)
1924- .... **CLC 6, 23, 36**
See also CA 49-52; CANR 3, 36; DLB 83;
MTCW; SATA 23

Tournimparte, Alessandra
See Ginzburg, Natalia

Towers, Ivar
See Kornbluth, C(yril) M.

Townsend, Sue   1946- .... **CLC 61**
See also CA 119; 127; MTCW; SATA 48,
55

Townshend, Peter (Dennis Blandford)
1945- .... **CLC 17, 42**
See also CA 107

Tozzi, Federigo   1883-1920 .... **TCLC 31**

Traill, Catharine Parr
1802-1899 .... **NCLC 31**
See also DLB 99

Trakl, Georg   1887-1914 .... **TCLC 5**
See also CA 104

Transtroemer, Tomas (Goesta)
1931- .... **CLC 52, 65**
See also CA 117; 129; CAAS 17

Transtromer, Tomas Gosta
See Transtroemer, Tomas (Goesta)

Traven, B.   (?)-1969 .... **CLC 8, 11**
See also CA 19-20; 25-28R; CAP 2; DLB 9,
56; MTCW

Treitel, Jonathan   1959- .... **CLC 70**

Tremain, Rose   1943- .... **CLC 42**
See also CA 97-100; DLB 14

Tremblay, Michel   1942- .... **CLC 29**
See also CA 116; 128; DLB 60; MTCW

Trevanian (a pseudonym)   1930(?)- ... **CLC 29**
See also CA 108

Trevor, Glen
See Hilton, James

Trevor, William
1928- .... **CLC 7, 9, 14, 25, 71**
See also Cox, William Trevor
See also DLB 14

Trifonov, Yuri (Valentinovich)
1925-1981 .... **CLC 45**
See also CA 126; 103; MTCW

Trilling, Lionel   1905-1975 .... **CLC 9, 11, 24**
See also CA 9-12R; 61-64; CANR 10;
DLB 28, 63; MTCW

Trimball, W. H.
See Mencken, H(enry) L(ouis)

Tristan
See Gomez de la Serna, Ramon

Tristram
See Housman, A(lfred) E(dward)

Trogdon, William (Lewis)   1939-
See Heat-Moon, William Least
See also CA 115; 119

Trollope, Anthony   1815-1882 .. **NCLC 6, 33**
See also CDBLB 1832-1890; DA; DLB 21,
57; SATA 22; WLC

Trollope, Frances   1779-1863 ..... **NCLC 30**
See also DLB 21

Trotsky, Leon   1879-1940 .... **TCLC 22**
See also CA 118

Trotter (Cockburn), Catharine
1679-1749 .... **LC 8**
See also DLB 84

Trout, Kilgore
See Farmer, Philip Jose

Trow, George W. S.   1943- .... **CLC 52**
See also CA 126

Troyat, Henri   1911- .... **CLC 23**
See also CA 45-48; CANR 2, 33; MTCW

Trudeau, G(arretson) B(eekman)   1948-
See Trudeau, Garry B.
See also CA 81-84; CANR 31; SATA 35

Trudeau, Garry B. .... **CLC 12**
See also Trudeau, G(arretson) B(eekman)
See also AAYA 10; AITN 2

Truffaut, Francois   1932-1984 ...... **CLC 20**
See also CA 81-84; 113; CANR 34

Trumbo, Dalton   1905-1976 .... **CLC 19**
See also CA 21-24R; 69-72; CANR 10;
DLB 26

Trumbull, John   1750-1831 ...... **NCLC 30**
See also DLB 31

Trundlett, Helen B.
See Eliot, T(homas) S(tearns)

Tryon, Thomas   1926-1991 .... **CLC 3, 11**
See also AITN 1; CA 29-32R; 135;
CANR 32; MTCW

Tryon, Tom
See Tryon, Thomas

Ts'ao Hsueh-ch'in   1715(?)-1763 .... **LC 1**

Tsushima, Shuji   1909-1948
See Dazai, Osamu
See also CA 107

Tsvetaeva (Efron), Marina (Ivanovna)
1892-1941 .... **TCLC 7, 35**
See also CA 104; 128; MTCW

Tuck, Lily   1938- .... **CLC 70**
See also CA 139

Tunis, John R(oberts)   1889-1975 ... **CLC 12**
See also CA 61-64; DLB 22; JRDA;
MAICYA; SATA 30, 37

Tuohy, Frank .... **CLC 37**
See also Tuohy, John Francis
See also DLB 14

Tuohy, John Francis   1925-
See Tuohy, Frank
See also CA 5-8R; CANR 3

Turco, Lewis (Putnam)   1934- ... **CLC 11, 63**
See also CA 13-16R; CANR 24; DLBY 84

Turgenev, Ivan
1818-1883 .... **NCLC 21; SSC 7**
See also DA; WLC

Turner, Frederick   1943- .... **CLC 48**
See also CA 73-76; CAAS 10; CANR 12,
30; DLB 40

Tusan, Stan   1936- .... **CLC 22**
See also CA 105

Tutu, Desmond M(pilo)   1931- ...... **CLC 80**
See also BLC 3; BW; CA 125

Tutuola, Amos   1920- .... **CLC 5, 14, 29**
See also BLC 3; BW; CA 9-12R; CANR 27;
DLB 125; MTCW

Twain, Mark
.... **TCLC 6, 12, 19, 36, 48; SSC 6**
See also Clemens, Samuel Langhorne
See also DLB 11, 12, 23, 64, 74; WLC

Tyler, Anne
1941- .... **CLC 7, 11, 18, 28, 44, 59**
See also BEST 89:1; CA 9-12R; CANR 11,
33; DLB 6; DLBY 82; MTCW; SATA 7

Tyler, Royall   1757-1826 .... **NCLC 3**
See also DLB 37

Vidal, Gore
1925- ..... **CLC 2, 4, 6, 8, 10, 22, 33, 72**
See also AITN 1; BEST 90:2; CA 5-8R;
CANR 13; DLB 6; MTCW

Viereck, Peter (Robert Edwin)
1916- .... **CLC 4**
See also CA 1-4R; CANR 1; DLB 5

Vigny, Alfred (Victor) de
1797-1863 .... **NCLC 7**
See also DLB 119

Vilakazi, Benedict Wallet
1906-1947 .... **TCLC 37**

**Villiers de l'Isle Adam, Jean Marie Mathias
Philippe Auguste Comte**
1838-1889 .... **NCLC 3**
See also DLB 123

Vincent, Gabrielle a pseudonym...... **CLC 13**
See also CA 126; CLR 13; MAICYA;
SATA 61

Vinci, Leonardo da   1452-1519 ...... **LC 12**

Vine, Barbara .... **CLC 50**
See also Rendell, Ruth (Barbara)
See also BEST 90:4

Vinge, Joan D(ennison)   1948- ...... **CLC 30**
See also CA 93-96; SATA 36

Violis, G.
See Simenon, Georges (Jacques Christian)

Visconti, Luchino   1906-1976 .... **CLC 16**
See also CA 81-84; 65-68; CANR 39

Vittorini, Elio   1908-1966 ..... **CLC 6, 9, 14**
See also CA 133; 25-28R

Vizinczey, Stephen   1933- .... **CLC 40**
See also CA 128

Vliet, R(ussell) G(ordon)
1929-1984 .... **CLC 22**
See also CA 37-40R; 112; CANR 18

Vogau, Boris Andreyevich   1894-1937(?)
See Pilnyak, Boris
See also CA 123

Vogel, Paula A(nne)   1951- .... **CLC 76**
See also CA 108

Voight, Ellen Bryant   1943- .... **CLC 54**
See also CA 69-72; CANR 11, 29; DLB 120

Voigt, Cynthia   1942- .... **CLC 30**
See also AAYA 3; CA 106; CANR 18, 37,
40; CLR 13; JRDA; MAICYA;
SATA 33, 48

Voinovich, Vladimir (Nikolaevich)
1932- .... **CLC 10, 49**
See also CA 81-84; CAAS 12; CANR 33;
MTCW

Voltaire   1694-1778 .... **LC 14; SSC 12**
See also DA; WLC

von Daeniken, Erich   1935- .... **CLC 30**
See also von Daniken, Erich
See also AITN 1; CA 37-40R; CANR 17

von Daniken, Erich................ **CLC 30**
See also von Daeniken, Erich

von Heidenstam, (Carl Gustaf) Verner
See Heidenstam, (Carl Gustaf) Verner von

von Heyse, Paul (Johann Ludwig)
See Heyse, Paul (Johann Ludwig von)

von Hofmannsthal, Hugo
See Hofmannsthal, Hugo von

von Horvath, Odon
See Horvath, Oedoen von

von Horvath, Oedoen
See Horvath, Oedoen von

von Liliencron, (Friedrich Adolf Axel) Detlev
See Liliencron, (Friedrich Adolf Axel)
Detlev von

Vonnegut, Kurt, Jr.
1922- ...... **CLC 1, 2, 3, 4, 5, 8, 12, 22,
40, 60; SSC 8**
See also AAYA 6; AITN 1; BEST 90:4;
CA 1-4R; CANR 1, 25;
CDALB 1968-1988; DA; DLB 2, 8;
DLBD 3; DLBY 80; MTCW; WLC

Von Rachen, Kurt
See Hubbard, L(afayette) Ron(ald)

von Rezzori (d'Arezzo), Gregor
See Rezzori (d'Arezzo), Gregor von

von Sternberg, Josef
See Sternberg, Josef von

Vorster, Gordon   1924- .... **CLC 34**
See also CA 133

Vosce, Trudie
See Ozick, Cynthia

Voznesensky, Andrei (Andreievich)
1933- .... **CLC 1, 15, 57**
See also CA 89-92; CANR 37; MTCW

Waddington, Miriam   1917- .... **CLC 28**
See also CA 21-24R; CANR 12, 30;
DLB 68

Wagman, Fredrica   1937- .... **CLC 7**
See also CA 97-100

Wagner, Richard   1813-1883....... **NCLC 9**
See also DLB 129

Wagner-Martin, Linda   1936- .... **CLC 50**

Wagoner, David (Russell)
1926- .... **CLC 3, 5, 15**
See also CA 1-4R; CAAS 3; CANR 2;
DLB 5; SATA 14

Wah, Fred(erick James)   1939- ...... **CLC 44**
See also CA 107; 141; DLB 60

Wahloo, Per   1926-1975 .... **CLC 7**
See also CA 61-64

Wahloo, Peter
See Wahloo, Per

Wain, John (Barrington)
1925- .... **CLC 2, 11, 15, 46**
See also CA 5-8R; CAAS 4; CANR 23;
CDBLB 1960 to Present; DLB 15, 27;
MTCW

Wajda, Andrzej   1926- .... **CLC 16**
See also CA 102

Wakefield, Dan   1932- .... **CLC 7**
See also CA 21-24R; CAAS 7

Wakoski, Diane
1937- .... **CLC 2, 4, 7, 9, 11, 40**
See also CA 13-16R; CAAS 1; CANR 9;
DLB 5

Wakoski-Sherbell, Diane
See Wakoski, Diane

Walcott, Derek (Alton)
1930- .... **CLC 2, 4, 9, 14, 25, 42, 67, 76**
See also BLC 3; BW; CA 89-92; CANR 26;
DLB 117; DLBY 81; MTCW

Waldman, Anne   1945- .... **CLC 7**
See also CA 37-40R; CAAS 17; CANR 34;
DLB 16

Waldo, E. Hunter
See Sturgeon, Theodore (Hamilton)

Waldo, Edward Hamilton
See Sturgeon, Theodore (Hamilton)

Walker, Alice (Malsenior)
1944- .... **CLC 5, 6, 9, 19, 27, 46, 58;
SSC 5**
See also AAYA 3; BEST 89:4; BLC 3; BW;
CA 37-40R; CANR 9, 27;
CDALB 1968-1988; DA; DLB 6, 33;
MTCW; SATA 31

Walker, David Harry   1911-1992.... **CLC 14**
See also CA 1-4R; 137; CANR 1; SATA 8;
SATA-Obit 71

Walker, Edward Joseph   1934-
See Walker, Ted
See also CA 21-24R; CANR 12, 28

Walker, George F.   1947- .... **CLC 44, 61**
See also CA 103; CANR 21, 43; DLB 60

Walker, Joseph A.   1935- .... **CLC 19**
See also BW; CA 89-92; CANR 26; DLB 38

Walker, Margaret (Abigail)
1915- .... **CLC 1, 6**
See also BLC 3; BW; CA 73-76; CANR 26;
DLB 76; MTCW

Walker, Ted..................... **CLC 13**
See also Walker, Edward Joseph
See also DLB 40

Wallace, David Foster   1962- .... **CLC 50**
See also CA 132

Wallace, Dexter
See Masters, Edgar Lee

Wallace, Irving   1916-1990 .... **CLC 7, 13**
See also AITN 1; CA 1-4R; 132; CAAS 1;
CANR 1, 27; MTCW

Wallant, Edward Lewis
1926-1962 .... **CLC 5, 10**
See also CA 1-4R; CANR 22; DLB 2, 28;
MTCW

Walpole, Horace   1717-1797.......... **LC 2**
See also DLB 39, 104

Walpole, Hugh (Seymour)
1884-1941 .... **TCLC 5**
See also CA 104; DLB 34

Walser, Martin   1927- .... **CLC 27**
See also CA 57-60; CANR 8; DLB 75, 124

Walser, Robert   1878-1956 .... **TCLC 18**
See also CA 118; DLB 66

Walsh, Jill Paton.................. **CLC 35**
See also Paton Walsh, Gillian
See also CLR 2; SAAS 3

Walter, William Christian
See Andersen, Hans Christian

Wambaugh, Joseph (Aloysius, Jr.)
1937- .... **CLC 3, 18**
See also AITN 1; BEST 89:3; CA 33-36R;
CANR 42; DLB 6; DLBY 83; MTCW

Ward, Arthur Henry Sarsfield   1883-1959
See Rohmer, Sax
See also CA 108

Wescott, Glenway 1901-1987...... **CLC 13**
See also CA 13-16R; 121; CANR 23;
DLB 4, 9, 102

Wesker, Arnold 1932-........ **CLC 3, 5, 42**
See also CA 1-4R; CAAS 7; CANR 1, 33;
CDBLB 1960 to Present; DLB 13;
MTCW

Wesley, Richard (Errol) 1945-...... **CLC 7**
See also BW; CA 57-60; CANR 27; DLB 38

Wessel, Johan Herman 1742-1785 .... **LC 7**

West, Anthony (Panther)
1914-1987 .... **CLC 50**
See also CA 45-48; 124; CANR 3, 19;
DLB 15

West, C. P.
See Wodehouse, P(elham) G(renville)

West, (Mary) Jessamyn
1902-1984 .... **CLC 7, 17**
See also CA 9-12R; 112; CANR 27; DLB 6;
DLBY 84; MTCW; SATA 37

West, Morris L(anglo) 1916-..... **CLC 6, 33**
See also CA 5-8R; CANR 24; MTCW

West, Nathanael
1903-1940 .... **TCLC 1, 14, 44**
See also CA 104; 125; CDALB 1929-1941;
DLB 4, 9, 28; MTCW

West, Owen
See Koontz, Dean R(ay)

West, Paul 1930- .... **CLC 7, 14**
See also CA 13-16R; CAAS 7; CANR 22;
DLB 14

West, Rebecca 1892-1983 .. **CLC 7, 9, 31, 50**
See also CA 5-8R; 109; CANR 19; DLB 36;
DLBY 83; MTCW

Westall, Robert (Atkinson)
1929-1993 .... **CLC 17**
See also CA 69-72; 141; CANR 18;
CLR 13; JRDA; MAICYA; SAAS 2;
SATA 23, 69; SATA-Obit 75

Westlake, Donald E(dwin)
1933- .... **CLC 7, 33**
See also CA 17-20R; CAAS 13; CANR 16

Westmacott, Mary
See Christie, Agatha (Mary Clarissa)

Weston, Allen
See Norton, Andre

Wetcheek, J. L.
See Feuchtwanger, Lion

Wetering, Janwillem van de
See van de Wetering, Janwillem

Wetherell, Elizabeth
See Warner, Susan (Bogert)

Whalen, Philip 1923- .... **CLC 6, 29**
See also CA 9-12R; CANR 5, 39; DLB 16

Wharton, Edith (Newbold Jones)
1862-1937 ...... **TCLC 3, 9, 27; SSC 6**
See also CA 104; 132; CDALB 1865-1917;
DA; DLB 4, 9, 12, 78; MTCW; WLC

Wharton, James
See Mencken, H(enry) L(ouis)

Wharton, William (a pseudonym)
.... **CLC 18, 37**
See also CA 93-96; DLBY 80

Wheatley (Peters), Phillis
1754(?)-1784 .... **LC 3; PC 3**
See also BLC 3; CDALB 1640-1865; DA;
DLB 31, 50; WLC

Wheelock, John Hall 1886-1978 .... **CLC 14**
See also CA 13-16R; 77-80; CANR 14;
DLB 45

White, E(lwyn) B(rooks)
1899-1985 .... **CLC 10, 34, 39**
See also AITN 2; CA 13-16R; 116;
CANR 16, 37; CLR 1, 21; DLB 11, 22;
MAICYA; MTCW; SATA 2, 29, 44

White, Edmund (Valentine III)
1940- .... **CLC 27**
See also AAYA 7; CA 45-48; CANR 3, 19,
36; MTCW

White, Patrick (Victor Martindale)
1912-1990 .. **CLC 3, 4, 5, 7, 9, 18, 65, 69**
See also CA 81-84; 132; CANR 43; MTCW

White, Phyllis Dorothy James 1920-
See James, P. D.
See also CA 21-24R; CANR 17, 43; MTCW

White, T(erence) H(anbury)
1906-1964 .... **CLC 30**
See also CA 73-76; CANR 37; JRDA;
MAICYA; SATA 12

White, Terence de Vere 1912-...... **CLC 49**
See also CA 49-52; CANR 3

White, Walter F(rancis)
1893-1955 .... **TCLC 15**
See also White, Walter
See also CA 115; 124; DLB 51

White, William Hale 1831-1913
See Rutherford, Mark
See also CA 121

Whitehead, E(dward) A(nthony)
1933- .... **CLC 5**
See also CA 65-68

Whitemore, Hugh (John) 1936-..... **CLC 37**
See also CA 132

Whitman, Sarah Helen (Power)
1803-1878 .... **NCLC 19**
See also DLB 1

Whitman, Walt(er)
1819-1892 .... **NCLC 4, 31; PC 3**
See also CDALB 1640-1865; DA; DLB 3,
64; SATA 20; WLC

Whitney, Phyllis A(yame) 1903-.... **CLC 42**
See also AITN 2; BEST 90:3; CA 1-4R;
CANR 3, 25, 38; JRDA; MAICYA;
SATA 1, 30

Whittemore, (Edward) Reed (Jr.)
1919- .... **CLC 4**
See also CA 9-12R; CAAS 8; CANR 4;
DLB 5

Whittier, John Greenleaf
1807-1892 .... **NCLC 8**
See also CDALB 1640-1865; DLB 1

Whittlebot, Hernia
See Coward, Noel (Peirce)

Wicker, Thomas Grey 1926-
See Wicker, Tom
See also CA 65-68; CANR 21

Wicker, Tom .... **CLC 7**
See also Wicker, Thomas Grey

Wideman, John Edgar
1941- .... **CLC 5, 34, 36, 67**
See also BLC 3; BW; CA 85-88; CANR 14,
42; DLB 33

Wiebe, Rudy (Henry) 1934-... **CLC 6, 11, 14**
See also CA 37-40R; CANR 42; DLB 60

Wieland, Christoph Martin
1733-1813 .... **NCLC 17**
See also DLB 97

Wieners, John 1934-............... **CLC 7**
See also CA 13-16R; DLB 16

Wiesel, Elie(zer) 1928-..... **CLC 3, 5, 11, 37**
See also AAYA 7; AITN 1; CA 5-8R;
CAAS 4; CANR 8, 40; DA; DLB 83;
DLBY 87; MTCW; SATA 56

Wiggins, Marianne 1947-......... **CLC 57**
See also BEST 89:3; CA 130

Wight, James Alfred 1916-
See Herriot, James
See also CA 77-80; SATA 44, 55

Wilbur, Richard (Purdy)
1921- .... **CLC 3, 6, 9, 14, 53**
See also CA 1-4R; CABS 2; CANR 2, 29;
DA; DLB 5; MTCW; SATA 9

Wild, Peter 1940-................. **CLC 14**
See also CA 37-40R; DLB 5

Wilde, Oscar (Fingal O'Flahertie Wills)
1854(?)-1900 .... **TCLC 1, 8, 23, 41;**
SSC 11
See also CA 104; 119; CDBLB 1890-1914;
DA; DLB 10, 19, 34, 57; SATA 24; WLC

Wilder, Billy .... **CLC 20**
See also Wilder, Samuel
See also DLB 26

Wilder, Samuel 1906-
See Wilder, Billy
See also CA 89-92

Wilder, Thornton (Niven)
1897-1975 ...... **CLC 1, 5, 6, 10, 15, 35;**
DC 1
See also AITN 2; CA 13-16R; 61-64;
CANR 40; DA; DLB 4, 7, 9; MTCW;
WLC

Wilding, Michael 1942-........... **CLC 73**
See also CA 104; CANR 24

Wiley, Richard 1944-............. **CLC 44**
See also CA 121; 129

Wilhelm, Kate .... **CLC 7**
See also Wilhelm, Katie Gertrude
See also CAAS 5; DLB 8

Wilhelm, Katie Gertrude 1928-
See Wilhelm, Kate
See also CA 37-40R; CANR 17, 36; MTCW

Wilkins, Mary
See Freeman, Mary Eleanor Wilkins

Willard, Nancy 1936-........... **CLC 7, 37**
See also CA 89-92; CANR 10, 39; CLR 5;
DLB 5, 52; MAICYA; MTCW;
SATA 30, 37, 71

Williams, C(harles) K(enneth)
1936- .... **CLC 33, 56**
See also CA 37-40R; DLB 5

Williams, Charles
See Collier, James L(incoln)

Wordsworth, Dorothy
1771-1855 .... **NCLC 25**
See also DLB 107

Wordsworth, William
1770-1850 .... **NCLC 12, 38; PC 4**
See also CDBLB 1789-1832; DA; DLB 93,
107; WLC

Wouk, Herman 1915- .... **CLC 1, 9, 38**
See also CA 5-8R; CANR 6, 33; DLBY 82;
MTCW

Wright, Charles (Penzel, Jr.)
1935- .... **CLC 6, 13, 28**
See also CA 29-32R; CAAS 7; CANR 23,
36; DLBY 82; MTCW

Wright, Charles Stevenson 1932- ... **CLC 49**
See also BLC 3; BW; CA 9-12R; CANR 26;
DLB 33

Wright, Jack R.
See Harris, Mark

Wright, James (Arlington)
1927-1980 .... **CLC 3, 5, 10, 28**
See also AITN 2; CA 49-52; 97-100;
CANR 4, 34; DLB 5; MTCW

Wright, Judith (Arandell)
1915- .... **CLC 11, 53**
See also CA 13-16R; CANR 31; MTCW;
SATA 14

Wright, L(aurali) R. 1939- .... **CLC 44**
See also CA 138

Wright, Richard (Nathaniel)
1908-1960 .... **CLC 1, 3, 4, 9, 14, 21, 48,
74; SSC 2**
See also AAYA 5; BLC 3; BW; CA 108;
CDALB 1929-1941; DA; DLB 76, 102;
DLBD 2; MTCW; WLC

Wright, Richard B(ruce) 1937- ...... **CLC 6**
See also CA 85-88; DLB 53

Wright, Rick 1945- .... **CLC 35**
See also Pink Floyd

Wright, Rowland
See Wells, Carolyn

Wright, Stephen 1946- .... **CLC 33**

Wright, Willard Huntington 1888-1939
See Van Dine, S. S.
See also CA 115

Wright, William 1930- .... **CLC 44**
See also CA 53-56; CANR 7, 23

Wu Ch'eng-en 1500(?)-1582(?) .... **LC 7**

Wu Ching-tzu 1701-1754 .... **LC 2**

Wurlitzer, Rudolph 1938(?)- ... **CLC 2, 4, 15**
See also CA 85-88

Wycherley, William 1641-1715 .... **LC 8, 21**
See also CDBLB 1660-1789; DLB 80

Wylie, Elinor (Morton Hoyt)
1885-1928 .... **TCLC 8**
See also CA 105; DLB 9, 45

Wylie, Philip (Gordon) 1902-1971... **CLC 43**
See also CA 21-22; 33-36R; CAP 2; DLB 9

Wyndham, John
See Harris, John (Wyndham Parkes Lucas)
Beynon

Wyss, Johann David Von
1743-1818 .... **NCLC 10**
See also JRDA; MAICYA; SATA 27, 29

Yakumo Koizumi
See Hearn, (Patricio) Lafcadio (Tessima
Carlos)

Yanez, Jose Donoso
See Donoso (Yanez), Jose

Yanovsky, Basile S.
See Yanovsky, V(assily) S(emenovich)

Yanovsky, V(assily) S(emenovich)
1906-1989 .... **CLC 2, 18**
See also CA 97-100; 129

Yates, Richard 1926-1992 ..... **CLC 7, 8, 23**
See also CA 5-8R; 139; CANR 10, 43;
DLB 2; DLBY 81, 92

Yeats, W. B.
See Yeats, William Butler

Yeats, William Butler
1865-1939 .... **TCLC 1, 11, 18, 31**
See also CA 104; 127; CDBLB 1890-1914;
DA; DLB 10, 19, 98; MTCW; WLC

Yehoshua, A(braham) B.
1936- .... **CLC 13, 31**
See also CA 33-36R; CANR 43

Yep, Laurence Michael 1948- ...... **CLC 35**
See also AAYA 5; CA 49-52; CANR 1;
CLR 3, 17; DLB 52; JRDA; MAICYA;
SATA 7, 69

Yerby, Frank G(arvin)
1916-1991 .... **CLC 1, 7, 22**
See also BLC 3; BW; CA 9-12R; 136;
CANR 16; DLB 76; MTCW

Yesenin, Sergei Alexandrovich
See Esenin, Sergei (Alexandrovich)

Yevtushenko, Yevgeny (Alexandrovich)
1933- .... **CLC 1, 3, 13, 26, 51**
See also CA 81-84; CANR 33; MTCW

Yezierska, Anzia 1885(?)-1970 ..... **CLC 46**
See also CA 126; 89-92; DLB 28; MTCW

Yglesias, Helen 1915- .... **CLC 7, 22**
See also CA 37-40R; CANR 15; MTCW

Yokomitsu Riichi 1898-1947 ...... **TCLC 47**

Yonge, Charlotte (Mary)
1823-1901 .... **TCLC 48**
See also CA 109; DLB 18; SATA 17

York, Jeremy
See Creasey, John

York, Simon
See Heinlein, Robert A(nson)

Yorke, Henry Vincent 1905-1974 ... **CLC 13**
See also Green, Henry
See also CA 85-88; 49-52

Young, Al(bert James) 1939- .... **CLC 19**
See also BLC 3; BW; CA 29-32R;
CANR 26; DLB 33

Young, Andrew (John) 1885-1971 .... **CLC 5**
See also CA 5-8R; CANR 7, 29

Young, Collier
See Bloch, Robert (Albert)

Young, Edward 1683-1765 .... **LC 3**
See also DLB 95

Young, Neil 1945- .... **CLC 17**
See also CA 110

Yourcenar, Marguerite
1903-1987 .... **CLC 19, 38, 50**
See also CA 69-72; CANR 23; DLB 72;
DLBY 88; MTCW

Yurick, Sol 1925- .... **CLC 6**
See also CA 13-16R; CANR 25

Zabolotskii, Nikolai Alekseevich
1903-1958 .... **TCLC 52**
See also CA 116

Zamiatin, Yevgenii
See Zamyatin, Evgeny Ivanovich

Zamyatin, Evgeny Ivanovich
1884-1937 .... **TCLC 8, 37**
See also CA 105

Zangwill, Israel 1864-1926........ **TCLC 16**
See also CA 109; DLB 10

Zappa, Francis Vincent, Jr. 1940-
See Zappa, Frank
See also CA 108

Zappa, Frank .... **CLC 17**
See also Zappa, Francis Vincent, Jr.

Zaturenska, Marya 1902-1982.... **CLC 6, 11**
See also CA 13-16R; 105; CANR 22

Zelazny, Roger (Joseph) 1937- ..... **CLC 21**
See also AAYA 7; CA 21-24R; CANR 26;
DLB 8; MTCW; SATA 39, 57

Zhdanov, Andrei A(lexandrovich)
1896-1948 .... **TCLC 18**
See also CA 117

Zhukovsky, Vasily 1783-1852 .... **NCLC 35**

Ziegenhagen, Eric .... **CLC 55**

Zimmer, Jill Schary
See Robinson, Jill

Zimmerman, Robert
See Dylan, Bob

Zindel, Paul 1936- .... **CLC 6, 26**
See also AAYA 2; CA 73-76; CANR 31;
CLR 3; DA; DLB 7, 52; JRDA;
MAICYA; MTCW; SATA 16, 58

Zinov'Ev, A. A.
See Zinoviev, Alexander (Aleksandrovich)

Zinoviev, Alexander (Aleksandrovich)
1922- .... **CLC 19**
See also CA 116; 133; CAAS 10

Zoilus
See Lovecraft, H(oward) P(hillips)

Zola, Emile (Edouard Charles Antoine)
1840-1902 .... **TCLC 1, 6, 21, 41**
See also CA 104; 138; DA; DLB 123; WLC

Zoline, Pamela 1941- .... **CLC 62**

Zorrilla y Moral, Jose 1817-1893.. **NCLC 6**

Zoshchenko, Mikhail (Mikhailovich)
1895-1958 .... **TCLC 15**
See also CA 115

Zuckmayer, Carl 1896-1977........ **CLC 18**
See also CA 69-72; DLB 56, 124

Zuk, Georges
See Skelton, Robin

Zukofsky, Louis
1904-1978 .... **CLC 1, 2, 4, 7, 11, 18**
See also CA 9-12R; 77-80; CANR 39;
DLB 5; MTCW

Zweig, Paul 1935-1984........ **CLC 34, 42**
See also CA 85-88; 113

Literary Criticism Series
Cumulative Topic Index

This index lists all topic entries in the Gale Literary Criticism Series *Classical and Medieval Literature Criticism, Contemporary Literary Criticism, Literature Criticism from 1400 to 1800, Nineteenth-Century Literature Criticism,* and *Twentieth-Century Literary Criticism.*

LC Cumulative Nationality Index

See *Vita di santa Caterina da Siena*
Life of Saint Thomas Aquinas (Aretino)
   12:13, 36
The Life of Samuel Johnson, LL. D. (Life of Johnson) (Boswell)   **4**:18-19, 21-6, 30, 36-7, 39-41, 46-8, 50, 53-4, 56-60, 65-71, 75, 77-9
"Life of Savage" (Johnson)
   See *An Account of the Life of Mr. Richard Savage, Son of Earl Rivers*
Life of Shakespeare (Rowe)
   See *Account of the Life of Shakespear*
Life of Sophocles (Lessing)   **8**:101, 109-10
The Life of the Countess de Gondez (Aubin)
   9:6
The Life of the Mother Teresa of Jesus (Teresa de Jesus)
   See *Libro de su vida*
"The Life of the Soul" (More)
   See "Psychozoia: or, A Christiano-Platonicall Display of Life"
Life of the Virgin Mary (Aretino)   **12**:13, 36
The Life of Thomas More (Roper)
   See *The Mirrour of Vertue in Worldly Greatnes; or, The Life of syr Thomas More Knight*
"Life of Waller" (Johnson)   **15**:225, 230
"Life of Watts" (Johnson)   **15**:225
Life's Progress through the Passions; or, The Adventures of Natura (Haywood)   **1**:291
Lilliput (Garrick)   **15**:101-03, 123-24
"The Lilly in a Christal" (Herrick)   **13**:350-51, 369, 380-82, 392-94
"Lines by Ladgate" (Chatterton)   **3**:119
"Lines to Sour-Faced Gila" (Juana Ines de la Cruz)   **5**:146
"Lines Written in Mezeray" (Prior)
   See "Written in the Beginning of Mezeray's History of France"
"Lisetta's Reply" (Prior)   **4**:461, 466
"The Litanie" (Donne)   **10**:40, 56, 84, 92; **24**:165, 167
"Litany" ("Letanie") (Herrick)   **13**:317, 320, 334, 336-38
Litany to the Germans (Hutten)   **16**:234
"Litany to the Holy Spirit" ("His Letanie, to the Holy Spirit"; "His Litany to the Holy Spirit") (Herrick)   **13**:314, 319, 328, 342, 357
Literaturbrief (Letters concerning Contemporary Literature) (Lessing)   **8**:70, 98, 100, 103-04, 106, 109-12, 115
Liter**** obscurorum Vivorum (Epistol**** Obscurorum Vivorum; Letters of Obscure Men; Obscure Men) (Hutten)   **16**:212, 214-15, 218-25, 228, 230-33, 235-37, 245
"A Litigious Man" (Butler)   **16**:50
Little Female Academy (Fielding)
   See *The Governess; or, Little Female Academy*
The Little Garden of Roses (Kempis)
   See *Hortulus rosarii de valle lachrymarum continens egreias & devotas sentecias*
"Little Red Riding Hood" (Perrault)
   See "Le petit chaperon rouge"
The Little Surgery (Paracelsus)
   See *Chirurgia minor quam Bertheoneam intitulaut*
"Little T. C." (Marvell)
   See "The Picture of Little T. C. in a Prospect of Flowers"
"La liturgie de Cythère" (Rousseau)   **9**:345

The Lives of Cleopatra and Octavia (Fielding)
   1:273
Lives of Do-wel, Do-bet, and Do-best (Langland)
   See *Piers Plowman*
The Lives of the Poets (Johnson)
   See *Prefaces, Biographical and Critical, to the Works of the English Poets*
"Living Flame of Love" (John of the Cross)
   See "Llama de amor viva"
The Living Flame of Love (John of the Cross)
   See *Llama de Amor Viva*
Le livre de la cité des dames (The Boke of the Cyte of Ladies) (Christine de Pizan)   **9**:23, 25, 28, 33-4, 38-9, 44-5
Le livre de la mutacion de fortune (Christine de Pizan)   **9**:24, 28, 34-5, 38-9, 48
Le livre de la paix (Christine de Pizan)   **9**:25, 48
Livre de la prod'hommie de l'homme (Christine de Pizan)   **9**:48
Le livre des fais et bonnes meurs du sage roy Charles V (Christine de Pizan)   **9**:23-4, 26, 48
Le livre des faits d'armes et de chevalerie (The Book of Fayttes of Armes and of Chyvalrye) (Christine de Pizan)   **9**:23, 25, 28-9, 35, 45, 47
Le livre du chemin de long estude (The Long Road of Learning) (Christine de Pizan)   **9**:24, 27, 46, 48
Le livre du corps de policie (The Body of Polycye) (Christine de Pizan)   **9**:25, 46-8
Le livre du dit de Poissy (The Debate of Poissy) (Christine de Pizan)   **9**:28, 41, 43
Le livre du duc des vrais amans (The Book of the Duke of True Lovers) (Christine de Pizan)   **9**:27, 42, 48
"Livret de Folastries" (Ronsard)   **6**:417, 431
"****lla: A Tragycal Enterlude" ("Dirge in ****lla") (Chatterton)   **3**:118-20, 123-24, 127, 129-30, 135
"Llama de amor viva" ("Living Flame of Love") (John of the Cross)   **18**:213, 216-17, 222, 224
Llama de Amor Viva (The Living Flame of Love) (John of the Cross)   **18**:202, 205, 221, 229-30
Loa a los años del rey (Juana Ines de la Cruz)   **5**:159
Loa en las huertas donde fue a divertirse la Excelentísima Señora Condesa de Paredes, Marquesa de la Laguna (Juana Ines de la Cruz)   **5**:159
La locandiera (Goldoni)   **4**:262, 264, 267, 273-74
The Logick Primer (Eliot)
   See *The Logick Primer, Some Logical Notions to Initiate the Indians in Knowledge of the Rule of Reason; and to Know How to Make Use Thereof*
The Logick Primer, Some Logical Notions to Initiate the Indians in Knowledge of the Rule of Reason; and to Know How to Make Use Thereof (The Logick Primer) (Eliot)   **5**:132, 134-35
Londinopolis; An Historical Discourse or Perlustration of the City of London (Howell)   **13**:424
"London: A Poem, In Imitation of the Third Satire of Juvenal" (Johnson)   **15**:187-90, 194, 206, 288, 291-95, 302-05

London Journal (Boswell)
   See *Boswell's London Journal*
London's Tempe (Dekker)   **22**:95, 130
"Longing" (Herbert)   **24**:272, 274
"Longing for Heaven" (Bradstreet)   **4**:85, 112
The Long Road of Learning (Christine de Pizan)
   See *Le livre du chemin de long estude*
"A Long Story" (Gray)   **4**:301, 312, 315-17, 333-34
"A Looking-Glasse" (Carew)   **13**:28
"A Loose Sarabande" (Lovelace)   **24**:303, 306, 315, 320, 347, 350, 354
"Lord Daer" (Burns)
   See "Meeting with Lord Daer"
"The Loss of his Mistresses" (Herrick)
   13:337
The Lost Lover; or, A Jealous Husband (Manley)   **1**:315
The Loud Secret (Calderon de la Barca)
   23:60, 64
"Love" (Herbert)   **24**:234, 268, 272, 274
"Love I" (Herbert)   **24**:234, 268, 272, 274
"Love II" (Herbert)   **24**:235, 238, 272, 282
"Love III" (Herbert)   **24**:230, 234, 252, 259, 262-64, 266, 269, 273, 275, 280, 282
Love and a Bottle (Love in a Bottle) (Farquhar)   **21**:128, 135-36, 139-40, 145-46, 148, 150-52, 154, 161-63, 170, 176
Love and Business (Farquhar)   **21**:130, 133, 142
Love and Honor (Davenant)   **13**:175-77, 181, 192, 196, 215
Love at a Loss; or, Most Votes Carry It (Trotter)   **8**:355, 357, 361, 368-69, 372-74
"Love Banish'd Heav'n, in Earth Was Held in Scorne" (Drayton)
   See "Sonnet 23"
"Love-Begotten Daughter" (Burns)
   See "A Poet's Welcome to His Love-Begotten Daughter"
"Love Conquered" (Lovelace)   **24**:350
"Love Disarm'd" (Prior)   **4**:459
Love Elegies (Donne)
   See *Elegies*
Love for Love (Congreve)   **5**:66, 68, 70-1, 74, 76, 78-9, 81, 83, 84, 86-90, 92, 94, 96-101, 105-06, 109, 111; **21**:4, 9-10, 15, 17, 22-3, 25-7, 29-32, 40-1, 43
Love in a Bottle (Farquhar)
   See *Love and a Bottle*
"Love, in a Humor, Play'd the Prodigall" (Drayton)
   See "Sonnet 7"
Love in a Wood; or, St. James's Park (Wycherley)   **8**:384, 388, 390-92, 395, 397, 402, 407, 410, 432-34; **21**:351-52, 354, 356, 359-60, 370-73, 376-78, 380-81, 391, 396-97
Love in Excess; or, The Fatal Enquiry (Haywood)   **1**:284-85, 290, 292, 295-300
"Love in Fantastic Triumph Sat" (Behn)
   1:31, 38
Love in Several Masques (Fielding)   **1**:250
"Love Joy" (Herbert)   **24**:255, 262, 266
Love Letters between a Nobleman and His Sister (Behn)   **1**:34, 43, 48
Love-Letters from King Henry VIII. to Anne Boleyn (Henry VIII)   **10**:119
Love Letters to a Gentleman (Behn)   **1**:38
"Love Made in the First Age" (Lovelace)
   24:316, 347
"The Love of Fame" (Young)